KT-556-472

OXFORD PAPERBACK REFERENCE

The Concise Oxford Dictionary of
# Quotations

# Oxford
## Paperback
## Reference

The most authoritative and up-to-date reference books for both students and the general reader.

The Concise
Oxford Dictionary of

# Quotations

**REVISED THIRD EDITION**

*Edited by*
**ANGELA PARTINGTON**

Oxford    New York
**OXFORD UNIVERSITY PRESS**

Oxford University Press, Great Clarendon Street, Oxford OX2 6DP

Oxford New York
Athens Auckland Bangkok Bogota Buenos Aires Calcutta
Cape Town Chennai Dar es Salaam Delhi Florence Hong Kong Istanbul
Karachi Kuala Lumpur Madrid Melbourne Mexico City Mumbai
Nairobi Paris São Paolo Singapore Taipei Tokyo Toronto Warsaw
and associated companies in
Berlin Ibadan

Oxford is a registered trade mark of Oxford University Press

First edition published 1964
Second edition published 1981
Third edition published 1993
Revised third edition published 1997

British Library Cataloguing in Publication Data
Data available

Library of Congress Cataloging in Publication Data
The Concise Oxford dictionary of quotations / edited by Angela
Partington.-Rev. ed.
p.   cm
Includes index.
1. Quotations.   I. Partington, Angela.
PN6080.C58   1997   082-dc21   97-15232
ISBN 0-19-280070-1

10 9 8 7 6 5

Printed in Great Britain by
Cox & Wyman Ltd
Reading, Berkshire

# FOREWORD

The *Oxford Dictionary of Quotations*, which first appeared in 1941, is now in its fourth edition, having been considerably expanded and revised in 1992. From this text the new *Concise Oxford Dictionary of Quotations* is drawn, a slimmed-down but decidedly well-toned version of its more substantial parent.

In making our selection, we have given priority to those quotations which we believe to be the best known, or, in the case of longer quotations—such as the big set pieces from Shakespeare—those parts which are the best known. In so doing, our object has been to make room for as many different quotations as possible, thereby enhancing the Dictionary's role as a key reference tool. To achieve this end, it has been necessary to trim selectively. In general, foreign language originals have been retained only for verse or where the words are known, and quoted, in their original language—'*Per ardua ad astra*', '*Plus ça change, plus c'est la même chose*'; occasionally they have been retained where the translation has proved the subject of dispute. Quotations from classical languages, inevitably, have been pruned back quite hard, as have some of the lengthier source notes which distinguish the more leisurely dimensions of the parent volume.

In their place we have inserted a handful of completely new quotations, which we felt made a case for inclusion in a genuinely contemporary work of reference—for instance 'Only the little people pay taxes', an observation which strikes a particularly mordant note in our times; and a further update on an idea originally put forward by Edmund Burke. We used to be 'economical with the truth', courtesy of Sir Robert Armstrong: now we are 'economical with the *actualité*'.

These are small considerations, however, measured against the ground swell of tradition which such a dictionary necessarily represents and reflects. Like its predecessors, the new *Concise Oxford Dictionary of Quotations* is the cumulative effort of many hands, stretching back in a long chain to that first edition of the *Oxford Dictionary of Quotations* in 1941. An acknowledgement of all those involved in the production of the parent text may be found in the 1992 edition; I should not wish to conclude, even so, without acknowledging here the extent to which this volume is indebted to them.

ANGELA PARTINGTON

*Oxford, May 1993*

# CONTENTS

Project Team

| | |
|---|---|
| Managing Editor | Freda Thornton |
| Editor | Angela Partington |
| Assistant Editor | Susan Ratcliffe |
| Research | Melinda Babcock |
| Data Capture and Validation | Helen McCurdy |
| | Patricia Moore |
| | Trish Stableford |

# PREFACE TO THE REVISED THIRD EDITION

This revised Third Edition has been brought up to date with the addition of a selection of 'Sayings of the 90s', reflecting current events and topics of interest. The appendices also take a broader approach, covering an extensive range of political and advertising slogans, with a note on their origins. 'Popular Misquotations' gathers together some of the best-known instances where popular culture has 'improved' on a remark, giving both the text as commonly quoted, and the original for comparison.

These appendices reflect and enhance the main body of quotations, as ideas and images from the earliest times to the present.

ELIZABETH KNOWLES
*Managing Editor*
*Oxford Quotations Dictionaries*

*Oxford, February 1997*

# HOW TO USE THE DICTIONARY

The sequence of entries is by alphabetical order of author, usually by surname but with occasional exceptions such as imperial or royal titles, authors known by a pseudonym ('Saki') or a nickname (Caligula). In general authors' names are given in the form by which they are best known, so we have George Eliot (not Mary Ann Evans), and T. S. Eliot (not Thomas Stearns Eliot). Collections such as Anonymous, Ballads, the Bible, the Book of Common Prayer, the Missal, and so forth, are included in the alphabetical sequence.

Within each author entry, quotations are arranged by alphabetical order of the titles of the works from which they are taken: books, plays, poems. These titles are given in italic type; titles of pieces which comprise part of a published volume or collection (e.g. essays, short stories, poems not published as volumes in their own right) are given in roman type inside inverted commas. For example, *Paradise Lost*, but 'Ode to Autumn'; often the two forms will be found together, e.g. *Cautionary Tales* (1907) 'Matilda'.

Quotations from diaries, letters, speeches, and so on are given in chronological order, and normally follow the literary or other published works quoted; in the case of political figures, for instance, speeches appear first, just as poetry quotations precede those in prose for poets, and vice versa for writers whose principal work was in prose. Quotations cited from secondary sources—biographies and other writers' works—are found towards the end of an author's entry, in alphabetical order of author, editor, or title of work (newspaper, journal, etc.). 'In' preceding a source, such as *The Times*, indicates that the quotation is cited there; where a reference reads, for instance, '*Guardian* 26 February 1972', this indicates the *origin* of the quotation.

All numbers in source references are given in arabic, with the exception of lower-case roman numerals denoting quotations from prefatory matter, whose page numbering is separate from that of the main text. The numbering itself relates to the beginning of the quotation, whether or not it runs on to another stanza or page in the original. Where possible, chapter numbers have been offered for prose works, since pagination varies from one edition to another. In very long prose works with minimal subdivisions, attempts have been made to provide page references to specified editions.

A date in brackets indicates first publication in volume form of the work cited. Unless otherwise stated, the dates thus offered are intended as chronological guides only and do not necessarily indicate the date of the text cited; where the latter is of significance, this has been stated. Where neither date of publication nor of composition is known, an approximate date (e.g. '*c*.1625') indicates the likely date of composition. Where there is a large discrepancy between date of composition (or performance) and of publication, in most cases the former only has been given (e.g. 'written 1725', 'performed 1622').

Spellings have been Anglicized and modernized except in those cases, such as ballads, where this would have been inappropriate; capitalization has been retained only for personifications; with rare exceptions, verse has been aligned with the left hand margin. Italic type has been used for all foreign-language originals.

## The Index

Both the keywords and the entries following each keyword, including those in foreign languages, are in strict alphabetical order. Singular and plural nouns (with their possessive forms) are grouped separately: for 'some old lover's ghost' see 'lover'; for 'at lovers' perjuries' see 'lovers'. Variant forms of common words (honey/hunny, luve/love) are grouped under a single heading: 'honey', 'love'.

The references show the author's name, usually in abbreviated form (SHAK/Shakespeare), followed by the page number and the number of the quotation on that page: 183:15 therefore means quotation 15 on page 183.

# Quotations

## Dannie Abse 1923–

1 I know the colour rose, and it is lovely,
But not when it ripens in a tumour;
And healing greens, leaves and grass, so
   springlike,
In limbs that fester are not springlike.
  'Pathology of Colours' (1968)

## Accius 170–c.86 BC

2 *Oderint, dum metuant.*
Let them hate, so long as they fear.
  From *Atreus*, in Seneca *Dialogues* bks. 3–5 *De
  Ira* bk. 1, sect. 20, subsect. 4

## Dean Acheson 1893–1971

3 Great Britain has lost an empire and has
not yet found a role.
  Speech at the Military Academy, West Point,
  5 December 1962, in *Vital Speeches* 1 January
  1963, p. 163

4 A memorandum is written not to inform
the reader but to protect the writer.
  In *Wall Street Journal* 8 September 1977

## Lord Acton 1834–1902

5 Power tends to corrupt and absolute power
corrupts absolutely.
  Letter to Bishop Mandell Creighton, 3 April
  1887, in L. Creighton *Life and Letters of
  Mandell Creighton* (1904) vol. 1, ch. 13.
  Cf. 249:4

## Giuseppe Adami 1878–1946 and Renato Simoni 1875–1952

6 *Nessun dorma.*
None shall sleep.
  *Turandot* (1926 opera, music by Puccini) *ad
  fin.* (after Gozzi's drama, 1762)

## Abigail Adams 1744–1818

7 These are times in which a genius would
wish to live. It is not in the still calm of
life, or the repose of a pacific station, that
great characters are formed ... Great
necessities call out great virtues.
  Letter to John Quincy Adams, 19 January
  1780, in Butterfield et al. (eds.) *The Book of
  Abigail and John Adams* (1975) p. 253

## Charles Francis Adams 1807–86

8 It would be superfluous in me to point out
to your lordship that this is war.
  Dispatch to Earl Russell, 5 September 1863,
  in C. F. Adams *Charles Francis Adams* (1900)
  ch. 17

## Douglas Adams 1952–

9 The Answer to the Great Question Of ...
Life, the Universe and Everything ... [is]
Forty-two.
  *The Hitch Hiker's Guide to the Galaxy* (1979)
  ch. 27

## Franklin P. Adams 1881–1960

10 Elections are won by men and women
chiefly because most people vote against
somebody rather than for somebody.
  *Nods and Becks* (1944) p. 206. Cf. 139:18

## Henry Brooks Adams 1838–1918

11 Politics ... has always been the systematic
organization of hatreds.
  *Education of Henry Adams* (1907) ch. 1

12 Accident counts for much in
companionship as in marriage.
  *Education of Henry Adams* (1907) ch. 4.
  Cf. 336:16

13 All experience is an arch to build upon.
  *Education of Henry Adams* (1907) ch. 6

14 A friend in power is a friend lost.
  *Education of Henry Adams* (1907) ch. 7

15 Chaos often breeds life, when order breeds
habit.
  *The Education of Henry Adams* (1907) ch. 16

16 A teacher affects eternity; he can never tell
where his influence stops.
  *The Education of Henry Adams* (1907) ch. 20

17 They know enough who know how to
learn.
  *The Education of Henry Adams* (1907) ch. 21

18 Morality is a private and costly luxury.
  *The Education of Henry Adams* (1907) ch. 22

19 Practical politics consists in ignoring facts.
  *The Education of Henry Adams* (1907) ch. 22

20 Nothing in education is so astonishing as
the amount of ignorance it accumulates in
the form of inert facts.
  *The Education of Henry Adams* (1907) ch. 25

21 No one means all he says, and yet very few
say all they mean, for words are slippery
and thought is viscous.
  *The Education of Henry Adams* (1907) ch. 31

## John Adams 1735–1826

22 A government of laws, and not of men.
  *Boston Gazette* (1774) no. 7, 'Novanglus' papers

23 In politics the middle way is none at all.
  Letter to Horatio Gates, 23 March 1776, in R.
  J. Taylor (ed.) *Papers of John Adams* 3rd series
  (1979) vol. 4

**1** The happiness of society is the end of government.
*Thoughts on Government* (1776)

**2** Fear is the foundation of most governments.
*Thoughts on Government* (1776)

**3** You and I ought not to die before we have explained ourselves to each other.
Letter to Thomas Jefferson, 15 July 1813, in L. J. Cappon (ed.) *The Adams–Jefferson Letters* (1959) vol. 2

## John Quincy Adams 1767–1848

**4** Think of your forefathers! Think of your posterity!
*Oration at Plymouth* 22 December 1802, p. 6

**5** *Fiat justitia, pereat coelum* [Let justice be done, though heaven fall]. My toast would be, may our country be always successful, but whether successful or otherwise, always right.
Letter to John Adams, 1 August 1816, in A. Koch and W. Peden (eds.) *Selected Writings of John and John Quincy Adams* (1946) p. 288. Cf. 115:10, 138:24

## Samuel Adams 1722–1803

**6** What a glorious morning is this.
On hearing gunfire at Lexington, 19 April 1775; in J. K. Hosmer *Samuel Adams* (1886) ch. 19 (traditionally quoted 'What a glorious morning for America')

**7** A nation of shop-keepers are very seldom so disinterested.
*Oration in Philadelphia* 1 August 1776 (of doubtful authenticity). Cf. 237:7, 308:23

## Sarah Flower Adams 1805–48

**8** Nearer, my God, to thee.
Title of hymn (1841)

## Harold Adamson 1906–80

**9** Comin' in on a wing and a pray'r.
Title of song (1943)

## Joseph Addison 1672–1719

**10** He more had pleased us, had he pleased us less.
*An Account of the Greatest English Poets* (1694); of Cowley

**11** And, pleased th' Almighty's orders to perform,
Rides in the whirl-wind, and directs the storm.
*The Campaign* (1705) l. 291

**12** And those who paint 'em truest praise 'em most.
*The Campaign* (1705) l. 476

**13** 'Tis not in mortals to command success,
But we'll do more, Sempronius; we'll deserve it.
*Cato* (1713) act 1, sc. 2, l. 43

**14** The pale, unripened beauties of the north.
*Cato* (1713) act 1, sc. 4, l. 134

**15** The woman that deliberates is lost.
*Cato* (1713) act 4, sc. 1, l. 31

**16**                      What pity is it
That we can die but once to serve our country!
*Cato* (1713) act 4, sc. 1, l. 258

**17** Content thyself to be obscurely good.
When vice prevails, and impious men bear sway,
The post of honour is a private station.
*Cato* (1713) act 4, sc. 1, l. 319

**18** Eternity! thou pleasing, dreadful thought!
*Cato* (1713) act 5, sc. 1, l. 10

**19** From hence, let fierce contending nations know
What dire effects from civil discord flow.
*Cato* (1713) act 5, sc. 1 *ad fin.*

**20** There is nothing more requisite in business than dispatch.
*The Drummer* (1716) act 5, sc. 1

**21** A painted meadow, or a purling stream.
*Letter from Italy* (1704)

**22** In all thy humours, whether grave or mellow,
Thou'rt such a touchy, testy, pleasant fellow;
Hast so much wit, and mirth, and spleen about thee,
There is no living with thee, nor without thee.
*The Spectator* no. 68 (18 May 1711). Cf. 220:7

**23** I have often thought, says Sir Roger, it happens very well that Christmas should fall out in the Middle of Winter.
*The Spectator* no. 269 (8 January 1712)

**24** Mirth is like a flash of lightning that breaks through a gloom of clouds, and glitters for a moment: cheerfulness keeps up a kind of day-light in the mind.
*The Spectator* no. 381 (17 May 1712)

**25** The spacious firmament on high,
With all the blue ethereal sky,
And spangled heavens, a shining frame,
Their great Original proclaim.
*The Spectator* no. 465 (23 August 1712) 'Ode'

**26** In Reason's ear they all rejoice,
And utter forth a glorious voice,
For ever singing, as they shine:
'The hand that made us is divine.'
*The Spectator* no. 465 (23 August 1712) 'Ode'

**27** If we may believe our logicians, man is distinguished from all other creatures by the faculty of laughter.
*The Spectator* no. 494 (26 September 1712)

**28** 'We are always doing,' says he, 'something for Posterity, but I would fain see Posterity do something for us.'
*The Spectator* no. 583 (20 August 1714)

### George Ade 1866–1944

1 It is no time for mirth and laughter,
The cold, grey dawn of the morning after.
*The Sultan of Sulu* (1903) act 2, p. 63

### Alfred Adler 1870–1937

2 The truth is often a terrible weapon of
aggression. It is possible to lie, and even to
murder, for the truth.
*The Problems of Neurosis* (1929) ch. 2

### Polly Adler 1900–62

3 A house is not a home.
Title of book (1954)

### Æ (George William Russell) 1867–1935

4 In ancient shadows and twilights
Where childhood had strayed,
The world's great sorrows were born
And its heroes were made.
In the lost boyhood of Judas
Christ was betrayed.
'Germinal' (1931)

### Herbert Agar 1897–1980

5 The truth which makes men free is for the
most part the truth which men prefer not
to hear.
*A Time for Greatness* (1942) ch. 7

### James Agate 1877–1947

6 My mind is not a bed to be made and
re-made.
*Ego 6* (1944) 9 June 1943

### Agathon b. *c*.445 BC

7 Even a god cannot change the past.
In Aristotle *Nicomachaean Ethics* bk. 6, 1139b
(literally 'The one thing which even a god
cannot do is to make undone what has been
done')

### Alfred Ainger 1837–1904

8 No flowers, by request.
Summarizing the principle of conciseness
for contributors to the *Dictionary of National
Biography*; in *Supplement 1901–1911* (1912)
p. 27

### Arthur Campbell Ainger 1841–1919

9 God is working his purpose out as year
succeeds to year;
God is working his purpose out and the
time is drawing near;
Nearer and nearer draws the time, the
time that shall surely be,
When the earth shall be filled with the
glory of God as the waters cover the sea.
'God is working his purpose out' (1894
hymn)

### Max Aitken

*See* LORD BEAVERBROOK

### Zoë Akins 1886–1958

10 The Greeks had a word for it.
Title of play (1930)

### Alain (Émile-Auguste Chartier) 1868–1951

11 Nothing is more dangerous than an idea,
when you have only one idea.
*Propos sur la religion* (1938) no. 74

### Edward Albee 1928–

12 Who's afraid of Virginia Woolf?
Title of play (1962)

### Scipione Alberti

13 *I pensieri stretti ed il viso sciolto* [Secret
thoughts and open countenance] will go
safely over the whole world.
On being asked how to behave in Rome; in
letter from Sir Henry Wotton to Milton,
13 April 1638; prefixed to Milton's *Comus* in
*Poems* (1645 ed.)

### Alcuin *c*.735–804

14 *Nec audiendi qui solent dicere, Vox populi, vox
Dei, quum tumultuositas vulgi semper insaniae
proxima sit.*
And those people should not be listened to
who keep saying the voice of the people is
the voice of God, since the riotousness of
the crowd is always very close to madness.
*Works* (1863) vol. 1, Letter 164

### Richard Aldington 1892–1962

15 Patriotism is a lively sense of collective
responsibility. Nationalism is a silly cock
crowing on its own dunghill.
*The Colonel's Daughter* (1931) pt. 1, ch. 6

### Brian Aldiss 1925–

16 Keep violence in the mind
Where it belongs.
*Barefoot in the Head* (1969) 'Charteris' *ad fin.*

### Thomas Bailey Aldrich 1836–1907

17 The fair, frail palaces,
The fading alps and archipelagoes,
And great cloud-continents of sunset-seas.
'Miracles' (1874)

### Buzz Aldrin 1930–

18 Houston, Tranquillity Base here. The Eagle
has landed.
In *The Times* 21 July 1969, p. 1

## Alexander the Great 356–323 BC

1 If I were not Alexander, I would be Diogenes.
In Plutarch *Parallel Lives* 'Alexander' ch. 14, sect. 3

## Cecil Frances Alexander 1818–95

2 All things bright and beautiful,
All creatures great and small,
All things wise and wonderful,
The Lord God made them all.
'All Things Bright and Beautiful' (1848)

3 The rich man in his castle,
The poor man at his gate,
God made them, high or lowly,
And ordered their estate.
'All Things Bright and Beautiful' (1848)

4 Once in royal David's city
Stood a lowly cattle-shed,
Where a mother laid her baby
In a manger for his bed.
'Once in royal David's city' (1848)

5 I bind unto myself to-day
The strong name of the Trinity,
By invocation of the same
The Three in One and One in Three.
Translation of 'St Patrick's Breastplate' (1889)

6 There is a green hill far away,
Without a city wall,
Where the dear Lord was crucified,
Who died to save us all.
'There is a green hill far away' (1848)

## Sir William Alexander, Earl of Stirling c.1567–1640

7 The weaker sex, to piety more prone.
'Doomsday' 5th Hour (1637)

## Alfonso 'the Wise', King of Castile 1221–84

8 Had I been present at the Creation, I would have given some useful hints for the better ordering of the universe.
On studying the Ptolemaic system (attributed)

## Nelson Algren 1909–

9 A walk on the wild side.
Title of novel (1956)

## Muhammad Ali (Cassius Clay) 1942–

10 Float like a butterfly, sting like a bee.
Summary of his boxing strategy, in G. Sullivan *Cassius Clay Story* (1964) ch. 8 (probably originated by Drew 'Bundini' Brown)

## Abbé d'Allainval 1700–53

11 *L'embarras des richesses.*
The embarrassment of riches.
Title of comedy (1726)

## Fred Allen 1894–1956

12 Committee—a group of men who individually can do nothing but as a group decide that nothing can be done.
Attributed

## Woody Allen 1935–

13 [Sex] was the most fun I ever had without laughing.
*Annie Hall* (1977 film, with Marshall Brickman)

14 Don't knock masturbation. It's sex with someone I love.
*Annie Hall* (1977 film, with Marshall Brickman)

15 Is sex dirty? Only if it's done right.
*Everything You Always Wanted to Know about Sex* (1972 film)

16 It's not that I'm afraid to die. I just don't want to be there when it happens.
*Death* (1975) p. 63

17 On bisexuality: It immediately doubles your chances for a date on Saturday night.
*New York Times* 1 December 1975, p. 33

## William Allingham 1824–89

18 Up the airy mountain,
Down the rushy glen,
We daren't go a-hunting,
For fear of little men.
'The Fairies' (1850)

## St Ambrose c.339–97

19 *Ubi Petrus, ibi ergo ecclesia.*
Where Peter is, there must be the Church.
'Explanatio psalmi 40' in *Corpus Scriptorum Ecclesiasticorum Latinorum* (1919) vol. 64

20 When I go to Rome, I fast on Saturday, but here [Milan] I do not. Do you also follow the custom of whatever church you attend, if you do not want to give or receive scandal.
In *St Augustine: Letters* vol. 1 (tr. Sister W. Parsons, 1951) 'Letter 54 to Januarius' (AD c.400); usually quoted 'When in Rome, do as the Romans do'

## Leo Amery 1873–1955

21 Speak for England.
To Arthur Greenwood in the House of Commons, 2 September 1939; *My Political Life* (1955) vol. 3, p. 324

## Fisher Ames 1758–1808

22 A monarchy is a merchantman which sails well, but will sometimes strike on a rock, and go to the bottom; whilst a republic is a raft which would never sink, but then your feet are always in the water.
Attributed to Ames, speaking in the House of Representatives, 1795, and quoted by R. W. Emerson in *Essays* (2nd series, 1844) no. 7

## Kingsley Amis 1922–95

1 The delusion that there are thousands of
young people about who are capable of
benefiting from university training, but
have somehow failed to find their way
there, is ... a necessary component of the
expansionist case ... More will mean
worse.
   *Encounter* July 1960

2 His mouth had been used as a latrine by
some small creature of the night, and then
as its mausoleum.
   *Lucky Jim* (1953) ch. 6

3 Alun's life was coming to consist more and
more exclusively of being told at dictation
speed what he knew.
   *The Old Devils* (1986) ch. 7

4 Outside every fat man there was an even
fatter man trying to close in.
   *One Fat Englishman* (1963) ch. 3. Cf. 106:28,
   241:25

5 Should poets bicycle-pump the human
heart
Or squash it flat?
Man's love is of man's life a thing apart;
Girls aren't like that.
   'A Bookshop Idyll' (1956). Cf. 86:4

6 Women are really much nicer than men:
No wonder we like them.
   'A Bookshop Idyll' (1956)

7 Death has got something to be said for it:
There's no need to get out of bed for it.
   'Delivery Guaranteed' (1979)

8 The women of that ever-fresh terrain,
The night after tonight.
   'A Dream of Fair Women' (1956)

## Anacharsis 6th century BC

9 Written laws are like spider's webs; they
will catch, it is true, the weak and poor,
but would be torn in pieces by the rich and
powerful.
   Plutarch *Parallel Lives* 'Solon' bk. 5, sect. 2.
   Cf. 319:19

## Anatolius 8th century

10 Fierce was the wild billow,
Dark was the night;
Oars laboured heavily,
Foam glimmered white;
Trembled the mariners,
Peril was nigh:
Then said the God of God,
'Peace! it is I.'
   'Fierce was the wild billow' (tr. J. M. Neale,
   1862)

## Hans Christian Andersen 1805–75

11 'But the Emperor has nothing on at all!'
cried a little child.
   *Danish Fairy Legends and Tales* (1846) 'The
   Emperor's New Clothes'

## Maxwell Anderson 1888–1959

12 But it's a long, long while
From May to December;
And the days grow short
When you reach September.
   'September Song' (1938 song)

## Maxwell Anderson 1888–1959 and Lawrence Stallings 1894–1968

13 What price glory?
   Title of play (1924)

## Robert Anderson 1917–

14 Tea and sympathy.
   Title of play (1957)

## Bishop Lancelot Andrewes 1555–1626

15 It was no summer progress. A cold coming
they had of it, at this time of the year; just,
the worst time of the year, to take a
journey, and specially a long journey, in.
The ways deep, the weather sharp, the days
short, the sun farthest off *in solstitio
brumali*, the very dead of Winter.
   *Of the Nativity* (1622) Sermon 15. Cf. 133:21

16 The nearer the Church the further from
God.
   *Of the Nativity* (1622) Sermon 15

## Sir Norman Angell 1872–1967

17 The great illusion.
   Title of book (1910) on the futility of war

## Anonymous
### English

18 An abomination unto the Lord, but a very
present help in time of trouble.
   Definition of a lie, an amalgamation of
   Proverbs 12.22 and Psalms 46.1, often
   attributed to Adlai Stevenson

19 Adam
Had 'em.
   On the antiquity of microbes (claimed to be
   the shortest poem)

20 All human beings are born free and equal
in dignity and rights.
   *Universal Declaration of Human Rights* (1948)
   article 1

21 All present and correct.
   *King's Regulations (Army)* Report of the
   Orderly Sergeant to the Officer of the Day

22 All this buttoning and unbuttoning.
   18th-century suicide note

23 The almighty dollar is the only object of
worship.
   *Philadelphia Public Ledger* 2 December 1836

1 Along the electric wire the message came:
He is not better—he is much the same.
> Parodic poem on the illness of the Prince of
> Wales, later King Edward VII, in F. H. Gribble
> *Romance of the Cambridge Colleges* (1913) p. 226;
> sometimes attributed to Alfred Austin
> (1835–1913)

2 Any officer who shall behave in a
scandalous manner, unbecoming the
character of an officer and a gentleman
shall ... be CASHIERED.
> *Articles of War* (1872) 'Disgraceful Conduct'
> Article 79; 'conduct unbecoming the
> character of an Officer' in Naval Discipline
> Act, 10 August 1860, Article 24

3 Appeal from Philip drunk to Philip sober.
> Traditional summary of the words of an
> unidentified woman in Valerius Maximus
> *Facta ac Dicta Memorabilia* (AD *c.*32) bk. 6, ch. 2

4 Are we downhearted? No!
> Expression much taken up by British
> soldiers during the First World War.
> Cf. 93:24

5 A-roving! A-roving!
Since roving's been my ru-i-n
I'll go no more a-roving
With you fair maid.
> 'A-roving' (traditional song)

6 A was an apple-pie;
B bit it;
C cut it.
> In J. Eachard *Some Observations* (1671) p. 140

7 A bayonet is a weapon with a worker at
each end.
> British pacifist slogan (1940)

8 A beast, but a just beast.
> Describing Dr Temple, Headmaster of Rugby
> School. See F. E. Kitchener *Rugby Memoir of
> Archbishop Temple 1857–1869* (1907) ch. 3

9 Be happy while y'er leevin,
For y'er a lang time deid.
> Scottish motto for a house. See *Notes and
> Queries* 9th series, vol. 8, 7 December 1901,
> p. 469

10 Between a rock and a hard place.
> Meaning to be in difficulty without a
> satisfactory alternative. See *Dialect Notes*
> (1921) no. 5, p. 113

11 Bigamy is having one husband too many.
Monogamy is the same.
> In Erica Jong *Fear of Flying* (1973) ch. 1
> (epigraph)

12 A bigger bang for a buck.
> Charles E. Wilson's defence policy, in
> *Newsweek* 22 March 1954

13 Black is beautiful.
> Slogan of American civil rights campaigners,
> mid-1960s

14 Burn, baby, burn.
> Black extremist slogan; Los Angeles riots,
> August 1965

15 Careless talk costs lives.
> Second World War security slogan

16 The cloud of unknowing.
> Title of mystical prose work (14th century)

17 Collapse of Stout Party.
> Standard dénouement in Victorian humour.
> See R. Pearsall *Collapse of Stout Party* (1975)
> introduction

18 For to-night we'll merry be,
To-morrow we'll be sober.
> 'Come, Landlord, Fill the Flowing Bowl'
> (traditional song)

19 Come lasses and lads, get leave of your
dads,
And away to the Maypole hie,
For every he has got him a she,
And the fiddler's standing by.
> 'Come Lasses and Lads' (traditional song,
> *c.*1670)

20 A committee is a group of the unwilling,
chosen from the unfit, to do the
unnecessary.
> Various attributions (origin unknown)

21 A Company for carrying on an undertaking
of Great Advantage, but no one to know
what it is.
> The South Sea Company Prospectus (1711);
> in V. Cowles *The Great Swindle* (1963) ch. 5

22 Conduct ... to the prejudice of good order
and military discipline.
> *Army Discipline and Regulation Act* (1879)
> Section 40

23 Coughs and sneezes spread diseases. Trap
the germs in your handkerchief.
> Second World War health slogan (1942)

24 Crisis? What Crisis?
> *Sun* headline, 11 January 1979, summarizing
> James Callaghan: 'I don't think other people
> in the world would share the view [that]
> there is mounting chaos'

25 [Death is] nature's way of telling you to
slow down.
> Life insurance proverb; in *Newsweek* 25 April
> 1960, p. 70

26 Do not fold, spindle or mutilate.
> Instruction on punched cards (1950s, and in
> differing forms from the 1930s)

27 Early one morning, just as the sun was
rising,
I heard a maid sing in the valley below:
'Oh, don't deceive me; Oh, never leave me!
How could you use a poor maiden so?'
> 'Early One Morning' (traditional song)

28 Earned a precarious living by taking in one
another's washing.
> Attributed to Mark Twain by William Morris,
> in *The Commonweal* 6 August 1887

29 The eternal triangle.
> Book review title, in *Daily Chronicle*
> 5 December 1907

30 Every country has its own constitution;
ours is absolutism moderated by
assassination.
> 'An intelligent Russian' quoted in *Political
> Sketches of the State of Europe, 1814–1867* (1868)
> p. 19

1 Everyman, I will go with thee, and be thy guide,
In thy most need to go by thy side.
   *Everyman* (c.1509–19) l. 522 (spoken by Knowledge)

2 Every picture tells a story.
   Advertisement for Doan's Backache Kidney Pills (early 1900s)

3 Expletive deleted.
   *Submission of Recorded Presidential Conversations ... by President Richard M. Nixon* 30 April 1974, appendix 1, p. 2

4 Exterminate ... the treacherous English, walk over General French's contemptible little army.
   Annexe to British Expeditionary Force Routine Orders, 24 September 1914 (allegedly quoting Kaiser Wilhelm II but probably fabricated by the British); in A. Ponsonby *Falsehood in Wartime* (1928) ch. 10

5 Faster than a speeding bullet! ... Look! Up in the sky! It's a bird! It's a plane! It's Superman! Yes, it's Superman! ... who—disguised as Clark Kent, mild-mannered reporter for a great metropolitan newspaper—fights a never ending battle for truth, justice and the American way!
   *Superman* (US radio show, 1940 onwards) preamble

6 Frankie and Albert were lovers, O Lordy, how they could love.
Swore to be true to each other, true as the stars above;
He was her man, but he done her wrong.
   'Frankie and Albert', in J. Huston *Frankie and Johnny* (1930) p. 95 (later better known as 'Frankie and Johnny')

7 From ghoulies and ghosties and long-leggety beasties
And things that go bump in the night,
Good Lord, deliver us!
   'The Cornish or West Country Litany', in F. T. Nettleingham *Polperro Proverbs and Others* (1926) 'Pokerwork Panels'

8 From shirtsleeves to shirtsleeves in three generations.
   In N. M. Butler *True and False Democracy* (1907) ch. 2 (often attributed to Andrew Carnegie)

9 A gentleman haranguing on the perfection of our law, and that it was equally open to the poor and the rich, was answered by another, 'So is the London Tavern'.
   *Tom Paine's Jests* (1794) no. 23; also attributed to John Horne Tooke (1736–1812) in W. Hazlitt *The Spirit of the Age* (1825) 'Mr Horne Tooke'. Cf. 222:7

10 Give me a child for the first seven years, and you may do what you like with him afterwards.
   Attributed as a Jesuit maxim, in *Lean's Collectanea* vol. 3 (1903) p. 472

11 God be in my head,
And in my understanding;
God be in my eyes,
And in my looking;
God be in my mouth,
And in my speaking;
God be in my heart,
And in my thinking;
God be at my end,
And at my departing.
   *Sarum Missal* (11th century)

12 God gave Noah the rainbow sign,
No more water, the fire next time.
   *Home in that Rock* (Negro spiritual)

13 God save our gracious king!
Long live our noble king!
God save the king!
   'God save the King', attributed to various authors, including Henry Carey (c.1687–1743). See P. Scholes *God save the King* (1942). Cf. 170:7

14 Confound their politics,
Frustrate their knavish tricks.
   'God save the King'

15 Greensleeves was all my joy,
Greensleeves was my delight,
Greensleeves was my heart of gold,
And who but Lady Greensleeves?
   'A new Courtly Sonnet of the Lady Greensleeves', in *A Handful of Pleasant Delights* (1584)

16 Happy is that city which in time of peace thinks of war.
   Inscription found in the armoury of Venice, in Robert Burton *Anatomy of Melancholy* (1621–51) pt. 2, sect. 3, member 6. Cf. 337:18

17 Here lies a poor woman who always was tired,
For she lived in a place where help wasn't hired.
Her last words on earth were, Dear friends I am going
Where washing ain't done nor sweeping nor sewing,
And everything there is exact to my wishes,
For there they don't eat and there's no washing of dishes ...
Don't mourn for me now, don't mourn for me never,
For I'm going to do nothing for ever and ever.
   Epitaph in Bushey churchyard, before 1860; destroyed by 1916

18 Here's tae us; wha's like us?
Gey few, and they're a' deid.
   Scottish toast (probably 19th-century)

19 Hierusalem, my happy home
When shall I come to thee?
When shall my sorrows have an end,
Thy joys when shall I see?
   'Hierusalem' (c.1600 hymn)

**1** How different, how very different from the home life of our own dear Queen!

Overheard at a performance by Sarah Bernhardt in the role of Cleopatra, in I. S. Cobb *A Laugh a Day* (1924)

**2** I don't like the family Stein!
There is Gert, there is Ep, there is Ein.
Gert's writings are punk,
Ep's statues are junk,
Nor can anyone understand Ein.

1920s rhyme, in R. Graves and A. Hodge *The Long Weekend* (1940) ch. 12

**3** I feel no pain dear mother now
But oh, I am so dry!
O take me to a brewery
And leave me there to die.

Parody of 'The Collier's Dying Child'. Cf. 138:13

**4** If it moves, salute it; if it doesn't move, pick it up; and if you can't pick it up, paint it.

1940s saying, in P. Dickson *The Official Rules* (1978) p. 21

**5** I'll hang my harp on a weeping willow-tree,
And may the world go well with thee.

'There is a Tavern in the Town' (traditional song)

**6** I'll sing you twelve O.
*Green grow the rushes O.*
What is your twelve O?
Twelve for the twelve apostles,
Eleven for the eleven who went to heaven,
Ten for the ten commandments,
Nine for the nine bright shiners,
Eight for the eight bold rangers,
Seven for the seven stars in the sky,
Six for the six proud walkers,
Five for the symbol at your door,
Four for the Gospel makers,
Three for the rivals,
Two, two, the lily-white boys,
Clothed all in green O,
One is one and all alone
And ever more shall be so.

'The Dilly Song'

**7** I'm armed with more than complete steel—The justice of my quarrel.

*Lust's Dominion* (1657) act 4, sc. 3 (attributed to Marlowe, though of doubtful authorship)

**8** I married my husband for life, not for lunch.

Origin unknown

**9** I met wid Napper Tandy, and he took me by the hand,
And he said, 'How's poor ould Ireland, and how does she stand?'
She's the most disthressful country that iver yet was seen,
For they're hangin' men an' women for the wearin' o' the Green.

'The Wearin' o' the Green' (*c.*1795 ballad)

**10** It became necessary to destroy the town to save it.

Statement issued by US Army, referring to Ben Tre in Vietnam; in *New York Times* 8 February 1968

**11** It'll play in Peoria.

Catch-phrase of the Nixon administration (early 1970s) meaning 'it will be acceptable to middle America', but originating in a standard music hall joke of the 1930s

**12** It's that man again ... ! At the head of a cavalcade of seven black motor cars Hitler swept out of his Berlin Chancellery last night on a mystery journey.

Headline in *Daily Express* 2 May 1939; the acronym ITMA became the title of a BBC radio show, from September 1939

**13** Jacques Brel is alive and well and living in Paris.

Title of musical entertainment (1968–72) which triggered numerous imitations

**14** John Brown's body lies a mould'ring in the grave,
His soul is marching on.

Song (1861), variously attributed to Charles Sprague Hall, Henry Howard Brownell, Thomas Brigham Bishop, and inspired by the hanging of John Brown, an abolitionist, on 2 December 1859

**15** Just when you thought it was safe to go back in the water.

*Jaws 2* (1978 film) advertising copy

**16** The King over the Water.

Jacobite toast (18th century)

**17** King's Moll Reno'd in Wolsey's Home Town.

US newspaper headline on Wallis Simpson's divorce proceedings in Ipswich; in F. Donaldson *Edward VIII* (1974) ch. 7

**18** Let's get out of these wet clothes and into a dry Martini.

Line coined in the 1920s by Robert Benchley's press agent and adopted by Mae West in *Every Day's a Holiday* (1937 film)

**19** Liberty is always unfinished business.

Title of 36th Annual Report of the American Civil Liberties Union, 1 July 1955–30 June 1956

**20** Life is a sexually transmitted disease.

Graffito found on the London Underground, in D. J. Enright (ed.) *Faber Book of Fevers and Frets* (1989) p. 345

**21** Little Englanders.

*Westminster Gazette* 1 August 1895, p. 2 (describing persons opposed to imperialism)

**22** Lizzie Borden took an axe
And gave her mother forty whacks;
When she saw what she had done
She gave her father forty-one!

Popular rhyme in circulation after the acquittal of Lizzie Borden, in June 1893, from the charge of murdering her father and stepmother

1 Lloyd George knew my father,
My father knew Lloyd George.

> Sung to the tune of 'Onward, Christian
> Soldiers'; possibly by Tommy Rhys Roberts
> (1910–75)

2 London, thou art the flower of cities all!
Gemme of all joy, jasper of jocunditie.

> 'London' (unknown authorship, previously
> attributed to William Dunbar, c.1465–c.1530)
> l. 16

3 Lousy but loyal.

> East End (London) slogan at George V's
> Jubilee (1935)

4 Love me little, love me long,
Is the burden of my song.

> 'Love me little, love me long' (1569–70)

5 Mademoiselle from Armenteers,
Hasn't been kissed for forty years,
Hinky, dinky, parley-voo.

> Song of the First World War, variously
> attributed to Edward Rowland and to Harry
> Carlton

6 CHILD: Mamma, are Tories born wicked, or
do they grow wicked afterwards?
MOTHER: They are born wicked, and grow
worse.

> In G. W. E. Russell *Collections and Recollections*
> (1898) ch. 10

7 The man you love to hate.

> Billing for Erich von Stroheim in the film *The
> Heart of Humanity* (1918)

8 Matthew, Mark, Luke, and John,
The bed be blest that I lie on.
Four angels to my bed,
Four angels round my head,
One to watch, and one to pray,
And two to bear my soul away.

> Traditional (the first two lines in Thomas
> Ady *A Candle in the Dark*, 1656)

9 The ministry of all the talents.

> Name given ironically to William Grenville's
> coalition of 1806 in G. W. Cooke *The History
> of Party* (1837) vol. 3, p. 460

10 Miss Buss and Miss Beale
Cupid's darts do not feel.
How different from us,
Miss Beale and Miss Buss.

> Of the Headmistress of the North London
> Collegiate School and the Principal of the
> Ladies' College, Cheltenham (c.1884)

11 Multiplication is vexation,
Division is as bad;
The Rule of Three doth puzzle me,
And Practice drives me mad.

> In *Lean's Collectanea* vol. 4 (1904) p. 53
> (possibly 16th century)

12 My name is George Nathaniel Curzon,
I am a most superior person.

> *The Masque of Balliol* (c.1870), in W. G. Hiscock
> *The Balliol Rhymes* (1939) p. 19. Cf. 32:6,
> 314:1

13 The nature of God is a circle of which the
centre is everywhere and the
circumference is nowhere.

> Said to have been traced to a lost treatise of
> Empedocles; quoted in the *Roman de la Rose*,
> and by St Bonaventura in *Itinerarius Mentis in
> Deum* ch. 5 *ad fin.*

14 The nearest thing to death in life
Is David Patrick Maxwell Fyfe,
Though underneath that gloomy shell
He does himself extremely well.

> In E. Grierson *Confessions of a Country
> Magistrate* (1972) p. 35 (current on the
> Northern circuit in the late 1930s)

15 *Nil carborundum illegitimi.*

> Cod Latin for 'Don't let the bastards grind
> you down', in circulation during the Second
> World War, though possibly of earlier
> origin; often quoted 'nil carborundum' or
> 'illegitimi non carborundum'

16 The noise, my dear! And the people!

> Of the retreat from Dunkirk, May 1940. See
> A. Rhodes *Sword of Bone* (1942) ch. 22 *ad fin.*

17 No more Latin, no more French,
No more sitting on a hard board bench.
No more beetles in my tea
Making googly eyes at me;
No more spiders in my bath
Trying hard to make me laugh.

> Children's rhyme for the end of school term,
> in Iona and Peter Opie *Lore and Language of
> Schoolchildren* (1959) ch. 13 (variants include
> 'No more Latin, no more Greek, / No more
> cares to make me squeak')

18 Nostalgia isn't what it used to be.

> Graffito (taken as title of book by Simone
> Signoret, 1978)

19 Not so much a programme, more a way of
life!

> Title of BBC television series, 1964

20 Now I lay me down to sleep;
I pray the Lord my soul to keep.
If I should die before I wake,
I pray the Lord my soul to take.

> First printed in a late edition of the *New
> England Primer* (1781)

21 O Death, where is thy sting-a-ling-a-ling,
O grave, thy victory?
The bells of Hell go ting-a-ling-a-ling
For you but not for me.

> 'For You But Not For Me', in S. Louis Guiraud
> (ed.) *Songs That Won the War* (1930).
> Cf. 55:22

22 O God, if there be a God, save my soul, if I
have a soul!

> Prayer of a common soldier before the battle
> of Blenheim (1704); in *Notes and Queries*
> vol. 173, no. 15 (9 October 1937) p. 264

23 Once again we stop the mighty roar of
London's traffic.

> *In Town Tonight* (BBC radio series, 1933–60)
> preamble

1 One Cartwright brought a Slave from
Russia, and would scourge him, for which
he was questioned: and it was resolved,
That England was too pure an Air for
Slaves to breathe in.
> 'In the 11th of Elizabeth' (1568–9); in J.
> Rushworth *Historical Collections* (1680–1722)
> vol. 2, p. 468. Cf. 110:7

2 O ye'll tak' the high road, and I'll tak' the
low road,
And I'll be in Scotland afore ye,
But me and my true love will never meet
again,
On the bonnie, bonnie banks o' Loch
Lomon'.
> 'The Bonnie Banks of Loch Lomon'
> (traditional song)

3 A place within the meaning of the Act.
> Usually taken to be a reference to the
> Betting Act 1853, sect. 2, which banned off-
> course betting on horse-races

4 Please do not shoot the pianist. He is doing
his best.
> Printed notice in a dancing saloon, in Oscar
> Wilde *Impressions of America* 'Leadville'
> (c.1882–3)

5 Please to remember the Fifth of November,
Gunpowder Treason and Plot.
> Traditional rhyme (1605)

6 Power to the people.
> Slogan of the Black Panther movement, from
> c.1968

7 The [or A] quick brown fox jumps over the
lazy dog.
> Used by keyboarders to ensure that all
> letters of the alphabet are functioning. See
> R. H. Templeton Jr. *The Quick Brown Fox* (1945)
> introduction

8 The rabbit has a charming face:
Its private life is a disgrace.
I really dare not name to you
The awful things that rabbits do.
> 'The Rabbit', in *The Week-End Book* (1925)
> p. 171

9 See the happy moron,
He doesn't give a damn,
I wish I were a moron,
My God! perhaps I am!
> *Eugenics Review* July 1929

10 Seven wealthy towns contend for HOMER
dead
Through which the living HOMER begged
his bread.
> Epilogue to *Aesop at Tunbridge* By No Person
> of Quality (1698). Cf. 168:9

11 She was poor but she was honest
Victim of a rich man's game.
First he loved her, then he left her,
And she lost her maiden name ...
It's the same the whole world over,
It's the poor wot gets the blame,
It's the rich wot gets the gravy.
Ain't it all a bleedin' shame?
> 'She was Poor but she was Honest' (sung by
> British soldiers in the First World War)

12 The singer not the song.
> From a West Indian calypso; title of a novel
> (1959) by Audrey Erskine Lindop

13 Some talk of Alexander, and some of
Hercules;
Of Hector and Lysander, and such great
names as these;
But of all the world's brave heroes, there's
none that can compare
With a tow, row, row, row, row, row, for
the British Grenadier.
> 'The British Grenadiers' (traditional song)

14 So much chewing gum for the eyes.
> Small boy's definition of certain television
> programmes, in J. B. Simpson *Best Quotes*
> (1957)

15 Sticks nix hick pix.
> Headline on the lack of enthusiasm for farm
> dramas among rural populations, in *Variety*
> 17 July 1935

16 Sumer is icumen in,
Lhude sing cuccu!
> 'Cuckoo Song' (c.1250)

17 Swing low, sweet chariot—
Comin' for to carry me home;
I looked over Jordan and what did I see?
A band of angels comin' after me—
Comin' for to carry me home.
> Negro spiritual (c.1850)

18 There is a lady sweet and kind,
Was never face so pleased my mind;
I did but see her passing by,
And yet I love her till I die.
> Latin verse by Thomas Naogeorgus,
> Englished by Barnabe Googe and printed in
> 1570 (sometimes attributed to Thomas
> Forde)

19 There is one thing stronger than all the
armies in the world; and that is an idea
whose time has come.
> *Nation* 15 April 1943. Cf. 176:2

20 There is so much good in the worst of us,
And so much bad in the best of us,
That it hardly becomes any of us
To talk about the rest of us.
> Attributed, among others, to E. W. Hoch
> (1849–1945) on the grounds of it having
> appeared in his Kansas publication, the
> *Marion Record*, though in fact disclaimed by
> him ('behooves' sometimes substituted for
> 'becomes')

21 There's no such thing as a free lunch.
> Colloquial axiom in US economics from the
> 1960s, much associated with Milton
> Friedman; first found in printed form in
> Robert Heinlein *The Moon is a Harsh Mistress*
> (1966) ch. 11

22 There was a young lady of Riga
Who went for a ride on a tiger;
They returned from the ride
With the lady inside,
And a smile on the face of the tiger.
> In R. L. Green (ed.) *A Century of Humorous
> Verse* (1959)

1 They come as a boon and a blessing to men,
The Pickwick, the Owl, and the Waverley pen.

Advertisement by MacNiven and H. Cameron Ltd. (c.1920); almost certainly inspired by J. C. Prince 'The Pen and the Press' in E. W. Cole (ed.) *The Thousand Best Poems in the World* (1891): 'It came as a boon and a blessing to men, / The peaceful, the pure, the victorious PEN!'

2 Thirty days hath September,
April, June, and November;
All the rest have thirty-one,
Excepting February alone,
And that has twenty-eight days clear
And twenty-nine in each leap year.

Stevins MS (c.1555)

3 This is a rotten argument, but it should be good enough for their lordships on a hot summer afternoon.

Annotation to a ministerial brief, said to have been read out inadvertently in the House of Lords; in Lord Home *The Way the Wind Blows* (1976) p. 204

4 Though I yield to no one in my admiration for Mr Coolidge, I do wish he did not look as if he had been weaned on a pickle.

Anonymous remark, in Alice Roosevelt Longworth *Crowded Hours* (1933) ch. 21

5 Thought shall be the harder, heart the keener, courage the greater, as our might lessens.

*The Battle of Maldon* (c.1000, tr. R. K. Gordon, 1926)

6 Three acres and a cow.

Associated with Jesse Collings and his land reform propaganda (*Hansard* 26 January 1886, col. 444), although used earlier by Joseph Chamberlain in a speech at Evesham (*The Times* 17 November 1885, p. 10), by which time it was already proverbial

7 To err is human but to really foul things up requires a computer.

*Farmers' Almanac for 1978* 'Capsules of Wisdom'

8 Too small to live in and too large to hang on a watch-chain.

Chiswick House described by a guest, in C. Roberts *And so to Bath* (1940) ch. 4

9 Vote early and vote often.

US election slogan, already current when quoted by William Porcher Miles in the House of Representatives; *Congressional Globe* 31 March 1858, appendix, p. 286

10 Wall St lays an egg.

Crash headline, *Variety* 30 October 1929

11 War will cease when men refuse to fight.

Pacifist slogan, from c.1936 (often quoted 'Wars will cease ... ')

12 We hold these truths to be self-evident, that all men are created equal, that they are endowed by their Creator with certain unalienable rights, that among these are life, liberty and the pursuit of happiness.

American Declaration of Independence, 4 July 1776. Cf. 180:18

13 We're here
Because
We're here.

Sung to the tune of 'Auld Lang Syne', in J. Brophy and E. Partridge *Songs and Slang of the British Soldier 1914–18* (1930)

14 Were you there when they crucified my Lord?

Title of Negro spiritual (1865)

15 We shall not be moved.

Title of labour and civil rights song (1931) adapted from an earlier gospel hymn

16 We shall overcome.

Title of song, originating from before the American Civil War, adapted as a Baptist hymn ('I'll Overcome Some Day', 1901) by C. A. Tindley; revived in 1946 as a protest song by black tobacco workers, and in 1963 during the black Civil Rights Campaign

17 We want eight, and we won't wait.

On the construction of Dreadnoughts. See George Wyndham's speech in *The Times* 29 March 1909

18 Western wind, when will thou blow,
The small rain down can rain?
Christ, if my love were in my arms
And I in my bed again!

'Western Wind' (16th century)

19 When Israel was in Egypt land,
Let my people go,
Oppressed so hard they could not stand,
Let my people go.
*Go down, Moses,*
*Way-down in Egypt land,*
*Tell old Pharaoh*
*To let my people go.*

'Go Down, Moses' (Negro spiritual). Cf. 39:34

20 Who dares wins.

Motto of the British Special Air Service regiment, from 1942

21 Whose finger do you want on the trigger?

*Daily Mirror* 21 September 1951 (referring to the atom bomb)

22 A willing foe and sea room.

Naval toast in the time of Nelson, in W. N. T. Beckett *A Few Naval Customs, Expressions, Traditions, and Superstitions* (1931) 'Customs'

23 With a heart of furious fancies,
Whereof I am commander;
With a burning spear,
And a horse of air,
To the wilderness I wander.

'Tom o' Bedlam'

24 Yankee Doodle came to town
Riding on a pony;
Stuck a feather in his cap
And called it Macaroni.

'Yankee Doodle' (song, 1755 or earlier)

1 You should make a point of trying every experience once, excepting incest and folk-dancing.

Sir Arnold Bax (1883–1953), quoting 'a sympathetic Scot' in *Farewell My Youth* (1943) p. 17

## French

2 *Ça ira.*

Things will work out.

Refrain of 'Carillon national', popular song of the French Revolution (c. July 1790). See W. Doyle *Oxford History of the French Revolution* (1989) p. 129

3 *Cet animal est très méchant,*
*Quand on l'attaque il se défend.*

This animal is very bad; when attacked it defends itself.

'La Ménagerie' (1868 song) by 'Théodore P. K.'

4 *Chevalier sans peur et sans reproche.*

Fearless, blameless knight.

Description in contemporary chronicles of Pierre Bayard (1476–1524)

5 *Honi soit qui mal y pense.*

Evil be to him who evil thinks.

Motto of the Order of the Garter, originated by Edward III, probably on 23 April 1348 or 1349

6 *Ils ne passeront pas.*

They shall not pass.

Slogan of the French army at the defence of Verdun 1916; variously attributed to Marshal Pétain and to General Robert Nivelle, and taken up by the Republicans in the Spanish Civil War. Cf. 178:2

7 *Je suis Marxiste—tendance Groucho.*

I am a Marxist—of the Groucho tendency.

Slogan found at Nanterre in Paris, 1968

8 *Il ne faut pas être plus royaliste que le roi.*
*Cette phrase n'est pas du moment; elle fut inventée sous Louis XVI: elle enchaîna les mains des fidèles, pour ne laisser libre que le bras du bourreau.*

You mustn't be more of a royalist than the king. This expression is not new; it was coined under Louis XVI: it chained up the hands of the loyal, leaving free only the arm of the hangman.

Chateaubriand *De la monarchie selon la charte* (1816) ch. 81

9 *Laissez-nous-faire.*

Allow us to do [it].

Dating from c.1664, in *Journal Oeconomique* Paris, April 1751: 'M. Colbert assembled several deputies of commerce at his house to ask what could be done for commerce; the most rational and the least flattering among them answered him in one word: "Laissez-nous-faire"'. Cf. 15:6

10 *Le monde est plein de fous, et qui n'en veut pas voir*
*Doit se tenir tout seul, et casser son miroir.*

The world is full of fools, and he who would not see it should live alone and smash his mirror.

Adaptation of an original form attributed to Claude Le Petit (1640–65) in *Discours satiriques* (1686)

11 *Liberté! Égalité! Fraternité!*

Freedom! Equality! Brotherhood!

Motto of the French Revolution, but of earlier origin. The Club des Cordeliers passed a motion (30 June 1793) 'that owners should be urged to paint on the front of their houses, in large letters, the words: Unity, indivisibility of the Republic, Liberty, Equality, Fraternity or death'; in *Journal de Paris* no. 182 (from 1795 the words 'ou la mort [or death]' were dropped). Cf. 94:5

12 *L'ordre règne à Varsovie.*

Order reigns in Warsaw.

After the brutal suppression of an uprising, the newspaper *Moniteur* reported (16 September 1831) 'Order and calm are completely restored in the capital'; on the same day Count Sebastiani, minister of foreign affairs, declared: 'Peace reigns in Warsaw'

13 *Nous n'irons plus aux bois, les lauriers sont coupés.*

We'll to the woods no more,
The laurels all are cut.

Nursery rhyme, quoted by Théodore de Banville in *Les Cariatides, les stalactites* (1842–6); translated by A. E. Housman in *Last Poems* (1922) introductory

14 *Revenons à ces moutons.*

Let us get back to these sheep [i.e. 'Let us get back to the subject'].

*Maistre Pierre Pathelin* (c.1470) l. 1191 (often quoted '*Retournons à nos moutons* [Let us return to our sheep]')

15 *Taisez-vous! Méfiez-vous! Les oreilles ennemies vous écoutent.*

Keep your mouth shut! Be on your guard! Enemy ears are listening to you.

Official notice in France, 1915

16 *Toujours perdrix!*

Always partridge!

Attributed to a confessor of Henri IV, who was served nothing but partridge, having rebuked the king for his sexual liaisons; in G. Büchmann *Geflügelte Worte* (1874 ed.) p. 240

17 *Tout passe, tout casse, tout lasse.*

Everything passes, everything perishes, everything palls.

C. Cahier *Quelques six mille proverbes* (1856) no. 1718

### German

**1** *Arbeit macht frei.*

Work liberates.
> Words inscribed on the gates of Dachau concentration camp, 1933, and subsequently on those of Auschwitz

**2** *Ein Reich, ein Volk, ein Führer.*

One realm, one people, one leader.
> Nazi Party slogan, early 1930s

**3** *Kommt der Krieg ins Land*
*Gibt's Lügen wie Sand.*

When war enters a country
It produces lies like sand.
> Epigraph to A. Ponsonby *Falsehood in Wartime* (1928) p. 11. Cf. 182:12

**4** *Vorsprung durch Technik.*

Progress through technology.
> Audi motors (advertising slogan, from 1986)

### Greek

**5** Know thyself.
> Inscribed on the temple of Apollo at Delphi; in *Protagoras* 343 b, Plato ascribes the saying to the Seven Wise Men

**6** Let no one enter who does not know geometry [mathematics].
> Inscription on Plato's door, probably at the Academy at Athens, in Elias Philosophus *In Aristotelis Categorias Commentaria* p. 118, l. 18; in A. Busse (ed.) *Commentaria in Aristotelem Graeca* (1900) vol. 18, pt. 1

**7** Nothing in excess.
> Inscribed on the temple of Apollo at Delphi, and variously ascribed to the Seven Wise Men

**8** Whenever God prepares evil for a man, He first damages his mind, with which he deliberates.
> Scholiastic annotation to Sophocles' *Antigone* l. 622. Cf. 129:11

### Latin

**9** *Adeste, fideles.*

O come, all ye faithful.
> 'Adeste, fideles' (c.1743); based on F. Oakeley's translation (1841)

**10** *Venite, adoremus Dominum.*

O come, let us adore him, Christ the Lord!
> 'Adeste, fideles'

**11** *Ad majorem Dei gloriam.*

To the greater glory of God.
> Motto of the Society of Jesus

**12** *Ave Caesar, morituri te salutant.*

Hail Caesar, those who are about to die salute you.
> Gladiators saluting the Roman Emperor. See Suetonius *Lives of the Caesars* 'Claudius' ch. 21

**13** *Ave Maria, gratia plena, Dominus tecum.*

Hail Mary, full of grace, the Lord is with thee.
> 'Ave Maria', also known as 'The Angelic Salutation' (11th century)

**14** *Ave verum corpus,*
*natum ex Maria Virgine.*

Hail the true body, born of the Virgin Mary.
> Eucharistic hymn (probably 14th century)

**15** *Et in Arcadia ego.*

And I too in Arcadia.
> Tomb inscription, of disputed meaning, often depicted in classical paintings

**16** *Gaudeamus igitur,*
*Juvenes dum sumus*
*Post jucundam juventutem,*
*Post molestam senectutem,*
*Nos habebit humus.*

Let us then rejoice,
While we are young.
After the pleasures of youth
And the burdens of old age
Earth will hold us.
> Medieval students' song (18th-century revision of 13th-century original)

**17** *Nemo me impune lacessit.*

No one provokes me with impunity.
> Motto of the Crown of Scotland and of all Scottish regiments

**18** *Per ardua ad astra.*

Through struggle to the stars.
> Motto of the Mulvany family, as translated by Rider Haggard in *The People of the Mist* (1894) ch. 1 (motto of the R.A.F.)

**19** *Post coitum omne animal triste.*

After coition every animal is sad.
> Post-classical saying

**20** *Quidquid agis, prudenter agas, et respice finem.*

Whatever you do, do cautiously, and look to the end.
> *Gesta Romanorum* no. 103

**21** *Salve, regina, mater misericordiae,*
*Vita, dulcedo et spes nostra, salve!*

Hail holy queen, mother of mercy, hail our life, our sweetness, and our hope!
> Attributed to various 11th-century authors. See *Analecta Hymnica* vol. 50 (1907) p. 318

**22** *Sic transit gloria mundi.*

Thus passes the glory of the world.
> Said at the coronation of a new Pope, while flax is burned; used at the coronation of Alexander V in Pisa, 7 July 1409, but earlier in origin. Cf. 329:28

**23** *Si monumentum requiris, circumspice.*

If you seek a monument, gaze around.
> Inscription in St Paul's Cathedral, London, attributed to the son of Sir Christopher Wren, its architect

1 *Te Deum laudamus: Te Dominum confitemur.*
We praise thee, God: we own thee Lord.
'Te Deum'; hymn traditionally attributed to
St Ambrose and St Augustine in AD 387,
though more recently to St Niceta (d. *c.*414).
Cf. 63:18

2 *Tempora mutantur, et nos mutamur in illis.*
Times change, and we change with them.
In William Harrison *Description of Britain*
(1577) bk. 3, ch. 3; attributed to Emperor
Lothar I (795–855) in the form '*Omnia
mutantur . . .* [All things change . . . ]'

3 *Vox et praeterea nihil.*
A voice and nothing more.
Describing a nightingale. See Plutarch
*Moralia* sect. 233a, no. 15

## Jean Anouilh 1910–87

4 God is on everyone's side . . . And, in the
last analysis, he is on the side of those
with plenty of money and large armies.
*L'Alouette* (1953) p. 120. Cf. 83:20, 340:23

5 The spring is wound up tight. It will uncoil
of itself. That is what is so convenient in
tragedy. The least little turn of the wrist
will do the job. Anything will set it going.
*Antigone* (1944, tr. L. Galantiere, 1957) p. 34

6 Tragedy is clean, it is restful, it is flawless.
*Antigone* (1944, tr. L. Galantiere, 1957) p. 34

7 There is love of course. And then there's
life, its enemy.
*Ardèle* (1949) p. 8

8 You know very well that love is, above all,
the gift of oneself!
*Ardèle* (1949) p. 79

9 Dying is nothing. So start by living. It's less
fun and it lasts longer.
*Roméo et Jeannette* (1946) act 3

## F. Anstey 1856–1934

10 Drastic measures is Latin for a whopping.
*Vice Versa* (1882) ch. 7

## Guillaume Apollinaire 1880–1918

11 *Les souvenirs sont cors de chasse
Dont meurt le bruit parmi le vent.*
Memories are hunting horns
Whose sound dies on the wind.
'Cors de Chasse' (1912)

12 *Sous le pont Mirabeau coule la Seine.
Et nos amours, faut-il qu'il m'en souvienne?
La joie venait toujours après la peine.*
Under Mirabeau Bridge flows the Seine.
And our loves, must I remember them?
Joy always came after pain.
'Le Pont Mirabeau' (1912)

13 *On ne peut pas porter partout le cadavre de son
père.*
One can't carry one's father's corpse about
everywhere.
In *Les peintres cubistes* (1965) 'Méditations
esthétiques: Sur la peinture' pt. 1

## Thomas Gold Appleton 1812–84

14 A Boston man is the east wind made flesh.
Attributed

15 Good Americans, when they die, go to
Paris.
In Oliver Wendell Holmes *The Autocrat of the
Breakfast-Table* (1858) ch. 6

## Arabian Nights

16 Who will change old lamps for new ones?
. . . new lamps for old ones?
'The History of Aladdin'

17 Open Sesame!
'The History of Ali Baba'

## William Arabin 1773–1841

18 If ever there was a case of clearer evidence
than this of persons acting together, this
case is that case.
In H. B. Churchill *Arabiniana* (1843) p. 9

19 They will steal the very teeth out of your
mouth as you walk through the streets. *I
know it from experience.*
On the citizens of Uxbridge, in Sir W.
Ballantine *Some Experiences of a Barrister's Life*
(1882) vol. 1, ch. 6

20 Prisoner, God has given you good abilities,
instead of which you go about the country
stealing ducks.
See Sir Frederick Pollock *Essays in the Law*
(1922) p. 298, where attribution to a Revd Mr
Alderson is preferred

## Louis Aragon 1897–1982

21 *Ô mois des floraisons mois des métamorphoses
Mai qui fut sans nuage et Juin poignardé
Je n'oublierai jamais les lilas ni les roses
Ni ceux que le printemps dans ses plis a gardé.*
O month of flowerings, month of
metamorphoses,
May without cloud and June that was
stabbed,
I shall never forget the lilac and the roses
Nor those whom spring has kept in its
folds.
'Les lilas et les roses' (1940)

## Dr Arbuthnot 1667–1735

22 Law is a bottomless pit.
*The History of John Bull* (1712) title of first
pamphlet

23 Hame's hame, be it never so hamely.
*The History of John Bull* (1712) 'John Bull Still
in His Senses' ch. 3

24 Curle (who is one of the new terrors of
Death) has been writing letters to every
body for memoirs of his life.
Letter to Jonathan Swift, 13 January 1733, in
H. Williams (ed.) *Correspondence of Jonathan
Swift* vol. 4 (1965). Cf. 212:19, 347:2

## Archilochus 7th century BC

**1** The fox knows many things—the hedgehog
one *big* one.
> E. Diehl (ed.) *Anthologia Lyrica Graeca* (3rd ed.,
> 1949–52) vol. 1, p. 241, no. 103. Cf. 36:4

## Archimedes *c.*287–212 BC

**2** *Eureka!*
I've got it!
> In Vitruvius Pollio *De Architectura* bk. 9,
> preface, sect. 10

**3** Give me but one firm spot on which to
stand, and I will move the earth.
> On the action of a lever, in Pappus *Synagoge*
> bk. 8, proposition 10, sect. 11

## Hannah Arendt 1906–75

**4** The fearsome, word-and-thought-defying
banality of evil.
> *Eichmann in Jerusalem* (1963) ch. 15

**5** The most radical revolutionary will become
a conservative on the day after the
revolution.
> *New Yorker* 12 September 1970, p. 88

## Marquis d'Argenson 1694–1757

**6** *Laisser-faire.*
No interference.
> *Mémoires et Journal Inédit* (1858 ed.) vol. 5,
> p. 364. Cf. 12:9

## Comte d'Argenson 1696–1764

**7** DESFONTAINES: I must live.
D'ARGENSON: I do not see the necessity.
> On Desfontaines having produced a
> pamphlet satirizing D'Argenson, his
> benefactor. See Voltaire *Alzire* (1736)
> 'Discours Préliminaire' in *Oeuvres Complètes
> Théâtre* vol. 2 (1877) p. 381

## Ludovico Ariosto 1474–1533

**8** *Natura il fece, e poi roppe la stampa.*
Nature made him, and then broke the
mould.
> *Orlando Furioso* (1532) canto 10, st. 84

## Aristophanes *c.*450–*c.*385 BC

**9** How about 'Cloudcuckooland'?
> Naming the capital city of the Birds in *The
> Birds* (414 BC) l. 819

**10** This Second Logic then, I mean the Worse
one,
They teach to talk unjustly, and—prevail.
> *The Clouds* (423 BC) l. 113 (tr. B. Rogers).
> Cf. 228:23

**11** Brekekekex koax koax.
> Cry of the Frogs in *The Frogs* (405 BC) l. 209
> and *passim*

## Aristotle 384–322 BC

**12** Every art and every investigation, and
likewise every practical pursuit or
undertaking, seems to aim at some good:
hence it has been well said that the Good
is That at which all things aim.
> *Nicomachean Ethics* bk. 1, 1094a 1–3

**13** Therefore, the good of man must be the
end [i.e. objective] of the science of politics.
> *Nicomachean Ethics* bk. 1, 1094b 6–7

**14** We make war that we may live in peace.
> *Nicomachean Ethics* bk. 10, 1177b 5–6 (tr. M.
> Ostwald). Cf. 337:18

**15** Tragedy is thus a representation of an
action that is worth serious attention,
complete in itself and of some amplitude
... by means of pity and fear bringing
about the purgation of such emotions.
> *Poetics* ch. 6, 1449b

**16** So poetry is something more philosophical
and more worthy of serious attention than
history.
> *Poetics* ch. 9, 1451b

**17** Probable impossibilities are to be preferred
to improbable possibilities.
> *Poetics* ch. 24, 1460a

**18** Man is by nature a political animal.
> *Politics* bk. 1, 1253a

**19** He who is unable to live in society, or who
has no need because he is sufficient for
himself, must be either a beast or a god.
> *Politics* bk. 1, 1253a

**20** Nature does nothing without purpose or
uselessly.
> *Politics* bk. 1, 1256b

**21** When he was asked 'What is a friend?' he
said 'One soul inhabiting two bodies.'
> In Diogenes Laertius *Lives of Philosophers* bk. 5,
> sect. 20

**22** *Amicus Plato, sed magis amica veritas.*
Plato is dear to me, but dearer still is
truth.
> Latin translation of a Greek original ascribed
> to Aristotle

## Lewis Addison Armistead 1817–63

**23** Give them the cold steel, boys!
> Attributed during the American Civil War,
> 1863

## Harry Armstrong 1879–1951

**24** There's an old mill by the stream, Nellie
Dean,
Where we used to sit and dream, Nellie
Dean.
And the waters as they flow
Seem to murmur sweet and low,
'You're my heart's desire; I love you, Nellie
Dean.'
> 'Nellie Dean' (1905 song)

## Dr John Armstrong 1709–79

1        Much had he read,
Much more had seen; he studied from the
     life,
And in th'original perused mankind.
    *The Art of Preserving Health* (1744) bk. 4, l. 231

2 'Tis not too late to-morrow to be brave.
    *The Art of Preserving Health* (1744) bk. 4, l. 460

## Louis Armstrong 1901–71

3 All music is folk music, I ain't never heard
no horse sing a song.
    In *New York Times* 7 July 1971, p. 41

4 If you still have to ask ... shame on you.
    When asked what jazz is, in Max Jones et al.
    *Salute to Satchmo* (1970) p. 25 (sometimes
    quoted 'Man, if you gotta ask you'll never
    know')

## Neil Armstrong 1930–

5 That's one small step for a man, one giant
leap for mankind.
    Landing on the moon; In *New York Times*
    21 July 1969, p. 5 (interference in
    transmission obliterated 'a')

## Sir Robert Armstrong 1927–

6 It contains a misleading impression, not a
lie. It was being economical with the truth.
    During the 'Spycatcher' trial, Supreme
    Court, New South Wales, in *Daily Telegraph*
    19 November 1986. See Edmund Burke *Two
    letters on Proposals for Peace* (1796) pt. 1, p. 137:
    'Falsehood and delusion are allowed in no
    case whatsoever: But, as in the exercise of
    all the virtues, there is an economy of truth'

## Sir Edwin Arnold 1832–1904

7 Nor ever once ashamed
So we be named
Press-men; Slaves of the Lamp; Servants of
Light.
    'The Tenth Muse' (1895) st. 18

## George Arnold 1834–65

8 The living need charity more than the
dead.
    'The Jolly Old Pedagogue' (1866)

## Matthew Arnold 1822–88

9 And we forget because we must
And not because we will.
    'Absence' (1852)

10 A bolt is shot back somewhere in our
breast,
And a lost pulse of feeling stirs again.
The eye sinks inward, and the heart lies
plain,
And what we mean, we say, and what we
would, we know.
    'The Buried Life' (1852) l. 84

11 The Sea of Faith
Was once, too, at the full, and round
     earth's shore
Lay like the folds of a bright girdle furled.
But now I only hear
Its melancholy, long, withdrawing roar,
Retreating, to the breath
Of the night-wind, down the vast edges
     drear
And naked shingles of the world.
    'Dover Beach' (1867) l. 21

12 And we are here as on a darkling plain
Swept with confused alarms of struggle
     and flight,
Where ignorant armies clash by night.
    'Dover Beach' (1867) l. 35

13 Be neither saint nor sophist-led, but be a
man.
    *Empedocles on Etna* (1852) act 1, sc. 2, l. 136

14 Is it so small a thing
To have enjoyed the sun,
To have lived light in the spring,
To have loved, to have thought, to have
     done.
    *Empedocles on Etna* (1852) act 1, sc. 2, l. 397

15 Because thou must not dream, thou needst
not then despair!
    *Empedocles on Etna* (1852) act 1, sc. 2, l. 426

16 Come, dear children, let us away;
Down and away below!
    'The Forsaken Merman' (1849) l. 1

17 Where great whales come sailing by,
Sail and sail, with unshut eye,
Round the world for ever and aye.
    'The Forsaken Merman' (1849) l. 43

18 Creep into thy narrow bed,
Creep, and let no more be said!
Vain thy onset! all stands fast.
Thou thyself must break at last.
Let the long contention cease!
Geese are swans, and swans are geese.
Let them have it how they will!
Thou art tired; best be still.
    'The Last Word' (1867)

19 He spoke, and loosed our heart in tears.
He laid us as we lay at birth
On the cool flowery lap of earth.
    'Memorial Verses, April 1850' (1852) l. 47 (of
    Wordsworth)

20 Ere the parting hour go by,
Quick, thy tablets, Memory!
    'A Memory Picture' (1849)

21 Say, has some wet bird-haunted English
lawn
Lent it the music of its trees at dawn?
    'Parting' (1852) l. 19

22 Eternal Passion!
Eternal Pain!
    'Philomela' (1853) l. 31

23 Cruel, but composed and bland,
Dumb, inscrutable and grand,
So Tiberius might have sat,
Had Tiberius been a cat.
    'Poor Matthias' (1885) l. 40

1 Her cabined ample Spirit,
It fluttered and failed for breath.
To-night it doth inherit
The vasty hall of death.
  'Requiescat' (1853)

2 Not deep the Poet sees, but wide.
  'Resignation' (1849) l. 214

3 Coldly, sadly descends
The autumn evening. The Field
Strewn with its dank yellow drifts
Of withered leaves, and the elms,
Fade into dimness apace,
Silent;—hardly a shout
From a few boys late at their play!
  'Rugby Chapel, November 1857' (1867)

4 Go, for they call you, Shepherd, from the
hill.
  'The Scholar-Gipsy' (1853) l. 1

5 All the live murmur of a summer's day.
  'The Scholar-Gipsy' (1853) l. 20

6 Tired of knocking at Preferment's door.
  'The Scholar-Gipsy' (1853) l. 35

7 Crossing the stripling Thames at Bab-lock-
hithe.
  'The Scholar-Gipsy' (1853) l. 74

8 Rapt, twirling in thy hand a withered
spray,
And waiting for the spark from heaven to
fall.
  'The Scholar-Gipsy' (1853) l. 119

9 The line of festal light in Christ-Church
hall.
  'The Scholar-Gipsy' (1853) l. 129

10 Thou waitest for the spark from heaven!
and we,
Light half-believers in our casual creeds ...
Who hesitate and falter life away,
And lose to-morrow the ground won to-
day.
  'The Scholar-Gipsy' (1853) l. 171

11 O born in days when wits were fresh and
clear,
And life ran gaily as the sparkling Thames;
Before this strange disease of modern life,
With its sick hurry, its divided aims,
Its heads o'ertaxed, its palsied hearts, was
rife—
Fly hence, our contact fear!
  'The Scholar-Gipsy' (1853) l. 201

12 Still nursing the unconquerable hope,
Still clutching the inviolable shade.
  'The Scholar-Gipsy' (1853) l. 211

13 Resolve to be thyself: and know, that he
Who finds himself, loses his misery.
  'Self-Dependence' (1852) l. 31

14 Others abide our question. Thou art free.
We ask and ask: Thou smilest and art still,
Out-topping knowledge.
  'Shakespeare' (1849)

15 Truth sits upon the lips of dying men.
  'Sohrab and Rustum' (1853) l. 656

16 Wandering between two worlds, one dead,
The other powerless to be born.
  'Stanzas from the Grande Chartreuse' (1855)
  l. 85

17 That sweet City with her dreaming spires.
  'Thyrsis' (1866) l. 19 (of Oxford)

18 So have I heard the cuckoo's parting cry,
From the wet field, through the vext
garden-trees,
Come with the volleying rain and tossing
breeze:
'The bloom is gone, and with the bloom go
I.'
  'Thyrsis' (1866) l. 57

19 Too quick despairer, wherefore wilt thou
go?
Soon will the high Midsummer pomps
come on,
Soon will the musk carnations break and
swell.
  'Thyrsis' (1866) l. 61

20 Who saw life steadily, and saw it whole:
The mellow glory of the Attic stage;
Singer of sweet Colonus, and its child.
  'To a Friend' (1849) (of Sophocles)

21 France, famed in all great arts, in none
supreme.
  'To a Republican Friend—Continued' (1849)

22 Yes! in the sea of life enisled,
With echoing straits between us thrown,
Dotting the shoreless watery wild,
We mortal millions live alone.
  'To Marguerite—Continued' (1852) l. 1

23 The unplumbed, salt, estranging sea.
  'To Marguerite—Continued' (1852) l. 24

24 Our society distributes itself into
Barbarians, Philistines, and Populace; and
America is just ourselves, with the
Barbarians quite left out. and the Populace
nearly.
  Culture and Anarchy (1869) preface

25 The pursuit of perfection, then, is the
pursuit of sweetness and light ... He who
works for sweetness and light united,
works to make reason and the will of God
prevail.
  Culture and Anarchy (1869) ch. 1. Cf. 319:18

26 When I want to distinguish clearly the
aristocratic class from the Philistines
proper, or middle class, [I] name the
former, in my own mind the Barbarians.
  Culture and Anarchy (1869) ch. 3

27 Marching where it likes, meeting where it
likes, bawling what it likes, breaking what
it likes—to this vast residuum we may
with great propriety give the name of
Populace.
  Culture and Anarchy (1869) ch. 3

1 Hebraism and Hellenism—between these
 two points of influence moves our world.
   *Culture and Anarchy* (1869) ch. 4

2 Whispering from her towers the last
 enchantments of the Middle Age . . . Home
 of lost causes, and forsaken beliefs.
   *Essays in Criticism* First Series (1865) preface
   (of Oxford)

3 The gloom, the smoke, the cold, the
 strangled illegitimate child! . . . And the
 final touch,—short, bleak and inhuman:
 *Wragg is in custody.*
   *Essays in Criticism* First Series (1865) 'The
   Function of Criticism at the Present Time'

4 In poetry, no less than in life, he is 'a
 beautiful and ineffectual angel, beating in
 the void his luminous wings in vain'.
   *Essays in Criticism* Second Series (1888)
   'Shelley' (quoting from his own essay on
   Byron in the same work)

5 The difference between genuine poetry and
 the poetry of Dryden, Pope, and all their
 school, is briefly this: their poetry is
 conceived and composed in their wits,
 genuine poetry is conceived and composed
 in the soul.
   *Essays in Criticism* Second Series (1888)
   'Thomas Gray'

6 Poetry is at bottom a criticism of life.
   *Essays in Criticism* Second Series (1888)
   'Wordsworth'

7 I am past thirty, and three parts iced over.
   H. F. Lowry (ed.) *Letters of Matthew Arnold to
   Arthur Hugh Clough* (1932) 12 February 1853

8 The true meaning of religion is thus not
 simply morality, but morality touched by
 emotion.
   *Literature and Dogma* (1873) ch. 1

9 Conduct is three-fourths of our life and its
 largest concern.
   *Literature and Dogma* (1873) ch. 1

10 But there remains the question: what
 righteousness really is. The method and
 secret and sweet reasonableness of Jesus.
   *Literature and Dogma* (1873) ch. 12

11 So we have the Philistine of genius in
 religion—Luther; the Philistine of genius
 in politics—Cromwell; the Philistine of
 genius in literature—Bunyan.
   *Mixed Essays* (1879) 'Lord Falkland'

12 Of these two literatures [French and
 German], as of the intellect of Europe in
 general, the main effort, for now many
 years, has been a *critical* effort . . . to see the
 object as in itself it really is.
   *On Translating Homer* (1861) Lecture 2

13 Have something to say, and say it as
 clearly as you can. That is the only secret
 of style.
   In G. W. E. Russell *Collections and Recollections*
   (1898) ch. 13

## Samuel James Arnold

14 England, home and beauty.
   'The Death of Nelson' (1811 song)

## Dr Thomas Arnold 1795–1842

15 My object will be, if possible, to form
 Christian men, for Christian boys I can
 scarcely hope to make.
   Letter to Revd John Tucker, 2 March 1828, on
   his appointment to the Headmastership of
   Rugby School; in A. P. Stanley *Life and
   Correspondence of Thomas Arnold* (1844) vol. 1,
   ch. 2

16 As for rioting, the old Roman way of
 dealing with that is always the right one;
 flog the rank and file, and fling the
 ringleaders from the Tarpeian rock.
   From an unpublished letter written before
   1828, quoted by Matthew Arnold in *Cornhill
   Magazine* August 1868 'Anarchy and
   Authority'

## George Asaf 1880–1951

17 What's the use of worrying?
 It never was worth while,
 So, pack up your troubles in your old kit-
     bag,
 And smile, smile, smile.
   'Pack up your Troubles' (1915 song)

## Roger Ascham 1515–68

18 I said . . . how, and why, young children,
 were sooner allured by love, than driven by
 beating, to attain good learning.
   *The Schoolmaster* (1570) preface

19 There is no such whetstone, to sharpen a
 good wit and encourage a will to learning,
 as is praise.
   *The Schoolmaster* (1570) bk. 1

## Daisy Ashford 1881–1972

20 Mr Salteena was an elderly man of 42.
   *The Young Visiters* (1919) ch. 1

21 You look rather rash my dear your colors
 dont quite match your face.
   *The Young Visiters* (1919) ch. 2

22 Not kind sir he muttered quite usual.
   *The Young Visiters* (1919) ch. 5

23 Oh I see said the Earl but my own idear is
 that these things are as piffle before the
 wind.
   *The Young Visiters* (1919) ch. 5

24 My life will be sour grapes and ashes
 without you.
   *The Young Visiters* (1919) ch. 8

25 Take me back to the Gaierty hotel.
   *The Young Visiters* (1919) ch. 9

## Isaac Asimov 1920–92

1 The three fundamental Rules of Robotics
... One, a robot may not injure a human
being, or, through inaction, allow a human
being to come to harm ... Two ... a robot
must obey the orders given it by human
beings except where such orders would
conflict with the First Law ... three, a
robot must protect its own existence as
long as such protection does not conflict
with the First or Second Laws.
  *I, Robot* (1950) 'Runaround'

## Herbert Asquith 1852–1928

2 We had better wait and see.
  Referring, in 1910, to the rumour that the
  House of Lords was to be flooded with new
  Liberal peers to ensure the passage of the
  Finance Bill. See Roy Jenkins *Asquith* (1964)
  ch. 14

3 It is fitting that we should have buried the
Unknown Prime Minister [Bonar Law] by
the side of the Unknown Soldier.
  In R. Blake *The Unknown Prime Minister* (1955)
  p. 531

4 [The War Office kept three sets of figures:]
one to mislead the public, another to
mislead the Cabinet, and the third to
mislead itself.
  In A. Horne *Price of Glory* (1962) ch. 2

## Margot Asquith 1864–1945

5 Kitchener is a great poster.
  *More Memories* (1933) ch. 6

6 The *t* is silent, as in *Harlow*.
  To Jean Harlow, who had mispronounced
  her name; in T. S. Matthews *Great Tom* (1973)
  ch. 7

## Mary Astell 1668–1731

7 If all men are born free, how is it that all
women are born slaves?
  *Some Reflections upon Marriage* (1706 ed.)
  preface

## Sir Jacob Astley 1579–1652

8 O Lord! thou knowest how busy I must be
this day: if I forget thee, do not thou forget
me.
  Prayer before the Battle of Edgehill, in Sir
  Philip Warwick *Memoires* (1701) p. 229

## Nancy Astor 1879–1964

9 I married beneath me, all women do.
  In *Dictionary of National Biography 1961–1970*

## Brooks Atkinson 1894–1984

10 After each war there is a little less
democracy to save.
  *Once Around the Sun* (1951) 7 January

## E. L. Atkinson 1882–1929 and
## Apsley Cherry-Garrard 1882–1959

11 Hereabouts died a very gallant gentleman,
Captain L. E. G. Oates of the Inniskilling
Dragoons. In March 1912, returning from
the Pole, he walked willingly to his death
in a blizzard to try and save his comrades,
beset by hardships.
  Epitaph on cairn erected in the Antarctic,
  15 November 1912; in Cherry-Garrard's *Worst
  Journey in the World* (1922) p. 487

## Clement Attlee 1883–1967

12 The voice we heard was that of Mr
Churchill but the mind was that of Lord
Beaverbrook.
  Speech on radio, 5 June 1945, in F. Williams
  *A Prime Minister Remembers* (1961) ch. 6

13 [Russian Communism is] the illegitimate
child of Karl Marx and Catherine the Great.
  Speech at Aarhus University, 11 April 1956,
  in *The Times* 12 April 1956

14 Democracy means government by
discussion, but it is only effective if you
can stop people talking.
  Speech at Oxford, 14 June 1957, in *The Times*
  15 June 1957

## Henriette Auber 1773–1862

15 He came in tongues of living flame,
To teach, convince, subdue;
All-powerful as the wind he came,
As viewless too.
  'Our blest Redeemer, ere he breathed' (1829
  hymn)

## John Aubrey 1626–97

16 How these curiosities would be quite
forgot, did not such idle fellows as I am
put them down.
  *Brief Lives* 'Venetia Digby'

17 He was wont to say that if he had read as
much as other men, he should have known
no more than other men.
  *Brief Lives* 'Thomas Hobbes'

18 And when he saw the cheese-cakes:—'What
have we here, *crinkum crankum?*'
  *Brief Lives* 'Ralph Kettel'

19 His harmonical and ingenious soul did
lodge in a beautiful and well proportioned
body. He was a spare man.
  *Brief Lives* 'John Milton'

20 Oval face. His eye a dark grey. He had
auburn hair. His complexion exceeding
fair—he was so fair that they called him
*the lady of* Christ's College.
  *Brief Lives* 'John Milton'

21 He pronounced the letter R (*littera canina*)
very hard—a certain sign of a satirical wit.
  *Brief Lives* 'John Milton'

1 Sciatica: he cured it, by boiling his buttock.
   *Brief Lives* 'Sir Jonas Moore'

2 He was a handsome, well-shaped man: very
   good company, and of a very ready and
   pleasant smooth wit.
   *Brief Lives* 'William Shakespeare'

## Auctoritates Aristotelis

*A compilation of medieval propositions drawn
from diverse classical and other sources (ed. J.
Hamesse, 1974)*

3 *Consuetudo est altera natura.*
   Habit is second nature.

4 *Contra negantem principia non est
   disputandum.*
   You cannot argue with someone who
   denies the first principles.

5 *Deus et natura nihil faciunt frustra.*
   God and nature do nothing in vain.

6 *Omnes homines naturaliter scire desiderant.*
   All men naturally desire to know.

7 *Parentes plus amant filios quam e converso.*
   Parents love their children more than
   children love their parents.

8 *Tempus est mensura motus rerum mobilium.*
   Time is the measure of movement.

## W. H. Auden 1907–73

9 Sob, heavy world,
   Sob as you spin
   Mantled in mist, remote from the happy.
   *The Age of Anxiety* (1947) pt. 4 'The Dirge'

10 Blessed Cecilia, appear in visions
   To all musicians, appear and inspire:
   Translated Daughter, come down and
   startle
   Composing mortals with immortal fire.
   *Anthem for St Cecilia's Day* (1941) pt. 1

11 I'll love you, dear, I'll love you
   Till China and Africa meet
   And the river jumps over the mountain
   And the salmon sing in the street,

   I'll love you till the ocean
   Is folded and hung up to dry
   And the seven stars go squawking
   Like geese about the sky.
   'As I Walked Out One Evening' (1940)

12 The glacier knocks in the cupboard,
   The desert sighs in the bed,
   And the crack in the tea-cup opens
   A lane to the land of the dead.
   'As I Walked Out One Evening' (1940)

13 At the far end of the enormous room
   An orchestra is playing to the rich.
   'At the far end of the enormous room' (1933)

14 August for the people and their favourite
   islands.
   Title of poem (1936)

15 The desires of the heart are as crooked as
   corkscrews
   Not to be born is the best for man.
   'Death's Echo' (1937). Cf. 311:13

16 Happy the hare at morning, for she cannot
   read
   The Hunter's waking thoughts.
   *Dog beneath the Skin* (with Christopher
   Isherwood, 1935) act 2, sc. 2

17 To save your world you asked this man to
   die:
   Would this man, could he see you now, ask
   why?
   'Epitaph for the Unknown Soldier' (1955)

18 When he laughed, respectable senators
   burst with laughter,
   And when he cried the little children died
   in the streets.
   'Epitaph on a Tyrant' (1940). Cf. 236:1

19 Altogether elsewhere, vast
   Herds of reindeer move across
   Miles and miles of golden moss,
   Silently and very fast.
   'The Fall of Rome' (1951)

20 To us he is no more a person
   now but a whole climate of opinion.
   'In Memory of Sigmund Freud' (1940) st. 17

21 The mercury sank in the mouth of the
   dying day.
   What instruments we have agree
   The day of his death was a dark cold day.
   'In Memory of W. B. Yeats' (1940) pt. 1

22 You were silly like us; your gift survived it
   all:
   The parish of rich women, physical decay,
   Yourself. Mad Ireland hurt you into poetry.
   'In Memory of W. B. Yeats' (1940) pt. 1

23 For poetry makes nothing happen: it
   survives
   In the valley of its saying where executives
   Would never want to tamper.
   'In Memory of W. B. Yeats' (1940) pt. 2

24 Earth, receive an honoured guest:
   William Yeats is laid to rest.
   Let the Irish vessel lie
   Emptied of its poetry.
   'In Memory of W. B. Yeats' (1940) pt. 3

25 I see it often since you've been away:
   The island, the veranda, and the fruit;
   The tiny steamer breaking from the bay;
   The literary mornings with its hoot;
   Our ugly comic servant; and then you,
   Lovely and willing every afternoon.
   'I see it often since you've been away' (1933)

26 Look, stranger, at this island now.
   Title of poem (1936)

27 Lay your sleeping head, my love,
   Human on my faithless arm.
   'Lullaby' (1940)

28 But in my arms till break of day
   Let the living creature lie,
   Mortal, guilty, but to me
   The entirely beautiful.
   'Lullaby' (1940)

1 About suffering they were never wrong,
The Old Masters.
'Musée des Beaux Arts' (1940)

2 Even the dreadful martyrdom must run its
course
Anyhow in a corner, some untidy spot
Where the dogs go on with their doggy life
and the torturer's horse
Scratches its innocent behind on a tree.
'Musée des Beaux Arts' (1940)

3 To the man-in-the-street, who, I'm sorry to
say,
Is a keen observer of life,
The word 'Intellectual' suggests straight
away
A man who's untrue to his wife.
New Year Letter (1941) l. 1277 n.

4 This is the Night Mail crossing the Border,
Bringing the cheque and the postal order,
Letters for the rich, letters for the poor,
The shop at the corner, the girl next door.
'Night Mail' (1936) pt. 1

5 And make us as Newton was, who in his
garden watching
The apple falling towards England, became
aware
Between himself and her of an eternal tie.
'O Love, the interest itself' (1936)

6 Private faces in public places
Are wiser and nicer
Than public faces in private places.
Orators (1932) dedication

7 Out on the lawn I lie in bed,
Vega conspicuous overhead.
'Out on the lawn I lie in bed' (1936)

8 Some thirty inches from my nose
The frontier of my Person goes,
And all the untilled air between
Is private pagus or demesne.
Stranger, unless with bedroom eyes
I beckon you to fraternize,
Beware of rudely crossing it:
I have no gun, but I can spit.
'Prologue: the Birth of Architecture' (1966)
postscript

9 My Dear One is mine as mirrors are lonely.
'The Sea and the Mirror' (1944) pt. 2
(Miranda)

10 I and the public know
What all schoolchildren learn,
Those to whom evil is done
Do evil in return.
'September 1, 1939' (1940)

11 All I have is a voice
To undo the folded lie,
The romantic lie in the brain
Of the sensual man-in-the-street
And the lie of Authority
Whose buildings grope the sky:
There is no such thing as the State
And no one exists alone;
Hunger allows no choice
To the citizen or the police;
We must love one another or die.
'September 1, 1939' (1940)

12 A shilling life will give you all the facts.
Title of poem (1936)

13 A poet's hope: to be,
like some valley cheese,
local, but prized elsewhere.
'Shorts II' (1976)

14 Harrow the house of the dead; look
shining at
New styles of architecture, a change of
heart.
'Sir, No Man's Enemy' (1930)

15 The stars are dead; the animals will not
look:
We are left alone with our day, and the
time is short and
History to the defeated
May say Alas but cannot help or pardon.
'Spain 1937' (1937) st. 23

16 To ask the hard question is simple.
Title of poem (1933)

17 Was he free? Was he happy? The question
is absurd:
Had anything been wrong, we should
certainly have heard.
'The Unknown Citizen' (1940)

18 When I find myself in the company of
scientists, I feel like a shabby curate who
has strayed by mistake into a drawing
room full of dukes.
The Dyer's Hand (1963) 'The Poet and the City'

19 What do you think about England, this
country of ours where nobody is well?
The Orators (1932) 'Address for a Prize-Day'

20 Art is born of humiliation.
In Stephen Spender World Within World
(1951) ch. 2

## Émile Augier 1820–89

21 La nostalgie de la boue!
Longing to be back in the mud!
Le Mariage d'Olympe (1855) act 1, sc. 1

## St Augustine of Hippo AD 354–430

22 Give me chastity and continency—but not
yet!
Confessions (AD 397–8) bk. 8, ch. 7

23 Tolle lege, tolle lege.
Take up and read, take up and read.
Confessions (AD 397–8) bk. 8, ch. 12

24 Sero te amavi, pulchritudo tam antiqua et tam
nova, sero te amavi!
Too late came I to love thee, O thou Beauty
both so ancient and so fresh, yea too late
came I to love thee.
Confessions (AD 397–8) bk. 10, ch. 27

25 You command continence; give what you
command, and command what you will.
Confessions (AD 397–8) bk. 10, ch. 29

26 There is no salvation outside the church.
De Baptismo contra Donatistas bk. 4, ch. 17,
sect. 24. Cf. 113:12, 113:14

1 *Audi partem alteram.*
  Hear the other side.
  *De Duabus Animabus contra Manicheos* ch. 14

2 *Dilige et quod vis fac.*
  Love and do what you will.
  *In Epistolam Joannis ad Parthos* (AD 413)
  tractatus 7, sect. 8 (often quoted 'Ama et fac
  quod vis')

3 To many, total abstinence is easier than
  perfect moderation.
  *On the Good of Marriage* (AD 401) ch. 21

4 *Cum dilectione hominum et odio vitiorum.*
  With love for mankind and hatred of sins.
  Letter 211 in J.-P. Migne (ed.) *Patrologiae
  Latinae* (1845) vol. 33 (often quoted 'Love the
  sinner but hate the sin')

5 *Roma locuta est; causa finita est.*
  Rome has spoken; the case is concluded.
  Traditional summary of words found in
  *Sermons* (Antwerp, 1702) no. 131, sect. 10

## Emperor Augustus 63 BC–AD 14

6 *Festina lente.*
  Make haste slowly.
  In Suetonius *Lives of the Caesars* 'Divus
  Augustus' sect. 25

7 He could boast that he inherited it brick
  and left it marble.
  Of the city of Rome; Suetonius *Lives of the
  Caesars* 'Divus Augustus' sect. 28

## Marcus Aurelius AD 121–80

8 Time is a violent torrent; no sooner is a
  thing brought to sight than it is swept by
  and another takes its place.
  *Meditations* bk. 4, sect. 43

9 Nothing happens to anybody which he is
  not fitted by nature to bear.
  *Meditations* bk. 5, sect. 18

10 Every instant of time is a pinprick of
  eternity.
  *Meditations* bk. 6, sect. 36

11 To change your mind and to follow him
  who sets you right is to be nonetheless the
  free agent that you were before.
  *Meditations* bk. 8, sect. 16

12 Mankind have been created for the sake of
  one another. Either instruct them,
  therefore, or endure them.
  *Meditations* bk. 8, sect. 59

## Jane Austen 1775–1817

13 An egg boiled very soft is not
  unwholesome.
  *Emma* (1816) ch. 3

14 One half of the world cannot understand
  the pleasures of the other.
  *Emma* (1816) ch. 9

15 The sooner every party breaks up the
  better.
  *Emma* (1816) ch. 25

16 Surprises are foolish things. The pleasure
  is not enhanced, and the inconvenience is
  often considerable.
  *Emma* (1816) ch. 26

17 One has no great hopes from Birmingham.
  I always say there is something direful in
  the sound.
  *Emma* (1816) ch. 36

18 There is not one in a hundred of either sex
  who is not taken in when they marry ... it
  is, of all transactions, the one in which
  people expect most from others, and are
  least honest themselves.
  *Mansfield Park* (1814) ch. 5

19 We do not look in great cities for our best
  morality.
  *Mansfield Park* (1814) ch. 9

20 A large income is the best recipe for
  happiness I ever heard of. It certainly may
  secure all the myrtle and turkey part of it.
  *Mansfield Park* (1814) ch. 22

21 Let other pens dwell on guilt and misery. I
  quit such odious subjects as soon as I can.
  *Mansfield Park* (1814) ch. 48

22 'Oh! it is only a novel!' ... only Cecilia, or
  Camilla, or Belinda:' or, in short, only some
  work in which the most thorough
  knowledge of human nature, the happiest
  delineation of its varieties, the liveliest
  effusions of wit and humour are conveyed
  to the world in the best chosen language.
  *Northanger Abbey* (1818) ch. 5

23 Where people wish to attach, they should
  always be ignorant. To come with a well-
  informed mind, is to come with an
  inability of administering to the vanity of
  others, which a sensible person would
  always wish to avoid. A woman especially,
  if she have the misfortune of knowing any
  thing, should conceal it as well as she can.
  *Northanger Abbey* (1818) ch. 14

24 From politics, it was an easy step to
  silence.
  *Northanger Abbey* (1818) ch. 14

25 Every man is surrounded by a
  neighbourhood of voluntary spies.
  *Northanger Abbey* (1818) ch. 34

26 She had been forced into prudence in her
  youth, she learned romance as she grew
  older—the natural sequel of an unnatural
  beginning.
  *Persuasion* (1818) ch. 4

27 Men have had every advantage of us in
  telling their own story. Education has been
  theirs in so much higher a degree; the pen
  has been in their hands.
  *Persuasion* (1818) ch. 23

28 All the privilege I claim for my own sex ...
  is that of loving longest, when existence or
  when hope is gone.
  *Persuasion* (1818) ch. 23

1 It was, perhaps, one of those cases in which advice is good or bad only as the event decides.
 *Persuasion* (1818) ch. 23

2 It is a truth universally acknowledged, that a single man in possession of a good fortune, must be in want of a wife.
 *Pride and Prejudice* (1813) ch. 1. Cf. 81:17

3 Mr Collins had only to change from Jane to Elizabeth—and it was soon done—done while Mrs Bennet was stirring the fire.
 *Pride and Prejudice* (1813) ch. 15

4 Marriage had always been her object; it was the only honourable provision for well-educated young women of small fortune, and however uncertain of giving happiness, must be their pleasantest preservative from want.
 *Pride and Prejudice* (1813) ch. 22

5 Are the shades of Pemberley to be thus polluted?
 *Pride and Prejudice* (1813) ch. 56

6 For what do we live, but to make sport for our neighbours, and laugh at them in our turn?
 *Pride and Prejudice* (1813) ch. 57

7 An annuity is a very serious business.
 *Sense and Sensibility* (1811) vol. 1, ch. 2

8 On every formal visit a child ought to be of the party, by way of provision for discourse.
 *Sense and Sensibility* (1811) vol. 2, ch. 6

9 3 or 4 families in a country village is the very thing to work on.
 Letter to Anna Austen, 9 September 1814, in R. W. Chapman (ed.) *Jane Austen's Letters* (1952)

10 The little bit (two inches wide) of ivory on which I work with so fine a brush, as produces little effect after much labour?
 Letter to J. Edward Austen, 16 December 1816, in R. W. Chapman (ed.) *Jane Austen's Letters* (1952)

11 Single women have a dreadful propensity for being poor—which is one very strong argument in favour of matrimony.
 Letter to Fanny Knight, 13 March 1817, in R. W. Chapman (ed.) *Jane Austen's Letters* (1952)

12 Pictures of perfection as you know make me sick and wicked.
 Letter to Fanny Knight, 23 March 1817, in R. W. Chapman (ed.) *Jane Austen's Letters* (1952)

## Earl of Avon

*See* Sir Anthony Eden

## Revd Awdry 1911–

13 You've a lot to learn about trucks, little Thomas. They are silly things and must be kept in their place. After pushing them about here for a few weeks you'll know almost as much about them as Edward. Then you'll be a Really Useful Engine.
 *Thomas the Tank Engine* (1946) p. 46

## Alan Ayckbourn 1939–

14 My mother used to say, Delia, if S-E-X ever rears its ugly head, close your eyes before you see the rest of it.
 *Bedroom Farce* (1978) act 2

## Pam Ayres 1947–

15 Medicinal discovery,
It moves in mighty leaps,
It leapt straight past the common cold
And gave it us for keeps.
 'Oh no, I got a cold' (1976)

## W. E. Aytoun 1813–65

16 The grim Geneva ministers
With anxious scowl drew near,
As you have seen the ravens flock
Around the dying deer.
 'The Execution of Montrose' (1849) st. 17

17 The deep, unutterable woe
Which none save exiles feel.
 'The Island of the Scots' (1849) st. 12

18 The earth is all the home I have,
The heavens my wide roof-tree.
 'The Wandering Jew' (1867) l. 49

## Charles Babbage 1792–1871

19 Every moment dies a man,
Every moment $1\frac{1}{16}$ is born.
 Parody of Tennyson's 'Vision of Sin' in an unpublished letter to the poet. See *New Scientist* 4 December 1958, p. 1428. Cf. 328:26

## Francis Bacon 1561–1626

20 If a man will begin with certainties, he shall end in doubts; but if he will be content to begin with doubts, he shall end in certainties.
 *The Advancement of Learning* (1605) bk. 1, ch. 5, sect. 8

21 Antiquities are history defaced, or some remnants of history which have casually escaped the shipwreck of time.
 *The Advancement of Learning* (1605) bk. 2, ch. 2, sect. 1

22 They are ill discoverers that think there is no land, when they can see nothing but sea.
 *The Advancement of Learning* (1605) bk. 2, ch. 7, sect. 5

23 Words are the tokens current and accepted for conceits, as moneys are for values.
 *The Advancement of Learning* (1605) bk. 2, ch. 16, sect. 3

24 A dance is a measured pace, as a verse is a measured speech.
 *The Advancement of Learning* (1605) bk. 2, ch. 16, sect. 5

1 But men must know, that in this theatre of man's life it is reserved only for God and angels to be lookers on.
*The Advancement of Learning* (1605) bk. 2, ch. 20, sect. 8

2 All good moral philosophy is but an handmaid to religion.
*The Advancement of Learning* (1605) bk. 2, ch. 22, sect. 14

3 It is in life as it is in ways, the shortest way is commonly the foulest, and surely the fairer way is not much about.
*The Advancement of Learning* (1605) bk. 2, ch. 23, sect. 45

4 That all things are changed, and that nothing really perishes, and that the sum of matter remains exactly the same, is sufficiently certain.
*Cogitationes de Natura Rerum* Cogitatio 5 in J. Spedding (ed.) *Works* vol. 5 (1858) p. 426

5 Ancient times were the youth of the world.
*De Dignitate et Augmentis Scientiarum* (1623) bk. 1 (tr. Gilbert Watts, 1640)

6 Riches are a good handmaid, but the worst mistress.
*De Dignitate et Augmentis Scientiarum* (1623) bk. 6, ch. 3, pt. 3 'The Antitheta of Things' no. 6 (tr. Gilbert Watts, 1640)

7 No term of moderation takes place with the vulgar.
*De Dignitate et Augmentis Scientiarum* (1623) bk. 6, ch. 3, pt. 3 'The Antitheta of Things' no. 30 (tr. Gilbert Watts, 1640)

8 Silence is the virtue of fools.
*De Dignitate et Augmentis Scientiarum* (1623) bk. 6, ch. 3, pt. 3 'The Antitheta of Things' no. 31 (tr. Gilbert Watts, 1640)

9 I hold every man a debtor to his profession.
*The Elements of the Common Law* (1596) preface

10 He is the fountain of honour.
*An Essay of a King* (1642)

11 Prosperity doth best discover vice, but adversity doth best discover virtue.
*Essays* (1625) 'Of Adversity'

12 A little philosophy inclineth man's mind to atheism, but depth in philosophy bringeth men's minds about to religion.
*Essays* (1625) 'Of Atheism'

13 Virtue is like a rich stone, best plain set.
*Essays* (1625) 'Of Beauty'

14 There is no excellent beauty that hath not some strangeness in the proportion.
*Essays* (1625) 'Of Beauty'

15 He said it that knew it best.
*Essays* (1625) 'Of Boldness' (referring to Demosthenes)

16 Mahomet called the hill to come to him again and again; and when the hill stood still, he was never a whit abashed, but said, 'If the hill will not come to Mahomet, Mahomet will go to the hill.'
*Essays* (1625) 'Of Boldness' (proverbially 'If the mountain will not come ... ')

17 Books will speak plain when counsellors blanch.
*Essays* (1625) 'Of Counsel'

18 In things that are tender and unpleasing, it is good to break the ice by some whose words are of less weight, and to reserve the more weighty voice to come in as by chance.
*Essays* (1625) 'Of Cunning'

19 I knew one that when he wrote a letter he would put that which was most material in the postscript, as if it had been a bymatter.
*Essays* (1625) 'Of Cunning'

20 Men fear death as children fear to go in the dark; and as that natural fear in children is increased with tales, so is the other.
*Essays* (1625) 'Of Death'

21 Revenge triumphs over death; love slights it; honour aspireth to it; grief flieth to it.
*Essays* (1625) 'Of Death'

22 It is as natural to die as to be born; and to a little infant, perhaps, the one is as painful as the other.
*Essays* (1625) 'Of Death'

23 A crowd is not company, and faces are but a gallery of pictures, and talk but a tinkling cymbal, where there is no love.
*Essays* (1625) 'Of Friendship'

24 It redoubleth joys, and cutteth griefs in halves.
*Essays* (1625) 'Of Friendship'

25 Cure the disease and kill the patient.
*Essays* (1625) 'Of Friendship'

26 God Almighty first planted a garden; and, indeed, it is the purest of human pleasures.
*Essays* (1625) 'Of Gardens'

27 Men in great place are thrice servants: servants of the sovereign or state, servants of fame, and servants of business.
*Essays* (1625) 'Of Great Place'

28 It is a strange desire to seek power and to lose liberty.
*Essays* (1625) 'Of Great Place'

29 All rising to great place is by a winding stair.
*Essays* (1625) 'Of Great Place'

30 As the births of living creatures at first are ill-shapen, so are all innovations, which are the births of time.
*Essays* (1625) 'Of Innovations'

31 He that will not apply new remedies must expect new evils; for time is the greatest innovator.
*Essays* (1625) 'Of Innovations'

32 It has been well said that 'the arch-flatterer with whom all the petty flatterers have intelligence is a man's self.'
*Essays* (1625) 'Of Love'

1 He that hath wife and children hath given hostages to fortune; for they are impediments to great enterprises, either of virtue or mischief.
*Essays* (1625) 'Of Marriage and the Single Life'. Cf. 211:26

2 Wives are young men's mistresses, companions for middle age, and old men's nurses.
*Essays* (1625) 'Of Marriage and the Single Life'

3 He was reputed one of the wise men that made answer to the question when a man should marry? 'A young man not yet, an elder man not at all.'
*Essays* (1625) 'Of Marriage and the Single Life'. Cf. 256:5

4 New nobility is but the act of power, but ancient nobility is the act of time.
*Essays* (1625) 'Of Nobility'

5 Nobility of birth commonly abateth industry.
*Essays* (1625) 'Of Nobility'

6 Children sweeten labours, but they make misfortunes more bitter.
*Essays* (1625) 'Of Parents and Children'

7 Fame is like a river, that beareth up things light and swollen, and drowns things weighty and solid.
*Essays* (1625) 'Of Praise'

8 Age will not be defied.
*Essays* (1625) 'Of Regimen of Health'

9 Revenge is a kind of wild justice, which the more man's nature runs to, the more ought law to weed it out.
*Essays* (1625) 'Of Revenge'

10 Money is like muck, not good except it be spread.
*Essays* (1625) 'Of Seditions and Troubles'

11 The remedy is worse than the disease.
*Essays* (1625) 'Of Seditions and Troubles'

12 The French are wiser than they seem, and the Spaniards seem wiser than they are.
*Essays* (1625) 'Of Seeming Wise'

13 Studies serve for delight, for ornament, and for ability.
*Essays* (1625) 'Of Studies'

14 Some books are to be tasted, others to be swallowed, and some few to be chewed and digested.
*Essays* (1625) 'Of Studies'

15 Reading maketh a full man; conference a ready man; and writing an exact man.
*Essays* (1625) 'Of Studies'

16 Histories make men wise; poets, witty; the mathematics, subtle; natural philosophy, deep; moral, grave; logic and rhetoric, able to contend.
*Essays* (1625) 'Of Studies'

17 Travel, in the younger sort, is a part of education; in the elder, a part of experience. He that travelleth into a country before he hath some entrance into the language, goeth to school, and not to travel.
*Essays* (1625) 'Of Travel'

18 What is truth? said jesting Pilate; and would not stay for an answer.
*Essays* (1625) 'Of Truth'. Cf. 54:1

19 All colours will agree in the dark.
*Essays* (1625) 'Of Unity in Religion'

20 It was prettily devised of Aesop, 'The fly sat upon the axletree of the chariot-wheel and said, what a dust do I raise.'
*Essays* (1625) 'Of Vain-Glory'

21 Be so true to thyself as thou be not false to others.
*Essays* (1625) 'Of Wisdom for a Man's Self'. Cf. 274:23

22 Lucid intervals and happy pauses.
*History of King Henry VII* (1622) para. 3 in J. Spedding (ed.) *Works* vol. 6 (1858) p. 32

23 I have taken all knowledge to be my province.
'To My Lord Treasurer Burghley' (1592) in J. Spedding (ed.) *Letters and Life* vol. 1 (1861) p. 109

24 Opportunity makes a thief.
'A Letter of Advice to the Earl of Essex ... ' (1598) in J. Spedding (ed.) *Letters and Life* vol. 2 (1862) p. 99

25 For also knowledge itself is power.
*Meditationes Sacrae* (1597) 'Of Heresies'

26 The end of our foundation is the knowledge of causes, and secret motions of things; and the enlarging of the bounds of human Empire, to the effecting of all things possible.
*New Atlantis* (1627)

27 That great mother of sciences [natural philosophy].
*Novum Organum* (1620) bk. 1, Aphorism 80 (tr. J. Spedding)

28 Printing, gunpowder, and the magnet [Mariner's Needle] ... these three have changed the whole face and state of things throughout the world.
*Novum Organum* (1620) bk. 1, Aphorism 129 (tr. J. Spedding). Cf. 90:9

29 Anger makes dull men witty, but it keeps them poor.
J. Spedding (ed.) *Works* vol. 7 (1859) 'Baconiana' (often attributed to Queen Elizabeth I)

30 The world's a bubble; and the life of man Less than a span.
*The World* (1629)

31 What then remains, but that we still should cry,
Not to be born, or being born, to die?
*The World* (1629)

## Lord Baden-Powell 1857–1941

1 The scouts' motto is founded on my initials, it is: BE PREPARED.

*Scouting for Boys* (1908) pt. 1

## Walter Bagehot 1826–77

2 A constitutional statesman is in general a man of common opinion and uncommon abilities.

*Biographical Studies* (1881) 'The Character of Sir Robert Peel'

3 In such constitutions [as England's] there are two parts ... first, those which excite and preserve the reverence of the population—the *dignified* parts ... and next, the *efficient* parts—those by which it, in fact, works and rules.

*The English Constitution* (1867) 'The Cabinet'

4 The Crown is, according to the saying, the 'fountain of honour'; but the Treasury is the spring of business.

*The English Constitution* (1867) 'The Cabinet'. Cf. 24:10

5 A cabinet is a combining committee—a *hyphen* which joins, a *buckle* which fastens, the legislative part of the state to the executive part of the state.

*The English Constitution* (1867) 'The Cabinet'

6 It has been said that England invented the phrase, 'Her Majesty's Opposition'; that it was the first government which made a criticism of administration as much a part of the polity as administration itself. This critical opposition is the consequence of cabinet government.

*The English Constitution* (1867) 'The Cabinet'

7 *The Times* has made many ministries.

*The English Constitution* (1867) 'The Cabinet'

8 It has been said, not truly, but with a possible approximation to truth, that in 1802 every hereditary monarch was insane.

*The English Constitution* (1867) 'Checks and Balances'

9 Nations touch at their summits.

*The English Constitution* (1867) 'The House of Lords'

10 As soon as we see that England is a disguised republic we must see too that the classes for whom the disguise is necessary must be tenderly dealt with.

*The English Constitution* (1867) 'Its History'

11 Women—one half the human race at least—care fifty times more for a marriage than a ministry.

*The English Constitution* (1867) 'The Monarchy'

12 Royalty is a government in which the attention of the nation is concentrated on one person doing interesting actions. A Republic is a government in which that attention is divided between many, who are all doing uninteresting actions. Accordingly, so long as the human heart is strong and the human reason weak, Royalty will be strong because it appeals to diffused feeling, and Republics weak because they appeal to the understanding.

*The English Constitution* (1867) 'The Monarchy'

13 We must not let in daylight upon magic.

*The English Constitution* (1867) 'The Monarchy (continued)'

14 The Sovereign has, under a constitutional monarchy such as ours, three rights—the right to be consulted, the right to encourage, the right to warn.

*The English Constitution* (1867) 'The Monarchy (continued)'

15 Writers, like teeth, are divided into incisors and grinders.

*Estimates of some Englishmen and Scotchmen* (1858) 'The First Edinburgh Reviewers'

16 He describes London like a special correspondent for posterity.

*National Review* 7 October 1858 'Charles Dickens'

17 Wordsworth, Tennyson and Browning; or, pure, ornate, and grotesque art in English poetry.

*National Review* November 1864 (essay title)

## Philip James Bailey 1816–1902

18 We should count time by heart-throbs.

*Festus* (1839) sc. 5

19 America, thou half-brother of the world; With something good and bad of every land.

*Festus* (1839) sc. 10

## Bruce Bairnsfather 1888–1959

20 Well, if you knows of a better 'ole, go to it.

*Fragments from France* (1915) p. 1

## Sir Henry Williams Baker 1821–77

21 Perverse and foolish oft I strayed, But yet in love he sought me, And on his shoulder gently laid, And home, rejoicing, brought me.

'The King of love my shepherd is' (1868 hymn)

## Michael Bakunin 1814–76

22 The urge for destruction is also a creative urge!

*Jahrbuch für Wissenschaft und Kunst* (1842) 'Die Reaktion in Deutschland' (under the pseudonym 'Jules Elysard')

**1** From each according to his faculties, to each according to his needs.

> Declaration signed by forty-seven anarchists on trial after the failure of their uprising at Lyons in 1870, in J. Morrison Davidson *The Old Order and the New* (1890). Cf. 221:9

## James Baldwin 1924–87

**2** Anyone who has ever struggled with poverty knows how extremely expensive it is to be poor.

> *Nobody Knows My Name* (1961) 'Fifth Avenue, Uptown: a letter from Harlem'

**3** Money, it turned out, was exactly like sex, you thought of nothing else if you didn't have it and thought of other things if you did.

> *Esquire* May 1961 'Black Boy looks at the White Boy'

**4** If they take you in the morning, they will be coming for us that night.

> *New York Review of Books* 7 January 1971 'Open Letter to my Sister, Angela Davis'

## Stanley Baldwin 1867–1947

**5** The bomber will always get through. The only defence is in offence, which means that you have to kill more women and children more quickly than the enemy if you want to save yourselves.

> Speech, *Hansard* 10 November 1932, col. 632

**6** Since the day of the air, the old frontiers are gone. When you think of the defence of England you no longer think of the chalk cliffs of Dover; you think of the Rhine.

> Speech, *Hansard* 30 July 1934, col. 2339

**7** I shall be but a short time tonight. I have seldom spoken with greater regret, for my lips are not yet unsealed. Were these troubles over I would make a case, and I guarantee that not a man would go into the lobby against us.

> Speech, *Hansard* 10 December 1935, col. 856, on the Abyssinian crisis (usually quoted 'My lips are sealed')

**8** Do not run up your nose dead against the Pope or the NUM!

> In Lord Butler *The Art of Memory* (1982) 'Iain Macleod'. Cf. 215:19

**9** They [parliament] are a lot of hard-faced men who look as if they had done very well out of the war.

> In J. M. Keynes *Economic Consequences of the Peace* (1919) ch. 5

**10** There are three classes which need sanctuary more than others—birds, wild flowers, and Prime Ministers.

> In *Observer* 24 May 1925

## Arthur James Balfour 1848–1930

**11** Christianity, of course ... but why journalism?

> Replying to Frank Harris's remark that 'all the faults of the age come from Christianity and journalism'; in Margot Asquith *Autobiography* (1920) vol. 1, ch. 10

**12** I thought he was a young man of promise, but it appears he is a young man of promises.

> Describing Churchill, in Winston Churchill *My Early Life* (1930) ch. 17

## Ballads

**13** O mother, mother, make my bed,
O make it saft and narrow:
My love has died for me to-day,
I'll die for him to-morrow.

> 'Barbara Allen's Cruelty'

**14** Ye Highlands and ye Lawlands,
O where hae ye been?
They hae slain the Earl of Murray,
And hae laid him on the green.

> 'The Bonny Earl of Murray'

**15** O lang will his Lady
Look owre the Castle Downe,
Ere she see the Earl of Murray
Come sounding through the town!

> 'The Bonny Earl of Murray'

**16** She hadna sailed a league, a league,
A league but barely three,
Till grim, grim grew his countenance
And gurly grew the sea.

> 'The Daemon Lover'

**17** I am a man upon the land,
I am a selkie in the sea;
When I am far and far from land,
My home it is the Sule Skerry.

> 'The Great Selkie of Sule Skerry'

**18** Where are your eyes that looked so mild
When my poor heart you first beguiled?
Why did you run from me and the child?
Och, Johnny, I hardly knew ye!

> 'Johnny, I hardly knew Ye'

**19** 'What gat ye to your dinner, Lord Randal,
my Son?
What gat ye to your dinner, my handsome
young man?'
'I gat eels boil'd in broo'; mother, make my
bed soon,
For I'm weary wi' hunting, and fain wald
lie down.'

> 'Lord Randal'

**20** This ae nighte, this ae nighte,
—*Every nighte and alle,*
Fire and fleet and candle-lighte,
*And Christe receive thy saule.*

> 'Lyke-Wake Dirge'

1 When captains courageous whom death
    could not daunt,
  Did march to the siege of the city of
    Gaunt,
  They mustered their soldiers by two and by
    three,
  And the foremost in battle was Mary
    Ambree.
    'Mary Ambree'

2 Yestreen the Queen had four Maries,
  The night she'll hae but three;
  There was Marie Seaton, and Marie Beaton,
  And Marie Carmichael, and me.
    'The Queen's Maries'

3 Fight on, my men, sayes Sir Andrew
    Bartton,
  I am hurt but I am not slain;
  Ile lay mee downe and bleed a while
  And then Ile rise and fight againe.
    'Sir Andrew Bartton'

4 The king sits in Dunfermline town
  Drinking the blude-red wine.
    'Sir Patrick Spens'

5 I saw the new moon late yestreen
  Wi' the auld moon in her arm;
  And if we gang to sea master,
  I fear we'll come to harm.
    'Sir Patrick Spens'

6 Half-owre, half-owre to Aberdour,
  'Tis fifty fathoms deep;
  And there lies good Sir Patrick Spens,
  Wi' the Scots lords at his feet!
    'Sir Patrick Spens'

7 And see ye not yon braid, braid road,
  That lies across the lily leven?
  That is the Path of Wickedness,
  Though some call it the Road to Heaven.
    'Thomas the Rhymer'

8 It was mirk, mirk night, there was nae
    starlight,
  They waded thro' red blude to the knee;
  For a' the blude that's shed on the earth
  Rins through the springs o' that countrie.
    'Thomas the Rhymer'

9 And naebody kens that he lies there
  But his hawk, his hound, and his lady fair.
    'The Twa Corbies'

10 O waly, waly, gin love be bonnie
  A little time while it is new!
  But when 'tis auld it waxeth cauld,
  And fades awa' like morning dew.
    'Waly, Waly'

11 Tom Pearse, Tom Pearse, lend me your
    grey mare,
  All along, down along, out along, lee.
  For I want for to go to Widdicombe Fair,
  Wi' Bill Brewer, Jan Stewer, Peter Gurney,
  Peter Davey, Dan'l Whiddon, Harry Hawk,
  Old Uncle Tom Cobbleigh and all.
    'Widdicombe Fair'

## Whitney Balliett 1926–

12 A critic is a bundle of biases held loosely
  together by a sense of taste.
    *Dinosaurs in the Morning* (1962) introductory
    note

13 The sound of surprise.
    Title of book on jazz (1959)

## Richard Bancroft 1544–1610

14 Where Christ erecteth his Church, the
  devil in the same churchyard will have his
  chapel.
    Sermon at Paul's Cross, 9 February 1588.
    Cf. 31:17, 212:9

## John Barbour c.1320–95

15 Storys to rede ar delitabill,
  Suppos that thai be nocht bot fabill.
    *The Bruce* (1375) bk. 1, l. 1

16 A! fredome is a noble thing!
  Fredome mayse man to haiff liking.
    *The Bruce* (1375) bk. 1, l. 225

## Alexander Barclay c.1475–1552

17 The lords will alway that people note and
    see
  Between them and servants some diversity,
  Though it to them turn to no profit at all;
  If they have pleasure, the servant shall
    have small.
    *Eclogues* (1514) no. 2, l. 791

## Revd R. H. B. Barham ('Thomas Ingoldsby') 1788–1845

18 And six little Singing-boys,—dear little
    souls!
  In nice clean faces, and nice white stoles.
    *The Ingoldsby Legends* (First Series, 1840) 'The
    Jackdaw of Rheims'

19 Never was heard such a terrible curse!
  But what gave rise
  To no little surprise,
  Nobody seemed one penny the worse!
    *The Ingoldsby Legends* (First Series, 1840) 'The
    Jackdaw of Rheims'

20 Heedless of grammar, they all cried, 'That's
    him!'
    *The Ingoldsby Legends* (First Series, 1840) 'The
    Jackdaw of Rheims'

21 Here's a corpse in the case with a sad
    swelled face,
  And a 'Crowner's Quest' is a queer sort of
    thing!
    *The Ingoldsby Legends* (First Series, 1840) 'A
    Lay of St Gengulphus' (in later editions: 'a
    Medical Crowner's a queer sort of thing!')

22 A servant's too often a negligent elf;
  —If it's business of consequence, DO IT
  YOURSELF!
    *The Ingoldsby Legends* (Second Series, 1842)
    'The Ingoldsby Penance!—Moral'

## Revd Sabine Baring-Gould
1834–1924

1 Onward, Christian soldiers,
  Marching as to war,
  With the cross of Jesus
  Going on before.
  'Onward, Christian Soldiers' (1864 hymn)

2 Through the night of doubt and sorrow
  Onward goes the pilgrim band,
  Singing songs of expectation,
  Marching to the Promised Land.
  'Through the night of doubt and sorrow'
  (1867 hymn); translated from the Danish of
  B. S. Ingemann (1789–1862)

## Frederick R. Barnard

3 One picture is worth ten thousand words.
  *Printers' Ink* 10 March 1927

## Julian Barnes 1946–

4 The land of embarrassment and breakfast?
  *Flaubert's Parrot* (1984) ch. 7 (of England)

5 Books say: she did this because. Life says:
  she did this. Books are where things are
  explained to you; life is where things
  aren't.
  *Flaubert's Parrot* (1984) ch. 13

6 Does history repeat itself, the first time as
  tragedy, the second time as farce? No,
  that's too grand, too considered a process.
  History just burps, and we taste again that
  raw-onion sandwich it swallowed centuries
  ago.
  *A History of the World in 10½ Chapters* (1989)
  'Parenthesis'. Cf. 221:10

## Richard Barnfield 1574–1627

7 The waters were his winding sheet, the sea
  was made his tomb;
  Yet for his fame the ocean sea, was not
  sufficient room.
  *The Encomion of Lady Pecunia* (1598) 'To the
  Gentlemen Readers' (on the death of Sir John
  Hawkins)

8 My flocks feed not, my ewes breed not,
  My rams speed not, all is amiss:
  Love in dying, Faith is defying,
  Heart's renying, causer of this.
  'The Unknown Shepherd's Complaint' in
  Nicholas Ling (ed.) *England's Helicon* (1600)

## Phineas T. Barnum 1810–91

9 There's a sucker born every minute.
  Attributed

## J. M. Barrie 1860–1937

10 His lordship may compel us to be equal
  upstairs, but there will never be equality in
  the servants' hall.
  *The Admirable Crichton* (performed 1902) act 1

11 When the first baby laughed for the first
  time, the laugh broke into a thousand
  pieces and they all went skipping about,
  and that was the beginning of fairies.
  *Peter Pan* (1928) act 1

12 Every time a child says 'I don't believe in
  fairies' there is a little fairy somewhere
  that falls down dead.
  *Peter Pan* (1928) act 1

13 To die will be an awfully big adventure.
  *Peter Pan* (1928) act 3. Cf. 146:6

14 Do you believe in fairies? Say quick that
  you believe! If you believe, clap your hands!
  *Peter Pan* (1928) act 4

15 That is ever the way. 'Tis all jealousy to the
  bride and good wishes to the corpse.
  *Quality Street* (performed 1901) act 1

16 Charm . . . it's a sort of bloom on a woman.
  If you have it, you don't need to have
  anything else; and if you don't have it, it
  doesn't much matter what else you have.
  *What Every Woman Knows* (performed 1908)
  act 1

17 There are few more impressive sights in
  the world than a Scotsman on the make.
  *What Every Woman Knows* (performed 1908)
  act 2

18 The tragedy of a man who has found
  himself out.
  *What Every Woman Knows* (performed 1908)
  act 4

## Roland Barthes 1915–80

19 I think that cars today are almost the exact
  equivalent of the great Gothic cathedrals:
  I mean the supreme creation of an era,
  conceived with passion by unknown
  artists, and consumed in image if not in
  usage by a whole population which
  appropriates them as a purely magical
  object.
  *Mythologies* (1957) 'La nouvelle Citroën' (tr. A.
  Lavers, 1972)

## Bernard Baruch 1870–1965

20 We are today in the midst of a cold war.
  Speech to South Carolina Legislature
  16 April 1947, in *New York Times* 17 April
  1947, p. 21 ('cold war' was suggested to him
  by H. B. Swope, former editor of the *New York
  World*)

21 Vote for the man who promises least; he'll
  be the least disappointing.
  In M. Berger *New York* (1960)

## Jacques Barzun 1907–

22 If it were possible to talk to the unborn,
  one could never explain to them how it
  feels to be alive, for life is washed in the
  speechless real.
  *The House of Intellect* (1959) ch. 6

## Edgar Bateman and George Le Brunn

1 Wiv a ladder and some glasses,
You could see to 'Ackney Marshes,
If it wasn't for the 'ouses in between.
'If it wasn't for the 'Ouses in between' (1894 song)

## Katherine Lee Bates 1859–1929

2 America! America!
God shed His grace on thee
And crown thy good with brotherhood
From sea to shining sea!
'America the Beautiful' (1893)

## Charles Baudelaire 1821–67

3 *Hypocrite lecteur,—mon semblable,—mon frère.*
Hypocrite reader—my likeness—my brother.
*Les fleurs du mal* (1857) 'Au Lecteur'

4 *Là, tout n'est qu'ordre et beauté,*
*Luxe, calme et volupté.*
Everything there is simply order and beauty, luxury, peace and sensual indulgence.
*Les fleurs du mal* (1857) 'L'Invitation au voyage'—'Spleen et idéal' no. 56

5 *Quelle est cette île triste et noire? C'est Cythère,*
*Nous dit-on, un pays fameux dans les chansons,*
*Eldorado banal de tous les vieux garçons.*
*Regardez, après tout, c'est un pauvre terre.*
What sad, black isle is that? It's Cythera, so they say, a land celebrated in song, the banal Eldorado of all the old fools. Look, after all, it's a land of poverty.
*Les fleurs du mal* (1857) 'Un voyage à Cythère'—'Les fleurs du mal' no. 121

6 *Au fond de l'Inconnu pour trouver du nouveau!*
Through the unknown, we'll find the new.
*Les fleurs du mal* (1857) 'Le voyage' no. 126 (tr. Robert Lowell)

7 *Il y a dans tout changement quelque chose d'infâme et d'agréable à la fois, quelque chose qui tient de l'infidelité et du déménagement. Cela suffit à expliquer la Révolution Française.*
There is in all change something at once sordid and agreeable, which smacks of infidelity and household removals. This is sufficient to explain the French Revolution.
*Journaux intimes* (1887) 'Mon coeur mis à nu' no. 4 (tr. Christopher Isherwood)

8 *La croyance au progrès est une doctrine de paresseux, une doctrine de Belges. C'est l'individu qui compte sur ses voisins pour faire sa besogne.*
Belief in progress is a doctrine of idlers and Belgians. It is the individual relying upon his neighbours to do his work.
*Journaux intimes* (1887) 'Mon coeur mis à nu' no. 9 (tr. Christopher Isherwood)

9 *Il faut épater le bourgeois.*
One must astonish the bourgeois.
Attributed. Also attributed to Privat d'Anglemont (c.1820–59) in the form '*Je les ai épatés, les bourgeois* [I flabbergasted them, the bourgeois]'

## L. Frank Baum 1856–1919

10 The road to the City of Emeralds is paved with yellow brick.
*The Wonderful Wizard of Oz* (1900) ch. 2 ('Follow the yellow brick road' in the 1939 screenplay)

## Vicki Baum 1888–1960

11 Marriage always demands the finest arts of insincerity possible between two human beings.
*Zwischenfall in Lohwinckel* (1930) (tr. M. Goldsmith as *Results of an Accident* (1931) p. 140)

## Sir Beverley Baxter 1891–1964

12 Beaverbrook is so pleased to be in the Government that he is like the town tart who has finally married the Mayor!
In Sir Henry Channon *Chips: the Diaries* (1967) 12 June 1940

## James Beattie 1735–1803

13 Some deemed him wondrous wise, and some believed him mad.
*The Minstrel* bk. 1 (1771) st. 16

## Lord Beatty 1871–1936

14 There's something wrong with our bloody ships today.
At the Battle of Jutland, 1916; in Winston Churchill *The World Crisis 1916–1918* (1927) pt. 1, p. 129

## Pierre-Augustin Caron de Beaumarchais 1732–99

15 Today if something is not worth saying, people sing it.
*The Barber of Seville* (1775) act 1, sc. 2

16 Drinking when we are not thirsty and making love all year round, madam; that is all there is to distinguish us from other animals.
*The Marriage of Figaro* (1785) act 2, sc. 21

17 Because you are a great lord, you believe yourself to be a great genius! ... You took the trouble to be born, but no more.
*The Marriage of Figaro* (1785) act 5, sc. 3

## Francis Beaumont 1584–1616

18          What things have we seen,
Done at the Mermaid!
'Letter to Ben Jonson'

## Francis Beaumont 1584–1616 and John Fletcher 1579–1625

1 Those have most power to hurt us that we love.
  *The Maid's Tragedy* (written 1610–11) act 5

2 PHILASTER: Oh, but thou dost not know
  What 'tis to die.
  BELLARIO: Yes, I do know, my Lord:
  'Tis less than to be born; a lasting sleep;
  A quiet resting from all jealousy,
  A thing we all pursue; I know besides,
  It is but giving over of a game,
  That must be lost.
  *Philaster* (written 1609) act 3

3 It would talk: Lord how it talk't!
  *The Scornful Lady* (1616) act 4

## Lord Beaverbrook (Max Aitken) 1879–1964

4 Now who is responsible for this work of development on which so much depends? To whom must the praise be given? To the boys in the back rooms. They do not sit in the limelight. But they are the men who do the work.
  *Listener* 27 March 1941

5 With the publication of his Private Papers in 1952, he committed suicide 25 years after his death.
  *Men and Power* (1956) p. xviii (of Earl Haig)

6 Our cock won't fight.
  Of Edward VIII, during the abdication crisis of 1936; in F. Donaldson *Edward VIII* (1974) ch. 22

## Samuel Beckett 1906–89

7 It is suicide to be abroad. But what is it to be at home, Mr Tyler, what is it to be at home? A lingering dissolution.
  *All That Fall* (1957) p. 10

8 We could have saved sixpence. We have saved fivepence. (*Pause*) But at what cost?
  *All That Fall* (1957) p. 25

9 CLOV: Do you believe in the life to come?
  HAMM: Mine was always that.
  *Endgame* (1958) p. 35

10 Nothing to be done.
  *Waiting for Godot* (1955) act 1

11 One of the thieves was saved. (*Pause*) It's a reasonable percentage.
  *Waiting for Godot* (1955) act 1

12 Nothing happens, nobody comes, nobody goes, it's awful!
  *Waiting for Godot* (1955) act 1

13 VLADIMIR: That passed the time.
  ESTRAGON: It would have passed in any case.
  VLADIMIR: Yes, but not so rapidly.
  *Waiting for Godot* (1955) act 1

14 We all are born mad. Some remain so.
  *Waiting for Godot* (1955) act 2

15 They give birth astride of a grave, the light gleams an instant, then it's night once more.
  *Waiting for Godot* (1955) act 2

16 Habit is a great deadener.
  *Waiting for Godot* (1955) act 2

## Thomas Becon 1512–67

17 For commonly, wheresoever God buildeth a church, the devil will build a chapel just by.
  *Catechism* (1560, ed. J. Ayre, 1844) p. 361. Cf. 28:14, 212:9

18 When the wine is in, the wit is out.
  *Catechism* (1560, ed. J. Ayre, 1844) p. 375

## Thomas Lovell Beddoes 1803–49

19 If there were dreams to sell,
  What would you buy?
  'Dream-Pedlary' (written 1830)

## The Venerable Bede AD 673–735

20 'Such,' he said, 'O King, seems to me the present life of men on earth, in comparison with that time which to us is uncertain, as if when on a winter's night you sit feasting with your ealdormen and thegns,—a single sparrow should fly swiftly into the hall, and coming in at one door, instantly fly out through another'.
  *Ecclesiastical History of the English People* (tr. B. Colgrave, 1969) bk. 2, ch. 13

## Harry Bedford and Terry Sullivan

21 I'm a bit of a ruin that Cromwell knocked about a bit.
  'It's a Bit of a Ruin that Cromwell Knocked about a Bit' (1920 song, written for Marie Lloyd)

## Barnard Elliott Bee 1823–61

22 There is Jackson with his Virginians, standing like a stone wall. Let us determine to die here, and we will conquer.
  Referring to General T. J. ('Stonewall') Jackson at the battle of Bull Run, 21 July, 1861 (in which Bee himself was killed); in B. Perley Poore *Perley's Reminiscences* (1886) vol. 2, ch. 7

## Sir Thomas Beecham 1879–1961

23 There are two golden rules for an orchestra: start together and finish together. The public doesn't give a damn what goes on in between.
  In H. Atkins and A. Newman *Beecham Stories* (1978) p. 27

**1** Two skeletons copulating on a corrugated tin roof.

> Describing the harpsichord, in H. Atkins and A. Newman *Beecham Stories* (1978) p. 34

**2** A kind of musical Malcolm Sargent.

> Of Herbert von Karajan, in H. Atkins and A. Newman *Beecham Stories* (1978) p. 61

**3** Too much counterpoint; what is worse, Protestant counterpoint.

> Of J. S. Bach, in *Guardian* 8 March 1971

**4** Madam, you have between your legs an instrument capable of giving pleasure to thousands—and all you can do is scratch it.

> To a cellist (attributed)

## Revd H. C. Beeching 1859–1919

**5** Not when the sense is dim,
But now from the heart of joy,
I would remember Him:
Take the thanks of a boy.

> 'Prayers' (1895)

**6** First come I; my name is Jowett.
There's no knowledge but I know it.
I am Master of this college:
What I don't know isn't knowledge.

> *The Masque of Balliol* (*c.*1870) in W. G. Hiscock (ed.) *The Balliol Rhymes* (1939). Cf. 9:12, 314:1

## Max Beerbohm 1872–1956

**7** They so very indubitably *are*, you know!

> *Christmas Garland* (1912) 'Mote in the Middle Distance'

**8** I was not unpopular [at school] ... It is Oxford that has made me insufferable.

> *More* (1899) 'Going Back to School'

**9** Enter Michael Angelo. Andrea del Sarto appears for a moment at a window. Pippa passes.

> *Seven Men* (1919) 'Savonarola Brown' act 3

**10** The fading signals and grey eternal walls of that antique station, which, familiar to them and insignificant, does yet whisper to the tourist the last enchantments of the Middle Age.

> *Zuleika Dobson* (1911) ch. 1. Cf. 18:2

**11** Women who love the same man have a kind of bitter freemasonry.

> *Zuleika Dobson* (1911) ch. 4

**12** The Socratic manner is not a game at which two can play.

> *Zuleika Dobson* (1911) ch. 15

**13** Fate wrote her a most tremendous tragedy, and she played it in tights.

> *The Yellow Book* (1894) vol. 3, p. 260 (of Queen Caroline of Brunswick)

## Ethel Lynn Beers 1827–79

**14** All quiet along the Potomac to-night,
No sound save the rush of the river,
While soft falls the dew on the face of the dead—
The picket's off duty forever.

> 'The Picket Guard' (1861) st. 6. Cf. 214:14

## Mrs Beeton 1836–65

**15** A place for everything and everything in its place.

> *Book of Household Management* (1861) ch. 2, sect. 55 (often attributed to Samuel Smiles)

## Brendan Behan 1923–64

**16** PAT: He was an Anglo-Irishman.
MEG: In the blessed name of God what's that?
PAT: A Protestant with a horse.

> *Hostage* (1958) act 1

**17** Meanwhile I'll sing that famous old song, 'The Hound that Caught the Pubic Hare'.

> *Hostage* (1958) act 1

**18** When I came back to Dublin, I was courtmartialled in my absence and sentenced to death in my absence, so I said they could shoot me in my absence.

> *Hostage* (1958) act 1

**19** There's no such thing as bad publicity except your own obituary.

> In Dominic Behan *My Brother Brendan* (1965) p. 158

## Aphra Behn 1640–89

**20** Oh, what a dear ravishing thing is the beginning of an Amour!

> *The Emperor of the Moon* (1687) act 1, sc. 1

**21** Love ceases to be a pleasure, when it ceases to be a secret.

> *The Lover's Watch* (1686) 'Four o' Clock. General Conversation'

**22** Come away; poverty's catching.

> *The Rover* pt. 2 (1681) act 1

**23** Money speaks sense in a language all nations understand.

> *The Rover* pt. 2 (1681) act 3

**24** The soft, unhappy sex.

> *The Wandering Beauty* (1698) para. 1

## John Hay Beith

*See* IAN HAY

## Hilaire Belloc 1870–1953

**25** Child! do not throw this book about;
Refrain from the unholy pleasure
Of cutting all the pictures out!

> *A Bad Child's Book of Beasts* (1896) dedication

1 I shoot the Hippopotamus
   With bullets made of platinum,
   Because if I use leaden ones
   His hide is sure to flatten 'em.
   *A Bad Child's Book of Beasts* (1896) 'The
   Hippopotamus'. Cf. 143:14

2 And mothers of large families (who claim
   to common sense)
   Will find a Tiger well repay the trouble and
   expense.
   *A Bad Child's Book of Beasts* (1896) 'The Tiger'

3 Believing Truth is staring at the sun.
   Title of poem (1938)

4 Physicians of the Utmost Fame
   Were called at once; but when they came
   They answered, as they took their Fees,
   'There is no Cure for this Disease.'
   *Cautionary Tales* (1907) 'Henry King'

5 And always keep a-hold of Nurse
   For fear of finding something worse.
   *Cautionary Tales* (1907) 'Jim'

6 In my opinion, Butlers ought
   To know their place, and not to play
   The Old Retainer night and day.
   *Cautionary Tales* (1907) 'Lord Lundy'

7 Sir! you have disappointed us!
   We had intended you to be
   The next Prime Minister but three:
   The stocks were sold; the Press was
   squared;
   The Middle Class was quite prepared.
   But as it is! . . . My language fails!
   Go out and govern New South Wales!
   *Cautionary Tales* (1907) 'Lord Lundy'

8 Matilda told such Dreadful Lies,
   It made one Gasp and Stretch one's Eyes.
   *Cautionary Tales* (1907) 'Matilda'

9 For every time She shouted 'Fire!'
   They only answered 'Little Liar!'
   *Cautionary Tales* (1907) 'Matilda'

10 A Trick that everyone abhors
   In Little Girls is slamming Doors.
   *Cautionary Tales* (1907) 'Rebecca'

11 She was not really bad at heart,
   But only rather rude and wild:
   She was an aggravating child.
   *Cautionary Tales* (1907) 'Rebecca'

12 I said to Heart, 'How goes it?' Heart
   replied:
   'Right as a Ribstone Pippin!' But it lied.
   'The False Heart' (1910)

13 I'm tired of Love: I'm still more tired of
   Rhyme.
   But Money gives me pleasure all the time.
   'Fatigued' (1923)

14 Strong brother in God and last companion,
   Wine.
   'Heroic Poem upon Wine' (1926)

15 The moral is (it is indeed!)
   You mustn't monkey with the Creed.
   *Ladies and Gentlemen* (1932) 'The Example'

16 Remote and ineffectual Don
   That dared attack my Chesterton.
   'Lines to a Don' (1910)

17 Dons admirable! Dons of Might!
   Uprising on my inward sight
   Compact of ancient tales, and port
   And sleep—and learning of a sort.
   'Lines to a Don' (1910)

18 Whatever happens we have got
   The Maxim Gun, and they have not.
   *The Modern Traveller* (1898) pt. 6

19 The Llama is a woolly sort of fleecy hairy
   goat,
   With an indolent expression and an
   undulating throat
   Like an unsuccessful literary man.
   *More Beasts for Worse Children* (1897) 'The
   Llama'

20 The Microbe is so very small
   You cannot make him out at all.
   *More Beasts for Worse Children* (1897) 'The
   Microbe'

21 Oh! let us never, never doubt
   What nobody is sure about!
   *More Beasts for Worse Children* (1897) 'The
   Microbe'

22 Lord Finchley tried to mend the Electric
   Light
   Himself. It struck him dead: And serve him
   right!
   It is the business of the wealthy man
   To give employment to the artisan.
   *More Peers* (1911) 'Lord Finchley'

23 Like many of the Upper Class
   He liked the Sound of Broken Glass.
   *New Cautionary Tales* (1930) 'About John'.
   Cf. 343:18

24 And even now, at twenty-five,
   He has to WORK to keep alive!
   Yes! All day long from 10 till 4!
   For half the year or even more;
   With but an hour or two to spend
   At luncheon with a city friend.
   *New Cautionary Tales* (1930) 'Peter Goole'

25 The accursed power which stands on
   Privilege
   (And goes with Women, and Champagne,
   and Bridge)
   Broke—and Democracy resumed her reign:
   (Which goes with Bridge, and Women and
   Champagne).
   'On a Great Election' (1923)

26 I am a sundial, and I make a botch
   Of what is done much better by a watch.
   'On a Sundial' (1938)

27 When I am dead, I hope it may be said:
   'His sins were scarlet, but his books were
   read.'
   'On His Books' (1923)

28 Pale Ebenezer thought it wrong to fight,
   But Roaring Bill (who killed him) thought
   it right.
   'The Pacifist' (1938)

1 Do you remember an Inn,
   Miranda?
   Do you remember an Inn? . . .
   And the fleas that tease in the High
   Pyrenees
   And the wine that tasted of the tar?
   'Tarantella' (1923)

2 Balliol made me, Balliol fed me,
   Whatever I had she gave me again:
   And the best of Balliol loved and led me.
   God be with you, Balliol men.
   'To the Balliol Men Still in Africa' (1910)

3 From quiet homes and first beginning,
   Out to the undiscovered ends,
   There's nothing worth the wear of
   winning,
   But laughter and the love of friends.
   *Verses* (1910) 'Dedicatory Ode'

## Saul Bellow 1915–

4 If I am out of my mind, it's all right with
   me, thought Moses Herzog.
   *Herzog* (1961) opening sentence

## De Belloy 1727–75

5 The more foreigners I saw, the more I
   loved my homeland.
   *Le Siège de Calais* (1765) act 2, sc. 3

## Robert Benchley 1889–1945

6 STREETS FLOODED. PLEASE ADVISE.
   Telegraph message on arriving in Venice, in
   R. E. Drennan (ed.) *Wits End* (1973) 'Robert
   Benchley'

## Julien Benda 1867–1956

7 *La trahison des clercs.*
   The treachery of the intellectuals.
   Title of book (1927)

## Stephen Vincent Benét 1898–1943

8 I have fallen in love with American names,
   The sharp, gaunt names that never get fat.
   'American Names' (1927)

9 Bury my heart at Wounded Knee.
   'American Names' (1927)

## George Bennard 1873–1958

10 I will cling to the old rugged cross,
   And exchange it some day for a crown.
   'The Old Rugged Cross' (1913 hymn)

## Alan Bennett 1934–

11 I don't want to give you the idea I'm trying
   to hide anything, or that anything
   unorthodox goes on between my wife and
   me. It doesn't. Nothing goes on at all . . .
   No foreplay. No afterplay. And fuck all in
   between.
   *Enjoy* (1980) act 1

12 I have never understood this liking for
   war. It panders to instincts already catered
   for within the scope of any respectable
   domestic establishment.
   *Forty Years On* (1969) act 1

13 Memories are not shackles, Franklin, they
   are garlands.
   *Forty Years On* (1969) act 2

14 Standards are always out of date. That is
   what makes them standards.
   *Forty Years On* (1969) act 2

15 We started off trying to set up a small
   anarchist community, but people wouldn't
   obey the rules.
   *Getting On* (1972) act 1

16 Here I sit, alone and sixty,
   Bald, and fat, and full of sin,
   Cold the seat and loud the cistern,
   As I read the Harpic tin.
   'Place Names of China'

## Arnold Bennett 1867–1931

17 The price of justice is eternal publicity.
   *Things that have Interested Me* (2nd series,
   1923) 'Secret Trials'

18 A cause may be inconvenient, but it's
   magnificent. It's like champagne or high
   heels, and one must be prepared to suffer
   for it.
   *The Title* (1918) act 1

## Jill Bennett 1931–90

19 Never marry a man who hates his mother,
   because he'll end up hating you.
   In *Observer* 12 September 1982 'Sayings of the
   Week'

## A. C. Benson 1862–1925

20 Land of Hope and Glory, Mother of the
   Free,
   How shall we extol thee who are born of
   thee?
   Wider still and wider shall thy bounds be
   set;
   God who made thee mighty, make thee
   mightier yet.
   'Land of Hope and Glory' written to be sung
   as the Finale to Elgar's *Coronation Ode* (1902)

## Stella Benson 1892–1933

21 Call no man foe, but never love a stranger.
   *This is the End* (1917) p. 63

## Jeremy Bentham 1748–1832

22 Natural rights is simple nonsense: natural
   and imprescriptible rights, rhetorical
   nonsense—nonsense upon stilts.
   *Anarchical Fallacies* in J. Bowring (ed.) *Works*
   vol. 2 (1843) p. 501

1 The greatest happiness of the greatest
   number is the foundation of morals and
   legislation.
   *Commonplace Book* in J. Bowring (ed.) *Works*
   vol. 10 (1843) p. 142, where Bentham claims
   that either Joseph Priestley (1733–1804) or
   Cesare Beccaria (1738–94) passed on 'the
   sacred truth'. Cf. 177:2

2 All punishment is mischief: all
   punishment in itself is evil.
   *Principles of Morals and Legislation* (1789)
   ch. 13, para. 2

3 Prose is when all the lines except the last
   go on to the end. Poetry is when some of
   them fall short of it.
   In M. Packe *Life of John Stuart Mill* (1954) bk. 1,
   ch. 2

4 He rather hated the ruling few than loved
   the suffering many.
   Of James Mill, in H. N. Pym (ed.) *Memories of
   Old Friends* (1882) 7 August 1840

## Edmund Clerihew Bentley
### 1875–1956

5 The Art of Biography
   Is different from Geography.
   Geography is about Maps,
   But Biography is about Chaps.
   *Biography for Beginners* (1905) introduction

6 What I like about Clive
   Is that he is no longer alive.
   There is a great deal to be said
   For being dead.
   'Clive' (1905)

7 George the Third
   Ought never to have occurred.
   One can only wonder
   At so grotesque a blunder.
   'George the Third' (1929)

8 Sir Humphrey Davy
   Abominated gravy.
   He lived in the odium
   Of having discovered Sodium.
   'Sir Humphrey Davy' (1905)

9 Sir Christopher Wren
   Said, 'I am going to dine with some men.
   If anybody calls
   Say I am designing St Paul's.'
   'Sir Christopher Wren' (1905)

## Richard Bentley 1662–1742

10 It would be port if it could.
   Describing claret, in R. C. Jebb *Bentley* (1902)
   ch. 12

## Pierre-Jean de Béranger
### 1780–1857

11 *Nos amis, les ennemis.*
   Our friends, the enemy.
   'L'Opinion de ces demoiselles' (written 1815)
   in *Chansons de De Béranger* (1832)

## Lord Charles Beresford 1846–1919

12 Very sorry can't come. Lie follows by post.
   Telegraphed message to the Prince of Wales,
   on being summoned to dine at the eleventh
   hour. See R. Nevill *World of Fashion 1837–1922*
   (1923) ch. 5

## Henri Bergson 1859–1941

13 The present contains nothing more than
   the past, and what is found in the effect
   was already in the cause.
   *L'Évolution créatrice* (1907) ch. 1

14 *L'élan vital.*
   The vital spirit.
   *L'Évolution créatrice* (1907) ch. 2 (section title)

## Bishop George Berkeley
### 1685–1753

15 They are neither finite quantities, or
   quantities infinitely small, nor yet nothing.
   May we not call them the ghosts of
   departed quantities?
   *The Analyst* (1734) sect. 35 (on Newton's
   infinitesimals)

16 [Tar water] is of a nature so mild and
   benign and proportioned to the human
   constitution, as to warm without heating,
   to cheer but not inebriate.
   *Siris* (1744) para. 217. Cf. 110:11

17 Truth is the cry of all, but the game of the
   few.
   *Siris* (1744) para. 368

18 We have first raised a dust and then
   complain we cannot see.
   *A Treatise Concerning the Principles of Human
   Knowledge* (1710) introduction, sect. 3

19 Westward the course of empire takes its
   way;
   The first four acts already past,
   A fifth shall close the drama with the day
   Time's noblest offspring is the last.
   'On the Prospect of Planting Arts and
   Learning in America' (1752) st. 6. See John
   Quincy Adams *Oration at Plymouth* (1802):
   'Westward the star of empire takes its way'

## Irving Berlin 1888–1989

20 There's no business like show business.
   'Annie Get Your Gun' (1946)

21 God bless America,
   Land that I love,
   Stand beside her and guide her
   Thru the night with a light from above.
   From the mountains to the prairies,
   To the oceans white with foam,
   God bless America,
   My home sweet home.
   'God Bless America' (1939)

22 There may be trouble ahead,
   But while there's moonlight and music and
   love and romance,
   Let's face the music and dance.
   'Let's Face the Music and Dance' (1936)

**1** A pretty girl is like a melody
That haunts you night and day.
'A Pretty Girl is like a Melody' (1919)

**2** The song is ended (but the melody lingers on).
Title of song (1927)

**3** I'm dreaming of a white Christmas,
Just like the ones I used to know.
'White Christmas' (1942)

## Sir Isaiah Berlin 1909–

**4** There exists a great chasm between those, on one side, who relate everything to a single central vision ... and, on the other side, those who pursue many ends, often unrelated and even contradictory ... The first kind of intellectual and artistic personality belongs to the hedgehogs, the second to the foxes.
*The Hedgehog and the Fox* (1953) ch. 1. Cf. 15:1

**5** [Rousseau] is the first militant lowbrow of history.
Unpublished lecture (1952); National Sound Archive T10145W

**6** Liberty is liberty, not equality or fairness or justice or human happiness or a quiet conscience.
*Two Concepts of Liberty* (1958) p. 10

## Georges Bernanos 1888–1948

**7** The wish for prayer is a prayer in itself.
*Journal d'un curé de campagne* (1936) ch. 2

**8** Hell, madam, is to love no more.
*Journal d'un curé de campagne* (1936) ch. 2

## Bernard of Chartres d. c.1130

**9** We are like dwarfs on the shoulders of giants, so that we can see more than they, and things at a greater distance, not by virtue of any sharpness of sight on our part, or any physical distinction, but because we are carried high and raised up by their giant size.
In John of Salisbury *The Metalogicon* (1159) bk. 3, ch. 4. Cf. 239:2

## Eric Berne 1910–70

**10** Games people play: the psychology of human relationships.
Title of book (1964)

## John Berryman 1914–72

**11**            People will take balls,
Balls will be lost always, little boy,
And no one buys a ball back.
'The Ball Poem' (1948)

**12** We must travel in the direction of our fear.
'A Point of Age' (1942)

**13** Life, friends, is boring. We must not say so ...
And moreover my mother taught me as a boy
(repeatingly) 'Ever to confess you're bored means you have no
Inner Resources.'
*77 Dream Songs* (1964) no. 14

**14** I seldom go to films. They are too exciting, said the Honourable Possum.
*77 Dream Songs* (1964) no. 53

## Theobald von Bethmann Hollweg 1856–1921

**15** Just for a word 'neutrality'—a word which in wartime has so often been disregarded—just for a scrap of paper, Great Britain is going to make war on a kindred nation who desires nothing better than to be friends with her.
Summary of a report by Sir Edward Goschen to Sir Edward Grey in *British Documents on Origins of the War 1898–1914* (1926) vol. 11, p. 351

## Sir John Betjeman 1906–84

**16** He sipped at a weak hock and seltzer
As he gazed at the London skies
Through the Nottingham lace of the curtains
Or was it his bees-winged eyes?
'The Arrest of Oscar Wilde at the Cadogan Hotel' (1937)

**17** And girls in slacks remember Dad,
And oafish louts remember Mum,
And sleepless children's hearts are glad,
And Christmas-morning bells say 'Come!'
'Christmas' (1954)

**18** And is it true? And is it true,
This most tremendous tale of all,
Seen in a stained-glass window's hue,
A Baby in an ox's stall?
'Christmas' (1954)

**19** Oh! Chintzy, Chintzy cheeriness,
Half dead and half alive!
'Death in Leamington' (1931)

**20** Spirits of well-shot woodcock, partridge, snipe
Flutter and bear him up the Norfolk sky.
'Death of King George V' (1937)

**21** Old men who never cheated, never doubted,
Communicated monthly, sit and stare
At the new suburb stretched beyond the run-way
Where a young man lands hatless from the air.
'Death of King George V' (1937)

**22** Whist upon whist upon whist upon whist drive, in Institute, Legion and Social Club.
Horny hands that hold the aces which this morning held the plough.
'Dorset' (1937)

1 Oh shall I see the Thames again?
  The prow-promoted gems again,
  As beefy ATS
  Without their hats
  Come shooting through the bridge?
  And 'cheerioh' or 'cheeri-bye'
  Across the waste of waters die
  And low the mists of evening lie
  And lightly skims the midge.
  'Henley-on-Thames' (1945)

2 Phone for the fish-knives, Norman
  As Cook is a little unnerved;
  You kiddies have crumpled the serviettes
  And I must have things daintily served.
  'How to get on in Society' (1954)

3 The Church's Restoration
  In eighteen-eighty-three
  Has left for contemplation
  Not what there used to be.
  'Hymn' (1931)

4 Think of what our Nation stands for,
  Books from Boots' and country lanes,
  Free speech, free passes, class distinction,
  Democracy and proper drains.
  'In Westminster Abbey' (1940)

5 In the licorice fields at Pontefract
  My love and I did meet
  And many a burdened licorice bush
  Was blooming round our feet.
  'The Licorice Fields at Pontefract' (1954)

6 Belbroughton Road is bonny, and pinkly
    bursts the spray
  Of prunus and forsythia across the public
    way.
  'May-Day Song for North Oxford' (1945)

7 Gaily into Ruislip Gardens
  Runs the red electric train,
  With a thousand Ta's and Pardon's
  Daintily alights Elaine;
  Hurries down the concrete station
  With a frown of concentration,
  Out into the outskirt's edges
  Where a few surviving hedges
  Keep alive our lost Elysium—rural
    Middlesex again.
  'Middlesex' (1954)

8 Pam, I adore you, Pam, you great big
    mountainous sports girl,
  Whizzing them over the net, full of the
    strength of five:
  That old Malvernian brother, you zephyr
    and khaki shorts girl,
  Although he's playing for Woking,
  Can't stand up to your wonderful
    backhand drive.
  'Pot Pourri from a Surrey Garden' (1940)

9 Come, friendly bombs, and fall on Slough!
  It isn't fit for humans now,
  There isn't grass to graze a cow.
  Swarm over, Death!
  'Slough' (1937)

10 Miss J. Hunter Dunn, Miss J. Hunter Dunn,
   Furnish'd and burnish'd by Aldershot sun.
   'A Subaltern's Love-Song' (1945)

11 Love-thirty, love-forty, oh! weakness of joy,
   The speed of a swallow, the grace of a boy,
   With carefullest carelessness, gaily you
     won,
   I am weak from your loveliness, Joan
     Hunter Dunn.
   'A Subaltern's Love-Song' (1945)

12 By roads 'not adopted', by woodlanded
     ways,
   She drove to the club in the late summer
     haze.
   'A Subaltern's Love-Song' (1945)

13 Oh! full Surrey twilight! importunate band!
   Oh! strongly adorable tennis-girl's hand!
   'A Subaltern's Love-Song' (1945)

14 The dread of beatings! Dread of being late!
   And, greatest dread of all, the dread of
     games!
   Summoned by Bells (1960) ch. 7

15 Broad of Church and 'broad of Mind',
   Broad before and broad behind,
   A keen ecclesiologist,
   A rather dirty Wykehamist.
   'The Wykehamist' (1931)

16 Ghastly good taste, or a depressing story of
   the rise and fall of English architecture.
   Title of book (1933)

## Aneurin Bevan 1897–1960

17 This island is made mainly of coal and
   surrounded by fish. Only an organizing
   genius could produce a shortage of coal
   and fish at the same time.
   Speech at Blackpool, 24 May 1945, in *Daily
   Herald* 25 May 1945

18 No amount of cajolery, and no attempts at
   ethical or social seduction, can eradicate
   from my heart a deep burning hatred for
   the Tory Party . . . So far as I am concerned
   they are lower than vermin.
   Speech at Manchester, 4 July 1948, in *The
   Times* 5 July 1948

19 The language of priorities is the religion of
   Socialism.
   Speech at Labour Party Conference, 8 June
   1949; in *Report of the 48th Annual Conference*
   (1949) p. 172

20 [Winston Churchill] does not talk the
   language of the 20th century but that of
   the 18th. He is still fighting Blenheim all
   over again. His only answer to a difficult
   situation is send a gun-boat.
   Speech at Labour Party Conference,
   2 October 1951, in *Daily Herald* 3 October
   1951

21 I am not going to spend any time
   whatsoever in attacking the Foreign
   Secretary . . . If we complain about the
   tune, there is no reason to attack the
   monkey when the organ grinder is present.
   During a debate on the Suez crisis, *Hansard*
   16 May 1957, col. 680

1 If you carry this resolution you will send
Britain's Foreign Secretary naked into the
conference chamber.

> Speech at Labour Party Conference,
> 3 October 1957, against a motion proposing
> unilateral nuclear disarmament by the UK;
> in *Daily Herald* 4 October 1957

2 I stuffed their mouths with gold.

> On his handling of the consultants during
> the establishment of the National Health
> Service, in B. Abel-Smith *The Hospitals
> 1800–1948* (1964) ch. 29

3 Listening to a speech by Chamberlain is
like paying a visit to Woolworth's:
everything in its place and nothing above
sixpence.

> In Michael Foot *Aneurin Bevan* (1962) vol. 1,
> ch. 8

4 Damn it all, you can't have the crown of
thorns *and* the thirty pieces of silver.

> In Michael Foot *Aneurin Bevan* (1973) vol. 2,
> ch. 13

5 We know what happens to people who
stay in the middle of the road. They get
run down.

> In *Observer* 6 December 1953

6 I read the newspapers avidly. It is my one
form of continuous fiction.

> In *The Times* 29 March 1960

# William Henry Beveridge
1879–1963

7 Want is one only of five giants on the road
of reconstruction ... the others are
Disease, Ignorance, Squalor and Idleness.

> *Social Insurance and Allied Services* (1942) pt. 7

# Ernest Bevin 1881–1951

8 The most conservative man in this world is
the British Trade Unionist when you want
to change him.

> Speech, 8 September 1927, in *Report of
> Proceedings of the Trades Union Congress* (1927)
> p. 298

9 My [foreign] policy is to be able to take
a ticket at Victoria Station and go
anywhere I damn well please.

> In *Spectator* 20 April 1951, p. 514

10 If you open that Pandora's Box, you never
know what Trojan 'orses will jump out.

> On the Council of Europe, in Sir Roderick
> Barclay *Ernest Bevin and the Foreign Office*
> (1975) ch. 3

11 I didn't ought never to have done it. It was
you, Willie, what put me up to it.

> To Lord Strang, after officially recognizing
> Communist China; in C. Parrott *Serpent and
> Nightingale* (1977) ch. 3

# The Bible
# (Authorized Version, 1611)

12 Upon the setting of that bright Occidental
Star, Queen Elizabeth of most happy
memory.

> The Epistle Dedicatory

## Old Testament: Genesis

13 In the beginning God created the heaven
and the earth. And the earth was without
form, and void; and darkness was upon
the face of the deep. And the Spirit of
God moved upon the face of the waters.
And God said, Let there be light: and there
was light.

> Genesis ch. 1, v. 1

14 And the evening and the morning were the
first day.

> Genesis ch. 1, v. 5

15 And God saw that it was good.

> Genesis ch. 1, v. 10

16 Male and female created he them.

> Genesis ch. 1, v. 27

17 Be fruitful, and multiply, and replenish the
earth, and subdue it.

> Genesis ch. 1, v. 28

18 And the Lord God planted a garden
eastward in Eden.

> Genesis ch. 2, v. 8

19 But of the tree of the knowledge of good
and evil, thou shalt not eat of it: for in
the day that thou eatest thereof thou
shalt surely die.

> Genesis ch. 2, v. 17

20 It is not good that the man should be
alone; I will make him an help meet for
him.

> Genesis ch. 2, v. 18

21 And the rib, which the Lord God had taken
from man, made he a woman.

> Genesis ch. 2, v. 22

22 Bone of my bones, and flesh of my flesh.

> Genesis ch. 2, v. 23

23 Therefore shall a man leave his father and
his mother, and shall cleave unto his
wife: and they shall be one flesh.

> Genesis ch. 2, v. 24

24 Now the serpent was more subtil than any
beast of the field.

> Genesis ch. 3, v. 1

25 Ye shall be as gods, knowing good and evil.

> Genesis ch. 3, v. 5

26 And they sewed fig leaves together, and
made themselves aprons.
And they heard the voice of the Lord God
walking in the garden in the cool of the
day.

> Genesis ch. 3, v. 7 ('and made themselves
> breeches' in the Geneva ['Breeches'] Bible,
> 1560)

27 The serpent beguiled me, and I did eat.

> Genesis ch. 3, v. 13

1 In sorrow thou shalt bring forth children.
Genesis ch. 3, v. 16

2 In the sweat of thy face shalt thou eat bread.
Genesis ch. 3, v. 19

3 For dust thou art, and unto dust shalt thou return.
Genesis ch. 3, v. 19

4 Am I my brother's keeper?
Genesis ch. 4, v. 9

5 And the Lord set a mark upon Cain.
Genesis ch. 4, v. 15

6 And Cain went out from the presence of the Lord, and dwelt in the land of Nod, on the east of Eden.
Genesis ch. 4, v. 16

7 There were giants in the earth in those days.
Genesis ch. 6, v. 4

8 There went in two and two unto Noah into the Ark, the male and the female.
Genesis ch. 7, v. 9

9 Whoso sheddeth man's blood, by man shall his blood be shed.
Genesis ch. 9, v. 6

10 I do set my bow in the cloud, and it shall be for a token of a covenant between me and the earth.
Genesis ch. 9, v. 13

11 Even as Nimrod the mighty hunter before the Lord.
Genesis ch. 10, v. 9

12 Thou shalt be buried in a good old age.
Genesis ch. 15, v. 15

13 His [Ishmael's] hand will be against every man, and every man's hand against him.
Genesis ch. 16, v. 12

14 Now Abraham and Sarah were old and well stricken in age; and it ceased to be with Sarah after the manner of women.
Genesis ch. 18, v. 11

15 But his wife looked back from behind him, and she became a pillar of salt.
Genesis ch. 19, v. 26

16 Behold behind him a ram caught in a thicket by his horns.
Genesis ch. 22, v. 13

17 Esau selleth his birthright for a mess of potage.
Genesis ch. 25 (chapter heading in Geneva Bible, 1560)

18 And he sold his birthright unto Jacob.
Genesis ch. 25, v. 33

19 Behold, Esau my brother is a hairy man, and I am a smooth man.
Genesis ch. 27, v. 11

20 The voice is Jacob's voice, but the hands are the hands of Esau.
Genesis ch. 27, v. 22

21 And he dreamed, and behold a ladder set up on the earth, and the top of it reached to heaven: and behold the angels of God ascending and descending on it.
Genesis ch. 28, v. 12

22 And Jacob served seven years for Rachel; and they seemed unto him but a few days, for the love he had to her.
Genesis ch. 29, v. 20

23 The Lord watch between me and thee, when we are absent one from another.
Genesis ch. 31, v. 49

24 Now Israel loved Joseph more than all his children, because he was the son of his old age; and he made him a coat of many colours.
Genesis ch. 37, v. 3

25 Behold, this dreamer cometh.
Genesis ch. 37, v. 19

26 Then shall ye bring down my grey hairs with sorrow to the grave.
Genesis ch. 42, v. 38

27 Ye shall eat the fat of the land.
Genesis ch. 45, v. 18

28 See that ye fall not out by the way.
Genesis ch. 45, v. 24

**Exodus**

29 I have been a stranger in a strange land.
Exodus ch. 2, v. 22. See Exodus ch. 18, v. 3

30 Behold, the bush burned with fire, and the bush was not consumed.
Exodus ch. 3, v. 2

31 Put off thy shoes from off thy feet, for the place whereon thou standest is holy ground.
Exodus ch. 3, v. 5

32 A land flowing with milk and honey.
Exodus ch. 3, v. 8

33 I AM THAT I AM.
Exodus ch. 3, v. 14

34 Let my people go.
Exodus ch. 7, v. 16

35 Stretch out thine hand toward heaven, that there may be darkness over the land of Egypt, even darkness which may be felt.
Exodus ch. 10, v. 21

36 And they shall eat the flesh in that night, roast with fire, and unleavened bread; and with bitter herbs they shall eat it.
Exodus ch. 12, v. 8

37 With your loins girded, your shoes on your feet, and your staff in your hand; and ye shall eat it in haste; it is the Lord's passover.
Exodus ch. 12, v. 11

38 And they spoiled the Egyptians.
Exodus ch. 12, v. 36

39 And the Lord went before them by day in a pillar of a cloud, to lead them the way; and by night in a pillar of fire, to give them light.
Exodus ch. 13, v. 21

1 Would to God we had died by the hand of
the Lord in the land of Egypt, when we
sat by the flesh pots, and when we did
eat bread to the full.
Exodus ch. 16, v. 3

2 I am the Lord thy God, which have brought
thee out of the land of Egypt, out of the
house of bondage.
Exodus ch. 20, v. 2

3 Thou shalt have no other gods before me.
Exodus ch. 20, v. 3

4 Thou shalt not make unto thee any graven
image.
Exodus ch. 20, v. 4

5 I the Lord thy God am a jealous God,
visiting the iniquity of the fathers upon
the children unto the third and fourth
generation of them that hate me.
Exodus ch. 20, v. 5

6 Thou shalt not take the name of the Lord
thy God in vain.
Exodus ch. 20, v. 7

7 Remember the sabbath day, to keep it holy.
Exodus ch. 20, v. 8

8 Honour thy father and thy mother.
Exodus ch. 20, v. 12

9 Thou shalt not kill.
Thou shalt not commit adultery.
Thou shalt not steal.
Thou shalt not bear false witness against
thy neighbour.
Thou shalt not covet thy neighbour's
house, thou shalt not covet thy
neighbour's wife, nor his manservant,
nor his maidservant, nor his ox, nor his
ass, nor any thing that is thy
neighbour's.
Exodus ch. 20, v. 13

10 Life for life,
Eye for eye, tooth for tooth.
Exodus ch. 21, v. 23

11 Thou art a stiffnecked people.
Exodus ch. 33, v. 3

12 There shall no man see me and live.
Exodus ch. 33, v. 20

### Leviticus

13 Let him go for a scapegoat into the
wilderness.
Leviticus ch. 16, v. 10

14 Thou shalt love thy neighbour as thyself.
Leviticus ch. 19, v. 18. See St Matthew ch. 19,
v. 19

### Numbers

15 The Lord bless thee, and keep thee:
The Lord make his face shine upon thee,
and be gracious unto thee:
The Lord lift up his countenance upon
thee, and give thee peace.
Numbers ch. 6, v. 24

16 These are the names of the men which
Moses sent to spy out the land.
Numbers ch. 13, v. 16

17 He whom thou blessest is blessed, and he
whom thou cursest is cursed.
Numbers ch. 22, v. 6

18 God is not a man, that he should lie.
Numbers ch. 23, v. 19

19 What hath God wrought!
Numbers ch. 23, v. 23 (quoted by Samuel
Morse in the first electric telegraph message,
24 May 1844)

20 Be sure your sin will find you out.
Numbers ch. 32, v. 23

### Deuteronomy

21 For the Lord thy God is a jealous God.
Deuteronomy ch. 6, v. 15. Cf. 40:5

22 If there arise among you a prophet, or a
dreamer of dreams ... Thou shalt not
hearken.
Deuteronomy ch. 13, v. 1

23 He found him in a desert land, and in the
waste howling wilderness; he led him
about, he instructed him, he kept him as
the apple of his eye.
Deuteronomy ch. 32, v. 10

24 For they are a very froward generation,
children in whom is no faith.
Deuteronomy ch. 32, v. 20

25 The eternal God is thy refuge, and
underneath are the everlasting arms.
Deuteronomy ch. 33, v. 27

### Joshua

26 Be strong and of a good courage; be not
afraid, neither be thou dismayed: for the
Lord thy God is with thee, whithersoever
thou goest.
Joshua ch. 1, v. 9

27 When the people heard the sound of the
trumpet, and the people shouted with a
great shout, that the wall fell down flat,
so that the people went up into the city.
Joshua ch. 6, v. 20

28 Let them live; but let them be hewers of
wood and drawers of water unto all the
congregation.
Joshua ch. 9, v. 21

29 I am going the way of all the earth.
Joshua ch. 23, v. 14

### Judges

30 He delivered them into the hands of
spoilers.
Judges ch. 2, v. 14

31 I arose a mother in Israel.
Judges ch. 5, v. 7

32 The stars in their courses fought against
Sisera.
Judges ch. 5, v. 20

33 She brought forth butter in a lordly dish.
Judges ch. 5, v. 25

34 Why tarry the wheels of his chariots?
Judges ch. 5, v. 28

35 The Lord is with thee, thou mighty man of
valour.
Judges ch. 6, v. 12

**1** Faint, yet pursuing.
Judges ch. 8, v. 4

**2** Then said they unto him, Say now Shibboleth: and he said Sibboleth: for he could not frame to pronounce it right.
Judges ch. 12, v. 6

**3** Out of the eater came forth meat, and out of the strong came forth sweetness.
Judges ch. 14, v. 14

**4** He smote them hip and thigh.
Judges ch. 15, v. 8

**5** With the jaw of an ass have I slain a thousand men.
Judges ch. 15, v. 16

**6** He did grind in the prison house.
Judges ch. 16, v. 21

**7** The people arose as one man.
Judges ch. 20, v. 8

### Ruth

**8** Intreat me not to leave thee, or to return from following after thee: for whither thou goest, I will go; and where thou lodgest, I will lodge: thy people shall be my people, and thy God my God.
Ruth ch. 1, v. 16

### I Samuel

**9** Speak, Lord; for thy servant heareth.
I Samuel ch. 3, v. 9

**10** Quit yourselves like men, and fight.
I Samuel ch. 4, v. 9

**11** And she named the child I-chabod, saying, The glory is departed from Israel.
I Samuel ch. 4, v. 21

**12** God save the king.
I Samuel ch. 10, v. 24

**13** A man after his own heart.
I Samuel ch. 13, v. 14

**14** I did but taste a little honey with the end of the rod that was in mine hand, and, lo, I must die.
I Samuel ch. 14, v. 43

**15** For the Lord seeth not as man seeth: for man looketh on the outward appearance, but the Lord looketh on the heart.
I Samuel ch. 16, v. 7

**16** Now he was ruddy, and withal of a beautiful countenance, and goodly to look to.
I Samuel ch. 16, v. 12

**17** I know thy pride, and the naughtiness of thine heart.
I Samuel ch. 17, v. 28

**18** And he took his staff in his hand and chose him five smooth stones out of the brook.
I Samuel ch. 17, v. 40

**19** Behold, I have played the fool.
I Samuel ch. 26, v. 21

### II Samuel

**20** The beauty of Israel is slain upon thy high places: how are the mighty fallen!
II Samuel ch. 1, v. 19

**21** Tell it not in Gath, publish it not in the streets of Askelon.
II Samuel ch. 1, v. 20

**22** Saul and Jonathan were lovely and pleasant in their lives, and in their death they were not divided: they were swifter than eagles, they were stronger than lions.
II Samuel ch. 1, v. 23

**23** Thy love to me was wonderful, passing the love of women.
How are the mighty fallen, and the weapons of war perished!
II Samuel ch. 1, v. 26

**24** The poor man had nothing, save one little ewe lamb.
II Samuel ch. 12, v. 3

**25** Come out, come out, thou bloody man.
II Samuel ch. 16, v. 7

**26** And when Ahithophel saw that his counsel was not followed, he saddled his ass, and arose, and gat him home to his house, to his city, and put his household in order, and hanged himself.
II Samuel ch. 17, v. 23

**27** O my son Absalom, my son, my son Absalom! would God I had died for thee, O Absalom, my son, my son!
II Samuel ch. 18, v. 33

**28** David . . . sweet psalmist of Israel.
II Samuel ch. 23, v. 1

### I Kings

**29** Then will I cut off Israel out of the land which I have given them; and this house, which I have hallowed for my name, will I cast out of my sight; and Israel shall be a proverb and a byword among all people.
I Kings ch. 9, v. 7

**30** Behold, the half was not told me.
I Kings ch. 10, v. 7

**31** Once in three years came the navy of Tharshish, bringing gold, and silver, ivory, and apes, and peacocks.
I Kings ch. 10, v. 22

**32** But king Solomon loved many strange women.
I Kings ch. 11, v. 1

**33** My little finger shall be thicker than my father's loins.
I Kings ch. 12, v. 10

**34** My father hath chastised you with whips, but I will chastise you with scorpions.
I Kings ch. 12, v. 11

**35** An handful of meal in a barrel, and a little oil in a cruse.
I Kings ch. 17, v. 12

**36** How long halt ye between two opinions?
I Kings ch. 18, v. 21

1 There is a sound of abundance of rain.
   I Kings ch. 18, v. 41

2 There ariseth a little cloud out of the sea,
   like a man's hand.
   I Kings ch. 18, v. 44

3 But the Lord was not in the wind: and
   after the wind an earthquake; but the
   Lord was not in the earthquake:
   And after the earthquake a fire: but the
   Lord was not in the fire: and after the
   fire a still small voice.
   I Kings ch. 19, v. 11

4 Elijah passed by him, and cast his mantle
   upon him.
   I Kings ch. 19, v. 19

5 Hast thou found me, O mine enemy?
   I Kings ch. 21, v. 20

6 Feed him with bread of affliction and with
   water of affliction, until I come in peace.
   I Kings ch. 22, v. 27

7 And a certain man drew a bow at a
   venture, and smote the king of Israel
   between the joints of the harness.
   I Kings ch. 22, v. 34

### II Kings

8 Go up, thou bald head.
   II Kings ch. 2, v. 23

9 Is it well with the child? And she
   answered, It is well.
   II Kings ch. 4, v. 26

10 There is death in the pot.
   II Kings ch. 4, v. 40

11 I bow myself in the house of Rimmon.
   II Kings ch. 5, v. 18

12 Is thy servant a dog, that he should do this
   great thing?
   II Kings ch. 8, v. 13

13 The driving is like the driving of Jehu, the
   son of Nimshi; for he driveth furiously.
   II Kings ch. 9, v. 20

14 She painted her face, and tired her head,
   and looked out at a window.
   II Kings ch. 9, v. 30

15 Who is on my side? who?
   II Kings ch. 9, v. 32

16 Thou trustest upon the staff of this bruised
   reed, even upon Egypt, on which if a man
   lean, it will go into his hand, and pierce
   it.
   II Kings ch. 18, v. 21

### I Chronicles

17 For we are strangers before thee, and
   sojourners, as were all our fathers: our
   days on the earth are as a shadow, and
   there is none abiding.
   I Chronicles ch. 29, v. 15

18 He died in a good old age, full of days,
   riches, and honour.
   I Chronicles ch. 29, v. 28

### Esther

19 And if I perish, I perish.
   Esther ch. 4, v. 16

20 Thus shall it be done to the man whom
   the king delighteth to honour.
   Esther ch. 6, v. 9

### Job

21 And the Lord said unto Satan, Whence
   comest thou? Then Satan answered the
   Lord, and said, From going to and fro in
   the earth, and from walking up and
   down in it.
   Job ch. 1, v. 7

22 The Lord gave, and the Lord hath taken
   away; blessed be the name of the Lord.
   Job ch. 1, v. 21

23 All that a man hath will he give for his
   life.
   Job ch. 2, v. 4

24 Curse God, and die.
   Job ch. 2, v. 9

25 Let the day perish wherein I was born, and
   the night in which it was said, There is a
   man child conceived.
   Job ch. 3, v. 3

26 Kings and counsellors of the earth, which
   built desolate places for themselves.
   Job ch. 3, v. 14

27 There the wicked cease from troubling, and
   there the weary be at rest.
   Job ch. 3, v. 17

28 Then a spirit passed before my face; the
   hair of my flesh stood up.
   Job ch. 4, v. 15

29 Man is born unto trouble, as the sparks fly
   upward.
   Job ch. 5, v. 7

30 My days are swifter than a weaver's
   shuttle.
   Job ch. 7, v. 6

31 He shall return no more to his house,
   neither shall his place know him any
   more.
   Job ch. 7, v. 10

32 Canst thou by searching find out God?
   Job ch. 11, v. 7

33 Man that is born of a woman is of few
   days, and full of trouble.
   He cometh forth like a flower, and is cut
   down: he fleeth also as a shadow, and
   continueth not.
   Job ch. 14, v. 1. Cf. 66:6

34 Miserable comforters are ye all.
   Job ch. 16, v. 2

35 I am escaped with the skin of my teeth.
   Job ch. 19, v. 20

36 I know that my redeemer liveth, and that
   he shall stand at the latter day upon the
   earth:
   Job ch. 19, v. 25

1 But where shall wisdom be found? and
where is the place of understanding?
Job ch. 28, v. 12

2 The price of wisdom is above rubies.
Job ch. 28, v. 18

3 I am a brother to dragons, and
a companion to owls.
Job ch. 30, v. 29

4 Canst thou bind the sweet influences of
Pleiades, or loose the bands of Orion?
Job ch. 38, v. 31

5 He saith among the trumpets, Ha, ha; and
he smelleth the battle afar off, the
thunder of the captains, and the
shouting.
Job ch. 39, v. 25

6 Canst thou draw out leviathan with an
hook?
Job ch. 41, v. 1

Proverbs

7 For whom the Lord loveth he correcteth.
Proverbs ch. 3, v. 12

8 Length of days is in her right hand; and in
her left hand riches and honour.
Proverbs ch. 3, v. 16

9 Her ways are ways of pleasantness, and all
her paths are peace.
Proverbs ch. 3, v. 17

10 Wisdom is the principal thing; therefore
get wisdom: and with all thy getting get
understanding.
Proverbs ch. 4, v. 7

11 Go to the ant thou sluggard; consider her
ways, and be wise.
Proverbs ch. 6, v. 6

12 Yet a little sleep, a little slumber, a little
folding of the hands to sleep.
Proverbs ch. 6, v. 10. See Proverbs ch. 24,
v. 33

13 He goeth after her straightway, as an ox
goeth to the slaughter.
Proverbs ch. 7, v. 22

14 Wisdom hath builded her house, she hath
hewn out her seven pillars.
Proverbs ch. 9, v. 1

15 Stolen waters are sweet, and bread eaten
in secret is pleasant.
Proverbs ch. 9, v. 17

16 A wise son maketh a glad father: but a
foolish son is the heaviness of his
mother.
Proverbs ch. 10, v. 1

17 The destruction of the poor is their
poverty.
Proverbs ch. 10, v. 15

18 He that is surety for a stranger shall smart
for it.
Proverbs ch. 11, v. 15

19 A virtuous woman is a crown to her
husband.
Proverbs ch. 12, v. 4

20 A righteous man regardeth the life of his
beast: but the tender mercies of the
wicked are cruel.
Proverbs ch. 12, v. 10

21 Hope deferred maketh the heart sick: but
when the desire cometh, it is a tree of
life.
Proverbs ch. 13, v. 12

22 The way of transgressors is hard.
Proverbs ch. 13, v. 15

23 He that spareth his rod hateth his son.
Proverbs ch. 13, v. 24

24 A soft answer turneth away wrath.
Proverbs ch. 15, v. 1

25 A merry heart maketh a cheerful
countenance.
Proverbs ch. 15, v. 13

26 Better is a dinner of herbs where love is,
than a stalled ox and hatred therewith.
Proverbs ch. 15, v. 17

27 A word spoken in due season, how good is
it!
Proverbs ch. 15, v. 23

28 Pride goeth before destruction, and an
haughty spirit before a fall.
Proverbs ch. 16, v. 18

29 A wounded spirit who can bear?
Proverbs ch. 18, v. 14

30 There is a friend that sticketh closer than a
brother.
Proverbs ch. 18, v. 24

31 Wine is a mocker, strong drink is raging.
Proverbs ch. 20, v. 1

32 It is better to dwell in a corner of the
housetop, than with a brawling woman
in a wide house.
Proverbs ch. 21, v. 9

33 Look not thou upon the wine when it is
red, when it giveth his colour in the cup
... At the last it biteth like a serpent, and
stingeth like an adder.
Proverbs ch. 23, v. 31

34 The heart of kings is unsearchable.
Proverbs ch. 25, v. 3

35 A word fitly spoken is like apples of gold in
pictures of silver.
Proverbs ch. 25, v. 11

36 If thine enemy be hungry, give him bread
to eat; and if he be thirsty, give him
water to drink.
For thou shalt heap coals of fire upon his
head, and the Lord shall reward thee.
Proverbs ch. 25, v. 21

37 As cold waters to a thirsty soul, so is good
news from a far country.
Proverbs ch. 25, v. 25

38 Answer not a fool according to his folly,
lest thou also be like unto him.
Answer a fool according to his folly, lest he
be wise in his own conceit.
Proverbs ch. 26, v. 4

1 A continual dropping in a very rainy day and a contentious woman are alike.
Proverbs ch. 27, v. 15

2 A fool uttereth all his mind.
Proverbs ch. 29, v. 11

3 Where there is no vision, the people perish.
Proverbs ch. 29, v. 18

4 There be three things which are too wonderful for me, yea, four which I know not:
The way of an eagle in the air; the way of a serpent upon a rock; the way of a ship in the midst of the sea; and the way of a man with a maid.
Proverbs ch. 30, v. 18

5 Give strong drink unto him that is ready to perish, and wine unto those that be of heavy hearts.
Proverbs ch. 31, v. 6

6 Who can find a virtuous woman? for her price is far above rubies.
Proverbs ch. 31, v. 10

### Ecclesiastes

7 Vanity of vanities; all is vanity.
Ecclesiastes ch. 1, v. 2

8 The thing that hath been, it is that which shall be; and that which is done is that which shall be done: and there is no new thing under the sun.
Ecclesiastes ch. 1, v. 9

9 All is vanity and vexation of spirit.
Ecclesiastes ch. 1, v. 14

10 He that increaseth knowledge increaseth sorrow.
Ecclesiastes ch. 1, v. 18

11 To every thing there is a season, and a time to every purpose under the heaven:
A time to be born, and a time to die; a time to plant, and a time to pluck up that which is planted.
Ecclesiastes ch. 3, v. 1

12 A time to weep, and a time to laugh; a time to mourn, and a time to dance.
Ecclesiastes ch. 3, v. 4

13 A time to love, and a time to hate; a time of war, and a time of peace.
Ecclesiastes ch. 3, v. 8

14 A threefold cord is not quickly broken.
Ecclesiastes ch. 4, v. 12

15 The sleep of a labouring man is sweet.
Ecclesiastes ch. 5, v. 12

16 As the crackling of thorns under a pot, so is the laughter of a fool.
Ecclesiastes ch. 7, v. 6

17 There is no discharge in that war.
Ecclesiastes ch. 8, v. 8

18 A man hath no better thing under the sun, than to eat, and to drink, and to be merry.
Ecclesiastes ch. 8, v. 15. Cf. 45:24, 52:18

19 Whatsoever thy hand findeth to do, do it with thy might; for there is no work, nor device, nor knowledge, nor wisdom, in the grave, whither thou goest.
Ecclesiastes ch. 9, v. 10

20 The race is not to the swift, nor the battle to the strong.
Ecclesiastes ch. 9, v. 11

21 He that diggeth a pit shall fall into it.
Ecclesiastes ch. 10, v. 8

22 Woe to thee, O land, when thy king is a child, and thy princes eat in the morning!
Ecclesiastes ch. 10, v. 16

23 Wine maketh merry: but money answereth all things.
Ecclesiastes ch. 10, v. 19

24 Cast thy bread upon the waters: for thou shalt find it after many days.
Ecclesiastes ch. 11, v. 1

25 Remember now thy Creator in the days of thy youth.
Ecclesiastes ch. 12, v. 1

26 And desire shall fail: because man goeth to his long home, and the mourners go about the streets:
Or ever the silver cord be loosed, or the golden bowl be broken, or the pitcher be broken at the fountain, or the wheel broken at the cistern.
Then shall the dust return to the earth as it was: and the spirit shall return unto God who gave it.
Ecclesiastes ch. 12, v. 5

27 Of making many books there is no end; and much study is a weariness of the flesh.
Ecclesiastes ch. 12, v. 12

28 Fear God, and keep his commandments: for this is the whole duty of man.
Ecclesiastes ch. 12, v. 13

### Song of Solomon

29 I am black, but comely.
Song of Solomon ch. 1, v. 5

30 A bundle of myrrh is my wellbeloved unto me.
Song of Solomon ch. 1, v. 13

31 I am the rose of Sharon, and the lily of the valleys.
Song of Solomon ch. 2, v. 1

32 The time of the singing of birds is come, and the voice of the turtle is heard in our land.
Song of Solomon ch. 2, v. 12

33 Take us the foxes, the little foxes, that spoil the vines.
Song of Solomon ch. 2, v. 15

34 Behold, thou art fair, my love; behold, thou art fair.
Song of Solomon ch. 4, v. 1

35 Thou art all fair, my love; there is no spot in thee.
Song of Solomon ch. 4, v. 7

1 Set me as a seal upon thine heart, as a seal upon thine arm.
Song of Solomon ch. 8, v. 6

2 Many waters cannot quench love, neither can the floods drown it.
Song of Solomon ch. 8, v. 7

## Isaiah

3 The daughter of Zion is left as a cottage in a vineyard, as a lodge in a garden of cucumbers.
Isaiah ch. 1, v. 8

4 Though your sins be as scarlet, they shall be as white as snow.
Isaiah ch. 1, v. 18

5 They shall beat their swords into plowshares, and their spears into pruninghooks: nation shall not lift up sword against nation, neither shall they learn war any more.
Isaiah ch. 2, v. 4. See also Micah ch. 4, v. 3, Joel ch. 3, v. 10

6 What mean ye that ye beat my people to pieces, and grind the faces of the poor?
Isaiah ch. 3, v. 15

7 My well-beloved hath a vineyard in a very fruitful hill.
Isaiah ch. 5, v. 1

8 Woe unto them that join house to house, that lay field to field, till there be no place.
Isaiah ch. 5, v. 8

9 Woe unto them that call evil good, and good evil.
Isaiah ch. 5, v. 20

10 I saw also the Lord sitting upon a throne, high and lifted up, and his train filled the temple.
Above it stood the seraphims: each one had six wings; with twain he covered his face, and with twain he covered his feet, and with twain he did fly.
And one cried unto another, and said, Holy, holy, holy, is the Lord of hosts: the whole earth is full of his glory.
Isaiah ch. 6, v. 1

11 Then said I, Woe is me! for I am undone; because I am a man of unclean lips, and I dwell in the midst of a people of unclean lips.
Isaiah ch. 6, v. 5

12 Whom shall I send, and who will go for us? Then said I, Here am I; send me.
Isaiah ch. 6, v. 8

13 Then said I, Lord, how long?
Isaiah ch. 6, v. 11

14 Behold, a virgin shall conceive, and bear a son, and shall call his name Immanuel.
Isaiah ch. 7, v. 14

15 The people that walked in darkness have seen a great light: they that dwell in the land of the shadow of death, upon them hath the light shined.
Isaiah ch. 9, v. 2. Cf. 269:10

16 For unto us a child is born, unto us a son is given: and the government shall be upon his shoulder: and his name shall be called Wonderful, Counsellor, The mighty God, The everlasting Father, The Prince of Peace.
Isaiah ch. 9, v. 6

17 The zeal of the Lord of hosts will perform this.
Isaiah ch. 9, v. 7

18 And there shall come forth a rod out of the stem of Jesse, and a branch shall grow out of his roots:
And the spirit of the Lord shall rest upon him, the spirit of wisdom and understanding, the spirit of counsel and might, the spirit of knowledge and of the fear of the Lord.
Isaiah ch. 11, v. 1

19 The wolf also shall dwell with the lamb, and the leopard shall lie down with the kid; and the calf and the young lion and the fatling together; and a little child shall lead them.
Isaiah ch. 11, v. 6

20 And the sucking child shall play on the hole of the asp, and the weaned child shall put his hand on the cockatrice' den.
They shall not hurt nor destroy in all my holy mountain: for the earth shall be full of the knowledge of the Lord, as the waters cover the sea.
Isaiah ch. 11, v. 8

21 Dragons in their pleasant palaces.
Isaiah ch. 13, v. 22

22 How art thou fallen from heaven, O Lucifer, son of the morning!
Isaiah ch. 14, v. 12

23 Watchman, what of the night? Watchman, what of the night?
The watchman said, The morning cometh, and also the night.
Isaiah ch. 21, v. 11

24 Let us eat and drink; for to morrow we shall die.
Isaiah ch. 22, v. 13. Cf. 44:18, 52:18

25 He will swallow up death in victory; and the Lord God will wipe away tears from off all faces.
Isaiah ch. 25, v. 8

26 We have as it were brought forth wind.
Isaiah ch. 26, v. 18

27 For precept must be upon precept, precept upon precept; line upon line, line upon line; here a little, and there a little.
Isaiah ch. 28, v. 10

28 We have made a covenant with death, and with hell are we at agreement.
Isaiah ch. 28, v. 15

29 Speak unto us smooth things, prophesy deceits.
Isaiah ch. 30, v. 10

1 The bread of adversity, and the waters of affliction.
Isaiah ch. 30, v. 20

2 This is the way, walk ye in it.
Isaiah ch. 30, v. 21

3 And thorns shall come up in her palaces, nettles and brambles in the fortresses thereof: and it shall be an habitation of dragons, and a court for owls.
Isaiah ch. 34, v. 13

4 The desert shall rejoice, and blossom as the rose.
Isaiah ch. 35, v. 1

5 Strengthen ye the weak hands, and confirm the feeble knees.
Isaiah ch. 35, v. 3

6 Set thine house in order: for thou shalt die, and not live.
Isaiah ch. 38, v. 1

7 Comfort ye, comfort ye my people, saith your God.
Speak ye comfortably to Jerusalem, and cry unto her, that her warfare is accomplished.
Isaiah ch. 40, v. 1

8 The voice of him that crieth in the wilderness, Prepare ye the way of the Lord.
Isaiah ch. 40, v. 3. Cf. 48:13

9 Every valley shall be exalted, and every mountain and hill shall be made low: and the crooked shall be made straight, and the rough places plain:
And the glory of the Lord shall be revealed, and all flesh shall see it together: for the mouth of the Lord hath spoken it.
Isaiah ch. 40, v. 3

10 All flesh is grass, and all the goodliness thereof is as the flower of the field:
The grass withereth, the flower fadeth: because the spirit of the Lord bloweth upon it: surely the people is grass.
Isaiah ch. 40, v. 6. Cf. 57:6

11 He shall feed his flock like a shepherd: he shall gather the lambs with his arm, and carry them in his bosom, and shall gently lead those that are with young.
Isaiah ch. 40, v. 11

12 Have ye not known? have ye not heard? hath it not been told you from the beginning?
Isaiah ch. 40, v. 21

13 They shall mount up with wings as eagles; they shall run, and not be weary; and they shall walk, and not faint.
Isaiah ch. 40, v. 31

14 There is no peace, saith the Lord, unto the wicked.
Isaiah ch. 48, v. 22

15 How beautiful upon the mountains are the feet of him that bringeth good tidings, that publisheth peace; that bringeth good tidings of good, that publisheth salvation.
Isaiah ch. 52, v. 7

16 For they shall see eye to eye, when the Lord shall bring again Zion.
Break forth into joy, sing together, ye waste places of Jerusalem.
Isaiah ch. 52, v. 8

17 He is despised and rejected of men; a man of sorrows, and acquainted with grief.
Isaiah ch. 53, v. 2

18 Surely he hath borne our griefs, and carried our sorrows.
Isaiah ch. 53, v. 3

19 But he was wounded for our transgressions, he was bruised for our iniquities: the chastisement of our peace was upon him; and with his stripes we are healed.
All we like sheep have gone astray; we have turned every one to his own way; and the Lord hath laid on him the iniquity of us all.
Isaiah ch. 53, v. 5

20 He is brought as a lamb to the slaughter.
Isaiah ch. 53, v. 7

21 He was cut off out of the land of the living.
Isaiah ch. 53, v. 8

22 For my thoughts are not your thoughts, neither are your ways my ways, saith the Lord.
Isaiah ch. 55, v. 8

23 Arise, shine; for thy light is come, and the glory of the Lord is risen upon thee.
Isaiah ch. 60, v. 1

24 To bind up the brokenhearted, to proclaim liberty to the captives, and the opening of the prison to them that are bound.
Isaiah ch. 61, v. 1

25 Stand by thyself, come not near to me; for I am holier than thou.
Isaiah ch. 65, v. 5

26 For, behold, I create new heavens and a new earth.
Isaiah ch. 65, v. 17

### Jeremiah

27 This people hath a revolting and a rebellious heart.
Jeremiah ch. 5, v. 23

28 They have healed also the hurt of the daughter of my people slightly, saying, Peace, peace; when there is no peace.
Jeremiah ch. 6, v. 14

29 Is there no balm in Gilead?
Jeremiah ch. 8, v. 22

30 Can the Ethiopian change his skin, or the leopard his spots?
Jeremiah ch. 13, v. 23

31 The heart is deceitful above all things, and desperately wicked.
Jeremiah ch. 17, v. 9

### Lamentations

32 Is it nothing to you, all ye that pass by? behold, and see if there be any sorrow like unto my sorrow.
Lamentations ch. 1, v. 12

1 Remembering mine affliction and my
misery, the wormwood and the gall.
Lamentations ch. 3, v. 19

2 It is good for a man that he bear the yoke
in his youth.
Lamentations ch. 3, v. 27

3 O Lord, thou hast seen my wrong: judge
thou my cause.
Lamentations ch. 4, v. 59

### Ezekiel

4 As is the mother, so is her daughter.
Ezekiel ch. 16, v. 44

5 The fathers have eaten sour grapes, and
the children's teeth are set on edge.
Ezekiel ch. 18, v. 2

6 When the wicked man turneth away from
his wickedness that he hath committed,
and doeth that which is lawful and right,
he shall save his soul alive.
Ezekiel ch. 18, v. 27

7 The king of Babylon stood at the parting of
the ways.
Ezekiel ch. 21, v. 21

8 The valley which was full of bones.
Ezekiel ch. 37, v. 1

9 Can these bones live?
Ezekiel ch. 37, v. 3

10 O ye dry bones, hear the word of the Lord.
Ezekiel ch. 37, v. 4

### Daniel

11 Cast into the midst of a burning fiery
furnace.
Daniel ch. 3, v. 6

12 And this is the writing that was written,
MENE, MENE, TEKEL, UPHARSIN.
This is the interpretation of the thing:
MENE; God hath numbered thy kingdom,
and finished it.
TEKEL; Thou art weighed in the balances
and art found wanting.
PERES; Thy kingdom is divided, and given
to the Medes and Persians.
Daniel ch. 5, v. 25

13 Now, O king, establish the decree, and sign
the writing, that it be not changed,
according to the law of the Medes and
Persians, which altereth not.
Daniel ch. 6, v. 8

14 The Ancient of days did sit, whose garment
was white as snow, and the hair of his
head like the pure wool.
Daniel ch. 7, v. 9

15 Ten thousand times ten thousand stood
before him: the judgement was set, and
the books were opened.
Daniel ch. 7, v. 10

16 O Daniel, a man greatly beloved.
Daniel ch. 10, v. 11

### Hosea

17 They have sown the wind, and they shall
reap the whirlwind.
Hosea ch. 8, v. 7

18 I drew them ... with bands of love.
Hosea ch. 11, v. 4

### Joel

19 I will restore to you the years that the
locust hath eaten.
Joel ch. 2, v. 25

20 Your sons and your daughters shall
prophesy, your old men shall dream
dreams, your young men shall see
visions.
Joel ch. 2, v. 28

21 Multitudes, multitudes in the valley of
decision.
Joel ch. 3, v. 14

### Micah

22 But thou, Bethlehem Ephratah, though
thou be little among the thousands of
Judah, yet out of thee shall he come forth
unto me that is to be ruler in Israel.
Micah ch. 5, v. 2

23 What doth the Lord require of thee, but to
do justly, and to love mercy, and to walk
humbly with thy God?
Micah ch. 6, v. 8

### Nahum

24 Woe to the bloody city!
Nahum ch. 3, v. 1

### Zephaniah

25 Woe to her that is filthy and polluted, to
the oppressing city!
Zephaniah ch. 3, v. 1

### Malachi

26 But unto you that fear my name shall the
Sun of righteousness arise with healing
in his wings.
Malachi ch. 4, v. 2

### Apocrypha

27 Great is Truth, and mighty above all
things.
I Esdras ch. 4, v. 41. Cf. 58:23

28 I shall light a candle of understanding in
thine heart, which shall not be put out.
II Esdras ch. 14, v. 25

29 And in the time of their visitation they
shall shine, and run to and fro like
sparks among the stubble.
Wisdom of Solomon ch. 3, v. 7

30 Even so we in like manner, as soon as we
were born, began to draw to our end.
Wisdom of Solomon ch. 5, v. 13

31 For the hope of the ungodly ... passeth
away as the remembrance of a guest that
tarrieth but a day.
Wisdom of Solomon ch. 5, v. 14

32 We will fall into the hands of the Lord, and
not into the hands of men: for as his
majesty is, so is his mercy.
Ecclesiasticus ch. 2, v. 18

33 Laugh no man to scorn in the bitterness of
his soul.
Ecclesiasticus ch. 7, v. 11

1 Judge none blessed before his death.
Ecclesiasticus ch. 11, v. 28. Cf. 310:27

2 He that toucheth pitch shall be defiled
therewith.
Ecclesiasticus ch. 13, v. 1

3 A merchant shall hardly keep himself from
doing wrong.
Ecclesiasticus ch. 26, v. 29

4 Leave off first for manners' sake.
Ecclesiasticus ch. 31, v. 17

5 He that sinneth before his Maker, let him
fall into the hand of the physician.
Ecclesiasticus ch. 38, v. 15

6 How can he get wisdom ... whose talk is
of bullocks?
Ecclesiasticus ch. 38, v. 25

7 Let us now praise famous men, and our
fathers that begat us.
Ecclesiasticus ch. 44, v. 1

8 And some there be, which have no
memorial ... and are become as though
they had never been born ...
But these were merciful men, whose
righteousness hath not been forgotten ...

Their seed shall remain for ever, and their
glory shall not be blotted out.
Their bodies are buried in peace; but their
name liveth for evermore.
Ecclesiasticus ch. 44, v. 9

### New Testament: St Matthew

9 There came wise men from the east to
Jerusalem,
Saying, Where is he that is born King of
the Jews? for we have seen his star in the
east, and are come to worship him.
St Matthew ch. 2, v. 1

10 They presented unto him gifts; gold, and
frankincense, and myrrh.
St Matthew ch. 2, v. 11

11 In Rama was there a voice heard,
lamentation, and weeping, and great
mourning, Rachel weeping for her
children, and would not be comforted,
because they are not.
St Matthew ch. 2, v. 18. See Jeremiah ch. 31,
v. 15

12 Repent ye: for the kingdom of heaven is at
hand.
St Matthew ch. 3, v. 2

13 The voice of one crying in the wilderness,
Prepare ye the way of the Lord, make his
paths straight.
St Matthew ch. 3, v. 3. Cf. 46:8

14 O generation of vipers, who hath warned
you to flee from the wrath to come?
St Matthew ch. 3, v. 7

15 This is my beloved Son, in whom I am well
pleased.
St Matthew ch. 3, v. 17

16 Man shall not live by bread alone, but by
every word that proceedeth out of the
mouth of God.
St Matthew ch. 4, v. 4. See Deuteronomy
ch. 8, v. 3

17 Thou shalt not tempt the Lord thy God.
St Matthew ch. 4, v. 7. See Deuteronomy
ch. 6, v. 16

18 Follow me, and I will make you fishers of
men.
St Matthew ch. 4, v. 19

19 Blessed are the poor in spirit: for theirs is
the kingdom of heaven.
Blessed are they that mourn: for they shall
be comforted.
Blessed are the meek: for they shall inherit
the earth.
Blessed are they which do hunger and
thirst after righteousness: for they shall
be filled.
Blessed are the merciful: for they shall
obtain mercy.
Blessed are the pure in heart: for they shall
see God.
Blessed are the peacemakers: for they shall
be called the children of God.
St Matthew ch. 5, v. 3

20 Ye are the salt of the earth: but if the salt
have lost his savour, wherewith shall it
be salted?
St Matthew ch. 5, v. 13

21 Ye are the light of the world. A city that is
set on an hill cannot be hid.
St Matthew ch. 5, v. 14

22 Let your light so shine before men, that
they may see your good works.
St Matthew ch. 5, v. 16

23 Resist not evil: but whosoever shall smite
thee on thy right cheek, turn to him the
other also.
St Matthew ch. 5, v. 39

24 He maketh his sun to rise on the evil and
on the good, and sendeth rain on the just
and on the unjust.
St Matthew ch. 5, v. 45

25 Be ye therefore perfect, even as your Father
which is in heaven is perfect.
St Matthew ch. 5, v. 48

26 When thou doest alms, let not thy left
hand know what thy right hand doeth.
St Matthew ch. 6, v. 3

27 After this manner therefore pray ye: Our
Father which art in heaven, Hallowed be
thy name.
Thy kingdom come. Thy will be done in
earth, as it is in heaven.
Give us this day our daily bread.
And forgive us our debts, as we forgive our
debtors.
And lead us not into temptation, but
deliver us from evil: For thine is the
kingdom, and the power, and the glory,
for ever. Amen.
St Matthew ch. 6, v. 9. See St Luke ch. 11, v. 2

1 Lay not up for yourselves treasures upon
earth, where moth and rust doth corrupt,
and where thieves break through and
steal:
But lay up for yourselves treasures in
heaven.
St Matthew ch. 6, v. 19

2 Where your treasure is, there will your
heart be also.
St Matthew ch. 6, v. 21

3 No man can serve two masters ... Ye
cannot serve God and mammon.
St Matthew ch. 6, v. 24

4 Consider the lilies of the field, how they
grow; they toil not, neither do they spin:
And yet I say unto you, That even Solomon
in all his glory was not arrayed like one
of these.
St Matthew ch. 6, v. 28

5 Take therefore no thought for the morrow:
for the morrow shall take thought for
the things of itself. Sufficient unto the
day is the evil thereof.
St Matthew ch. 6, v. 34

6 Judge not, that ye be not judged.
St Matthew ch. 7, v. 1

7 Why beholdest thou the mote that is in
thy brother's eye, but considerest not the
beam that is in thine own eye?
St Matthew ch. 7, v. 3

8 Neither cast ye your pearls before swine.
St Matthew ch. 7, v. 6

9 Ask, and it shall be given you; seek, and ye
shall find; knock, and it shall be opened
unto you.
St Matthew ch. 7, v. 7

10 Or what man is there of you, whom if his
son ask bread, will he give him a stone?
St Matthew ch. 7, v. 9

11 Therefore all things whatsoever ye would
that men should do to you, do ye even so
to them: for this is the law and the
prophets.
St Matthew ch. 7, v. 12

12 Wide is the gate, and broad is the way,
that leadeth to destruction, and many
there be that go in thereat.
St Matthew ch. 7, v. 13

13 Strait is the gate, and narrow is the way,
which leadeth unto life, and few there be
that find it.
St Matthew ch. 7, v. 14

14 Beware of false prophets, which come to
you in sheep's clothing, but inwardly
they are ravening wolves.
St Matthew ch. 7, v. 15

15 By their fruits ye shall know them.
St Matthew ch. 7, v. 20

16 Lord I am not worthy that thou shouldest
come under my roof.
St Matthew ch. 8, v. 8

17 I am a man under authority, having
soldiers under me: and I say to this man,
Go, and he goeth; and to another, Come,
and he cometh; and to my servant, Do
this, and he doeth it.
St Matthew ch. 8, v. 9

18 But the children of the kingdom shall be
cast out into outer darkness: there shall
be weeping and gnashing of teeth.
St Matthew ch. 8, v. 12

19 The foxes have holes, and the birds of the
air have nests; but the Son of man hath
not where to lay his head.
St Matthew ch. 8, v. 20

20 Let the dead bury their dead.
St Matthew ch. 8, v. 22

21 Why eateth your Master with publicans
and sinners?
St Matthew ch. 9, v. 11

22 They that be whole need not a physician,
but they that are sick.
St Matthew ch. 9, v. 12

23 I am not come to call the righteous, but
sinners to repentance.
St Matthew ch. 9, v. 13

24 Neither do men put new wine into old
bottles.
St Matthew ch. 9, v. 17

25 Thy faith hath made thee whole.
St Matthew ch. 9, v. 22

26 The maid is not dead, but sleepeth.
St Matthew ch. 9, v. 24

27 Freely ye have received, freely give.
St Matthew ch. 10, v. 8

28 When ye depart out of that house or city,
shake off the dust of your feet.
St Matthew ch. 10, v. 14

29 Be ye therefore wise as serpents, and
harmless as doves.
St Matthew ch. 10, v. 16

30 The very hairs of your head are all
numbered.
St Matthew ch. 10, v. 30

31 I came not to send peace, but a sword.
St Matthew ch. 10, v. 34

32 A man's foes shall be they of his own
household.
St Matthew ch. 10, v. 36

33 He that findeth his life shall lose it: and he
that loseth his life for my sake shall find
it.
St Matthew ch. 10, v. 39

34 What went ye out into the wilderness to
see? A reed shaken with the wind?
St Matthew ch. 11, v. 7

35 Come unto me, all ye that labour and are
heavy laden, and I will give you rest.
St Matthew ch. 11, v. 28

36 For my yoke is easy, and my burden is
light.
St Matthew ch. 11, v. 30

1 He that is not with me is against me.
St Matthew ch. 12, v. 30 and St Luke ch. 11, v. 23

2 Behold, a greater than Solomon is here.
St Matthew ch. 12, v. 42

3 Then he saith, I will return into my house from whence I came out; and when he is come, he findeth it empty, swept, and garnished.
St Matthew ch. 12, v. 44

4 Behold, a sower went forth to sow;
And when he sowed, some seeds fell by the wayside.
St Matthew ch. 13, v. 3

5 The kingdom of heaven is like to a grain of mustard seed.
St Matthew ch. 13, v. 31

6 The kingdom of heaven is like unto a merchant man, seeking goodly pearls:
Who, when he had found one pearl of great price, went and sold all that he had, and bought it.
St Matthew ch. 13, v. 45

7 A prophet is not without honour, save in his own country, and in his own house.
St Matthew ch. 13, v. 57

8 Be of good cheer; it is I; be not afraid.
St Matthew ch. 14, v. 27

9 O thou of little faith, wherefore didst thou doubt?
St Matthew ch. 14, v. 31

10 If the blind lead the blind, both shall fall into the ditch.
St Matthew ch. 15, v. 14

11 The dogs eat of the crumbs which fall from their masters' table.
St Matthew ch. 15, v. 27

12 Can ye not discern the signs of the times?
St Matthew ch. 16, v. 3

13 Thou art Peter, and upon this rock I will build my church.
St Matthew ch. 16, v. 18

14 Get thee behind me, Satan.
St Matthew ch. 16, v. 23

15 Except ye be converted, and become as little children, ye shall not enter into the kingdom of heaven.
St Matthew ch. 18, v. 3

16 Whoso shall offend one of these little ones which believe in me, it were better for him that a millstone were hanged about his neck, and that he were drowned in the depth of the sea.
St Matthew ch. 18, v. 6. See also St Luke ch. 17, v. 2

17 If thine eye offend thee, pluck it out, and cast it from thee.
St Matthew ch. 18, v. 9

18 For where two or three are gathered together in my name, there am I in the midst of them.
St Matthew ch. 18, v. 20

19 Lord, how oft shall my brother sin against me, and I forgive him? till seven times?
Jesus saith unto him I say not unto thee, Until seven times: but Until seventy times seven.
St Matthew ch. 18, v. 21

20 What therefore God hath joined together, let not man put asunder.
St Matthew ch. 19, v. 6

21 If thou wilt be perfect, go and sell that thou hast, and give to the poor, and thou shalt have treasure in heaven.
St Matthew ch. 19, v. 21

22 It is easier for a camel to go through the eye of a needle, than for a rich man to enter into the kingdom of God.
St Matthew ch. 19, v. 24. See also St Luke ch. 18, v. 24

23 With God all things are possible.
St Matthew ch. 19, v. 26

24 But many that are first shall be last; and the last shall be first.
St Matthew ch. 19, v. 30

25 The burden and heat of the day.
St Matthew ch. 20, v. 12

26 I will give unto this last, even as unto thee.
St Matthew ch. 20, v. 14

27 It is written, My house shall be called the house of prayer; but ye have made it a den of thieves.
St Matthew ch. 21, v. 13. See Isaiah ch. 56, v. 7

28 For many are called, but few are chosen.
St Matthew ch. 22, v. 14

29 Render therefore unto Caesar the things which are Caesar's; and unto God the things that are God's.
St Matthew ch. 22, v. 21

30 For in the resurrection they neither marry, nor are given in marriage.
St Matthew ch. 22, v. 30

31 Ye blind guides, which strain at a gnat, and swallow a camel.
St Matthew ch. 23, v. 24

32 Ye are like unto whited sepulchres.
St Matthew ch. 23, v. 27

33 Ye shall hear of wars and rumours of wars.
St Matthew ch. 24, v. 6

34 For nation shall rise against nation, and kingdom against kingdom.
St Matthew ch. 24, v. 7

35 The abomination of desolation, spoken of by Daniel.
St Matthew ch. 24, v. 15. See Daniel ch. 12, v. 11

36 Wheresoever the carcase is, there will the eagles be gathered together.
St Matthew ch. 24, v. 28

37 Heaven and earth shall pass away, but my words shall not pass away.
St Matthew ch. 24, v. 35

38 Watch therefore: for ye know not what hour your Lord doth come.
St Matthew ch. 24, v. 42

1 Well done, thou good and faithful servant.
St Matthew ch. 25, v. 21

2 Lord, I knew thee that thou art an hard man, reaping where thou hast not sown, and gathering where thou hast not strawed.
St Matthew ch. 25, v. 24

3 Unto every one that hath shall be given, and he shall have abundance: but from him that hath not shall be taken away even that which he hath.
St Matthew ch. 25, v. 29

4 And he shall set the sheep on his right hand, but the goats on the left.
St Matthew ch. 25, v. 33

5 I was a stranger, and ye took me in.
St Matthew ch. 25, v. 35

6 Inasmuch as ye have done it unto one of the least of these my brethren, ye have done it unto me.
St Matthew ch. 25, v. 40

7 And they covenanted with him for thirty pieces of silver.
St Matthew ch. 26, v. 15

8 It had been good for that man if he had not been born.
St Matthew ch. 26, v. 24

9 Jesus took bread, and blessed it, and brake it, and gave it to the disciples, and said, Take, eat; this is my body.
St Matthew ch. 26, v. 26

10 This night, before the cock crow, thou shalt deny me thrice.
St Matthew ch. 26, v. 34

11 If it be possible, let this cup pass from me.
St Matthew ch. 26, v. 39

12 What, could ye not watch with me one hour?
St Matthew ch. 26, v. 40

13 Watch and pray, that ye enter not into temptation: the spirit indeed is willing but the flesh is weak.
St Matthew ch. 26, v. 41

14 All they that take the sword shall perish with the sword.
St Matthew ch. 26, v. 52

15 He saved others; himself he cannot save.
St Matthew ch. 27, v. 42

16 Eli, Eli, lama sabachthani? ... My God, my God, why hast thou forsaken me?
St Matthew ch. 27, v. 46

17 And, lo, I am with you alway, even unto the end of the world.
St Matthew ch. 28, v. 20

**St Mark**

18 The sabbath was made for man, and not man for the sabbath.
St Mark ch. 2, v. 27

19 If a house be divided against itself, that house cannot stand.
St Mark ch. 3, v. 25

20 He that hath ears to hear, let him hear.
St Mark ch. 4, v. 9

21 My name is Legion: for we are many.
St Mark ch. 5, v. 9

22 I see men as trees, walking.
St Mark ch. 8, v. 24

23 For what shall it profit a man, if he shall gain the whole world, and lose his own soul?
St Mark ch. 8, v. 36. See also St Matthew ch. 16, v. 26

24 Lord, I believe; help thou mine unbelief.
St Mark ch. 9, v. 24

25 Suffer the little children to come unto me, and forbid them not: for of such is the kingdom of God.
St Mark ch. 10, v. 14

26 Go ye into all the world, and preach the gospel to every creature.
St Mark ch. 16, v. 15

**St Luke**

27 Hail, thou that art highly favoured, the Lord is with thee: blessed art thou among women.
St Luke ch. 1, v. 28

28 My soul doth magnify the Lord,
And my spirit hath rejoiced in God my Saviour.
For he hath regarded the low estate of his handmaiden: for, behold, from henceforth all generations shall call me blessed.
St Luke ch. 1, v. 46 ('Tell out my soul, the greatness of the Lord' in *New English Bible*). Cf. 58:16

29 He hath shewed strength with his arm; he hath scattered the proud in the imagination of their hearts.
He hath put down the mighty from their seats, and exalted them of low degree.
He hath filled the hungry with good things; and the rich he hath sent empty away.
St Luke ch. 1, v. 51

30 To give light to them that sit in darkness and in the shadow of death, to guide our feet into the way of peace.
St Luke ch. 1, v. 79

31 And it came to pass in those days, that there went out a decree from Caesar Augustus, that all the world should be taxed.
St Luke ch. 2, v. 1

32 She brought forth her firstborn son, and wrapped him in swaddling clothes, and laid him in a manger; because there was no room for them in the inn.
And there were in the same country shepherds abiding in the field, keeping watch over their flock by night.
And, lo, the angel of the Lord came upon them, and the glory of the Lord shone round about them: and they were sore afraid.
St Luke ch. 2, v. 7

1 Behold, I bring you good tidings of great joy.
St Luke ch. 2, v. 10

2 Glory to God in the highest, and on earth peace, good will toward men.
St Luke ch. 2, v. 14

3 Lord, now lettest thou thy servant depart in peace, according to thy word.
St Luke ch. 2, v. 29. Cf. 58:17

4 Wist ye not that I must be about my Father's business?
St Luke ch. 2, v. 49

5 Physician, heal thyself.
St Luke ch. 4, v. 23

6 Love your enemies, do good to them which hate you.
St Luke ch. 6, v. 27

7 Give, and it shall be given unto you; good measure, pressed down, and shaken together, and running over, shall men give into your bosom.
St Luke ch. 6, v. 38

8 Her sins, which are many, are forgiven; for she loved much.
St Luke ch. 7, v. 47

9 No man, having put his hand to the plough, and looking back, is fit for the kingdom of God.
St Luke ch. 9, v. 62

10 For the labourer is worthy of his hire.
St Luke ch. 10, v. 7

11 A certain man went down from Jerusalem to Jericho, and fell among thieves.
St Luke ch. 10, v. 30

12 He passed by on the other side.
St Luke ch. 10, v. 31

13 Go, and do thou likewise.
St Luke ch. 10, v. 37

14 But Martha was cumbered about much serving.
St Luke ch. 10, v. 40

15 No man, when he hath lighted a candle, putteth it in a secret place, neither under a bushel.
St Luke ch. 11, v. 33

16 Woe unto you, lawyers! for ye have taken away the key of knowledge.
St Luke ch. 11, v. 52

17 Are not five sparrows sold for two farthings, and not one of them is forgotten before God?
St Luke ch. 12, v. 6. See also St Matthew ch. 10, v. 29

18 Soul, thou hast much goods laid up for many years; take thine ease, eat, drink, and be merry.
St Luke ch. 12, v. 19. Cf. 44:18, 45:24

19 Thou fool, this night thy soul shall be required of thee.
St Luke ch. 12, v. 13

20 Let your loins be girded about, and your lights burning.
St Luke ch. 12, v. 35

21 Friend, go up higher.
St Luke ch. 14, v. 10

22 For whosoever exalteth himself shall be abased; and he that humbleth himself shall be exalted.
St Luke ch. 14, v. 11. See also St Matthew ch. 23, v. 12

23 I have married a wife, and therefore I cannot come.
St Luke ch. 14, v. 20

24 Bring in hither the poor, and the maimed, and the halt, and the blind.
St Luke ch. 14, v. 21

25 Go out into the highways and hedges, and compel them to come in.
St Luke ch. 14, v. 23

26 Leave the ninety and nine in the wilderness.
St Luke ch. 15, v. 4

27 Rejoice with me; for I have found my sheep which was lost.
St Luke ch. 15, v. 6

28 Joy shall be in heaven over one sinner that repenteth, more than over ninety and nine just persons, which need no repentance.
St Luke ch. 15, v. 7

29 Wasted his substance with riotous living.
St Luke ch. 15, v. 13

30 I will arise and go to my father, and will say unto him, Father, I have sinned against heaven, and before thee,
And am no more worthy to be called thy son: make me as one of thy hired servants.
St Luke ch. 15, v. 18

31 Bring hither the fatted calf, and kill it.
St Luke ch. 15, v. 23

32 This my son was dead, and is alive again; he was lost, and is found.
St Luke ch. 15, v. 24

33 The children of this world are in their generation wiser than the children of light.
St Luke ch. 16, v. 8

34 The crumbs which fell from the rich man's table.
St Luke ch. 16, v. 21

35 Between us and you there is a great gulf fixed.
St Luke ch. 16, v. 26

36 The kingdom of God is within you.
St Luke ch. 17, v. 21

37 Remember Lot's wife.
St Luke ch. 17, v. 32

38 God, I thank thee, that I am not as other men are.
St Luke ch. 18, v. 11

39 God be merciful to me a sinner.
St Luke ch. 18, v. 13

40 He shall show you a large upper room furnished.
St Luke ch. 22, v. 12

1 Not my will, but thine, be done.
St Luke ch. 22, v. 42

2 Father, forgive them: for they know not
what they do.
St Luke ch. 23, v. 34

3 To day shalt thou be with me in paradise.
St Luke ch. 23, v. 43

4 Father, into thy hands I commend my
spirit.
St Luke ch. 23, v. 46. Cf. 66:23

5 He was a good man, and a just.
St Luke ch. 23, v. 50

**St John**

6 In the beginning was the Word, and the
Word was with God, and the Word was
God.
St John ch. 1, v. 1

7 All things were made by him; and without
him was not any thing made that was
made.
St John ch. 1, v. 3

8 And the light shineth in darkness; and the
darkness comprehended it not.
St John ch. 1, v. 5

9 He was not that Light, but was sent to bear
witness of that Light.
St John ch. 1, v. 8

10 He was in the world, and the world was
made by him, and the world knew him
not.
He came unto his own, and his own
received him not.
St John ch. 1, v. 10

11 And the Word was made flesh, and dwelt
among us.
St John ch. 1, v. 14

12 He it is, who coming after me is preferred
before me, whose shoe's latchet I am not
worthy to unloose.
St John ch. 1, v. 27

13 Behold the Lamb of God, which taketh
away the sin of the world.
St John ch. 1, v. 29

14 Can there any good thing come out of
Nazareth?
St John ch. 1, v. 46

15 Behold an Israelite indeed, in whom is no
guile!
St John ch. 1, v. 47

16 Woman, what have I to do with thee? mine
hour is not yet come.
St John ch. 2, v. 4

17 Except a man be born again, he cannot see
the kingdom of God.
St John ch. 3, v. 3

18 The wind bloweth where it listeth.
St John ch. 3, v. 8

19 God so loved the world, that he gave his
only begotten Son, that whosoever
believeth in him should not perish, but
have everlasting life.
St John ch. 3, v. 16

20 Except ye see signs and wonders, ye will
not believe.
St John ch. 4, v. 48

21 Rise, take up thy bed, and walk.
St John ch. 5, v. 8

22 I am the bread of life: he that cometh to
me shall never hunger; and he that
believeth on me shall never thirst.
St John ch. 6, v. 35

23 Him that cometh to me I will in no wise
cast out.
St John ch. 6, v. 37

24 Verily, verily, I say unto you, He that
believeth on me hath everlasting life.
St John ch. 6, v. 47

25 And the scribes and the Pharisees brought
unto him a woman taken in adultery.
St John ch. 8, v. 3

26 He that is without sin among you, let him
first cast a stone at her.
St John ch. 8, v. 7

27 Neither do I condemn thee: go, and sin no
more.
St John ch. 8, v. 11

28 And ye shall know the truth, and the truth
shall make you free.
St John ch. 8, v. 32

29 I am the door.
St John ch. 10, v. 9

30 I am the good shepherd: the good
shepherd giveth his life for the sheep.
St John ch. 10, v. 11

31 Though ye believe not me, believe the
works.
St John ch. 10, v. 38

32 I am the resurrection, and the life.
St John ch. 11, v. 25

33 Jesus wept.
St John ch. 11, v. 35

34 It is expedient for us, that one man should
die for the people, and that the whole
nation perish not.
St John ch. 11, v. 50

35 The poor always ye have with you.
St John ch. 12, v. 8

36 Let not your heart be troubled: ye believe
in God, believe also in me.
St John ch. 14, v. 1

37 In my Father's house are many mansions
... I go to prepare a place for you.
St John ch. 14, v. 2

38 I am the way, the truth, and the life: no
man cometh unto the Father, but by me.
St John ch. 14, v. 6

39 Peace I leave with you, my peace I give
unto you.
St John ch. 14, v. 27

40 Greater love hath no man than this, that a
man lay down his life for his friends.
St John ch. 15, v. 13

1 Pilate saith unto him, What is truth?
St John ch. 18, v. 38

2 Now Barabbas was a robber.
St John ch. 18, v. 40

3 What I have written I have written.
St John ch. 19, v. 22

4 Woman, behold thy son! ...
Behold thy mother!
St John ch. 19, v. 26

5 It is finished.
St John ch. 19, v. 30. Cf. 58:21

6 Touch me not.
St John ch. 20, v. 17. Cf. 58:22

7 Feed my sheep.
St John ch. 21, v. 16

### Acts of the Apostles

8 And suddenly there came a sound from
heaven as of a rushing mighty wind.
Acts of the Apostles ch. 2, v. 2

9 Silver and gold have I none; but such as I
have give I thee.
Acts of the Apostles ch. 3, v. 6

10 Walking, and leaping, and praising God.
Acts of the Apostles ch. 3, v. 8

11 Saul, Saul, why persecutest thou me?
Acts of the Apostles ch. 9, v. 4

12 It is hard for thee to kick against the
pricks.
Acts of the Apostles ch. 9, v. 5

13 The street which is called Straight.
Acts of the Apostles ch. 9, v. 11

14 Dorcas: this woman was full of good
works.
Acts of the Apostles ch. 9, v. 36

15 God is no respecter of persons.
Acts of the Apostles ch. 10, v. 34. See also
Romans ch. 2, v. 11

16 Come over into Macedonia, and help us.
Acts of the Apostles ch. 16, v. 9

17 What must I do to be saved?
Acts of the Apostles ch. 16, v. 30

18 Certain lewd fellows of the baser sort.
Acts of the Apostles ch. 17, v. 5

19 What will this babbler say?
Acts of the Apostles ch. 17, v. 18

20 I found an altar with this inscription, TO
THE UNKNOWN GOD.
Acts of the Apostles ch. 17, v. 23

21 For in him we live, and move, and have our
being.
Acts of the Apostles ch. 17, v. 28

22 It is more blessed to give than to receive.
Acts of the Apostles ch. 20, v. 35

23 But Paul said, I am a man which am a Jew
of Tarsus, a city in Cilicia, a citizen of no
mean city.
Acts of the Apostles ch. 21, v. 39

24 And the chief captain answered, With a
great sum obtained I this freedom. And
Paul said, But I was free born.
Acts of the Apostles ch. 22, v. 28

25 Hast thou appealed unto Caesar? unto
Caesar shalt thou go.
Acts of the Apostles ch. 25, v. 12

26 Paul, thou art beside thyself; much
learning doth make thee mad.
Acts of the Apostles ch. 26, v. 24

27 Almost thou persuadest me to be a
Christian.
Acts of the Apostles ch. 26, v. 28

### Romans

28 Patient continuance in well doing.
Romans ch. 2, v. 7

29 Let God be true, but every man a liar.
Romans ch. 3, v. 4

30 Let us do evil, that good may come.
Romans ch. 3, v. 8

31 Where no law is, there is no transgression.
Romans ch. 4, v. 15

32 Who against hope believed in hope.
Romans ch. 4, v. 18 (of Abraham)

33 Shall we continue in sin, that grace may
abound?
Romans ch. 6, v. 1

34 We also should walk in newness of life.
Romans ch. 6, v. 4

35 Christ being raised from the dead dieth no
more; death hath no more dominion over
him.
Romans ch. 6, v. 9

36 The wages of sin is death.
Romans ch. 6, v. 23

37 I had not known sin, but by the law.
Romans ch. 7, v. 7

38 For the good that I would I do not: but the
evil which I would not, that I do.
Romans ch. 7, v. 19. Cf. 243:15

39 To be carnally minded is death.
Romans ch. 8, v. 6

40 All things work together for good to them
that love God.
Romans ch. 8, v. 28

41 If God be for us, who can be against us?
Romans ch. 8, v. 31

42 For I am persuaded, that neither death, nor
life, nor angels, nor principalities, nor
powers, nor things present, nor things to
come,
Nor height, nor depth, nor any other
creature, shall be able to separate us
from the love of God, which is in Christ
Jesus our Lord.
Romans ch. 8, v. 38

43 Present your bodies a living sacrifice, holy,
acceptable unto God.
Romans ch. 12, v. 1

44 Be not wise in your own conceits.
Romans ch. 12, v. 16

45 Vengeance is mine; I will repay, saith the
Lord.
Romans ch. 12, v. 19

1 Let us therefore cast off the works of darkness, and let us put on the armour of light.
   Romans ch. 13, v. 12

2 Salute one another with an holy kiss.
   Romans ch. 16, v. 16

## I Corinthians

3 I have planted, Apollos watered; but God gave the increase.
   I Corinthians ch. 3, v. 6

4 Your body is the temple of the Holy Ghost.
   I Corinthians ch. 6, v. 19

5 It is better to marry than to burn.
   I Corinthians ch. 7, v. 9

6 The fashion of this world passeth away.
   I Corinthians ch. 7, v. 31

7 Knowledge puffeth up, but charity edifieth.
   I Corinthians ch. 8, v. 1

8 I am made all things to all men.
   I Corinthians ch. 9, v. 22

9 For the earth is the Lord's and the fulness thereof.
   I Corinthians ch. 10, v. 26. Cf. 66:19

10 Doth not even nature itself teach you, that if a man have long hair, it is a shame unto him?
   But if a woman have long hair, it is a glory to her.
   I Corinthians ch. 11, v. 14

11 Though I speak with the tongues of men and of angels, and have not charity, I am become as sounding brass, or a tinkling cymbal.
   And though I have the gift of prophecy, and understand all mysteries, and all knowledge; and though I have all faith; so that I could remove mountains; and have not charity, I am nothing.
   I Corinthians ch. 13, v. 1

12 Charity suffereth long, and is kind; charity envieth not; charity vaunteth not itself, is not puffed up ...
   Beareth all things, believeth all things, hopeth all things, endureth all things.
   Charity never faileth.
   I Corinthians ch. 13, v. 4

13 For we know in part, and we prophesy in part.
   I Corinthians ch. 13, v. 9

14 When I was a child, I spake as a child, I understood as a child, I thought as a child: but when I became a man, I put away childish things.
   For now we see through a glass, darkly; but then face to face: now I know in part; but then shall I know even as also I am known.
   And now abideth faith, hope, charity, these three; but the greatest of these is charity.
   I Corinthians ch. 13, v. 11

15 Let all things be done decently and in order.
   I Corinthians ch. 14, v. 40

16 Last of all he was seen of me also, as of one born out of due time.
   I Corinthians ch. 15, v. 8

17 But now is Christ risen from the dead, and become the first fruits of them that slept.
   For since by man came death, by man came also the resurrection of the dead.
   For as in Adam all die, even so in Christ shall all be made alive.
   I Corinthians ch. 15, v. 20

18 The last enemy that shall be destroyed is death.
   I Corinthians ch. 15, v. 26

19 Evil communications corrupt good manners.
   I Corinthians ch. 15, v. 33

20 The first man is of the earth, earthy.
   I Corinthians ch. 15, v. 47

21 Behold, I shew you a mystery; We shall not all sleep, but we shall all be changed,
   In a moment, in the twinkling of an eye, at the last trump; for the trumpet shall sound, and the dead shall be raised incorruptible, and we shall be changed.
   I Corinthians ch. 15, v. 51

22 O death, where is thy sting? O grave, where is thy victory?
   I Corinthians ch. 15, v. 55

## II Corinthians

23 The letter killeth, but the spirit giveth life.
   II Corinthians ch. 3, v. 6

24 We have a building of God, an house not made with hands, eternal in the heavens.
   II Corinthians ch. 5, v. 1

25 Behold, now is the accepted time; behold; now is the day of salvation.
   II Corinthians ch. 6, v. 2

26 God loveth a cheerful giver.
   II Corinthians ch. 9, v. 7

27 For ye suffer fools gladly, seeing ye yourselves are wise.
   II Corinthians ch. 9, v. 19

28 There was given to me a thorn in the flesh, the messenger of Satan to buffet me.
   II Corinthians ch. 12, v. 7

## Galatians

29 Ye are fallen from grace.
   Galatians ch. 5, v. 4

30 Be not deceived; God is not mocked: for whatsoever a man soweth, that shall he also reap.
   Galatians ch. 6, v. 7

## Ephesians

31 The unsearchable riches of Christ.
   Ephesians ch. 3, v. 8

32 We are members one of another.
   Ephesians ch. 4, v. 25

33 Be ye angry and sin not: let not the sun go down upon your wrath.
   Ephesians ch. 4, v. 26

**1** See then that ye walk circumspectly, not as fools, but as wise,

Redeeming the time, because the days are evil.

Ephesians ch. 5, v. 15

**2** Ye fathers, provoke not your children to wrath.

Ephesians ch. 6, v. 4

**3** Put on the whole armour of God.

Ephesians ch. 6, v. 11

**4** For we wrestle not against flesh and blood, but against principalities, against powers, against the rulers of the darkness of this world, against spiritual wickedness in high places.

Wherefore take unto you the whole armour of God, that ye may be able to withstand in the evil day, and having done all, to stand.

Stand therefore, having your loins girt about with truth, and having on the breastplate of righteousness.

Ephesians ch. 6, v. 12

### Philippians

**5** At the name of Jesus every knee should bow.

Philippians ch. 2, v. 10

**6** Work out your own salvation with fear and trembling.

Philippians ch. 2, v. 12

**7** Rejoice in the Lord alway: and again I say, Rejoice.

Philippians ch. 4, v. 4

**8** The peace of God, which passeth all understanding, shall keep your hearts and minds through Christ Jesus.

Philippians ch. 4, v. 7

**9** Whatsoever things are true, whatsoever things are honest, whatsoever things are just, whatsoever things are pure, whatsoever things are lovely, whatsoever things are of good report; if there be any virtue and if there be any praise, think on these things.

Philippians ch. 4, v. 8

**10** I can do all things through Christ which strengtheneth me.

Philippians ch. 4, v. 13

### Colossians

**11** Husbands, love your wives, and be not bitter against them.

Colossians ch. 3, v. 19

**12** Let your speech be alway with grace, seasoned with salt.

Colossians ch. 4, v. 6

### I Thesssalonians

**13** Remembering without ceasing your work of faith and labour of love.

I Thesssalonians ch. 1, v. 3

**14** Prove all things; hold fast that which is good.

1 Thessalonians ch. 5, v. 21

### II Thesssalonians

**15** If any would not work, neither should he eat.

II Thesssalonians ch. 3, v. 10

### I Timothy

**16** A bishop then must be blameless, the husband of one wife, vigilant, sober, of good behaviour, given to hospitality, apt to teach;

Not given to wine, no striker, not greedy of filthy lucre; but patient, not a brawler, not covetous.

I Timothy ch. 3, v. 2

**17** Refuse profane and old wives' fables.

I Timothy ch. 4, v. 7

**18** For we brought nothing into this world, and it is certain we can carry nothing out.

I Timothy ch. 6, v. 7

**19** The love of money is the root of all evil.

I Timothy ch. 6, v. 10

**20** Fight the good fight of faith, lay hold on eternal life.

I Timothy ch. 6, v. 12

### II Timothy

**21** I have fought a good fight, I have finished my course, I have kept the faith.

II Timothy ch. 4, v. 7

### Titus

**22** Unto the pure all things are pure.

Titus ch. 1, v. 15

### Hebrews

**23** God, who at sundry times and in divers manners spake in time past unto the fathers by the prophets.

Hebrews ch. 1, v. 1

**24** Without shedding of blood is no remission.

Hebrews ch. 9, v. 22

**25** It is a fearful thing to fall into the hands of the living God.

Hebrews ch. 10, v. 31

**26** Faith is the substance of things hoped for, the evidence of things not seen.

Hebrews ch. 11, v. 1

**27** Wherefore seeing we also are compassed about with so great a cloud of witnesses, let us lay aside every weight, and the sin which doth so easily beset us, and let us run with patience the race that is set before us,

Looking unto Jesus the author and finisher of our faith.

Hebrews ch. 12, v. 1

**28** Whom the Lord loveth he chasteneth.

Hebrews ch. 12, v. 6

**29** Be not forgetful to entertain strangers: for thereby some have entertained angels unawares.

Hebrews ch. 13, v. 2

**30** Jesus Christ the same yesterday, and to day, and for ever.

Hebrews ch. 13, v. 8

1 For here have we no continuing city, but we seek one to come.
  Hebrews ch. 13, v. 14

## James

2 Be ye doers of the word, and not hearers only.
  James ch. 1, v. 22

3 Faith without works is dead.
  James ch. 2, v. 20

4 Ye have heard of the patience of Job.
  James ch. 5, v. 11

5 Let your yea be yea; and your nay, nay.
  James ch. 5, v. 12

## I Peter

6 All flesh is as grass, and all the glory of man as the flower of grass. The grass withereth, and the flower thereof falleth away.
  I Peter ch. 1, v. 24. Cf. 46:10

7 As newborn babes, desire the sincere milk of the word, that ye may grow thereby: If so be ye have tasted that the Lord is gracious.
  I Peter ch. 2, v. 2

8 But ye are a chosen generation, a royal priesthood, an holy nation, a peculiar people.
  I Peter ch. 2, v. 9

9 Honour all men. Love the brotherhood. Fear God. Honour the king.
  I Peter ch. 2, v. 17

10 Giving honour unto the wife, as unto the weaker vessel.
  I Peter ch. 3, v. 7

11 Charity shall cover the multitude of sins.
  I Peter ch. 4, v. 8

12 Be sober, be vigilant; because your adversary the devil, as a roaring lion, walketh about, seeking whom he may devour.
  I Peter ch. 5, v. 8

## II Peter

13 The dog is turned to his own vomit again.
  II Peter ch. 2, v. 22

## I John

14 If we say that we have no sin, we deceive ourselves, and the truth is not in us.
  I John ch. 1, v. 8

15 He that loveth not knoweth not God; for God is love.
  I John ch. 4, v. 8

16 There is no fear in love; but perfect love casteth out fear.
  I John ch. 4, v. 18

17 If a man say, I love God, and hateth his brother, he is a liar: for he that loveth not his brother whom he hath seen, how can he love God whom he hath not seen?
  I John ch. 4, v. 20

## III John

18 He that doeth good is of God: but he that doeth evil hath not seen God.
  III John v. 11

## Revelation

19 I am Alpha and Omega, the beginning and the ending, saith the Lord.
  Revelation ch. 1, v. 8

20 I have somewhat against thee, because thou hast left thy first love.
  Revelation ch. 2, v. 4

21 Be thou faithful unto death, and I will give thee a crown of life.
  Revelation ch. 2, v. 10

22 Because thou art lukewarm, and neither cold nor hot, I will spew thee out of my mouth.
  Revelation ch. 3, v. 16

23 Behold, I stand at the door, and knock.
  Revelation ch. 3, v. 20

24 Holy, holy, holy, Lord God Almighty, which was, and is, and is to come.
  Revelation ch. 4, v. 8

25 And I looked, and behold a pale horse: and his name that sat on him was Death.
  Revelation ch. 6, v. 8

26 These are they which came out of great tribulation, and have washed their robes, and made them white in the blood of the Lamb.
  Revelation ch. 7, v. 14

27 They shall hunger no more, neither thirst any more.
  Revelation ch. 7, v. 16

28 God shall wipe away all tears from their eyes.
  Revelation ch. 7, v. 17. Cf. 58:5

29 And when he had opened the seventh seal, there was silence in heaven about the space of half an hour.
  Revelation ch. 8, v. 1

30 And there appeared a great wonder in heaven; a woman clothed with the sun, and the moon under her feet, and upon her head a crown of twelve stars.
  Revelation ch. 12, v. 1

31 And there was war in heaven: Michael and his angels fought against the dragon; and the dragon fought and his angels.
  Revelation ch. 12, v. 7

32 And that no man might buy or sell, save he that had the mark, or the name of the beast, or the number of his name.
  Revelation ch. 13, v. 17

33 Let him that hath understanding count the number of the beast: for it is the number of a man; and his number is Six hundred threescore and six.
  Revelation ch. 13, v. 18

34 Babylon is fallen, is fallen, that great city.
  Revelation ch. 14, v. 8

1 Behold, I come as a thief.
  Revelation ch. 16, v. 15

2 And upon her forehead was a name
  written, MYSTERY, BABYLON THE GREAT, THE
  MOTHER OF HARLOTS AND ABOMINATIONS
  OF THE EARTH.
  Revelation ch. 17, v. 5

3 And the sea gave up the dead which were
  in it.
  Revelation ch. 20, v. 13

4 And I saw a new heaven and a new earth:
  for the first heaven and the first earth
  were passed away; and there was no
  more sea.
  And I John saw the holy city, new
  Jerusalem, coming down from God out of
  heaven, prepared as a bride adorned for
  her husband.
  Revelation ch. 21, v. 1

5 And God shall wipe away all tears from
  their eyes; and there shall be no more
  death, neither sorrow, nor crying, neither
  shall there be any more pain: for the
  former things are passed away.
  And he that sat upon the throne said,
  Behold, I make all things new.
  Revelation ch. 21, v. 4

6 I will give unto him that is athirst of the
  fountain of the water of life freely.
  Revelation ch. 21, v. 6

7 And the leaves of the tree were for the
  healing of the nations.
  Revelation ch. 22, v. 2

8 Amen. Even so, come, Lord Jesus.
  Revelation ch. 22, v. 20

## Vulgate

9 *Dominus illuminatio mea, et salus mea, quem
  timebo?*
  The Lord is the source of my light and my
  safety, so whom shall I fear?
  Psalm 26, v. 1

10 *Jubilate Deo, omnis terra; servite Domino in
   laetitia.*
   Sing joyfully to God, all the earth; serve the
   Lord with gladness.
   Psalm 99, v. 2 (Psalm 100, v. 2 in the
   Authorized Version). Cf. 68:5

11 *Beatus vir qui timet Dominum, in mandatis ejus
   volet nimis!*
   Happy is the man who fears the Lord, who
   is only too willing to follow his orders.
   Psalm 111, v. 1 (Psalm 112, v. 1 in the
   Authorized Version)

12 *Non nobis, Domine, non nobis; sed nomini tuo
   da gloriam.*
   Not unto us, Lord, not unto us; but to thy
   name give glory.
   Psalm 113 (second part), v. 1 (Psalm 115, v. 1
   in the Authorized Version). Cf. 68:17

13 *Nisi Dominus custodierit civitatem, frustra
   vigilat qui custodit eam.*
   Unless the Lord guards the city, the
   watchman watches in vain.
   Psalm 126, v. 2 (Psalm 127, v. 2 in the
   Authorized Version; contracted to '*Nisi
   Dominus frustra*' for the motto of the city of
   Edinburgh). Cf. 68:30

14 *De profundis clamavi ad te, Domine; Domine,
   exaudi vocem meam.*
   Up from the depths I have cried to thee,
   Lord; Lord, hear my voice.
   Psalm 129, v. 1 (Psalm 130, v. 1 in the
   Authorized Version). Cf. 68:33

15 *Vanitas vanitatum, dixit Ecclesiastes; vanitas
   vanitatum, et omnia vanitas.*
   Vanity of vanities, said the preacher; vanity
   of vanities, and everything is vanity.
   Ecclesiastes ch. 1, v. 2. Cf. 44:7

16 *Magnificat anima mea Dominum.*
   My soul doth magnify the Lord.
   St Luke ch. 1, v. 46. Cf. 51:28

17 *Nunc dimittis servum tuum, Domine, secundum
   verbum tuum in pace.*
   Lord, now lettest thou thy servant depart
   in peace: according to thy word.
   St Luke ch. 2, v. 29. Cf. 52:3

18 *Pax Vobis.*
   Peace be unto you.
   St Luke ch. 24, v. 36

19 *Quo vadis?*
   Where are you going?
   St John ch. 16, v. 5

20 *Ecce homo.*
   Behold the man.
   St John ch. 19, v. 5

21 *Consummatum est.*
   It is achieved.
   St John ch. 19, v. 30. Cf. 54:5

22 *Noli me tangere.*
   Do not touch me.
   St John ch. 20, v. 17. Cf. 54:6

23 *Magna est veritas, et praevalet.*
   Great is truth, and it prevails.
   III Esdras ch. 4, v. 41. Cf. 47:27
   *See also* BOOK OF COMMON PRAYER (Psalms)

## Isaac Bickerstaffe 1733–c.1808

24 And this the burthen of his song,
   For ever used to be,
   I care for nobody, not I,
   If no one cares for me.
   *Love in a Village* (1762) act 1, sc. 2 'The Miller
   of Dee'

## E. H. Bickersteth 1825–1906

25 Peace, perfect peace, in this dark world of
   sin?
   The Blood of Jesus whispers peace within.
   *Songs in the House of Pilgrimage* (1875) 'Peace,
   perfect peace'

## Georges Bidault 1899–1983

1 The weak have one weapon: the errors of those who think they are strong.
   In *Observer* 15 July 1962 'Sayings of the Week'

## Ambrose Bierce 1842–c.1914

2 ALLIANCE, *n.* In international politics, the union of two thieves who have their hands so deeply inserted in each other's pocket that they cannot separately plunder a third.
   *The Cynic's Word Book* (1906) p. 16

3 APPLAUSE, *n.* The echo of a platitude.
   *The Cynic's Word Book* (1906) p. 19

4 BATTLE, *n.* A method of untying with the teeth a political knot that would not yield to the tongue.
   *The Cynic's Word Book* (1906) p. 30

5 CONSERVATIVE, *n.* A statesman who is enamoured of existing evils, as distinguished from the Liberal, who wishes to replace them with others.
   *The Cynic's Word Book* (1906) p. 56

6 HISTORY, *n.* An account, mostly false, of events, mostly unimportant, which are brought about by rulers, mostly knaves, and soldiers, mostly fools.
   *The Cynic's Word Book* (1906) p. 161

7 PEACE, *n.* In international affairs, a period of cheating between two periods of fighting.
   *The Devil's Dictionary* (1911) p. 248

8 PREJUDICE, *n.* A vagrant opinion without visible means of support.
   *The Devil's Dictionary* (1911) p. 264

9 SAINT, *n.* A dead sinner revised and edited.
   *The Devil's Dictionary* (1911) p. 306

## Josh Billings 1818–85

10 Love iz like the meazles; we kant have it bad but onst, and the latter in life we hav it the tuffer it goes with us.
   *Josh Billings' Wit and Humour* (1874) p. 146

11 Natur never makes enny blunders. When she makes a phool she means it.
   *Josh Billings' Wit and Humour* (1874) p. 174

## Laurence Binyon 1869–1943

12 They shall grow not old, as we that are left grow old.
   Age shall not weary them, nor the years condemn.
   At the going down of the sun and in the morning
   We will remember them.
   'For the Fallen' (1914)

13 Now is the time for the burning of the leaves.
   'The Ruins' (1942)

## Nigel Birch 1906–81

14 My God! They've shot our fox!
   On hearing of the resignation of Hugh Dalton, Chancellor of the Exchequer in the Labour Government, 13 November 1947; in Harold Macmillan *Tides of Fortune* (1969) ch. 3

## Earl of Birkenhead

*See* F. E. SMITH

## Augustine Birrell 1850–1933

15 That great dust-heap called 'history'.
   *Obiter Dicta* (1884) 'Carlyle'

## Elizabeth Bishop 1911–79

16 The armoured cars of dreams, contrived to let us do
   so many a dangerous thing.
   'Sleeping Standing Up' (1946)

## Prince Otto von Bismarck 1815–98

17 Politics is the art of the possible.
   In conversation with Meyer von Waldeck, 11 August 1867, in H. Amelung *Bismarck-Worte* (1918) p. 19

18 I do not regard the procuring of peace as a matter in which we should play the role of arbiter between different opinions ... more that of an honest broker who really wants to press the business forward.
   Speech to the Reichstag, 19 February 1878, in L. Hahn (ed.) *Fürst Bismarck. Sein politisches Leben und Wirken* vol. 3 (1881) p. 90

19 This policy cannot succeed through speeches, and shooting-matches, and songs; it can only be carried out through blood and iron.
   Speech in the Prussian House of Deputies, 28 January 1886, in *Fürst Bismarck als Redner. Vollständige Sammlung der parlamentarischen Reden* (1885–91) vol. 15, p. 157. In an earlier speech, 30 September 1862, Bismarck used the form 'iron and blood'

20 If there is ever another war in Europe, it will come out of some damned silly thing in the Balkans.
   Quoted in the House of Commons; *Hansard* 16 August 1945, col. 84

21 A lath of wood painted to look like iron.
   Describing Lord Salisbury; attributed, but vigorously denied by Sidney Whitman in *Personal Reminiscences of Prince Bismarck* (1902) ch. 14

## Valentine Blacker 1728–1823

22 Put your trust in God, my boys, and keep your powder dry.
   'Oliver's Advice' in E. Hayes *Ballads of Ireland* (1856) vol. 1 (often attributed to Oliver Cromwell himself)

## Sir William Blackstone 1723–80

1 The king never dies.
   *Commentaries on the Laws of England* (1765)
   bk. 1, ch. 7

2 That the king can do no wrong, is a
   necessary and fundamental principle of the
   English constitution.
   *Commentaries on the Laws of England* (1765)
   bk. 3, ch. 17

3 It is better that ten guilty persons escape
   than one innocent suffer.
   *Commentaries on the Laws of England* (1765)
   bk. 4, ch. 27

## Eubie Blake 1883–1983

4 If I'd known I was gonna live this long, I'd
   have taken better care of myself.
   On reaching the age of 100; in *Observer*
   13 February 1983 'Sayings of the Week'

## William Blake 1757–1827

5 To see a world in a grain of sand
   And a heaven in a wild flower
   Hold infinity in the palm of your hand
   And eternity in an hour.
   'Auguries of Innocence' (*c*.1803) l. 1

6 A robin red breast in a cage
   Puts all Heaven in a rage.
   'Auguries of Innocence' (*c*.1803) l. 5

7 A truth that's told with bad intent
   Beats all the lies you can invent.
   'Auguries of Innocence' (*c*.1803) l. 53

8 The strongest poison ever known
   Came from Caesar's laurel crown.
   'Auguries of Innocence' (*c*.1803) l. 97

9 The whore and gambler by the State
   Licensed build that nation's fate
   The harlot's cry from street to street
   Shall weave old England's winding sheet.
   'Auguries of Innocence' (*c*.1803) l. 113

10 Does the eagle know what is in the pit?
   Or wilt thou go ask the mole:
   Can wisdom be put in a silver rod?
   Or love in a golden bowl?
   *The Book of Thel* (1789) plate i 'Thel's Motto'

11 The Vision of Christ that thou dost see
   Is my vision's greatest enemy
   Thine has a great hook nose like thine
   Mine has a snub nose like to mine.
   *The Everlasting Gospel* (*c*.1818) (a) l. 1

12 Humility is only doubt
   And does the sun and moon blot out
   Rooting over with thorns and stems
   The buried soul and all its gems
   This life's dim windows of the soul
   Distorts the heavens from pole to pole
   And leads you to believe a lie
   When you see with not through the eye.
   *The Everlasting Gospel* (*c*.1818) (d) l. 99

13 Was Jesus chaste or did he
   Give any lessons of chastity
   The morning blushed fiery red
   Mary was found in adulterous bed.
   *The Everlasting Gospel* (*c*.1818) (e) l. 1

14 I am sure this Jesus will not do
   Either for Englishman or Jew.
   *The Everlasting Gospel* (*c*.1818) (f) l. 1

15 Truly, my Satan, thou art but a dunce,
   And dost not know the garment from the
   man;
   Every harlot was a virgin once,
   Nor can'st thou ever change Kate into Nan.
   Tho' thou art worshipped by the names
   divine
   Of Jesus and Jehovah, thou art still
   The Son of Morn in weary Night's decline,
   The lost traveller's dream under the hill.
   *For the Sexes: The Gates of Paradise* 'To the
   Accuser who is The God of This World'
   [epilogue]

16 Mournful ever weeping Paddington.
   *Jerusalem* (1815) 'Chapter 1' (plate 12, l. 27)

17 The fields from Islington to Marybone,
   To Primrose Hill and Saint John's Wood
   Were builded over with pillars of gold;
   And there Jerusalem's pillars stood.
   *Jerusalem* (1815) 'To the Jews' (plate 27, l. 1)
   "The fields from Islington to Marybone"

18 For a tear is an intellectual thing;
   And a sigh is the sword of an Angel King.
   *Jerusalem* (1815) 'To the Deists' (plate 52, l. 25)
   "I saw a Monk of Charlemaine"

19 He who would do good to another, must
   do it in minute particulars.
   *Jerusalem* (1815) 'Chapter 3' (plate 55, l. 60)

20 I give you the end of a golden string;
   Only wind it into a ball:
   It will lead you in at Heaven's gate,
   Built in Jerusalem's wall.
   *Jerusalem* (1815) 'To the Christians' (plate 77)
   "I give you the end of a golden string"

21 England! awake! awake! awake!
   Jerusalem thy sister calls!
   Why wilt thou sleep the sleep of death,
   And close her from thy ancient walls?
   *Jerusalem* (1815) 'To the Christians' (plate 77)
   "England! awake! ... "

22 I care not whether a man is good or evil;
   all that I care
   Is whether he is a wise man or a fool. Go!
   put off holiness
   And put on Intellect.
   *Jerusalem* (1815) 'Chapter 4' (plate 91, l. 54)

23              May God us keep
   From Single vision and Newton's sleep!
   'Letter to Thomas Butts, 22 November 1802'

24 Energy is Eternal Delight.
   *The Marriage of Heaven and Hell* (1790–3) 'The
   voice of the Devil'

25 The reason Milton wrote in fetters when
   he wrote of Angels and God, and at liberty
   when he wrote of Devils and Hell, is because he was
   a true Poet, and of the Devil's party
   without knowing it.
   *The Marriage of Heaven and Hell* (1790–3) 'The
   voice of the Devil' (note)

1 The road of excess leads to the palace of wisdom.
*The Marriage of Heaven and Hell* (1790–3) 'Proverbs of Hell'

2 Prudence is a rich, ugly, old maid courted by Incapacity.
*The Marriage of Heaven and Hell* (1790–3) 'Proverbs of Hell'

3 He who desires but acts not, breeds pestilence.
*The Marriage of Heaven and Hell* (1790–3) 'Proverbs of Hell'

4 A fool sees not the same tree that a wise man sees.
*The Marriage of Heaven and Hell* (1790–3) 'Proverbs of Hell'

5 Eternity is in love with the productions of time.
*The Marriage of Heaven and Hell* (1790–3) 'Proverbs of Hell'

6 If the fool would persist in his folly he would become wise.
*The Marriage of Heaven and Hell* (1790–3) 'Proverbs of Hell'

7 Prisons are built with stones of Law, brothels with bricks of Religion.
*The Marriage of Heaven and Hell* (1790–3) 'Proverbs of Hell'

8 The tigers of wrath are wiser than the horses of instruction.
*The Marriage of Heaven and Hell* (1790–3) 'Proverbs of Hell'

9 Damn braces: Bless relaxes.
*The Marriage of Heaven and Hell* (1790–3) 'Proverbs of Hell'

10 Sooner murder an infant in its cradle than nurse unacted desires.
*The Marriage of Heaven and Hell* (1790–3) 'Proverbs of Hell'

11 If the doors of perception were cleansed everything would appear to man as it is, infinite.
*The Marriage of Heaven and Hell* (1790–3) 'A Memorable Fancy' plate 14

12 And did those feet in ancient time
Walk upon England's mountains green?
And was the holy Lamb of God
On England's pleasant pastures seen?

And did the Countenance Divine
Shine forth upon our clouded hills?
And was Jerusalem builded here
Among these dark Satanic mills?

Bring me my bow of burning gold:
Bring me my arrows of desire:
Bring me my spear: O clouds, unfold!
Bring me my chariot of fire.

I will not cease from mental fight,
Nor shall my sword sleep in my hand,
Till we have built Jerusalem,
In England's green and pleasant land.
*Milton* (1804–10) preface 'And did those feet in ancient time'

13 Mock on mock on Voltaire Rousseau
Mock on mock on tis all in vain
You throw the sand against the wind
And the wind blows it back again.
*MS Note-Book* p. 7

14 The atoms of Democritus
And Newton's particles of light
Are sands upon the Red sea shore
Where Israel's tents do shine so bright.
*MS Note-Book* p. 7

15 Great things are done when men and mountains meet
This is not done by jostling in the street.
*MS Note-Book* p. 43

16 He who binds to himself a joy
Doth the winged life destroy
But he who kisses the joy as it flies
Lives in Eternity's sunrise.
*MS Note-Book* p. 99 'Several Questions Answered'

17 What is it men in women do require
The lineaments of gratified desire
What is it women do in men require
The lineaments of gratified desire.
*MS Note-Book* p. 99 'Several Questions Answered'

18 Piping down the valleys wild
Piping songs of pleasant glee
On a cloud I saw a child.
*Songs of Innocence* (1789) introduction

19 Your chimneys I sweep and in soot I sleep.
*Songs of Innocence* (1789) 'The Chimney Sweeper'

20 To Mercy Pity Peace and Love,
All pray in their distress.
*Songs of Innocence* (1789) 'The Divine Image'

21 For Mercy has a human heart
Pity a human face:
And Love, the human form divine,
And Peace, the human dress.
*Songs of Innocence* (1789) 'The Divine Image'

22 Then cherish pity, lest you drive an angel from your door.
*Songs of Innocence* (1789) 'Holy Thursday'

23 Little Lamb who made thee
Dost thou know who made thee.
*Songs of Innocence* (1789) 'The Lamb'

24 My mother bore me in the southern wild,
And I am black, but O! my soul is white;
White as an angel is the English child:
But I am black as if bereaved of light.
*Songs of Innocence* (1789) 'The Little Black Boy'

25 When the voices of children are heard on the green
And laughing is heard on the hill.
*Songs of Innocence* (1789) 'Nurse's Song'

26 Hear the voice of the Bard!
Who present, past, and future, sees.
*Songs of Experience* (1794) introduction

1 Love seeketh not itself to please,
Nor for itself hath any care;
But for another gives its ease,
And builds a Heaven in Hell's despair.
*Songs of Experience* (1794) 'The Clod and the
Pebble'

2 Love seeketh only Self to please,
To bind another to its delight,
Joys in another's loss of ease,
And builds a Hell in Heaven's despite.
*Songs of Experience* (1794) 'The Clod and the
Pebble'

3 My mother groaned! my father wept.
Into the dangerous world I leapt:
Helpless, naked, piping loud;
Like a fiend hid in a cloud.
*Songs of Experience* (1794) 'Infant Sorrow'

4 O Rose, thou art sick!
The invisible worm
That flies in the night,
In the howling storm:
Has found out thy bed
Of crimson joy:
And his dark secret love
Does thy life destroy.
*Songs of Experience* (1794) 'The Sick Rose'

5 Tiger Tiger, burning bright,
In the forests of the night;
What immortal hand or eye,
Could frame thy fearful symmetry?
*Songs of Experience* (1794) 'The Tiger'

6 When the stars threw down their spears
And watered heaven with their tears:
Did he smile his work to see?
Did he who made the Lamb make thee?
*Songs of Experience* (1794) 'The Tiger'

7 Cruelty has a human heart,
And Jealousy a human face;
Terror the human form divine,
And Secrecy the human dress.
'A Divine Image'; etched but not included in
*Songs of Experience* (1794)

## Susanna Blamire 1747–94

8 I've gotten a rock, I've gotten a reel,
I've gotten a wee bit spinning-wheel;
An' by the whirling rim I've found
How the weary, weary warl goes round.
'I've Gotten a Rock, I've Gotten a Reel'
(c.1790) l. 1

## Lesley Blanch 1907–

9 The wilder shores of love.
Title of book (1954)

## Philip Paul Bliss 1838–76

10 Hold the fort, for I am coming.
*Gospel Hymns and Sacred Songs* (1875) no. 14
(suggested by a flag message from General
Sherman near Atlanta, October 1864)

## Karen Blixen

*See* ISAK DINESEN

## Gebhard Lebrecht Blücher
1742–1819

11 *Was für Plunder!*
What rubbish!
Of London, as seen from the Monument in
June 1814; in Evelyn Princess Blücher
*Memoirs of Prince Blücher* (1932) p. 33 (often
misquoted '*Was für plündern* [What a place to
plunder]!')

## Edmund Blunden 1896–1974

12 All things they have in common being so
poor,
And their one fear, Death's shadow at the
door.
'Almswomen' (1920)

13 I am for the woods against the world,
But are the woods for me?
'The Kiss' (1931)

14 Dance on this ball-floor thin and wan,
Use him as though you love him;
Court him, elude him, reel and pass,
And let him hate you through the glass.
'Midnight Skaters' (1925)

15 I have been young, and now am not too
old;
And I have seen the righteous forsaken,
His health, his honour and his quality
taken.
This is not what we were formerly told.
'Report on Experience' (1929)

## John Ernest Bode 1816–74

16 O let me hear thee speaking
In accents clear and still,
Above the storms of passion,
The murmurs of self-will.
'O Jesus, I have promised' (1869 hymn)

## Boethius AD c.476–524

17 For in every ill-turn of fortune the most
unhappy sort of unfortunate man is the
one who has been happy.
*De Consolatione Philosophiae* bk. 2, prose 4

## Louise Bogan 1897–1970

18 Women have no wilderness in them,
They are provident instead,
Content in the tight hot cell of their hearts
To eat dusty bread.
'Women' (1923)

## John B. Bogart 1848–1921

19 When a dog bites a man, that is not news,
because it happens so often. But if a man
bites a dog, that is news.
In F. M. O'Brien *Story of the* [New York] *Sun*
(1918) ch. 10 (often attributed to Charles A.
Dana)

## Niels Bohr 1885–1962

1 One of the favourite maxims of my father
was the distinction between the two sorts
of truths, profound truths recognized by
the fact that the opposite is also
a profound truth, in contrast to trivialities
where opposites are obviously absurd.
*S. Rozental* Niels Bohr *(1967) p. 328*

## Alan Bold 1943–

2 Scotland, land of the omnipotent No.
'A Memory of Death' (1969)

## Henry St John, 1st Viscount Bolingbroke 1678–1751

3 They make truth serve as a stalking-horse
to error.
*Letters on the Study and Use of History (1752)
No. 4, pt. 1*

4 Nations, like men, have their infancy.
*On the Study of History letter 5, in* Works *(1809)
vol. 3, p. 414*

5 Truth lies within a little and certain
compass, but error is immense.
*Reflections upon Exile (1716)*

6 What a world is this, and how does fortune
banter us!
Letter to Jonathan Swift, 3 August 1714; in
H. Williams (ed.) *Correspondence of Jonathan
Swift* (1963) vol. 2

7 The greatest art of a politician is to render
vice serviceable to the cause of virtue.
Comment (c.1728), in Joseph Spence
*Observations, Anecdotes, and Characters* (1820,
ed. J. M. Osborn, 1966) Anecdote 882

## Robert Bolt 1924–

8 It profits a man nothing to give his soul
for the whole world ... But for Wales—!
*A Man for All Seasons (1960) act 2*

## Carrie Jacobs Bond 1862–1946

9 When you come to the end of a perfect
day,
And you sit alone with your thought,
While the chimes ring out with a carol gay
For the joy that the day has brought,
Do you think what the end of a perfect day
Can mean to a tired heart,
When the sun goes down with a flaming
ray,
And the dear friends have to part?
'A Perfect Day' (1910 song)

## Sir David Bone 1874–1959

10 It's 'Damn you, Jack — I'm all right!' with
you chaps.
*Brassbounder* (1910) ch. 3

## Dietrich Bonhoeffer 1906–45

11 It is the nature, and the advantage, of
strong people that they can bring out the
crucial questions and form a clear opinion
about them. The weak always have to
decide between alternatives that are not
their own.
*Widerstand und Ergebung (1951) p. 255 (tr. R.
Fuller)*

## The Book of Common Prayer 1662

12 Dearly beloved brethren, the Scripture
moveth us in sundry places to
acknowledge and confess our manifold sins
and wickedness.
*Morning Prayer Sentences of the Scriptures*

13 We have erred, and strayed from thy ways
like lost sheep. We have followed too much
the devices and desires of our own hearts.
*Morning Prayer General Confession*

14 We have left undone those things which
we ought to have done; And we have done
those things which we ought not to have
done; And there is no health in us.
*Morning Prayer General Confession*

15 And grant, O most merciful Father, for his
sake; That we may hereafter live a godly,
righteous, and sober life.
*Morning Prayer General Confession*

16 And forgive us our trespasses, As we
forgive them that trespass against us.
*Morning Prayer The Lord's Prayer. Cf. 48:27*

17 Glory be to the Father, and to the Son: and
to the Holy Ghost; As it was in the
beginning, is now, and ever shall be: world
without end. Amen.
*Morning Prayer Gloria*

18 We praise thee, O God: we acknowledge
thee to be the Lord.
All the earth doth worship thee: the Father
everlasting.
To thee all Angels cry aloud: the Heavens,
and all the Powers therein.
*Morning Prayer Te Deum. Cf. 14:1*

19 The glorious company of the Apostles:
praise thee.
The goodly fellowship of the Prophets:
praise thee.
The noble army of Martyrs: praise thee.
*Morning Prayer Te Deum. Cf. 14:1*

20 When thou hadst overcome the sharpness
of death: thou didst open the Kingdom of
Heaven to all believers.
*Morning Prayer Te Deum. Cf. 14:1*

21 Day by day: we magnify thee;
And we worship thy Name: ever world
without end.
*Morning Prayer Te Deum. Cf. 14:1*

22 O Lord, in thee have I trusted: let me never
be confounded.
*Morning Prayer Te Deum. Cf. 14:1*

1 O all ye Green Things upon the Earth, bless
ye the Lord.
*Morning Prayer* Benedicite

2 O ye Whales, and all that move in the
Waters, bless ye the Lord.
*Morning Prayer* Benedicite

3 I believe in the Holy Ghost; The holy
Catholic Church; The Communion of
Saints; The Forgiveness of sins; The
Resurrection of the body, And the life
everlasting. Amen.
*Morning Prayer* The Apostles' Creed. Cf. 65:5

4 Give peace in our time, O Lord.
*Morning Prayer* Versicle

5 O God, who art the author of peace and
lover of concord, in knowledge of whom
standeth our eternal life, whose service is
perfect freedom; Defend us thy humble
servants in all assaults of our enemies.
*Morning Prayer* The Second Collect, for Peace

6 Grant that this day we fall into no sin,
neither run into any kind of danger.
*Morning Prayer* The Third Collect, for Grace

7 In Quires and Places where they sing.
*Morning Prayer* rubric following Third Collect

8 Almighty God, the fountain of all
goodness.
*Morning Prayer* Prayer for the Royal Family

9 And that they may truly please thee, pour
upon them the continual dew of thy
blessing.
*Morning Prayer* Prayer for the Clergy and
People

10 Almighty God, who hast given us grace at
this time with one accord to make our
common supplications unto thee; and dost
promise, that when two or three are
gathered together in thy Name thou wilt
grant their requests: Fulfil now, O Lord, the
desires and petitions of thy servants, as
may be most expedient for them.
*Morning Prayer* Prayer of St Chrysostom

11 O God, from whom all holy desires, all
good counsels, and all just works do
proceed; Give unto thy servants that peace
which the world cannot give.
*Evening Prayer* Second Collect

12 Lighten our darkness, we beseech thee,
O Lord; and by thy great mercy defend us
from all perils and dangers of this night.
*Evening Prayer* Third Collect

13 Have mercy upon us miserable sinners.
*The Litany*

14 From all blindness of heart; from pride,
vain-glory, and hypocrisy; from envy,
hatred, and malice, and from all
uncharitableness,
Good Lord, deliver us.
*The Litany*

15 From all the deceits of the world, the flesh,
and the devil,
Good Lord, deliver us.
*The Litany*

16 In the hour of death, and in the day of
judgement,
Good Lord, deliver us.
*The Litany*

17 That it may please thee to defend, and
provide for, the fatherless children, and
widows, and all that are desolate and
oppressed.
*The Litany*

18 O God, the Creator and Preserver of all
mankind, we humbly beseech thee for all
sorts and conditions of men.
*Prayers . . . upon Several Occasions* 'Collect or
Prayer for all Conditions of Men'

19 We commend to thy fatherly goodness all
those, who are any ways afflicted, or
distressed, in mind, body, or estate; that it
may please thee to comfort and relieve
them, according to their several
necessities, giving them patience under
their sufferings, and a happy issue out of
all their afflictions.
*Prayers . . . upon Several Occasions* 'Collect or
Prayer for all Conditions of Men'

20 O God our heavenly Father, who by thy
gracious providence dost cause the former
and the latter rain to descend upon the
earth.
*Thanksgivings* For Rain

21 Almighty God, give us grace that we may
cast away the works of darkness, and put
upon us the armour of light.
*Collects* 1st Sunday in Advent

22 Blessed Lord, who hast caused all holy
Scriptures to be written for our learning;
Grant that we may in such wise hear
them, read, mark, learn, and inwardly
digest them.
*Collects* 2nd Sunday in Advent

23 The sundry and manifold changes of the
world.
*Collects* 4th Sunday after Easter

24 O God, the protector of all that trust in
thee, without whom nothing is strong,
nothing is holy.
*Collects* 4th Sunday after Trinity

25 Lord of all power and might, who art the
author and giver of all good things; Graft
in our hearts the love of thy Name,
increase in us true religion, nourish us
with all goodness, and of thy great mercy
keep us in the same.
*Collects* 7th Sunday after Trinity

26 O God, forasmuch as without thee we are
not able to please thee.
*Collects* 19th Sunday after Trinity

27 Grant that those things which we ask
faithfully we may obtain effectually.
*Collects* 23rd Sunday after Trinity

28 Stir up, we beseech thee, O Lord, the wills
of thy faithful people.
*Collects* 25th Sunday after Trinity

29 An open and notorious evil liver.
*Holy Communion* introductory rubric

1 His former naughty life.
   *Holy Communion* introductory rubric

2 Almighty God, unto whom all hearts be
   open, all desires known, and from whom
   no secrets are hid.
   *Holy Communion* The Collect

3 Incline our hearts to keep this law.
   *Holy Communion* The Ten Commandments
   (response)

4 Thou shalt do no murder.
   *Holy Communion* The Ten Commandments.
   Cf. 40:9

5 I believe in one God the Father Almighty,
   Maker of heaven and earth, And of all
   things visible and invisible:
   And in one Lord Jesus Christ, the only-
   begotten Son of God, Begotten of his
   Father before all worlds, God of God,
   Light of Light, Very God of very God,
   Begotten, not made, Being of one
   substance with the Father, By whom all
   things were made.
   *Holy Communion* Nicene Creed. Cf. 64:3,
   231:15

6 And I believe one Catholick and Apostolick
   Church.
   *Holy Communion* Nicene Creed

7 Let us pray for the whole state of Christ's
   Church militant here in earth.
   *Holy Communion* Prayer for the Church
   Militant

8 We humbly beseech thee most mercifully
   to accept our alms and oblations.
   *Holy Communion* Prayer for the Church
   Militant

9 Inspire continually the universal Church
   with the spirit of truth, unity, and concord.
   *Holy Communion* Prayer for the Church
   Militant

10 Give grace, O heavenly Father, to all
   Bishops and Curates, that they may both
   by their life and doctrine set forth thy true
   and lively Word.
   *Holy Communion* Prayer for the Church
   Militant

11 We do earnestly repent, And are heartily
   sorry for these our misdoings; The
   remembrance of them is grievous unto us;
   The burden of them is intolerable.
   *Holy Communion* General Confession

12 Hear what comfortable words our Saviour
   Christ saith unto all that truly turn to him.
   *Holy Communion* Comfortable Words
   (preamble)

13 Lift up your hearts.
   *Holy Communion* versicles and responses

14 It is meet and right so to do.
   *Holy Communion* versicles and responses

15 It is very meet, right, and our bounden
   duty, that we should at all times, and in
   all places, give thanks unto thee.
   *Holy Communion* Hymn of Praise

16 Who made there (by his one oblation of
   himself once offered) a full, perfect, and
   sufficient sacrifice.
   *Holy Communion* Prayer of Consecration

17 We beseech thee to accept this our
   bounden duty and service; not weighing
   our merits, but pardoning our offences.
   *Holy Communion* First Prayer of Oblation

18 Among all the changes and chances of this
   mortal life.
   *Holy Communion* Collects after the Offertory

19 O merciful God, grant that the old Adam in
   this Child may be so buried, that the new
   man may be raised up in him.
   *Public Baptism of Infants* Invocation of blessing
   on the child

20 QUESTION: Who gave you this Name?
   ANSWER: My Godfathers and Godmothers in
   my Baptism; wherein I was made a
   member of Christ, the child of God, and
   an inheritor of the kingdom of heaven.
   *Catechism*

21 I should renounce the devil and all his
   works, the pomps and vanity of this
   wicked world, and all the sinful lusts of
   the flesh.
   *Catechism*

22 To keep my hands from picking and
   stealing.
   *Catechism*

23 QUESTION: What meanest thou by this
   word *Sacrament*?
   ANSWER: I mean an outward and visible
   sign of an inward and spiritual grace.
   *Catechism*

24 Lord, hear our prayers.
   And let our cry come unto thee.
   *Order of Confirmation*

25 If any of you know cause, or just
   impediment, why these two persons
   should not be joined together in holy
   Matrimony, ye are to declare it. This is the
   first [*second*, or *third*] time of asking.
   *Solemnization of Matrimony* The Banns

26 Not by any to be enterprised, nor taken in
   hand, unadvisedly, lightly, or wantonly, to
   satisfy men's carnal lusts and appetites,
   like brute beasts that have no
   understanding.
   *Solemnization of Matrimony* Exhortation

27 If any man can shew any just cause, why
   they may not lawfully be joined together,
   let him now speak, or else hereafter for
   ever hold his peace.
   *Solemnization of Matrimony* Exhortation

28 Wilt thou love her, comfort her, honour,
   and keep her in sickness and in health;
   and, forsaking all other, keep thee only
   unto her, so long as ye both shall live?
   *Solemnization of Matrimony* Betrothal

1 To have and to hold from this day forward, for better for worse, for richer for poorer, in sickness and in health, to love, cherish, and to obey, till death us do part.
*Solemnization of Matrimony* Betrothal

2 With this Ring I thee wed, with my body I thee worship, and with all my worldly goods I thee endow.
*Solemnization of Matrimony* Wedding ('All that I am I give to you, and all that I have I share with you' in *Alternative Service Book*)

3 Those whom God hath joined together let no man put asunder.
*Solemnization of Matrimony* Wedding. Cf. 50:20

4 And thereto have given and pledged their troth either to other, and have declared the same by giving and receiving of a Ring, and by joining of hands.
*Solemnization of Matrimony* Minister's Declaration

5 The Office ensuing is not to be used for any that die unbaptized, or excommunicate, or have laid violent hands upon themselves.
*The Burial of the Dead* introductory rubric

6 Man that is born of a woman hath but a short time to live, and is full of misery.
*The Burial of the Dead* First Anthem. Cf. 42:33

7 In the midst of life we are in death.
*The Burial of the Dead* First Anthem

8 Forasmuch as it hath pleased Almighty God of his great mercy to take unto himself the soul of our dear brother here departed, we therefore commit his body to the ground; earth to earth, ashes to ashes, dust to dust; in sure and certain hope of the Resurrection to eternal life.
*The Burial of the Dead* Interment

9 Why do the heathen so furiously rage together: and why do the people imagine a vain thing?
Psalm 2, v. 1

10 Out of the mouth of very babes and sucklings hast thou ordained strength, because of thine enemies.
Psalm 8, v. 2

11 Up, Lord, and let not man have the upper hand.
Psalm 9, v. 19

12 The fool hath said in his heart: There is no God.
Psalm 14, v. 1

13 Lord, who shall dwell in thy tabernacle: or who shall rest upon thy holy hill?
Psalm 15, v. 1

14 He that hath not given his money upon usury: nor taken reward against the innocent.
Psalm 15, v. 6

15 The lot is fallen unto me in a fair ground: yea, I have a goodly heritage.
Psalm 16, v. 7 ('The lines are fallen unto me in pleasant places' in the Authorized Version of the Bible, v. 6)

16 They part my garments among them: and cast lots upon my vesture.
Psalm 22, v. 18

17 The Lord is my shepherd: therefore can I lack nothing.
He shall feed me in a green pasture: and lead me forth beside the waters of comfort.
Psalm 23, v. 1. Cf. 269:8

18 Yea, though I walk through the valley of the shadow of death, I will fear no evil: for thou art with me; thy rod and thy staff comfort me.
Thou shalt prepare a table before me against them that trouble me: thou hast anointed my head with oil, and my cup shall be full.
But thy loving-kindness and mercy shall follow me all the days of my life: and I will dwell in the house of the Lord for ever.
Psalm 23, v. 4. Cf. 269:9

19 The earth is the Lord's, and all that therein is.
Psalm 24, v. 1

20 Lift up your heads, O ye gates, and be ye lift up, ye everlasting doors: and the King of glory shall come in.
Psalm 24, v. 7

21 O remember not the sins and offences of my youth.
Psalm 25, v. 6

22 For his wrath endureth but the twinkling of an eye, and in his pleasure is life: heaviness may endure for a night, but joy cometh in the morning.
Psalm 30, v. 4

23 Into thy hands I commend my spirit.
Psalm 31, v. 6. Cf. 53:4

24 Sing unto the Lord a new song: sing praises lustily unto him with a good courage.
Psalm 33, v. 3

25 Keep thy tongue from evil: and thy lips, that they speak no guile.
Eschew evil, and do good: seek peace, and ensue it.
Psalm 34, v. 13

26 Fret not thyself because of the ungodly.
Psalm 37, v. 1

27 I have been young, and now am old: and yet saw I never the righteous forsaken, nor his seed begging their bread.
Psalm 37, v. 25

28 I myself have seen the ungodly in great power: and flourishing like a green bay-tree.
Psalm 37, v. 36

**1** Lord, let me know mine end, and the number of my days: that I may be certified how long I have to live.
Psalm 39, v. 3

**2** Mine own familiar friend, whom I trusted.
Psalm 41, v. 9

**3** Like as the hart desireth the water-brooks: so longeth my soul after thee, O God.
Psalm 42, v. 1 ('As the hart panteth after the water brooks, so panteth my soul after thee, O God' in the Authorized Version of the Bible)

**4** One deep calleth another, because of the noise of the water-pipes: all thy waves and storms are gone over me.
Psalm 42, v. 9

**5** My heart is inditing of a good matter: I speak of the things which I have made unto the King.
My tongue is the pen: of a ready writer.
Psalm 45, v. 1

**6** God is our hope and strength: a very present help in trouble.
Psalm 46, v. 1

**7** Be still then, and know that I am God.
Psalm 46, v. 10

**8** God is gone up with a merry noise: and the Lord with the sound of the trump.
Psalm 47, v. 5

**9** Thou shalt purge me with hyssop, and I shall be clean: thou shalt wash me, and I shall be whiter than snow.
Psalm 51, v. 7

**10** Make me a clean heart, O God: and renew a right spirit within me.
Psalm 51, v. 10

**11** O that I had wings like a dove: for then would I flee away, and be at rest.
Psalm 55, v. 6

**12** It was even thou, my companion: my guide, and mine own familiar friend.
Psalm 55, v. 14

**13** They are as venomous as the poison of a serpent: even like the deaf adder that stoppeth her ears;
Which refuseth to hear the voice of the charmer: charm he never so wisely.
Psalm 58, v. 4

**14** Moab is my wash-pot; over Edom will I cast out my shoe.
Psalm 60, v. 8

**15** Let them fall upon the edge of the sword: that they may be a portion for foxes.
Psalm 63, v. 11

**16** That thy way may be known upon earth: thy saving health among all nations.
Psalm 67, v. 2

**17** Thou art gone up on high, thou hast led captivity captive.
Psalm 68, v. 18

**18** For promotion cometh neither from the east, nor from the west: nor yet from the south.
Psalm 75, v. 7

**19** O how amiable are thy dwellings: thou Lord of hosts!
Psalm 84, v. 1

**20** Yea, the sparrow hath found her an house, and the swallow a nest where she may lay her young: even thy altars, O Lord of hosts.
Psalm 84, v. 3

**21** Blessed is the man whose strength is in thee: in whose heart are thy ways.
Who going through the vale of misery use it for a well: and the pools are filled with water.
Psalm 84, v. 5

**22** For one day in thy courts: is better than a thousand.
I had rather be a door-keeper in the house of my God: than to dwell in the tents of ungodliness.
Psalm 84, v. 10

**23** Mercy and truth are met together: righteousness and peace have kissed each other.
Psalm 85, v. 10

**24** Very excellent things are spoken of thee: thou city of God.
Psalm 87, v. 2

**25** For a thousand years in thy sight are but as yesterday: seeing that is past as a watch in the night.
Psalm 90, v. 4

**26** The days of our age are threescore years and ten; and though men be so strong that they come to fourscore years: yet is their strength then but labour and sorrow; so soon passeth it away, and we are gone.
Psalm 90, v. 10

**27** So teach us to number our days: that we may apply our hearts unto wisdom.
Psalm 90, v. 12

**28** For he shall deliver thee from the snare of the hunter.
Psalm 91, v. 3

**29** Thou shalt not be afraid for any terror by night: nor for the arrow that flieth by day;
For the pestilence that walketh in darkness: nor for the sickness that destroyeth in the noon-day.
Psalm 91, v. 5

**30** For he shall give his angels charge over thee: to keep thee in all thy ways.
They shall bear thee in their hands: that thou hurt not thy foot against a stone.
Psalm 91, v. 11

**31** Let us come before his presence with thanksgiving: and shew ourselves glad in him with psalms.
Psalm 95, v. 2

1 To-day if ye will hear his voice, harden not your hearts: as in the provocation, and as in the day of temptation in the wilderness.
Psalm 95, v. 8

2 O worship the Lord in the beauty of holiness: let the whole earth stand in awe of him.
Psalm 96, v. 9

3 O sing unto the Lord a new song: for he hath done marvellous things.
Psalm 98, v. 1

4 With righteousness shall he judge the world: and the people with equity.
Psalm 98, v. 10

5 O be joyful in the Lord, all ye lands: serve the Lord with gladness, and come before his presence with a song.
Be ye sure that the Lord he is God: it is he that hath made us, and not we ourselves; we are his people, and the sheep of his pasture.
Psalm 100, v. 1. Cf. 58:10

6 The Lord is full of compassion and mercy: long-suffering, and of great goodness.
He will not alway be chiding: neither keepeth he his anger for ever.
Psalm 103, v. 8

7 The days of man are but as grass: for he flourisheth as a flower of a field.
For as soon as the wind goeth over it, it is gone: and the place thereof shall know it no more.
Psalm 103, v. 15

8 Man goeth forth to his work, and to his labour: until the evening.
Psalm 104, v. 23

9 The iron entered into his soul.
Psalm 105, v. 18

10 That he might inform his princes after his will: and teach his senators wisdom.
Psalm 105, v. 22

11 Thus were they stained with their own works: and went a whoring with their own inventions.
Psalm 106, v. 38

12 They that go down to the sea in ships: and occupy their business in great waters.
Psalm 107, v. 23

13 They reel to and fro, and stagger like a drunken man: and are at their wit's end.
Psalm 107, v. 27

14 The Lord said unto my Lord: Sit thou on my right hand, until I make thine enemies thy footstool.
Psalm 110, v. 1

15 The fear of the Lord is the beginning of wisdom.
Psalm 111, v. 10

16 The mountains skipped like rams: and the little hills like young sheep.
Psalm 114, v. 4

17 Not unto us, O Lord, not unto us, but unto thy Name give the praise.
Psalm 115, v. 1. Cf. 58:12

18 They have mouths, and speak not: eyes have they, and see not.
They have ears, and hear not: noses have they, and smell not.
They have hands, and handle not: feet have they, and walk not: neither speak they through their throat.
Psalm 115, v. 5

19 The snares of death compassed me round about: and the pains of hell gat hold upon me.
Psalm 116, v. 3

20 Thou hast delivered my soul from death: mine eyes from tears, and my feet from falling.
Psalm 116, v. 8

21 I said in my haste, All men are liars.
Psalm 116, v. 10

22 The same stone which the builders refused: is become the head-stone in the corner.
Psalm 118, v. 22

23 Blessed be he that cometh in the Name of the Lord.
Psalm 118, v. 26

24 Thy word is a lantern unto my feet: and a light unto my paths.
Psalm 119, v. 105

25 I will lift up mine eyes unto the hills: from whence cometh my help.
Psalm 121, v. 1

26 So that the sun shall not burn thee by day: neither the moon by night.
Psalm 121, v. 6

27 The Lord shall preserve thy going out, and thy coming in: from this time forth for evermore.
Psalm 121, v. 8

28 I was glad when they said unto me: We will go into the house of the Lord.
Psalm 122, v. 1

29 They that sow in tears: shall reap in joy.
Psalm 126, v. 6

30 Except the Lord build the house: their labour is but lost that build it.
Except the Lord keep the city: the watchman waketh but in vain.
Psalm 127, v. 1. Cf. 58:13

31 Like as the arrows in the hand of the giant: even so are the young children.
Happy is the man that hath his quiver full of them.
Psalm 127, v. 5

32 Thy wife shall be as the fruitful vine: upon the walls of thine house.
Thy children like the olive-branches: round about thy table.
Psalm 128, v. 3

33 Out of the deep have I called unto thee, O Lord: Lord, hear my voice.
Psalm 130, v. 1. Cf. 58:14

1 O give thanks unto the Lord, for he is
  gracious: and his mercy endureth for
  ever.
  *Psalm 136, v. 1*

2 By the waters of Babylon we sat down and
  wept: when we remembered thee, O Sion.
  *Psalm 137, v. 1*

3 How shall we sing the Lord's song: in a
  strange land?
  *Psalm 137, v. 4*

4 If I forget thee, O Jerusalem: let my right
  hand forget her cunning.
  *Psalm 137, v. 5*

5 O Lord, thou hast searched me out, and
  known me: thou knowest my down-
  sitting, and mine up-rising.
  *Psalm 139, v. 1*

6 If I take the wings of the morning: and
  remain in the uttermost parts of the sea;
  Even there also shall thy hand lead me:
  and thy right hand shall hold me.
  *Psalm 139, v. 8*

7 I will give thanks unto thee, for I am
  fearfully and wonderfully made.
  *Psalm 139, v. 13*

8 Let the lifting up of my hands be an
  evening sacrifice.
  *Psalm 141, v. 2*

9 O put not your trust in princes.
  *Psalm 146, v. 2*

10 He hath no pleasure in the strength of an
   horse: neither delighteth he in any man's
   legs.
   *Psalm 147, v. 10*

11 To bind their kings in chains: and their
   nobles with links of iron.
   *Psalm 149, v. 8*

12 Praise him upon the well-tuned cymbals:
   praise him upon the loud cymbals.
   *Psalm 150, v. 5*

13 Be pleased to receive into thy Almighty
   and most gracious protection the persons
   of us thy servants, and the Fleet in which
   we serve.
   *Forms of Prayer to be Used at Sea* First Prayer

14 That we may be ... a security for such as
   pass on the seas upon their lawful
   occasions.
   *Forms of Prayer to be Used at Sea* First Prayer

15 We therefore commit his body to the deep,
   to be turned into corruption, looking for
   the resurrection of the body (when the Sea
   shall give up her dead).
   *Forms of Prayer to be Used at Sea* At the Burial
   of their Dead at Sea

16 Come, Holy Ghost, our souls inspire,
   And lighten with celestial fire.
   Thou the anointing Spirit art,
   Who dost thy seven-fold gifts impart.
   *Ordering of Priests* 'Veni, Creator Spiritus' (tr.
   Bishop John Cosin, 1627, from 9th-century
   original)

17 Man is very far gone from original
   righteousness.
   *Articles of Religion* (1562) no. 9

18 It is a thing plainly repugnant to the Word
   of God, and the custom of the Primitive
   Church, to have publick Prayer in the
   Church, or to minister the Sacraments in a
   tongue not understood of the people.
   *Articles of Religion* (1562) no. 24

19 A Man may not marry his Mother.
   *A Table of Kindred and Affinity*

## John Wilkes Booth 1838–65

20 *Sic semper tyrannis!* The South is avenged.
   Having shot President Lincoln, 14 April 1865
   ('*Sic semper tyrannis* [Thus always to
   tyrants]'—motto of the State of Virginia). See
   *New York Times* 15 April 1865

## General William Booth 1829–1912

21 The Submerged Tenth.
   *In Darkest England* (1890) pt. 1, title of ch. 2
   ('three million men, women, and children, a
   vast despairing multitude in a condition
   nominally free, but really enslaved')

## Jorge Luis Borges 1899–1986

22 The original is unfaithful to the
   translation.
   Of Henley's translation, in *Sobre el 'Vathek' de
   William Beckford*; in *Obras Completas* (1974)
   p. 730

23 For one of those gnostics, the visible
   universe was an illusion or, more precisely,
   a sophism. Mirrors and fatherhood are
   abominable because they multiply it and
   extend it.
   *Tlön, Uqbar, Orbis Tertius* (1941) in *Obras
   Completas* (1974) p. 431

24 The Falklands thing was a fight between
   two bald men over a comb.
   In *Time* 14 February 1983

## Cesare Borgia 1476–1507

25 *Aut Caesar, aut nihil.*
   Caesar or nothing.
   Motto inscribed on his sword. See J. L.
   Garner *Caesar Borgia* (1912) p. 309

## George Borrow 1803–81

26 A losing trade, I assure you, sir: literature
   is a drug.
   *Lavengro* (1851) ch. 30

27 Youth will be served, every dog has his day,
   and mine has been a fine one.
   *Lavengro* (1851) ch. 92

## Pierre Bosquet 1810–61

28 *C'est magnifique, mais ce n'est pas la guerre.*
   It is magnificent, but it is not war.
   On the charge of the Light Brigade at
   Balaclava, 25 October 1854; in C. Woodham-
   Smith *The Reason Why* (1953) ch. 12

## John Collins Bossidy 1860–1928

1 And this is good old Boston,
  The home of the bean and the cod,
  Where the Lowells talk to the Cabots
  And the Cabots talk only to God.
>  Verse spoken at Holy Cross College alumni
>  dinner in Boston, Massachusetts, 1910; in
>  *Springfield Sunday Republican* 14 December
>  1924

## Jacques-Bénigne Bossuet 1627–1704

2 *L'Angleterre, ah, la perfide Angleterre, que le
  rempart de ses mers rendait inaccessible aux
  Romains, la foi du Sauveur y est abordée.*
  England, ah, faithless England, which the
  protection afforded by its seas rendered
  inaccessible to the Romans, the faith of the
  Saviour spread even there.
>  First sermon on the feast of the
>  Circumcision, in *Oeuvres de Bossuet* (1816)
>  vol. 11, p. 469. Cf. 358:9

## James Boswell 1740–95

3 I am, I flatter myself, completely a citizen
  of the world.
>  *Journal of a Tour to the Hebrides* (ed. F. A. Pottle,
>  1936) 14 August 1773

4 A page of my Journal is like a cake of
  portable soup. A little may be diffused into
  a considerable portion.
>  *Journal of a Tour to the Hebrides* (ed. F. A. Pottle,
>  1936) 13 September 1773

5 Most vices may be committed very
  genteelly: a man may debauch his friend's
  wife genteelly: he may cheat at cards
  genteelly.
>  *Life of Samuel Johnson* (1934 ed.) vol. 2, p. 340
>  (6 April 1775)

## Gordon Bottomley 1874–1948

6 Your worship is your furnaces,
  Which, like old idols, lost obscenes,
  Have molten bowels; your vision is
  Machines for making more machines.
>  'To Ironfounders and Others' (1912)

## Horatio Bottomley 1860–1933

7 What poor education I have received has
  been gained in the University of Life.
>  Speech at the Oxford Union, 2 December
>  1920; in Beverley Nichols *25* (1926) ch. 7

## Dion Boucicault 1820–90

8 Men talk of killing time, while time quietly
  kills them.
>  *London Assurance* (1841) act 2, sc. 1. Cf. 307:22

## Antoine Boulay de la Meurthe 1761–1840

9 *C'est pire qu'un crime, c'est une faute.*
  It is worse than a crime, it is a blunder.
>  On hearing of the execution of the Duc
>  d'Enghien, 1804; in C.-A. Sainte-Beuve
>  *Nouveaux Lundis* (1870) vol. 12, p. 52

## Sir Harold Edwin Boulton 1859–1935

10 Speed, bonnie boat, like a bird on the wing,
   'Onward,' the sailors cry;
   Carry the lad that's born to be king,
   Over the sea to Skye.
>  'Skye Boat Song' (1908)

## Matthew Boulton 1728–1809

11 I sell here, Sir, what all the world desires
   to have—POWER.
>  Speaking to Boswell of his engineering
>  works; in James Boswell *Life of Samuel Johnson*
>  (1934 ed.) vol. 2, p. 459 (22 March 1776)

## F. W. Bourdillon 1852–1921

12 The night has a thousand eyes,
   And the day but one.
>  *Among the Flowers* (1878) 'Light'. Cf. 212:18

## Lord Bowen 1835–94

13 When I hear of an 'equity' in a case like
   this, I am reminded of a blind man in a
   dark room—looking for a black
   hat—which isn't there.
>  In J. A. Foote *Pie-Powder* (1911) p. 25

14 The rain, it raineth on the just
   And also on the unjust fella:
   But chiefly on the just, because
   The unjust steals the just's umbrella.
>  In W. Sichel *Sands of Time* (1923) ch. 4

## E. E. Bowen 1836–1901

15 Forty years on, when afar and asunder
   Parted are those who are singing to-day.
>  'Forty Years On' (Harrow School Song,
>  published 1886)

16 Follow up! Follow up! Follow up! Follow up!
   Follow up!
   Till the field ring again and again,
   With the tramp of the twenty-two men.
>  'Forty Years On'

## Elizabeth Bowen 1899–1973

17 There is no end to the violations
   committed by children on children, quietly
   talking alone.
>  *The House in Paris* (1935) pt. 1, ch. 2

18 Fate is not an eagle, it creeps like a rat.
>  *The House in Paris* (1935) pt. 2, ch. 2

1 Jealousy is no more than feeling alone
against smiling enemies.
*The House in Paris* (1935) pt. 2, ch. 8

2 A high altar on the move.
Describing Edith Sitwell, in V. Glendinning
*Edith Sitwell* (1981) ch. 25

## Sir Maurice Bowra 1898–1971

3 I'm a man more dined against than dining.
In John Betjeman *Summoned by Bells* (1960)
ch. 9. Cf. 283:10

4 My dear fellow, buggers can't be choosers.
On being told he should not marry anyone
as plain as his fiancée; in H. Lloyd-Jones
*Maurice Bowra: a Celebration* (1974) p. 150
(possibly apocryphal)

## Charles Brackett 1892–1969 and Billy Wilder 1906–

5 JOE GILLIS: You used to be in pictures. You
used to be big.
NORMA DESMOND: I am big. It's the pictures
that got small.
*Sunset Boulevard* (1950 film, with D. M.
Marshman Jr.)

## John Bradford c.1510–55

6 But for the grace of God there goes John
Bradford.
On seeing a group of criminals being led to
their execution; in *Dictionary of National
Biography* (1917– ) p. 1067 (usually quoted
'There but for the grace of God go I')

## F. H. Bradley 1846–1924

7 Metaphysics is the finding of bad reasons
for what we believe upon instinct.
*Appearance and Reality* (1893) preface

8 The world is the best of all possible worlds,
and everything in it is a necessary evil.
*Appearance and Reality* (1893) preface

9 Where everything is bad it must be good
to know the worst.
*Appearance and Reality* (1893) preface

## Omar Bradley 1893–1981

10 We have grasped the mystery of the atom
and rejected the Sermon on the Mount.
Speech on Armistice Day, 1948, in *Collected
Writings* (1967) vol. 1, p. 588

## John Bradshaw 1602–59

11 Rebellion to tyrants is obedience to God.
Suppositious epitaph. See H. S. Randall *Life of
Thomas Jefferson* (1865) vol. 3, appendix 4,
p. 585

## Anne Bradstreet c.1612–72

12 I am obnoxious to each carping tongue,
Who says my hand a needle better fits.
'The Prologue' (1650)

## James Bramston c.1694–1744

13 What's not destroyed by Time's devouring
hand?
Where's Troy, and where's the Maypole in
the Strand?
*The Art of Politics* (1729) l. 71

## Georges Braque 1882–1963

14 Art is meant to disturb, science reassures.
*Le Jour et la nuit: Cahiers 1917–52* p. 11.
Cf. 236:11

15 Truth exists; only lies are invented.
*Le Jour et la nuit: Cahiers 1917–52* p. 20

## Richard Brathwaite c.1588–1673

16 To Banbury came I, O profane one!
Where I saw a Puritane-one
Hanging of his cat on Monday
For killing of a mouse on Sunday.
*Barnabee's Journal* (1638) pt. 1, st. 4

## Bertolt Brecht 1898–1956

17 The resistible rise of Arturo Ui.
Title of play (1941)

18 Oh, the shark has pretty teeth, dear,
And he shows them pearly white.
Just a jack-knife has Macheath, dear
And he keeps it out of sight.
*The Threepenny Opera* (1928) prologue

19 Food comes first, then morals.
*The Threepenny Opera* (1928) act 2, sc. 3

20 They have gone too long without a war
here. Where is morality to come from in
such a case, I ask? Peace is nothing but
slovenliness, only war creates order.
*Mother Courage* (1939) sc. 1

21 Don't tell me peace has broken out, when
I've just bought fresh supplies.
*Mother Courage* (1939) sc. 8

## Jane Brereton 1685–1740

22 The picture, placed the busts between,
Adds to the thought much strength:
Wisdom and Wit are little seen,
But Folly's at full length.
'On Mr Nash's Picture at Full Length,
between the Busts of Sir Isaac Newton and
Mr Pope' (1744)

## Nicholas Breton c.1545–1626

23 I wish my deadly foe, no worse
Than want of friends, and empty purse.
'A Farewell to Town' (1577)

## Robert Bridges 1844–1930

24 All my hope on God is founded.
Title of hymn (1899)

1 When men were all asleep the snow came
  flying,
  In large white flakes falling on the city
  brown,
  Stealthily and perpetually settling and
  loosely lying,
  Hushing the latest traffic of the drowsy
  town.
    'London Snow' (1890)

## John Bright 1811–89

2 The angel of death has been abroad
  throughout the land; you may almost hear
  the beating of his wings.
    On the effects of the Crimean war; in
    *Hansard*, 23 February 1855, col. 1761

3 I am for 'Peace, retrenchment, and reform',
  the watchword of the great Liberal party
  30 years ago.
    Speech at Birmingham, 28 April 1859, in *The
    Times* 29 April 1859; the 'watchword' may be
    found in Samuel Warren's novel *Ten
    Thousand a Year* (1841) bk. 7, ch. 1

4 My opinion is that the Northern States will
  manage somehow to muddle through.
    During the American Civil War; in J.
    McCarthy *Reminiscences* (1899) vol. 1, ch. 5

5 England is the mother of Parliaments.
    Speech at Birmingham, 18 January 1865, in
    *The Times* 19 January 1865

6 Force is not a remedy.
    Speech, 16 November 1880, in *The Times*
    17 November 1880

## Anthelme Brillat-Savarin
1755–1826

7 Tell me what you eat and I will tell you
  what you are.
    *Physiologie du Goût* (1825) 'Aphorismes pour
    servir de prolégomènes' no. 4. Cf. 139:1

## Alexander Brome 1620–66

8 Come, blessed peace, we once again
  implore,
  And let our pains be less, or power more.
    *Songs and Other Poems* (1661) 'The Riddle'

## Jacob Bronowski 1908–74

9 The world can only be grasped by action,
  not by contemplation ... The hand is the
  cutting edge of the mind.
    *The Ascent of Man* (1973) ch. 3

10 The essence of science: ask an impertinent
   question, and you are on the way to a
   pertinent answer.
    *The Ascent of Man* (1973) ch. 4

11 The wish to hurt, the momentary
   intoxication with pain, is the loophole
   through which the pervert climbs into the
   minds of ordinary men.
    *The Face of Violence* (1954) ch. 5

## Charlotte Brontë 1816–55

12 Reader, I married him.
    *Jane Eyre* (1847) ch. 38

13 Of late years an abundant shower of
   curates has fallen upon the North of
   England.
    *Shirley* (1849) ch. 1

14 Be a governess! Better be a slave at once!
    *Shirley* (1849) ch. 13

15 It is rustic all through. It is moorish, and
   wild, and knotty as a root of heath.
    On the setting of Emily Brontë's *Wuthering
    Heights*, in her own preface to the 1850
    edition

## Emily Brontë 1818–48

16 No coward soul is mine,
   No trembler in the world's storm-troubled
   sphere:
   I see Heaven's glories shine,
   And faith shines equal, arming me from
   fear.
    'No coward soul is mine' (1846)

17 My love for Heathcliff resembles the
   eternal rocks beneath:—a source of little
   visible delight, but necessary.
    *Wuthering Heights* (1847) ch. 9

18 I lingered round them, under that benign
   sky: watched the moths fluttering among
   the heath and hare-bells; listened to the
   soft wind breathing through the grass; and
   wondered how any one could ever imagine
   unquiet slumbers for the sleepers in that
   quiet earth.
    *Wuthering Heights* (1847) *ad fin.*

## Patrick Brontë 1777–1861

19 No quailing, Mrs Gaskell! no drawing back!
    Apropos her undertaking to write the life of
    Charlotte Brontë; in J. A. V. Chapple and A.
    Pollard (eds.) *Letters of Mrs Gaskell* (1966)
    no. 257

## Rupert Brooke 1887–1915

20 Blow out, you bugles, over the rich Dead!
   There's none of these so lonely and poor of
   old,
   But, dying, has made us rarer gifts than
   gold.
   These laid the world away; poured out the
   red
   Sweet wine of youth; gave up the years to
   be
   Of work and joy, and that unhoped serene,
   That men call age; and those that would
   have been,
   Their sons, they gave, their immortality.
    'The Dead' (1914)

21 Honour has come back, as a king, to earth,
   And paid his subjects with a royal wage;
   And Nobleness walks in our ways again;
   And we have come into our heritage.
    'The Dead' (1914)

**1** ... The cool kindliness of sheets, that soon
Smooth away trouble; and the rough male
kiss
Of blankets.
'The Great Lover' (1914)

**2** Fish say, they have their stream and pond;
But is there anything beyond?
'Heaven' (1915)

**3** Just now the lilac is in bloom,
All before my little room.
'The Old Vicarage, Grantchester' (1915)

**4** Unkempt about those hedges blows
An English unofficial rose.
'The Old Vicarage, Grantchester' (1915)

**5** Curates, long dust, will come and go
On lissom, clerical, printless toe;
And oft between the boughs is seen
The sly shade of a Rural Dean.
'The Old Vicarage, Grantchester' (1915)

**6** God! I will pack, and take a train,
And get me to England once again!
For England's the one land, I know,
Where men with Splendid Hearts may go.
'The Old Vicarage, Grantchester' (1915)

**7** For Cambridge people rarely smile,
Being urban, squat, and packed with guile.
'The Old Vicarage, Grantchester' (1915)

**8** Stands the Church clock at ten to three?
And is there honey still for tea?
'The Old Vicarage, Grantchester' (1915)

**9** Now, God be thanked Who has matched us
with His hour,
And caught our youth, and wakened us
from sleeping,
With hand made sure, clear eye, and
sharpened power,
To turn, as swimmers into cleanness
leaping.
'Peace' (1914)

**10** If I should die, think only this of me:
That there's some corner of a foreign field
That is for ever England. There shall be
In that rich earth a richer dust concealed;
A dust whom England bore, shaped, made
aware,
Gave, once, her flowers to love, her ways to
roam,
A body of England's, breathing English air,
Washed by the rivers, blest by suns of
home.

And think, this heart, all evil shed away,
A pulse in the eternal mind, no less
Gives somewhere back the thoughts by
England given;
Her sights and sounds; dreams happy as
her day;
And laughter, learnt of friends; and
gentleness,
In hearts at peace, under an English
heaven.
'The Soldier' (1914)

## Anita Brookner 1938–

**11** Good women always think it is their fault
when someone else is being offensive. Bad
women never take the blame for anything.
*Hotel du Lac* (1984) ch. 7

**12** They were reasonable people, and no one
was to be hurt, not even with words.
*Hotel du Lac* (1984) ch. 9

**13** Dr Weiss, at forty, knew that her life had
been ruined by literature.
*A Start in Life* (1981) ch. 1

## Thomas Brooks 1608–80

**14** For (*magna est veritas et praevalebit*) great is
truth, and shall prevail.
*The Crown and Glory of Christianity* (1662)
p. 407. Cf. 58:23

## H. Rap Brown 1943–

**15** I say violence is necessary. It is as
American as cherry pie.
Speech, 27 July 1967, in *Washington Post*
28 July 1967, p. A7

## John Brown 1715–66

**16** I have seen some extracts from Johnson's
Preface to his 'Shakespeare' ... No feeling
nor pathos in him! Altogether upon the
high horse, and blustering about Imperial
Tragedy!
Letter to Garrick, 27 October 1765, in *Private
Correspondence of David Garrick* (1831) vol. 1

## Lew Brown 1893–1958

**17** Life is just a bowl of cherries.
Title of song (1931)

## Thomas Brown 1663–1704

**18** I do not love thee, Dr Fell.
The reason why I cannot tell;
But this I know, and know full well,
I do not love thee, Dr Fell.
Written while an undergraduate at Christ
Church, Oxford, of which Dr Fell was Dean;
in A. L. Hayward (ed.) *Amusements Serious and
Comical by Tom Brown* (1927) p. xiii.
Cf. 220:4

## T. E. Brown 1830–97

**19** A garden is a lovesome thing, God wot!
'My Garden' (1893)

**20** O blackbird, what a boy you are!
How you do go it!
'Vespers' (1900)

## Cecil Browne 1932–

**21** But not so odd
As those who choose
A Jewish God,
But spurn the Jews.
Reply to verse by William Norman Ewer.
Cf. 138:2

## Sir Thomas Browne 1605–82

1 He who discommendeth others obliquely
commendeth himself.
*Christian Morals* (1716) pt. 1, sect. 34

2 Life itself is but the shadow of death, and
souls departed but the shadows of the
living.
*The Garden of Cyrus* (1658) ch. 4

3 Old mortality, the ruins of forgotten times.
*Hydriotaphia* (Urn Burial, 1658) Epistle
Dedicatory

4 Men have lost their reason in nothing so
much as their religion, wherein stones and
clouts make martyrs.
*Hydriotaphia* (Urn Burial, 1658) ch. 4

5 The long habit of living indisposeth us for
dying.
*Hydriotaphia* (Urn Burial, 1658) ch. 5

6 Generations pass while some trees stand,
and old families last not three oaks.
*Hydriotaphia* (Urn Burial, 1658) ch. 5

7 Man is a noble animal, splendid in ashes,
and pompous in the grave.
*Hydriotaphia* (Urn Burial, 1658) ch. 5

8 Ready to be any thing, in the ecstasy of
being ever.
*Hydriotaphia* (Urn Burial, 1658) ch. 5

9 Many from ... an inconsiderate zeal unto
truth, have too rashly charged the troops
of error, and remain as trophies unto the
enemies of truth.
*Religio Medici* (1643) pt. 1, sect. 6

10 As for those wingy mysteries in divinity
and airy subtleties in religion, which have
unhinged the brains of better heads, they
never stretched the *pia mater* of mine;
methinks there be not impossibilities
enough in religion for an active faith.
*Religio Medici* (1643) pt. 1, sect. 9

11 I love to lose myself in a mystery, to
pursue my reason to an *O altitudo!*
*Religio Medici* (1643) pt. 1, sect. 9

12 I have often admired the mystical way of
Pythagoras, and the secret magic of
numbers.
*Religio Medici* (1643) pt. 1, sect. 12

13 We carry within us the wonders we seek
without us: there is all Africa and her
prodigies in us.
*Religio Medici* (1643) pt. 1, sect. 15

14 All things are artificial, for nature is the
art of God.
*Religio Medici* (1643) pt. 1, sect. 16

15 Obstinacy in a bad cause, is but constancy
in a good.
*Religio Medici* (1643) pt. 1, sect. 25

16 Persecution is a bad and indirect way to
plant religion.
*Religio Medici* (1643) pt. 1, sect. 25

17 Certainly there is no happiness within this
circle of flesh, nor is it in the optics of
these eyes to behold felicity; the first day
of our Jubilee is death.
*Religio Medici* (1643) pt. 1, sect. 44

18 This trivial and vulgar way of coition; it is
the foolishest act a wise man commits in
all his life, nor is there any thing that will
more deject his cooled imagination, when
he shall consider what an odd and
unworthy piece of folly he hath
committed.
*Religio Medici* (1643) pt. 2, sect. 9

19 We all labour against our own cure, for
death is the cure of all diseases.
*Religio Medici* (1643) pt. 2, sect. 9

20 For the world, I count it not an inn, but an
hospital, and a place, not to live, but to die
in.
*Religio Medici* (1643) pt. 2, sect. 11

21 There is surely a piece of divinity in us,
something that was before the elements,
and owes no homage unto the sun.
*Religio Medici* (1643) pt. 2, sect. 11

22 We term sleep a death, and yet it is
waking that kills us, and destroys those
spirits which are the house of life.
*Religio Medici* (1643) pt. 2, sect. 12

23 That children dream not in the first half
year, that men dream not in some
countries, are to me sick men's dreams,
dreams out of the ivory gate, and visions
before midnight.
S. Wilkin (ed.) *Works* (1835) vol. 4, p. 359 'On
Dreams'

## William Browne c.1590–1643

24 Underneath this sable hearse
Lies the subject of all verse;
Sidney's sister, Pembroke's mother,
Death, ere thou hast slain another,
Fair and learn'd, and good as she,
Time shall throw a dart at thee.
'Epitaph on the Countess Dowager of
Pembroke' (1623)

## Sir William Browne 1692–1774

25 The King to Oxford sent a troop of horse,
For Tories own no argument but force:
With equal skill to Cambridge books he
sent,
For Whigs admit no force but argument.
Reply to Trapp's epigram, in J. Nichols
*Literary Anecdotes* vol. 3 (1812) p. 330.
Cf. 334:3

## Elizabeth Barrett Browning 1806–61

26 The devil's most devilish when respectable.
*Aurora Leigh* (1857) bk. 7, l. 105

27 And kings crept out again to feel the sun.
'Crowned and Buried' (1844) st. 11

1 And lips say, 'God be pitiful,'
Who ne'er said, 'God be praised.'
'The Cry of the Human' (1844) st. 1

2 I tell you, hopeless grief is passionless.
'Grief' (1844)

3 Or from Browning some 'Pomegranate',
which, if cut deep down the middle,
Shows a heart within blood-tinctured, of a
veined humanity.
'Lady Geraldine's Courtship' (1844) st. 41

4 What was he doing, the great god Pan,
Down in the reeds by the river?
'A Musical Instrument' (1862)

5 How do I love thee? Let me count the ways.
Sonnets from the Portuguese (1850) no. 43

6 Thou large-brained woman and large-
hearted man.
'To George Sand—A Desire' (1844)

## Sir Frederick Browning
### 1896–1965

7 I think we might be going a bridge too far.
Expressing reservations about the Arnhem
'Market Garden' operation, 10 September
1944; in R. E. Urquhart Arnhem (1958) p. 4

## Robert Browning 1812–89

8 The high that proved too high, the heroic
for earth too hard,
The passion that left the ground to lose
itself in the sky,
Are music sent up to God by the lover and
the bard;
Enough that he heard it once: we shall
hear it by-and-by.
'Abt Vogler' (1864) st. 10

9 ... I feel for the common chord again ...
The C Major of this life.
'Abt Vogler' (1864) st. 12

10 Ah, but a man's reach should exceed his
grasp,
Or what's a heaven for?
'Andrea del Sarto' (1855) l. 97

11 One who never turned his back but
marched breast forward,
Never doubted clouds would break,
Never dreamed, though right were
worsted, wrong would triumph,
Held we fall to rise, are baffled to fight
better,
Sleep to wake.
Asolando (1889) 'Epilogue'

12 Greet the unseen with a cheer!
Asolando (1889) 'Epilogue'

13 Just when we are safest, there's a sunset-
touch,
A fancy from a flower-bell, some one's
death,
A chorus-ending from Euripides.
'Bishop Blougram's Apology' (1855) l. 182

14 The grand Perhaps!
'Bishop Blougram's Apology' (1855) l. 190

15 Our interest's on the dangerous edge of
things.
'Bishop Blougram's Apology' (1855) l. 395

16 He said true things, but called them by
wrong names.
'Bishop Blougram's Apology' (1855) l. 996

17 Boot, saddle, to horse, and away!
'Boot and Saddle' (1842)

18 And I turn the page, and I turn the page,
Not verse now, only prose!
'By the Fireside' (1855) st. 2

19 Oh, the little more, and how much it is!
And the little less, and what worlds away!
'By the Fireside' (1855) st. 39

20 The raree-show of Peter's successor.
'Christmas-Eve' (1850) l. 1242

21 We loved, sir—used to meet:
How sad and bad and mad it was—
But then, how it was sweet!
'Confessions' (1864) st. 9

22 Stung by the splendour of a sudden
thought.
'A Death in the Desert' (1864) l. 59

23 Progress, man's distinctive mark alone,
Not God's, and not the beasts': God is, they
are,
Man partly is and wholly hopes to be.
'A Death in the Desert' (1864) l. 586

24 Open my heart and you will see
Graved inside of it, 'Italy'.
'De Gustibus' (1855) pt. 2, l. 39

25 Reads verse and thinks she understands.
'Dîs Aliter Visum' (1864) st. 4

26 Sure of the Fortieth spare Arm-chair
When gout and glory seat me there.
'Dîs Aliter Visum' (1864) st. 12

27              'Tis well averred,
A scientific faith's absurd.
'Easter-Day' (1850) l. 123

28 Beautiful Evelyn Hope is dead!
'Evelyn Hope' (1855)

29 You will wake, and remember, and
understand.
'Evelyn Hope' (1855)

30 If you get simple beauty and naught else,
You get about the best thing God invents.
'Fra Lippo Lippi' (1855) l. 217

31              This world's no blot for us,
Nor blank; it means intensely, and means
good.
'Fra Lippo Lippi' (1855) l. 313

32 He said, 'What's time? Leave Now for dogs
and apes!
Man has Forever.'
'A Grammarian's Funeral' (1855) l. 83

33 That low man seeks a little thing to do,
Sees it and does it:
This high man, with a great thing to
pursue,
Dies ere he knows it.
'A Grammarian's Funeral' (1855) l. 113

1 Oh, to be in England
  Now that April's there.
  'Home-Thoughts, from Abroad' (1845)

2 That's the wise thrush; he sings each song
  twice over,
  Lest you should think he never could
  recapture
  The first fine careless rapture!
  'Home-Thoughts, from Abroad' (1845)

3 Nobly, nobly Cape Saint Vincent to the
  North-west died away;
  Sunset ran, one glorious blood-red, reeking
  into Cadiz Bay.
  'Home-Thoughts, from the Sea' (1845)

4 Here and here did England help me: how
  can I help England?
  'Home-Thoughts, from the Sea' (1845)

5 I sprang to the stirrup, and Joris, and he;
  I galloped, Dirck galloped, we galloped all
  three.
  'How they brought the Good News from
  Ghent to Aix' (1845) l. 1

6 A man can have but one life and one
  death,
  One heaven, one hell.
  'In a Balcony' (1855) l. 13

7          I count life just a stuff
  To try the soul's strength on, educe the
  man.
  'In a Balcony' (1855) l. 651

8 'You're wounded!' 'Nay,' the soldier's pride
  Touched to the quick, he said:
  'I'm killed, Sire!' And his chief beside,
  Smiling the boy fell dead.
  'Incident of the French Camp' (1842) st. 5

9 Ignorance is not innocence but sin.
  The Inn Album (1875) canto 5

10 The swallow has set her six young on the
   rail,
   And looks sea-ward.
   'James Lee's Wife' (1864) pt. 3, st. 1

11 Who knows but the world may end
   tonight?
   'The Last Ride Together' (1855) st. 2

12 'Tis an awkward thing to play with souls,
   And matter enough to save one's own.
   'A Light Woman' (1855) st. 12

13 Just for a handful of silver he left us,
   Just for a riband to stick in his coat.
   'The Lost Leader' (1845) (of Wordsworth)

14 We that had loved him so, followed him,
   honoured him,
   Lived in his mild and magnificent eye,
   Learned his great language, caught his
   clear accents,
   Made him our pattern to live and to die!
   Shakespeare was of us, Milton was for us,
   Burns, Shelley, were with us—they watch
   from their graves!
   'The Lost Leader' (1845)

15 Never glad confident morning again!
   'The Lost Leader' (1845)

16 Oppression makes the wise man mad.
   Luria (1846) act 4, l. 16

17 A tap at the pane, the quick sharp scratch
   And blue spurt of a lighted match,
   And a voice less loud, through its joys and
   fears,
   Than the two hearts beating each to each!
   'Meeting at Night' (1845)

18 Ah, did you once see Shelley plain,
   And did he stop and speak to you
   And did you speak to him again?
   How strange it seems, and new!
   'Memorabilia' (1855)

19          She had
   A heart—how shall I say?—too soon made
   glad,
   Too easily impressed; she liked whate'er
   She looked on, and her looks went
   everywhere.
   'My Last Duchess' (1842) l. 21

20 Never the time and the place
   And the loved one all together!
   'Never the Time and the Place' (1883)

21          What's come to perfection
   perishes.
   Things learned on earth, we shall practise
   in heaven:
   Works done least rapidly, Art most
   cherishes.
   'Old Pictures in Florence' (1855) st. 17

22 Measure your mind's height by the shade
   it casts!
   Paracelsus (1835) pt. 3, l. 821

23 Round the cape of a sudden came the sea,
   And the sun looked over the mountain's
   rim:
   And straight was a path of gold for him,
   And the need of a world of men for me.
   'Parting at Morning' (1849)

24 It was roses, roses, all the way.
   'The Patriot' (1855)

25 The air broke into a mist with bells.
   'The Patriot' (1855)

26 Rats!
   They fought the dogs and killed the cats,
   And bit the babies in the cradles ...
   And even spoiled the women's chats
   By drowning their speaking
   With shrieking and squeaking
   In fifty different sharps and flats.
   'The Pied Piper of Hamelin' (1842) st. 2

27 So munch on, crunch on, take your
   nuncheon,
   Breakfast, supper, dinner, luncheon!
   'The Pied Piper of Hamelin' (1842) st. 7

28 The year's at the spring
   And day's at the morn;
   Morning's at seven;
   The hill-side's dew-pearled;
   The lark's on the wing;
   The snail's on the thorn:
   God's in his heaven—
   All's right with the world!
   Pippa Passes (1841) pt. 1, l. 221

1 All service ranks the same with God—
With God, whose puppets, best and worst,
Are we: there is no last nor first.
*Pippa Passes* (1841) epilogue

2 Fear death?—to feel the fog in my throat,
The mist in my face.
'Prospice' (1864)

3 Grow old along with me!
The best is yet to be.
'Rabbi Ben Ezra' (1864) st. 1

4 Fancies that broke through language and
escaped.
'Rabbi Ben Ezra' (1864) st. 25

5 O lyric Love, half-angel and half-bird
And all a wonder and a wild desire.
*The Ring and the Book* (1868–9) bk. 1, l. 1391

6         So, Pietro craved an heir,
(The story always old and always new).
*The Ring and the Book* (1868–9) bk. 2, l. 213

7         Go practise if you please
With men and women: leave a child alone
For Christ's particular love's sake!
*The Ring and the Book* (1868–9) bk. 3, l. 88

8 In the great right of an excessive wrong.
*The Ring and the Book* (1868–9) bk. 3, l. 1055

9 Faultless to a fault.
*The Ring and the Book* (1868–9) bk. 9, l. 1175

10 White shall not neutralize the black, nor
good
Compensate bad in man, absolve him so:
Life's business being just the terrible
choice.
*The Ring and the Book* (1868–9) bk. 10, l. 1235

11 I want to know a butcher paints,
A baker rhymes for his pursuit.
'Shop' (1876) st. 21

12 There's a great text in Galatians,
Once you trip on it, entails
Twenty-nine distinct damnations,
One sure, if another fails.
'Soliloquy of the Spanish Cloister' (1842) st. 7

13 Sidney's self, the starry paladin.
*Sordello* (1840) bk. 1, l. 69

14 Still more labyrinthine buds the rose.
*Sordello* (1840) bk. 1, l. 476

15         Any nose
May ravage with impunity a rose.
*Sordello* (1840) bk. 6, l. 881

16 The unlit lamp and the ungirt loin.
'The Statue and the Bust' (1863 revision)
l. 247

17 Hark, the dominant's persistence till it
must be answered to!
'A Toccata of Galuppi's' (1855) st. 8

18 What of soul was left, I wonder, when the
kissing had to stop?
'A Toccata of Galuppi's' (1855) st. 14

19 Dear dead women, with such hair,
too—what's become of all the gold
Used to hang and brush their bosoms? I
feel chilly and grown old.
'A Toccata of Galuppi's' (1855) st. 15

20 I would that you were all to me,
You that are just so much, no more.
'Two in the Campagna' (1855) st. 8

21         I pluck the rose
And love it more than tongue can speak—
Then the good minute goes.
'Two in the Campagna' (1855) st. 10

## Robert Bruce 1554–1631

22 Now, God be with you, my children: I have
breakfasted with you and shall sup with
my Lord Jesus Christ this night.
In Robert Fleming *The Fulfilling of the Scripture*
(3rd ed., 1693) p. 372

## Beau Brummell 1778–1840

23 He [Brummell] always liked to have the
morning well-aired before he got up.
C. Macfarlane *Reminiscences of a Literary Life*
(1917) ch. 27

24 No perfumes, but very fine linen, plenty of
it, and country washing.
In *Memoirs of Harriette Wilson* (1825) vol. 1,
p. 42

## Frank Bruno 1961–

25 Boxing's just showbusiness with blood.
In *Observer* 29 December 1991 'Sayings of the
Year'

## John Buchan (Baron Tweedsmuir) 1875–1940

26 It's a great life if you don't weaken.
*Mr Standfast* (1919) ch. 5

27 An atheist is a man who has no invisible
means of support.
In H. E. Fosdick *On Being a Real Person* (1943)
ch. 10

## Robert Buchanan 1841–1901

28         She just wore
Enough for modesty—no more.
'White Rose and Red' (1873) pt. 1, sect. 5, l. 60

29 The sweet post-prandial cigar.
'De Berny' (1874)

## Frank Buchman 1878–1961

30 There is enough in the world for
everyone's need, but not enough for
everyone's greed.
*Remaking the World* (1947) p. 56

## Gene Buck 1885–1957 and Herman Ruby 1891–1959

31 That Shakespearian rag—
Most intelligent, very elegant.
'That Shakespearian Rag' (1912 song).
Cf. 134:24

## George Villiers, 2nd Duke of Buckingham 1628–87

**1** The world is made up for the most part of fools and knaves, both irreconcilable foes to truth.
*Dramatic Works* (1715) vol. 2 'To Mr Clifford On his Humane Reason'

**2** Ay, now the plot thickens very much upon us.
*The Rehearsal* (1672) act 3, sc. 2

## H. J. Buckoll 1803–71

**3** Lord, dismiss us with Thy blessing,
Thanks for mercies past receive.
Pardon all, their faults confessing;
Time that's lost may all retrieve.
*Psalms and Hymns for the Use of Rugby School Chapel* (1850) 'Lord, Dismiss us with Thy Blessing'

## Eustace Budgell 1686–1737

**4** What Cato did, and Addison approved,
Cannot be wrong.
Of suicide, in Colley Cibber *Lives of the Poets* (1753) vol. 5 'Life of Eustace Budgell'

## Comte de Buffon 1707–88

**5** Style is the man.
*Discours sur le style* (address given to the Académie Française, 25 August 1753)

**6** Genius is only a greater aptitude for patience.
In H. de Séchelles *Voyage à Montbar* (1803) p. 15

## Arthur Buller 1874–1944

**7** There was a young lady named Bright,
Whose speed was far faster than light;
She set out one day
In a relative way
And returned on the previous night.
'Relativity' in *Punch* 19 December 1923

## Prince Bernhard von Bülow 1849–1929

**8** We desire to throw no one into the shade [in East Asia], but we also demand our own place in the sun.
Reichstag, 6 December 1897, in *Graf Bülows Reden* (1903) p. 8. Cf. 350:25

## Edward George Bulwer-Lytton (Baron Lytton) 1803–73

**9** The brilliant chief, irregularly great,
Frank, haughty, rash,—the Rupert of Debate!
Of Edward Stanley, 14th Earl of Derby, in *The New Timon* (1846) pt. 1, sect. 3, l. 203. Cf. 121:8

**10** Out-babying Wordsworth and out-glittering Keats.
Of Tennyson, in *The New Timon* (1846) pt. 2, sect. 1, l. 62

**11** Beneath the rule of men entirely great
The pen is mightier than the sword.
*Richelieu* (1839) act 2, sc. 2, l. 307. Cf. 83:9

**12** There is no man so friendless but what he can find a friend sincere enough to tell him disagreeable truths.
*What will he do with it?* (1857) vol. 1, bk. 3, ch. 15

## Edward Robert Bulwer, Earl of Lytton
*See* OWEN MEREDITH

## Alfred 'Poet' Bunn *c.*1796–1860

**13** I dreamed that I dwelt in marble halls
With vassals and serfs at my side.
*The Bohemian Girl* (1843) act 2 'The Gipsy Girl's Dream'

## Basil Bunting 1900–85

**14** Praise the green earth. Chance has appointed her
home, workshop, larder, middenpit.
Her lousy skin scabbed here and there by cities provides us with name and nation.
'Attis: or, Something Missing' (1931) pt. 1

**15** Dance tiptoe, bull,
black against may.
'Briggflatts' (1965) pt. 1

## Luis Buñuel 1900–83

**16** The discreet charm of the bourgeoisie.
Title of film (1972)

## John Bunyan 1628–88

**17** As I walked through the wilderness of this world.
*The Pilgrim's Progress* (1678) pt. 1, opening words

**18** The name of the slough was Despond.
*The Pilgrim's Progress* (1678) pt. 1, p. 12

**19** It is an hard matter for a man to go down into the valley of Humiliation ... and to catch no slip by the way.
*The Pilgrim's Progress* (1678) pt. 1, p. 46

**20** A foul Fiend coming over the field to meet him; his name is Apollyon.
*The Pilgrim's Progress* (1678) pt. 1, p. 46

**21** It beareth the name of Vanity-Fair, because the town where 'tis kept, is lighter than vanity.
*The Pilgrim's Progress* (1678) pt. 1, p. 72

**22** Hanging is too good for him, said Mr Cruelty.
*The Pilgrim's Progress* (1678) pt. 1, p. 79

1 Yet my great-grandfather was but a water-man, looking one way, and rowing another.
   *The Pilgrim's Progress* (1678) pt. 1, p. 81.
   Cf. 83:7

2 They are for religion when in rags and contempt; but I am for him when he walks in his golden slippers, in the sunshine and with applause.
   *The Pilgrim's Progress* (1678) pt. 1, p. 83

3 Now Giant Despair had a wife, and her name was Diffidence.
   *The Pilgrim's Progress* (1678) pt. 1, p. 93

4 Sleep is sweet to the labouring man.
   *The Pilgrim's Progress* (1678) pt. 1, p. 111.
   Cf. 44:15

5 So I awoke, and behold it was a dream.
   *The Pilgrim's Progress* (1678) pt. 1, p. 133

6 A man that could look no way but downwards, with a muckrake in his hand.
   *The Pilgrim's Progress* (1684) pt. 2, p. 164.
   Cf. 262:18

7 He that is down needs fear no fall,
   He that is low no pride.
   He that is humble ever shall
   Have God to be his guide.
   *The Pilgrim's Progress* (1684) pt. 2, p. 197
   'Shepherd Boy's Song'

8 Mercy ... laboured much for the poor ... an ornament to her profession.
   *The Pilgrim's Progress* (1684) pt. 2, p. 231

9 Who would true valour see,
   Let him come hither;
   One here will constant be,
   Come wind, come weather.
   There's no discouragement
   Shall make him once relent
   His first avowed intent
   To be a pilgrim.

   Who so beset him round
   With dismal stories,
   Do but themselves confound—
   His strength the more is.
   *The Pilgrim's Progress* (1684) pt. 2, p. 247

10 My sword, I give to him that shall succeed me in my pilgrimage, and my courage and skill to him that can get it.
   *The Pilgrim's Progress* (1684) pt. 2, p. 259 (Mr Valiant-for-Truth)

11 So he passed over, and the trumpets sounded for him on the other side.
   *The Pilgrim's Progress* (1684) pt. 2, p. 260

## Samuel Dickinson Burchard 1812–91

12 We are Republicans and don't propose to leave our party and identify ourselves with the party whose antecedents are rum, Romanism, and rebellion.
   Speech, 29 October 1884, in *New York World* 30 October 1884

## Anthony Burgess 1917–93

13 A clockwork orange.
   Title of novel (1962)

14 It was the afternoon of my eighty-first birthday, and I was in bed with my catamite when Ali announced that the archbishop had come to see me.
   *Earthly Powers* (1980) p. 7

15 He said it was artificial respiration, but now I find I am to have his child.
   *Inside Mr Enderby* (1963) pt. 1, ch. 4

## Gelett Burgess 1866–1951

16 I never saw a Purple Cow,
   I never hope to see one;
   But I can tell you, anyhow,
   I'd rather see than be one!
   *The Burgess Nonsense Book* (1914) 'The Purple Cow'

## John William Burgon 1813–88

17 A rose-red city—half as old as Time!
   *Petra* (1845) l. 132. Cf. 261:19

## Edmund Burke 1729–97

18 The conduct of a losing party never appears right: at least it never can possess the only infallible criterion of wisdom to vulgar judgements—success.
   *Letter to a Member of the National Assembly* (1791) p. 7

19 Tyrants seldom want pretexts.
   *Letter to a Member of the National Assembly* (1791) p. 25

20 You can never plan the future by the past.
   *Letter to a Member of the National Assembly* (1791) p. 73

21 The king, and his faithful subjects, the lords and commons of this realm,—the triple cord, which no man can break.
   *A Letter to a Noble Lord* (1796) p. 54. Cf. 44:14

22 I know many have been taught to think that moderation, in a case like this, is a sort of treason.
   *Letter to the Sheriffs of Bristol* (1777) p. 30

23 Liberty too must be limited in order to be possessed.
   *Letter to the Sheriffs of Bristol* (1777) p. 55

24 It is the nature of all greatness not to be exact; and great trade will always be attended with considerable abuses.
   *On American Taxation* (1775) p. 26

25 Falsehood has a perennial spring.
   *On American Taxation* (1775) p. 30

26 To tax and to please, no more than to love and to be wise, is not given to men.
   *On American Taxation* (1775) p. 49

27 The concessions of the weak are concessions of fear.
   *On Conciliation with America* (1775) p. 7

1 The use of force alone is but *temporary*. It may subdue for a moment; but it does not remove the necessity of subduing again; and a nation is not governed, which is perpetually to be conquered.
  *On Conciliation with America* (1775) p. 14

2 I do not know the method of drawing up an indictment against an whole people.
  *On Conciliation with America* (1775) p. 28

3 Instead of a standing revenue, you will have therefore a perpetual quarrel.
  *On Conciliation with America* (1775) p. 57

4 Slavery they can have anywhere. It is a weed that grows in every soil.
  *On Conciliation with America* (1775) p. 61

5 Magnanimity in politics is not seldom the truest wisdom; and a great empire and little minds go ill together.
  *On Conciliation with America* (1775) p. 62

6 By adverting to the dignity of this high calling, our ancestors have turned a savage wilderness into a glorious empire: and have made the most extensive, and the only honourable conquests; not by destroying, but by promoting the wealth, the number, the happiness of the human race.
  *On Conciliation with America* (1775) p. 62

7 No passion so effectually robs the mind of all its powers of acting and reasoning as fear.
  *On the Sublime and Beautiful* (1757) pt. 2, sect. 2

8 Custom reconciles us to everything.
  *On the Sublime and Beautiful* (1757) pt. 4, sect. 18

9 Whenever our neighbour's house is on fire, it cannot be amiss for the engines to play a little on our own.
  *Reflections on the Revolution in France* (1790) p. 10

10 A state without the means of some change is without the means of its conservation.
  *Reflections on the Revolution in France* (1790) p. 29

11 Make the Revolution a parent of settlement, and not a nursery of future revolutions.
  *Reflections on the Revolution in France* (1790) p. 38

12 People will not look forward to posterity, who never look backward to their ancestors.
  *Reflections on the Revolution in France* (1790) p. 47

13 Whatever each man can separately do, without trespassing upon others, he has a right to do for himself; and he has a right to a fair portion of all which society, with all its combinations of skill and force, can do in his favour.
  *Reflections on the Revolution in France* (1790) p. 87

14 The age of chivalry is gone.— That of sophisters, economists, and calculators, has succeeded; and the glory of Europe is extinguished for ever.
  *Reflections on the Revolution in France* (1790) p. 113

15 This barbarous philosophy, which is the offspring of cold hearts and muddy understandings.
  *Reflections on the Revolution in France* (1790) p. 115

16 Kings will be tyrants from policy when subjects are rebels from principle.
  *Reflections on the Revolution in France* (1790) p. 116

17 Society is indeed a contract ... it becomes a partnership not only between those who are living, but between those who are living, those who are dead, and those who are to be born.
  *Reflections on the Revolution in France* (1790) p. 143

18 Superstition is the religion of feeble minds.
  *Reflections on the Revolution in France* (1790) p. 234

19 By hating vices too much, they come to love men too little.
  *Reflections on the Revolution in France* (1790) p. 251

20 We begin our public affections in our families. No cold relation is a zealous citizen.
  *Reflections on the Revolution in France* (1790) p. 286

21 Good order is the foundation of all good things.
  *Reflections on the Revolution in France* (1790) p. 351

22 Your representative owes you, not his industry only, but his judgement; and he betrays, instead of serving you, if he sacrifices it to your opinion.
  Speech, 3 November 1774, in *Speeches at his Arrival at Bristol* (1774) p. 14

23 The people are the masters.
  Speech, *Hansard* 11 February 1780, col. 67

24 Bad laws are the worst sort of tyranny.
  *Speech at Bristol, previous to the Late Election* (1780)

25 The people never give up their liberties except under some delusion.
  Speech at County Meeting of Buckinghamshire, 1784; attributed in E. Latham *Famous Sayings* (1904)

26 An event has happened, upon which it is difficult to speak, and impossible to be silent.
  Speech, 5 May 1789, in E. A. Bond (ed.) *Speeches ... in the Trial of Warren Hastings* (1859) vol. 2

27 Dying in the last dyke of prevarication.
  Speech, 7 May 1789, in E. A. Bond (ed.) *Speeches ... in the Trial of Warren Hastings* (1859) vol. 2

1 Old religious factions are volcanoes burnt
out.
>   Speech on the Petition of the Unitarians,
>   11 May 1792, in *Works* vol. 5 (1812).
>   Cf. 121:16

2 Dangers by being despised grow great.
>   Speech on the Petition of the Unitarians,
>   11 May 1792, in *Works* vol. 5 (1812)

3 And having looked to government for
bread, on the very first scarcity they will
turn and bite the hand that fed them.
>   *Thoughts and Details on Scarcity* (1800) p. 31

4 When bad men combine, the good must
associate; else they will fall, one by one, an
unpitied sacrifice in a contemptible
struggle.
>   *Thoughts on the Cause of the Present Discontents*
>   (1770) p. 71

5 So to be patriots, as not to forget we are
gentlemen.
>   *Thoughts on the Cause of the Present Discontents*
>   (1770) p. 77

6 Laws, like houses, lean on one another.
>   *A Tract on the Popery Laws* (planned *c*.1765)
>   ch. 3, pt. 1; in *Works* vol. 5 (1812)

7 All men that are ruined are ruined on the
side of their natural propensities.
>   *Two Letters on the Proposals for Peace with the
>   Regicide Directory* (9th ed., 1796) p. 69

8 Well is it known that ambition can creep
as well as soar.
>   *Third Letter ... on the Proposals for Peace with the
>   Regicide Directory* (1797) p. 38

9 People crushed by law have no hopes but
from power. If laws are their enemies, they
will be enemies to laws; and those, who
have much to hope and nothing to lose,
will always be dangerous, more or less.
>   Letter to Charles James Fox, 8 October 1777,
>   in *Correspondence of Edmund Burke* vol. 3 (1961)

10 The silent touches of time.
>   Letter to William Smith, 29 January 1795, in
>   *Correspondence of Edmund Burke* vol. 8 (1969)

11 Not merely a chip of the old 'block', but
the old block itself.
>   On the younger Pitt's maiden Speech,
>   February 1781; in N. W. Wraxall *Historical
>   Memoirs of My Own Time* (1904 ed.) pt. 2, p. 377

12 The cold neutrality of an impartial judge.
>   J. P. Brissot *To his Constituents* (1794)
>   'Translator's Preface' (written by Burke)

13 It is necessary only for the good man to do
nothing for evil to triumph.
>   Attributed (in a number of forms) to Burke,
>   but not found in his writings. Cf. 81:4

## Johnny Burke 1908–64

14 Every time it rains, it rains
Pennies from heaven.
Don't you know each cloud contains
Pennies from heaven?
>   'Pennies from Heaven' (1936 song)

15 Like Webster's Dictionary, we're Morocco
bound.
>   *The Road to Morocco* (1942 film) title song

## Fanny Burney 1752–1840

16 A little alarm now and then keeps life
from stagnation.
>   *Camilla* (1796) bk. 3, ch. 11

17 'The whole of this unfortunate business,'
said Dr Lyster, 'has been the result of PRIDE
AND PREJUDICE.'
>   *Cecilia* (1782) bk. 10, ch. 10

18 The delusive seduction of martial music.
>   In J. Hemlow et al. (eds.) *Journals and Letters of
>   Fanny Burney* vol. 5 (1975) 'Paris Journal'

19 O! how short a time does it take to put an
end to a woman's liberty!
>   Of a wedding; L. E. Troide (ed.) *Early Journals
>   and Letters* (1988) vol. 1 (Journal, 20 July 1768)

## John Burns 1858–1943

20 The Thames is liquid history.
>   To an American, who had compared the
>   Thames disparagingly with the Mississippi;
>   in *Daily Mail* 25 January 1943

## Robert Burns 1759–96

21 Then gently scan your brother man,
Still gentler sister woman;
Tho' they may gang a kennin wrang,
To step aside is human.
>   'Address to the Unco Guid' (1787)

22 Ae fond kiss, and then we sever;
Ae fareweel, and then for ever!
>   'Ae fond Kiss' (1792)

23 Flow gently, sweet Afton, among thy green
braes,
Flow gently, I'll sing thee a song in thy
praise.
>   'Afton Water' (1792)

24 Should auld acquaintance be forgot
And never brought to mind?
>   'Auld Lang Syne' (1796)

25 We'll tak a cup o' kindness yet,
For auld lang syne.
>   'Auld Lang Syne' (1796)

26 Freedom and Whisky gang thegither!
>   'The Author's Earnest Cry and Prayer' (1786)
>   l. 185

27 Ye banks and braes o' bonny Doon,
How can ye bloom sae fresh and fair;
How can ye chant, ye little birds,
And I sae weary fu' o' care!
>   'The Banks o' Doon' (1792)

28 Thou minds me o' departed joys,
Departed, never to return.
>   'The Banks o' Doon' (1792)

29 Gin a body meet a body
Comin thro' the rye,
Gin a body kiss a body
Need a body cry?
>   'Comin thro' the rye' (1796)

1 They never sought in vain that sought the
   Lord aright.
   'The Cotter's Saturday Night' (1786) st. 6

2 The healsome porritch, chief of Scotia's
   food.
   'The Cotter's Saturday Night' (1786) st. 11

3 I wasna fou, but just had plenty.
   'Death and Dr Hornbook' (1787) st. 3

4 On ev'ry hand it will allow'd be,
   He's just—nae better than he shou'd be.
   'A Dedication to G[avin] H[amilton]' (1786)
   l. 25

5 I waive the quantum o'the sin;
   The hazard of concealing;
   But och! it hardens a' within,
   And petrifies the feeling!
   'Epistle to a Young Friend' (1786) st. 6

6 An atheist-laugh's a poor exchange
   For Deity offended!
   'Epistle to a Young Friend' (1786) st. 9

7 The rank is but the guinea's stamp,
   The man's the gowd for a' that!
   'For a' that and a' that' (1790)

8 A man's a man for a' that.
   'For a' that and a' that' (1790)

9 Green grow the rashes, O,
   Green grow the rashes, O;
   The sweetest hours that e'er I spend,
   Are spent among the lasses, O.
   'Green Grow the Rashes' (1787)

10 There's death in the cup—so beware!
   'Inscription on a Goblet' (published 1834)

11 John Anderson my jo, John,
   When we were first acquent,
   Your locks were like the raven,
   Your bonny brow was brent.
   'John Anderson my Jo' (1790)

12 I once was a maid, tho' I cannot tell when,
   And still my delight is in proper young
   men.
   'The Jolly Beggars' (1799) l. 57, also known as
   'Love and Liberty—A Cantata'

13 Life is all a VARIORUM,
   We regard not how it goes;
   Let them cant about DECORUM,
   Who have characters to lose.
   'The Jolly Beggars' (1799) l. 270

14 Some have meat and cannot eat,
   Some cannot eat that want it:
   But we have meat and we can eat,
   Sae let the Lord be thankit.
   'The Kirkcudbright Grace' (1790), also known
   as 'The Selkirk Grace'

15 May coward shame distain his name,
   The wretch that dares not die!
   'McPherson's Farewell' (1788)

16 Man's inhumanity to man
   Makes countless thousands mourn!
   'Man was made to Mourn' (1786) st. 7

17 O Death! the poor man's dearest friend,
   The kindest and the best!
   'Man was made to Mourn' (1786) st. 11

18 My heart's in the Highlands, my heart is
   not here;
   My heart's in the Highlands a-chasing the
   deer.
   'My Heart's in the Highlands' (1790)

19 O whistle, an' I'll come to you, my lad.
   Title of poem (1788). Cf. 142:6

20 O, my Luve's like a red, red rose
   That's newly sprung in June;
   O my Luve's like the melodie
   That's sweetly play'd in tune.
   'A Red Red Rose' (1796) (derived from various
   folk-songs)

21 Scots, wha hae wi' Wallace bled,
   Scots, wham Bruce has aften led,
   Welcome to your gory bed,—
   Or to victorie.
   'Robert Bruce's March to Bannockburn'
   (1799)

22 Liberty's in every blow!
   Let us do—or die!!!
   'Robert Bruce's March to Bannockburn'
   (1799)

23 As Tammie glowr'd, amaz'd, and curious,
   The mirth and fun grew fast and furious.
   'Tam o' Shanter' (1791) l. 143

24 Fair fa' your honest, sonsie face,
   Great chieftain o' the puddin'-race!
   'To a Haggis' (1787)

25 O wad some Pow'r the giftie gie us
   To see oursels as others see us!
   It wad frae mony a blunder free us,
   And foolish notion.
   'To a Louse' (1786)

26 Wee, sleekit, cow'rin', tim'rous beastie,
   O what a panic's in thy breastie!
   'To a Mouse' (1786)

27 The best laid schemes o' mice an' men
   Gang aft a-gley.
   'To a Mouse' (1786)

28 Fareweel dear, deluding woman.
   'To J. S[mith]' (1786) st. 14

29 Their sighan', cantan', grace-proud faces,
   Their three-mile prayers, and half-mile
   graces.
   'To the Rev. John M'Math' (1808)

30 Don't let the awkward squad fire over me.
   Shortly before his death, in A. Cunningham
   *Works of Robert Burns* vol. 1 (1834) p. 344

## William S. Burroughs 1914–

31 The face of 'evil' is always the face of total
   need.
   *The Naked Lunch* (1959) introduction

## Sir Fred Burrows 1887–1973

32 Unlike my predecessors I have devoted
   more of my life to shunting and hooting
   than to hunting and shooting.
   Speech as last Governor of undivided Bengal
   (1946–7), having been a former President of
   the National Union of Railwaymen. See *Daily
   Telegraph* 24 April 1973, obituary notice

## Benjamin Hapgood Burt
1880–1950

1 'You can tell a man who "boozes" by the
company he chooses'
And the pig got up and slowly walked
away.
   'The Pig Got Up and Slowly Walked Away'
   (1933 song)

2 When you're all dressed up and no place to
go.
   Title of song (1913)

## Nat Burton

3 There'll be bluebirds over the white cliffs
of Dover,
Tomorrow, just you wait and see.
   'The White Cliffs of Dover' (1941 song)

## Sir Richard Burton 1821–90

4 Don't be frightened; I am recalled. Pay,
pack, and follow at convenience.
   Note to his wife, 19 August 1871, on being
   replaced as British Consul to Damascus; in
   Isabel Burton Life of Captain Sir Richard F.
   Burton (1893) vol. 1, ch. 21

## Robert Burton 1577–1640

5 All my joys to this are folly,
Naught so sweet as Melancholy.
   Anatomy of Melancholy (1621–51) 'The Author's
   Abstract of Melancholy'

6 A loose, plain, rude writer . . . I call a spade
a spade.
   Anatomy of Melancholy (1621–51) 'Democritus
   to the Reader' (p. 31, Everyman ed., 1932)

7 Like watermen, that row one way and look
another.
   Anatomy of Melancholy (1621–51) 'Democritus
   to the Reader' (p. 55, Everyman ed., 1932).
   Cf. 79:1

8 All poets are mad.
   Anatomy of Melancholy (1621–51) 'Democritus
   to the Reader' (p. 112, Everyman ed., 1932).
   Cf. 356:17

9 The pen is worse than the sword.
   Anatomy of Melancholy (1621–51) pt. 1, sect. 2,
   member 4, subsect. 4. Cf. 78:11

10 What is a ship but a prison?
   Anatomy of Melancholy (1621–51) pt. 2, sect. 3,
   member 4, subsect. 1. Cf. 184:5

11 All places are distant from Heaven alike.
   Anatomy of Melancholy (1621–51) pt. 2, sect. 3,
   member 4, subsect. 1

12 To enlarge or illustrate this power and
effect of love is to set a candle in the sun.
   Anatomy of Melancholy (1621–51) pt. 3, sect. 2,
   member 1, subsect. 2. Cf. 306:14, 360:16

13 England is a paradise for women, and hell
for horses: Italy a paradise for horses, hell
for women, as the diverb goes.
   Anatomy of Melancholy (1621–51) pt. 3, sect. 3,
   member 1, subsect. 2. Cf. 142:13

14 One religion is as true as another.
   Anatomy of Melancholy (1621–51) pt. 3, sect. 4,
   member 2, subsect. 1

15 Be not solitary, be not idle.
   Anatomy of Melancholy (1621–51) ad fin.

## Hermann Busenbaum 1600–68

16 Cum finis est licitus, etiam media sunt licita.
The end justifies the means.
   Medulla Theologiae Moralis (1650); literally
   'When the end is allowed, the means also
   are allowed'

## George Bush 1924–

17 Oh, the vision thing.
   Responding to the suggestion that he turn
   his attention from short-term campaign
   objectives and look to the longer term; in
   Time 26 January 1987, p. 20

18 Read my lips: no new taxes.
   Campaign pledge on taxation, in New York
   Times 19 August 1988

## Comte de Bussy-Rabutin 1618–93

19 L'absence est à l'amour ce qu'est au feu le vent;
Il éteint le petit, il allume le grand.
Absence is to love what wind is to fire;
It extinguishes the small, it kindles the
great.
   Histoire Amoureuse des Gaules: Maximes d'Amour
   (1665) pt. 2. Cf. 145:5, 201:24

20 As you know, God is usually on the side of
the big squadrons against the small.
   Letter to the Comte de Limoges, 18 October
   1677, in Lettres de . . . Comte de Bussy (1697)
   vol. 4. Cf. 14:4, 322:8, 340:23

## Nicholas Murray Butler
1862–1947

21 An expert is one who knows more and
more about less and less.
   Commencement address at Columbia
   University (attributed)

## Samuel ('Hudibras') Butler
1612–80

22 What ever sceptic could inquire for;
For every why he had a wherefore.
   Hudibras pt. 1 (1663), canto 1, l. 131

23 He knew what's what, and that's as high
As metaphysic wit can fly.
   Hudibras pt. 1 (1663), canto 1, l. 149

24 Compound for sins, they are inclined to,
By damning those they have no mind to.
   Hudibras pt. 1 (1663), canto 1, l. 213

25 For rhyme the rudder is of verses,
With which like ships they steer their
courses.
   Hudibras pt. 1 (1663), canto 1, l. 457

1 Cleric before, and Lay behind;
   A lawless linsy-woolsy brother,
   Half of one order, half another.
   *Hudibras* pt. 1 (1663), canto 3, l. 1226

2 Learning, that cobweb of the brain,
   Profane, erroneous, and vain.
   *Hudibras* pt. 1 (1663), canto 3, l. 1339

3 Love is a boy, by poets styled,
   Then spare the rod, and spoil the child.
   *Hudibras* pt. 2 (1664), canto 1, l. 843

4 Oaths are but words, and words but wind.
   *Hudibras* pt. 2 (1664), canto 2, l. 107

5 What makes all doctrines plain and clear?
   About two hundred pounds a year.
   And that which was proved true before,
   Prove false again? Two hundred more.
   *Hudibras* pt. 3 (1680), canto 1, l. 1277

6 He that complies against his will,
   Is of his own opinion still.
   *Hudibras* pt. 3 (1680), canto 3, l. 547

7 For Justice, though she's painted blind,
   Is to the weaker side inclined.
   *Hudibras* pt. 3 (1680), canto 3, l. 709

8 The law can take a purse in open court,
   Whilst it condemns a less delinquent for't.
   *Genuine Remains* (1759) 'Miscellaneous
   Thoughts'

## Samuel Butler 1835–1902

9 The advantage of doing one's praising for
   oneself is that one can lay it on so thick
   and exactly in the right places.
   *The Way of All Flesh* (1903) ch. 34

10 The best liar is he who makes the smallest
   amount of lying go the longest way.
   *The Way of All Flesh* (1903) ch. 39

11 'Tis better to have loved and lost than
   never to have lost at all.
   *The Way of All Flesh* (1903) ch. 67. Cf. 325:4

12 It was very good of God to let Carlyle and
   Mrs Carlyle marry one another and so
   make only two people miserable instead of
   four.
   *Letters between Samuel Butler and Miss E. M. A.
   Savage 1871–1885* (1935) 21 November 1884

13 Life is one long process of getting tired.
   *Notebooks* (1912) ch. 1

14 The history of art is the history of revivals.
   *Notebooks* (1912) ch. 8

15 An apology for the Devil: It must be
   remembered that we have only heard one
   side of the case. God has written all the
   books.
   *Notebooks* (1912) ch. 14

16 A definition is the enclosing a wilderness
   of idea within a wall of words.
   *Notebooks* (1912) ch. 14

17 To live is like to love — all reason is
   against it, and all healthy instinct for it.
   *Notebooks* (1912) ch. 14

18 The three most important things a man
   has are, briefly, his private parts, his
   money, and his religious opinions.
   *Further Extracts from Notebooks* (1934) p. 93

19 Jesus! with all thy faults I love thee still.
   *Further Extracts from Notebooks* (1934) p. 117

20 Conscience is thoroughly well-bred and
   soon leaves off talking to those who do not
   wish to hear it.
   *Further Extracts from Notebooks* (1934) p. 279

21 Yet meet we shall, and part, and meet
   again
   Where dead men meet, on lips of living
   men.
   'Not on sad Stygian shore' (1904)

## William Butler 1535–1618

22 Doubtless God could have made a better
   berry, but doubtless God never did.
   On the strawberry, in Izaak Walton *The
   Compleat Angler* (3rd ed., 1661) pt. 1, ch. 5

## John Byrom 1692–1763

23 Christians, awake! Salute the happy morn,
   Whereon the Saviour of the world was
   born.
   Hymn (c.1750)

24 Some say, that Signor Bononcini,
   Compared to Handel's a mere ninny;
   Others aver, that to him Handel
   Is scarcely fit to hold a candle.
   Strange! that such high dispute should be
   'Twixt Tweedledum and Tweedledee.
   'On the Feuds between Handel and
   Bononcini' (1727)

## Lord Byron 1788–1824

25 Year after year they voted cent per cent
   Blood, sweat, and tear-wrung
   millions—why? for rent!
   'The Age of Bronze' (1823) st. 14

26 It glides along the water looking blackly,
   Just like a coffin clapt in a canoe.
   *Beppo* (1818) st. 19 (a gondola)

27 In short, he was a perfect cavaliero,
   And to his very valet seemed a hero.
   *Beppo* (1818) st. 33. Cf. 108:9

28 His heart was one of those which most
   enamour us,
   Wax to receive, and marble to retain.
   *Beppo* (1818) st. 34

29 Our cloudy climate, and our chilly women.
   *Beppo* (1818) st. 49

30 None are so desolate but something dear,
   Dearer than self, possesses or possessed
   A thought, and claims the homage of a
   tear.
   *Childe Harold's Pilgrimage* (1812–18) canto 2,
   st. 24

1 Hereditary bondsmen! know ye not
   Who would be free themselves must strike
   the blow?
   *Childe Harold's Pilgrimage* (1812–18) canto 2,
   st. 76

2 There was a sound of revelry by night,
   And Belgium's capital had gathered then
   Her beauty and her chivalry, and bright
   The lamps that shone o'er fair women and
   brave men;
   A thousand hearts beat happily; and when
   Music arose with its voluptuous swell,
   Soft eyes looked love to eyes which spake
   again,
   And all went merry as a marriage bell;
   But hush! hark! a deep sound strikes like a
   rising knell!
   *Childe Harold's Pilgrimage* (1812–18) canto 3,
   st. 21

3 On with the dance! let joy be unconfined;
   No sleep till morn, when Youth and
   Pleasure meet
 . To chase the glowing Hours with flying
   feet.
   *Childe Harold's Pilgrimage* (1812–18) canto 3,
   st. 22

4 Quiet to quick bosoms is a hell.
   *Childe Harold's Pilgrimage* (1812–18) canto 3,
   st. 42

5 To fly from, need not be to hate, mankind.
   *Childe Harold's Pilgrimage* (1812–18) canto 3,
   st. 69

6 Sapping a solemn creed with solemn sneer.
   *Childe Harold's Pilgrimage* (1812–18) canto 3,
   st. 107 (of Edward Gibbon)

7 Italia! oh Italia! thou who hast
   The fatal gift of beauty.
   *Childe Harold's Pilgrimage* (1812–18) canto 4,
   st. 42

8 Oh Rome! my country! city of the soul!
   *Childe Harold's Pilgrimage* (1812–18) canto 4,
   st. 78

9 Of its own beauty is the mind diseased.
   *Childe Harold's Pilgrimage* (1812–18) canto 4,
   st. 122

10 *There* were his young barbarians all at play,
   *There* was their Dacian mother— he, their
   sire,
   Butchered to make a Roman holiday.
   *Childe Harold's Pilgrimage* (1812–18) canto 4,
   st. 141

11 While stands the Coliseum, Rome shall
   stand;
   When falls the Coliseum, Rome shall fall;
   And when Rome falls—the World.
   *Childe Harold's Pilgrimage* (1812–18) canto 4,
   st. 145

12 There is a pleasure in the pathless woods,
   There is a rapture on the lonely shore,
   There is society, where none intrudes,
   By the deep sea, and music in its roar:
   I love not man the less, but nature more.
   *Childe Harold's Pilgrimage* (1812–18) canto 4,
   st. 178

13 Roll on, thou deep and dark blue
   Ocean—roll!
   Ten thousand fleets sweep over thee in
   vain;
   Man marks the earth with ruin—his
   control
   Stops with the shore.
   *Childe Harold's Pilgrimage* (1812–18) canto 4,
   st. 179

14 Without a grave, unknelled, uncoffined,
   and unknown.
   *Childe Harold's Pilgrimage* (1812–18) canto 4,
   st. 179

15 The glory and the nothing of a name.
   'Churchill's Grave' (1816)

16            The spirit burning but unbent,
   May writhe, rebel—the weak alone repent!
   *The Corsair* (1814) canto 2, st. 10

17 Oh! too convincing—dangerously dear—
   In woman's eye the unanswerable tear!
   *The Corsair* (1814) canto 2, st. 15

18            And she for him had given
   Her all on earth, and more than all in
   heaven!
   *The Corsair* (1814) canto 3, st. 17

19 He left a Corsair's name to other times,
   Linked with one virtue, and a thousand
   crimes.
   *The Corsair* (1814) canto 3, st. 24

20 Slow sinks, more lovely ere his race be run,
   Along Morea's hills the setting sun;
   Not, as in northern climes, obscurely
   bright,
   But one unclouded blaze of living light.
   'The Curse of Minerva' (1812) l. 1 and *The
   Corsair* (1814) canto 3, st. 1

21 A land of meanness, sophistry, and mist.
   'The Curse of Minerva' (1812) l. 138 (of
   Scotland)

22 The Assyrian came down like the wolf on
   the fold,
   And his cohorts were gleaming in purple
   and gold;
   And the sheen of their spears was like
   stars on the sea,
   When the blue wave rolls nightly on deep
   Galilee.
   'The Destruction of Sennacherib' (1815) st. 1

23 Married, charming, chaste, and twenty-
   three.
   *Don Juan* (1819–24) canto 1, st. 59

24 What men call gallantry, and gods
   adultery,
   Is much more common where the
   climate's sultry.
   *Don Juan* (1819–24) canto 1, st. 63

25 Christians have burnt each other, quite
   persuaded
   That all the Apostles would have done as
   they did.
   *Don Juan* (1819–24) canto 1, st. 83

1 A little still she strove, and much repented,
And whispering 'I will ne'er
consent'—consented.
*Don Juan* (1819–24) canto 1, st. 117

2 Sweet is revenge—especially to women.
*Don Juan* (1819–24) canto 1, st. 124

3 Pleasure's a sin, and sometimes sin's a
pleasure.
*Don Juan* (1819–24) canto 1, st. 133

4 Man's love is of man's life a thing apart,
'Tis woman's whole existence.
*Don Juan* (1819–24) canto 1, st. 194

5 There's nought, no doubt, so much the
spirit calms
As rum and true religion.
*Don Juan* (1819–24) canto 2, st. 34

6 Let us have wine and women, mirth and
laughter,
Sermons and soda-water the day after.
*Don Juan* (1819–24) canto 2, st. 178

7 Man, being reasonable, must get drunk;
The best of life is but intoxication.
*Don Juan* (1819–24) canto 2, st. 179

8 And thus they form a group that's quite
antique,
Half naked, loving, natural, and Greek.
*Don Juan* (1819–24) canto 2, st. 194

9 In her first passion woman loves her lover,
In all the others all she loves is love.
*Don Juan* (1819–24) canto 3, st. 3

10 ... Love and marriage rarely can combine,
Although they both are born in the same
clime.
*Don Juan* (1819–24) canto 3, st. 5

11 Think you, if Laura had been Petrarch's
wife,
He would have written sonnets all his life?
*Don Juan* (1819–24) canto 3, st. 8

12 All tragedies are finished by a death,
All comedies are ended by a marriage;
The future states of both are left to faith.
*Don Juan* (1819–24) canto 3, st. 9

13 The isles of Greece, the isles of Greece!
Where burning Sappho loved and sung,
Where grew the arts of war and peace,
Where Delos rose, and Phoebus sprung!
Eternal summer gilds them yet,
But all, except their sun, is set!
*Don Juan* (1819–24) canto 3, st. 86 (1)

14 The mountains look on Marathon—
And Marathon looks on the sea;
And musing there an hour alone,
I dreamed that Greece might still be free.
*Don Juan* (1819–24) canto 3, st. 86 (3)

15 Milton's the prince of poets—so we say;
A little heavy, but no less divine.
*Don Juan* (1819–24) canto 3, st. 91

16 A drowsy frowzy poem, called the
'Excursion',
Writ in a manner which is my aversion.
*Don Juan* (1819–24) canto 3, st. 94

17 We learn from Horace, Homer sometimes
sleeps;
We feel without him: Wordsworth
sometimes wakes.
*Don Juan* (1819–24) canto 3, st. 98. Cf. 173:3

18 Ave Maria! 'tis the hour of prayer!
Ave Maria! 'tis the hour of love!
*Don Juan* (1819–24) canto 3, st. 103

19 Now my sere fancy 'falls into the yellow
Leaf,' and imagination droops her pinion.
*Don Juan* (1819–24) canto 4, st. 3. Cf. 288:1

20 That all-softening, overpowering knell,
The tocsin of the soul—the dinner bell.
*Don Juan* (1819–24) canto 5, st. 49

21 A lady of a 'certain age', which means
Certainly aged.
*Don Juan* (1819–24) canto 6, st. 69

22 That water-land of Dutchmen and of
ditches.
*Don Juan* (1819–24) canto 10, st. 63

23 And, after all, what is a lie? 'Tis but
The truth in masquerade.
*Don Juan* (1819–24) canto 11, st. 37

24　　　　　　Merely innocent flirtation,
Not quite adultery, but adulteration.
*Don Juan* (1819–24) canto 12, st. 63

25 Now hatred is by far the longest pleasure;
Men love in haste, but they detest at
leisure.
*Don Juan* (1819–24) canto 13, st. 4. Cf. 106:13

26 The English winter—ending in July,
To recommence in August.
*Don Juan* (1819–24) canto 13, st. 42

27 Society is now one polished horde,
Formed of two mighty tribes, the *Bores* and
*Bored*.
*Don Juan* (1819–24) canto 13, st. 95

28 Of all the horrid, hideous notes of woe,
Sadder than owl-songs or the midnight
blast,
Is that portentous phrase, 'I told you so.'
*Don Juan* (1819–24) canto 14, st. 50

29 'Tis strange—but true; for truth is always
strange;
Stranger than fiction.
*Don Juan* (1819–24) canto 14, st. 101

30 How little do we know that which we are!
How less what we may be!
*Don Juan* (1819–24) canto 15, st. 99

31 A man must serve his time to every trade
Save censure—critics all are ready made.
Take hackneyed jokes from Miller, got by
rote,
With just enough of learning to misquote.
*English Bards and Scotch Reviewers* (1809) l. 63

32 The petrifactions of a plodding brain.
*English Bards and Scotch Reviewers* (1809) l. 416

33 Then let Ausonia, skilled in every art
To soften manners, but corrupt the heart,
Pour her exotic follies o'er the town,
To sanction Vice, and hunt Decorum down.
*English Bards and Scotch Reviewers* (1809) l. 618

1 Friendship is Love without his wings!
  'L'Amitié est l'amour sans ailes' (written
  1806)

2 Old man! 'tis not so difficult to die.
  *Manfred* (2nd ed., 1819) act 3, sc. 4, l. 151

3           You have deeply ventured;
  But all must do so who would greatly win.
  *Marino Faliero* (1821) act 1, sc. 2

4 The Cincinnatus of the West.
  'Ode to Napoleon Bonaparte' (1814) st. 19 (of
  George Washington)

5 My hair is grey, but not with years,
  Nor grew it white
  In a single night,
  As men's have grown from sudden fears.
  *The Prisoner of Chillon* (1816) st. 1

6 She walks in beauty, like the night
  Of cloudless climes and starry skies;
  And all that's best of dark and bright
  Meet in her aspect and her eyes.
  'She Walks in Beauty' (1815) st. 1

7 Eternal spirit of the chainless mind!
  Brightest in dungeons, Liberty! thou art.
  'Sonnet on Chillon' (1816)

8 So, we'll go no more a-roving
  So late into the night,
  Though the heart be still as loving,
  And the moon be still as bright.
  'So we'll go no more a-roving' (written 1817)

9 There's not a joy the world can give like
  that it takes away.
  'Stanzas for Music' (1816)

10 Oh, talk not to me of a name great in
   story;
   The days of our youth are the days of our
   glory;
   And the myrtle and ivy of sweet two-and-
   twenty
   Are worth all your laurels, though ever so
   plenty.
   'Stanzas Written on the Road between
   Florence and Pisa, November 1821'

11 I knew it was love, and I felt it was glory.
   'Stanzas Written on the Road between
   Florence and Pisa, November 1821'

12 Still I can't contradict, what so oft has
   been said,
   'Though women are angels, yet wedlock's
   the devil.'
   'To Eliza' (1806)

13           Satan met his ancient friend
   With more hauteur, as might an old
   Castilian
   Poor noble meet a mushroom rich civilian.
   *The Vision of Judgement* (1822) st. 36

14 When we two parted
   In silence and tears,
   Half broken-hearted
   To sever for years,
   Pale grew thy cheek and cold,
   Colder thy kiss.
   'When we two parted' (1816)

15 My Princess of Parallelograms.
   Of Annabella Milbanke, a keen amateur
   mathematician, in a letter to Lady
   Melbourne, 18 October 1812; in L. A.
   Marchand (ed.) *Letters and Journals* vol. 2
   (1973)

16 What is hope? nothing but the paint on
   the face of Existence; the least touch of
   truth rubs it off, and then we see what a
   hollow-cheeked harlot we have got hold of.
   Letter to Thomas Moore, 28 October 1815, in
   L. A. Marchand (ed.) *Letters and Journals* vol. 4
   (1975)

17 Love in this part of the world is no
   sinecure.
   Letter to John Murray from Venice,
   27 December 1816, in L. A. Marchand (ed.)
   *Letters and Journals* vol. 5 (1976)

18 Pure invention is but the talent of a liar.
   Letter to John Murray, 2 April 1817; in L. A.
   Marchand (ed.) *Letters and Journals* vol. 5
   (1976)

19 Is it not *life*, is it not *the thing*?
   Of *Don Juan*, in a letter to Douglas Kinnaird,
   26 October 1819; in L. A. Marchand (ed.)
   *Letters and Journals* vol. 6 (1978)

20 The reading or non-reading a book—will
   never keep down a single petticoat.
   Letter to Richard Hoppner, 29 October 1819,
   in L. A. Marchand (ed.) *Letters and Journals*
   vol. 6 (1978)

21 I awoke one morning and found myself
   famous.
   On the instantaneous success of *Childe
   Harold*, in Thomas Moore *Letters and Journals
   of Lord Byron* (1830) vol. 1, p. 346

22 You should have a softer pillow than my
   heart.
   To his wife, who had rested her head on his
   breast, in E. C. Mayne (ed.) *Life and Letters of
   Anne Isabella, Lady Noel Byron* (1929) ch. 11

## James Branch Cabell 1879–1958

23 The optimist proclaims that we live in the
   best of all possible worlds; and the
   pessimist fears this is true.
   *The Silver Stallion* (1926) bk. 4, ch. 26

## Augustus Caesar
See AUGUSTUS

## Julius Caesar 100–44 BC

24 *Gallia est omnis divisa in partes tres.*
   Gaul as a whole is divided into three parts.
   *De Bello Gallico* bk. 1, sect. 1

25 Caesar's wife must be above suspicion.
   Oral tradition, based on Plutarch *Parallel Lives*
   'Julius Caesar' ch. 10, sect. 9

26 [Caesar] had rather be first in a village
   than second at Rome.
   Francis Bacon *Advancement of Learning* pt. 2,
   ch. 23, sect. 36 (based on Plutarch *Parallel
   Lives* 'Julius Caesar' ch. 11)

**1** The die is cast.
> At the crossing of the Rubicon, in Suetonius *Lives of the Caesars* 'Divus Julius' sect. 32 (often quoted '*Iacta alea est*' but originally spoken in Greek)

**2** *Veni, vidi, vici.*
> I came, I saw, I conquered.
> Inscription displayed in Caesar's Pontic triumph, according to Suetonius *Lives of the Caesars* 'Divus Julius' sect. 37; or, according to Plutarch *Parallel Lives* 'Julius Caesar' ch. 50, sect. 2, written in a letter by Caesar, announcing the victory of Zela which concluded the Pontic campaign

**3** *Et tu, Brute?*
> You too, Brutus?
> Traditional rendering of Suetonius *Lives of the Caesars* 'Divus Julius' sect. 82 Cf. 281:10

## John Cage 1912–92

**4**              I have nothing to say
          and I am saying it    and that is
poetry.
> 'Lecture on nothing' (1961)

## Callimachus *c.*305–*c.*240 BC

**5** A great book is like great evil.
> In R. Pfeiffer (ed.) *Callimachus* (1949–53) Fragment 465 (proverbially 'Great book, great evil')

## Charles Alexandre de Calonne 1734–1802

**6** Madam, if a thing is possible, consider it done; the impossible? that will be done.
> In J. Michelet *Histoire de la Révolution Française* (1847) vol. 1, pt. 2, sect. 8; better known as the US Armed Forces' slogan: 'The difficult we do immediately; the impossible takes a little longer.'

## C. S. Calverley 1831–84

**7** The farmer's daughter hath soft brown hair;
> (*Butter and eggs and a pound of cheese*)
> And I met with a ballad, I can't say where,
> Which wholly consisted of lines like these.
> 'Ballad' (1872)

**8** O Beer! O Hodgson, Guinness, Allsopp, Bass! Names that should be on every infant's tongue!
> 'Beer' (1861)

**9** Life is with such all beer and skittles; They are not difficult to please About their victuals.
> 'Contentment' (1872)

**10** For king-like rolls the Rhine, And the scenery's divine, And the victuals and the wine Rather good.
> 'Dover to Munich' (1861)

## Pierre, Baron de Cambronne 1770–1842

**11** *La Garde meurt, mais ne se rend pas.*
> The Guards die but do not surrender.
> Attributed to Cambronne when called upon to surrender at Waterloo, 1815, but later denied by him. See H. Houssaye *La Garde meurt et ne se rend pas* (1907)

## William Camden 1551–1623

**12** Betwixt the stirrup and the ground Mercy I asked, mercy I found.
> *Remains Concerning Britain* (1605) 'Epitaphs' (for a man who fell from his horse)

## Jane Montgomery Campbell 1817–78

**13** We plough the fields, and scatter The good seed on the land, But it is fed and watered By God's almighty hand.
> 'We plough the fields, and scatter' (1861 hymn); translated from the German of Matthias Claudius (1740–1815)

## Mrs Patrick Campbell 1865–1940

**14** It doesn't matter what you do in the bedroom as long as you don't do it in the street and frighten the horses.
> In Daphne Fielding *Duchess of Jermyn Street* (1964) ch. 2

**15** The deep, deep peace of the double-bed after the hurly-burly of the chaise-longue.
> On her recent marriage, in Alexander Woollcott *While Rome Burns* (1934) 'The First Mrs Tanqueray'

## Roy Campbell 1901–57

**16** You praise the firm restraint with which they write—
> I'm with you there, of course:
> They use the snaffle and the curb all right,
> But where's the bloody horse?
> 'On Some South African Novelists' (1930)

## Thomas Campbell 1777–1844

**17** O leave this barren spot to me! Spare, woodman, spare the beechen tree.
> 'The Beech-Tree's Petition' (1800). Cf. 235:13

**18** To-morrow let us do or die!
> 'Gertrude of Wyoming' (1809) pt. 3, st. 37

**19** 'Tis distance lends enchantment to the view, And robes the mountain in its azure hue.
> *Pleasures of Hope* (1799) pt. 1, l. 7

**20** What millions died—that Caesar might be great!
> *Pleasures of Hope* (1799) pt. 2, l. 174

**1** Now Barabbas was a publisher.

Attributed, in Samuel Smiles *A Publisher and his Friends* (1891) vol. 1, ch. 14; also attributed, wrongly, to Byron. See *Notes and Queries* 11th series, vol. 2, 30 July 1910, p. 92. Cf. 54:2

## Thomas Campion 1567–1620

**2** My sweetest Lesbia let us live and love,
And though the sager sort our deeds reprove,
Let us not weigh them: Heav'n's great lamps do dive
Into their west, and straight again revive,
But soon as once set is our little light,
Then must we sleep one ever-during night.

*A Book of Airs* (1601) no. 1 'My sweetest Lesbia' (translation of Catullus *Carmina* no. 5). Cf. 93:2

**3** Good thoughts his only friends,
His wealth a well-spent age,
The earth his sober inn
And quiet pilgrimage.

*A Book of Airs* (1601) no. 18

## Albert Camus 1913–60

**4** An intellectual is someone whose mind watches itself.

*Notebooks 1935–42* (1963) p. 15

**5** You know what charm is: a way of getting the answer yes without having asked any clear question.

*The Fall* (1957) p. 43

**6** I'll tell you a big secret, *mon cher*. Don't wait for the last judgement. It takes place every day.

*The Fall* (1957) p. 83

**7** What is a rebel? A man who says no.

*The Rebel* (1953) p. 19

**8** All modern revolutions have ended in a reinforcement of the State.

*The Rebel* (1953) p. 148

## Elias Canetti 1905–94

**9** All the things one has forgotten scream for help in dreams.

*Die Provinz der Menschen* (1973) p. 269

## George Canning 1770–1827

**10** In matters of commerce the fault of the Dutch
Is offering too little and asking too much.
The French are with equal advantage content,
So we clap on Dutch bottoms just twenty per cent.

Dispatch, in cipher, to the English ambassador at the Hague, 31 January 1826; in Sir Harry Poland *Mr Canning's Rhyming 'Dispatch' to Sir Charles Bagot* (1905)

**11** A steady patriot of the world alone,
The friend of every country but his own.

Of the Jacobin, in 'New Morality' (1821) l. 113. Cf. 121:17, 243:8

**12** Give me the avowed, erect and manly foe;
Firm I can meet, perhaps return the blow;
But of all plagues, good Heaven, thy wrath can send,
Save me, oh, save me, from the candid friend.

'New Morality' (1821) l. 207

**13** Away with the cant of 'Measures not men'!—the idle supposition that it is the harness and not the horses that draw the chariot along. If the comparison must be made, if the distinction must be taken, men are everything, measures comparatively nothing.

Speech on the Army estimates, 8 December 1802, in *Speeches* (1828) vol. 2, p. 61. 'Measures not men' appears as early as 1742 (in a letter from Chesterfield to Dr Chevenix, 6 March); also Goldsmith *The Good Natured Man* (1768) act 2, sc. 1

**14** I called the New World into existence, to redress the balance of the Old.

Speech on the affairs of Portugal, in *Hansard* 12 December 1826, col. 397

## Truman Capote 1924–84

**15** Other voices, other rooms.

Title of novel (1948)

## Al Capp 1907–79

**16** A product of the untalented, sold by the unprincipled to the utterly bewildered.

On abstract art, in *National Observer* 1 July 1963. Cf. 361:1

## Francesco Caracciolo 1752–99

**17** In England there are sixty different religions, and only one sauce.

Attributed. See *Notes and Queries* December 1968

## Richard Carew 1555–1620

**18** Will you have all in all for prose and verse? Take the miracle of our age, Sir Philip Sidney.

In William Camden *Remains concerning Britain* (1614) 'The Excellency of the English Tongue'

## Thomas Carew c.1595–1640

**19** Here lies a king, that ruled as he thought fit
The universal monarchy of wit.

'An Elegy upon the Death of Dr John Donne' (1640)

**20** Ask me no more where Jove bestows,
When June is past, the fading rose.

'A Song' (1640)

## Henry Carey c.1687–1743

1 Let the verse the subject fit,
Little subject, little wit.
'Namby-Pamby' (1725)

2 Of all the girls that are so smart
There's none like pretty Sally,
She is the darling of my heart,
And she lives in our alley.
'Sally in our Alley' (1729)

## Jane Carlyle 1801–66

3 I am not at all the sort of person you and I
took me for.
Letter to Thomas Carlyle, 7 May 1822, in C. R.
Sanders et al. (eds.) Collected Letters of Thomas
and Jane Welsh Carlyle (1970) vol. 2

## Thomas Carlyle 1795–1881

4 In epochs when cash payment has become
the sole nexus of man to man.
Chartism (1839) ch. 6

5 The foul sluggard's comfort: 'It will last my
time.'
Critical and Miscellaneous Essays (1838) 'Count
Cagliostro. Flight Last'

6 History is the essence of innumerable
biographies.
Critical and Miscellaneous Essays (1838) 'On
History'

7 A well-written Life is almost as rare as a
well-spent one.
Critical and Miscellaneous Essays (1838) 'Jean
Paul Friedrich Richter'

8 To the very last he [Napoleon] had a kind
of idea; that, namely, of La carrière ouverte
aux talents, The tools to him that can
handle them.
Critical and Miscellaneous Essays (1838) 'Sir
Walter Scott'. Cf. 237:6

9 The three great elements of modern
civilization, Gunpowder, Printing, and the
Protestant Religion.
Critical and Miscellaneous Essays (1838) 'The
State of German Literature'. Cf. 25:28

10 'Genius' (which means transcendent
capacity of taking trouble, first of all).
History of Frederick the Great (1858–65) bk. 4,
ch. 3. Cf. 78:6

11 A whiff of grapeshot.
History of the French Revolution (1837) vol. 1,
bk. 5, ch. 3

12 History [is] a distillation of rumour.
History of the French Revolution (1837) vol. 1,
bk. 7, ch. 5

13 The seagreen Incorruptible.
History of the French Revolution (1837) vol. 2,
bk. 4, ch. 4 (of Robespierre)

14 France was long a despotism tempered by
epigrams.
History of the French Revolution (1837) vol. 3,
bk. 7, ch. 7

15 Aristocracy of the Moneybag.
History of the French Revolution (1837) vol. 3,
bk. 7, ch. 7

16 The true University of these days is a
collection of books.
On Heroes, Hero-Worship, and the Heroic (1841)
'The Hero as Man of Letters'

17 A Parliament speaking through reporters
to Buncombe and the twenty-seven
millions mostly fools.
Latter-Day Pamphlets (1850) 'Parliaments'.
Cf. 341:6

18 The Dismal Science.
Latter-Day Pamphlets (1850) 'The Present Time'
(of political economy)

19 Transcendental moonshine.
Life of John Sterling (1851) pt. 1, ch. 15 (on the
influence of a romantic imagination in
motivating Sterling to enter the priesthood)

20 Captains of industry.
Past and Present (1843) bk. 4, ch. 4 (title)

21 Man is a tool-using animal ... Without
tools he is nothing, with tools he is all.
Sartor Resartus (1834) bk. 1, ch. 5

22 The everlasting No.
Sartor Resartus (1834) bk. 2, ch. 7 (title)

23 'Gad! she'd better!'
On hearing that Margaret Fuller 'accept[ed]
the universe'; in William James Varieties of
Religious Experience (1902) lecture 2, p. 41

24 Macaulay is well for a while, but one
wouldn't live under Niagara.
In R. M. Milnes Notebook (1838) p. 157

25 Cobden is an inspired bagman, who
believes in a calico millennium.
In T. W. Reid Life, Letters and Friendships of
Richard Monckton (1890) vol. 1, ch. 10

26 If Jesus Christ were to come to-day, people
would not even crucify him. They would
ask him to dinner, and hear what he had
to say, and make fun of it.
In D. A. Wilson Carlyle at his Zenith (1927)
p. 238

## Andrew Carnegie 1835–1919

27 The man who dies ... rich dies disgraced.
North American Review June 1889 'Wealth'

## Dale Carnegie 1888–1955

28 How to win friends and influence people.
Title of book (1936)

## Julia A. Carney 1823–1908

29 Little drops of water,
Little grains of sand,
Make the mighty ocean
And the beauteous land.
'Little Things' (1845)

## J. L. Carr 1912–

30 You have not had thirty years' experience
... You have had one year's experience 30
times.
The Harpole Report (1972) p. 128

## Lewis Carroll 1832–98

1 'What is the use of a book,' thought Alice,
'without pictures or conversations?'
*Alice's Adventures in Wonderland* (1865) ch. 1

2 'Curiouser and curiouser!' cried Alice.
*Alice's Adventures in Wonderland* (1865) ch. 2

3 How doth the little crocodile
Improve his shining tail,
And pour the waters of the Nile
On every golden scale!
*Alice's Adventures in Wonderland* (1865) ch. 2.
Cf. 343:5

4 'You are old, Father William,' the young
man said,
'And your hair has become very white;
And yet you incessantly stand on your
head—
Do you think, at your age, it is right?'
*Alice's Adventures in Wonderland* (1865) ch. 5.
Cf. 312:1

5 Speak roughly to your little boy,
And beat him when he sneezes;
He only does it to annoy,
Because he knows it teases.
*Alice's Adventures in Wonderland* (1865) ch. 6

6 'Then you should say what you mean,' the
March Hare went on. 'I do,' Alice hastily
replied; 'at least—at least I mean what I
say—that's the same thing, you know.'
'Not the same thing a bit!' said the Hatter.
'Why, you might just as well say that "I see
what I eat" is the same thing as "I eat
what I see!"'
*Alice's Adventures in Wonderland* (1865) ch. 7

7 Twinkle, twinkle, little bat!
How I wonder what you're at!
Up above the world you fly!
Like a teatray in the sky.
*Alice's Adventures in Wonderland* (1865) ch. 7.
Cf. 323:3

8 'Take some more tea,' the March Hare said
to Alice, very earnestly. 'I've had nothing
yet,' Alice replied in an offended tone, 'so I
can't take more.' 'You mean you can't take
*less*,' said the Hatter: 'it's very easy to take
*more* than nothing.'
*Alice's Adventures in Wonderland* (1865) ch. 7

9 Take care of the sense, and the sounds will
take care of themselves.
*Alice's Adventures in Wonderland* (1865) ch. 9.
Cf. 211:21

10 'That's the reason they're called lessons,'
the Gryphon remarked: 'because they
lessen from day to day.'
*Alice's Adventures in Wonderland* (1865) ch. 9

11 'Will you walk a little faster?' said a
whiting to a snail,
'There's a porpoise close behind us, and
he's treading on my tail.'
*Alice's Adventures in Wonderland* (1865) ch. 10

12 Will you, won't you, will you, won't you,
will you join the dance?
*Alice's Adventures in Wonderland* (1865) ch. 10

13 'Begin at the beginning,' the King said,
gravely, 'and go on till you come to the
end: then stop.'
*Alice's Adventures in Wonderland* (1865) ch. 12

14 No! No! Sentence first—verdict afterwards.
*Alice's Adventures in Wonderland* (1865) ch. 12

15 'Twas brillig, and the slithy toves
Did gyre and gimble in the wabe;
All mimsy were the borogoves,
And the mome raths outgrabe.
'Beware the Jabberwock, my son!
The jaws that bite, the claws that catch!'
*Through the Looking-Glass* (1872) ch. 1

16 O frabjous day! Callooh! Callay!'
*Through the Looking-Glass* (1872) ch. 1

17 Curtsey while you're thinking what to say.
It saves time.
*Through the Looking-Glass* (1872) ch. 2

18 Now, *here*, you see, it takes all the running
*you* can do, to keep in the same place. If
you want to get somewhere else, you must
run at least twice as fast as that!
*Through the Looking-Glass* (1872) ch. 2

19 Speak in French when you can't think of
the English for a thing.
*Through the Looking-Glass* (1872) ch. 2

20 If it was so, it might be; and if it were so,
it would be: but as it isn't, it ain't. That's
logic.
*Through the Looking-Glass* (1872) ch. 4

21 The Walrus and the Carpenter
Were walking close at hand;
They wept like anything to see
Such quantities of sand:
'If this were only cleared away,'
They said, 'it would be grand!'
'If seven maids with seven mops
Swept it for half a year,
Do you suppose,' the Walrus said,
'That they could get it clear?'
*Through the Looking-Glass* (1872) ch. 4

22 'The time has come,' the Walrus said,
'To talk of many things:
Of shoes—and ships—and sealing wax—
Of cabbages—and kings—
And why the sea is boiling hot—
And whether pigs have wings.'
*Through the Looking-Glass* (1872) ch. 4

23 The rule is, jam to-morrow and jam
yesterday—but never jam today.
*Through the Looking-Glass* (1872) ch. 5

24 Why, sometimes I've believed as many as
six impossible things before breakfast.
*Through the Looking-Glass* (1872) ch. 5

25 They gave it me,—for an un-birthday
present.
*Through the Looking-Glass* (1872) ch. 6

26 'When *I* use a word,' Humpty Dumpty said
in a rather scornful tone, 'it means just
what I choose it to mean—neither more
nor less.'
*Through the Looking-Glass* (1872) ch. 6

1 'The question is,' said Humpty Dumpty,
'which is to be master—that's all.'
*Through the Looking-Glass* (1872) ch. 6

2 You see it's like a portmanteau—there are
two meanings packed up into one word.
*Through the Looking-Glass* (1872) ch. 6

3 He's an Anglo-Saxon Messenger—and those
are Anglo-Saxon attitudes.
*Through the Looking-Glass* (1872) ch. 7

4 It's as large as life, and twice as natural!
*Through the Looking-Glass* (1872) ch. 7

5 No admittance till the week after next!
*Through the Looking-Glass* (1872) ch. 9

6 What I tell you three times is true.
*The Hunting of the Snark* (1876) 'Fit the First:
The Landing'

7 'What's the good of *Mercator's* North Poles
and Equators,
Tropics, Zones and Meridian lines?'
So the Bellman would cry: and the crew
would reply,
'They are merely conventional signs!'
*The Hunting of the Snark* (1876) 'Fit the
Second: The Bellman's Speech'

8 But oh, beamish nephew, beware of the
day,
If your Snark be a Boojum! For then
You will softly and suddenly vanish away,
And never be met with again!
*The Hunting of the Snark* (1876) 'Fit the Third:
The Baker's Tale'

9 They sought it with thimbles, they sought
it with care;
They pursued it with forks and hope;
They threatened its life with a railway-
share;
They charmed it with smiles and soap.
*The Hunting of the Snark* (1876) 'Fit the Fifth:
The Beaver's Lesson'

## William Herbert Carruth
1859–1924

10 Some call it evolution,
And others call it God.
'Each In His Own Tongue' (1908)

## Edward Carson 1854–1935

11 My only great qualification for being put at
the head of the Navy is that I am very
much at sea.
In I. Colvin *Life of Lord Carson* (1936) vol. 3,
ch. 23

## Henry Carter d. 1806

12 True patriots we; for be it understood,
We left our country for our country's good.
Prologue, written for, but not recited at, the
opening of the Playhouse, Sydney, New
South Wales, 16 January 1796, when the
actors were principally convicts. See A. W.
Jose and H. J. Carter (eds.) *The Australian
Encyclopaedia* (1927) p. 139. Previously
attributed to George Barrington (b. 1755).
Cf. 140:3

## Sydney Carter 1915–

13 Dance then wherever you may be,
I am the Lord of the Dance, said he,
And I'll lead you all, wherever you may be
And I'll lead you all in the dance, said he.
'Lord of the Dance' (1967)

## John Cartwright 1740–1824

14 One man shall have one vote.
*The People's Barrier Against Undue Influence*
(1780) ch. 1 'Principles, maxims, and primary
rules of politics' no. 68

## Ted Castle 1907–79

15 In place of strife.
Title of Labour Government White Paper,
17 January 1969. See Barbara Castle *Diaries*
(1984) 15 January 1969

## Fidel Castro 1926–

16 History will absolve me.
Title of pamphlet (1953)

## Edward Caswall 1814–78

17 Jesu, the very thought of Thee
With sweetness fills the breast.
'Jesu, the very thought of thee' (1849 hymn);
translation of '*Jesu dulcis memoria*', usually
attributed to St Bernard (1090–1153)

18 Hail, thou ever-blessèd morn!
Hail, redemption's happy dawn!
'See, amid the winter's snow' (1858 hymn)

19 When morning gilds the skies.
Title of hymn (1854)

## A Catechism of Christian Doctrine ('Penny Catechism')
1898

20 Who made you? God made me.
Why did God make you? God made me to
know Him, love him, and serve Him in
this world, and to be happy with Him for
ever in the next.
Ch. 1

## Empress Catherine the Great
1729–96

21 I shall be an autocrat: that's my trade. And
the good Lord will forgive me: that's his.
Attributed. Cf. 165:3

## Cato the Elder 234–149 BC

22 *Delenda est Carthago.*
Carthage must be destroyed.
In Pliny the Elder *Naturalis Historia* bk. 15,
ch. 74

23 *Rem tene; verba sequentur.*
Grasp the subject, the words will follow.
In Caius Julius Victor *Ars Rhetorica* 'De
inventione'

## Catullus c.84–c.54 BC

1 *Lugete, O Veneres Cupidinesque,*
*Et quantum est hominum venustiorum.*
*Passer mortuus est meae puellae,*
*Passer, deliciae meae puellae.*
Mourn, you powers of Charm and Desire,
and all you who are endowed with charm.
My lady's sparrow is dead, the sparrow
which was my lady's darling.
*Carmina* no. 3

2 *Vivamus, mea Lesbia, atque amemus.*
Let us live, my Lesbia, and let us love.
*Carmina* no. 5. Cf. 89:2

3 *Paene insularum, Sirmio, insularumque*
*Ocelle.*
Sirmio, bright eye of peninsulas and
islands.
*Carmina* no. 31

4 *Nam risu inepto res ineptior nulla est.*
For there is nothing sillier than a silly
laugh.
*Carmina* no. 39

5 *Difficile est longum subito deponere amorem.*
It is difficult suddenly to lay aside a long-
cherished love.
*Carmina* no. 76

6 *Si vitam puriter egi.*
If I have led a pure life.
*Carmina* no. 76

7 *Odi et amo: quare id faciam, fortasse requiris.*
*Nescio, sed fieri sentio et excrucior.*
I hate and I love: why I do so you may well
ask. I do not know, but I feel it happen and
am in agony.
*Carmina* no. 85

8 *Atque in perpetuum, frater, ave atque vale.*
And so, my brother, hail, and farewell
evermore!
*Carmina* no. 101

## Charles Causley 1917–

9 Timothy Winters comes to school
With eyes as wide as a football-pool,
Ears like bombs and teeth like splinters:
A blitz of a boy is Timothy Winters.
'Timothy Winters' (1957)

## Constantine Cavafy 1863–1933

10 When you set out for Ithaka
Ask that your way be long.
'Ithaka' (1911) (tr. E. Keeley and P. Sherrard)

11 And now, what will become of us without
the barbarians?
Those people were a kind of solution.
'Waiting for the Barbarians' (1904) (tr. E.
Keeley and P. Sherrard)

## Edith Cavell 1865–1915

12 Patriotism is not enough. I must have no
hatred or bitterness towards anyone.
On the eve of her execution, in *The Times*
23 October 1915

## Margaret Cavendish (Duchess of Newcastle) c.1624–74

13 Marriage is the grave or tomb of wit.
*Plays* (1662) 'Nature's Three Daughters' pt. 2,
act 5, sc. 20

## Count Cavour 1810–61

14 We are ready to proclaim throughout Italy
this great principle: a free church in a free
state.
Speech, 27 March 1861, in William de la Rive
*Reminiscences of the Life and Character of Count
Cavour* (1862) ch. 18

## Susannah Centlivre c.1669–1723

15 Nothing to be done without a bribe I find,
in love as well as law.
*The Perjured Husband* (1700) act 3, sc. 2

## Cervantes 1547–1616

16 The Knight of the Doleful Countenance.
*Don Quixote* (1605) pt. 1, ch. 19

17 Hunger is the best sauce in the world.
*Don Quixote* (1605) pt. 2, ch. 5

18 There are only two families in the world,
as a grandmother of mine used to say: the
haves and the have-nots.
*Don Quixote* (1605) pt. 2, ch. 20

19 Patience, and shuffle the cards.
*Don Quixote* (1605) pt. 2, ch. 23

20 Good painters imitate nature, bad ones
spew it up.
*El Licenciado Vidriera* in *Novelas Ejemplares*
(1613)

21 With one foot already in the stirrup.
Apprehending his own, imminent death; *Los
Trabajos de Persiles y Sigismunda* (1617) preface

## Joseph Chamberlain 1836–1914

22 Provided that the City of London remains,
as it is at present, the clearing-house of the
world, any other nation may be its
workshop.
Speech at the Guildhall, London, 19 January
1904; in *The Times* 20 January 1904

23 The day of small nations has long passed
away. The day of Empires has come.
Speech at Birmingham, 12 May 1904, in *The
Times* 13 May 1904

24 We are not downhearted. The only trouble
is we cannot understand what is
happening to our neighbours.
Speech at Smethwick, 18 January 1906
(referring to a constituency which had
remained unaffected by an electoral
landslide); in *The Times* 19 January 1906

## Neville Chamberlain 1869–1940

25 In war, whichever side may call itself the
victor, there are no winners, but all are
losers.
Speech at Kettering, 3 July 1938, in *The Times*
4 July 1938

1 How horrible, fantastic, incredible it is that
we should be digging trenches and trying
on gas-masks here because of a quarrel in
a far away country between people of
whom we know nothing.
   On Germany's annexation of the
   Sudetenland; radio broadcast, 27 September
   1938, in *The Times* 28 September 1938

2 This is the second time in our history that
there has come back from Germany to
Downing Street peace with honour. I
believe it is peace for our time.
   Speech from 10 Downing Street,
   30 September 1938, in *The Times* 1 October
   1938. Cf. 121:18, 265:6

3 [Hitler] missed the bus.
   Speech at Central Hall, Westminster, 4 April
   1940, in *The Times* 5 April 1940

## Nicolas-Sébastien Chamfort
## 1741–94

4 The poor are Europe's blacks.
   *Maximes et Pensées* (1796) ch. 8

5 *Sois mon frère, ou je te tue.*
Be my brother, or I kill you.
   His interpretation of 'Fraternité ou la mort
   [Fraternity or death]', in P. R. Anguis (ed.)
   *Oeuvres Complètes* (1824) vol. 1 'Notice
   Historique sur la Vie et les Écrits de
   Chamfort'. Cf. 12:11

## John Chandler 1806–76

6 Conquering kings their titles take.
   Title of hymn (1837)

## Raymond Chandler 1888–1959

7 It was a blonde. A blonde to make a bishop
kick a hole in a stained glass window.
   *Farewell, My Lovely* (1940) ch. 13

8 A big hard-boiled city with no more
personality than a paper cup.
   *The Little Sister* (1949) ch. 26 (Los Angeles)

9 Down these mean streets a man must go
who is not himself mean, who is neither
tarnished nor afraid.
   *Atlantic Monthly* December 1944 'The Simple
   Art of Murder'

10 If my books had been any worse, I should
not have been invited to Hollywood, and if
they had been any better, I should not have
come.
   Letter to Charles W. Morton, 12 December
   1945, in D. Gardiner and K. S. Walker
   *Raymond Chandler Speaking* (1962) p. 126

11 When I split an infinitive, God damn it, I
split it so it will stay split.
   Letter to Edward Weeks, 18 January 1947; in
   F. MacShane *Life of Raymond Chandler* (1976)
   ch. 7

## Charlie Chaplin 1889–1977

12 All I need to make a comedy is a park, a
policeman and a pretty girl.
   *My Autobiography* (1964) ch. 10

## Arthur Chapman 1873–1935

13 Out where the handclasp's a little stronger,
Out where the smile dwells a little longer,
That's where the West begins.
   *Out Where the West Begins* (1916) p. 1

## George Chapman c.1559–1634

14          An Englishman,
Being flattered, is a lamb; threatened, a
lion.
   *Alphonsus, Emperor of Germany* (1654) act 1

15 Man is a torch borne in the wind; a dream
But of a shadow, summed with all his
substance.
   *Bussy D'Ambois* (1607–8) act 1, sc. 1

16 Who to himself is law, no law doth need,
Offends no law, and is a king indeed.
   *Bussy D'Ambois* (1607–8) act 2, sc. 1

17 We have watered our houses in Helicon.
   *May-Day* (1611) act 3, sc. 3; occasionally
   misread 'We have watered our horses in
   Helicon'. See A. Holaday (ed.) *Plays of George
   Chapman: Comedies* (1970) p. 383

18 I am ashamed the law is such an ass.
   *Revenge for Honour* (1654) act 3, sc. 2.
   Cf. 119:20

19 A poem, whose subject is not truth, but
things like truth.
   *The Revenge of Bussy D'Ambois* (1613)
   dedication

20 Danger, the spur of all great minds.
   *The Revenge of Bussy D'Ambois* (1613) act 5, sc. 1

21 And let a scholar all Earth's volumes carry,
He will be but a walking dictionary.
   *The Tears of Peace* (1609) l. 530

## Charles I 1600–49

22 Never make a defence or apology before
you are accused.
   Letter to Lord Wentworth, 3 September 1636,
   in Sir Charles Petrie (ed.) *Letters of King
   Charles I* (1935)

23 I see all the birds are flown.
   In the House of Commons, 4 January 1642,
   after attempting to arrest the Five Members;
   *Hansard Parliamentary History to the year 1803*
   vol. 2 (1807) col. 1010

24 You manifestly wrong even the poorest
ploughman, if you demand not his free
consent.
   The King's Reasons for declining the
   jurisdiction of the High Court of Justice,
   21 January 1649; in S. R. Gardiner
   *Constitutional Documents of the Puritan
   Revolution* (1906 ed.) p. 375

25 A subject and a sovereign are clean
different things.
   Speech on the scaffold, 30 January 1649. See
   J. Rushworth *Historical Collections* pt. 4, vol. 2
   (1701) p. 1429

## Charles II 1630–85

1 It is upon the navy under the good
Providence of God that the safety, honour,
and welfare of this realm do chiefly
depend.
'Articles of War' preamble, in Sir Geoffrey
Callender *The Naval Side of British History*
(1952) pt. 1, ch. 8

2 This is very true: for my words are my
own, and my actions are my ministers'.
Reply to Lord Rochester's epitaph on him, in
*Thomas Hearne: Remarks and Collections*
(1885–1921) 17 November 1706. Cf. 261:4

3 Better than a play.
On the debates in the House of Lords on
Lord Ross's Divorce Bill, 1670; in A. Bryant
*King Charles II* (1931) p. 209

4 Let not poor Nelly starve.
Of Nell Gwyn, his mistress, in Bishop Gilbert
Burnet *History of My Own Time* (1724) vol. 1,
bk. 3, p. 609

5 Never *in* the way, and never *out* of the way.
Of Lord Godolphin, who had been raised as
page to the king; in *Dictionary of National
Biography* (1917– ) vol. 8, p. 43

6 He had been, he said, an unconscionable
time dying; but he hoped that they would
excuse it.
Lord Macaulay *History of England* (1849) vol. 1,
ch. 4

## Emperor Charles V 1500–58

7 To God I speak Spanish, to women Italian,
to men French, and to my horse—German.
Attributed. See Lord Chesterfield *Letters to his
Son* (ed. Dobrée, 1932) vol. 4, p. 1497

## Charles, Prince of Wales 1948–

8 A monstrous carbuncle on the face of a
much-loved and elegant friend.
Speech on the proposed extension to the
National Gallery, London, 30 May 1984; in
*The Times* 31 May 1984. Cf. 312:22

## Pierre Charron 1541–1603

9 The true science and study of man is man.
*De la Sagesse* (1601) bk. 1, preface. Cf. 252:17

## Geoffrey Chaucer c.1343–1400

10 Whan that Aprill with his shoures soote
The droghte of March hath perced to the
roote.
*The Canterbury Tales* 'General Prologue' l. 1

11 And smale foweles maken melodye,
That slepen al the nyght with open ye
(So priketh hem nature in hir corages),
Thanne longen folk to goon on
pilgrimages.
*The Canterbury Tales* 'General Prologue' l. 9

12 He was a verray, parfit gentil knyght.
*The Canterbury Tales* 'General Prologue' l. 72

13 He was as fressh as is the month of May.
*The Canterbury Tales* 'General Prologue' l. 92

14 Curteis he was, lowely, and servysable,
And carf biforn his fader at the table.
*The Canterbury Tales* 'General Prologue' l. 99

15 And Frenssh she spak ful faire and fetisly,
After the scole of Stratford atte Bowe,
For Frenssh of Parys was to hire unknowe.
*The Canterbury Tales* 'General Prologue' l. 124

16 And theron heng a brooch of gold ful
sheene,
On which ther was first write a crowned A,
And after *Amor vincit omnia*.
*The Canterbury Tales* 'General Prologue' l. 160.
Cf. 340:4

17 A Clerk there was of Oxenford also,
That unto logyk hadde longe ygo.
*The Canterbury Tales* 'General Prologue' l. 285

18 And gladly wolde he lerne and gladly teche.
*The Canterbury Tales* 'General Prologue' l. 308

19 Nowher so bisy a man as he ther nas,
And yet he semed bisier than he was.
*The Canterbury Tales* 'General Prologue' l. 321

20 Housbondes at chirche dore she hadde
fyve,
Withouten oother compaignye in youth.
*The Canterbury Tales* 'General Prologue' l. 460

21 This noble ensample to his sheep he yaf,
That first he wroghte, and afterward he
taughte.
*The Canterbury Tales* 'General Prologue' l. 496

22 If gold ruste, what shall iren do?
*The Canterbury Tales* 'General Prologue' l. 500

23 His walet, biforn him in his lappe,
Bretful of pardoun, comen from Rome al
hoot.
*The Canterbury Tales* 'General Prologue' l. 686

24 O stormy peple! Unsad and evere untrewe!
*The Canterbury Tales* 'The Clerk's Tale' l. 995

25 Love wol nat been constreyned by
maistrye.
When maistrie comth, the God of Love
anon
Beteth his wynges, and farewel, he is gon!
*The Canterbury Tales* 'The Franklin's Tale' l. 764

26 The bisy larke, messager of day.
*The Canterbury Tales* 'The Knight's Tale' l. 1491

27 The smylere with the knyf under the cloke.
*The Canterbury Tales* 'The Knight's Tale' l. 1999

28 And what is bettre than wisedoom?
Womman. And
what is bettre than a good womman?
Nothyng.
*The Canterbury Tales* 'The Tale of Melibee'
l. 1107

29 Mordre wol out; that se we day by day.
*The Canterbury Tales* 'The Nun's Priest's Tale'
l. 3052

30 O wombe! O bely! O stynkyng cod
Fulfilled of dong and of corrupcioun!
*The Canterbury Tales* 'The Pardoner's Tale'
l. 534

1 And lightly as it comth, so wol we spende.
*The Canterbury Tales* 'The Pardoner's Tale'
l. 781

2 The gretteste clerkes been noght wisest
men.
*The Canterbury Tales* 'The Reeve's Tale' l. 4054

3 So was hir joly whistle wel ywet.
*The Canterbury Tales* 'The Reeve's Tale' l. 4155

4 'By God,' quod he, 'for pleynly, at a word,
Thy drasty rymyng is nat worth a toord!'
*The Canterbury Tales* 'Sir Thopas' l. 929

5 Experience, though noon auctoritee
Were in this world, is right ynogh for me
To speke of wo that is in mariage.
*The Canterbury Tales* 'The Wife of Bath's
Prologue' l. 1

6 A likerous mouth moste han a likerous
tayl.
*The Canterbury Tales* 'The Wife of Bath's
Prologue' l. 466

7 But yet I hadde alwey a coltes tooth.
Gat-tothed I was, and that bicam me weel.
*The Canterbury Tales* 'The Wife of Bath's
Prologue' l. 602

8 Wommen desiren to have sovereynetee
As wel over hir housbond as hir love.
*The Canterbury Tales* 'The Wife of Bath's Tale'
l. 1038

9 Farewel my bok and my devocioun!
*The Legend of Good Women* 'The Prologue' l. 39

10 That wel by reson men it calle may
The 'dayesye,' or elles the 'ye of day,'
The emperice and flour of floures alle.
*The Legend of Good Women* 'The Prologue'
l. 183

11 And she was fayr as is the rose in May.
*The Legend of Good Women* 'Cleopatra' l. 613

12 That lyf so short, the craft so long to lerne.
*The Parliament of Fowls* l. 1. Cf. 168:19

13 O blynde world, O blynde entencioun!
How often falleth al the effect contraire
Of surquidrie and foul presumpcioun.
*Troilus and Criseyde* bk. 1, l. 211

14 But love a womman that she woot it
nought,
And she wol quyte it that thow shalt nat
fele;
Unknowe, unkist, and lost, that is
unsought.
*Troilus and Criseyde* bk. 1, l. 807

15 So longe mote ye lyve, and alle proude,
Til crowes feet be growe under youre yë.
*Troilus and Criseyde* bk. 2, l. 402

16 For I have seyn of a ful misty morwe
Folowen ful ofte a myrie someris day.
*Troilus and Criseyde* bk. 3, l. 1060

17 Right as an aspes leef she gan to quake.
*Troilus and Criseyde* bk. 3, l. 1200

18 For of fortunes sharpe adversitee
The worst kynde of infortune is this,
A man to han ben in prosperitee,
And it remembren, whan it passed is.
*Troilus and Criseyde* bk. 3, l. 1625. Cf. 62:17,
113:21

19 Oon ere it herde, at tother out it wente.
*Troilus and Criseyde* bk. 4, l. 434

20 Go, litel bok, go, litel myn tragedye.
*Troilus and Criseyde* bk. 5, l. 1786

21 And down from thennes faste he gan avyse
This litel spot of erthe, that with the se
Embraced is.
*Troilus and Criseyde* bk. 5, l. 1814

22 O yonge, fresshe folkes, he or she,
In which that love up groweth with youre
age.
*Troilus and Criseyde* bk. 5, l. 1835

23 O moral Gower, this book I directe
To the.
*Troilus and Criseyde* bk. 5, l. 1856

## Anton Chekhov 1860–1904

24 If a lot of cures are suggested for a disease,
it means that the disease is incurable.
*The Cherry Orchard* (1904) act 1 (tr. E. Fen)

25 MEDVEDENKO: Why do you wear black all
the time?
MASHA: I'm in mourning for my life, I'm
unhappy.
*The Seagull* (1896) act 1

26 Women can't forgive failure.
*The Seagull* (1896) act 2

27 I'm a seagull. No, that's wrong. Remember
you shot a seagull? A man happened to
come along, saw it and killed it, just to
pass the time. A plot for a short story.
*The Seagull* (1896) act 4

28 A woman can become a man's friend only
in the following stages—first an
acquaintance, next a mistress, and only
then a friend.
*Uncle Vanya* (1897) act 2

29 When a woman isn't beautiful, people
always say, 'You have lovely eyes, you have
lovely hair.'
*Uncle Vanya* (1897) act 3

30 Medicine is my lawful wife and literature
is my mistress. When I get tired of one I
spend the night with the other.
Letter to A. S. Suvorin, 11 September 1888, in
L. S. Friedland (ed.) *Anton Chekhov: Letters on
the Short Story ...* (1964)

31 Brevity is the sister of talent.
Letter to Alexander Chekhov, 11 April 1889,
in L. S. Friedland (ed.) *Anton Chekhov: Letters on
the Short Story ...* (1964)

1 In *Anna Karenina* and *Onegin* not a single problem is solved, but they satisfy you completely just because all their problems are correctly presented. The court is obliged to submit the case fairly, but let the jury do the deciding, each according to its own judgement.

Letter to Alexei Suvorin, 27 October 1888, in L. Hellman (ed.) *Selected Letters of Anton Chekhov* (1955, tr. S. Lederer)

## Lord Chesterfield 1694–1773

2 Unlike my subject will I frame my song, It shall be witty and it sha'n't be long.

Epigram on 'Long' Sir Thomas Robinson, in *Dictionary of National Biography* (1917– ) vol. 17, p. 51

3 Religion is by no means a proper subject of conversation in a mixed company.

*Letters . . . to his Godson and Successor* (1890) Letter 142

4 Cunning is the dark sanctuary of incapacity.

*Letters . . . to his Godson and Successor* (1890) 'Letter . . . to be delivered after his own death'

5 An injury is much sooner forgotten than an insult.

*Letters to his Son* (1774) 9 October 1746

6 Courts and camps are the only places to learn the world in.

*Letters to his Son* (1774) 2 October 1747

7 Take the tone of the company that you are in.

*Letters to his Son* (1774) 16 October 1747

8 I recommend to you to take care of minutes: for hours will take care of themselves.

*Letters to his Son* (1774) 6 November 1747. Cf. 211:21

9 Advice is seldom welcome; and those who want it the most always like it the least.

*Letters to his Son* (1774) 29 January 1748

10 Wear your learning, like your watch in a private pocket: and do not merely pull it out and strike it, merely to show that you have one.

*Letters to his Son* (1774) 22 February 1748

11 Women, then, are only children of a larger growth.

*Letters to his Son* (1774) 5 September 1748. Cf. 127:25

12 It must be owned, that the Graces do not seem to be natives of Great Britain; and I doubt, the best of us here have more of rough than polished diamond.

*Letters to his Son* (1774) 18 November 1748

13 Idleness is only the refuge of weak minds.

*Letters to his Son* (1774) 20 July 1749

14 Putting moral virtues at the highest, and religion at the lowest, religion must still be allowed to be a collateral security, at least, to virtue; and every prudent man will sooner trust to two securities than to one.

*Letters to his Son* (1774) 8 January 1750

15 It is commonly said, and more particularly by Lord Shaftesbury, that ridicule is the best test of truth.

*Letters to his Son* (1774) 6 February 1752. Cf. 270:21, 270:22

16 Knowledge may give weight, but accomplishments give lustre, and many more people see than weigh.

*Maxims*, in *Letters to his Son* (3rd ed., 1774) vol. 4, p. 304

17 The chapter of knowledge is a very short, but the chapter of accidents is a very long one.

Letter to Solomon Dayrolles, 16 February 1753, in M. Maty (ed.) *Miscellaneous Works* vol. 2 (1778) no. 79

18 The pleasure is momentary, the position ridiculous, and the expense damnable.

Of sex (attributed)

## G. K. Chesterton 1874–1936

19 I tell you naught for your comfort, Yea, naught for your desire.

*The Ballad of the White Horse* (1911) bk. 1, p. 18

20 For the great Gaels of Ireland Are the men that God made mad, For all their wars are merry, And all their songs are sad.

*The Ballad of the White Horse* (1911) bk. 2, p. 35

21 The thing on the blind side of the heart, On the wrong side of the door, The green plant groweth, menacing Almighty lovers in the Spring; There is always a forgotten thing, And love is not secure.

*The Ballad of the White Horse* (1911) bk. 3, p. 52

22 Fools! For I also had my hour; One far fierce hour and sweet: There was a shout about my ears, And palms before my feet.

'The Donkey' (1900)

23 They died to save their country and they only saved the world.

'English Graves' (1922)

24 From all that terror teaches, From lies of tongue and pen, From all the easy speeches That comfort cruel men, From sale and profanation Of honour and the sword, From sleep and from damnation, Deliver us, good Lord!

'A Hymn' (1915)

25 Strong gongs groaning as the guns boom far, Don John of Austria is going to the war.

'Lepanto' (1915)

1 Before the Roman came to Rye or out to
Severn strode,
The rolling English drunkard made the
rolling English road.
'The Rolling English Road' (1914)

2 A merry road, a mazy road, and such as we
did tread
The night we went to Birmingham by way
of Beachy Head.
'The Rolling English Road' (1914)

3 For there is good news yet to hear and fine
things to be seen,
Before we go to Paradise by way of Kensal
Green.
'The Rolling English Road' (1914)

4 Smile at us, pay us, pass us; but do not
quite forget.
For we are the people of England, that
never have spoken yet.
'The Secret People' (1915)

5 They haven't got no noses,
The fallen sons of Eve.
'The Song of Quoodle' (1914)

6 And goodness only knowses
The Noselessness of Man.
'The Song of Quoodle' (1914)

7 And Noah he often said to his wife when
he sat down to dine,
'I don't care where the water goes if it
doesn't get into the wine.'
'Wine and Water' (1914)

8 An adventure is only an inconvenience
rightly considered. An inconvenience is
only an adventure wrongly considered.
*All Things Considered* (1908) 'On Running after
one's Hat'

9 Literature is a luxury; fiction is a necessity.
*The Defendant* (1901) 'A Defence of Penny
Dreadfuls'

10 Bigotry may be roughly defined as the
anger of men who have no opinions.
*Heretics* (1905) ch. 20

11 Thieves respect property. They merely wish
the property to become their property that
they may more perfectly respect it.
*The Man who was Thursday* (1908) ch. 4

12 Democracy means government by the
uneducated, while aristocracy means
government by the badly educated.
*New York Times* 1 February 1931, pt. 5, p. 1

13 Tradition means giving votes to the most
obscure of all classes, our ancestors. It is
the democracy of the dead.
*Orthodoxy* (1908) ch. 4

14 Democrats object to men being
disqualified by the accident of birth;
tradition objects to their being disqualified
by the accident of death.
*Orthodoxy* (1908) ch. 4

15 The Christian ideal has not been tried and
found wanting. It has been found difficult;
and left untried.
*What's Wrong with the World* (1910) pt. 1 'The
Unfinished Temple'

16 The prime truth of woman, the universal
mother ... that if a thing is worth doing, it
is worth doing badly.
*What's Wrong with the World* (1910) pt. 4 'Folly
and Female Education'

## Rufus Choate 1799–1859

17 Its constitution the glittering and
sounding generalities of natural right
which make up the Declaration of
Independence.
Letter to the Maine Whig State Central
Committee, 9 August 1856, in S. G. Brown
*Works of Rufus Choate* (1862) vol. 1, p. 215.
Cf. 137:2

## Noam Chomsky 1928–

18 Colourless green ideas sleep furiously.
*Syntactic Structures* (1957) ch. 2 (illustrating
that grammatical structure is independent
of meaning)

## Chuang-tzu (or Zhuangzi)
c.369–286 BC

19 I do not know whether I was then a man
dreaming I was a butterfly, or whether I
am now a butterfly dreaming I am a man.
*Chuang Tzu* (1889) ch. 2 (tr. H. A. Giles)

## Charles Churchill 1731–64

20 The danger chiefly lies in acting well;
No crime's so great as daring to excel.
*An Epistle to William Hogarth* (1763) l. 51

21                 Be England what she will,
With all her faults, she is my country still.
*The Farewell* (1764) l. 27. Cf. 110:8

22 And adepts in the speaking trade
Keep a cough by them ready made.
*The Ghost* (1763) bk. 2, l. 545

23 Just to the windward of the law.
*The Ghost* (1763) bk. 3, l. 56

24 Old-age, a second child, by Nature cursed
With more and greater evils than the first,
Weak, sickly, full of pains; in ev'ry breath
Railing at life, and yet afraid of death.
*Gotham* (1764) bk. 1, l. 215

25 Keep up appearances; there lies the test;
The world will give thee credit for the rest.
Outward be fair, however foul within;
Sin if thou wilt, but then in secret sin.
*Night* (1761) l. 311

26 Grave without thought, and without
feeling gay.
*The Prophecy of Famine* (1763) l. 60 (on
pretentious poets)

27 Apt Alliteration's artful aid.
*The Prophecy of Famine* (1763) l. 86

28 A pert, prim prater of the northern race.
*The Rosciad* (1761) l. 71

29 Learned without sense, and venerably dull.
*The Rosciad* (1761) l. 592

## Lord Randolph Churchill 1849–94

**1** The forest laments in order that Mr Gladstone may perspire.

On Gladstone's fondness for felling trees; speech in Blackpool, 24 January 1884, in F. Banfield (ed.) *Life and Speeches of Lord Randolph Churchill* (1884)

**2** Ulster will fight; Ulster will be right.

Public letter, 7 May 1886, in R. F. Foster *Lord Randolph Churchill* (1981) p. 258

**3** An old man in a hurry.

Of Gladstone, in an address to the electors of South Paddington, 19 June 1886; in W. S. Churchill *Lord Randolph Churchill* (1906) vol. 2, p. 491

## Sir Winston Churchill 1874–1965

**4** It cannot in the opinion of His Majesty's Government be classified as slavery in the extreme acceptance of the word without some risk of terminological inexactitude.

Speech, *Hansard* 22 February 1906, col. 555

**5** He [Lord Charles Beresford] is one of those orators of whom it was well said, 'Before they get up, they do not know what they are going to say; when they are speaking, they do not know what they are saying; and when they have sat down, they do not know what they have said.'

Speech, *Hansard* 20 December 1912, col. 1893

**6** Business carried on as usual during alterations on the map of Europe.

Speech at Guildhall, 9 November 1914, in *Complete Speeches* (1974) vol. 3 (on the self-adopted 'motto' of the British people)

**7** The whole map of Europe has been changed ... but as the deluge subsides and the waters fall short we see the dreary steeples of Fermanagh and Tyrone emerging once again.

Speech, *Hansard* 16 February 1922, col. 1270

**8** I have waited 50 years to see the boneless wonder [Ramsay Macdonald] sitting on the Treasury Bench.

Speech, *Hansard* 28 January 1931, col. 1021

**9** [The Government] go on in strange paradox, decided only to be undecided, resolved to be irresolute, adamant for drift, solid for fluidity.

Speech, *Hansard* 12 November 1936, col. 1107

**10** I cannot forecast to you the action of Russia. It is a riddle wrapped in a mystery inside an enigma.

Radio broadcast, 1 October 1939, in *Into Battle* (1941) p. 131

**11** I have nothing to offer but blood, toil, tears and sweat.

Speech, *Hansard* 13 May 1940, col. 1502

**12** What is our policy? ... to wage war against a monstrous tyranny, never surpassed in the dark, lamentable catalogue of human crime.

Speech, *Hansard* 13 May 1940, col. 1502

**13** We shall not flag or fail. We shall go on to the end. We shall fight in France, we shall fight on the seas and oceans, we shall fight with growing confidence and growing strength in the air, we shall defend our island, whatever the cost may be. We shall fight on the beaches, we shall fight on the landing grounds, we shall fight in the fields and in the streets, we shall fight in the hills; we shall never surrender.

Speech, *Hansard* 4 June 1940, col. 796

**14** Let us therefore brace ourselves to our duty, and so bear ourselves that, if the British Empire and its Commonwealth lasts for a thousand years, men will still say, 'This was their finest hour.'

Speech, *Hansard* 18 June 1940, col. 60

**15** Never in the field of human conflict was so much owed by so many to so few.

Speech, *Hansard* 20 August 1940, col. 1166 (on the Battle of Britain)

**16** Give us the tools and we will finish the job.

Radio broadcast, 9 February 1941, in *Complete Speeches* (1974) vol. 6 (addressing President Roosevelt)

**17** When I warned them [the French Government] that Britain would fight on alone whatever they did, their generals told their Prime Minister and his divided Cabinet, 'In three weeks England will have her neck wrung like a chicken.' Some chicken! Some neck!

Speech to Canadian Parliament, 30 December 1941, in *Complete Speeches* (1974) vol. 6

**18** Now this is not the end. It is not even the beginning of the end. But it is, perhaps, the end of the beginning.

Speech at the Mansion House, London, 10 November 1942, in *The End of the Beginning* (1943) p. 214 (on the Battle of Egypt)

**19** We make this wide encircling movement in the Mediterranean, having for its primary object the recovery of the command of that vital sea, but also having for its object the exposure of the under-belly of the Axis, especially Italy, to heavy attack.

Speech, *Hansard* 11 November 1942, col. 28 (often misquoted 'the soft under-belly of the Axis')

**20** National compulsory insurance for all classes for all purposes from the cradle to the grave.

Radio broadcast, 21 March 1943, in *Complete Speeches* (1974) vol. 7

**21** There is no finer investment for any community than putting milk into babies.

Radio broadcast, 21 March 1943, in *Complete Speeches* (1974) vol. 7

1 From Stettin in the Baltic to Trieste in the Adriatic an iron curtain has descended across the Continent.

Speech at Westminster College, Fulton, Missouri, 5 March 1946, in *Complete Speeches* (1974) vol. 7. 'Iron curtain' previously had been applied by others to the Soviet Union or her sphere of influence, e.g. Ethel Snowden *Through Bolshevik Russia* (1920), Dr Goebbels *Das Reich* (25 February 1945), and by Churchill himself in a cable to President Truman (4 June 1945)

2 Democracy is the worst form of Government except all those other forms that have been tried from time to time.

Speech, *Hansard* 11 November 1947, col. 206

3 To jaw-jaw is always better than to war-war.

Speech at White House, 26 June 1954, in *New York Times* 27 June 1954, p. 1

4 In war: resolution. In defeat: defiance. In victory: magnanimity. In peace: goodwill.

*The Second World War* vol. 1 (1948) epigraph

5 This is the sort of English up with which I will not put.

In Ernest Gowers *Plain Words* (1948) 'Troubles with Prepositions'

6 Don't talk to me about naval tradition. It's nothing but rum, sodomy, and the lash.

In Sir Peter Gretton *Former Naval Person* (1968) ch. 1

7 A sheep in sheep's clothing.

Of Clement Attlee, in Lord Home *The Way the Wind Blows* (1976) ch. 6. Cf. 155:25

8 Take away that pudding — it has no theme.

In Lord Home *The Way the Wind Blows* (1976) ch. 16

9 In defeat unbeatable: in victory unbearable.

Of Viscount Montgomery, in E. Marsh *Ambrosia and Small Beer* (1964) ch. 5

10 The candle in that great turnip has gone out.

Of Stanley Baldwin, in *Harold Nicolson: Diaries and Letters 1945–62* (1968) Diary 17 August 1950

11 I have taken more out of alcohol than alcohol has taken out of me.

In Quentin Reynolds *By Quentin Reynolds* (1964) ch. 11

## Count Galeazzo Ciano 1903–44

12 *La vittoria trova cento padri, e nessuno vuole riconoscere l'insuccesso.*

Victory has a hundred fathers, but defeat is an orphan.

*Diary* (1946) vol. 2, 9 September 1942 (literally 'no-one wants to recognize defeat as his own')

## Colley Cibber 1671–1757

13 Oh! how many torments lie in the small circle of a wedding-ring!

*The Double Gallant* (1707) act 1, sc. 2

14 One had as good be out of the world, as out of the fashion.

*Love's Last Shift* (1696) act 2

15 Off with his head—so much for Buckingham.

*Richard III* (1700) act 4 (adapted from Shakespeare)

16 Perish the thought!

*Richard III* (1700) act 5 (adapted from Shakespeare)

17 Conscience avaunt, Richard's himself again.

*Richard III* (1700) act 5 (adapted from Shakespeare)

18 Stolen sweets are best.

*The Rival Fools* (1709) act 1, sc. 1

## Cicero 106–43 BC

19 There is nothing so absurd but some philosopher has said it.

*De Divinatione* bk. 2, ch. 119

20 *Salus populi suprema est lex.*

The good of the people is the chief law.

*De Legibus* bk. 3, ch. 8

21 *'Ipse dixit.' 'Ipse' autem erat Pythagoras.*

'He himself said,' and this 'himself' was Pythagoras.

*De Natura Deorum* bk. 1, ch. 10

22 *Summum bonum.*

The highest good.

*De Officiis* bk. 1, ch. 5

23 Let war yield to peace, laurels to paeans.

*De Officiis* bk. 1, ch. 77

24 Never less idle than when wholly idle, nor less alone than when wholly alone.

*De Officiis* bk. 3, ch. 1

25 *O tempora, O mores!*

Oh, the times! Oh, the manners!

*In Catilinam* Speech 1, ch. 1

26 *Abiit, excessit, evasit, erupit.*

He departed, he withdrew, he strode off, he broke forth.

*In Catilinam* Speech 2, ch. 1

27 *Civis Romanus sum.*

I am a Roman citizen.

*In Verrem* Speech 5, ch. 147

28 *Quod di omen avertant.* May the gods avert this omen.

*Third Philippic* ch. 35

29 *Nervos belli, pecuniam infinitam.*

The sinews of war, unlimited money.

*Fifth Philippic* ch. 5

30 Laws are silent in time of war.

*Pro Milone* ch. 11

31 *Cui bono?*

To whose profit?

*Pro Roscio Amerino* ch. 84 and *Pro Milone* ch. 12, sect. 32 (quoting L. Cassius Longinus Ravilla)

32 *Cum dignitate otium.*

Leisure with honour.

*Pro Sestio* ch. 98

**1** I would rather be wrong, by God, with
Plato ... than be correct with those men.
*Tusculanae Disputationes* bk. 1, ch. 39 (of
Pythagoreans)

**2** O happy Rome, born when I was consul!
In Juvenal *Satires* poem 10, l. 122

## John Clare 1793–1864

**3** He could not die when the trees were
green,
For he loved the time too well.
'The Dying Child'

**4** My life hath been one chain of
contradictions,
Madhouses, prisons, whore-shops.
'Child Harold' (written 1841) l. 146

**5** Hopeless hope hopes on and meets no end,
Wastes without springs and homes
without a friend.
'Child Harold' (written 1841) l. 1018

**6** A quiet, pilfering, unprotected race.
'The Gipsy Camp' (1841)

**7** I long for scenes where man hath never
trod
A place where woman never smiled or
wept
There to abide with my Creator God
And sleep as I in childhood sweetly slept,
Untroubling and untroubled where I lie
The grass below, above, the vaulted sky.
'I Am' (1848)

**8** The present is the funeral of the past,
And man the living sepulchre of life.
'The present is the funeral of the past'
(written 1845)

## Edward Hyde, Earl of Clarendon
1609–74

**9** Without question, when he first drew the
sword, he threw away the scabbard.
*History of the Rebellion* (1703, ed. W. D. Macray,
1888) vol. 3, bk. 7, sect. 84 (of Hampden)

**10** He had a head to contrive, a tongue to
persuade, and a hand to execute any
mischief.
*History of the Rebellion* (1703, ed. W. D. Macray,
1888) vol. 3, bk. 7, sect. 84 (of Hampden).
Cf. 150:12

**11** So enamoured on peace that he would
have been glad the King should have
bought it at any price.
*History of the Rebellion* (1703, ed. W. D. Macray,
1888) vol. 3, bk. 7, sect. 233 (of Falkland)

**12** He will be looked upon by posterity as a
brave bad man.
*History of the Rebellion* (1703, ed. W. D. Macray,
1888) vol. 6, bk. 15, *ad fin.* (of Cromwell)

## Alan Clark 1928–

**13** Our old friend economical ... with the
*actualité.*
Under cross-examination at the Old Bailey
during the Matrix Churchill case; in
*Independent* 10 November 1992, p. 1. Cf. 16:6

## Arthur C. Clarke 1917–

**14** If an elderly but distinguished scientist
says that something is possible he is
almost certainly right, but if he says that it
is impossible he is very probably wrong.
In *New Yorker* 9 August 1969

## John Clarke d. 1658

**15** Home is home, though it be never so
homely.
*Paraemiologia Anglo-Latina* (1639) 'Domi vivere'

## Karl von Clausewitz 1780–1831

**16** War is nothing but a continuation of
politics with the admixture of other
means.
*Vom Kriege* (1832–4) bk. 8, ch. 6, sect. B
(commonly rendered 'War is the
continuation of politics by other means')

## Henry Clay 1777–1852

**17** The gentleman [Josiah Quincy] can not
have forgotten his own sentiment, uttered
even on the floor of this House, 'peaceably
if we can, forcibly if we must'.
Speech in Congress, 8 January 1813, in C.
Colton (ed.) *Works of Henry Clay* (1904) vol. 1,
p. 197. Cf. 257:9

**18** I had rather be right than be President.
To Senator Preston of South Carolina, 1839.
See S. W. McCall *Life of Thomas Brackett Reed*
(1914) ch. 14

## Eldridge Cleaver 1935–

**19** You're either part of the solution or you're
part of the problem.
Speech in San Francisco, 1968, in R. Scheer
*Eldridge Cleaver, Post Prison Writings and
Speeches* (1969) p. 32

## John Cleland 1710–89

**20** Truth! stark naked truth, is the word.
*Memoirs of a Woman of Pleasure* (also known as
*Fanny Hill*, 1749) vol. 1

## Georges Clemenceau 1841–1929

**21** War is too serious a matter to entrust to
military men.
Attributed to Clemenceau, e.g. in Hampden
Jackson *Clemenceau and the Third Republic*
(1946) p. 228, but also to Briand and
Talleyrand

1 My home policy: I wage war; my foreign
policy: I wage war. All the time I wage war.
   Speech to French Chamber of Deputies,
   8 March 1918, in *Discours de Guerre* (1968)
   p. 172

2 It is easier to make war than to make
peace.
   Speech at Verdun, 20 July 1919, in *Discours de
   Paix* (1938) p. 122

## Pope Clement XIII 1693–1769

3 *Sint ut sunt aut non sint.*
   Let them be as they are or not be at all.
   Replying to a request for changes in the
   constitutions of the Society of Jesus, in J. A.
   M. Crétineau-Joly *Clément XIV et les Jésuites*
   (1847) p. 370 n.

## Grover Cleveland 1837–1908

4 I have considered the pension list of the
republic a roll of honour.
   Veto of Dependent Pension Bill, 5 July 1888,
   in *Compilation of the Messages and Papers of the
   Presidents* vol. 11 (1897) p. 5269

## Bill Clinton 1946–

5 I experimented with marijuana a time or
two. And I didn't like it, and I didn't inhale.
   In *Washington Post* 30 March 1992, p. A1

## Lord Clive 1725–74

6 By God, Mr Chairman, at this moment I
stand astonished at my own moderation!
   During Parliamentary cross-examination,
   1773, in G. R. Gleig *Life of Robert, First Lord
   Clive* (1848) ch. 29

## Arthur Hugh Clough 1819–61

7 Am I prepared to lay down my life for the
British female?
   Really, who knows? . . .
   Ah, for a child in the street I could strike;
   for the full-blown lady—
   Somehow, Eustace, alas! I have not felt the
   vocation.
   *Amours de Voyage* (1858) canto 2, pt. 4

8 I do not like being moved: for the will is
excited; and action
   Is a most dangerous thing.
   *Amours de Voyage* (1858) canto 2, pt. 11

9 Mild monastic faces in quiet collegiate
cloisters.
   *Amours de Voyage* (1858) canto 3, pt. 9

10 Sesquipedalian blackguard.
   *The Bothie of Tober-na-Vuolich* (1848) pt. 2, l. 223

11 Grace is given of God, but knowledge is
bought in the market.
   *The Bothie of Tober-na-Vuolich* (1848) pt. 4, l. 159

12 Afloat. We move: Delicious! Ah,
   What else is like the gondola?
   *Dipsychus* (1865) sc. 5

13 This world is bad enough may-be;
   We do not comprehend it;
   But in one fact can all agree
   God won't, and we can't mend it.
   *Dipsychus* (1865) sc. 5

14 My pleasure of thought is the pleasure of
thinking
   How pleasant it is to have money, heigh
   ho!
   How pleasant it is to have money.
   *Dipsychus* (1865) sc. 5

15 And almost every one when age,
   Disease, or sorrows strike him,
   Inclines to think there is a God,
   Or something very like Him.
   *Dipsychus* (1865) sc. 6

16 Thou shalt have one God only; who
   Would be at the expense of two?
   'The Latest Decalogue' (1862)

17 Thou shalt not kill; but need'st not strive
   Officiously to keep alive.
   'The Latest Decalogue' (1862)

18 Do not adultery commit;
   Advantage rarely comes of it.
   'The Latest Decalogue' (1862)

19 Thou shalt not steal; an empty feat,
   When it's so lucrative to cheat.
   'The Latest Decalogue' (1862)

20 Thou shalt not covet; but tradition
   Approves all forms of competition.
   'The Latest Decalogue' (1862)

21 'Tis better to have fought and lost,
   Than never to have fought at all.
   'Peschiera' (1854). Cf. 325:4

22 Say not the struggle naught availeth,
   The labour and the wounds are vain,
   The enemy faints not, nor faileth,
   And as things have been, things remain.
   'Say not the struggle naught availeth' (1855)

23 If hopes were dupes, fears may be liars.
   'Say not the struggle naught availeth' (1855)

24 In front the sun climbs slow, how slowly,
   But westward, look, the land is bright.
   'Say not the struggle naught availeth' (1855)

## William Cobbett 1762–1835

25 The slavery of the tea and coffee and other
slop-kettle.
   *Advice to Young Men* (1829) letter 1, sect. 31

26 The great wen of all.
   *Rural Rides: The Kentish Journal* in *Cobbett's
   Weekly Political Register* 5 January 1822,
   vol. 40, col. 1609 (of London)

## Alison Cockburn 1713–94

27 O fickle Fortune, why this cruel sporting?
   Why thus torment us poor sons of day?
   Nae mair your smiles can cheer me, nae
   mair your frowns can fear me,
   For the flowers of the forest are a' *wade*
   away.
   'The Flowers of the Forest' (1765); *wade*
   weeded (often quoted 'For the flowers of the
   forest are withered away')

## Claud Cockburn 1904–81

1 Small earthquake in Chile. Not many dead.
  Winning entry for a dullest headline
  competition at *The Times*; *In Time of Trouble*
  (1956) ch. 10

## Jean Cocteau 1889–1963

2 Life is a horizontal fall.
  *Opium* (1930) p. 37

3 Victor Hugo was a madman who thought
  he was Victor Hugo.
  *Opium* (1930) p. 77

4 Being tactful in audacity is knowing how
  far one can go too far.
  *Le Rappel à l'ordre* (1926) 'Le Coq et l'Arlequin'
  p. 2

## George M. Cohan 1878–1942

5 I'm a Yankee Doodle Dandy,
  A Yankee Doodle, do or die;
  A real live nephew of my Uncle Sam's,
  Born on the fourth of July.
  'Yankee Doodle Boy' (1904 song). Cf. 11:24

## Desmond Coke 1879–1931

6 As the race wore on . . . his oar was dipping
  into the water nearly *twice* as often as any
  other.
  *Sandford of Merton* (1903) ch. 12 (usually
  misquoted 'All rowed fast, but none so fast
  as stroke')

## Sir Edward Coke 1552–1634

7 How long soever it hath continued, if it be
  against reason, it is of no force in law.
  *First Part of the Institutes of the Laws of England*
  (1628) bk. 1, ch. 10, sect. 80, p. 62 recto

8 For a man's house is his castle, *et domus
  sua cuique est tutissimum refugium* [and each
  man's home is his safest refuge].
  *Third Part of the Institutes of the Laws of England*
  (1628) ch. 73

9 They [corporations] cannot commit
  treason, nor be outlawed, nor
  excommunicate, for they have no souls.
  *Reports of Sir Edward Coke* (1658) vol. 5, pt. 10
  'The case of Sutton's Hospital' p. 32 verso.
  Cf. 332:19

10 Magna Charta is such a fellow, that he will
  have no sovereign.
  On the Lords' Amendment to the Petition of
  Right, 17 May 1628, in J. Rushworth *Historical
  Collections* (1659) vol. 1, p. 562

## Hartley Coleridge 1796–1849

11 But what is Freedom? Rightly understood,
  A universal licence to be good.
  'Liberty' (1833)

## Samuel Taylor Coleridge
1772–1834

12 Behold! her bosom and half her side—
  A sight to dream of, not to tell!
  'Christabel' (1816) pt. 1, l. 252

13 A little child, a limber elf,
  Singing, dancing to itself.
  'Christabel' (1816) pt. 2, conclusion, l. 656

14 I see them all so excellently fair,
  I see, not feel, how beautiful they are!
  'Dejection: an Ode' (1802) st. 2

15 But oh! each visitation
  Suspends what nature gave me at my
  birth,
  My shaping spirit of imagination.
  'Dejection: an Ode' (1802) st. 6. Cf. 104:24

16 And the Devil did grin, for his darling sin
  Is pride that apes humility.
  'The Devil's Thoughts' (1799)

17 What is an Epigram? a dwarfish whole,
  Its body brevity, and wit its soul.
  'Epigram' (1809)

18 The frost performs its secret ministry,
  Unhelped by any wind.
  'Frost at Midnight' (1798) l. 1

19 With all the numberless goings-on of life,
  Inaudible as dreams!
  'Frost at Midnight' (1798) l. 12

20 Only that film, which fluttered on the
  grate,
  Still flutters there, the sole unquiet thing.
  'Frost at Midnight' (1798) l. 15

21 At this moment he was unfortunately
  called out by a person on business from
  Porlock.
  'Kubla Khan' (1816) preliminary note

22 In Xanadu did Kubla Khan
  A stately pleasure-dome decree:
  Where Alph, the sacred river, ran
  Through caverns measureless to man
  Down to a sunless sea.
  So twice five miles of fertile ground
  With walls and towers were girdled round.
  'Kubla Khan' (1816)

23 A savage place! as holy and enchanted
  As e'er beneath a waning moon was
  haunted
  By woman wailing for her demon-lover!
  And from this chasm, with ceaseless
  turmoil seething,
  As if this earth in fast thick pants were
  breathing,
  A mighty fountain momently was forced.
  'Kubla Khan' (1816)

24 It was a miracle of rare device,
  A sunny pleasure-dome with caves of ice.
  'Kubla Khan' (1816)

25 And 'mid this tumult Kubla heard from far
  Ancestral voices prophesying war!
  'Kubla Khan' (1816)

1 And all should cry, Beware! Beware!
His flashing eyes, his floating hair!
Weave a circle round him thrice,
And close your eyes with holy dread,
For he on honey-dew hath fed,
And drunk the milk of Paradise.
'Kubla Khan' (1816)

2 With Donne, whose muse on dromedary
trots,
Wreathe iron pokers into true-love knots.
'On Donne's Poetry' (1818)

3 It is an ancient Mariner,
And he stoppeth one of three.
'By thy long grey beard and glittering eye,
Now wherefore stopp'st thou me?'
'The Rime of the Ancient Mariner' (1798)
pt. 1

4 And ice, mast-high, came floating by,
As green as emerald.
'The Rime of the Ancient Mariner' (1798)
pt. 1

5 We were the first that ever burst
Into that silent sea.
'The Rime of the Ancient Mariner' (1798)
pt. 2

6 As idle as a painted ship
Upon a painted ocean.
'The Rime of the Ancient Mariner' (1798)
pt. 2

7 Water, water, everywhere,
And all the boards did shrink;
Water, water, everywhere,
Nor any drop to drink.
'The Rime of the Ancient Mariner' (1798)
pt. 2

8 The Night-mare LIFE-IN-DEATH was she,
Who thicks man's blood with cold.
'The Rime of the Ancient Mariner' (1798)
pt. 3

9 The Sun's rim dips; the stars rush out;
At one stride comes the dark.
'The Rime of the Ancient Mariner' (1798)
pt. 3

10 The hornèd Moon, with one bright star
Within the nether tip.
'The Rime of the Ancient Mariner' (1798)
pt. 3

11 I fear thee, ancient Mariner!
I fear thy skinny hand!
And thou art long, and lank, and brown,
As is the ribbed sea-sand.
'The Rime of the Ancient Mariner' (1798)
pt. 4

12 And a thousand thousand slimy things
Lived on; and so did I.
'The Rime of the Ancient Mariner' (1798)
pt. 4

13 Oh Sleep! it is a gentle thing,
Beloved from pole to pole.
'The Rime of the Ancient Mariner' (1798)
pt. 5

14 We were a ghastly crew.
'The Rime of the Ancient Mariner' (1798)
pt. 5

15 Like one, that on a lonesome road
Doth walk in fear and dread,
And having once turned round walks on,
And turns no more his head;
Because he knows, a frightful fiend
Doth close behind him tread.
'The Rime of the Ancient Mariner' (1798)
pt. 6

16 No voice; but oh! the silence sank
Like music on my heart.
'The Rime of the Ancient Mariner' (1798)
pt. 6

17 I pass, like night, from land to land;
I have strange power of speech.
'The Rime of the Ancient Mariner' (1798)
pt. 7

18 He prayeth well, who loveth well
Both man and bird and beast.

He prayeth best, who loveth best
All things both great and small.
'The Rime of the Ancient Mariner' (1798)
pt. 7

19 A sadder and a wiser man,
He rose the morrow morn.
'The Rime of the Ancient Mariner' (1798)
pt. 7

20 So for the mother's sake the child was
dear,
And dearer was the mother for the child.
'Sonnet to a Friend Who Asked How I Felt
When the Nurse First Presented My Infant to
Me' (1797)

21          When the last rook
Beat its straight path along the dusky air.
'This Lime-Tree Bower my Prison' (1800) l. 68

22 Work without hope draws nectar in a
sieve,
And hope without an object cannot live.
'Work without Hope' (1828)

23 He who begins by loving Christianity
better than Truth will proceed by loving
his own sect or church better than
Christianity, and end by loving himself
better than all.
Aids to Reflection (1825) 'Moral and Religious
Aphorisms' no. 25

24 That willing suspension of disbelief for the
moment, which constitutes poetic faith.
Biographia Literaria (1817) ch. 14

25 To see him act, is like reading Shakespeare
by flashes of lightning.
Table Talk (1835) 27 April 1823 (on Edmund
Kean)

26 Prose = words in their best order;—poetry
= the best words in the best order.
Table Talk (1835) 12 July 1827

27 The man's desire is for the woman; but the
woman's desire is rarely other than for the
desire of the man.
Table Talk (1835) 23 July 1827

28 In politics, what begins in fear usually
ends in folly.
Table Talk (1835) 5 October 1830

1 Youth and Hope—those twin realities of this phantom world!

Table Talk (1835) 10 July 1834

2 Summer has set in with its usual severity.

Letter to Vincent Novello, 9 May 1826, in A. Ainger (ed.) Letters of Charles Lamb (1888) vol. 2

## William Collingbourne d. 1484

3 The Cat, the Rat, and Lovell our dog
Rule all England under a hog.

Referring to Sir William Catesby (d. 1485), Sir Richard Ratcliffe (d. 1485), Lord Lovell (1454–c.1487), whose crest was a dog, and King Richard III, whose emblem was a wild boar. See Robert Fabyan Concordance of Chronicles (ed. H. Ellis, 1811) p. 672

## Admiral Collingwood 1748–1810

4 Now, gentlemen, let us do something today which the world may talk of hereafter.

Before the Battle of Trafalgar, 21 October 1805; in G. L. Newnham Collingwood (ed.) Selection from the Correspondence of Lord Collingwood (1828) vol. 1, p. 168

## R. G. Collingwood 1889–1943

5 Perfect freedom is reserved for the man who lives by his own work and in that work does what he wants to do.

Speculum Mentis (1924) p. 25. Cf. 153:1

## Charles Collins

6 Any old iron, any old iron,
Any any old old iron?
You look neat
Talk about a treat,
You look dapper from your napper to your feet.
Dressed in style, brand new tile,
And your father's old green tie on,
But I wouldn't give you tuppence for your old watch chain;
Old iron, old iron?

'Any Old Iron' (1911 song, with E. A. Sheppard and Fred Terry); the second line often sung 'Any any any old iron?'

7 My old man said, 'Follow the van,
Don't dilly-dally on the way!'
Off went the cart with the home packed in it,
I walked behind with my old cock linnet.
But I dillied and dallied, dallied and dillied,
Lost the van and don't know where to roam.
You can't trust the 'specials' like the old time 'coppers'
When you can't find your way home.

'Don't Dilly-Dally on the Way' (1919 song, with Fred Leigh); popularized by Marie Lloyd

## Michael Collins 1890–1922

8 Early this morning I signed my death warrant.

On signing the treaty establishing the Irish Free State; letter, 6 December 1921, in T. R. Dwyer Michael Collins and the Treaty (1981) ch. 4

## William Collins 1721–59

9 To fair Fidele's grassy tomb
Soft maids and village hinds shall bring
Each opening sweet of earliest bloom,
And rifle all the breathing spring.

'Dirge' (1744); occasionally included in 18th-century performances of Shakespeare's Cymbeline

10 Now air is hushed, save where the weak-eyed bat,
With short shrill shriek flits by on leathern wing.

'Ode to Evening' (1747)

11 How sleep the brave, who sink to rest,
By all their country's wishes blest!

'Ode Written in the Year 1746' (1748)

## George Colman, the Elder 1732–94 and David Garrick 1717–79

12 Love and a cottage! Eh, Fanny! Ah, give me indifference and a coach and six!

The Clandestine Marriage (1766) act 1

## George Colman, the Younger 1762–1836

13 Oh, London is a fine town,
A very famous city,
Where all the streets are paved with gold,
And all the maidens pretty.

The Heir at Law (performed 1797) act 1, sc. 2

14 Says he, 'I am a handsome man, but I'm a gay deceiver.'

Love Laughs at Locksmiths (1808) act 2

15 Johnson hewed passages through the Alps, while Gibbon levelled walks through parks and gardens.

Random Records (1830) vol. 1, p. 122

## Charles Caleb Colton c.1780–1832

16 When you have nothing to say, say nothing.

Lacon (1820) vol. 1, no. 183

17 Examinations are formidable even to the best prepared, for the greatest fool may ask more than the wisest man can answer.

Lacon (1820) vol. 1, no. 322

18 If you would be known, and not know, vegetate in a village; if you would know, and not be known, live in a city.

Lacon (1820) vol. 1, no. 334

1 Man is an embodied paradox, a bundle of
contradictions.
*Lacon* (1820) vol. 1, no. 408

## Betty Comden 1919– and Adolph Green 1915–

2 The party's over, it's time to call it a day.
'The Party's Over' (1956 song)

## Ivy Compton-Burnett 1884–1969

3 Well, of course, people are only human ...
But it really does not seem much for them
to be.
*A Family and a Fortune* (1939) ch. 2

4 People don't resent having nothing nearly
as much as too little.
*A Family and a Fortune* (1939) ch. 4

5 There are different kinds of wrong. The
people sinned against are not always the
best.
*The Mighty and their Fall* (1961) ch. 7

## William Congreve 1670–1729

6 Retired to their tea and scandal, according
to their ancient custom.
*The Double Dealer* (1694) act 1, sc. 1

7 See how love and murder will out.
*The Double Dealer* (1694) act 4, sc. 6

8 I came upstairs into the world; for I was
born in a cellar.
*Love for Love* (1695) act 2, sc. 7

9 I know that's a secret, for it's whispered
every where.
*Love for Love* (1695) act 3, sc. 3

10 'Tis well enough for a servant to be bred at
an University. But the education is a little
too pedantic for a gentleman.
*Love for Love* (1695) act 5, sc. 3

11 Music has charms to soothe a savage
breast.
*The Mourning Bride* (1697) act 1, sc. 1

12 Heaven has no rage, like love to hatred
turned,
Nor Hell a fury, like a woman scorned.
*The Mourning Bride* (1697) act 3, sc. 8

13 SHARPER: Thus grief still treads upon the
heels of pleasure:
Married in haste, we may repent at leisure.
SETTER: Some by experience find those
words mis-placed:
At leisure married, they repent in haste.
*The Old Bachelor* (1693) act 5, sc. 1

14 Courtship to marriage, as a very witty
prologue to a very dull play.
*The Old Bachelor* (1693) act 5, sc. 10

15 They come together like the Coroner's
Inquest, to sit upon the murdered
reputations of the week.
*The Way of the World* (1700) act 1, sc. 1

16 Say what you will, 'tis better to be left than
never to have been loved.
*The Way of the World* (1700) act 2, sc. 1.
Cf. 325:4

17 Here she comes i' faith full sail, with her
fan spread and streamers out, and a shoal
of fools for tenders.
*The Way of the World* (1700) act 2, sc. 4

18 WITWOUD: Madam, do you pin up your hair
with all your letters?
MILLAMANT: Only those in verse, Mr
Witwoud. I never pin up my hair with
prose.
*The Way of the World* (1700) act 2, sc. 4

19 A little disdain is not amiss; a little scorn
is alluring.
*The Way of the World* (1700) act 3, sc. 5

20 Let us be very strange and well-bred: Let us
be as strange as if we had been married a
great while, and as well-bred as if we were
not married at all.
*The Way of the World* (1700) act 4, sc. 5

21 These articles subscribed, if I continue to
endure you a little longer, I may by
degrees dwindle into a wife.
*The Way of the World* (1700) act 4, sc. 5

22 For 'tis some virtue, virtue to commend.
'To Sir Godfrey Kneller'

## James M. Connell 1852–1929

23 Then raise the scarlet standard high!
Within its shade we'll live or die.
Tho' cowards flinch and traitors sneer,
We'll keep the red flag flying here.
'The Red Flag' (1889) in H. E. Piggott *Songs
that made History* (1937) ch. 6

## Cyril Connolly 1903–74

24 Whom the gods wish to destroy they first
call promising.
*Enemies of Promise* (1938) ch. 13

25 There is no more sombre enemy of good
art than the pram in the hall.
*Enemies of Promise* (1938) ch. 14

26 The Mandarin style ... is beloved by
literary pundits, by those who would make
the written word as unlike as possible to
the spoken one.
*Enemies of Promise* (1938) ch. 20

27 It is closing time in the gardens of the
West and from now on an artist will be
judged only by the resonance of his
solitude or the quality of his despair.
*Horizon* December 1949–January 1950,
p. 362

28 Imprisoned in every fat man a thin one is
wildly signalling to be let out.
*The Unquiet Grave* (1944) pt. 2. Cf. 241:25

29 The true index of a man's character is the
health of his wife.
*The Unquiet Grave* (1944) pt. 2

1 Our memories are card-indexes consulted,
and then put back in disorder by
authorities whom we do not control.
*The Unquiet Grave* (1944) pt. 3

2 Perfect fear casteth out love.
In *Observer* 1 December 1974; obituary notice
by Philip Toynbee, to whom Connolly
addressed the remark during the Blitz

## James Connolly 1868–1916

3 The worker is the slave of capitalist
society, the female worker is the slave of
that slave.
*The Re-conquest of Ireland* (1915) p. 38

## Joseph Conrad 1857–1924

4 Exterminate all the brutes!
*Heart of Darkness* (1902) ch. 2

5 The horror! The horror!
*Heart of Darkness* (1902) ch. 3

6 Mistah Kurtz—he dead.
*Heart of Darkness* (1902) ch. 3

7 To the destructive element submit
yourself.
*Lord Jim* (1900) ch. 20

8 Action is consolatory. It is the enemy of
thought and the friend of flattering
illusions.
*Nostromo* (1904) pt. 1, ch. 6

9 The terrorist and the policeman both come
from the same basket.
*The Secret Agent* (1907) ch. 4

## Shirley Conran 1932–

10 Life is too short to stuff a mushroom.
*Superwoman* (1975) p. 15

## John Constable 1776–1837

11 *I never saw an ugly thing in my life*: for let the
form of an object be what it may,—light,
shade, and perspective will always make it
beautiful.
In C. R. Leslie *Memoirs of the Life of John
Constable* (1843) ch. 17

12 In Claude's landscape all is lovely—all
amiable—all is amenity and repose;—the
calm sunshine of the heart.
Lecture, 2 June 1836, in C. R. Leslie *Memoirs
of the Life of John Constable* (1843) ch. 18

## Benjamin Constant 1767–1834

13 Art for art's sake, with no purpose, for any
purpose perverts art. But art achieves a
purpose which is not its own.
*Journal intime* 11 February 1804, in *Revue
Internationale* 10 January 1887 p. 96.
Cf. 108:17

## Emperor Constantine
AD *c.*288–337

14 *In hoc signo vinces.*
In this sign shalt thou conquer.
Traditional form of Constantine's vision
(AD 312); in Eusebius *Life of Constantine* bk. 1,
ch. 28

## A. J. Cook 1885–1931

15 Not a penny off the pay, not a second on
the day.
Speech at York, 3 April 1926, as Secretary of
the Miners' Federation of Great Britain; in
*The Times* 5 April 1926 (often quoted with
'minute' substituted for 'second')

## Dan Cook

16 The opera ain't over 'til the fat lady sings.
In *Washington Post* 3 June 1978. See *Concise
Oxford Dictionary of Proverbs* under 'opera'

## Eliza Cook 1818–89

17 Better build schoolrooms for 'the boy',
Than cells and gibbets for 'the man'.
'A Song for the Ragged Schools' (1853)

## Calvin Coolidge 1872–1933

18 Civilization and profits go hand in hand.
Speech in New York, 27 November 1920, in
*New York Times* 28 November 1920, p. 20

19 The chief business of the American people
is business.
Speech in Washington, 17 January 1925, in
*New York Times* 18 January 1925, p. 19

20 They hired the money, didn't they?
On war debts incurred by England and
others; in J. H. McKee *Coolidge: Wit and
Wisdom* (1933) p. 118

## Duff Cooper 1890–1954

21 Your two stout lovers frowning at one
another across the hearth rug, while your
small, but perfectly formed one kept the
party in a roar.
Letter to Lady Diana Manners, later his wife,
October 1914; in Artemis Cooper *Durable Fire*
(1983) p. 17

## Wendy Cope 1945–

22 Bloody men are like bloody buses—
You wait for about a year
And as soon as one approaches your stop
Two or three others appear.
'Bloody Men' (1992)

## Bishop Richard Corbet 1582–1635

23 Farewell, rewards and Fairies,
Good housewives now may say,
For now foul sluts in dairies
Do fare as well as they.
'The Fairies' Farewell'

## Pierre Corneille 1606–84

1 When there is no peril in the fight, there is no glory in the triumph.
   *Le Cid* (1637) act 2, sc. 2

2 Do your duty, and leave the outcome to the Gods.
   *Horace* (1640) act 2, sc. 8

3 A first impulse was never a crime.
   *Horace* (1640) act 5, sc. 3. Cf. 234:1

## Bernard Cornfeld 1927–

4 Do you sincerely want to be rich?
   Stock question to salesmen. See C. Raw et al. *Do You Sincerely Want to be Rich?* (1971) p. 67

## Frances Cornford 1886–1960

5 How long ago Hector took off his plume,
   Not wanting that his little son should cry,
   Then kissed his sad Andromache goodbye—
   And now we three in Euston waiting-room.
   'Parting in Wartime' (1948)

6 O fat white woman whom nobody loves,
   Why do you walk through the fields in gloves ...
   Missing so much and so much?
   'To a Fat Lady seen from the Train' (1910)

7 A young Apollo, golden-haired,
   Stands dreaming on the verge of strife,
   Magnificently unprepared
   For the long littleness of life.
   'Youth' (1910) (of Rupert Brooke)

## Francis M. Cornford 1874–1943

8 Every public action, which is not customary, either is wrong, or, if it is right, is a dangerous precedent. It follows that nothing should ever be done for the first time.
   *Microcosmographia Academica* (1908) ch. 7

## Mme Cornuel 1605–94

9 No man is a hero to his valet.
   In *Lettres de Mlle Aïssé à Madame C* (1787) Letter 13 'De Paris, 1728'

## Coronation Service

10 Here is wisdom; this is the royal Law; these are the lively Oracles of God.
   The Presenting of the Holy Bible. See L. G. Wickham Legge *English Coronation Records* (1901) p. 334

## William Cory 1823–92

11 Jolly boating weather,
   And a hay harvest breeze,
   Blade on the feather,
   Shade off the trees
   Swing, swing together
   With your body between your knees.
   'Eton Boating Song' in *Eton Scrap Book* (1865)

12 Nothing in life shall sever
   The chain that is round us now.
   'Eton Boating Song' (1865)

13 They told me, Heraclitus, they told me you were dead,
   They brought me bitter news to hear and bitter tears to shed.
   I wept as I remembered how often you and I
   Had tired the sun with talking and sent him down the sky.
   'Heraclitus' (1858); translation of Callimachus 'Epigram 2' in R. Pfeiffer (ed.) *Callimachus* (1949–53)

14 Your chilly stars I can forgo,
   This warm kind world is all I know.
   'Mimnermus in Church' (1858)

## Baron Pierre de Coubertin 1863–1937

15 The important thing in life is not the victory but the contest; the essential thing is not to have won but to have fought well.
   Speech in London, 24 July 1908; in T. A. Cook *Fourth Olympiad* (1909) p. 793

## Émile Coué 1857–1926

16 Every day, in every way, I am getting better and better.
   To be said 15 to 20 times, morning and evening, in *De la suggestion et de ses applications* (1915) p. 17

## Victor Cousin 1792–1867

17 We must have religion for religion's sake, morality for morality's sake, as with art for art's sake ... the beautiful cannot be the way to what is useful, or to what is good, or to what is holy; it leads only to itself.
   *Du Vrai, du beau, et du bien* [Sorbonne lecture, 1818] (1853) pt. 2, p. 197. Cf. 107:13

## Thomas Coventry 1578–1640

18 The dominion of the sea, as it is an ancient and undoubted right of the crown of England, so it is the best security of the land ... The wooden walls are the best walls of this kingdom.
   Speech to the Judges, 17 June 1635, in J. Rushworth *Historical Collections* (1680) vol. 2, p. 297 (*wooden walls* ships). See Herodotus *Histories* bk. 7, ch. 141–3

## Noël Coward 1899–1973

19 Dance, dance, dance, little lady!
   Leave tomorrow behind.
   'Dance, Little Lady' (1928 song)

20 Don't let's be beastly to the Germans
   When our Victory is ultimately won.
   'Don't Let's Be Beastly to the Germans' (1943 song)

1 I believe that since my life began
The most I've had is just
A talent to amuse.
'If Love Were All' (1929 song)

2 I'll see you again,
Whenever spring breaks through again.
'I'll See You Again' (1929 song)

3 Mad about the boy.
Title of song (1932)

4 Mad dogs and Englishmen
Go out in the midday sun.
The Japanese don't care to,
The Chinese wouldn't dare to,
The Hindus and Argentines sleep firmly
from twelve to one,
But Englishmen detest a siesta.
'Mad Dogs and Englishmen' (1931 song)

5 Don't put your daughter on the stage, Mrs
Worthington,
Don't put your daughter on the stage.
'Mrs Worthington' (1935 song)

6 Poor little rich girl
You're a bewitched girl,
Better beware!
'Poor Little Rich Girl' (1925 song)

7 Someday I'll find you,
Moonlight behind you,
True to the dream I am dreaming.
'Someday I'll Find You' (1930 song)

8 The Stately Homes of England,
How beautiful they stand,
To prove the upper classes
Have still the upper hand.
'The Stately Homes of England' (1938 song).
Cf. 165:10

9 Very flat, Norfolk.
Private Lives (1930) act 1

10 Extraordinary how potent cheap music is.
Private Lives (1930) act 1

11 Certain women should be struck regularly,
like gongs.
Private Lives (1930) act 3

12 Two wise acres and a cow.
Describing the Sitwells, in J. Pearson Façades
(1978) ch. 10. Cf. 11:6

## Abraham Cowley 1618–67

13 God the first garden made, and the first
city Cain.
Essays, in Verse and Prose (1668) 'The Garden'.
Cf. 110:6

14 In all her outward parts Love's always
seen;
But, oh, he never went within.
The Mistress (1647) 'The Change'

15 The world's a scene of changes, and to be
Constant, in Nature were inconstancy.
The Mistress (1647) 'Inconstancy'

16 Lukewarmness I account a sin
As great in love as in religion.
The Mistress (1647) 'The Request'

17 Life is an incurable disease.
'To Dr Scarborough' (1656) st. 6

## Hannah Cowley 1743–1809

18 Five minutes! Zounds! I have been five
minutes too late all my life-time!
The Belle's Stratagem (1780) act 1, sc. 1

19 Vanity, like murder, will out.
The Belle's Stratagem (1780) act 1, sc. 4

## William Cowper 1731–1800

20 We perished, each alone:
But I beneath a rougher sea,
And whelmed in deeper gulfs than he.
'The Castaway' (written 1799) l. 61

21 Pernicious weed! whose scent the fair
annoys,
Unfriendly to society's chief joys.
'Conversation' (1782) l. 251 (of tobacco)

22 His wit invites you by his looks to come,
But when you knock it never is at home.
'Conversation' (1782) l. 303

23 John Gilpin was a citizen
Of credit and renown,
A train-band captain eke was he
Of famous London town.
'John Gilpin' (1785) l. 1

24 My sister and my sister's child,
Myself and children three,
Will fill the chaise; so you must ride
On horseback after we.
'John Gilpin' (1785) l. 13

25 God moves in a mysterious way
His wonders to perform;
He plants his footsteps in the sea,
And rides upon the storm.
Olney Hymns (1779) 'Light Shining out of
Darkness'

26 Behind a frowning providence
He hides a smiling face.
Olney Hymns (1779) 'Light Shining out of
Darkness'

27 Oh! for a closer walk with God,
A calm and heav'nly frame;
A light to shine upon the road
That leads me to the Lamb!
Olney Hymns (1779) 'Walking with God'

28 Toll for the brave—
The brave! that are no more:
All sunk beneath the wave,
Fast by their native shore.
'On the Loss of the Royal George' (written
1782)

29 I shall not ask Jean Jacques Rousseau,
If birds confabulate or no.
'Pairing Time Anticipated' (1795)

30 The poplars are felled, farewell to the
shade
And the whispering sound of the cool
colonnade.
'The Poplar-Field' (written 1784)

1 Oh, laugh or mourn with me the rueful
jest,
A cassocked huntsman and a fiddling
priest!
'The Progress of Error' (1782) l. 110

2 Remorse, the fatal egg by pleasure laid.
'The Progress of Error' (1782) l. 239

3 Thou god of our idolatry, the press ...
Thou fountain, at which drink the good
and wise;
Thou ever-bubbling spring of endless lies;
Like Eden's dread probationary tree,
Knowledge of good and evil is from thee.
'The Progress of Error' (1782) l. 461

4 The disencumbered Atlas of the state.
'Retirement' (1782) l. 394 (of the statesman)

5 Admirals extolled for standing still,
Or doing nothing with a deal of skill.
'Table Talk' (1782) l. 192

6 God made the country, and man made the
town.
The Task (1785) bk. 1 'The Sofa' l. 749.
Cf. 109:13

7 Slaves cannot breathe in England, if their
lungs
Receive our air, that moment they are free;
They touch our country, and their shackles
fall.
The Task (1785) bk. 2 'The Timepiece' l. 40.
Cf. 10:1

8 England, with all thy faults, I love thee
still—
My country!
The Task (1785) bk. 2 'The Timepiece' l. 206.
Cf. 98:21

9 Variety's the very spice of life,
That gives it all its flavour.
The Task (1785) bk. 2 'The Timepiece' l. 606

10 Studious of laborious ease.
The Task (1785) bk. 3 'The Garden' l. 361

11 Now stir the fire, and close the shutters
fast,
Let fall the curtains, wheel the sofa round,
And, while the bubbling and loud-hissing
urn
Throws up a steamy column, and the cups,
That cheer but not inebriate, wait on each,
So let us welcome peaceful evening in.
The Task (1785) bk. 4 'The Winter Evening'
l. 34. Cf. 35:16

12 I crown thee king of intimate delights,
Fire-side enjoyments, home-born
happiness.
The Task (1785) bk. 4 'The Winter Evening'
l. 139

13 Public schools 'tis public folly feeds.
'Tirocinium' (1785) l. 250

14 The parson knows enough who knows a
duke.
'Tirocinium' (1785) l. 403

15        A priest,
A piece of mere church furniture at best.
'Tirocinium' (1785) l. 425

16        Tenants of life's middle state,
Securely placed between the small and
great.
'Tirocinium' (1785) l. 807

17 He has no hope that never had a fear.
'Truth' (1782) l. 298

18 I am monarch of all I survey,
My right there is none to dispute.
'Verses Supposed to be Written by Alexander
Selkirk' (1782)

## George Crabbe 1754-1832

19 The Town small-talk flows from lip to lip;
Intrigues half-gathered, conversation-
scraps,
Kitchen-cabals, and nursery-mishaps.
The Borough (1810) Letter 3 'The Vicar' l. 70

20 Habit with him was all the test of truth,
'It must be right: I've done it from my
youth.'
The Borough (1810) Letter 3 'The Vicar' l. 138

21 Lo! the poor toper whose untutored sense,
Sees bliss in ale, and can with wine
dispense;
Whose head proud fancy never taught to
steer,
Beyond the muddy ecstasies of beer.
'Inebriety' (in imitation of Pope, 1775) pt. 1,
l. 132. Cf. 252:13

22 With awe, around these silent walks I
tread;
These are the lasting mansions of the dead.
'The Library' (1808) l. 105

23 Coldly profane and impiously gay.
'The Library' (1808) l. 265

24 The murmuring poor, who will not fast in
peace.
'The Newspaper' (1785) l. 158

25 A master passion is the love of news.
'The Newspaper' (1785) l. 279

26 That all was wrong because not all was
right.
Tales (1812) 'The Convert' l. 313

27 He tried the luxury of doing good.
Tales of the Hall (1819) 'Boys at School' l. 139

28 'The game,' said he, 'is never lost till won.'
Tales of the Hall (1819) 'Gretna Green' l. 334

29 The face the index of a feeling mind.
Tales of the Hall (1819) 'Lady Barbara' l. 124

30 The cold charities of man to man.
The Village (1783) bk. 1, l. 245

## Hart Crane 1899-1932

31 Stars scribble on our eyes the frosty sagas,
The gleaming cantos of unvanquished
space.
'Cape Hatteras' (1930)

32 We have seen
The moon in lonely alleys make
A grail of laughter of an empty ash can.
'Chaplinesque' (1926)

1 Ah, madame! truly it's not right
When one isn't the real Gioconda,
To adapt her methods and deportment
For snaring the poor world in a blue funk.
'Locutions des Pierrots' (1933)

2            So the 20th Century—so
whizzed the Limited—roared by and left
three men, still hungry on the tracks,
  ploddingly
watching the tail lights wizen and
  converge, slipping
gimleted and neatly out of sight.
'The River' (1930)

## Stephen Crane 1871–1900

3 The red badge of courage.
Title of novel (1895)

## Thomas Cranmer 1489–1556

4 This was the hand that wrote it [his
recantation], therefore it shall suffer first
punishment.
At the stake, 21 March 1556; in J. R. Green
*Short History of the English People* (1874) ch. 7,
sect. 2

## Richard Crashaw c.1612–49

5 Lord, what is man, that thou hast
  overbought
So much a thing of nought?
'Caritas Nimia, or The Dear Bargain' (1648)

6 *Nympha pudica Deum vidit, et erubuit.*
The conscious water saw its God, and
  blushed.
*Epigrammata Sacra* (1634) 'Aquae in vinum
versae' (Dryden's translation; literally 'the
chaste nymph saw . . . ')

7 Love's passives are his activ'st part.
The wounded is the wounding heart.
'The Flaming Heart upon the Book of Saint
Teresa' (1652) l. 73

8 By all the eagle in thee, all the dove.
'The Flaming Heart upon the Book of Saint
Teresa' (1652) l. 95

9 Love, thou art absolute sole Lord
Of life and death.
'Hymn to the Name and Honour of the
Admirable Saint Teresa' (1652) l. 1

10 Poor World (said I) what wilt thou do
To entertain this starry stranger?
'Hymn of the Nativity' (1652)

11 Welcome, all wonders in one sight!
Eternity shut in a span.
'Hymn of the Nativity' (1652)

12 Lo here a little volume, but large book.
'On a Prayer book' (1646)

13 I would be married, but I'd have no wife,
I would be married to a single life.
'On Marriage' (1646)

14 Two walking baths; two weeping motions;
Portable, and compendious oceans.
'Saint Mary Magdalene, or The Weeper'
(1652) st. 19

15 And when life's sweet fable ends,
Soul and body part like friends;
No quarrels, murmurs, no delay;
A kiss, a sigh, and so away.
'Temperance' (1652)

16 That not impossible she
That shall command my heart and me.
'Wishes to His (Supposed) Mistress' (1646)

## James Creelman 1901–41 and Ruth Rose

17 Oh no, it wasn't the aeroplanes. It was
Beauty killed the Beast.
*King Kong* (1933 film)

## Bishop Mandell Creighton 1843–1901

18 No people do so much harm as those who
go about doing good.
In *Life and Letters of Mandell Creighton* by his
wife (1904) vol. 2, p. 503

## Francis Crick 1916–

19 Almost all aspects of life are engineered at
the molecular level, and without
understanding molecules we can only have
a very sketchy understanding of life itself.
*What Mad Pursuit* (1988) ch. 5

## Quentin Crisp 1908–

20 There was no need to do any housework at
all. After the first four years the dirt
doesn't get any worse.
*The Naked Civil Servant* (1968) ch. 15

21 An autobiography is an obituary in serial
form with the last instalment missing.
*The Naked Civil Servant* (1968) ch. 29

## Julian Critchley 1930–

22 The only safe pleasure for a
parliamentarian is a bag of boiled sweets.
*Listener* 10 June 1982

## Richmal Crompton 1890–1969

23 I'll thcream and thcream and thcream till
I'm thick.
*Still—William* (1925) ch. 8 (Violet Elizabeth)

## Oliver Cromwell 1599–1658

24 I would rather have a plain russet-coated
captain that knows what he fights for, and
loves what he knows, than that which you
call 'a gentleman' and is nothing else.
Letter to Sir William Spring, September
1643, in Thomas Carlyle *Oliver Cromwell's
Letters and Speeches* (2nd ed., 1846)

1 Cruel necessity.
   On the execution of Charles I, in Joseph
   Spence *Anecdotes* (1820) p. 286

2 I beseech you, in the bowels of Christ,
   think it possible you may be mistaken.
   Letter to the General Assembly of the Kirk of
   Scotland, 3 August 1650, in Thomas Carlyle
   *Oliver Cromwell's Letters and Speeches* (1845)

3 The dimensions of this mercy are above
   my thoughts. It is, for aught I know, a
   crowning mercy.
   Letter to William Lenthall, Speaker of the
   Parliament of England, 4 September 1651, in
   Thomas Carlyle *Oliver Cromwell's Letters and
   Speeches* (1845)

4 You have sat too long here for any good
   you have been doing. Depart, I say, and let
   us have done with you. In the name of
   God, go!
   Addressing the Rump Parliament, 20 April
   1653 (oral tradition; quoted by Leo Amery,
   *Hansard* 7 May 1940, col. 1150). See Bulstrode
   Whitelock *Memorials of the English Affairs*
   (1732 ed.) p. 529

5 Take away that fool's bauble, the mace.
   At the dismissal of the Rump Parliament,
   20 April 1653, in Bulstrode Whitelock
   *Memorials of the English Affairs* (1732 ed.)
   p. 529 (often quoted 'Take away these
   baubles')

6 Necessity hath no law. Feigned necessities,
   imaginary necessities ... are the greatest
   cozenage that men can put upon the
   Providence of God, and make pretences to
   break known rules by.
   Speech to Parliament, 12 September 1654, in
   Thomas Carlyle *Oliver Cromwell's Letters and
   Speeches* (1845). Cf. 256:2

7 Remark all these roughnesses, pimples,
   warts, and everything as you see me;
   otherwise I will never pay a farthing for it.
   To Lely, on the painting of his portrait; in
   Horace Walpole *Anecdotes of Painting in
   England* vol. 3 (1763) ch. 1 (commonly quoted
   'warts and all')

8 My design is to make what haste I can to
   be gone.
   Last words, in J. Morley *Oliver Cromwell* (1900)
   bk. 5, ch. 10

## Bing Crosby 1903–77

9 Where the blue of the night meets the
   gold of the day.
   Title of song, with Roy Turk and Fred Ahlert
   (1931)

## Douglas Cross

10 I left my heart in San Francisco
   High on a hill it calls to me.
   To be where little cable cars climb half-way
   to the stars,
   The morning fog may chill the air—
   I don't care!
   'I Left My Heart in San Francisco' (1954 song)

## Richard Assheton, Viscount Cross 1823–1914

11 I hear a smile.
   When the House of Lords laughed at his
   speech in favour of Spiritual Peers, in G. W.
   E. Russell *Collections and Recollections* (1898)
   ch. 29

## Richard Crossman 1907–74

12 The Civil Service is profoundly deferential
   — 'Yes, Minister! No, Minister! If you wish
   it, Minister!'
   *Diaries of a Cabinet Minister* vol. 1 (1975)
   22 October 1964

## Samuel Crossman 1624–83

13 My song is love unknown,
   My saviour's love for me,
   Love to the loveless shown,
   That they might lovely be.
   O, who am I,
   That for my sake
   My Lord should take
   Frail flesh and die?
   'My song is love unknown' (1664)

## Aleister Crowley 1875–1947

14 Do what thou wilt shall be the whole of
   the Law.
   *Book of the Law* (1909) l. 40. Cf. 257:12

## Bishop Richard Cumberland 1631–1718

15 It is better to wear out than to rust out.
   In George Horne *The Duty of Contending for the
   Faith* (1786) p. 21 n.

## e. e. cummings 1894–1962

16 anyone lived in a pretty how town
   (with up so floating many bells down)
   spring summer autumn winter
   he sang his didn't he danced his did.
   *50 Poems* (1949) no. 29

17 'next to of course god america i
   love you land of the pilgrims' and so forth.
   *is 5* (1926) p. 62

18 a politician is an arse upon
   which everyone has sat except a man.
   *1 x 1* (1944) no. 10

19 plato told
   him: he couldn't
   believe it (jesus
   told him; he
   wouldn't believe
   it).
   *1 x 1* (1944) no. 13

20 pity this busy monster, manunkind,
   not. Progress is a comfortable disease.
   *1 x 1* (1944) no. 14

**1** We doctors know
a hopeless case if—listen: there's a hell
of a good universe next door; let's go.
> *1 x 1* (1944) no. 14

**2** when man determined to destroy
himself he picked the was
of shall and finding only why
smashed it into because.
> *1 x 1* (1944) no. 26

**3** nobody, not even the rain, has such small
hands.
> 'somewhere I have never travelled' (1931)

**4** i like my body when it is with your
body. It is so quite new a thing.
Muscles better and nerves more.
> 'Sonnets–Actualities' no. 8 (1925)

**5** the Cambridge ladies who live in furnished
souls
are unbeautiful and have comfortable
minds.
> 'Sonnets–Realities' no. 1 (1923)

## William Thomas Cummings
1903–45

**6** There are no atheists in the foxholes.
> In C. P. Romulo *I Saw the Fall of the Philippines*
(1943) ch. 15

## Allan Cunningham 1784–1842

**7** A wet sheet and a flowing sea,
A wind that follows fast
And fills the white and rustling sail
And bends the gallant mast.
> 'A Wet Sheet and a Flowing Sea' (1825)

## John Philpot Curran 1750–1817

**8** The condition upon which God hath given
liberty to man is eternal vigilance.
> Speech on the right of election of the Lord
Mayor of Dublin, 10 July 1790; in T. Davis
(ed.) *Speeches* (1845) p. 94

**9** Like the silver plate on a coffin.
> Describing Sir Robert Peel's smile; quoted by
Daniel O'Connell, *Hansard* 26 February 1835,
col. 397

## Michael Curtiz 1888–1962

**10** Bring on the empty horses!
> While directing *The Charge of the Light Brigade*
(1936 film); in David Niven *Bring on the Empty
Horses* (1975) ch. 6

## Lord Curzon 1859–1925

**11** Gentlemen do not take soup at luncheon.
> In E. L. Woodward *Short Journey* (1942) ch. 7

## St Cyprian c.AD 200–258

**12** He cannot have God for his father who has
not the church for his mother.
> *De Ecclesiae Catholicae Unitate* sect. 6. Cf. 21:26

**13** *Fratres nostros non esse lugendos arcessitione
dominica de saeculo liberatos, cum sciamus non
amitti sed praemitti.*
Our brethren who have been freed from
the world by the summons of the Lord
should not be mourned, since we know
that they are not lost but sent before.
> *De Mortalite* ch. 20 (ed. M. L. Hannam, 1933)

**14** There cannot be salvation for any, except
in the Church.
> *Epistle Ad Pomponium, De Virginibus* sect. 4.
Cf. 21:26, 113:12

## Samuel Daniel 1563–1619

**15** Care-charmer Sleep, son of the sable Night,
Brother to Death, in silent darkness born.
> *Delia* (1592) Sonnet 54

**16**                But years hath done this
wrong,
To make me write too much, and live too
long.
> *Philotas* (1605) 'To the Prince' (dedication)
l. 108

## Dante Alighieri 1265–1321

**17** *Nel mezzo del cammin di nostra vita.*
Midway along the path of our life.
> *Divina Commedia* 'Inferno' canto 1, l. 1

**18** LASCIATE OGNI SPERANZA VOI CH'ENTRATE!
Abandon all hope, you who enter!
> *Divina Commedia* 'Inferno' canto 3, l. 1
(inscription at the entrance to Hell)

**19** *Non ragioniam di lor, ma guarda, e passa.*
Let us not speak of them, but look, and
pass on.
> *Divina Commedia* 'Inferno' canto 3, l. 51

**20** *Il gran rifiuto.*
The great refusal.
> *Divina Commedia* 'Inferno' canto 3, l. 60

**21** ... *Nessun maggior dolore,*
*Che ricordarsi del tempo felice*
*Nella miseria.*
There is no greater pain than to remember
a happy time when one is in misery.
> *Divina Commedia* 'Inferno' canto 5, l. 121.
Cf. 62:17

**22** *E'n la sua volontade è nostra pace.*
In His will is our peace.
> *Divina Commedia* 'Paradiso' canto 3, l. 85

**23** *Tu proverai sì come sa di sale*
*Lo pane altrui, e com'è duro calle*
*Lo scendere e'l salir per l'altrui scale.*
You shall find out how salt is the taste of
another man's bread, and how hard is the
way up and down another man's stairs.
> *Divina Commedia* 'Paradiso' canto 17, l. 58

**24** *L'amor che muove il sole e l'altre stelle.*
The love that moves the sun and the other
stars.
> *Divina Commedia* 'Paradiso' canto 33, l. 145

## Georges Jacques Danton 1759–94

1 *De l'audace, et encore de l'audace, et toujours de l'audace!*

Boldness, and again boldness, and always boldness!

 Speech to the Legislative Committee of General Defence, 2 September 1792; in *Le Moniteur* 4 September 1792

## Joe Darion 1917–

2 Dream the impossible dream.
 'The Quest' (1965 song)

## Charles Darwin 1809–82

3 I have called this principle, by which each slight variation, if useful, is preserved, by the term of Natural Selection.
 *On the Origin of Species* (1859) ch. 3

4 We will now discuss in a little more detail the Struggle for Existence.
 *On the Origin of Species* (1859) ch. 3

5 What a book a devil's chaplain might write on the clumsy, wasteful, blundering, low, and horridly cruel works of nature!
 Letter to J. D. Hooker, 13 July 1856; in *Correspondence of Charles Darwin* vol. 6 (1990)

6 Animals, whom we have made our slaves, we do not like to consider our equal.
 Notebook B (1837–8) in P. H. Barrett et al. (eds.) *Charles Darwin's Notebooks 1836–1844* (1987) p. 228

## Sir Francis Darwin 1848–1925

7 In science the credit goes to the man who convinces the world, not to the man to whom the idea first occurs.
 *Eugenics Review* April 1914 'Francis Galton'

## Charles D'Avenant 1656–1714

8 Custom, that unwritten law,
By which the people keep even kings in awe.
 *Circe* (1677) act 2, sc. 3

## Sir William D'Avenant 1606–68

9 In every grave make room, make room!
The world's at an end, and we come, we come.
 *The Law against Lovers* (1673) act 3, sc. 1
 'Viola's Song'

10 The lark now leaves his wat'ry nest
And, climbing, shakes his dewy wings.
 'Song: The Lark' (1638)

## John Davidson 1857–1909

11 A runnable stag, a kingly crop.
 'A Runnable Stag' (1906)

12 The race is to the swift,
The battle to the strong.
 'War Song' (1899) st. 1

## Sir John Davies 1569–1626

13 Wedlock, indeed, hath oft compared been
To public feasts where meet a public rout,
Where they that are without would fain go in
And they that are within would fain go out.
 'A Contention Betwixt a Wife, a Widow, and a Maid for Precedence' (1608) l. 193

14 I know my life's a pain and but a span,
I know my sense is mocked in every thing;
And to conclude, I know myself a man,
Which is a proud and yet a wretched thing.
 'Nosce Teipsum' (1599) st. 45

15 This wondrous miracle did Love devise,
For dancing is love's proper exercise.
 'Orchestra, or a Poem of Dancing' (1596) st. 18

## Scrope Davies c.1783–1852

16 Babylon in all its desolation is a sight not so awful as that of the human mind in ruins.
 Letter to Thomas Raikes, May 1835, in *A Portion of the Journal kept by Thomas Raikes* (1856) vol. 2, p. 113. Addison, in *The Spectator* no. 421 (3 July 1712), also remarked of 'a distracted person' that 'Babylon in ruins is not so melancholy a spectacle'

## W. H. Davies 1871–1940

17 And hear the pleasant cuckoo, loud and long—
The simple bird that thinks two notes a song.
 'April's Charms' (1916)

18 A rainbow and a cuckoo's song
May never come together again;
May never come
This side the tomb.
 'A Great Time' (1914)

19 It was the Rainbow gave thee birth,
And left thee all her lovely hues.
 'Kingfisher' (1910)

20 What is this life if, full of care,
We have no time to stand and stare.
 'Leisure' (1911)

21 Come, lovely Morning, rich in frost
On iron, wood and glass.
 'Silver Hours' (1932)

22 Sweet Stay-at-Home, sweet Well-content,
Thou knowest of no strange continent:
Thou hast not felt thy bosom keep
A gentle motion with the deep.
 'Sweet Stay-At-Home' (1913)

## Sammy Davis Jnr. 1925–90

23 Being a star has made it possible for me to get insulted in places where the average Negro could never *hope* to go and get insulted.
 *Yes I Can* (1965) pt. 3, ch. 23

## Thomas Davis 1814–45

1 Come in the evening, or come in the
  morning,
  Come when you're looked for, or come
  without warning.
  'The Welcome' (1846)

## Richard Dawkins 1941–

2 [Natural selection] has no vision, no
  foresight, no sight at all. If it can be said to
  play the role of watchmaker in nature, it is
  the *blind* watchmaker.
  *The Blind Watchmaker* (1986) ch. 1

3 However many ways there may be of being
  alive, it is certain that there are vastly
  more ways of being dead.
  *The Blind Watchmaker* (1986) ch. 1

4 The essence of life is statistical
  improbability on a colossal scale.
  *The Blind Watchmaker* (1986) ch. 11

## Lord Dawson of Penn 1864–1945

5 The King's life is moving peacefully
  towards its close.
  Bulletin, 20 January 1936; in K. Rose *King
  George V* (1983) ch. 10

## C. Day-Lewis 1904–72

6 It is the logic of our times,
  No subject for immortal verse—
  That we who lived by honest dreams
  Defend the bad against the worse.
  'Where are the War Poets?' (1943)

## Percy Dearmer 1867–1936

7 Jesu, good above all other,
  Gentle Child of gentle Mother,
  In a stable born our Brother,
  Give us grace to persevere.
  'Jesu, good above all other' (1906 hymn)

## Simone de Beauvoir 1908–86

8 One is not born a woman: one becomes
  one.
  *The Second Sex* (1949) vol. 2, pt. 1, ch. 1

## Eugene Victor Debs 1855–1926

9 While there is a lower class, I am in it;
  while there is a criminal element, I am of
  it; while there is a soul in prison, I am not
  free.
  Speech at his trial for sedition in Cleveland,
  Ohio, 14 September 1918; in *Liberator*
  November 1918, p. 12

## Stephen Decatur 1779–1820

10 Our country! In her intercourse with
  foreign nations, may she always be in the
  right; but our country, right or wrong.
  Toast at Norfolk, Virginia, April 1816; in A. S.
  Mackenzie *Life of Stephen Decatur* (1846) ch. 14

## Daniel Defoe 1660–1731

11 Pleasure is a *thief* to business.
  *The Complete English Tradesman* (1725) vol. 1,
  ch. 9

12 Vice came in always at the door of
  necessity, not at the door of inclination.
  *Moll Flanders* (1721, ed. G. A. Starr, 1971)
  p. 128

13 Give me not poverty lest I steal.
  *Review* vol. 8, no. 75 (15 September 1711);
  later incorporated into *Moll Flanders* (1721)

14 He told me ... that mine was the middle
  state, or what might be called the upper
  station of low life, which he had found by
  long experience was the best state in the
  world, the most suited to human
  happiness.
  *Robinson Crusoe* (1719, ed. J. D. Crowley, 1972)
  p. 4

15 My man Friday.
  *Robinson Crusoe* (1719, ed. J. D. Crowley, 1972)
  p. 207

16 Necessity makes an honest man a knave.
  *The Serious Reflections of Robinson Crusoe* (1720)
  ch. 2

17 The best of men cannot suspend their fate:
  The good die early, and the bad die late.
  'Character of the late Dr S. Annesley' (1697)

18 We loved the doctrine for the teacher's
  sake.
  'Character of the late Dr S. Annesley' (1697)

19 Actions receive their tincture from the
  times,
  And as they change are virtues made or
  crimes.
  *A Hymn to the Pillory* (1703) l. 29

20 Nature has left this tincture in the blood,
  That all men would be tyrants if they
  could.
  *The History of the Kentish Petition* (1712–13)
  addenda, l. 11

21 Fools out of favour grudge at knaves in
  place.
  *The True-Born Englishman* (1701) introduction,
  l. 7

22 Wherever God erects a house of prayer,
  The Devil always builds a chapel there;
  And 'twill be found, upon examination,
  The latter has the largest congregation.
  *The True-Born Englishman* (1701) pt. 1, l. 1.
  Cf. 28:14, 212:9

23 In their religion they are so uneven,
  That each one goes his own by-way to
  heaven.
  *The True-Born Englishman* (1701) pt. 1, l. 104

24 Your Roman-Saxon-Danish-Norman
  English.
  *The True-Born Englishman* (1701) pt. 1, l. 139

25 And of all plagues with which mankind are
  curst,
  Ecclesiastic tyranny's the worst.
  *The True-Born Englishman* (1701) pt. 2, l. 299

1 Titles are shadows, crowns are empty
   things,
   The good of subjects is the end of kings.
   *The True-Born Englishman* (1701) pt. 2, l. 315

## Edgar Degas 1834–1917

2 Art is vice. You don't marry it legitimately,
   you rape it.
   In P. Lafond *Degas* (1918) p. 140

## Charles de Gaulle 1890–1970

3 France has lost a battle. But France has not
   lost the war!
   Proclamation, 18 June 1940, in *Discours,
   messages et déclarations du Général de Gaulle*
   (1941) p. 15

4 Treaties, you see, are like girls and roses:
   they last while they last.
   Speech at Elysée Palace, 2 July 1963, in A.
   Passeron *De Gaulle parle 1962–6* (1966) p. 340

5 Authority doesn't work without prestige,
   or prestige without distance.
   *Le Fil de l'épée* (1932) 'Du caractère' sect. 2

6 The sword is the axis of the world and its
   power is absolute.
   *Vers l'armée de métier* (1934) 'Comment?'
   Commandement 3

7 How can you govern a country which has
   246 varieties of cheese?
   In E. Mignon *Les Mots du Général* (1962) p. 57

## Thomas Dekker 1570–1641

8 That great fishpond (the sea).
   *The Honest Whore* (1604) pt. 1, act 1, sc. 2

9 Honest labour bears a lovely face.
   *Patient Grissil* (1603) act 1, sc. 1

10 Golden slumbers kiss your eyes,
   Smiles awake you when you rise:
   Sleep, pretty wantons, do not cry,
   And I will sing a lullaby.
   *Patient Grissil* (1603) act 4, sc. 2

## Walter de la Mare 1873–1956

11 Ann, Ann!
   Come! quick as you can!
   There's a fish that *talks*
   In the frying-pan.
   'Alas, Alack' (1913)

12 Oh, no man knows
   Through what wild centuries
   Roves back the rose.
   'All That's Past' (1912)

13 He is crazed with the spell of far Arabia,
   They have stolen his wits away.
   'Arabia' (1912)

14 Beauty vanishes; beauty passes.
   'Epitaph' (1912)

15 Look thy last on all things lovely,
   Every hour.
   'Fare Well' (1918)

16 Nought but vast Sorrow was there —
   The sweet cheat gone.
   'The Ghost' (1918)

17 Three jolly gentlemen,
   In coats of red,
   Rode their horses
   Up to bed.
   'The Huntsmen' (1913)

18 'Is there anybody there?' said the Traveller,
   Knocking on the moonlit door.
   'The Listeners' (1912)

19 'Tell them I came, and no one answered,
   That I kept my word,' he said.
   'The Listeners' (1912)

20 And how the silence surged softly
   backward,
   When the plunging hoofs were gone.
   'The Listeners' (1912)

21 Softly along the road of evening,
   In a twilight dim with rose,
   Wrinkled with age, and drenched with
   dew,
   Old Nod, the shepherd, goes.
   'Nod' (1912)

22 Slowly, silently, now the moon
   Walks the night in her silver shoon.
   'Silver' (1913)

23 Behind the blinds I sit and watch
   The people passing—passing by;
   And not a single one can see
   My tiny watching eye.
   'The Window' (1913)

## Walter de Leon and Paul M. Jones

24 It's a funny old world—a man's lucky if he
   gets out of it alive.
   *You're Telling Me* (1934 film); spoken by W. C.
   Fields

## Jack Dempsey 1895–1983

25 Honey, I just forgot to duck.
   To his wife, on losing the World
   Heavyweight title, 23 September 1926, in J.
   and B. P. Dempsey *Dempsey* (1977) p. 202.
   After a failed attempt on his life in 1981,
   Ronald Reagan quipped 'I forgot to duck'

## Sir John Denham 1615–69

26 Youth, what man's age is like to be doth
   show;
   We may our ends by our beginnings know.
   'Of Prudence' (1668) l. 225

## Lord Denman 1779–1854

27 Trial by jury itself, instead of being a
   security to persons who are accused, will
   be a delusion, a mockery, and a snare.
   Speech in the House of Lords, 4 September
   1844; in E. W. Cox (ed.) *Reports of Cases in
   Criminal Law* (1846) vol. 1, p. 519

### John Dennis 1657–1734

1 A man who could make so vile a pun
would not scruple to pick a pocket.
*The Gentleman's Magazine* (1781) p. 324
(editorial note)

2 Damn them! They will not let my play run,
but they steal my thunder!
On hearing his new thunder effects used at
a performance of *Macbeth*, following the
withdrawal of one of his own plays after
only a short run; in W. S. Walsh *Handy-Book
of Literary Curiosities* (1893) p. 1052

### Thomas De Quincey 1785–1859

3 Oxford Street, stony-hearted stepmother,
thou that listenest to the sighs of orphans,
and drinkest the tears of children.
*Confessions of an English Opium Eater* (1822,
ed. 1856) pt. 1

4 A duller spectacle this earth of ours has
not to show than a rainy Sunday in
London.
*Confessions of an English Opium Eater* (1822,
ed. 1856) pt. 2

5 Murder considered as one of the fine arts.
*Blackwood's Magazine* February 1827 (essay
title)

### Edward Stanley, 14th Earl of Derby 1799–1869

6 The duty of an Opposition [is] very simple
. . . to oppose everything, and propose
nothing.
Quoting 'Mr Tierney, a great Whig
authority', in *Hansard* 4 June 1841, col. 1188

7 Meddle and muddle.
Summarizing Earl Russell's foreign policy, in
Speech on the Address, *Hansard* (Lords)
4 February 1864, col. 28

### René Descartes 1596–1650

8 Common sense is the best distributed
commodity in the world, for every man is
convinced that he is well supplied with it.
*Le Discours de la méthode* (1637) pt. 1

9 *Cogito, ergo sum.*
I think, therefore I am.
*Le Discours de la méthode* (1637) pt. 4

### Philippe Néricault Destouches 1680–1754

10 The absent are always in the wrong.
*L'Obstacle imprévu* (1717) act 1, sc. 6

### Robert Devereux, Earl of Essex

*See* ESSEX

### Bernard De Voto 1897–1955

11 The proper union of gin and vermouth is a
great and sudden glory; it is one of the
happiest marriages on earth, and one of
the shortest lived.
*Harper's Magazine* December 1949, p. 70

### Peter De Vries 1910–

12 The value of marriage is not that adults
produce children but that children produce
adults.
*The Tunnel of Love* (1954) ch. 8

### Sir James Dewar 1842–1923

13 Minds are like parachutes. They only
function when they are open.
Attributed

### Lord Dewar 1864–1930

14 [There are] only two classes of pedestrians
in these days of reckless motor traffic—the
quick, and the dead.
In George Robey *Looking Back on Life* (1933)
ch. 28

### Sergei Diaghilev 1872–1929

15 *Étonne-moi.*
Astonish me.
To Jean Cocteau, in W. Fowlie (ed.) *Journals of
Jean Cocteau* (1956) ch. 1

### Porfirio Diaz 1830–1915

16 Poor Mexico, so far from God and so close
to the United States.
Attributed

### Charles Dibdin 1745–1814

17 Did you ever hear of Captain Wattle?
He was all for love, and a little for the
bottle.
'Captain Wattle and Miss Roe' (1797)

18 In every mess I finds a friend,
In every port a wife.
'Jack in his Element' (1790)

19 Here, a sheer hulk, lies poor Tom Bowling,
The darling of our crew.
'Tom Bowling' (1790)

### Thomas Dibdin 1771–1841

20 Oh! what a snug little Island,
A right little, tight little Island!
'The Snug Little Island' (1833)

### Charles Dickens 1812–70

21 There are strings . . . in the human heart
that had better not be wibrated.
*Barnaby Rudge* (1841) ch. 22 (Mr Tappertit)

1 Jarndyce and Jarndyce still drags its dreary length before the Court, perennially hopeless.
   *Bleak House* (1853) ch. 1

2 This is a London particular ... A fog, miss.
   *Bleak House* (1853) ch. 3

3 'It is,' says Chadband, 'the ray of rays, the sun of suns, the moon of moons, the star of stars. It is the light of Terewth.'
   *Bleak House* (1853) ch. 25

4 The one great principle of the English law is, to make business for itself.
   *Bleak House* (1853) ch. 39

5 O let us love our occupations,
   Bless the squire and his relations,
   Live upon our daily rations,
   And always know our proper stations.
   *The Chimes* (1844) 'The Second Quarter'

6 'Bah,' said Scrooge. 'Humbug!'
   *A Christmas Carol* (1843) stave 1

7 'God bless us every one!' said Tiny Tim, the last of all.
   *A Christmas Carol* (1843) stave 3

8 I am a lone lorn creetur ... and everythink goes contrary with me.
   *David Copperfield* (1850) ch. 3 (Mrs Gummidge)

9 Barkis is willin'.
   *David Copperfield* (1850) ch. 5

10 I live on broken wittles—and I sleep on the coals.
   *David Copperfield* (1850) ch. 5 (The Waiter)

11 I have known him come home to supper with a flood of tears, and a declaration that nothing was now left but a jail; and go to bed making a calculation of the expense of putting bow-windows to the house, 'in case anything turned up,' which was his favourite expression.
   *David Copperfield* (1850) ch. 11 (of Mr Micawber)

12 Annual income twenty pounds, annual expenditure nineteen nineteen six, result happiness. Annual income twenty pounds, annual expenditure twenty pounds ought and six, result misery.
   *David Copperfield* (1850) ch. 12 (Mr Micawber)

13 We live in a numble abode.
   *David Copperfield* (1850) ch. 16 (Uriah Heep)

14 We are so very 'umble.
   *David Copperfield* (1850) ch. 17 (Uriah Heep)

15 I only ask for information.
   *David Copperfield* (1850) ch. 20 (Miss Rosa Dartle)

16 Accidents will occur in the best-regulated families.
   *David Copperfield* (1850) ch. 28 (Mr Micawber)

17 It's only my child-wife.
   *David Copperfield* (1850) ch. 44 (of Dora)

18 I'm Gormed—and I can't say no fairer than that!
   *David Copperfield* (1850) ch. 63 (Mr Peggotty)

19 None of your live languages for Miss Blimber. They must be dead—stone dead—and then Miss Blimber dug them up like a Ghoul.
   *Dombey and Son* (1848) ch. 11

20 In the Proverbs of Solomon you will find the following words, 'May we never want a friend in need, nor a bottle to give him!' When found, make a note of.
   *Dombey and Son* (1848) ch. 15 (Captain Cuttle)

21 If you could see my legs when I take my boots off, you'd form some idea of what unrequited affection is.
   *Dombey and Son* (1848) ch. 48 (Mr Toots)

22 'He calls the knaves, Jacks, this boy,' said Estella with disdain.
   *Great Expectations* (1861) ch. 8

23 In the little world in which children have their existence, whosoever brings them up, there is nothing so finely perceived and so finely felt, as injustice.
   *Great Expectations* (1861) ch. 8

24 Her bringing me up by hand, gave her no right to bring me up by jerks.
   *Great Expectations* (1861) ch. 8

25 It is a most miserable thing to feel ashamed of home.
   *Great Expectations* (1861) ch. 14

26 On the Rampage, Pip, and off the Rampage, Pip; such is Life!
   *Great Expectations* (1861) ch. 15 (Joe Gargery)

27 Now, what I want is, Facts ... Facts alone are wanted in life.
   *Hard Times* (1854) bk. 1, ch. 1 (Mr Gradgrind)

28 People mutht be amuthed.
   *Hard Times* (1854) bk. 3, ch. 8 (Mr Sleary)

29 Whatever was required to be done, the Circumlocution Office was beforehand with all the public departments in the art of perceiving—HOW NOT TO DO IT.
   *Little Dorrit* (1857) bk. 1, ch. 10

30 I revere the memory of Mr F. as an estimable man and most indulgent husband, only necessary to mention Asparagus and it appeared or to hint at any little delicate thing to drink and it came like magic in a pint bottle it was not ecstasy but it was comfort.
   *Little Dorrit* (1857) bk. 1, ch. 24 (Flora Finching)

31 As to marriage on the part of a man, my dear, Society requires that he should retrieve his fortunes by marriage. Society requires that he should gain by marriage. Society requires that he should found a handsome establishment by marriage. Society does not see, otherwise, what he has to do with marriage.
   *Little Dorrit* (1857) bk. 1, ch. 33 (Mrs Merdle)

1 Father is rather vulgar, my dear. The word
Papa, besides, gives a pretty form to the
lips. Papa, potatoes, poultry, prunes, and
prism, are all very good words for the lips:
especially prunes and prism.
*Little Dorrit* (1857) bk. 2, ch. 5 (Mrs General)

2 Affection beaming in one eye, and
calculation shining out of the other.
*Martin Chuzzlewit* (1844) ch. 8 (Mrs Todgers)

3 Here's the rule for bargains: 'Do other
men, for they would do you.' That's the
true business precept.
*Martin Chuzzlewit* (1844) ch. 11 (Jonas
Chuzzlewit)

4 Brought reg'lar and draw'd mild.
*Martin Chuzzlewit* (1844) ch. 25 (Mrs Gamp on
her 'half a pint of porter')

5 He'd make a lovely corpse.
*Martin Chuzzlewit* (1844) ch. 25 (Mrs Gamp)

6 We never knows wot's hidden in each
other's hearts; and if we had glass winders
there, we'd need keep the shutters up,
some on us, I do assure you!
*Martin Chuzzlewit* (1844) ch. 29 (Mrs Gamp)

7 Howls the sublime, and softly sleeps the
calm Ideal, in the whispering chambers of
Imagination.
*Martin Chuzzlewit* (1844) ch. 34

8 His 'owls was organs.
*Martin Chuzzlewit* (1844) ch. 49 (Mrs Gamp)

9 The words she spoke of Mrs Harris, lambs
could not forgive ... nor worms forget.
*Martin Chuzzlewit* (1844) ch. 49 (Mrs Gamp)

10 EDUCATION.—At Mr Wackford Squeers's
Academy, Dotheboys Hall, at the delightful
village of Dotheboys, near Greta Bridge in
Yorkshire, Youth are boarded, clothed,
booked, furnished with pocket-money,
provided with all necessaries, instructed in
all languages living and dead ... Terms,
twenty guineas per annum. No extras, no
vacations, and diet unparalleled.
*Nicholas Nickleby* (1839) ch. 3

11 He had but one eye, and the popular
prejudice runs in favour of two.
*Nicholas Nickleby* (1839) ch. 4 (Mr Squeers)

12 Here's richness!
*Nicholas Nickleby* (1839) ch. 5 (Mr Squeers)

13 C-l-e-a-n, clean, verb active, to make bright,
to scour. W-i-n, win, d-e-r, der, winder, a
casement. When the boy knows this out of
the book, he goes and does it.
*Nicholas Nickleby* (1839) ch. 8 (Mr Squeers)

14 As she frequently remarked when she
made any such mistake, it would be all the
same a hundred years hence.
*Nicholas Nickleby* (1839) ch. 9 (Mrs Squeers)

15 There are only two styles of portrait
painting; the serious and the smirk.
*Nicholas Nickleby* (1839) ch. 10 (Miss La Creevy)

16 Language was not powerful enough to
describe the infant phenomenon.
*Nicholas Nickleby* (1839) ch. 23

17 All is gas and gaiters.
*Nicholas Nickleby* (1839) ch. 49 (The Gentleman
in the Small-clothes)

18 Please, sir, I want some more.
*Oliver Twist* (1838) ch. 2 (Oliver)

19 I only know two sorts of boys. Mealy boys,
and beef-faced boys.
*Oliver Twist* (1838) ch. 14 (Mr Grimwig)

20 'If the law supposes that ... the law is a
ass—a idiot.'
*Oliver Twist* (1838) ch. 51 (Bumble). Cf. 94:18

21 A literary man—*with* a wooden leg.
*Our Mutual Friend* (1865) bk. 1, ch. 5 (Mr
Boffin, of Silas Wegg)

22 There is in the Englishman a combination
of qualities, a modesty, an independence, a
responsibility, a repose, combined with an
absence of everything calculated to call a
blush into the cheek of a young person,
which one would seek in vain among the
Nations of the Earth.
*Our Mutual Friend* (1865) bk. 1, ch. 11 (Mr
Podsnap)

23 A slap-up gal in a bang-up chariot.
*Our Mutual Friend* (1865) bk. 2, ch. 8

24 He'd be sharper than a serpent's tooth, if
he wasn't as dull as ditch water.
*Our Mutual Friend* (1865) bk. 3, ch. 10 (Fanny
Cleaver)

25 I want to be something so much worthier
than the doll in the doll's house.
*Our Mutual Friend* (1865) bk. 4, ch. 5 (Bella)

26 Kent, sir—everybody knows Kent—apples,
cherries, hops, and women.
*Pickwick Papers* (1837) ch. 2 (Jingle)

27 I wants to make your flesh creep.
*Pickwick Papers* (1837) ch. 8 (The Fat Boy)

28 'It's always best on these occasions to do
what the mob do.' 'But suppose there are
two mobs?' suggested Mr Snodgrass. 'Shout
with the largest,' replied Mr Pickwick.
*Pickwick Papers* (1837) ch. 13

29 Battledore and shuttlecock's a wery good
game, vhen you an't the shuttlecock and
two lawyers the battledores, in which case
it gets too excitin' to be pleasant.
*Pickwick Papers* (1837) ch. 20 (Mr Weller)

30 Poverty and oysters always seem to go
together.
*Pickwick Papers* (1837) ch. 22 (Sam Weller)

31 Dumb as a drum vith a hole in it, sir.
*Pickwick Papers* (1837) ch. 25 (Sam Weller)

32 A double glass o' the inwariable.
*Pickwick Papers* (1837) ch. 33 (Mr Weller)

33 'Do you spell it with a "V" or a "W"?' ...
'That depends upon the taste and fancy of
the speller, my Lord.'
*Pickwick Papers* (1837) ch. 34 (Sam Weller)

34 'You must not tell us what the soldier, or
any other man, said, sir,' interposed the
judge; 'it's not evidence.'
*Pickwick Papers* (1837) ch. 34

1 A good uniform must work its way with
the women, sooner or later.
*Pickwick Papers* (1837) ch. 37 (The Gentleman
in Blue)

2 'And a bird-cage, sir,' says Sam. 'Veels
vithin veels, a prison in a prison.'
*Pickwick Papers* (1837) ch. 40

3 The have-his-carcase, next to the perpetual
motion, is vun of the blessedest things as
wos ever made.
*Pickwick Papers* (1837) ch. 43 (Sam Weller)

4 'Never ... see ... a dead postboy, did you?'
inquired Sam ... 'No,' rejoined Bob, 'I never
did.' 'No!' rejoined Sam triumphantly. 'Nor
never vill; and there's another thing that
no man never see, and that's a dead
donkey.'
*Pickwick Papers* (1837) ch. 51

5 Minerva House ... where some twenty girls
... acquired a smattering of everything,
and a knowledge of nothing.
*Sketches by Boz* (1839) Tales, ch. 3 'Sentiment'

6 It was the best of times, it was the worst
of times.
*A Tale of Two Cities* (1859) bk. 1, ch. 1

7 It is a far, far better thing that I do, than I
have ever done; it is a far, far better rest
that I go to, than I have ever known.
*A Tale of Two Cities* (1859) bk. 3, ch. 15

## Emily Dickinson 1830–86

8 After great pain, a formal feeling comes.
Title of poem (1862)

9 Because I could not stop for Death—
He kindly stopped for me—
The Carriage held but just Ourselves—
And Immortality.
'Because I could not stop for Death' (c.1863)

10 The Bustle in a House
The Morning after Death
Is solemnest of industries
Enacted upon Earth—

The Sweeping up the Heart
And putting Love away
We shall not want to use again
Until Eternity.
'The Bustle in a House' (c.1866)

11 My life closed twice before its close;
It yet remains to see
If Immortality unveil
A third event to me.
'My life closed twice before its close'

12 Parting is all we know of heaven,
And all we need of hell.
'My life closed twice before its close'

13 Success is counted sweetest
By those who ne'er succeed.
To comprehend a nectar
Requires sorest need.
'Success is counted sweetest' (1859)

14 There's a certain Slant of light,
Winter Afternoons—
That oppresses like the Heft
Of Cathedral Tunes.
'There's a certain Slant of light' (c.1861)

15 They shut me up in prose—
As when a little girl
They put me in the closet—
Because they liked me 'still'.
'They shut me up in prose' (c.1862)

16 This is my letter to the world.
Title of poem (c.1862)

17 This quiet Dust was Gentlemen and Ladies
And Lads and Girls—
Was laughter and ability and Sighing
And Frocks and Curls.
'This quiet Dust was Gentlemen and Ladies'
(c.1864)

## John Dickinson 1732–1808

18 By uniting we stand, by dividing we fall.
'The Liberty Song' (1768), in *Writings of John
Dickinson* vol. 1 (1895) p. 421

## Paul Dickson 1939–

19 Rowe's Rule: the odds are five to six that
the light at the end of the tunnel is the
headlight of an oncoming train.
*Washingtonian* November 1978. Cf. 211:18

## Denis Diderot 1713–84

20 *L'esprit de l'escalier.*
Staircase wit.
The witty riposte one thinks of only when
one has left the drawing-room and is already
on the way downstairs; in *Paradoxe sur le
Comédien* (written 1773–8)

## Joan Didion 1934–

21 Was there ever in anyone's life span a
point free in time, devoid of memory, a
night when choice was any more than the
sum of all the choices gone before?
*Run River* (1963) ch. 4

## Wentworth Dillon, Earl of Roscommon c.1633–1685

22 Choose an author as you choose a friend.
*Essay on Translated Verse* (1684) l. 96

23 Immodest words admit of no defence,
For want of decency is want of sense.
*Essay on Translated Verse* (1684) l. 113

24 The multitude is always in the wrong.
*Essay on Translated Verse* (1684) l. 183

## Ernest Dimnet

25 Architecture, of all the arts, is the one
which acts the most slowly, but the most
surely, on the soul.
*What We Live By* (1932) pt. 2, ch. 12

## Isak Dinesen (Karen Blixen)
### 1885–1962

1 A herd of elephant ... pacing along as if
they had an appointment at the end of the
world.
*Out of Africa* (1937) pt. 1, ch. 1

2 What is man, when you come to think
upon him, but a minutely set, ingenious
machine for turning, with infinite
artfulness, the red wine of Shiraz into
urine?
*Seven Gothic Tales* (1934) 'The Dreamers'

## Diogenes *c.*400–*c.*325 BC

3 Alexander ... asked him if he lacked
anything. 'Yes,' said he, 'that I do: that you
stand out of my sun a little.'
Plutarch *Parallel Lives* 'Alexander' ch. 14,
sect. 4 (tr. T. North, 1579)

## Dionysius of Halicarnassus
### fl. 30–7 BC

4 History is philosophy from examples.
*Ars Rhetorica* ch. 11, sect. 2

## Benjamin Disraeli 1804–81

5 Though I sit down now, the time will come
when you will hear me.
Maiden speech in the House of Commons;
*Hansard* 7 December 1837, col. 807

6 The Continent will [not] suffer England to
be the workshop of the world.
Speech, *Hansard* 15 March 1838, col. 940

7 Thus you have a starving population, an
absentee aristocracy, and an alien Church,
and in addition the weakest executive in
the world. That is the Irish Question.
Speech, *Hansard* 16 February 1844, col. 1016

8 The noble Lord is the Prince Rupert of
Parliamentary discussion.
Speech, *Hansard* 24 April 1844, col. 248 (of
Lord Stanley). Cf. 78:9

9 The right hon. Gentleman caught the
Whigs bathing, and walked away with
their clothes.
Speech, *Hansard* 28 February 1845, col. 154
(on Sir Robert Peel's abandoning protection
in favour of free trade, traditionally the
policy of the [Whig] Opposition)

10 Protection is not a principle, but an
expedient.
Speech, *Hansard* 17 March 1845, col. 1023

11 A Conservative Government is an
organized hypocrisy.
Speech, *Hansard* 17 March 1845, col. 1028

12 Justice is truth in action.
Speech, *Hansard* 11 February 1851, col. 412

13 England does not love coalitions.
Speech, *Hansard* 16 December 1852, col. 1666

14 Party is organized opinion.
Speech at Oxford, 25 November 1864, in *The
Times* 26 November 1864

15 Is man an ape or an angel? Now I am on
the side of the angels.
Speech at Oxford, 25 November 1864, in *The
Times* 26 November 1864

16 You behold a range of exhausted volcanoes.
Speaking of the Treasury Bench at
Manchester, 3 April 1872; in *The Times* 4 April
1872. Cf. 81:1

17 Cosmopolitan critics, men who are the
friends of every country save their own.
Speech at Guildhall, 9 November 1877, in *The
Times* 10 November 1877. Cf. 89:11, 243:8

18 Lord Salisbury and myself have brought
you back peace—but a peace I hope with
honour.
Speech on returning from the Congress of
Berlin, 16 July 1878, in *The Times* 17 July
1878. Cf. 94:2, 265:6

19 A series of congratulatory regrets.
Describing Lord Harrington's Resolution on
the Berlin Treaty, 27 July 1878; in *The Times*
29 July 1878

20 A sophistical rhetorician, inebriated with
the exuberance of his own verbosity.
Of Gladstone, in *The Times* 29 July 1878

21 One of the greatest of Romans, when asked
what were his politics, replied, *Imperium et
Libertas*. That would not make a bad
programme for a British Ministry.
Speech, 10 November 1879, paraphrasing
Tacitus *Agricola* ch. 3. See *Notes and Queries*
(8th series) vol. 10, p. 453

22 The key of India is London.
Speech, *Hansard* 4 March 1881, col. 299

23 No Government can be long secure
without a formidable Opposition.
*Coningsby* (1844) bk. 2, ch. 1

24 A government of statesmen or of clerks?
Of Humbug or Humdrum?
*Coningsby* (1844) bk. 2, ch. 4

25 'A sound Conservative government,' said
Taper, musingly. 'I understand: Tory men
and Whig measures.'
*Coningsby* (1844) bk. 2, ch. 6

26 Youth is a blunder; Manhood a struggle;
Old Age a regret.
*Coningsby* (1844) bk. 3, ch. 1

27 It seems to me a barren thing this
Conservatism—an unhappy cross-breed,
the mule of politics that engenders
nothing.
*Coningsby* (1844) bk. 3, ch. 5

28 Read no history: nothing but biography,
for that is life without theory.
*Contarini Fleming* (1832) pt. 1, ch. 23.
Cf. 136:22

29 His Christianity was muscular.
*Endymion* (1880) ch. 14

1 Said Waldershare, 'Sensible men are all of the same religion.' 'And pray what is that?' ... 'Sensible men never tell.'
*Endymion* (1880) ch. 81. Cf. 270:20

2 The sweet simplicity of the three per cents.
*Endymion* (1880) ch. 91. Cf. 318:9

3 Time is the great physician.
*Henrietta Temple* (1837) bk. 6, ch. 9

4 The blue ribbon of the turf.
*Lord George Bentinck* (1852) ch. 26 (of the Derby)

5 London: a nation, not a city.
*Lothair* (1870) ch. 27

6 'Two nations; between whom there is no intercourse and no sympathy; who are as ignorant of each other's habits, thoughts, and feelings, as if they were dwellers in different zones, or inhabitants of different planets ... ' 'You speak of—' said Egremont, hesitatingly, 'THE RICH AND THE POOR.'
*Sybil* (1845) bk. 2, ch. 5. Cf. 144:8

7 That fatal drollery called a representative government.
*Tancred* (1847) bk. 2, ch. 13

8 The East is a career.
*Tancred* (1847) bk. 2, ch. 14

9 Experience is the child of Thought, and Thought is the child of Action. We cannot learn men from books.
*Vivian Grey* (1826) bk. 5, ch. 1

10 All power is a trust.
*Vivian Grey* (1826) bk. 6, ch. 7

11 'The age of chivalry is past,' said May Dacre. 'Bores have succeeded to dragons.'
*The Young Duke* (1831) bk. 2, ch. 5

12 We came here for fame.
To John Bright, in the House of Commons; in R. Blake *Disraeli* (1966) ch. 4

13 The school of Manchester.
Describing the free trade politics of Cobden and Bright; in R. Blake *Disraeli* (1966) ch. 10

14 I will not go down to posterity talking bad grammar.
Correcting proofs of his last Parliamentary speech, 31 March 1881; in R. Blake *Disraeli* (1966) ch. 32

15 Damn your principles! Stick to your party.
Attributed to Disraeli and believed to have been said to Edward Bulwer-Lytton; in E. Latham *Famous Sayings and their Authors* (1904) p. 11

16 Pray remember, Mr Dean, no dogma, no Dean.
In Monypenny and Buckle *Life of Disraeli* vol. 4 (1916) ch. 10

17 I have climbed to the top of the greasy pole.
On becoming Prime Minister, in Monypenny and Buckle *Life of Disraeli* vol. 4 (1916) ch. 16

18 I am dead; dead, but in the Elysian fields.
To a peer, on his elevation to the House of Lords; in Monypenny and Buckle *Life of Disraeli* vol. 5 (1920) ch. 13

19 Never complain and never explain.
In J. Morley *Life of Gladstone* (1903) vol. 1, p. 123. Cf. 139:24, 175:13

20 Everyone likes flattery; and when you come to Royalty you should lay it on with a trowel.
To Matthew Arnold, in G. W. E. Russell *Collections and Recollections* (1898) ch. 23

21 There are three kinds of lies: lies, damned lies and statistics.
Attributed to Disraeli in Mark Twain *Autobiography* (1924) vol. 1, p. 246

22 She would only ask me to take a message to Albert.
On his death-bed, declining the proposal of a visit from Queen Victoria; in R. Blake *Disraeli* (1966) ch. 32

## Isaac D'Israeli 1766–1848

23 He wreathed the rod of criticism with roses.
*Curiosities of Literature* (9th ed., 1834) vol. 1, p. 20 (of Pierre Bayle)

## William Chatterton Dix 1837–98

24 As with gladness men of old
Did the guiding star behold,
As with joy they hailed its light,
Leading onward, beaming bright.
'As with gladness men of old' (1861 hymn)

## Henry Austin Dobson 1840–1921

25 All passes. Art alone
Enduring stays to us;
The Bust outlasts the throne,—
The Coin, Tiberius.
'Ars Victrix' (1876); translation of Théophile Gautier's 'L'Art'

26 Fame is a food that dead men eat,—
I have no stomach for such meat.
'Fame is a Food' (1906)

27 The ladies of St James's!
They're painted to the eyes;
Their white it stays for ever,
Their red it never dies.
'The Ladies of St James's' (1883)

28 Time goes, you say? Ah no!
Alas, Time stays, *we* go.
'The Paradox of Time' (1877)

## Ken Dodd 1931–

29 The trouble with Freud is that he never had to play the old Glasgow Empire on a Saturday night after Rangers and Celtic had both lost.
*Guardian* 30 April 1991, p. 19 (quoted in many forms since the mid-1960s)

## Philip Doddridge 1702–51

30 Ye servants of the Lord,
Each in his office wait,
Observant of his heavenly word
And watchful at his gate.
*Hymns* (1755) 'The active Christian'

## Aelius Donatus 4th century

1 Confound those who have said our
remarks before us.

> In St Jerome *Commentary on Ecclesiastes* bk 1;
> J.-P. Migne *Patrologiae Latinae* vol. 23, col. 1019

## J. P. Donleavy 1926–

2 When you don't have any money, the
problem is food. When you have money,
it's sex. When you have both, it's health.

> *The Ginger Man* (1955) ch. 5

## John Donne 1572–1631

3 Love built on beauty, soon as beauty, dies.

> *Elegies* 'The Anagram' (c.1595)

4 Whoever loves, if he do not propose
The right true end of love, he's one that
goes
To sea for nothing but to make him sick.

> *Elegies* 'Love's Progress' (c.1600)

5 Our first strange and fatal interview.

> *Elegies* 'On His Mistress' (c.1600)

6 Licence my roving hands, and let them go,
Behind, before, above, between, below.
O my America, my new found land,
My kingdom, safeliest when with one man
manned.

> *Elegies* 'To His Mistress Going to Bed' (c.1595)

7 At the round earth's imagined corners,
blow
Your trumpets, angels, and arise, arise
From death, you numberless infinities
Of souls, and to your scattered bodies go.

> *Holy Sonnets* (1609) no. 4 (ed. J. Carey, 1990)

8 Death be not proud, though some have
called thee
Mighty and dreadful, for thou art not so.

> *Holy Sonnets* (1609) no. 6 (ed. J. Carey, 1990)

9 One short sleep past, we wake eternally,
And death shall be no more; Death thou
shalt die.

> *Holy Sonnets* (1609) no. 6 (ed. J. Carey, 1990)

10 Batter my heart, three-personed God; for,
you
As yet but knock, breathe, shine, and seek
to mend.

> *Holy Sonnets* (after 1609) no. 10 (ed. J. Carey, 1990)

11 Take me to you, imprison me, for I
Except you enthral me, never shall be free,
Nor ever chaste, except you ravish me.

> *Holy Sonnets* (after 1609) no. 10 (ed. J. Carey, 1990)

12 I am a little world made cunningly
Of elements, and an angelic sprite.

> *Holy Sonnets* (after 1609) no. 15 (ed. J. Carey, 1990)

13 What if this present were the world's last
night?

> *Holy Sonnets* (after 1609) no. 19 (ed. J. Carey, 1990)

14         As thou
Art jealous, Lord, so I am jealous now,
Thou lov'st not, till from loving more, thou
free
My soul; who ever gives, takes liberty.

> 'A Hymn to Christ, at the Author's last going
> into Germany' (1619)

15 Seal then this bill of my divorce to all.

> 'A Hymn to Christ, at the Author's last going
> into Germany' (1619)

16 Since I am coming to that holy room,
Where, with thy choir of saints for
evermore,
I shall be made thy music; as I come
I tune the instrument here at the door,
And what I must do then, think now
before.

> 'Hymn to God my God, in my Sickness'
> (1623)

17 Wilt thou forgive that sin where I begun,
Which is my sin, though it were done
before?
Wilt thou forgive those sins, through
which I run
And do them still: though still I do
deplore?
When thou hast done, thou hast not done,
For, I have more.

> 'A Hymn to God the Father' (1623)

18 Immensity cloistered in thy dear womb,
Now leaves his well-beloved imprisonment.

> *La Corona* (1609) 'Nativity'

19 Think then, my soul, that death is but a
groom,
Which brings a taper to the outward room.

> *Of the Progress of the Soul: The Second
> Anniversary* (1612) l. 85

20 Nature's great masterpiece, an elephant,
The only harmless great thing.

> 'The Progress of the Soul' (1601) st. 39

21         Just such disparity
As is 'twixt air and angels' purity,
'Twixt women's love, and men's will ever
be.

> *Songs and Sonnets* 'Air and Angels'

22 All other things, to their destruction draw,
Only our love hath no decay;
This, no tomorrow hath, nor yesterday,
Running it never runs from us away,
But truly keeps his first, last, everlasting
day.

> *Songs and Sonnets* 'The Anniversary'

23 Come live with me, and be my love,
And we will some new pleasures prove
Of golden sands, and crystal brooks,
With silken lines, and silver hooks.

> *Songs and Sonnets* 'The Bait'. Cf. 219:3, 253:20

24 For God's sake hold your tongue, and let
me love.

> *Songs and Sonnets* 'The Canonization'

1 Dear love, for nothing less than thee
Would I have broke this happy dream,
It was a theme
For reason, much too strong for fantasy.
*Songs and Sonnets* 'The Dream' ('Dear love, for
nothing less than thee')

2 Where, like a pillow on a bed,
A pregnant bank swelled up, to rest
The violet's reclining head,
Sat we two, one another's best.
*Songs and Sonnets* 'The Ecstasy'

3 But O alas, so long, so far
Our bodies why do we forbear?
They're ours, though they're not we, we
are
The intelligencies, they the sphere.
*Songs and Sonnets* 'The Ecstasy'

4 So must pure lovers' souls descend
T'affections, and to faculties,
Which sense may reach and apprehend,
Else a great prince in prison lies.
*Songs and Sonnets* 'The Ecstasy'

5 I wonder by my troth, what thou, and I
Did, till we loved, were we not weaned till
then?
But sucked on country pleasures,
childishly?
Or snorted we in the seven sleepers den?
*Songs and Sonnets* 'The Good-Morrow'

6 Love is a growing or full constant light;
And his first minute, after noon, is night.
*Songs and Sonnets* 'A Lecture in the Shadow'

7 'Tis the year's midnight, and it is the day's.
*Songs and Sonnets* 'A Nocturnal upon St Lucy's
Day'

8 The world's whole sap is sunk:
The general balm th'hydroptic earth hath
drunk.
*Songs and Sonnets* 'A Nocturnal upon St Lucy's
Day'

9 When my grave is broke up again
Some second guest to entertain,
(For graves have learnt that woman-head
To be to more than one a bed)
And he that digs it, spies
A bracelet of bright hair about the bone,
Will he not let us alone?
*Songs and Sonnets* 'The Relic'

10 Go, and catch a falling star,
Get with child a mandrake root,
Tell me, where all past years are,
Or who cleft the Devil's foot.
*Songs and Sonnets* 'Song: Go and catch a
falling star'

11 Busy old fool, unruly sun,
Why dost thou thus,
Through windows, and through curtains
call on us?
*Songs and Sonnets* 'The Sun Rising'

12 Love, all alike, no season knows, nor clime,
Nor hours, days, months, which are the
rags of time.
*Songs and Sonnets* 'The Sun Rising'

13 This bed thy centre is, these walls thy
sphere.
*Songs and Sonnets* 'The Sun Rising'

14 I am two fools, I know,
For loving, and for saying so
In whining poetry.
*Songs and Sonnets* 'The Triple Fool'

15 So let us melt, and make no noise,
No tear-floods, nor sigh-tempests move,
'Twere profanation of our joys
To tell the laity our love.
*Songs and Sonnets* 'A Valediction: forbidding
mourning'

16          O more than moon,
Draw not up seas to drown me in thy
sphere,
Weep me not dead, in thine arms, but
forbear
To teach the sea what it may do too soon.
*Songs and Sonnets* 'A Valediction: of Weeping'

17 Sir, more than kisses, letters mingle souls.
'To Sir Henry Wotton' (1597–8)

18 But I do nothing upon my self, and yet I
am mine own *Executioner*.
*Devotions upon Emergent Occasions* (1624)
'Meditation XII'

19 No man is an Island, entire of it self.
*Devotions upon Emergent Occasions* (1624)
'Meditation XVII'

20 Any man's death diminishes me, because I
am involved in Mankind; And therefore
never send to know for whom the bell
tolls; it tolls for thee.
*Devotions upon Emergent Occasions* (1624)
'Meditation XVII'

21 I throw myself down in my Chamber, and I
call in, and invite God, and his Angels
thither, and when they are there, I neglect
God and his Angels, for the noise of a fly,
for the rattling of a coach, for the whining
of a door.
*LXXX Sermons* (1640) 12 December 1626 'At
the Funeral of Sir William Cokayne'

22 Poor intricated soul! Riddling, perplexed,
labyrinthical soul!
*LXXX Sermons* (1640) 25 January 1628/9

23 John Donne, Anne Donne, Un-done.
In a letter to his wife, on being dismissed
from the service of his father-in-law, Sir
George More; in Izaak Walton *Life of Dr Donne*
(first printed in *LXXX Sermons*, 1640)

## Sir Reginald Dorman-Smith
1899–1977

24 Dig for victory
Radio broadcast as Minister of Agriculture
and Fisheries, 3 October 1939; in *The Times*
4 October 1939

## Fedor Dostoevsky 1821–81

1 If you were to destroy in mankind the belief in immortality, not only love but every living force maintaining the life of the world would at once be dried up.
*The Brothers Karamazov* (1879–80) bk. 2, ch. 6

2 Beauty is mysterious as well as terrible. God and devil are fighting there, and the battlefield is the heart of man.
*The Brothers Karamazov* (1879–80) bk. 3, ch. 3

3 If the devil doesn't exist, but man has created him, he has created him in his own image and likeness.
*The Brothers Karamazov* (1879–80) bk. 5, ch. 4

4 Too high a price is asked for harmony; it's beyond our means to pay so much to enter. And so I hasten to give back my entrance ticket ... It's not God that I don't accept, Alyosha, only I most respectfully return Him the ticket.
*The Brothers Karamazov* (1879–80) bk. 5, ch. 4

5 Money is coined liberty.
*House of the Dead* (1862) pt. 1, ch. 1 (tr. Constance Garnett)

## Lord Alfred Douglas 1870–1945

6 I am the Love that dare not speak its name.
'Two Loves' (1896)

## James Douglas, 4th Earl of Morton *c*.1516–81

7 Here lies he who neither feared nor flattered any flesh.
Of John Knox, said as he was buried, 26 November 1572; in G. R. Preedy *Life of John Knox* (1940) ch. 7

## Keith Douglas 1920–44

8 And all my endeavours are unlucky explorers
come back, abandoning the expedition.
'On Return from Egypt, 1943–4' (1946)

9 Remember me when I am dead
And simplify me when I'm dead.
'Simplify me when I'm Dead' (1941)

10 For here the lover and killer are mingled
who had one body and one heart.
And death, who had the soldier singled
has done the lover mortal hurt.
'Vergissmeinnicht, 1943'

## Lorenzo Dow 1777–1834

11 You will be damned if you do—And you will be damned if you don't.
*Reflections on the Love of God* (1836) ch. 6 (on 'the doctrine of Particular Election')

## Ernest Dowson 1867–1900

12 I have forgot much, Cynara! gone with the wind,
Flung roses, roses, riotously, with the throng,
Dancing, to put thy pale, lost lilies out of mind;
But I was desolate and sick of an old passion,
Yea, all the time, because the dance was long:
I have been faithful to thee, Cynara! in my fashion.
'Non Sum Qualis Eram' (1896). Cf. 173:30

13 They are not long, the days of wine and roses.
'Vitae Summa Brevis' (1896)

## Sir Arthur Conan Doyle 1859–1930

14 Singularity is almost invariably a clue. The more featureless and commonplace a crime is, the more difficult is it to bring it home.
*Adventures of Sherlock Holmes* (1892) 'The Boscombe Valley Mystery'

15 It is quite a three-pipe problem.
*Adventures of Sherlock Holmes* (1892) 'The Red-Headed League'

16 You see, but you do not observe.
*The Adventures of Sherlock Holmes* (1892) 'Scandal in Bohemia'

17 Matilda Briggs ... was a ship which is associated with the giant rat of Sumatra, a story for which the world is not yet prepared.
*Case-Book of Sherlock Homes* (1927) 'The Sussex Vampire'

18 Good old Watson! You are the one fixed point in a changing age.
*His Last Bow* (1917) title story

19 'Excellent,' I cried. 'Elementary,' said he.
*Memoirs of Sherlock Holmes* (1894) 'The Crooked Man'. 'Elementary, my dear Watson' is not found in any book by Conan Doyle, although a review of the film *The Return of Sherlock Holmes* in *New York Times* 19 October 1929, p. 22, states: 'In the final scene Dr Watson is there with his "Amazing, Holmes", and Holmes comes forth with his "Elementary, my dear Watson, elementary" '

20 Ex-Professor Moriarty of mathematical celebrity ... is the Napoleon of crime.
*Memoirs of Sherlock Holmes* (1894) 'The Final Problem'

21 'The curious incident of the dog in the night-time.'
'The dog did nothing in the night-time.'
'That was the curious incident.
*Memoirs of Sherlock Holmes* (1894) 'Silver Blaze'

1 When you have eliminated the impossible,
whatever remains, *however improbable*, must
be the truth.
*The Sign of Four* (1890) ch. 6

2 You know my methods. Apply them.
*The Sign of Four* (1890) ch. 6

3 It is the unofficial force—the Baker Street
irregulars.
*The Sign of Four* (1890) ch. 8

4 London, that great cesspool into which all
the loungers and idlers of the Empire are
irresistibly drained.
*A Study in Scarlet* (1888) ch. 1

5 It is a capital mistake to theorize before
you have all the evidence. It biases the
judgement.
*A Study in Scarlet* (1888) ch. 3

6 Where there is no imagination there is no
horror.
*A Study in Scarlet* (1888) ch. 5

7 The vocabulary of 'Bradshaw' is nervous
and terse, but limited.
*The Valley of Fear* (1915) ch. 1

8 Mediocrity knows nothing higher than
itself, but talent instantly recognizes
genius.
*The Valley of Fear* (1915) ch. 1

## Margaret Drabble 1939–

9 England's not a bad country ... It's just a
mean, cold, ugly, divided, tired, clapped-
out, post-imperial, post-industrial slag-heap
covered in polystyrene hamburger cartons.
*A Natural Curiosity* (1989) p. 308

## Sir Francis Drake c.1540–96

10 There must be a beginning of any great
matter, but the continuing unto the end
until it be thoroughly finished yields the
true glory.
Dispatch to Sir Francis Walsingham, 17 May
1587, in *Navy Records Society* vol. 11 (1898)
p. 134

11 The singeing of the King of Spain's Beard.
On the expedition to Cadiz, 1587, in Francis
Bacon *Considerations touching a War with Spain*
(1629)

12 I must have the gentleman to haul and
draw with the mariner, and the mariner
with the gentleman ... I would know him,
that would refuse to set his hand to a rope,
but I know there is not any such here.
In J. S. Corbett *Drake and the Tudor Navy*
(1898) vol. 1, ch. 9

13 There is plenty of time to win this game,
and to thrash the Spaniards too.
Attributed, in *Dictionary of National Biography*
(1917– ) vol. 5, p. 1342

## Milton Drake et al.

14 Mares eat oats
And does eat oats
And little lambs eat ivy.
'Mairzy Doats' (1943 song)

## Michael Drayton 1563–1631

15 Ill news hath wings, and with the wind
doth go,
Comfort's a cripple and comes ever slow.
*The Barons' Wars* (1603) canto 2, st. 28

16 Since there's no help, come let us kiss and
part,
Nay, I have done: you get no more of me,
And I am glad, yea glad with all my heart,
That thus so cleanly, I myself can free,
Shake hands for ever, cancel all our vows,
And when we meet at any time again,
Be it not seen in either of our brows,
That we one jot of former love retain.
*Idea* (1619) Sonnet 61

17 That shire which we the Heart of England
well may call.
*Poly-Olbion* (1612–22) Song 13, l. 2 (of
Warwickshire)

18 And thus began th'exordium of our woes,
The fatal dumb-show of our misery.
*The Shepherd's Garland* (1593) Eclogue 8

19 For that fine madness still he did retain
Which rightly should possess a poet's
brain.
'To Henry Reynolds, of Poets and Poesy'
(1627) l. 109 (of Marlowe)

20 Next these, learn'd Jonson, in this list I
bring,
Who had drunk deep of the Pierian spring.
'To Henry Reynolds, of Poets and Poesy'
(1627) l. 129. Cf. 251:28

21 These poor half-kisses kill me quite.
'To His Coy Love' (1619)

22 Fair stood the wind for France
When we our sails advance,
Nor now to prove our chance
Longer will tarry.
*To the Cambro-Britons* (1619) 'Agincourt'

## William Drennan 1754–1820

23 Nor one feeling of vengeance presume to
defile
The cause, or the men, of the Emerald Isle.
*Erin* (1795) st. 3

## John Drinkwater 1882–1937

24 Deep is the silence, deep
On moon-washed apples of wonder.
'Moonlit Apples' (1917)

## Thomas Drummond 1797–1840

25 Property has its duties as well as its rights.
Letter to the Earl of Donoughmore, 22 May
1838; in R. B. O'Brien *Thomas Drummond ...
Life and Letters* (1889) p. 284

## William Drummond of Hawthornden 1585–1649

1 Phoebus, arise,
And paint the sable skies,
With azure, white, and red.
'Song: Phoebus, arise' (1614)

## John Dryden 1631–1700

2 In pious times, ere priestcraft did begin,
Before polygamy was made a sin.
*Absalom and Achitophel* (1681) pt. 1, l. 1

3 Then Israel's monarch, after Heaven's own heart,
His vigorous warmth did, variously, impart
To wives and slaves: and, wide as his command,
Scattered his Maker's image through the land.
*Absalom and Achitophel* (1681) pt. 1, l. 7

4 Plots, true or false, are necessary things,
To raise up commonwealths and ruin kings.
*Absalom and Achitophel* (1681) pt. 1, l. 83

5 Of these the false Achitophel was first,
A name to all succeeding ages curst.
*Absalom and Achitophel* (1681) pt. 1, l. 150

6 A fiery soul, which working out its way,
Fretted the pigmy body to decay:
And o'er informed the tenement of clay.
*Absalom and Achitophel* (1681) pt. 1, l. 156

7 Great wits are sure to madness near allied,
And thin partitions do their bounds divide.
*Absalom and Achitophel* (1681) pt. 1, l. 163

8 Bankrupt of life, yet prodigal of ease.
*Absalom and Achitophel* (1681) pt. 1, l. 168

9 And all to leave what with his toil he won
To that unfeathered two-legged thing, a son.
*Absalom and Achitophel* (1681) pt. 1, l. 169

10 All empire is no more than power in trust.
*Absalom and Achitophel* (1681) pt. 1, l. 411

11 But far more numerous was the herd of such
Who think too little and who talk too much.
*Absalom and Achitophel* (1681) pt. 1, l. 533

12 A man so various that he seemed to be
Not one, but all mankind's epitome.
Stiff in opinions, always in the wrong;
Was everything by starts, and nothing long.
*Absalom and Achitophel* (1681) pt. 1, l. 545

13 In squandering wealth was his peculiar art:
Nothing went unrewarded, but desert.
*Absalom and Achitophel* (1681) pt. 1, l. 559

14 And pity never ceases to be shown
To him, who makes the people's wrongs his own.
*Absalom and Achitophel* (1681) pt. 1, l. 725

15 Nor is the people's judgement always true:
The most may err as grossly as the few.
*Absalom and Achitophel* (1681) pt. 1, l. 781

16 Never was patriot yet, but was a fool.
*Absalom and Achitophel* (1681) pt. 1, l. 968

17 Beware the fury of a patient man.
*Absalom and Achitophel* (1681) pt. 1, l. 1005

18 Free from all meaning, whether good or bad,
And in one word, heroically mad.
*Absalom and Achitophel* (1681) pt. 2, l. 416

19 None but the brave deserves the fair.
*Alexander's Feast* (1697) l. 7

20 Sweet is pleasure after pain.
*Alexander's Feast* (1697) l. 60

21 War, he sung, is toil and trouble;
Honour but an empty bubble.
Never ending, still beginning,
Fighting still, and still destroying,
If the world be worth thy winning,
Think, oh think, it worth enjoying.
*Alexander's Feast* (1697) l. 97

22 Sighed and looked, and sighed again.
*Alexander's Feast* (1697) l. 120

23 Errors, like straws, upon the surface flow;
He who would search for pearls must dive below.
*All for Love* (1678) prologue

24 My love's a noble madness.
*All for Love* (1678) act 2, sc. 1

25 Men are but children of a larger growth;
Our appetites as apt to change as theirs,
And full as craving too, and full as vain.
*All for Love* (1678) act 4, sc. 1. Cf. 97:11

26 I am as free as nature first made man,
Ere the base laws of servitude began,
When wild in woods the noble savage ran.
*The Conquest of Granada* (1670) pt. 1, act 1, sc. 1

27 Thou strong seducer, opportunity!
*The Conquest of Granada* (1670) pt. 2, act 4, sc. 3

28 Bold knaves thrive without one grain of sense,
But good men starve for want of impudence.
*Constantine the Great* (1684) epilogue

29 My manhood, long misled by wandering fires,
Followed false lights.
*The Hind and the Panther* (1687) pt. 1, l. 72

30 Either be wholly slaves or wholly free.
*The Hind and the Panther* (1687) pt. 2, l. 285

31 Much malice mingled with a little wit.
*The Hind and the Panther* (1687) pt. 3, l. 1

32 For present joys are more to flesh and blood
Than a dull prospect of a distant good.
*The Hind and the Panther* (1687) pt. 3, l. 364

33 And love's the noblest frailty of the mind.
*The Indian Emperor* (1665) act 2, sc. 2.
Cf. 270:18

34 Repentance is the virtue of weak minds.
*The Indian Emperor* (1665) act 3, sc. 1

35 For all the happiness mankind can gain
Is not in pleasure, but in rest from pain.
*The Indian Emperor* (1665) act 4, sc. 1

**1** War is the trade of kings.
 *King Arthur* (1691) act 2, sc. 2

**2** Fairest Isle, all isles excelling,
 Seat of pleasures, and of loves;
 Venus here will choose her dwelling,
 And forsake her Cyprian groves.
 *King Arthur* (1691) act 5 'Song of Venus'

**3** Ovid, the soft philosopher of love.
 *Love Triumphant* (1694) act 2, sc. 1

**4** All human things are subject to decay,
 And, when fate summons, monarchs must
 obey.
 *MacFlecknoe* (1682) l. 1

**5** The rest to some faint meaning make
 pretence,
 But Shadwell never deviates into sense.
 Some beams of wit on other souls may fall,
 Strike through and make a lucid interval;
 But Shadwell's genuine night admits no
 ray,
 His rising fogs prevail upon the day.
 *MacFlecknoe* (1682) l. 19

**6** And torture one poor word ten thousand
 ways.
 *MacFlecknoe* (1682) l. 208

**7** I am to be married within these three
 days; married past redemption.
 *Marriage à la Mode* (1672) act 1, sc. 1

**8** But treason is not owned when 'tis
 descried;
 Successful crimes alone are justified.
 *The Medal* (1682) l. 207

**9** But love's a malady without a cure.
 *Palamon and Arcite* (1700) bk. 2, l. 110

**10** Antony, who lost the world for love.
 *Palamon and Arcite* (1700) bk. 2, l. 607

**11** Repentance is but want of power to sin.
 *Palamon and Arcite* (1700) bk. 3, l. 813

**12** Like pilgrims to th'appointed place we
 tend;
 The world's an inn, and death the journey's
 end.
 *Palamon and Arcite* (1700) bk. 3, l. 887

**13** A virgin-widow, and a *mourning bride*.
 *Palamon and Arcite* (1700) bk. 3, l. 927

**14** And this unpolished rugged verse I chose
 As fittest for discourse and nearest prose.
 *Religio Laici* (1682) l. 453

**15** A very merry, dancing, drinking,
 Laughing, quaffing, and unthinking time.
 *The Secular Masque* (1700) l. 39

**16** For secrets are edged tools,
 And must be kept from children and from
 fools.
 *Sir Martin Mar-All* (1667) act 2, sc. 2

**17** What passion cannot Music raise and
 quell?
 *A Song for St Cecilia's Day* (1687) st. 2

**18** The soft complaining flute.
 *A Song for St Cecilia's Day* (1687) st. 4

**19**          There is a pleasure sure,
 In being mad, which none but madmen
 know!
 *The Spanish Friar* (1681) act 1, sc. 1

**20** Mute and magnificent, without a tear.
 *Threnodia Augustalis* (1685) st. 2

**21**          Wit will shine
 Through the harsh cadence of a rugged
 line.
 'To the Memory of Mr Oldham' (1684)

**22** All delays are dangerous in war.
 *Tyrannic Love* (1669) act 1, sc. 1

**23** I can enjoy her while she's kind;
 But when she dances in the wind,
 And shakes the wings, and will not stay,
 I puff the prostitute away.
 Translation of Horace *Odes* bk. 3, no. 29 (of
 Fortune)

**24** She knows her man, and when you rant
 and swear,
 Can draw you to her *with a single hair*.
 Translation of Persius *Satires* no. 5, l. 246

**25** Arms, and the man I sing, who, forced by
 fate,
 And haughty Juno's unrelenting hate,
 Expelled and exiled, left the Trojan shore.
 Translation of Virgil *Aeneid* (*Aeneis*, 1697)
 bk. 1, l. 1. Cf. 338:23

**26** We must beat the iron while it is hot, but
 we may polish it at leisure.
 *Aeneis* (1697) dedication

**27** A thing well said will be wit in all
 languages.
 *Essay of Dramatic Poesy* (1668)

**28** He is many times flat, insipid; his comic
 wit degenerating into clenches, his serious
 swelling into bombast. But he is always
 great.
 *Essay of Dramatic Poesy* (1668) of Shakespeare

**29** He invades authors like a monarch; and
 what would be theft in other poets, is only
 victory in him.
 *Essay of Dramatic Poesy* (1668) of Ben Jonson

**30** 'Tis sufficient to say [of Chaucer], according
 to the proverb, that here is God's plenty.
 *Fables Ancient and Modern* (1700) preface

## Alexander Dubček 1921–92

**31** In the service of the people we followed
 such a policy that socialism would not lose
 its human face.
 In *Rudé Právo* 19 July 1968

## Joachim Du Bellay 1522–60

**32** *France, mère des arts, des armes et des lois.*
 France, mother of arts, of warfare, and of
 laws.
 *Les Regrets* (1558) Sonnet 9

**33** *Heureux qui comme Ulysse a fait un beau
 voyage.*
 Happy he who like Ulysses has made a
 great journey.
 *Les Regrets* (1558) Sonnet 31

## Mme Du Deffand 1697–1780

1 The distance is nothing; it is only the first step that is difficult.
  Commenting on the legend that St Denis, carrying his head in his hands, walked two leagues: letter to Jean Le Rond d'Alembert, 7 July 1763, in G. Maugras *Trois mois à la cour de Frédéric* (1886) p. 28

## John Foster Dulles 1888–1959

2 The ability to get to the verge without getting into the war is the necessary art ... We walked to the brink and we looked it in the face.
  In *Life* 16 January 1956

## Alexandre Dumas 1802–70

3 *Cherchons la femme.*
  Let us look for the woman.
  *Les Mohicans de Paris* (1854–5) passim; attributed to Joseph Fouché (1763–1820) in the form '*Cherchez la femme*'

4 *Tous pour un, un pour tous.*
  All for one, one for all.
  *Les Trois Mousquetaires* (1844) ch. 9

## Daphne Du Maurier 1907–89

5 Last night I dreamt I went to Manderley again.
  *Rebecca* (1938) ch. 1

## General Dumouriez 1739–1823

6 The courtiers who surround him have forgotten nothing and learnt nothing.
  Of Louis XVIII, in *Examen impartial d'un Écrit intitulé Déclaration de Louis XVIII* (1795) p. 40

## Paul Lawrence Dunbar 1872–1906

7 I know why the caged bird sings!
  'Sympathy' st. 3. Cf. 344:27

## William Dunbar c.1465–c.1513

8 *Timor mortis conturbat me.*
  The fear of death disquiets me.
  'Lament for the Makaris [poets]'

## Ian Dunlop 1925–

9 The shock of the new.
  Title of book about modern art (1972)

## John Dunning, Baron Ashburton 1731–83

10 The influence of the Crown has increased, is increasing, and ought to be diminished.
  Resolution passed in the House of Commons, 6 April 1780; in *Parliamentary History of England* (T. C. Hansard, 1814) vol. 21, col. 347

## James Duport 1606–79

11 *Quem Jupiter vult perdere, dementat prius.*
  Whom God would destroy He first sends mad.
  *Homeri Gnomologia* (1660) p. 282. Cf. 13:8

## Richard Duppa 1770–1831

12 In language, the ignorant have prescribed laws to the learned.
  *Maxims* (1830) no. 252

## Leo Durocher 1906–91

13 Nice guys. Finish last.
  Casual remark at a baseball ground, July 1946; in *Nice Guys Finish Last* (as the remark generally is quoted, 1975) pt. 1, p. 14

## Ian Dury 1942–

14 Sex and drugs and rock and roll.
  Title of song (1977)

## Sir Edward Dyer d. 1607

15 Silence augmenteth grief, writing increaseth rage,
  Staled are my thoughts, which loved and lost, the wonder of our age.
  'Elegy on the Death of Sir Philip Sidney' (1593) (formerly attributed to Fulke Greville, 1554–1628)

16 My mind to me a kingdom is.
  Such perfect joy therein I find
  That it excels all other bliss
  That world affords or grows by kind.
  Though much I want which most would have,
  Yet still my mind forbids to crave.
  'In praise of a contented mind' (1588)

## John Dyer 1700–58

17 But transient is the smile of fate:
  A little rule, a little sway,
  A sunbeam in a winter's day,
  Is all the proud and mighty have
  Between the cradle and the grave.
  *Grongar Hill* (1726) l. 88

## John Dyer

18 And he that will this health deny,
  Down among the dead men let him lie.
  'Down among the Dead Men' (c.1700)

## Bob Dylan 1941–

19 How many roads must a man walk down
  Before you can call him a man? ...
  The answer, my friend, is blowin' in the wind,
  The answer is blowin' in the wind.
  'Blowin' in the Wind' (1962 song)

20 And Ezra Pound and T. S. Eliot
  Fighting in the captain's tower.
  'Desolation Row' (1965 song)

**1** Don't think twice, it's all right.
   Title of song (1963)

**2** A hard rain's a gonna fall.
   Title of song (1963)

**3** Money doesn't talk, it swears.
   'It's Alright, Ma (I'm Only Bleeding)' (1965 song)

**4** She knows there's no success like failure
   And that failure's no success at all.
   'Love Minus Zero / No Limit' (1965 song)

**5** Hey! Mr Tambourine Man, play a song for me.
   I'm not sleepy and there is no place I'm going to.
   'Mr Tambourine Man' (1965 song)

**6** Ah, but I was so much older then,
   I'm younger than that now.
   'My Back Pages' (1964 song)

**7** Señor, señor, do you know where we're headin'?
   Lincoln County Road or Armageddon?
   'Señor (Tale of Yankee Power)' (1978 song)

**8** All that foreign oil controlling American soil.
   'Slow Train' (1979 song)

**9** Come mothers and fathers,
   Throughout the land
   And don't criticize
   What you can't understand.
   'The Times They Are A-Changing' (1964 song)

## Sir Arthur Eddington 1882–1944

**10** I shall use the phrase 'time's arrow' to express this one-way property of time which has no analogue in space.
   *The Nature of the Physical World* (1928) ch. 4

**11** If your theory is found to be against the second law of thermodynamics I can give you no hope; there is nothing for it but to collapse in deepest humiliation.
   *The Nature of the Physical World* (1928) ch. 14

**12** I ask you to look both ways. For the road to a knowledge of the stars leads through the atom; and important knowledge of the atom has been reached through the stars.
   *Stars and Atoms* (1928) Lecture 1

**13** Science is an edged tool, with which men play like children, and cut their own fingers.
   Attributed in R. L. Weber *More Random Walks in Science* (1982) p. 48

## Sir Anthony Eden (Earl of Avon) 1897–1977

**14** We are in an armed conflict; that is the phrase I have used. There has been no declaration of war.
   Speech, *Hansard* 1 November 1956, col. 1641 (on the Suez crisis)

## Marriott Edgar 1880–1951

**15** There's a famous seaside place called Blackpool,
   That's noted for fresh air and fun,
   And Mr and Mrs Ramsbottom
   Went there with young Albert, their son.
   'The Lion and Albert' (1932)

## Maria Edgeworth 1768–1849

**16** Well! some people talk of morality, and some of religion, but give me a little snug property.
   *The Absentee* (1812) ch. 2

**17** Business was his aversion; pleasure was his business.
   *The Contrast* (1804) ch. 2

**18** Man is to be held only by the *slightest* chains, with the idea that he can break them at pleasure, he submits to them in sport.
   *Letters for Literary Ladies* (1795) 'Letters of Julia and Caroline' no. 1

## Thomas Alva Edison 1847–1931

**19** Genius is one per cent inspiration, ninety-nine per cent perspiration.
   Said *c.*1903, in *Harper's Monthly Magazine* September 1932. Cf. 78:6

## John Maxwell Edmonds 1875–1958

**20** When you go home, tell them of us and say,
   'For your tomorrows these gave their today.'
   *Inscriptions Suggested for War Memorials* (1919)

## Edward III 1312–77

**21** Also say to them, that they suffre hym this day to wynne his spurres, for if god be pleased, I woll this journey be his, and the honoure therof.
   Speaking of the Black Prince at Crécy, 1346 (commonly quoted 'Let the boy win his spurs'); in *Chronicle of Froissart* (tr. Sir John Bourchier, Lord Berners, 1523–5) ch. 130

## Edward VII 1841–1910

**22** I thought everyone must know that a *short* jacket is always worn with a silk hat at a private view in the morning.
   To Sir Frederick Ponsonby, who had proposed accompanying him in a tail-coat; in Sir Philip Magnus *Edward VII* (1964) ch. 19

## Edward VIII (Duke of Windsor)
### 1894–1972

1 These works brought all these people here. Something should be done to get them at work again.

>Speaking at the derelict Dowlais Iron and Steel Works, 18 November 1936; in *Western Mail* 19 November 1936 (generally quoted 'Something must be done')

2 At long last I am able to say a few words of my own ... you must believe me when I tell you that I have found it impossible to carry the heavy burden of responsibility and to discharge my duties as King as I would wish to do without the help and support of the woman I love.

>Radio broadcast following his abdication, 11 December 1936; in *The Times* 12 December 1936

## Jonathan Edwards 1703–58

3 I ... once saw a very large spider to my surprise swimming in the air ... and others have assured me that they often have seen spiders fly, the appearance is truly very pretty and pleasing.

>*The Flying Spider—Observations by Jonathan Edwards when a boy* 'Of Insects'; in *Andover Review* vol. 13 (1890) p. 5

4 The bodies of those that made such a noise and tumult when alive, when dead, lie as quietly among the graves of their neighbours as any others.

>Sermon on procrastination (*Miscellaneous Discourses*) in *Works* (1834) vol. 2, p. 241

## Oliver Edwards 1711–91

5 I have tried too in my time to be a philosopher; but, I don't know how, cheerfulness was always breaking in.

>In James Boswell *Life of Samuel Johnson* (1934 ed.) vol. 3, p. 305 (17 April 1778)

6 For my part now, I consider supper as a turnpike through which one must pass, in order to get to bed.

>In James Boswell *Life of Samuel Johnson* (1934 ed.) vol. 3, p. 306 (17 April 1778)

## John Ehrlichman 1925–

7 I think we ought to let him hang there. Let him twist slowly, slowly in the wind.

>Speaking of Patrick Gray (regarding his nomination as director of the FBI); in *Washington Post* 27 July 1973, p. A27

## Albert Einstein 1879–1955

8 God is subtle but he is not malicious.

>Remark made at Princeton University, May 1921; in R. W. Clark *Einstein* (1973) ch. 14

9 I am convinced that *He* [God] does not play dice.

>Letter to Max Born, 4 December 1926; in *Einstein und Born Briefwechsel* (1969) p. 130

10 If $A$ is a success in life, then $A$ equals $x$ plus $y$ plus $z$. Work is $x$; $y$ is play; and $z$ is keeping your mouth shut.

>In *Observer* 15 January 1950

11 Science without religion is lame, religion without science is blind.

>*Science, Philosophy and Religion* (1941) ch. 13

12 Equations are more important to me, because politics is for the present, but an equation is something for eternity.

>In Stephen Hawking *A Brief History of Time* (1988) p. 178. See also C. P. Snow 'Einstein' in M. Goldsmith et al. (eds.) *Einstein* (1980)

13 I never think of the future. It comes soon enough.

>In an interview, given on the *Belgenland*, December 1930

## Dwight D. Eisenhower 1890–1969

14 This world in arms is not spending money alone. It is spending the sweat of its labourers, the genius of its scientists, the hopes of its children.

>Speech in Washington, 16 April 1953; in *Public Papers of Presidents 1953* (1960) p. 182

15 You have broader considerations that might follow what you might call the 'falling domino' principle. You have a row of dominoes set up. You knock over the first one, and what will happen to the last one is that it will go over very quickly.

>Speech at press conference, 7 April 1954; in *Public Papers of Presidents 1954* (1960) p. 383

16 I think that people want peace so much that one of these days governments had better get out of the way and let them have it.

>Broadcast discussion, 31 August 1959; in *Public Papers of Presidents 1959* (1960) p. 625

## Sir Edward Elgar 1857–1934

17 To my friends pictured within.

>*Enigma Variations* (1899) dedication

18 There is music in the air.

>In R. J. Buckley *Sir Edward Elgar* (1905) ch. 4

## George Eliot (Mary Ann Evans) 1819–80

19 We hand folks over to God's mercy, and show none ourselves.

>*Adam Bede* (1859) ch. 42

20 Gossip is a sort of smoke that comes from the dirty tobacco-pipes of those who diffuse it: it proves nothing but the bad taste of the smoker.

>*Daniel Deronda* (1876) bk. 2, ch. 13

1 A difference of taste in jokes is a great
   strain on the affections.
   *Daniel Deronda* (1876) bk. 2, ch. 15

2 There is a great deal of unmapped country
   within us which would have to be taken
   into account in an explanation of our
   gusts and storms.
   *Daniel Deronda* (1876) bk. 3, ch. 24

3 Half the sorrows of women would be
   averted if they could repress the speech
   they know to be useless; nay, the speech
   they have resolved not to make.
   *Felix Holt* (1866) ch. 2

4 An election is coming. Universal peace is
   declared, and the foxes have a sincere
   interest in prolonging the lives of the
   poultry.
   *Felix Holt* (1866) ch. 5

5 A woman can hardly ever choose ... she is
   dependent on what happens to her. She
   must take meaner things, because only
   meaner things are within her reach.
   *Felix Holt* (1866) ch. 27

6 'Abroad', that large home of ruined
   reputations.
   *Felix Holt* (1866) epilogue

7 Debasing the moral currency.
   *The Impressions of Theophrastus Such* (1879)
   essay title

8 A woman dictates before marriage in order
   that she may have an appetite for
   submission afterwards.
   *Middlemarch* (1871–2) bk. 1, ch. 9

9 He said he should prefer not to know the
   sources of the Nile, and that there should
   be some unknown regions preserved as
   hunting-grounds for the poetic
   imagination.
   *Middlemarch* (1871–2) bk. 1, ch. 9

10 If we had a keen vision and feeling of all
   ordinary human life, it would be like
   hearing the grass grow and the squirrel's
   heart beat, and we should die of that roar
   which lies on the other side of silence.
   *Middlemarch* (1871–2) bk. 2, ch. 20

11 We do not expect people to be deeply
   moved by what is not unusual. That
   element of tragedy which lies in the very
   fact of frequency, has not yet wrought
   itself into the coarse emotion of mankind.
   *Middlemarch* (1871–2) bk. 2, ch. 20

12 Anger and jealousy can no more bear to
   lose sight of their objects than love.
   *The Mill on the Floss* (1860) bk. 1, ch. 10

13 The dead level of provincial existence.
   *The Mill on the Floss* (1860) bk. 5, ch. 3

14 The happiest women, like the happiest
   nations, have no history.
   *The Mill on the Floss* (1860) bk. 6, ch. 3.
   Cf. 233:22

15 'Character' says Novalis, in one of his
   questionable aphorisms—'character is
   destiny.'
   *The Mill on the Floss* (1860) bk. 6, ch. 6.
   Cf. 240:12

16 In every parting there is an image of
   death.
   *Scenes of Clerical Life* (1858) 'Amos Barton'
   ch. 10

17 Oh may I join the choir invisible
   Of those immortal dead who live again
   In minds made better by their presence.
   'Oh May I Join the Choir Invisible' (1867)

## T. S. Eliot 1888–1965

18 Because I do not hope to turn again
   Because I do not hope
   Because I do not hope to turn.
   *Ash-Wednesday* (1930) pt. 1

19 Teach us to care and not to care
   Teach us to sit still.
   *Ash-Wednesday* (1930) pt. 1

20 Lady, three white leopards sat under a
   juniper-tree
   In the cool of the day.
   *Ash-Wednesday* (1930) pt. 2

21 What is hell?
   Hell is oneself,
   Hell is alone, the other figures in it
   Merely projections.
   *The Cocktail Party* (1950) act 1, sc. 3. Cf. 267:4

22 Over buttered scones and crumpets
   Weeping, weeping multitudes
   Droop in a hundred A.B.C.'s.
   'Cooking Egg' (1920)

23 Success is relative:
   It is what we can make of the mess we
   have made of things.
   *The Family Reunion* (1939) pt. 2, sc. 3

24 Round and round the circle
   Completing the charm
   So the knot be unknotted
   The cross be uncrossed
   The crooked be made straight
   And the curse be ended.
   *The Family Reunion* (1939) pt. 2, sc. 3

25 Time present and time past
   Are both perhaps present in time future,
   And time future contained in time past.
   *Four Quartets* 'Burnt Norton' (1936) pt. 1

26 Footfalls echo in the memory
   Down the passage which we did not take
   Towards the door we never opened
   Into the rose-garden.
   *Four Quartets* 'Burnt Norton' (1936) pt. 1

27            Human kind
   Cannot bear very much reality.
   *Four Quartets* 'Burnt Norton' (1936) pt. 1.

28 At the still point of the turning world.
   *Four Quartets* 'Burnt Norton' (1936) pt. 2

**1**         Words strain,
Crack and sometimes break, under the
    burden,
Under the tension, slip, slide, perish,
Decay with imprecision, will not stay in
    place,
Will not stay still.
*Four Quartets* 'Burnt Norton' (1936) pt. 5

**2** In my beginning is my end.
*Four Quartets* 'East Coker' (1940) pt. 1.
Cf. 221:16

**3**         The intolerable wrestle
With words and meanings.
*Four Quartets* 'East Coker' (1940) pt. 2

**4** The houses are all gone under the sea.
The dancers are all gone under the hill.
*Four Quartets* 'East Coker' (1940) pt. 2

**5** The wounded surgeon plies the steel
That questions the distempered part;
Beneath the bleeding hands we feel
The sharp compassion of the healer's art
Resolving the enigma of the fever chart.
*Four Quartets* 'East Coker' (1940) pt. 4

**6**         Each venture
Is a new beginning, a raid on the
    inarticulate
With shabby equipment always
    deteriorating
In the general mess of imprecision of
    feeling.
*Four Quartets* 'East Coker' (1940) pt. 5

**7**         I think that the river
Is a strong brown god.
*Four Quartets* 'The Dry Salvages' (1941) pt. 1

**8** Ash on an old man's sleeve
Is all the ash the burnt roses leave.
*Four Quartets* 'Little Gidding' (1942) pt. 2

**9**         Speech impelled us
To purify the dialect of the tribe.
*Four Quartets* 'Little Gidding' (1942) pt. 2

**10** And the end of all our exploring
Will be to arrive where we started
And know the place for the first time.
*Four Quartets* 'Little Gidding' (1942) pt. 5

**11** What we call the beginning is often the
    end
And to make an end is to make a
    beginning.
The end is where we start from.
*Four Quartets* 'Little Gidding' (1942) pt. 5

**12**         So, while the light fails
On a winter's afternoon, in a secluded
    chapel
History is now and England.
*Four Quartets* 'Little Gidding' (1942) pt. 5

**13** And all shall be well and
All manner of thing shall be well
When the tongues of flame are in-folded
Into the crowned knot of fire
And the fire and the rose are one.
*Four Quartets* 'Little Gidding' (1942) pt. 5.
Cf. 188:21

**14** Here I am, an old man in a dry month
Being read to by a boy, waiting for rain.
'Gerontion' (1920)

**15** After such knowledge, what forgiveness?
'Gerontion' (1920)

**16** Tenants of the house,
Thoughts of a dry brain in a dry season.
'Gerontion' (1920)

**17** We are the hollow men
We are the stuffed men
Leaning together
Headpiece filled with straw. Alas!
'The Hollow Men' (1925)

**18** Here we go round the prickly pear
Prickly pear prickly pear.
'The Hollow Men' (1925)

**19** Between the idea
And the reality
Between the motion
And the act
Falls the Shadow.
'The Hollow Men' (1925)

**20** This is the way the world ends
Not with a bang but a whimper.
'The Hollow Men' (1925)

**21** A cold coming we had of it,
Just the worst time of the year
For a journey, and such a long journey:
The ways deep and the weather sharp,
The very dead of winter.
'Journey of the Magi' (1927). Cf. 5:15

**22**         I had seen birth and death
But had thought they were different.
'Journey of the Magi' (1927)

**23** An alien people clutching their gods.
'Journey of the Magi' (1927)

**24** Let us go then, you and I,
When the evening is spread out against
    the sky
Like a patient etherized upon a table.
'Love Song of J. Alfred Prufrock' (1917)

**25** In the room the women come and go
Talking of Michelangelo.
'Love Song of J. Alfred Prufrock' (1917)

**26** The yellow fog that rubs its back upon the
    window-panes.
'Love Song of J. Alfred Prufrock' (1917)

**27** I have measured out my life with coffee
    spoons.
'Love Song of J. Alfred Prufrock' (1917)

**28** I should have been a pair of ragged claws
Scuttling across the floors of silent seas.
'Love Song of J. Alfred Prufrock' (1917)

**29** I have seen the moment of my greatness
    flicker,
And I have seen the eternal Footman hold
    my coat, and snicker,
And in short, I was afraid.
'Love Song of J. Alfred Prufrock' (1917)

1 No! I am not Prince Hamlet, nor was
  meant to be;
  Am an attendant lord, one that will do
  To swell a progress, start a scene or two,
  Advise the prince.
  'Love Song of J. Alfred Prufrock' (1917)

2 I grow old ... I grow old ...
  I shall wear the bottoms of my trousers
  rolled.
  'Love Song of J. Alfred Prufrock' (1917)

3 Shall I part my hair behind? Do I dare to
  eat a peach?
  'Love Song of J. Alfred Prufrock' (1917)

4 I am aware of the damp souls of
  housemaids
  Sprouting despondently at area gates.
  'Morning at the Window' (1917)

5 The sapient sutlers of the Lord.
  'Mr Eliot's Sunday Morning Service' (1919)

6 Yet we have gone on living,
  Living and partly living.
  Murder in the Cathedral (1935) pt. 1

7 The last temptation is the greatest treason:
  To do the right deed for the wrong reason.
  Murder in the Cathedral (1935) pt. 1

8 Clear the air! clean the sky! wash the wind!
  Murder in the Cathedral (1935) pt. 1

9 He always has an alibi, and one or two to
  spare:
  At whatever time the deed took place—
  MACAVITY WASN'T THERE!
  Old Possum's Book of Practical Cats (1939)
  'Macavity: the Mystery Cat'

10 The winter evening settles down
   With smell of steaks in passageways.
   Six o'clock.
   The burnt-out ends of smoky days.
   'Preludes' (1917)

11 Midnight shakes the memory
   As a madman shakes a dead geranium.
   'Rhapsody on a Windy Night' (1917)

12 Where is the wisdom we have lost in
   knowledge?
   Where is the knowledge we have lost in
   information?
   The Rock (1934) pt. 1

13 ... Here were decent godless people:
   Their only monument the asphalt road
   And a thousand lost golf balls.
   The Rock (1934) pt. 1

14 Birth, and copulation, and death.
   That's all the facts when you come to brass
   tacks.
   Sweeney Agonistes (1932) 'Fragment of an
   Agon'

15 Any man has to, needs to, wants to
   Once in a lifetime, do a girl in.
   Sweeney Agonistes (1932) 'Fragment of an
   Agon'

16 I gotta use words when I talk to you.
   Sweeney Agonistes (1932) 'Fragment of an
   Agon'

17 The nightingales are singing near
   The Convent of the Sacred Heart,
   And sang within the bloody wood
   When Agamemnon cried aloud
   And let their liquid siftings fall
   To stain the stiff dishonoured shroud.
   'Sweeney among the Nightingales' (1919)

18 April is the cruellest month, breeding
   Lilacs out of the dead land.
   The Waste Land (1922) pt. 1

19 I read, much of the night, and go south in
   the winter.
   The Waste Land (1922) pt. 1

20 I will show you fear in a handful of dust.
   The Waste Land (1922) pt. 1

21 A crowd flowed over London Bridge, so
   many,
   I had not thought death had undone so
   many.
   The Waste Land (1922) pt. 1

22 And still she cried, and still the world
   pursues,
   'Jug Jug' to dirty ears.
   The Waste Land (1922) pt. 2. Cf. 212:17

23 I think we are in rats' alley
   Where the dead men lost their bones.
   The Waste Land (1922) pt. 2

24 O O O O that Shakespeherian Rag—
   It's so elegant
   So intelligent
   The Waste Land (1922) pt. 2. Cf. 77:31

25 Hurry up please it's time.
   The Waste Land (1922) pt. 2

26 O the moon shone bright on Mrs Porter
   And on her daughter
   They wash their feet in soda water.
   The Waste Land (1922) pt. 3

27 At the violet hour, when the eyes and back
   Turn upward from the desk, when the
   human engine waits
   Like a taxi throbbing waiting.
   The Waste Land (1922) pt. 3

28 I Tiresias, old man with wrinkled dugs.
   The Waste Land (1922) pt. 3

29 One of the low on whom assurance sits
   As a silk hat on a Bradford millionaire.
   The Waste Land (1922) pt. 3

30 Bats with baby faces in the violet light.
   The Waste Land (1922) pt. 5

31 These fragments I have shored against my
   ruins.
   The Waste Land (1922) pt. 5

32 Webster was much possessed by death
   And saw the skull beneath the skin.
   'Whispers of Immortality' (1919)

33 Uncorseted, her friendly bust
   Gives promise of pneumatic bliss.
   'Whispers of Immortality' (1919)

1 The only way of expressing emotion in the form of art is by finding an 'objective correlative'; in other words, a set of objects, a situation, a chain of events which shall be the formula of that *particular* emotion; such that when the external facts, which must terminate in sensory experience, are given, the emotion is immediately evoked.

> *The Sacred Wood* (1920) 'Hamlet and his Problems'

2 Immature poets imitate; mature poets steal.

> *The Sacred Wood* (1920) 'Philip Massinger'

3 Poets in our civilization, as it exists at present, must be *difficult*.

> *Selected Essays* (1932) 'The Metaphysical Poets' (1921)

4 [*The Waste Land*] was only the relief of a personal and wholly insignificant grouse against life; it is just a piece of rhythmical grumbling.

> *The Waste Land* (ed. Valerie Eliot, 1971) epigraph

## Elizabeth I 1533–1603

5 I know what it is to be a subject, what to be a Sovereign, what to have good neighbours, and sometimes meet evil-willers.

> Speech, 12 November 1586, in Sir John Neale *Elizabeth I and her Parliaments 1584–1601* (1957) p. 118. The traditional version concludes: 'In trust I have found treason'

6 I know I have the body of a weak and feeble woman, but I have the heart and stomach of a king, and of a king of England too.

> Speech to the troops at Tilbury on the approach of the Armada, 1588; in Lord Somers *A Third Collection of Scarce and Valuable Tracts* (1751) p. 196

7 Though God hath raised me high, yet this I count the glory of my crown: that I have reigned with your loves.

> The Golden Speech, 1601, in *Journals of All the Parliaments . . .* Collected by Sir Simonds D'Ewes (1682) p. 659

8 I will make you shorter by the head.

> To the leaders of her Council, who were opposing her course towards Mary Queen of Scots; in F. Chamberlin *Sayings of Queen Elizabeth* (1923)

9 If thy heart fails thee, climb not at all.

> Lines after Sir Walter Ralegh, written on a window-pane; in Thomas Fuller *Worthies of England* vol. 1, p. 419. Cf. 257:24

10 Must! Is *must* a word to be addressed to princes? Little man, little man! thy father, if he had been alive, durst not have used that word.

> To Robert Cecil, on his saying she must go to bed; in J. R. Green *A Short History of the English People* (1874) ch. 7

11 God may pardon you, but I never can.

> To the dying Countess of Nottingham, in David Hume *History of England under the House of Tudor* (1759) vol. 2, ch. 7

12 The queen of Scots is this day leichter of a fair son, and I am but a barren stock.

> To her ladies, in Sir James Melville *Memoirs of His Own Life* (1827 ed.) p. 159

13 The daughter of debate, that eke discord doth sow.

> Of Mary Queen of Scots, in George Puttenham (ed.) *Art of English Poesie* (1589) bk. 3, ch. 20

14 I would not open windows into men's souls.

> Oral tradition, in J. B. Black *Reign of Elizabeth 1558–1603* (1936) p. 19 (the words possibly originating in a letter drafted by Bacon). See J. Spedding (ed.) *Works of Francis Bacon* (1862) vol. 8, p. 98

15 All my possessions for a moment of time.

> Last words (attributed, probably apocryphal)

## Elizabeth II 1926–

16 I think everybody really will concede that on this, of all days, I should begin my speech with the words 'My husband and I'.

> Speech at Guildhall, London, on her 25th wedding anniversary; in *The Times* 21 November 1972

17 In the words of one of my more sympathetic correspondents, it has turned out to be an 'annus horribilis'.

> Speech at Guildhall, London, 24 November 1992; in *The Times* 25 November 1992, p. 3

## Queen Elizabeth, the Queen Mother 1900–

18 I'm glad we've been bombed. It makes me feel I can look the East End in the face.

> To a London policeman, 13 September 1940; in J. Wheeler-Bennett *King George VI* (1958) pt. 3, ch. 6

19 The Princesses would never leave without me and I couldn't leave without the King, and the King will never leave.

> On the suggestion that the royal family be evacuated during the Blitz; in P. Mortimer *Queen Elizabeth* (1986) ch. 25

## Alf Ellerton

20 Belgium put the kibosh on the Kaiser.

> Title of song (1914)

## John Ellerton 1826–93

21 The day Thou gavest, Lord, is ended,
The darkness falls at Thy behest.

> Hymn (1870)

## Emily Elizabeth Steele Elliot
1836–97

1 O come to my heart, Lord Jesus!
There is room in my heart for thee.
  'Thou didst leave thy throne and thy kingly
  crown' (1870 hymn)

## Charlotte Elliott 1789–1871

2 Just as I am, without one plea.
  *Invalid's Hymn Book* (1834) 'Just as I am'

## Ebenezer Elliott 1781–1849

3 What is a communist? One who hath
yearnings
For equal division of unequal earnings.
  'Epigram' (1850)

## George Ellis 1753–1815

4 Snowy, Flowy, Blowy,
Showery, Flowery, Bowery,
Hoppy, Croppy, Droppy,
Breezy, Sneezy, Freezy.
  'The Twelve Months'

## Havelock Ellis 1859–1939

5 What we call 'progress' is the exchange of
one nuisance for another nuisance.
  *Impressions and Comments* (1914) 31 July 1912

6 All civilization has from time to time
become a thin crust over a volcano of
revolution.
  *Little Essays of Love and Virtue* (1922) ch. 7

## Friar Elstow

7 With thanks to God we know the way to
heaven, to be as ready by water as by land,
and therefore we care not which way we
go.
  When threatened with drowning by Henry
  VIII; in John Stow *Annals of England* (1615)
  p. 543. Cf. 151:3

## Paul Éluard 1895–1952

8 *L'espoir ne fait pas de poussière.*
Hope raises no dust.
  'Ailleurs, ici, partout' (1946)

9 *Adieu tristesse*
*Bonjour tristesse.*
Farewell sadness
Good-day sadness.
  'À peine défigurée' (1932)

## Ralph Waldo Emerson 1803–82

10 If the red slayer think he slays,
Or if the slain think he is slain,
They know not well the subtle ways
I keep, and pass, and turn again.
  'Brahma' (1867)

11 I am the doubter and the doubt.
  'Brahma' (1867)

12 By the rude bridge that arched the flood,
Their flag to April's breeze unfurled,
Here once the embattled farmers stood,
And fired the shot heard round the world.
  'Concord Hymn' (1837)

13 Things are in the saddle,
And ride mankind.
  'Ode' Inscribed to W. H. Channing (1847)

14 I like a church; I like a cowl;
I love a prophet of the soul.
  'The Problem' (1847)

15 He builded better than he knew;—
The conscious stone to beauty grew.
  'The Problem' (1847)

16 The frolic architecture of the snow.
  'The Snowstorm' (1847)

17 Make yourself necessary to someone.
  *The Conduct of Life* (1860) 'Considerations by
  the way'

18 All sensible people are selfish, and nature
is tugging at every contract to make the
terms of it fair.
  *The Conduct of Life* (1860) 'Considerations by
  the way'

19 Art is a jealous mistress.
  *The Conduct of Life* (1860) 'Wealth'

20 The louder he talked of his honour, the
faster we counted our spoons.
  *The Conduct of Life* (1860) 'Worship'. Cf. 184:11,
  301:23

21 The only reward of virtue is virtue; the
only way to have a friend is to be one.
  *Essays* (1841) 'Friendship'

22 There is properly no history; only
biography.
  *Essays* (1841) 'History'. Cf. 121:28

23 The faith that stands on authority is not
faith.
  *Essays* (1841) 'The Over-Soul'

24 A foolish consistency is the hobgoblin of
little minds.
  *Essays* (1841) 'Self-Reliance'

25 To be great is to be misunderstood.
  *Essays* (1841) 'Self-Reliance'

26 To fill the hour—that is happiness.
  *Essays. Second Series* (1844) 'Experience'

27 Every man is wanted, and no man is
wanted much.
  *Essays. Second Series* (1844) 'Nominalist and
  Realist'

28 Language is fossil poetry.
  *Essays. Second Series* (1844) 'The Poet'

29 What is a weed? A plant whose virtues
have not been discovered.
  *Fortune of the Republic* (1878) p. 3

30 Every hero becomes a bore at last.
  *Representative Men* (1850) 'Uses of Great Men'

31 Hitch your wagon to a star.
  *Society and Solitude* (1870) 'Civilization'

32 We boil at different degrees.
  *Society and Solitude* (1870) 'Eloquence'

1 America is a country of young men.
   *Society and Solitude* (1870) 'Old Age'

2 Glittering generalities! They are blazing ubiquities.
   On Rufus Choate (attributed). Cf. 98:17

3 If a man write a better book, preach a better sermon, or make a better mouse-trap than his neighbour, tho' he build his house in the woods, the world will make a beaten path to his door.
   Attributed to Emerson in Sarah Yule *Borrowings* (1889), but claimed also by Elbert Hubbard

## William Empson 1906–84

4 Waiting for the end, boys, waiting for the end.
   'Just a smack at Auden' (1940)

5 You don't want madhouse and the whole thing there.
   'Let it Go' (1955)

6 Slowly the poison the whole blood stream fills.
   It is not the effort nor the failure tires.
   The waste remains, the waste remains and kills.
   'Missing Dates' (1935)

7 Seven types of ambiguity.
   Title of book (1930)

## Friedrich Engels 1820–95

8 *Der Staat wird nicht 'abgeschafft', er stirbt ab.*
   The State is not 'abolished', *it withers away.*
   *Anti-Dühring* (1878) pt. 3, ch. 2

See also KARL MARX and FRIEDRICH ENGELS

## Julius J. Epstein 1909– et al.

9 Of all the gin joints in all the towns in all the world, she walks into mine.
   *Casablanca* (1942 film)

10 If she can stand it, I can. Play it!
   *Casablanca* (1942 film). Spoken by Humphrey Bogart and usually quoted 'Play it again, Sam'

11 Here's looking at you, kid.
   *Casablanca* (1942 film)

12 Major Strasser has been shot. Round up the usual suspects.
   *Casablanca* (1942 film)

## Olaudah Equiano c.1745–c.1797

13 A nation of dancers, singers and poets.
   *Narrative of the Life of Olaudah Equiano* (1789) ch. 1 (the Ibo people)

## Erasmus c.1469–1536

14 *In regione caecorum rex est luscus.*
   In the country of the blind the one-eyed man is king.
   *Adages* bk. 3, century 4, no. 96

## Susan Ertz 1894–1985

15 Millions long for immortality who don't know what to do with themselves on a rainy Sunday afternoon.
   *Anger in the Sky* (1943) p. 137

## Robert Devereux, 2nd Earl of Essex 1566–1601

16 Reasons are not like garments, the worse for wearing.
   Letter to Lord Willoughby, 4 January 1599; in *Notes and Queries* 10th Series, vol. 2 (1904) p. 23

## Henri Estienne 1531–98

17 *Si jeunesse savait; si vieillesse pouvait.*
   If youth knew; if age could.
   *Les Prémices* (1594) bk. 4, epigram 4

## Sir George Etherege (or Etheredge) c.1635–91

18 I walk within the purlieus of the Law.
   *Love in a Tub* (1664) act 1, sc. 3

## Euclid fl. c.300 BC

19 *Quod erat demonstrandum*
   Which was to be proved.
   Latin translation from the Greek of *Elementa* bk. 1, proposition 5 and *passim*

20 A line is length without breadth.
   *Elementa* bk. 1, definition 2

21 There is no 'royal road' to geometry.
   Addressed to Ptolemy I, in Proclus *Commentary on the First Book of Euclid's Elementa* prologue, pt. 2

## Euripides c.485–c.406 BC

22 My tongue swore, but my mind's unsworn.
   *Hippolytus* l. 612 (lamenting the breaking of an oath)

## Abel Evans 1679–1737

23 Under this stone, Reader, survey
   Dead Sir John Vanbrugh's house of clay.
   Lie heavy on him, Earth! for he
   Laid many heavy loads on thee!
   'Epitaph on Sir John Vanbrugh, Architect of Blenheim Palace'

## David Everett 1769–1813

24 Large streams from little fountains flow,
   Tall oaks from little acorns grow.
   'Lines Written for a School Declamation' (aged 7)

## Viscount Eversley

*See* CHARLES SHAW-LEFEVRE

## William Norman Ewer 1885–1976

1 I gave my life for freedom—This I know:
For those who bade me fight had told me
so.
'Five Souls' (1917)

2 How odd
Of God
To choose
The Jews.
In *Week-End Book* (1924) p. 117. Cf. 73:21

## F. W. Faber 1814–63

3 My God, how wonderful Thou art!
Thy Majesty how bright!
'The Eternal Father' (1854 hymn)

4 The music of the Gospel leads us home.
'The Pilgrims of the Night' (1854 hymn)

5 There's a wideness in God's mercy
Like the wideness of the sea.
'Souls of men, why will ye scatter' (1854
hymn)

## Robert Fabyan d. 1513

6 Finally he paid the debt of nature.
*New Chronicles of England and France* (1516)
vol. 1, ch. 41

7 Ranulphe says he took a surfeit by eating
of a lamprey, and thereof died.
*New Chronicles of England and France* (1516)
vol. 1, ch. 229 (of Henry I)

8 The Duke of Clarence ... then being a
prisoner in the Tower, was secretly put to
death and drowned in a barrel of
Malmesey wine.
*New Chronicles of England and France* (1516)
vol. 2 ('1478')

## Clifton Fadiman 1904–

9 Milk's leap toward immortality.
*Any Number Can Play* (1957) p. 105 (of cheese)

10 The mama of dada.
*Party of One* (1955) p. 90 (of Gertrude Stein)

## Lucius Cary, Viscount Falkland
1610–43

11 When it is not necessary to change, it is
necessary not to change.
*Discourses of Infallibility* (1660) 'A Speech
concerning Episcopacy' (1641)

## Eleanor Farjeon 1881–1965

12 Morning has broken
Like the first morning,
Blackbird has spoken
Like the first bird.
'A Morning Song (for the First Day of
Spring)' (1957)

## Edward Farmer *c.*1809–76

13 I have no pain, dear mother, now;
But oh! I am so dry:
Just moisten poor Jim's lips once more;
And, mother, do not cry!
'The Collier's Dying Child'. Cf. 8:3

## King Farouk 1920–65

14 Soon there will be only five Kings left—the
King of England, the King of Spades, the
King of Clubs, the King of Hearts and the
King of Diamonds.
In Lord Boyd-Orr *As I Recall* (1966) ch. 21
(Cairo, 1948)

## George Farquhar 1678–1707

15 There is no scandal like rags, nor any
crime so shameful as poverty.
*The Beaux' Stratagem* (1707) act 1, sc. 1

16 No woman can be a beauty without a
fortune.
*The Beaux' Stratagem* (1707) act 2, sc. 2

17 Crimes, like virtues, are their own rewards.
*The Inconstant* (1702) act 4, sc. 2

18 Money is the sinews of love, as of war.
*Love and a Bottle* (1698) act 2, sc. 1. Cf. 100:29

19 Poetry's a mere drug, Sir.
*Love and a Bottle* (1698) act 3, sc. 2. Cf. 211:3

20 Hanging and marriage, you know, go by
Destiny.
*The Recruiting Officer* (1706) act 3, sc. 2

21 A lady, if undressed at Church, looks silly,
One cannot be devout in dishabilly.
*The Stage Coach* (1704) prologue

## Guy Fawkes 1570–1606

22 A desperate disease requires a dangerous
remedy.
6 November 1605. See *Dictionary of National
Biography* (1917– ) vol. 6, p. 1132. Cf. 276:27

## James Fenton 1949–

23 It is not what they built. It is what they
knocked down.
It is not the houses. It is the spaces
between the houses.
It is not the streets that exist. It is the
streets that no longer exist.
*German Requiem* (1981) p. 1

## Emperor Ferdinand I 1503–64

24 *Fiat justitia et pereat mundus.*
Let justice be done, though the world
perish.
Motto. See Johannes Manlius *Locorum
Communium Collectanea* (1563) vol. 2 'De Lege:
Octatum Praeceptum'. Cf. 342:25

## Ludwig Feuerbach 1804–72

1 *Der Mensch ist, was er isst.*
Man is what he eats.
In Jacob Moleschott *Lehre der Nahrungsmittel: Für das Volk* (1850) 'Advertisement'. Cf. 72:7

## Eugene Field 1850–95

2 Wynken, Blynken, and Nod one night
Sailed off in a wooden shoe—
Sailed on a river of crystal light,
Into a sea of dew.
'Wynken, Blynken, and Nod' (1889)

3 He played the King as though under momentary apprehension that someone else was about to play the ace.
Of Creston Clarke as King Lear; review attributed to Field, in *Denver Tribune c.*1880

## Henry Fielding 1707–54

4 One fool at least in every married couple.
*Amelia* (1751) bk. 9, ch. 4

5 The dusky night rides down the sky,
And ushers in the morn;
The hounds all join in glorious cry,
The huntsman winds his horn:
And a-hunting we will go.
*Don Quixote in England* (1733) act 2, sc. 5
'A-Hunting We Will Go'

6 Oh! The roast beef of England,
And old England's roast beef.
*The Grub Street Opera* (1731) act 3, sc. 3

7 He in a few minutes ravished this fair creature, or at least would have ravished her, if she had not, by a timely compliance, prevented him.
*Jonathan Wild* (1743) bk. 3, ch. 7

8 Public schools are the nurseries of all vice and immorality.
*Joseph Andrews* (1742) bk. 3, ch. 5

9 Love and scandal are the best sweeteners of tea.
*Love in Several Masques* (1728) act 4, sc. 11

10 What is commonly called love, namely the desire of satisfying a voracious appetite with a certain quantity of delicate white human flesh.
*Tom Jones* (1749) bk. 6, ch. 1

11 His designs were strictly honourable, as the phrase is; that is, to rob a lady of her fortune by way of marriage.
*Tom Jones* (1749) bk. 11, ch. 4

12 That monstrous animal, a husband and wife.
*Tom Jones* (1749) bk. 15, ch. 9

13 All Nature wears one universal grin.
*Tom Thumb the Great* (1731) act 1, sc. 1

## Dorothy Fields 1905–74

14 A fine romance with no kisses.
A fine romance, my friend, this is.
'A Fine Romance' (1936 song)

15 Grab your coat, and get your hat,
Leave your worry on the doorstep,
Just direct your feet
To the sunny side of the street.
'On the Sunny Side of the Street' (1930 song)

## W. C. Fields 1880–1946

16 Never give a sucker an even break.
Title of a W. C. Fields film (1941); the catch-phrase (Fields's own) is said to have originated in the musical comedy *Poppy* (1923)

17 It ain't a fit night out for man or beast.
Adopted by Fields but claimed by him not to be original. See Letter, 8 February 1944, in *W. C. Fields by Himself* (1974) pt. 2

18 Hell, I never vote *for* anybody. I always vote *against*.
In R. L. Taylor *W. C. Fields* (1950) p. 228. Cf. 1:10

*See also* LEO ROSTEN

## Ronald Firbank 1886–1926

19 I remember the average curate at home as something between a eunuch and a snigger.
*The Flower Beneath the Foot* (1923) ch. 4

20 There was a pause—just long enough for an angel to pass, flying slowly.
*Vainglory* (1915) ch. 6

21 All millionaires love a baked apple.
*Vainglory* (1915) ch. 13

## H. A. L. Fisher 1856–1940

22 Europe is a continent of energetic mongrels.
*A History of Europe* (1935) ch. 1

## Lord Fisher 1841–1920

23 Sack the lot!
Letter to *The Times*, 2 September 1919 (on government overmanning and overspending)

24 Never contradict. Never explain. Never apologize.
Letter to *The Times*, 5 September 1919. Cf. 122:19, 175:13

25 Yours till Hell freezes.
Attributed to Fisher, but not original. See F. Ponsonby *Reflections of Three Reigns* (1951) p. 131

## Marve Fisher

26 I like Chopin and Bizet, and the voice of Doris Day,
Gershwin songs and old forgotten carols.
But the music that excels is the sound of oil wells
As they slurp, slurp, slurp into the barrels.
'An Old-Fashioned Girl' (1954 song)

1 I want an old-fashioned house
With an old-fashioned fence
And an old-fashioned millionaire.
'An Old-Fashioned Girl' (1954 song)

## Albert H. Fitz

2 You are my honey, honeysuckle, I am the
bee.
'The Honeysuckle and the Bee' (1901 song)

## Charles Fitzgeffrey c.1575–1638

3 And bold and hard adventures t' undertake,
Leaving his country for his country's sake.
*Sir Francis Drake* (1596) st. 213

## Edward Fitzgerald 1809–83

4 Awake! for Morning in the bowl of night
Has flung the stone that puts the stars to
flight:
And Lo! the Hunter of the East has caught
The Sultan's turret in a noose of light.
*The Rubáiyát of Omar Khayyám* (1859) st. 1

5 Each morn a thousand roses brings, you
say;
Yes, but where leaves the rose of
yesterday?
*The Rubáiyát of Omar Khayyám* (4th ed., 1879)
st. 9

6 Here with a loaf of bread beneath the
bough,
A flask of wine, a book of verse—and Thou
Beside me singing in the wilderness—
And wilderness is paradise enow.
*The Rubáiyát of Omar Khayyám* (1859) st. 11. 'A
book of verses underneath the bough, / A
jug of wine, a loaf of bread—and Thou /
Beside me singing in the wilderness— / Oh,
wilderness were paradise enow!' in 4th ed.
(1879) st. 12

7 Ah, take the cash in hand and waive the
rest;
Oh, the brave music of a *distant* drum!
*The Rubáiyát of Omar Khayyám* (1859) st. 12.
'Ah, take the cash and let the credit go, / Nor
heed the rumble of a distant drum!' in 4th
ed. (1879) st. 13

8 I sometimes think that never blows so red
The rose as where some buried Caesar
bled.
*The Rubáiyát of Omar Khayyám* (1859) st. 18

9 Dust into dust, and under dust, to lie,
Sans wine, sans song, sans singer,
and—sans End!
*The Rubáiyát of Omar Khayyám* (1859) st. 23

10 One thing is certain, and the rest is lies;
The flower that once hath blown for ever
dies.
*The Rubáiyát of Omar Khayyám* (1859) st. 26

11 Ah, fill the cup:—what boots it to repeat
How time is slipping underneath our feet:
Unborn TO-MORROW, and dead YESTERDAY,
Why fret about them if TO-DAY be sweet!
*The Rubáiyát of Omar Khayyám* (1859) st. 37

12 'Tis all a chequer-board of nights and days
Where Destiny with Men for pieces plays:
Hither and thither moves, and mates, and
slays,
And one by one back in the closet lays.
*The Rubáiyát of Omar Khayyám* (1859) st. 49.
'But helpless pieces of the game he plays /
Upon this chequer-board of nights and
days; / Hither and thither moves, and
checks, and slays, / And one by one back
in the closet lays' in 4th ed. (1879) st. 69

13 The ball no question makes of Ayes and
Noes,
But here or there as strikes the player
goes;
And he that tossed you down into the field,
He knows about it all—HE knows—HE
knows!
*The Rubáiyát of Omar Khayyám* (4th ed., 1879)
st. 70

14 The moving finger writes; and, having writ,
Moves on: nor all thy piety nor wit
Shall lure it back to cancel half a line,
Nor all thy tears wash out a word of it.
*The Rubáiyát of Omar Khayyám* (1859) st. 51

15 That inverted bowl we call The Sky.
*The Rubáiyát of Omar Khayyám* (1859) st. 52

16 'Who *is* the potter, pray, and who the pot?'
*The Rubáiyát of Omar Khayyám* (1859) st. 60

17 Indeed the idols I have loved so long
Have done my credit in this world much
wrong:
Have drowned my glory in a shallow cup
And sold my reputation for a song.
*The Rubáiyát of Omar Khayyám* (4th ed., 1879)
st. 93

18 Alas, that spring should vanish with the
rose!
*The Rubáiyát of Omar Khayyám* (1859) st. 72

19 Taste is the feminine of genius.
To J. R. Lowell, October 1877, in A. and A.
Terhune (eds.) *Letters* (1980) vol. 4

## F. Scott Fitzgerald 1896–1940

20 Let me tell you about the very rich. They
are different from you and me.
*All the Sad Young Men* (1926) 'Rich Boy' (to
which Ernest Hemingway replied, 'Yes, they
have more money')

21 Her voice is full of money.
*The Great Gatsby* (1925) ch. 7 (of Daisy)

22 In a real dark night of the soul it is always
three o'clock in the morning.
'Handle with Care' in *Esquire* March 1936.
'Dark night of the soul' being a translation
of the Spanish title of a work (1578–80) by
St John of the Cross

23 There are no second acts in American lives.
Edmund Wilson (ed.) *The Last Tycoon* (1941)
'Hollywood, etc.'

## Robert Fitzsimmons 1862–1917

1 The bigger they are, the further they have to fall.

> Prior to a boxing match, in *Brooklyn Daily Eagle* 11 August 1900 (similar forms found in proverbs since the 15th century)

## Bud Flanagan 1896–1968

2 Underneath the Arches,
I dream my dreams away,
Underneath the Arches,
On cobble-stones I lay.

> 'Underneath the Arches' (1932 song)

## Michael Flanders 1922–75 and Donald Swann 1923–

3 Have Some Madeira, M'dear.

> Title of song (c.1956)

4 Mud! Mud! Glorious mud!
Nothing quite like it for cooling the blood.

> 'The Hippopotamus' (1952)

5 Eating people is wrong!

> 'The Reluctant Cannibal' (1956 song)

6 That monarch of the road,
Observer of the Highway Code,
That big six-wheeler
Scarlet-painted
London Transport
Diesel-engined
Ninety-seven horse power
Omnibus!

> 'A Transport of Delight' (c.1956 song)

## Gustave Flaubert 1821–80

7 Human speech is like a cracked kettle on which we tap crude rhythms for bears to dance to, while we long to make music that will melt the stars.

> *Madame Bovary* (1857) pt. 1, ch. 12 (tr. F. Steegmuller)

8 You can calculate the worth of a man by the number of his enemies, and the importance of a work of art by the harm that is spoken of it.

> Letter to Louise Colet, 14 June 1853, in M. Nadeau (ed.) *Correspondence 1853–56* (1964)

9 Poetry is a subject as precise as geometry.

> Letter to Louise Colet, 14 August 1853, in M. Nadeau (ed.) *Correspondence 1853–56* (1964)

10 Style is life! It is the very life-blood of thought!

> Letter to Louise Colet, 7 September 1853, in M. Nadeau (ed.) *Correspondence 1853–56* (1964)

11 The artist must be in his work as God is in creation, invisible and all-powerful; one must sense him everywhere but never see him.

> Letter to Mlle Leroyer de Chantepie, 18 March 1857, in M. Nadeau (ed.) *Correspondence 1857–64* (1965)

12 Books are made not like children but like pyramids ... and they're just as useless! and they stay in the desert! ... Jackals piss at their foot and the bourgeois climb up on them.

> Letter to Ernest Feydeau, November/ December 1857, in M. Nadeau (ed.) *Correspondence 1857–64* (1965)

13 Human life is a sad show, undoubtedly: ugly, heavy and complex. Art has no other end, for people of feeling, than to conjure away the burden and bitterness.

> Letter to Amelie Bosquet, July 1864, in M. Nadeau (ed.) *Correspondence 1857–64* (1965)

## James Elroy Flecker 1884–1915

14 West of these out to seas colder than the Hebrides
I must go
Where the fleet of stars is anchored and the young
Star captains glow.

> 'The Dying Patriot' (1913)

15 The dragon-green, the luminous, the dark, the serpent-haunted sea.

> 'The Gates of Damascus' (1913)

16 We who with songs beguile your pilgrimage
And swear that beauty lives though lilies die.

> *The Golden Journey to Samarkand* (1913) 'Prologue'

17 For lust of knowing what should not be known,
We take the Golden Road to Samarkand.

> *The Golden Journey to Samarkand* (1913) pt. 1, 'Epilogue'

18 I have seen old ships sail like swans asleep
Beyond the village which men still call Tyre,
With leaden age o'ercargoed, dipping deep
For Famagusta and the hidden sun
That rings black Cyprus with a lake of fire.

> 'Old Ships' (1915)

19 A ship, an isle, a sickle moon—
With few but with how splendid stars
The mirrors of the sea are strewn
Between their silver bars!

> 'A Ship, an Isle, and a Sickle Moon' (1913)

20 O friend unseen, unborn, unknown,
Student of our sweet English tongue,
Read out my words at night, alone.

> 'To a Poet a Thousand Years Hence' (1910)

## Ian Fleming 1908–64

21 A medium Vodka dry Martini—with a slice of lemon peel. Shaken and not stirred.

> *Dr No* (1958) ch. 14

## Marjory Fleming 1803–11

22 The most devilish thing is 8 times 8 and 7 times 7 it is what nature itselfe cant endure.

> *Journals, Letters and Verses* (ed. A. Esdaile, 1934) p. 47

1 His noses cast is of the roman
He is a very pretty weoman
I could not get a rhyme for roman
And was obliged to call it weoman.
'Sonnet'

## Robert, Marquis de Flers
1872–1927 and Arman de
Caillavet 1869–1915

2 Democracy is the name we give the people
whenever we need them.
*L'habit vert* act 1, sc. 12

## Andrew Fletcher of Saltoun
1655–1716

3 If a man were permitted to make all the
ballads, he need not care who should make
the laws of a nation.
*Political Works* (1732) pt. 7 'Account of a
Conversation concerning a Right Regulation
of Government for the Good of Mankind ... '
(1704)

## John Fletcher 1579–1625

4 Death hath so many doors to let out life.
*The Custom of the Country* (with Massinger)
act 2, sc. 2. Cf. 222:6, 270:8

5 Care-charming Sleep, thou easer of all
woes,
Brother to Death.
*Valentinian* (performed *c.*1610–14) act 5, sc. 7
'Song'

6 Whistle and she'll come to you.
*Wit Without Money* act 4, sc. 4. Cf. 82:19

7 Charity and beating begins at home.
*Wit Without Money* act 5, sc. 2

*See also* FRANCIS BEAUMONT and JOHN FLETCHER,
SHAKESPEARE *Henry VIII*

## Phineas Fletcher 1582–1650

8 Drop, drop, slow tears,
And bathe those beauteous feet,
Which brought from Heaven
The news and Prince of Peace.
'An Hymn'(1633)

9 Love's tongue is in the eyes.
*Piscatory Eclogues* (1633) no. 5, st. 13

10 Love is like linen often changed, the
sweeter.
*Sicelides* (performed 1614) act 3, sc. 5

11 The coward's weapon, poison.
*Sicelides* (performed 1614) act 5, sc. 3

## Jean-Pierre Claris de Florian
1755–94

12 *Plaisir d'amour ne dure qu'un moment,
Chagrin d'amour dure toute la vie.*
Love's pleasure lasts but a moment; love's
sorrow lasts all through life.
*Célestine* (1784) Cf. 217:2

## John Florio *c.*1553–1625

13 England is the paradise of women, the
purgatory of men, and the hell of horses.
*Second Frutes* (1591) ch. 12

## Ferdinand Foch 1851–1929

14 My centre is giving way, my right is
retreating, situation excellent, I am
attacking.
Message during the first Battle of the Marne,
September 1914; in R. Recouly *Foch* (1919)
ch. 6

15 This is not a peace treaty, it is an armistice
for twenty years.
At the signing of the Treaty of Versailles,
1919; in P. Reynaud *Mémoires* (1963) vol. 2,
p. 457

## J. Foley 1906–1970

16 Old soldiers never die,
They simply fade away.
'Old Soldiers Never Die' (1920 song)

## Michael Foot 1913–

17 Think of it! A second Chamber selected by
the Whips. A seraglio of eunuchs.
Speech, *Hansard* 3 February 1969, col. 88

18 It is not necessary that every time he rises
he should give his famous imitation of a
semi-house-trained polecat.
Speech, *Hansard* 2 March 1978, col. 668 (of
Norman Tebbit)

## Samuel Foote 1720–77

19 Born in a cellar ... and living in a garret.
*The Author* (1757) act 2

20 So she went into the garden to cut a
cabbage-leaf to make an apple-pie; and at
the same time a great she-bear coming up
the street, pops its head into the shop.
'What! no soap?' So he died, and she very
imprudently married the barber; and there
were present the Picninnies, and the
Joblillies, and the Garyulies, and the grand
Panjandrum himself, with the little round
button at top; and they all fell to playing
the game of catch as catch can, till the gun
powder ran out at the heels of their boots.
Nonsense composed to test the vaunted
memory of the actor Charles Macklin; in
Maria Edgeworth *Harry and Lucy* (1825) vol. 2,
p. 152. See *Quarterly Review* (1854) vol. 95,
p. 516

**1** He is not only dull in himself, but the cause of dullness in others.

Of a dull law lord, in James Boswell *Life of Samuel Johnson* (1934 ed.) vol. 4, p. 178 (1783). Cf. 278:16

## Miss C. F. Forbes 1817–1911

**2** The sense of being well-dressed gives a feeling of inward tranquillity which religion is powerless to bestow.

In R. W. Emerson *Letters and Social Aims* (1876) p. 79

## Gerald Ford 1909–

**3** I am a Ford, not a Lincoln.

On taking the vice-presidential oath, 6 December 1973; in *Washington Post* 7 December 1973

**4** Our long national nightmare is over.

On being sworn in as President, 9 August 1974; in G. J. Lankevich *Gerald R. Ford* (1977)

**5** If the Government is big enough to give you everything you want, it is big enough to take away everything you have.

In J. F. Parker *If Elected* (1960) p. 193

## Henry Ford 1863–1947

**6** History is more or less bunk.

In *Chicago Tribune* 25 May 1916

**7** Any customer can have a car painted any colour that he wants so long as it is black.

In Henry Ford, Samuel Crowther *My Life and Work* (1922) ch. 4

**8** What we call evil is simply ignorance bumping its head in the dark.

In *Observer* 16 March 1930

## John Ford 1586–after 1639

**9** I am ... a mushroom
On whom the dew of heaven drops now and then.

*The Broken Heart* (1633) act 1, sc. 3

**10** He hath shook hands with time.

*The Broken Heart* (1633) act 5, sc. 2

**11**          Why, I hold fate
Clasped in my fist, and could command the course
Of time's eternal motion, hadst thou been
One thought more steady than an ebbing sea.

*'Tis Pity She's a Whore* (1633) act 5, sc. 4

## Lena Guilbert Ford 1870–1916

**12** Keep the Home-fires burning,
While your hearts are yearning,
Though your lads are far away
They dream of Home.
There's a silver lining
Through the dark cloud shining;
Turn the dark cloud inside out,
Till the boys come Home.

'Till the Boys Come Home!' (1914 song); music by Ivor Novello

## Howell Forgy 1908–83

**13** Praise the Lord and pass the ammunition.

At Pearl Harbor, 7 December 1941, while sailors passed ammunition by hand to the deck; in *New York Times* 1 November 1942 (later title of song by Frank Loesser, 1942)

## E. M. Forster 1879–1970

**14** American women shoot the hippopotamus with eyebrows made of platinum.

*Abinger Harvest* (1936) 'Mickey and Minnie'. Cf. 33:1

**15** They go forth into it [the world] with well-developed bodies, fairly developed minds, and undeveloped hearts.

*Abinger Harvest* (1936) 'Notes on English Character' (of public-school men)

**16** Yes—oh dear yes—the novel tells a story.

*Aspects of the Novel* (1927) ch. 2

**17** The test of a round character is whether it is capable of surprising in a convincing way. If it never surprises, it is flat. If it does not convince, it is flat pretending to be round.

*Aspects of the Novel* (1927) ch. 4

**18** A dogged attempt to cover the universe with mud, an inverted Victorianism, an attempt to make crossness and dirt succeed where sweetness and light failed.

*Aspects of the Novel* (1927) ch. 6 (of James Joyce's *Ulysses*)

**19** Railway termini. They are our gates to the glorious and the unknown. Through them we pass out into adventure and sunshine, to them, alas! we return.

*Howards End* (1910) ch. 2

**20** Personal relations are the important thing for ever and ever, and not this outer life of telegrams and anger.

*Howards End* (1910) ch. 19

**21** Only connect! ... Only connect the prose and the passion.

*Howards End* (1910) ch. 22

**22** There is much good luck in the world, but it is luck. We are none of us safe. We are children, playing or quarrelling on the line.

*The Longest Journey* (1907) ch. 12

**23** Very notable was his distinction between coarseness and vulgarity (coarseness, revealing something; vulgarity, concealing something).

*The Longest Journey* (1907) ch. 26

**24** The so-called white races are really pinko-grey.

*A Passage to India* (1924) ch. 7

**25** Pathos, piety, courage—they exist, but are identical, and so is filth. Everything exists, nothing has value.

*A Passage to India* (1924) ch. 14

**26** Where there is officialism every human relationship suffers.

*A Passage to India* (1924) ch. 24

1 Like all gossip—it's merely one of those half-alive things that try to crowd out real life.

    *A Passage to India* (1924) ch. 31

2 If I had to choose between betraying my country and betraying my friend, I hope I should have the guts to betray my country.

    *Two Cheers for Democracy* (1951) 'What I Believe'

3 So Two cheers for Democracy: one because it admits variety and two because it permits criticism. Two cheers are quite enough: there is no occasion to give three. Only Love the Beloved Republic deserves that.

    *Two Cheers for Democracy* (1951) 'What I Believe' ('Love, the beloved republic' borrowed from Swinburne's poem 'Hertha')

## Venantius Fortunatus AD
c.530–c.610

4 *Pange, lingua, gloriosi*
*Proelium certaminis.*
Sing, my tongue, of the battle in the glorious struggle.

    'Pange lingua gloriosi' (Passiontide hymn: 'Sing, my tongue, the glorious battle')

5 *Vexilla regis prodeunt,*
*Fulget crucis mysterium.*
The banners of the king advance, the mystery of the cross shines bright.

    'Vexilla Regis' (hymn: 'The royal banners forward go')

## Charles Foster 1828–1904

6 Isn't this a billion dollar country?

    At the 51st Congress, responding to a Democratic gibe about a 'million dollar Congress'; also attributed to Thomas B. Reed, who reported the exchange in *North American Review* March 1892, vol. 154, p. 319

## Sir George Foster 1847–1931

7 These somewhat troublesome days when the great Mother Empire stands splendidly isolated in Europe.

    In *Official Report of the Debates of the House of Commons of the Dominion of Canada* (1896) vol. 41, col. 176 (16 January 1896). On 22 January 1896, *The Times* referred to this speech under the heading 'Splendid Isolation'

## John Foster 1770–1843

8 But the two classes [the educated and the uneducated] so beheld in contrast, might they not seem to belong to two different nations?

    *Essay on the Evils of Popular Ignorance* (1820) p. 277. Cf. 122:6

## Stephen Collins Foster 1826–64

9 Beautiful dreamer, wake unto me,
Starlight and dewdrop are waiting for thee.

    'Beautiful Dreamer' (1864 song)

10 Gwine to run all night!
Gwine to run all day!
I'll bet my money on de bobtail nag—
Somebody bet on de bay.

    'De Camptown Races' (1850) chorus

11 I dream of Jeanie with the light brown hair,
Floating, like a vapour, on the soft summer air.

    'Jeanie with the Light Brown Hair' (1854)

12 Way down upon the Swanee River,
Far, far, away,
There's where my heart is turning ever;
There's where the old folks stay.

    'The Old Folks at Home' (1851)

13 All the world is sad and dreary
Everywhere I roam,
Oh! darkies, how my heart grows weary,
Far from the old folks at home.

    'The Old Folks at Home' (1851) chorus

## Charles Fourier 1772–1837

14 The extension of women's rights is the basic principle of all social progress.

    *Théorie des Quatre Mouvements* (1808) vol. 2, ch. 4

## Charles James Fox 1749–1806

15 He was uniformly of an opinion ... that the right of governing was not property but a trust.

    On the younger Pitt's scheme of Parliamentary Reform, 1785; in J. L. Hammond *Charles James Fox* (1903) ch. 4

16 How much the greatest event it is that ever happened in the world! and how much the best!

    On the fall of the Bastille; letter to R. Fitzpatrick, 30 July 1789, in Lord John Russell *Life and Times of C. J. Fox* vol. 2 (1859) p. 361

## George Fox 1624–91

17 I saw also that there was an ocean of darkness and death, but an infinite ocean of light and love, which flowed over the ocean of darkness.

    *Journal* 1647 (ed. J. L. Nickalls, 1952) p. 19

18 Walk cheerfully over the world, answering that of God in every one.

    *Journal* 1656 (ed. J. L. Nickalls, 1952) p. 263

## Henry Fox
*See* 1ST LORD HOLLAND

## Anatole France 1844–1924

1 In every well-governed state, wealth is a sacred thing; in democracies it is the only sacred thing.
L'Île des pingouins (1908) pt. 6, ch. 2

2 They [the poor] have to labour in the face of the majestic equality of the law, which forbids the rich as well as the poor to sleep under bridges, to beg in the streets, and to steal bread.
Le Lys rouge (1894) ch. 7

3 The good critic is he who relates the adventures of his soul in the midst of masterpieces.
La Vie littéraire (1888) dedicatory letter

## Francis I 1494–1547

4 De toutes choses ne m'est demeuré que l'honneur et la vie qui est saulve.
Of all I had, only honour and life have been spared.
Letter to his mother following his defeat at Pavia, 1525; in Collection des Documents Inédits sur l'Histoire de France (1847) vol. 1, p. 129 (usually quoted 'Tout est perdu fors l'honneur [All is lost save honour]')

## St Francis de Sales 1567–1622

5 Big fires flare up in a wind, but little ones are blown out unless they are carried in under cover.
Introduction à la vie dévote (1609) pt. 3, ch. 34. Cf. 83:19, 201:24

6 Quantum ore dixerimus, sane cor cordi loquitur, lingua non nisi aures pulsat.
It has been well said, that heart speaks to heart, whereas language only speaks to the ears.
Latin translation of a letter to the Archbishop of Bourges, 5 October 1604, paraphrased for his motto by John Henry Newman as 'cor ad cor loquitur [heart speaks to heart]'

## St Francis of Assisi 1181–1226

7 Lord, make me an instrument of Your peace!
Where there is hatred let me sow love;
Where there is injury, pardon;
Where there is doubt, faith;
Where there is despair, hope;
Where there is darkness, light;
Where there is sadness, joy.
'Prayer of St Francis' (attributed)

## Benjamin Franklin 1706–90

8 Remember that time is money.
Advice to a Young Tradesman (1748)

9 Some are weather-wise, some are otherwise.
Poor Richard's Almanac (1735) February

10 Necessity never made a good bargain.
Poor Richard's Almanac (1735) April

11 He that lives upon hope will die fasting.
Poor Richard's Almanac (1758) preface

12 A little neglect may breed mischief ... for want of a nail, the shoe was lost; for want of a shoe the horse was lost; and for want of a horse the rider was lost.
Poor Richard's Almanac (1758) preface

13 We must indeed all hang together, or, most assuredly, we shall all hang separately.
At the Signing of the Declaration of Independence, 4 July 1776 (possibly not original). See P. M. Zall Ben Franklin (1980) p. 154

14 There never was a good war, or a bad peace.
Letter to Josiah Quincy, 11 September 1783, in Works (1882) vol. 10, p. 11

15 In this world nothing can be said to be certain, except death and taxes.
Letter to Jean Baptiste Le Roy, 13 November 1789, in Works (1817) ch. 6.

16 Man is a tool-making animal.
In James Boswell Life of Samuel Johnson (1934 ed.) vol. 3, p. 245 (7 April 1778)

17 What is the use of a new-born child?
When asked what was the use of a new invention; in J. Parton Life and Times of Benjamin Franklin (1864) pt. 4, ch. 17

## Frederick the Great 1712–86

18 Drive out prejudices through the door, and they will return through the window.
Letter to Voltaire, 19 March 1771, in Oeuvres Complètes (1790) vol. 12

19 My people and I have come to an agreement which satisfies us both. They are to say what they please, and I am to do what I please.
His interpretation of benevolent despotism (attributed)

20 Rascals, would you live for ever?
To hesitant Guards at Kolin, 18 June 1757 (attributed)

## E. A. Freeman 1823–92

21 History is past politics, and politics is present history.
Methods of Historical Study (1886) p. 44

## John Hookham Frere 1769–1846

22 The feathered race with pinions skim the air—
Not so the mackerel, and still less the bear!
'The Progress of Man' (1798) canto 1, l. 34

## Sigmund Freud 1856–1939

23 Anatomy is destiny.
Collected Writings (1924) vol. 5, p. 210

**1** The interpretation of dreams is the royal road to a knowledge of the unconscious activities of the mind.

*The Interpretation of Dreams* (2nd ed., 1909) ch. 7, sect. E (often quoted 'Dreams are the royal road to the unconscious')

**2** 'Itzig, where are you riding to?' 'Don't ask me, ask the horse.'

Letter to W. Fliess, 7 July 1898, in *Origins of Psychoanalysis* (1950) p. 275

**3** What does a woman want?

Letter to Marie Bonaparte, in E. Jones *Sigmund Freud* (1955) vol. 2, pt. 3, ch. 16

**4** All that matters is love and work.

Attributed

## Max Frisch 1911–

**5** Technology . . . the knack of so arranging the world that we need not experience it.

*Homo Faber* (1957) pt. 2

## Charles Frohman 1860–1915

**6** Why fear death? It is the most beautiful adventure in life.

Last words before drowning in the *Lusitania*, 7 May 1915; in I. F. Marcosson and D. Frohman *Charles Frohman* (1916) ch. 19. Cf. 29:13

## Erich Fromm 1900–80

**7** In the nineteenth century the problem was that *God is dead*; in the twentieth century the problem is that *man is dead*.

*The Sane Society* (1955) ch. 9

## Robert Frost 1874–1963

**8** . . . Earth's the right place for love:
I don't know where it's likely to go better.

'Birches' (1916)

**9** Most of the change we think we see in life
Is due to truths being in and out of favour.

'The Black Cottage' (1914)

**10** Forgive, O Lord, my little jokes on Thee
And I'll forgive Thy great big one on me.

'Cluster of Faith' (1962)

**11** 'Home is the place where, when you have to go there,
They have to take you in.'
'I should have called it
Something you somehow haven't to deserve.'

'The Death of the Hired Man' (1914)

**12** Some say the world will end in fire,
Some say in ice.

'Fire and Ice' (1923)

**13** The land was ours before we were the land's.

'The Gift Outright' (1942)

**14** Happiness makes up in height for what it lacks in length.

Title of poem (1942)

**15** Something there is that doesn't love a wall.

'Mending Wall' (1914)

**16** My apple trees will never get across
And eat the cones under his pines, I tell him.
He only says, 'Good fences make good neighbours.'

'Mending Wall' (1914)

**17** Before I built a wall I'd ask to know
What I was walling in or walling out,
And to whom I was like to give offence.

'Mending Wall' (1914)

**18** I never dared be radical when young
For fear it would make me conservative when old.

'Precaution' (1936)

**19** Two roads diverged in a wood, and I—
I took the one less travelled by,
And that has made all the difference.

'The Road Not Taken' (1916)

**20** We dance round in a ring and suppose,
But the Secret sits in the middle and knows.

'The Secret Sits' (1942)

**21** Pressed into service means pressed out of shape.

'The Self-Seeker' (1914)

**22** The best way out is always through.

'A Servant to Servants' (1914)

**23** The woods are lovely, dark and deep.
But I have promises to keep,
And miles to go before I sleep.

'Stopping by Woods on a Snowy Evening' (1923)

**24** The figure a poem makes. It begins in delight and ends in wisdom.

*Collected Poems* (1939) 'The Figure a Poem Makes'

**25** Like a piece of ice on a hot stove the poem must ride on its own melting. A poem may be worked over once it is in being, but may not be worried into being.

*Collected Poems* (1939) 'The Figure a Poem Makes'

**26** I'd as soon write free verse as play tennis with the net down.

In E. Lathem *Interviews with Robert Frost* (1966) p. 203

**27** Poetry is a way of taking life by the throat.

In E. S. Sergeant *Robert Frost* (1960) ch. 18

**28** Poetry is what is lost in translation. It is also what is lost in interpretation.

In L. Untermeyer *Robert Frost* (1964) p. 18

## Christopher Fry 1907–

**29** The dark is light enough.

Title of play (1954)

**30**  What after all
Is a halo? It's only one more thing to keep clean.

*The Lady's not for Burning* (1949) act 1

**1** Where in this small-talking world can I
find
A longitude with no platitude?
*The Lady's not for Burning* (1949) act 3

**2**                 The best
Thing we can do is to make wherever we're
lost in
Look as much like home as we can.
*The Lady's not for Burning* (1949) act 3

## Roger Fry 1866–1934

**3** Art is significant deformity.
In Virginia Woolf *Roger Fry* (1940) ch. 8

## R. Buckminster Fuller 1895–1983

**4** God, to me, it seems,
is a verb
not a noun,
proper or improper.
*No More Secondhand God* (1963) p. 28 (untitled
poem written in 1940). Cf. 175:24

## Thomas Fuller 1608–61

**5** Anger is one of the sinews of the soul.
*The Holy State and the Profane State* bk. 3 'Of
Anger'

**6** Light (God's eldest daughter) is a principal
beauty in building.
*The Holy State and the Profane State* bk. 3 'Of
Building'

## Thomas Fuller 1654–1734

**7** We are all Adam's children but silk makes
the difference.
*Gnomologia* (1732) no. 5425

## Alfred Funke b. 1869

**8** *Gott strafe England!*
God punish England!
*Schwert und Myrte* (1914) p. 78

## Sir David Maxwell Fyfe 1900–67

*See* LORD KILMUIR

## Rose Fyleman 1877–1957

**9** There are fairies at the bottom of our
garden!
*Fairies and Chimneys* (1918) 'The Fairies'

## Thomas Gainsborough 1727–88

**10** We are all going to Heaven, and Vandyke is
of the company.
Attributed last words, in W. B. Boulton
*Thomas Gainsborough* (1905) ch. 9

## Hugh Gaitskell 1906–63

**11** There are some of us ... who will fight and
fight and fight again to save the Party we
love.
Speech at Labour Party Conference,
5 October 1960; in *Report of 59th Annual
Conference* p. 201

**12** It means the end of a thousand years of
history.
On a European federation; Speech at Labour
Party Conference, 3 October 1962, in *Report of
61st Annual Conference* p. 159

## Gaius (or Caius) AD *c.*110–*c.*180

**13** *Damnosa hereditas.*
Ruinous inheritance.
*The Institutes* bk. 2, ch. 163

## J. K. Galbraith 1908–

**14** These are the days when men of all social
disciplines and all political faiths seek the
comfortable and the accepted ... in minor
modification of the scriptural parable, the
bland lead the bland.
*The Affluent Society* (1958) ch. 1, sect. 3

**15** The greater the wealth, the thicker will be
the dirt.
*The Affluent Society* (1958) ch. 18, sect. 2

## Galileo Galilei 1564–1642

**16** *Eppur si muove.*
But it does move.
Attributed to Galileo after his recantation,
that the earth moves around the sun, in
1632

## John Galsworthy 1867–1933

**17** He was afflicted by the thought that where
Beauty was, nothing ever ran quite
straight, which, no doubt, was why so
many people looked on it as immoral.
*In Chancery* (1920) pt. 1, ch. 13

**18** A man of action forced into a state of
thought is unhappy until he can get out of
it.
*Maid in Waiting* (1931) ch. 3

## John Galt 1779–1839

**19** From the lone shieling of the misty island
Mountains divide us, and the waste of
seas—
Yet still the blood is strong, the heart is
Highland,
And we in dreams behold the Hebrides!
'Canadian Boat Song', attributed to Galt and
translated from the Gaelic in *Blackwoods
Edinburgh Magazine* September 1829 'Noctes
Ambrosianae' no. 46

## Greta Garbo 1905–90

1 I want to be alone.
   *Grand Hotel* (1932 film)

## Federico García Lorca 1899–1936

2 *A las cinco de la tarde.*
   *Eran las cinco en punto de la tarde.*
   *Un niño trajo la blanca sábana*
   *a las cinco de la tarde.*
   At five in the afternoon.
   It was exactly five in the afternoon.
   A boy brought the white sheet
   at five in the afternoon.
   *Llanto por Ignacio Sánchez Mejías* (1935) 'La
   Cogida y la muerte'

3 *Verde que te quiero verde.*
   *Verde viento. Verdes ramas.*
   *El barco sobre la mar*
   *y el caballo en la montaña.*
   Green how I love you green.
   Green wind.
   Green boughs.
   The ship on the sea
   and the horse on the mountain.
   *Romance sonámbulo* (1924–7)

## Richard Gardiner b. c.1533

4 Sowe Carrets in your Gardens, and humbly
   praise God for them, as for a singular and
   great blessing.
   *Profitable Instructions for the Manuring, Sowing
   and Planting of Kitchen Gardens* (1599)

## Ed Gardner 1901–63

5 Opera is when a guy gets stabbed in the
   back and, instead of bleeding, he sings.
   In *Duffy's Tavern* (US radio programme, 1940s)

## James A. Garfield 1831–81

6 Fellow-citizens: God reigns, and the
   Government at Washington lives!
   Speech on the assassination of President
   Lincoln, 1865. See *Death of President Garfield*
   (1881) p. 24

## John Nance Garner 1868–1967

7 The vice-presidency isn't worth a pitcher of
   warm piss.
   In O. C. Fisher *Cactus Jack* (1978) ch. 11

## David Garrick 1717–79

8 Heart of oak are our ships,
   Heart of oak are our men:
   We always are ready;
   Steady, boys, steady;
   We'll fight and we'll conquer again and
   again.
   *Harlequin's Invasion* (1759) 'Heart of Oak'
   (song)

9 Here lies Nolly Goldsmith, for shortness
   called Noll,
   Who wrote like an angel, but talked like
   poor Poll.
   'Impromptu Epitaph' (written 1773/4).
   Cf. 155:1

10 A fellow-feeling makes one wond'rous
   kind.
   'An Occasional Prologue on Quitting the
   Theatre' 10 June 1776

11 Heaven sends us good meat, but the Devil
   sends cooks.
   'On Doctor Goldsmith's Characteristical
   Cookery' (1777)
   *See also* GEORGE COLMAN and DAVID GARRICK

## William Lloyd Garrison 1805–79

12 I am in earnest—I will not equivocate—I
   will not excuse—I will not retreat a single
   inch—and I will be heard!
   *The Liberator* 1 January 1831 'Salutatory
   Address'

13 The compact which exists between the
   North and the South is 'a covenant with
   death and an agreement with hell'.
   Resolution adopted by the Massachusetts
   Anti-Slavery Society, 27 January 1843; in A.
   H. Grimke *William Lloyd Garrison* (1891)
   ch. 16. Cf. 45:28

## Sir Samuel Garth 1661–1719

14 Hard was their lodging, homely was their
   food;
   For all their luxury was doing good.
   'Claremont' (1715) l. 148

15 A barren superfluity of words.
   *The Dispensary* (1699) canto 2, l. 82

## Elizabeth Gaskell 1810–65

16 A man ... is *so* in the way in the house!
   *Cranford* (1853) ch. 1

17 Bombazine would have shown a deeper
   sense of her loss.
   *Cranford* (1853) ch. 7

18 I'll not listen to reason ... Reason always
   means what someone else has got to say.
   *Cranford* (1853) ch. 14

19 We donnot want dainties, we want bellyfulls.
   *Mary Barton* (1848) ch. 16

20 That kind of patriotism which consists in
   hating all other nations.
   *Sylvia's Lovers* (1863) ch. 1

## Gavarni 1804–66

21 *Les enfants terribles.*
   The little terrors.
   Title of a series of prints (1842)

## John Gay 1685–1732

1 O ruddier than the cherry,
O sweeter than the berry.
*Acis and Galatea* (performed 1718) pt. 2

2 How, like a moth, the simple maid
Still plays about the flame!
*The Beggar's Opera* (1728) act 1, sc. 4, air 4

3 Do you think your mother and I should
have lived comfortably so long together, if
ever we had been married?
*The Beggar's Opera* (1728) act 1, sc. 8

4 The comfortable estate of widowhood, is
the only hope that keeps up a wife's
spirits.
*The Beggar's Opera* (1728) act 1, sc. 10

5 If with me you'd fondly stray
Over the hills and far away.
*The Beggar's Opera* (1728) act 1, sc. 13, air 16

6 Youth's the season made for joys;
Love is then our duty.
*The Beggar's Opera* (1728) act 2, sc. 4, air 22

7 How happy could I be with either,
Were t'other dear charmer away!
*The Beggar's Opera* (1728) act 2, sc. 13, air 35

8 She who has never loved, has never lived.
*The Captives* (1724) act 2, sc. 2

9 She who trifles with all
Is less likely to fall
Than she who but trifles with one.
'The Coquet Mother and the Coquet
Daughter' (1727)

10 And when a lady's in the case,
You know, all other things give place.
*Fables* (1727) 'The Hare and Many Friends'
l. 41

11 An open foe may prove a curse,
But a pretended friend is worse.
*Fables* (1727) 'The Shepherd's Dog and the
Wolf' l. 33

12 Studious of elegance and ease,
Myself alone I seek to please.
*Fables* (1738) 'The Man, the Cat, the Dog, and
the Fly' l. 127

13 Give me, kind heaven, a private station,
A mind serene for contemplation.
*Fables* (1738) 'The Vulture, the Sparrow, and
Other Birds' l. 69

14 Behold the bright original appear.
'A Letter to a Lady' (1714) l. 85

15 Life is a jest; and all things show it.
I thought so once; but now I know it.
'My Own Epitaph' (1720)

16 An inconstant woman, tho' she has no
chance to be very happy, can never be very
unhappy.
'Polly' (1729) act 1, sc. 14

17 All in the Downs the fleet was moored,
The streamers waving in the wind,
When black-eyed Susan came aboard.
'Sweet William's Farewell to Black-Eyed
Susan' (1720)

## Noel Gay 1898–1954

18 I'm leaning on a lamp-post at the corner of
the street,
In case a certain little lady comes by.
'Leaning on a Lamp-Post' (1937); sung by
George Formby

## Sir Eric Geddes 1875–1937

19 The Germans ... are going to be squeezed
as a lemon is squeezed—until the pips
squeak.
Speech at Cambridge, 10 December 1918, in
*Cambridge Daily News* 11 December 1918

## George I 1660–1727

20 I hate all Boets and Bainters.
In John Campbell *Lives of the Chief Justices*
(1849) 'Lord Mansfield'

## George II 1683–1760

21 *Non, j'aurai des maîtresses.*
No, I shall have mistresses.
When Queen Caroline, on her deathbed,
urged him to marry again; in J. Hervey
*Memoirs of the Reign of George II* (1848) vol. 2.
The Queen replied, 'Ah! mon dieu! cela
n'empêche pas [Oh, my God! That won't make
any difference]'

22 Mad, is he? Then I hope he will *bite* some
of my other generals.
Replying to the Duke of Newcastle, who had
complained that General Wolfe was a
madman; in H. B. Willson *Life and Letters of
James Wolfe* (1909) ch. 17

## George III 1738–1820

23 Born and educated in this country, I glory
in the name of Briton.
*The King's Speech on Opening the Session* in
*Hansard* 18 November 1760, col. 942

24 Was there ever such stuff as great part of
Shakespeare? Only one must not say so!
In *Diary and Letters of Madame d'Arblay* [Fanny
Burney] vol. 2 (1842) Diary, 19 December
1785

## George V 1865–1936

25 The Old Country must wake up if she
intends to maintain her old position of
pre-eminence in her Colonial trade against
foreign competitors.
Speech at Guildhall, 5 December 1901, in *The
Times* 6 December 1901; reprinted in 1911
with the title 'Wake up, England'

26 No more coals to Newcastle, no more
Hoares to Paris
Following Samuel Hoare's resignation as
Foreign Secretary on 18 December 1935; in
Earl of Avon *Facing the Dictators* (1962) pt. 2,
ch. 1

1 After I am dead, the boy will ruin himself
in twelve months.
> Of his son, the future Edward VIII; in K.
> Middlemas and J. Barnes *Baldwin* (1969)
> ch. 34

2 Bugger Bognor.
> Possibly on his deathbed. See K. Rose *King
> George V* (1983) ch. 9

3 How's the Empire?
> To his private secretary on the morning of
> his death; in K. Rose *King George V* (1983)
> ch. 10

## George VI 1895–1952

4 Abroad is bloody.
> In W. H. Auden *A Certain World* (1970)
> 'Royalty'. Cf. 232:10

5 I feel happier now that we have no allies
to be polite to and to pamper.
> To Queen Mary, 27 June 1940; in J. Wheeler-
> Bennett *King George VI* (1958) pt. 3, ch. 6

## Daniel George

6 O Freedom, what liberties are taken in thy
name!
> *The Perpetual Pessimist* (1963) p. 58. Cf. 262:3

## David Lloyd George

*See* LLOYD GEORGE

## Ira Gershwin 1896–1983

7 In time the Rockies may crumble,
Gibraltar may tumble,
They're only made of clay,
But our love is here to stay.
> 'Love is Here to Stay' (1938 song)

8 Holding hands at midnight
'Neath a starry sky,
Nice work if you can get it,
And you can get it if you try.
> 'Nice Work If You Can Get It' (1937 song)

## Giuseppe Giacosa 1847–1906 and Luigi Illica 1857–1919

9 *Che gelida manina.*
Your tiny hand is frozen.
> *La Bohème* (1896) act 1 (Rodolfo to Mimi);
> music by Puccini

## Edward Gibbon 1737–94

10 The various modes of worship, which
prevailed in the Roman world, were all
considered by the people as equally true;
by the philosopher, as equally false; and by
the magistrate, as equally useful. And thus
toleration produced not only mutual
indulgence, but even religious concord.
> *Decline and Fall of the Roman Empire* (1776–88)
> ch. 2

11 History ... is, indeed, little more than the
register of the crimes, follies, and
misfortunes of mankind.
> *Decline and Fall of the Roman Empire* (1776–88)
> ch. 3. Cf. 340:20

12 In every deed of mischief he had a heart to
resolve, a head to contrive, and a hand to
execute.
> *Decline and Fall of the Roman Empire* (1776–88)
> ch. 48 (of Comnenus). Cf. 101:10

13 To the University of Oxford I acknowledge
no obligation; and she will as cheerfully
renounce me for a son, as I am willing to
disclaim her for a mother. I spent fourteen
months at Magdalen College: they proved
the fourteen months the most idle and
unprofitable of my whole life.
> *Memoirs of My Life* (1796) ch. 3

14 I sighed as a lover, I obeyed as a son.
> *Memoirs of My Life* (1796) ch. 4 n.

15 Crowds without company, and dissipation
without pleasure.
> *Memoirs of My Life* (1796) ch. 5

16 My English text is chaste, and all licentious
passages are left in the obscurity of a
learned language.
> *Memoirs of My Life* (1796) ch. 8 (parodied as
> 'decent obscurity' in the *Anti-Jacobin*, 1797–8)

## Stella Gibbons 1902–89

17 Something nasty in the woodshed.
> *Cold Comfort Farm* (1932) ch. 10

## Wolcott Gibbs 1902–58

18 Backward ran sentences until reeled the
mind.
> *New Yorker* 28 November 1936 'Time ...
> Fortune ... Life ... Luce' (satirizing the style
> of *Time* magazine)

## Kahlil Gibran 1883–1931

19 Your children are not your children.
They are the sons and daughters of Life's
longing for itself.
They came through you but not from you
And though they are with you yet they
belong not to you.
> *The Prophet* (1923) 'On Children'

20 Work is love made visible.
> *The Prophet* (1923) 'On Work'

21 An exaggeration is a truth that has lost its
temper.
> *Sand and Foam* (1926) p. 59

## Wilfrid Wilson Gibson 1878–1962

22 But we, how shall we turn to little things
And listen to the birds and winds and
streams
Made holy by their dreams,
Nor feel the heart-break in the heart of
things?
> 'Lament' (1918)

## André Gide 1869–1951

1 The great secret of Stendhal, his great
shrewdness, consisted in writing *at once* ...
thought charged with emotion.
*Journal* (1939) vol. 3, 3 September 1937 (tr. J.
O'Brien)

2 Hugo—alas!
When asked who was the greatest 19th-
century poet; in C. Martin *La Maturité d'André
Gide* (1977) p. 502

## Sir Humphrey Gilbert *c*.1537–83

3 We are as near to heaven by sea as by
land!
In Richard Hakluyt *Third and Last Volume of
the Voyages ... of the English Nation* (1600)
p. 159. Cf. 136:7

## W. S. Gilbert 1836–1911

4 That celebrated,
Cultivated,
Underrated
Nobleman,
The Duke of Plaza Toro!
*The Gondoliers* (1889) act 1

5 Of that there is no manner of doubt—
No probable, possible shadow of doubt—
No possible doubt whatever.
*The Gondoliers* (1889) act 1

6 But the privilege and pleasure
That we treasure beyond measure
Is to run on little errands for the Ministers
of State.
*The Gondoliers* (1889) act 2

7 Take a pair of sparkling eyes.
*The Gondoliers* (1889) act 2

8 When every one is somebodee,
Then no one's anybody.
*The Gondoliers* (1889) act 2

9 Bow, bow, ye lower middle classes!
Bow, bow, ye tradesmen, bow, ye masses.
*Iolanthe* (1882) act 1

10 The Law is the true embodiment
Of everything that's excellent.
It has no kind of fault or flaw,
And I, my Lords, embody the Law.
*Iolanthe* (1882) act 1

11 Hearts just as pure and fair
May beat in Belgrave Square
As in the lowly air
Of Seven Dials.
*Iolanthe* (1882) act 1

12 I often think it's comical
How Nature always does contrive
That every boy and every gal,
That's born into the world alive,
Is either a little Liberal,
Or else a little Conservative!
*Iolanthe* (1882) act 2

13 The prospect of a lot
Of dull MPs in close proximity,
All thinking for themselves is what
No man can face with equanimity.
*Iolanthe* (1882) act 2

14 The House of Peers, throughout the war,
Did nothing in particular,
And did it very well.
*Iolanthe* (1882) act 2

15 When you're lying awake with a dismal
headache, and repose is taboo'd by
anxiety,
I conceive you may use any language you
choose to indulge in, without
impropriety.
*Iolanthe* (1882) act 2

16 For you dream you are crossing the
Channel, and tossing about in a steamer
from Harwich—
Which is something between a large
bathing machine and a very small second
class carriage.
*Iolanthe* (1882) act 2

17 A wandering minstrel I—
A thing of shreds and patches.
Of ballads, songs and snatches,
And dreamy lullaby!
*The Mikado* (1885) act 1. Cf. 276:21

18 I can trace my ancestry back to a
protoplasmal primordial atomic globule.
Consequently, my family pride is
something in-conceivable. I can't help it. I
was born sneering.
*The Mikado* (1885) act 1

19 As some day it may happen that a victim
must be found,
I've got a little list—I've got a little list
Of society offenders who might well be
under ground
And who never would be missed—who
never would be missed!
*The Mikado* (1885) act 1

20 The idiot who praises, with enthusiastic
tone,
All centuries but this, and every country
but his own.
*The Mikado* (1885) act 1. Cf. 89:11, 121:17,
243:8

21 Three little maids from school are we.
*The Mikado* (1885) act 1

22 Life is a joke that's just begun.
*The Mikado* (1885) act 1

23 Three little maids who, all unwary,
Come from a ladies' seminary.
*The Mikado* (1885) act 1

24 Modified rapture!
*The Mikado* (1885) act 1

25 Awaiting the sensation of a short, sharp
shock,
From a cheap and chippy chopper on a big
black block.
*The Mikado* (1885) act 1

26 Here's a how-de-doo!
*The Mikado* (1885) act 2

27 Here's a state of things!
*The Mikado* (1885) act 2

1 My object all sublime
I shall achieve in time—
To let the punishment fit the crime—
The punishment fit the crime.
*The Mikado* (1885) act 2

2 And there he plays extravagant matches
In fitless finger-stalls
On a cloth untrue
With a twisted cue
And elliptical billiard balls.
*The Mikado* (1885) act 2

3 I have a left shoulder-blade that is a
miracle of loveliness. People come miles to
see it. My right elbow has a fascination
that few can resist.
*The Mikado* (1885) act 2

4 Something lingering, with boiling oil in it,
I fancy.
*The Mikado* (1885) act 2

5 Merely corroborative detail, intended to
give artistic verisimilitude to an otherwise
bald and unconvincing narrative.
*The Mikado* (1885) act 2

6 The flowers that bloom in the spring,
Tra la,
Have nothing to do with the case.
*The Mikado* (1885) act 2

7 On a tree by a river a little tom-tit
Sang 'Willow, titwillow, titwillow!'
*The Mikado* (1885) act 2

8 There's a fascination frantic
In a ruin that's romantic;
Do you think you are sufficiently decayed?
*The Mikado* (1885) act 2

9 If you're anxious for to shine in the high
aesthetic line as a man of culture rare.
*Patience* (1881) act 1

10 The meaning doesn't matter if it's only idle
chatter of a transcendental kind.
*Patience* (1881) act 1

11 An attachment à la Plato for a bashful
young potato, or a not too French French
bean!
*Patience* (1881) act 1

12 Francesca di Rimini, miminy, piminy,
*Je-ne-sais-quoi* young man!
*Patience* (1881) act 2

13 A greenery-yallery, Grosvenor Gallery,
Foot-in-the-grave young man!
*Patience* (1881) act 2

14 I'm called Little Buttercup—dear Little
Buttercup,
Though I could never tell why.
*HMS Pinafore* (1878) act 1

15 What, never?
No, never!
What, *never*?
Hardly ever!
*HMS Pinafore* (1878) act 1

16 Though 'Bother it' I may
Occasionally say,
I never use a big, big D—
*HMS Pinafore* (1878) act 1

17 And so do his sisters, and his cousins and
his aunts!
His sisters and his cousins,
Whom he reckons up by dozens,
And his aunts!
*HMS Pinafore* (1878) act 1

18 I cleaned the windows and I swept the
floor,
And I polished up the handle of the big
front door.
I polished up that handle so carefullee
That now I am the Ruler of the Queen's
Navee!
*HMS Pinafore* (1878) act 1

19 I always voted at my party's call,
And I never thought of thinking for myself
at all.
*HMS Pinafore* (1878) act 1

20 Stick close to your desks and never go to
sea,
And you all may be Rulers of the Queen's
Navee!
*HMS Pinafore* (1878) act 1

21 For he might have been a Roosian,
A French, or Turk, or Proosian,
Or perhaps Ital-ian!
But in spite of all temptations
To belong to other nations,
He remains an Englishman!
*HMS Pinafore* (1878) act 2

22 It is, it is a glorious thing
To be a Pirate King.
*The Pirates of Penzance* (1879) act 1

23 In short, in matters vegetable, animal, and
mineral,
I am the very model of a modern Major-
General.
*The Pirates of Penzance* (1879) act 1

24 When constabulary duty's to be done,
A policeman's lot is not a happy one.
*The Pirates of Penzance* (1879) act 2

25 Man is Nature's sole mistake!
*Princess Ida* (1884) act 2

26 He combines the manners of a Marquess
with the morals of a Methodist.
*Ruddigore* (1887) act 1

27 Some word that teems with hidden
meaning—like Basingstoke.
*Ruddigore* (1887) act 2

28 This particularly rapid, unintelligible
patter
Isn't generally heard, and if it is it doesn't
matter.
*Ruddigore* (1887) act 2

29 I was a pale young curate then.
*The Sorcerer* (1877) act 1

30 So I fell in love with a rich attorney's
Elderly ugly daughter.
*Trial by Jury* (1875)

31 She may very well pass for forty-three
In the dusk with a light behind her!
*Trial by Jury* (1875)

## Eric Gill 1882–1940

**1** That state is a state of slavery in which a man does what he likes to do in his spare time and in his working time that which is required of him.

*Art-nonsense and Other Essays* (1929) 'Slavery and Freedom'. Cf. 105:5

## Allen Ginsberg 1926–

**2** What if someone gave a war & Nobody came?

'Graffiti' (1972). Cf. 266:16

**3** I saw the best minds of my generation destroyed by madness, starving hysterical naked.

*Howl* (1956) p. 9

## George Gipp d. 1920

**4** Win just one for the Gipper.

Gipp being an American football legend, the catch-phrase later became associated with Ronald Reagan, who uttered the immortal words in the 1940 film *Knute Rockne, All American*

## Jean Giraudoux 1882–1944

**5** As soon as war is declared it will be impossible to hold the poets back. Rhyme is still the most effective drum.

*La Guerre de Troie n'aura pas lieu* (1935) act 2, sc. 4 (translated by Christopher Fry as *Tiger at the Gates*, 1955)

**6** No poet ever interpreted nature as freely as a lawyer interprets the truth.

*La Guerre de Troie n'aura pas lieu* (1935) act 2, sc. 5 (tr. Christopher Fry)

## W. E. Gladstone 1809–98

**7** Finance is, as it were, the stomach of the country, from which all the other organs take their tone.

Article on finance, 1858, in H. C. G. Matthew *Gladstone 1809–1874* (1986) ch. 5

**8** You cannot fight against the future. Time is on our side.

Speech on the Reform Bill, in *Hansard* 27 April 1866, col. 152

**9** We have been borne down in a torrent of gin and beer.

Letter to his brother, 6 February 1874, in J. Morley *Life of Gladstone* (1903) vol. 2, ch. 14

**10** [The Turks] one and all, bag and baggage, shall I hope clear out from the province they have desolated and profaned.

*Bulgarian Horrors and the Question of the East* (1876) p. 61

**11** Our first site in Egypt, be it by larceny or be it by emption, will be the almost certain egg of a North African Empire.

*Aggression on Egypt and Freedom in the East* (1884) p. 16

**12** The resources of civilization against its enemies are not yet exhausted.

Speech, 7 October 1881, in H. W. Lucy (ed.) *Speeches of . . . Gladstone* (1885) p. 57

**13** All the world over, I will back the masses against the classes.

Speech in Liverpool, 28 June 1886, in *The Times* 29 June 1886

**14** It is not a Life at all. It is a Reticence, in three volumes.

On J. W. Cross's *Life of George Eliot*; in E. F. Benson *As We Were* (1930) ch. 6

**15** I absorb the vapour and return it as a flood.

On public speaking, in Lord Riddell *Some Things That Matter* (1927 ed.) p. 69

## Hannah Glasse fl. 1747

**16** Take your hare when it is cased.

*The Art of Cookery Made Plain and Easy* (1747) ch. 1 (*cased* skinned). The proverbial 'First catch your hare' dates from *c*.1300

## Duke of Gloucester 1743–1805

**17** Another damned, thick, square book! Always scribble, scribble, scribble! Eh! Mr Gibbon?

In Henry Best *Personal and Literary Memorials* (1829) p. 68 (also attributed to the Duke of Cumberland and George III)

## Jean-Luc Godard 1930–

**18** Photography is truth. The cinema is truth 24 times per second.

*Le Petit Soldat* (1960 film)

**19** 'Movies should have a beginning, a middle and an end,' harrumphed French film maker Georges Franju . . . 'Certainly,' replied Jean-Luc Godard. 'But not necessarily in that order.'

*Time* 14 September 1981

## A. D. Godley 1856–1925

**20** What is this that roareth thus?
Can it be a Motor Bus?
Yes, the smell and hideous hum
Indicat Motorem Bum!

Letter, 10 January 1914, in *Reliquiae* (1926) vol. 1, p. 292

## Joseph Goebbels 1897–1945

**21** If we are attacked we can only defend ourselves with guns not with butter.

Speech in Berlin, 17 January 1936, in *Deutsche Allgemeine Zeitung* 18 January 1936. Cf. 153:22

## Hermann Goering 1893–1946

**22** Would you rather have butter or guns? . . . preparedness makes us powerful. Butter merely makes us fat.

Speech at Hamburg, 1936, in W. Frischauer *Goering* (1951) ch. 10. Cf. 153:21

**1** I herewith commission you to carry out all preparations with regard to ... a *total solution* of the Jewish question in those territories of Europe which are under German influence.

Instructions to Heydrich, 31 July 1941; in W. L. Shirer *Rise and Fall of the Third Reich* (1962) bk. 5, ch. 27

## Johann Wolfgang von Goethe
### 1749–1832

**2** Elective affinities.

Title of novel (1809)

**3** *Es irrt der Mensch, so lang er strebt.*

Man will err while yet he strives.

*Faust* pt. 1 (1808) 'Prolog im Himmel'

**4** *Entbehren sollst Du! sollst entbehren!*
*Das ist der ewige Gesang.*

Deny yourself! You must deny yourself!
That is the song that never ends.

*Faust* pt. 1 (1808) 'Studierzimmer'

**5** *Grau, teurer Freund, ist alle Theorie*
*Und grün des Lebens goldner Baum.*

All theory, dear friend, is grey, but the golden tree of actual life springs ever green.

*Faust* pt. 1 (1808) 'Studierzimmer'

**6** *Meine Ruh' ist hin,*
*Mein Herz ist schwer.*

My peace is gone,
My heart is heavy.

*Faust* pt. 1 (1808) 'Gretchen am Spinnrad'

**7** *Die Tat ist alles, nichts der Ruhm.*

The deed is all, the glory nothing.

*Faust* pt. 2 (1832) 'Hochgebirg'

**8** *Das Ewig-Weibliche zieht uns hinan.*

Eternal Woman draws us upward.

*Faust* pt. 2 (1832) 'Hochgebirg' *ad fin.*

**9** In art the best is good enough.

*Italienische Reise* (1816–17) 3 March 1787

**10** *Der Aberglaube ist die Poesie des Lebens.*

Superstition is the poetry of life.

*Maximen und Reflexionen* (1819) 'Literatur und Sprache' no. 908

**11** *Es bildet ein Talent sich in der Stille,*
*Sich ein Charakter in dem Strom der Welt.*

Talent develops in quiet places, character in the full current of human life.

*Torquato Tasso* (1790) act 1, sc. 2

**12** *Über allen Gipfeln*
*Ist Ruh'.*

Over all the mountain tops is peace.

*Wanderers Nachtlied* (1821)

**13** *Kennst du das Land, wo die Zitronen blühn?*

Know you the land where the lemon-trees bloom?

*Wilhelm Meisters Lehrjahre* (1795–6) bk. 3, ch. 1

**14** I do not know myself, and God forbid that I should.

J. P. Eckermann *Gespräche mit Goethe* (1836–48) 10 April 1829. Cf. 13:5

**15** More light!

Attributed dying words (actually 'Open the second shutter, so that more light can come in')

## Isaac Goldberg 1887–1938

**16** Diplomacy is to do and say
The nastiest thing in the nicest way.

*The Reflex* October 1927, p. 77

## Oliver Goldsmith 1730–74

**17** Sweet Auburn, loveliest village of the plain.

*The Deserted Village* (1770) l. 1

**18** Ill fares the land, to hast'ning ills a prey,
Where wealth accumulates, and men decay;
Princes and lords may flourish, or may fade;
A breath can make them, as a breath has made;
But a bold peasantry, their country's pride,
When once destroyed, can never be supplied.

*The Deserted Village* (1770) l. 51

**19** How happy he who crowns in shades like these,
A youth of labour with an age of ease.

*The Deserted Village* (1770) l. 99

**20** The loud laugh that spoke the vacant mind.

*The Deserted Village* (1770) l. 122

**21** A man he was to all the country dear,
And passing rich with forty pounds a year.

*The Deserted Village* (1770) l. 141

**22** Truth from his lips prevailed with double sway,
And fools, who came to scoff, remained to pray.

*The Deserted Village* (1770) l. 179

**23** Well had the boding tremblers learned to trace
The day's disasters in his morning face.

*The Deserted Village* (1770) l. 199

**24** And still they gazed, and still the wonder grew,
That one small head could carry all he knew.

*The Deserted Village* (1770) l. 215

**25** How wide the limits stand
Between a splendid and a happy land.

*The Deserted Village* (1770) l. 267

**26** In all the silent manliness of grief.

*The Deserted Village* (1770) l. 384

**27** Man wants but little here below,
Nor wants that little long.

'Edwin and Angelina, or the Hermit' (1766). Cf. 360:22

**28** The man recovered of the bite,
The dog it was that died.

'Elegy on the Death of a Mad Dog' (1766)

**1** Our Garrick's a salad; for in him we see
Oil, vinegar, sugar, and saltness agree.
*Retaliation* (1774) l. 11

**2** Too nice for a statesman, too proud for a
wit.
*Retaliation* (1774) l. 32 (of Edmund Burke)

**3** An abridgement of all that was pleasant in
man.
*Retaliation* (1774) l. 93 (of Garrick)

**4** Such is the patriot's boast, where'er we
roam,
His first, best country ever is, at home.
*The Traveller* (1764) l. 73

**5** Laws grind the poor, and rich men rule the
law.
*The Traveller* (1764) l. 386

**6** Friendship is a disinterested commerce
between equals; love, an abject intercourse
between tyrants and slaves.
*The Good-Natured Man* (1768) act 1

**7** Silence is become his mother tongue.
*The Good-Natured Man* (1768) act 2

**8** Let schoolmasters puzzle their brain,
With grammar, and nonsense, and
learning,
Good liquor, I stoutly maintain,
Gives genius a better discerning.
*She Stoops to Conquer* (1773) act 1, sc. 1 'Song'

**9** The very pink of perfection.
*She Stoops to Conquer* (1773) act 1

**10** This is Liberty-Hall, gentlemen.
*She Stoops to Conquer* (1773) act 2

**11** I . . . chose my wife, as she did her wedding
gown, not for a fine glossy surface, but
such qualities as would wear well.
*The Vicar of Wakefield* (1766) ch. 1

**12** All our adventures were by the fire-side,
and all our migrations from the blue bed
to the brown.
*The Vicar of Wakefield* (1766) ch. 1

**13** When lovely woman stoops to folly
And finds too late that men betray,
What charm can soothe her melancholy,
What art can wash her guilt away?
*The Vicar of Wakefield* (1766) ch. 29

**14** There is no arguing with Johnson; for
when his pistol misses fire, he knocks you
down with the butt end of it.
In James Boswell *Life of Samuel Johnson* (1934
ed.) vol. 2, p. 100 (26 October 1769)

### Barry Goldwater 1909–

**15** I would remind you that extremism in the
defence of liberty is no vice! And let me
remind you also that moderation in the
pursuit of justice is no virtue!
Accepting the presidential nomination,
16 July 1964, in *New York Times* 17 July 1964,
p. 1

### Sam Goldwyn 1882–1974

**16** Gentlemen, include me out.
Resigning from the Motion Picture
Producers and Distributors of America,
October 1933; in M. Freedland *The Goldwyn
Touch* (1986) ch. 10

**17** A verbal contract isn't worth the paper it
is written on.
In A. Johnston *The Great Goldwyn* (1937) ch. 1

**18** Pictures are for entertainment, messages
should be delivered by Western Union.
In A. Marx *Goldwyn* (1976) ch. 15

### Ivan Goncharov 1812–91

**19** No devastating or redeeming fires have
ever burnt in my life . . . My life began by
flickering out.
*Oblomov* (1859) pt. 2, ch. 4 (tr. D. Magarshak)

**20** You lost your ability for doing things in
childhood . . . It all began with your
inability to put on your socks and ended by
your inability to live.
*Oblomov* (1859) pt. 4, ch. 2 (tr. D. Magarshak)

### Adam Lindsay Gordon 1833–70

**21** Life is mostly froth and bubble,
Two things stand like stone,
Kindness in another's trouble,
Courage in your own.
*Ye Wearie Wayfarer* (1866) 'Fytte 8'

### Mack Gordon 1904–59

**22** Dinner in the diner nothing could be finer
Than to have your ham'n eggs in Carolina.
'Chattanooga Choo-choo' (1941 song)

### Stuart Gorrell 1902–63

**23** Georgia, Georgia, no peace I find,
Just an old sweet song keeps Georgia on
my mind.
'Georgia on my Mind' (1930 song)

### Lord Goschen 1831–1907

**24** I have the courage of my opinions, but I
have not the temerity to give a political
blank cheque to Lord Salisbury.
Speech, *Hansard* 19 February 1884, col. 1420

### Edmund Gosse 1849–1928

**25** A sheep in sheep's clothing.
Of the 'woolly-bearded poet' Sturge Moore,
in F. Greenslet *Under the Bridge* (1943) ch. 10.
Cf. 100:7

### Edward Meyrick Goulburn
1818–97

**26** Let the scintillations of your wit be like the
coruscations of summer lightning, lambent
but innocuous.
Sermon at Rugby School, in W. Tuckwell
*Reminiscences of Oxford* (2nd ed., 1907) p. 272

## Goya 1746–1828

1 The dream of reason produces monsters.
   *Los Caprichos* (1799) plate 43 (title)

## D. M. Graham 1911–

2 That this House will in no circumstances
   fight for its King and Country.
   Motion worded by Graham for a debate at
   the Oxford Union, 9 February 1933

## Harry Graham 1874–1936

3 'There's been an accident,' they said,
   'Your servant's cut in half; he's dead!'
   'Indeed!' said Mr Jones, 'and please,
   Send me the half that's got my keys.'
   *Ruthless Rhymes for Heartless Homes* (1899) 'Mr
   Jones' (attributed to 'G.W.')

4 Billy, in one of his nice new sashes,
   Fell in the fire and was burnt to ashes;
   Now, although the room grows chilly,
   I haven't the heart to poke poor Billy.
   *Ruthless Rhymes for Heartless Homes* (1899)
   'Tender-Heartedness'

## Kenneth Grahame 1859–1932

5 There is *nothing*—absolutely nothing—half
   so much worth doing as simply messing
   about in boats.
   *The Wind in the Willows* (1908) ch. 1

6 The poetry of motion! The *real* way to
   travel! The *only* way to travel! Here
   today—in next week tomorrow!
   *The Wind in the Willows* (1908) ch. 2. Cf. 190:5

## James Grainger c.1721–66

7 What is fame? an empty bubble;
   Gold? a transient, shining trouble.
   'Solitude' (1755) l. 96

## Sir Robert Grant 1785–1838

8 O worship the King, all-glorious above;
   O gratefully sing his power and his love:
   Our Shield and Defender, the Ancient of
   Days,
   Pavilioned in splendour, and girded with
   praise.
   'O worship the King, all glorious above' (1833
   hymn)

## Ulysses S. Grant 1822–85

9 I know no method to secure the repeal of
   bad or obnoxious laws so effective as their
   stringent execution.
   Inaugural Address, 4 March 1869, in P. C.
   Headley *Life and Campaigns of General U. S.
   Grant* (1869) ch. 29

## George Granville, Baron Lansdowne 1666–1735

10 Bright as the day, and like the morning,
   fair,
   Such Cloe is ... and common as the air.
   'Cloe' (1712)

11 Cowards in scarlet pass for men of war.
   *The She Gallants* (1696) act 5

## John Woodcock Graves 1795–1886

12 D'ye ken John Peel with his coat so grey?
   D'ye ken John Peel at the break of the day?
   D'ye ken John Peel when he's far far away
   With his hounds and his horn in the
   morning?
   'Twas the sound of his horn called me
   from my bed,
   And the cry of his hounds has me oft-times
   led;
   For Peel's view-hollo would waken the
   dead,
   Or a fox from his lair in the morning.
   'John Peel' (1820)

## Robert Graves 1895–1985

13 Children are dumb to say how hot the day
   is,
   How hot the scent is of the summer rose.
   'The Cool Web' (1927)

14 There's a cool web of language winds us in,
   Retreat from too much joy or too much
   fear.
   'The Cool Web' (1927)

15 Truth-loving Persians do not dwell upon
   The trivial skirmish fought near Marathon.
   'The Persian Version' (1945)

16 As you are woman, so be lovely:
   As you are lovely, so be various.
   'Pygmalion to Galatea' (1927)

17 Goodbye to all that.
   Title of autobiography (1929)

## John Chipman Gray 1839–1915

18 Dirt is only matter out of place; and what
   is a blot on the escutcheon of the Common
   Law may be a jewel in the crown of the
   Social Republic.
   *Restraints on the Alienation of Property* (2nd ed.,
   1895) preface

## Patrick, 6th Lord Gray d. 1612

19 A dead woman bites not.
   Oral tradition, Gray being said to have
   pressed hard for the execution of Mary
   Queen of Scots in 1587, with the words
   'Mortua non mordet [Being dead, she will bite
   no more]'; in A. Darcy's 1625 translation of
   William Camden's *Annals of the Reign of Queen
   Elizabeth* (1615) vol. 1, p. 196

## Thomas Gray 1716–71

1 Ruin seize thee, ruthless King!
Confusion on thy banners wait,
Tho' fanned by Conquest's crimson wing
They mock the air with idle state.
*The Bard* (1757) l. 1

2 Weave the warp, and weave the woof,
The winding-sheet of Edward's race.
Give ample room, and verge enough
The characters of hell to trace.
*The Bard* (1757) l. 49

3 In gallant trim the gilded vessel goes;
Youth on the prow, and Pleasure at the
helm.
*The Bard* (1757) l. 73

4 The curfew tolls the knell of parting day,
The lowing herd wind slowly o'er the lea,
The ploughman homeward plods his weary
way,
And leaves the world to darkness and to
me.

Now fades the glimmering landscape on
the sight,
And all the air a solemn stillness holds,
Save where the beetle wheels his droning
flight,
And drowsy tinklings lull the distant folds.
*Elegy Written in a Country Churchyard* (1751)
l. 1

5 Save that from yonder ivy-mantled tow'r,
The moping owl does to the moon
complain.
*Elegy Written in a Country Churchyard* (1751)
l. 9

6 Beneath those rugged elms, that yew-tree's
shade,
Where heaves the turf in many a
mouldering heap,
Each in his narrow cell for ever laid,
The rude forefathers of the hamlet sleep.
*Elegy Written in a Country Churchyard* (1751)
l. 13

7 Let not ambition mock their useful toil,
Their homely joys, and destiny obscure;
Nor grandeur hear with a disdainful smile,
The short and simple annals of the poor.

The boast of heraldry, the pomp of pow'r,
And all that beauty, all that wealth e'er
gave,
Awaits alike th' inevitable hour,
The paths of glory lead but to the grave.
*Elegy Written in a Country Churchyard* (1751)
l. 29

8 Can storied urn or animated bust
Back to its mansion call the fleeting
breath?
Can honour's voice provoke the silent dust,
Or flatt'ry soothe the dull cold ear of
death?
*Elegy Written in a Country Churchyard* (1751)
l. 41

9 Full many a gem of purest ray serene,
The dark unfathomed caves of ocean bear:
Full many a flower is born to blush
unseen,
And waste its sweetness on the desert air.
Some village-Hampden, that with dauntless
breast
The little tyrant of his fields withstood;
Some mute inglorious Milton here may
rest,
Some Cromwell guiltless of his country's
blood.
*Elegy Written in a Country Churchyard* (1751)
l. 53

10 Far from the madding crowd's ignoble
strife,
Their sober wishes never learned to stray;
Along the cool sequestered vale of life
They kept the noiseless tenor of their way.
*Elegy Written in a Country Churchyard* (1751)
l. 73

11 Ye distant spires, ye antique towers,
That crown the wat'ry glade.
*Ode on a Distant Prospect of Eton College* (1747)
l. 1

12 Alas, regardless of their doom,
The little victims play!
No sense have they of ills to come,
Nor care beyond to-day.
*Ode on a Distant Prospect of Eton College* (1747)
l. 51

13 To each his suff'rings, all are men,
Condemned alike to groan;
The tender for another's pain,
Th' unfeeling for his own.
*Ode on a Distant Prospect of Eton College* (1747)
l. 91

14 Where ignorance is bliss,
'Tis folly to be wise.
*Ode on a Distant Prospect of Eton College* (1747)
l. 99

15 Not all that tempts your wand'ring eyes
And heedless hearts, is lawful prize;
Nor all, that glisters, gold.
'Ode on the Death of a Favourite Cat' (1748)

16 In thy green lap was Nature's darling laid.
*The Progress of Poesy* (1757) l. 84 (of
Shakespeare)

17 He saw; but blasted with excess of light,
Closed his eyes in endless night.
*The Progress of Poesy* (1757) l. 95 (of Milton)

18 Thoughts, that breathe, and words, that
burn.
*The Progress of Poesy* (1757) l. 110

19 Beyond the limits of a vulgar fate,
Beneath the good how far—but far above
the great.
*The Progress of Poesy* (1757) l. 122

## Horace Greeley 1811–72

20 Go West, young man, and grow up with
the country.
*Hints toward Reforms* (1850). Cf. 311:17

## Hannah Green

1 I never promised you a rose garden.
   Title of novel (1964)

## Graham Greene 1904–91

2 Catholics and Communists have
   committed great crimes, but at least they
   have not stood aside, like an established
   society, and been indifferent. I would
   rather have blood on my hands than water
   like Pilate.
   *The Comedians* (1966) pt. 3, ch. 4

3 He gave her a bright fake smile; so much
   of life was a putting-off of unhappiness for
   another time. Nothing was ever lost by
   delay.
   *The Heart of the Matter* (1948) bk. 1, pt. 1, ch. 1

4 They had been corrupted by money, and he
   had been corrupted by sentiment.
   Sentiment was the more dangerous,
   because you couldn't name its price. A
   man open to bribes was to be relied upon
   below a certain figure, but sentiment
   might uncoil in the heart at a name, a
   photograph, even a smell remembered.
   *The Heart of the Matter* (1948) bk. 1, pt. 1, ch. 2

5 He felt the loyalty we all feel to
   unhappiness—the sense that that is where
   we really belong.
   *The Heart of the Matter* (1948) bk. 2, pt. 2, ch. 1

6 There is always one moment in childhood
   when the door opens and lets the future
   in.
   *The Power and the Glory* (1940) pt. 1, ch. 1

7 Innocence always calls mutely for
   protection, when we would be so much
   wiser to guard ourselves against it:
   innocence is like a dumb leper who has
   lost his bell, wandering the world meaning
   no harm.
   *The Quiet American* (1955) pt. 1, ch. 3

## Robert Greene c.1560–92

8 Hangs in the uncertain balance of proud
   time.
   *Friar Bacon and Friar Bungay* (1594) act 3, sc. 1

9 Ah! what is love! It is a pretty thing,
   As sweet unto a shepherd as a king.
   'The Shepherd's Wife's Song' (1590)

## Germaine Greer 1939–

10 You can now see the Female Eunuch the
   world over ... spreading herself wherever
   blue jeans and Coca-Cola may go.
   Wherever you see nail varnish, lipstick,
   brassieres, and high heels, the Eunuch has
   set up her camp.
   *The Female Eunuch* (20th anniversary ed.,
   1991) foreword

11 I didn't fight to get women out from
   behind the vacuum cleaner to get them
   onto the board of Hoover.
   In *Guardian* 27 October 1986

## Pope Gregory the Great
AD c.540–604

12 *Non Angli sed Angeli.*
   Not Angles but Angels.
   Oral tradition. See Bede *Historia Ecclesiastica*
   bk. 2, sect. 1

## Pope Gregory VII c.1020–85

13 I have loved justice and hated iniquity:
   therefore I die in exile.
   Last words, in J. W. Bowden *Life and
   Pontificate of Gregory VII* (1840) vol. 2, bk. 3,
   ch. 20

## Stephen Grellet 1773–1855

14 I expect to pass through this world but
   once; any good thing therefore that I can
   do, or any kindness that I can show to any
   fellow-creature, let me do it now; let me
   not defer or neglect it, for I shall not pass
   this way again.
   Attributed. See John o' London *Treasure Trove*
   (1925) p. 48 for some of the many other
   claimants to authorship

## Joyce Grenfell 1910–79

15 So gay the band,
   So giddy the sight,
   Full evening dress is a must,
   But the zest goes out of a beautiful waltz
   When you dance it bust to bust.
   'Stately as a Galleon' (1978 song)

## Julian Grenfell 1888–1915

16 And Life is Colour and Warmth and Light
   And a striving evermore for these;
   And he is dead, who will not fight;
   And who dies fighting has increase.
   'Into Battle' in *The Times* 28 May 1915

## Frances Greville c.1724–89

17 Far as distress the soul can wound
   'Tis pain in each degree;
   Bliss goes but to a certain bound,
   Beyond is agony.
   'A Prayer for Indifference' (1759)

## Fulke Greville 1554–1628

18 Life is a top which whipping Sorrow
   driveth.
   *Caelica* (1633) 'The earth with thunder torn,
   with fire blasted'

19 O wearisome condition of humanity!
   Born under one law, to another bound;
   Vainly begot, and yet forbidden vanity;
   Created sick, commanded to be sound.
   *Mustapha* (1609) act 5, sc. 4

## Lord Grey of Fallodon 1862–1933

1 The lamps are going out all over Europe;
we shall not see them lit again in our
lifetime.
*25 Years* (1925) vol. 2, ch. 18 (on the eve of the
First World War)

## Mervyn Griffith-Jones 1909–79

2 Is it a book you would even wish your wife
or your servants to read?
Of D. H. Lawrence's *Lady Chatterley's Lover*,
while appearing for the prosecution at the
Old Bailey; in *The Times* 21 October 1960

## George and Weedon Grossmith
1847–1912, 1854–1919

3 What's the good of a home if you are never
in it?
*Diary of a Nobody* (1894) ch. 1

4 I left the room with silent dignity, but
caught my foot in the mat.
*Diary of a Nobody* (1894) ch. 12

## Philip Guedalla 1889–1944

5 Any stigma, as the old saying is, will serve
to beat a dogma.
*Masters and Men* (1923) 'Ministers of State'

6 The little ships, the unforgotten Homeric
catalogue of *Mary Jane* and *Peggy IV*, of
*Folkestone Belle*, *Boy Billy*, and *Ethel Maud*, of
*Lady Haig* and *Skylark* . . . the little ships of
England brought the Army home.
*Mr Churchill* (1941) ch. 7 (on the evacuation of
Dunkirk)

7 The work of Henry James has always
seemed divisible by a simple dynastic
arrangement into three reigns: James I,
James II, and the Old Pretender.
*Supers and Supermen* (1920) 'Some Critics'

## Hervé Guibert 1955–91

8 [AIDS was] an illness in stages, a very long
flight of steps that led assuredly to death,
but whose every step represented a unique
apprenticeship. It was a disease that gave
death time to live and its victims time to
die, time to discover time, and in the end
to discover life.
*To the Friend who did not Save my Life* (1991)
ch. 61 (tr. Linda Coverdale)

## Texas Guinan 1884–1933

9 Fifty million Frenchmen can't be wrong.
In *New York World–Telegram* 21 March 1931,
p. 25, which asserts that Guinan used the
phrase at least six or seven years previously;
it was the title of a 1927 song by Billy Rose
and Willie Raskin

## Dorothy Frances Gurney
1858–1932

10 The kiss of the sun for pardon,
The song of the birds for mirth,
One is nearer God's Heart in a garden
Than anywhere else on earth.
'God's Garden' (1913)

## John Hampden Gurney 1802–62

11 My soul, bear thou thy part,
Triumph in God above,
And with a well-tuned heart
Sing thou the songs of love.
'Ye holy angels bright' (1838 hymn)

## Woody Guthrie 1912–67

12 This land is your land, this land is my land,
From California to the New York Island.
From the redwood forest to the Gulf
Stream waters
This land was made for you and me.
'This Land is Your Land' (1956 song)

## Nell Gwyn 1650–87

13 Pray, good people, be civil. I am the
Protestant whore.
At Oxford, during the Popish Terror, 1681; in
B. Bevan *Nell Gwyn* (1969) ch. 13

## Emperor Hadrian AD 76–138

14 *Animula vagula blandula,*
*Hospes comesque corporis.*
Ah! gentle, fleeting, wav'ring sprite,
Friend and associate of this clay!
In J. W. Duff (ed.) *Minor Latin Poets* (1934)
p. 445 (translated by Byron as 'Adrian's
Address to His Soul When Dying')

## Rider Haggard 1856–1925

15 She who must be obeyed.
*She* (1887) ch. 6 and *passim*

## Earl Haig 1861–1928

16 A very weak-minded fellow I am afraid,
and, like the feather pillow, bears the
marks of the last person who has sat on
him!
Describing the 17th Earl of Derby in a letter
to Lady Haig, 14 January 1918; in R. Blake
*Private Papers of Douglas Haig* (1952) ch. 16

17 Every position must be held to the last
man: there must be no retirement. With
our backs to the wall, and believing in the
justice of our cause, each one of us must
fight on to the end.
Order to British troops, 12 April 1918; in A.
Duff Cooper *Haig* (1936) vol. 2, ch. 23

## Lord Hailsham (Quintin Hogg)
1907–

**1** A great party is not to be brought down because of a scandal by a woman of easy virtue and a proved liar.

BBC television interview on the Profumo affair; in *The Times* 14 June 1963

## J. B. S. Haldane 1892–1964

**2** Now, my own suspicion is that the universe is not only queerer than we suppose, but queerer than we *can* suppose.

*Possible Worlds* (1927) title essay

**3** The Creator, if He exists, has a special preference for beetles.

Observing that there are 400,000 species of beetle; in *Journal of the British Interplanetary Society* (1951) vol. 10, p. 156

## Edward Everett Hale 1822–1909

**4** 'Do you pray for the senators, Dr Hale?' 'No, I look at the senators and I pray for the country.'

Van Wyck Brooks *New England Indian Summer* (1940) p. 418 n.

## Sir Matthew Hale 1609–76

**5** Christianity is part of the laws of England.

Sir William Blackstone's summary of Hale's words (Taylor's case, 1676) in *Commentaries* (1769) vol. 4, p. 59

## Nathan Hale 1755–76

**6** I only regret that I have but one life to lose for my country.

Prior to his execution by the British for spying, 22 September 1776; in H. P. Johnston *Nathan Hale, 1776* (1914) ch. 7. Cf. 2:16

## Sarah Josepha Hale 1788–1879

**7** Mary had a little lamb,
Its fleece was white as snow,
And everywhere that Mary went
The lamb was sure to go.

*Poems for Our Children* (1830) 'Mary's Little Lamb'

## George Savile, Marquess of Halifax 1633–95

**8** Malice is of a low stature, but it hath very long arms.

*Political, Moral, and Miscellaneous Thoughts* (1750) 'Of Malice and Envy'

**9** When the people contend for their liberty, they seldom get anything by their victory but new masters.

*Political, Moral, and Miscellaneous Thoughts* (1750) 'Of Prerogative, Power and Liberty'

**10** Power is so apt to be insolent and Liberty to be saucy, that they are very seldom upon good terms.

*Political, Moral, and Miscellaneous Thoughts* (1750) 'Of Prerogative, Power and Liberty'

**11** Men are not hanged for stealing horses, but that horses may not be stolen.

*Political, Moral, and Miscellaneous Thoughts* (1750) 'Of Punishment'

**12** [Halifax] had heard of many that kicked down stairs, but never of any that was kicked up stairs before.

Gilbert Burnet *History of My Own Time* vol. 1 (1724) p. 592

## Bishop Joseph Hall 1574–1656

**13** Perfection is the child of Time.

*Works* (1625) p. 670

## Radclyffe Hall 1883–1943

**14** You're neither unnatural, nor abominable, nor mad; you're as much a part of what people call nature as anyone else; only you're unexplained as yet—you've not got your niche in creation.

*The Well of Loneliness* (1928) bk. 2, ch. 20, sect. 3

## Friedrich Halm 1806–71

**15** *Zwei Seelen und ein Gedanke,*
*Zwei Herzen und ein Schlag!*
Two souls with but a single thought,
Two hearts that beat as one.

*Der Sohn der Wildnis* (1842) act 2 *ad fin.*

## Alex Hamilton 1936–

**16** Those who stand for nothing fall for anything.

'Born Old' (radio broadcast), in *Listener* 9 November 1978

## Sir William Hamilton 1788–1856

**17** Truth, like a torch, the more it's shook it shines.

*Discussions on Philosophy* (1852) title page (epigram)

**18** On earth there is nothing great but man; in man there is nothing great but mind.

*Lectures on Metaphysics and Logic* (ed. Mamsel and Veitch, 1859) vol. 1, p. 24; attributed in a Latin form to Favorinus (2nd century AD)

## Oscar Hammerstein II 1895–1960

**19** Fish got to swim and birds got to fly
I got to love one man till I die,
Can't help lovin' dat man of mine.

'Can't Help Lovin' Dat Man of Mine' (1927 song)

**1** The last time I saw Paris
Her heart was warm and gay,
I heard the laughter of her heart in ev'ry
street café.
'The Last Time I saw Paris' (1941 song)

**2** The corn is as high as an elephant's eye,
An' it looks like it's climbin' clear up to the
sky.
'Oh, What a Beautiful Mornin' ' (1943 song)

**3** Ol' man river, dat ol' man river,
He must know sumpin', but don't say
nothin',
He jus' keeps rollin',
He jus' keeps rollin' along.
'Ol' Man River' (1927 song)

**4** I'm as corny as Kansas in August,
High as a flag on the Fourth of July!
'A Wonderful Guy' (1949 song)

## Christopher Hampton 1946–

**5** A definition of capitalism . . . the process
whereby American girls turn into
American women.
*Savages* (1974) sc. 16

## Minnie Hanff 1880–1942

**6** High o'er the fence leaps Sunny Jim
'Force' is the food that raises him.
Advertising slogan for breakfast cereal
(1903)

## Kate Hankey 1834–1911

**7** Tell me the old, old story.
Title of hymn (1867)

## Brian Hanrahan 1949–

**8** I counted them all out and I counted them
all back.
On the number of British aeroplanes joining
the raid on Port Stanley; BBC broadcast
report, 1 May 1982, in *Battle for the Falklands*
(1982) p. 21

## Edmond Haraucourt 1856–1941

**9** *Partir c'est mourir un peu,*
*C'est mourir à ce qu'on aime.*
To go away is to die a little, to that which
one loves it is to die.
*Seul* (1891) 'Rondel de l'Adieu'

## Otto Harbach 1873–1963

**10** Now laughing friends deride tears I cannot
hide,
So I smile and say 'When a lovely flame
dies,
Smoke gets in your eyes.'
'Smoke Gets in your Eyes' (1933 song)

## E. Y. ('Yip') Harburg 1898–1981

**11** Brother can you spare a dime?
Title of song (1932)

**12** Say, it's only a paper moon,
Sailing over a cardboard sea.
'It's Only a Paper Moon' (1933 song, with
Billy Rose)

**13** Wanna cry, wanna croon.
Wanna laugh like a loon.
It's that Old Devil Moon in your eyes.
'Old Devil Moon' (1946 song)

**14** Somewhere over the rainbow
Way up high,
There's a land that I heard of
Once in a lullaby.
'Over the Rainbow' (1939 song)

## Sir William Harcourt 1827–1904

**15** We are all socialists now.
During the passage of Lord Goschen's 1888
budget, noted for the reduction of the
national debt (attributed). See H. Bland
'The Outlook' in G. B. Shaw (ed.) *Fabian
Essays in Socialism* (1889)

## D. W. Harding 1906–

**16** Regulated hatred.
Title of an article on the novels of Jane
Austen, in *Scrutiny* March 1940

## Philip Yorke, Earl of Hardwicke
1690–1764

**17** His doubts are better than most people's
certainties.
Of *Dirleton's Doubts*, in James Boswell *Life of
Samuel Johnson* (1934 ed.) vol. 3, p. 205

## Godfrey Harold Hardy 1877–1947

**18** Beauty is the first test: there is no
permanent place in the world for ugly
mathematics.
*A Mathematician's Apology* (1940) p. 25

## Thomas Hardy 1840–1928

**19** A local thing called Christianity.
*The Dynasts* (1904) pt. 1, act 1, sc. 6

**20** War makes rattling good history; but Peace
is poor reading.
*The Dynasts* (1904) pt. 1, act 2, sc. 5

**21** A lover without indiscretion is no lover at
all.
*The Hand of Ethelberta* (1876) ch. 20

**22** Done because we are too menny.
*Jude the Obscure* (1896) pt. 6, ch. 2

**23** Dialect words—those terrible marks of the
beast to the truly genteel.
*The Mayor of Casterbridge* (1886) ch. 20

**24** Happiness was but the occasional episode
in a general drama of pain.
*The Mayor of Casterbridge* (1886) ch. 45 *ad fin.*

**25** 'Justice' was done, and the President of the
Immortals (in Aeschylean phrase) had
ended his sport with Tess.
*Tess of the D'Urbervilles* (1891) ch. 59

1 Good, but not religious-good.
  *Under the Greenwood Tree* (1872) ch. 2

2 When the Present has latched its postern
    behind my tremulous stay,
  And the May month flaps its glad green
    leaves like wings,
  Delicate-filmed as new-spun silk, will the
    neighbours say,
  'He was a man who used to notice such
    things'?
  'Afterwards' (1917)

3 The bower we shrined to Tennyson,
    Gentlemen,
  Is roof-wrecked; damps there drip upon
  Sagged seats, the creeper-nails are rust,
  The spider is sole denizen.
  'An Ancient to Ancients' (1922)

4 After two thousand years of mass
  We've got as far as poison-gas.
  'Christmas: 1924' (1928)

5 The Immanent Will that stirs and urges
    everything.
  'Convergence of the Twain' (1914)

6 An aged thrush, frail, gaunt, and small,
  In blast-beruffled plume.
  'The Darkling Thrush' (1902)

7 So little cause for carollings
  Of such ecstatic sound
  Was written on terrestrial things
  Afar or nigh around,
  That I could think there trembled through
  His happy good-night air
  Some blessed Hope, whereof he knew
  And I was unaware.
  'The Darkling Thrush' (1902)

8 If way to the Better there be, it exacts a full
  look at the worst.
  'De Profundis' (1902)

9 Well, World, you have kept faith with me,
    Kept faith with me;
  Upon the whole you have proved to be
  Much as you said you were.
  'He Never Expected Much' (1928)

10 I am the family face;
  Flesh perishes, I live on,
  Projecting trait and trace
  Through time to times anon,
  And leaping from place to place
  Over oblivion.
  'Heredity' (1917)

11 Only a man harrowing clods
  In a slow silent walk
  With an old horse that stumbles and nods
  Half asleep as they stalk.
  'In Time of "The Breaking of Nations" '
  (1917)

12 Yonder a maid and her wight
  Come whispering by:
  War's annals will cloud into night
  Ere their story die.
  'In Time of "The Breaking of Nations" '
  (1917)

13 Yes; quaint and curious war is!
  You shoot a fellow down
  You'd treat if met where any bar is,
  Or help to half-a-crown.
  'The Man he Killed' (1909)

14 In the third-class seat sat the journeying
    boy
  And the roof-lamp's oily flame
  Played down on his listless form and face,
  Bewrapt past knowing to what he was
    going,
  Or whence he came.
  'Midnight on the Great Western' (1917)

15 Woman much missed, how you call to me,
    call to me.
  'The Voice' (1914)

16 This is the weather the cuckoo likes,
  And so do I.
  'Weathers' (1922)

17 And drops on gate-bars hang in a row,
  And rooks in families homeward go.
  'Weathers' (1922)

18 When I set out for Lyonnesse,
  A hundred miles away,
  The rime was on the spray,
  And starlight lit my lonesomeness.
  'When I set out for Lyonnesse' (1914)

## Maurice Evan Hare 1886–1967

19 There once was an old man who said,
    'Damn!
  It is borne in upon me I am
  An engine that moves
  In determinate grooves,
  I'm not even a bus, I'm a tram.'
  'Limerick' (1905)

## W. F. Hargreaves 1846–1919

20 I'm Burlington Bertie
  I rise at ten thirty and saunter along like
    a toff,
  I walk down the Strand with my gloves on
    my hand,
  Then I walk down again with them off.
  'Burlington Bertie from Bow' (1915 song)

21 I acted so tragic the house rose like magic,
  The audience yelled 'You're sublime.'
  They made me a present of Mornington
    Crescent
  They threw it a brick at a time.
  'The Night I Appeared as Macbeth' (1922
  song)

## Sir John Harington 1561–1612

22 Treason doth never prosper, what's the
    reason?
  For if it prosper, none dare call it treason.
  *Epigrams* (1618) bk. 4, no. 5

## Lord Harlech 1918–85

1 Britain will be honoured by historians
more for the way she disposed of an
empire than for the way in which she
acquired it.
In *New York Times* 28 October 1962, sect. 4,
p. 11

## Jimmy Harper et al.

2 The biggest aspidistra in the world.
Title of song (1938); popularized by Gracie
Fields

## Joel Chandler Harris 1848–1908

3 All by my own-alone self.
*Nights with Uncle Remus* (1883) ch. 36

4 I'm sickly but sassy.
*Nights with Uncle Remus* (1883) ch. 50

5 Bred en bawn in a brier-patch!
*Uncle Remus and His Legends* ... (1881) 'How
Mr Rabbit was too Sharp for Mr Fox'

6 Tar-baby ain't sayin' nuthin', en Brer Fox,
he lay low.
*Uncle Remus and His Legends* ... (1881) 'The
Wonderful Tar-Baby Story'

## Lorenz Hart 1895–1943

7 Bewitched, bothered, and bewildered am I.
'Bewitched' (1941 song)

8 When love congeals
It soon reveals
The faint aroma of performing seals.
'I Wish I Were in Love Again' (1937 song)

9 I get too hungry for dinner at eight.
I like the theatre, but never come late.
I never bother with people I hate.
That's why the lady is a tramp.
'The Lady is a Tramp' (1937 song)

10 In a mountain greenery
Where God paints the scenery—
Just two crazy people together.
'Mountain Greenery' (1926 song)

11 Thou swell! Thou witty!
Thou sweet! Thou grand!
Wouldst kiss me pretty?
Wouldst hold my hand?
'Thou Swell' (1927 song)

## Bret Harte 1836–1902

12 If, of all words of tongue and pen,
The saddest are, 'It might have been,'
More sad are these we daily see:
'It is, but hadn't ought to be!'
'Mrs Judge Jenkins' (1867). Cf. 349:1

13 And he smiled a kind of sickly smile, and
curled up on the floor,
And the subsequent proceedings interested
him no more.
'The Society upon the Stanislaus' (1868) st. 7

## L. P. Hartley 1895–1972

14 The past is a foreign country: they do
things differently there.
*The Go-Between* (1953) prologue. Cf. 235:7

## F. W. Harvey b. 1888

15 From troubles of the world
I turn to ducks
Beautiful comical things.
'Ducks' (1919)

## Minnie Louise Haskins 1875–1957

16 And I said to the man who stood at the
gate of the year: 'Give me a light that I may
tread safely into the unknown.' And he
replied: 'Go out into the darkness and put
your hand into the Hand of God. That shall
be to you better than light and safer than
a known way.'
*Desert* (1908) 'God Knows' (quoted by George
VI in his Christmas broadcast, 1939)

## R. S. Hawker 1803–75

17 And have they fixed the where and when?
And shall Trelawny die?
Here's twenty thousand Cornish men
Will know the reason why!
'The Song of the Western Men' (last three
lines traditional since the 17th century)

## Stephen Hawking 1942–

18 If we find the answer to that [why it is that
we and the universe exist], it would be the
ultimate triumph of human reason—for
then we would know the mind of God.
*A Brief History of Time* (1988) ch. 11

## Nathaniel Hawthorne 1804–64

19 Dr Johnson's morality was as English an
article as a beefsteak.
*Our Old Home* (1863) 'Lichfield and Uttoxeter'

## Ian Hay 1876–1952

20 What do you mean, funny? Funny-peculiar
or funny ha-ha?
*The Housemaster* (1938) act 3

## J. Milton Hayes 1884–1940

21 There's a one-eyed yellow idol to the north
of Khatmandu,
There's a little marble cross below the
town,
There's a broken-hearted woman tends the
grave of Mad Carew,
And the Yellow God forever gazes down.
'The Green Eye of the Yellow God' (1911)

## William Hazlitt 1778–1830

22 His sayings are generally like women's
letters; all the pith is in the postscript.
*Conversations of James Northcote* (1826–7) (of
Charles Lamb)

**1** He talked on for ever; and you wished him to talk on for ever.
   *Lectures on the English Poets* (1818) 'On the Living Poets' (of Coleridge)

**2** I have wanted only one thing to make me happy, but wanting that have wanted everything.
   *Literary Remains* (1836) 'My First Acquaintance with Poets'

**3** There is nothing good to be had in the country, or if there is, they will not let you have it.
   *The Round Table* (1817) 'Observations on ... The Excursion'

**4** Of all footmen the lowest class is *literary footmen.*
   *Sketches and Essays* (1839) 'Footmen'

**5** Rules and models destroy genius and art.
   *Sketches and Essays* (1839) 'On Taste'

**6** His worst is better than any other person's best.
   *The Spirit of the Age* (1825) 'Sir Walter Scott'

**7** We can scarcely hate any one that we know.
   *Table Talk* vol. 2 (1822) 'On Criticism'

**8** Give me the clear blue sky over my head, and the green turf beneath my feet, a winding road before me, and a three hours' march to dinner—and then to thinking! It is hard if I cannot start some game on these lone heaths.
   *Table Talk* vol. 2 (1822) 'On Going a Journey'

**9** Well, I've had a happy life.
   Last words, in W. C. Hazlitt *Memoirs of William Hazlitt* (1867)

## Denis Healey 1917–

**10** Like being savaged by a dead sheep.
   On being criticized by Sir Geoffrey Howe in the House of Commons; *Hansard* 14 June 1978, col. 1027

## Seamus Heaney 1939–

**11**           The famous
   Northern reticence, the tight gag of place
   And times.
   'Whatever You Say Say Nothing' (1975)

## Edward Heath 1916–

**12** The unpleasant and unacceptable face of capitalism.
   *Hansard* 15 May 1973, col. 1243 (on the Lonrho affair)

## John Heath-Stubbs 1918–

**13** Venerable Mother Toothache
   Climb down from the white battlements,
   Stop twisting in your yellow fingers
   The fourfold rope of nerves.
   'A Charm Against the Toothache' (1954)

## Bishop Reginald Heber 1783–1826

**14** Brightest and best of the sons of the morning,
   Dawn on our darkness and lend us thine aid.
   'Brightest and best' (1827 hymn)

**15** From Greenland's icy mountains,
   From India's coral strand,
   Where Afric's sunny fountains
   Roll down their golden sand.
   'From Greenland's icy mountains' (1821 hymn)

**16** What though the spicy breezes
   Blow soft o'er Ceylon's isle;
   Though every prospect pleases,
   And only man is vile:
   In vain with lavish kindness
   The gifts of God are strown;
   The heathen in his blindness
   Bows down to wood and stone.
   'From Greenland's icy mountains' (1821 hymn). 'Ceylon' later altered to 'Java'. Cf. 196:10

**17** Holy, Holy, Holy! all the saints adore thee,
   Casting down their golden crowns around the glassy sea,
   Cherubim and Seraphim falling down before thee,
   Which wert, and art, and evermore shalt be.
   'Holy, Holy, Holy! Lord God Almighty!' (1826 hymn)

## G. W. F. Hegel 1770–1831

**18** What experience and history teach is this—that nations and governments have never learned anything from history, or acted upon any lessons they might have drawn from it.
   *Lectures on the Philosophy of World History: Introduction* (1830, tr. H. B. Nisbet)

**19** Only in the state does man have a rational existence ... Man owes his entire existence to the state, and has his being within it alone.
   *Lectures on the Philosophy of World History: Introduction* (1830, tr. H. B. Nisbet) p. 94

**20** When philosophy paints its grey on grey, then has a shape of life grown old. By philosophy's grey on grey it cannot be rejuvenated but only understood. The owl of Minerva spreads its wings only with the falling of the dusk.
   *Philosophy of Right* (1821, tr. T. M. Knox) p. 13

## Heinrich Heine 1797–1856

**21**           *Dort, wo man Bücher*
   *Verbrennt, verbrennt man auch am Ende Menschen.*
   Wherever books will be burned, men also, in the end, are burned.
   *Almansor* (1823) l. 245

**1** *Auf Flügeln des Gesanges.*
On wings of song.
Title of song (1823)

**2** Maximilien Robespierre was nothing but
the hand of Jean Jacques Rousseau, the
bloody hand that drew from the womb of
time the body whose soul Rousseau had
created.
*Zur Geschichte der Religion und Philosophie in
Deutschland* (1834) bk. 3, para. 3

**3** *Dieu me pardonnera, c'est son métier.*
God will pardon me, it is His trade.
On his deathbed, in A. Meissner *Heinrich
Heine. Erinnerungen* (1856) ch. 5. Cf. 92:21

## Werner Heisenberg 1901–76

**4** An expert is someone who knows some of
the worst mistakes that can be made in his
subject and who manages to avoid them.
*Der Teil und das Ganze* (1969) ch. 17 (tr. A. J.
Pomerans as *Physics and Beyond*, 1971)

## Joseph Heller 1923–

**5** There was only one catch and that was
Catch-22, which specified that a concern
for one's own safety in the face of dangers
that were real and immediate was the
process of a rational mind ... Orr would be
crazy to fly more missions and sane if he
didn't, but if he was sane he had to fly
them. If he flew them he was crazy and
didn't have to; but if he didn't want to he
was sane and had to.
*Catch-22* (1961) ch. 5

**6** Some men are born mediocre, some men
achieve mediocrity, and some men have
mediocrity thrust upon them. With Major
Major it had been all three.
*Catch-22* (1961) ch. 9. Cf. 298:3

## Lillian Hellman 1905–84

**7** I cannot and will not cut my conscience to
fit this year's fashions.
Letter to John S. Wood, 19 May 1952, in *US
Congress Committee Hearing on Un-American
Activities* (1952) pt. 8, p. 3546

## Leona Helmsley c.1920–

**8** Only the little people pay taxes.
Addressed to her housekeeper in 1983, and
reported at her trial for tax evasion; in *New
York Times* 12 July 1989, p. B2

## Felicia Hemans 1793–1835

**9** The boy stood on the burning deck
Whence all but he had fled;
The flame that lit the battle's wreck
Shone round him o'er the dead.
'Casabianca' (1849)

**10** The stately homes of England,
How beautiful they stand!
'The Homes of England' (1849)

## John Heming 1556–1630 and Henry Condell d. 1627

**11** His mind and hand went together: And
what he thought, he uttered with that
easiness, that we have scarce received from
him a blot.
First Folio Shakespeare (1623) preface.
Cf. 187:32, 252:30

## Ernest Hemingway 1899–1961

**12** But did thee feel the earth move?
*For Whom the Bell Tolls* (1940) ch. 13

**13** Paris is a movable feast.
*A Movable Feast* (1964) epigraph

**14** The sun also rises.
Title of novel (1926)

**15** Grace under pressure.
When asked what he meant by 'guts' in an
interview with Dorothy Parker; in *New Yorker*
30 November 1929
*See also* F. SCOTT FITZGERALD

## Arthur W. D. Henley

**16** Nobody loves a fairy when she's forty.
Title of song (1934)

## W. E. Henley 1849–1903

**17** Under the bludgeonings of chance
My head is bloody, but unbowed.
'Invictus. In Memoriam R.T.H.B.' (1888)

**18** I am the master of my fate:
I am the captain of my soul.
'Invictus. In Memoriam R.T.H.B.' (1888)

**19** What have I done for you,
England, my England?
'Pro Rege Nostro' (1900)

## Henri IV 1553–1610

**20** I want there to be no peasant in my
kingdom so poor that he is unable to have
a chicken in his pot every Sunday.
In Hardouin de Péréfixe *Histoire de Henri le
Grand* (1681)

**21** Paris is well worth a mass.
Attributed to Henri IV; alternatively to his
minister Sully, in conversation with him

**22** The wisest fool in Christendom.
Of James I of England (attributed both to
Henri IV and Sully)

## Henry II 1133–89

**23** Will no one rid me of this turbulent
priest?
Of Thomas Becket, Archbishop of
Canterbury, murdered in Canterbury
Cathedral, December 1170 (oral tradition,
conflating a number of variant forms)

## Henry VIII 1491–1547

1 The King found her [Anne of Cleves] so different from her picture ... that ... he swore they had brought him a Flanders mare.

Tobias Smollett *Complete History of England* (3rd ed., 1759) vol. 6, p. 68

## Matthew Henry 1662–1714

2 The better day, the worse deed.

*Exposition on the Old and New Testament* (1710) Genesis ch. 3, v. 6, gloss 2

3 They that die by famine die by inches.

*Exposition on the Old and New Testament* (1710) Psalm 59, v. 15, gloss 5 (referring incorrectly to v. 13)

## O. Henry 1862–1910

4 It was beautiful and simple as all truly great swindles are.

*Gentle Grafter* (1908) 'Octopus Marooned'

## Patrick Henry 1736–99

5 Caesar had his Brutus—Charles the First, his Cromwell—and George the Third—('Treason,' cried the Speaker) ... *may profit by their example. If this be treason, make the most of it.*

Speech in the Virginia assembly, May 1765; in W. Wirt *Patrick Henry* (1818) sect. 2, p. 65

6 I know not what course others may take; but as for me, give me liberty, or give me death!

Speech, 23 March 1775; in W. Wirt *Patrick Henry* (1818) sect. 4, p. 123

## Philip Henry 1631–96

7 All this, and heaven too!

In Matthew Henry *Life of Mr Philip Henry* (1698) ch. 5

## Heraclitus *c.*540–*c.*480 BC

8 You can't step twice into the same river.

In Plato *Cratylus* 402a

9 A man's character is his fate.

*On the Universe* fragment 121 (tr. W. H. S. Jones). Cf. 132:15, 240:12

10 The road up and the road down are one and the same.

In H. Diels and W. Kranz *Die Fragmente der Vorsokratiker* (7th ed., 1954) fragment 60

## A. P. Herbert 1890–1971

11 The Farmer will never be happy again;
He carries his heart in his boots;
For either the rain is destroying his grain
Or the drought is destroying his roots.

'The Farmer' (1922)

12 As my poor father used to say
In 1863,
Once people start on all this Art
Goodbye, moralitee!

'Lines for a Worthy Person' (1930)

13 Other people's babies—
That's my life!
Mother to dozens,
And nobody's wife.

'Other People's Babies' (1930)

14 This high official, all allow,
Is grossly overpaid;
There wasn't any Board, and now
There isn't any Trade.

'The President of the Board of Trade' (1922)

15 Nothing is wasted, nothing is in vain:
The seas roll over but the rocks remain.

*Tough at the Top* (operetta *c.*1949)

16 Holy deadlock.

Title of novel (1934)

17 People must not do things for fun. We are not here for fun. There is no reference to fun in any Act of Parliament.

*Uncommon Law* (1935) 'Is it a Free Country?'

18 The critical period in matrimony is breakfast-time.

*Uncommon Law* (1935) 'Is Marriage Lawful?'

## Lord Herbert of Cherbury 1583–1648

19 Now that the April of your youth adorns
The garden of your face.

'Ditty: Now that the April' (1665)

## George Herbert 1593–1633

20 Let all the world in ev'ry corner sing
My God and King.

'Antiphon' (1633)

21 A verse may find him, who a sermon flies,
And turn delight into a sacrifice.

'The Church Porch' (1633) st. 1

22 I struck the board, and cried, 'No more.
I will abroad.'

'The Collar' (1633)

23 But as I raved and grew more fierce and wild
At every word,
Methought I heard one calling, 'Child';
And I replied, 'My Lord.'

'The Collar' (1633)

24 I got me flowers to strew Thy way.

'Easter' (1633)

25 Teach me, my God and King,
In all things Thee to see,
And what I do in any thing
To do it as for Thee.

'The Elixir' (1633)

26 A servant with this clause
Makes drudgery divine:
Who sweeps a room as for Thy laws
Makes that and th' action fine.

'The Elixir' (1633)

1 Who says that fictions only and false hair
  Become a verse? Is there in truth no
    beauty?
  Is all good structure in a winding stair?
  'Jordan (1)' (1633)

2 Love bade me welcome: yet my soul drew
    back,
  Guilty of dust and sin.
  'Love: Love bade me welcome' (1633)

3 'You must sit down,' says Love, 'and taste
    my meat.'
  So I did sit and eat.
  'Love: Love bade me welcome' (1633)

4 The land of spices; something understood.
  'Prayer the Church's banquet' (1633)

5 When God at first made man,
  Having a glass of blessings standing by;
  Let us (said he) pour on him all we can:
  Let the world's riches, which dispersed lie,
  Contract into a span.
  'The Pulley' (1633)

6 But who does hawk at eagles with a dove?
  'The Sacrifice' (1633) l. 91

7 Bibles laid open, millions of surprises.
  'Sin: Lord, with what care Thou hast begirt
  us round!' (1633)

8 Sweet spring, full of sweet days and roses,
  A box where sweets compacted lie.
  'Virtue' (1633)

9 He that makes a good war makes a good
    peace.
  *Outlandish Proverbs* (1640) no. 420

10 He that lives in hope danceth without
    music.
  *Outlandish Proverbs* (1640) no. 1006

## Robert Herrick 1591–1674

11 Here a little child I stand,
  Heaving up my either hand;
  Cold as paddocks though they be,
  Here I lift them up to Thee,
  For a benison to fall
  On our meat, and on us all. Amen.
  'Another Grace for a Child' (1647)

12 I sing of brooks, of blossoms, birds, and
    bowers:
  Of April, May, of June, and July-flowers.
  I sing of May-poles, Hock-carts, wassails,
    wakes,
  Of bride-grooms, brides, and of their
    bridal-cakes.
  'The Argument of his Book' from *Hesperides*
  (1648)

13 Cherry-ripe, ripe, ripe, I cry,
  Full and fair ones; come and buy:
  If so be, you ask me where
  They do grow? I answer, there,
  Where my Julia's lips do smile;
  There's the land, or cherry-isle.
  'Cherry-Ripe' (1648)

14 So when or you or I are made
  A fable, song, or fleeting shade;
  All love, all liking, all delight
  Lies drowned with us in endless night.
  'Corinna's Going a-Maying' (1648)

15 A sweet disorder in the dress
  Kindles in clothes a wantonness:
  A lawn about the shoulders thrown
  Into a fine distraction . . .
  A careless shoe-string, in whose tie
  I see a wild civility:
  Do more bewitch me, than when Art
  Is too precise in every part.
  'Delight in Disorder' (1648)

16 It is the end that crowns us, not the fight.
  'The End' (1648)

17 In prayer the lips ne'er act the winning
    part,
  Without the sweet concurrence of the
    heart.
  'The Heart' (1647)

18 Night makes no difference 'twixt the Priest
    and Clerk;
  Joan as my Lady is as good i' th' dark.
  'No Difference i' th' Dark' (1648)

19 Made us nobly wild, not mad.
  'An Ode for him [Ben Jonson]' (1648)

20 Fain would I kiss my Julia's dainty leg,
  Which is as white and hairless as an egg.
  'On Julia's Legs' (1648)

21 Praise they that will times past, I joy to see
  My self now live: this age best pleaseth me.
  'The Present Time Best Pleaseth' (1648)

22 A little saint best fits a little shrine,
  A little prop best fits a little vine,
  As my small cruse best fits my little wine.
  'A Ternary of Littles, upon a Pipkin of Jelly
  sent to a Lady' (1648)

23 Fair daffodils, we weep to see
  You haste away so soon.
  'To Daffodils' (1648)

24 Gather ye rosebuds while ye may,
  Old Time is still a-flying:
  And this same flower that smiles to-day,
  To-morrow will be dying.
  'To the Virgins, to Make Much of Time'
  (1648)

25 Then be not coy, but use your time;
  And while ye may, go marry:
  For having lost but once your prime,
  You may for ever tarry.
  'To the Virgins, to Make Much of Time'
  (1648)

26 Whenas in silks my Julia goes,
  Then, then (methinks) how sweetly flows
  That liquefaction of her clothes.
  'Upon Julia's Clothes' (1648)

## Lord Hervey 1696–1743

27 Whoever would lie usefully should lie
    seldom.
  *Memoirs of the Reign of George II* (ed. J. W.
  Croker, 1848) vol. 1, ch. 19

**1** I am fit for nothing but to carry candles and set chairs all my life.
  Letter to Sir Robert Walpole, 1737, in *Memoirs of the Reign of George II* (ed. J. W. Croker, 1848) vol. 2, ch. 40

## Hesiod *c.*700 BC

**2** The half is greater than the whole.
  *Works and Days* l. 40

## Hermann Hesse 1877–1962

**3** If you hate a person, you hate something in him that is part of yourself. What isn't part of ourselves doesn't disturb us.
  *Demian* (1919) ch. 6

## Lord Hewart 1870–1943

**4** Justice should not only be done, but should manifestly and undoubtedly be seen to be done.
  *Rex v Sussex Justices*, 9 November 1923, in *Law Reports King's Bench Division* (1924) vol. 1, p. 259

## Du Bose Heyward 1885–1940 and Ira Gershwin 1896–1983

**5** It ain't necessarily so,
De t'ings dat yo' li'ble
To read in de Bible
It ain't necessarily so.
  'It ain't necessarily so' (1935 song)

**6** Summer time an' the livin' is easy,
Fish are jumpin' an' the cotton is high.
  'Summertime' (1935 song)

**7** A woman is a sometime thing.
  Title of song (1935)

## John Heywood *c.*1497–*c.*1580

**8** All a green willow, willow;
All a green willow is my garland.
  'The Green Willow'. Cf. 292:26

## Thomas Heywood *c.*1574–1641

**9** Seven cities warred for Homer, being dead,
Who, living, had no roof to shroud his head.
  'The Hierarchy of the Blessed Angels' (1635). Cf. 10:10

## J. R. Hicks 1904–

**10** The best of all monopoly profits is a quiet life.
  *Econometrica* (1935) 'The Theory of Monopoly'

## Aaron Hill 1685–1750

**11** Tender-handed stroke a nettle,
And it stings you for your pains;
Grasp it like a man of mettle,
And it soft as silk remains.
  'Verses Written on a Window in Scotland'

## Joe Hill 1879–1915

**12** Work and pray, live on hay,
You'll get pie in the sky when you die.
  'Preacher and the Slave' in *Songs of the Workers* (Industrial Workers of the World, 1911)

**13** I will die like a true-blue rebel. Don't waste any time in mourning—organize.
  Farewell telegram prior to his death by firing squad; in *Salt Lake* (Utah) *Tribune* 19 November 1915

## Rowland Hill 1744–1833

**14** He [Hill] did not see any reason why the devil should have all the good tunes.
  E. W. Broome *Rowland Hill* (1881) ch. 7

## Sir Edmund Hillary 1919–

**15** Well, we knocked the bastard off!
  On conquering Mount Everest; in *Nothing Venture, Nothing Win* (1975) ch. 10. Cf. 216:22

## Fred Hillebrand 1893–

**16** Home James, and don't spare the horses.
  Title of song (1934)

## Lady Hillingdon 1857–1940

**17** When I hear his steps outside my door I lie down on my bed, close my eyes, open my legs, and think of England.
  *Journal* 1912, in J. Gathorne-Hardy *The Rise and Fall of the British Nanny* (1972) ch. 3

## James Hilton 1900–54

**18** Nothing really wrong with him—only anno domini, but that's the most fatal complaint of all, in the end.
  *Goodbye, Mr Chips* (1934) ch. 1

## Hippocrates *c.*460–357 BC

**19** Life is short, the art long.
  *Aphorisms* sect. 1, para. 1; often quoted 'Ars longa, vita brevis'. See Seneca *De Brevitate Vitae* sect. 1. Cf. 96:12

## Alfred Hitchcock 1899–1980

**20** Television has brought back murder into the home—where it belongs.
  In *Observer* 19 December 1965

## Adolf Hitler 1889–1945

**21** The night of the long knives.
  Referring to the massacre of Ernst Roehm and his associates by Hitler on 29–30 June 1934 (subsequently associated with Harold Macmillan's Cabinet dismissals of 13 July 1962). See S. H. Roberts *The House Hitler Built* (1937) pt. 2, ch. 3

**1** I go the way that Providence dictates with the assurance of a sleepwalker.

Speech in Munich, 15 March 1936; in M. Domarus (ed.) *Hitler: Reden und Proklamationen 1932–1945* (1962) p. 606

**2** It is the last territorial claim which I have to make in Europe.

On the Sudetenland; Speech in Berlin, 26 September 1938, in M. Domarus (ed.) *Hitler: Reden und Proklamationen 1932–1945* (1962) p. 927

**3** The broad mass of a nation ... will more easily fall victim to a big lie than to a small one.

*Mein Kampf* (1925) vol. 1, ch. 10

**4** Is Paris burning?

25 August 1944, in L. Collins and D. Lapierre *Is Paris Burning?* (1965) ch. 5

## Thomas Hobbes 1588–1679

**5** True and False are attributes of speech, not of things. And where speech is not, there is neither Truth nor Falsehood.

*Leviathan* (1651) pt. 1, ch. 4

**6** Words are wise men's counters, they do but reckon by them.

*Leviathan* (1651) pt. 1, ch. 4

**7** They that approve a private opinion, call it opinion; but they that mislike it, heresy: and yet heresy signifies no more than private opinion.

*Leviathan* (1651) pt. 1, ch. 11

**8** During the time men live without a common power to keep them all in awe, they are in that condition which is called war; and such a war as is of every man against every man.

*Leviathan* (1651) pt. 1, ch. 13

**9** For as the nature of foul weather, lieth not in a shower or two of rain; but in an inclination thereto of many days together: so the nature of war consisteth not in actual fighting, but in the known disposition thereto during all the time there is no assurance to the contrary.

*Leviathan* (1651) pt. 1, ch. 13

**10** No arts; no letters; no society; and which is worst of all, continual fear and danger of violent death; and the life of man, solitary, poor, nasty, brutish, and short.

*Leviathan* (1651) pt. 1, ch. 13

**11** I am about to take my last voyage, a great leap in the dark.

Last words. See John Watkins *Anecdotes of Men of Learning* (1808) p. 276

## John Cam Hobhouse 1786–1869

**12** When I invented the phrase 'His Majesty's Opposition' [Canning] paid me a compliment on the fortunate hit.

*Recollections of a Long Life* (1865) vol. 2, ch. 12

## Ralph Hodgson 1871–1962

**13** 'Twould ring the bells of Heaven
The wildest peal for years,
If Parson lost his senses
And people came to theirs,
And he and they together
Knelt down with angry prayers
For tamed and shabby tigers
And dancing dogs and bears,
And wretched, blind, pit ponies,
And little hunted hares.

'Bells of Heaven' (1917)

**14** Reason has moons, but moons not hers,
Lie mirrored on her sea,
Confounding her astronomers,
But, O! delighting me.

'Reason Has Moons' (1917)

**15** Time, you old gipsy man,
Will you not stay,
Put up your caravan
Just for one day?

'Time, You Old Gipsy Man' (1917)

## August Heinrich Hoffmann 1798–1874

**16** *Deutschland über alles.*

Germany above all.

Title of poem (1841)

## Max Hoffmann 1869–1927

**17** Lions led by donkeys.

Of British soldiers during the First World War; in Alan Clark *The Donkeys* (1961) epigraph also attributed to Napoleon and others

## Heinrich Hoffmann 1809–94

**18** O take the nasty soup away!
I won't have any soup today.'

*Struwwelpeter* (1848) 'Augustus'

**19** But fidgety Phil,
He won't sit still;
He wriggles
And giggles,
And then, I declare,
Swings backwards and forwards,
And tilts up his chair.

*Struwwelpeter* (1848) 'Fidgety Philip'

**20** Look at little Johnny there,
Little Johnny Head-In-Air!

*Struwwelpeter* (1848) 'Johnny Head-In-Air'

**21** The door flew open, in he ran,
The great, long, red-legged scissor-man.

*Struwwelpeter* (1848) 'The Little Suck-a-Thumb'

**22** Snip! Snap! Snip! They go so fast
That both his thumbs are off at last.

*Struwwelpeter* (1848) 'The Little Suck-a-Thumb'

1 The hare sits snug in leaves and grass,
   And laughs to see the green man pass.
   *Struwwelpeter* (1848) 'The Man Who Went Out
   Shooting'

2 And now she's trying all she can,
   To shoot the sleepy, green-coat man.
   *Struwwelpeter* (1848) 'The Man Who Went Out
   Shooting'

3 The hare's own child, the little hare.
   *Struwwelpeter* (1848) 'The Man Who Went Out
   Shooting'

4 Anything to me is sweeter
   Than to see Shock-headed Peter.
   *Struwwelpeter* (1848) 'Shock-Headed Peter'
   (title poem)

## Gerard Hoffnung 1925–59

5 Standing among savage scenery, the hotel
   offers stupendous revelations. There is
   a French widow in every bedroom,
   affording delightful prospects.
   Supposedly quoting a letter from a Tyrolean
   landlord; in speech at the Oxford Union,
   4 December 1958

## Lancelot Hogben 1895–1975

6 This is not the age of pamphleteers. It is
   the age of the engineers. The spark-gap is
   mightier than the pen.
   *Science for the Citizen* (1938) epilogue

## James Hogg 1770–1835

7 Where the pools are bright and deep
   Where the grey trout lies asleep,
   Up the river and o'er the lea
   That's the way for Billy and me.
   'A Boy's Song' (1838)

8 God bless our lord the king!
   God save our lord the king!
   God save the king!
   Make him victorious,
   Happy, and glorious,
   Long to reign over us:
   God save the king!
   'The King's Anthem' in *Jacobite Relics of
   Scotland* Second Series (1821) p. 50. Cf. 7:13

## Paul Henri, Baron d'Holbach 1723–89

9 If ignorance of nature gave birth to the
   Gods, knowledge of nature is destined to
   destroy them.
   *Système de la Nature* (1770) pt. 2, ch. 1

## Billie Holiday 1915–59

10 Mama may have, papa may have,
   But God bless the child that's got his own!
   'God Bless the Child' (1941 song, with Arthur
   Herzog Jnr.)

## Henry Fox, 1st Lord Holland 1705–74

11 If Mr Selwyn calls again, shew him up: if I
   am alive I shall be delighted to see him;
   and if I am dead he would like to see me.
   During his last illness; in J. H. Jesse *George
   Selwyn and his Contemporaries* (1844) vol. 3,
   p. 50

## Henry Scott Holland 1847–1918

12 Death is nothing at all; it does not count. I
   have only slipped away into the next room.
   Sermon preached on Whitsunday, 1910; *Facts
   of the Faith* (1919) 'The King of Terrors'

## John H. Holmes 1879–1964

13 This, now, is the judgement of our
   scientific age—the third reaction of man
   upon the universe! This universe is not
   hostile, nor yet is it friendly. It is simply
   indifferent.
   *The Sensible Man's View of Religion* (1932) ch. 4

## Oliver Wendell Holmes 1809–94

14 The axis of the earth sticks out visibly
   through the centre of each and every town
   or city.
   *The Autocrat of the Breakfast-Table* (1858) ch. 6

15 It is the province of knowledge to speak
   and it is the privilege of wisdom to listen.
   *The Poet at the Breakfast-Table* (1872) ch. 10

16 Lean, hungry, savage anti-everythings.
   'A Modest Request' (1848)

17 Man wants but little drink below,
   But wants that little strong.
   'A Song of other Days' (1848). Cf. 154:27

## John Home 1722–1808

18 My name is Norval; on the Grampian hills
   My father feeds his flocks; a frugal swain,
   Whose constant cares were to increase his
   store
   And keep his only son, myself, at home.
   *Douglas* (1756) act 2, sc. 1

19 Like Douglas conquer, or like Douglas die.
   *Douglas* (1756) act 5

## Homer 8th century BC

20 Winged words.
   *The Iliad* bk. 1, l. 201

21 Like that of leaves is a generation of men.
   *The Iliad* bk. 6, l. 146

22 Smiling through her tears.
   *The Iliad* bk. 6, l. 484

23 It lies in the lap of the gods.
   *The Iliad* bk. 17, l. 514 and *passim*

1 Tell me, Muse, of the man of many devices,
who wandered far and wide after he had
sacked Troy's sacred city, and saw the
towns of many men and knew their mind.
*The Odyssey* bk. 1, l. 1 (of Odysseus)

2 Rosy-fingered dawn.
*The Odyssey* bk. 2, l. 1 and *passim*

3 I would rather be tied to the soil as
another man's serf, even a poor man's,
who hadn't much to live on himself, than
be King of all these the dead and
destroyed.
*The Odyssey* bk. 11, l. 489

## Thomas Hood 1799–1845

4 Ben Battle was a soldier bold,
And used to war's alarms:
But a cannon-ball took off his legs,
So he laid down his arms!
'Faithless Nelly Gray' (1826)

5 For here I leave my second leg,
And the Forty-second Foot!
'Faithless Nelly Gray' (1826)

6 The love that loves a scarlet coat
Should be more uniform.
'Faithless Nelly Gray' (1826)

7 His death, which happened in his berth,
At forty-odd befell:
They went and told the sexton, and
The sexton tolled the bell.
'Faithless Sally Brown' (1826)

8 I remember, I remember,
The house where I was born,
The little window where the sun
Came peeping in at morn.
'I Remember' (1826)

9 No sun—no moon!
No morn—no noon
No dawn—no dusk—no proper time of
day.
'No!' (1844)

10 No shade, no shine, no butterflies, no bees,
No fruits, no flowers, no leaves, no birds,—
November!
'No!' (1844)

11 She stood breast high amid the corn,
Clasped by the golden light of morn.
'Ruth' (1827). Cf. 192:5

12 Stitch! stitch! stitch!
In poverty, hunger, and dirt.
And still with a voice of dolorous pitch
She sang the 'Song of the Shirt'.
'The Song of the Shirt' (1843)

13 Oh! God! that bread should be so dear,
And flesh and blood so cheap!
'The Song of the Shirt' (1843)

14 The sedate, sober, silent, serious, sad-
coloured sect.
*Comic Annual* (1839) 'The Doves and the
Crows' (of Quakers)

## Richard Hooker c.1554–1600

15 Alteration though it be from worse to
better hath in it inconveniences, and those
weighty.
*Of the Laws of Ecclesiastical Polity* (1593) bk. 4,
ch. 14, sect. 1. Cf. 182:3

## Ellen Sturgis Hooper 1816–41

16 I slept, and dreamed that life was beauty;
I woke, and found that life was duty.
'Beauty and Duty' (1840)

## Herbert Hoover 1874–1964

17 The American system of rugged
individualism.
Speech, 22 October 1928, in *New Day* (1928)
p. 154

18 The grass will grow in the streets of
a hundred cities, a thousand towns.
Speech, 31 October 1932, in *State Papers of
Herbert Hoover* (1934) vol. 2 (on proposals 'to
reduce the protective tariff to a competitive
tariff for revenue')

## Anthony Hope 1863–1933

19 Economy is going without something you
do want in case you should, some day,
want something you probably won't want.
*The Dolly Dialogues* (1894) no. 12

20 His foe was folly and his weapon wit.
Inscription for W. S. Gilbert's memorial on
the Victoria Embankment, London (1915)

21 Oh, for an hour of Herod!
At the first night of *Peter Pan* (1904); in D.
Mackail *Story of JMB* (1941) ch. 17

## Laurence Hope (Adela Florence Nicolson) 1865–1904

22 Pale hands I loved beside the Shalimar,
Where are you now? Who lies beneath
your spell?
*The Garden of Kama* (1901) 'Kashmiri Song'

23 Less than the dust, beneath thy Chariot
wheel,
Less than the rust, that never stained thy
Sword . . .
Less than the need thou hast in life of me.
Even less am I.
*The Garden of Kama* (1901) 'Less than the
Dust'

## Gerard Manley Hopkins 1844–89

24 Ten or twelve, only ten or twelve
Strokes of havoc únselve.
'Binsey Poplars' (written 1879)

25 Not, I'll not, carrion comfort, Despair, not
feast on thee;
Not untwist—slack they may be—these
last strands of man
In me or, most weary, cry *I can no more*. I
can;
Can something, hope, wish day come, not
choose not to be.
'Carrion Comfort' (written 1885)

1          That night, that year
Of now done darkness I wretch lay
wrestling with (my God!) my God.
'Carrion Comfort' (written 1885)

2 Towery city and branchy between towers.
'Duns Scotus's Oxford' (written 1879)

3 The world is charged with the grandeur of
God.
'God's Grandeur' (written 1877)

4 And all is seared with trade; bleared,
smeared with toil;
And wears man's smudge and shares
man's smell.
'God's Grandeur' (written 1877)

5 Elected Silence, sing to me
And beat upon my whorlèd ear.
'The Habit of Perfection' (written 1866)

6 Palate, the hutch of tasty lust,
Desire not to be rinsed with wine.
'The Habit of Perfection' (written 1866)

7 I have desired to go
Where springs not fail,
To fields where flies no sharp and sided
hail
And a few lilies blow.
'Heaven-Haven' (written 1864)

8 What would the world be, once bereft
Of wet and wildness? Let them be left,
O let them be left, wildness and wet;
Long live the weeds and the wilderness yet.
'Inversnaid' (written 1881)

9 No worst, there is none. Pitched past pitch
of grief,
More pangs will, schooled at forepangs,
wilder wring.
Comforter, where, where is your
comforting?
'No worst, there is none' (written 1885)

10 O the mind, mind has mountains; cliffs of
fall
Frightful, sheer, no-man-fathomed.
'No worst, there is none' (written 1885)

11                                    All
Life death does end and each day dies with
sleep.
'No worst, there is none' (written 1885)

12 Glory be to God for dappled things.
'Pied Beauty' (written 1877)

13 All things counter, original, spare, strange;
Whatever is fickle, freckled (who knows
how?)
With swift, slow; sweet, sour; adazzle, dim;
He fathers-forth whose beauty is past
change:
Praise him.
'Pied Beauty' (written 1877)

14 Márgarét, áre you gríeving
Over Goldengrove unleaving?
'Spring and Fall: to a young child' (written
1880)

15 Though worlds of wanwood leafmeal lie.
'Spring and Fall: to a young child' (written
1880)

16 Look at the stars! look, look up at the
skies!
O look at all the fire-folk sitting in the air!
The bright boroughs, the circle-citadels
there!
'The Starlight Night' (written 1877)

17 This piece-bright paling shuts the spouse
Christ home, Christ and his mother and all
his hallows.
'The Starlight Night' (written 1877)

18 Thou art indeed just, Lord, if I contend
With thee; but, sir, so what I plead is just.
Why do sinners' ways prosper? and why
must
Disappointment all I endeavour end?
'Thou art indeed just, Lord' (written 1889)

19 Birds build—but not I build; no, but strain,
Time's eunuch, and not breed one work
that wakes.
'Thou art indeed just, Lord' (written 1889)

20 I caught this morning morning's minion,
kingdom of daylight's dauphin, dapple-
dawn-drawn Falcon.
'The Windhover' (written 1877)

21          My heart in hiding
Stirred for a bird,—the achieve of, the
mastery of the thing!
'The Windhover' (written 1877)

22 To lift up the hands in prayer gives God
glory, but a man with a dungfork in his
hand, a woman with a slop-pail, give him
glory too.
G. Roberts (ed.) *Gerard Manley Hopkins. Selected
Prose* (1980) 'The Principle or Foundation'
(1882) *ad fin.*

## Horace 65–8 BC

23 *Inceptis gravibus plerumque et magna professis
Purpureus, late qui splendeat, unus et alter
Adsuitur pannus.*
Works of serious purpose and grand
promises often have a purple patch or two
stitched on, to shine far and wide.
*Ars Poetica* l. 14

24          *Brevis esse laboro,
Obscurus fio.*
I strive to be brief, and I become obscure.
*Ars Poetica* l. 25

25 *Grammatici certant et adhuc sub iudice lis est.*
Scholars dispute, and the case is still
before the courts.
*Ars Poetica* l. 78

26 *Proicit ampullas et sesquipedalia verba.*
He throws aside his paint-pots and his
words a foot and a half long.
*Ars Poetica* l. 97

27 *Parturient montes, nascetur ridiculus mus.*
Mountains will go into labour, and a silly
little mouse will be born.
*Ars Poetica* l. 139

1 *Semper ad eventum festinat et in medias res*
*Non secus ac notas auditorem rapit.*
He always hurries to the main event and
whisks his audience into the middle of
things as though they knew already.
*Ars Poetica l. 148*

2 *Difficilis, querulus, laudator temporis acti.*
Tiresome, complaining, a praiser of past
times.
*Ars Poetica l. 173*

3 *Indignor quandoque bonus dormitat Homerus.*
I'm aggrieved when sometimes even
excellent Homer nods.
*Ars Poetica l. 359*

4 *Ut pictura poesis.*
A poem is like a painting.
*Ars Poetica l. 361*

5 *Nullius addictus iurare in verba magistri,*
*Quo me cumque rapit tempestas, deferor hospes.*
Not bound to swear allegiance to any
master, wherever the wind takes me I
travel as a visitor.
*Epistles bk. 1, no. 1, l. 14. 'Nullius in verba' is*
the motto of the Royal Society

6 *Si possis recte, si non, quocumque modo rem.*
If possible honestly, if not, somehow, make
money.
*Epistles bk. 1, no. 1, l. 66*

7 *Nos numerus sumus et fruges consumere nati.*
We are just statistics, born to consume
resources.
*Epistles bk. 1, no. 2, l. 27*

8 *Dimidium facti qui coepit habet: sapere aude.*
To have begun is half the job: be bold and
be sensible.
*Epistles bk. 1, no. 2, l. 40*

9 *Ira furor brevis est.*
Anger is a short madness.
*Epistles bk. 1, no. 2, l. 62*

10 *Nil admirari prope res est una, Numici,*
*Solaque quae possit facere et servare beatum.*
To marvel at nothing is just about the one
and only thing, Numicius, that can make a
man happy and keep him that way.
*Epistles bk. 1, no. 6, l. 1*

11 *Naturam expelles furca, tamen usque recurret.*
You may drive out nature with a pitchfork,
yet she'll be constantly running back.
*Epistles bk. 1, no. 10, l. 24*

12 *Concordia discors.*
Discordant harmony.
*Epistles bk. 1, no. 12, l. 19*

13 *Et semel emissum volat irrevocabile verbum.*
And once sent out, a word takes wing
beyond recall.
*Epistles bk. 1, no. 18, l. 71*

14 *Nam tua res agitur, paries cum proximus ardet.*
For it is your business, when the wall next
door catches fire.
*Epistles bk. 1, no. 18, l. 84*

15 *O imitatores, servum pecus.*
O imitators, you slavish herd.
*Epistles bk. 1, no. 19, l. 19*

16 *Scribimus indocti doctique poemata passim.*
Skilled or unskilled, we all scribble poems.
*Epistles bk. 2, no. 1, l. 117. Cf. 252:29*

17 *Atque inter silvas Academi quaerere verum.*
And seek for truth in the groves of
Academe.
*Epistles bk. 2, no. 2, l. 45*

18 *Multa fero, ut placem genus irritabile vatum.*
I have to put up with a lot, to please the
touchy breed of poets.
*Epistles bk. 2, no. 2, l. 102*

19 *Nil desperandum.*
Never despair.
*Odes bk. 1, no. 7, l. 27*

20 *Dum loquimur, fugerit invida*
*Aetas: carpe diem, quam minimum credula*
*postero.*
While we're talking, envious time is
fleeing: seize the day, put no trust in the
future.
*Odes bk. 1, no. 11, l. 7*

21 *Integer vitae scelerisque purus.*
Wholesome of life and free of crimes.
*Odes bk. 1, no. 22, l. 1*

22 *Auream quisquis mediocritatem*
*Diligit.*
Someone who loves the golden mean.
*Odes bk. 2, no. 10, l. 5*

23 *Eheu fugaces, Postume, Postume,*
*Labuntur anni.*
Ah me, Postumus, Postumus, the fleeting
years are slipping by.
*Odes bk. 2, no. 14, l. 1*

24 *Credite posteri.*
Believe me, you who come after me!
*Odes bk. 2, no. 19, l. 2*

25 *Post equitem sedet atra Cura.*
Black Care sits behind the horseman.
*Odes bk. 3, no. 1, l. 40*

26 *Dulce et decorum est pro patria mori.*
Lovely and honourable it is to die for one's
country.
*Odes bk. 3, no. 2, l. 13*

27 *Splendide mendax et in omne virgo*
*Nobilis aevum.*
Gloriously deceitful and a virgin renowned
for ever.
*Odes bk. 3, no. 11, l. 35 (of the Danaid*
Hypermestra)

28 *Exegi monumentum aere perennius.*
I have erected a monument more lasting
than bronze.
*Odes bk. 3, no. 30, l. 1*

29 *Non omnis moriar.*
I shall not altogether die.
*Odes bk. 3, no. 30, l. 6*

30 *Non sum qualis eram bonae*
*Sub regno Cinarae.*
I am not as I was when good Cinara was
my queen.
*Odes bk. 4, no. 1, l. 3*

**1** *Misce stultitiam consiliis brevem:*
*Dulce est desipere in loco.*
Mix a little foolishness with your
prudence: it's good to be silly at the right
moment.
> *Odes* bk. 4, no. 12, l. 27

**2** *Est modus in rebus.*
There is moderation in everything.
> *Satires* bk. 1, no. 1, l. 106

**3** *Etiam disiecti membra poetae.*
Even though broken up, the limbs of a
poet.
> *Satires* bk. 1, no. 4, l. 62 (of Ennius)

**4** *Hoc erat in votis: modus agri non ita magnus,*
*Hortus ubi et tecto vicinus iugis aquae fons*
*Et paulum silvae super his foret.*
This was among my prayers: a piece of
land not so very large, where a garden
should be and a spring of ever-flowing
water near the house, and a bit of
woodland as well as these.
> *Satires* bk. 2, no. 6, l. 1

## Bishop Samuel Horsley 1733–1806

**5** In this country ... the individual subject
... 'has nothing to do with the laws but to
obey them.'
> *Hansard* (Lords) 13 November 1795, col. 268
> (defending a maxim he had earlier used in
> committee)

## A. E. Housman 1859–1936

**6** And wherefore is he wearing such
a conscience-stricken air?
Oh they're taking him to prison for the
colour of his hair.
> *Collected Poems* (1939) 'Additional Poems'
> no. 18

**7** Mud's sister, not himself, adorns my legs.
> *Fragment of a Greek Tragedy* (Bromsgrovian
> vol. 2, no. 5, 1883)

**8** The Grizzly Bear is huge and wild;
He has devoured the infant child.
The infant child is not aware
He has been eaten by the bear.
> 'Infant Innocence' (1938)

**9** Pass me the can, lad; there's an end of
May.
> *Last Poems* (1922) no. 9

**10** But men at whiles are sober
And think by fits and starts,
And if they think, they fasten
Their hands upon their hearts.
> *Last Poems* (1922) no. 10

**11** I, a stranger and afraid
In a world I never made.
> *Last Poems* (1922) no. 12

**12** The candles burn their sockets,
The blinds let through the day,
The young man feels his pockets
And wonders what's to pay.
> *Last Poems* (1922) no. 21

**13** Their shoulders held the sky suspended;
They stood, and earth's foundations stay;
What God abandoned, these defended,
And saved the sum of things for pay.
> *Last Poems* (1922) no. 37 'Epitaph on an Army
> of Mercenaries'

**14** For nature, heartless, witless nature,
Will neither care nor know
What stranger's feet may find the meadow
And trespass there and go,
Nor ask amid the dews of morning
If they are mine or no.
> *Last Poems* (1922) no. 40

**15** The rainy Pleiads wester,
Orion plunges prone.
> *More Poems* (1936) no. 11

**16** Loveliest of trees, the cherry now
Is hung with bloom along the bough,
And stands about the woodland ride
Wearing white for Eastertide.
> *A Shropshire Lad* (1896) no. 2

**17** And since to look at things in bloom
Fifty springs are little room,
About the woodlands I will go
To see the cherry hung with snow.
> *A Shropshire Lad* (1896) no. 2

**18** Clay lies still, but blood's a rover;
Breath's a ware that will not keep.
Up, lad: when the journey's over
There'll be time enough to sleep.
> *A Shropshire Lad* (1896) no. 4

**19** A neck God made for other use
Than strangling in a string.
> *A Shropshire Lad* (1896) no. 9

**20** In summertime on Bredon
The bells they sound so clear;
Round both the shires they ring them
In steeples far and near,
A happy noise to hear.
Here of a Sunday morning
My love and I would lie,
And see the coloured counties,
And hear the larks so high
About us in the sky.
> *A Shropshire Lad* (1896) no. 21

**21** The lads for the girls and the lads for the
liquor are there,
And there with the rest are the lads that
will never be old.
> *A Shropshire Lad* (1896) no. 23

**22** On Wenlock Edge the wood's in trouble.
> *A Shropshire Lad* (1896) no. 31

**23** To-day the Roman and his trouble
Are ashes under Uricon.
> *A Shropshire Lad* (1896) no. 31

**24** What are those blue remembered hills,
What spires, what farms are those?
That is the land of lost content,
I see it shining plain,
The happy highways where I went
And cannot come again.
> *A Shropshire Lad* (1896) no. 40

**25** The beautiful and death-struck year.
> *A Shropshire Lad* (1896) no. 41

1 Clunton and Clunbury,
  Clungunford and Clun,
  Are the quietest places
  Under the sun.
     *A Shropshire Lad* (1896) no. 50 (epigraph)

2 By brooks too broad for leaping
  The lightfoot boys are laid.
     *A Shropshire Lad* (1896) no. 54

3 Say, for what were hop-yards meant,
  Or why was Burton built on Trent?
     *A Shropshire Lad* (1896) no. 62

4 And malt does more than Milton can
  To justify God's ways to man.
     *A Shropshire Lad* (1896) no. 62. Cf. 228:9

5 Mithridates, he died old.
     *A Shropshire Lad* (1896) no. 62

6 This great College, of this ancient
  University, has seen some strange sights. It
  has seen Wordsworth drunk and Porson
  sober. And here am I, a better poet than
  Porson, and a better scholar than
  Wordsworth, betwixt and between.
     Speech at Trinity College, Cambridge, in G.
     K. Chesterton *Autobiography* (1936) ch. 12

## Julia Ward Howe 1819–1910

7 Mine eyes have seen the glory of the
  coming of the Lord:
  He is trampling out the vintage where the
  grapes of wrath are stored;
  He hath loosed the fateful lightning of his
  terrible swift sword:
  His truth is marching on.
     'Battle Hymn of the Republic' (1862)

## James Howell *c.*1593–1666

8 Some hold translations not unlike to be
  The wrong side of a Turkey tapestry.
     *Familiar Letters* (1645–55) bk. 1, no. 6

9 One hair of a woman can draw more than
  a hundred pair of oxen.
     *Familiar Letters* (1645–55) bk. 2, no. 4

## Mary Howitt 1799–1888

10 Buttercups and daisies,
   Oh, the pretty flowers;
   Coming ere the springtime,
   To tell of sunny hours.
      'Buttercups and Daisies' (1838)

11 'Will you walk into my parlour?' said a
   spider to a fly:
   ''Tis the prettiest little parlour that ever
   you did spy.'
      'The Spider and the Fly' (1834)

## Edmond Hoyle 1672–1769

12 When in doubt, win the trick.
      *Hoyle's Games Improved* (ed. Charles Jones,
      1790) 'Twenty-four Short Rules for Learners'
      (possibly Jones's addition)

## Elbert Hubbard 1859–1915

13 Never explain—your friends do not need it
   and your enemies will not believe you
   anyway.
      *The Motto Book* (1907) p. 31. Cf. 352:21

14 Life is just one damned thing after
   another.
      *Philistine* December 1909, p. 32 (often
      attributed to Frank Ward O'Malley)

15 Editor: a person employed by a newspaper,
   whose business it is to separate the wheat
   from the chaff, and to see that the chaff is
   printed.
      *The Roycroft Dictionary* (1914) p. 46
   *See also* RALPH WALDO EMERSON

## Frank McKinney ('Kin') Hubbard 1868–1930

16 Classic music is th'kind that we keep
   thinkin'll turn into a tune.
      *Comments of Abe Martin and His Neighbors*
      (1923)

17 It's no disgrace t'be poor, but it might as
   well be.
      *Short Furrows* (1911) p. 42

## Jimmy Hughes and Frank Lake

18 Bless 'em all! Bless 'em all! The long and
   the short and the tall.
      'Bless 'Em All' (1940 song)

## Langston Hughes 1902–67

19 I, too, sing America.
      'I, Too' in *Survey Graphic* March 1925

## Ted Hughes 1930–

20 It took the whole of Creation
   To produce my foot, my each feather:
   Now I hold Creation in my foot.
      'Hawk Roosting' (1960)

21 Adam ate the apple.
   Eve ate Adam.
   The serpent ate Eve.
   This is the dark intestine.
      'Theology' (1967)

22 Grape is my mulatto mother
   In this frozen whited country.
      'Wino' (1967)

## Thomas Hughes 1822–96

23 It's more than a game. It's an institution.
      *Tom Brown's Schooldays* (1857) pt. 2, ch. 7 (of
      cricket)

## Victor Hugo 1802–85

24 The word is the Verb, and the Verb is God.
      *Contemplations* (1856) bk. 1, no. 8

1 If suffer we must, let's suffer on the heights.

> *Contemplations* (1856) bk. 5, no. 26 'Les Malheureux'

2 A stand can be made against invasion by an army; no stand can be made against invasion by an idea.

> *Histoire d'un Crime* (written 1851–2, published 1877) pt. 5, sect. 10

## David Hume 1711–76

3 Custom, then, is the great guide of human life.

> *An Enquiry Concerning Human Understanding* (1748) sect. 5, pt. 1

4 If we take in our hand any volume; of divinity or school metaphysics, for instance; let us ask, *Does it contain any abstract reasoning concerning quantity or number?* No. *Does it contain any experimental reasoning, concerning matter of fact and existence?* No. Commit it then to the flames: for it can contain nothing but sophistry and illusion.

> *Enquiry Concerning Human Understanding* (1748) sect. 12, pt. 3

5 Avarice, the spur of industry.

> *Essays: Moral and Political* (1741–2) 'Of Civil Liberty'

6 Money ... is none of the wheels of trade: it is the oil which renders the motion of the wheels more smooth and easy.

> *Essays: Moral and Political* (1741–2) 'Of Money'

7 A little miss, dressed in a new gown for a dancing-school ball, receives as complete enjoyment as the greatest orator, who ... governs the passions and resolutions of a numerous assembly.

> *Essays: Moral and Political* (1741–2) 'The Sceptic'

8 In all ages of the world, priests have been enemies of liberty.

> *Essays, Moral, Political, and Literary* (ed. Green and Grose, 1875) 'Of the Parties of Great Britain' (1741–2)

9 Beauty is no quality in things themselves. It exists merely in the mind which contemplates them.

> *Essays, Moral, Political, and Literary* (ed. Green and Grose, 1875) 'Of the Standard of Taste' (1757)

10 Never literary attempt was more unfortunate than my Treatise of Human Nature. It fell *dead-born from the press.*

> *My Own Life* (1777) ch. 1

11 It is not contrary to reason to prefer the destruction of the whole world to the scratching of my finger.

> *A Treatise upon Human Nature* (1739) bk. 2, pt. 3

## Leigh Hunt 1784–1859

12 Abou Ben Adhem (may his tribe increase!) Awoke one night from a deep dream of peace.

> 'Abou Ben Adhem' (1838)

13 Write me as one that loves his fellow-men.

> 'Abou Ben Adhem' (1838)

14 The laughing queen that caught the world's great hands.

> 'The Nile' (1818); of Cleopatra

15 Jenny kissed me when we met, Jumping from the chair she sat in; Time, you thief, who love to get Sweets into your list, put that in.

> 'Rondeau' (1838)

16 Stolen sweets are always sweeter, Stolen kisses much completer, Stolen looks are nice in chapels, Stolen, stolen, be your apples.

> 'Song of Fairies Robbing an Orchard' (1830)

17 The two divinest things this world has got, A lovely woman in a rural spot!

> 'The Story of Rimini' (1816) canto 3, l. 257

18 A mere gossiping entertainment: a few child's squalls, a few mumbled amens, and a few mumbled cakes, and a few smirks accompanied by a few fees.

> Of a christening; letter to Marianne Kent, February 1806, in T. L. Hunt *Correspondence of Leigh Hunt* (1862) vol. 1

## Anne Hunter 1742–1821

19 My mother bids me bind my hair With bands of rosy hue, Tie up my sleeves with ribbons rare, And lace my bodice blue.

> 'A Pastoral Song' (1794)

## Herman Hupfeld 1894–1951

20 You must remember this, a kiss is still a kiss, A sigh is just a sigh; The fundamental things apply, As time goes by.

> 'As Time Goes By' (1931 song)

## John Huss c.1372–1415

21 *O sancta simplicitas!* O holy simplicity!

> At the stake, seeing an aged peasant bringing a bundle of twigs to throw on the pile; in J. W. Zincgreff and J. L. Weidner *Apophthegmata* (Amsterdam, 1653) pt. 3, p. 383. Cf. 181:6

## Saddam Hussein 1937–

22 The mother of battles.

> Popular interpretation of his description of the approaching Gulf War, given in a speech in Baghdad, 6 January 1991; *The Times*, 7 January 1991, reported that he was ready for the 'mother of all wars'

## Francis Hutcheson 1694–1746

1 Wisdom denotes the pursuing of the best ends by the best means.
*Inquiry into the Original of our Ideas of Beauty and Virtue* (1725) Treatise 1, sect. 5, subsect. 16

2 That action is best, which procures the greatest happiness for the greatest numbers.
*Inquiry into the Original ...* (1725) Treatise 2, sect. 3, subsect. 8. Cf. 35:1

## Aldous Huxley 1894–1963

3 There are few who would not rather be taken in adultery than in provincialism.
*Antic Hay* (1923) ch. 10

4 The saxophones wailed like melodious cats under the moon.
*Brave New World* (1932) ch. 5

5 The proper study of mankind is books.
*Crome Yellow* (1921) ch. 28. Cf. 252:17

6 Consistency is contrary to nature, contrary to life. The only completely consistent people are the dead.
*Do What You Will* (1929) 'Wordsworth in the Tropics'

7 Chastity—the most unnatural of all the sexual perversions.
*Eyeless in Gaza* (1936) ch. 27

8 I can sympathize with people's pains, but not with their pleasures. There is something curiously boring about somebody else's happiness.
*Limbo* (1920) 'Cynthia'

9 Several excuses are always less convincing than one.
*Point Counter Point* (1928) ch. 1

10 Brought up in an epoch when ladies apparently rolled along on wheels, Mr Quarles was peculiarly susceptible to calves.
*Point Counter Point* (1928) ch. 20

11 A million million spermatozoa,
All of them alive:
Out of their cataclysm but one poor Noah
Dare hope to survive.
And among that billion minus one
Might have chanced to be
Shakespeare, another Newton, a new Donne—
But the One was Me.
'Fifth Philosopher's Song' (1920)

12              When the wearied Band
Swoons to a waltz, I take her hand,
And there we sit in peaceful calm,
Quietly sweating palm to palm.
'Frascati's' (1920)

13 Beauty for some provides escape,
Who gain a happiness in eyeing
The gorgeous buttocks of the ape
Or Autumn sunsets exquisitely dying.
'Ninth Philosopher's Song' (1920)

## Sir Julian Huxley 1887–1975

14 Operationally, God is beginning to resemble not a ruler but the last fading smile of a cosmic Cheshire cat.
*Religion without Revelation* (1957 ed.) ch. 3

## T. H. Huxley 1825–95

15 The great tragedy of Science—the slaying of a beautiful hypothesis by an ugly fact.
*Collected Essays* (1893–4) 'Biogenesis and Abiogenesis'

16 Science is nothing but trained and organized common sense, differing from the latter only as a veteran may differ from a raw recruit: and its methods differ from those of common sense only as far as the guardsman's cut and thrust differ from the manner in which a savage wields his club.
*Collected Essays* (1893–4) 'The Method of Zadig'

17 If a little knowledge is dangerous, where is the man who has so much as to be out of danger?
*Collected Essays* vol. 3 (1895) 'On Elementary Instruction in Physiology' (written 1877)

18 It is the customary fate of new truths to begin as heresies and to end as superstitions.
*Science and Culture and Other Essays* (1881) 'The Coming of Age of the Origin of Species'

19 Irrationally held truths may be more harmful than reasoned errors.
*Science and Culture and Other Essays* (1881) 'The Coming of Age of the Origin of Species'

20 Logical consequences are the scarecrows of fools and the beacons of wise men.
*Science and Culture and Other Essays* (1881) 'On the Hypothesis that Animals are Automata'

21 A man has no reason to be ashamed of having an ape for his grandfather. If there were an ancestor whom I should feel shame in recalling it would rather be a *man*—a man of restless and versatile intellect—who, not content with an equivocal success in his own sphere of activity, plunges into scientific questions with which he has no real acquaintance, only to obscure them by an aimless rhetoric, and distract the attention of his hearers from the real point at issue by eloquent digressions and skilled appeals to religious prejudice.
Replying to Samuel Wilberforce in a debate on Darwin's theory of evolution at Oxford, 30 June 1860. See L. Huxley (ed.) *Life and Letters of T. H. Huxley* (1900) vol. 1, p. 185. Cf. 349:7

22 I am too much of a sceptic to deny the possibility of anything.
Letter to H. Spencer, 22 March 1886, in L. Huxley (ed.) *Life and Letters of T. H. Huxley* (1900) vol. 2, ch. 8

## Edward Hyde
*See* EARL OF CLARENDON

## Dolores Ibarruri ('La Pasionaria')
1895–1989

1 It is better to die on your feet than to live on your knees.
   Speech in Paris, 3 September 1936; in *L'Humanité* 4 September 1936 (also attributed to Emiliano Zapata)

2 *No pasarán.*
   They shall not pass.
   Radio broadcast, Madrid, 19 July 1936, in *Speeches and Articles 1936–38* (1938) p. 7. Cf. 12:6

## Henrik Ibsen 1828–1906

3 You should never have your best trousers on when you go out to fight for freedom and truth.
   *An Enemy of the People* (1882) act 5

4 Mother, give me the sun.
   *Ghosts* (1881) act 3

5 But good God, people don't do such things!
   *Hedda Gabler* (1890) act 4

6 Castles in the air—they are so easy to take refuge in. And easy to build, too.
   *The Master Builder* (1892) act 3

7 Take the life-lie away from the average man and straight away you take away his happiness.
   *The Wild Duck* (1884) act 5

## St Ignatius Loyola 1491–1556

8 Teach us, good Lord, to serve Thee as Thou deservest:
   To give and not to count the cost;
   To fight and not to heed the wounds;
   To toil and not to seek for rest;
   To labour and not to ask for any reward
   Save that of knowing that we do Thy will.
   'Prayer for Generosity' (1548)

## Ivan Illich 1926–

9 In a consumer society there are inevitably two kinds of slaves: the prisoners of addiction and the prisoners of envy.
   *Tools for Conviviality* (1973) ch. 3

## Dean Inge 1860–1954

10 The enemies of Freedom do not argue; they shout and they shoot.
   *End of an Age* (1948) ch. 4

11 The effect of boredom on a large scale in history is underestimated. It is a main cause of revolutions, and would soon bring to an end all the static Utopias and the farmyard civilization of the Fabians.
   *End of an Age* (1948) ch. 6

12 To become a popular religion, it is only necessary for a superstition to enslave a philosophy.
   *Idea of Progress* (Romanes Lecture, 27 May 1920) p. 9

13 Many people believe that they are attracted by God, or by Nature, when they are only repelled by man.
   *More Lay Thoughts of a Dean* (1931) pt. 4, ch. 1

14 A man may build himself a throne of bayonets, but he cannot sit on it.
   *Philosophy of Plotinus* (1923) vol. 2, Lecture 22 (quoted by Boris Yeltsin at the time of the failed military coup in Russia, August 1991)

## Robert G. Ingersoll 1833–99

15 An honest God is the noblest work of man.
   *The Gods* (1876) pt. 1, p. 2. Cf. 252:22

16 In nature there are neither rewards nor punishments—there are consequences.
   *Some Reasons Why* (1881) pt. 8 'The New Testament'

## J. A. D. Ingres 1780–1867

17 *Le dessin est la probité de l'art.*
   Drawing is the true test of art.
   *Pensées d'Ingres* (1922) p. 70

## Weldon J. Irvine

18 Young, gifted and black.
   Title of song (1969)

## Washington Irving 1783–1859

19 A ... sharp tongue is the only edged tool that grows keener with constant use.
   *The Sketch Book* (1820) 'Rip Van Winkle'

20 There is a certain relief in change, even though it be from bad to worse ... it is often a comfort to shift one's position and be bruised in a new place.
   *Tales of a Traveller* (1824) 'To the Reader'

## Christopher Isherwood 1904–86

21 The common cormorant (or shag)
   Lays eggs inside a paper bag,
   You follow the idea, no doubt?
   It's to keep the lightning out.
   But what these unobservant birds
   Have never thought of, is that herds
   Of wandering bears might come with buns
   And steal the bags to hold the crumbs.
   'The Common Cormorant' (written c.1925)

22 I am a camera with its shutter open, quite passive, recording, not thinking.
   *Goodbye to Berlin* (1939) 'Berlin Diary' Autumn 1930

## Alec Issigonis (1906–88)

23 A camel is a horse designed by a committee.
   On his dislike of working in teams, in *Guardian* 14 January 1991 'Notes and Queries' (attributed)

## Holbrook Jackson 1874–1948

24 Pedantry is the dotage of knowledge.
   *Anatomy of Bibliomania* (1930) vol. 1, p. 150

## Joe Jacobs 1896–1940

**1** We was robbed!
> After Jack Sharkey beat Max Schmeling (of
> whom Jacobs was manager) in the
> heavyweight title fight, 21 June 1932; in P.
> Heller *In This Corner* (1975) p. 44

**2** I should of stood in bed.
> After leaving his sick-bed to attend the
> World Baseball Series in Detroit, 1935, and
> betting on the losers; in J. Lardner *Strong
> Cigars* (1951) p. 61

## Jacopone da Todi *c.*1230–1306

**3** *Stabat Mater dolorosa,*
> *Iuxta crucem lacrimosa.*
> At the cross her station keeping,
> Stood the mournful Mother weeping.
> 'Stabat Mater dolorosa' (tr. E. Caswall 1849);
> also attributed to Pope Innocent III and
> others

## Mick Jagger 1943– and Keith Richards 1943–

**4** Get off of my cloud.
> Title of song (1966)

**5** And though she's not really ill,
> There's a little yellow pill:
> She goes running for the shelter
> Of a mother's little helper.
> 'Mother's Little Helper' (1966 song)

**6** I can't get no satisfaction
> I can't get no girl reaction.
> '(I Can't Get No) Satisfaction' (1965 song)

**7** Ev'rywhere I hear the sound of marching,
> charging feet, boy.
> 'Street Fighting Man' (1968 song)

## Richard Jago 1715–81

**8** With leaden foot time creeps along
> While Delia is away.
> 'Absence'

## James I (James VI of Scotland) 1566–1625

**9** A custom loathsome to the eye, hateful to
> the nose, harmful to the brain, dangerous
> to the lungs, and in the black, stinking
> fume thereof, nearest resembling the
> horrible Stygian smoke of the pit that is
> bottomless.
> *A Counterblast to Tobacco* (1604)

**10** The king is truly *parens patriae*, the polite
> father of his people.
> Speech to Parliament, 21 March 1610, in
> *Works* (1616) p. 529

**11** No bishop, no King.
> To a deputation of Presbyterians from the
> Church of Scotland, seeking religious
> tolerance in England; in W. Barlow *Sum and
> Substance of the Conference* (1604) p. 82

**12** I will govern according to the common
> weal, but not according to the common
> will.
> December, 1621, in J. R. Green *History of the
> English People* vol. 3 (1879) bk. 7, ch. 4

**13** Dr Donne's verses are like the peace of
> God; they pass all understanding.
> Remark recorded by Archdeacon Plume
> (1630–1704)

## James V 1512–42

**14** It came with a lass, and it will pass with a
> lass.
> Of the crown of Scotland, on learning of the
> birth of Mary Queen of Scots, December
> 1542; in Robert Lindsay of Pitscottie
> (*c.*1500–65) *History of Scotland* (1728) p. 176

## Henry James 1843–1916

**15** The historian, essentially, wants more
> documents than he can really use; the
> dramatist only wants more liberties than
> he can really take.
> *The Aspern Papers* (1909 ed.) preface

**16** Most English talk is a quadrille in a sentry-
> box.
> *The Awkward Age* (1899) bk. 5, ch. 19

**17** Vereker's secret, my dear man—the
> general intention of his books: the string
> the pearls were strung on, the buried
> treasure, the figure in the carpet.
> *The Figure in the Carpet* (1896) ch. 11

**18** It takes a great deal of history to produce
> a little literature.
> *Hawthorne* (1879) ch. 1

**19** He was ... worse than provincial—he was
> parochial.
> *Hawthorne* (1879) ch. 4 (of H. D. Thoreau)

**20** The black and merciless things that are
> behind the great possessions.
> *The Ivory Tower* (1917) notes p. 287

**21** I could come back to America ... to
> die—but never, never to live.
> Letter to Mrs William James, 1 April 1913, in
> Leon Edel (ed.) *Letters* vol. 4 (1984) p. 657

**22** Cats and monkeys—monkeys and cats—all
> human life is there!
> *The Madonna of the Future* (1879) vol. 1, p. 59
> ('All human life is there' became the slogan
> of the *News of the World* from the late 1950s)

**23** We work in the dark—we do what we
> can—we give what we have. Our doubt is
> our passion and our passion is our task.
> The rest is the madness of art.
> 'The Middle Years' (short story, 1893)

**24** What is character but the determination of
> incident? What is incident but the
> illustration of character?
> *Partial Portraits* (1888) 'The Art of Fiction'

**25** The house of fiction has in short not one
> window, but a million ... but they are,
> singly or together, as nothing without the
> posted presence of the watcher.
> *The Portrait of a Lady* (1908 ed.) preface

**1** The note I wanted; that of the strange and sinister embroidered on the very type of the normal and easy.
*Prefaces* (1909) 'The Altar of the Dead'

**2** The fatal futility of Fact.
*The Spoils of Poynton* (1909 ed.) preface

**3** We were alone with the quiet day, and his little heart, dispossessed, had stopped.
*The Turn of the Screw* (1898) p. 169

**4** Of course, of course.
On hearing that Rupert Brooke had died on a Greek island; in C. Hassall *Rupert Brooke* (1964) ch. 14

**5** Summer afternoon—summer afternoon … the two most beautiful words in the English language.
In Edith Wharton *A Backward Glance* (1934) ch. 10

**6** So here it is at last, the distinguished thing!
On experiencing his first stroke; in Edith Wharton *A Backward Glance* (1934) ch. 14

## William James 1842–1910

**7** The moral flabbiness born of the exclusive worship of the bitch-goddess *success.*
Letter to H. G. Wells, 11 September 1906, in *Letters* (1920) vol. 2

**8** There is no more miserable human being than one in whom nothing is habitual but indecision.
*Principles of Psychology* (1890) vol. 1, ch. 4

**9** The art of being wise is the art of knowing what to overlook.
*Principles of Psychology* (1890) vol. 2, ch. 22

**10** There is no worse lie than a truth misunderstood by those who hear it.
*Varieties of Religious Experience* (1902) p. 355

**11** Hogamus, higamus
Man is polygamous
Higamus, hogamus
Woman monogamous.
In *Oxford Book of Marriage* (1990) p. 195

## Randall Jarrell 1914–65

**12** To Americans, English manners are far more frightening than none at all.
*Pictures from an Institution* (1954) pt. 1, ch. 4

**13** It is better to entertain an idea than to take it home to live with you for the rest of your life.
*Pictures from an Institution* (1954) pt. 1, ch. 4

## Douglas Jay 1907–

**14** Fair shares for all, is Labour's call.
*Change and Fortune* (1980) ch. 7 (slogan for the North Battersea by-election, 1946)

**15** In the case of nutrition and health, just as in the case of education, the gentleman in Whitehall really does know better what is good for people than the people know themselves.
*The Socialist Case* (1939) ch. 30

## Jean Paul
*See* JOHANN PAUL FRIEDRICH RICHTER

## Sir James Jeans 1877–1946

**16** Life exists in the universe only because the carbon atom possesses certain exceptional properties.
*The Mysterious Universe* (1930) ch. 1

**17** From the intrinsic evidence of his creation, the Great Architect of the Universe now begins to appear as a pure mathematician.
*The Mysterious Universe* (1930) ch. 5

## Thomas Jefferson 1743–1826

**18** We hold these truths to be sacred and undeniable; that all men are created equal and independent, that from that equal creation they derive rights inherent and inalienable, among which are the preservation of life, and liberty, and the pursuit of happiness.
'Rough Draft' of the American Declaration of Independence, in J. P. Boyd et al. *Papers of Thomas Jefferson* vol. 1 (1950) p. 423. Cf. 11:12

**19** Peace, commerce, and honest friendship with all nations—entangling alliances with none.
*Speech* [First Inaugural Address] … on the 4th of March, 1801

**20** A little rebellion now and then is a good thing.
Letter to James Madison, 30 January 1787, in *Papers* vol. 11 (1955)

**21** The tree of liberty must be refreshed from time to time with the blood of patriots and tyrants. It is its natural manure.
Letter to W. S. Smith, 13 November 1787, in *Papers* vol. 12 (1955)

**22** If a due participation of office is a matter of right, how are vacancies to be obtained? Those by death are few; by resignation none.
Letter to E. Shipman and others, 12 July 1801 (usually quoted 'Few die and none resign'); in P. L. Ford (ed.) *Writings of T. Jefferson* vol. 8 (1897)

**23** To attain all this [universal republicanism], however, rivers of blood must yet flow, and years of desolation pass over; yet the object is worth rivers of blood, and years of desolation.
Letter to John Adams, 4 September 1823, in P. L. Ford *Writings of T. Jefferson* vol. 10 (1899). Cf. 255:3, 339:11

**24** Indeed I tremble for my country when I reflect that God is just.
*Notes on the State of Virginia* (1781–5) Query 18

**25** We have the wolf by the ears; and we can neither hold him, nor safely let him go. Justice is in one scale, and self-preservation in the other.
On slavery, in a letter to John Holmes, 22 April 1820; in A. Lipscome and A. Berg (eds.) *Writings of T. Jefferson* (1903) vol. 15

1 When a man assumes a public trust, he should consider himself as public property.
   To Baron von Humboldt, 1807, in B. L. Rayner *Life of Jefferson* (1834) p. 356

## Francis, Lord Jeffrey 1773–1850

2 This will never do.
   On Wordsworth's *The Excursion* (1814) in *Edinburgh Review* November 1814

## David Jenkins, Bishop of Durham 1925–

3 An imported, elderly American.
   Referring to Ian MacGregor, Chairman of the National Coal Board; in *The Times* 22 September 1984

4 I am not clear that God manoeuvres physical things ... After all, a conjuring trick with bones only proves that it is as clever as a conjuring trick with bones.
   On the Resurrection, in 'Poles Apart' (BBC radio, 4 October 1984)

## Paul Jennings 1918–89

5 Resistentialism is concerned with what Things think about men.
   *Even Oddlier* (1952) 'Developments in Resistentialism'

## St Jerome AD *c*.342–420

6 *Venerationi mihi semper fuit non verbosa rusticitas, sed sancta simplicitas.*
   I have revered always not crude verbosity, but holy simplicity.
   Letter 'Ad Pammachium' in *Patrologiae Latinae* vol. 22 (1864) col. 579

## Jerome K. Jerome 1859–1927

7 It is impossible to enjoy idling thoroughly unless one has plenty of work to do.
   *Idle Thoughts of an Idle Fellow* (1886) 'On Being Idle'

8 I want a house that has got over all its troubles; I don't want to spend the rest of my life bringing up a young and inexperienced house.
   *They and I* (1909) ch. 11

## William Jerome 1865–1932

9 Any old place I can hang my hat is home sweet home to me.
   Title of song (1901)

## Douglas Jerrold 1803–57

10 Religion's in the heart, not in the knees.
   *The Devil's Ducat* (1830) act 1, sc. 2

11 The best thing I know between France and England is—the sea.
   *Wit and Opinions* (1859) 'The Anglo-French Alliance'

12 Earth is here so kind, that just tickle her with a hoe and she laughs with a harvest.
   *Wit and Opinions* (1859) 'A Land of Plenty' (Australia)

13 Love's like the measles—all the worse when it comes late in life.
   *Wit and Opinions* (1859) 'Love'

## Bishop John Jewel 1522–71

14 In old time we had treen chalices and golden priests, but now we have treen priests and golden chalices.
   *Certain Sermons Preached Before the Queen's Majesty* (1609) p. 176

## C. E. M. Joad 1891–1953

15 It all depends what you mean by ...
   Replying to questions on 'The Brains Trust' (formerly 'Any Questions'), BBC radio (1941–8)

## St John of the Cross 1542–91

16 *Muero porque no muero.*
   I die because I do not die.
   'Coplas del alma que pena por ver a Dios' (*c*.1578); also in St Teresa of Ávila 'Versos nacidos del fuego del amor de Dios' (*c*.1571–3)

## Lionel Johnson 1867–1902

17 Alone he rides, alone,
   The fair and fatal king.
   'By the Statue of King Charles I at Charing Cross' (1895)

18 I know you: solitary griefs,
   Desolate passions, aching hours.
   'The Precept of Silence' (1895)

## Lyndon Baines Johnson 1908–73

19 I am a free man, an American, a United States Senator, and a Democrat, in that order.
   *Texas Quarterly* Winter 1958

20 I don't want loyalty. I want *loyalty*. I want him to kiss my ass in Macy's window at high noon and tell me it smells like roses. I want his pecker in my pocket.
   In D. Halberstam *The Best and the Brightest* (1972) ch. 20 (discussing a prospective assistant)

21 Better to have him inside the tent pissing out, than outside pissing in.
   Of J. Edgar Hoover, in D. Halberstam *The Best and the Brightest* (1972) ch. 20

22 So dumb he can't fart and chew gum at the same time.
   Of Gerald Ford, in R. Reeves *A Ford, not a Lincoln* (1975) ch. 2

## Philander Chase Johnson
### 1866–1939

1 Cheer up! the worst is yet to come!
*Everybody's Magazine* May 1920

## Philip Johnson 1906–

2 Architecture is the art of how to waste space.
*New York Times* 27 December 1964, p. 9

## Samuel Johnson 1709–84

3 Change is not made without inconvenience, even from worse to better.
*Dictionary of the English Language* (1755) preface. Cf. 171:15

4 I am not yet so lost in lexicography as to forget that words are the daughters of earth, and that things are the sons of heaven. Language is only the instrument of science, and words are but the signs of ideas.
*Dictionary of the English Language* (1755) preface. Cf. 216:14

5 Every quotation contributes something to the stability or enlargement of the language.
*Dictionary of the English Language* (1755) preface (on citations of usage in a dictionary)

6 *Dull*. To make dictionaries is dull work.
*Dictionary of the English Language* (1755) 'dull' (8th definition)

7 *Excise*. A hateful tax levied upon commodities.
*Dictionary of the English Language* (1755)

8 *Lexicographer*. A writer of dictionaries, a harmless drudge.
*Dictionary of the English Language* (1755)

9 *Oats*. A grain, which in England is generally given to horses, but in Scotland supports the people.
*Dictionary of the English Language* (1755)

10 *Patron*. Commonly a wretch who supports with insolence, and is paid with flattery.
*Dictionary of the English Language* (1755)

11 When two Englishmen meet, their first talk is of the weather.
*The Idler* no. 11 (24 June 1758)

12 Among the calamities of war may be jointly numbered the diminution of the love of truth, by the falsehoods which interest dictates and credulity encourages.
*The Idler* no. 30 (11 November 1758); possibly the source of 'When war is declared, Truth is the first casualty', epigraph to Arthur Ponsonby's *Falsehood in Wartime* (1928); attributed also to Hiram Johnson, speaking in the US Senate, 1918

13 Promise, large promise, is the soul of an advertisement.
*The Idler* no. 40 (20 January 1759)

14 A Scotchman must be a very sturdy moralist, who does not love Scotland better than truth.
*A Journey to the Western Islands of Scotland* (1775) 'Ostig in Sky'

15 Grief is a species of idleness.
Letter to Mrs Thrale, 17 March 1773, in R. W. Chapman (ed.) *Letters* (1952) vol. 1

16 He is gone, and we are going.
Letter to Mrs Thrale on the death of her son, Harry, 25 March 1776; in R. W. Chapman (ed.) *Letters* (1952) vol. 3

17 When I rise my breakfast is solitary, the black dog waits to share it, from breakfast to dinner he continues barking, except that Dr Brocklesby for a little keeps him at a distance.
Letter to Mrs Thrale, 28 June 1783, in R. W. Chapman (ed.) *Letters* (1952) vol. 3 (on his melancholia; Winston Churchill later used the words 'black dog' to refer to his own bouts of depression)

18 The true genius is a mind of large general powers, accidentally determined to some particular direction.
*Lives of the English Poets* (1779–81) 'Cowley'

19 Language is the dress of thought.
*Lives of the English Poets* (1779–81) 'Cowley'. Cf. 252:2, 346:18

20 The father of English criticism.
*Lives of the English Poets* (1779–81) 'Dryden'

21 In the character of his Elegy I rejoice to concur with the common reader; for by the common sense of readers uncorrupted with literary prejudices ... must be finally decided all claim to poetical honours.
*Lives of the English Poets* (1779–81) 'Gray'

22 An exotic and irrational entertainment.
*Lives of the English Poets* (1779–81) 'Hughes' (of Italian opera)

23 I am disappointed by that stroke of death, which has eclipsed the gaiety of nations and impoverished the public stock of harmless pleasure.
*Lives of the English Poets* (1779–81) 'Edmund Smith' (on the death of Garrick)

24 Nothing can please many, and please long, but just representations of general nature.
*Plays of William Shakespeare ...* (1765) preface (Yale ed., p. 61)

25 Love is only one of many passions.
*Plays of William Shakespeare ...* (1765) preface (Yale ed., p. 63)

26 I have always suspected that the reading is right, which requires many words to prove it wrong; and the emendation wrong, that cannot without so much labour appear to be right.
*Plays of William Shakespeare ...* (1765) preface (Yale ed., p. 108)

27 This world where much is to be done and little to be known.
*Prayers and Meditations* (1785) no. 170 'Against inquisitive and perplexing Thoughts' 12 August 1784

1 No place affords a more striking conviction of the vanity of human hopes, than a public library.
   *The Rambler* no. 106 (23 March 1751)

2 The business of a poet, said Imlac, is to examine, not the individual, but the species; to remark general properties and appearances.
   *Rasselas* (1759) ch. 10

3 He [the poet] must write as the interpreter of nature, and the legislator of mankind.
   *Rasselas* (1759) ch. 10. Cf. 305:19

4 Human life is everywhere a state in which much is to be endured, and little to be enjoyed.
   *Rasselas* (1759) ch. 11

5 Marriage has many pains, but celibacy has no pleasures.
   *Rasselas* (1759) ch. 26

6 Example is always more efficacious than precept.
   *Rasselas* (1759) ch. 30

7 I consider this mighty structure [the pyramids] as a monument of the insufficiency of human enjoyments.
   *Rasselas* (1759) ch. 32

8 Here falling houses thunder on your head,
   And here a female atheist talks you dead.
   *London* (1738) l. 17

9 This mournful truth is ev'rywhere confessed,
   Slow rises worth, by poverty depressed.
   *London* (1738) l. 176

10 The stage but echoes back the public voice.
   The drama's laws the drama's patrons give,
   For we that live to please, must please to live.
   'Prologue spoken at the Opening of the Theatre in Drury Lane' (1747)

11 Let observation with extensive view,
   Survey mankind, from China to Peru.
   *The Vanity of Human Wishes* (1749) l. 1

12 There mark what ills the scholar's life assail,
   Toil, envy, want, the patron, and the jail.
   *The Vanity of Human Wishes* (1749) l. 159

13 A frame of adamant, a soul of fire,
   No dangers fright him, and no labours tire.
   *The Vanity of Human Wishes* (1749) l. 193 (Charles XII of Sweden)

14 He left the name, at which the world grew pale,
   To point a moral, or adorn a tale.
   *The Vanity of Human Wishes* (1749) l. 221 (Charles XII of Sweden)

15 Hides from himself his state, and shuns to know,
   That life protracted is protracted woe.
   *The Vanity of Human Wishes* (1749) l. 257

16 Must helpless man, in ignorance sedate,
   Roll darkling down the torrent of his fate?
   *The Vanity of Human Wishes* (1749) l. 345

17 A lawyer has no business with the justice or injustice of the cause which he undertakes, unless his client asks his opinion, and then he is bound to give it honestly. The justice or injustice of the cause is to be decided by the judge.
   In James Boswell *Journal of a Tour to the Hebrides* (1785) 15 August 1773

18 I am always sorry when any language is lost, because languages are the pedigree of nations.
   In ... *Tour to the Hebrides* (1785) 18 September 1773

19 A cucumber should be well sliced, and dressed with pepper and vinegar, and then thrown out, as good for nothing.
   In ... *Tour to the Hebrides* (1785) 5 October 1773

20 I am sorry I have not learned to play at cards. It is very useful in life: it generates kindness and consolidates society.
   In ... *Tour to the Hebrides* (1785) 21 November 1773

**The Life of Samuel Johnson** (1791) by James Boswell (references are to G. B. Hill's edition, 1934, revised by L. F. Powell, 1964)

21 [JOHNSON] I had no notion that I was wrong or irreverent to my tutor.
   [BOSWELL] That, Sir, was great fortitude of mind.
   [JOHNSON] No, Sir; stark insensibility.
   Boswell *Life* vol. 1, p. 60 (31 October 1728)

22 Sir, we are a nest of singing birds.
   Boswell *Life* vol. 1, p. 75 (1730) of Pembroke College, Oxford

23 He was a vicious man, but very kind to me. If you call a dog *Hervey*, I shall love him.
   Boswell *Life* vol. 1, p. 106 (1737)

24 I'll come no more behind your scenes, David; for the silk stockings and white bosoms of your actresses excite my amorous propensities.
   Boswell *Life* vol. 1, p. 201 (1750)

25 I had done all that I could; and no man is well pleased to have his all neglected, be it ever so little.
   Boswell *Life* vol. 1, p. 261 (7 February 1755) letter to Lord Chesterfield

26 Is not a Patron, my Lord, one who looks with unconcern on a man struggling for life in the water, and, when he has reached ground, encumbers him with help?
   Boswell *Life* vol. 1, p. 262 (7 February 1755) letter to Lord Chesterfield

27 A fly, Sir, may sting a stately horse and make him wince; but one is but an insect, and the other is a horse still.
   Boswell *Life* vol. 1, p. 263, n. 3 (1754)

28 This man [Lord Chesterfield] I thought had been a Lord among wits; but, I find, he is only a wit among Lords.
   Boswell *Life* vol. 1, p. 266 (1754)

1 They [the *Letters* of Lord Chesterfield] teach the morals of a whore, and the manners of a dancing master.
   Boswell *Life* vol. 1, p. 266 (1754)

2 Ignorance, madam, pure ignorance.
   Boswell *Life* vol. 1, p. 293 (1755); on being asked why he had defined *pastern* as the 'knee' of a horse

3 Dictionaries are like watches, the worst is better than none, and the best cannot be expected to go quite true.
   Boswell *Life* vol. 1, p. 293, n. 3 (letter to Francesco Sastres, 21 August 1784)

4 If a man does not make new acquaintance as he advances through life, he will soon find himself left alone. A man, Sir, should keep his friendship in constant repair.
   Boswell *Life* vol. 1, p. 300 (1755)

5 No man will be a sailor who has contrivance enough to get himself into a jail; for being in a ship is being in a jail, with the chance of being drowned ... A man in a jail has more room, better food, and commonly better company.
   Boswell *Life* vol. 1, p. 348 (16 March 1759). Cf. 83:10

6 [BOSWELL:] I do indeed come from Scotland, but I cannot help it ...
   [JOHNSON:] That, Sir, I find, is what a very great many of your countrymen cannot help.
   Boswell *Life* vol. 1, p. 392 (16 May 1763)

7 You *may* abuse a tragedy, though you cannot write one. You may scold a carpenter who has made you a bad table, though you cannot make a table. It is not your trade to make tables.
   Boswell *Life* vol. 1, p. 409 (25 June 1763); on literary criticism

8 He never passes a church without pulling off his hat. This shows that he has good principles.
   Boswell *Life* vol. 1, p. 418 (1 July 1763)

9 The noblest prospect which a Scotchman ever sees, is the high road that leads him to England!
   Boswell *Life* vol. 1, p. 425 (6 July 1763)

10 A man ought to read just as inclination leads him; for what he reads as a task will do him little good.
   Boswell *Life* vol. 1, p. 428 (14 July 1763)

11 But if he does really think that there is no distinction between virtue and vice, why, Sir, when he leaves our houses, let us count our spoons.
   Boswell *Life* vol. 1, p. 432 (14 July 1763)

12 Truth, Sir, is a cow, that will yield such people [sceptics] no more milk, and so they are gone to milk the bull.
   Boswell *Life* vol. 1, p. 444 (21 July 1763)

13 Your levellers wish to level *down* as far as themselves; but they cannot bear levelling *up* to themselves.
   Boswell *Life* vol. 1, p. 448 (21 July 1763)

14 Why, Sir, Sherry [Thomas Sheridan] is dull, naturally dull; but it must have taken him a great deal of pains to become what we now see him. Such an excess of stupidity, Sir, is not in Nature.
   Boswell *Life* vol. 1, p. 453 (28 July 1763)

15 It is burning a farthing candle at Dover, to shew light at Calais.
   Boswell *Life* vol. 1, p. 454 (28 July 1763); on Thomas Sheridan's influence on the English language. Cf. 360:16

16 A woman's preaching is like a dog's walking on his hinder legs. It is not done well; but you are surprised to find it done at all.
   Boswell *Life* vol. 1, p. 463 (31 July 1763)

17 I refute it *thus*.
   Boswell *Life* vol. 1, p. 471 (6 August 1763); kicking a large stone by way of refuting Bishop Berkeley's theory of the non-existence of matter

18 Sir John, Sir, is a very unclubbable man.
   Boswell *Life* vol. 1, p. 480 n. 1 (Spring 1764)

19 It was not for me to bandy civilities with my Sovereign.
   Boswell *Life* vol. 2, p. 35 (February 1767)

20 We *know* our will is free, and *there's* an end on't.
   Boswell *Life* vol. 2, p. 82 (16 October 1769)

21 In the description of night in Macbeth, the beetle and the bat detract from the general idea of darkness,—inspissated gloom.
   Boswell *Life* vol. 2, p. 90 (16 October 1769)

22 Most schemes of political improvement are very laughable things.
   Boswell *Life* vol. 2, p. 102 (26 October 1769)

23 That fellow seems to me to possess but one idea, and that is a wrong one.
   Boswell *Life* vol. 2, p. 126 (1770)

24 The triumph of hope over experience.
   Boswell *Life* vol. 2, p. 128 (1770); of a man who remarried immediately after the death of a wife with whom he had been unhappy

25 He has, indeed, done it very well; but it is a foolish thing well done.
   Boswell *Life* vol. 2, p. 210 (3 April 1773); on a public apology for assault issued by Goldsmith

26 [ELPHINSTON:] What, have you not read it through?
   [JOHNSON:] No, Sir, do *you* read books *through*?
   Boswell *Life* vol. 2, p. 226 (19 April 1773)

27 Read over your compositions, and where ever you meet with a passage which you think is particularly fine, strike it out.
   Boswell *Life* vol. 2, p. 237 (30 April 1773); quoting a college tutor

28 He was dull in a new way, and that made many people think him *great*.
   Boswell *Life* vol. 2, p. 327 (28 March 1775); of Thomas Gray

1 The full tide of human existence is at Charing-Cross.
  Boswell *Life* vol. 2, p. 337 (2 April 1775)

2 It is wonderful, when a calculation is made, how little the mind is actually employed in the discharge of any profession.
  Boswell *Life* vol. 2, p. 344 (6 April 1775)

3 A man will turn over half a library to make one book.
  Boswell *Life* vol. 2, p. 344 (6 April 1775)

4 Patriotism is the last refuge of a scoundrel.
  Boswell *Life* vol. 2, p. 348 (7 April 1775)

5 Knowledge is of two kinds. We know a subject ourselves, or we know where we can find information upon it.
  Boswell *Life* vol. 2, p. 365 (18 April 1775)

6 In lapidary inscriptions a man is not upon oath.
  Boswell *Life* vol. 2, p. 407 (1775)

7 Nothing odd will do long. *Tristram Shandy* did not last.
  Boswell *Life* vol. 2, p. 449 (20 March 1776)

8 There is nothing which has yet been contrived by man, by which so much happiness is produced as by a good tavern or inn.
  Boswell *Life* vol. 2, p. 452 (21 March 1776)

9 We would all be idle if we could.
  Boswell *Life* vol. 3, p. 13 (3 April 1776)

10 No man but a blockhead ever wrote, except for money.
  Boswell *Life* vol. 3, p. 19 (5 April 1776)

11 [BOSWELL:] Sir, what is poetry?
  [JOHNSON:] Why Sir, it is much easier to say what it is not. We all *know* what light is; but it is not easy to *tell* what it is.
  Boswell *Life* vol. 3, p. 38 (12 April 1776)

12 To Oliver Goldsmith, A Poet, Naturalist, and Historian, who left scarcely any style of writing untouched, and touched none that he did not adorn.
  Boswell *Life* vol. 3, p. 82 (22 June 1776); translation of his Latin epitaph on Goldsmith

13 If I had no duties, and no reference to futurity, I would spend my life in driving briskly in a post-chaise with a pretty woman.
  Boswell *Life* vol. 3, p. 162 (19 September 1777)

14 Depend upon it, Sir, when a man knows he is to be hanged in a fortnight, it concentrates his mind wonderfully.
  Boswell *Life* vol. 3, p. 167 (19 September 1777)

15 When a man is tired of London, he is tired of life.
  Boswell *Life* vol. 3, p. 178 (20 September 1777)

16 John Wesley's conversation is good, but he is never at leisure. He is always obliged to go at a certain hour. This is very disagreeable to a man who loves to fold his legs and have out his talk, as I do.
  Boswell *Life* vol. 3, p. 230 (31 March 1778)

17 The more contracted that power is, the more easily it is destroyed. A country governed by a despot is an inverted cone.
  Boswell *Life* vol. 3, p. 283 (14 April 1778)

18 So it is in travelling; a man must carry knowledge with him, if he would bring home knowledge.
  Boswell *Life* vol. 3, p. 302 (17 April 1778)

19 Sir, the insolence of wealth will creep out.
  Boswell *Life* vol. 3, p. 316 (18 April 1778)

20 All censure of a man's self is oblique praise. It is in order to shew how much he can spare.
  Boswell *Life* vol. 3, p. 323 (25 April 1778)

21 Were it not for imagination, Sir, a man would be as happy in the arms of a chambermaid as of a Duchess.
  Boswell *Life* vol. 3, p. 341 (9 May 1778)

22 Claret is the liquor for boys; port, for men; but he who aspires to be a hero (smiling) must drink brandy.
  Boswell *Life* vol. 3, p. 381 (7 April 1779)

23 All tricks are either knavish or childish.
  Boswell *Life* vol. 3, p. 396 (letter, 9 September 1779)

24 Worth seeing, yes; but not worth going to see.
  Boswell *Life* vol. 3, p. 410 (12 October 1779); of the Giant's Causeway

25 If you are idle, be not solitary; if you are solitary, be not idle.
  Boswell *Life* vol. 3, p. 415 (letter to Boswell, 27 October 1779). Cf. 83:15

26 Every man has a right to utter what he thinks truth, and every other man has a right to knock him down for it. Martyrdom is the test.
  Boswell *Life* vol. 4, p. 12 (1780)

27 They are forced plants, raised in a hot-bed; and they are poor plants; they are but cucumbers after all.
  Boswell *Life* vol. 4, p. 13 (1780); of Thomas Gray's *Odes*

28 This merriment of parsons is mighty offensive.
  Boswell *Life* vol. 4, p. 76 (March 1781)

29 We are not here to sell a parcel of boilers and vats, but the potentiality of growing rich, beyond the dreams of avarice.
  Boswell *Life* vol. 4, p. 87 (6 April 1781); at the sale of Thrale's brewery. Cf. 234:5

30 Classical quotation is the *parole* of literary men all over the world.
  Boswell *Life* vol. 4, p. 102 (8 May 1781)

31 Resolve not to be poor: whatever you have, spend less. Poverty is a great enemy to human happiness; it certainly destroys liberty, and it makes some virtues impracticable, and others extremely difficult.
  Boswell *Life* vol. 4, p. 157 (letter to Boswell, 7 December 1782)

1 I hate a fellow whom pride, or cowardice, or laziness drives into a corner, and who does nothing when he is there but sit and *growl*; let him come out as I do, and *bark*.
Boswell *Life* vol. 4, p. 161, n. 3 (10 October 1782)

2 Sir, there is no settling the point of precedency between a louse and a flea.
Boswell *Life* vol. 4, p. 192 (1783) on the relative merits of two minor poets

3 My dear friend, clear your *mind* of cant . . . You may *talk* in this manner; it is a mode of talking in Society: but don't *think* foolishly.
Boswell *Life* vol. 4, p. 221 (15 May 1783)

4 Milton, Madam, was a genius that could cut a Colossus from a rock; but could not carve heads upon cherry-stones.
Boswell *Life* vol. 4, p. 305 (13 June 1784); to Hannah More, who had expressed a wonder that the poet who had written *Paradise Lost* should write such poor sonnets

5 Sir, I have found you an argument; but I am not obliged to find you an understanding.
Boswell *Life* vol. 4, p. 313 (June 1784)

6 No man is a hypocrite in his pleasures.
Boswell *Life* vol. 4, p. 316 (June 1784).
Cf. 251:21

7 Sir, I look upon every day to be lost, in which I do not make a new acquaintance.
Boswell *Life* vol. 4, p. 374 (November 1784)

8 We shall receive no letters in the grave.
Boswell *Life* vol. 4, p. 413 (December 1784)

9 Love is the wisdom of the fool and the folly of the wise.
In W. Cooke *Life of Samuel Foote* (1805) vol. 2, p. 154

10 Of music Dr Johnson used to say that it was the only sensual pleasure without vice.
In *European Magazine* (1795) p. 82

11 Fly fishing may be a very pleasant amusement; but angling or float fishing I can only compare to a stick and a string, with a worm at one end and a fool at the other.
Attributed, in Hawker *Instructions to Young Sportsmen* (1859) p. 197; attributed to Jonathan Swift in *The Indicator* 27 October 1819, p. 44

12 Corneille is to Shakespeare . . . as a clipped hedge is to a forest.
In Hester Lynch Piozzi *Anecdotes of . . . Johnson* (1786) p. 59

13 If the man who turnips cries,
Cry not when his father dies,
'Tis a proof that he had rather
Have a turnip than his father.
In Hester Lynch Piozzi *Anecdotes of . . . Johnson* (1786) p. 67

14 Abstinence is as easy to me, as temperance would be difficult.
In W. Roberts (ed.) *Memoirs of . . . Mrs Hannah More* (1834) vol. 1, p. 251

15 What is written without effort is in general read without pleasure.
In W. Seward *Biographia* (1799) p. 260

16 Difficult do you call it, Sir? I wish it were impossible.
On the performance of a celebrated violinist, in W. Seward *Supplement to the Anecdotes of Distinguished Persons* (1797) p. 267

## John Benn Johnstone 1803–91

17 I want you to assist me in forcing her on board the lugger; once there, I'll frighten her into marriage.
*The Gipsy Farmer* (performed 1845); since quoted 'Once aboard the lugger and the maid is mine'

## Hanns Johst 1890–1978

18 Whenever I hear the word culture . . . I release the safety-catch of my Browning!
*Schlageter* (1933) act 1, sc. 1 (often attributed to Hermann Goering, and quoted 'Whenever I hear the word culture, I reach for my pistol!')

## Al Jolson 1886–1950

19 You think that's noise—you ain't heard nuttin' yet!
In a café, competing with the din from a neighbouring building site; in M. Abramson *Real Story of Al Jolson* (1950) p. 12 (later title of a Jolson song, 'You Ain't Heard Nothing Yet')

## Henry Arthur Jones 1851–1929 and Henry Herman 1832–94

20 O God! Put back Thy universe and give me yesterday.
*The Silver King* (1907) act 2, sc. 4

## John Paul Jones 1747–92

21 I have not yet begun to fight.
As his ship was sinking, 23 September 1779, having been asked whether he had lowered his flag; in Mrs Reginald De Koven *Life and Letters of John Paul Jones* (1914) vol. 1, p. 455

## Ben Jonson c.1573–1637

22 Fortune, that favours fools.
*The Alchemist* (1610) prologue

23             Think
What a young wife and a good brain may do:
Stretch age's truth sometimes, and crack it too.
*The Alchemist* (1610) act 5, sc. 2

24 The very womb and bed of enormity.
*Bartholomew Fair* (1614) act 2, sc. 1 (of Ursula, the 'pig-woman')

25 Neither do thou lust after that tawney weed tobacco.
*Bartholomew Fair* (1614) act 2, sc. 6

1 The voice of Rome is the consent of
   heaven!
   *Catiline his Conspiracy* (1611) act 3, sc. 1

2 Slow, slow, fresh fount, keep time with my
   salt tears.
   *Cynthia's Revels* (1600) act 1, sc. 1

3 Queen and huntress, chaste and fair,
   Now the sun is laid to sleep,
   Seated in thy silver chair,
   State in wonted manner keep:
   Hesperus entreats thy light,
   Goddess, excellently bright.
   *Cynthia's Revels* (1600) act 5, sc. 3

4 This is Mab, the Mistress-Fairy
   That doth nightly rob the dairy.
   *The Entertainment at Althorpe* (1603)

5 Lady, it is to be presumed,
   Though art's hid causes are not found,
   All is not sweet, all is not sound.
   *Epicene* (1609) act 1, sc. 1

6 Such sweet neglect more taketh me,
   Than all the adulteries of art;
   They strike mine eyes, but not my heart.
   *Epicene* (1609) act 1, sc. 1

7 And to these courteous eyes oppose a
   mirror,
   As large as is the stage whereon we act;
   Where they shall see the time's deformity
   Anatomised in every nerve, and sinew.
   *Every Man out of His Humour* (1600) Induction

8              Blind Fortune still
   Bestows her gifts on such as cannot use
   them.
   *Every Man out of His Humour* (1599) act 2, sc. 2

9 Ramp up my genius, be not retrograde;
   But boldly nominate a spade a spade.
   *The Poetaster* (1601) act 5, sc. 1

10 Detraction is but baseness' varlet;
   And apes are apes, though clothed in
   scarlet.
   *The Poetaster* (1601) act 5, sc. 1

11 'Twas only fear first in the world made
   gods.
   *Sejanus* (1603) act 2, sc. 2

12              I glory
   More in the cunning purchase of my
   wealth
   Than in the glad possession.
   *Volpone* (1606) act 1, sc. 1

13 I have been at my book, and am now past
   the craggy paths of study, and come to the
   flowery plains of honour and reputation.
   *Volpone* (1606) act 2, sc. 1

14 Calumnies are answered best with silence.
   *Volpone* (1605) act 2, sc. 2

15 Suns, that set, may rise again;
   But if once we lose this light,
   'Tis with us perpetual night.
   *Volpone* (1605) act 3, sc. 5. Cf. 89:2

16 Come, my Celia, let us prove,
   While we can, the sports of love.
   *Volpone* (1605) act 3, sc. 5. Cf. 93:2

17 You have a gift, sir, (thank your education),
   Will never let you want, while there are
   men,
   And malice, to breed causes.
   *Volpone* (1605) act 5, sc. 1 (to a lawyer)

18 The voice so sweet, the words so fair,
   As some soft chime had stroked the air;
   And though the sound were parted thence,
   Still left an echo in the sense.
   'Eupheme' (1640) no. 4 'The Mind'

19 Rest in soft peace, and, asked, say here
   doth lie
   Ben Jonson his best piece of poetry.
   'On My First Son' (1616)

20 This figure that thou here seest put,
   It was for gentle Shakespeare cut,
   Wherein the graver had a strife
   With Nature, to out-do the life.
   'On the Portrait of Shakespeare' (1623)

21              Reader, look
   Not on his picture, but his book.
   'On the Portrait of Shakespeare' (1623)

22 So court a mistress, she denies you;
   Let her alone, she will court you.
   Say, are not women truly then
   Styled but the shadows of us men?
   'That Women are but Men's Shadows' (1616)

23 Drink to me only with thine eyes,
   And I will pledge with mine;
   Or leave a kiss but in the cup,
   And I'll not look for wine.
   'To Celia' (1616)

24 In small proportions we just beauty see,
   And in short measures life may perfect be.
   'To the Immortal Memory [of] Sir Lucius
   Carey and Sir H. Morison' (1640)

25              Soul of the Age!
   The applause, delight, the wonder of our
   stage!
   'To the Memory of My Beloved, the Author,
   Mr William Shakespeare' (1623)

26              How far thou didst our Lyly
   outshine,
   Or sporting Kyd, or Marlowe's mighty line.
   'To the Memory of ... Shakespeare' (1623)

27 Thou hadst small Latin, and less Greek.
   'To the Memory of ... Shakespeare' (1623)

28 He was not of an age, but for all time!
   'To the Memory of ... Shakespeare' (1623)

29 Sweet Swan of Avon!
   'To the Memory of ... Shakespeare' (1623)

30 The blushing apricot and woolly peach
   Hang on thy walls, that every child may
   reach.
   'To Penshurst' (1616) l. 43

31 Donne, for not keeping of accent, deserved
   hanging ... Shakespeare wanted art.
   In *Conversations with William Drummond of
   Hawthornden* (written 1619) no. 3

32 Whatsoever he [Shakespeare] penned, he
   never blotted out a line. My answer hath
   been 'Would he had blotted a thousand'.
   *Timber* (1641) l. 658. Cf. 165:11, 252:30

## John Jortin 1698–1770

1 *Palmam qui meruit, ferat.*
Let him who has won it bear the palm.
*Lusus Poetici* (3rd ed., 1748) 'Ad Ventos' (motto
of Lord Nelson)

## Benjamin Jowett 1817–93

2 The lie in the soul is a true lie.
Introduction to his translation (1871) of
Plato's *Republic* bk. 2

## James Joyce 1882–1941

3 riverrun, past Eve and Adam's, from
swerve of shore to bend of bay, brings us
by a commodious vicus of recirculation
back to Howth Castle and Environs.
*Finnegans Wake* (1939) pt. 1, p. 3

4 All moanday, tearsday, wailsday,
thumpsday, frightday, shatterday till the
fear of the Law.
*Finnegans Wake* (1939) pt. 2, p. 301

5 Three quarks for Muster Mark!
*Finnegans Wake* (1939) pt. 2, p. 383

6 Once upon a time and a very good time it
was there was a moocow coming down
along the road and this moocow that was
down along the road met a nicens little boy
named baby tuckoo.
*A Portrait of the Artist as a Young Man* (1916)
ch. 1

7 Ireland is the old sow that eats her farrow.
*A Portrait of the Artist as a Young Man* (1916)
ch. 5

8 The artist, like the God of the creation,
remains within or behind or beyond or
above his handiwork, invisible, refined out
of existence, indifferent, paring his
fingernails.
*A Portrait of the Artist as a Young Man* (1916)
ch. 5

9 The only arms I allow myself to use,
silence, exile, and cunning.
*A Portrait of the Artist as a Young Man* (1916)
ch. 5

10 By an epiphany he meant a sudden
spiritual manifestation, whether in
vulgarity of speech or of gesture or in a
memorable phase of the mind itself.
*Stephen Hero* (1944) ch. 25

11 The snotgreen sea. The scrotumtightening
sea.
*Ulysses* (1922) p. 5

12 It is a symbol of Irish art. The cracked
lookingglass of a servant.
*Ulysses* (1922) p. 7

13 I fear those big words, Stephen said, which
make us so unhappy.
*Ulysses* (1922) p. 31

14 History, Stephen said, is a nightmare from
which I am trying to awake.
*Ulysses* (1922) p. 34

15 Lawn Tennyson, gentleman poet.
*Ulysses* (1922) p. 50

16 [He] saw the dark tangled curls of his bush
floating, floating hair of the stream around
the limp father of thousands.
*Ulysses* (1922) p. 83

17 Plenty to see and hear and feel yet. Feel
live warm beings near you ... Warm beds:
warm full blooded life.
*Ulysses* (1922) p. 102

18 Greater love than this, he said, no man
hath that a man lay down his wife for his
friend.
*Ulysses* (1922) p. 375

19 The heaventree of stars hung with humid
nightblue fruit.
*Ulysses* (1922) p. 651

## Emperor Julian the Apostate
AD *c.*332–63

20 *Vicisti, Galilaee.*
You have won, Galilean.
Supposed dying words, though in fact a late
embellishment of Theodoret *Ecclesiastical
History* (AD *c.*450) bk. 3, ch. 25

## Julian of Norwich 1343–after 1416

21 Sin is behovely, but all shall be well and all
shall be well and all manner of thing shall
be well.
*Revelations of Divine Love* (the long text) ch. 27,
Revelation 13

## Carl Gustav Jung 1875–1961

22 A man who has not passed through the
inferno of his passions has never overcome
them.
*Memories, Dreams, Reflections* (1962) ch. 9

23 As far as we can discern, the sole purpose
of human existence is to kindle a light in
the darkness of mere being.
*Memories, Dreams, Reflections* (1962) ch. 11

24 Every form of addiction is bad, no matter
whether the narcotic be alcohol or
morphine or idealism.
*Memories, Dreams, Reflections* (1962) ch. 12

## 'Junius' 18th century

25 The liberty of the press is the *Palladium* of
all the civil, political, and religious rights
of an Englishman.
*Letters of Junius* (1772 ed.) 'Dedication to the
English Nation'

26 There is a holy mistaken zeal in politics as
well as in religion. By persuading others,
we convince ourselves.
*Public Advertiser* 19 December 1769, Letter 35

## Sir John Junor 1919–

27 Pass the sick bag, Alice.
Catch-phrase; in *Sunday Express* 28 December
1980 and elsewhere

## Juvenal AD *c*.60–*c*.130

1 Honesty is praised and left to shiver.
   *Satires* no. 1, l. 74 (tr. G. Ramsay)

2 Even if nature says no, indignation makes
   me write verse.
   *Satires* no. 1, l. 79

3 No one ever suddenly became depraved.
   *Satires* no. 2, l. 83

4 The misfortunes of poverty carry with
   them nothing harder to bear than that it
   makes men ridiculous.
   *Satires* no. 3, l. 152

5 They do not easily rise out of obscurity
   whose talents straitened circumstances
   obstruct at home.
   *Satires* no. 3, l. 164

6 ... *Omnia Romae*
   *Cum pretio.*
   Everything in Rome has its price.
   *Satires* no. 3, l. 183

7 *Rara avis in terris nigroque simillima cycno.*
   A rare bird on this earth, like nothing so
   much as a black swan.
   *Satires* no. 6, l. 165

8 *Hoc volo, sic iubeo, sit pro ratione voluntas.*
   I will have this done, so I order it done; let
   my will replace reasoned judgement.
   *Satires* no. 6, l. 223

9 *Quis custodiet ipsos custodes?*
   Who is to guard the guards themselves?
   *Satires* no. 6, l. 347

10 Many suffer from the incurable disease of
   writing, and it becomes chronic in their
   sick minds.
   *Satires* no. 7, l. 51

11 Travel light and you can sing in the
   robber's face.
   *Satires* no. 10, l. 22

12 ... *Duas tantum res anxius optat,*
   *Panem et circenses.*
   Only two things does he [the modern
   citizen] anxiously wish for—bread and the
   big match.
   *Satires* no. 10, l. 80 (usually quoted 'bread and
   circuses')

13 *Mens sana in corpore sano.*
   A sound mind in a sound body.
   *Satires* no. 10, l. 356

14 ... *Prima est haec ultio, quod se*
   *Iudice nemo nocens absolvitur.*
   This is the first of punishments, that no
   guilty man is acquitted if judged by
   himself.
   *Satires* no. 13, l. 2

15 A child is owed the greatest respect; if you
   ever have something disgraceful in mind,
   don't ignore your son's tender years.
   *Satires* no. 14, l. 47

## Franz Kafka 1883–1924

16 When Gregor Samsa awoke one morning
   from uneasy dreams he found himself
   transformed in his bed into a gigantic
   insect.
   *The Metamorphosis* (1915) ch. 1

17 You may object that it is not a trial at all;
   you are quite right, for it is only a trial if I
   recognize it as such.
   *The Trial* (1925) ch. 2

18 It's often better to be in chains than to be
   free.
   *The Trial* (1925) ch. 8

## Gus Kahn 1886–1941 and Raymond B. Egan 1890–1952

19 There's nothing surer,
   The rich get rich and the poor get children.
   'Ain't We Got Fun' (1921 song)

## Bert Kalmar et al. 1884–1947

20 Remember, you're fighting for this
   woman's honour ... which is probably
   more than she ever did.
   *Duck Soup* (1933 film); spoken by Groucho
   Marx

21 If you can't leave in a taxi you can leave in
   a huff. If that's too soon, you can leave in
   a minute and a huff.
   *Duck Soup* (1933 film); spoken by Groucho
   Marx

## Immanuel Kant 1724–1804

22 Two things fill the mind with ever new and
   increasing wonder and awe, the more
   often and the more seriously reflection
   concentrates upon them: the starry heaven
   above me and the moral law within me.
   *Critique of Practical Reason* (1788) p. 2

23 There is an imperative which commands a
   certain conduct immediately, without
   having as its condition any other purpose
   to be attained by it. This imperative is
   Categorical ... This imperative may be
   called that of Morality.
   *Fundamental Principles of the Metaphysics of
   Ethics* (1785) sect. 2 (tr. T. K. Abbott)

24 Happiness is not an ideal of reason but of
   imagination.
   *Fundamental Principles of the Metaphysics of
   Ethics* (1785) sect. 2 (translated by T. K.
   Abbott)

25 Out of the crooked timber of humanity no
   straight thing can ever be made.
   *Idee zu einer allgemeinen Geschichte in
   weltbürgerlicher Absicht* (1784) Proposition 6

## Alphonse Karr 1808–90

1 *Si l'on veut abolir la peine de mort en ce cas,
que MM les assassins commencent.*
In that case, if we are to abolish the death
penalty, let the murderers take the first
step.
Les Guêpes January 1849 (6th series, 1859)
p. 304

2 *Plus ça change, plus c'est la même chose.*
The more things change, the more they are
the same.
Les Guêpes January 1849 (6th series, 1859)
p. 305

## George S. Kaufman 1889–1961

3 Satire is what closes Saturday night.
In Scott Meredith *George S. Kaufman and his
Friends* (1974) ch. 6

## Gerald Kaufman 1930–

4 The longest suicide note in history.
On the Labour Party's *New Hope for Britain*
(1983); in Denis Healey *The Time of My Life*
(1989) ch. 23

## Paul Kaufman and Mike Anthony

5 Poetry in motion.
Title of song (1960). Cf. 156:6

## Christoph Kaufmann 1753–95

6 *Sturm und Drang.*
Storm and stress.
Title suggested by Kaufmann for a romantic
drama by F. M. Klinger (1775)

## Patrick Kavanagh 1905–67

7 But the weak, washy way of true tragedy—
A sick horse nosing around the meadow
for a clean place to die.
'The Great Hunger' (1947)

## Paul Keating 1944–

8 Even as it [Great Britain] walked out on
you and joined the Common Market, you
were still looking for your MBEs and your
knighthoods, and all the rest of the regalia
that comes with it. You would take
Australia right back down the time tunnel
to the cultural cringe where you have
always come from.
Addressing Conservative supporters of Great
Britain, 27 February 1992; *House of
Representatives Weekly Hansard* [Australia]
(1992) no. 1, p. 374

9 These are the same old fogies who doffed
their lids and tugged the forelock to the
British establishment.
Of Britain's Conservative supporters in
Australia, 27 February 1992; *House of
Representatives Weekly Hansard* (1992) no. 1,
p. 374

## John Keats 1795–1821

10 The moving waters at their priestlike task
Of pure ablution round earth's human
shores.
'Bright star, would I were steadfast as thou
art' (written 1819)

11 A thing of beauty is a joy for ever:
Its loveliness increases; it will never
Pass into nothingness.
*Endymion* (1818) bk. 1, l. 1

12 They alway must be with us, or we die.
*Endymion* (1818) bk. 1, l. 33

13           Their smiles,
Wan as primroses gathered at midnight
By chilly fingered spring.
*Endymion* (1818) bk. 4, l. 969

14 St Agnes' Eve—Ah, bitter chill it was!
The owl, for all his feathers, was a-cold;
The hare limped trembling through the
frozen grass,
And silent was the flock in woolly fold.
'The Eve of St Agnes' (1820) st. 1

15 The sculptured dead, on each side, seem to
freeze,
Emprisoned in black, purgatorial rails.
'The Eve of St Agnes' (1820) st. 2

16 The silver, snarling trumpets 'gan to chide.
'The Eve of St Agnes' (1820) st. 4

17 And soft adorings from their loves receive
Upon the honeyed middle of the night.
'The Eve of St Agnes' (1820) st. 6

18           By degrees
Her rich attire creeps rustling to her
knees.
'The Eve of St Agnes' (1820) st. 26

19 Trembling in her soft and chilly nest.
'The Eve of St Agnes' (1820) st. 27

20 As though a rose should shut, and be a
bud again.
'The Eve of St Agnes' (1820) st. 27

21 And still she slept an azure-lidded sleep,
In blanchèd linen, smooth, and lavendered.
'The Eve of St Agnes' (1820) st. 30

22 And the long carpets rose along the gusty
floor.
'The Eve of St Agnes' (1820) st. 40

23 And they are gone: aye, ages long ago
These lovers fled away into the storm.
'The Eve of St Agnes' (1820) st. 42

24 Fanatics have their dreams, wherewith
they weave
A paradise for a sect.
'The Fall of Hyperion' (written 1819) l. 1

25 The poet and the dreamer are distinct,
Diverse, sheer opposite, antipodes.
The one pours out a balm upon the world,
The other vexes it.
'The Fall of Hyperion' (written 1819) l. 199

26 Ever let the fancy roam,
Pleasure never is at home.
'Fancy' (1820) l. 1

1 O aching time! O moments big as years!
  'Hyperion: A Fragment' (1820) bk. 1, l. 64

2 Knowledge enormous makes a god of me.
  'Hyperion: A Fragment' (1820) bk. 3, l. 113

3 I had a dove and the sweet dove died;
  And I have thought it died of grieving:
  O, what could it grieve for? Its feet were
  tied,
  With a silken thread of my own hand's
  weaving.
  'I had a dove and the sweet dove died'
  (written 1818)

4 ............ 'For cruel 'tis,' said she,
  'To steal my Basil-pot away from me.'
  'Isabella; or, The Pot of Basil' (1820) st. 62

5 A little noiseless noise among the leaves,
  Born of the very sigh that silence heaves.
  'I stood tip-toe upon a little hill' (1817) l. 11

6 Here are sweet peas, on tip-toe for a flight.
  'I stood tip-toe upon a little hill' (1817) l. 57

7 Oh, what can ail thee knight at arms
  Alone and palely loitering?
  'La belle dame sans merci' (1820) st. 1

8 I see a lily on thy brow
  With anguish moist and fever dew,
  And on thy cheeks a fading rose
  Fast withereth too.
  'La belle dame sans merci' (1820) st. 3

9 I met a lady in the meads
  Full beautiful, a faery's child
  Her hair was long, her foot was light
  And her eyes were wild.
  'La belle dame sans merci' (1820) st. 4

10 ... La belle dame sans merci
  Thee hath in thrall.
  'La belle dame sans merci' (1820) st. 10

11 Love in a hut, with water and a crust,
  Is—Love, forgive us!—cinders, ashes, dust.
  'Lamia' (1820) pt. 2, l. 1

12 That purple-linèd palace of sweet sin.
  'Lamia' (1820) pt. 2, l. 31

13 In pale contented sort of discontent.
  'Lamia' (1820) pt. 2, l. 135

14 ............ Do not all charms fly
  At the mere touch of cold philosophy?
  'Lamia' (1820) pt. 2, l. 229

15 Philosophy will clip an Angel's wings.
  'Lamia' (1820) pt. 2, l. 234

16 Souls of poets dead and gone,
  What Elysium have ye known,
  Happy field or mossy cavern,
  Choicer than the Mermaid Tavern?
  'Lines on the Mermaid Tavern' (1820)

17 Thou still unravished bride of quietness,
  Thou foster-child of silence and slow time.
  'Ode on a Grecian Urn' (1820) st. 1

18 What men or gods are these? What
  maidens loth?
  What mad pursuit? What struggle to
  escape?
  'Ode on a Grecian Urn' (1820) st. 1

19 Heard melodies are sweet, but those
  unheard
  Are sweeter.
  'Ode on a Grecian Urn' (1820) st. 2

20 For ever piping songs for ever new.
  'Ode on a Grecian Urn' (1820) st. 3

21 For ever warm and still to be enjoyed,
  For ever panting, and for ever young.
  'Ode on a Grecian Urn' (1820) st. 3

22 O Attic shape! Fair attitude!
  'Ode on a Grecian Urn' (1820) st. 5

23 Thou, silent form, dost tease us out of
  thought
  As doth eternity: Cold Pastoral!
  'Ode on a Grecian Urn' (1820) st. 5

24 'Beauty is truth, truth beauty,'—that is all
  Ye know on earth, and all ye need to know.
  'Ode on a Grecian Urn' (1820) st. 5

25 No, no, go not to Lethe, neither twist
  Wolf's-bane, tight-rooted, for its poisonous
  wine.
  'Ode on Melancholy' (1820) st. 1

26 Then glut thy sorrow on a morning rose,
  Or on the rainbow of the salt sand-wave,
  Or on the wealth of globèd peonies;
  Or if thy mistress some rich anger shows,
  Emprison her soft hand, and let her rave,
  And feed deep, deep upon her peerless
  eyes.
  'Ode on Melancholy' (1820) st. 2

27 She dwells with Beauty—Beauty that must
  die;
  And Joy, whose hand is ever at his lips
  Bidding adieu.
  'Ode on Melancholy' (1820) st. 3

28 My heart aches, and a drowsy numbness
  pains
  My sense, as though of hemlock I had
  drunk,
  Or emptied some dull opiate to the drains.
  'Ode to a Nightingale' (1820) st. 1

29 O, for a draught of vintage! that hath been
  Cooled a long age in the deep-delvèd earth,
  Tasting of Flora and the country green.
  'Ode to a Nightingale' (1820) st. 2

30 O for a beaker full of the warm South,
  Full of the true, the blushful Hippocrene,
  With beaded bubbles winking at the brim,
  And purple-stainèd mouth.
  'Ode to a Nightingale' (1820) st. 2

31 Fade far away, dissolve, and quite forget
  What thou among the leaves hast never
  known,
  The weariness, the fever, and the fret.
  'Ode to a Nightingale' (1820) st. 3

32 Where youth grows pale, and spectre-thin,
  and dies.
  'Ode to a Nightingale' (1820) st. 3

1 Away! away! for I will fly to thee,
Not charioted by Bacchus and his pards,
But on the viewless wings of Poesy,
Though the dull brain perplexes and
retards:
Already with thee! tender is the night.
'Ode to a Nightingale' (1820) st. 4

2 And mid-May's eldest child,
The coming musk-rose, full of dewy wine,
The murmurous haunt of flies on summer
eves.
'Ode to a Nightingale' (1820) st. 5

3 Darkling I listen; and, for many a time
I have been half in love with easeful Death,
Called him soft names in many a musèd
rhyme,
To take into the air my quiet breath;
Now more than ever seems it rich to die,
To cease upon the midnight with no pain.
'Ode to a Nightingale' (1820) st. 6

4 Thou wast not born for death, immortal
bird!
'Ode to a Nightingale' (1820) st. 7

5 Perhaps the self-same song that found a
path
Through the sad heart of Ruth, when, sick
for home,
She stood in tears amid the alien corn;
The same that oft-times hath
Charmed magic casements, opening on the
foam
Of perilous seas, in faery lands forlorn.
'Ode to a Nightingale' (1820) st. 7

6 Forlorn! the very word is like a bell
To toll me back from thee to my sole self!
'Ode to a Nightingale' (1820) st. 8

7 Was it a vision, or a waking dream?
Fled is that music:—do I wake or sleep?
'Ode to a Nightingale' (1820) st. 8

8 Nor virgin-choir to make delicious moan
Upon the midnight hours.
'Ode to Psyche' (1820) st. 2

9 A bright torch, and a casement ope at
night,
To let the warm Love in!
'Ode to Psyche' (1820) st. 4

10 Much have I travelled in the realms of
gold,
And many goodly states and kingdoms
seen.
'On First Looking into Chapman's Homer'
(1817)

11 Then felt I like some watcher of the skies
When a new planet swims into his ken;
Or like stout Cortez when with eagle eyes
He stared at the Pacific—and all his men
Looked at each other with a wild
surmise—
Silent, upon a peak in Darien.
'On First Looking into Chapman's Homer'
(1817)

12 And they shall be accounted poet kings
Who simply tell the most heart-easing
things.
'Sleep and Poetry' (1817) l. 267

13 Turn the key deftly in the oilèd wards,
And seal the hushèd casket of my soul.
'Sonnet to Sleep' (written 1819)

14 Season of mists and mellow fruitfulness,
Close bosom-friend of the maturing sun;
Conspiring with him how to load and bless
With fruit the vines that round the thatch-
eaves run.
'To Autumn' (1820) st. 1

15 Where are the songs of Spring? Ay, where
are they?
Think not of them, thou hast thy music
too.
'To Autumn' (1820) st. 3

16 Then in a wailful choir the small gnats
mourn
Among the river sallows, borne aloft
Or sinking as the light wind lives or dies.
'To Autumn' (1820) st. 3

17 How soon the film of death obscured that
eye,
Whence genius wildly flashed.
'To Chatterton' (written 1815)

18               It is a flaw
In happiness, to see beyond our bourn.
'To J. H. Reynolds, Esq.' (written 1818)

19 When I have fears that I may cease to be
Before my pen has gleaned my teeming
brain.
'When I have fears that I may cease to be'
(written 1818)

20 When I behold, upon the night's starred
face
Huge cloudy symbols of a high romance.
'When I have fears that I may cease to be'
(written 1818)

21               Then on the shore
Of the wide world I stand alone and think
Till love and fame to nothingness do sink.
'When I have fears that I may cease to be'
(written 1818)

22 A long poem is a test of invention which I
take to be the polar star of poetry, as fancy
is the sails, and imagination the rudder.
Letter to Bailey, 8 October 1817, in H. E.
Rollins (ed.) Letters (1958) vol. 1

23 I am certain of nothing but the holiness of
the heart's affections and the truth of
imagination—what the imagination seizes
as beauty must be truth—whether it
existed before or not.
Letter to Bailey, 22 November 1817, in H. E.
Rollins (ed.) Letters (1958) vol. 1. Cf. 191:24

24 O for a life of sensations rather than of
thoughts!
Letter to Bailey, 22 November 1817, in H. E.
Rollins (ed.) Letters (1958) vol. 1

1 The excellence of every art is its intensity, capable of making all disagreeables evaporate, from their being in close relationship with beauty and truth.
> Letter to George and Thomas Keats, 21 December 1817, in H. E. Rollins (ed.) *Letters* (1958) vol. 1

2 Negative Capability, that is when man is capable of being in uncertainties, mysteries, doubts, without any irritable reaching after fact and reason.
> Letter to George and Thomas Keats, 21 December 1817, in H. E. Rollins (ed.) *Letters* (1958) vol. 1

3 There is nothing stable in the world—uproar's your only music.
> Letter to George and Thomas Keats, 13 January 1818, in H. E. Rollins (ed.) *Letters* (1958) vol. 1

4 If poetry comes not as naturally as the leaves to a tree it had better not come at all.
> Letter to Taylor, 27 February 1818, in H. E. Rollins (ed.) *Letters* (1958) vol. 1

5 Scenery is fine—but human nature is finer.
> Letter to Bailey, 13 March 1818, in H. E. Rollins (ed.) *Letters* (1958) vol. 1

6 It is impossible to live in a country which is continually under hatches ... Rain! Rain! Rain!
> Letter to Reynolds from Devon, 10 April 1818, in H. E. Rollins (ed.) *Letters* (1958) vol. 1

7 I am in that temper that if I were under water I would scarcely kick to come to the top.
> Letter to Bailey, 25 May 1818, in H. E. Rollins (ed.) *Letters* (1958) vol. 1

8 The Wordsworthian or egotistical sublime.
> Letter to Woodhouse, 27 October 1818, in H. E. Rollins (ed.) *Letters* (1958) vol. 1

9 The roaring of the wind is my wife and the stars through the window pane are my children.
> Letter to George and Georgiana Keats, 24 October 1818, in H. E. Rollins (ed.) *Letters* (1958) vol. 1

10 Call the world if you please 'The vale of soul-making'.
> Letter to George and Georgiana Keats, 21 April 1819, in H. E. Rollins (ed.) *Letters* (1958) vol. 2

11 I have met with women whom I really think would like to be married to a poem and to be given away by a novel.
> Letter to Fanny Brawne, 8 July 1819, in H. E. Rollins (ed.) *Letters* (1958) vol. 2

12 Fine writing is next to fine doing the top thing in the world.
> Letter to Reynolds, 24 August 1819, in H. E. Rollins (ed.) *Letters* (1958) vol. 2

13 All clean and comfortable I sit down to write.
> Letter to George and Georgiana Keats, 17 September 1819, in H. E. Rollins (ed.) *Letters* (1958) vol. 2

14 'Load every rift' of your subject with ore.
> Letter to Shelley, August 1820, in H. E. Rollins (ed.) *Letters* (1958) vol. 2 (Spenser *Faerie Queen* (1596) bk. 2, canto 7, st. 28: 'And with rich metal loaded every rift')

15 Here lies one whose name was writ in water.
> Epitaph for himself, in R. Monckton Milnes *Life, Letters and Literary Remains of John Keats* (1848) vol. 2, p. 91. Cf. 280:22

## John Keble 1792–1866

16 New every morning is the love
Our wakening and uprising prove;
Through sleep and darkness safely brought,
Restored to life, and power, and thought.
> *The Christian Year* (1827) 'Morning'

17 The trivial round, the common task,
Would furnish all we ought to ask;
Room to deny ourselves; a road
To bring us, daily, nearer God.
> *The Christian Year* (1827) 'Morning'

18 The voice that breathed o'er Eden,
That earliest wedding-day.
> 'Holy Matrimony' (1857 hymn)

## Thomas Kelly 1769–1855

19 The head that once was crowned with thorns
Is crowned with glory now;
A royal diadem adorns
The mighty Victor's brow.
> 'The head that once was crowned with thorns' (1820 hymn)

## Thomas à Kempis

See THOMAS

## Bishop Thomas Ken 1637–1711

20 Awake, my soul, and with the sun
Thy daily stage of duty run.
Shake off dull sloth, and joyful rise
To pay thy morning sacrifice.
> 'Morning Hymn' in Winchester College *Manual of Prayers* (1695)

21 Redeem thy mis-spent time that's past,
And live this day as if thy last.
> 'Morning Hymn' (1709 ed.) v. 2

22 Teach me to live, that I may dread
The grave as little as my bed.
> 'Evening Hymn' (1695) v. 3

## Jimmy Kennedy and Michael Carr

23 We're gonna hang out the washing on the Siegfried Line.
> Title of song (1939)

## John F. Kennedy 1917–63

1 We stand today on the edge of a new frontier.

Speech accepting the Democratic nomination, 15 July 1960, in *Vital Speeches* 1 August 1960

2 The torch has been passed to a new generation of Americans—born in this century, tempered by war, disciplined by a hard and bitter peace.

Inaugural address, 20 January 1961, in *Vital Speeches* 1 February 1961

3 We shall pay any price, bear any burden, meet any hardship, support any friend, oppose any foe to assure the survival and the success of liberty.

Inaugural address, 20 January 1961, in *Vital Speeches* 1 February 1961

4 Let us never negotiate out of fear. But let us never fear to negotiate.

Inaugural address, 20 January 1961, in *Vital Speeches* 1 February 1961

5 All this will not be finished in the first 100 days. Nor will it be finished in the first 1,000 days, nor in the life of this Administration, nor even perhaps in our lifetime on this planet. But let us begin.

Inaugural address, 20 January 1961, in *Vital Speeches* 1 February 1961

6 And so, my fellow Americans: ask not what your country can do for you—ask what you can do for your country.

Inaugural address, 20 January 1961, in *Vital Speeches* 1 February 1961

7 There are no 'white' or 'coloured' signs on the foxholes or graveyards of battle.

Message to Congress on proposed Civil Rights Bill, 19 June 1963; in *New York Times* 20 June 1963, p. 16

8 *Ich bin ein Berliner.*

I am a Berliner.

Speech in West Berlin, 26 June 1963; in *New York Times* 27 June 1963, p. 12

9 It was involuntary. They sank my boat.

On being asked how he became a war hero; in A. M. Schlesinger Jnr. *A Thousand Days* (1965) ch. 4

## Joseph P. Kennedy 1888–1969

10 When the going gets tough, the tough get going.

In J. H. Cutler *Honey Fitz* (1962) p. 291 (also attributed to Knute Rockne)

## William Kethe d. 1594

11 O enter then his gates with praise, Approach with joy his courts unto.

'All people that on earth do dwell' (metrical Psalm, 1561)

## Francis Scott Key 1779–1843

12 'Tis the star-spangled banner; O long may it wave
O'er the land of the free, and the home of the brave!

'The Star-Spangled Banner' (1814)

## John Maynard Keynes 1883–1946

13 I work for a Government I despise for ends I think criminal.

Letter to Duncan Grant, 15 December 1917, in *British Library Add. MSS 57931* fo. 119

14 Lenin was right. There is no subtler, no surer means of overturning the existing basis of society than to debauch the currency.

*Economic Consequences of the Peace* (1919) ch. 6

15 I do not know which makes a man more conservative—to know nothing but the present, or nothing but the past.

*The End of Laissez-Faire* (1926) pt. 1

16 If the Treasury were to fill old bottles with banknotes, bury them at suitable depths in disused coalmines which are then filled up to the surface with town rubbish, and leave it to private enterprise on well-tried principles of *laissez-faire* to dig the notes up again ... there need be no more unemployment and, with the help of the repercussions, the real income of the community, and its capital wealth also, would probably become a good deal greater than it actually is.

*General Theory* (1936) bk. 3, ch. 10

17 *In the long run* we are all dead.

*A Tract on Monetary Reform* (1923) ch. 3

## Nikita Khrushchev 1894–1971

18 If anyone believes that our smiles involve abandonment of the teaching of Marx, Engels and Lenin he deceives himself. Those who wait for that must wait until a shrimp learns to whistle.

Speech in Moscow, 17 September 1955; in *New York Times* 18 September 1955, p. 19

19 If you don't like us, don't accept our invitations and don't invite us to come to see you. Whether you like it or not, history is on our side. We will bury you.

Speech to Western diplomats in Moscow, 18 November 1956; in *The Times* 19 November 1956

20 If one cannot catch the bird of paradise, better take a wet hen.

In *Time* 6 January 1958

21 If you start throwing hedgehogs under me, I shall throw a couple of porcupines under you.

In *New York Times* 7 November 1963

## Joyce Kilmer 1886–1918

22 I think that I shall never see
A poem lovely as a tree.

'Trees' (1914)

**1** Poems are made by fools like me,
But only God can make a tree.
'Trees' (1914)

## Lord Kilmuir (Sir David Maxwell Fyfe) 1900–67

**2** Loyalty is the Tory's secret weapon.
In Anthony Sampson *Anatomy of Britain*
(1962) ch. 6. Cf. 9:14

## Francis Kilvert 1840–79

**3** Of all noxious animals, too, the most
noxious is a tourist. And of all tourists the
most vulgar, ill-bred, offensive and
loathsome is the British tourist.
W. Plomer (ed.) *Selections from the Diary of the
Revd Francis Kilvert* (1938–40) 5 April 1870

## Benjamin Franklin King 1857–94

**4** Nothing to do but work,
Nothing to eat but food,
Nothing to wear but clothes
To keep one from going nude.
'The Pessimist'

## Bishop Henry King 1592–1669

**5** Sleep on (my Love!) in thy cold bed
Never to be disquieted.
My last Good-night! Thou wilt not wake
Till I thy fate shall overtake:
Till age, or grief, or sickness must
Marry my body to that dust
It so much loves; and fill the room
My heart keeps empty in thy tomb.
Stay for me there: I will not fail
To meet thee in that hollow vale.
'An Exequy' (1657) l. 81 (written for his wife
Anne, d. 1624)

**6** But hark! My pulse, like a soft drum
Beats my approach, tells thee I come.
'An Exequy' (1657) l. 111

## Martin Luther King 1929–68

**7** I want to be the white man's brother, not
his brother-in-law.
In *New York Journal-American* 10 September
1962, p. 1

**8** If a man hasn't discovered something he
will die for, he isn't fit to live.
Speech in Detroit, 23 June 1963; in J. Bishop
*The Days of Martin Luther King* (1971) ch. 4

**9** I have a dream that one day on the red
hills of Georgia the sons of former slaves
and the sons of former slave owners will
be able to sit down together at the table of
brotherhood.
Speech at Civil Rights March in Washington,
28 August 1963; in *New York Times* 29 August
1963

**10** We must learn to live together as brothers
or perish together as fools.
Speech at St Louis, 22 March 1964; in *St Louis
Post-Dispatch* 23 March 1964

**11** A riot is at bottom the language of the
unheard.
*Where Do We Go From Here?* (1967) ch. 4

## Stoddard King 1889–1933

**12** There's a long, long trail awinding
Into the land of my dreams.
'There's a Long, Long Trail' (1913 song)

## Charles Kingsley 1819–75

**13** Be good, sweet maid, and let who will be
clever.
'A Farewell' (1858)

**14** Do the work that's nearest,
Though it's dull at whiles,
Helping, when we meet them,
Lame dogs over stiles.
'The Invitation. To Tom Hughes' (1856)

**15** 'Tis the hard grey weather
Breeds hard English men.
'Ode to the North-East Wind' (1858)

**16** For men must work, and women must
weep,
And there's little to earn, and many to
keep,
Though the harbour bar be moaning.
'The Three Fishers' (1858)

**17** When all the world is young, lad,
And all the trees are green;
And every goose a swan, lad,
And every lass a queen;
Then hey for boot and horse, lad,
And round the world away:
Young blood must have its course, lad,
And every dog his day.
'Young and Old' (from *The Water Babies*, 1863)

**18** We have used the Bible as if it was a
constable's handbook—an opium-dose for
keeping beasts of burden patient while
they are being overloaded.
*Letters to the Chartists* no. 2. Cf. 221:8

## Hugh Kingsmill 1889–1949

**19** What still alive at twenty-two,
A clean upstanding chap like you?
Sure, if your throat 'tis hard to slit,
Slit your girl's, and swing for it.
'Two Poems, after A. E. Housman' (1933)
no. 1

**20** But bacon's not the only thing
That's cured by hanging from a string.
'Two Poems, after A. E. Housman' (1933)
no. 1

## Neil Kinnock 1942–

1 I warn you not to be ordinary, I warn you
   not to be young, I warn you not to fall ill,
   and I warn you not to grow old.
   On the prospect of a Conservative re-
   election; speech at Bridgend, 7 June 1983, in
   *Guardian* 8 June 1983

## Rudyard Kipling 1865–1936

2 When you've shouted 'Rule Britannia',
   when you've sung 'God save the Queen'—
   When you've finished killing Kruger with
   your mouth—
   Will you kindly drop a shilling in my little
   tambourine
   For a gentleman in *Kharki* ordered South?
   'The Absent-Minded Beggar' (1899) st. 1

3 England's on the anvil—hear the hammers
   ring—
   Clanging from the Severn to the Tyne!
   'The Anvil' (1927)

4 Oh, East is East, and West is West, and
   never the twain shall meet,
   Till Earth and Sky stand presently at God's
   great Judgement Seat.
   'The Ballad of East and West' (1892)

5 Four things greater than all things are,—
   Women and Horses and Power and War.
   'The Ballad of the King's Jest' (1892)

6 Foot—foot—foot—foot—sloggin' over
   Africa—
   (Boots—boots—boots—boots—movin' up
   and down again!)
   'Boots' (1903)

7 If any question why we died,
   Tell them, because our fathers lied.
   'Common Form' (1919)

8 It's clever, but is it Art?
   'The Conundrum of the Workshops' (1892)

9 They've taken of his buttons off an' cut his
   stripes away,
   An' they're hangin' Danny Deever in the
   mornin'.
   'Danny Deever' (1892)

10 The 'eathen in 'is blindness must end
   where 'e began.
   But the backbone of the Army is the non-
   commissioned man!
   'The 'Eathen' (1896). Cf. 164:16

11 What should they know of England who
   only England know?
   'The English Flag' (1892)

12 The female of the species is more deadly
   than the male.
   'The Female of the Species' (1919)

13 What stands if freedom fall?
   Who dies if England live?
   *For All We Have and Are* (1914) p. 2

14 So 'ere's *to* you, Fuzzy-Wuzzy, at your 'ome
   in the Soudan:
   You're a pore benighted 'eathen but a first-
   class fightin' man.
   'Fuzzy-Wuzzy' (1892)

15 Gentlemen-rankers out on the spree,
   Damned from here to Eternity.
   'Gentlemen-Rankers' (1892)

16 Our England is a garden, and such gardens
   are not made
   By singing:—'Oh, how beautiful!' and
   sitting in the shade.
   'The Glory of the Garden' (1911)

17 Though I've belted you and flayed you,
   By the livin' Gawd that made you,
   You're a better man than I am, Gunga Din!
   'Gunga Din' (1892)

18 The flannelled fools at the wicket or the
   muddied oafs at the goals.
   'The Islanders' (1903)

19 For the Colonel's Lady an' Judy O'Grady
   Are sisters under their skins!
   'The Ladies' (1896)

20 Down to Gehenna or up to the Throne,
   He travels the fastest who travels alone.
   'L'Envoi' (from *The Story of the Gadsbys*, 1890)

21 Come you back to Mandalay,
   Where the old flotilla lay:
   Can't you 'ear their paddles chunkin' from
   Rangoon to Mandalay?
   On the road to Mandalay,
   Where the flyin'-fishes play,
   An' the dawn comes up like thunder outer
   China 'crost the Bay!
   'Mandalay' (1892)

22 A-wastin' Christian kisses on an 'eathen
   idol's foot.
   'Mandalay' (1892)

23 Ship me somewheres east of Suez, where
   the best is like the worst.
   'Mandalay' (1892)

24 And the epitaph drear: 'A fool lies here
   who tried to hustle the East.'
   *The Naulahka* (1892) ch. 5

25 A Nation spoke to a Nation,
   A Throne sent word to a Throne:
   'Daughter am I in my mother's house,
   But mistress in my own.'
   'Our Lady of the Snows' (1898)

26 The toad beneath the harrow knows
   Exactly where each tooth-point goes;
   The butterfly upon the road
   Preaches contentment to that toad.
   'Pagett, MP' (1886)

27 Brothers and Sisters, I bid you beware
   Of giving your heart to a dog to tear.
   'The Power of the Dog' (1909)

28 Five and twenty ponies,
   Trotting through the dark—
   Brandy for the Parson,
   'Baccy for the Clerk;
   Laces for a lady, letters for a spy,
   Watch the wall, my darling, while the
   Gentlemen go by!
   *Puck of Pook's Hill* (1906) 'A Smuggler's Song'

1 Of all the trees that grow so fair,
   Old England to adorn,
   Greater are none beneath the Sun,
   Than Oak, and Ash, and Thorn.
   *Puck of Pook's Hill* (1906) 'A Tree Song'

2 The tumult and the shouting dies—
   The captains and the kings depart—
   Still stands Thine ancient Sacrifice,
   An humble and a contrite heart.
   Lord God of Hosts, be with us yet,
   Lest we forget—lest we forget!
   'Recessional' (1897). Cf. 43:5

3 Lo, all our pomp of yesterday
   Is one with Nineveh, and Tyre!
   'Recessional' (1897)

4 Such boasting as the Gentiles use,
   Or lesser breeds without the Law.
   'Recessional' (1897)

5 If you can keep your head when all about
   you
   Are losing theirs and blaming it on you.
   *Rewards and Fairies* (1910) 'If—'

6 If you can meet with triumph and disaster
   And treat those two imposters just the
   same.
   *Rewards and Fairies* (1910) 'If—'

7 If you can talk with crowds and keep your
   virtue,
   Or walk with Kings—nor lose the common
   touch . . .
   If you can fill the unforgiving minute
   With sixty seconds' worth of distance run,
   Yours is the Earth and everything that's in
   it,
   And—which is more—you'll be a Man, my
   son!
   *Rewards and Fairies* (1910) 'If—'

8 They shut the road through the woods
   Seventy years ago.
   Weather and rain have undone it again,
   And now you would never know
   There was once a road through the woods.
   *Rewards and Fairies* (1910) 'The Way through
   the Woods'

9 If blood be the price of admiralty,
   Lord God, we ha' paid in full!
   'The Song of the Dead' (1896)

10 For the sin ye do by two and two ye must
   pay for one by one!
   'Tomlinson' (1892)

11 Then it's Tommy this, an' Tommy that, an'
   'Tommy 'ow's yer soul?'
   But it's 'Thin red line of 'eroes' when the
   drums begin to roll.
   'Tommy' (1892)

12 A rag and a bone and a hank of hair
   (We called her the woman who did not
   care).
   'The Vampire' st. 1

13 But each for the joy of the working, and
   each, in his separate star,
   Shall draw the Thing as he sees It for the
   God of Things as They are!
   'When Earth's Last Picture is Painted' (1896)

14 When 'Omer smote 'is bloomin' lyre,
   He'd 'eard men sing by land an' sea;
   An' what he thought 'e might require,
   'E went an' took—the same as me!
   'When 'Omer smote 'is bloomin' lyre' (1896)

15 Take up the White Man's burden—
   Send forth the best ye breed—
   Go, bind your sons to exile
   To serve your captives' need.
   'The White Man's Burden' (1899)

16 What the horses o' Kansas think to-day,
   the horses of America will think
   tomorrow; an' I tell *you* that when the
   horses of America rise in their might, the
   day o' the Oppressor is ended.
   *The Day's Work* (1898) 'A Walking Delegate'

17 Lalun is a member of the most ancient
   profession in the world.
   *In Black and White* (1888) 'On the City Wall'

18 Brother, thy tail hangs down behind!
   *The Jungle Book* (1894) 'Road Song of the
   Bandar-Log'

19 Yes, weekly from Southampton,
   Great steamers, white and gold,
   Go rolling down to Rio
   (Roll down—roll down to Rio!).
   *Just So Stories* (1902) 'The Beginning of the
   Armadilloes'

20 He walked by himself, and all places were
   alike to him.
   *Just So Stories* (1902) 'The Cat that Walked by
   Himself'

21 An Elephant's Child—who was full of
   'satiable curtiosity.
   *Just So Stories* (1902) 'The Elephant's Child'

22 The cure for this ill is not to sit still,
   Or frowst with a book by the fire;
   But to take a large hoe and a shovel also,
   And dig till you gently perspire.
   *Just So Stories* (1902) 'How the Camel got his
   Hump'

23 You must *not* forget the suspenders, Best
   Beloved.
   *Just So Stories* (1902) 'How the Whale got his
   Throat'

24 He was a man of infinite-resource-and-
   sagacity.
   *Just So Stories* (1902) 'How the Whale got his
   Throat'

25 Little Friend of all the World.
   *Kim* (1901) ch. 1 (Kim's nickname)

26 The mad all are in God's keeping.
   *Kim* (1901) ch. 2

27 The man who would be king.
   Title of story (1888)

28 The silliest woman can manage a clever
   man; but it takes a very clever woman to
   manage a fool.
   *Plain Tales from the Hills* (1888) 'Three and—an
   Extra'

1 Now this is the Law of the Jungle—as old
and as true as the sky;
And the Wolf that shall keep it may
prosper, but the Wolf that shall break it
must die.
*Second Jungle Book* (1895) 'The Law of the
Jungle'

2 A Flopshus Cad, an Outrageous Stinker, a
Jelly-bellied Flag-flapper.
*Stalky & Co.* (1899) p. 214

3 Being kissed by a man who *didn't* wax his
moustache was—like eating an egg
without salt.
*Story of the Gadsbys* (1889) 'Poor Dear Mamma'

4 'Tisn't beauty, so to speak, nor good talk
necessarily. It's just It. Some women'll stay
in a man's memory if they once walked
down a street.
*Traffics and Discoveries* (1904) 'Mrs Bathurst'

5 Power without responsibility: the
prerogative of the harlot throughout the
ages.
Summing up Lord Beaverbrook's political
standpoint *vis-à-vis* the *Daily Express*; in
*Kipling Journal* vol. 38, no. 180, December
1971, p. 6 (quoted by Stanley Baldwin,
18 March 1931)

## Henry Kissinger 1923–

6 Power is the great aphrodisiac.
In *New York Times* 19 January 1971, p. 12

7 We are the President's men.
In M. and B. Kalb *Kissinger* (1974) ch. 7

## Lord Kitchener 1850–1916

8 Do your duty bravely. Fear God. Honour
the King.
Message to soldiers of the British
Expeditionary Force (1914); in *The Times*
19 August 1914

9 I don't mind your being killed, but I object
to your being taken prisoner.
To the Prince of Wales during the First
World War; in *Journals and Letters of Viscount
Esher* vol. 3 (1938) p. 198 (18 December 1914)

## Paul Klee 1879–1940

10 Art does not reproduce the visible; rather,
it makes visible.
*Inward Vision* (1958) 'Creative Credo' (1920)

11 An active line on a walk, moving freely
without a goal. A walk for walk's sake.
*Pedagogical Sketchbook* (1925) p. 6

## Friedrich Klopstock 1724–1803

12 God and I both knew what it meant once;
now God alone knows.
In C. Lombroso *The Man of Genius* (1891) pt. 1,
ch. 2 (also attributed to Browning, apropos
*Sordello*, in the form 'When it was written,
God and Robert Browning knew what it
meant; now only God knows')

## Charles Knight and Kenneth Lyle

13 When there's trouble brewing,
When there's something doing,
Are we downhearted?
No! Let 'em all come!
'Here we are! Here we are again!!' (1914
song). Cf. 6:4

## Frank H. Knight 1885–1973

14 Costs merely register competing
attractions.
*Risk, Uncertainty and Profit* (1921) p. 159

## Mary Knowles 1733–1807

15 He gets at the substance of a book directly;
he tears out the heart of it.
Of Johnson, in James Boswell *Life of Samuel
Johnson* (1934 ed.) vol. 3, p. 284 (15 April 1778)

## John Knox c.1505–72

16 The First Blast of the Trumpet Against the
Monstrous Regiment of Women.
Title of Pamphlet (1558)

## Monsignor Ronald Knox
## 1888–1957

17 When suave politeness, tempering bigot
zeal,
Corrected *I believe* to *One does feel.*
'Absolute and Abitofhell' (1913)

18 There once was a man who said, 'God
Must think it exceedingly odd
If he finds that this tree
Continues to be
When there's no one about in the Quad.'
In L. Reed *Complete Limerick Book* (1924), to
which came the anonymous reply: 'Dear
Sir, / Your astonishment's odd: / I am
always about in the Quad. / And that's why
the tree / Will continue to be, / Since
observed by / Yours faithfully, / God'

19 The baby doesn't understand English and
the Devil knows Latin.
On being asked to perform a baptism in
English; in Evelyn Waugh *Ronald Knox* (1959)
pt. 1, ch. 5

20 A loud noise at one end and no sense of
responsibility at the other.
Definition of a baby (attributed)

## Vicesimus Knox 1752–1821

21 Can anything be more absurd than
keeping women in a state of ignorance,
and yet so vehemently to insist on their
resisting temptation?
In Mary Wollstonecraft *A Vindication of the
Rights of Woman* (1792) ch. 7

## Ted Koehler

22 Stormy weather,
Since my man and I ain't together.
'Stormy Weather' (1933 song)

## Arthur Koestler 1905–83

1 One may not regard the world as a sort of metaphysical brothel for emotions.
*Darkness at Noon* (1940) 'The Second Hearing' pt. 7

2 God seems to have left the receiver off the hook, and time is running out.
*The Ghost in the Machine* (1967) ch. 18

3 A writer's ambition should be ... to trade a hundred contemporary readers for ten readers in ten years' time and for one reader in a hundred years.
In *New York Times Book Review* 1 April 1951, p. 24

## Jiddu Krishnamurti d. 1986

4 Religion is the frozen thought of men out of which they build temples.
In *Observer* 22 April 1928 'Sayings of the Week'

## Kris Kristofferson 1936–

5 Freedom's just another word for nothin' left to lose,
Nothin' ain't worth nothin', but it's free.
'Me and Bobby McGee' (1969 song, with Fred Foster)

## Jeremy Joe Kronsberg

6 Every which way but loose.
Title of film (1978); starring Clint Eastwood

## Stanley Kubrick 1928–

7 The great nations have always acted like gangsters, and the small nations like prostitutes.
In *Guardian* 5 June 1963

## Milan Kundera 1929–

8 The unbearable lightness of being.
Title of novel (1984)

## Thomas Kyd 1558–94

9 Thus must we toil in other men's extremes,
That know not how to remedy our own.
*The Spanish Tragedy* (1592) act 3, sc. 6, l. 1

10 My son—and what's a son? A thing begot Within a pair of minutes, thereabout,
A lump bred up in darkness.
*The Spanish Tragedy* (1592) act 3, sc. 11, The Third Addition (1602 ed.) l. 5

11 For what's a play without a woman in it?
*The Spanish Tragedy* (1592) act 4, sc. 1, l. 97

## Henry Labouchere 1831–1912

12 He [Labouchere] did not object to the old man always having a card up his sleeve, but he did object to his insinuating that the Almighty had placed it there.
On Gladstone's 'frequent appeals to a higher power'; in Earl Curzon *Modern Parliamentary Eloquence* (1913) p. 25

## Jean de la Bruyère 1645–96

13 The people have little intelligence, the great no heart ... if I had to choose I should have no hesitation: I would be of the people.
*The Characters, or The Manners of the Age* (1688) 'The Great'

14 Man has but three events in his life: to be born, to live, and to die. He is not conscious of his birth, he suffers at his death and he forgets to live.
*The Characters, or The Manners of the Age* (1688) 'Of Man'

## Nivelle de la Chaussée 1692–1754

15 When everyone is wrong, everyone is right.
*La Gouvernante* (1747) act 1, sc. 3

## Jean de la Fontaine 1621–95

16 Help yourself, and heaven will help you.
*Fables* bk. 6 (1668) 'Le Chartier Embourbé'

17 I bend and I break not.
*Fables* bk. 1 (1668) 'Le Chêne et le Roseau'

18 The reason of the strongest is always the best.
*Fables* bk. 1 (1668) 'Le Loup et l'Agneau'

19 Death never takes the wise man by surprise; he is always ready to go.
*Fables* bk. 8 (1678–9) 'La Mort et le Mourant'.
Cf. 233:8

## Jules Laforgue 1860–87

20 *Ah! que la vie est quotidienne.*
Oh, what a day-to-day business life is.
*Complainte sur certains ennuis* (1885)

## Alphonse de Lamartine 1790–1869

21 *Ô temps! suspend ton vol, et vous, heures propices! Suspendez votre cours.*
O Time! arrest your flight, and you, propitious hours, stay your course.
*Le Lac* (1820) st. 6

## Lady Caroline Lamb 1785–1828

22 Mad, bad, and dangerous to know.
Writing of Byron in her journal, March 1812; in E. Jenkins *Lady Caroline Lamb* (1932) ch. 6

## Charles Lamb 1775–1834

23 Ceremony is an invention to take off the uneasy feeling which we derive from knowing ourselves to be less the object of love and esteem with a fellow-creature than some other person is.
*Essays of Elia* (1823) 'A Bachelor's Complaint of the Behaviour of Married People'

24 Presents, I often say, endear Absents.
*Essays of Elia* (1823) 'A Dissertation upon Roast Pig'

**1** The human species, according to the best theory I can form of it, is composed of two distinct races, *the men who borrow*, and *the men who lend*.
Essays of Elia (1823) 'The Two Races of Men'

**2** Your *borrowers of books*—those mutilators of collections, spoilers of the symmetry of shelves, and creators of odd volumes.
Essays of Elia (1823) 'The Two Races of Men'

**3** Not many sounds in life ... exceed in interest a knock at the door.
Essays of Elia (1823) 'Valentine's Day'

**4** Things in books' clothing.
Last Essays of Elia (1833) 'Detached Thoughts on Books and Reading'

**5** A poor relation—is the most irrelevant thing in nature.
Last Essays of Elia (1833) 'Poor Relations'

**6** [A pun] is a pistol let off at the ear; not a feather to tickle the intellect.
Last Essays of Elia (1833) 'Popular Fallacies' no. 9

**7** The man must have a rare recipe for melancholy, who can be dull in Fleet Street.
Letter to Manning, 15 February 1802, in E. W. Marrs (ed.) Letters of Charles and Mary Lamb vol. 2 (1976)

**8** An Archangel a little damaged.
Of Coleridge; letter to Wordsworth, 26 April 1816, in E. W. Marrs (ed.) Letters of Charles and Mary Lamb vol. 3 (1978)

**9** Fanny Kelly's divine plain face.
Letter to Mary Wordsworth, 18 February 1818, in H. Harper (ed.) Letters of Charles Lamb (1905) vol. 4

**10** The ever-haunting importunity
Of business.
Letter to Barton, 11 September 1822, in H. Harper (ed.) Letters of Charles Lamb (1905) vol. 4

**11** The greatest pleasure I know, is to do a good action by stealth, and to have it found out by accident.
'Table Talk by the late Elia' in The Athenaeum 4 January 1834

**12**                    Gone before
To that unknown and silent shore.
'Hester' (1803) st. 7

**13** I have had playmates, I have had companions,
In my days of childhood, in my joyful school-days,—
All, all are gone, the old familiar faces.
'The Old Familiar Faces'

**14** A child's a plaything for an hour.
'Parental Recollections' (1809); often attributed to Lamb's sister Mary

**15** I toiled after it, sir, as some men toil after virtue.
On being asked 'how he had acquired his power of smoking at such a rate'; in T. Talfourd Memoirs of Charles Lamb (1892) p. 262

## John George Lambton, 1st Earl of Durham 1792–1840

**16** £40,000 a year a moderate income—such a one as a man *might jog on with*.
In Sir Herbert Maxwell (ed.) The Creevey Papers (1903) vol. 2, p. 32 (letter, 13 September 1821)

## George Lamming b. 1927

**17** In the castle of my skin.
Title of novel (1953)

## Norman Lamont 1942–

**18** Rising unemployment and the recession have been the price that we've had to pay to get inflation down. [Labour shouts] That is a price well worth paying.
Speech in House of Commons, 16 May 1991; in Independent 17 May 1991, p. 1

## Giuseppe di Lampedusa 1896–1957

**19** If we want things to stay as they are, things will have to change.
The Leopard (1957) p. 33

## Sir Osbert Lancaster 1908–86

**20** Fan-vaulting ... from an aesthetic standpoint frequently belongs to the 'Last-supper-carved-on-a-peach-stone' class of masterpiece.
Pillar to Post (1938) 'Perpendicular'

## Bert Lance 1931–

**21** If it ain't broke, don't fix it.
In Nation's Business May 1977, p. 27

## Walter Savage Landor 1775–1864

**22** I strove with none; for none was worth my strife;
Nature I loved, and, next to Nature, Art.
'Dying Speech of an Old Philosopher' (1853)

**23** Ah, what avails the sceptred race!
Ah, what the form divine!
'Rose Aylmer' (1806)

**24** George the First was always reckoned
Vile, but viler George the Second;
And what mortal ever heard
Any good of George the Third?
When from earth the Fourth descended
God be praised the Georges ended!
Epigram in The Atlas, 28 April 1855

**25** Fleas know not whether they are upon the body of a giant or upon one of ordinary size.
Imaginary Conversations (1824) 'Southey and Porson'

## Andrew Lang 1844–1912

1 St Andrews by the Northern sea,
A haunted town it is to me!
'Almae Matres' (1884)

2 *I* am the batsman and the bat,
*I* am the bowler and the ball,
The umpire, the pavilion cat,
The roller, pitch, and stumps, and all.
'Brahma'. Cf. 136:11

3 They hear like ocean on a western beach
The surge and thunder of the Odyssey.
'The Odyssey' (1881)

## Julia Lang 1921–

4 Are you sitting comfortably? Then I'll
begin.
*Listen with Mother* (BBC radio programme for
children, 1950–82); sometimes 'Then we'll
begin'

## William Langland *c*.1330–*c*.1400

5 In a somer seson, whan softe was the
sonne.
*The Vision of Piers Plowman* B text (ed. Schmidt,
1987) prologue l. 1

6 Ac on a May morwenynge on Malverne
hilles
Me bifel a ferly, of Fairye me thoghte.
*The Vision of Piers Plowman* B text (ed. Schmidt,
1987) prologue l. 5 ('Ac on a May mornyng
on Maluerne hulles / Me biful for to slepe,
for werynesse of-walked' in C text (ed., 1978)
prologue l. 6)

7 A faire feeld ful of folk fond I ther bitwene.
*The Vision of Piers Plowman* B text (ed. Schmidt,
1987) prologue l. 17

8 Grammer, the ground of al.
*The Vision of Piers Plowman* B text (ed. Schmidt,
1987) Passus 15, l. 370

9 'After sharpest shoures,' quath Pees 'most
shene is the sonne;
Is no weder warmer than after watry
cloudes.'
*The Vision of Piers Plowman* B text (ed. Schmidt,
1987) Passus 18, l. 411 (*Pees* Peace)

## Stephen Langton d. 1228

10 *Veni, Sancte Spiritus,*
*Et emitte coelitus*
*Lucis tuae radium.*
Come, Holy Spirit, and send out from
heaven the beam of your light.
The 'Golden Sequence' for Whit Sunday
(attributed also to Pope Innocent III, among
others)

## Lao-tsu *c*.604–*c*.531 BC

11 Heaven and Earth are not ruthful;
To them the Ten Thousand Things are but
as straw dogs.
*Tao-Tê-Ching* ch. 5 (tr. A. Waley in *The Way and
its Power*, 1934)

## Philip Larkin 1922–85

12 Sexual intercourse began
In nineteen sixty-three
(Which was rather late for me)—
Between the end of the *Chatterley* ban
And the Beatles' first LP.
'Annus Mirabilis' (1974)

13 What are days for?
Days are where we live.
'Days' (1964)

14 Life is first boredom, then fear.
Whether or not we use it, it goes,
And leaves what something hidden from
us chose,
And age, and then the only end of age.
'Dockery & Son' (1964)

15 Nothing, like something, happens
anywhere.
'I Remember, I Remember' (1955)

16 Perhaps being old is having lighted rooms
Inside your head, and people in them,
acting.
People you know, yet can't quite name.
'The Old Fools' (1974)

17 They fuck you up, your mum and dad.
They may not mean to, but they do.
They fill you with the faults they had
And add some extra, just for you.
'This Be The Verse' (1974)

18 Man hands on misery to man.
It deepens like a coastal shelf.
Get out as early as you can,
And don't have any kids yourself.
'This Be The Verse' (1974)

19 Why should I let the toad *work*
Squat on my life?
Can't I use my wit as a pitchfork
And drive the brute off?
'Toads' (1955)

20 A beginning, a muddle, and an end.
*New Fiction* no. 15, January 1978 (on the
'classic formula' for a novel)

## Duc de la Rochefoucauld 1613–80

21 We are all strong enough to bear the
misfortunes of others.
*Maximes* (1678) no. 19

22 There are good marriages, but no
delightful ones.
*Maximes* (1678) no. 113

23 Hypocrisy is a tribute which vice pays to
virtue.
*Maximes* (1678) no. 218

24 Absence diminishes commonplace passions
and increases great ones, as the wind
extinguishes candles and kindles fire.
*Maximes* (1678) no. 276. Cf. 83:19, 145:5

25 In most of mankind gratitude is merely a
secret hope for greater favours.
*Maximes* (1678) no. 298

**1** The accent of one's birthplace lingers in the mind and in the heart as it does in one's speech.
> *Maximes* (1678) no. 342

**2** In the misfortune of our best friends, we always find something which is not displeasing to us.
> *Réflexions ou Maximes Morales* (1665) maxim 99

## Hugh Latimer c.1485–1555

**3** The drop of rain maketh a hole in the stone, not by violence, but by oft falling.
> *Second Sermon preached before the King's Majesty* (19 April 1549). Cf. 243:12

**4** Be of good comfort Master Ridley, and play the man. We shall this day light such a candle by God's grace in England, as (I trust) shall never be put out.
> Prior to being burned for heresy, 16 October 1555; in John Foxe *Actes and Monuments* (1570 ed.) p. 1937

## Sir Harry Lauder 1870–1950

**5** Keep right on to the end of the road,
Keep right on to the end.
Tho' the way be long, let your heart be strong,
Keep right on round the bend.
> 'The End of the Road' (1924 song)

**6** I love a lassie, a bonnie, bonnie lassie.
She's as pure as the lily in the dell.
She's as sweet as the heather, the bonnie bloomin' heather—
Mary, ma Scotch Bluebell.
> 'I Love a Lassie' (1905 song)

**7** Roamin' in the gloamin'.
> Title of song (1911)

## Stan Laurel 1890–1965

**8** Another nice mess you've gotten me into.
> *Another Fine Mess* (1930 film) and many other Laurel and Hardy films; spoken by Oliver Hardy

## D. H. Lawrence 1885–1930

**9** To the Puritan all things are impure, as somebody says.
> *Etruscan Places* (1932) 'Cerveteri'. Cf. 56:22

**10** John Thomas says good-night to Lady Jane, a little droopingly, but with a hopeful heart.
> *Lady Chatterley's Lover* (1928) ch. 19

**11** If you try to nail anything down in the novel, either it kills the novel, or the novel gets up and walks away with the nail.
> *Phoenix* (1936) 'Morality and the Novel'

**12** Morality in the novel is the trembling instability of the balance. When the novelist puts his thumb in the scale, to pull down the balance to his own predilection, that is immorality.
> *Phoenix* (1936) 'Morality and the Novel'

**13** Pornography is the attempt to insult sex, to do dirt on it.
> *Phoenix* (1936) 'Pornography and Obscenity' ch. 3

**14** The novel is the one bright book of life.
> *Phoenix* (1936) 'Why the novel matters'

**15** Never trust the artist. Trust the tale.
> *Studies in Classic American Literature* (1923) ch. 1

**16** Be a good animal, true to your instincts.
> *The White Peacock* (1911) pt. 2, ch. 2

**17** Don't you find it a beautiful clean thought, a world empty of people, just uninterrupted grass, and a hare sitting up?
> *Women in Love* (1920) ch. 11

**18** How beastly the bourgeois is
Especially the male of the species.
> 'How Beastly the Bourgeois Is' (1929)

**19** While we have sex in the mind, we truly have none in the body.
> 'Leave Sex Alone' (1929)

**20** Men! The only animal in the world to fear!
> 'Mountain Lion' (1923)

**21** I never saw a wild thing
Sorry for itself.
> 'Self-Pity' (1929)

**22** And so, I missed my chance with one of the lords
Of life.
And I have something to expiate:
A pettiness.
> 'Snake' (1923)

**23** Not I, not I, but the wind that blows through me!
> 'Song of a Man who has Come Through' (1917)

**24** When I read Shakespeare I am struck with wonder
That such trivial people should muse and thunder
In such lovely language.
> 'When I Read Shakespeare' (1929)

**25** Tragedy ought really to be a great kick at misery.
> Letter to A. W. McLeod, 6 October 1912, in H. T. Moore (ed.) *Collected Letters* (1962) vol. 1

**26** The dead don't die. They look on and help.
> Letter to J. Middleton Murry, 2 February 1923, in H. T. Moore (ed.) *Collected Letters* (1962) vol. 2

## T. E. Lawrence 1888–1935

**27** Many men would take the death-sentence without a whimper to escape the life-sentence which fate carries in her other hand.
> *The Mint* (1955) pt. 1, ch. 4

**28** The trumpets came out brazenly with the last post … A man hates to be moved to folly by a noise.
> *The Mint* (1955) pt. 3, ch. 9

1 I loved you, so I drew these tides of men
into my hands and wrote my will across
the sky in stars.
*Seven Pillars of Wisdom* (1926) dedication

## Emma Lazarus 1849–87

2 Give me your tired, your poor,
Your huddled masses yearning to breathe
free.
'The New Colossus' (1883); inscribed on the
Statue of Liberty, New York

## Stephen Leacock 1869–1944

3 I am what is called a *professor emeritus*—
from the Latin *e*, 'out', and *meritus*, 'so he
ought to be'.
*Here are my Lectures* (1938) ch. 14

4 A sportsman is a man who, every now and
then, simply has to get out and kill
something. Not that he's cruel. He
wouldn't hurt a fly. It's not big enough.
*My Remarkable Uncle* (1942) p. 73

5 Lord Ronald said nothing; he flung himself
from the room, flung himself upon his
horse and rode madly off in all directions.
*Nonsense Novels* (1911) 'Gertrude the
Governess'

## Mary Leapor 1722–46

6 In spite of all romantic poets sing,
This gold, my dearest, is an useful thing.
'Mira to Octavia'

## Edward Lear 1812–88

7 On the coast of Coromandel
Where the early pumpkins blow,
In the middle of the woods,
Lived the Yonghy-Bonghy-Bó.
'The Courtship of the Yonghy-Bonghy-Bó'
(1871)

8 When awful darkness and silence reign
Over the great Gromboolian plain.
'The Dong with a Luminous Nose' (1871)

9 When storm-clouds brood on the towering
heights
Of the Hills of the Chankly Bore.
'The Dong with a Luminous Nose' (1871)

10 Far and few, far and few,
Are the lands where the Jumblies live;
Their heads are green, and their hands are
blue,
And they went to sea in a Sieve.
'The Jumblies' (1871)

11 The Owl and the Pussy-Cat went to sea
In a beautiful pea-green boat.
They took some honey, and plenty of
money,
Wrapped up in a five-pound note.
'The Owl and the Pussy-Cat' (1871)

12 They sailed away for a year and a day,
To the land where the Bong-tree grows,
And there in a wood a Piggy-wig stood
With a ring at the end of his nose.
'The Owl and the Pussy-Cat' (1871)

13 They dined on mince, and slices of quince,
Which they ate with a runcible spoon;
And hand in hand, on the edge of the sand,
They danced by the light of the moon.
'The Owl and the Pussy-Cat' (1871)

14 The Pobble who has no toes
Had once as many as we;
When they said, 'Some day you may lose
them all';—
He replied,—'Fish fiddle de-dee!'
'The Pobble Who Has No Toes' (1871)

15 He has gone to fish, for his Aunt Jobiska's
Runcible Cat with crimson whiskers!
'The Pobble Who Has No Toes' (1871)

16 There was an old man of Thermopylae,
Who never did anything properly;
But they said, 'If you choose
To boil eggs in your shoes,
You shall never remain in Thermopylae.'
'There was an old man of Thermopylae'
(1872)

17 There was an Old Man with a beard,
Who said, 'It is just as I feared!—
Two Owls and a Hen,
Four Larks and a Wren,
Have all built their nests in my beard!'
'There was an Old Man with a beard' (1846)

18 When they asked,—'Does it trot?'—
He said, 'Certainly not!
He's a Moppsikon Floppsikon bear.'
'There was an old person of Ware' (1872)

## Timothy Leary 1920–96

19 Turn on, tune in and drop out.
*The Politics of Ecstasy* (1968) ch. 21

## Mary Elizabeth Lease 1853–1933

20 Kansas had better stop raising corn and
begin raising hell.
In E. J. James et al. *Notable American Women
1607–1950* (1971) vol. 2, p. 381

## F. R. Leavis 1895–1978

21 The common pursuit.
Title of book (1952)

22 Like Keats's vulgarity with a Public School
accent.
*New Bearings in English Poetry* (1932) ch. 2 (of
Rupert Brooke's verse)

23 Self-contempt, well-grounded.
On the foundation of T. S. Eliot's work, in
*Times Literary Supplement* 21 October 1988,
p. 1177

## Fran Lebowitz 1946–

24 There is no such thing as inner peace.
There is only nervousness or death.
*Metropolitan Life* (1978) p. 6

## Stanislaw Lec 1909–66

1 Is it progress if a cannibal uses knife and fork?
   *Unkempt Thoughts* (1962) p. 78

## John le Carré 1931–

2 The spy who came in from the cold.
   Title of novel (1963)

## Le Corbusier 1887–1965

3 A house is a machine for living in.
   *Vers une architecture* (1923) p. ix. Cf. 333:12

## Alexandre Auguste Ledru-Rollin 1807–74

4 *Eh! je suis leur chef, il fallait bien les suivre.*
   Ah well! I am their leader, I really had to follow them!
   In E. de Mirecourt *Les Contemporains* vol. 14 (1857) 'Ledru-Rollin'

## Gypsy Rose Lee 1914–70

5 God is love, but get it in writing.
   Attributed

## Harper Lee 1926–

6 Shoot all the bluejays you want, if you can hit 'em, but remember it's a sin to kill a mockingbird.
   *To Kill a Mockingbird* (1960) ch. 10

## Henry Lee ('Light-Horse Harry') 1756–1818

7 A citizen, first in war, first in peace, and first in the hearts of his countrymen.
   *Funeral Oration on the death of General Washington* (1800) p. 14

## Nathaniel Lee c.1653–92

8 Then he will talk, Good Gods,
   How he will talk.
   *The Rival Queens* (1677) act 3

9 When Greeks joined Greeks, then was the tug of war!
   *The Rival Queens* (1677) act 4, sc. 2

10 Philip fought men, but Alexander women.
   *The Rival Queens* (1677) act 4, sc. 2

## Robert E. Lee 1807–70

11 It is well that war is so terrible. We should grow too fond of it.
   After the battle of Fredericksburg, December 1862 (attributed)

## Richard Le Gallienne 1866–1947

12 The cry of the Little Peoples goes up to God in vain,
   For the world is given over to the cruel sons of Cain.
   'The Cry of the Little Peoples' (1899)

## Ernest Lehman 1920–

13 Sweet smell of success.
   Title of book and film (1957)

## Tom Lehrer 1928–

14 Plagiarize! Let no one else's work evade your eyes,
   Remember why the good Lord made your eyes.
   'Lobachevski' (1953 song)

## Gottfried Wilhelm Leibniz 1646–1716

15 *Nihil est sine ratione.*
   There is nothing without a reason.
   *Studies in Physics and the Nature of Body* (1671) in *Leibniz: Philosophical Papers and Letters* (tr. L. E. Loemker, 1969) p. 142

16 *Eadem sunt quorum unum potest substitui alteri salva veritate.*
   Two things are identical if one can be substituted for the other without affecting the truth.
   'Table de définitions' (1704) in L. Coutourat (ed.) *Opuscules et fragments inédits de Leibniz* (1903)

## Fred W. Leigh d. 1924

17 Can't get away to marry you today,
   My wife won't let me!
   'Waiting at the Church' (1906 song)

18 Why am I always the bridesmaid,
   Never the blushing bride?
   'Why Am I Always the Bridesmaid?' (1917 song, with Charles Collins and Lily Morris)

## Henry Sambrooke Leigh 1837–83

19 The rapturous, wild, and ineffable pleasure Of drinking at somebody else's expense.
   *Carols of Cockayne* (1869) 'Stanzas to an Intoxicated Fly'

## Curtis E. LeMay 1906–90

20 We're going to bomb them back into the Stone Age.
   On the North Vietnamese, in *Mission with LeMay* (1965) p. 565

## Lenin (Vladimir Ilich Ulyanov)
### 1870–1924

1 Communism is Soviet power plus the electrification of the whole country.
Report to 8th Congress, 1920, in *Collected Works* (ed. 5) vol. 42, p. 30

2 Imperialism is the monopoly stage of capitalism.
*Imperialism as the Last Stage of Capitalism* (1916) ch. 7

3 What is to be done?
Title of pamphlet (1902); originally the title of a novel (1863) by N. G. Chernyshevsky

4 Who? Whom?
Definition of political science, meaning 'Who will outstrip whom?'; in *Polnoe Sobranie Sochinenii* vol. 44 (1970) p. 161 (17 October 1921) and *passim*

5 A good man fallen among Fabians.
Of G. B. Shaw, in A. Ransome *Six Weeks in Russia in 1919* (1919) 'Notes of Conversations with Lenin'

6 Liberty is precious—so precious that it must be rationed.
In Sidney and Beatrice Webb *Soviet Communism* (1936) p. 1036

## John Lennon 1940–80

7 Imagine there's no heaven,
It's easy if you try,
No hell below us,
Above us only sky.
'Imagine' (1971 song)

8 We're more popular than Jesus now; I don't know which will go first—rock 'n' roll or Christianity.
Interview in *Evening Standard* 4 March 1966 (of The Beatles)

9 Will the people in the cheaper seats clap your hands? All the rest of you, if you'll just rattle your jewellery.
At Royal Variety Performance, 4 November 1963; in R. Colman *John Winston Lennon* (1984) pt. 1, ch. 11

## John Lennon 1940–80 and Paul McCartney 1942–

10 Back in the USSR.
Title of song (1968)

11 For I don't care too much for money,
For money can't buy me love.
'Can't Buy Me Love' (1964 song)

12 All the lonely people, where do they all come from?
'Eleanor Rigby' (1966 song)

13 Give peace a chance.
Title of song (1969)

14 It's been a hard day's night,
And I've been working like a dog.
'A Hard Day's Night' (1964 song)

15 Strawberry fields forever.
Title of song (1967)

16 She's got a ticket to ride, but she don't care.
'Ticket to Ride' (1965 song)

17 Will you still need me, will you still feed me,
When I'm sixty four?
'When I'm Sixty Four' (1967 song)

18 Oh I get by with a little help from my friends,
Mm, I get high with a little help from my friends.
'With a Little Help From My Friends' (1967 song)

## Dan Leno 1860–1904

19 Ah! what is man? Wherefore does he why? Whence did he whence? Whither is he withering?
*Dan Leno Hys Booke* (1901) ch. 1

## Speaker William Lenthall
### 1591–1662

20 I have neither eye to see, nor tongue to speak here, but as the House is pleased to direct me.
To Charles I, 4 January 1642, on being asked if he had seen any of the five MPs whom the King had ordered to be arrested; in John Rushworth *Historical Collections. The Third Part* vol. 2 (1692) p. 478

## Leonardo da Vinci 1452–1519

21 Life well spent is long.
E. McCurdy (ed. and trans.) *Leonardo da Vinci's Notebooks* (1906) bk. 1, p. 65

22 In her [Nature's] inventions nothing is lacking, and nothing is superfluous.
E. McCurdy (ed. and trans.) *Leonardo da Vinci's Notebooks* (1906) bk. 1, p. 171

23 Every man at three years old is half his height.
I. Richter (ed.) *Selections from the Notebooks of Leonardo da Vinci* (World's Classics, 1952) p. 149

## Mikhail Lermontov 1814–41

24 Of two close friends, one is always the slave of the other.
*A Hero of our Time* (1840) 'Princess Mary' (tr. P. Longworth)

25 I am like a man yawning at a ball; the only reason he does not go home to bed is that his carriage has not arrived yet.
*A Hero of our Time* (1840) 'Princess Mary' (tr. P. Longworth)

## Alan Jay Lerner 1918–86

26 Why can't a woman be more like a man?
Men are so honest, so thoroughly square;
Eternally noble, historically fair.
*My Fair Lady* (1956) 'A Hymn to Him'

1 In Hertford, Hereford, and Hampshire,
Hurricanes hardly happen.
*My Fair Lady* (1956) 'The Rain in Spain'

2 Oozing charm from every pore,
He oiled his way around the floor.
*My Fair Lady* (1956) 'You Did It'

## Doris Lessing 1919–

3 What of October, that ambiguous month,
the month of tension, the unendurable
month?
*Martha Quest* (1952) pt. 4, sect. 1

4 What is charm then? . . . something extra,
superfluous, unnecessary, essentially a
power thrown away.
*Particularly Cats* (1967) ch. 9

## G. E. Lessing 1729–81

5 One single grateful thought raised to
heaven is the most perfect prayer.
*Minna von Barnhelm* (1767) act 2, sc. 7

## Ada Leverson 1865–1936

6 He seemed at ease and to have the look of
the last gentleman in Europe.
*Letters to the Sphinx* (1930) p. 34 (of Oscar
Wilde)

## Bernard Levin 1928–

7 The Stag at Bay with the mentality of a fox
at large.
Of Harold Macmillan, in *The Pendulum Years*
(1970) ch. 12

8 Whom the mad would destroy, they first
make gods.
Of Mao Tse-tung in 1967; Levin quoting
himself in *The Times* 21 September 1987.
Cf. 129:11

## Duc de Lévis 1764–1830

9 *Noblesse oblige.*
Nobility has its obligations.
*Maximes et Réflexions* (1812 ed.) 'Morale:
Maximes et Préceptes' no. 73

10 *Gouverner, c'est choisir.*
To govern is to choose.
*Maximes et Réflexions* (1812 ed.) 'Politique:
Maximes de Politique' no. 19

## C. S. Lewis 1898–1963

11 We have trained them [men] to think of
the Future as a promised land which
favoured heroes attain—not as something
which everyone reaches at the rate of sixty
minutes an hour, whatever he does,
whoever he is.
*The Screwtape Letters* (1942) no. 25

12 She's the sort of woman who lives for
others—you can always tell the others by
their hunted expression.
*The Screwtape Letters* (1942) no. 26

13 Courage is not simply *one* of the virtues
but the form of every virtue at the testing
point.
In Cyril Connolly *The Unquiet Grave* (1944)
ch. 3

## Esther Lewis fl. 1747–89

14 Why are the needle and the pen
Thought incompatible by men?
'A Mirror for Detractors' (1754) l. 149

## Sir George Cornewall Lewis 1806–63

15 Life would be tolerable but for its
amusements.
In *The Times* 18 September 1872, p. 4

## John Lewis 1885–1963

16 Never knowingly undersold.
Motto (from *c.*1920) of the John Lewis
Partnership; in *Partnership for All* (1948) ch. 29

## Sam M. Lewis 1885–1959 and Joe Young 1889–1939

17 How 'ya gonna keep 'em down on the farm
(after they've seen Paree)?
Title of song (1919)

## Sinclair Lewis 1885–1951

18 Our American professors like their
literature clear and cold and pure and very
dead.
*The American Fear of Literature* (Nobel Prize
Address, 12 December 1930)

19 She did her work with the thoroughness of
a mind which reveres details and never
quite understands them.
*Babbitt* (1922) ch. 18

## Robert Ley 1890–1945

20 *Kraft durch Freude.*
Strength through joy.
German Labour Front slogan, from 1933

## George Leybourne d. 1884

21 He'd fly through the air with the greatest
of ease,
A daring young man on the flying trapeze.
'The Flying Trapeze' (1868 song)

## Liberace 1919–87

22 I cry all the way to the bank.
On bad reviews; *Autobiography* (1973) ch. 2
(from the mid-1950s)

## Georg Christoph Lichtenberg
### 1742–99

1 The journalists have constructed for themselves a little wooden chapel, which they also call the Temple of Fame, in which they put up and take down portraits all day long and make such a hammering you can't hear yourself speak.

In A. Leitzmann *Georg Christoph Lichtenberg Aphorismen* (1904) p. 108

## Charles-Joseph, Prince de Ligne
### 1735–1814

2 *Le congrès ne marche pas, il danse.*
The Congress makes no progress; it dances.

In A. de la Garde-Chambonas *Souvenirs du Congrès de Vienne* (1820) ch. 1

## George Lillo 1693–1739

3 There's sure no passion in the human soul, But finds its food in music.

*The Fatal Curiosity* (1736) act 1, sc. 2

## Abraham Lincoln 1809–65

4 To give victory to the right, not bloody bullets, but peaceful ballots only, are necessary.

Speech, 18 May 1858, in R. P. Basler (ed.) *Collected Works of Abraham Lincoln* (1953) vol. 2 (usually quoted 'The ballot is stronger than the bullet')

5 'A house divided against itself cannot stand.' I believe this government cannot endure permanently, half slave and half free.

Speech, 16 June 1858, in R. P. Basler (ed.) *Collected Works* (1953) vol. 2. Cf. 51:19

6 In giving freedom to the slave, we assure freedom to the free—honourable alike in what we give and what we preserve. We shall nobly save, or meanly lose, the last, best hope of earth.

Annual Message to Congress, 1 December 1862, in R. P. Basler (ed.) *Collected Works* (1953) vol. 5

7 With malice toward none; with charity for all; with firmness in the right, as God gives us to see the right, let us strive on to finish the work we are in.

Second Inaugural Address, 4 March 1865, in R. P. Basler (ed.) *Collected Works* (1953) vol. 8

8 Fourscore and seven years ago our fathers brought forth upon this continent a new nation, conceived in liberty, and dedicated to the proposition that all men are created equal ... We here highly resolve that the dead shall not have died in vain, that this nation, under God, shall have a new birth of freedom; and that government of the people, by the people, and for the people, shall not perish from the earth.

Address at the Dedication of the National Cemetery at Gettysburg, 19 November 1863, in R. P. Basler (ed.) *Collected Works* (1953) vol. 7 (the Lincoln Memorial inscription reads 'by the people, for the people')

9 I claim not to have controlled events, but confess plainly that events have controlled me.

Letter to A. G. Hodges, 4 April 1864, in R. P. Basler (ed.) *Collected Works* (1953) vol. 7

10 You may fool all the people some of the time; you can even fool some of the people all the time; but you can't fool all of the people all the time.

In A. McClure *Lincoln's Yarns and Stories* (1904); also attributed to Phineas Barnum

11 The Lord prefers common-looking people. That is why he makes so many of them.

Attributed. See J. Morgan *Our Presidents* (1928) ch. 6

12 People who like this sort of thing will find this the sort of thing they like.

Judgement of a book, in G. W. E. Russell *Collections and Recollections* (1898) ch. 30

13 So you're the little woman who wrote the book that made this great war!

On meeting Harriet Beecher Stowe, author of *Uncle Tom's Cabin* (1852); in C. Sandburg *Abraham Lincoln: The War Years* (1936) vol. 2, ch. 39

14 As President, I have no eyes but constitutional eyes; I cannot see you.

Reply to the South Carolina Commissioners (attributed). Cf. 205:20

## R. M. Lindner 1914–56

15 Rebel without a cause.

Title of book (1944) and film (1955) starring James Dean

## Vachel Lindsay 1879–1931

16 Booth led boldly with his big bass drum— (Are you washed in the blood of the Lamb?)

'General William Booth Enters into Heaven' (1913). Cf. 57:26

## Eric Linklater 1899–1974

17 'There won't be any revolution in America,' said Isadore. Nikitin agreed. 'The people are all too clean. They spend all their time changing their shirts and washing themselves. You can't feel fierce and revolutionary in a bathroom.'

*Juan in America* (1931) bk. 5, pt. 3

## Art Linkletter 1912–

18 The four stages of man are infancy, childhood, adolescence and obsolescence.

*A Child's Garden of Misinformation* (1965) ch. 8

## George Linley 1798–1865

1 Among our ancient mountains,
And from our lovely vales,
Oh, let the prayer re-echo:
'God bless the Prince of Wales!'
   'God Bless the Prince of Wales' (1862 song);
   translated from the Welsh original by J. C.
   Hughes (1837–87)

## Richard Littledale 1833–90

2 Let holy charity
Mine outward vesture be,
And lowliness become mine inner clothing.
   'Come down, O Love divine' (1867 hymn);
   translation of 'Discendi, Amor santo' by
   Bianco da Siena (c.1350–1434)

## Joan Littlewood 1914– and Charles Chilton 1914–

3 Oh what a lovely war.
   Title of stage show (1963)

## Maxim Litvinov 1876–1951

4 Peace is indivisible.
   Note to the Allies, 25 February 1920, in A. U.
   Pope *Maxim Litvinoff* (1943) p. 234

## Livy 59 BC–AD 17

5 *Vae victis.*
   Down with the defeated!
   Cry (already proverbial) of the Gallic king,
   Brennus, on capturing Rome in 390 BC; in *Ab
   Urbe Condita* bk. 5, ch. 48, sect. 9

## Richard Llewellyn 1907–83

6 How green was my valley.
   Title of book (1939)

## Robert Lloyd

7 All the art of Imitation,
Is pilf'ring from the first creation.
   'Shakespeare' (1762)

## David Lloyd George 1863–1945

8 A mastiff? It is the right hon. Gentleman's
poodle.
   On the House of Lords and Lord Balfour
   respectively; in *Hansard* 26 June 1907,
   col. 1429

9 A fully-equipped duke costs as much to
keep up as two Dreadnoughts; and dukes
are just as great a terror and they last
longer.
   Speech at Newcastle, 9 October 1909, in *The
   Times* 11 October 1909

10 I hope we may say that thus, this fateful
morning, came to an end all wars.
   Speech, *Hansard* 11 November 1918,
   col. 2463. Cf. 345:24

11 What is our task? To make Britain a fit
country for heroes to live in.
   Speech at Wolverhampton, 23 November
   1918, in *The Times* 25 November 1918

12 The world is becoming like a lunatic
asylum run by lunatics.
   In *Observer* 8 January 1933. Cf. 264:1

## John Locke 1632–1704

13 New opinions are always suspected, and
usually opposed, without any other reason
but because they are not already common.
   *Essay concerning Human Understanding* (1690)
   'Dedicatory Epistle'

14 No man's knowledge here can go beyond
his experience.
   *Essay concerning Human Understanding* (1690)
   bk. 2, ch. 1, sect. 19

15 It is one thing to show a man that he is in
error, and another to put him in
possession of truth.
   *Essay concerning Human Understanding* (1690)
   bk. 4, ch. 7, sect. 11

16 Reason is natural revelation.
   *Essay concerning Human Understanding* (1690)
   bk. 4, ch. 19, sect. 4

17 Crooked things may be as stiff and
unflexible as straight: and men may be as
positive in error as in truth.
   *Essay concerning Human Understanding* (1690)
   bk. 4, ch. 19, sect. 11

18 All men are liable to error; and most men
are, in many points, by passion or interest,
under temptation to it.
   *Essay concerning Human Understanding* (1690)
   bk. 4, ch. 20, sect. 17

19 Whatsoever ... [man] removes out of the
state that nature hath provided and left it
in, he hath mixed his labour with, and
joined to it something that is his own, and
thereby makes it his property.
   *Second Treatise of Civil Government* (1690) ch. 5,
   sect. 27

20 The end of law is, not to abolish or
restrain, but to preserve and enlarge
freedom.
   *Second Treatise of Civil Government* (1690) ch. 6,
   sect. 57

21 This power to act according to discretion
for the public good, without the
prescription of the law, and sometimes
even against it, is that which is called
prerogative.
   *Second Treatise of Civil Government* (1690)
   ch. 14, sect. 160

## Frederick Locker-Lampson 1821–95

22 The world's as ugly, ay, as sin,
And almost as delightful.
   'The Jester's Plea' (1868)

1 And many are afraid of God—
  And more of Mrs Grundy.
    'The Jester's Plea' (1868)

## John Gibson Lockhart 1794–1854

2 It is a better and a wiser thing to be
  a starved apothecary than a starved poet;
  so back to the shop Mr John, back to
  'plasters, pills, and ointment boxes.'
    Reviewing Keats's *Endymion* in *Blackwood's*
    *Edinburgh Magazine* August 1818

3 Here lies that peerless paper peer Lord
  Peter,
  Who broke the laws of God and man and
  metre.
    Epitaph for Patrick ('Peter'), Lord Robertson;
    in *Journal of Sir Walter Scott* (1890) vol. 1,
    p. 259, n. 2

## David Lodge 1935–

4 Literature is mostly about having sex and
  not much about having children. Life is the
  other way round.
    *The British Museum is Falling Down* (1965) ch. 4

## Frank Loesser 1910–69

5 See what the boys in the back room will
  have
  And tell them I'm having the same.
    'Boys in the Back Room' (1939 song)

6 Isn't it grand! Isn't it fine! Look at the cut,
  the style, the line!
  The suit of clothes is altogether, but
  altogether it's altogether
  The most remarkable suit of clothes that I
  have ever seen.
    'The King's New Clothes' (1952 song)

## Jack London 1876–1916

7 The call of the wild.
    Title of novel (1903)

## Huey Long 1893–1935

8 I can go Mr Wilson one better; I was born
  barefoot.
    In T. Harry Williams *Huey Long* (1969) p. 250
    (replying to the claim that an opponent had
    gone barefoot as a boy)

9 The time has come for all good men to rise
  above principle.
    Attributed

## Henry Wadsworth Longfellow
1807–82

10 I shot an arrow into the air,
  It fell to earth, I knew not where.
    'The Arrow and the Song' (1845)

11 Thou, too, sail on, O Ship of State!
  Sail on, O Union, strong and great!
    'The Building of the Ship' (1849)

12 Between the dark and the daylight,
  When the night is beginning to lower,
  Comes a pause in the day's occupations,
  That is known as the Children's Hour.
    'The Children's Hour' (1859)

13 The cares that infest the day
  Shall fold their tents, like the Arabs,
  And as silently steal away.
    'The Day is Done' (1844)

14 If you would hit the mark, you must aim
  a little above it;
  Every arrow that flies feels the attraction
  of earth.
    'Elegiac Verse' (1880)

15 This is the forest primeval.
    *Evangeline* (1847) introduction

16 Sorrow and silence are strong, and patient
  endurance is godlike.
    *Evangeline* (1847) pt. 2, l. 60

17 A youth, who bore, 'mid snow and ice,
  A banner with the strange device,
  Excelsior!
    'Excelsior' (1841)

18                  Giotto's tower,
  The lily of Florence blossoming in stone.
    'Giotto's Tower' (1866)

19 I like that ancient Saxon phrase, which
  calls
  The burial-ground God's-Acre!
    'God's-Acre' (1841)

20 The holiest of all holidays are those
  Kept by ourselves in silence and apart;
  The secret anniversaries of the heart.
    'Holidays' (1877)

21 A boy's will is the wind's will
  And the thoughts of youth are long, long
  thoughts.
    'My Lost Youth' (1858)

22 Life is real! Life is earnest!
  And the grave is not its goal;
  Dust thou art, to dust returnest,
  Was not spoken of the soul.
    'A Psalm of Life' (1838). Cf. 39:3

23 Lives of great men all remind us
  We can make our lives sublime,
  And, departing, leave behind us
  Footprints on the sands of time.
    'A Psalm of Life' (1838)

24 Though the mills of God grind slowly, yet
  they grind exceeding small;
  Though with patience He stands waiting,
  with exactness grinds He all.
    'Retribution' (1870); translation of Friedrich
    von Logau *Sinnegedichte* (1654) no. 3224,
    being itself a translation of an anonymous
    line in Sextus Empiricus *Adversus*
    *Mathematicos* bk. 1, sect. 287

25 A Lady with a Lamp shall stand
  In the great history of the land,
  A noble type of good,
  Heroic womanhood.
    'Santa Filomena' (1857); of Florence
    Nightingale

1 By the shore of Gitche Gumee,
  By the shining Big-Sea-Water,
  Stood the wigwam of Nokomis,
  Daughter of the Moon, Nokomis.
  *The Song of Hiawatha* (1855) 'Hiawatha's
  Childhood'

2 From the waterfall he named her,
  Minnehaha, Laughing Water.
  *The Song of Hiawatha* (1855) 'Hiawatha and
  Mudjekeewis'

3 Ships that pass in the night, and speak
  each other in passing;
  Only a signal shown and a distant voice in
  the darkness;
  So on the ocean of life we pass and speak
  one another,
  Only a look and a voice; then darkness
  again and a silence.
  *Tales of a Wayside Inn* pt. 3 (1874) 'The
  Theologian's Tale' pt. 4

4 Under a spreading chestnut tree
  The village smithy stands;
  The smith, a mighty man is he,
  With large and sinewy hands.
  'The Village Blacksmith' (1839)

5 It was the schooner Hesperus,
  That sailed the wintry sea.
  'The Wreck of the Hesperus' (1839)

6 There was a little girl
  Who had a little curl
  Right in the middle of her forehead,
  When she was good
  She was very, very good,
  But when she was bad she was horrid.
  Composed for his second daughter *c.*1850.
  See B. R. Tucker-Macchetta *Home Life of
  Longfellow* (1882) ch. 5

## Anita Loos 1893–1981

7 So this gentleman said a girl with brains
  ought to do something with them besides
  think.
  *Gentlemen Prefer Blondes* (1925) ch. 1

8 She said she always believed in the old
  addage, 'Leave them while you're looking
  good.'
  *Gentlemen Prefer Blondes* (1925) ch. 1

9 Fun is fun but no girl wants to laugh all of
  the time.
  *Gentlemen Prefer Blondes* (1925) ch. 4

## Frederico García Lorca

*See* García Lorca

## Edward N. Lorenz

10 Predictability: Does the flap of a butterfly's
   wings in Brazil set off a tornado in Texas?
   Title of paper given to the American
   Association for the Advancement of Science,
   Washington, 29 December 1979. See James
   Gleick *Chaos* (1988) p. 322

## Konrad Lorenz 1903–89

11 It is a good morning exercise for a research
   scientist to discard a pet hypothesis every
   day before breakfast.
   *On Aggression* (1966) ch. 2 (tr. M. Latzke)

## Louis XIV 1638–1715

12 *L'État c'est moi.*
   I am the State.
   Before the Parlement de Paris, 13 April 1655;
   in J. A. Dulaure *Histoire de Paris* (1834) vol. 6,
   p. 298 (probably apocryphal)

13 *J'ai failli attendre.*
   I was nearly kept waiting.
   Attribution queried, among others, by E.
   Fournier in *L'Esprit dans l'Histoire* (1857)
   ch. 48

14 Every time I create an appointment,
   I create a hundred malcontents and one
   ingrate.
   In Voltaire *Siècle de Louis XIV* (1768 ed.) vol. 2,
   ch. 26

15 *Il n'y a plus de Pyrénées.*
   The Pyrenees are no more.
   On the accession of his grandson to the
   throne of Spain in 1700; in Voltaire *Siècle de
   Louis XIV* (1753) ch. 26. Attributed to the
   Spanish Ambassador to France in *Mercure
   Galant* (Paris) November 1700, p. 237

## Louis XVIII 1755–1824

16 Remember that there is not one of you
   who does not carry in his cartridge-pouch
   the marshal's baton of the duke of Reggio;
   it is up to you to bring it forth.
   Speech to Saint-Cyr cadets, 9 August 1819, in
   *Moniteur Universel* 10 August 1819

17 *L'exactitude est la politesse des rois.*
   Punctuality is the politeness of kings.
   In *Souvenirs de J. Lafitte* (1844) bk. 1, ch. 3
   (attributed)

## Richard Lovelace 1618–58

18 Lucasta that bright northern star.
   'Amyntor from Beyond the Sea to Alexis'
   (1649)

19 Stone walls do not a prison make,
   Nor iron bars a cage.
   'To Althea, From Prison' (1649)

20 Tell me not, Sweet, I am unkind,
   That from the nunnery
   Of thy chaste breast, and quiet mind,
   To war and arms I fly.
   'To Lucasta, Going to the Wars' (1649)

21 I could not love thee, Dear, so much,
   Loved I not honour more.
   'To Lucasta, Going to the Wars' (1649)

## Samuel Lover 1797–1868

22 When once the itch of literature comes
   over a man, nothing can cure it but the
   scratching of a pen.
   *Handy Andy* (1842) ch. 36

## Robert Lowe, Viscount
## Sherbrooke 1811–92

1 The Chancellor of the Exchequer is a man
whose duties make him more or less of
a taxing machine. He is intrusted with
a certain amount of misery which it is his
duty to distribute as fairly as he can.
Speech, *Hansard* 11 April 1870, col. 1639

## Amy Lowell 1874–1925

2 And the softness of my body will be
   guarded by embrace
By each button, hook, and lace.
For the man who should loose me is dead,
Fighting with the Duke in Flanders,
In a pattern called a war.
Christ! What are patterns for?
'Patterns' (1916)

3 All books are either dreams or swords,
You can cut, or you can drug, with words.
'Sword Blades and Poppy Seed' (1914).
Cf. 138:19

## James Russell Lowell 1819–91

4 An' you've gut to git up airly
Ef you want to take in God.
*The Biglow Papers* (First Series, 1848) no. 1 'A
Letter'

5 Blessèd are the horny hands of toil!
'A Glance Behind the Curtain' (1844)

6 Before Man made us citizens, great Nature
made us men.
'On the Capture of Fugitive Slaves' (1854)

7 Once to every man and nation comes the
moment to decide.
'The Present Crisis' (1845)

8 Truth forever on the scaffold, Wrong
forever on the throne.
'The Present Crisis' (1845)

9 New occasions teach new duties: Time
makes ancient good uncouth;
They must upward still, and onward, who
would keep abreast of Truth.
'The Present Crisis' (1845)

10 May is a pious fraud of the almanac.
'Under the Willows' (1869) l. 21

## Robert Lowell 1917–77

11 Terrible that old life of decency
without unseemly intimacy
or quarrels, when the unemancipated
woman
still had her Freudian papa and maids!
'During Fever' (1959)

12 The aquarium is gone. Everywhere,
giant finned cars nose forward like fish;
a savage servility
slides by on grease.
'For the Union Dead' (1964)

13 Their monument sticks like a fishbone
in the city's throat.
'For the Union Dead' (1964)

14 These are the tranquillized *Fifties*,
and I am forty.
'Memories of West Street and Lepke' (1956)

15 At forty-five,
What next, what next?
At every corner,
I meet my Father,
my age, still alive.
'Middle Age' (1964)

16                  This is death.
To die and know it. This is the Black
Widow, death.
'Mr Edwards and the Spider' (1950)

17 The Lord survives the rainbow of His will.
'The Quaker Graveyard in Nantucket' (1950)

18 If we see light at the end of the tunnel,
It's the light of the oncoming train.
'Since 1939' (1977). Cf. 120:19

19 But I suppose even God was born
too late to trust the old religion.
'Tenth Muse' (1964)

20 The present, yes,
we are in it,
it's the infection
of things gone.
'We Took Our Paradise' (1977)

## William Lowndes 1652–1724

21 Take care of the pence, and the pounds
will take care of themselves.
In Lord Chesterfield *Letters to his Son* (1774)
5 February 1750

## Malcolm Lowry 1909–57

22 How alike are the groans of love to those
of the dying.
*Under the Volcano* (1947) ch. 12

## Lucan AD 39–65

23 The winning cause pleased the gods, but
the losing one pleased Cato.
*Pharsalia* bk. 1, l. 126

24 There stands the ghost of a great name.
*Pharsalia* bk. 1, l. 135 (of Pompey)

25 Thinking nothing done while anything
remained to be done.
*Pharsalia* bk. 2, l. 657

26 I have a wife, I have sons: we have given so
many hostages to the fates.
*Pharsalia* bk. 6, l. 661. Cf. 25:1

## George Lucas 1944–

27 The Empire strikes back.
Title of film (1980)

28 Man your ships, and may the force be with
you.
*Star Wars* (1977 film)

## Lucilius *c*.180–102 BC

1  *Maior erat natu; non omnia possumus omnes.*
   He was older; we cannot all do everything.
   In Macrobius *Saturnalia* bk. 6, ch. 1, sect. 35.
   Cf. 340:2

## Lucretius *c*.94–55 BC

2  *Tantum religio potuit suadere malorum.*
   So much wrong could religion induce.
   *De Rerum Natura* bk. 1, l. 101

3  *... Nil posse creari*
   *De nilo.*
   Nothing can be created out of nothing.
   *De Rerum Natura* bk. 1, l. 155

4  *Suave, mari magno turbantibus aequora ventis,*
   *E terra magnum alterius spectare laborem.*
   Lovely it is, when the winds are churning
   up the waves on the great sea, to gaze out
   from the land on the great efforts of
   someone else.
   *De Rerum Natura* bk. 2, l. 1

5  *Inque brevi spatio mutantur saecla animantum*
   *Et quasi cursores vitai lampada tradunt.*
   And in a short while the generations of
   living creatures are changed and like
   runners relay the torch of life.
   *De Rerum Natura* bk. 2, l. 7

6  *Vitaque mancipio, nulli datur, omnibus usu.*
   And life is given to none freehold, but it is
   leasehold for all.
   *De Rerum Natura* bk. 3, l. 971

## Fray Luis de León *c*.1527–91

7  We were saying yesterday ...
   On resuming a lecture in 1577, after five
   years' imprisonment; in A. Bell *Luis de León*
   (1925) ch. 8

## Martin Luther 1483–1546

8  Here stand I. I can do no other. God help
   me. Amen.
   Speech at the Diet of Worms, 18 April 1521
   (attributed)

9  For, where God built a church, there the
   devil would also build a chapel ... In such
   sort is the devil always God's ape.
   *Colloquia Mensalia* (1566) ch. 2 (translated by
   H. Bell as *Martin Luther's Divine Discourses*,
   1652). Cf. 28:14, 31:17

10 *Eine feste Burg ist unser Gott,*
   *Ein gute Wehr und Waffen.*
   A safe stronghold our God is still,
   A trusty shield and weapon.
   'Eine feste Burg ist unser Gott' (1529, tr.
   Thomas Carlyle)

11 Who loves not woman, wine, and song
   Remains a fool his whole life long.
   Attributed (later inscribed, in German, in the
   Luther room in the Wartburg)

## Rosa Luxemburg 1871–1919

12 Freedom is always and exclusively freedom
   for the one who thinks differently.
   *Die Russische Revolution* (1918) sect. 4

## John Lydgate *c*.1370–*c*.1451

13 Off oure language he was the lodesterre.
   *The Fall of Princes* (1431–8) prologue l. 252 (of
   Chaucer)

14 Comparisouns doon offte gret greuaunce.
   *The Fall of Princes* (1431–8) bk. 3, l. 2188

15 Woord is but wynd; leff woord and tak the
   dede.
   *Secrets of Old Philosophers* l. 1224

## John Lyly *c*.1554–1606

16 Cupid and my Campaspe played
   At cards for kisses, Cupid paid.
   *Campaspe* (1584) act 3, sc. 5

17 What bird so sings, yet so does wail?
   O 'tis the ravished nightingale.
   Jug, jug, jug, jug, tereu, she cries,
   And still her woes at midnight rise.
   *Campaspe* (1584) act 5, sc. 1

18 Night hath a thousand eyes.
   *The Maydes Metamorphosis* (1600) act 3, sc. 1

## Baron Lyndhurst 1772–1863

19 Campbell has added another terror to
   death.
   On Lord Campbell's *Lives of the Lord
   Chancellors* being written without the consent
   of heirs or executors; in E. Bowen-Rowlands
   *Seventy-Two Years At the Bar* (1924) ch. 10.
   Cf. 14:24, 347:2

## Henry Francis Lyte 1793–1847

20 Abide with me: fast falls the eventide;
   The darkness deepens; Lord, with me abide:
   When other helpers fail, and comforts flee,
   Help of the helpless, O abide with me.

   Swift to its close ebbs out life's little day;
   Earth's joys grow dim, its glories pass
   away;
   Change and decay in all around I see;
   O Thou, who changest not, abide with me.
   'Abide with Me' (*c*.1847)

21 Praise my soul, the King of heaven;
   To his feet thy tribute bring.
   Ransomed, healed, restored, forgiven,
   Who like me his praise should sing?
   'Praise, my soul, the King of heaven' (1834
   hymn)

## E. R. Bulwer, 1st Earl of Lytton

*See* OWEN MEREDITH

## General Douglas MacArthur
1880–1964

1 I came through and I shall return.
On reaching Australia, 20 March 1942,
having broken through Japanese lines en
route from Corregidor; in *New York Times*
21 March 1942

## Rose Macaulay 1881–1958

2 'Take my camel, dear,' said my aunt Dot, as
she climbed down from this animal on her
return from High Mass.
*The Towers of Trebizond* (1956) p. 9

## Lord Macaulay 1800–59

3 The business of everybody is the business
of nobody.
*Essays* [*Edinburgh Review*] (1843) vol. 1
'Hallam'

4 The gallery in which the reporters sit has
become a fourth estate of the realm.
*Essays* [*Edinburgh Review*] (1843) vol. 1
'Hallam'

5 Boswell is the first of biographers.
*Essays* [*Edinburgh Review*] (1843) vol. 1
'Samuel Johnson'

6 The gigantic body, the huge massy face,
seamed with the scars of disease.
*Essays* [*Edinburgh Review*] (1843) vol. 1
'Samuel Johnson'

7 As civilization advances, poetry almost
necessarily declines.
*Essays* [*Edinburgh Review*] (1843) vol. 1
'Milton'

8 If men are to wait for liberty till they
become wise and good in slavery, they may
indeed wait for ever.
*Essays* [*Edinburgh Review*] (1843) vol. 1
'Milton'

9 We know no spectacle so ridiculous as the
British public in one of its periodical fits of
morality.
*Essays* [*Edinburgh Review*] (1843) vol. 1 'Moore's
*Life of Lord Byron*'

10 We have heard it said that five per cent is
the natural interest of money.
*Essays* [*Edinburgh Review*] (1843) vol. 1
'Southey's Colloquies'

11 An acre in Middlesex is better than a
principality in Utopia.
*Essays* [*Edinburgh Review*] (1843) vol. 2 'Lord
Bacon'

12 The reluctant obedience of distant
provinces generally costs more than it is
worth.
*Essays* [*Edinburgh Review*] (1843) vol. 2 'The
War of Succession in Spain'

13 Every schoolboy knows who imprisoned
Montezuma, and who strangled Atahualpa.
*Essays* [*Edinburgh Review*] (1843) vol. 3 'Lord
Clive'

14 That temple of silence and reconciliation
where the enmities of twenty generations
lie buried.
*Essays* [*Edinburgh Review*] (1843) vol. 3 'Warren
Hastings' (of Westminster Abbey)

15 She [the Roman Catholic Church] may still
exist in undiminished vigour when some
traveller from New Zealand shall, in the
midst of a vast solitude, take his stand on
a broken arch of London Bridge to sketch
the ruins of St Paul's.
*Essays* [*Edinburgh Review*] (1843) vol. 3 'Von
Ranke'

16 She [the Church of Rome] thoroughly
understands what no other church has
ever understood, how to deal with
enthusiasts.
*Essays* [*Edinburgh Review*] (1843) vol. 3 'Von
Ranke'

17 Persecution produced its natural effect on
them [Puritans and Calvinists]. It found
them a sect; it made them a faction.
*History of England* vol. 1 (1849) ch. 1

18 It was a crime in a child to read by the
bedside of a sick parent one of those
beautiful collects which had soothed the
griefs of forty generations of Christians.
*History of England* vol. 1 (1849) ch. 2

19 The Puritan hated bear-baiting, not
because it gave pain to the bear, but
because it gave pleasure to the spectators.
*History of England* vol. 1 (1849) ch. 2

20 The English Bible, a book which, if
everything else in our language should
perish, would alone suffice to show the
whole extent of its beauty and power.
T. F. Ellis (ed.) *Miscellaneous Writings of Lord
Macaulay* (1860) 'John Dryden' (1828)

21 His imagination resembled the wings of an
ostrich. It enabled him to run, though not
to soar.
T. F. Ellis (ed.) *Miscellaneous Writings* (1860)
'John Dryden' (1828)

22 This province of literature [history] is a
debatable line. It lies on the confines of
two distinct territories ... It is sometimes
fiction. It is sometimes theory.
T. F. Ellis (ed.) *Miscellaneous Writings* (1860)
vol. 1 'History' (1828)

23 Thank you, madam, the agony is abated.
Aged four, having had hot coffee spilt over
his legs; in G. O. Trevelyan *Life and Letters of
Lord Macaulay* (1876) ch. 1

24 The rugged miners poured to war from
Mendip's sunless caves.
'The Armada' (1833)

25 Oh, wherefore come ye forth in triumph
from the north,
With your hands, and your feet, and your
raiment all red?
'The Battle of Naseby' (1824)

1 By those white cliffs I never more must
    see,
  By that dear language which I spake like
    thee,
  Forget all feuds, and shed one English tear
  O'er English dust. A broken heart lies here.
    'A Jacobite's Epitaph' (1845)

2 Lars Porsena of Clusium
  By the nine gods he swore
  That the great house of Tarquin
  Should suffer wrong no more.
    *Lays of Ancient Rome* (1842) 'Horatius' st. 1

3 To every man upon this earth
  Death cometh soon or late.
  And how can man die better
  Than facing fearful odds,
  For the ashes of his fathers,
  And the temples of his Gods?
    *Lays of Ancient Rome* (1842) 'Horatius' st. 27

4 Now who will stand on either hand,
  And keep the bridge with me?
    *Lays of Ancient Rome* (1842) 'Horatius' st. 29

5 Then none was for a party;
  Then all were for the state.
    *Lays of Ancient Rome* (1842) 'Horatius' st. 32

6 Was none who would be foremost
  To lead such dire attack;
  But those behind cried 'Forward!'
  And those before cried 'Back!'
    *Lays of Ancient Rome* (1842) 'Horatius' st. 50

7 Oh, Tiber! father Tiber
  To whom the Romans pray,
  A Roman's life, a Roman's arms,
  Take thou in charge this day!
    *Lays of Ancient Rome* (1842) 'Horatius' st. 59

8 And even the ranks of Tuscany
  Could scarce forbear to cheer.
    *Lays of Ancient Rome* (1842) 'Horatius' st. 60

## General Anthony McAuliffe
1898–1975

9 Nuts!
    Replying to the German demand for
    surrender at Bastogne, Belgium,
    22 December 1944; in *New York Times*
    28 December 1944, p. 4

## Mary McCarthy 1912–89

10 Europe is the unfinished negative of which
   America is the proof.
    *On the Contrary* (1961) 'America the Beautiful'

11 In violence, we forget who we are.
    *On the Contrary* (1961) 'Characters in Fiction'

12 Every word she writes is a lie, including
   'and' and 'the'.
    Quoting herself on Lillian Hellman in *New
    York Times* 16 February 1980, p. 12

## Paul McCartney 1942–

13 Ballads and babies. That's what happened
   to me.
    On reaching the age of fifty; in *Time* 8 June
    1992, p. 84

## General George B. McClellan
1826–85

14 All quiet along the Potomac.
    Said at the time of the American Civil War
    (attributed). Cf. 32:14

## David McCord 1897–

15 By and by
   God caught his eye.
    'Remainders' (1935); epitaph for a waiter

## Horace McCoy 1897–1955

16 They shoot horses don't they.
    Title of novel (1935)

## John McCrae 1872–1918

17 In Flanders fields the poppies blow
   Between the crosses, row on row.
    'In Flanders Fields' (1915)

## George MacDonald 1824–1905

18 Where did you come from, baby dear?
   Out of the everywhere into here.
    *At the Back of the North Wind* (1871) ch. 33
    'Song'

## William McGonagall c.1825–1902

19 Beautiful Railway Bridge of the Silv'ry Tay!
   Alas, I am very sorry to say
   That ninety lives have been taken away
   On the last Sabbath day of 1879,
   Which will be remembered for a very long
     time.
    'The Tay Bridge Disaster'

## Roger McGough 1937–

20 You will put on a dress of guilt
   and shoes with broken high ideals.
    'Comeclose and Sleepnow' (1967)

21 Let me die a youngman's death
   Not a clean & in-between-
   The-sheets, holy-water death.
    'Let Me Die a Youngman's Death' (1967)

## Jimmy McGregor

22 Oh, he's football crazy, he's football mad
   And the football it has robbed him o' the
     wee bit sense he had.
   And it would take a dozen skivvies, his
     clothes to wash and scrub,
   Since our Jock became a member of that
     terrible football club.
    'Football Crazy' (1960 song)

## Niccolò Machiavelli 1469–1527

23 Men should be either treated generously or
   destroyed, because they take revenge for
   slight injuries—for heavy ones they
   cannot.
    *The Prince* (1513) ch. 3 (tr. A. Gilbert)

**1** It is much safer for a prince to be feared than loved, if he is to fail in one of the two.
*The Prince* (1513) ch. 8 (tr. A. Gilbert)

**2** Let no one oppose this belief of mine with that well-worn proverb: 'He who builds on the people builds on mud.'
*The Prince* (1513) ch. 9 (tr. A. Gilbert)

**3** The prince must be a fox, therefore, to recognize the traps and a lion to frighten the wolves.
*The Prince* (1513) ch. 18 (tr. A. Gilbert)

## Fritz Machlup 1902–83

**4** Let us remember the unfortunate econometrician who, in one of the major functions of his system, had to use a proxy for risk and a dummy for sex.
In *Journal of Political Economy* July/August 1974, p. 892

## Sir James Mackintosh 1765–1832

**5** The Commons, faithful to their system, remained in a wise and masterly inactivity.
*Vindiciae Gallicae* (1791) sect. 1

## Alexander Maclaren 1826–1910

**6** 'The Church is an anvil which has worn out many hammers', and the story of the first collision is, in essentials, the story of all.
*Expositions of Holy Scripture: Acts of the Apostles* (1907) ch. 4

## Don McLean 1945–

**7** Something touched me deep inside
The day the music died.
'American Pie' (1972 song, on the death of Buddy Holly)

**8** So, bye, bye, Miss American Pie,
Drove my Chevy to the levee
But the levee was dry.
Them good old boys was drinkin' whiskey and rye
Singin' 'This'll be the day that I die.'
'American Pie' (1972 song)

## Archibald MacLeish 1892–1982

**9** A poem should not mean
But be.
'Ars Poetica' (1926)

## Fiona McLeod (William Sharp) 1855–1905

**10** My heart is a lonely hunter that hunts on a lonely hill.
'The Lonely Hunter' (1896) st. 6

## Marshall McLuhan 1911–80

**11** The new electronic interdependence recreates the world in the image of a global village.
*The Gutenberg Galaxy* (1962) p. 31

**12** The medium is the message.
*Understanding Media* (1964) ch. 1 (title)

## Comte de Macmahon 1808–93

**13** *J'y suis, j'y reste.*
Here I am, and here I stay.
At the taking of the Malakoff fortress, 8 September 1855. See G. Hanotaux *Histoire de la France Contemporaine* (1903–8) vol. 2, ch. 1, sect. 1

## Harold Macmillan 1894–1986

**14** Forever poised between a cliché and an indiscretion.
In *Newsweek* 30 April 1956 (on the life of a Foreign Secretary)

**15** Let us be frank about it: most of our people have never had it so good.
Speech at Bedford, 20 July 1957, in *The Times* 22 July 1957 ('You Never Had It So Good' was the Democratic Party slogan during the 1952 US election campaign)

**16** I thought the best thing to do was to settle up these little local difficulties, and then turn to the wider vision of the Commonwealth.
Statement at London airport on leaving for a Commonwealth tour, 7 January 1958, following the resignation of the Chancellor of the Exchequer and others; in *The Times* 8 January 1958

**17** The wind of change is blowing through this continent, and, whether we like it or not, this growth of [African] national consciousness is a political fact.
Speech at Cape Town, 3 February 1960, in *Pointing the Way* (1972) p. 475

**18** I was determined that no British government should be brought down by the action of two tarts.
Comment on the Profumo affair, July 1963; in A. Sampson *Macmillan* (1967) p. 243

**19** There are three bodies no sensible man directly challenges: the Roman Catholic Church, the Brigade of Guards and the National Union of Mineworkers.
In *Observer* 22 February 1981. Cf. 27:8

**20** First of all the Georgian silver goes, and then all that nice furniture that used to be in the saloon. Then the Canalettos go.
Speech on privatization to the Tory Reform Group, 8 November 1985; in *The Times* 9 November 1985

## Louis MacNeice 1907–63

**21** Better authentic mammon than a bogus god.
*Autumn Journal* (1939) p. 49

**1** It's no go the merrygoround, it's no go the
rickshaw,
All we want is a limousine and a ticket for
the peepshow.
'Bagpipe Music' (1938)

**2** It's no go the picture palace, it's no go the
stadium,
It's no go the country cot with a pot of
pink geraniums,
It's no go the Government grants, it's no
go the elections,
Sit on your arse for fifty years and hang
your hat on a pension.
'Bagpipe Music' (1938)

**3** The glass is falling hour by hour, the glass
will fall for ever,
But if you break the bloody glass you won't
hold up the weather.
'Bagpipe Music' (1938)

**4** Crumbling between the fingers, under the
feet,
Crumbling behind the eyes,
Their world gives way and dies
And something twangs and breaks at the
end of the street.
'Débâcle' (1941)

**5** Time was away and somewhere else,
There were two glasses and two chairs
And two people with the one pulse.
'Meeting Point' (1941)

**6** I am not yet born; O fill me
With strength against those who would
freeze my
humanity.
'Prayer Before Birth' (1944)

**7** Let them not make me a stone and let
them not spill me,
Otherwise kill me.
'Prayer Before Birth' (1944)

**8** The drunkenness of things being various.
'Snow' (1935)

**9** Down the road someone is practising
scales,
The notes like little fishes vanish with
a wink of tails,
Man's heart expands to tinker with his car
For this is Sunday morning, Fate's great
bazaar.
'Sunday Morning' (1935)

**10** The sunlight on the garden
Hardens and grows cold,
We cannot cage the minute
Within its net of gold.
'Sunlight on the Garden' (1938)

**11** By a high star our course is set,
Our end is Life. Put out to sea.
'Thalassa' (1964)

### Geoffrey Madan 1895–1947

**12** The great tragedy of the classical
languages is to have been born twins.
*Geoffrey Madan's Notebooks* (1981) p. 67

**13** The dust of exploded beliefs may make
a fine sunset.
*Livre sans nom: Twelve Reflections* (privately
printed 1934) no. 12

### Samuel Madden 1686–1765

**14** Words are men's daughters, but God's sons
are things.
*Boulter's Monument* (1745) l. 377. Cf. 182:4

### Maurice Maeterlinck 1862–1949

**15** *Il n'y a pas de morts.*
There are no dead.
*L'Oiseau bleu* (1909) act 4

### Magna Carta 1215

**16** Except by the lawful judgement of his
peers or by the law of the land.
Clause 39

**17** To no man will we sell, or deny, or delay,
right or justice.
Clause 40

### Josephe de Maistre 1753–1821

**18** Every country has the government it
deserves.
*Lettres et Opuscules Inédits* (1851) vol. 1, letter
53 (15 August 1811)

### John Major 1943–

**19** Society needs to condemn a little more and
understand a little less.
Interview with *Mail on Sunday* 21 February
1993

### Stéphane Mallarmé 1842–98

**20** *La chair est triste, hélas! et j'ai lu tous les livres.*
The flesh, alas, is wearied; and I have read
all the books there are.
'Brise Marin' (1887)

### David Mallet (or Malloch)
*c.*1705–65

**21** O grant me, Heaven, a middle state,
Neither too humble nor too great;
More than enough, for nature's ends,
With something left to treat my friends.
'Imitation of Horace'. Cf. 174:4

### George Leigh Mallory 1886–1924

**22** Because it's there.
On being asked why he wanted to climb
Mount Everest; in *New York Times* 18 March
1923

### Sir Thomas Malory d. 1471

**23** Whoso pulleth out this sword of this stone
and anvil is rightwise King born of all
England.
*Le Morte D'Arthur* (finished 1470, printed by
Caxton 1485) bk. 1, ch. 4

1 Ah, my little son, thou hast murdered thy mother! ... When he is christened let call him Tristram, that is as much to say as a sorrowful birth.
   *Le Morte D'Arthur* (1485) bk. 8, ch. 1

2 God defend me, said Dinadan, for the joy of love is too short, and the sorrow thereof, and what cometh thereof, dureth over long.
   *Le Morte D'Arthur* (1485) bk. 10, ch. 56

3 Therefore all ye that be lovers call unto your remembrance the month of May, like as did Queen Guenevere, for whom I make here a little mention, that while she lived she was a true lover, and therefore she had a good end.
   *Le Morte D'Arthur* (1485) bk. 18, ch. 25

## André Malraux 1901–76

4 *L'art est un anti-destin.*
   Art is a revolt against fate.
   *Les Voix du silence* (1951) pt. 4, ch. 7

## Thomas Robert Malthus 1766–1834

5 Population, when unchecked, increases in a geometrical ratio. Subsistence only increases in an arithmetical ratio.
   *Essay on the Principle of Population* (1798) ch. 1

6 The perpetual struggle for room and food.
   *Essay on the Principle of Population* (1798) ch. 3

## Lord Mancroft 1914–87

7 Cricket—a game which the English, not being a spiritual people, have invented in order to give themselves some conception of eternity.
   *Bees in Some Bonnets* (1979) p. 185

## W. R. Mandale

8 Up and down the City Road,
   In and out the Eagle,
   That's the way the money goes—
   Pop goes the weasel!
   'Pop Goes the Weasel' (1853 song); also attributed to Charles Twiggs

## Winnie Mandela 1934–

9 With that stick of matches, with our necklace, we shall liberate this country.
   Speech in black townships, 14 April 1986; in *Guardian* 15 April 1986

## Osip Mandelstam 1892–1938

10 The age is rocking the wave
   with human grief
   to a golden beat, and an adder
   is breathing in time with it in the grass.
   'The Age' (1923, tr. C. M. Bowra)

11 Perhaps my whisper was already born before my lips.
   *Selected Poems* (1973, tr. D. McDuff) 'Poems Published Posthumously' (written 1934)

## Joseph L. Mankiewicz 1909–

12 Fasten your seat-belts, it's going to be a bumpy night.
   *All About Eve* (1950 film); spoken by Bette Davis

## Thomas Mann 1875–1955

13 We come out of the dark and go into the dark again, and in between lie the experiences of our life.
   *The Magic Mountain* (1924) ch. 6, sect. 8 (tr. H. T. Lowe-Porter)

14 A man's dying is more the survivors' affair than his own.
   *The Magic Mountain* (1924) ch. 6, sect. 8 (tr. H. T. Lowe-Porter)

## Katherine Mansfield 1888–1923

15 Whenever I prepare for a journey I prepare as though for death. Should I never return, all is in order.
   *Journal* (1927) p. 224 (29 January 1922)

## Lord Mansfield 1705–93

16 Consider what you think justice requires, and decide accordingly. But never give your reasons; for your judgement will probably be right, but your reasons will certainly be wrong.
   In Lord Campbell *Lives of the Chief Justices of England* (1849) vol. 2, ch. 40

## Richard Mant 1776–1848

17 Bright the vision that delighted
   Once the sight of Judah's seer;
   Sweet the countless tongues united
   To entrance the prophet's ear.
   'Bright the vision that delighted' (1837 hymn)

## Mao Tse-tung 1893–1976

18 Politics is war without bloodshed while war is politics with bloodshed.
   Lecture, 1938, in *Selected Works* (1965) vol. 2, p. 153

19 Every Communist must grasp the truth, 'Political power grows out of the barrel of a gun'.
   Speech, 6 November 1938, in *Selected Works* (1965) vol. 2, p. 224

20 The atom bomb is a paper tiger which the United States reactionaries use to scare people. It looks terrible, but in fact it isn't ... All reactionaries are paper tigers.
   Interview, 1946, in *Selected Works* (1961) vol. 4, p. 100

1 Letting a hundred flowers blossom and a hundred schools of thought contend is the policy for promoting progress in the arts and the sciences and a flourishing socialist culture in our land.

> Speech in Peking, 27 February 1957, in *Quotations of Chairman Mao* (1966) p. 302

## William Learned Marcy
1786–1857

2 The politicians of New York ... see nothing wrong in the rule, that to the victor belong the spoils of the enemy.

> Speech, 25 January 1832, in J. Parton *Life of Andrew Jackson* (1860) vol. 3, ch. 29

## Marie-Antoinette 1755–93

3 *Qu'ils mangent de la brioche.*
Let them eat cake.

> On being told that her people had no bread. In *Confessions* (1740) Rousseau refers to a similar remark being a well-known saying; in *Relation d'un Voyage à Bruxelles et à Coblentz en 1791* (1823) p. 59, Louis XVIII attributes 'Why don't they eat pastry?' to Marie-Thérèse (1638–83), wife of Louis XIV

## Edwin Markham 1852–1940

4 A thing that grieves not and that never hopes,
Stolid and stunned, a brother to the ox?

> 'The Man with the Hoe' (1899)

## Sarah, Duchess of Marlborough
1660–1744

5 The Duke returned from the wars today and did pleasure me in his top-boots.

> Attributed in various forms. See I. Butler *Rule of Three* (1967) ch. 7

## Bob Marley 1945–81

6 Get up, stand up
Stand up for your rights
Get up, stand up
Never give up the fight.

> 'Get up, Stand up' (1973 song)

7 I shot the sheriff
But I swear it was in self-defence
I shot the sheriff
And they say it is a capital offence.

> 'I Shot the Sheriff' (1974 song)

## Christopher Marlowe 1564–93

8 I'll have them fly to India for gold,
Ransack the ocean for orient pearl.

> *Doctor Faustus* (1604) act 1, sc. 1

9 Why, this is hell, nor am I out of it.

> *Doctor Faustus* (1604) act 1, sc. 3

10 Hell hath no limits nor is circumscribed
In one self place, where we are is Hell,
And to be short, when all the world dissolves,
And every creature shall be purified,
All places shall be hell that are not heaven.

> *Doctor Faustus* (1604) act 2, sc. 1

11 Was this the face that launched a thousand ships,
And burnt the topless towers of Ilium?
Sweet Helen, make me immortal with a kiss!

> *Doctor Faustus* (1604) act 5, sc. 1

12 Now hast thou but one bare hour to live,
And then thou must be damned perpetually.
Stand still, you ever-moving spheres of heaven,
That time may cease, and midnight never come.

> *Doctor Faustus* (1604) act 5, sc. 2

13 *O lente lente currite noctis equi.*
The stars move still, time runs, the clock will strike,
The devil will come, and Faustus must be damned.
O I'll leap up to my God: who pulls me down?
See, see, where Christ's blood streams in the firmament.
One drop would save my soul, half a drop, ah my Christ.

> *Doctor Faustus* (1604) act 5, sc. 2

14 Cut is the branch that might have grown full straight,
And burnèd is Apollo's laurel bough,
That sometime grew within this learned man.

> *Doctor Faustus* (1604) epilogue

15 My men, like satyrs grazing on the lawns,
Shall with their goat feet dance an antic hay.

> *Edward II* (1593) act 1, sc. 1

16 Base Fortune, now I see, that in thy wheel
There is a point, to which when men aspire,
They tumble headlong down.

> *Edward II* (1593) act 5, sc. 6

17 It lies not in our power to love, or hate,
For will in us is over-ruled by fate.

> *Hero and Leander* (1598) First Sestiad, l. 167

18 Where both deliberate, the love is slight;
Who ever loved that loved not at first sight?

> *Hero and Leander* (1598) First Sestiad, l. 175.
> Cf. 273:7

19 I count religion but a childish toy,
And hold there is no sin but ignorance.

> *The Jew of Malta* (c.1592) prologue

**1** Thus methinks should men of judgement
   frame
   Their means of traffic from the vulgar
   trade,
   And, as their wealth increaseth, so enclose
   Infinite riches in a little room.
   *The Jew of Malta* (c.1592) act 1, sc. 1

**2** BARNARDINE: Thou hast committed—
   BARABAS: Fornication? But that was in
   another country: and besides, the wench
   is dead.
   *The Jew of Malta* (c.1592) act 4, sc. 1

**3** Come live with me, and be my love,
   And we will all the pleasures prove,
   That valleys, groves, hills and fields,
   Woods or steepy mountain yields.
   'The Passionate Shepherd to his Love'.
   Cf. 123:23, 257:20

**4** From jigging veins of rhyming mother-
   wits,
   And such conceits as clownage keeps in
   pay,
   We'll lead you to the stately tents of war.
   *Tamburlaine the Great* (1590) pt. 1, prologue

**5** Our swords shall play the orators for us.
   *Tamburlaine the Great* (1590) pt. 1, act 1, sc. 2

**6** His looks do menace heaven and dare the
   Gods.
   *Tamburlaine the Great* (1590) pt. 1, act 1, sc. 2

**7** Is it not passing brave to be a king,
   And ride in triumph through Persepolis?
   *Tamburlaine the Great* (1590) pt. 1, act 2, sc. 5

**8** The ripest fruit of all,
   That perfect bliss and sole felicity,
   The sweet fruition of an earthly crown.
   *Tamburlaine the Great* (1590) pt. 1, act 2, sc. 7

**9** Virtue is the fount whence honour springs.
   *Tamburlaine the Great* (1590) pt. 1, act 4, sc. 4

**10** Ah fair Zenocrate, divine Zenocrate,
   Fair is too foul an epithet for thee.
   *Tamburlaine the Great* (1590) pt. 1, act 5, sc. 5

**11** Now walk the angels on the walls of
   heaven,
   As sentinels to warn th' immortal souls,
   To entertain divine Zenocrate.
   *Tamburlaine the Great* (1590) pt. 2, act 2, sc. 4

**12** Yet let me kiss my Lord before I die,
   And let me die with kissing of my Lord.
   *Tamburlaine the Great* (1590) pt. 2, act 2, sc. 4

**13** More childish valorous than manly wise.
   *Tamburlaine the Great* (1590) pt. 2, act 4, sc. 1

**14** Holla, ye pampered jades of Asia!
   What, can ye draw but twenty miles a day?
   *Tamburlaine the Great* (1590) pt. 2, act 4, sc. 3

## Don Marquis 1878–1937

**15** procrastination is the
   art of keeping
   up with yesterday.
   *archy and mehitabel* (1927) 'certain maxims of
   archy'

**16** an optimist is a guy
   that has never had
   much experience.
   *archy and mehitabel* (1927) 'certain maxims of
   archy'

**17** it s cheerio
   my deario that
   pulls a lady through.
   *archy and mehitabel* (1927) 'cheerio, my deario'

**18** I have got you out here
   in the great open spaces
   where cats are cats.
   *archy and mehitabel* (1927) 'mehitabel has an
   adventure'

**19** but wotthehell archy wotthehell
   jamais triste archy jamais triste
   that is my motto.
   *archy and mehitabel* (1927) 'mehitabel sees
   paris'

**20** boss there is always
   a comforting thought
   in time of trouble when
   it is not our trouble.
   *archy does his part* (1935) 'comforting
   thoughts'

**21** now and then
   there is a person born
   who is so unlucky
   that he runs into accidents
   which started to happen
   to somebody else.
   *archys life of mehitabel* (1933) 'archy says'

**22** Writing a book of poetry is like dropping
   a rose petal down the Grand Canyon and
   waiting for the echo.
   In E. Anthony *O Rare Don Marquis* (1962)
   p. 146

**23** The art of newspaper paragraphing is to
   stroke a platitude until it purrs like an
   epigram.
   In E. Anthony *O Rare Don Marquis* (1962)
   p. 354

## John Marriot 1780–1825

**24** Thou, whose eternal Word
   Chaos and darkness heard,
   And took their flight,
   Hear us, we humbly pray,
   And, where the Gospel-day
   Sheds not its glorious ray,
   Let there be light!
   'Thou, whose eternal Word' (hymn written
   c.1813); 'almighty' substituted for 'eternal'
   from 1861

## Captain Marryat 1792–1848

**25** There's no getting blood out of a turnip.
   *Japhet, in Search of a Father* (1836) ch. 4

**26** As savage as a bear with a sore head.
   *The King's Own* (1830) vol. 2, ch. 6

**27** If you please, ma'am, it was a very little
   one.
   *Mr Midshipman Easy* (1836) ch. 3 (the nurse,
   excusing her illegitimate baby)

1 All zeal, Mr Easy.
  *Mr Midshipman Easy* (1836) ch. 9

## Arthur Marshall 1910–89

2 What, knocked a tooth out? Never mind, dear, laugh it off, laugh it off; it's all part of life's rich pageant.
  *The Games Mistress* (recorded monologue, 1937)

## Thomas R. Marshall 1854–1925

3 What this country needs is a really good 5-cent cigar.
  In *New York Tribune* 4 January 1920, pt. 7, p. 1

## Martial AD c.40–c.104

4 *Non amo te, Sabidi, nec possum dicere quare: Hoc tantum possum dicere, non amo te.*
  I don't love you, Sabidius, and I can't tell you why; all I can tell you is this, that I don't love you.
  *Epigrammata* bk. 1, no. 32. Cf. 73:18

5 *Laudant illa sed ista legunt.*
  They praise those works, but read these.
  *Epigrammata* bk. 4, no. 49

6 *Non est vivere, sed valere vita est.*
  Life's not just being alive, but being well.
  *Epigrammata* bk. 6, no. 70

7 *Difficilis facilis, iucundus acerbus es idem: Nec tecum possum vivere nec sine te.*
  Difficult or easy, pleasant or bitter, you are the same you: I cannot live with you—or without you.
  *Epigrammata* bk. 12, no. 46 (47)

8 *Rus in urbe.*
  Country in the town.
  *Epigrammata* bk. 12, no. 57

## Andrew Marvell 1621–78

9 Where the remote Bermudas ride
  In the ocean's bosom unespied.
  'Bermudas' (*c.*1653)

10 He hangs in shades the orange bright,
  Like golden lamps in a green night.
  'Bermudas' (*c.*1653)

11 Echo beyond the Mexique Bay.
  'Bermudas' (*c.*1653)

12 My love is of a birth as rare
  As 'tis for object strange and high:
  It was begotten by Despair
  Upon Impossibility.

  Magnanimous Despair alone
  Could show me so divine a thing,
  Where feeble Hope could ne'er have flown
  But vainly flapped its tinsel wing.
  'The Definition of Love' (1681)

13 As lines (so loves) oblique may well
  Themselves in every angle greet:
  But ours so truly parallel,
  Though infinite, can never meet.

  Therefore the love which us doth bind,
  But Fate so enviously debars,
  Is the conjunction of the mind,
  And opposition of the stars.
  'The Definition of Love' (1681)

14 How vainly men themselves amaze
  To win the palm, the oak, or bays.
  'The Garden' (1681) st. 1

15 What wondrous life is this I lead!
  Ripe apples drop about my head;
  The luscious clusters of the vine
  Upon my mouth do crush their wine;
  The nectarine, and curious peach,
  Into my hands themselves do reach;
  Stumbling on melons, as I pass,
  Ensnared with flowers, I fall on grass.
  'The Garden' (1681) st. 5

16 Annihilating all that's made
  To a green thought in a green shade.
  'The Garden' (1681) st. 6

17 Two paradises 'twere in one
  To live in paradise alone.
  'The Garden' (1681) st. 8

18 *He* nothing common did or mean
  Upon that memorable scene.
  'An Horatian Ode upon Cromwell's Return from Ireland' (written 1650) l. 57 (on the execution of Charles I)

19 So much one man can do,
  That does both act and know.
  'An Horatian Ode upon Cromwell's Return from Ireland' (1650) l. 75

20 Ye living lamps, by whose dear light
  The nightingale does sit so late.
  'The Mower to the Glow-worms' (1681)

21 Ye country comets, that portend
  No war, nor prince's funeral.
  'The Mower to the Glow-worms' (1681)

22 Had we but world enough, and time,
  This coyness, lady, were no crime.
  'To His coy Mistress' (1681) l. 1

23             I would
  Love you ten years before the flood:
  And you should, if you please, refuse
  Till the conversion of the Jews.
  My vegetable love should grow
  Vaster than empires, and more slow.
  'To His coy Mistress' (1681) l. 7

24 But at my back I always hear
  Time's wingèd chariot hurrying near:
  And yonder all before us lie
  Deserts of vast eternity.
  'To His coy Mistress' (1681) l. 21

25 The grave's a fine and private place,
  But none, I think, do there embrace.
  'To His Coy Mistress' (1681) l. 31

1 Let us roll all our strength, and all
Our sweetness, up into one ball;
And tear our pleasures with rough strife,
Thorough the iron gates of life.
Thus, though we cannot make our sun
Stand still, yet we will make him run.
'To His Coy Mistress' (1681) l. 41

2 'Tis not what once it was, the world,
But a rude heap together hurled.
'Upon Appleton House' (1681) st. 96

3 But now the salmon-fishers moist
Their leathern boats begin to hoist;
And, like Antipodes in shoes,
Have shod their heads in their canoes.
How tortoise-like, but not so slow,
These rational amphibii go!
'Upon Appleton House' (1681) st. 97

## Holt Marvell 1901–69

4 A cigarette that bears a lipstick's traces,
An airline ticket to romantic places.
'These Foolish Things Remind Me of You'
(1935 song)

## Groucho Marx 1895–1977

5 PLEASE ACCEPT MY RESIGNATION. I DON'T
WANT TO BELONG TO ANY CLUB THAT WILL
ACCEPT ME AS A MEMBER.
*Groucho and Me* (1959) ch. 26

6 Either he's dead, or my watch has stopped.
In *A Day at the Races* (1937 film; script by
Robert Pirosh, George Seaton, and George
Oppenheimer)

7 I never forget a face, but in your case I'll be
glad to make an exception.
In Leo Rosten *People I have Loved, Known or
Admired* (1970) 'Groucho'
*See also* BERT KALMAR

## Karl Marx 1818–83

8 Religion ... is the opium of the people.
*A Contribution to the Critique of Hegel's
Philosophy of Right* (1843–4) introduction.
Cf. 195:18

9 From each according to his abilities, to
each according to his needs.
*Critique of the Gotha Programme* (written 1875,
but of earlier origin). See Morelly *Code de la
nature* (1755) pt. 4, p. 190, and J. Blanc
*Organisation du travail* (1839) p. 126.
Cf. 27:1

10 Hegel says somewhere that all great events
and personalities in world history reappear
in one fashion or another. He forgot to
add: the first time as tragedy, the second
as farce.
*Eighteenth Brumaire of Louis Bonaparte* (1852)
sect. 1. Cf. 164:18

11 The philosophers have only interpreted the
world in various ways; the point is to
change it.
*Theses on Feuerbach* (written 1845) no. 11

12 The class struggle necessarily leads to the
dictatorship of the proletariat.
Letter to Weydemeyer, 5 March 1852. Marx
claimed that 'dictatorship of the proletariat'
had been coined by Auguste Blanqui
(1805–81), but it has not been found in his
work

## Karl Marx 1818–83 and Friedrich Engels 1820–95

13 A spectre is haunting Europe—the spectre
of Communism.
*The Communist Manifesto* (1848) opening words

14 The history of all hitherto existing society
is the history of class struggles.
*The Communist Manifesto* (1848) pt. 1

15 The proletarians have nothing to lose but
their chains. They have a world to win.
WORKING MEN OF ALL COUNTRIES, UNITE!
*The Communist Manifesto* (1848) *ad fin.* (from
the 1888 translation by Samuel Moore,
edited by Engels and commonly rendered
'Workers of the world, unite!')

## Mary, Queen of Scots 1542–87

16 *En ma fin git mon commencement.*
In my end is my beginning.
Motto. Cf. 133:2

## Mary Tudor 1516–58

17 When I am dead and opened, you shall find
'Calais' lying in my heart.
*Holinshed's Chronicles* vol. 4 (1808 ed.) p. 137

## John Masefield 1878–1967

18 Quinquireme of Nineveh from distant
Ophir
Rowing home to haven in sunny Palestine,
With a cargo of ivory,
And apes and peacocks,
Sandalwood, cedarwood, and sweet white
wine.
'Cargoes' (1903). Cf. 41:31

19 Dirty British coaster with a salt-caked
smoke stack,
Butting through the Channel in the mad
March days,
With a cargo of Tyne coal,
Road-rails, pig lead,
Firewood, ironware, and cheap tin trays.
'Cargoes' (1903)

20 And fifteen arms went round her waist.
(And then men ask, Are Barmaids Chaste?)
'The Everlasting Mercy' (1911) st. 26

21 I must go down to the sea again, to the
lonely sea and the sky,
And all I ask is a tall ship and a star to
steer her by.
'Sea Fever' (misprinted 'I must down to the
seas' in the 1902 original)

1 I must go down to the sea again, for the
call of the running tide
Is a wild call and a clear call that may not
be denied.
'Sea Fever' (1902)

2 I must go down to the sea again, to the
vagrant gypsy life,
To the gull's way and the whale's way
where the wind's like a whetted knife;
And all I ask is a merry yarn from
a laughing fellow-rover,
And quiet sleep and a sweet dream when
the long trick's over.
'Sea Fever' (1902)

## Philip Massinger 1583–1640

3 Ambition, in a private man a vice,
Is in a prince the virtue.
The Bashful Lover (licensed 1636) act 1, sc. 2

4         Pray enter
You are learned Europeans and we worse
Than ignorant Americans.
The City Madam (licensed 1632) act 3, sc. 3

5 Oh that thou hadst like others been all
words,
And no performance.
The Parliament of Love (1624) act 4, sc. 2

6 Death has a thousand doors to let out life.
A Very Woman (licensed 1634) act 5, sc. 4.
Cf. 142:4, 270:8, 344:18

## Sir James Mathew 1830–1908

7 In England, justice is open to all—like the
Ritz Hotel.
In R. E. Megarry Miscellany-at-Law (1955)
p. 254. Cf. 7:9

## W. Somerset Maugham 1874–1965

8 The most useful thing about a principle is
that it can always be sacrificed to
expediency.
The Circle (1921) act 3

9 Impropriety is the soul of wit.
The Moon and Sixpence (1919) ch. 4

10 A woman can forgive a man for the harm
he does her, but she can never forgive him
for the sacrifices he makes on her account.
The Moon and Sixpence (1919) ch. 41

11 Money is like a sixth sense without which
you cannot make a complete use of the
other five.
Of Human Bondage (1915) ch. 51

12 Few misfortunes can befall a boy which
bring worse consequences than to have
a really affectionate mother.
A Writer's Notebook (1949) p. 27 (written in
1896)

## Bill Mauldin 1921–

13 I feel like a fugitive from th' law of
averages.
Cartoon caption in Up Front (1945)

## James Maxton 1885–1946

14 All I say is, if you cannot ride two horses
you have no right in the circus.
Opposing disaffiliation of the Scottish
Independent Labour Party from the Labour
Party, in Daily Herald 12 January 1931
(usually quoted ' . . . no right in the bloody
circus')

## Vladimir Mayakovsky 1893–1930

15 If you wish—
. . . I'll be irreproachably tender;
not a man, but—a cloud in trousers!
'The Cloud in Trousers' (1915) (tr. S.
Charteris)

16 The poet is always indebted to the
universe, paying interest and fines on
sorrow.
'Conversation with an Inspector of Taxes
about Poetry' (1926) (tr. D. Obolensky)

## Shepherd Mead 1914–

17 How to succeed in business without really
trying.
Title of book (1952)

## Hughes Mearns 1875–1965

18 As I was walking up the stair
I met a man who wasn't there.
He wasn't there again today.
I wish, I wish he'd stay away.
Lines written for an amateur play The
Psycho-ed (1910) and set to music in 1939 as
'The Little Man Who Wasn't There'

## Dame Nellie Melba 1861–1931

19 Sing 'em muck! It's all they can
understand!
Advice to Dame Clara Butt, prior to her
departure for Australia; in W. H. Ponder
Clara Butt (1928) ch. 12

## Lord Melbourne 1779–1848

20 Now, is it to lower the price of corn, or
isn't it? It is not much matter which we
say, but mind, we must all say the same.
Attributed, in Walter Bagehot The English
Constitution (1867) ch. 1, p. 16 n.

21 God help the Minister that meddles with
art!
In Lord David Cecil Lord M (1954) ch. 3

22 What I want is men who will support me
when I am in the wrong.
Replying to a politician who said 'I will
support you as long as you are in the right';
in Lord David Cecil Lord M (1954) ch. 4

23 Things have come to a pretty pass when
religion is allowed to invade the sphere of
private life.
On hearing an evangelical sermon; in
G. W. E. Russell Collections and Recollections
(1898) ch. 6

## Herman Melville 1819–91

1 Call me Ishmael.
*Moby Dick* (1851) ch. 1

2 Delight,—top-gallant delight is to him, who acknowledges no law or lord, but the Lord his God, and is only a patriot to heaven.
*Moby Dick* (1851) ch. 9

3 A whaleship was my Yale College and my Harvard.
*Moby Dick* (1851) ch. 24

4 Towards thee I roll, thou all-destroying but unconquering whale ... from hell's heart I stab at thee.
*Moby Dick* (1851) ch. 135

## Menander 342–c.292 BC

5 Whom the gods love dies young.
*Dis Exapaton* fragment 4, in F. H. Sandbach (ed.) *Menandri Reliquiae Selectae* (1990)

## H. L. Mencken 1880–1956

6 Love is the delusion that one woman differs from another.
*Chrestomathy* (1949) ch. 30

7 Puritanism. The haunting fear that someone, somewhere, may be happy.
*Chrestomathy* (1949) ch. 30

8 Conscience: the inner voice which warns us that someone may be looking.
*A Little Book in C major* (1916) p. 42

## Johnny Mercer 1909–76

9 You've got to ac-cent-tchu-ate the positive
Elim-my-nate the negative
Latch on to the affirmative
Don't mess with Mister In-between.
'Ac-cent-tchu-ate the Positive' (1944 song)

10 Jeepers Creepers—where you get them peepers?
'Jeepers Creepers' (1938 song)

11 We're drinking my friend,
To the end of a brief episode,
Make it one for my baby
And one more for the road.
'One For My Baby' (1943 song)

## George Meredith 1828–1909

12 A witty woman is a treasure; a witty beauty is a power.
*Diana of the Crossways* (1885) ch. 1

13 'Tis Ireland gives England her soldiers, her generals too.
*Diana of the Crossways* (1885) ch. 2

14 Cynicism is intellectual dandyism without the coxcomb's feathers.
*The Egoist* (1879) ch. 7

15 None of your dam punctilio.
*One of Our Conquerors* (1891) ch. 1

16 I expect that Woman will be the last thing civilized by Man.
*The Ordeal of Richard Feverel* (1859) ch. 1

17 Kissing don't last: cookery do!
*The Ordeal of Richard Feverel* (1859) ch. 28

18 Speech is the small change of silence.
*The Ordeal of Richard Feverel* (1859) ch. 34

19 The lark ascending.
Title of poem (1881)

20 She whom I love is hard to catch and conquer,
Hard, but O the glory of the winning were she won!
'Love in the Valley' st. 2

21 On a starred night Prince Lucifer uprose. Tired of his dark dominion swung the fiend.
'Lucifer in Starlight' (1883)

22 Around the ancient track marched, rank on rank,
The army of unalterable law.
'Lucifer in Starlight' (1883)

23 'I play for Seasons; not Eternities!'
Says Nature.
*Modern Love* (1862) st. 13

24 Ah, what a dusty answer gets the soul
When hot for certainties in this our life!
*Modern Love* (1862) st. 50

## Owen Meredith (Earl of Lytton) 1831–91

25 Genius does what it must, and Talent does what it can.
'Last Words of a Sensitive Second-Rate Poet' (1868)

## Dixon Lanier Merritt 1879–1972

26 Oh, a wondrous bird is the pelican!
His beak holds more than his belican.
He takes in his beak
Food enough for a week.
But I'll be darned if I know how the helican.
In *Nashville Banner* 22 April 1913

## Le Curé Meslier c.1664–1733

27 An ignorant, uneducated man [said he wished] that all the great men in the world and all the nobility could be hanged, and strangled with the guts of priests.
*Testament* (ed. R. Charles, 1864) vol. 1, ch. 2 (often quoted 'I should like ... the last of the kings to be strangled with the guts of the last priest')

## Methodist Service Book 1975

28 I am no longer my own, but yours. Put me to what you will, rank me with whom you will; put me to doing, put me to suffering.
The Covenant Prayer (based on the words of Richard Alleine in the First Covenant Service, 1782)

## Prince Metternich 1773–1859

1 The Emperor is everything, Vienna is
nothing.
  Letter to Count Bombelles, 5 June 1848, in
  *Aus Metternich's Nachgelassene Papieren* (ed. A.
  von Klinkowström, 1880) vol. 8, p. 426

2 Error has never approached my spirit.
  Addressed to Guizot in 1848, in F. Guizot
  *Mémoires* (1858–67) vol. 4, p. 21

3 Italy is a geographical expression.
  Discussing the Italian question with
  Palmerston in 1847; in *Mémoires, Documents,
  etc. de Metternich publiés par son fils* (1883)
  vol. 7, p. 415

## Sir Anthony Meyer 1920–

4 I question the right of that great Moloch,
national sovereignty, to burn its children
to save its pride.
  Speaking against the Falklands War, 1982; in
  *Listener* 27 September 1990, p. 31

## Thomas Middleton c.1580–1627

5 Anything for a quiet life.
  Title of play (c.1620, possibly with John
  Webster)

6 I could not get the ring without the finger.
  *The Changeling* (with William Rowley, c.1622)
  act 3, sc. 4

7 Y'are the deed's creature.
  *The Changeling* (with William Rowley, c.1622)
  act 3, sc. 4

8 My study's ornament, thou shell of death,
Once the bright face of my betrothèd lady.
  *The Revenger's Tragedy* (1607, previously
  attributed to Cyril Tourneur, c.1575–1626)
  act 1, sc. 1

9 Does the silk-worm expend her yellow
labours
For thee? for thee does she undo herself?
  *The Revenger's Tragedy* (1607) act 3, sc. 5

## George Mikes 1912–

10 On the Continent people have good food;
in England people have good table
manners.
  *How to be an Alien* (1946) p. 10

11 Continental people have sex life; the
English have hot-water bottles.
  *How to be an Alien* (1946) p. 25

12 An Englishman, even if he is alone, forms
an orderly queue of one.
  *How to be an Alien* (1946) p. 44

## John Stuart Mill 1806–73

13 Ask yourself whether you are happy, and
you cease to be so.
  *Autobiography* (1873) ch. 5

14 Detention by the State of the unearned
increment of rent.
  *Dissertations and Discussions* vol. 4 (1875) 'The
  Right of Property in Land'

15 The only purpose for which power can be
rightfully exercised over any member of a
civilized community, against his will, is to
prevent harm to others. His own good,
either physical or moral, is not a sufficient
warrant.
  *On Liberty* (1859) ch. 1

16 The liberty of the individual must be thus
far limited; he must not make himself a
nuisance to other people.
  *On Liberty* (1859) ch. 3

17 Liberty consists in doing what one desires.
  *On Liberty* (1859) ch. 5

18 Everyone who desires power, desires it
most over those who are nearest to him,
with whom his life is passed, with whom
he has most concerns in common, and in
whom any independence of his authority is
oftenest likely to interfere with his
individual preferences.
  *The Subjection of Women* (1869) ch. 1

19 The laws of most countries are far worse
than the people who execute them, and
many of them are only able to remain laws
by being seldom or never carried into
effect. If married life were all that it might
be expected to be, looking to the laws
alone, society would be a hell upon earth.
  *The Subjection of Women* (1869) ch. 2

20 The true virtue of human beings is fitness
to live together as equals; claiming
nothing for themselves but what they as
freely concede to everyone else; regarding
command of any kind as an exceptional
necessity, and in all cases a temporary one.
  *The Subjection of Women* (1869) ch. 2

## Edna St Vincent Millay 1892–1950

21 Childhood is the kingdom where nobody
dies.
Nobody that matters, that is.
  'Childhood is the Kingdom where Nobody
  dies' (1934)

22 My candle burns at both ends;
It will not last the night;
But ah, my foes, and oh, my friends—
It gives a lovely light.
  *A Few Figs From Thistles* (1920) 'First Fig'

23 After all, my erstwhile dear,
My no longer cherished,
Need we say it was not love,
Now that love is perished?
  'Passer Mortuus Est' (1921)

## Alice Duer Miller 1874–1942

24 I am American bred,
I have seen much to hate here—much to
forgive,
But in a world where England is finished
and dead,
I do not wish to live.
  *The White Cliffs* (1940) p. 70

## Arthur Miller 1915–

1 A suicide kills two people, Maggie, that's
what it's for!
*After the Fall* (1964) act 2

2 The world is an oyster, but you don't crack
it open on a mattress.
*Death of a Salesman* (1949) act 1

3 Willy Loman never made a lot of money.
His name was never in the paper. He's not
the finest character that ever lived. But
he's a human being, and a terrible thing is
happening to him. So attention must be
paid.
*Death of a Salesman* (1949) act 1

4 He's a man way out there in the blue,
riding on a smile and a shoeshine. And
when they start not smiling back—that's
an earthquake ... A salesman is got to
dream, boy. It comes with the territory.
*Death of a Salesman* (1949) 'Requiem'

5 This is Red Hook, not Sicily ... This is the
gullet of New York swallowing the tonnage
of the world.
*A View from the Bridge* (1955) act 1

6 A good newspaper, I suppose, is a nation
talking to itself.
In *Observer* 26 November 1961

## Henry Miller 1891–1980

7 Every man with a bellyful of the classics is
an enemy to the human race.
*Tropic of Cancer* (1934) p. 280

## Jonathan Miller 1934–

8 I'm not really a *Jew*. Just Jew-*ish*. Not the
whole hog, you know.
*Beyond the Fringe* (1960 review) 'Real Class'

## William Miller 1810–72

9 Wee Willie Winkie rins through the town,
Up stairs and down stairs in his nicht-
gown.
'Willie Winkie' (1841)

## Spike Milligan 1918–

10 You silly twisted boy.
*The Goon Show* (BBC radio series) 'The
Dreaded Batter Pudding Hurler' (12 October
1954)

11 Money couldn't buy friends but you got
a better class of enemy.
*Puckoon* (1963) ch. 6

## A. J. Mills et al.

12 Take me back to dear old Blighty.
Title of song (1916)

## Henry Hart Milman 1791–1868

13 Ride on! ride on in majesty!
The wingèd squadrons of the sky
Look down with sad and wond'ring eyes
To see the approaching sacrifice.
'Ride on! ride on in majesty!' (1827 hymn)

## A. A. Milne 1882–1956

14 The more he looked inside the more Piglet
wasn't there.
*The House at Pooh Corner* (1928) ch. 1

15 When you are a Bear of Very Little Brain,
and you Think of Things, you find
sometimes that a Thing which seemed very
Thingish inside you is quite different when
it gets out into the open and has other
people looking at it.
*The House at Pooh Corner* (1928) ch. 6

16 Time for a little something.
*Winnie-the-Pooh* (1926) ch. 6

17 My spelling is Wobbly. It's good spelling
but it Wobbles, and the letters get in the
wrong places.
*Winnie-the-Pooh* (1926) ch. 6

18 Owl hasn't exactly got Brain, but he Knows
Things.
*Winnie-the-Pooh* (1926) ch. 9

19 They're changing guard at Buckingham
Palace—
Christopher Robin went down with Alice.
Alice is marrying one of the guard.
'A soldier's life is terrible hard,'
Says Alice.
'Buckingham Palace' (1924)

20 James James
Morrison Morrison
Weatherby George Dupree
Took great
Care of his Mother,
Though he was only three.
James James
Said to his Mother,
'Mother,' he said, said he;
'You must never go down to the end of the
town, if you don't go down with me.'
'Disobedience' (1924)

21 There once was a Dormouse who lived in a
bed
Of delphiniums (blue) and geraniums (red),
And all the day long he'd a wonderful view
Of geraniums (red) and delphiniums (blue).
'The Dormouse and the Doctor' (1924)

22 The King asked
The Queen, and
The Queen asked
The Dairymaid:
'Could we have some butter for
The Royal slice of bread?'
'The King's Breakfast' (1924)

23 *What* is the matter with Mary Jane?
She's perfectly well and she hasn't a pain,
*And it's lovely rice pudding for dinner again!*
What *is* the matter with Mary Jane?
'Rice Pudding' (1924)

1 Little Boy kneels at the foot of the bed,
Droops on the little hands little gold head.
Hush! Hush! Whisper who dares!
Christopher Robin is saying his prayers.
  'Vespers' (1924)

## Lord Milner 1854–1925

2 If we believe a thing to be bad, and if we
have a right to prevent it, it is our duty to
try to prevent it and to damn the
consequences.
  Speech, 26 November 1909, in *The Times*
  27 November 1909

## John Milton 1608–74

3 Such sweet compulsion doth in music lie.
  'Arcades' (1645) l. 68

4 Blest pair of Sirens, pledges of heaven's joy,
Sphere-born harmonious sisters, Voice, and
Verse.
  'At a Solemn Music' (1645)

5 Above the smoke and stir of this dim spot,
Which men call earth.
  *Comus* (1637) l. 5

6 An old and haughty nation proud in arms.
  *Comus* (1637) l. 33

7 And the gilded car of day
His glowing axle doth allay
In the steep Atlantic stream.
  *Comus* (1637) l. 95

8 What hath night to do with sleep?
  *Comus* (1637) l. 122

9 Come, knit hands, and beat the ground,
In a light fantastic round.
  *Comus* (1637) l. 143. Cf. 227:2

10 Sweet Echo, sweetest nymph that liv'st
unseen
Within thy airy shell
By slow Meander's margent green,
And in the violet-embroidered vale.
  *Comus* (1637) l. 230

11 Virtue could see to do what Virtue would
By her own radiant light, though sun and
moon
Were in the flat sea sunk.
  *Comus* (1637) l. 373

12 He that has light within his own clear
breast
May sit i' the centre, and enjoy bright day,
But he that hides a dark soul, and foul
thoughts
Benighted walks under the midday sun;
Himself is his own dungeon.
  *Comus* (1637) l. 381

13 Yet where an equal poise of hope and fear
Does arbitrate the event, my nature is
That I incline to hope, rather than fear,
And gladly banish squint suspicion.
  *Comus* (1637) l. 410

14 'Tis chastity, my brother, chastity:
She that has that, is clad in complete steel.
  *Comus* (1637) l. 420

15 How charming is divine philosophy!
Not harsh and crabbèd, as dull fools
suppose,
But musical as is Apollo's lute.
  *Comus* (1637) l. 475

16 Storied of old in high immortal verse
Of dire chimeras and enchanted isles,
And rifted rocks whose entrance leads to
hell.
  *Comus* (1637) l. 516

17 And filled the air with barbarous
dissonance.
  *Comus* (1637) l. 550

18                     Against the threats
Of malice or of sorcery, or that power
Which erring men call chance, this I hold
firm,
Virtue may be assailed, but never hurt,
Surprised by unjust force, but not
enthralled.
  *Comus* (1637) l. 586

19 Those budge doctors of the Stoic fur.
  *Comus* (1637) l. 707

20 Beauty is Nature's brag, and must be
shown
In courts, at feasts, and high solemnities
Where most may wonder at the
workmanship.
  *Comus* (1637) l. 745

21 Sabrina fair,
Listen where thou art sitting
Under the glassy, cool, translucent wave,
In twisted braids of lilies knitting
The loose train of thy amber-dropping hair.
  *Comus* (1637) l. 859 'Song'

22 Hence, vain deluding joys,
The brood of folly without father bred.
  'Il Penseroso' (1645) l. 1

23 As thick and numberless
As the gay motes that people the
sunbeams.
  'Il Penseroso' (1645) l. 7

24 Come, pensive nun, devout and pure,
Sober, steadfast, and demure.
  'Il Penseroso' (1645) l. 31

25 Where glowing embers through the room
Teach light to counterfeit a gloom,
Far from all resort of mirth,
Save the cricket on the hearth.
  'Il Penseroso' (1645) l. 79

26 Hide me from day's garish eye.
  'Il Penseroso' (1645) l. 141

27 Hence, loathèd Melancholy,
Of Cerberus, and blackest Midnight born,
In Stygian cave forlorn
'Mongst horrid shapes, and shrieks, and
sights unholy.
  'L'Allegro' (1645) l. 1

28 So buxom, blithe, and debonair.
  'L'Allegro' (1645) l. 24

1 Haste thee nymph, and bring with thee
Jest and youthful jollity,
Quips and cranks, and wanton wiles,
Nods, and becks, and wreathèd smiles.
'L'Allegro' (1645) l. 25

2 Sport that wrinkled Care derides,
And Laughter holding both his sides.
Come, and trip it as ye go
On the light fantastic toe.
'L'Allegro' (1645) l. 31. Cf. 226:9

3 Where perhaps some beauty lies,
The cynosure of neighbouring eyes.
'L'Allegro' (1645) l. 79

4 And the jocund rebecks sound
To many a youth, and many a maid,
Dancing in the chequered shade.
'L'Allegro' (1645) l. 94

5 Then to the spicy nut-brown ale.
'L'Allegro' (1645) l. 100

6 Towered cities please us then,
And the busy hum of men.
'L'Allegro' (1645) l. 117

7 Such sights as youthful poets dream
On summer eves by haunted stream.
'L'Allegro' (1645) l. 129

8 Then to the well-trod stage anon,
If Jonson's learnèd sock be on,
Or sweetest Shakespeare fancy's child,
Warble his native wood-notes wild.
'L'Allegro' (1645) l. 131

9 Let us with a gladsome mind
Praise the Lord, for he is kind,
For his mercies ay endure,
Ever faithful, ever sure.
'Let us with a gladsome mind' (1645);
paraphrase of Psalm 136

10 Yet once more, O ye laurels, and once more
Ye myrtles brown, with ivy never sere.
'Lycidas' (1638) l. 1

11 He must not float upon his watery bier
Unwept, and welter to the parching wind,
Without the meed of some melodious tear.
'Lycidas' (1638) l. 12

12 For we were nursed upon the self-same
hill.
'Lycidas' (1638) l. 23

13                    The woods, and desert caves,
With wild thyme and the gadding vine
o'ergrown.
'Lycidas' (1638) l. 39

14 Were it not better done as others use,
To sport with Amaryllis in the shade,
Or with the tangles of Neaera's hair?
Fame is the spur that the clear spirit doth
raise
(That last infirmity of noble mind)
To scorn delights, and live laborious days.
'Lycidas' (1638) l. 67

15                    Their lean and flashy songs
Grate on their scrannel pipes of wretched
straw.
'Lycidas' (1638) l. 123

16 But that two-handed engine at the door
Stands ready to smite once, and smite no
more.
'Lycidas' (1638) l. 130

17 Look homeward angel now, and melt with
ruth.
'Lycidas' (1638) l. 163

18 So sinks the day-star in the ocean bed,
And yet anon repairs his drooping head,
And tricks his beams, and with new
spangled ore,
Flames in the forehead of the morning sky.
'Lycidas' (1638) l. 168

19 While the still morn went out with sandals
grey.
'Lycidas' (1638) l. 187

20 Tomorrow to fresh woods, and pastures
new.
'Lycidas' (1638) l. 193

21 What needs my Shakespeare for his
honoured bones,
The labour of an age in pilèd stones.
'On Shakespeare' (1632)

22 O fairest flower no sooner blown but
blasted.
'On the Death of a Fair Infant Dying of a
Cough' (1673) st. 1

23 For what can war, but endless war still
breed?
'On the Lord General Fairfax at the Siege of
Colchester' (written 1648)

24 The star-led wizards haste with odours
sweet.
'On the Morning of Christ's Nativity' (1645)
st. 4

25 It was the winter wild,
While the heaven-born-child
All meanly wrapped in the rude manger
lies;
Nature in awe to him
Had doffed her gaudy trim,
With her great master so to sympathize.
'On the Morning of Christ's Nativity' (1645)
'The Hymn' st. 1

26 No war, or battle's sound
Was heard the world around.
'On the Morning of Christ's Nativity' (1645)
'The Hymn' st. 4

27 Time will run back, and fetch the age of
gold.
'On the Morning of Christ's Nativity' (1645)
'The Hymn' st. 14

28 And hell itself will pass away,
And leave her dolorous mansions to the
peering day.
'On the Morning of Christ's Nativity' (1645)
'The Hymn' st. 14

29 So when the sun in bed,
Curtained with cloudy red,
Pillows his chin upon an orient wave.
'On the Morning of Christ's Nativity' (1645)
'The Hymn' st. 26

1 Time is our tedious song should here have
   ending.
   'On the Morning of Christ's Nativity' (1645)
   'The Hymn' st. 27

2 New *Presbyter* is but old *Priest* writ large.
   'On the New Forcers of Conscience under the
   Long Parliament' (1646)

3 Fly envious Time, till thou run out thy
   race,
   Call on the lazy leaden-stepping hours.
   'On Time' (1645)

4 If any ask for him, it shall be said,
   Hobson has supped, and's newly gone to
   bed.
   'On the University Carrier' (1645)

5 Rhyme being ... but the invention of a
   barbarous age, to set off wretched matter
   and lame metre.
   *Paradise Lost* (1667) 'The Verse' (preface, 1668)

6 The troublesome and modern bondage of
   rhyming.
   *Paradise Lost* (1667) 'The Verse' (preface, 1668)

7 Of man's first disobedience, and the fruit
   Of that forbidden tree, whose mortal taste
   Brought death into the world, and all our
   woe,
   With loss of Eden.
   *Paradise Lost* (1667) bk. 1, l. 1

8 Things unattempted yet in prose or rhyme.
   *Paradise Lost* (1667) bk. 1, l. 16

9          What in me is dark
   Illumine, what is low raise and support;
   That to the height of this great argument
   I may assert eternal providence,
   And justify the ways of God to men.
   *Paradise Lost* (1667) bk. 1, l. 22

10 No light, but rather darkness visible
   Served only to discover sights of woe.
   *Paradise Lost* (1667) bk. 1, l. 63

11 And out of good still to find means of evil.
   *Paradise Lost* (1667) bk. 1, l. 165

12 The mind is its own place, and in itself
   Can make a heaven of hell, a hell of
   heaven.
   *Paradise Lost* (1667) bk. 1, l. 254

13 Better to reign in hell, than serve in
   heaven.
   *Paradise Lost* (1667) bk. 1, l. 263

14 Thick as autumnal leaves that strew the
   brooks
   In Vallombrosa, where the Etrurian shades
   High overarched imbower.
   *Paradise Lost* (1667) bk. 1, l. 302

15          When night
   Darkens the streets, then wander forth the
   sons
   Of Belial, flown with insolence and wine.
   *Paradise Lost* (1667) bk. 1, l. 500

16 A shout that tore hell's concave, and
   beyond
   Frighted the reign of Chaos and old Night.
   *Paradise Lost* (1667) bk. 1, l. 542

17 In dim eclipse disastrous twilight sheds
   On half the nations, and with fear of
   change
   Perplexes monarchs.
   *Paradise Lost* (1667) bk. 1, l. 597

18          Who overcomes
   By force, hath overcome but half his foe.
   *Paradise Lost* (1667) bk. 1, l. 648

19          Let none admire
   That riches grow in hell; that soil may best
   Deserve the precious bane.
   *Paradise Lost* (1667) bk. 1, l. 690

20          From morn
   To noon he fell, from noon to dewy eve,
   A summer's day; and with the setting sun
   Dropped from the zenith like a falling star.
   *Paradise Lost* (1667) bk. 1, l. 742

21 ... Pandemonium, the high capital
   Of Satan and his peers.
   *Paradise Lost* (1667) bk. 1, l. 756

22 His trust was with the eternal to be
   deemed
   Equal in strength, and rather than be less
   Cared not to be at all.
   *Paradise Lost* (1667) bk. 2, l. 46

23 But all was false and hollow; though his
   tongue
   Dropped manna, and could make the
   worse appear
   The better reason.
   *Paradise Lost* (1667) bk. 2, l. 112. Cf. 15:10

24 To perish rather, swallowed up and lost
   In the wide womb of uncreated night,
   Devoid of sense and motion.
   *Paradise Lost* (1667) bk. 2, l. 149

25 Unrespited, unpitied, unreprieved,
   Ages of hopeless end.
   *Paradise Lost* (1667) bk. 2, l. 185

26 Our torments also may in length of time
   Become our elements.
   *Paradise Lost* (1667) bk. 2, l. 274

27          With grave
   Aspect he rose, and in his rising seemed
   A pillar of state; deep on his front
   engraven
   Deliberation sat and public care;
   And princely counsel in his face yet shone,
   Majestic though in ruin.
   *Paradise Lost* (1667) bk. 2, l. 300

28          To sit in darkness here
   Hatching vain empires.
   *Paradise Lost* (1667) bk. 2, l. 377

29 And through the palpable obscure find out
   His uncouth way.
   *Paradise Lost* (1667) bk. 2, l. 406

30          Long is the way
   And hard, that out of hell leads up to light.
   *Paradise Lost* (1667) bk. 2, l. 432

31 Eloquence the soul, song charms the sense.
   *Paradise Lost* (1667) bk. 2, l. 556

32 Sable-vested Night, eldest of things.
   *Paradise Lost* (1667) bk. 2, l. 962

1 With ruin upon ruin, rout on rout,
Confusion worse confounded.
*Paradise Lost* (1667) bk. 2, l. 995

2 So he with difficulty and labour hard
Moved on, with difficulty and labour he.
*Paradise Lost* (1667) bk. 2, l. 1021

3 Die he or justice must.
*Paradise Lost* (1667) bk. 3, l. 210

4 Dark with excessive bright.
*Paradise Lost* (1667) bk. 3, l. 380

5 Hypocrisy, the only evil that walks
Invisible, except to God alone.
*Paradise Lost* (1667) bk. 3, l. 683

6 Me miserable! which way shall I fly
Infinite wrath, and infinite despair?
Which way I fly is hell; myself am hell.
*Paradise Lost* (1667) bk. 4, l. 73

7 Farewell remorse! All good to me is lost;
Evil, be thou my good.
*Paradise Lost* (1667) bk. 4, l. 109

8 Flowers of all hue, and without thorn the
rose.
*Paradise Lost* (1667) bk. 4, l. 256

9 He for God only, she for God in him.
*Paradise Lost* (1667) bk. 4, l. 299

10 These two
Emparadised in one another's arms
The happier Eden, shall enjoy their fill
Of bliss on bliss.
*Paradise Lost* (1667) bk. 4, l. 505

11 Sweet the coming on
Of grateful evening mild, then silent night
With this her solemn bird and this fair
moon,
And these the gems of heaven, her starry
train.
*Paradise Lost* (1667) bk. 4, l. 646

12 Sleep on
Blest pair; and O yet happiest if ye seek
No happier state, and know to know no
more.
*Paradise Lost* (1667) bk. 4, l. 773

13 Him there they found
Squat like a toad, close at the ear of Eve.
*Paradise Lost* (1667) bk. 4, l. 799

14 But wherefore thou alone? Wherefore with
thee
Came not all hell broke loose?
*Paradise Lost* (1667) bk. 4, l. 917

15 My fairest, my espoused, my latest found,
Heaven's last best gift, my ever new
delight.
*Paradise Lost* (1667) bk. 5, l. 18

16 Best image of myself and dearer half.
*Paradise Lost* (1667) bk. 5, l. 95

17 Nor jealousy
Was understood, the injured lover's hell.
*Paradise Lost* (1667) bk. 5, l. 449

18 What if earth
Be but the shadow of heaven, and things
therein
Each to other like, more than on earth is
thought?
*Paradise Lost* (1667) bk. 5, l. 574

19 Still govern thou my song,
Urania, and fit audience find, though few.
*Paradise Lost* (1667) bk. 7, l. 30

20 So absolute she seems
And in herself complete, so well to know
Her own, that what she wills to do or say
Seems wisest, virtuousest, discreetest, best.
*Paradise Lost* (1667) bk. 8, l. 547

21 And dictates to me slumbering, or inspires
Easy my unpremeditated verse.
*Paradise Lost* (1667) bk. 9, l. 23

22 The serpent subtlest beast of all the field.
*Paradise Lost* (1667) bk. 9, l. 86

23 As one who long in populous city pent,
Where houses thick and sewers annoy the
air,
Forth issuing on a summer's morn to
breathe
Among the pleasant villages and farms
Adjoined, from each thing met conceives
delight.
*Paradise Lost* (1667) bk. 9, l. 445

24 She fair, divinely fair, fit love for gods.
*Paradise Lost* (1667) bk. 9, l. 489

25 God so commanded, and left that
command
Sole daughter of his voice; the rest, we live
Law to our selves, our reason is our law.
*Paradise Lost* (1667) bk. 9, l. 652

26 Earth felt the wound, and Nature from her
seat
Sighing through all her works gave signs
of woe
That all was lost.
*Paradise Lost* (1

27 O fairest of creation, last and best
Of all God's works.
*Paradise Lost* (1667) bk. 9, l. 896

28 Flesh of flesh,
Bone of my bone thou art, and from thy
state
Mine never shall be parted, bliss or woe.
*Paradise Lost* (1667) bk. 9, l. 914

29 ... Yet I shall temper so
Justice with mercy.
*Paradise Lost* (1667) bk. 10, l. 77

30 This novelty on earth, this fair defect
Of nature.
*Paradise Lost* (1667) bk. 10, l. 891

31 Demoniac frenzy, moping melancholy
And moon-struck madness.
*Paradise Lost* (1667) bk. 11, l. 485

32 ... The evening star,
Love's harbinger.
*Paradise Lost* (1667) bk. 11, l. 588

1  In me is no delay; with thee to go,
   Is to stay here; without thee here to stay,
   Is to go hence unwilling.
   *Paradise Lost* (1667) bk. 12, l. 615

2  The world was all before them, where to
   choose
   Their place of rest, and Providence their
   guide:
   They hand in hand, with wandering steps
   and slow,
   Through Eden took their solitary way.
   *Paradise Lost* (1667) bk. 12, l. 646

3  Of whom to be dispraised were no small
   praise.
   *Paradise Regained* (1671) bk. 3, l. 56

4  But on occasion's forelock watchful wait.
   *Paradise Regained* (1671) bk. 3, l. 173

5  He who seeking asses found a kingdom.
   *Paradise Regained* (1671) bk. 3, l. 242 (of Saul).
   See Samuel ch. 9, v. 3

6  Athens, the eye of Greece, mother of arts
   And eloquence . . .
   See there the olive grove of Academe,
   Plato's retirement, where the Attic bird
   Trills her thick-warbled notes the summer
   long.
   *Paradise Regained* (1671) bk. 4, l. 240

7  The first and wisest of them all professed
   To know this only, that he nothing knew.
   *Paradise Regained* (1671) bk. 4, l. 293.
   Cf. 310:21

8  Deep-versed in books and shallow in
   himself.
   *Paradise Regained* (1671) bk. 4, l. 327

9  But headlong joy is ever on the wing.
   'The Passion' (1645) st. 1

10 Ask for this great deliverer now, and find
   him
   Eyeless in Gaza at the mill with slaves.
   *Samson Agonistes* (1671) l. 40

11 O dark, dark, dark, amid the blaze of noon,
   Irrecoverably dark, total eclipse
   Without all hope of day!
   *Samson Agonistes* (1671) l. 80

12 The sun to me is dark
   And silent as the moon,
   When she deserts the night
   Hid in her vacant interlunar cave.
   *Samson Agonistes* (1671) l. 86

13 To live a life half dead, a living death.
   *Samson Agonistes* (1671) l. 100

14 Just are the ways of God,
   And justifiable to men;
   Unless there be who think not God at all.
   *Samson Agonistes* (1671) l. 293

15 Love-quarrels oft in pleasing concord end.
   *Samson Agonistes* (1671) l. 1008

16 Lords are lordliest in their wine.
   *Samson Agonistes* (1671) l. 1418

17              Samson hath quit himself
   Like Samson, and heroically hath finished
   A life heroic.
   *Samson Agonistes* (1671) l. 1709

18 Nothing is here for tears.
   *Samson Agonistes* (1671) l. 1721

19 Calm of mind, all passion spent.
   *Samson Agonistes* (1671) l. 1758

20 Time the subtle thief of youth.
   Sonnet 7 'How soon hath time' (1645)

21 Licence they mean when they cry liberty;
   For who loves that, must first be wise and
   good.
   Sonnet 12 'I did but prompt the age' (1673)

22 When I consider how my light is spent,
   E're half my days, in this dark world and
   wide,
   And that one talent which is death to hide
   Lodged with me useless.
   Sonnet 16 'When I consider how my light is
   spent' (1673)

23 They also serve who only stand and wait.
   Sonnet 16 'When I consider how my light is
   spent' (1673)

24 Methought I saw my late espousèd saint
   Brought to me like Alcestis from the grave.
   Sonnet 19 'Methought I saw my late espousèd
   saint' (1673)

25 But oh as to embrace me she inclined
   I waked, she fled, and day brought back my
   night.
   Sonnet 19 'Methought I saw my late espousèd
   saint' (1673)

26 Cromwell, our chief of men.
   'To the Lord General Cromwell' (written
   1652)

27 . . . Peace hath her victories
   No less renowned than war.
   'To the Lord General Cromwell' (written
   1652)

28 He who would not be frustrate of his hope
   to write well hereafter in laudable things,
   ought himself to be a true poem.
   *An Apology for Smectymnuus* (1642)
   introduction, p. 16

29 As good almost kill a man as kill a good
   book: who kills a man kills a reasonable
   creature, God's image; but he who destroys
   a good book, kills reason itself, kills the
   image of God, as it were in the eye.
   *Areopagitica* (1644) p. 4

30 A good book is the precious life-blood of a
   master spirit.
   *Areopagitica* (1644) p. 4

31 I cannot praise a fugitive and cloistered
   virtue, unexercised and unbreathed, that
   never sallies out and sees her adversary,
   but slinks out of the race, where that
   immortal garland is to be run for, not
   without dust and heat . . . that which
   purifies us is trial, and trial is by what is
   contrary.
   *Areopagitica* (1644) p. 12

32 If we think to regulate printing, thereby to
   rectify manners, we must regulate all
   recreations and pastimes, all that is
   delightful to man.
   *Areopagitica* (1644) p. 16

1 And who shall silence all the airs and
madrigals, that whisper softness in
chambers?
*Areopagitica* (1644) p. 16

2 What does he [God] then but reveal
Himself to his servants, and as his manner
is, first to his Englishmen?
*Areopagitica* (1644) p. 31

3 City of refuge, the mansion-house of
liberty.
*Areopagitica* (1644) p. 31 (of London)

4 Opinion in good men is but knowledge in
the making.
*Areopagitica* (1644) p. 31

5 Let not England forget her precedence of
teaching nations how to live.
*The Doctrine and Discipline of Divorce* (1643) 'To
the Parliament of England'

6 What I have spoken, is the language of
that which is not called amiss *The good old
Cause.*
*The Ready and Easy Way to Establish a Free
Commonwealth* (2nd ed., 1660) p. 106

7 None can love freedom heartily, but good
men; the rest love not freedom, but
licence.
*The Tenure of Kings and Magistrates* (1649)

## Comte de Mirabeau 1749–91

8 War is the national industry of Prussia.
Attributed to Mirabeau by Albert Sorel
(1842–1906), on the basis of Mirabeau's
introduction to *De la monarchie prussienne sous
Frédéric le Grand* (1788)

## The Missal

9 *Dominus vobiscum.
Et cum spiritu tuo.*
The Lord be with you.
And with thy spirit.
*Ordinary of the Mass*

10 *In Nomine Patris, et Filii, et Spiritus Sancti.*
In the Name of the Father, and of the Son,
and of the Holy Ghost.
*Ordinary of the Mass*

11 *Peccavi nimis cogitatione, verbo, et opere, mea
culpa, mea culpa, mea maxima culpa.*
I have sinned exceedingly in thought,
word, and deed, through my fault, through
my fault, through my most grievous fault.
*Ordinary of the Mass*

12 *Kyrie eleison ... Christe eleison.*
Lord, have mercy upon us ... Christ, have
mercy upon us.
*Ordinary of the Mass*

13 *Gloria in excelsis Deo, et in terra pax hominibus
bonae voluntatis.*
Glory be to God on high, and on earth
peace to men of good will.
*Ordinary of the Mass.* Cf. 52:2

14 *Deo gratias.*
Thanks be to God.
*Ordinary of the Mass*

15 *Credo in unum Deum.*
I believe in one God.
*The Ordinary of the Mass* 'The Nicene Creed'.
Cf. 65:5

16 *Et homo factus est.*
And was made man.
*Ordinary of the Mass* 'The Nicene Creed'

17 *Sanctus, sanctus, sanctus, Dominus Deus
Sabaoth. Pleni sunt coeli et terra gloria tua.
Hosanna in excelsis. Benedictus qui venit in
nomine Domini.*
Holy, holy, holy, Lord God of Hosts. Heaven
and earth are full of thy glory. Hosanna in
the highest. Blessed is he that cometh in
the name of the Lord.
*Ordinary of the Mass*

18 *Pater noster, qui es in coelis, sanctificetur nomen
tuum.*
Our Father, who art in heaven, hallowed be
thy name.
*Ordinary of the Mass.* Cf. 48:27

19 *Agnus Dei, qui tollis peccata mundi, miserere
nobis.*
Lamb of God, who takest away the sins of
the world, have mercy on us.
*Ordinary of the Mass*

20 *Ite missa est.*
Go, you are dismissed.
*Ordinary of the Mass* (commonly interpreted as
'Go, the Mass is ended')

21 *Verbum caro factum est.*
The word was made flesh.
*Ordinary of the Mass.* Cf. 53:11

22 *Requiem aeternam dona eis, Domine: et lux
perpetua luceat eis.*
Grant them eternal rest, O Lord; and let
perpetual light shine on them.
*Order of Mass for the Dead*

23 *Dies irae, dies illa,
Solvet saeclum in favilla,
Teste David cum Sibylla.*
That day, the day of wrath, will turn the
universe to ashes, as David foretells (and
the Sibyl too).
*Order of Mass for the Dead* 'Sequentia'
(commonly known as *'Dies Irae'*) l. 1
(attributed to Thomas of Celano,
c.1190–1260)

24 *Rex tremendae maiestatis,
Qui salvandos salvas gratis,
Salva me, fons pietatis!*
O King of tremendous majesty, who freely
saves those who should be saved, save me,
O source of pity!
*Order of Mass for the Dead* 'Sequentia' l. 22

25 *Requiescant in pace.*
May they rest in peace.
*Order of Mass for the Dead*

**1** *O felix culpa, quae talem ac tantum meruit habere Redemptorem.*

O happy fault, which has earned such a mighty Redeemer.

'Exsultet' on Holy Saturday

## Adrian Mitchell 1932–

**2** Most people ignore most poetry
because
most poetry ignores most people.
*Poems* (1964) p. 8

## Joni Mitchell 1945–

**3** I've looked at life from both sides now,
From win and lose and still somehow
It's life's illusions I recall;
I really don't know life at all.
'Both Sides Now' (1967 song)

**4** We are stardust,
We are golden,
And we got to get ourselves
Back to the garden.
'Woodstock' (1969 song)

## Margaret Mitchell 1900–49

**5** Death and taxes and childbirth! There's never any convenient time for any of them.
*Gone with the Wind* (1936) ch. 38. Cf. 145:15

**6** I wish I could care what you do or where you go but I can't ... My dear, I don't give a damn.
*Gone with the Wind* (1936) ch. 57 (Rhett Butler to Scarlett). 'Frankly, my dear, I don't give a damn!' in Sidney Howard's 1939 screenplay

**7** After all, tomorrow is another day.
*Gone with the Wind* (1936) *ad fin.*

## Nancy Mitford 1904–73

**8** An aristocracy in a republic is like a chicken whose head has been cut off: it may run about in a lively way, but in fact it is dead.
*Noblesse Oblige* (1956) 'The English Aristocracy'

**9** Wooing, so tiring.
*The Pursuit of Love* (1945) ch. 4

**10** Abroad is unutterably bloody and foreigners are fiends.
*The Pursuit of Love* (1945) ch. 15. Cf. 150:4

## Wilson Mizner 1876–1933

**11** Be nice to people on your way up because you'll meet 'em on your way down.
In A. Johnston *The Legendary Mizners* (1953) ch. 4

**12** If you steal from one author, it's plagiarism; if you steal from many, it's research.
In A. Johnston *The Legendary Mizners* (1953) ch. 4

**13** A trip through a sewer in a glass-bottomed boat.
Of Hollywood, in A. Johnston *The Legendary Mizners* (1953) ch. 4

## Molière 1622–73

**14** One should eat to live, and not live to eat.
*L'Avare* (1669) act 3, sc. 1

**15** All that is not prose is verse; and all that is not verse is prose.
*Le Bourgeois Gentilhomme* (1671) act 2, sc. 4

**16** Good heavens! For more than forty years I have been speaking prose without knowing it.
*Le Bourgeois Gentilhomme* (1671) act 2, sc. 4

**17** One dies only once, and it's for such a long time!
*Le Dépit amoureux* (performed 1656) act 5, sc. 3

**18** A knowledgeable fool is a greater fool than an ignorant fool.
*Les Femmes savantes* (1672) act 4, sc. 3

**19** GÉRONTE: It seems to me you are locating them wrongly: the heart is on the left and the liver is on the right.
SGANARELLE: Yes, in the old days that was so, but we have changed all that.
*Le Médecin malgré lui* (1667) act 2, sc. 4

**20** What's needed in this world is an accommodating sort of virtue.
*Le Misanthrope* (1666) act 1, sc. 1

**21** Here they hang a man first, and try him afterwards.
*Monsieur de Pourceaugnac* (1670) act 1, sc. 5

**22** Assassination is the quickest way.
*Le Sicilien* (1668) sc. 12

**23** *Le ciel défend, de vrai, certains contentements, Mais on trouve avec lui des accommodements.*
God, it is true, does some delights condemn,
But 'tis not hard to come to terms with Him.
*Le Tartuffe* (1669) act 4, sc. 5

**24** *Le scandale du monde est ce qui fait l'offense, Et ce n'est pas pécher que pécher en silence.*
It is public scandal that constitutes offence, and to sin in secret is not to sin at all.
*Le Tartuffe* (1669) act 4, sc. 5

**25** *L'homme est, je vous l'avoue, un méchant animal.*
Man, I can assure you, is a nasty creature.
*Le Tartuffe* (1669) act 5, sc. 6

## William Cosmo Monkhouse 1840–1901

**26** There once was an old man of Lyme
Who married three wives at a time,
When asked 'Why a third?'
He replied, 'One's absurd!
And bigamy, Sir, is a crime!'
*Nonsense Rhymes* (1902)

## Duke of Monmouth 1649–85

1 Do not hack me as you did my Lord Russell.

> To his executioner, in T. B. Macaulay *History of England* vol. 1 (1849) ch. 5

## John Samuel Bewley Monsell 1811–75

2 Run the straight race through God's good grace,
Lift up thine eyes and seek his face;
Life with its way before us lies,
Christ is the path and Christ the prize.

> 'Fight the good fight with all thy might' (1863 hymn)

3 With gold of obedience and incense of lowliness,
Kneel and adore him: the Lord is his name.

> 'O worship the Lord in the beauty of holiness' (1863 hymn)

## Lady Mary Wortley Montagu 1689–1762

4 And we meet with champagne and a chicken at last.

> *Six Town Eclogues* (1747) 'The Lover' l. 25

5 Civility costs nothing and buys everything.

> Letter to her daughter, 30 May 1756, in R. Halsband (ed.) *Complete Letters* vol. 3 (1967)

6 People wish their enemies dead—but I do not; I say give them the gout, give them the stone!

> In W. S. Lewis et al. (eds.) *Horace Walpole's Correspondence* vol. 35 (1973) p. 489

## C. E. Montague 1867–1928

7 War hath no fury like a non-combatant.

> *Disenchantment* (1922) ch. 16

## Montaigne 1533–92

8 One should always have one's boots on, and be ready to leave.

> *Essais* (1580, ed. M. Rat, 1958) bk. 1, ch. 20. Cf. 199:13

9 I want death to find me planting my cabbages, but caring little for it, and even less about the imperfections of my garden.

> *Essais* (1580, ed. M. Rat, 1958) bk. 1, ch. 20

10 The ceaseless labour of your life is to build the house of death.

> *Essais* (1580, ed. M. Rat, 1958) bk. 1, ch. 20

11 It should be noted that children at play are not playing about; their games should be seen as their most serious-minded activity.

> *Essais* (1580, ed. M. Rat, 1958) bk. 1, ch. 23

12 If I am pressed to say why I loved him, I feel it can only be explained by replying: 'Because it was he; because it was me.'

> *Essais* (1580, ed. M. Rat, 1958) bk. 1, ch. 28

13 There is scarcely any less bother in the running of a family than in that of an entire state. And domestic business is no less importunate for being less important.

> *Essais* (1580, ed. M. Rat, 1958) bk. 1, ch. 39

14 A man should keep for himself a little back shop, all his own, quite unadulterated, in which he establishes his true freedom and chief place of seclusion and solitude.

> *Essais* (1580, ed. M. Rat, 1958) bk. 1, ch. 39

15 The greatest thing in the world is to know how to be oneself.

> *Essais* (1580, ed. M. Rat, 1958) bk. 1, ch. 39

16 *Mon métier et mon art c'est vivre.*
Living is my job and my art.

> *Essais* (1580, ed. M. Rat, 1958) bk. 2, ch. 6

17 When I play with my cat, who knows whether she isn't amusing herself with me more than I am with her?

> *Essais* (1580, ed. M. Rat, 1958) bk. 2, ch. 12

18 *Que sais-je?*
What do I know?

> *Essais* (1580, ed. M. Rat, 1958) bk. 2, ch. 12 (on the position of the sceptic)

19 It could be said of me that in this book I have only made up a bunch of other men's flowers, providing of my own only the string that ties them together.

> *Essais* (1580, ed. M. Rat, 1958) bk. 3, ch. 12

## Montesquieu 1689–1755

20 Men should be bewailed at their birth, and not at their death.

> *Lettres Persanes* (1721) no. 40 (tr. J. Ozell, 1722)

21 If the triangles were to make a God they would give him three sides.

> *Lettres Persanes* (1721) no. 59 (tr. J. Ozell, 1722)

22 Happy the people whose annals are blank in history-books!

> Attributed to Montesquieu by Thomas Carlyle in *History of Frederick the Great* bk. 16, ch. 1. Cf. 132:14

## Field Marshal Montgomery 1887–1976

23 Rule 1, on page 1 of the book of war, is: 'Do not march on Moscow' . . . [Rule 2] is: 'Do not go fighting with your land armies in China.'

> *Hansard* (Lords) 30 May 1962, col. 227

24 I have heard some say . . . [homosexual] practices are allowed in France and in other NATO countries. We are not French, and we are not other nationals. We are British, thank God!

> Speaking on the 2nd reading of the Sexual Offences Bill; in *Hansard* (Lords) 24 May 1965, col. 648

## Robert Montgomery 1807–55

25 The solitary monk who shook the world.

> *Luther: a Poem* (1842) ch. 3 'Man's Need and God's Supply'

## Casimir, Comte de Montrond
### 1768–1843

1 Have no truck with first impulses for they
are always generous ones.
  Attributed, in Comte J. d'Estourmel *Derniers
  Souvenirs* (1860) p. 319 (where the alternative
  attribution to Talleyrand is denied). Cf. 108:3

## Percy Montrose

2 In a cavern, in a canyon,
Excavating for a mine,
Dwelt a miner, Forty-niner,
And his daughter, Clementine.
  'Clementine' (1884 song)

## Clement C. Moore 1779–1863

3 'Twas the night before Christmas, when all
through the house
Not a creature was stirring, not even a
mouse.
  'A Visit from St Nicholas' (December 1823)

## Edward Moore 1712–57

4 This is adding insult to injuries.
  *The Foundling* (1748) act 5, sc. 5

5 I am rich beyond the dreams of avarice.
  *The Gamester* (1753) act 2, sc. 2. Cf. 185:29

## George Moore 1852–1933

6 All reformers are bachelors.
  *The Bending of the Bough* (1900) act 1

7 A man travels the world in search of what
he needs and returns home to find it.
  *The Brook Kerith* (1916) ch. 11

## Marianne Moore 1887–1972

8 Imaginary gardens with real toads in them.
  'Poetry' (1935)

9 My father used to say,
'Superior people never make long visits,
have to be shown Longfellow's grave
or the glass flowers at Harvard.'
  'Silence' (1935)

## Thomas Moore 1779–1852

10 Though an angel should write, still 'tis
*devils* must print.
  *The Fudges in England* (1835) Letter 3, l. 65

11 Believe me, if all those endearing young
charms,
Which I gaze on so fondly today,
Were to change by tomorrow, and fleet in
my arms,
Like fairy gifts fading away!
  *Irish Melodies* (1807) 'Believe me, if all those
  endearing young charms'

12 'Twas from Kathleen's eyes he flew,
Eyes of most unholy blue!
  *Irish Melodies* (1807) 'By that Lake'

13 You may break, you may shatter the vase,
if you will,
But the scent of the roses will hang round
it still.
  *Irish Melodies* (1807) 'Farewell!—but
  whenever'

14 The harp that once through Tara's halls
The soul of music shed,
Now hangs as mute on Tara's walls
As if that soul were fled.
  *Irish Melodies* (1807) 'The harp that once
  through Tara's halls'

15 No, there's nothing half so sweet in life
As love's young dream.
  *Irish Melodies* (1807) 'Love's Young Dream'

16 The Minstrel Boy to the war is gone,
In the ranks of death you'll find him;
His father's sword he has girded on,
And his wild harp slung behind him.
  *Irish Melodies* (1807) 'The Minstrel Boy'

17 Rich and rare were the gems she wore,
And a bright gold ring on her wand she
bore.
  *Irish Melodies* (1807) 'Rich and rare were the
  gems she wore'

18 'Tis the last rose of summer
Left blooming alone;
All her lovely companions
Are faded and gone.
  *Irish Melodies* (1807) ''Tis the last rose of
  summer'

19 I never nursed a dear gazelle,
To glad me with its soft black eye,
But when it came to know me well,
And love me, it was sure to die!
  *Lalla Rookh* (1817) 'The Fire-Worshippers'
  pt. 1, l. 283

20 Oft, in the stilly night,
Ere Slumber's chain has bound me,
Fond Memory brings the light
Of other days around me.
  *National Airs* (1815) 'Oft in the Stilly Night'

## Thomas Osbert Mordaunt
### 1730–1809

21 One crowded hour of glorious life
Is worth an age without a name.
  'A Poem, said to be written by Major
  Mordaunt during the last German War', in
  *The Bee* 12 October 1791

## Hannah More 1745–1833

22 How much it is to be regretted, that the
British ladies should ever sit down
contented to polish, when they are able to
reform; to entertain, when they might
instruct; and to dazzle for an hour, when
they are candidates for eternity!
  *Essays on Various Subjects . . . for Young Ladies*
  (1777) 'On Dissipation'

## Sir Thomas More 1478–1535

1 After his head was upon the block, [he] lift it up again, and gently drew his beard aside, and said, *This hath not offended the king.*

Francis Bacon *Apophthegms New and Old* (1625) no. 22

2 Is not this house [the Tower of London] as nigh heaven as my own?

In William Roper *Life of Sir Thomas More* (Everyman ed., 1963) p. 41

3 I pray you, master Lieutenant, see me safe up, and my coming down let me shift for my self.

On mounting the scaffold; in William Roper *Life of Sir Thomas More* p. 50

4 Fare well my dear child and pray for me, and I shall for you and all your friends that we may merrily meet in heaven.

Letter to his daughter Margaret, 5 July 1535, on the eve of his execution; in E. F. Rogers (ed.) *Correspondence of Sir Thomas More* (1947)

## Thomas Morell 1703–84

5 See, the conquering hero comes! Sound the trumpets, beat the drums!

*Judas Maccabeus* (1747) 'A Chorus of youths'; also *Joshua* (1748) pt. 3

## Robin Morgan 1941–

6 Sisterhood is powerful.

Title of book (1970)

## Christopher Morley 1890–1957

7 Life is a foreign language: all men mispronounce it.

*Thunder on the Left* (1925) ch. 14. Cf. 163:14

## Lord Morley 1838–1923

8 The golden Gospel of Silence is effectively compressed in thirty fine volumes.

*Critical Miscellanies* (1886) 'Carlyle' (on Carlyle's *History of Frederick the Great* (1858–65), Carlyle having written of his subject as 'that strong, silent man')

9 You have not converted a man, because you have silenced him.

*On Compromise* (1874) ch. 5

## Countess Morphy fl. 1930–50

10 The tragedy of English cooking is that 'plain' cooking cannot be entrusted to 'plain' cooks.

*English Recipes* (1935) p. 17

## Charles Morris 1745–1838

11 But a house is much more to my mind than a tree,
And for groves, O! a good grove of chimneys for me.

'Country and Town' (1840)

## Desmond Morris 1928–

12 The city is not a concrete jungle, it is a human zoo.

*The Human Zoo* (1969) introduction

## George Pope Morris 1802–64

13 Woodman, spare that tree!
Touch not a single bough!
In youth it sheltered me,
And I'll protect it now.

'Woodman, Spare That Tree' (1830). Cf. 88:17

## William Morris 1834–96

14 The idle singer of an empty day.

*The Earthly Paradise* (1868–70) 'An Apology'

15 Dreamer of dreams, born out of my due time,
Why should I strive to set the crooked straight?

*The Earthly Paradise* (1868–70) 'An Apology'

16 Forget six counties overhung with smoke,
Forget the snorting steam and piston stroke,
Forget the spreading of the hideous town;
Think rather of the pack-horse on the down,
And dream of London, small and white and clean,
The clear Thames bordered by its gardens green.

*The Earthly Paradise* (1868–70) 'Prologue: The Wanderers' l. 1

17 Fellowship is heaven, and lack of fellowship is hell.

*A Dream of John Ball* (1888) ch. 4

18 Have nothing in your houses that you do not know to be useful, or believe to be beautiful.

*Hopes and Fears for Art* (1882) 'Making the Best of It'

## Jim Morrison 1943–71

19 C'mon, baby, light my fire.

'Light My Fire' (1967 song, with Robby Krieger)

20 We want the world and we want it now!

'When the Music's Over' (1967 song)

## John Mortimer 1923–

21 No brilliance is needed in the law. Nothing but common sense, and relatively clean finger nails.

*A Voyage Round My Father* (1971) act 1

22 Champagne socialist.

Description of himself (attributed)

## Thomas Morton c.1764–1838

23 Always ding, dinging Dame Grundy into my ears—what will Mrs Grundy zay? What will Mrs Grundy think?

*Speed the Plough* (1798) act 1, sc. 1

## John Lothrop Motley 1814–77

1 As long as he lived, he was the guiding-star
of a whole brave nation, and when he died
the little children cried in the streets.
   Of William of Orange; in *The Rise of the Dutch
   Republic* (1856) pt. 6, ch. 7. Cf. 20:18

2 Give us the luxuries of life, and we will
dispense with its necessities.
   In Oliver Wendell Holmes *Autocrat of the
   Breakfast-Table* (1857–8) ch. 6

## Peter Anthony Motteux
1660–1718

3 The devil was sick, the devil a monk would
be;
The devil was well, and the devil a monk
he'd be.
   Translation of Rabelais *Gargantua and
   Pantagruel* (1693) bk. 4 (1708 ed.) ch. 24
   (variant of a medieval Latin proverb)

## Earl Mountbatten of Burma
1900–79

4 The nuclear arms race has no military
purpose. Wars cannot be fought with
nuclear weapons. Their existence only adds
to our perils.
   Speech at Strasbourg, 11 May 1979; in P.
   Ziegler *Mountbatten* (1985) ch. 52

## Malcolm Muggeridge 1903–90

5 He was not only a bore; he bored for
England.
   *Tread Softly* (1966) p. 147 (of Sir Anthony
   Eden)

## Edwin Muir 1887–1959

6 And without fear the lawless roads
Ran wrong through all the land.
   *Journeys and Places* (1937) 'Hölderlin's Journey'

## Ethel Watts Mumford et al.
1878–1940

7 In the midst of life we are in debt.
   *Altogether New Cynic's Calendar* (1907). Cf. 66:7

## Lewis Mumford 1895–1982

8 Our national flower is the concrete
cloverleaf.
   *Quote Magazine* 8 October 1961

## Iris Murdoch 1919–

9 Dora Greenfield left her husband because
she was afraid of him. She decided six
months later to return to him for the same
reason.
   *The Bell* (1958) ch. 1

10 One doesn't have to get anywhere in a
marriage. It's not a public conveyance.
   *A Severed Head* (1961) ch. 3

11 Anything that consoles is fake.
   In R. Harries *Prayer and the Pursuit of
   Happiness* (1985) p. 113. Cf. 71:14

## C. W. Murphy and Will Letters

12 Has anybody here seen Kelly?
Kelly from the Isle of Man?
   'Has Anybody Here Seen Kelly?' (1909 song)

## Ed Murrow 1908–65

13 He [Winston Churchill] mobilized the
English language and sent it into battle to
steady his fellow countrymen and hearten
those Europeans upon whom the long dark
night of tyranny had descended.
   Broadcast, 30 November 1954, in *In Search of
   Light* (1967) p. 276

14 Anyone who isn't confused doesn't really
understand the situation.
   On the Vietnam War, in Walter Bryan *The
   Improbable Irish* (1969) ch. 1

## Alfred de Musset 1810–57

15 *Je ne puis:—malgré moi l'infini me tourmente.*
I can't help it:—in spite of myself, infinity
torments me.
   'L'Espoir en Dieu' (1838)

16 *Le seul bien qui me reste au monde
Est d'avoir quelquefois pleuré.*
The only good thing left to me is that I
have sometimes wept.
   'Tristesse' (1841)

17 *Je suis venu trop tard dans un monde trop
vieux.*
I have come too late into a world too old.
   *Rollo* (1833)

## Vladimir Nabokov 1899–1977

18 Lolita, light of my life, fire of my loins. My
sin, my soul. Lo-lee-ta: the tip of the
tongue taking a trip of three steps down
the palate to tap, at three, on the teeth. Lo.
Lee. Ta.
   *Lolita* (1955) ch. 1

19 The cradle rocks above an abyss, and
common sense tells us that our existence
is but a brief crack of light between two
eternities of darkness.
   *Speak, Memory* (1951) ch. 1

20 I think like a genius, I write like
a distinguished author, and I speak like
a child.
   *Strong Opinions* (1973) foreword

## Ralph Nader 1934–

21 Unsafe at any speed.
   Title of book (1965)

## Napoléon I 1769–1821

1 [The Channel] is a mere ditch, and will be
crossed as soon as someone has the
courage to attempt it.
   Letter to Consul Cambacérès, 16 November
   1803, in *Correspondance de Napoléon Ier*
   (1858–69) vol. 9

2 There is only one step from the sublime to
the ridiculous.
   Following the retreat from Moscow in 1812;
   in D. G. De Pradt *Histoire de l'Ambassade dans
   le grand-duché de Varsovie en 1812* (1815) p. 215.
   Cf. 244:8

3 Think of it, soldiers; from the summit of
these pyramids, forty centuries look down
upon you.
   Speech before the Battle of the Pyramids
   21 July 1798; in G. Gourgaud *Mémoires* (1823)
   vol. 2

4 As to moral courage, I have very rarely met
with two o'clock in the morning courage: I
mean instantaneous courage.
   In E. A. de Las Cases *Mémorial de Ste-Hélène*
   (1823) vol. 1, pt. 2, 4–5 December 1815

5 An army marches on its stomach.
   Attributed, but probably condensed from a
   long passage in E. A. de Las Cases *Mémorial
   de Ste-Hélène* (1823) vol. 4, 14 November 1816

6 *La carrière ouverte aux talents.*
   The career open to the talents.
   In B. O'Meara *Napoleon in Exile* (1822) vol. 1,
   p. 103

7 England is a nation of shopkeepers.
   In B. O'Meara *Napoleon in Exile* (1822) vol. 2,
   p. 81. Cf. 2:7, 308:23

8 Not tonight, Josephine.
   Attributed, but probably apocryphal. See
   R. H. Horne *History of Napoleon* (1841) vol. 2,
   ch. 8

## Ogden Nash 1902–71

9 The turtle lives 'twixt plated decks
Which practically conceal its sex.
I think it clever of the turtle
In such a fix to be so fertile.
   'Autres Bêtes, Autres Moeurs' (1931)

10 The cow is of the bovine ilk;
One end is moo, the other, milk.
   'The Cow' (1931)

11 One would be in less danger
From the wiles of the stranger
If one's own kin and kith
Were more fun to be with.
   'Family Court' (1931)

12 Professional men, they have no cares;
Whatever happens, they get theirs.
   'I Yield to My Learned Brother' (1935)

13 Beneath this slab
John Brown is stowed.
He watched the ads,
And not the road.
   'Lather as You Go' (1942)

14 Do you think my mind is maturing late,
Or simply rotted early?
   'Lines on Facing Forty' (1942)

15 Candy
Is dandy
But liquor
Is quicker.
   'Reflections on Ice-breaking' (1931)

16 I test my bath before I sit,
And I'm always moved to wonderment
That what chills the finger not a bit
Is so frigid upon the fundament.
   'Samson Agonistes' (1942)

17 I think that I shall never see
A billboard lovely as a tree.
Perhaps, unless the billboards fall,
I'll never see a tree at all.
   'Song of the Open Road' (1933). Cf. 194:22

18 Sure, deck your lower limbs in pants;
Yours are the limbs, my sweeting.
You look divine as you advance—
Have you seen yourself retreating?
   'What's the Use?' (1940)

## Thomas Nashe 1567–1601

19 Brightness falls from the air;
Queens have died young and fair;
Dust hath closed Helen's eye.
I am sick, I must die.
Lord have mercy on us.
   *Summer's Last Will and Testament* (1600) l. 1588

## James Ball Naylor 1860–1945

20 King David and King Solomon
Led merry, merry lives,
With many, many lady friends,
And many, many wives;
But when old age crept over them—
With many, many qualms!—
King Solomon wrote the Proverbs
And King David wrote the Psalms.
   'King David and King Solomon' (1935)

## John Mason Neale 1818–66

21 All glory, laud, and honour
To thee, Redeemer, King,
To whom the lips of children
Made sweet hosannas ring.
   'All glory, laud, and honour' (1851 hymn)

22 Jerusalem the golden,
With milk and honey blessed,
Beneath thy contemplation
Sink heart and voice oppressed.
   'Jerusalem the golden' (1858 hymn);
   translated from the Latin of St Bernard of
   Cluny (b. *c*.1100)

## Horatio, Lord Nelson 1758–1805

23 Before this time to-morrow I shall have
gained a peerage, or Westminster Abbey.
   Before the battle of the Nile, in R. Southey
   *Life of Nelson* (1813) ch. 5

1 I have only one eye,—I have a right to be
  blind sometimes ... I really do not see the
  signal!
    At the battle of Copenhagen, in R. Southey
    *Life of Nelson* (1813) ch. 7

2 When I came to explain to them the '*Nelson
  touch*', it was like an electric shock.
    Letter to Lady Hamilton, 1 October 1805, in
    R. Southey *Life of Nelson* (1813) ch. 9

3 England expects that every man will do his
  duty.
    At the battle of Trafalgar, in R. Southey *Life
    of Nelson* (1813) ch. 9

4 This is too warm work, Hardy, to last long.
    At the battle of Trafalgar, in R. Southey *Life
    of Nelson* (1813) ch. 9

5 Thank God, I have done my duty.
    At the battle of Trafalgar, in R. Southey *Life
    of Nelson* (1813) ch. 9

6 Kiss me, Hardy.
    At the battle of Trafalgar, in R. Southey *Life
    of Nelson* (1813) ch. 9

## Emperor Nero AD 37–68

7 *Qualis artifex pereo!*
  What an artist dies with me!
    In Suetonius *Lives of the Caesars* 'Nero' sect. 49

## Gérard de Nerval 1808–55

8 *Je suis le ténébreux,—le veuf,—l'inconsolé,
  Le prince d'Aquitaine à la tour abolie.*
  I am the darkly shaded, the bereaved, the
  inconsolate, the prince of Aquitaine, with
  the blasted tower.
    *Les Chimères* (1854) 'El Desdichado'

## Allan Nevins 1890–1971

9 Offering Germany too little, and offering
  even that too late.
    In *Current History* (New York) May 1935,
    p. 178

## Sir Henry Newbolt 1862–1938

10 Take my drum to England, hang et by the
   shore,
   Strike et when your powder's runnin' low;
   If the Dons sight Devon, I'll quit the port o'
   Heaven,
   An' drum them up the Channel as we
   drummed them long ago.
     'Drake's Drum' (1897)

11 Drake he's in his hammock till the great
   Armadas come.
   (Capten, art tha sleepin' there below?)
     'Drake's Drum' (1897)

12 Now the sunset breezes shiver,
   And she's fading down the river,
   But in England's song for ever
   She's the Fighting Téméraire.
     'The Fighting Téméraire' (1897)

13 There's a breathless hush in the Close to-
   night—
   Ten to make and the match to win—
   A bumping pitch and a blinding light,
   An hour to play and the last man in.
   And it's not for the sake of a ribboned
   coat,
   Or the selfish hope of a season's fame,
   But his Captain's hand on his shoulder
   smote—
   'Play up! play up! and play the game!'
     'Vitaï Lampada' (1897)

## Anthony Newley 1931– and Leslie Bricusse 1931–

14 Stop the world, I want to get off.
     Title of musical (1961)

## Cardinal Newman 1801–90

15 He has attempted (as I may call it) to *poison
   the wells.*
     *Apologia pro Vita Sua* (1864) 'Mr Kingsley's
     Method of Disputation'

16 Ten thousand difficulties do not make one
   doubt.
     *Apologia pro Vita Sua* (1864) 'Position of my
     Mind since 1845'

17 It is almost a definition of a gentleman to
   say that he is one who never inflicts pain.
     *The Idea of a University* (1852) 'Knowledge and
     Religious Duty'

18 If I am obliged to bring religion into after-
   dinner toasts (which indeed does not seem
   quite the thing) I shall drink ... to
   Conscience first, and to the Pope
   afterwards.
     *Letter Addressed to the Duke of Norfolk* ...
     (1875) sect. 5

19 Firmly I believe and truly
   God is Three, and God is One;
   And I next acknowledge duly
   Manhood taken by the Son.
     *The Dream of Gerontius* (1865)

20 Praise to the Holiest in the height,
   And in the depth be praise;
   In all his words most wonderful,
   Most sure in all His ways.
     *The Dream of Gerontius* (1865)

21 Lead, kindly Light, amid the encircling
   gloom,
   Lead thou me on;
   The night is dark, and I am far from home,
   Lead thou me on.
   Keep Thou my feet; I do not ask to see
   The distant scene; one step enough for me.
     'Lead, kindly Light' (1834)

22 I loved the garish day, and spite of fears,
   Pride ruled my will: remember not past
   years.
     'Lead, kindly Light' (1834). Cf. 226:26

**1** *We can believe what we choose.* We are
answerable for what we choose to believe.
> Letter to Mrs William Froude, 27 June 1848,
> in C. S. Dessain (ed.) *Letters and Diaries of John
> Henry Newman* vol. 12 (1962)

## Sir Isaac Newton 1642–1727

**2** If I have seen further it is by standing on
the shoulders of giants.
> Letter to Robert Hooke, 5 February 1676, in
> H. W. Turnbull (ed.) *Correspondence* vol. 1
> (1959) p. 416. Cf. 36:9

**3** Every body continues in its state of rest, or
of uniform motion in a right line, unless it
is compelled to change that state by forces
impressed upon it.
> *Principia Mathematica* (1687) Laws of Motion 1
> (tr. A. Motte, 1729)

**4** To every action there is always opposed an
equal reaction.
> *Principia Mathematica* (1687) Laws of Motion 3
> (tr. A. Motte, 1729)

**5** *Hypotheses non fingo.*
I do not feign hypotheses.
> *Principia Mathematica* (1713 ed.) 'Scholium
> Generale'

**6** I don't know what I may seem to the
world, but as to myself, I seem to have
been only like a boy playing on the sea-
shore and diverting myself in now and
then finding a smoother pebble or a
prettier shell than ordinary, whilst the
great ocean of truth lay all undiscovered
before me.
> In Joseph Spence *Anecdotes* (ed. J. Osborn,
> 1966) no. 1259

## John Newton 1725–1807

**7** Amazing grace! how sweet the sound
That saved a wretch like me!
> *Olney Hymns* (1779) 'Amazing grace'

**8** Glorious things of thee are spoken,
Zion, city of our God!
> *Olney Hymns* (1779) 'Glorious things of thee
> are spoken'

**9** How sweet the name of Jesus sounds
In a believer's ear!
> *Olney Hymns* (1779) 'How sweet the name of
> Jesus sounds'

## Emperor Nicholas I of Russia 1796–1855

**10** Turkey is a dying man. We may endeavour
to keep him alive, but we shall not
succeed. He will, he must die.
> In F. Max Müller (ed.) *Memoirs of Baron
> Stockmar* (tr. G. Müller, 1873) vol. 2, p. 107

**11** Russia has two generals in whom she can
confide—Generals Janvier [January] and
Février [February].
> Attributed. See *Punch* 10 March 1855

## Sir Harold Nicolson 1886–1968

**12** We shall have to walk and live a
Woolworth life hereafter.
> Anticipating the aftermath of the Second
> World War, in *Diaries and Letters 1939–45*
> (1967) 4 June 1941

**13** For seventeen years he did nothing at all
but kill animals and stick in stamps.
> Of King George V, in *Diaries and Letters
> 1945–62* (1968) 17 August 1949

## Reinhold Niebuhr 1892–1971

**14** Man's capacity for justice makes
democracy possible, but man's inclination
to injustice makes democracy necessary.
> *Children of Light and Children of Darkness* (1944)
> foreword

## Martin Niemöller 1892–1984

**15** When Hitler attacked the Jews I was not
a Jew, therefore, I was not concerned. And
when Hitler attacked the Catholics, I was
not a Catholic, and therefore, I was not
concerned. And when Hitler attacked the
unions and the industrialists, I was not
a member of the unions and I was not
concerned. Then, Hitler attacked me and
the Protestant church—and there was
nobody left to be concerned.
> In *Congressional Record* 14 October 1968,
> p. 31636

## Friedrich Nietzsche 1844–1900

**16** I teach you the superman. Man is
something to be surpassed.
> *Also Sprach Zarathustra* (1883) prologue, sect. 3

**17** You are going to women? Do not forget the
whip!
> *Also Sprach Zarathustra* (1883) bk. 1 'Von Alten
> und jungen Weiblein'

**18** Woman was God's second blunder.
> *Der Antichrist* (1888) aphorism 48

**19** What I understand by 'philosopher': a
terrible explosive in the presence of which
everything is in danger.
> *Ecce Homo* (1908) 'Die Unzeitgemässen' sect. 3

**20** Morality is the herd-instinct in the
individual.
> *Die fröhliche Wissenschaft* (1882) bk. 3, sect. 116

**21** Believe me! The secret of reaping the
greatest fruitfulness and the greatest
enjoyment from life is *to live dangerously!*
> *Die fröhliche Wissenschaft* (1882) bk. 4,
> sect. 283

**22** Master-morality and slave-morality.
> *Jenseits von Gut und Böse* ch. 9, no. 260

**23** Wit is the epitaph of an emotion.
> *Menschliches, Allzumenschliches* (1867–80) vol. 2,
> sect. 1, no. 202

## Florence Nightingale 1820–1910

1 Too kind, too kind.
   On the Order of Merit being brought to her
   at her home, 5 December 1907; in E. Cook
   *Life of Florence Nightingale* (1913) vol. 2, pt. 7,
   ch. 9

## Richard Nixon 1913–

2 There can be no whitewash at the White
   House.
   Television speech on Watergate, 30 April
   1973, in *New York Times* 1 May 1973, p. 31

3 People have got to know whether or not
   their President is a crook. Well, I'm not
   a crook.
   Speech, 17 November 1973, in *New York Times*
   18 November 1973, p. 62

4 I brought myself down. I gave them
   a sword. And they stuck it in.
   Television interview, 19 May 1977, in David
   Frost *I Gave Them a Sword* (1978) ch. 10

## Thomas Noel 1799–1861

5 Rattle his bones over the stones;
   He's only a pauper, whom nobody owns!
   'The Pauper's Drive' (1841)

## Christopher North (John Wilson) 1785–1854

6 His Majesty's dominions, on which the sun
   never sets.
   *Blackwood's Magazine* (April 1829) 'Noctes
   Ambrosianae' no. 42. Cf. 267:19

7 Laws were made to be broken.
   *Blackwood's Magazine* (May 1830) 'Noctes
   Ambrosianae' no. 49

## Lord Northcliffe 1865–1922

8 The power of the press is very great, but
   not so great as the power of suppress.
   Office message, *Daily Mail* 1918, in R. Rose
   and G. Harmsworth *Northcliffe* (1959) ch. 22

9 When I want a peerage, I shall buy it like
   an honest man.
   In Tom Driberg *Swaff* (1974) ch. 2

## Caroline Norton 1808–77

10 And all our calm is in that balm—
   Not lost but gone before.
   'Not Lost but Gone Before'. Cf. 113:13

## Jack Norworth 1879–1959

11 Oh, shine on, shine on, harvest moon
   Up in the sky.
   I ain't had no lovin'
   Since April, January, June, or July.
   'Shine On, Harvest Moon' (1908 song)

## Novalis (Friedrich von Hardenberg) 1772–1801

12 Fate and character are the same concept.
   *Heinrich von Ofterdingen* (1802) bk. 2 (often
   quoted 'Character is destiny' or 'Character is
   fate'). Cf. 132:15, 166:9

13 A God-intoxicated man.
   Of Spinoza (attributed)

## Alfred Noyes 1880–1958

14 Look for me by moonlight;
   Watch for me by moonlight;
   I'll come to thee by moonlight, though hell
   should bar the way!
   'The Highwayman' (1907)

## Bill Nye

15 I have been told that Wagner's music is
   better than it sounds.
   In Mark Twain *Autobiography* (1924) vol. 1,
   p. 338

## Charles Edward Oakley 1832–65

16 Hills of the North, rejoice:
   River and mountain-spring,
   Hark to the advent voice!
   Valley and lowland, sing!
   'Hills of the North, rejoice' (1870 hymn)

## Captain Lawrence Oates 1880–1912

17 I am just going outside and may be some
   time.
   Last words, in *Scott's Last Expedition* (1913)
   ch. 20 (Scott's diary entry, 16–17 March 1912)

## Edna O'Brien 1936–

18 August is a wicked month.
   Title of novel (1965)

## Flann O'Brien 1911–66

19 The conclusion of your syllogism, I said
   lightly, is fallacious, being based upon
   licensed premises.
   *At Swim-Two-Birds* (1939) ch. 1

20 A pint of plain is your only man.
   *At Swim-Two-Birds* (1939) 'The Workman's
   Friend'

## Sean O'Casey 1880–1964

21 He's an oul' butty o' mine—oh, he's
   a darlin' man, a daarlin' man.
   *Juno and the Paycock* (1925) act 1

22 The whole worl's in a state o' chassis!
   *Juno and the Paycock* (1925) act 1

23 English literature's performing flea.
   In P. G. Wodehouse *Performing Flea* (1953)
   p. 217 (describing the author)

## Adolph S. Ochs 1858–1935

**1** All the news that's fit to print.
Motto of the *New York Times*, from 1896

## David Ogilvy 1911–

**2** The consumer isn't a moron; she is your wife.
*Confessions of an Advertising Man* (1963) ch. 5

## James Ogilvy, 1st Earl of Seafield 1664–1730

**3** Now there's ane end of ane old song.
As he signed the engrossed exemplification of the Act of Union, 1706, in *The Lockhart Papers* (1817) vol. 1, p. 223

## Theodore O'Hara 1820–67

**4** Sons of the dark and bloody ground.
'The Bivouac of the Dead' (1847) st. 1

## John O'Keeffe 1747–1833

**5** Amo, amas, I love a lass,
As a cedar tall and slender;
Sweet cowslip's grace
Is her nom'native case,
And she's of the feminine gender.
*The Agreeable Surprise* (1781) act 2, sc. 2

**6** Fat, fair and forty were all the toasts of the young men.
*The Irish Mimic* (1795) sc. 2

## Dennis O'Kelly *c.*1720–87

**7** Eclipse first, the rest nowhere.
Comment at Epsom, 3 May 1769, in *Annals of Sporting* vol. 2 (1822) p. 271

## Laurence Olivier 1907–89

**8** The tragedy of a man who could not make up his mind.
Introduction to his 1948 screen adaptation of *Hamlet*

## Frank Ward O'Malley

See ELBERT HUBBARD

## Eugene O'Neill 1888–1953

**9** For de little stealin' dey gits you in jail soon or late. For de big stealin' dey makes you Emperor and puts you in de Hall o' Fame when you croaks.
*The Emperor Jones* (1921) sc. 1

**10** The iceman cometh.
Title of play (1946)

**11** A long day's journey into night.
Title of play (written 1940–1)

**12** The sea hates a coward!
*Mourning becomes Electra* (1931) pt. 2, act 4

## Yoko Ono 1933–

**13** Woman is the nigger of the world.
Interview for *Nova* magazine (1968); adopted by John Lennon as song title (1972)

## J. Robert Oppenheimer 1904–67

**14** The physicists have known sin; and this is a knowledge which they cannot lose.
*Open Mind* (1955) ch. 5 (lecture, 1947)

## Susie Orbach 1946–

**15** Fat is a feminist issue.
Title of book (1978)

## Roy Orbison and Joe Melsom

**16** Only the lonely (know the way I feel).
Title of song (1960)

## Baroness Orczy 1865–1947

**17** We seek him here, we seek him there,
Those Frenchies seek him everywhere.
Is he in heaven?—Is he in hell?
That demmed, elusive Pimpernel?
*The Scarlet Pimpernel* (1905) ch. 12

## Meta Orred

**18** In the gloaming, Oh my darling!
When the lights are dim and low,
And the quiet shadows falling
Softly come and softly go.
'In the Gloaming' (1877 song)

## Joe Orton 1933–67

**19** I'd the upbringing a nun would envy . . .
Until I was fifteen I was more familiar with Africa than my own body.
*Entertaining Mr Sloane* (1964) act 1

**20** It's all any reasonable child can expect if the dad is present at the conception.
*Entertaining Mr Sloane* (1964) act 3

**21** You were born with your legs apart. They'll send you to the grave in a Y-shaped coffin.
*What the Butler Saw* (1969) act 1

## George Orwell 1903–50

**22** Four legs good, two legs bad.
*Animal Farm* (1945) ch. 3

**23** All animals are equal but some animals are more equal than others.
*Animal Farm* (1945) ch. 10

**24** At 50, everyone has the face he deserves.
Last words in his notebook, 17 April 1949; *Collected Essays, Journalism and Letters . . .* (1968) vol. 4, p. 515

**25** I'm fat, but I'm thin inside. Has it ever struck you that there's a thin man inside every fat man, just as they say there's a statue inside every block of stone?
*Coming up For Air* (1939) pt. 1, ch. 3. Cf. 5:4

1 Down here it was still the England I had known in my childhood: the railway cuttings smothered in wild flowers ... the red buses, the blue policemen—all sleeping the deep, deep sleep of England, from which I sometimes fear that we shall never wake till we are jerked out of it by the roar of bombs.

  *Homage to Catalonia* (1938) ch. 14

2 Keep the aspidistra flying.

  Title of novel (1936)

3 It [England] is a family in which the young are generally thwarted and most of the power is in the hands of irresponsible uncles and bed-ridden aunts. Still, it is a family. It has its private language and its common memories, and at the approach of an enemy it closes its ranks. A family with the wrong members in control.

  *The Lion and the Unicorn* (1941) pt. 1 'England Your England'

4 Probably the battle of Waterloo *was* won on the playing-fields of Eton, but the opening battles of all subsequent wars have been lost there.

  *The Lion and the Unicorn* (1941) pt. 1 'England Your England'. Cf. 345:10

5 It was a bright cold day in April, and the clocks were striking thirteen.

  *Nineteen Eighty-Four* (1949) pt. 1, ch. 1

6 BIG BROTHER IS WATCHING YOU.

  *Nineteen Eighty-Four* (1949) pt. 1, ch. 1

7 War is peace. Freedom is slavery. Ignorance is strength.

  *Nineteen Eighty-Four* (1949) pt. 1, ch. 1

8 Who controls the past controls the future: who controls the present controls the past.

  *Nineteen Eighty-Four* (1949) pt. 1, ch. 3

9 Freedom is the freedom to say that two plus two make four. If that is granted, all else follows.

  *Nineteen Eighty-Four* (1949) pt. 1, ch. 7

10 *Doublethink* means the power of holding two contradictory beliefs in one's mind simultaneously, and accepting both of them.

  *Nineteen Eighty-Four* (1949) pt. 2, ch. 9

11 If you want a picture of the future, imagine a boot stamping on a human face—for ever.

  *Nineteen Eighty-Four* (1949) pt. 3, ch. 3

12 The quickest way of ending a war is to lose it.

  *Polemic* May 1946 'Second Thoughts on James Burnham'

13 To the ordinary working man, the sort you would meet in any pub on Saturday night, Socialism does not mean much more than better wages and shorter hours and nobody bossing you about.

  *The Road to Wigan Pier* (1937) ch. 11

14 We of the sinking middle class ... may sink without further struggles into the working class where we belong, and probably when we get there it will not be so dreadful as we feared, for, after all, we have nothing to lose but our aitches.

  *The Road to Wigan Pier* (1937) ch. 13. Cf. 221:15

15 Political language ... is designed to make lies sound truthful and murder respectable, and to give an appearance of solidity to pure wind.

  *Shooting an Elephant* (1950) 'Politics and the English Language'

16 Advertising is the rattling of a stick inside a swill bucket.

  Attributed

## Dorothy Osborne 1627–95

17 All letters, methinks, should be free and easy as one's discourse, not studied as an oration, nor made up of hard words like a charm.

  *Letters of Dorothy Osborne to William Temple* (ed. G. C. Moore Smith, 1928) September 1653

## John Osborne 1929–

18 Don't clap too hard—it's a very old building.

  *The Entertainer* (1957) no. 7

19 Thank God we're normal,
   Yes, this is our finest shower!

  *The Entertainer* (1957) no. 7

20 But I have a go, lady, don't I? I 'ave a go. I do.

  *The Entertainer* (1957) no. 7

21 His knowledge of life and ordinary human beings is so hazy, he really deserves some sort of decoration for it—a medal inscribed 'For Vaguery in the Field'.

  *Look Back in Anger* (1956) act 1

22 Slamming their doors, stamping their high heels, banging their irons and saucepans—the eternal flaming racket of the female.

  *Look Back in Anger* (1956) act 1

23 Reason and Progress, the old firm, is selling out!

  *Look Back in Anger* (1956) act 2, sc. 1

24 They spend their time mostly looking forward to the past.

  *Look Back in Anger* (1956) act 2, sc. 1

25 She's like the old line about justice—not only must be done, but must be seen to be done.

  *Time Present* (1968) act 1

26 Royalty is the gold filling in a mouthful of decay.

  'They call it cricket' in T. Maschler (ed.) *Declaration* (1957)

## Arthur O'Shaughnessy 1844–81

1 We are the music makers,
We are the dreamers of dreams …
We are the movers and shakers
Of the world for ever, it seems.
'Ode' (1874)

2 For each age is a dream that is dying,
Or one that is coming to birth.
'Ode' (1874)

## Sir William Osler 1849–1919

3 One finger in the throat and one in the
rectum makes a good diagnostician.
*Aphorisms from his Bedside Teachings* (1961)
p. 104

## John L. O'Sullivan 1813–95

4 The best government is that which governs
least.
*United States Magazine and Democratic Review*
(1837) introduction

5 A torchlight procession marching down
your throat.
Of whisky, in G. W. E. Russell *Collections and
Recollections* (1898) ch. 19

## James Otis 1725–83

6 Taxation without representation is
tyranny.
Watchword (coined *c*.1761) of the American
Revolution. See *Dictionary of American
Biography* vol. 14, p. 102

## Thomas Otway 1652–85

7 No praying, it spoils business.
*Venice Preserved* (1682) act 2, l. 87

## Sir Thomas Overbury 1581–1613

8 He disdains all things above his reach, and
preferreth all countries before his own.
*Miscellaneous Works* (1632) 'An Affected
Traveller'. Cf. 89:11, 121:17, 151:20

## Ovid 43 BC–AD c.17

9 *Procul hinc, procul este, severae!*
Far hence, keep far from me, you grim
women!
*Amores* bk. 2, no. 1, l. 3

10 *Iuppiter ex alto periuria ridet amantum.*
Jupiter from on high laughs at lovers'
perjuries.
*Ars Amatoria* bk. 1, l. 633

11 *Expedit esse deos, et, ut expedit, esse putemus.*
It is convenient that there be gods, and, as
it is convenient, let us believe that there
are.
*Ars Amatoria* bk. 1, l. 637

12 *Gutta cavat lapidem, consumitur anulus usu.*
Dripping water hollows out a stone, a ring
is worn away by use.
*Epistulae Ex Ponto* bk. 4, no. 10, l. 5. Cf. 202:3

13 *Medio tutissimus ibis.*
You will go most safely by the middle way.
*Metamorphoses* bk. 2, l. 137

14 *Inopem me copia fecit.*
Plenty has made me poor.
*Metamorphoses* bk. 3, l. 466

15 *Video meliora, proboque;
Deteriora sequor.*
I see the better things, and approve; I
follow the worse.
*Metamorphoses* bk. 7, l. 20

16 *Tempus edax rerum.*
Time the devourer of everything.
*Metamorphoses* bk. 15, l. 234

## John Owen c.1563–1622

17 God and the doctor we alike adore
But only when in danger, not before;
The danger o'er, both are alike requited,
God is forgotten, and the Doctor slighted.
*Epigrams.* Cf. 256:27

## Robert Owen 1771–1858

18 All the world is queer save thee and me,
and even thou art a little queer.
To his partner W. Allen, on severing
business relations at New Lanark, 1828
(attributed)

## Wilfred Owen 1893–1918

19 My subject is War, and the pity of War.
The Poetry is in the pity.
*Poems* (1963) preface (written 1918)

20 All a poet can do today is warn.
*Poems* (1963) preface (written 1918)

21 What passing-bells for these who die as
cattle?
Only the monstrous anger of the guns.
'Anthem for Doomed Youth' (written 1917)

22 The shrill, demented choirs of wailing
shells;
And bugles calling for them from sad
shires.
'Anthem for Doomed Youth' (written 1917)

23 The pallor of girls' brows shall be their
pall;
Their flowers the tenderness of patient
minds,
And each slow dusk a drawing-down of
blinds.
'Anthem for Doomed Youth' (written 1917)

24 Move him into the sun—
Gently its touch awoke him once,
At home, whispering of fields half-sown.
'Futility' (written 1918)

1 Red lips are not so red
As the stained stones kissed by the English dead.
'Greater Love' (written 1917)

2 It seemed that out of battle I escaped
Down some profound dull tunnel, long since scooped
Through granites which titanic wars had groined.
'Strange Meeting' (written 1918)

3 I am the enemy you killed, my friend.
I knew you in this dark.
'Strange Meeting' (written 1918)

4 Let us sleep now.
'Strange Meeting' (written 1918)

## Count Oxenstierna 1583–1654

5 Dost thou not know, my son, with how little wisdom the world is governed?
Letter to his son, 1648, in J. F. af Lundblad *Svensk Plutark* (1826) pt. 2, p. 95. In *Table Talk* (1689) John Selden quotes 'a certain Pope': 'Thou little thinkest what *a little foolery governs the whole world!*'

## Thomas Paine 1737–1809

6 It is necessary to the happiness of man that he be mentally faithful to himself. Infidelity does not consist in believing, or in disbelieving, it consists in professing to believe what one does not believe.
*The Age of Reason* pt. 1 (1794) p. 2

7 Any system of religion that has any thing in it that shocks the mind of a child cannot be a true system.
*The Age of Reason* pt. 1 (1794) p. 39

8 The sublime and the ridiculous are often so nearly related, that it is difficult to class them separately. One step above the sublime, makes the ridiculous; and one step above the ridiculous, makes the sublime again.
*The Age of Reason* pt. 2 (1795) p. 20

9 Government, even in its best state, is but a necessary evil; in its worst state, an intolerable one. Government, like dress, is the badge of lost innocence; the palaces of kings are built upon the ruins of the bowers of paradise.
*Common Sense* (1776) ch. 1

10 As to religion, I hold it to be the indispensable duty of government to protect all conscientious professors thereof, and I know of no other business which government hath to do therewith.
*Common Sense* (1776) ch. 4

11 These are the times that try men's souls. The summer soldier and the sunshine patriot will, in this crisis, shrink from the service of their country; but he that stands it *now*, deserves the love and thanks of men and women.
*The Crisis* (December 1776) introduction

12 As he rose like a rocket, he fell like the stick.
On Edmund Burke losing the debate on the French Revolution to Charles James Fox, in the House of Commons; in *Letter to the Addressers on the late Proclamation* (1792) p. 4

13 When, in countries that are called civilized, we see age going to the workhouse and youth to the gallows, something must be wrong in the system of government.
*The Rights of Man* pt. 2 (1792, ed. P. S. Foner, 1945) p. 404

14 My country is the world, and my religion is to do good.
*The Rights of Man* pt. 2 (1792, ed. P. S. Foner, 1945) p. 414

15 A share in two revolutions is living to some purpose.
In E. Foner *Tom Paine and Revolutionary America* (1976) ch. 7

## José de Palafox 1780–1847

16 *Guerra a cuchillo.*
War to the knife.
At the siege of Saragossa, 4 August 1808, replying to the suggestion that he should surrender (as reported). He actually said '*Guerra y cuchillo* [War and the knife]'. See José Gòmez de Arteche y Moro *Guerra de la Independencia* (1875) vol. 2, ch. 4

## William Paley 1743–1805

17 Who can refute a sneer?
*Principles of Moral and Political Philosophy* (1785) bk. 5, ch. 9

## Lord Palmerston 1784–1865

18 We have no eternal allies and we have no perpetual enemies. Our interests are eternal and perpetual, and those interests it is our duty to follow.
Speech, *Hansard* 1 March 1848, col. 122

19 You may call it combination, you may call it the accidental and fortuitous concurrence of atoms.
On a projected Palmerston–Disraeli coalition, in *Hansard* 5 March 1857, col. 1934

20 What is merit? The opinion one man entertains of another.
In T. Carlyle *Shooting Niagara: and After?* (1867) ch. 8

21 [Palmerston] once said that only three men in Europe had ever understood [the Schleswig-Holstein question], and of these the Prince Consort was dead, a Danish statesman (unnamed) was in an asylum, and he himself had forgotten it.
In R. W. Seton-Watson *Britain in Europe 1789–1914* (1937) ch. 11

22 Die, my dear Doctor, that's the last thing I shall do!
Last words, in E. Latham *Famous Sayings and their Authors* (1904) p. 12

## Norman Panama 1914– and Melvin Frank 1913–88

1 The pellet with the poison's in the vessel with the pestle. The chalice from the palace has the brew that is true.
   *The Court Jester* (1955 film); spoken by Danny Kaye

## Emmeline Pankhurst 1858–1928

2 The argument of the broken window pane is the most valuable argument in modern politics.
   In G. Dangerfield *The Strange Death of Liberal England* (1936) pt. 2, ch. 3, sect. 4

## Mitchell Parish d. 1993

3 When the deep purple falls over sleepy garden walls.
   'Deep Purple' (1939 song)

## Dorothy Parker 1893–1967

4 Oh, life is a glorious cycle of song,
   A medley of extemporanea;
   And love is a thing that can never go wrong;
   And I am Marie of Roumania.
   'Comment' (1937)

5 Four be the things I'd been better without:
   Love, curiosity, freckles, and doubt.
   'Inventory' (1937)

6 Men seldom make passes
   At girls who wear glasses.
   'News Item' (1937)

7 Why is it no one ever sent me yet
   One perfect limousine, do you suppose?
   Ah no, it's always just my luck to get
   One perfect rose.
   'One Perfect Rose' (1937)

8 Guns aren't lawful;
   Nooses give;
   Gas smells awful;
   You might as well live.
   'Résumé' (1937)

9 By the time you say you're his,
   Shivering and sighing
   And he vows his passion is
   Infinite, undying—
   Lady, make a note of this:
   One of you is lying.
   'Unfortunate Coincidence' (1937)

10 And I'll stay off Verlaine too; he was always chasing Rimbauds.
   *Here Lies* (1939) 'The Little Hours'

11 Sorrow is tranquillity remembered in emotion.
   *Here Lies* (1939) 'Sentiment'. Cf. 357:12

12 How do they know?
   On being told that Calvin Coolidge had died; in M. Cowley *Writers at Work* 1st Series (1958) p. 65

13 *House Beautiful* is play lousy.
   *New Yorker* review (1933), in P. Hartnoll *Plays and Players* (1984) p. 89

14 You can lead a horticulture, but you can't make her think.
   In J. Keats *You Might as well Live* (1970) p. 46

15 It serves me right for putting all my eggs in one bastard.
   On her abortion; in J. Keats *You Might as well Live* (1970) pt. 2, ch. 3

16 She ran the whole gamut of the emotions from A to B.
   Of Katharine Hepburn at a Broadway first night (attributed)

## Martin Parker d. c.1656

17 You gentlemen of England
   Who live at home at ease,
   How little do you think
   On the dangers of the seas.
   'The Valiant Sailors'. See *Early Naval Ballads* (Percy Society, 1841)

18 But all's to no end, for the times will not mend
   Till the King enjoys his own again.
   'Upon Defacing of Whitehall' (1671)

## Ross Parker 1914–74 and Hugh Charles 1907–

19 There'll always be an England
   While there's a country lane,
   Wherever there's a cottage small
   Beside a field of grain.
   'There'll always be an England' (1939 song)

## C. Northcote Parkinson 1909–93

20 Expenditure rises to meet income.
   *The Law and the Profits* (1960) ch. 1

21 Work expands so as to fill the time available for its completion.
   *Parkinson's Law* (1958) ch. 1

22 Time spent on any item of the agenda will be in inverse proportion to the sum involved.
   *Parkinson's Law* (1958) ch. 3

## Charles Stewart Parnell 1846–91

23 No man has a right to fix the boundary of the march of a nation; no man has a right to say to his country—thus far shalt thou go and no further.
   Speech, 21 January 1885, in *The Times* 22 January 1885

## Blaise Pascal 1623–62

24 I have made this [letter] longer than usual, only because I have not had the time to make it shorter.
   *Lettres Provinciales* (1657) no. 16

1 When we see a natural style, we are quite
surprised and delighted, for we expected to
see an author and we find a man.
  *Pensées* (1670, ed. L. Brunschvicg, 1909) sect. 1,
  no. 29

2 Had Cleopatra's nose been shorter, the
whole face of the world would have
changed.
  *Pensées* (1670) sect. 2, no. 162

3 The eternal silence of these infinite spaces
[the heavens] terrifies me.
  *Pensées* (1670) sect. 2, no. 206

4 We shall die alone.
  *Pensées* (1670) sect. 3, no. 211

5 The heart has its reasons which reason
knows nothing of.
  *Pensées* (1670) sect. 4, no. 277

6 Man is only a reed, the weakest thing in
nature; but he is a thinking reed.
  *Pensées* (1670) sect. 6, no. 347

7 The self is hateful.
  *Pensées* (1670) sect. 7, no. 455

8 Comfort yourself, you would not seek me if
you had not found me.
  *Pensées* (1670) sect. 7, no. 553

## Boris Pasternak 1890–1960

9 Man is born to live, not to prepare for life.
  *Doctor Zhivago* (1958) pt. 2, ch. 9, sect. 14

10 Yet the order of the acts is planned
And the end of the way inescapable.
I am alone; all drowns in the Pharisees'
hypocrisy.
To live your life is not as simple as to cross
a field.
  *Doctor Zhivago* (1958) 'Hamlet' (tr. M. Hayward
  and M. Harari)

## Louis Pasteur 1822–95

11 Where observation is concerned, chance
favours only the prepared mind.
  Address, 7 December 1854; in R. Vallery-
  Radot *La Vie de Pasteur* (1900) ch. 4

12 There are no such things as applied
sciences, only applications of science.
  Address, 11 September 1872, in *Comptes
  rendus des travaux du Congrès viticole et séricicole
  de Lyon, 9–14 septembre 1872*

## Walter Pater 1839–94

13 She is older than the rocks among which
she sits.
  *Studies in the History of the Renaissance* (1873)
  'Leonardo da Vinci' (of the *Mona Lisa*)

14 All art constantly aspires towards the
condition of music.
  *Studies in the History of the Renaissance* (1873)
  'The School of Giorgione'

15 To burn always with this hard, gemlike
flame, to maintain this ecstasy, is success
in life.
  *Studies in the History of the Renaissance* (1873)
  'Conclusion'

## 'Banjo' Paterson 1864–1941

16 Once a jolly swagman camped by
a billabong,
Under the shade of a coolibah tree;
And he sang as he watched and waited till
his 'Billy' boiled:
'You'll come a-waltzing, Matilda, with me.'
  'Waltzing Matilda' (1903 song)

## Coventry Patmore 1823–96

17 'I saw you take his kiss!' ''Tis true.'
'O modesty!' ''Twas strictly kept:
He thought me asleep; at least, I knew
He thought I thought he thought I slept.'
  *The Angel in the House* (1854–62) bk. 2, canto 8,
  'The Kiss'

18 Some dish more sharply spiced than this
Milk-soup men call domestic bliss.
  'Olympus' l. 15

## Alan Paton 1903–

19 Cry, the beloved country.
  Title of novel (1948)

## James Payn 1830–98

20 I had never had a piece of toast
Particularly long and wide,
But fell upon the sanded floor,
And always on the buttered side.
  *Chambers's Journal* 2 February 1884. Cf. 234:19

## J. H. Payne 1791–1852

21 Mid pleasures and palaces though we may
roam,
Be it ever so humble, there's no place like
home.
  *Clari, or, The Maid of Milan* (1823 opera)
  'Home, Sweet Home'

## Thomas Love Peacock 1785–1866

22 Where they [the Greeks] had anything that
exalts, delights, or adorns humanity, we
have nothing but cant, cant, cant.
  *Crotchet Castle* (1831) ch. 7

23 My house has been broken open on the
most scientific principles.
  *Crotchet Castle* (1831) ch. 17

24 Marriage may often be a stormy lake, but
celibacy is almost always a muddy
horsepond.
  *Melincourt* (1817) ch. 7

25 Laughter is pleasant, but the exertion is
too much for me.
  *Nightmare Abbey* (1818) ch. 5

## Hesketh Pearson 1887–1964

26 There is no stronger craving in the world
than that of the rich for titles, except
perhaps that of the titled for riches.
  *The Pilgrim Daughters* (1961) ch. 6

### George Peele c.1556–96

1 What thing is love for (well I wot) love is a thing.
   It is a prick, it is a sting,
   It is a pretty, pretty thing.
   *The Hunting of Cupid* (c.1591)

2 When as the rye reach to the chin,
   And chopcherry, chopcherry ripe within,
   Strawberries swimming in the cream,
   And schoolboys playing in the stream,
   Then O, then O, then O, my true love said,
   Till that time come again,
   She could not live a maid.
   *The Old Wive's Tale* (1595) l. 75 'Song'

3 His golden locks time hath to silver turned;
   O time too swift, O swiftness never ceasing!
   *Polyhymnia* (1590) *ad fin.* 'Sonnet'

### Charles Péguy 1873–1914

4 Tyranny is always better organised than freedom.
   *Basic Verities* (1943) 'War and Peace'

### William Herbert, 1st Earl of Pembroke c.1501–70

5 Out ye whores, to work, to work, ye whores, go spin.
   In A. Clark (ed.) *'Brief Lives ... by John Aubrey'* (1898) vol. 1 (commonly quoted 'Go spin, you jades, go spin')

### Henry Herbert, 2nd Earl of Pembroke c.1534–1601

6 A parliament can do any thing but make a man a woman, and a woman a man.
   Quoted by his son, the 4th Earl, in a speech on 11 April 1648; in *Harleian Miscellany* (1745) vol. 5, p. 106

### Henry Herbert, 10th Earl of Pembroke 1734–94

7 Dr Johnson's sayings would not appear so extraordinary, were it not for his bow-wow way.
   In James Boswell *Life of Samuel Johnson* (1934 ed.) vol. 2, p. 326 n. (27 March 1775)

### Vladimir Peniakoff 1897–1951

8 A message came on the wireless for me. It said: 'SPREAD ALARM AND DESPONDENCY' ...
   The date was, I think, May 18th, 1942.
   *Private Army* (1950) pt. 2, ch. 5 ('reports calculated to create unnecessary alarm or despondency' derives from the Army Act of 1879)

### William Penn 1644–1718

9 No pain, no palm; no thorns, no throne; no gall, no glory; no cross, no crown.
   *No Cross, No Crown* (1669 pamphlet)

10 Men are generally more careful of the breed of their horses and dogs than of their children.
   *Some Fruits of Solitude* (1693) pt. 1, no. 85

### Roger Penrose 1931–

11 Consciousness ... is the phenomenon whereby the universe's very existence is made known.
   *The Emperor's New Mind* (1989) ch. 10 'Conclusion'

### Samuel Pepys 1633–1703

12 And so to bed.
   *Diary* 20 April 1660

13 I went out to Charing Cross, to see Major-general Harrison hanged, drawn, and quartered; which was done there, he looking as cheerful as any man could do in that condition.
   *Diary* 13 October 1660

14 A good honest and painful sermon.
   *Diary* 17 March 1661

15 I see it is impossible for the King to have things done as cheap as other men.
   *Diary* 21 July 1662

16 My wife, who, poor wretch, is troubled with her lonely life.
   *Diary* 19 December 1662

17 Pretty witty Nell.
   *Diary* 3 April 1665 (of Nell Gwyn)

18 Strange to say what delight we married people have to see these poor fools decoyed into our condition.
   *Diary* 25 December 1665

19 Music and women I cannot but give way to, whatever my business is.
   *Diary* 9 March 1666

20 But it is pretty to see what money will do.
   *Diary* 21 March 1667

21 This day my wife made it appear to me that my late entertainment this week cost me above £12, an expense which I am almost ashamed of, though it is but once in a great while, and is the end for which, in the most part, we live, to have such a merry day once or twice in a man's life.
   *Diary* 6 March 1669

22 And so I betake myself to that course, which is almost as much as to see myself go into my grave—for which, and all the discomforts that will accompany my being blind, the good God prepare me!
   *Diary* 31 May 1669

### S. J. Perelman 1904–79

23 Crazy like a fox.
   Title of book (1944)

## Pericles c.495–429 BC

1 Our love of what is beautiful does not lead
to extravagance; our love of the things of
the mind does not make us soft.
   Funeral Oration, Athens, 430 BC, in
   Thucydides *History of the Peloponnesian War*
   bk. 2, ch. 40, sect. 1 (tr. R. Warner)

2 Famous men have the whole earth as their
memorial.
   In Thucydides *History of the Peloponnesian War*
   bk. 2, ch. 43, sect. 3 (tr. R. Warner)

3 The greatest glory of a woman is to be
least talked about by men.
   In Thucydides *History of the Peloponnesian War*
   bk. 2, ch. 45, sect. 2 (tr. R. Warner)

## Edward Perronet 1726–92

4 All hail the power of Jesus' Name;
Let Angels prostrate fall;
Bring forth the royal diadem
To crown Him Lord of all.
   'All hail the power of Jesus' Name' (1780
   hymn)

## Jimmy Perry

5 Who do you think you are kidding, Mister
Hitler?
   Theme song of *Dad's Army*, BBC television
   (1968–77)

## Ted Persons

6 Things ain't what they used to be.
   Title of song (1941)

## Marshal Pétain 1856–1951

7 To write one's memoirs is to speak ill of
everybody except oneself.
   In *Observer* 26 May 1946

## Laurence Peter 1919–

8 In a hierarchy every employee tends to rise
to his level of incompetence.
   *The Peter Principle* (1969) ch. 1

## Petronius d. AD 65

9 *Abiit ad plures.*
   He's gone to join the majority [the dead].
   *Satyricon* 'Cena Trimalchionis' ch. 42, sect. 5

10 *Foeda est in coitu et brevis voluptas
Et taedet Veneris statim peractae.*
Delight of lust is gross and brief
And weariness treads on desire.
   In A. Baehrens *Poetae Latini Minores* (1882)
   vol. 4, no. 101 (tr. H. Waddell)

## Edward John Phelps 1822–1900

11 The man who makes no mistakes does not
usually make anything.
   Speech, 24 January 1889; in *The Times*
   25 January 1889, p. 10

## Kim Philby 1912–88

12 To betray, you must first belong.
   In *Sunday Times* 17 December 1967, p. 2

## 'Jack' Philip 1840–1900

13 Don't cheer, men; those poor devils are
dying.
   At the Battle of Santiago, 4 July 1898; in
   *Dictionary of American Biography* vol. 14 (1934)
   'John Woodward Philip'

## Ambrose Philips c.1675–1749

14 The flowers anew, returning seasons bring;
But beauty faded has no second spring.
   *The First Pastoral* (1708) 'Lobbin' l. 47

15 There solid billows of enormous size,
Alps of green ice, in wild disorder rise.
   'A Winter-Piece' in *The Tatler* (7 May 1709)

## Stephen Phillips 1864–1915

16 Behold me now
A man not old, but mellow, like good wine.
Not over-jealous, yet an eager husband.
   *Ulysses* (1902) act 3, sc. 2

## Eden Phillpotts 1862–1960

17 A little dreamin', a little dyin',
A little lew corner of airth to lie in.
   'Gaffer's Song' (1942)

## Pablo Picasso 1881–1973

18 God is really only another artist. He
invented the giraffe, the elephant, and the
cat. He has no real style. He just goes on
trying other things.
   In F. Gilot and C. Lake *Life With Picasso* (1964)
   pt. 1

19 Every positive value has its price in
negative terms ... The genius of Einstein
leads to Hiroshima.
   In F. Gilot and C. Lake *Life With Picasso* (1964)
   pt. 2

## Harold Pinter 1930–

20 If only I could get down to Sidcup! I've
been waiting for the weather to break. He's
got my papers, this man I left them with,
it's got it all down there, I could prove
everything.
   *The Caretaker* (1960) act 1

21 Apart from the known and the unknown,
what else is there?
   *The Homecoming* (1965) act 2, sc. 1

22 The weasel under the cocktail cabinet.
   On being asked what his plays were about,
   in J. Russell Taylor *Anger and After* (1962)
   p. 231

## Luigi Pirandello 1867–1936

1 Six characters in search of an author.
   Title of play (1921)

## Robert M. Pirsig 1928–

2 That's the classical mind at work, runs fine
   inside but looks dingy on the surface.
   *Zen and the Art of Motorcycle Maintenance* (1974)
   pt. 3, ch. 26

## William Pitt, Earl of Chatham
1708–78

3 The atrocious crime of being a young man
   ... I shall neither attempt to palliate nor
   deny.
   Speech, *Hansard* 2 March 1741, col. 115

4 Unlimited power is apt to corrupt the
   minds of those who possess it.
   Speech, *Hansard* (Lords) 9 January 1770,
   col. 665. Cf. 1:5

5 I invoke the genius of the Constitution!
   Speech, *Hansard* (Lords) 18 November 1777,
   col. 369

6 The parks are the lungs of London.
   In *Hansard* 30 June 1808, col. 1124 (quoted by
   William Windham)

## William Pitt 1759–1806

7 Necessity is the plea for every
   infringement of human freedom: it is the
   argument of tyrants; it is the creed of
   slaves.
   Speech, *Hansard* 18 November 1783, col. 1209

8 England has saved herself by her exertions,
   and will, as I trust, save Europe by her
   example.
   In R. Coupland *War Speeches of William Pitt*
   (1915) p. 35 (9 November 1805)

9 Roll up that map; it will not be wanted
   these ten years.
   Of a map of Europe, on hearing of
   Napoleon's victory at Austerlitz, December
   1805; in Earl Stanhope *Life of the Rt. Hon.
   William Pitt* vol. 4 (1862) ch. 43

10 Oh, my country! how I leave my country!
   Last words, in Earl Stanhope *Life of the Rt.
   Hon. William Pitt* vol. 3 (1879) ch. 43 ('How I
   love my country' in the 1st ed., vol. 4 (1862)
   ch. 43). G. Rose *Diaries and Correspondence*
   (1860) vol. 2, cites 'My country! oh, my
   country!'; oral tradition reports 'I think I
   could eat one of Bellamy's veal pies'

## Pope Pius VII 1742–1823

11 We are prepared to go to the gates of
   Hell—but no further.
   Attempting to reach an agreement with
   Napoleon, *c*.1800–1, in J. M. Robinson
   *Cardinal Consalvi* (1987) p. 66

## Max Planck 1858–1947

12 A new scientific truth does not triumph by
   convincing its opponents and making
   them see the light, but rather because its
   opponents eventually die, and a new
   generation grows up that is familiar with
   it.
   *A Scientific Autobiography* (1949) p. 33 (tr. F.
   Gaynor)

## Sylvia Plath 1932–63

13 Is there no way out of the mind?
   'Apprehensions' (1971)

14 Every woman adores a Fascist,
   The boot in the face, the brute
   Brute heart of a brute like you.
   'Daddy' (1963)

15 Dying,
   Is an art, like everything else.
   'Lady Lazarus' (1963)

16 Love set you going like a fat gold watch.
   'Morning Song' (1965)

17 Widow. The word consumes itself.
   'Widow' (1971)

## Plato 429–347 BC

18 Socrates, he says, breaks the law by
   corrupting young men and not recognizing
   the gods that the city recognizes, but some
   other new deities.
   *Apologia* 24b

19 Is that which is holy loved by the gods
   because it is holy, or is it holy because it is
   loved by the gods?
   *Euthyphro* 10

20 This was the end, Echekrates, of our friend;
   a man of whom we may say that of all
   whom we met at that time he was the
   wisest and justest and best.
   *Phaedo* 118a (on the death of Socrates)

21 What I say is that 'just' or 'right' means
   nothing but what is in the interest of the
   stronger party.
   Spoken by Thrasymachus in *The Republic*
   bk. 1, 338c (tr. F. M. Cornford)

## Plautus *c*.250–184 BC

22 *Dictum sapienti sat est.*
   A sentence is enough for a sensible man.
   *Persa* l. 729 (proverbially '*Verbum sapienti sat
   est* [A word is enough for the wise]')

## Pliny the Elder AD 23–79

23 *Semper aliquid novi Africam adferre.*
   Africa always brings [us] something new.
   *Historia Naturalis* bk. 8, sect. 42 (often quoted
   '*Ex Africa semper aliquid novi* [Always
   something new out of Africa]')

## William Plomer 1903-73

1 With first-rate sherry flowing into second-
rate whores,
And third-rate conversation without one
single pause:
Just like a young couple
Between the wars.
'Father and Son: 1939' (1945)

## Plutarch AD c.46-c.120

2 He who cheats with an oath acknowledges
that he is afraid of his enemy, but that he
thinks little of God.
*Parallel Lives* 'Lysander' ch. 8

## Edgar Allan Poe 1809-49

3 I was a child and she was a child,
In this kingdom by the sea;
But we loved with a love which was more
than love—
I and my Annabel Lee.
'Annabel Lee' (1849)

4 Keeping time, time, time,
In a sort of Runic rhyme,
To the tintinnabulation that so musically
wells
From the bells, bells, bells, bells.
'The Bells' (1849) st. 1

5 All that we see or seem
Is but a dream within a dream.
'A Dream within a Dream' (1849)

6 The fever called 'Living'
Is conquered at last.
'For Annie' (1849)

7 Take thy beak from out my heart, and take
thy form from off my door!
Quoth the Raven, 'Nevermore'.
'The Raven' (1845) st. 17

8 Helen, thy beauty is to me
Like those Nicean barks of yore.
'To Helen' (1831)

9 Thy Naiad airs have brought me home,
To the glory that was Greece
And the grandeur that was Rome.
'To Helen' (1831)

## Henri Poincaré 1854-1912

10 Science is built up of facts, as a house is
built of stones; but an accumulation of
facts is no more a science than a heap of
stones is a house.
*Science and Hypothesis* (1905) ch. 9

## Madame de Pompadour 1721-64

11 *Après nous le déluge.*
After us the deluge.
In Mme du Hausset *Mémoires* (1824) p. 19

## Georges Pompidou 1911-74

12 A statesman is a politician who places
himself at the service of the nation.
A politician is a statesman who places the
nation at his service.
In *Observer* 30 December 1973 'Sayings of the
Year'

## Alexander Pope 1688-1744

13 Gentle Dullness ever loves a joke.
*The Dunciad* (1742) bk. 2, l. 34

14 A brain of feathers, and a heart of lead.
*The Dunciad* (1742) bk. 2, l. 44

15 Flow Welsted, flow! like thine inspirer,
Beer,
Tho' stale, not ripe; tho' thin, yet never
clear;
So sweetly mawkish, and so smoothly dull;
Heady, not strong; o'erflowing tho' not full.
*The Dunciad* (1742) bk. 3, l. 169

16 'Till Isis' elders reel, their pupils' sport,
And Alma mater lie dissolved in port!
*The Dunciad* (1742) bk. 3, l. 337

17 A wit with dunces, and a dunce with wits.
*The Dunciad* (1742) bk. 4, l. 90

18 The Right Divine of Kings to govern wrong.
*The Dunciad* (1742) bk. 4, l. 187

19 With the same cement, ever sure to bind,
We bring to one dead level ev'ry mind.
*The Dunciad* (1742) bk. 4, l. 267

20 Stretched on the rack of a too easy chair.
*The Dunciad* (1742) bk. 4, l. 342

21 Thy truffles, Perigord! thy hams, Bayonne!
*The Dunciad* (1742) bk. 4, l. 558

22 Lo! thy dread empire, Chaos! is restored;
Light dies before thy uncreating word:
Thy hand, great Anarch! lets the curtain
fall;
And universal darkness buries all.
*The Dunciad* (1742) bk. 4, l. 653

23 Is there no bright reversion in the sky,
For those who greatly think, or bravely
die?
'Elegy to the Memory of an Unfortunate
Lady' (1717) l. 9

24 Ambition first sprung from your blest
abodes;
The glorious fault of angels and of gods.
'Elegy to the Memory of an Unfortunate
Lady' (1717) l. 13

25 How shall I lose the sin, yet keep the sense,
And love th'offender, yet detest th'offence?
'Eloisa to Abelard' (1717) l. 191. Cf. 22:4

26 How happy is the blameless Vestal's lot!
The world forgetting, by the world forgot.
'Eloisa to Abelard' (1717) l. 207

27 You beat your pate, and fancy wit will
come:
Knock as you please, there's nobody at
home.
'Epigram: You beat your pate' (1732)

1 I am his Highness' dog at Kew;
   Pray, tell me sir, whose dog are you?
   'Epigram Engraved on the Collar of a Dog
   which I gave to his Royal Highness' (1738)

2 Sir, I admit your gen'ral rule
   That every poet is a fool:
   But you yourself may serve to show it,
   That every fool is not a poet.
   'Epigram from the French' (1732)

3 You think this cruel? take it for a rule,
   No creature smarts so little as a fool.
   'An Epistle to Dr Arbuthnot' (1735) l. 83.

4 The Muse but served to ease some friend,
      not wife,
   To help me through this long disease, my
      life.
   'An Epistle to Dr Arbuthnot' (1735) l. 131

5 And he, whose fustian's so sublimely bad,
   It is not poetry, but prose run mad.
   'An Epistle to Dr Arbuthnot' (1735) l. 187

6 Damn with faint praise, assent with civil
      leer,
   And without sneering, teach the rest to
      sneer.
   'An Epistle to Dr Arbuthnot' (1735) l. 201.
   Cf. 358:6

7 Satire or sense, alas! can Sporus feel?
   Who breaks a butterfly upon a wheel?'
   'An Epistle to Dr Arbuthnot' (1735) l. 307

8 Yet let me flap this bug with gilded wings,
   This painted child of dirt that stinks and
      stings.
   'An Epistle to Dr Arbuthnot' (1735) l. 309

9 Unlearn'd, he knew no schoolman's subtle
      art,
   No language, but the language of the
      heart.
   'An Epistle to Dr Arbuthnot' (1735) l. 398

10 Virtue she finds too painful an endeavour,
   Content to dwell in decencies for ever.
   Epistles to Several Persons 'To a Lady' (1735)
   l. 163

11 See how the world its veterans rewards!
   A youth of frolics, an old age of cards.
   Epistles to Several Persons 'To a Lady' (1735)
   l. 241

12 Woman's at best a contradiction still.
   Epistles to Several Persons 'To a Lady' (1735)
   l. 270

13 Die, and endow a college, or a cat.
   Epistles to Several Persons 'To Lord Bathurst'
   (1733) l. 98

14 The ruling passion, be it what it will,
   The ruling passion conquers reason still.
   Epistles to Several Persons 'To Lord Bathurst'
   (1733) l. 155. Cf. 251:21

15 Consult the genius of the place in all.
   Epistles to Several Persons 'To Lord Burlington'
   (1731) l. 57. Cf. 339:18

16 To rest, the cushion and soft Dean invite,
   Who never mentions Hell to ears polite.
   Epistles to Several Persons 'To Lord Burlington'
   (1731) l. 149

17 Deep harvests bury all his pride has
      planned,
   And laughing Ceres re-assume the land.
   Epistles to Several Persons 'To Lord Burlington'
   (1731) l. 175

18 'Tis use alone that sanctifies expense,
   And splendour borrows all her rays from
      sense.
   Epistles to Several Persons 'To Lord Burlington'
   (1731) l. 179

19 Like following life thro' creatures you
      dissect,
   You lose it in the moment you detect.
   Epistles to Several Persons 'To Lord Cobham'
   (1734) l. 39

20 'Tis from high life high characters are
      drawn;
   A saint in crape is twice a saint in lawn.
   Epistles to Several Persons 'To Lord Cobham'
   (1734) l. 87

21 Search then the Ruling Passion: There,
      alone,
   The wild are constant, and the cunning
      known;
   The fool consistent, and the false sincere.
   Epistles to Several Persons 'To Lord Cobham'
   (1734) l. 174. Cf. 251:14

22 Odious! in woollen! 'twould a saint
      provoke!
   Epistles to Several Persons 'To Lord Cobham'
   (1734) l. 242

23 Old politicians chew on wisdom past,
   And totter on in business to the last.
   Epistles to Several Persons 'To Lord Cobham'
   (1734) l. 248

24 She went, to plain-work, and to purling
      brooks,
   Old-fashioned halls, dull aunts, and
      croaking rooks.
   'Epistle to Miss Blount, on her leaving the
   Town, after the Coronation' (1717)

25 Or o'er cold coffee trifle with the spoon,
   Court the slow clock, and dine exact at
      noon.
   'Epistle to Miss Blount, on her leaving the
   Town . . . ' (1717)

26 Nature, and Nature's laws lay hid in night.
   God said, Let Newton be! and all was light.
   'Epitaph: Intended for Sir Isaac Newton'
   (1730). Cf. 314:4

27 Some have at first for wits, then poets
      passed,
   Turned critics next, and proved plain fools
      at last.
   An Essay on Criticism (1711) l. 36

28 A little learning is a dangerous thing;
   Drink deep, or taste not the Pierian spring:
   There shallow draughts intoxicate the
      brain,
   And drinking largely sobers us again.
   An Essay on Criticism (1711) l. 215. Cf. 126:20

29 Whoever thinks a faultless piece to see,
   Thinks what ne'er was, nor is, nor e'er
      shall be.
   An Essay on Criticism (1711) l. 253

1 True wit is Nature to advantage dressed,
  What oft was thought, but ne'er so well
  expressed.
  *An Essay on Criticism* (1711) l. 297

2 Expression is the dress of thought.
  *An Essay on Criticism* (1711) l. 318. Cf. 346:18

3              As some to church repair,
  Not for the doctrine, but the music there.
  *An Essay on Criticism* (1711) l. 342

4 A needless Alexandrine ends the song,
  That, like a wounded snake, drags its slow
  length along.
  *An Essay on Criticism* (1711) l. 356

5 But let a Lord once own the happy lines,
  How the wit brightens! how the style
  refines!
  *An Essay on Criticism* (1711) l. 420

6 Some praise at morning what they blame
  at night;
  But always think the last opinion right.
  *An Essay on Criticism* (1711) l. 430

7 To err is human; to forgive, divine.
  *An Essay on Criticism* (1711) l. 525

8 Men must be taught as if you taught them
  not,
  And things unknown proposed as things
  forgot.
  *An Essay on Criticism* (1711) l. 574

9 The bookful blockhead, ignorantly read,
  With loads of learned lumber in his head.
  *An Essay on Criticism* (1711) l. 612

10 Fools rush in where angels fear to tread.
   *An Essay on Criticism* (1711) l. 625

11 Eye Nature's walks, shoot Folly as it flies,
   And catch the Manners living as they rise.
   Laugh where we must, be candid where we
   can;
   But vindicate the ways of God to man.
   *An Essay on Man* Epistle 1 (1733) l. 13.
   Cf. 228:9

12 Hope springs eternal in the human breast:
   Man never Is, but always To be blest.
   *An Essay on Man* Epistle 1 (1733) l. 95

13 Lo! the poor Indian, whose untutored mind
   Sees God in clouds, or hears him in the
   wind.
   *An Essay on Man* Epistle 1 (1733) l. 99

14 Why has not man a microscopic eye?
   For this plain reason, man is not a fly.
   *An Essay on Man* Epistle 1 (1733) l. 193

15 The spider's touch, how exquisitely fine!
   Feels at each thread, and lives along the
   line.
   *An Essay on Man* Epistle 1 (1733) l. 217

16 And, spite of Pride, in erring Reason's
   spite,
   One truth is clear, 'Whatever IS, is RIGHT.'
   *An Essay on Man* Epistle 1 (1733) l. 293

17 Know then thyself, presume not God to
   scan;
   The proper study of mankind is man.
   *An Essay on Man* Epistle 2 (1733) l. 1.
   Cf. 95:9

18 Created half to rise, and half to fall;
   Great lord of all things, yet a prey to all;
   Sole judge of truth, in endless error hurled;
   The glory, jest, and riddle of the world!
   *An Essay on Man* Epistle 2 (1733) l. 15

19 Behold the child, by Nature's kindly law
   Pleased with a rattle, tickled with a straw.
   *An Essay on Man* Epistle 2 (1733) l. 275

20 For forms of government let fools contest;
   Whate'er is best administered is best.
   *An Essay on Man* Epistle 3 (1733) l. 303

21 Thus God and nature linked the gen'ral
   frame,
   And bade self-love and social be the same.
   *An Essay on Man* Epistle 3 (1733) l. 317. See
   also *An Essay on Man* Epistle 4 (1734) l. 396

22 An honest man's the noblest work of God.
   *An Essay on Man* Epistle 4 (1734) l. 248

23 All our knowledge is, ourselves to know.
   *An Essay on Man* Epistle 4 (1734) l. 398

24 For I, who hold sage Homer's rule the best,
   Welcome the coming, speed the going
   guest.
   *Imitations of Horace* Horace bk. 2, Satire 2
   (1734) l. 159 ('speed the parting guest' in
   Pope's translation of *The Odyssey* (1725–6)
   bk. 15, l. 84)

25 Get place and wealth, if possible, with
   grace;
   If not, by any means get wealth and place.
   *Imitations of Horace* Horace bk. 1, Epistle 1
   (1738) l. 103. Cf. 173:6

26 Not to admire, is all the art I know,
   To make men happy, and to keep them so.
   *Imitations of Horace* Horace bk. 1, Epistle 6
   (1738) l. 1. Cf. 173:10

27 The worst of madmen is a saint run mad.
   *Imitations of Horace* Horace bk. 1, Epistle 6
   (1738) l. 27

28              The people's voice is odd,
   It is, and it is not, the voice of God.
   *Imitations of Horace* Horace bk. 2, Epistle 1
   (1737) l. 89. Cf. 3:14

29 But those who cannot write, and those
   who can,
   All rhyme, and scrawl, and scribble, to a
   man.
   *Imitations of Horace* Horace bk. 2, Epistle 1
   (1737) l. 187. Cf. 173:16

30 Ev'n copious Dryden, wanted, or forgot,
   The last and greatest art, the art to blot.
   *Imitations of Horace* Horace bk. 2, Epistle 1
   (1737) l. 280. Cf. 165:11, 187:32

31 Let humble Allen, with an awkward shame,
   Do good by stealth, and blush to find it
   fame.
   *Imitations of Horace* Epilogue to the Satires
   (1738) Dialogue 1, l. 135

32 Ask you what provocation I have had?
   The strong antipathy of good to bad.
   *Imitations of Horace* Epilogue to the Satires
   (1738) Dialogue 2, l. 197

1 Where'er you walk, cool gales shall fan the glade,
Trees, where you sit, shall crowd into a shade.
*Pastorals* (1709) 'Summer' l. 73

2 What dire offence from am'rous causes springs.
*The Rape of the Lock* (1714) canto 1, l. 1

3 They shift the moving toyshop of their heart.
*The Rape of the Lock* (1714) canto 1, l. 100

4 Fair tresses man's imperial race insnare,
And beauty draws us with a single hair.
*The Rape of the Lock* (1714) canto 2, l. 27

5 Belinda smiled, and all the world was gay.
*The Rape of the Lock* (1714) canto 2, l. 52

6 Here thou, great Anna! whom three realms obey,
Dost sometimes counsel take—and sometimes tea.
*The Rape of the Lock* (1714) canto 3, l. 7

7 At ev'ry word a reputation dies.
*The Rape of the Lock* (1714) canto 3, l. 16

8 The hungry judges soon the sentence sign,
And wretches hang that jury-men may dine.
*The Rape of the Lock* (1714) canto 3, l. 21

9 Coffee, (which makes the politician wise,
And see thro' all things with his half-shut eyes).
*The Rape of the Lock* (1714) canto 3, l. 117

10 Not louder shrieks to pitying heav'n are cast,
When husbands or when lapdogs breathe their last.
*The Rape of the Lock* (1714) canto 3, l. 157

11 Party-spirit, which at best is but the madness of many for the gain of a few.
Letter to E. Blount, 27 August 1714, in G. Sherburn (ed.) *Correspondence of Alexander Pope* (1956) vol. 1

12 To endeavour to work upon the vulgar with fine sense, is like attempting to hew blocks with a razor.
*Miscellanies* (1727) vol. 2 'Thoughts on Various Subjects'

13 A man should never be ashamed to own he has been in the wrong, which is but saying, in other words, that he is wiser to-day than he was yesterday.
*Miscellanies* (1727) vol. 2 'Thoughts on Various Subjects'

14 Here am I, dying of a hundred good symptoms.
To Lord Lyttelton, 15 May 1744, in Joseph Spence *Anecdotes* (ed. J. Osborn, 1966) no. 637

## Sir Karl Popper 1902–94

15 We may become the makers of our fate when we have ceased to pose as its prophets.
*The Open Society and its Enemies* (1945) introduction

16 Science must begin with myths, and with the criticism of myths.
'The Philosophy of Science' in C. A. Mace (ed.) *British Philosophy in the Mid-Century* (1957)

## Cole Porter 1891–1964

17 In olden days a glimpse of stocking
Was looked on as something shocking
Now, heaven knows,
Anything goes.
'Anything Goes' (1934 song)

18 When they begin the Beguine
It brings back the sound of music so tender,
It brings back a night of tropical splendour,
It brings back a memory ever green.
'Begin the Beguine' (1935 song)

19 There's no love song finer,
But how strange the change from major to minor
Every time we say goodbye.
'Every Time We Say Goodbye' (1944 song)

20 I get no kick from champagne,
Mere alcohol doesn't thrill me at all.
'I Get a Kick Out of You' (1934 song)

21 So goodbye dear, and Amen,
Here's hoping we meet now and then,
It was great fun,
But it was just one of those things.
'Just One of Those Things' (1935 song)

22 Birds do it, bees do it,
Even educated fleas do it.
Let's do it, let's fall in love.
'Let's Do It' (1954 song; words added to the 1928 original)

23 Miss Otis regrets (she's unable to lunch today).
Title of song (1934)

24 My heart belongs to Daddy.
Title of song (1938)

25 Night and day, you are the one,
Only you beneath the moon and under the sun.
'Night and Day' (1932 song)

## Beilby Porteus 1731–1808

26 ... One murder made a villain,
Millions a hero.
*Death* (1759) l. 154. Cf. 263:12

27            Teach him how to live,
And, oh! still harder lesson! how to die.
*Death* (1759) l. 319

## Francis Pott 1832–1909

28 The strife is o'er, the battle done;
Now is the Victor's triumph won.
Hymn (1861); translation of 'Finita iam sunt praelia' (*c.*1695)

## Beatrix Potter 1866–1943

1 I am worn to a ravelling ... I am undone
and worn to a thread-paper, for I have NO
MORE TWIST.
   *The Tailor of Gloucester* (1903) p. 22

2 It is said that the effect of eating too much
lettuce is 'soporific'.
   *The Tale of the Flopsy Bunnies* (1909) p. 9

3 Don't go into Mr McGregor's garden: your
father had an accident there, he was put
into a pie by Mrs McGregor.
   *The Tale of Peter Rabbit* (1902) p. 10

## Stephen Potter 1900–69

4 *How to be one up*—how to make the other
man feel that something has gone wrong,
however slightly.
   *Lifemanship* (1950) p. 14

5 'Yes, but not in the South', with slight
adjustments, will do for any argument
about any place, if not about any person.
   *Lifemanship* (1950) p. 43

6 A good general rule is to state that the
bouquet is better than the taste, and vice
versa.
   *One-Upmanship* (1952) ch. 14 (on wine-tasting)

7 The theory and practice of gamesmanship
or The art of winning games without
actually cheating.
   Title of book (1947)

## Ezra Pound 1885–1972

8 Winter is icummen in,
Lhude sing Goddamm,
Raineth drop and staineth slop,
And how the wind doth ramm!
Sing: Goddamm.
   'Ancient Music' (1917). Cf. 10:16

9 With usura hath no man a house of good
stone
each block cut smooth and well fitting.
   *Cantos* (1954) no. 45

10 Tching prayed on the mountain and
wrote MAKE IT NEW
on his bath tub.
   *Cantos* (1954) no. 53

11 Bah! I have sung women in three cities,
But it is all the same;
And I will sing of the sun.
   'Cino' (1908)

12 Hang it all, Robert Browning,
There can be but the one 'Sordello'.
   *Draft of XXX Cantos* (1930) no. 2

13 And even I can remember
A day when the historians left blanks in
their writings,
I mean for things they didn't know.
   *Draft of XXX Cantos* (1930) no. 13

14 For three years, out of key with his time,
He strove to resuscitate the dead art
Of poetry; to maintain 'the sublime'
In the old sense. Wrong from the start.
   *Hugh Selwyn Mauberley* (1920) 'E. P. Ode pour
   l'élection de son sépulcre' pt. 1

15 His true Penelope was Flaubert,
He fished by obstinate isles;
Observed the elegance of Circe's hair
Rather than the mottoes on sundials.
   *Hugh Selwyn Mauberley* (1920) 'E. P. Ode ... '
   pt. 1

16 The age demanded an image
Of its accelerated grimace,
Something for the modern stage,
Not, at any rate, an Attic grace.
   *Hugh Selwyn Mauberley* (1920) 'E. P. Ode ... '
   pt. 2

17 Christ follows Dionysus,
Phallic and ambrosial
Made way for macerations;
Caliban casts out Ariel.
   *Hugh Selwyn Mauberley* (1920) 'E. P. Ode ... '
   pt. 3

18 Died some, pro patria,
non 'dulce' non 'et decor' ...
walked eye-deep in hell
believing in old men's lies, the unbelieving
came home, home to a lie.
   *Hugh Selwyn Mauberley* (1920) 'E. P. Ode ... '
   pt. 4. Cf. 173:26

19 There died a myriad,
And of the best, among them,
For an old bitch gone in the teeth,
For a botched civilization.
   *Hugh Selwyn Mauberley* (1920) 'E. P. Ode ... '
   pt. 5

20 The apparition of these faces in the crowd;
Petals on a wet, black bough.
   'In a Station of the Metro' (1916)

21 Pull down thy vanity
Thou art a beaten dog beneath the hail,
A swollen magpie in a fitful sun,
Half black half white
Nor knowst'ou wing from tail.
   *pisan Cantos* (1948) no. 81

22 Music begins to atrophy when it departs
too far from the dance ... poetry begins to
atrophy when it gets too far from music.
   *The ABC of Reading* (1934) 'Warning'

23 Literature is news that STAYS news.
   *The ABC of Reading* (1934) ch. 2

24 Poetry must be *as well written as prose*.
   Letter to Harriet Monroe, January 1915, in D.
   Paige (ed.) *Selected Letters* (1950)

## Anthony Powell 1905–

25 Books do furnish a room.
   Title of novel (1971). Cf. 310:2

26 He's so wet you could shoot snipe off him.
   *A Question of Upbringing* (1951) ch. 1

1 Growing old is like being increasingly
penalized for a crime you haven't
committed.
*Temporary Kings* (1973) ch. 1

## Enoch Powell 1912–

2 History is littered with the wars which
everybody knew would never happen.
Speech, 19 October 1967, in *The Times*
20 October 1967

3 As I look ahead, I am filled with
foreboding. Like the Roman, I seem to see
'the River Tiber foaming with much blood'.
Speech, 20 April 1968, in *Observer* 21 April
1968. Cf. 339:11

## John O'Connor Power b. 1846

4 The mules of politics: without pride of
ancestry, or hope of posterity.
Of the Liberal Unionists, in H. H. Asquith
*Memories and Reflections* (1928) vol. 1, ch. 16

## Keith Preston 1884–1927

5 Of all the literary scenes
Saddest this sight to me:
The graves of little magazines
Who died to make verse free.
'The Liberators'

## Jacques Prévert 1900–77

6 *C'est tellement simple, l'amour.*
It's so simple, love.
*Les Enfants du Paradis* (1945 film)

## J. B. Priestley 1894–1984

7 First you take their faces from 'em by
calling 'em the masses and then you
accuse 'em of not having any faces.
*Saturn Over the Water* (1961) ch. 2

8 Our great-grand-children, when they learn
how we began this war by snatching glory
out of defeat, and then swept on to victory,
may also learn how the little holiday
steamers made an excursion to hell and
came back glorious.
Radio broadcast, 5 June 1940, following the
evacuation of Dunkirk; in *Listener* 13 June
1940

## Matthew Prior 1664–1721

9 Be to her virtues very kind;
Be to her faults a little blind;
Let all her ways be unconfined;
And clap your padlock—on her mind.
'An English Padlock' (1705) l. 79

10 Nobles and heralds, by your leave,
Here lies what once was Matthew Prior,
The son of Adam and of Eve,
Can Stuart or Nassau go higher?
'Epitaph' (1702)

11 Cured yesterday of my disease,
I died last night of my physician.
'The Remedy Worse than the Disease' (1727)

12 No, no; for my virginity,
When I lose that, says Rose, I'll die:
Behind the elms last night, cried Dick,
Rose, were you not extremely sick?
'A True Maid' (1718)

## Adelaide Ann Procter 1825–64

13 Seated one day at the organ,
I was weary and ill at ease,
And my fingers wandered idly
Over the noisy keys.
'A Lost Chord' (1858)

14 But I struck one chord of music,
Like the sound of a great Amen.
'A Lost Chord' (1858)

## Protagoras b. c.485 BC

15 Man is the measure of all things.
In Plato *Theaetetus* 160d

## Pierre-Joseph Proudhon 1809–65

16 *La propriété c'est le vol.*
Property is theft.
*Qu'est-ce que la propriété?* (1840) ch. 1

## Marcel Proust 1871–1922

17 *A la recherche du temps perdu.*
In search of lost time.
Title of novel (1913–27, translated by C. K.
Scott-Moncrieff and S. Hudson, 1922–31, as
*Remembrance of things past*). Cf. 299:16

18 And suddenly the memory revealed itself.
The taste was that of the little piece of
madeleine which ... my aunt Léonie used
to give me, dipping it first in her own cup
of tea or tisane.
*Swann's Way* (1913, ed. T. Kilmartin, 1981)
'Overture'

19 One becomes moral as soon as one is
unhappy.
*Within a Budding Grove* (1918, ed. T. Kilmartin,
1981) 'Madame Swann at Home'

20 I have a horror of sunsets, they're so
romantic, so operatic.
*Cities of the Plain* (1922, ed. T. Kilmartin, 1981)
pt. 2, ch. 2

21 The true paradises are the paradises that
we have lost.
*Time Regained* (1926, ed. T. Kilmartin, 1981)
vol. 3, p. 903

## Publilius Syrus 1st century BC

22 A beautiful face is a mute
recommendation.
*Sententiae* no. 199, in J. and A. Duff *Minor
Latin Poets* (Loeb ed., 1934); tr. Thomas
Tenison in *Baconiana* (1679) 'Ornamenta
Rationalia' no. 12

1 *Inopi beneficium bis dat qui dat celeriter.*
He gives the poor man twice as much good
who gives quickly.
*Sententiae* no. 274, in J. and A. Duff *Minor
Latin Poets* (proverbially '*Bis dat qui cito dat*
[He gives twice who gives soon]')

2 *Necessitas dat legem non ipsa accipit.*
Necessity gives the law without itself
acknowledging one.
*Sententiae* no. 444, in J. and A. Duff *Minor
Latin Poets* (proverbially '*Necessitas non habet
legem* [Necessity has no law]')

## John Pudney 1909–77

3 Do not despair
For Johnny-head-in-air;
He sleeps as sound
As Johnny underground.
'For Johnny' (1942)

## William Pulteney, Earl of Bath
1684–1764

4 For Sir Ph—p well knows
That innuendos
Will serve him no longer in verse or in
prose,
Since twelve honest men have decided the
cause,
And were judges of fact, tho' not judges of
laws.
'The Honest Jury' (1729) st. 3 (on Sir Philip
Yorke's unsuccessful prosecution of *The
Craftsman*, 1729)

## Punch 1841–1992

5 Advice to persons about to marry.—'Don't.'
vol. 8, p. 1 (1845)

6 You pays your money and you takes your
choice.
vol. 10, p. 17 (1846)

7 The Half-Way House to Rome, Oxford.
vol. 16, p. 36 (1849)

8 Never do to-day what you can put off till
to-morrow.
vol. 17, p. 241 (1849)

9 Who's 'im, Bill?
A stranger!
'Eave 'arf a brick at 'im.
vol. 26, p. 82 (1854)

10 What is Matter?—Never mind.
What is Mind?—No matter.
vol. 29, p. 19 (1855)

11 It ain't the 'unting as 'urts 'im, it's the
'ammer, 'ammer, 'ammer along the 'ard
'igh road.
vol. 30, p. 218 (1856)

12 Mun, a had na' been the-erre abune two
hours when—*bang*—went saxpence!!!
vol. 54, p. 235 (1868)

13 Go directly—see what she's doing, and tell
her she mustn't.
vol. 63, p. 202 (1872)

14 There was one poor tiger that hadn't *got* a
Christian.
vol. 68, p. 143 (1875)

15 It's worse than wicked, my dear, it's vulgar.
Almanac (1876)

16 I used your soap two years ago; since then
I have used no other.
vol. 86, p. 197 (1884)

17 Don't look at me, Sir, with—ah—in that
tone of voice.
vol. 87, p. 38 (1884)

18 Botticelli isn't a wine, you Juggins!
Botticelli's a *cheese*!
vol. 106, p. 270 (1894)

19 I'm afraid you've got a bad egg, Mr Jones.
Oh no, my Lord, I assure you! Parts of it
are excellent!
vol. 109, p. 222 (1895)

20 Look here, Steward, if this is coffee, I want
tea; but if this is tea, then I wish for coffee.
vol. 123, p. 44 (1902)

21 Sometimes I sits and thinks, and then
again I just sits.
vol. 131, p. 297 (1906)

## Alexander Pushkin 1799–1837

22 A tedious season they await
Who hear November at the gate.
*Eugene Onegin* (1833) ch. 4, st. 40 (tr. B.
Deutsch)

23 Moscow: those syllables can start
A tumult in the Russian heart.
*Eugene Onegin* (1833) ch. 7, st. 36 (tr. B.
Deutsch)

## Israel Putnam 1718–90

24 Don't one of you fire until you see the
white of their eyes.
At Bunker Hill, 1775, in R. Frothingham
*History of the Siege of Boston* (1873) ch. 5 n.
(also attributed to William Prescott,
1726–95)

## Mario Puzo 1920–

25 I'll make him an offer he can't refuse.
*The Godfather* (1969) ch. 1

26 A lawyer with his briefcase can steal more
than a hundred men with guns.
*The Godfather* (1969) ch. 1

## Francis Quarles 1592–1644

27 Our God and soldiers we alike adore
Ev'n at the brink of danger; not before:
After deliverance, both alike requited,
Our God's forgotten, and our soldiers
slighted.
*Divine Fancies* (1632) 'Of Common Devotion'.
Cf. 243:17

1 My soul, sit thou a patient looker-on;
Judge not the play before the play is done:
Her plot hath many changes; every day
Speaks a new scene; the last act crowns
the play.
*Emblems* (1635) bk. 1, no. 15 'Respice Finem'

2 We spend our midday sweat, our midnight
oil:
We tire the night in thought, the day in
toil.
*Emblems* (1635) bk. 2, no. 2, l. 33

3 Be wisely worldly, be not worldly wise.
*Emblems* (1635) bk. 2, no. 2, l. 46

4 Man is man's A.B.C. There is none that can
Read God aright, unless he first spell Man.
*Hieroglyphics of the Life of Man* (1638) no. 1, l. 1

5 We'll cry both arts and learning down,
And hey! then up go we!
*The Shepherd's Oracles* (1646) Eclogue 11 'Song
of Anarchus'

## Peter Quennell 1905–93

6 An elderly fallen angel travelling incognito.
*The Sign of the Fish* (1960) ch. 2 (of André Gide)

## Sir Arthur Quiller-Couch
1863–1944

7 The best is the best, though a hundred
judges have declared it so.
*Oxford Book of English Verse* (1900) preface

8 O pastoral heart of England! like a psalm
Of green days telling with a quiet beat.
'Ode upon Eckington Bridge' (1896)

## Josiah Quincy 1772–1864

9 As it will be the right of all, so it will be
the duty of some, definitely to prepare for
a separation, amicably if they can, violently
if they must.
*Abridgement of Debates of Congress* vol. 4, p. 327
(14 January 1811). Cf. 101:17

## François Rabelais c.1494–c.1553

10 The appetite grows by eating.
*Gargantua* (1534) bk. 1, ch. 5

11 Nature abhors a vacuum.
*Gargantua* (1534) bk. 1, ch. 5 (quoting an
article of ancient wisdom)

12 *Fais ce que voudras.*
Do what you like.
*Gargantua* (1534) bk. 1, ch. 57

13 I am going to seek a great perhaps . . .
Bring down the curtain, the farce is played
out.
Last words (attributed)

## Jean Racine 1639–99

14 *Je l'ai trop aimé pour ne le point haïr!*
I have loved him too much not to feel any
hatred for him.
*Andromaque* (1667) act 2, sc. 1

15 *Elle flotte, elle hésite; en un mot, elle est femme.*
She floats, she hesitates; in a word, she's a
woman.
*Athalie* (1691) act 3, sc. 3

16 *Ce n'est plus une ardeur dans mes veines cachée:
C'est Vénus tout entière à sa proie attachée.*
It's no longer a burning within my veins:
it's Venus entire latched onto her prey.
*Phèdre* (1677) act 1, sc. 3

17 *Point d'argent, point de Suisse, et ma porte était
close.*
No money, no service, and my door stayed
shut.
*Les Plaideurs* (1668) act 1, sc. 1

## James Rado 1939– and Gerome
Ragni 1942–

18 When the moon is in the seventh house,
And Jupiter aligns with Mars . . .
This is the dawning of the age of Aquarius.
*Hair* (1967) 'Aquarius'

## Thomas Rainborowe d. 1648

19 The poorest he that is in England hath a
life to live as the greatest he.
During the Army debates at Putney,
29 October 1647; in C. H. Firth (ed.) *Clarke
Papers* vol. 1, Camden Society, New Series 49
(1891) p. 301

## Sir Walter Ralegh c.1552–1618

20 If all the world and love were young,
And truth in every shepherd's tongue,
These pretty pleasures might me move
To live with thee, and be thy love.
'Answer to Marlow'. Cf. 123:23, 219:3

21 Go, Soul, the body's guest,
Upon a thankless arrant:
Fear not to touch the best;
The truth shall be thy warrant:
Go, since I needs must die,
And give the world the lie.
'The Lie' (1608)

22 We die in earnest, that's no jest.
'On the Life of Man'

23 Give me my scallop-shell of quiet,
My staff of faith to walk upon,
My scrip of joy, immortal diet,
My bottle of salvation,
My gown of glory, hope's true gage,
And thus I'll take my pilgrimage.
'The Passionate Man's Pilgrimage' (1604)

24 Fain would I climb, yet fear I to fall.
Line written on a window-pane, in Thomas
Fuller *Worthies of England* (1662) 'Devonshire'
p. 261. Cf. 135:9

1 Even such is Time, which takes in trust
Our youth, our joys, and all we have,
And pays us but with age and dust;
Who in the dark and silent grave,
When we have wandered all our ways,
Shuts up the story of our days:
And from which earth, and grave, and
    dust,
The Lord shall raise me up, I trust.
   Written the night before his death. See V. B.
   Heltzel 'Ralegh's "Even such is time" ' in
   *Huntingdon Library Bulletin* no. 10 (October
   1936)

2 O eloquent, just, and mighty Death! ...
thou hast drawn together all the
farstretched greatness, all the pride,
cruelty, and ambition of man, and covered
it all over with these two narrow words,
*Hic jacet* [Here lies].
   *The History of the World* (1614) bk. 5, ch. 6

3 'Tis a sharp remedy, but a sure one for all
ills.
   On feeling the edge of the axe prior to his
   execution, in D. Hume *History of Great Britain*
   (1754) vol. 1, ch. 4

4 So the heart be right, it is no matter which
way the head lies.
   At his execution, on being asked which way
   he preferred to lay his head; in W. Stebbing
   *Sir Walter Raleigh* (1891) ch. 30

## Sir Walter Raleigh 1861–1922

5 In examinations those who do not wish to
know ask questions of those who cannot
tell.
   *Laughter from a Cloud* (1923) 'Some Thoughts
   on Examinations'

6 I wish I loved the Human Race;
I wish I loved its silly face;
I wish I liked the way it walks;
I wish I liked the way it talks;
And when I'm introduced to one
I wish I thought *What Jolly Fun!*
   'Wishes of an Elderly Man' (1923)

## Arthur Ransome 1884–1967

7 BETTER DROWNED THAN DUFFERS IF NOT
DUFFERS WONT DROWN.
   *Swallows and Amazons* (1930) ch. 1

## Terence Rattigan 1911–77

8 You can be in the Horseguards and still be
common, dear.
   *Separate Tables* (1954) 'Table Number Seven'
   sc. 1

## Sir Herbert Read 1893–1968

9 Art is ... pattern informed by sensibility.
   *The Meaning of Art* (1955) ch. 1

## Charles Reade 1814–84

10 *Courage, mon ami, le diable est mort!*
Take courage, my friend, the devil is dead!
   *The Cloister and the Hearth* (1861) ch. 24, and
   *passim*

11 Sow an act, and you reap a habit. Sow a
habit and you reap a character. Sow a
character, and you reap a destiny.
   Attributed. See *Notes and Queries* (9th Series)
   vol. 12 (17 October 1903) p. 309

## Ronald Reagan 1911–

12 You can tell a lot about a fellow's character
by his way of eating jellybeans.
   In *New York Times* 15 January 1981

## Erell Reaves

13 Lady of Spain, I adore you.
Right from the night I first saw you,
My heart has been yearning for you,
What else could any heart do?
   'Lady of Spain' (1913 song)

## Henry Reed 1914–86

14 As we get older we do not get any younger.
Seasons return, and today I am fifty-five,
And this time last year I was fifty-four,
And this time next year I shall be sixty-two.
   'Chard Whitlow (Mr Eliot's Sunday Evening
   Postscript)' (1946)

15 Today we have naming of parts. Yesterday,
We had daily cleaning. And tomorrow
    morning,
We shall have what to do after firing. But
today,
Today we have naming of parts.
   'Lessons of the War: 1, Naming of Parts'
   (1946)

16 They call it easing the Spring: it is
perfectly easy
If you have any strength in your thumb:
like the bolt,
And the breech, and the cocking-piece, and
the point of balance,
Which in our case we have not got.
   'Lessons of the War: 1, Naming of Parts'
   (1946)

17                    And as for war, my wars
Were global from the start.
   'Lessons of the War: 3, Unarmed Combat'
   (1946)

18 In a civil war, a general must know—and
I'm afraid it's a thing rather of instinct
than of practice—he must know exactly
when to move over to the other side.
   *Not a Drum was Heard: The War Memoirs of
   General Gland* (unpublished radio play, 1959)

19 And the sooner the tea's out of the way,
the sooner we can get out the gin, eh?
   *Private Life of Hilda Tablet* (1954 radio play) in
   *Hilda Tablet and Others* (1971) p. 60

20 Modest? My word, no ... He was an all-the-
lights-on man.
   *A Very Great Man Indeed* (1953 radio play) in
   *Hilda Tablet and Others* (1971) p. 23

21 I have known her pass the whole evening
without mentioning a single book, or *in
fact anything unpleasant, at all.*
   *A Very Great Man Indeed* (1953 radio play) in
   *Hilda Tablet and Others* (1971) p. 45

## John Reed 1887–1920

**1** Ten days that shook the world.
  Title of book (1919)

## Max Reger 1873–1916

**2** I am sitting in the smallest room of my
house. I have your review before me. In
a moment it will be behind me.
  Responding to a savage review by Rudolf
  Louis in *Münchener Neueste Nachrichten*,
  7 February 1906; in N. Slonimsky *Lexicon of
  Musical Invective* (1953) p. 139

## Keith Reid 1946–

**3** Her face, at first ... just ghostly
Turned a whiter shade of pale.
  'A Whiter Shade of Pale' (1967 song)

## Erich Maria Remarque 1898–1970

**4** All quiet on the western front.
  English title of *Im Westen nichts Neues* (1929
  novel). Cf. 32:14, 214:14

## Montague John Rendall
1862–1950

**5** Nation shall speak peace unto nation.
  Motto of the BBC (1927). Cf. 45:5

## Pierre Auguste Renoir 1841–1919

**6** I paint with my prick.
  Much quoted, but possibly an inversion of
  'It's with my brush that I make love'; in A.
  André *Renoir* (1919) p. 10

## Frederic Reynolds 1764–1841

**7** It is better to have written a damned play,
than no play at all—it snatches a man
from obscurity.
  *The Dramatist* (1789) act 1, sc. 1

## Sir Joshua Reynolds 1723–92

**8** If you have great talents, industry will
improve them: if you have but moderate
abilities, industry will supply their
deficiency.
  *Discourses on Art* (ed. R. Wark, 1975) no. 2
  (11 December 1769)

**9** A mere copier of nature can never produce
anything great.
  *Discourses on Art* (ed. R. Wark, 1975) no. 3
  (14 December 1770)

**10** Genius ... is the child of imitation.
  *Discourses on Art* (ed. R. Wark, 1975) no. 6
  (10 December 1774)

## Malvina Reynolds 1900–78

**11** Little boxes on the hillside ...
And they're all made out of ticky-tacky
And they all look just the same.
  'Little Boxes' (1962 song); on the tract
  houses in the hills to the south of San
  Francisco

## Cecil Rhodes 1853–1902

**12** So little done, so much to do.
  On the day of his death, in L. Michell *Life of
  Rhodes* (1910) vol. 2, ch. 39. Cf. 325:14

## Jean Rhys c.1890–1979

**13** We can't all be happy, we can't all be rich,
we can't all be lucky ... Some must cry so
that others may be able to laugh the more
heartily.
  *Good Morning, Midnight* (1939) pt. 1

**14** The perpetual hunger to be beautiful and
that thirst to be loved which is the real
curse of Eve.
  *The Left Bank* (1927) 'Illusion'

**15** A doormat in a world of boots.
  Describing herself; in *Guardian* 6 December
  1990, p. 24

## David Ricardo 1772–1823

**16** Rent is that portion of the earth, which is
paid to the landlord for the use of the
original and indestructible powers of the
soil.
  *On the Principles of Political Economy and
  Taxation* (1817) ch. 2

## Grantland Rice 1880–1954

**17** For when the One Great Scorer comes to
mark against your name,
He writes—not that you won or lost—but
how you played the Game.
  'Alumnus Football' (1941)

**18** All wars are planned by old men
In council rooms apart.
  'The Two Sides of War' (1955)

## Sir Stephen Rice 1637–1715

**19** I will drive a coach and six horses through
the Act of Settlement.
  In W. King *State of the Protestants of Ireland*
  (1672) ch. 3, sect. 8, p. 6

## Mandy Rice-Davies 1944–

**20** He would, wouldn't he?
  At the trial of Stephen Ward, 29 June 1963,
  on hearing that Lord Astor denied her
  allegations, concerning himself and his
  house parties at Cliveden; in *Guardian* 1 July
  1963

## Frank Richards 1876–1961

1 The fat greedy owl of the Remove.
  'Billy Bunter' in the *Magnet* (1909) vol. 3,
  no. 72 'The Greyfriars Photographer'

## Samuel Richardson 1689–1761

2 Mine is the most plotting heart in the
  world.
  *Clarissa* (1747–8) Letter 171

3 I love to write to the moment.
  *Clarissa* (1747–8) Letter 224

4 His [Fielding's] spurious brat, Tom Jones.
  Letter to Thomas Edwards, 21 February 1752,
  in J. Carroll (ed.) *Selected Letters* (1964)

## Hans Richter 1843–1916

5 Up with your damned nonsense will I put
  twice, or perhaps once, but sometimes
  always, by God, never.
  Attributed

## Johann Paul Friedrich Richter ('Jean Paul') 1763–1825

6 Providence has given to the French the
  empire of the land, to the English that of
  the sea, and to the Germans that of—the
  air!
  In Thomas Carlyle 'Jean Paul Friedrich
  Richter' in *Edinburgh Review* no. 91 (1827)

## Rainer Maria Rilke 1875–1926

7 *So leben wir und nehmen immer Abschied.*
  We live our lives, for ever taking leave.
  *Duineser Elegien* (tr. J. B. Leishman and
  Stephen Spender, 1948) no. 8

## Arthur Rimbaud 1854–91

8 . . . *Je me suis baigné dans le Poème
  De la Mer.*
  I have bathed in the Poem of the Sea.
  'Le Bâteau ivre' (1883)

9 *Je regrette l'Europe aux anciens parapets!*
  I pine for Europe of the ancient parapets!
  'Le Bâteau ivre' (1883)

10 *Ô saisons, ô châteaux!
  Quelle âme est sans défauts?*
  O seasons, O castles! What soul is without
  fault?
  'Ô saisons, ô châteaux' (1872)

11 *A noir, E blanc, I rouge, U vert, O bleu: voyelles,
  Je dirais quelque jour vos naissances latentes.*
  A black, E white, I red, U green, O blue:
  vowels, some day I will tell of the births
  that may be yours.
  'Voyelles' (1870)

## Hal Riney 1932–

12 It's morning again in America.
  Ronald Reagan's election campaign slogan
  (1984); in *Newsweek* 6 August 1984

## César Ritz 1850–1918

13 The customer is never wrong.
  In R. Nevill and C. E. Jerningham *Piccadilly to
  Pall Mall* (1908) p. 94

## Antoine de Rivarol 1753–1801

14 *Ce qui n'est pas clair n'est pas français.*
  What is not clear is not French.
  *Discours sur l'Universalité de la Langue Française*
  (1784)

## Lord Robbins 1898–1984

15 Economics is the science which studies
  human behaviour as a relationship
  between ends and scarce means which
  have alternative uses.
  *Essay on the Nature and Significance of Economic
  Science* (1932) ch. 1, sect. 3

## Maximilien Robespierre 1758–94

16 Any law which violates the inalienable
  rights of man is essentially unjust and
  tyrannical; it is not a law at all.
  *Déclaration des droits de l'homme* 24 April 1793,
  article 6

17 Any institution which does not suppose
  the people good, and the magistrate
  corruptible, is evil.
  *Déclaration des droits de l'homme* 24 April 1793,
  article 25

## Leo Robin 1900–

18 A kiss on the hand may be quite
  continental,
  But diamonds are a girl's best friend.
  'Diamonds are a Girl's Best Friend' (1949
  song); from the film *Gentlemen Prefer Blondes*

19 Thanks for the memory.
  Title of song (with Ralph Rainger, 1937)

## Edwin Arlington Robinson 1869–1935

20 I shall have more to say when I am dead.
  'John Brown' (1920)

## Bishop John Robinson 1919–83

21 Honest to God.
  Title of book (1963)

## Mary Robinson 1758–1800

22 Pavement slippery, people sneezing,
  Lords in ermine, beggars freezing;
  Titled gluttons dainties carving,
  Genius in a garret starving.
  'January, 1795'

## Sir Boyle Roche 1743–1807

1 Mr Speaker, I smell a rat; I see him
forming in the air and darkening the sky;
but I'll nip him in the bud.
*Attributed*

## John Wilmot, Earl of Rochester 1647–80

2 Tell me no more of constancy,
that frivolous pretence,
Of cold age, narrow jealousy,
disease and want of sense.
'Against Constancy' (1676)

3         'Is there then no more?'
She cries. 'All this to love and rapture's
due;
Must we not pay a debt to pleasure too?'
'The Imperfect Enjoyment' (1680)

4 Here lies a great and mighty king
Whose promise none relies on;
He never said a foolish thing,
Nor ever did a wise one.
'The King's Epitaph' (alternatively 'Here lies
our sovereign lord the King'); in C. E. Doble
et al. *Thomas Hearne: Remarks and Collections*
(1885–1921) 17 November 1706. Cf. 95:2

5 ... Natural freedoms are but just:
There's something generous in mere lust.
'A Ramble in St James' Park' (1680)

6 Reason, an *ignis fatuus* of the mind,
Which leaves the light of nature, sense,
behind.
'A Satire against Mankind' (1679) l. 11

7 All men would be cowards if they durst.
'A Satire against Mankind' (1679) l. 158

8 A merry monarch, scandalous and poor.
'A Satire on King Charles II' (1697)

9 Ancient person, for whom I
All the flattering youth defy,
Long be it ere thou grow old,
Aching, shaking, crazy, cold;
But still continue as thou art,
Ancient person of my heart.
'A Song of a Young Lady to her Ancient
Lover' (1691)

10 Ere time and place were, time and place
were not;
Where primitive nothing something
straight begot,
Then all proceeded from the great united
what.
'Upon Nothing' (1680)

## John D. Rockefeller 1839–1937

11 The growth of a large business is merely
a survival of the fittest ... The American
beauty rose can be produced in the
splendour and fragrance which bring cheer
to its beholder only by sacrificing the early
buds which grow up around it.
In W. J. Ghent *Our Benevolent Feudalism* (1902)
p. 29 ('American Beauty Rose' became the
title of a 1950 song by Hal David and
others). Cf. 312:17

## Gene Roddenberry 1921–91

12 These are the voyages of the starship
*Enterprise*. Its five-year mission ... to boldly
go where no man has gone before.
*Star Trek* (television series, from 1966)

13 Beam us up, Mr Scott.
*Star Trek* 'Gamesters of Triskelion' (usually
quoted 'Beam me up, Scotty')

## Theodore Roethke 1908–63

14 I have known the inexorable sadness of
pencils,
Neat in their boxes, dolour of pad and
paper-weight,
All the misery of manilla folders and
mucilage,
Desolation in immaculate public places.
'Dolour' (1948)

15 The body and the soul know how to play
In that dark world where gods have lost
their way.
'Four for Sir John Davies' (1953) no. 2

16         O who can be
Both moth and flame? The weak moth
blundering by.
Whom do we love? I thought I knew the
truth;
Of grief I died, but no one knew my death.
'The Sequel' (1964)

## Samuel Rogers 1763–1855

17 Think nothing done while aught remains
to do.
'Human Life' (1819) l. 49. Cf. 211:25

18 But there are moments which he calls his
own,
Then, never less alone than when alone,
Those whom he loved so long and sees no
more,
Loved and still loves—not dead—but gone
before,
He gathers round him.
'Human Life' (1819) l. 755

19 By many a temple half as old as Time.
*Italy* (1838 ed.) epilogue. Cf. 79:17

20 It doesn't much signify whom one marries,
for one is sure to find next morning that it
was someone else.
In A. Dyce (ed.) *Table Talk of Samuel Rogers*
(1860)

## Will Rogers 1879–1935

21 Income Tax has made more Liars out of
the American people than Golf.
*The Illiterate Digest* (1924) 'Helping the Girls
with their Income Taxes'

22 Everything is funny as long as it is
happening to Somebody Else.
*The Illiterate Digest* (1924) 'Warning to Jokers:
lay off the prince'

1 Well, all I know is what I read in the
   papers.
   *New York Times* 30 September 1923

2 You can't say civilization don't advance,
   however, for in every war they kill you in
   a new way.
   *New York Times* 23 December 1929

## Mme Roland 1754–93

3 O liberty! what crimes are committed in
   thy name!
   In A. de Lamartine *Histoire des Girondins*
   (1847) bk. 51, ch. 8

## Richard Rolle de Hampole
## c.1290–1349

4 When Adam dalfe and Eve spane ...
   Where was than the pride of man?
   In G. G. Perry *Religious Pieces* (EETS no. 26,
   1914 ed.). Taken in the form 'When Adam
   delved and Eve span, who was then the
   gentleman?' by John Ball as the text of his
   revolutionary sermon on the outbreak of the
   Peasants' Revolt, 1381

## Pierre de Ronsard 1524–85

5 *Quand vous serez bien vieille, au soir, à la*
   *chandelle,*
   *Assise auprès du feu, dévidant et filant,*
   *Direz, chantant mes vers, en vous émerveillant,*
   *Ronsard me célébrait du temps que j'étais belle.*
   When you are very old, and sit in the
   candle-light at evening spinning by the
   fire, you will say, as you murmur my
   verses, a wonder in your eyes, 'Ronsard
   sang of me in the days when I was fair.'
   *Sonnets pour Hélène* (1578) bk. 2, no. 42

## Eleanor Roosevelt 1884–1962

6 No one can make you feel inferior without
   your consent.
   In *Catholic Digest* August 1960, p. 102

## Franklin D. Roosevelt 1882–1945

7 The forgotten man at the bottom of the
   economic pyramid.
   Radio address, 7 April 1932, in *Public Papers*
   (1938) vol. 1

8 I pledge you, I pledge myself, to a new deal
   for the American people.
   Speech, 2 July 1932, accepting the
   presidential nomination; in *Public Papers*
   (1938) vol. 1

9 The only thing we have to fear is fear
   itself.
   Inaugural address, 4 March 1933, in *Public
   Papers* (1938) vol. 2

10 In the field of world policy I would dedicate
   this Nation to the policy of the good
   neighbour.
   Inaugural address, 4 March 1933, in *Public
   Papers* (1938) vol. 2

11 I see one-third of a nation ill-housed, ill-
   clad, ill-nourished.
   Second inaugural address, 20 January 1937,
   in *Public Papers* (1941) vol. 6

12 We must be the great arsenal of
   democracy.
   Broadcast, 29 December 1940, in *Public Papers*
   (1941) vol. 9

13 We look forward to a world founded upon
   four essential human freedoms. The first is
   freedom of speech and expression—
   everywhere in the world. The second is
   freedom of every person to worship
   God in his own way—everywhere in the
   world. The third is freedom from want...
   The fourth is freedom from fear.
   Message to Congress, 6 January 1941, in
   *Public Papers* (1941) vol. 9

14 Yesterday, December 7, 1941—a date which
   will live in infamy—the United States of
   America was suddenly and deliberately
   attacked by naval and air forces of the
   Empire of Japan.
   Address to Congress, 8 December 1941, in
   *Public Papers* (1950) vol. 10

## Theodore Roosevelt 1858–1919

15 I wish to preach, not the doctrine of
   ignoble ease, but the doctrine of the
   strenuous life.
   Speech, 10 April 1899, in *Works* (Memorial
   ed., 1923–6), vol. 15

16 Speak softly and carry a big stick; you will
   go far.
   Speech, 3 April 1903, in *New York Times*
   4 April 1903 (quoting an 'old adage')

17 A man who is good enough to shed his
   blood for the country is good enough to be
   given a square deal afterwards.
   Speech, 4 June 1903, in *Addresses and
   Presidential Messages 1902–4* (1904)

18 The men with the muck-rakes are often
   indispensable to the well-being of society;
   but only if they know when to stop raking
   the muck.
   Speech, 14 April 1906, in *Works* (Memorial
   ed., 1923–6) vol. 18. Cf. 79:6

19 There is no room in this country for
   hyphenated Americanism.
   Speech, 12 October 1915, in *Works* (Memorial
   ed., 1923–6) vol. 20

## Lord Rosebery 1847–1929

20 Men who sit still with the fly-blown
   phylacteries bound round their obsolete
   policy.
   On certain members of the Liberal Party;
   speech at Chesterfield, 16 December 1901, in
   *The Times* 17 December 1901, p. 10

## Christina Rossetti 1830–94

21 Because the birthday of my life
   Is come, my love is come to me.
   'A Birthday' (1862)

**1** Come to me in the silence of the night;
Come in the speaking silence of a dream.
'Echo' (1862)

**2** In the bleak mid-winter
Frosty wind made moan,
Earth stood hard as iron,
Water like a stone;
Snow had fallen, snow on snow,
Snow on snow,
In the bleak mid-winter,
Long ago.
'Mid-Winter' (1875)

**3** Oh roses for the flush of youth,
And laurel for the perfect prime;
But pluck an ivy branch for me
Grown old before my time.
'Oh roses for the flush of youth' (1862)

**4** Better by far you should forget and smile
Than that you should remember and be
sad.
'Remember' (1862)

**5** Does the road wind up-hill all the way?
Yes, to the very end.
Will the day's journey take the whole long
day?
From morn to night, my friend.
'Up-Hill' (1862)

## Dante Gabriel Rossetti 1828–82

**6** The blessed damozel leaned out
From the gold bar of Heaven;
Her eyes were deeper than the depth
Of waters stilled at even;
She had three lilies in her hand,
And the stars in her hair were seven.
'The Blessed Damozel' (1870) st. 1

**7** A sonnet is a moment's monument,—
Memorial from the Soul's eternity
To one dead deathless hour.
*The House of Life* (1881) pt. 1, introduction

**8** Look in my face; my name is Might-have-
been;
I am also called No-more, Too-late,
Farewell.
*The House of Life* (1881) pt. 2 'A Superscription'

**9** Sleepless with cold commemorative eyes.
*The House of Life* (1881) pt. 2 'A Superscription'

**10** I have been here before,
But when or how I cannot tell:
I know the grass beyond the door,
The sweet keen smell,
The sighing sound, the lights around the
shore.
'Sudden Light' (1870)

## Gioacchino Rossini 1792–1868

**11** Wagner has lovely moments but awful
quarters of an hour.
In E. Naumann *Italienische Tondichter* (1883)
vol. 4, p. 541 (April 1867)

## Jean Rostand 1894–1977

**12** Kill a man, and you are an assassin. Kill
millions of men, and you are a conqueror.
Kill everyone, and you are a god.
*Pensées d'un biologiste* (1939) p. 116. Cf. 253:26,
360:15

## Leo Rosten 1908–

**13** Any man who hates dogs and babies can't
be all bad.
Of W. C. Fields, and often attributed to him,
in speech at Masquers' Club dinner,
16 February 1939. See letter in *Times Literary
Supplement* 24 January 1975, p. 85

## Philip Roth 1933–

**14** A Jewish man with parents alive is
a fifteen-year-old boy, and will remain
a fifteen-year-old boy until *they die*!
*Portnoy's Complaint* (1967) p. 111

**15** Doctor, my doctor, what do you say, LET'S
PUT THE ID BACK IN YID!
*Portnoy's Complaint* (1967) p. 124

## Claude-Joseph Rouget de Lisle 1760–1836

**16** *Allons, enfants de la patrie,
Le jour de gloire est arrivé . . .
Aux armes, citoyens!
Formez vos bataillons!*
Come, children of our country, the day of
glory has arrived . . . To arms, citizens!
Form your battalions!
'La Marseillaise' (25 April 1792)

## Charles Roupell

**17** To play billiards well is a sign of an ill-
spent youth.
Attributed, in D. Duncan *Life of Herbert
Spencer* (1908) ch. 20

## Jean-Jacques Rousseau 1712–78

**18** Man was born free, and everywhere he is
in chains.
*Du Contrat social* (1762) ch. 1

## Martin Joseph Routh 1755–1854

**19** You will find it a very good practice always
to verify your references, sir!
In J. W. Burgon *Lives of Twelve Good Men* (1888
ed.) vol. 1, p. 73

## Nicholas Rowe 1674–1718

**20** Is this that haughty, gallant, gay Lothario?
*The Fair Penitent* (1703) act 5, sc. 1

## Helen Rowland 1875–1950

**21** A husband is what is left of a lover, after
the nerve has been extracted.
*A Guide to Men* (1922) p. 19

## Richard Rowland c.1881–1947

1 The lunatics have taken charge of the
asylum.

On the take-over of United Artists by Charles
Chaplin and others, in T. Ramsaye *A Million
and One Nights* (1926) vol. 2, ch. 79. Cf. 208:12

## Maude Royden 1876–1956

2 The Church [of England] should go forward
along the path of progress and be no
longer satisfied only to represent the
Conservative Party at prayer.

In *The Times* 17 July 1917

## Naomi Royde-Smith c.1875–1964

3 I know two things about the horse
And one of them is rather coarse.

*Weekend Book* (1928) p. 231

## Paul Alfred Rubens 1875–1917

4 Oh! we don't want to lose you but we think
you ought to go
For your King and your Country both need
you so.

'Your King and Country Want You' (1914
song)

## Richard Rumbold c.1622–85

5 I never could believe that Providence had
sent a few men into the world, ready
booted and spurred to ride, and millions
ready saddled and bridled to be ridden.

On the scaffold, in T. B. Macaulay *History of
England* vol. 1 (1849) ch. 1

## Damon Runyon 1884–1946

6 I do see her in tough joints more than
somewhat.

*Collier's* 22 May 1930, 'Social Error'

7 I long ago come to the conclusion that all
life is 6 to 5 against.

*Collier's* 8 September 1934, 'A Nice Price'

8 'My boy,' he says, 'always try to rub up
against money, for if you rub up against
money long enough, some of it may rub
off on you.'

*Cosmopolitan* August 1929, 'A Very
Honourable Guy'

## Dean Rusk 1909–94

9 We're eyeball to eyeball, and I think the
other fellow just blinked.

On the Cuban missile crisis, 24 October
1962, in *Saturday Evening Post* 8 December
1962

## John Ruskin 1819–1900

10 I have seen, and heard, much of Cockney
impudence before now; but never expected
to hear a coxcomb ask two hundred
guineas for flinging a pot of paint in the
public's face.

*Fors Clavigera* (1871–84) Letter 79, 18 June
1877 (on Whistler's *Nocturne in Black and
Gold*). Cf. 347:13

11 Life without industry is guilt, and industry
without art is brutality.

*Lectures on Art* (1870) Lecture 3 'The Relation
of Art to Morals' sect. 95

12 All violent feelings ... produce in us a
falseness in all our impressions of external
things, which I would generally
characterize as the 'Pathetic Fallacy'.

*Modern Painters* (1856) vol. 3, pt. 4, ch. 12

13 Mountains are the beginning and the end
of all natural scenery.

*Modern Painters* (1856) vol. 4, pt. 5, ch. 20

14 All books are divisible into two classes, the
books of the hour, and the books of all
time.

*Sesame and Lilies* (1865) p. 16 'Of Kings'
Treasuries'

15 Which of us ... is to do the hard and dirty
work for the rest—and for what pay? Who
is to do the pleasant and clean work, and
for what pay?

*Sesame and Lilies* (1865) p. 69 n. 'Of Kings'
Treasuries'

16 When we build, let us think that we build
for ever.

*Seven Lamps of Architecture* (1849) 'The Lamp of
Memory' sect. 10

17 Remember that the most beautiful things
in the world are the most useless; peacocks
and lilies for instance.

*Stones of Venice* vol. 1 (1851) ch. 2, sect. 17

18 Labour without joy is base. Labour without
sorrow is base. Sorrow without labour is
base. Joy without labour is base.

*Time and Tide* (1867) Letter 5

19 The first duty of a State is to see that every
child born therein shall be well housed,
clothed, fed and educated, till it attain
years of discretion.

*Time and Tide* (1867) Letter 13

20 There is no wealth but life.

*Unto this Last* (1862) Essay 4, p. 156

## Bertrand Russell 1872–1970

21 Boredom is ... a vital problem for the
moralist, since half the sins of mankind
are caused by the fear of it.

*The Conquest of Happiness* (1930) ch. 4

22 To be able to fill leisure intelligently is the
last product of civilization.

*The Conquest of Happiness* (1930) ch. 14

**1** Work is of two kinds: first, altering the position of matter at or near the earth's surface relatively to other such matter; second, telling other people to do so. The first kind is unpleasant and ill paid; the second is pleasant and highly paid.

*In Praise of Idleness and Other Essays* (1986) title essay (1932)

**2** Mathematics may be defined as the subject in which we never know what we are talking about, nor whether what we are saying is true.

*Mysticism and Logic* (1918) ch. 4

**3** Mathematics, rightly viewed, possesses not only truth, but supreme beauty—a beauty cold and austere, like that of sculpture.

*Philosophical Essays* (1910) no. 4

**4** It is obvious that 'obscenity' is not a term capable of exact legal definition; in the practice of the Courts, it means 'anything that shocks the magistrate'.

*Sceptical Essays* (1928) 'The Recrudescence of Puritanism'

## George William Russell

*See Æ*

## Lord John Russell 1792–1878

**5** It is impossible that the whisper of a faction should prevail against the voice of a nation.

Reply to an Address from a meeting of 150,000 persons at Birmingham on the defeat of the second Reform Bill, October 1831; in S. Walpole *Life of Lord John Russell* (1889) vol. 1, ch. 7

**6** If peace cannot be maintained with honour, it is no longer peace.

Speech at Greenock, 19 September 1853, in *The Times* 21 September 1853, p. 7. Cf. 94:2

## Sir William Howard Russell 1820–1907

**7** They dashed on towards that thin red line tipped with steel.

Of the Russians charging the British, in *The British Expedition to the Crimea* (1877) p. 156. Russell's original dispatch to *The Times*, 14 November 1854, reads 'That thin red streak tipped with a line of steel'

## Ernest Rutherford 1871–1937

**8** All science is either physics or stamp collecting.

In J. B. Birks *Rutherford at Manchester* (1962) p. 108

**9** We haven't got the money, so we've got to think!

In *Bulletin of the Institute of Physics* (1962) vol. 13, p. 102 (as recalled by R. V. Jones)

## Gilbert Ryle 1900–76

**10** Philosophy is the replacement of category-habits by category-disciplines.

*The Concept of Mind* (1949) introduction

**11** The dogma of the Ghost in the Machine.

*The Concept of Mind* (1949) ch. 1 (on the mental-conduct concepts of Descartes)

## Vita Sackville-West 1892–1962

**12** The greater cats with golden eyes
Stare out between the bars.

*The King's Daughter* (1929) pt. 2, no. 1

## Françoise Sagan 1935–

**13** To jealousy, nothing is more frightful than laughter.

*La Chamade* (1965) ch. 9

## Charles-Augustin Sainte-Beuve 1804–69

**14** Et Vigny plus secret,
Comme en sa tour d'ivoire, avant midi rentrait.

And Vigny more discreet, as if in his ivory tower, returned before noon.

*Les Pensées d'Août, à M. Villemain* (1837) p. 152

## Antoine de Saint-Exupéry 1900–44

**15** Grown-ups never understand anything for themselves, and it is tiresome for children to be always and forever explaining things to them.

*Le Petit Prince* (1943) ch. 1

## Saki (H. H. Munro) 1870–1916

**16** Waldo is one of those people who would be enormously improved by death.

*Beasts and Super-Beasts* (1914) 'The Feast of Nemesis'

**17** The people of Crete unfortunately make more history than they can consume locally.

*Chronicles of Clovis* (1911) 'The Jesting of Arlington Stringham'

**18** The cook was a good cook, as cooks go; and as good cooks go, she went.

*Reginald* (1904) 'Reginald on Besetting Sins'

**19** I always say beauty is only sin deep.

*Reginald* (1904) 'Reginald's Choir Treat'

**20** You can't expect a boy to be vicious till he's been to a good school.

*Reginald in Russia* (1910) 'The Baker's Dozen'

**21** Addresses are given to us to conceal our whereabouts.

*Reginald in Russia* (1910) 'Cross Currents'

**22** We all know that Prime Ministers are wedded to the truth, but like other married couples they sometimes live apart.

*The Unbearable Bassington* (1912) ch. 13

## J. D. Salinger 1919–

1 I keep picturing all these little kids playing some game in this big field of rye and all ... I mean if they're running and they don't look where they're going I have to come out from somewhere and catch them. That's all I'd do all day. I'd just be the catcher in the rye.

*The Catcher in the Rye* (1951) ch. 22

## Lord Salisbury 1830–1903

2 English policy is to float lazily downstream, occasionally putting out a diplomatic boathook to avoid collisions.

Letter, 9 March 1877; in Lady Gwendolen Cecil *Life of Robert, Marquis of Salisbury* (1921–32) vol. 2, p. 130

3 A great deal of misapprehension arises from the popular use of maps on a small scale ... If the noble Lord would use a larger map—say one on the scale of the Ordnance Map of England—he would find that the distance between Russia and British India is not to be measured by the finger and thumb, but by a rule.

Speech, *Hansard* 11 June 1877, col. 1565

4 We are part of the community of Europe and we must do our duty as such.

Speech at Caernarvon, 10 April 1888, in *The Times* 11 April 1888

5 Horny-handed sons of toil.

*Quarterly Review* October 1873, p. 543 (later popularized in the US by Denis Kearney, 1847–1907). Cf. 211:5

6 By office boys for office boys.

Of the *Daily Mail*, in H. Hamilton Fyfe *Northcliffe* (1930) ch. 4

## Lord Salisbury 1893–1972

7 Too clever by half.

Of Iain Macleod, Colonial Secretary; in *Hansard* (Lords) 7 March 1961, col. 307

## Sallust 86–35 BC

8 A venal city ripe to perish, if a buyer can be found.

*Jugurtha* ch. 35 (of Rome)

9 *Punica fide.*

With Carthaginian trustworthiness.

*Jugurtha* ch. 108, sect. 3 (meaning treachery)

## Lord Samuel 1870–1963

10 A library is thought in cold storage.

*A Book of Quotations* (1947) p. 10

## Paul A. Samuelson 1915–

11 The consumer, so it is said, is the king ... each is a voter who uses his money as votes to get the things done that he wants done.

*Economics* (8th ed., 1970) p. 55

## Carl Sandburg 1878–1967

12 Hog Butcher for the World,
Tool Maker, Stacker of Wheat,
Player with Railroads and the Nation's
    Freight Handler;
Stormy, husky, brawling,
City of the Big Shoulders.

'Chicago' (1916)

13 The fog comes
on little cat feet.

It sits looking
over harbour and city
on silent haunches
and then moves on.

'Fog' (1916)

14 Pile the bodies high at Austerlitz and
    Waterloo.
Shovel them under and let me work—
I am the grass; I cover all.

'Grass' (1918)

15 I tell you the past is a bucket of ashes.

'Prairie' (1918)

16 Little girl ... Sometime they'll give a war and nobody will come.

*The People, Yes* (1936). 'Suppose They Gave a War and No One Came?' was the title of a piece by Charlotte Keyes in *McCall's* October 1966; 'Suppose They Gave a War and Nobody Came?' was the title of a 1970 film. Cf. 153:2

17 Poetry is the achievement of the synthesis of hyacinths and biscuits.

*Atlantic Monthly* March 1923 'Poetry Considered'

18 Slang is a language that rolls up its sleeves, spits on its hands and goes to work.

In *New York Times* 13 February 1959, p. 21

## Henry 'Red' Sanders

19 Sure, winning isn't everything. It's the only thing.

In *Sports Illustrated* 26 December 1955 (often attributed to Vince Lombardi)

## Martha Sansom 1690–1736

20 Foolish eyes, thy streams give over,
Wine, not water, binds the lover.

'Song' (written *c.*1726)

## George Santayana 1863–1952

21 Fanaticism consists in redoubling your effort when you have forgotten your aim.

*The Life of Reason* (1905) vol. 1, introduction

22 Those who cannot remember the past are condemned to repeat it.

*The Life of Reason* (1905) vol. 1, ch. 12

## John Singer Sargent 1856–1925

23 Every time I paint a portrait I lose a friend.

In N. Bentley and E. Esar *Treasury of Humorous Quotations* (1951)

## Leslie Sarony 1897–1985

1 Ain't it grand to be blooming well dead?
  Title of song (1932)

## Jean-Paul Sartre 1905–80

2 I am condemned to be free.
  *L'Être et le néant* (1943) pt. 4, ch. 1

3 Man is a useless passion.
  *L'Être et le néant* (1943) pt. 4, ch. 2

4 Hell is other people.
  *Huis Clos* (1944) sc. 5. Cf. 132:21

5 I confused things with their names: that is belief.
  *Les Mots* (1964) 'Écrire'

6 Human life begins on the far side of despair.
  *Les Mouches* (1943) act 3, sc. 2

7 I hate victims who respect their executioners.
  *Les Séquestrés d'Altona* (1960) act 1, sc. 1

## Siegfried Sassoon 1886–1967

8 If I were fierce, and bald, and short of breath,
  I'd live with scarlet Majors at the Base,
  And speed glum heroes up the line to death.
  'Base Details' (1918)

9 Does it matter?—losing your sight? . . .
  There's such splendid work for the blind;
  And people will always be kind,
  As you sit on the terrace remembering
  And turning your face to the light.
  'Does it Matter?' (1918)

10 Soldiers are citizens of death's grey land,
  Drawing no dividend from time's tomorrows.
  'Dreamers' (1918)

11 Everyone suddenly burst out singing.
  'Everyone Sang' (1919)

12 The song was wordless; the singing will never be done.
  'Everyone Sang' (1919)

13 'He's a cheery old card,' grunted Harry to Jack
  As they slogged up to Arras with rifle and pack.
  But he did for them both by his plan of attack.
  'The General' (1918)

14 Here was the world's worst wound.
  'On Passing the New Menin Gate' (1928)

## George Savile

*See* 1ST MARQUESS OF HALIFAX

## Dorothy L. Sayers 1893–1957

15 I admit it is better fun to punt than to be punted, and that a desire to have all the fun is nine-tenths of the law of chivalry.
  *Gaudy Night* (1935) ch. 14

## Al Scalpone

16 The family that prays together stays together.
  Motto devised for the Roman Catholic Family Rosary Crusade, 1947

## Friedrich von Schelling 1775–1854

17 Architecture in general is frozen music.
  *Philosophie der Kunst* (1809) in *Werke* (1916) vol. 3, p. 24

## Friedrich von Schiller 1759–1805

18 *Freude, schöner Götterfunken,*
  *Tochter aus Elysium.*
  Joy, beautiful radiance of the gods, daughter of Elysium.
  'An die Freude' (1785)

19 The sun does not set in my dominions.
  *Don Carlos* (1787) act 1, sc. 6 (Philip II).
  Cf. 240:6

20 With stupidity the gods themselves struggle in vain.
  *Die Jungfrau von Orleans* (1801) act 3, sc. 6

21 *Die Weltgeschichte ist das Weltgericht.*
  The world's history is the world's judgement.
  'Resignation' (1786) st. 19

## Moritz Schlick

22 The meaning of a proposition is the method of its verification.
  *Philosophical Review* (1936) vol. 45, p. 341

## Artur Schnabel 1882–1951

23 Too easy for children, and too difficult for artists.
  Of Mozart's sonatas, in Nat Shapiro (ed.) *Encyclopaedia of Quotations about Music* (1978) p. 58. In *My Life and Music* (1961) p. 122, Schnabel says: 'Children are given Mozart because of the small *quantity* of the notes; grown-ups avoid Mozart because of the great *quality* of the notes'

## Budd Schulberg 1914–

24 I could have had class. I could have been a contender.
  *On the Waterfront* (1954 film); spoken by Marlon Brando

## E. F. Schumacher 1911–77

25 Small is beautiful.
  Title of book (1973)

## J. A. Schumpeter 1883–1950

26 The cold metal of economic theory is in Marx's pages immersed in such a wealth of steaming phrases as to acquire a temperature not naturally its own.
  *Capitalism, Socialism and Democracy* (1942) p. 21

## Carl Schurz 1829–1906

1 My country, right or wrong; if right, to be kept right; and if wrong, to be set right!
Speech, US Senate, 29 February 1872, in *Congressional Globe* vol. 45, p. 1287. Cf. 115:10

## Kurt Schwitters 1887–1948

2 I am a painter and I nail my pictures together.
In R. Hausmann *Am Anfang war Dada* (1972) p. 63

## C. P. Scott 1846–1932

3 Comment is free, but facts are sacred.
*Manchester Guardian* 5 May 1921

## Robert Falcon Scott 1868–1912

4 Great God! this is an awful place.
Of the South Pole; Journal, 17 January 1912, in *Scott's Last Expedition* (1913) vol. 1, ch. 18

5 For God's sake look after our people.
Last journal entry, 29 March 1912, in *Scott's Last Expedition* (1913) vol. 1, ch. 20

## Sir Walter Scott 1771–1832

6 The valiant Knight of Triermain
Rung forth his challenge-blast again,
But answer came there none.
*The Bridal of Triermain* (1813) canto 3, st. 10

7 Come fill up my cup, come fill up my can,
Come saddle your horses, and call up your men;
Come open the West Port, and let me gang free,
And it's room for the bonnets of Bonny Dundee!
*The Doom of Devorgoil* (1830) act 2, sc. 2 'Bonny Dundee'

8 Yet seemed that tone, and gesture bland,
Less used to sue than to command.
*The Lady of the Lake* (1810) canto 1, st. 21

9 Respect was mingled with surprise,
And the stern joy which warriors feel
In foemen worthy of their steel.
*The Lady of the Lake* (1810) canto 5, st. 10

10 If thou would'st view fair Melrose aright,
Go visit it by the pale moonlight.
*The Lay of the Last Minstrel* (1805) canto 2, st. 1

11 It is the secret sympathy,
The silver link, the silken tie,
Which heart to heart, and mind to mind,
In body and in soul can bind.
*The Lay of the Last Minstrel* (1805) canto 5, st. 13

12 Breathes there the man, with soul so dead,
Who never to himself hath said,
This is my own, my native land!
*The Lay of the Last Minstrel* (1805) canto 6, st. 1

13 And, doubly dying, shall go down
To the vile dust, from whence he sprung,
Unwept, unhonoured, and unsung.
*The Lay of the Last Minstrel* (1805) canto 6, st. 1

14 O Caledonia! stern and wild,
Meet nurse for a poetic child!
*The Lay of the Last Minstrel* (1805) canto 6, st. 2

15 O! many a shaft, at random sent,
Finds mark the archer little meant!
And many a word, at random spoken,
May soothe or wound a heart that's broken.
*The Lord of the Isles* (1813) canto 5, st. 18

16 Had'st thou but lived, though stripped of power,
A watchman on the lonely tower.
*Marmion* (1808) introduction to canto 1, st. 8

17 And come he slow, or come he fast,
It is but Death who comes at last.
*Marmion* (1808) canto 2, st. 30

18 O, young Lochinvar is come out of the west,
Through all the wide Border his steed was the best.
*Marmion* (1808) canto 5, st. 12 ('Lochinvar' st. 1)

19 So faithful in love, and so dauntless in war,
There never was knight like the young Lochinvar.
*Marmion* (1808) canto 5, st. 12 ('Lochinvar' st. 1)

20 For a laggard in love, and a dastard in war,
Was to wed the fair Ellen of brave Lochinvar.
*Marmion* (1808) canto 5, st. 12 ('Lochinvar' st. 2)

21 O what a tangled web we weave,
When first we practise to deceive!
*Marmion* (1808) canto 6, st. 17

22 O Woman! in our hours of ease,
Uncertain, coy, and hard to please,
And variable as the shade
By the light quivering aspen made;
When pain and anguish wring the brow,
A ministering angel thou!
*Marmion* (1808) canto 6, st. 30. Cf. 277:10

23 Still from the sire the son shall hear
Of the stern strife, and carnage drear,
Of Flodden's fatal field,
Where shivered was fair Scotland's spear,
And broken was her shield!
*Marmion* (1808) canto 6, st. 34

24 Vacant heart and hand, and eye,—
Easy live and quiet die.
*The Bride of Lammermoor* (1819) ch. 2

25 Touch not the cat but a glove.
*The Fair Maid of Perth* (1828) ch. 34 (*but without*)

26 It's ill taking the breeks aff a wild Highlandman.
*The Fortunes of Nigel* (1822) ch. 5

27 The hour is come, but not the man.
*The Heart of Midlothian* (1818) ch. 4, title

1 Proud Maisie is in the wood,
Walking so early,
Sweet Robin sits in the bush,
Singing so rarely.
*The Heart of Midlothian* (1818) ch. 40

2 March, march, Eskdale and Liddesdale,
All the Blue Bonnets are bound for the
Border.
*The Monastery* (1820) ch. 25

3 But with the morning cool repentance
came.
*Rob Roy* (1817) ch. 12

4 There's a gude time coming.
*Rob Roy* (1817) ch. 32

5 The play-bill, which is said to have
announced the tragedy of Hamlet, the
character of the Prince of Denmark being
left out.
*The Talisman* (1825) introduction (commonly
alluded to as 'Hamlet without the Prince')

6 The Big Bow-Wow strain I can do myself
like any now going; but the exquisite
touch, which renders ordinary
commonplace things and characters
interesting, from the truth of the
description and the sentiment, is denied to
me.
On Jane Austen, in W. Anderson (ed.) *Journals
of Sir Walter Scott* (1972) 14 March 1826.
Cf. 247:7

7 Too many flowers ... too little fruit.
Of Felicia Hemans's literary style; letter to
Joanna Baillie, 18 July 1823, in *Letters*
(Centenary ed.) vol. 8

## Scottish Metrical Psalms 1650

8 The Lord's my shepherd, I'll not want.
He makes me down to lie
In pastures green: he leadeth me
the quiet waters by.
Psalm 23, v. 1. Cf. 66:17

9 My head thou dost with oil anoint,
and my cup overflows.
Psalm 23, v. 2. Cf. 66:18

10 The race that long in darkness pined
have seen a glorious light.
Paraphrase 19. Cf. 45:15

## Edmund Hamilton Sears 1810–76

11 It came upon the midnight clear,
That glorious song of old,
From Angels bending near the earth
To touch their harps of gold.
*The Christian Register* (1850) 'That Glorious
Song of Old'

## Sir Charles Sedley *c.*1639–1701

12 Phyllis, without frown or smile,
Sat and knotted all the while.
'Phyllis Knotting' (1694)

## Alan Seeger 1888–1916

13 I have a rendezvous with Death
At some disputed barricade.
'I Have a Rendezvous with Death' (1916)

## Pete Seeger 1919–

14 Where have all the flowers gone?
Title of song (1961)

## Sir John Seeley 1834–95

15 We [the English] seem, as it were, to have
conquered and peopled half the world in a
fit of absence of mind.
*The Expansion of England* (1883) Lecture 1

## John Selden 1584–1654

16 *Scrutamini scripturas* [Let us look at the
scriptures]. These two words have undone
the world.
*Table Talk* (1689) 'Bible Scripture'

17 Ignorance of the law excuses no man; not
that all men know the law, but because 'tis
an excuse every man will plead, and no
man can tell how to confute him.
*Table Talk* (1689) 'Law'

18 Take a straw and throw it up into the air,
you shall see by that which way the wind
is.
*Table Talk* (1689) 'Libels'

19 There never was a merry world since the
fairies left off dancing, and the Parson left
conjuring.
*Table Talk* (1689) 'Parson'

20 Pleasure is nothing else but the
intermission of pain.
*Table Talk* (1689) 'Pleasure'

21 Syllables govern the world.
*Table Talk* (1689) 'Power: State'

## Arthur Seldon 1916–

22 Government of the busy by the bossy for
the bully.
*Capitalism* (1990) p. 111 (subheading on over-
government)

## W. C. Sellar 1898–1951 and R. J. Yeatman 1898–1968

23 History is not what you thought. *It is what
you can remember.*
*1066 and All That* (1930) 'Compulsory Preface'

24 The Roman Conquest was, however, a *Good
Thing,* since the Britons were only natives
at the time.
*1066 and All That* (1930) ch. 1

25 'Honi soie qui mal y pense' ('Honey, your
silk stocking's hanging down').
*1066 and All That* (1930) ch. 24. Cf. 12:5

1 The cruel Queen died and a post-mortem examination revealed the word 'CALLOUS' engraved on her heart.
   *1066 and All That* (1930) ch. 32. Cf. 221:17

2 The Cavaliers (Wrong but Wromantic) and the Roundheads (Right but Repulsive).
   *1066 and All That* (1930) ch. 35

3 The Rump Parliament—so called because it had been sitting for such a long time.
   *1066 and All That* (1930) ch. 35

4 The National Debt is a very Good Thing and it would be dangerous to pay it off, for fear of Political Economy.
   *1066 and All That* (1930) ch. 38

5 AMERICA was thus clearly top nation, and History came to a.
   *1066 and All That* (1930) ch. 62

## Seneca ('the Younger') *c.*4 BC–AD 65

6 *Homines dum docent discunt.*
   Even while they teach, men learn.
   *Epistulae Morales* no. 7, sect. 8

7 If one does not know to which port one is sailing, no wind is favourable.
   *Epistulae Morales* no. 71, sect. 3

8 Anyone can stop a man's life, but no one his death; a thousand doors open on to it.
   *Phoenissae* l. 152

## Robert W. Service 1874–1958

9 A promise made is a debt unpaid, and the trail has its own stern code.
   'The Cremation of Sam McGee' (1907)

10 Ah! the clock is always slow;
   It is later than you think.
   'It Is Later Than You Think' (1921)

11 This is the law of the Yukon, that only the Strong shall thrive;
   That surely the Weak shall perish, and only the Fit survive.
   'The Law of the Yukon' (1907)

12 When we, the Workers, all demand: 'What are WE fighting for?' ...
   Then, then we'll end that stupid crime, that devil's madness—War.
   'Michael' (1921)

13 Back of the bar, in a solo game, sat Dangerous Dan McGrew,
   And watching his luck was his light-o'-love, the lady that's known as Lou.
   'The Shooting of Dan McGrew' (1907)

## Edward Sexby d. 1658

14 Killing no murder briefly discourst in three questions.
   Title of pamphlet (an apology for tyrannicide, 1657)

## Anne Sexton 1928–74

15 In a dream you are never eighty.
   'Old' (1962)

## James Seymour and Rian James

16 You're going out a youngster but you've *got* to come back a star.
   *42nd Street* (1933 film)

## Thomas Shadwell *c.*1642–92

17 Words may be false and full of art,
   Sighs are the natural language of the heart.
   *Psyche* (1675) act 3

18 And wit's the noblest frailty of the mind.
   *A True Widow* (1679) act 2, sc. 1. Cf. 127:33

## Peter Shaffer 1926–

19 The Normal is the good smile in a child's eyes—all right. It is also the dead stare in a million adults. It both sustains and kills—like a God. It is the Ordinary made beautiful; it is also the Average made lethal.
   *Equus* (1983 ed.) act 1, sc. 19

## 1st Earl of Shaftesbury 1621–83

20 'Men of sense are really but of one religion.' ... 'Pray, my lord, what religion is that which men of sense agree in?' 'Madam,' says the earl immediately, 'men of sense never tell it.'
   Bishop Gilbert Burnet *History of My Own Time* vol. 1 (1724) bk. 2, ch. 1 n.

## 3rd Earl of Shaftesbury 1671–1713

21 How comes it to pass, then, that we appear such cowards in reasoning, and are so afraid to stand the test of ridicule?
   *A Letter Concerning Enthusiasm* (1708) sect. 2

22 Truth ... may bear all lights.
   *Sensus Communis* (1709) pt. 1, sect. 1

## William Shakespeare 1564–1616

The line number is given without brackets where the scene is all verse up to the quotation and the line number is certain, and in square brackets where prose makes it variable. All references are to the Oxford Standard Authors edition in one volume

### All's Well that Ends Well (1603–4)

23          It were all one
   That I should love a bright particular star
   And think to wed it, he is so above me.
   *All's Well that Ends Well* act 1, sc. 1, l. [97]

24 Our remedies oft in ourselves do lie
   Which we ascribe to heaven.
   *All's Well that Ends Well* act 1, sc. 1, l. [232]

25 It is like a barber's chair that fits all buttocks.
   *All's Well that Ends Well* act 2, sc. 2, l. [18]

1 A young man married is a man that's
marred.
*All's Well that Ends Well* act 2, sc. 3, l. [315]

2 I know a man that had this trick of
melancholy sold a goodly manor for a
song.
*All's Well that Ends Well* act 3, sc. 2, l. [8]

## Antony and Cleopatra (1606–7)

3 The triple pillar of the world transformed
Into a strumpet's fool.
*Antony and Cleopatra* act 1, sc. 1, l. 12

4 ANTONY: There's beggary in the love that
can be reckoned.           ,
CLEOPATRA: I'll set a bourn how far to be
beloved.
ANTONY: Then must thou needs find out
new heaven, new earth.
*Antony and Cleopatra* act 1, sc. 1, l. 15

5 Let Rome in Tiber melt, and the wide arch
Of the ranged empire fall. Here is my
space.
*Antony and Cleopatra* act 1, sc. 1, l. 33

6 A Roman thought hath struck him.
*Antony and Cleopatra* act 1, sc. 2, l. [91]

7 There's a great spirit gone!
*Antony and Cleopatra* act 1, sc. 2, l. [131]

8 In time we hate that which we often fear.
*Antony and Cleopatra* act 1, sc. 3, l. 12

9 O! my oblivion is a very Antony,
And I am all forgotten.
*Antony and Cleopatra* act 1, sc. 3, l. 90

10 O happy horse, to bear the weight of
Antony!
*Antony and Cleopatra* act 1, sc. 5, l. 21

11 Where's my serpent of old Nile?
*Antony and Cleopatra* act 1, sc. 5, l. 25

12              My salad days,
When I was green in judgement.
*Antony and Cleopatra* act 1, sc. 5, l. 73

13 I do not much dislike the matter, but
The manner of his speech.
*Antony and Cleopatra* act 2, sc. 2, l. 117

14 The barge she sat in, like a burnished
throne,
Burned on the water; the poop was beaten
gold,
Purple the sails, and so perfumed, that
The winds were love-sick with them, the
oars were silver,
Which to the tune of flutes kept stroke,
and made
The water which they beat to follow faster,
As amorous of their strokes. For her own
person,
It beggared all description.
*Antony and Cleopatra* act 2, sc. 2, l. [199]

15 Her gentlewomen, like the Nereides,
So many mermaids, tended her i' the eyes,
And made their bends adornings.
*Antony and Cleopatra* act 2, sc. 2, l. [214]

16              I saw her once
Hop forty paces through the public street;
And having lost her breath, she spoke, and
panted
That she did make defect perfection,
And, breathless, power breathe forth.
*Antony and Cleopatra* act 2, sc. 2, l. [236]

17 Age cannot wither her, nor custom stale
Her infinite variety; other women cloy
The appetites they feed, but she makes
hungry
Where most she satisfies; for vilest things
Become themselves in her, that the holy
priests
Bless her when she is riggish.
*Antony and Cleopatra* act 2, sc. 2, l. [243]

18              Egypt, thou knew'st too well
My heart was to thy rudder tied by th'
strings,
And thou shouldst tow me after.
*Antony and Cleopatra* act 3, sc. 9, l. 56

19 Let's have one other gaudy night: call to
me
All my sad captains; fill our bowls once
more;
Let's mock the midnight bell.
*Antony and Cleopatra* act 3, sc. 11, l. 182

20 To business that we love we rise betime,
And go to 't with delight.
*Antony and Cleopatra* act 4, sc. 4, l. 20

21 O infinite virtue! com'st thou smiling from
The world's great snare uncaught?
*Antony and Cleopatra* act 4, sc. 8, l. 17

22              The hearts
That spanieled me at heels, to whom I gave
Their wishes, do discandy, melt their
sweets
On blossoming Caesar.
*Antony and Cleopatra* act 4, sc. 10, l. 33

23 The soul and body rive not more in parting
Than greatness going off.
*Antony and Cleopatra* act 4, sc. 11, l. 5

24 I am dying, Egypt, dying.
*Antony and Cleopatra* act 4, sc. 13, l. 18

25              O! see my women,
The crown o' the earth doth melt. My lord!
O! withered is the garland of the war,
The soldier's pole is fall'n; young boys and
girls
Are level now with men; the odds is gone,
And there is nothing left remarkable
Beneath the visiting moon.
*Antony and Cleopatra* act 4, sc. 13, l. 62

26              What's brave, what's noble,
Let's do it after the high Roman fashion,
And make death proud to take us.
*Antony and Cleopatra* act 4, sc. 13, l. 86

27              A rarer spirit never
Did steer humanity; but you, gods, will
give us
Some faults to make us men.
*Antony and Cleopatra* act 5, sc. 1, l. 31

**1** My desolation does begin to make
A better life.
  *Antony and Cleopatra* act 5, sc. 2, l. 1

**2**                    And it is great
To do that thing that ends all other deeds,
Which shackles accidents, and bolts up
change.
  *Antony and Cleopatra* act 5, sc. 2, l. 4

**3** He words me, girls, he words me.
  *Antony and Cleopatra* act 5, sc. 2, l. 190

**4** Finish, good lady; the bright day is done,
And we are for the dark.
  *Antony and Cleopatra* act 5, sc. 2, l. 192

**5**           Antony
Shall be brought drunken forth, and I shall
see
Some squeaking Cleopatra boy my
greatness
I' the posture of a whore.
  *Antony and Cleopatra* act 5, sc. 2, l. 217

**6** I wish you all joy of the worm.
  *Antony and Cleopatra* act 5, sc. 2, l. [260]

**7** Give me my robe, put on my crown; I have
Immortal longings in me.
  *Antony and Cleopatra* act 5, sc. 2, l. [282]

**8**                    Come, thou mortal wretch,
With thy sharp teeth this knot intrinsicate
Of life at once untie.
  *Antony and Cleopatra* act 5, sc. 2, l. [305]

**9**           Peace! peace!
Dost thou not see my baby at my breast,
That sucks the nurse asleep?
  *Antony and Cleopatra* act 5, sc. 2, l. [310]

**10** Now boast thee, death, in thy possession
lies
A lass unparalleled.
  *Antony and Cleopatra* act 5, sc. 2, l. [317]

**11** She hath pursued conclusions infinite
Of easy ways to die.
  *Antony and Cleopatra* act 5, sc. 2, l. [356]

**As You Like It** (1599)

**12** Fleet the time carelessly, as they did in the
golden world.
  *As You Like It* act 1, sc. 1, l. [126]

**13** Hereafter, in a better world than this,
I shall desire more love and knowledge of
you.
  *As You Like It* act 1, sc. 2, l. [301]

**14** Sweet are the uses of adversity,
Which like the toad, ugly and venomous,
Wears yet a precious jewel in his head;
And this our life, exempt from public
haunt,
Finds tongues in trees, books in the
running brooks,
Sermons in stones, and good in everything.
  *As You Like It* act 2, sc. 1, l. 12

**15** Unregarded age in corners thrown.
  *As You Like It* act 2, sc. 3, l. 42

**16** Therefore my age is as a lusty winter,
Frosty, but kindly.
  *As You Like It* act 2, sc. 3, l. 52

**17** Thou art not for the fashion of these times,
Where none will sweat but for promotion.
  *As You Like It* act 2, sc. 3, l. 59

**18** In thy youth thou wast as true a lover
As ever sighed upon a midnight pillow.
  *As You Like It* act 2, sc. 4, l. [26]

**19** Under the greenwood tree
Who loves to lie with me,
And turn his merry note
Unto the sweet bird's throat,
Come hither, come hither, come hither:
Here shall he see
No enemy
But winter and rough weather.
  *As You Like It* act 2, sc. 5, l. 1

**20** I can suck melancholy out of a song as a
weasel sucks eggs.
  *As You Like It* act 2, sc. 5, l. [12]

**21** Who doth ambition shun
And loves to live i' the sun,
Seeking the food he eats,
And pleased with what he gets.
  *As You Like It* act 2, sc. 5, l. [38]

**22** And so, from hour to hour, we ripe and
ripe,
And then from hour to hour, we rot and
rot:
And thereby hangs a tale.
  *As You Like It* act 2, sc. 7, l. 26

**23** A worthy fool! Motley's the only wear.
  *As You Like It* act 2, sc. 7, l. 34

**24** All the world's a stage,
And all the men and women merely
players:
They have their exits and their entrances;
And one man in his time plays many parts,
His acts being seven ages.
  *As You Like It* act 2, sc. 7, l. 139

**25**           At first the infant,
Mewling and puking in the nurse's arms.
And then the whining schoolboy, with his
satchel,
And shining morning face, creeping like
snail
Unwillingly to school.
  *As You Like It* act 2, sc. 7, l. 143

**26**           A soldier,
Full of strange oaths, and bearded like the
pard,
Jealous in honour, sudden and quick in
quarrel,
Seeking the bubble reputation
Even in the cannon's mouth.
  *As You Like It* act 2, sc. 7, l. 149

**27**           The sixth age shifts
Into the lean and slippered pantaloon,
With spectacles on nose and pouch on
side.
  *As You Like It* act 2, sc. 7, l. 157

**28** Second childishness, and mere oblivion,
Sans teeth, sans eyes, sans taste, sans
everything.
  *As You Like It* act 2, sc. 7, l. 165

1 Blow, blow, thou winter wind,
Thou art not so unkind
As man's ingratitude.
*As You Like It* act 2, sc. 7, l. 174

2 Run, run, Orlando: carve on every tree
The fair, the chaste, and unexpressive she.
*As You Like It* act 3, sc. 2, l. 9

3 Let us make an honourable retreat; though
not with bag and baggage, yet with scrip
and scrippage.
*As You Like It* act 3, sc. 2, l. [170]

4 O wonderful, wonderful, and most
wonderful wonderful! and yet again
wonderful, and after that, out of all
whooping!
*As You Like It* act 3, sc. 2, l. [202]

5 I do desire we may be better strangers.
*As You Like It* act 3, sc. 2, l. [276]

6 Down on your knees,
And thank heaven, fasting, for a good
man's love.
*As You Like It* act 3, sc. 5, l. 57

7 Dead shepherd, now I find thy saw of
might:
'Who ever loved that loved not at first
sight?'
*As You Like It* act 3, sc. 5, l. [81]. Cf. 218:18

8 Come, woo me, woo me; for now I am in a
holiday humour, and like enough to
consent.
*As You Like It* act 4, sc. 1, l. [70]

9 Men are April when they woo, December
when they wed: maids are May when they
are maids, but the sky changes when they
are wives.
*As You Like It* act 4, sc. 1, l. [153]

10 It was a lover and his lass,
With a hey, and a ho, and a hey nonino,
That o'er the green cornfield did pass,
In the spring time, the only pretty ring
time,
When birds do sing, hey ding a ding, ding;
Sweet lovers love the spring.
*As You Like It* act 5, sc. 3, l. [18]

11 A poor virgin, sir, an ill-favoured thing, sir,
but mine own.
*As You Like It* act 5, sc. 4, l. [60]

12 The retort courteous ... the quip modest
... the reply churlish ... the reproof
valiant ... the countercheck quarrelsome
... the lie circumstantial ... the lie direct.
*As You Like It* act 5, sc. 4, l. [96] (of the degrees
of a lie)

13 Your 'if' is the only peace-maker; much
virtue in 'if'.
*As You Like It* act 5, sc. 4, l. [108]

14 He uses his folly like a stalking-horse, and
under the presentation of that he shoots
his wit.
*As You Like It* act 5, sc. 4, l. [112]

## Coriolanus (1608)

15 He's a very dog to the commonalty.
*Coriolanus* act 1, sc. 1, l. [29]

16 Bid them wash their faces,
And keep their teeth clean.
*Coriolanus* act 2, sc. 1, l. [65]

17 My gracious silence, hail!
*Coriolanus* act 2, sc. 1, l. [194]

18 Hear you this Triton of the minnows?
mark you
His absolute 'shall'?
*Coriolanus* act 3, sc. 1, l. 88

19 What is the city but the people?
*Coriolanus* act 3, sc. 1, l. 198

20 Despising,
For you, the city, thus I turn my back:
There is a world elsewhere.
*Coriolanus* act 3, sc. 3, l. 131

21 I'll never
Be such a gosling to obey instinct, but
stand
As if a man were author of himself
And knew no other kin.
*Coriolanus* act 5, sc. 3, l. 34

22 Thou hast never in thy life
Showed thy dear mother any courtesy;
When she—poor hen! fond of no second
brood—
Has clucked thee to the wars, and safely
home,
Loaden with honour.
*Coriolanus* act 5, sc. 3, l. 160

## Cymbeline (1609–10)

23 Boldness be my friend!
Arm me, audacity.
*Cymbeline* act 1, sc. 6, l. 18

24 But kiss: one kiss! Rubies unparagoned,
How dearly they do't!
*Cymbeline* act 2, sc. 2, l. 17

25 Hark! hark! the lark at heaven's gate sings.
*Cymbeline* act 2, sc. 3, l. [22]

26 Is there no way for men to be, but women
Must be half-workers?
*Cymbeline* act 2, sc. 5, l. 1

27 Fear no more the heat o' the sun,
Nor the furious winter's rages;
Thou thy worldly task hast done,
Home art gone and ta'en thy wages:
Golden lads and girls all must,
As chimney-sweepers, come to dust.
*Cymbeline* act 4, sc. 2, l. 258

28 No exorciser harm thee!
Nor no witchcraft charm thee!
Ghost unlaid forbear thee!
Nothing ill come near thee!
Quiet consummation have:
And renowned be thy grave!
*Cymbeline* act 4, sc. 2, l. 276

## Hamlet (1601)

29 You come most carefully upon your hour.
*Hamlet* act 1, sc. 1, l. 6

30 For this relief much thanks; 'tis bitter cold
And I am sick at heart.
*Hamlet* act 1, sc. 1, l. 8

1 In the most high and palmy state of Rome,
A little ere the mightiest Julius fell,
The graves stood tenantless and the
sheeted dead
Did squeak and gibber in the Roman
streets.
*Hamlet* act 1, sc. 1, l. 113

2 Some say that ever 'gainst that season
comes
Wherein our Saviour's birth is celebrated,
The bird of dawning singeth all night long;
And then, they say, no spirit can walk
abroad.
*Hamlet* act 1, sc. 1, l. 158

3 But, look, the morn, in russet mantle clad,
Walks o'er the dew of yon high eastern
hill.
*Hamlet* act 1, sc. 1, l. 166

4 The head is not more native to the heart,
The hand more instrumental to the brain,
Than is the throne of Denmark to thy
father.
*Hamlet* act 1, sc. 2, l. 47

5 A little more than kin, and less than kind.
*Hamlet* act 1, sc. 2, l. 65

6 Not so, my lord; I am too much i' the sun.
*Hamlet* act 1, sc. 2, l. 67

7 Seems, madam! Nay, it is; I know not
'seems'.
*Hamlet* act 1, sc. 2, l. 76

8 But I have that within which passeth
show;
These but the trappings and the suits of
woe.
*Hamlet* act 1, sc. 2, l. 85

9 O! that this too too solid flesh would melt,
Thaw, and resolve itself into a dew.
*Hamlet* act 1, sc. 2, l. 129

10 How weary, stale, flat, and unprofitable
Seem to me all the uses of this world.
Fie on't! O fie! 'tis an unweeded garden,
That grows to seed; things rank and gross
in nature
Possess it merely.
*Hamlet* act 1, sc. 2, l. 133

11 So excellent a king; that was, to this,
Hyperion to a satyr.
*Hamlet* act 1, sc. 2, l. 139

12                    Frailty, thy name is woman!
A little month; or ere those shoes were old
With which she followed my poor father's
body,
Like Niobe, all tears; why she, even she,—
O God! a beast, that wants discourse of
reason,
Would have mourned longer.
*Hamlet* act 1, sc. 2, l. 146

13 It is not, nor it cannot come to good;
But break, my heart, for I must hold my
tongue!
*Hamlet* act 1, sc. 2, l. 158

14 A truant disposition, good my lord.
*Hamlet* act 1, sc. 2, l. 169

15 We'll teach you to drink deep ere you
depart.
*Hamlet* act 1, sc. 2, l. 175

16 Thrift, thrift, Horatio! the funeral baked
meats
Did coldly furnish forth the marriage
tables.
Would I had met my dearest foe in heaven
Ere I had ever seen that day, Horatio!
*Hamlet* act 1, sc. 2, l. 180

17 He was a man, take him for all in all,
I shall not look upon his like again.
*Hamlet* act 1, sc. 2, l. 187

18 But answer made it none.
*Hamlet* act 1, sc. 2, l. 215

19 A countenance more in sorrow than in
anger.
*Hamlet* act 1, sc. 2, l. 231

20 Do not, as some ungracious pastors do,
Show me the steep and thorny way to
heaven,
Whiles, like a puffed and reckless libertine,
Himself the primrose path of dalliance
treads,
And recks not his own rede.
*Hamlet* act 1, sc. 3, l. 47

21 The apparel oft proclaims the man.
*Hamlet* act 1, sc. 3, l. 72

22 Neither a borrower, nor a lender be.
*Hamlet* act 1, sc. 3, l. 73

23 This above all: to thine own self be true,
And it must follow, as the night the day,
Thou canst not then be false to any man.
*Hamlet* act 1, sc. 3, l. 76

24 Ay, springes to catch woodcocks.
*Hamlet* act 1, sc. 3, l. 115

25 It is a nipping and an eager air.
*Hamlet* act 1, sc. 4, l. 2

26 But to my mind,—though I am native here,
And to the manner born,—it is a custom
More honoured in the breach than the
observance.
*Hamlet* act 1, sc. 4, l. 14

27 Angels and ministers of grace defend us!
*Hamlet* act 1, sc. 4, l. 39

28 I do not set my life at a pin's fee.
*Hamlet* act 1, sc. 4, l. 65

29 Something is rotten in the state of
Denmark.
*Hamlet* act 1, sc. 4, l. 90

30 I could a tale unfold whose lightest word
Would harrow up thy soul, freeze thy
young blood,
Make thy two eyes, like stars, start from
their spheres.
*Hamlet* act 1, sc. 5, l. 15

31 Murder most foul, as in the best it is;
But this most foul, strange, and unnatural.
*Hamlet* act 1, sc. 5, l. 27

32                    O my prophetic soul!
My uncle!
*Hamlet* act 1, sc. 5, l. 40

1 But, soft! methinks I scent the morning air.
   *Hamlet* act 1, sc. 5, l. 58

2 O, horrible! O, horrible! most horrible!
   *Hamlet* act 1, sc. 5, l. 80

3 There are more things in heaven and
   earth, Horatio,
   Than are dreamt of in your philosophy.
   *Hamlet* act 1, sc. 5, l. 166

4 To put an antic disposition on.
   *Hamlet* act 1, sc. 5, l. 172

5 Rest, rest, perturbèd spirit.
   *Hamlet* act 1, sc. 5, l. 182

6 The time is out of joint; O cursèd spite,
   That ever I was born to set it right!
   *Hamlet* act 1, sc. 5, l. 188

7 By indirections find directions out.
   *Hamlet* act 2, sc. 1, l. 66

8 Brevity is the soul of wit.
   *Hamlet* act 2, sc. 2, l. 90

9          To define true madness,
   What is't but to be nothing else but mad?
   *Hamlet* act 2, sc. 2, l. 93

10 More matter with less art.
   *Hamlet* act 2, sc. 2, l. 95

11 POLONIUS: What do you read, my lord?
   HAMLET: Words, words, words.
   *Hamlet* act 2, sc. 2, l. [195]

12 Though this be madness, yet there is
   method in't.
   *Hamlet* act 2, sc. 2, l. [211]

13 HAMLET: Then you live about her waist, or
   in the middle of her favours?
   GUILDENSTERN: Faith, her privates, we.
   HAMLET: In the secret parts of Fortune? O!
   most true; she is a strumpet.
   *Hamlet* act 2, sc. 2, l. [240]

14 There is nothing either good or bad, but
   thinking makes it so.
   *Hamlet* act 2, sc. 2, l. [259]

15 O God! I could be bounded in a nut-shell,
   and count myself a king of infinite space,
   were it not that I have bad dreams.
   *Hamlet* act 2, sc. 2, l. [263]

16 What a piece of work is a man! How noble
   in reason! how infinite in faculty! in form,
   in moving, how express and admirable! in
   action how like an angel! in apprehension
   how like a god! the beauty of the world!
   the paragon of animals! And yet, to me,
   what is this quintessence of dust? man
   delights not me; no, nor woman neither,
   though, by your smiling, you seem to say
   so.
   *Hamlet* act 2, sc. 2, l. [323]

17 I am but mad north-north-west; when the
   wind is southerly, I know a hawk from a
   handsaw.
   *Hamlet* act 2, sc. 2, l. [405]

18 The play, I remember, pleased not the
   million; 'twas caviare to the general.
   *Hamlet* act 2, sc. 2, l. [465]

19 Good my lord, will you see the players well
   bestowed? Do you hear, let them be well
   used; for they are the abstracts and brief
   chronicles of the time.
   *Hamlet* act 2, sc. 2, l. [553]

20 Use every man after his desert, and who
   should 'scape whipping?
   *Hamlet* act 2, sc. 2, l. [561]

21 O, what a rogue and peasant slave am I.
   *Hamlet* act 2, sc. 2, l. [584]

22 What's Hecuba to him or he to Hecuba
   That he should weep for her?
   *Hamlet* act 2, sc. 2, l. [593]

23          He would drown the stage with
   tears,
   And cleave the general ear with horrid
   speech,
   Make mad the guilty, and appal the free,
   Confound the ignorant, and amaze, indeed,
   The very faculties of eyes and ears.
   *Hamlet* act 2, sc. 2, l. [596]

24          The play's the thing
   Wherein I'll catch the conscience of the
   king.
   *Hamlet* act 2, sc. 2, l. [641]

25 To be, or not to be: that is the question:
   Whether 'tis nobler in the mind to suffer
   The slings and arrows of outrageous
   fortune,
   Or to take arms against a sea of troubles,
   And by opposing end them? To die: to
   sleep;
   No more; and, by a sleep to say we end
   The heart-ache and the thousand natural
   shocks
   That flesh is heir to, 'tis a consummation
   Devoutly to be wished. To die, to sleep;
   To sleep: perchance to dream: ay, there's
   the rub;
   For in that sleep of death what dreams
   may come
   When we have shuffled off this mortal coil,
   Must give us pause.
   *Hamlet* act 3, sc. 1, l. 56

26 ... The dread of something after death,
   The undiscovered country from whose
   bourn
   No traveller returns, puzzles the will,
   And makes us rather bear those ills we
   have,
   Than fly to others that we know not of?
   Thus conscience doth make cowards of us
   all;
   And thus the native hue of resolution
   Is sicklied o'er with the pale cast of
   thought.
   *Hamlet* act 3, sc. 1, l. 78

27          Nymph, in thy orisons
   Be all my sins remembered.
   *Hamlet* act 3, sc. 1, l. 89

28 Get thee to a nunnery.
   *Hamlet* act 3, sc. 1, l. [124]

29 Be thou as chaste as ice, as pure as snow,
   thou shalt not escape calumny.
   *Hamlet* act 3, sc. 1, l. [142]

1 I say, we will have no more marriages.
  *Hamlet* act 3, sc. 1, l. [156]

2 O! what a noble mind is here o'erthrown:
  The courtier's, soldier's, scholar's, eye,
     tongue, sword;
  The expectancy and rose of the fair state,
  The glass of fashion, and the mould of
     form,
  The observed of all observers, quite, quite,
     down!
  *Hamlet* act 3, sc. 1, l. [159]

3             O! woe is me,
  To have seen what I have seen, see what I
     see!
  *Hamlet* act 3, sc. 1, l. [169]

4 Speak the speech, I pray you, as I
  pronounced it to you, trippingly on the
  tongue; but if you mouth it, as many of
  your players do, I had as lief the town-crier
  spoke my lines. Nor do not saw the air too
  much with your hand, thus; but use all
  gently.'
  *Hamlet* act 3, sc. 2, l. 1

5 I would have such a fellow whipped for
  o'erdoing Termagant; it out-herods Herod.
  *Hamlet* act 3, sc. 2, l. 14

6 Suit the action to the word, the word to
  the action.
  *Hamlet* act 3, sc. 2, l. [20]

7             Give me that man
  That is not passion's slave, and I will wear
     him
  In my heart's core, ay, in my heart of
     heart,
  As I do thee.
  *Hamlet* act 3, sc. 2, l. [76]

8 Here's metal more attractive.
  *Hamlet* act 3, sc. 2, l. [117]

9 The lady doth protest too much, methinks.
  *Hamlet* act 3, sc. 2, l. [242]

10 Let the galled jade wince, our withers are
  unwrung.
  *Hamlet* act 3, sc. 2, l. [256]

11 What! frighted with false fire?
  *Hamlet* act 3, sc. 2, l. [282]

12 Why, let the stricken deer go weep,
  The hart ungallèd play;
  For some must watch, while some must
     sleep:
  So runs the world away.
  *Hamlet* act 3, sc. 2, l. [287]

13 You would play upon me; you would seem
  to know my stops; you would pluck out
  the heart of my mystery; you would sound
  me from my lowest note to the top of my
  compass.
  *Hamlet* act 3, sc. 2, l. [387]

14 They fool me to the top of my bent.
  *Hamlet* act 3, sc. 2, l. [408]

15 'Tis now the very witching time of night.
  *Hamlet* act 3, sc. 2, l. [413]

16 O! my offence is rank, it smells to heaven.
  *Hamlet* act 3, sc. 3, l. 36

17 Now might I do it pat, now he is praying.
  *Hamlet* act 3, sc. 3, l. 73

18 My words fly up, my thoughts remain
     below:
  Words without thoughts never to heaven
     go.
  *Hamlet* act 3, sc. 3, l. 97

19 How now! a rat? Dead, for a ducat, dead!
  *Hamlet* act 3, sc. 4, l. 23

20 Thou wretched, rash, intruding fool,
     farewell!
  I took thee for thy better.
  *Hamlet* act 3, sc. 4, l. 31

21 A king of shreds and patches.
  *Hamlet* act 3, sc. 4, l. 102

22             Mother, for love of grace,
  Lay not that flattering unction to your
     soul.
  *Hamlet* act 3, sc. 4, l. 142

23 Assume a virtue, if you have it not.
  *Hamlet* act 3, sc. 4, l. 160

24 I must be cruel only to be kind.
  *Hamlet* act 3, sc. 4, l. 178

25 For 'tis the sport to have the enginer
  Hoist with his own petar.
  *Hamlet* act 3, sc. 4, l. 206

26 I'll lug the guts into the neighbour room.
  *Hamlet* act 3, sc. 4, l. 212

27             Diseases desperate grown,
  By desperate appliances are relieved
  Or not at all.
  *Hamlet* act 4, sc. 2, l. 9

28 We go to gain a little patch of ground,
  That hath in it no profit but the name.
  *Hamlet* act 4, sc. 4, l. 18

29 How all occasions do inform against me.
  *Hamlet* act 4, sc. 4, l. 32

30             Some craven scruple
  Of thinking too precisely on the event.
  *Hamlet* act 4, sc. 4, l. 40

31             Rightly to be great
  Is not to stir without great argument,
  But greatly to find quarrel in a straw
  When honour's at the stake.
  *Hamlet* act 4, sc. 4, l. 53

32 How should I your true love know
  From another one?
  By his cockle hat and staff,
  And his sandal shoon.
  *Hamlet* act 4, sc. 5, l. [23]

33 Lord! we know what we are, but know not
  what we may be.
  *Hamlet* act 4, sc. 5, l. [43]

34 Come, my coach! Good-night, ladies; good-
  night, sweet ladies; good-night, good-night.
  *Hamlet* act 4, sc. 5, l. [72]

35 When sorrows come, they come not single
     spies,
  But in battalions.
  *Hamlet* act 4, sc. 5, l. [78]

1 There's such divinity doth hedge a king,
That treason can but peep to what it
would.
  *Hamlet* act 4, sc. 5, l. [123]

2 There's rosemary, that's for remembrance;
pray, love, remember: and there is pansies,
that's for thoughts.
  *Hamlet* act 4, sc. 5, l. [174]

3 There's rue for you; and here's some for
me; we may call it herb of grace o'
Sundays. O! you must wear your rue with a
difference.
  *Hamlet* act 4, sc. 5, l. [180]

4 And where the offence is let the great axe
fall.
  *Hamlet* act 4, sc. 5, l. [218]

5 A very riband in the cap of youth.
  *Hamlet* act 4, sc. 7, l. 77

6 There is a willow grows aslant a brook,
That shows his hoar leaves in the glassy
stream.
  *Hamlet* act 4, sc. 7, l. 167

7 There, on the pendent boughs her coronet
weeds
Clambering to hang, an envious sliver
broke,
When down her weedy trophies and
herself
Fell in the weeping brook.
  *Hamlet* act 4, sc. 7, l. 173

8 Alas, poor Yorick. I knew him, Horatio; a
fellow of infinite jest, of most excellent
fancy.
  *Hamlet* act 5, sc. 1, l. [201]

9 Imperious Caesar, dead, and turned to clay,
Might stop a hole to keep the wind away.
  *Hamlet* act 5, sc. 1, l. [235]

10 A ministering angel shall my sister be,
When thou liest howling.
  *Hamlet* act 5, sc. 1, l. [260]

11 Sweets to the sweet: farewell!
  *Hamlet* act 5, sc. 1, l. [265]

12 There's a divinity that shapes our ends,
Rough-hew them how we will.
  *Hamlet* act 5, sc. 2, l. 10

13 Not a whit, we defy augury; there's a
special providence in the fall of a sparrow.
If it be now, 'tis not to come; if it be not to
come, it will be now; if it be not now, yet it
will come: the readiness is all.
  *Hamlet* act 5, sc. 2, l. [232]

14 A hit, a very palpable hit.
  *Hamlet* act 5, sc. 2, l. [295]

15          This fell sergeant, death,
Is swift in his arrest.
  *Hamlet* act 5, sc. 2, l. [350]

16 I am more an antique Roman than a Dane.
  *Hamlet* act 5, sc. 2, l. [355]

17 If thou didst ever hold me in thy heart,
Absent thee from felicity awhile,
And in this harsh world draw thy breath in
pain,
To tell my story.
  *Hamlet* act 5, sc. 2, l. [360]

18 The rest is silence.
  *Hamlet* act 5, sc. 2, l. [372]

19 Now cracks a noble heart. Good-night,
sweet prince,
And flights of angels sing thee to thy rest!
  *Hamlet* act 5, sc. 2, l. [373]

20 Rosencrantz and Guildenstern are dead.
  *Hamlet* act 5, sc. 2, l. [385]

**Henry IV, Part 1 (1597)**

21 So shaken as we are, so wan with care.
  *Henry IV, Part 1* act 1, sc. 1, l. 1

22 Let us be Diana's foresters, gentlemen of
the shade, minions of the moon.
  *Henry IV, Part 1* act 1, sc. 2, l. [28]

23 What, in thy quips and thy quiddities?
  *Henry IV, Part 1* act 1, sc. 2, l. [50]

24 The rusty curb of old father antick, the
law.
  *Henry IV, Part 1* act 1, sc. 2, l. [68]

25 If all the year were playing holidays,
To sport would be as tedious as to work;
But when they seldom come, they wished
for come.
  *Henry IV, Part 1* act 1, sc. 2, l. [226]

26 To put down Richard, that sweet lovely
rose,
And plant this thorn, this canker,
Bolingbroke.
  *Henry IV, Part 1* act 1, sc. 3, l. 175

27 By heaven methinks it were an easy leap
To pluck bright honour from the pale-faced
moon,
Or dive into the bottom of the deep,
Where fathom-line could never touch the
ground,
And pluck up drownèd honour by the
locks.
  *Henry IV, Part 1* act 1, sc. 3, l. 201

28 It would be argument for a week, laughter
for a month, and a good jest for ever.
  *Henry IV, Part 1* act 2, sc. 2, l. [104]

29          Falstaff sweats to death
And lards the lean earth as he walks along.
  *Henry IV, Part 1* act 2, sc. 2, l. [119]

30 Out of this nettle, danger, we pluck this
flower, safety.
  *Henry IV, Part 1* act 2, sc. 3, l. [11]

31 We must have bloody noses and cracked
crowns.
  *Henry IV, Part 1* act 2, sc. 3, l. [98]

32 Fie upon this quiet life! I want work.
  *Henry IV, Part 1* act 2, sc. 4, l. [119]

33 Nay that's past praying for.
  *Henry IV, Part 1* act 2, sc. 4, l. [214]

1 Banish not him thy Harry's company:
banish plump Jack and banish all the
world.
*Henry IV, Part 1 act 2, sc. 4, l. [533]*

2 O monstrous! but one half-pennyworth of
bread to this intolerable deal of sack!
*Henry IV, Part 1 act 2, sc. 4, l. [598]*

3 GLENDOWER: I can call spirits from the
vasty deep.
HOTSPUR: Why, so can I, or so can any man;
But will they come when you do call for
them?
*Henry IV, Part 1 act 3, sc. 1, l. [53]*

4 That would set my teeth nothing on edge,
Nothing so much as mincing poetry:
'Tis like the forced gait of a shuffling nag.
*Henry IV, Part 1 act 3, sc. 1, l. [132]*

5 Now I perceive the devil understands
Welsh.
*Henry IV, Part 1 act 3, sc. 1, l. [233]*

6 He was but as the cuckoo is in June,
Heard, not regarded.
*Henry IV, Part 1 act 3, sc. 2, l. 75*

7 My near'st and dearest enemy.
*Henry IV, Part 1 act 3, sc. 2, l. 123*

8 Company, villainous company, hath
been the spoil of me.
*Henry IV, Part 1 act 3, sc. 3, l. [10]*

9 Thou seest I have more flesh than another
man, and therefore more frailty.
*Henry IV, Part 1 act 3, sc. 3, l. [187]*

10 Greatness knows itself.
*Henry IV, Part 1 act 4, sc. 3, l. 74*

11 Rebellion lay in his way, and he found it.
*Henry IV, Part 1 act 5, sc. 1, l. 28*

12 What is honour? A word. What is that
word, honour? Air. A trim reckoning! Who
hath it? He that died o' Wednesday.
*Henry IV, Part 1 act 5, sc. 1, l. [136]*

13 Two stars keep not their motion in one
sphere.
*Henry IV, Part 1 act 5, sc. 4, l. 65*

14 But thought's the slave of life, and life
time's fool;
And time, that takes survey of all the
world,
Must have a stop.
*Henry IV, Part 1 act 5, sc. 4, l. [81]*

15 Poor Jack, farewell!
I could have better spared a better man.
*Henry IV, Part 1 act 5, sc. 4, l. [103]*

**Henry IV, Part 2 (1597)**

16 I am not only witty in myself, but the
cause that wit is in other men.
*Henry IV, Part 2 act 1, sc. 2, l. [10]*

17 It is the disease of not listening, the
malady of not marking, that I am troubled
withal.
*Henry IV, Part 2 act 1, sc. 2, l. [139]*

18 I am as poor as Job, my lord, but not so
patient.
*Henry IV, Part 2 act 1, sc. 2, l. [145]*

19 I can get no remedy against this
consumption of the purse: borrowing only
lingers and lingers it out, but the disease is
incurable.
*Henry IV, Part 2 act 1, sc. 2, l. [268]*

20 Away, you scullion! you rampallion! you
fustilarian! I'll tickle your catastrophe.
*Henry IV, Part 2 act 2, sc. 1, l. [67]*

21 Pack-horses,
And hollow pampered jades of Asia,
Which cannot go but thirty miles a day.
*Henry IV, Part 2 act 2, sc. 4, l. [176]. Cf. 219:14*

22 Is it not strange that desire should so
many years outlive performance?
*Henry IV, Part 2 act 2, sc. 4, l. [283]*

23 Uneasy lies the head that wears a crown.
*Henry IV, Part 2 act 3, sc. 1, l. 31*

24 We have heard the chimes at midnight.
*Henry IV, Part 2 act 3, sc. 2, l. [231]*

25 I care not; a man can die but once; we owe
God a death.
*Henry IV, Part 2 act 3, sc. 2, l. [253]*

26 O polished perturbation! golden care!
*Henry IV, Part 2 act 4, sc. 5, l. 22*

27 Thy wish was father, Harry, to that
thought.
*Henry IV, Part 2 act 4, sc. 5, l. 91*

28 Commit
The oldest sins the newest kind of ways.
*Henry IV, Part 2 act 4, sc. 5, l. 124*

29 This is the English, not the Turkish court;
Not Amurath an Amurath succeeds,
But Harry, Harry.
*Henry IV, Part 2 act 5, sc. 2, l. 47*

30 My father is gone wild into his grave.
*Henry IV, Part 2 act 5, sc. 2, l. 123*

31 'Tis merry in hall when beards wag all.
*Henry IV, Part 2 act 5, sc. 3, l. [35]*

32 How ill white hairs become a fool and
jester!
*Henry IV, Part 2 act 5, sc. 5, l. [53]*

**Henry V (1599)**

33 O! for a Muse of fire, that would ascend
The brightest heaven of invention.
*Henry V chorus, l. 1*

34 Can this cockpit hold
The vasty fields of France? or may we cram
Within this wooden O the very casques
That did affright the air at Agincourt?
*Henry V chorus, l. 11*

35 Consideration like an angel came,
And whipped the offending Adam out of
him.
*Henry V act 1, sc. 1, l. 28*

36 When he speaks,
The air, a chartered libertine, is still.
*Henry V act 1, sc. 1, l. 47*

1  When we have matched our rackets to
   these balls,
   We will in France, by God's grace, play a
   set
   Shall strike his father's crown into the
   hazard.
   *Henry V* act 1, sc. 2, l. 261

2  Now all the youth of England are on fire,
   And silken dalliance in the wardrobe lies.
   *Henry V* act 2, chorus, l. 1

3  He's in Arthur's bosom, if ever man went
   to Arthur's bosom.
   *Henry V* act 2, sc. 3, l. [9]

4  His nose was as sharp as a pen, and a'
   babbled of green fields.
   *Henry V* act 2, sc. 3, l. [17]

5  Once more unto the breach, dear friends,
   once more;
   Or close the wall up with our English dead!
   In peace there's nothing so becomes a man
   As modest stillness and humility:
   But when the blast of war blows in our
   ears,
   Then imitate the action of the tiger;
   Stiffen the sinews, summon up the blood,
   Disguise fair nature with hard-favoured
   rage;
   Then lend the eye a terrible aspect.
   *Henry V* act 3, sc. 1, l. 1

6  I see you stand like greyhounds in the
   slips,
   Straining upon the start. The game's afoot:
   Follow your spirit; and, upon this charge
   Cry 'God for Harry! England and Saint
   George!'
   *Henry V* act 3, sc. 1, l. 31

7  Now entertain conjecture of a time
   When creeping murmur and the poring
   dark
   Fills the wide vessel of the universe.
   *Henry V* act 4, chorus, l. 1

8  A little touch of Harry in the night.
   *Henry V* act 4, chorus, l. 47

9  Discuss unto me; art thou officer?
   Or art thou base, common and popular?
   *Henry V* act 4, sc. 1, l. 37

10 The king's a bawcock, and a heart of gold,
   A lad of life, an imp of fame,
   Of parents good, of fist most valiant:
   I kiss his dirty shoe, and from my heart-
   string
   I love the lovely bully.
   *Henry V* act 4, sc. 1, l. 44

11 Though it appear a little out of fashion,
   There is much care and valour in this
   Welshman.
   *Henry V* act 4, sc. 1, l. [86]

12 I think the king is but a man, as I am: the
   violet smells to him as it doth to me.
   *Henry V* act 4, sc. 1, l. [106]

13 I am afeard there are few die well that die
   in a battle; for how can they charitably
   dispose of any thing when blood is their
   argument?
   *Henry V* act 4, sc. 1, l. [149]

14 Every subject's duty is the king's; but every
   subject's soul is his own.
   *Henry V* act 4, sc. 1, l. [189]

15 And what have kings that privates have
   not too,
   Save ceremony, save general ceremony?
   *Henry V* act 4, sc. 1, l. [258]

16 'Tis not the balm, the sceptre and the ball,
   The sword, the mace, the crown imperial,
   The intertissued robe of gold and pearl,
   The farcèd title running 'fore the king,
   The throne he sits on, nor the tide of pomp
   That beats upon the high shore of this
   world,
   No, not all these, thrice-gorgeous
   ceremony,
   Not all these, laid in bed majestical,
   Can sleep so soundly as the wretched slave,
   Who with a body filled and vacant mind
   Gets him to rest, crammed with distressful
   bread.
   *Henry V* act 4, sc. 1, l. [280]

17 If we are marked to die, we are enow
   To do our country loss; and if to live,
   The fewer men, the greater share of
   honour.
   *Henry V* act 4, sc. 3, l. 20

18 He which hath no stomach to this fight,
   Let him depart; his passport shall be made,
   And crowns for convoy put into his purse:
   We would not die in that man's company
   That fears his fellowship to die with us.
   This day is called the feast of Crispian:
   He that outlives this day and comes safe
   home,
   Will stand a tip-toe when this day is
   named,
   And rouse him at the name of Crispian.
   *Henry V* act 4, sc. 3, l. 35

19 Old men forget: yet all shall be forgot,
   But he'll remember with advantages
   What feats he did that day.
   *Henry V* act 4, sc. 3, l. 49

20 And Crispin Crispian shall ne'er go by,
   From this day to the ending of the world,
   But we in it shall be rememberèd;
   We few, we happy few, we band of
   brothers;
   For he to-day that sheds his blood with me
   Shall be my brother; be he ne'er so vile
   This day shall gentle his condition:
   And gentlemen in England, now a-bed
   Shall think themselves accursed they were
   not here,
   And hold their manhoods cheap whiles any
   speaks
   That fought with us upon Saint Crispin's
   day.
   *Henry V* act 4, sc. 3, l. 57

**1**  But now behold,
In the quick forge and working-house of thought,
How London doth pour out her citizens.
*Henry V* act 5, chorus, l. 22

**2** ... The naked, poor, and manglèd Peace,
Dear nurse of arts, plenties, and joyful births.
*Henry V* act 5, sc. 2, l. 34

**Henry VI, Part 1 (1592)**

**3** Expect Saint Martin's summer, halcyon days.
*Henry VI, Part 1* act 1, sc. 2, l. 131

**4**  Unbidden guests
Are often welcomest when they are gone.
*Henry VI, Part 1* act 2, sc. 2, l. 55

**5** I owe him little duty and less love.
*Henry VI, Part 1* act 4, sc. 4, l. 34

**6** She's beautiful and therefore to be wooed;
She is a woman, therefore to be won.
*Henry VI, Part 1* act 5, sc. 3, l. 78. Cf. 296:25

**Henry VI, Part 2 (1592)**

**7** She bears a duke's revenues on her back,
And in her heart she scorns our poverty.
*Henry VI, Part 2* act 1, sc. 3, l. [83]

**8** Thrice is he armed that hath his quarrel just.
*Henry VI, Part 2* act 3, sc. 2, l. 233

**9** The gaudy, blabbing, and remorseful day
Is crept into the bosom of the sea.
*Henry VI, Part 2* act 4, sc. 1, l. 1

**10** The first thing we do, let's kill all the lawyers.
*Henry VI, Part 2* act 4, sc. 2, l. [86]

**11** And Adam was a gardener.
*Henry VI, Part 2* act 4, sc. 2, l. [146]

**12** Away with him! away with him! he speaks Latin.
*Henry VI, Part 2* act 4, sc. 7, l. [62]

**Henry VI, Part 3 (1592)**

**13** O tiger's heart wrapped in a woman's hide!
*Henry VI, Part 3* act 1, sc. 4, l. 137

**Henry VIII (with John Fletcher, 1613)**

**14** Go with me, like good angels, to my end;
And, as the long divorce of steel falls on me,
Make of your prayers one sweet sacrifice,
And lift my soul to heaven.
*Henry VIII* act 2, sc. 1, l. 75

**15**  Heaven will one day open
The king's eyes, that so long have slept upon
This bold bad man.
*Henry VIII* act 2, sc. 2, l. [42]. Cf. 313:8

**16** Orpheus with his lute made trees,
And the mountain-tops that freeze,
Bow themselves when he did sing.
*Henry VIII* act 3, sc. 1, l. 3

**17**  I shall fall
Like a bright exhalation in the evening,
And no man see me more.
*Henry VIII* act 3, sc. 2, l. 226

**18** Farewell! a long farewell, to all my greatness!
This is the state of man: to-day he puts forth
The tender leaves of hope; to-morrow blossoms,
And bears his blushing honours thick upon him;
The third day comes a frost, a killing frost;
And, when he thinks, good easy man, full surely
His greatness is a-ripening, nips his root,
And then he falls, as I do. I have ventured,
Like little wanton boys that swim on bladders,
This many summers in a sea of glory,
But far beyond my depth.
*Henry VIII* act 3, sc. 2, l. 352

**19** Cromwell, I charge thee, fling away ambition:
By that sin fell the angels.
*Henry VIII* act 3, sc. 2, l. 441

**20** Love thyself last: cherish those hearts that hate thee;
Corruption wins not more than honesty.
*Henry VIII* act 3, sc. 2, l. 444

**21** Had I but served my God with half the zeal
I served my king, he would not in mine age
Have left me naked to mine enemies.
*Henry VIII* act 3, sc. 2, l. 456

**22** Men's evil manners live in brass; their virtues
We write in water.
*Henry VIII* act 4, sc. 2, l. 45

**23** Some come to take their ease
And sleep an act or two.
*Henry VIII* act 5, epilogue, l. 2

**Julius Caesar (1599)**

**24** You blocks, you stones, you worse than senseless things!
O you hard hearts, you cruel men of Rome,
Knew you not Pompey?
*Julius Caesar* act 1, sc. 1, l. [39]

**25** Beware the ides of March.
*Julius Caesar* act 1, sc. 2, l. 18

**26** Well, honour is the subject of my story.
I cannot tell what you and other men
Think of this life: but, for my single self,
I had as lief not be as live to be
In awe of such a thing as I myself.
*Julius Caesar* act 1, sc. 2, l. 92

**27** Why, man, he doth bestride the narrow world
Like a Colossus; and we petty men
Walk under his huge legs, and peep about
To find ourselves dishonourable graves.
Men at some time are masters of their fates:
The fault, dear Brutus, is not in our stars,
**But in ourselves, that we are underlings.**
*Julius Caesar* act 1, sc. 2, l. 134

1 Let me have men about me that are fat;
  Sleek-headed men and such as sleep o'
    nights;
  Yond Cassius has a lean and hungry look;
  He thinks too much: such men are
    dangerous.
  *Julius Caesar* act 1, sc. 2, l. 191

2 It is the bright day that brings forth the
    adder.
  *Julius Caesar* act 2, sc. 1, l. 14

3 Between the acting of a dreadful thing
  And the first motion, all the interim is
  Like a phantasma, or a hideous dream.
  *Julius Caesar* act 2, sc. 1, l. 63

4 Let's carve him as a dish fit for the gods,
  Not hew him as a carcass fit for hounds.
  *Julius Caesar* act 2, sc. 1, l. 173

5 But when I tell him he hates flatterers,
  He says he does, being then most flattered.
  *Julius Caesar* act 2, sc. 1, l. 207

6                    What! is Brutus sick,
  And will he steal out of his wholesome bed
  To dare the vile contagion of the night?
  *Julius Caesar* act 2, sc. 1, l. 263

7 PORTIA: Dwell I but in the suburbs
  Of your good pleasure? If it be no more,
  Portia is Brutus' harlot, not his wife.
  BRUTUS: You are my true and honourable
    wife,
  As dear to me as are the ruddy drops
  That visit my sad heart.
  *Julius Caesar* act 2, sc. 1, l. 285

8 CALPHURNIA: When beggars die, there are
    no comets seen;
  The heavens themselves blaze forth the
    death of princes.
  CAESAR: Cowards die many times before
    their deaths;
  The valiant never taste of death but once.
  *Julius Caesar* act 2, sc. 2, l. 30

9 But I am constant as the northern star,
  Of whose true-fixed and resting quality
  There is no fellow in the firmament.
  *Julius Caesar* act 3, sc. 1, l. 60

10 *Et tu, Brute?*
  *Julius Caesar* act 3, sc. 1, l. 77. Cf. 88:3

11 Ambition's debt is paid.
  *Julius Caesar* act 3, sc. 1, l. 83

12                    Live a thousand years,
  I shall not find myself so apt to die:
  No place will please me so, no mean of
    death,
  As here by Caesar, and by you cut off,
  The choice and master spirits of this age.
  *Julius Caesar* act 3, sc. 1, l. 159

13 O! pardon me, thou bleeding piece of
    earth,
  That I am meek and gentle with these
    butchers.
  *Julius Caesar* act 3, sc. 1, l. 254

14 Cry, 'Havoc!' and let slip the dogs of war.
  *Julius Caesar* act 3, sc. 1, l. 273

15 Not that I loved Caesar less, but that I
    loved Rome more.
  *Julius Caesar* act 3, sc. 2, l. [22]

16 As he was valiant, I honour him: but, as he
    was ambitious, I slew him.
  *Julius Caesar* act 3, sc. 2, l. [27]

17 Who is here so base that would be a
    bondman? If any, speak; for him have I
    offended.
  *Julius Caesar* act 3, sc. 2, l. [31]

18 Friends, Romans, countrymen, lend me
    your ears;
  I come to bury Caesar, not to praise him.
  The evil that men do lives after them,
  The good is oft interrèd with their bones.
  *Julius Caesar* act 3, sc. 2, l. [79]

19 For Brutus is an honourable man.
  *Julius Caesar* act 3, sc. 2, l. [88]

20 When that the poor have cried, Caesar
    hath wept;
  Ambition should be made of sterner stuff.
  *Julius Caesar* act 3, sc. 2, l. [97]

21 But yesterday the word of Caesar might
  Have stood against the world; now lies he
    there,
  And none so poor to do him reverence.
  *Julius Caesar* act 3, sc. 2, l. [124]

22 If you have tears, prepare to shed them
    now.
  *Julius Caesar* act 3, sc. 2, l. [174]

23 This was the most unkindest cut of all.
  *Julius Caesar* act 3, sc. 2, l. [188]

24 O! what a fall was there, my countrymen;
  Then I, and you, and all of us fell down,
  Whilst bloody treason flourished over us.
  *Julius Caesar* act 3, sc. 2, l. [195]

25 I am no orator, as Brutus is;
  But, as you know me all, a plain, blunt
    man,
  That love my friend.
  *Julius Caesar* act 3, sc. 2, l. [221]

26                    But were I Brutus,
  And Brutus Antony, there were an Antony
  Would ruffle up your spirits, and put a
    tongue
  In every wound of Caesar, that should
    move
  The stones of Rome to rise and mutiny.
  *Julius Caesar* act 3, sc. 2, l. [230]

27 Tear him for his bad verses.
  *Julius Caesar* act 3, sc. 3, l. [34]

28 He shall not live; look, with a spot I damn
    him.
  *Julius Caesar* act 4, sc. 1, l. 6

29 Let me tell you, Cassius, you yourself
  Are much condemned to have an itching
    palm.
  *Julius Caesar* act 4, sc. 3, l. 7

30 Away, slight man!
  *Julius Caesar* act 4, sc. 3, l. 37

1 There is a tide in the affairs of men,
Which, taken at the flood, leads on to
fortune;
Omitted, all the voyage of their life
Is bound in shallows and in miseries.
*Julius Caesar* act 4, sc. 3, l. 217

2 This was the noblest Roman of them all;
All the conspirators save only he
Did that they did in envy of great Caesar;
He only in a general honest thought
And common good to all, made one of
them.
His life was gentle, and the elements
So mixed in him that Nature might stand
up
And say to all the world, 'This was a man!'
*Julius Caesar* act 5, sc. 5, l. 68

**King John** (1591–8)

3 And if his name be George, I'll call him
Peter;
For new-made honour doth forget men's
names.
*King John* act 1, sc. 1, l. 186

4 Mad world! mad kings! mad composition!
*King John* act 2, sc. 1, l. 561

5 Well, whiles I am a beggar, I will rail,
And say there is no sin, but to be rich;
And, being rich, my virtue then shall be,
To say there is no vice, but beggary.
*King John* act 2, sc. 1, l. 593

6 Old Time the clock-setter, that bald sexton,
Time.
*King John* act 3, sc. 1, l. 324

7 Bell, book, and candle shall not drive me
back,
When gold and silver becks me to come
on.
*King John* act 3, sc. 3, l. 12

8 Grief fills the room up of my absent child,
Lies in his bed, walks up and down with
me,
Puts on his pretty looks, repeats his words,
Remembers me of all his gracious parts,
Stuffs out his vacant garments with his
form:
Then have I reason to be fond of grief.
*King John* act 3, sc. 4, l. 93

9 Life is as tedious as a twice-told tale,
Vexing the dull ear of a drowsy man.
*King John* act 3, sc. 4, l. 108

10 To gild refinèd gold, to paint the lily,
To throw a perfume on the violet,
To smooth the ice, or add another hue
Unto the rainbow, or with taper light
To seek the beauteous eye of heaven to
garnish,
Is wasteful and ridiculous excess.
*King John* act 4, sc. 2, l. 11

11 Another lean unwashed artificer
Cuts off his tale and talks of Arthur's
death.
*King John* act 4, sc. 2, l. 201

12 How oft the sight of means to do ill deeds
Makes ill deeds done!
*King John* act 4, sc. 2, l. 219

13 Heaven take my soul, and England keep my
bones!
*King John* act 4, sc. 3, l. 10

14        I do not ask you much:
I beg cold comfort.
*King John* act 5, sc. 7, l. 41

15 This England never did, nor never shall,
Lie at the proud foot of a conqueror,
But when it first did help to wound itself.
Now these her princes are come home
again,
Come the three corners of the world in
arms,
And we shall shock them: nought shall
make us rue,
If England to itself do rest but true.
*King John* act 5, sc. 7, l. 112

**King Lear** (1605–6)

16 Nothing will come of nothing: speak again.
*King Lear* act 1, sc. 1, l. [92]

17 LEAR: So young, and so untender?
CORDELIA: So young, my lord, and true.
*King Lear* act 1, sc. 1, l. [108]

18        I want that glib and oily art
To speak and purpose not.
*King Lear* act 1, sc. 1, l. [227]

19 Fairest Cordelia, that art most rich, being
poor;
Most choice, forsaken; and most loved,
despised!
*King Lear* act 1, sc. 1, l. [253]

20        Why bastard? wherefore base?
When my dimensions are as well compact,
My mind as generous, and my shape as
true,
As honest madam's issue?
*King Lear* act 1, sc. 2, l. 6

21 I grow, I prosper;
Now, gods, stand up for bastards!
*King Lear* act 1, sc. 2, l. 21

22 This is the excellent foppery of the world,
that, when we are sick in fortune,—often
the surfeit of our own behaviour,— we
make guilty of our own disasters the sun,
the moon, and the stars; as if we were
villains by necessity, fools by heavenly
compulsion, knaves, thieves, and treachers
by spherical predominance, drunkards,
liars, and adulterers by an enforced
obedience of planetary influence.
*King Lear* act 1, sc. 2, l. [132]

23 Who is it that can tell me who I am?
*King Lear* act 1, sc. 4, l. 230

24 Ingratitude, thou marble-hearted fiend,
More hideous, when thou show'st thee in a
child,
Than the sea-monster.
*King Lear* act 1, sc. 4, l. [283]

25 How sharper than a serpent's tooth it is
To have a thankless child!
*King Lear* act 1, sc. 4, l. [312]

1 O! let me not be mad, not mad, sweet
heaven;
Keep me in temper; I would not be mad!
  *King Lear* act 1, sc. 5, l. [51]

2 Thou whoreson zed! thou unnecessary
letter!
  *King Lear* act 2, sc. 2, l. [68]

3              O, sir! you are old;
Nature in you stands on the very verge
Of her confine.
  *King Lear* act 2, sc. 4, l. [148]

4 O reason not the need! Our basest beggars
Are in the poorest thing superfluous.
  *King Lear* act 2, sc. 4, l. 264

5 I will do such things,—
What they are yet I know not,—but they
shall be
The terrors of the earth.
  *King Lear* act 2, sc. 4, l. [283]

6 Blow, winds, and crack your cheeks! rage!
blow!
You cataracts and hurricanoes, spout
Till you have drenched our steeples,
drowned the cocks!
You sulphurous and thought-executing
fires,
Vaunt-couriers to oak-cleaving
thunderbolts,
Singe my white head! And thou, all-shaking
thunder,
Strike flat the thick rotundity o' the world!
  *King Lear* act 3, sc. 2, l. 1

7 Rumble thy bellyful! Spit, fire! Spout, rain!
Nor rain, wind, thunder, fire, are my
daughters:
I tax not you, you elements, with
unkindness.
  *King Lear* act 3, sc. 2, l. 14

8 There was never yet fair woman but she
made mouths in a glass.
  *King Lear* act 3, sc. 2, l. [35]

9 No, I will be the pattern of all patience; I
will say nothing.
  *King Lear* act 3, sc. 2, l. [37]

10            I am a man
More sinned against than sinning.
  *King Lear* act 3, sc. 2, l. [57]

11 O! that way madness lies; let me shun that.
  *King Lear* act 3, sc. 4, l. 21

12            Take physic, pomp;
Expose thyself to feel what wretches feel.
  *King Lear* act 3, sc. 4, l. 33

13 Keep thy foot out of brothels, thy hand out
of plackets, thy pen from lenders' books,
and defy the foul fiend.
  *King Lear* act 3, sc. 4, l. [96]

14 Thou art the thing itself; unaccommodated
man is no more but such a poor, bare,
forked animal as thou art.
  *King Lear* act 3, sc. 4, l. [109]

15 The green mantle of the standing pool.
  *King Lear* act 3, sc. 4, l. [136]

16 The prince of darkness is a gentleman.
  *King Lear* act 3, sc. 4, l. [148]

17 Poor Tom's a-cold.
  *King Lear* act 3, sc. 4, l. [151]

18 Child Roland to the dark tower came,
His word was still, Fie, foh, and fum,
I smell the blood of a British man.
  *King Lear* act 3, sc. 4, l. [185]

19            Out, vile jelly!
Where is thy lustre now?
  *King Lear* act 3, sc. 7, l. [83]

20            The worst is not,
So long as we can say, 'This is the worst.'
  *King Lear* act 4, sc. 1, l. 27

21 As flies to wanton boys, are we to the gods;
They kill us for their sport.
  *King Lear* act 4, sc. 1, l. 36

22 GLOUCESTER: Is't not the king?
LEAR: Ay, every inch a king.
  *King Lear* act 4, sc. 6, l. [110]

23            Die; die for adultery! No:
The wren goes to't, and the small gilded fly
Does lecher in my sight.
Let copulation thrive.
  *King Lear* act 4, sc. 6, l. [114]

24 GLOUCESTER: O! let me kiss that hand!
LEAR: Let me wipe it first; it smells of
mortality.
GLOUCESTER: O ruined piece of nature! This
great world
Should so wear out to nought.
  *King Lear* act 4, sc. 6, l. [136]

25 Why dost thou lash that whore? Strip
thine own back;
Thou hotly lust'st to use her in that kind
For which thou whipp'st her.
  *King Lear* act 4, sc. 6, l. [166]

26            Get thee glass eyes;
And, like a scurvy politician, seem
To see the things thou dost not.
  *King Lear* act 4, sc. 6, l. [175]

27 When we are born we cry that we are
come
To this great stage of fools.
  *King Lear* act 4, sc. 6, l. [187]

28            Mine enemy's dog,
Though he had bit me, should have stood
that night
Against my fire.
  *King Lear* act 4, sc. 7, l. 36

29 I am a very foolish, fond old man,
Fourscore and upward, not an hour more
or less;
And, to deal plainly,
I fear I am not in my perfect mind.
  *King Lear* act 4, sc. 7, l. 60

30            Men must endure
Their going hence, even as their coming
hither:
Ripeness is all.
  *King Lear* act 5, sc. 2, l. 9

**1**          Come, let's away to prison;
We two alone will sing like birds i' the cage:
When thou dost ask me blessing, I'll kneel down,
And ask of thee forgiveness.
*King Lear* act 5, sc. 3, l. 8. Cf. 344:27

**2** The gods are just, and of our pleasant vices
Make instruments to plague us.
*King Lear* act 5, sc. 3, l. [172]

**3** The wheel is come full circle.
*King Lear* act 5, sc. 3, l. [176]

**4** Howl, howl, howl, howl! O! you are men of stones:
Had I your tongue and eyes, I'd use them so
That heaven's vaults should crack. She's gone for ever!
*King Lear* act 5, sc. 3, l. [259]

**5**          Her voice was ever soft,
Gentle and low, an excellent thing in woman.
*King Lear* act 5, sc. 3, l. [274]

**6** And my poor fool is hanged! No, no, no life!
Why should a dog, a horse, a rat, have life,
And thou no breath at all? Thou'lt come no more,
Never, never, never, never, never!
Pray you, undo this button.
*King Lear* act 5, sc. 3, l. [307]

**7** Vex not his ghost: O! let him pass; he hates him
That would upon the rack of this tough world
Stretch him out longer.
*King Lear* act 5, sc. 3, l. [314]

**8** The oldest hath borne most: we that are young,
Shall never see so much, nor live so long.
*King Lear* act 5, sc. 3, l. [327]

### Love's Labour's Lost (1595)

**9** Cormorant devouring Time.
*Love's Labour's Lost* act 1, sc. 1, l. 4

**10** Study is like the heaven's glorious sun,
That will not be deep-searched with saucy looks;
*Love's Labour's Lost* act 1, sc. 1, l. 84

**11** At Christmas I no more desire a rose
Than wish a snow in May's new-fangled mirth;
But like of each thing that in season grows.
*Love's Labour's Lost* act 1, sc. 1, l. 105

**12** Warble, child; make passionate my sense of hearing.
*Love's Labour's Lost* act 3, sc. 1, l. 1

**13** This wimpled, whining, purblind, wayward boy,
This senior-junior, giant-dwarf, Dan Cupid.
*Love's Labour's Lost* act 3, sc. 1, l. [189]

**14** A wightly wanton with a velvet brow,
With two pitch balls stuck in her face for eyes;
Ay, and, by heaven, one that will do the deed
Though Argus were her eunuch and her guard.
*Love's Labour's Lost* act 3, sc. 1, l. [206]

**15** He hath not fed of the dainties that are bred in a book; he hath not eat paper, as it were; he hath not drunk ink.
*Love's Labour's Lost* act 4, sc. 2, l. [25]

**16** From women's eyes this doctrine I derive:
They are the ground, the books, the academes,
From whence doth spring the true Promethean fire.
*Love's Labour's Lost* act 4, sc. 3, l. [302]. See also act 4, sc. 3, l. [350]

**17** They have been at a great feast of languages, and stolen the scraps.
*Love's Labour's Lost* act 5, sc. 1, l. [39]

**18** Taffeta phrases, silken terms precise.
*Love's Labour's Lost* act 5, sc. 2, l. 407

**19** Henceforth my wooing mind shall be expressed
In russet yeas and honest kersey noes.
*Love's Labour's Lost* act 5, sc. 2, l. 413

**20** A jest's prosperity lies in the ear
Of him that hears it, never in the tongue
Of him that makes it.
*Love's Labour's Lost* act 5, sc. 2, l. [869]

**21** When daisies pied and violets blue
And lady-smocks all silver-white
And cuckoo-buds of yellow hue
Do paint the meadows with delight,
The cuckoo then, on every tree,
Mocks married men.
*Love's Labour's Lost* act 5, sc. 2, l. [902]

**22** Cuckoo, cuckoo; O, word of fear,
Unpleasing to a married ear!
*Love's Labour's Lost* act 5, sc. 2, l. [909]

**23** When icicles hang by the wall,
And Dick the shepherd blows his nail,
And Tom bears logs into the hall,
And milk comes frozen home in pail,
When blood is nipped and ways be foul,
Then nightly sings the staring owl,
Tu-who;
Tu-whit, tu-who—a merry note,
While greasy Joan doth keel the pot.
*Love's Labour's Lost* act 5, sc. 2, l. [920]

**24** The words of Mercury are harsh after the songs of Apollo.
*Love's Labour's Lost* act 5, sc. 2, l. [938]

### Macbeth (1606)

**25** FIRST WITCH: When shall we three meet again
In thunder, lightning, or in rain?
SECOND WITCH: When the hurly-burly's done,
When the battle's lost and won.
*Macbeth* act 1, sc. 1, l. 1

1 Fair is foul, and foul is fair:
Hover through the fog and filthy air.
*Macbeth* act 1, sc. 1, l. 11

2 What bloody man is that?
*Macbeth* act 1, sc. 2, l. 1

3 'Aroint thee, witch!' the rump-fed ronyon
cries.
Her husband's to Aleppo gone, master o'
the Tiger:
But in a sieve I'll thither sail,
And, like a rat without a tail,
I'll do, I'll do, and I'll do.
*Macbeth* act 1, sc. 3, l. 6

4 Sleep shall neither night nor day
Hang upon his pent-house lid.
He shall live a man forbid.
Weary se'nnights nine times nine
Shall he dwindle, peak, and pine:
Though his bark cannot be lost,
Yet it shall be tempest-tost.
*Macbeth* act 1, sc. 3, l. 19

5 The weird sisters, hand in hand,
Posters of the sea and land,
Thus do go about, about.
*Macbeth* act 1, sc. 3, l. 32

6 So foul and fair a day I have not seen.
*Macbeth* act 1, sc. 3, l. 38

7 If you can look into the seeds of time,
And say which grain will grow and which
will not.
*Macbeth* act 1, sc. 3, l. 58

8 Say, from whence
You owe this strange intelligence? or why
Upon this blasted heath you stop our way
With such prophetic greeting?
*Macbeth* act 1, sc. 3, l. 72

9 What! can the devil speak true?
*Macbeth* act 1, sc. 3, l. 107

10 Two truths are told,
As happy prologues to the swelling act
Of the imperial theme.
*Macbeth* act 1, sc. 3, l. 127

11 Present fears
Are less than horrible imaginings.
*Macbeth* act 1, sc. 3, l. 137

12 Come what come may,
Time and the hour runs through the
roughest day.
*Macbeth* act 1, sc. 3, l. 146

13 Nothing in his life
Became him like the leaving it.
*Macbeth* act 1, sc. 4, l. 7

14 There's no art
To find the mind's construction in the face.
*Macbeth* act 1, sc. 4, l. 11

15 Glamis thou art, and Cawdor; and shalt be
What thou art promised. Yet I do fear thy
nature;

It is too full o' the milk of human kindness
To catch the nearest way; thou wouldst be
great,
Art not without ambition; but without
The illness should attend it; what thou
wouldst highly,
That thou wouldst holily; wouldst not play
false,
And yet wouldst wrongly win.
*Macbeth* act 1, sc. 5, l. [16]

16 The raven himself is hoarse
That croaks the fatal entrance of Duncan
Under my battlements.
*Macbeth* act 1, sc. 5, l. [39]

17 Unsex me here,
And fill me from the crown to the toe top
full
Of direst cruelty; make thick my blood,
Stop up the access and passage to remorse,
That no compunctious visitings of nature
Shake my fell purpose.
*Macbeth* act 1, sc. 5, l. [42]

18 Come to my woman's breasts,
And take my milk for gall, you murdering
ministers.
*Macbeth* act 1, sc. 5, l. [48]

19 Come, thick night,
And pall thee in the dunnest smoke of hell,
That my keen knife see not the wound it
makes.
*Macbeth* act 1, sc. 5, l. [51]

20 Your face, my thane, is as a book where
men
May read strange matters.
*Macbeth* act 1, sc. 5, l. [63]

21 This guest of summer,
The temple-haunting martlet.
*Macbeth* act 1, sc. 6, l. 3

22 If it were done when 'tis done, then 'twere
well
It were done quickly: if the assassination
Could trammel up the consequence, and
catch
With his surcease success; that but this
blow
Might be the be-all and the end-all here,
But here, upon this bank and shoal of
time,
We'd jump the life to come.
*Macbeth* act 1, sc. 7, l. 1

23 We but teach
Bloody instructions, which, being taught,
return,
To plague the inventor.
*Macbeth* act 1, sc. 7, l. 8

24 Besides, this Duncan
Hath borne his faculties so meek, hath
been
So clear in his great office, that his virtues
Will plead like angels trumpet-tongued,
against
The deep damnation of his taking-off.
*Macbeth* act 1, sc. 7, l. 16

1           I have no spur
To prick the sides of my intent, but only
Vaulting ambition, which o'erleaps itself,
And falls on the other.
   *Macbeth* act 1, sc. 7, l. 25

2 He hath honoured me of late; and I have
bought
Golden opinions from all sorts of people.
   *Macbeth* act 1, sc. 7, l. 32

3           Was the hope drunk,
Wherein you dressed yourself?
   *Macbeth* act 1, sc. 7, l. 35

4 Letting 'I dare not' wait upon 'I would',
Like the poor cat i' the adage.
   *Macbeth* act 1, sc. 7, l. 44

5 I dare do all that may become a man;
Who dares do more is none.
   *Macbeth* act 1, sc. 7, l. 46

6 LADY MACBETH: I have given suck, and know
How tender 'tis to love the babe that
milks me:
I would, while it was smiling in my face,
Have plucked my nipple from his
boneless gums,
And dash'd the brains out, had I so sworn
as you
Have done to this.
MACBETH: If we should fail,—
LADY MACBETH: We fail!
But screw your courage to the sticking-
place,
And we'll not fail.
   *Macbeth* act 1, sc. 7, l. 54

7 Bring forth men-children only.
   *Macbeth* act 1, sc. 7, l. 72

8 False face must hide what the false heart
doth know.
   *Macbeth* act 1, sc. 7, l. 82

9           There's husbandry in heaven;
Their candles are all out.
   *Macbeth* act 2, sc. 1, l. 4

10 Is this a dagger which I see before me,
The handle toward my hand? Come, let me
clutch thee:
I have thee not, and yet I see thee still.
Art thou not, fatal vision, sensible
To feeling as to sight? or art thou but
A dagger of the mind, a false creation,
Proceeding from the heat-oppressèd brain?
   *Macbeth* act 2, sc. 1, l. 33

11           The bell invites me.
Hear it not, Duncan; for it is a knell
That summons thee to heaven or to hell.
   *Macbeth* act 2, sc. 1, l. 62

12 That which hath made them drunk hath
made me bold.
   *Macbeth* act 2, sc. 2, l. 1

13           The attempt and not the deed,
Confounds us.
   *Macbeth* act 2, sc. 2, l. 12

14           Had he not resembled
My father as he slept I had done't.
   *Macbeth* act 2, sc. 2, l. 14

15 Methought I heard a voice cry, 'Sleep no
more!
Macbeth does murder sleep,' the innocent
sleep,
Sleep that knits up the ravelled sleave of
care.
   *Macbeth* act 2, sc. 2, l. 36

16 Glamis hath murdered sleep, and therefore
Cawdor
Shall sleep no more, Macbeth shall sleep
no more!
   *Macbeth* act 2, sc. 2, l. 43

17           Infirm of purpose!
Give me the daggers. The sleeping and the
dead
Are but as pictures; 'tis the eye of
childhood
That fears a painted devil.
   *Macbeth* act 2, sc. 2, l. 53

18 Will all great Neptune's ocean wash this
blood
Clean from my hand? No, this my hand
will rather
The multitudinous seas incarnadine,
Making the green one red.
   *Macbeth* act 2, sc. 2, l. 61

19 A little water clears us of this deed.
   *Macbeth* act 2, sc. 2, l. 68

20 Here's a farmer that hanged himself on the
expectation of plenty.
   *Macbeth* act 2, sc. 3, l. 5

21 Drink, sir, is a great provoker ...
Lechery, sir, it provokes, and unprovokes; it
provokes the desire, but it takes away the
performance.
   *Macbeth* act 2, sc. 3, l. [28]

22 The labour we delight in physics pain.
   *Macbeth* act 2, sc. 3, l. [56]

23 Confusion now hath made his masterpiece!
   *Macbeth* act 2, sc. 3, l. [72]

24 Shake off this downy sleep, death's
counterfeit,
And look on death itself!
   *Macbeth* act 2, sc. 3, l. [83]

25 MACDUFF: Our royal master's murdered!
LADY MACBETH: Woe, alas!
What! in our house?
   *Macbeth* act 2, sc. 3, l. [95]

26 There's nothing serious in mortality:
All is but toys; renown and grace is dead,
The wine of life is drawn, and the mere
lees
Is left this vault to brag of.
   *Macbeth* act 2, sc. 3, l. [100]

27 There's daggers in men's smiles: the near
in blood,
The nearer bloody.
   *Macbeth* act 2, sc. 3, l. [147]

28 A falcon, towering in her pride of place,
Was by a mousing owl hawked at and
killed.
   *Macbeth* act 2, sc. 4, l. 12

1 BANQUO: Go not my horse the better,
I must become a borrower of the night
For a dark hour or twain.
MACBETH: Fail not our feast.
*Macbeth* act 3, sc. 1, l. 26

2 Leave no rubs nor botches in the work.
*Macbeth* act 3, sc. 1, l. 134

3 LADY MACBETH: Things without all remedy
Should be without regard: what's done is
done.
MACBETH: We have scotched the snake, not
killed it:
She'll close and be herself, whilst our
poor malice
Remains in danger of her former tooth.
*Macbeth* act 3, sc. 2, l. 11

4                   Duncan is in his grave;
After life's fitful fever he sleeps well;
Treason has done his worst: nor steel, nor
poison,
Malice domestic, foreign levy, nothing,
Can touch him further.
*Macbeth* act 3, sc. 2, l. 22

5                   Ere the bat hath flown
His cloistered flight, ere, to black Hecate's
summons
The shard-borne beetle with his drowsy
hums
Hath rung night's yawning peal, there
shall be done
A deed of dreadful note.
*Macbeth* act 3, sc. 2, l. 40

6                   Come, seeling night,
Scarf up the tender eye of pitiful day,
And with thy bloody and invisible hand,
Cancel and tear to pieces that great bond
Which keeps me pale!
*Macbeth* act 3, sc. 2, l. 46

7 Now spurs the lated traveller apace
To gain the timely inn.
*Macbeth* act 3, sc. 3, l. 6

8 Ourself will mingle with society
And play the humble host.
*Macbeth* act 3, sc. 4, l. 3

9 ... Now I am cabined, cribbed, confined,
bound in
To saucy doubts and fears.
*Macbeth* act 3, sc. 4, l. 24

10 Now good digestion wait on appetite,
And health on both!
*Macbeth* act 3, sc. 4, l. 38

11 Thou canst not say I did it: never shake
Thy gory locks at me.
*Macbeth* act 3, sc. 4, l. 50

12 Stand not upon the order of your going.
*Macbeth* act 3, sc. 4, l. 119

13 It will have blood, they say; blood will have
blood.
*Macbeth* act 3, sc. 4, l. 122

14                   I am in blood
Stepped in so far that, should I wade no
more,
Returning were as tedious as go o'er.
*Macbeth* act 3, sc. 4, l. 136

15 Double, double toil and trouble;
Fire burn and cauldron bubble.
*Macbeth* act 4, sc. 1, l. 10

16 Eye of newt, and toe of frog.
*Macbeth* act 4, sc. 1, l. 14

17 Liver of blaspheming Jew,
Gall of goat, and slips of yew.
*Macbeth* act 4, sc. 1, l. 26

18                   By the pricking of my thumbs,
Something wicked this way comes.
*Macbeth* act 4, sc. 1, l. 44

19 MACBETH: How now, you secret, black, and
midnight hags!
What is't you do?
WITCHES: A deed without a name.
*Macbeth* act 4, sc. 1, l. 48

20 Be bloody, bold, and resolute.
*Macbeth* act 4, sc. 1, l. 79

21 But yet, I'll make assurance double sure,
And take a bond of fate.
*Macbeth* act 4, sc. 1, l. 83

22 His flight was madness: when our actions
do not,
Our fears do make us traitors.
*Macbeth* act 4, sc. 2, l. 3

23                   He loves us not;
He wants the natural touch.
*Macbeth* act 4, sc. 2, l. 8

24 Stands Scotland where it did?
*Macbeth* act 4, sc. 3, l. 164

25 Give sorrow words: the grief that does not
speak
Whispers the o'er-fraught heart, and bids it
break.
*Macbeth* act 4, sc. 3, l. 209

26 What! all my pretty chickens and their
dam,
At one fell swoop?
*Macbeth* act 4, sc. 3, l. 218

27 Out, damned spot!
*Macbeth* act 5, sc. 1, l. [38]

28 Who would have thought the old man to
have had so much blood in him?
*Macbeth* act 5, sc. 1, l. [42]

29 The Thane of Fife had a wife: where is she
now? What! will these hands ne'er be
clean? No more o' that, my lord, no more
o' that: you mar all with this starting.
*Macbeth* act 5, sc. 1, l. [46]

30 Here's the smell of the blood still: all the
perfumes of Arabia will not sweeten this
little hand.
*Macbeth* act 5, sc. 1, l. [55]

31 What's done cannot be undone.
*Macbeth* act 5, sc. 1, l. [74]

32 Bring me no more reports; let them fly all:
Till Birnam wood remove to Dunsinane
I cannot taint with fear.
*Macbeth* act 5, sc. 3, l. 1

33 The devil damn thee black, thou cream-
faced loon!
Where gott'st thou that goose look?
*Macbeth* act 5, sc. 3, l. 11

1 I have lived long enough: my way of life
Is fall'n into the sear, the yellow leaf.
*Macbeth* act 5, sc. 3, l. 22

2 Canst thou not minister to a mind
diseased?
*Macbeth* act 5, sc. 3, l. 40

3 Throw physic to the dogs; I'll none of it.
*Macbeth* act 5, sc. 3, l. 47

4 I have supped full with horrors.
*Macbeth* act 5, sc. 5, l. 13

5 She should have died hereafter;
There would have been a time for such a
word,
To-morrow, and to-morrow, and to-
morrow,
Creeps in this petty pace from day to day,
To the last syllable of recorded time;
And all our yesterdays have lighted fools
The way to dusty death. Out, out, brief
candle!
Life's but a walking shadow, a poor player,
That struts and frets his hour upon the
stage,
And then is heard no more; it is a tale
Told by an idiot, full of sound and fury,
Signifying nothing.
*Macbeth* act 5, sc. 5, l. 16

6 I bear a charmèd life.
*Macbeth* act 5, sc. 7, l. 41

7 Macduff was from his mother's womb
Untimely ripped.
*Macbeth* act 5, sc. 7, l. 44

8 Lay on, Macduff;
And damned be him that first cries, 'Hold,
enough!'
*Macbeth* act 5, sc. 7, l. 62

**Measure for Measure** (1604)

9 And liberty plucks justice by the nose.
*Measure for Measure* act 1, sc. 3, l. 29

10 I hold you as a thing enskyed and sainted.
*Measure for Measure* act 1, sc. 4, l. 34

11 A man whose blood
Is very snow-broth; one who never feels
The wanton stings and motions of the
sense.
*Measure for Measure* act 1, sc. 4, l. 57

12 We must not make a scarecrow of the law.
*Measure for Measure* act 2, sc. 1, l. 1

13 O! it is excellent
To have a giant's strength, but it is
tyrannous
To use it like a giant.
*Measure for Measure* act 2, sc. 2, l. 107

14 Man, proud man,
Drest in a little brief authority.
*Measure for Measure* act 2, sc. 2, l. 117

15 That in the captain's but a choleric word,
Which in the soldier is flat blasphemy.
*Measure for Measure* act 2, sc. 2, l. 130

16 Ever till now
When men were fond, I smiled and
wondered how.
*Measure for Measure* act 2, sc. 2, l. 186

17 The miserable have no other medicine
But only hope.
*Measure for Measure* act 3, sc. 1, l. 2

18 Be absolute for death; either death or life
Shall thereby be the sweeter. Reason thus
with life:
If I do lose thee, I do lose a thing
That none but fools would keep.
*Measure for Measure* act 3, sc. 1, l. 5

19 A breath thou art
Servile to all the skyey influences.
*Measure for Measure* act 3, sc. 1, l. 8

20 If I must die,
I will encounter darkness as a bride,
And hug it in mine arms.
*Measure for Measure* act 3, sc. 1, l. 81

21 CLAUDIO: Death is a fearful thing.
ISABELLA: And shamed life a hateful.
CLAUDIO: Ay, but to die, and go we know
not where;
To lie in cold obstruction and to rot;
This sensible warm motion to become
A kneaded clod; and the delighted spirit
To bathe in fiery floods or to reside
In thrilling region of thick-ribbèd ice.
*Measure for Measure* act 3, sc. 1, l. 114

22 There, at the moated grange, resides this
dejected Mariana.
*Measure for Measure* act 3, sc. 1, l. [279]

23 When he makes water his urine is
congealed ice.
*Measure for Measure* act 3, sc. 2, l. [119]

24 Insensible of mortality, and desperately
mortal.
*Measure for Measure* act 4, sc. 2, l. [151]

25 I am a kind of burr; I shall stick.
*Measure for Measure* act 4, sc. 3, l. [193]

26 They say best men are moulded out of
faults,
And, for the most, become much more the
better
For being a little bad: so may my husband.
*Measure for Measure* act 5, sc. 1, l. [440]

**The Merchant of Venice** (1596–8)

27 I hold the world but as the world,
Gratiano;
A stage where every man must play a part,
And mine a sad one.
*The Merchant of Venice* act 1, sc. 1, l. 77

28 They are as sick that surfeit with too
much, as they that starve with nothing.
*The Merchant of Venice* act 1, sc. 2, l. [5]

29 If to do were as easy as to know what were
good to do, chapels had been churches, and
poor men's cottages princes' palaces.
*The Merchant of Venice* act 1, sc. 2, l. [13]

30 God made him, and therefore let him pass
for a man.
*The Merchant of Venice* act 1, sc. 2, l. [59]

31 I will buy with you, sell with you, talk with
you, walk with you, and so following; but I
will not eat with you, drink with you, nor
pray with you. What news on the Rialto?
*The Merchant of Venice* act 1, sc. 3, l. [36]

1 How like a fawning publican he looks!
*The Merchant of Venice* act 1, sc. 3, l. [42]

2 If I can catch him once upon the hip,
I will feed fat the ancient grudge I bear
him.
*The Merchant of Venice* act 1, sc. 3, l. [47]

3 The devil can cite Scripture for his
purpose.
*The Merchant of Venice* act 1, sc. 3, l. [99]

4 Still have I borne it with a patient shrug,
For sufferance is the badge of all our tribe.
*The Merchant of Venice* act 1, sc. 3, l. [110]

5 You call me misbeliever, cut-throat dog,
And spit upon my Jewish gabardine,
And all for use of that which is mine own.
*The Merchant of Venice* act 1, sc. 3, l. [112]

6 Mislike me not for my complexion,
The shadowed livery of the burnished sun,
To whom I am a neighbour and near bred.
*The Merchant of Venice* act 2, sc. 1, l. 1

7 It is a wise father that knows his own
child.
*The Merchant of Venice* act 2, sc. 2, l. [83]

8 Truth will come to light; murder cannot be
hid long.
*The Merchant of Venice* act 2, sc. 2, l. [86]

9 There is some ill a-brewing towards my
rest.
For I did dream of money-bags to-night.
*The Merchant of Venice* act 2, sc. 5, l. 17

10 Let not the sound of shallow foppery enter
My sober house.
*The Merchant of Venice* act 2, sc. 5, l. [35]

11 What! must I hold a candle to my shames?
*The Merchant of Venice* act 2, sc. 6, l. 41

12 My daughter! O my ducats! O my daughter!
*The Merchant of Venice* act 2, sc. 8, l. 15

13                    Like the martlet,
Builds in the weather on the outward wall,
Even in the force and road of casualty.
*The Merchant of Venice* act 2, sc. 9, l. 28

14 The portrait of a blinking idiot.
*The Merchant of Venice* act 2, sc. 9, l. 54

15 Let him look to his bond.
*The Merchant of Venice* act 3, sc. 1, l. [51]

16 Hath not a Jew eyes? hath not a Jew hands,
organs, dimensions, senses, affections,
passions?
*The Merchant of Venice* act 3, sc. 1, l. [63]

17 If you prick us, do we not bleed? if you
tickle us, do we not laugh? if you poison
us, do we not die? and if you wrong us,
shall we not revenge?
*The Merchant of Venice* act 3, sc. 1, l. [69]

18 The villainy you teach me I will execute,
and it shall go hard but I will better the
instruction.
*The Merchant of Venice* act 3, sc. 1, l. [76]

19                    He makes a swan-like end,
Fading in music.
*The Merchant of Venice* act 3, sc. 2, l. 44

20 Tell me where is fancy bred.
Or in the heart or in the head?
*The Merchant of Venice* act 3, sc. 2, l. 63

21 So may the outward shows be least
themselves:
The world is still deceived with ornament.
*The Merchant of Venice* act 3, sc. 2, l. 73

22                    An unlessoned girl, unschooled,
unpractised;
Happy in this, she is not yet so old
But she may learn; happier than this,
She is not bred so dull but she can learn.
*The Merchant of Venice* act 3, sc. 2, l. 160

23 I pray thee, understand a plain man in his
plain meaning.
*The Merchant of Venice* act 3, sc. 5, l. [63]

24 I am a tainted wether of the flock,
Meetest for death: the weakest kind of
fruit
Drops earliest to the ground.
*The Merchant of Venice* act 4, sc. 1, l. 114

25 I never knew so young a body with so old a
head.
*The Merchant of Venice* act 4, sc. 1, l. [163]

26 The quality of mercy is not strained,
It droppeth as the gentle rain from heaven
Upon the place beneath: it is twice blessed;
It blesseth him that gives and him that
takes:
'Tis mightiest in the mightiest: it becomes
The thronèd monarch better than his
crown.
*The Merchant of Venice* act 4, sc. 1, l. [182]

27 Though justice be thy plea, consider this,
That in the course of justice none of us
Should see salvation: we do pray for mercy,
And that same prayer doth teach us all to
render
The deeds of mercy.
*The Merchant of Venice* act 4, sc. 1, l. [197]

28 Wrest once the law to your authority:
To do a great right, do a little wrong.
*The Merchant of Venice* act 4, sc. 1, l. [215]

29 A Daniel come to judgement! yea, a Daniel!
*The Merchant of Venice* act 4, sc. 1, l. [223]

30 He is well paid that is well satisfied.
*The Merchant of Venice* act 4, sc. 1, l. [416]

31 The moon shines bright: in such a night as
this ...
Troilus methinks mounted the Troyan
walls,
And sighed his soul toward the Grecian
tents,
Where Cressid lay that night.
*The Merchant of Venice* act 5, sc. 1, l. 1

32                    In such a night
Stood Dido with a willow in her hand
Upon the wild sea-banks, and waft her love
To come again to Carthage.
*The Merchant of Venice* act 5, sc. 1, l. 9

1 How sweet the moonlight sleeps upon this
   bank.
   Here will we sit, and let the sounds of
   music
   Creep in our ears; soft stillness and the
   night
   Become the touches of sweet harmony.
   *The Merchant of Venice* act 5, sc. 1, l. 54

2                 Look, how the floor of heaven
   Is thick inlaid with patines of bright gold.
   *The Merchant of Venice* act 5, sc. 1, l. 58

3 The man that hath no music in himself,
   Nor is not moved with concord of sweet
   sounds,
   Is fit for treasons, stratagems, and spoils.
   *The Merchant of Venice* act 5, sc. 1, l. 79

4 How far that little candle throws his
   beams!
   So shines a good deed in a naughty world.
   *The Merchant of Venice* act 5, sc. 1, l. 90

5 How many things by season seasoned are
   To their right praise and true perfection!
   *The Merchant of Venice* act 5, sc. 1, l. 107

6 This night methinks is but the daylight
   sick.
   *The Merchant of Venice* act 5, sc. 1, l. 124

**The Merry Wives of Windsor** (1597)

7 I will make a Star-Chamber matter of it.
   *The Merry Wives of Windsor* act 1, sc. 1, l. 1

8 She has brown hair, and speaks small like
   a woman.
   *The Merry Wives of Windsor* act 1, sc. 1, l. [48]

9 Why, then the world's mine oyster,
   Which I with sword will open.
   *The Merry Wives of Windsor* act 2, sc. 2, l. 2

10 O, what a world of vile ill-favoured faults
   Looks handsome in three hundred pounds
   a year!
   *The Merry Wives of Windsor* act 3, sc. 4, l. [32]

11 There is divinity in odd numbers, either in
   nativity, chance or death.
   *The Merry Wives of Windsor* act 5, sc. 1, l. 3

**A Midsummer Night's Dream** (1595–6)

12 To live a barren sister all your life,
   Chanting faint hymns to the cold fruitless
   moon.
   *A Midsummer Night's Dream* act 1, sc. 1, l. 72

13 The course of true love never did run
   smooth.
   *A Midsummer Night's Dream* act 1, sc. 1, l. 134

14 Swift as a shadow, short as any dream,
   Brief as the lightning in the collied night.
   *A Midsummer Night's Dream* act 1, sc. 1, l. 144

15 So quick bright things come to confusion.
   *A Midsummer Night's Dream* act 1, sc. 1, l. 149

16 Things base and vile, holding no quantity,
   Love can transpose to form and dignity.
   Love looks not with the eyes, but with the
   mind,
   And therefore is winged Cupid painted
   blind.
   *A Midsummer Night's Dream* act 1, sc. 1, l. 232

17 Masters, spread yourselves.
   *A Midsummer Night's Dream* act 1, sc. 2, l. [16]

18 I could play Ercles rarely, or a part to tear
   a cat in, to make all split.
   *A Midsummer Night's Dream* act 1, sc. 2, l. [31]

19 Over hill, over dale,
   Thorough bush, thorough brier,
   Over park, over pale,
   Thorough flood, thorough fire,
   I do wander everywhere.
   *A Midsummer Night's Dream* act 2, sc. 1, l. 2

20 I must go seek some dew-drops here,
   And hang a pearl in every cowslip's ear.
   *A Midsummer Night's Dream* act 2, sc. 1, l. 14

21 The wisest aunt, telling the saddest tale.
   *A Midsummer Night's Dream* act 2, sc. 1, l. 51

22 Ill met by moonlight, proud Titania.
   *A Midsummer Night's Dream* act 2, sc. 1, l. 60

23 The seasons alter: hoary-headed frosts
   Fall in the fresh lap of the crimson rose.
   *A Midsummer Night's Dream* act 2, sc. 1, l. 107

24 And the imperial votaress passed on,
   In maiden meditation, fancy-free.
   *A Midsummer Night's Dream* act 2, sc. 1, l. 163

25 I'll put a girdle round about the earth
   In forty minutes.
   *A Midsummer Night's Dream* act 2, sc. 1, l. 175

26 I know a bank whereon the wild thyme
   blows,
   Where oxlips and the nodding violet grows
   Quite over-canopied with luscious
   woodbine,
   With sweet musk-roses, and with
   eglantine.
   *A Midsummer Night's Dream* act 2, sc. 1, l. 249

27 And there the snake throws her enamelled
   skin,
   Weed wide enough to wrap a fairy in.
   *A Midsummer Night's Dream* act 2, sc. 1, l. 255

28 You spotted snakes with double tongue,
   Thorny hedge-hogs, be not seen.
   *A Midsummer Night's Dream* act 2, sc. 2, l. 9

29 Weaving spiders come not here;
   Hence you long-legged spinners, hence!
   *A Midsummer Night's Dream* act 2, sc. 2, l. 20

30 Look in the almanack; find out moonshine.
   *A Midsummer Night's Dream* act 3, sc. 1, l. [55]

31 What hempen home-spuns have we
   swaggering here?
   *A Midsummer Night's Dream* act 3, sc. 1, l. [82]

32 Lord, what fools these mortals be!
   *A Midsummer Night's Dream* act 3, sc. 2, l. 115

33 She was a vixen when she went to school:
   And though she be but little, she is fierce.
   *A Midsummer Night's Dream* act 3, sc. 2, l. 323

34                 Ghosts, wandering here and
   there,
   Troop home to churchyards.
   *A Midsummer Night's Dream* act 3, sc. 2, l. 381

35 Let us have the tongs and the bones.
   *A Midsummer Night's Dream* act 4, sc. 1, l. [33]

1 I have an exposition of sleep come upon
me.
*A Midsummer Night's Dream* act 4, sc. 1, l. [43]

2 So musical a discord, such sweet thunder.
*A Midsummer Night's Dream* act 4, sc. 1, l. [121]

3 The lunatic, the lover, and the poet,
Are of imagination all compact.
*A Midsummer Night's Dream* act 5, sc. 1, l. 7

4 The poet's eye, in a fine frenzy rolling,
Doth glance from heaven to earth, from
earth to heaven;
And, as imagination bodies forth
The forms of things unknown, the poet's
pen
Turns them to shapes, and gives to airy
nothing
A local habitation and a name.
*A Midsummer Night's Dream* act 5, sc. 1, l. 12

5 Merry and tragical! tedious and brief!
That is, hot ice and wondrous strange
snow.
*A Midsummer Night's Dream* act 5, sc. 1, l. 58

6                    To show our simple skill,
That is the true beginning of our end.
*A Midsummer Night's Dream* act 5, sc. 1, l. [110]

7 Whereat, with blade, with bloody blameful
blade,
He bravely broached his boiling bloody
breast.
*A Midsummer Night's Dream* act 5, sc. 1, l. [148]

8 The best in this kind are but shadows, and
the worst are no worse, if imagination
amend them.
*A Midsummer Night's Dream* act 5, sc. 1, l. [215]

9 The iron tongue of midnight hath told
twelve.
*A Midsummer Night's Dream* act 5, sc. 1, l. [372]

10                    Not a mouse
Shall disturb this hallowed house:
I am sent with broom before,
To sweep the dust behind the door.
*A Midsummer Night's Dream* act 5, sc. 2, l. 17

### Much Ado About Nothing (1598–9)

11 He hath indeed better bettered expectation
than you must expect of me to tell you
how.
*Much Ado About Nothing* act 1, sc. 1, l. [15]

12 He is a very valiant trencher-man.
*Much Ado About Nothing* act 1, sc. 1, l. [52]

13 I see, lady, the gentleman is not in your
books.
*Much Ado About Nothing* act 1, sc. 1, l. [79]

14 In time the savage bull doth bear the yoke.
*Much Ado About Nothing* act 1, sc. 1, l. [271]

15 Lord! I could not endure a husband with a
beard on his face: I had rather lie in the
woollen.
*Much Ado About Nothing* act 2, sc. 1, l. [31]

16 Speak low, if you speak love.
*Much Ado About Nothing* act 2, sc. 1, l. [104]

17 Friendship is constant in all other things
Save in the office and affairs of love.
*Much Ado About Nothing* act 2, sc. 1, l. [184]

18 There was a star danced, and under that
was I born.
*Much Ado About Nothing* act 2, sc. 1, l. [348]

19 Sigh no more, ladies, sigh no more,
Men were deceivers ever.
*Much Ado About Nothing* act 2, sc. 3, l. [65]

20 Sits the wind in that corner?
*Much Ado About Nothing* act 2, sc. 3, l. [108]

21 He hath a heart as sound as a bell, and his
tongue is the clapper; for what his heart
thinks his tongue speaks.
*Much Ado About Nothing* act 3, sc. 2, l. [12]

22 Every one can master a grief but he that
has it.
*Much Ado About Nothing* act 3, sc. 2, l. [28]

23 Comparisons are odorous.
*Much Ado About Nothing* act 3, sc. 5, l. [18]

24 You have stayed me in a happy hour.
*Much Ado About Nothing* act 4, sc. 1, l. [283]

25 Patch grief with proverbs.
*Much Ado About Nothing* act 5, sc. 1, l. 17

26 No, I was not born under a rhyming
planet.
*Much Ado About Nothing* act 5, sc. 2, l. [40]

27                    The gentle day,
Before the wheels of Phoebus, round about
Dapples the drowsy east with spots of grey.
*Much Ado About Nothing* act 5, sc. 3, l. 25

### Othello (1602–4)

28 But I will wear my heart upon my sleeve
For daws to peck at: I am not what I am.
*Othello* act 1, sc. 1, l. 64

29 Even now, now, very now, an old black ram
Is tupping your white ewe.
*Othello* act 1, sc. 1, l. 88

30 Your daughter and the Moor are now
making the beast with two backs.
*Othello* act 1, sc. 1, l. [117]

31 Keep up your bright swords, for the dew
will rust them.
*Othello* act 1, sc. 2, l. 59

32 The wealthy curlèd darlings of our nation.
*Othello* act 1, sc. 2, l. 67

33                    Rude am I in my speech,
And little blessed with the soft phrase of
peace.
*Othello* act 1, sc. 3, l. 81

34 I will a round unvarnished tale deliver.
*Othello* act 1, sc. 3, l. 90

35 She loved me for the dangers I had passed,
And I loved her that she did pity them.
*Othello* act 1, sc. 3, l. 167

36 I do perceive here a divided duty.
*Othello* act 1, sc. 3, l. 181

37 The robbed that smiles steals something
from the thief.
*Othello* act 1, sc. 3, l. 208

38 But words are words; I never yet did hear
That the bruised heart was piercèd
through the ear.
*Othello* act 1, sc. 3, l. 218

1 The tyrant custom, most grave senators,
Hath made the flinty and steel couch of
war
My thrice-driven bed of down.
*Othello* act 1, sc. 3, l. [230]

2              If I be left behind,
A moth of peace, and he go to the war,
The rites for which I love him are bereft
me.
*Othello* act 1, sc. 3, l. [257]

3 Our great captain's captain.
*Othello* act 2, sc. 1, l. 74

4 To suckle fools and chronicle small beer.
*Othello* act 2, sc. 1, l. 163

5              If it were now to die,
'Twere now to be most happy.
*Othello* act 2, sc. 1, l. [192]

6 A slipper and subtle knave.
*Othello* act 2, sc. 1, l. [247]

7 Silence that dreadful bell! it frights the isle
From her propriety.
*Othello* act 2, sc. 3, l. [177]

8 O! I have lost my reputation. I have lost
the immortal part of myself, and what
remains is bestial.
*Othello* act 2, sc. 3, l. [264]

9 O! thereby hangs a tail.
*Othello* act 3, sc. 1, l. [8]

10 Excellent wretch! Perdition catch my soul
But I do love thee! and when I love thee
not,
Chaos is come again.
*Othello* act 3, sc. 3, l. 90

11 Good name in man and woman, dear my
lord,
Is the immediate jewel of their souls;
Who steals my purse steals trash; 'tis
something, nothing;
'Twas mine, 'tis his, and has been slave to
thousands;
But he that filches from me my good name
Robs me of that which not enriches him,
And makes me poor indeed.
*Othello* act 3, sc. 3, l. 155

12              O! beware, my lord, of jealousy;
It is the green-eyed monster which doth
mock
The meat it feeds on.
*Othello* act 3, sc. 3, l. 165

13 Foh! one may smell in such, a will most
rank,
Foul disposition, thoughts unnatural.
*Othello* act 3, sc. 3, l. 232

14              If I do prove her haggard,
Though that her jesses were my dear
heart-strings,
I'd whistle her off and let her down the
wind,
To prey at fortune.
*Othello* act 3, sc. 3, l. 260

15              I am black,
And have not those soft parts of
conversation
That chamberers have.
*Othello* act 3, sc. 3, l. 263

16              I am declined
Into the vale of years.
*Othello* act 3, sc. 3, l. 265

17              I had rather be a toad,
And live upon the vapour of a dungeon,
Than keep a corner in the thing I love
For others' uses.
*Othello* act 3, sc. 3, l. 270

18              Trifles light as air
Are to the jealous confirmations strong
As proofs of holy writ.
*Othello* act 3, sc. 3, l. 323

19 Farewell the tranquil mind; farewell
content!
Farewell the plumèd troop and the big
wars
That make ambition virtue!
*Othello* act 3, sc. 3, l. 349

20 Pride, pomp, and circumstance of glorious
war.
*Othello* act 3, sc. 3, l. 355

21 Othello's occupation's gone!
*Othello* act 3, sc. 3, l. 358

22 Jealous souls will not be answered so;
They are not ever jealous for the cause,
But jealous for they are jealous.
*Othello* act 3, sc. 4, l. 158

23 But yet the pity of it, Iago! O! Iago, the pity
of it, Iago!
*Othello* act 4, sc. 1, l. [205]

24              But, alas! to make me
The fixèd figure for the time of scorn
To point his slow and moving finger at.
*Othello* act 4, sc. 2, l. 46

25 Heaven stops the nose at it and the moon
winks.
*Othello* act 4, sc. 2, l. 76

26 The poor soul sat sighing by a sycamore
tree.
Sing all a green willow;
Her hand on her bosom, her head on her
knee,
Sing willow, willow, willow:
*Othello* act 4, sc. 3, l. [41]. Cf. 168:8

27              This is the night
That either makes me or fordoes me quite.
*Othello* act 5, sc. 1, l. 128

28 It is the cause, it is the cause, my soul;
Let me not name it to you, you chaste
stars!
It is the cause.
*Othello* act 5, sc. 2, l. 1

29 Put out the light, and then put out the
light.
*Othello* act 5, sc. 2, l. 7

**1**  One more, and this the last:
So sweet was ne'er so fatal.
*Othello* act 5, sc. 2, l. 19

**2**  Murder's out of tune,
And sweet revenge grows harsh.
*Othello* act 5, sc. 2, l. 113

**3**  May his pernicious soul
Rot half a grain a day!
*Othello* act 5, sc. 2, l. 153

**4**  Here is my journey's end, here is my butt,
And very sea-mark of my utmost sail.
*Othello* act 5, sc. 2, l. 266

**5**  I have done the state some service, and
they know 't;
No more of that. I pray you, in your letters,
When you shall these unlucky deeds relate,
Speak of me as I am; nothing extenuate,
Nor set down aught in malice: then, must
you speak
Of one that loved not wisely but too well;
Of one not easily jealous, but, being
wrought,
Perplexed in the extreme; of one whose
hand,
Like the base Indian, threw a pearl away
Richer than all his tribe.
*Othello* act 5, sc. 2, l. 338

**6**  I kissed thee ere I killed thee, no way but
this,
Killing myself to die upon a kiss.
*Othello* act 5, sc. 2, l. 357

### Richard II (1595)

**7**  The purest treasure mortal times afford
Is spotless reputation; that away,
Men are but gilded loam or painted clay.
*Richard II* act 1, sc. 1, l. 177

**8**  Mine honour is my life; both grow in one;
Take honour from me, and my life is done.
*Richard II* act 1, sc. 1, l. 182

**9**  We were not born to sue, but to command.
*Richard II* act 1, sc. 1, l. 196

**10**  How long a time lies in one little word!
*Richard II* act 1, sc. 3, l. 213

**11**  Things sweet to taste prove in digestion
sour.
*Richard II* act 1, sc. 3, l. 236

**12**  Must I not serve a long apprenticehood
To foreign passages, and in the end,
Having my freedom, boast of nothing else
But that I was a journeyman to grief?
*Richard II* act 1, sc. 3, l. 271

**13**  Teach thy necessity to reason thus;
There is no virtue like necessity.
*Richard II* act 1, sc. 3, l. 277

**14**  O, no! the apprehension of the good
Gives but the greater feeling to the worse.
*Richard II* act 1, sc. 3, l. 300

**15**  More are men's ends marked than their
lives before.
*Richard II* act 2, sc. 1, l. 11

**16**  This royal throne of kings, this sceptred
isle,
This earth of majesty, this seat of Mars,
This other Eden, demi-paradise,
This fortress built by Nature for herself
Against infection and the hand of war,
This happy breed of men, this little world,
This precious stone set in the silver sea,
Which serves it in the office of a wall,
Or as a moat defensive to a house,
Against the envy of less happier lands,
This blessèd plot, this earth, this realm,
this England,
This nurse, this teeming womb of royal
kings,
Feared by their breed and famous by their
birth.
*Richard II* act 2, sc. 1, l. 40

**17**  I am a stranger here in Gloucestershire:
These high wild hills and rough uneven
ways
Draw out our miles and make them
wearisome.
*Richard II* act 2, sc. 3, l. 2

**18**  Grace me no grace, nor uncle me no uncle.
*Richard II* act 2, sc. 3, l. 87

**19**  The caterpillars of the commonwealth.
*Richard II* act 2, sc. 3, l. 166

**20**  Things past redress are now with me past
care.
*Richard II* act 2, sc. 3, l. 171

**21**  Eating the bitter bread of banishment.
*Richard II* act 3, sc. 1, l. 21

**22**  Not all the water in the rough rude sea
Can wash the balm from an anointed king.
*Richard II* act 3, sc. 2, l. 54

**23**  If angels fight,
Weak men must fall, for heaven still
guards the right.
*Richard II* act 3, sc. 2, l. 61

**24**  O! call back yesterday, bid time return.
*Richard II* act 3, sc. 2, l. 69

**25**  The worst is death, and death will have his
day.
*Richard II* act 3, sc. 2, l. 103

**26**  Let's talk of graves, of worms, and
epitaphs;
Make dust our paper, and with rainy eyes
Write sorrow on the bosom of the earth.
Let's choose executors, and talk of wills.
*Richard II* act 3, sc. 2, l. 145

**27**  For God's sake, let us sit upon the ground
And tell sad stories of the death of kings.
*Richard II* act 3, sc. 2, l. 155

**28**  Within the hollow crown
That rounds the mortal temples of a king
Keeps Death his court.
*Richard II* act 3, sc. 2, l. 160

**29**  See, see, King Richard doth himself appear,
As doth the blushing discontented sun
From out the fiery portal of the east.
*Richard II* act 3, sc. 3, l. 62

1 The purple testament of bleeding war.
   *Richard II act 3, sc. 3, l. 94*

2 What must the king do now? Must he
   submit?
   The king shall do it: must he be deposed?
   The king shall be contented: must he lose
   The name of king? o' God's name, let it go.
   I'll give my jewels for a set of beads,
   My gorgeous palace for a hermitage,
   My gay apparel for an almsman's gown,
   My figured goblets for a dish of wood,
   My sceptre for a palmer's walking staff,
   My subjects for a pair of carved saints,
   And my large kingdom for a little grave,
   A little little grave, an obscure grave.
   *Richard II act 3, sc. 3, l. 143*

3 Shall we play the wantons with our woes,
   And make some pretty match with
   shedding tears?
   *Richard II act 3, sc. 3, l. 164*

4 God save the king! Will no man say, amen?
   Am I both priest and clerk? Well then,
   amen.
   *Richard II act 4, sc. 1, l. 172*

5 You may my glories and my state depose,
   But not my griefs; still am I king of those.
   *Richard II act 4, sc. 1, l. 192*

6              I am sworn brother, sweet,
   To grim Necessity, and he and I
   Will keep a league till death.
   *Richard II act 5, sc. 1, l. 20*

7 That were some love but little policy.
   *Richard II act 5, sc. 1, l. 84*

8              Who are the violets now
   That strew the green lap of the new come
   spring?
   *Richard II act 5, sc. 2, l. 46*

9 He prays but faintly and would be denied.
   *Richard II act 5, sc. 3, l. 103*

10 I have been studying how I may compare
   This prison where I live unto the world.
   *Richard II act 5, sc. 5, l. 1*

11             How sour sweet music is,
   When time is broke, and no proportion
   kept!
   So is it in the music of men's lives.
   *Richard II act 5, sc. 5, l. 42*

12 I wasted time, and now doth time waste
   me.
   *Richard II act 5, sc. 5, l. 49*

   Richard III (1591)

13 Now is the winter of our discontent
   Made glorious summer by this sun of York.
   *Richard III act 1, sc. 1, l. 1*

14 In this weak piping time of peace.
   *Richard III act 1, sc. 1, l. 24*

15 Was ever woman in this humour wooed?
   Was ever woman in this humour won?
   *Richard III act 1, sc. 2, l. 229*

16 Woe to the land that's governed by a child!
   *Richard III act 2, sc. 3, l. 11. Cf. 44:22*

17 So wise so young, they say, do never live
   long.
   *Richard III act 3, sc. 1, l. 79*

18 I am not in the giving vein to-day.
   *Richard III act 4, sc. 2, l. 115*

19 Harp not on that string.
   *Richard III act 4, sc. 4, l. 365*

20 The king's name is a tower of strength.
   *Richard III act 5, sc. 3, l. 12*

21 A horse! a horse! my kingdom for a horse!
   *Richard III act 5, sc. 4, l. 7*

   Romeo and Juliet (1595)

22 From forth the fatal loins of these two foes
   A pair of star-crossed lovers take their life.
   *Romeo and Juliet prologue*

23 The two hours' traffick of our stage.
   *Romeo and Juliet prologue*

24 O! then, I see, Queen Mab hath been with
   you ...
   She is the fairies' midwife, and she comes
   In shape no bigger than an agate-stone
   On the forefinger of an alderman,
   Drawn with a team of little atomies
   Athwart men's noses as they lie asleep.
   *Romeo and Juliet act 1, sc. 4, l. 53*

25 You and I are past our dancing days.
   *Romeo and Juliet act 1, sc. 5, l. [35]*

26 O! she doth teach the torches to burn
   bright.
   It seems she hangs upon the cheek of
   night
   Like a rich jewel in an Ethiop's ear;
   Beauty too rich for use, for earth too dear.
   *Romeo and Juliet act 1, sc. 5, l. [48]*

27 We have a trifling foolish banquet towards.
   *Romeo and Juliet act 1, sc. 5, l. [126]*

28 My only love sprung from my only hate!
   Too early seen unknown, and known too
   late!
   *Romeo and Juliet act 1, sc. 5, l. [142]*

29 He jests at scars, that never felt a wound.
   But, soft! what light through yonder
   window breaks?
   It is the east, and Juliet is the sun.
   *Romeo and Juliet act 2, sc. 2, l. 1*

30 O Romeo, Romeo! wherefore art thou
   Romeo?
   *Romeo and Juliet act 2, sc. 2, l. 33*

31 What's in a name? that which we call a
   rose
   By any other name would smell as sweet.
   *Romeo and Juliet act 2, sc. 2, l. 43*

32 For stony limits cannot hold love out,
   And what love can do that dares love
   attempt.
   *Romeo and Juliet act 2, sc. 2, l. 66*

33 O! swear not by the moon, the inconstant
   moon,
   That monthly changes in her circled orb,
   Lest that thy love prove likewise variable.
   *Romeo and Juliet act 2, sc. 2, l. 109*

1 It is too rash, too unadvised, too sudden.
  *Romeo and Juliet* act 2, sc. 2, l. 118

2 Love goes toward love, as schoolboys from
  their books;
  But love from love, toward school with
  heavy looks.
  *Romeo and Juliet* act 2, sc. 2, l. 156

3 How silver-sweet sound lovers' tongues by
  night,
  Like softest music to attending ears!
  *Romeo and Juliet* act 2, sc. 2, l. 165

4 Good-night, good-night! parting is such
  sweet sorrow
  That I shall say good-night till it be
  morrow.
  *Romeo and Juliet* act 2, sc. 2, l. 184

5 O flesh, flesh, how art thou fishified!
  *Romeo and Juliet* act 2, sc. 4, l. [41]

6 I am the very pink of courtesy.
  *Romeo and Juliet* act 2, sc. 4, l. [63]

7 No, 'tis not so deep as a well, nor so wide
  as a church door; but 'tis enough, 'twill
  serve.
  *Romeo and Juliet* act 3, sc. 1, l. [100]

8 A plague o' both your houses!
  *Romeo and Juliet* act 3, sc. 1, l. [112]

9 O! I am Fortune's fool.
  *Romeo and Juliet* act 3, sc. 1, l. [142]

10 Gallop apace, you fiery-footed steeds,
   Towards Phoebus' lodging.
   *Romeo and Juliet* act 3, sc. 2, l. 1

11 Spread thy close curtain, love-performing
   night!
   *Romeo and Juliet* act 3, sc. 2, l. 5

12              Come, civil night,
   Thou sober-suited matron, all in black.
   *Romeo and Juliet* act 3, sc. 2, l. 10

13 Come, night! come, Romeo! come, thou day
   in night!
   *Romeo and Juliet* act 3, sc. 2, l. 17

14 Give me my Romeo: and, when he shall
   die,
   Take him and cut him out in little stars,
   And he will make the face of heaven so
   fine
   That all the world will be in love with
   night,
   And pay no worship to the garish sun.
   *Romeo and Juliet* act 3, sc. 2, l. 21

15 Affliction is enamoured of thy parts,
   And thou art wedded to calamity.
   *Romeo and Juliet* act 3, sc. 3, l. 2

16 Adversity's sweet milk, philosophy.
   *Romeo and Juliet* act 3, sc. 3, l. 54

17 It was the nightingale, and not the lark,
   That pierced the fearful hollow of thine
   ear.
   *Romeo and Juliet* act 3, sc. 5, l. 1

18 Night's candles are burnt out, and jocund
   day
   Stands tiptoe on the misty mountain tops.
   *Romeo and Juliet* act 3, sc. 5, l. 9

19 I have more care to stay than will to go.
   *Romeo and Juliet* act 3, sc. 5, l. 23

20 Thank me no thankings, nor proud me no
   prouds.
   *Romeo and Juliet* act 3, sc. 5, l. 153

21 Death lies on her like an untimely frost.
   *Romeo and Juliet* act 4, sc. 5, l. 28

22 Tempt not a desperate man.
   *Romeo and Juliet* act 5, sc. 3, l. 59

23 How oft when men are at the point of
   death
   Have they been merry! which their keepers
   call
   A lightning before death.
   *Romeo and Juliet* act 5, sc. 3, l. 88

24              Beauty's ensign yet
   Is crimson in thy lips and in thy cheeks,
   And death's pale flag is not advancèd there.
   *Romeo and Juliet* act 5, sc. 3, l. 94

25              Seal with a righteous kiss
   A dateless bargain to engrossing death!
   *Romeo and Juliet* act 5, sc. 3, l. 114

26 Seal up the mouth of outrage for a while,
   Till we can clear these ambiguities.
   *Romeo and Juliet* act 5, sc. 3, l. 216

## The Taming of the Shrew (1592)

27 Kiss me Kate, we will be married o'
   Sunday.
   *The Taming of the Shrew* act 2, sc. 1, l. 318

28 This is the way to kill a wife with kindness.
   *The Taming of the Shrew* act 4, sc. 1, l. [211]

29              O vile,
   Intolerable, not to be endured!
   *The Taming of the Shrew* act 5, sc. 2, l. 93

30 A woman moved is like a fountain
   troubled,
   Muddy, ill-seeming, thick, bereft of beauty.
   *The Taming of the Shrew* act 5, sc. 2, l. 143

## The Tempest (1611)

31 He hath no drowning mark upon him; his
   complexion is perfect gallows.
   *The Tempest* act 1, sc. 1, l. [33]

32 Now would I give a thousand furlongs of
   sea for an acre of barren ground.
   *The Tempest* act 1, sc. 1, l. [70]

33              What seest thou else
   In the dark backward and abysm of time?
   *The Tempest* act 1, sc. 2, l. 49

34 The still-vexed Bermoothes.
   *The Tempest* act 1, sc. 2, l. 229

35 You taught me language; and my profit
   on't
   Is, I know how to curse.
   *The Tempest* act 1, sc. 2, l. 363

36 Come unto these yellow sands,
   And then take hands.
   *The Tempest* act 1, sc. 2, l. 375

1 Full fathom five thy father lies;
Of his bones are coral made:
Those are pearls that were his eyes:
Nothing of him that doth fade,
But doth suffer a sea-change
Into something rich and strange.
*The Tempest* act 1, sc. 2, l. 394

2 The fringèd curtains of thine eye advance,
And say what thou seest yond.
*The Tempest* act 1, sc. 2, l. 405

3 What's past is prologue.
*The Tempest* act 2, sc. 1, l. [261]

4 When they will not give a doit to relieve a
lame beggar, they will lay out ten to see a
dead Indian.
*The Tempest* act 2, sc. 2, l. [33]

5 Misery acquaints a man with strange
bedfellows.
*The Tempest* act 2, sc. 2, l. [42]

6 Thou deboshed fish thou.
*The Tempest* act 3, sc. 2, l. [30]

7 Flout 'em, and scout 'em; and scout 'em,
and flout 'em;
Thought is free.
*The Tempest* act 3, sc. 2, l. [133]

8 He that dies pays all debts.
*The Tempest* act 3, sc. 2, l. [143]

9 Be not afeard: the isle is full of noises,
Sounds and sweet airs, that give delight,
and hurt not.
*The Tempest* act 3, sc. 2, l. [147]

10 Our revels now are ended. These our
actors,
As I foretold you, were all spirits and
Are melted into air, into thin air:
And, like the baseless fabric of this vision,
The cloud-capped towers, the gorgeous
palaces,
The solemn temples, the great globe itself,
Yea, all which it inherit, shall dissolve
And, like this insubstantial pageant faded,
Leave not a rack behind. We are such stuff
As dreams are made on, and our little life
Is rounded with a sleep.
*The Tempest* act 4, sc. 1, l. 148

11 I do begin to have bloody thoughts.
*The Tempest* act 4, sc. 1, l. [221]

12              But this rough magic
I here abjure.
*The Tempest* act 5, sc. 1, l. 50

13              I'll break my staff,
Bury it certain fathoms in the earth,
And, deeper than did ever plummet sound,
I'll drown my book.
*The Tempest* act 5, sc. 1, l. 54

14 Where the bee sucks, there suck I
In a cowslip's bell I lie;
There I couch when owls do cry.
On the bat's back I do fly
After summer merrily:
Merrily, merrily shall I live now
Under the blossom that hangs on the
bough.
*The Tempest* act 5, sc. 1, l. 88

15 How beauteous mankind is! O brave new
world,
That has such people in't.
*The Tempest* act 5, sc. 1, l. 183

**Timon of Athens** (*c.*1607)

16 'Tis not enough to help the feeble up,
But to support him after.
*Timon of Athens* act 1, sc. 1, l. 108

17 I wonder men dare trust themselves with
men.
*Timon of Athens* act 1, sc. 2, l. [45]

18 Like madness is the glory of this life.
*Timon of Athens* act 1, sc. 2, l. [141]

19 Men shut their doors against a setting sun.
*Timon of Athens* act 1, sc. 2, l. [152]

20 You fools of fortune, trencher-friends,
time's flies.
*Timon of Athens* act 3, sc. 6, l. [107]

21 We have seen better days.
*Timon of Athens* act 4, sc. 2, l. 27

22              Never learned
The icy precepts of respect.
*Timon of Athens* act 4, sc. 3, l. 258

23              The moon's an arrant thief,
And her pale fire she snatches from the
sun.
*Timon of Athens* act 4, sc. 3, l. 443

24 Timon hath made his everlasting mansion
Upon the beachèd verge of the salt flood.
*Timon of Athens* act 5, sc. 1, l. [220]

**Titus Andronicus** (1590)

25 She is a woman, therefore may be wooed;
She is a woman, therefore may be won.
*Titus Andronicus* act 2, sc. 1, l. 82. Cf. 280:6

26              More water glideth by the mill
Than wots the miller of.
*Titus Andronicus* act 2, sc. 1, l. 85

27 Come, and take choice of all my library,
And so beguile thy sorrow.
*Titus Andronicus* act 4, sc. 1, l. 34

**Troilus and Cressida** (1602)

28 I have had my labour for my travail.
*Troilus and Cressida* act 1, sc. 1, l. [73]

29 Things won are done; joy's soul lies in the
doing.
*Troilus and Cressida* act 1, sc. 2, l. [311]

30 Take but degree away, untune that string,
And, hark! what discord follows; each thing
meets
In mere oppugnancy.
*Troilus and Cressida* act 1, sc. 3, l. 109

31              An envious fever
Of pale and bloodless emulation.
*Troilus and Cressida* act 1, sc. 3, l. 129

32 The baby figure of the giant mass
Of things to come at large.
*Troilus and Cressida* act 1, sc. 3, l. 343

33              Thus to persist
In doing wrong extenuates not wrong,
But makes it much more heavy.
*Troilus and Cressida* act 2, sc. 2, l. 186

1 I am giddy, expectation whirls me round.
*Troilus and Cressida* act 3, sc. 2, l. [17]

2 This is the monstruosity in love, lady, that
the will is infinite, and the execution
confined; that the desire is boundless, and
the act a slave to limit.
*Troilus and Cressida* act 3, sc. 2, l. [85]

3          To be wise, and love,
Exceeds man's might.
*Troilus and Cressida* act 3, sc. 2, l. [163]

4 Time hath, my lord, a wallet at his back,
Wherein he puts alms for oblivion.
*Troilus and Cressida* act 3, sc. 3, l. 145

5          Perseverance, dear my lord,
Keeps honour bright.
*Troilus and Cressida* act 3, sc. 3, l. 150

6 One touch of nature makes the whole
world kin.
*Troilus and Cressida* act 3, sc. 3, l. 175

7 How my achievements mock me!
*Troilus and Cressida* act 4, sc. 2, l. [72]

8 What a pair of spectacles is here!
*Troilus and Cressida* act 4, sc. 4, l. [13]
(Pandarus, of the lovers)

9          Fie, fie upon her!
There's language in her eye, her cheek, her
lip,
Nay, her foot speaks; her wanton spirits
look out
At every joint and motive of her body.
*Troilus and Cressida* act 4, sc. 5, l. 54

10 What's past, and what's to come is strewed
with husks
And formless ruin of oblivion.
*Troilus and Cressida* act 4, sc. 5, l. 165

11          The end crowns all,
And that old common arbitrator, Time,
Will one day end it.
*Troilus and Cressida* act 4, sc. 5, l. 223

12 Words, words, mere words, no matter from
the heart.
*Troilus and Cressida* act 5, sc. 3, l. [109]

**Twelfth Night** (1601)

13 If music be the food of love, play on;
Give me excess of it, that, surfeiting,
The appetite may sicken, and so die.
*Twelfth Night* act 1, sc. 1, l. 1

14 That strain again! it had a dying fall.
*Twelfth Night* act 1, sc. 1, l. 4

15 I am a great eater of beef, and I believe
that does harm to my wit.
*Twelfth Night* act 1, sc. 3, l. [92]

16 I would I had bestowed that time in the
tongues that I have in fencing, dancing,
and bear-baiting. O! had I but followed the
arts!
*Twelfth Night* act 1, sc. 3, l. [99]

17 Is it a world to hide virtues in?
*Twelfth Night* act 1, sc. 3, l. [142]

18 Many a good hanging prevents a bad
marriage.
*Twelfth Night* act 1, sc. 5, l. [20]

19 A plague o' these pickle herring!
*Twelfth Night* act 1, sc. 5, l. [127]

20 He is very well-favoured, and he speaks
very shrewishly: one would think his
mother's milk were scarce out of him.
*Twelfth Night* act 1, sc. 5, l. [170]

21 Make me a willow cabin at your gate,
And call upon my soul within the house;
Write loyal cantons of contemnèd love,
And sing them loud even in the dead of
night;
Halloo your name to the reverberate hills,
And make the babbling gossip of the air
Cry out, 'Olivia!'
*Twelfth Night* act 1, sc. 5, l. [289]

22 Not to be a-bed after midnight is to be up
betimes.
*Twelfth Night* act 2, sc. 3, l. 1

23 O mistress mine! where are you roaming?
O! stay and hear; your true love's coming,
That can sing both high and low.
Trip no further, pretty sweeting;
Journeys end in lovers meeting,
Every wise man's son doth know ...

What is love? 'tis not hereafter;
Present mirth hath present laughter;
What's to come is still unsure:
In delay there lies no plenty;
Then come kiss me, sweet and twenty,
Youth's a stuff will not endure.
*Twelfth Night* act 2, sc. 3, l. [42]

24 He does it with a better grace, but I do it
more natural.
*Twelfth Night* act 2, sc. 3, l. [91]

25 Is there no respect of place, persons, nor
time, in you?
*Twelfth Night* act 2, sc. 3, l. [100]

26 Dost thou think, because thou art virtuous,
there shall be no more cakes and ale?
*Twelfth Night* act 2, sc. 3, l. [124]

27 My purpose is, indeed, a horse of that
colour.
*Twelfth Night* act 2, sc. 3, l. [184]

28 I was adored once too.
*Twelfth Night* act 2, sc. 3, l. [200]

29 These most brisk and giddy-pacèd times.
*Twelfth Night* act 2, sc. 4, l. 6

30          Let still the woman take
An elder than herself, so wears she to him,
So sways she level in her husband's heart.
*Twelfth Night* act 2, sc. 4, l. 29

31 The spinsters and the knitters in the sun.
*Twelfth Night* act 2, sc. 4, l. 44

32 Come away, come away, death,
And in sad cypress let me be laid.
*Twelfth Night* act 2, sc. 4, l. 51

33 Now, the melancholy god protect thee, and
the tailor make thy doublet of changeable
taffeta, for thy mind is a very opal.
*Twelfth Night* act 2, sc. 4, l. [74]

**1**　　　　　She never told her love,
But let concealment, like a worm i' the
　bud,
Feed on her damask cheek: she pined in
　thought;
And with a green and yellow melancholy,
She sat like patience on a monument,
Smiling at grief.
　*Twelfth Night* act 2, sc. 4, l. [112]

**2** I am all the daughters of my father's
　house,
And all the brothers too.
　*Twelfth Night* act 2, sc. 4, l. [122]

**3** But be not afraid of greatness: some men
are born great, some achieve greatness,
and some have greatness thrust upon
them.
　*Twelfth Night* act 2, sc. 5, l. [158]

**4** Remember who commended thy yellow
stockings, and wished to see thee ever
cross-gartered.
　*Twelfth Night* act 2, sc. 5, l. [168]

**5** O world! how apt the poor are to be proud.
　*Twelfth Night* act 3, sc. 1, l. [141]

**6** O! what a deal of scorn looks beautiful
In the contempt and anger of his lip.
　*Twelfth Night* act 3, sc. 1, l. [159]

**7** Love sought is good, but giv'n unsought is
better.
　*Twelfth Night* act 3, sc. 1, l. [170]

**8** In the south suburbs, at the Elephant,
Is best to lodge.
　*Twelfth Night* act 3, sc. 3, l. 39

**9** Why, this is very midsummer madness.
　*Twelfth Night* act 3, sc. 4, l. [62]

**10** If this were played upon a stage now, I
could condemn it as an improbable fiction.
　*Twelfth Night* act 3, sc. 4, l. [142]

**11** More matter for a May morning.
　*Twelfth Night* act 3, sc. 4, l. [158]

**12** Still you keep o' the windy side of the law.
　*Twelfth Night* act 3, sc. 4, l. [183]

**13** Leave thy vain bibble-babble.
　*Twelfth Night* act 4, sc. 2, l. [106]

**14** Thus the whirligig of time brings in his
revenges.
　*Twelfth Night* act 5, sc. 1, l. [388]

**15** When that I was and a little tiny boy,
With hey, ho, the wind and the rain;
A foolish thing was but a toy,
For the rain it raineth every day.
　*Twelfth Night* act 5, sc. 1, l. [401]

**The Two Gentlemen of Verona** (1592–3)

**16** Home-keeping youth have ever homely
wits.
　*The Two Gentlemen of Verona* act 1, sc. 1, l. 2

**17** Fie, fie! how wayward is this foolish love
That, like a testy babe, will scratch the
　nurse
And presently all humbled kiss the rod!
　*The Two Gentlemen of Verona* act 1, sc. 2, l. 55

**18** O! how this spring of love resembleth
The uncertain glory of an April day.
　*The Two Gentlemen of Verona* act 1, sc. 3, l. 84

**19** Who is Silvia? what is she,
That all our swains commend her?
　*The Two Gentlemen of Verona* act 4, sc. 2, l. 40

**20**　　　　　O heaven! were man
But constant, he were perfect.
　*The Two Gentlemen of Verona* act 5, sc. 4, l. 110

**The Winter's Tale** (1610–11)

**21** Two lads that thought there was no more
　behind
But such a day to-morrow as to-day,
And to be boy eternal.
　*The Winter's Tale* act 1, sc. 2, l. 63

**22** A sad tale's best for winter.
　*The Winter's Tale* act 2, sc. 1, l. 24

**23** I have drunk, and seen the spider.
　*The Winter's Tale* act 2, sc. 1, l. 39

**24** What's gone and what's past help
Should be past grief.
　*The Winter's Tale* act 3, sc. 2, l. [223]

**25** Exit, pursued by a bear.
　*The Winter's Tale* act 3, sc. 3 (stage direction)

**26** When daffodils begin to peer,
With heigh! the doxy, over the dale,
Why, then comes in the sweet o' the year;
For the red blood reigns in the winter's
　pale.
　*The Winter's Tale* act 4, sc. 2, l. 1

**27** A snapper-up of unconsidered trifles.
　*The Winter's Tale* act 4, sc. 2, l. [26]

**28** Jog on, jog on, the foot-path way,
And merrily hent the stile-a:
A merry heart goes all the day,
Your sad tires in a mile-a.
　*The Winter's Tale* act 4, sc. 2, l. [133]

**29** For you there's rosemary and rue; these
　keep
Seeming and savour all the winter long.
　*The Winter's Tale* act 4, sc. 3, l. 74

**30**　　　　　I'll not put
The dibble in earth to set one slip of them.
　*The Winter's Tale* act 4, sc. 3, l. 99

**31** The marigold, that goes to bed wi' the sun,
And with him rises weeping.
　*The Winter's Tale* act 4, sc. 3, l. 105

**32**　　　　　Daffodils,
That come before the swallow dares, and
　take
The winds of March with beauty.
　*The Winter's Tale* act 4, sc. 3, l. 118

**33**　　　　　Pale prime-roses,
That die unmarried, ere they can behold
Bright Phoebus in his strength,—a malady
Most incident to maids.
　*The Winter's Tale* act 4, sc. 3, l. 122

**34**　　　　　Each your doing,
So singular in each particular,
Crowns what you are doing in the present
　deed,
That all your acts are queens.
　*The Winter's Tale* act 4, sc. 3, l. 144

1                    I'll queen it no inch further,
But milk my ewes and weep.
   *The Winter's Tale* act 4, sc. 3, l. [463]

2 Though I am not naturally honest, I am so
sometimes by chance.
   *The Winter's Tale* act 4, sc. 3, l. [734]

3                    Stars, stars!
And all eyes else dead coals.
   *The Winter's Tale* act 5, sc. 1, l. 67

4                    O! she's warm.
If this be magic, let it be an art
Lawful as eating.
   *The Winter's Tale* act 5, sc. 3, l. 109

**The Passionate Pilgrim** (1599,
attribution doubtful)

5 Crabbed age and youth cannot live
together:
Youth is full of pleasance, age is full of
care.
   *The Passionate Pilgrim* no. 12

6 Age, I do abhor thee, youth, I do adore
thee.
   *The Passionate Pilgrim* no. 12

**The Rape of Lucrece** (1594)

7 Beauty itself doth of itself persuade
The eyes of men without an orator.
   *The Rape of Lucrece* l. 29

8 Who buys a minute's mirth to wail a
week?
Or sells eternity to get a toy?
For one sweet grape who will the vine
destroy?
   *The Rape of Lucrece* l. 213

9 And now this pale swan in her watery nest
Begins the sad dirge of her certain ending.
   *The Rape of Lucrece* l. 1611

**Sonnets** (1609)

10 To the onlie begetter of these insuing
sonnets, Mr. W. H.
   Dedication (also attributed to Thomas
   Thorpe, the publisher)

11 From fairest creatures we desire increase,
That thereby beauty's rose might never die.
   Sonnet 1

12 Shall I compare thee to a summer's day?
Thou art more lovely and more temperate:
Rough winds do shake the darling buds of
May,
And summer's lease hath all too short a
date.
   Sonnet 18

13 But thy eternal summer shall not fade.
   Sonnet 18

14 Desiring this man's art, and that man's
scope,
With what I most enjoy contented least.
   Sonnet 29

15 Haply I think on thee,—and then my state,
Like to the lark at break of day arising
From sullen earth, sings hymns at heaven's
gate.
   Sonnet 29

16 When to the sessions of sweet silent
thought
I summon up remembrance of things past.
   Sonnet 30

17 Full many a glorious morning have I seen
Flatter the mountain-tops with sovereign
eye,
Kissing with golden face the meadows
green,
Gilding pale streams with heavenly
alchemy.
   Sonnet 33

18 What is your substance, whereof are you
made,
That millions of strange shadows on you
tend?
   Sonnet 53

19 Not marble, nor the gilded monuments
Of princes, shall outlive this powerful
rhyme.
   Sonnet 55

20 So true a fool is love that in your will,
Though you do anything, he thinks no ill.
   Sonnet 57

21 Like as the waves make towards the
pebbled shore,
So do our minutes hasten to their end.
   Sonnet 60

22 Time doth transfix the flourish set on
youth
And delves the parallels in beauty's brow.
   Sonnet 60

23 No longer mourn for me when I am dead
Than you shall hear the surly sullen bell
Give warning to the world that I am fled
From this vile world, with vilest worms to
dwell.
   Sonnet 71

24 That time of year thou mayst in me behold
When yellow leaves, or none, or few, do
hang
Upon those boughs which shake against
the cold,
Bare ruined choirs, where late the sweet
birds sang.
   Sonnet 73

25 So all my best is dressing old words new,
Spending again what is already spent.
   Sonnet 76

26 Time's thievish progress to eternity.
   Sonnet 77

27 Farewell! thou art too dear for my
possessing,
And like enough thou know'st thy
estimate:
The charter of thy worth gives thee
releasing;
My bonds in thee are all determinate.
   Sonnet 87

28 Thus have I had thee, as a dream doth
flatter,
In sleep a king, but, waking, no such
matter.
   Sonnet 87

1 Ah, do not, when my heart hath 'scaped
    this sorrow,
  Come in the rearward of a conquered woe;
  Give not a windy night a rainy morrow,
  To linger out a purposed overthrow.
    Sonnet 90

2 For sweetest things turn sourest by their
    deeds;
  Lilies that fester smell far worse than
    weeds.
    Sonnet 94

3 What freezings have I felt, what dark days
    seen!
  What old December's bareness everywhere!
    Sonnet 97

4 When in the chronicle of wasted time
  I see descriptions of the fairest wights,
  And beauty making beautiful old rime,
  In praise of ladies dead and lovely knights.
    Sonnet 106

5 For we, which now behold these present
    days,
  Have eyes to wonder, but lack tongues to
    praise.
    Sonnet 106

6 Alas! 'tis true I have gone here and there,
  And made myself a motley to the view.
    Sonnet 110

7          My nature is subdued
  To what it works in, like the dyer's hand.
    Sonnet 111

8 Let me not to the marriage of true minds
  Admit impediments. Love is not love
  Which alters when it alteration finds.
    Sonnet 116

9 Love alters not with his brief hours and
    weeks,
  But bears it out even to the edge of doom.
  If this be error, and upon me proved,
  I never writ, nor no man ever loved.
    Sonnet 116

10 The expense of spirit in a waste of shame
  Is lust in action.
    Sonnet 129

11 My mistress' eyes are nothing like the sun;
  Coral is far more red than her lips' red:
  If snow be white, why then her breasts are
    dun;
  If hairs be wires, black wires grow on her
    head.
    Sonnet 130

12 Whoever hath her wish, thou hast thy Will,
  And Will to boot, and Will in over-plus.
    Sonnet 135

13 Two loves I have of comfort and despair,
  Which like two spirits do suggest me still:
  The better angel is a man right fair,
  The worser spirit a woman, coloured ill.
    Sonnet 144

14 Why so large cost, having so short a lease,
  Dost thou upon thy fading mansion spend?
    Sonnet 146

15 So shalt thou feed on Death, that feeds on
    men,
  And Death once dead, there's no more
    dying then.
    Sonnet 146

16 For I have sworn thee fair, and thought
    thee bright,
  Who art as black as hell, as dark as night.
    Sonnet 147

**Venus and Adonis** (1593)

17 Love is a spirit all compact of fire,
  Not gross to sink, but light, and will
    aspire.
    *Venus and Adonis* l. 145

18 Love comforteth like sunshine after rain.
    *Venus and Adonis* l. 799

19 For he being dead, with him is beauty
    slain,
  And, beauty dead, black chaos comes again.
    *Venus and Adonis* l. 1019

20 Good friend, for Jesu's sake forbear
  To dig the dust enclosed here.
  Blest be the man that spares these stones,
  And curst be he that moves my bones.
    Epitaph on his tomb, probably composed by
    himself

21 Item, I give unto my wife my second best
  bed, with the furniture.
    Will, 1616. See E. K. Chambers *William
    Shakespeare* (1930) vol. 2, p. 169

# Bill Shankly 1914–81

22 Some people think football is a matter of
  life and death ... I can assure them it is
  much more serious than that.
    In *Sunday Times* 4 October 1981

# George Bernard Shaw 1856–1950

23 All great truths begin as blasphemies.
    *Annajanska* (1919) p. 262

24 Oh, you are a very poor soldier—a
  chocolate cream soldier!
    *Arms and the Man* (1898) act 1

25 When a stupid man is doing something he
  is ashamed of, he always declares that it is
  his duty.
    *Caesar and Cleopatra* (1901) act 3

26 We have no more right to consume
  happiness without producing it than to
  consume wealth without producing it.
    *Candida* (1898) act 1

27 It is easy—terribly easy— to shake a man's
  faith in himself. To take advantage of that
  to break a man's spirit is devil's work.
    *Candida* (1898) act 1

28 I'm only a beer teetotaller, not
  a champagne teetotaller.
    *Candida* (1898) act 3

29 Martyrdom ... the only way in which
  a man can become famous without ability.
    *The Devil's Disciple* (1901) act 3

1 The British soldier can stand up to anything except the British War Office.
*The Devil's Disciple* (1901) act 3

2 Stimulate the phagocytes.
*The Doctor's Dilemma* (1911) act 1

3 All professions are conspiracies against the laity.
*The Doctor's Dilemma* (1911) act 1

4 The one point on which all women are in furious secret rebellion against the existing law is the saddling of the right to a child with the obligation to become the servant of a man.
*Getting Married* (1911) preface 'The Right to Motherhood'

5 Go anywhere in England where there are natural, wholesome, contented, and really nice English people; and what do you always find? That the stables are the real centre of the household.
*Heartbreak House* (1919) act 3

6 A man who has no office to go to—I don't care who he is—is a trial of which you can have no conception.
*The Irrational Knot* (1905) ch. 18

7 There are only two qualities in the world: efficiency and inefficiency, and only two sorts of people: the efficient and the inefficient.
*John Bull's Other Island* (1907) act 4

8 The greatest of evils and the worst of crimes is poverty.
*Major Barbara* (1907) preface

9 I am a Millionaire. That is my religion.
*Major Barbara* (1907) act 2

10 I can't talk religion to a man with bodily hunger in his eyes.
*Major Barbara* (1907) act 2

11 Wot prawce Selvytion nah?
*Major Barbara* (1907) act 2

12 Alcohol is a very necessary article ... It enables Parliament to do things at eleven at night that no sane person would do at eleven in the morning.
*Major Barbara* (1907) act 2

13 He knows nothing; and he thinks he knows everything. That points clearly to a political career.
*Major Barbara* (1907) act 3

14 Nothing is ever done in this world until men are prepared to kill one another if it is not done.
*Major Barbara* (1907) act 3

15 But a lifetime of happiness! No man alive could bear it: it would be hell on earth.
*Man and Superman* (1903) act 1

16 The more things a man is ashamed of, the more respectable he is.
*Man and Superman* (1903) act 1

17 Vitality in a woman is a blind fury of creation.
*Man and Superman* (1903) act 1

18 Of all human struggles there is none so treacherous and remorseless as the struggle between the artist man and the mother woman.
*Man and Superman* (1903) act 1

19 Hell is full of musical amateurs: music is the brandy of the damned.
*Man and Superman* (1903) act 3

20 Englishmen never will be slaves: they are free to do whatever the Government and public opinion allow them to do.
*Man and Superman* (1903) act 3

21 An Englishman thinks he is moral when he is only uncomfortable.
*Man and Superman* (1903) act 3

22 In the arts of peace Man is a bungler.
*Man and Superman* (1903) act 3

23 When the military man approaches, the world locks up its spoons and packs off its womankind.
*Man and Superman* (1903) act 3

24 What is virtue but the Trade Unionism of the married?
*Man and Superman* (1903) act 3

25 Beauty is all very well at first sight; but who ever looks at it when it has been in the house three days?
*Man and Superman* (1903) act 4

26 The art of government is the organization of idolatry.
*Man and Superman* (1903) 'Maxims: Idolatry'

27 Democracy substitutes election by the incompetent many for appointment by the corrupt few.
*Man and Superman* (1903) 'Maxims: Democracy'

28 Liberty means responsibility. That is why most men dread it.
*Man and Superman* (1903) 'Maxims: Liberty and Equality'

29 He who can, does. He who cannot, teaches.
*Man and Superman* (1903) 'Maxims: Education'

30 Marriage is popular because it combines the maximum of temptation with the maximum of opportunity.
*Man and Superman* (1903) 'Maxims: Marriage'

31 Titles distinguish the mediocre, embarrass the superior, and are disgraced by the inferior.
*Man and Superman* (1903) 'Maxims: Titles'

32 If you strike a child take care that you strike it in anger, even at the risk of maiming it for life. A blow in cold blood neither can nor should be forgiven.
*Man and Superman* (1903) 'Maxims: How to Beat Children'

33 Beware of the man whose god is in the skies.
*Man and Superman* (1903) 'Maxims: Religion'

34 Self-denial is not a virtue: it is only the effect of prudence on rascality.
*Man and Superman* (1903) 'Maxims: Virtues and Vice'

1 The reasonable man adapts himself to the world: the unreasonable one persists in trying to adapt the world to himself. Therefore all progress depends on the unreasonable man.
  *Man and Superman* (1903) 'Maxims: Reason'

2 The man who listens to Reason is lost: Reason enslaves all whose minds are not strong enough to master her.
  *Man and Superman* (1903) 'Maxims: Reason'

3 Decency is Indecency's conspiracy of silence.
  *Man and Superman* (1903) 'Maxims: Decency'

4 Home is the girl's prison and the woman's workhouse.
  *Man and Superman* (1903) 'Maxims: Women in the Home'

5 Every man over forty is a scoundrel.
  *Man and Superman* (1903) 'Maxims: Stray Sayings'

6 Youth, which is forgiven everything, forgives itself nothing: age, which forgives itself everything, is forgiven nothing.
  *Man and Superman* (1903) 'Maxims: Stray Sayings'

7 Take care to get what you like or you will be forced to like what you get.
  *Man and Superman* (1903) 'Maxims: Stray Sayings'

8 Beware of the man who does not return your blow: he neither forgives you nor allows you to forgive yourself.
  *Man and Superman* (1903) 'Maxims: Stray Sayings'

9 You will never find an Englishman in the wrong. He does everything on principle ... he supports his king on loyal principles and cuts off his king's head on republican principles.
  *The Man of Destiny* (1898) p. 201

10 Anarchism is a game at which the police can beat you.
  *Misalliance* (1914) p. 85

11 The only way for a woman to provide for herself decently is for her to be good to some man that can afford to be good to her.
  *Mrs Warren's Profession* (1898) act 2

12 A great devotee of the Gospel of Getting On.
  *Mrs Warren's Profession* (1898) act 4

13 You'll never have a quiet world till you knock the patriotism out of the human race.
  *O'Flaherty V.C.* (1919) p. 178

14 A perpetual holiday is a good working definition of hell.
  *Parents and Children* (1914) 'Children's Happiness'

15 There is only one religion, though there are a hundred versions of it.
  *Plays Pleasant and Unpleasant* (1898) vol. 2, preface

16 It is impossible for an Englishman to open his mouth without making some other Englishman hate or despise him.
  *Pygmalion* (1916) preface

17 I don't want to talk grammar, I want to talk like a lady.
  *Pygmalion* (1916) act 2

18 Gin was mother's milk to her.
  *Pygmalion* (1916) act 3

19 Walk! Not bloody likely.
  *Pygmalion* (1916) act 3

20 No Englishman is ever fairly beaten.
  *Saint Joan* (1924) sc. 4

21 Must then a Christ perish in torment in every age to save those that have no imagination?
  *Saint Joan* (1924) epilogue

22 Assassination is the extreme form of censorship.
  *The Showing-Up of Blanco Posnet* (1911) 'Limits to Toleration'

23 The great advantage of a hotel is that it's a refuge from home life.
  *You Never Can Tell* (1898) act 2

24 The younger generation is knocking at the door, and as I open it there steps spritely in the incomparable Max.
  *Saturday Review* 21 May 1898 'Valedictory' (on handing over the theatre column to Max Beerbohm)

25 The trouble, Mr Goldwyn, is that you are only interested in art and I am only interested in money.
  Telegraphed version of the outcome of a conversation between Shaw and Sam Goldwyn; in A. Johnson *The Great Goldwyn* (1937) ch. 3

26 [Dancing is] a perpendicular expression of a horizontal desire.
  In *New Statesman* 23 March 1962 (attributed)

27 England and America are two countries divided by a common language.
  Attributed in this and other forms, but not found in Shaw's published writings

## Sir Hartley Shawcross 1902–

28 We are the masters at the moment, and not only at the moment, but for a very long time to come.
  Speech, *Hansard* 2 April 1946, col. 1213 (often quoted 'We are the masters now'). Cf. 92:1

## Charles Shaw-Lefevre, Viscount Eversley 1794–1888

29 What is that fat gentleman in such a passion about?
  As a child, hearing Charles James Fox speak in Parliament; in G. W. E. Russell *Collections and Recollections* (1898) ch. 11

## Patrick Shaw-Stewart 1888–1917

**1** I saw a man this morning
Who did not wish to die;
I ask and cannot answer
If otherwise wish I.

Poem (1916) in M. Baring *Have You Anything to Declare?* (1936) p. 39

## Percy Bysshe Shelley 1792–1822

**2** The cemetery is an open space among the ruins, covered in winter with violets and daisies. It might make one in love with death, to think that one should be buried in so sweet a place.

*Adonais* (1821) preface

**3** I weep for Adonais—he is dead!
O, weep for Adonais! though our tears
Thaw not the frost which binds so dear a head!

*Adonais* (1821) st. 1

**4** To that high Capital, where kingly Death
Keeps his pale court in beauty and decay,
He came.

*Adonais* (1821) st. 7

**5**         The quick Dreams,
The passion-wingèd Ministers of thought.

*Adonais* (1821) st. 9

**6** She faded, like a cloud which had outwept its rain.

*Adonais* (1821) st. 10

**7** Ah, woe is me! Winter is come and gone,
But grief returns with the revolving year.

*Adonais* (1821) st. 18

**8** Alas! that all we loved of him should be,
But for our grief, as if it had not been,
And grief itself be mortal!

*Adonais* (1821) st. 21

**9** A pardlike Spirit, beautiful and swift.

*Adonais* (1821) st. 32

**10** And in mad trance, strike with our spirit's knife
Invulnerable nothings.

*Adonais* (1821) st. 39

**11** He has out-soared the shadow of our night;
Envy and calumny and hate and pain,
And that unrest which men miscall delight,
Can touch him not and torture not again;
From the contagion of the world's slow stain
He is secure, and now can never mourn
A heart grown cold, a head grown grey in vain.

*Adonais* (1821) st. 40

**12** He is a portion of the loveliness
Which once he made more lovely.

*Adonais* (1821) st. 43

**13** The One remains, the many change and pass;
Heaven's light forever shines, Earth's shadows fly;
Life, like a dome of many-coloured glass,
Stains the white radiance of Eternity,
Until Death tramples it to fragments.

*Adonais* (1821) st. 52

**14** A widow bird sat mourning for her love
Upon a wintry bough;
The frozen wind crept on above,
The freezing stream below.

*Charles the First* (1822) sc. 5, l. 9

**15** I never was attached to that great sect,
Whose doctrine is that each one should select
Out of the crowd a mistress or a friend,
And all the rest, though fair and wise, commend
To cold oblivion.

'Epipsychidion' (1821) l. 149

**16**         The beaten road
Which those poor slaves with weary footsteps tread,
Who travel to their home among the dead
By the broad highway of the world, and so
With one chained friend, perhaps a jealous foe,
The dreariest and the longest journey go.

'Epipsychidion' (1821) l. 154

**17** Let there be light! said Liberty,
And like sunrise from the sea,
Athens arose!

*Hellas* (1822) l. 682

**18** The world's great age begins anew,
The golden years return.

*Hellas* (1822) l. 1060

**19** O cease! must hate and death return?
Cease! must men kill and die?

*Hellas* (1822) l. 1096

**20**         I love all waste
And solitary places.

'Julian and Maddalo' (1818) l. 14

**21** Thou Paradise of exiles, Italy!

'Julian and Maddalo' (1818) l. 57

**22**         Most wretched men
Are cradled into poetry by wrong:
They learn in suffering what they teach in song.

'Julian and Maddalo' (1818) l. 544

**23** A cloud-encircled meteor of the air,
A hooded eagle among blinking owls.

'Letter to Maria Gisborne' (1820) l. 207 (of Coleridge)

**24** When the lamp is shattered
The light in the dust lies dead—
When the cloud is scattered
The rainbow's glory is shed.
When the lute is broken,
Sweet tones are remembered not;
When the lips have spoken,
Loved accents are soon forgot.

'Lines: When the lamp' (1824)

1 Underneath Day's azure eyes
Ocean's nursling, Venice lies,
A peopled labyrinth of walls,
Amphitrite's destined halls.
   'Lines written amongst the Euganean Hills'
   (1818) l. 94

2 Sun-girt city, thou hast been
Ocean's child, and then his queen;
Now is come a darker day,
And thou soon must be his prey.
   'Lines written amongst the Euganean Hills'
   (1818) l. 115 (of Venice)

3 Nothing in the world is single;
All things, by a law divine,
In one spirit meet and mingle.
   'Love's Philosophy' (written 1819)

4 I met Murder on the way—
He had a mask like Castlereagh.
   'The Mask of Anarchy' (1819) st. 2

5 His big tears, for he wept well,
Turned to mill-stones as they fell.
   'The Mask of Anarchy' (1819) st. 4

6 O wild West Wind, thou breath of
Autumn's being,
Thou, from whose unseen presence the
leaves dead
Are driven, like ghosts from an enchanter
fleeing,
Yellow, and black, and pale, and hectic red,
Pestilence-stricken multitudes.
   'Ode to the West Wind' (1819) l. 1

7 The sea-blooms and the oozy woods which
wear
The sapless foliage of the ocean.
   'Ode to the West Wind' (1819) l. 39

8 Oh, lift me as a wave, a leaf, a cloud!
I fall upon the thorns of life! I bleed!
   'Ode to the West Wind' (1819) l. 53

9 Make me thy lyre, even as the forest is.
   'Ode to the West Wind' (1819) l. 57

10    O, Wind,
If Winter comes, can Spring be far behind?
   'Ode to the West Wind' (1819) l. 69

11 I met a traveller from an antique land
Who said: Two vast and trunkless legs of
stone
Stand in the desert.
   'Ozymandias' (1819)

12 My name is Ozymandias, king of kings:
Look on my works, ye Mighty, and despair!
   'Ozymandias' (1819)

13 Hell is a city much like London.
   'Peter Bell the Third' (1819) pt. 3, st. 1

14 But from the first 'twas Peter's drift
To be a kind of moral eunuch,
He touched the hem of Nature's shift,
Felt faint—and never dared uplift
The closest, all-concealing tunic.
   'Peter Bell the Third' (1819) pt. 4, st. 11

15    Ere Babylon was dust,
The Magus Zoroaster, my dead child,
Met his own image walking in the garden.
   Prometheus Unbound (1819) act 1, l. 191

16 Grief for awhile is blind, and so was mine.
   Prometheus Unbound (1820) act 1, l. 304

17 The good want power, but to weep barren
tears.
The powerful goodness want: worse need
for them.
The wise want love; and those who love
want wisdom.
   Prometheus Unbound (1820) act 1, l. 625

18    Peace is in the grave.
The grave hides all things beautiful and
good:
I am a God and cannot find it there.
   Prometheus Unbound (1820) act 1, l. 638

19 The dust of creeds outworn.
   Prometheus Unbound (1820) act 1, l. 697

20 He gave man speech, and speech created
thought,
Which is the measure of the universe.
   Prometheus Unbound (1820) act 2, sc. 4, l. 72

21 My soul is an enchanted boat,
Which, like a sleeping swan, doth float
Upon the silver waves of thy sweet singing.
   Prometheus Unbound (1820) act 2, sc. 5, l. 72

22 The loathsome mask has fallen, the man
remains
Sceptreless, free, uncircumscribed, but
man
Equal, unclassed, tribeless, and nationless.
   Prometheus Unbound (1820) act 3, sc. 4, l. 193

23 Pinnacled dim in the intense inane.
   Prometheus Unbound (1820) act 3, sc. 4, l. 204

24 A traveller from the cradle to the grave
Through the dim night of this immortal
day.
   Prometheus Unbound (1820) act 4, l. 551

25 To love, and bear; to hope till Hope creates
From its own wreck the thing it
contemplates.
   Prometheus Unbound (1820) act 4, l. 573

26 How wonderful is Death,
Death and his brother Sleep!
   Queen Mab (1813) canto 1, l. 1

27 That sweet bondage which is freedom's
self.
   Queen Mab (1813) canto 9, l. 76

28 I dreamed that, as I wandered by the way,
Bare Winter suddenly was changed to
Spring.
   'The Question' (1822)

29 Daisies, those pearled Arcturi of the earth,
The constellated flower that never sets.
   'The Question' (1822)

30 A Sensitive Plant in a garden grew.
   'The Sensitive Plant' (1820) pt. 1, l. 1

31 And the jessamine faint, and the sweet
tuberose,
The sweetest flower for scent that blows.
   'The Sensitive Plant' (1820) pt. 1, l. 37

32 Rarely, rarely, comest thou,
Spirit of Delight!
   'Song' (1824)

1 Men of England, wherefore plough
For the lords who lay ye low?
'Song to the Men of England' (written 1819)

2 Lift not the painted veil which those who
live
Call Life.
'Sonnet' (1824)

3 An old, mad, blind, despised, and dying
king.
'Sonnet: England in 1819' (of George III)

4 Music, when soft voices die,
Vibrates in the memory—
Odours, when sweet violets sicken,
Live within the sense they quicken.
'To—: Music, when soft voices die' (1824)

5 The desire of the moth for the star,
Of the night for the morrow,
The devotion to something afar
From the sphere of our sorrow.
'To—: One word is too often profaned' (1824)

6 Hail to thee, blithe Spirit!
Bird thou never wert,
That from Heaven, or near it,
Pourest thy full heart
In profuse strains of unpremeditated art.
'To a Skylark' (1819)

7 And singing still dost soar, and soaring
ever singest.
'To a Skylark' (1819)

8 Thou art unseen, but yet I hear thy shrill
delight.
'To a Skylark' (1819)

9 Like a Poet hidden
In the light of thought,
Singing hymns unbidden.
'To a Skylark' (1819)

10 Our sincerest laughter
With some pain is fraught;
Our sweetest songs are those that tell of
saddest thought.
'To a Skylark' (1819)

11 Teach me half the gladness
That thy brain must know,
Such harmonious madness
From my lips would flow
The world should listen then—as I am
listening now.
'To a Skylark' (1819)

12 Swiftly walk o'er the western wave,
Spirit of Night!
'To Night' (1824)

13 Death will come when thou art dead,
Soon, too soon.
'To Night' (1824)

14 Art thou pale for weariness
Of climbing heaven, and gazing on the
earth,
Wandering companionless
Among the stars that have a different
birth.
'To the Moon' (1824)

15 And like a dying lady, lean and pale,
Who totters forth, wrapped in a gauzy veil.
'The Waning Moon' (1824)

16 A lovely lady, garmented in light
From her own beauty.
'The Witch of Atlas' (written 1820) st. 5

17 For she was beautiful—her beauty made
The bright world dim, and everything
beside
Seemed like the fleeting image of a shade.
'The Witch of Atlas' (written 1820) st. 12

18 Poetry is the record of the best and
happiest moments of the happiest and best
minds.
A Defence of Poetry (written 1821)

19 Poets are the unacknowledged legislators
of the world.
A Defence of Poetry (written 1821). Cf. 183:3

## William Shenstone 1714–63

20 A fool and his words are soon parted.
Works (1764) vol. 2 'On Reserve'

21 The world may be divided into people that
read, people that write, people that think,
and fox-hunters.
Works (1764) vol. 2 'On Writing and Books'

## Philip Henry Sheridan 1831–88

22 The only good Indian is a dead Indian.
At Fort Cobb, January 1869 (attributed)

## Richard Brinsley Sheridan 1751–1816

23 If it is abuse,—why one is always sure to
hear of it from one damned goodnatured
friend or another!
The Critic (1779) act 1, sc. 1

24 O Lord, Sir—when a heroine goes mad she
always goes into white satin.
The Critic (1779) act 3, sc. 1

25 An oyster may be crossed in love!
The Critic (1779) act 3, sc. 1

26 Illiterate him, I say, quite from your
memory.
The Rivals (1775) act 1, sc. 2

27 'Tis safest in matrimony to begin with a
little aversion.
The Rivals (1775) act 1, sc. 2

28 He is the very pineapple of politeness!
The Rivals (1775) act 3, sc. 3

29 If I reprehend any thing in this world, it is
the use of my oracular tongue, and a nice
derangement of epitaphs!
The Rivals (1775) act 3, sc. 3

30 She's as headstrong as an allegory on the
banks of the Nile.
The Rivals (1775) act 3, sc. 3

31 Too civil by half.
The Rivals (1775) act 3, sc. 4

**1** No caparisons, Miss, if you
please!—Caparisons don't become a young
woman.
*The Rivals* (1775) act 4, sc. 2

**2** You are not like Cerberus, three gentlemen
at once, are you?
*The Rivals* (1775) act 4, sc. 2

**3** You shall see them on a beautiful quarto
page where a neat rivulet of text shall
meander through a meadow of margin.
*The School for Scandal* (1777) act 1, sc. 1

**4** Here is the whole set! a character dead at
every word.
*The School for Scandal* (1777) act 2, sc. 2.
Cf. 253:7

**5** I'm called away by particular
business—but I leave my character behind
me.
*The School for Scandal* (1777) act 2, sc. 2

**6** Here's to the maiden of bashful fifteen
Here's to the widow of fifty
Here's to the flaunting, extravagant quean;
And here's to the housewife that's thrifty.
*The School for Scandal* (1777) act 3, sc. 3

**7** An unforgiving eye, and a damned
disinheriting countenance!
*The School for Scandal* (1777) act 4, sc. 1

**8** You write with ease, to show your
breeding,
But easy writing's vile hard reading.
'Clio's Protest' (written 1771)

## General Sherman 1820–91

**9** There is many a boy here to-day who looks
on war as all glory, but, boys, it is all hell.
Speech at Columbus, Ohio, 11 August 1880;
in L. Lewis *Sherman, Fighting Prophet* (1932)

## James Shirley 1596–1666

**10** The glories of our blood and state
Are shadows, not substantial things.
*The Contention of Ajax and Ulysses* (1659) act 1,
sc. 3

**11** Only the actions of the just
Smell sweet, and blossom in their dust.
*The Contention of Ajax and Ulysses* (1659) act 1,
sc. 3

**12**                How little room
Do we take up in death, that, living know
No bounds?
*The Wedding* (1629) act 4, sc. 4

## The Shorter Catechism (1647)

**13** 'What is the chief end of man?'
'To glorify God and to enjoy him for ever'.

## Algernon Sidney 1622–83

**14** 'Tis not necessary to light a candle to the
sun.
*Discourses concerning Government* (1698) ch. 2,
sect. 23. Cf. 83:12, 360:16

## Sir Philip Sidney 1554–86

**15** My true love hath my heart and I have his,
By just exchange one for the other giv'n.
*Arcadia* ('Old Arcadia', completed 1581) bk. 3

**16** Words came halting forth, wanting
Invention's stay.
*Astrophil and Stella* (1591) sonnet 1

**17** Biting my truant pen, beating myself for
spite,
'Fool,' said my Muse to me; 'look in thy
heart and write.'
*Astrophil and Stella* (1591) sonnet 1

**18** With how sad steps, O Moon, thou climb'st
the skies;
How silently, and with how wan a face.
*Astrophil and Stella* (1591) sonnet 31

**19**                O moon, tell me,
Is constant love deemed there but want of
wit?
*Astrophil and Stella* (1591) sonnet 31

**20** Come, sleep, O sleep, the certain knot of
peace,
The baiting place of wit, the balm of woe.
*Astrophil and Stella* (1591) sonnet 39

**21** That sweet enemy, France.
*Astrophil and Stella* (1591) sonnet 41

**22** Dumb swans, not chattering pies, do lovers
prove;
They love indeed who quake to say they
love.
*Astrophil and Stella* (1591) sonnet 54

**23** I am no pick-purse of another's wit.
*Astrophil and Stella* (1591) sonnet 74

**24** Highway, since you my chief Parnassus be.
*Astrophil and Stella* (1591) sonnet 84

**25** If thou praise not, all other praise is
shame.
*Astrophil and Stella* (1591) sonnet 90

**26** Poetry [is] a speaking picture, with this
end: to teach and delight.
*The Defence of Poetry* (1595)

**27** [The poet] cometh unto you, with a tale
which holdeth children from play, and old
men from the chimney corner.
*The Defence of Poetry* (1595)

**28** Comedy is an imitation of the common
errors of our life.
*The Defence of Poetry* (1595)

**29** Delight hath a joy in it either permanent
or present. Laughter hath only a scornful
tickling.
*The Defence of Poetry* (1595)

**30** Thy necessity is yet greater than mine.
On giving his water-bottle to a dying soldier
on the battle-field of Zutphen, 1586; in Sir
Fulke Greville *Life of Sir Philip Sidney* (1652)
ch. 12 (commonly quoted 'thy need is greater
than mine')

## Abbé Emmanuel Joseph Sieyès
1748–1836

1 *J'ai vécu.*
  I survived.
    When asked what he had done during the
    French Revolution. See F. Mignet *Notice
    historique sur la vie et les travaux de M. le Comte
    de Sieyès* (1836)

## Maurice Sigler 1901–61 and Al Hoffman 1902–60

2 Little man, you've had a busy day.
    Title of song (1934)

## Alan Sillitoe 1928–

3 The loneliness of the long-distance runner.
    Title of novel (1959)

## Georges Simenon 1903–89

4 Writing is not a profession but a vocation
  of unhappiness.
    Interview in *Paris Review* Summer 1955

## Paul Simon 1942–

5 Like a bridge over troubled water
  I will lay me down.
    'Bridge over Troubled Water' (1970 song)

6 And here's to you, Mrs Robinson
  Jesus loves you more than you will know.
    'Mrs Robinson' (1967 song, from the film *The
    Graduate*)

7 People talking without speaking
  People hearing without listening . . .
  'Fools,' said I, 'You do not know
  Silence like a cancer grows.'
    'Sound of Silence' (1964 song)

8 Improvisation is too good to leave to
  chance.
    In *Observer* 30 December 1990 'Sayings of the
    Year'

## Simonides *c.*556–468 BC

9 Go, tell the Spartans, thou who passest by,
  That here obedient to their laws we lie.
    In Herodotus *Histories* bk. 7, ch. 228
    (attributed)

## Harold Simpson

10 Down in the forest something stirred:
   It was only the note of a bird.
     'Down in the Forest' (1906 song)

## Kirke Simpson

11 [Warren] Harding of Ohio was chosen by
   a group of men in a smoke-filled room
   early today as Republican candidate for
   President.
     News report, filed 12 June 1920 (usually
     attributed to Harry Daugherty, one of
     Harding's supporters, who appears merely to
     have concurred with this version of events,
     when pressed for comment by Simpson). See
     W. Safire *New Language of Politics* (1968)

## N. F. Simpson 1919–

12 Knocked down a doctor? With an
   ambulance? How could she? It's
   a contradiction in terms.
     *One Way Pendulum* (1960) act 1

13 A problem left to itself dries up or goes
   rotten. But fertilize a problem with a
   solution—you'll hatch out dozens.
     *A Resounding Tinkle* (1958) act 1, sc. 1

## George R. Sims 1847–1922

14 It is Christmas Day in the Workhouse.
     'In the Workhouse—Christmas Day' (1879)

## C. H. Sisson 1914–

15 Here lies a civil servant. He was civil
   To everyone, and servant to the devil.
     In *The London Zoo* (1961) p. 29

## Dame Edith Sitwell 1887–1964

16 Jane, Jane,
   Tall as a crane,
   The morning light creaks down again.
     *Façade* (1923) 'Aubade'

17 The fire was furry as a bear.
     *Façade* (1923) 'Dark Song'

18 When
   Sir
   Beelzebub called for his syllabub in the
     hotel in Hell
   Where Proserpine first fell,
   Blue as the gendarmerie were the waves of
     the sea,
   (Rocking and shocking the barmaid).
     *Façade* (1923) 'Sir Beelzebub'

19 Still falls the Rain—
   Dark as the world of man, black as our
     loss—
   Blind as the nineteen hundred and forty
     nails
   Upon the Cross.
     'Still Falls the Rain' (1942)

20 Daisy and Lily,
   Lazy and silly,
   Walk by the shore of the wan grassy sea.
     'Waltz' (1948)

## Sir Osbert Sitwell 1892–1969

21 The British Bourgeoise
   Is not born,
   And does not die,
   But, if it is ill,
   It has a frightened look in its eyes.
     *At the House of Mrs Kinfoot* (1921) p. 8

22 In reality, killing time
   Is only the name for another of the
     multifarious ways
   By which Time kills us.
     'Milordo Inglese' (1958). Cf. 70:8

1 On the coast of Coromandel
Dance they to the tunes of Handel.
  'On the Coast of Coromandel' (1943)

## John Skelton c.1460–1529

2 With solace and gladness,
Much mirth and no madness,
All good and no badness;
So joyously,
So maidenly,
So womanly,
Her demeaning.
  *The Garland of Laurel* (1523) 'To Mistress
  Margaret Hussey'

3 ... Merry Margaret,
This midsummer flower,
Gentle as falcon
Or hawk of the tower.
  *The Garland of Laurel* (1523) 'To Mistress
  Margaret Hussey'

4 I blunder, I bluster, I blow, and I blother,
I make on the one day, and I mar on the
other.
  *Magnificence* (1530) l. 1037

## B. F. Skinner 1904–90

5 The real question is not whether machines
think but whether men do.
  *Contingencies of Reinforcement* (1969) ch. 9

6 Education is what survives when what has
been learned has been forgotten.
  *New Scientist* 21 May 1964

## Christopher Smart 1722–71

7 For I will consider my Cat Jeoffry.
For he is the servant of the Living God duly
and daily serving him.
  *Jubilate Agno* (*c*.1758–63) Fragment B, l. 695

8 For he counteracts the powers of darkness
by his electrical skin and glaring eyes.
For he counteracts the Devil, who is death,
by brisking about the life.
  *Jubilate Agno* (*c*.1758–63) Fragment B, l. 719

9 Nature's decorations glisten
Far above their usual trim;
Birds on box and laurels listen,
As so near the cherubs hymn.
  'The Nativity of Our Lord and Saviour Jesus
  Christ' (1765)

10 Strong is the lion—like a coal
His eye-ball—like a bastion's mole
His chest against his foes.
  *A Song to David* (1763) st. 76

11 And in the seat to faith assigned,
Where ask is have, where seek is find,
Where knock is open wide.
  *A Song to David* (1763) st. 77

12 Beauteous the garden's umbrage mild,
Walk, water, meditated wild,
And all the bloomy beds.
  *A Song to David* (1763) st. 78

13 Glorious the northern lights astream;
Glorious the song, when God's the theme;
Glorious the thunder's roar.
  *A Song to David* (1763) st. 85

14 And now the matchless deed's achieved,
Determined, dared, and done.
  *A Song to David* (1763) st. 86

## Elizabeth Smart 1913–86

15 By Grand Central Station I sat down and
wept.
  Title of book (1945). Cf. 69:2

## Samuel Smiles 1812–1904

16 We each day dig our graves with our teeth.
  *Duty* (1880) ch. 16

17 The spirit of self-help is the root of all
genuine growth in the individual.
  *Self-Help* (1859) ch. 1

18 The shortest way to do many things is to
do only one thing at once.
  *Self-Help* (1859) ch. 9

19 Cheerfulness gives elasticity to the spirit.
Spectres fly before it.
  *Self-Help* (1859) ch. 12

## Adam Smith 1723–90

20 And thus, *Place*, that great object which
divides the wives of aldermen, is the end of
half the labours of human life; and is the
cause of all the tumult and bustle, all the
rapine and injustice, which avarice and
ambition have introduced into this world.
  *Theory of Moral Sentiments* (1759) pt. 1, sect. 3,
  ch. 2

21 People of the same trade seldom meet
together, even for merriment and
diversion, but the conversation ends in a
conspiracy against the public, or in some
contrivance to raise prices.
  *Wealth of Nations* (1776) bk. 1, ch. 10, pt. 2

22 The chief enjoyment of riches consists in
the parade of riches.
  *Wealth of Nations* (1776) bk. 1, ch. 11

23 To found a great empire for the sole
purpose of raising up a people of
customers, may at first sight appear a
project fit only for a nation of shopkeepers.
It is, however, a project altogether unfit for
a nation of shopkeepers; but extremely fit
for a nation whose government is
influenced by shopkeepers.
  *Wealth of Nations* (1776) bk. 4, ch. 7, pt. 3.
  Cf. 2:7, 237:7

24 Consumption is the sole end and purpose
of production; and the interest of the
producer ought to be attended to only so
far as it may be necessary for promoting
that of the consumer.
  *Wealth of Nations* (1776) bk. 4, ch. 8

1 There is no art which one government
sooner learns of another than that of
draining money from the pockets of the
people.
*Wealth of Nations* (1776) bk. 5, ch. 2

## Alfred Emanuel Smith 1873–1944

2 All the ills of democracy can be cured by
more democracy.
Speech, 27 June 1933, in *New York Times*
28 June 1933

## Sir Cyril Smith 1928–

3 The longest running farce in the West End.
Of the House of Commons, in *Big Cyril* (1977)
ch. 8

## Dodie Smith 1896–1990

4 The family—that dear octopus from whose
tentacles we never quite escape.
*Dear Octopus* (1938) p. 120

## Edgar Smith 1857–1938

5 You may tempt the upper classes
With your villainous demi-tasses,
But; Heaven will protect a working-girl!
'Heaven Will Protect the Working-Girl' (1909
song)

## F. E. Smith (1st Earl of Birkenhead) 1872–1930

6 The world continues to offer glittering
prizes to those who have stout hearts and
sharp swords.
Rectorial Address, Glasgow University,
7 November 1923; in *The Times* 8 November
1923

7 JUDGE: You are extremely offensive, young
man.
SMITH: As a matter of fact, we both are, and
the only difference between us is that
I am trying to be, and you can't help it.
In 2nd Earl of Birkenhead *Earl of Birkenhead*
(1933) vol. 1, ch. 9

8 JUDGE DARLING: And who is George Robey?
SMITH: Mr George Robey is the Darling of
the music halls, m'lud.
In A. E. Wilson *The Prime Minister of Mirth*
(1956) ch. 1

## Ian Smith 1919–

9 I don't believe in black majority rule in
Rhodesia—not in a thousand years.
Broadcast speech, 20 March 1976, in *Sunday
Times* 21 March 1976

## Logan Pearsall Smith 1865–1946

10 There is more felicity on the far side of
baldness than young men can possibly
imagine.
*Afterthoughts* (1931) 'Age and Death'

11 The test of a vocation is the love of the
drudgery it involves.
*Afterthoughts* (1931) 'Art and Letters'

12 A best-seller is the gilded tomb of
a mediocre talent.
*Afterthoughts* (1931) 'Art and Letters'

13 People say that life is the thing, but
I prefer reading.
*Afterthoughts* (1931) 'Myself'

14 Most people sell their souls, and live with
a good conscience on the proceeds.
*Afterthoughts* (1931) 'Other People'

15 All Reformers, however strict their social
conscience, live in houses just as big as
they can pay for.
*Afterthoughts* (1931) 'Other People'

## Samuel Francis Smith 1808–95

16 My country, 'tis of thee,
Sweet land of liberty,
Of thee I sing.
'America' (1831)

## Stevie Smith 1902–71

17 Oh I am a cat that likes to
Gallop about doing good.
'The Galloping Cat' (1972)

18 A good time was had by all.
Title of book (1937)

19 I was much too far out all my life
And not waving but drowning.
'Not Waving but Drowning' (1957)

20 Private Means is dead
God rest his soul, officers and fellow-
rankers said.
'Private Means is Dead' (1962)

21 This Englishwoman is so refined
She has no bosom and no behind.
'This Englishwoman' (1937)

22 If there wasn't death, I think you couldn't
go on.
In *Observer* 9 November 1969, p. 21

## Revd Sydney Smith 1771–1845

23 A Curate—there is something which
excites compassion in the very name of a
Curate!!!
'Persecuting Bishops' in *Edinburgh Review*
(1822)

24 What bishops like best in their clergy is a
dropping-down-deadness of manner.
*Works* (1859) vol. 2 'First Letter to
Archdeacon Singleton, 1837' p. 271 n.

25 I have no relish for the country; it is a kind
of healthy grave.
Letter to Miss G. Harcourt, 1838, in *Letters of
Sydney Smith* (1953)

26 That knuckle-end of England—that land of
Calvin, oat-cakes, and sulphur.
In Lady Holland *Memoir* (1855) vol. 1, ch. 2 (of
Scotland)

1 Take short views, hope for the best, and trust in God.

   In Lady Holland *Memoir* (1855) vol. 1, ch. 6

2 No furniture so charming as books.

   In Lady Holland *Memoir* (1855) vol. 1, ch. 9. Cf. 254:25

3 Not body enough to cover his mind decently with; his intellect is improperly exposed.

   In Lady Holland *Memoir* (1855) vol. 1, ch. 9

4 As the French say, there are three sexes—men, women, and clergymen.

   In Lady Holland *Memoir* (1855) vol. 1, ch. 9

5 My definition of marriage ... it resembles a pair of shears, so joined that they cannot be separated; often moving in opposite directions, yet always punishing anyone who comes between them.

   In Lady Holland *Memoir* (1855) vol. 1, ch. 11

6 He [Macaulay] has occasional flashes of silence, that make his conversation perfectly delightful.

   In Lady Holland *Memoir* (1855) vol. 1, ch. 11

7 Serenely full, the epicure would say,
   Fate cannot harm me, I have dined to-day.

   In Lady Holland *Memoir* (1855) vol. 1, ch. 11 'Receipt for a Salad'

8 Deserves to be preached to death by wild curates.

   In Lady Holland *Memoir* (1855) vol. 1, ch. 11

9 I never read a book before reviewing it; it prejudices a man so.

   In H. Pearson *The Smith of Smiths* (1934) ch. 3

10 Minorities ... are almost always in the right.

   In H. Pearson *The Smith of Smiths* (1934) ch. 9

11 My idea of heaven is, eating *pâté de foie gras* to the sound of trumpets.

   In H. Pearson *The Smith of Smiths* (1934) ch. 10

12 What a pity it is that we have no amusements in England but vice and religion!

   In H. Pearson *The Smith of Smiths* (1934) ch. 10

13 What two ideas are more inseparable than Beer and Britannia?

   In H. Pearson *The Smith of Smiths* (1934) ch. 11

14 I am just going to pray for you at St Paul's, but with no very lively hope of success.

   In H. Pearson *The Smith of Smiths* (1934) ch. 13

## Walter Chalmers Smith
### 1824–1908

15 Unresting, unhasting, and silent as light,
   Nor wanting, nor wasting, thou rulest in might.

   'Immortal, invisible, God only wise' (1867 hymn)

## Tobias Smollett 1721–71

16 What you imagine to be the new light of grace, (said his master) I take to be a deceitful vapour, glimmering through a crack in your upper storey.

   *Humphry Clinker* (1771) vol. 2 (letter from Jery Melford, 10 June)

17 That great Cham of literature, Samuel Johnson.

   Letter to John Wilkes, 16 March 1759, in James Boswell *Life of Samuel Johnson* (1934 ed.) vol. 1

## C. P. Snow 1905–80

18 The official world, the corridors of power.

   *Homecomings* (1956) ch. 22

19 The two cultures and the scientific revolution.

   Title of The Rede Lecture (1959)

## Socrates 469–399 BC

20 How many things I can do without!

   On looking at a multitude of wares exposed for sale, in Diogenes Laertius *Lives of the Philosophers* bk. 2, sect. 25

21 I know nothing except the fact of my ignorance.

   In Diogenes Laertius *Lives of the Philosophers* bk. 2, sect. 32

22 The unexamined life is not worth living.

   In Plato *Apology* 38a

23 It is never right to do wrong or to requite wrong with wrong, or when we suffer evil to defend ourselves by doing evil in return.

   In Plato *Crito* 49d

24 But, my dearest Agathon, it is truth which you cannot contradict; you can without any difficulty contradict Socrates.

   In Plato *Symposium* 201d

25 Crito, we owe a cock to Aesculapius; please pay it and don't forget it.

   Last words, in Plato *Phaedo* 118

## Solon c.640–after 556 BC

26 I grow old ever learning many things.

   T. Bergk (ed.) *Poetae Lyrici Graeci* (1843) no. 18

27 Call no man happy before he dies, he is at best but fortunate.

   In Herodotus *Histories* bk. 1, ch. 32. Cf. 48:1

## Alexander Solzhenitsyn 1918–

28 You only have power over people as long as you don't take *everything* away from them. But when you've robbed a man of *everything* he's no longer in your power—he's free again.

   *The First Circle* (1968) ch. 17

1 The thoughts of a prisoner—they're not
free either. They keep returning to the
same things.
*One Day in the Life of Ivan Denisovich* (1962)
p. 34 (tr. R. Parker)

## William Somerville 1675–1742

2 The chase, the sport of kings;
Image of war, without its guilt.
*The Chase* (1735) bk. 1, l. 14. Cf. 319:8

3 Hail, happy Britain! highly favoured isle,
And Heaven's peculiar care!
*The Chase* (1735) bk. 1, l. 84

## Anastasio Somoza 1925–80

4 You won the elections, but I won the count.
Replying to an accusation of ballot-rigging,
in *Guardian* 17 June 1977. Cf. 317:28

## Stephen Sondheim 1930–

5 Everything's coming up roses.
*Title of song* (1959)

6 Ev'ry day a little death
On the lips and in the eyes,
In the murmurs, in the pauses,
In the gestures, in the sighs.
'Every Day a Little Death' (1973 song)

7 Isn't it rich?
Are we a pair?
Me here at last on the ground, you in mid-
air.
'Send in the Clowns' (1973 song)

8 I like to be in America!
OK by me in America!
Ev'rything free in America
For a small fee in America!
'America' (1957 song)

## Susan Sontag 1933–

9 Interpretation is the revenge of the
intellect upon art.
*Evergreen Review* December 1964

10 Illness is the night-side of life, a more
onerous citizenship. Everyone who is born
holds dual citizenship, in the kingdom of
the well and in the kingdom of the sick.
*New York Review of Books* 26 January 1978

## Lord Soper 1903–

11 It is, I think, good evidence of life after
death.
On the quality of debate in the House of
Lords, in *Listener* 17 August 1978

## Sophocles c.496–406 BC

12 There are many wonderful things, and
nothing is more wonderful than man.
*Antigone* l. 333

13 Not to be born is, past all prizing, best.
*Oedipus Coloneus* l. 1225 (tr. R. C. Jebb)

14 Someone asked Sophocles, 'How is your
sex-life now? Are you still able to have a
woman?' He replied, 'Hush, man; most
gladly indeed am I rid of it all, as though I
had escaped from a mad and savage
master.'
In Plato *Republic* bk. 1, 329b

## Charles Hamilton Sorley
1895–1915

15 We swing ungirded hips,
And lightened are our eyes,
The rain is on our lips,
We do not run for prize.
'Song of the Ungirt Runners' (1916)

16 When you see millions of the mouthless
dead
Across your dreams in pale battalions go,
Say not soft things as other men have said,
That you'll remember. For you need not so.
Give them not praise. For, deaf, how
should they know
It is not curses heaped on each gashed
head?
'A Sonnet' (1916)

## John L. B. Soule 1815–91

17 Go West, young man, go West!
*Terre Haute* [Indiana] *Express* (1851) editorial.
Cf. 157:20

## Robert Southey 1774–1843

18 It was a summer evening,
Old Kaspar's work was done,
And he before his cottage door
Was sitting in the sun.
'The Battle of Blenheim' (1800)

19 Now tell us all about the war,
And what they fought each other for.
'The Battle of Blenheim' (1800)

20 'And everybody praised the Duke,
Who this great fight did win.'
'But what good came of it at last?'
Quoth little Peterkin.
'Why that I cannot tell,' said he,
'But 'twas a famous victory.'
'The Battle of Blenheim' (1800)

21 Curses are like young chickens, they
always come home to roost.
*The Curse of Kehama* (1810) motto

22 No stir in the air, no stir in the sea,
The ship was still as she could be.
'The Inchcape Rock'

23 My name is Death: the last best friend
am I.
'The Lay of the Laureate' (1816) st. 87

24 We wage no war with women nor with
priests.
*Madoc* (1805) pt. 1, canto 15 'The
Excommunication' l. 65

1 You are old, Father William, the young
man cried,
The few locks which are left you are grey;
You are hale, Father William, a hearty old
man,
Now tell me the reason, I pray.
'The Old Man's Comforts' (1799). Cf. 91:4

2 In the days of my youth I remembered my
God!
And He hath not forgotten my age.
'The Old Man's Comforts' (1799)

3 The arts babblative and scribblative.
Colloquies on the Progress and Prospects of Society
(1829) no. 10, pt. 2

4 The march of intellect.
Colloquies on the Progress and Prospects of Society
(1829) no. 14

5 Men started at the intelligence, and turned
pale, as if they had heard of the loss of a
dear friend.
The Life of Nelson (1813) ch. 9 (on Nelson's
death)

6 She has made me in love with a cold
climate, and frost and snow, with a
northern moonlight.
On Mary Wollstonecraft's letters from
Sweden and Norway; letter, 28 April 1797, in
Charles Southey Life and Correspondence of
Robert Southey vol. 1 (1849)

## Robert Southwell c.1561–95

7 Man's mind a mirror is of heavenly sights,
A brief wherein all marvels summèd lie.
'Look Home' (1595)

8 Good is best when soonest wrought,
Lingered labours come to naught.
'Loss in Delays' (1595)

9 Times go by turns, and chances change by
course,
From foul to fair, from better hap to
worse.
'Times go by Turns' (1595). Cf. 14:2

## Muriel Spark 1918–

10 The one certain way for a woman to hold a
man is to leave him for religion.
The Comforters (1957) ch. 1

11 I am putting old heads on your young
shoulders … all my pupils are the crème
de la crème.
The Prime of Miss Jean Brodie (1961) ch. 1

12 Give me a girl at an impressionable age,
and she is mine for life.
The Prime of Miss Jean Brodie (1961) ch. 1.
Cf. 7:10

13 One's prime is elusive. You little girls,
when you grow up, must be on the alert to
recognise your prime at whatever time of
your life it may occur.
The Prime of Miss Jean Brodie (1961) ch. 1

## John Sparrow 1906–92

14 That indefatigable and unsavoury engine of
pollution, the dog.
Letter to The Times 30 September 1975

## Herbert Spencer 1820–1903

15 Science is organized knowledge.
Education (1861) ch. 2

16 People are beginning to see that the first
requisite to success in life is to be a good
animal.
Education (1861) ch. 2

17 Survival of the fittest implies
multiplication of the fittest.
Principles of Biology (1865) pt. 3, ch. 12,
sect. 164

18 How often misused words generate
misleading thoughts.
Principles of Ethics (1879) bk. 1, pt. 2, ch. 8,
sect. 152

19 Progress, therefore, is not an accident, but
a necessity … It is a part of nature.
Social Statics (1850) pt. 1, ch. 2, sect. 4

20 A clever theft was praiseworthy amongst
the Spartans; and it is equally so amongst
Christians, provided it be on a sufficiently
large scale.
Social Statics (1850) pt. 2, ch. 16, sect. 3

21 No one can be perfectly free till all are
free; no one can be perfectly moral till all
are moral; no one can be perfectly happy
till all are happy.
Social Statics (1850) pt. 4, ch. 30, sect. 16
See also CHARLES ROUPELL

## Raine, Countess Spencer 1929–

22 Alas, for our towns and cities. Monstrous
carbuncles of concrete have erupted in
gentle Georgian Squares.
The Spencers on Spas (1983) p. 14. Cf. 95:8

## Stephen Spender 1909–

23 After the first powerful plain manifesto
The black statement of pistons, without
more fuss
But gliding like a queen, she leaves the
station.
'The Express' (1933)

24 Born of the sun they travelled a short
while towards the sun,
And left the vivid air signed with their
honour.
'I think continually of those who were truly
great' (1933)

25 My parents kept me from children who
were rough
And who threw words like stones and who
wore torn clothes.
'My parents kept me from children who
were rough' (1933)

1 Never being, but always at the edge of
Being.
Title of poem (1933)

2 Hearts wound up with love, like little
watch springs.
'The Past Values' (1939)

3 Pylons, those pillars
Bare like nude, giant girls that have no
secret.
'The Pylons' (1933)

## Edmund Spenser c.1552–99

4 Vain man, said she, that dost in vain assay,
A mortal thing so to immortalize.
*Amoretti* (1595) sonnet 75

5 Wake now, my love, awake; for it is time.
The rosy morn long since left Tithones bed,
All ready to her silver coach to climb,
And Phoebus gins to shew his glorious
head.
'Epithalamion' (1595) l. 74

6 Ah! when will this long weary day have
end,
And lend me leave to come unto my love?
'Epithalamion' (1595) l. 278

7 A gentle knight was pricking on the plain.
*The Faerie Queen* (1596) bk. 1, canto 1, st. 1

8 A bold bad man, that dared to call by name
Great Gorgon, Prince of darkness and dead
night.
*The Faerie Queen* (1596) bk. 1, canto 1, st. 37.
Cf. 280:15

9 Sleep after toil, port after stormy seas,
Ease after war, death after life does greatly
please.
*The Faerie Queen* (1596) bk. 1, canto 9, st. 40

10 So double was his pains, so double be his
praise.
*The Faerie Queen* (1596) bk. 2, canto 2, st. 25

11 And all for love, and nothing for reward.
*The Faerie Queen* (1596) bk. 2, canto 8, st. 2

12 Gather therefore the rose, whilst yet is
prime,
For soon comes age, that will her pride
deflower.
*The Faerie Queen* (1596) bk. 2, canto 12, st. 75

13 And painful pleasure turns to pleasing
pain.
*The Faerie Queen* (1596) bk. 3, canto 10, st. 60

14 Be bold, be bold, and everywhere Be bold.
*The Faerie Queen* (1596) bk. 3, canto 11, st. 54

15 O sacred hunger of ambitious minds.
*The Faerie Queen* (1596) bk. 5, canto 12, st. 1

16 Of such deep learning little had he need,
Ne yet of Latin, ne of Greek that breed
Doubts 'mongst Divines, and difference of
texts,
From whence arise diversity of sects,
And hateful heresies.
'Prosopopoia or Mother Hubbard's Tale'
(1591) l. 385

17 With that, I saw two swans of goodly hue,
Come softly swimming down along the
Lee.
*Prothalamion* (1596) l. 37

18 Sweet Thames, run softly, till I end my
song.
*Prothalamion* (1596) l. 54

19 Uncouth unkist, said the old famous poet
Chaucer.
*The Shepherd's Calendar* (1579) 'Letter to
Gabriel Harvey'

20 So now they have made our English tongue
a gallimaufry or hodgepodge of all other
speeches.
*The Shepherd's Calendar* (1579) 'Letter to
Gabriel Harvey'

## Steven Spielberg 1947–

21 Close encounters of the third kind.
Title of film (1977)

## Baruch Spinoza 1632–77

22 *Deus, sive Natura.*
God, or in other words, Nature.
*Ethics* (1677) pt. 1, para. 6

23 I have striven not to laugh at human
actions, not to weep at them, nor to hate
them, but to understand them.
*Tractatus Politicus* (1677) ch. 1, sect. 4

## Revd W. A. Spooner 1844–1930

24 Mr Huxley assures me that it's no farther
from the north coast of Spitzbergen to the
North Pole than it is from Land's End to
John of Gaunt.
Quoted by Julian Huxley in *SEAC* (Calcutta)
27 February 1944

25 You will find as you grow older that the
weight of rages will press harder and
harder upon the employer.
In William Hayter *Spooner* (1977) ch. 6

## Sir Cecil Spring-Rice 1859–1918

26 I vow to thee, my country—all earthly
things above—
Entire and whole and perfect, the service
of my love,
The love that asks no question: the love
that stands the test,
That lays upon the altar the dearest and
the best:
The love that never falters, the love that
pays the price,
The love that makes undaunted the final
sacrifice.
'I Vow to Thee, My Country' (written on the
eve of his departure from Washington,
12 January 1918)

27 Her ways are ways of gentleness and all
her paths are Peace.
'I Vow to Thee, My Country' (1918). Cf. 43:9

**1** I am the Dean of Christ Church, Sir:
There's my wife; look well at her.
She's the Broad and I'm the High;
We are the University.

> *The Masque of Balliol* (1870) in W. G. Hiscock
> (ed.) *The Balliol Rhymes* (1939) p. 29
> (unofficially altered to 'I am the Dean, and
> this is Mrs Liddell; / She the first, and I the
> second fiddle'). Cf. 9:12, 32:6

## C. H. Spurgeon 1834–92

**2** It is well said in the old proverb, 'a lie will
go round the world while truth is pulling
its boots on'.

> *Gems from Spurgeon* (1859) p. 74

## Sir J. C. Squire 1884–1958

**3** I'm not so think as you drunk I am.
> 'Ballade of Soporific Absorption' (1931)

**4** It did not last: the Devil howling 'Ho!
Let Einstein be!' restored the status quo.
> 'In continuation of Pope on Newton' (1926).
> Cf. 251:26

## Mme de Staël 1766–1817

**5** *Tout comprendre rend très indulgent.*
To be totally understanding makes one
very indulgent.

> *Corinne* (1807) bk. 18, ch. 5

**6** A man can brave opinion, a woman must
submit to it.

> *Delphine* (1802) epigraph

**7** Speech happens not to be his language.
> On being asked what she found to talk
> about with her new lover, a hussar
> (attributed)

## Joseph Stalin 1879–1953

**8** The Pope! How many divisions has *he* got?
> On being asked to encourage Catholicism in
> Russia by way of conciliating the Pope,
> 13 May 1935; in W. S. Churchill *The Gathering
> Storm* (1948) ch. 8

## Sir Henry Morton Stanley 1841–1904

**9** Dr Livingstone, I presume?
> *How I found Livingstone* (1872) ch. 11

## Charles E. Stanton 1859–1933

**10** *Lafayette, nous voilà!*
Lafayette, we are here.
> At the tomb of Lafayette in Paris, 4 July
> 1917; in *New York Tribune* 6 September 1917

## Frank L. Stanton 1857–1927

**11** Sweetes' li'l' feller,
Everybody knows;
Dunno what to call him,
But he's mighty lak' a rose!
> 'Mighty Lak' a Rose' (1901 song)

## John Stark 1728–1822

**12** We beat them to-day or Molly Stark's a
widow.
> Before the Battle of Bennington, 16 August
> 1777; in *Cyclopaedia of American Biography*
> vol. 5

## Christina Stead 1902–83

**13** A self-made man is one who believes in
luck and sends his son to Oxford.
> *House of All Nations* (1938) 'Credo'

## Sir Richard Steele 1672–1729

**14** The insupportable labour of doing nothing.
> *The Spectator* no. 54 (2 May 1711)

**15** A woman seldom writes her mind but in
her postscript.
> *The Spectator* no. 79 (31 May 1711). Cf. 24:19

**16** To love her is a liberal education.
> *The Tatler* no. 49 (2 August 1709); of Lady
> Elizabeth Hastings

**17** Reading is to the mind what exercise is to
the body.
> *The Tatler* no. 147 (18 March 1710)

**18** It was very prettily said, that we may learn
the little value of fortune by the persons
on whom heaven is pleased to bestow it.
> *The Tatler* no. 203 (27 July 1710)

## Lincoln Steffens 1866–1936

**19** I have seen the future; and it works.
> Following a visit to the Soviet Union in 1919,
> in *Letters* (1938) vol. 1, p. 463

## Gertrude Stein 1874–1946

**20** Remarks are not literature.
> *Autobiography of Alice B. Toklas* (1933) ch. 7

**21** Pigeons on the grass alas.
> *Four Saints in Three Acts* (1934) act 3, sc. 2

**22** Rose is a rose is a rose is a rose, is a rose.
> *Sacred Emily* (1913) p. 187

**23** You are all a lost generation.
> Of the young who served in the First World
> War; subsequently taken by Ernest
> Hemingway as epigraph to *The Sun Also Rises*
> (1926)

## John Steinbeck 1902–68

**24** Okie use' ta mean you was from
Oklahoma. Now it means you're a dirty
son-of-a-bitch. Okie means you're scum.
Don't mean nothing itself, it's the way they
say it.
> *The Grapes of Wrath* (1939) ch. 18

## Gloria Steinem 1934–

**25** We are becoming the men we wanted to
marry.
> *Ms* July/August 1982

1 Outrageous acts and everyday rebellions.
   Title of book (1983)

2 A woman without a man is like a fish
   without a bicycle.
   Attributed

## Stendhal 1783–1842

3 A novel is a mirror which passes over a
   highway. Sometimes it reflects to your eyes
   the blue of the skies, at others the
   churned-up mud of the road.
   *Le Rouge et le noir* (1830) bk. 2, ch. 19

## J. K. Stephen 1859–92

4 Two voices are there: one is of the deep . . .
   And one is of an old half-witted sheep
   Which bleats articulate monotony,
   And indicates that two and one are three.
   'A Sonnet' (1891); of Wordsworth. Cf. 357:6

5 When the Rudyards cease from kipling
   And the Haggards ride no more.
   'To R.K.' (1891)

## James Stephens 1882–1950

6 Finality is death. Perfection is finality.
   Nothing is perfect. There are lumps in it.
   *The Crock of Gold* (1912) bk. 1, ch. 4

7 I hear a sudden cry of pain!
   There is a rabbit in a snare:
   Now I hear the cry again,
   But I cannot tell from where . . .
   Little one! Oh, little one!
   I am searching everywhere.
   'The Snare' (1915)

## Laurence Sterne 1713–68

8 They order, said I, this matter better in
   France.
   *A Sentimental Journey* (1768) opening words

9 If ever I do a mean action, it must be in
   some interval betwixt one passion and
   another.
   *A Sentimental Journey* (1768) 'Montriul'

10 There are worse occupations in this world
   than feeling a woman's pulse.
   *A Sentimental Journey* (1768) 'The Pulse. Paris'

11 God tempers the wind, said Maria, to the
   shorn lamb.
   *A Sentimental Journey* (1768) 'Maria' (from a
   French proverb)

12 I wish either my father or my mother, or
   indeed both of them, as they were in duty
   both equally bound to it, had minded what
   they were about when they begot me.
   *Tristram Shandy* (1759–67) opening words

13 'Pray, my dear,' quoth my mother, 'have
   you not forgot to wind up the
   clock?'—'Good G—!' cried my father,
   making an exclamation, but taking care to
   moderate his voice at the same time,—'Did
   ever woman, since the creation of the
   world, interrupt a man with such a silly
   question?'
   *Tristram Shandy* (1759–67) bk. 1, ch. 1

14 'Tis known by the name of perseverance in
   a good cause,—and of obstinacy in a bad
   one.
   *Tristram Shandy* (1759–67) bk. 1, ch. 17

15 Digressions, incontestably, are the
   sunshine;—they are the life, the soul of
   reading.
   *Tristram Shandy* (1759–67) bk. 1, ch. 22

16 I should have no objection to this method,
   but that I think it must smell too strong of
   the lamp.
   *Tristram Shandy* (1759–67) bk. 1, ch. 23

17 Writing, when properly managed . . . is but
   a different name for conversation.
   *Tristram Shandy* (1759–67) bk. 2, ch. 11

18 It is the nature of an hypothesis, when
   once a man has conceived it, that it
   assimilates every thing to itself, as proper
   nourishment; and, from the first moment
   of your begetting it, it generally grows the
   stronger by every thing you see, hear, read,
   or understand.
   *Tristram Shandy* (1759–67) bk. 2, ch. 19

19 Is this a fit time, said my father to himself,
   to talk of Pensions and Grenadiers?
   *Tristram Shandy* (1759–67) bk. 4, ch. 5

20 'Tis better in battle than in bed,' said my
   uncle Toby.
   *Tristram Shandy* (1759–67) bk. 5, ch. 3

21 There is a North-west passage to the
   intellectual World.
   *Tristram Shandy* (1759–67) bk. 5, ch. 42

22 'The poor soul will die:—' 'He shall not die,
   by G—,' cried my uncle Toby.—The
   Accusing Spirit, which flew up to heaven's
   chancery with the oath, blushed as he gave
   it in;—and the Recording Angel, as he
   wrote it down, dropped a tear upon the
   word, and blotted it out for ever.
   *Tristram Shandy* (1759–67) bk. 6, ch. 8

23 My brother Toby, quoth she, is going to be
   married to Mrs Wadman.Then he will
   never, quoth my father, lie *diagonally* in his
   bed again as long as he lives.
   *Tristram Shandy* (1759–67) bk. 6, ch. 39

24 And who are you? said he.—Don't puzzle
   me, said I.
   *Tristram Shandy* (1759–67) bk. 7, ch. 33

25 'A soldier,' cried my Uncle Toby,
   interrupting the corporal, 'is no more
   exempt from saying a foolish thing, Trim,
   than a man of letters.'—'But not so often,
   an' please your honour,' replied the
   corporal.
   *Tristram Shandy* (1759–67) bk. 8, ch. 19

26 —d! said my mother, 'what is all this story
   about?'— 'A Cock and a Bull,' said Yorick.
   *Tristram Shandy* (1759–67) bk. 9, ch. 33

27 This sad vicissitude of things.
   *Sermons* (1767) no. 16 'The character of
   Shimei'

## Brooks Stevens

1 Our whole economy is based on planned obsolescence.
   In V. Packard *The Waste Makers* (1960) ch. 6

## Jocelyn Stevens 1932–

2 If I were a snob I wouldn't be living with Mrs Duffield, and Mrs Duffield has asked me to tell you that if I were a bore she wouldn't be living with me.
   Telephone conversation with the editor of the *Independent*, which had accused him of being a snob and a bore; in *Independent on Sunday* 15 November 1992, Review p. 3

## Wallace Stevens 1879–1955

3 The poet is the priest of the invisible.
   'Adagia' (1957)

4 Chieftain Iffucan of Azcan in caftan
   Of tan with henna hackles, halt!
   'Bantams in Pine Woods' (1923)

5 Call the roller of big cigars,
   The muscular one, and bid him whip
   In kitchen cups concupiscent curds.
   'The Emperor of Ice-Cream' (1923)

6 Let be be finale of seem.
   The only emperor is the emperor of ice-cream.
   'The Emperor of Ice-Cream' (1923)

7 Frogs Eat Butterflies. Snakes Eat Frogs. Hogs Eat Snakes. Men Eat Hogs.
   Title of poem (1923)

8 Poetry is the supreme fiction, madame.
   'A High-Toned old Christian Woman' (1923)

9 They said, 'You have a blue guitar,
   You do not play things as they are.'
   The man replied, 'Things as they are
   Are changed upon the blue guitar.'
   'The Man with the Blue Guitar' (1937)

10 Music is feeling, then, not sound.
   'Peter Quince at the Clavier' (1923) pt. 1

11 Beauty is momentary in the mind—
   The fitful tracing of a portal;
   But in the flesh it is immortal.
   The body dies; the body's beauty lives.
   'Peter Quince at the Clavier' (1923) pt. 4

12 Complacencies of the peignoir, and late
   Coffee and oranges in a sunny chair,
   And the green freedom of a cockatoo
   Upon a rug mingle to dissipate
   The holy hush of ancient sacrifice.
   'Sunday Morning' (1923) st. 1

13 I do not know which to prefer,
   The beauty of inflections
   Or the beauty of innuendoes,
   The blackbird whistling
   Or just after.
   'Thirteen Ways of Looking at a Blackbird' (1923)

## Adlai Stevenson 1900–65

14 I suppose flattery hurts no one, that is, if he doesn't inhale.
   Television broadcast, 30 March 1952, in N. F. Busch *Adlai E. Stevenson* (1952) ch. 5

15 If they [the Republicans] will stop telling lies about the Democrats, we will stop telling the truth about them.
   Speech during 1952 Presidential campaign; in J. B. Martin *Adlai Stevenson and Illinois* (1976) ch. 8

16 Let's talk sense to the American people. Let's tell them the truth, that there are no gains without pains.
   Speech of Acceptance at the Democratic National Convention, 26 July 1952; in *Speeches* (1952)

17 In America any boy may become President.
   Speech in Indianapolis, 26 September 1952; in *Major Campaign Speeches . . . 1952* (1953)

18 A free society is a society where it is safe to be unpopular.
   Speech in Detroit, 7 October 1952; in *Major Campaign Speeches . . . 1952* (1953)

19 The young man [Richard Nixon] who asks you to set him one heart-beat from the Presidency of the United States.
   Speech at Cleveland, Ohio, 23 October 1952, in *New York Times* 24 October 1952, p. 14 (commonly quoted 'just a heart-beat away . . . ')

20 We hear the Secretary of State boasting of his brinkmanship—the art of bringing us to the edge of the abyss.
   Speech in Hartford, Connecticut, 25 February 1956; in *New York Times* 26 February 1956, p. 64 (of John Foster Dulles)

21 She would rather light a candle than curse the darkness, and her glow has warmed the world.
   On learning of Eleanor Roosevelt's death; in *New York Times* 8 November 1962

## Anne Stevenson 1933–

22 Blackbirds are the cellos of the deep farms.
   'Green Mountain, Black Mountain' (1982)

## Robert Louis Stevenson 1850–94

23 Every one lives by selling something.
   *Across the Plains* (1892) 'Beggars' pt. 3

24 Politics is perhaps the only profession for which no preparation is thought necessary.
   *Familiar Studies of Men and Books* (1882) 'Yoshida-Torajiro'

25 Am I no a bonny fighter?
   *Kidnapped* (1886) ch. 10

26 I've a grand memory for forgetting, David.
   *Kidnapped* (1886) ch. 18

27 For my part, I travel not to go anywhere, but to go. I travel for travel's sake. The great affair is to move.
   *Travels with a Donkey* (1879) 'Cheylard and Luc'

1 If landscapes were sold, like the sheets of
characters of my boyhood, one penny plain
and twopence coloured, I should go the
length of twopence every day of my life.
*Travels with a Donkey* (1879) 'Father
Apollinaris'

2 Fifteen men on the dead man's chest
Yo-ho-ho, and a bottle of rum!
Drink and the devil had done for the rest—
Yo-ho-ho, and a bottle of rum!
*Treasure Island* (1883) ch. 1

3 Tip me the black spot.
*Treasure Island* (1883) ch. 3

4 Many's the long night I've dreamed of
cheese—toasted, mostly.
*Treasure Island* (1883) ch. 15

5 Old and young, we are all on our last
cruise.
*Virginibus Puerisque* (1881) 'Crabbed Age and
Youth'

6 To travel hopefully is a better thing than
to arrive, and the true success is to labour.
*Virginibus Puerisque* (1881) 'El Dorado'

7 Even if we take matrimony at its lowest,
even if we regard it as no more than a sort
of friendship recognised by the police.
*Virginibus Puerisque* (1881) title essay, pt. 1

8 Marriage is like life in this—that it is a
field of battle, and not a bed of roses.
*Virginibus Puerisque* (1881) title essay, pt. 1

9 The cruellest lies are often told in silence.
*Virginibus Puerisque* (1881) title essay, pt. 4

10 What hangs people . . . is the unfortunate
circumstance of guilt.
*The Wrong Box* (with Lloyd Osbourne, 1889)
ch. 7

11 Nothing like a little judicious levity.
*The Wrong Box* (with Lloyd Osbourne, 1889)
ch. 7

12 In winter I get up at night
And dress by yellow candle-light.
In summer, quite the other way,—
I have to go to bed by day.
*A Child's Garden of Verses* (1885) 'Bed in
Summer'

13 The world is so full of a number of things,
I'm sure we should all be as happy as
kings.
*A Child's Garden of Verses* (1885) 'Happy
Thought'

14 I was the giant great and still
That sits upon the pillow-hill,
And sees before him, dale and plain,
The pleasant land of counterpane.
*A Child's Garden of Verses* (1885) 'The Land of
Counterpane'

15 Let us arise and go like men,
And face with an undaunted tread
The long black passage up to bed.
*A Child's Garden of Verses* (1885) 'North-West
Passage. Good-Night'

16 A child should always say what's true,
And speak when he is spoken to,
And behave mannerly at table:
At least as far as he is able.
*A Child's Garden of Verses* (1885) 'Whole Duty
of Children'

17 Go, little book, and wish to all
Flowers in the garden, meat in the hall,
A bin of wine, a spice of wit,
A house with lawns enclosing it.
'Envoy' (1887). Cf. 96:20

18 In the highlands, in the country places,
Where the old plain men have rosy faces.
'In the highlands . . . ' (1896)

19 I will make you brooches and toys for your
delight
Of bird-song at morning and star-shine at
night.
'I will make you brooches . . . ' (1896)

20 Trusty, dusky, vivid, true,
With eyes of gold and bramble-dew,
Steel-true and blade-straight,
The great artificer
Made my mate.
'My Wife' (1896)

21 Under the wide and starry sky
Dig the grave and let me lie.
'Requiem' (1887)

22 Home is the sailor, home from sea,
And the hunter home from the hill.
'Requiem' (1887)

23 Sing me a song of a lad that is gone,
Say, could that lad be I?
Merry of soul he sailed on a day
Over the sea to Skye.
'Sing me a song of a lad that is gone' (1896)

24 Give to me the life I love,
Let the lave go by me,
Give the jolly heaven above
And the byway nigh me.
'The Vagabond' (1896)

25 Wealth I seek not, hope nor love,
Nor a friend to know me;
All I seek, the heaven above
And the road below me.
'The Vagabond' (1896)

## Joseph C. Stinson 1947–

26 Go ahead, make my day.
*Sudden Impact* (1983 film); spoken by Clint
Eastwood

## Samuel John Stone 1839–1900

27 The Church's one foundation
Is Jesus Christ, her Lord;
She is his new creation
By water and the word.
'The Church's one foundation' (1866 hymn)

## Tom Stoppard 1937–

28 It's not the voting that's democracy, it's
the counting.
*Jumpers* (1972) act 1. Cf. 311:4

1 The House of Lords, an illusion to which
I have never been able to subscribe—
responsibility without power, the
prerogative of the eunuch throughout the
ages.
*Lord Malquist and Mr Moon* (1966) pt. 6.
Cf. 198:5

2 I'm with you on the free press. It's the
newspapers I can't stand.
*Night and Day* (1978) act 1

3 Comment is free but facts are on expenses.
*Night and Day* (1978) act 2. Cf. 268:3

4 Eternity's a terrible thought. I mean,
where's it all going to end?
*Rosencrantz and Guildenstern are Dead* (1967)
act 2

5 The bad end unhappily, the good unluckily.
That is what tragedy means.
*Rosencrantz and Guildenstern are Dead* (1967)
act 2. Cf. 349:20

6 Life is a gamble at terrible odds—if it was
a bet, you wouldn't take it.
*Rosencrantz and Guildenstern are Dead* (1967)
act 3

7 War is capitalism with the gloves off.
*Travesties* (1975) act 1

## Harriet Beecher Stowe 1811–96

8 I s'pect I growed. Don't think nobody never
made me.
*Uncle Tom's Cabin* (1852) ch. 20 (Topsy)

## Lord Stowell 1745–1836

9 The elegant simplicity of the three per
cents.
In Lord Campbell *Lives of the Lord Chancellors*
(1857) vol. 10, ch. 212. Cf. 122:2

10 A precedent embalms a principle.
An opinion, while Advocate-General, 1788,
quoted by Disraeli in *Hansard* 22 February
1848, col. 1066

## Lytton Strachey 1880–1932

11 He was no striped frieze; he was shot silk.
*Elizabeth and Essex* (1928) ch. 5 (of Francis
Bacon)

12 The time was out of joint, and he was only
too delighted to have been born to set it
right.
*Eminent Victorians* (1918) 'Cardinal Manning'
pt. 2 (of Hurrell Froude). Cf. 275:6

13 Her conception of God was certainly not
orthodox. She felt towards Him as she
might have felt towards a glorified sanitary
engineer; and in some of her speculations
she seems hardly to distinguish between
the Deity and the Drains.
*Eminent Victorians* (1918) 'Florence
Nightingale' pt. 4

14 [CHAIRMAN OF MILITARY TRIBUNAL:] What
would you do if you saw a German
soldier trying to violate your sister?
[STRACHEY:] I would try to get between
them.
In Robert Graves *Good-bye to All That* (1929)
ch. 23 (otherwise rendered 'I should
interpose my body')

15 Discretion is not the better part of
biography.
In M. Holroyd *Lytton Strachey* vol. 1 (1967)
preface

16 If this is dying, then I don't think much of
it.
On his deathbed; in M. Holroyd *Lytton
Strachey* vol. 2 (1968) pt. 2, ch. 6

## Jan Struther 1901–53

17 Lord of all hopefulness, Lord of all joy,
Whose trust, ever childlike, no cares could
destroy,
Be there at our waking, and give us, we
pray,
Your bliss in our hearts, Lord, at the break
of the day.
'All Day Hymn' (1931)

## G. A. Studdert Kennedy 1883–1929

18 Waste of Blood, and waste of Tears,
Waste of youth's most precious years,
Waste of ways the saints have trod,
Waste of Glory, waste of God,
War!
*More Rough Rhymes of a Padre* by 'Woodbine
Willie' (1919) 'Waste'

19 When Jesus came to Birmingham they
simply passed Him by,
They never hurt a hair of Him, they only
let Him die.
*Peace Rhymes of a Padre* (1921) 'Indifference'

## Sir John Suckling 1609–42

20 Why so pale and wan, fond lover?
Prithee, why so pale?
Will, when looking well can't move her,
Looking ill prevail?
*Aglaura* (1637) act 4, sc. 1 'Song'

21 Her feet beneath her petticoat,
Like little mice, stole in and out,
As if they feared the light.
'A Ballad upon a Wedding' (1646) st. 8

22 Love is the fart
Of every heart:
It pains a man when 'tis kept close,
And others doth offend, when 'tis let loose.
'Love's Offence' (1646)

23 Sure beauty's empires, like to greater
states,
Have certain periods set, and hidden fates.
'Sonnet' (1646)

## Louis Henri Sullivan 1856–1924

1 Form follows function.
*The Tall Office Building Artistically Considered*
(1896)

## Terry Sullivan

2 She sells sea-shells on the sea-shore,
The shells she sells are sea-shells, I'm sure,
For if she sells sea-shells on the sea-shore,
Then I'm sure she sells sea-shore shells.
'She Sells Sea-Shells' (1908 song)

*See also* HARRY BEDFORD and TERRY SULLIVAN

## Maximilien de Béthune, Duc de Sully 1559–1641

3 *Labourage et pâturage sont les deux mamelles*
*dont la France est alimenteé.*
Tilling and grazing are the two breasts by
which France is fed.
*Mémoires* (1638) pt. 1, ch. 15

4 The English take their pleasures sadly after
the fashion of their country.
Attributed

## Edith Summerskill 1901–80

5 Nagging is the repetition of unpalatable
truths.
Speech to the Married Women's Association,
14 July 1960; in *The Times* 15 July 1960

## Henry Howard, Earl of Surrey
*c.*1517–47

6 Martial, the things for to attain
The happy life be these, I find:
The riches left, not got with pain;
The fruitful ground, the quiet mind.
'The Happy Life' (1547); translation of
Martial *Epigrams* bk. 10, no. 47

## R. S. Surtees 1805–64

7 The only infallible rule we know is, that
the man who is always talking about being
a gentleman never is one.
*Ask Mamma* (1858) ch. 1

8 'Unting is all that's worth living for—all
time is lost wot is not spent in 'unting—it
is like the hair we breathe—if we have it
not we die—it's the sport of kings, the
image of war without its guilt, and only
five-and-twenty per cent of its danger.
*Handley Cross* (1843) ch. 7. Cf. 311:2

9 I'll fill hup the chinks wi' cheese.
*Handley Cross* (1843) ch. 15

10 It ar'n't that I loves the fox less, but that I
loves the 'ound more.
*Handley Cross* (1843) ch. 16

11 Three things I never lends—my 'oss, my
wife, and my name.
*Hillingdon Hall* (1845) ch. 33

12 Better be killed than frightened to death.
*Mr Facey Romford's Hounds* (1865) ch. 32

13 Life would be very pleasant if it were not
for its enjoyments.
*Mr Facey Romford's Hounds* (1865) ch. 32.
Cf. 206:15

14 Everyone knows that the real business of a
ball is either to look out for a wife, to look
after a wife, or to look after somebody
else's wife.
*Mr Facey Romford's Hounds* (1865) ch. 56

15 He was a gentleman who was generally
spoken of as having nothing a-year, paid
quarterly.
*Mr Sponge's Sporting Tour* (1853) ch. 24

## Hannen Swaffer 1879–1962

16 Freedom of the press in Britain means
freedom to print such of the proprietor's
prejudices as the advertisers don't object
to.
In Tom Driberg *Swaff* (1974) ch. 2

## Jonathan Swift 1667–1745

17 Satire is a sort of glass, wherein beholders
do generally discover everybody's face but
their own.
*The Battle of the Books* (1704) preface

18 Instead of dirt and poison we have rather
chosen to fill our hives with honey and
wax; thus furnishing mankind with the
two noblest of things, which are sweetness
and light.
*The Battle of the Books* (1704). Cf. 17:25

19 Laws are like cobwebs, which may catch
small flies, but let wasps and hornets
break through.
*A Critical Essay upon the Faculties of the Mind*
(1709). Cf. 5:9

20 I have heard of a man who had a mind to
sell his house, and therefore carried a
piece of brick in his pocket, which he
showed as a pattern to encourage
purchasers.
*The Drapier's Letters* (1724) no. 2

21 And he gave it for his opinion, that
whoever could make two ears of corn or
two blades of grass to grow upon a spot of
ground where only one grew before, would
deserve better of mankind, and do more
essential service to his country than the
whole race of politicians put together.
*Gulliver's Travels* (1726) 'A Voyage to
Brobdingnag' ch. 7

22 He had been eight years upon a project for
extracting sun-beams out of cucumbers,
which were to be put into vials
hermetically sealed, and let out to warm
the air in raw inclement summers.
*Gulliver's Travels* (1726) 'A Voyage to Laputa,
etc.' ch. 5

1 He replied that I must needs be mistaken,
   or that I *said the thing which was not*. (For
   they have no word in their language to
   express lying or falsehood.)
   *Gulliver's Travels* (1726) 'A Voyage to the
   Houyhnhnms' ch. 3

2 We are so fond of one another, because
   our ailments are the same.
   *Journal to Stella* (in *Works*, 1768) 1 February
   1711

3 Will she pass in a crowd? Will she make a
   figure in a country church?
   *Journal to Stella* (in *Works*, 1768) 9 February
   1711

4 Proper words in proper places, make the
   true definition of a style.
   *Letter to a Young Gentleman lately entered into
   Holy Orders* (9 January 1720)

5 Not die here in a rage, like a poisoned rat
   in a hole.
   Letter to Bolingbroke, 21 March 1730, in H.
   Williams (ed.) *Correspondence of Jonathan Swift*
   vol. 3 (1963)

6 Surely mortal man is a broomstick!
   *A Meditation upon a Broomstick* (1710)

7 She wears her clothes, as if they were
   thrown on her with a pitchfork.
   *Polite Conversation* (1738) Dialogue 1

8 I always love to begin a journey on
   Sundays, because I shall have the prayers
   of the church, to preserve all that travel by
   land, or by water.
   *Polite Conversation* (1738) Dialogue 2

9 I never saw, heard, nor read, that the
   clergy were beloved in any nation where
   Christianity was the religion of the
   country. Nothing can render them popular,
   but some degree of persecution.
   *Thoughts on Religion* (1765)

10 We have just enough religion to make us
    hate, but not enough to make us love one
    another.
    *Thoughts on Various Subjects* (1711)

11 When a true genius appears in the world,
    you may know him by this sign, that the
    dunces are all in confederacy against him.
    *Thoughts on Various Subjects* (1711)

12 The stoical scheme of supplying our wants,
    by lopping off our desires, is like cutting
    off our feet when we want shoes.
    *Thoughts on Various Subjects* (1711)

13 Every man desires to live long; but no man
    would be old.
    *Thoughts on Various Subjects* (1727 ed.)

14 A coming shower your shooting corns
    presage.
    'A Description of a City Shower' (1710) l. 9

15 How haughtily he lifts his nose,
    To tell what every schoolboy knows.
    'The Journal' (1727) l. 81

16 Convey a libel in a frown,
    And wink a reputation down.
    'The Journal of a Modern Lady' (1729) l. 192

17 Hail, fellow, well met,
    All dirty and wet:
    Find out, if you can,
    Who's master, who's man.
    'My Lady's Lamentation' (written 1728) l. 165

18 Philosophy! the lumber of the schools.
    'Ode to Sir W. Temple' (written 1692)

19 Say, Britain, could you ever boast,—
    Three poets in an age at most?
    Our chilling climate hardly bears
    A sprig of bays in fifty years.
    'On Poetry' (1733) l. 5

20 As learned commentators view
    In Homer more than Homer knew.
    'On Poetry' (1733) l. 103

21 So geographers, in Afric-maps,
    With savage-pictures fill their gaps;
    And o'er unhabitable downs
    Place elephants for want of towns.
    'On Poetry' (1733) l. 177

22 Hobbes clearly proves, that every creature
    Lives in a state of war by nature.
    'On Poetry' (1733) l. 319

23 So, naturalists observe, a flea
    Hath smaller fleas that on him prey;
    And these have smaller fleas to bite 'em,
    And so proceed *ad infinitum*.
    Thus every poet, in his kind,
    Is bit by him that comes behind.
    'On Poetry' (1733) l. 337

24 Yet malice never was his aim;
    He lashed the vice, but spared the name;
    No individual could resent,
    Where thousands equally were meant.
    'Verses on the Death of Dr Swift' (1731)
    l. 512. Cf. 250:25

25 Good God! what a genius I had when I
    wrote that book.
    Of *A Tale of a Tub*, in Sir Walter Scott (ed.)
    *Works of Swift* (1814) vol. 1, p. 90

26 I shall be like that tree, I shall die at the
    top.
    In Sir Walter Scott (ed.) *Works of Swift* (1814)
    vol. 1, p. 443

27 *Ubi saeva indignatio ulterius cor lacerare
    nequit.*
    Where fierce indignation can no longer
    tear his heart.
    Swift's epitaph. See S. Leslie *The Skull of Swift*
    (1928) ch. 15

## Algernon Charles Swinburne
1837–1909

28 Maiden, and mistress of the months and
    stars
    Now folded in the flowerless fields of
    heaven.
    *Atalanta in Calydon* (1865) l. 1

1 When the hounds of spring are on winter's
  traces,
  The mother of months in meadow or plain
  Fills the shadows and windy places
  With lisp of leaves and ripple of rain;
  And the brown bright nightingale amorous
  Is half assuaged for Itylus,
  For the Thracian ships and the foreign
  faces,
  The tongueless vigil and all the pain.
  *Atalanta in Calydon* (1865) chorus 'When the
  hounds of spring'

2 For winter's rains and ruins are over,
  And all the season of snows and sins;
  The days dividing lover and lover,
  The light that loses, the night that wins;
  And time remembered is grief forgotten,
  And frosts are slain and flowers begotten,
  And in green underwood and cover
  Blossom by blossom the spring begins.
  *Atalanta in Calydon* (1865) chorus 'When the
  hounds of spring'

3 Before the beginning of years
  There came to the making of man
  Time with a gift of tears,
  Grief with a glass that ran.
  *Atalanta in Calydon* (1865) chorus 'Before the
  beginning of years'

4 The deep division of prodigious breasts,
  The solemn slope of mighty limbs asleep.
  'Ave atque Vale' (1878) st. 6

5 Villon, our sad bad glad mad brother's
  name.
  'Ballad of François Villon' (1878)

6 We shift and bedeck and bedrape us,
  Thou art noble and nude and antique.
  'Dolores' (1866) st. 7

7             Change in a trice
  The lilies and languors of virtue
  For the raptures and roses of vice.
  'Dolores' (1866) st. 9

8 O splendid and sterile Dolores,
  Our Lady of Pain.
  'Dolores' (1866) st. 9

9 No thorns go as deep as a rose's,
  And love is more cruel than lust.
  'Dolores' (1866) st. 20

10 As a god self-slain on his own strange
   altar,
   Death lies dead.
   'A Forsaken Garden' (1878)

11 Glory to Man in the highest! for Man is the
   master of things.
   'Hymn of Man' (1871)

12 Yea, is not even Apollo, with hair and
   harpstring of gold,
   A bitter God to follow, a beautiful God to
   behold?
   'Hymn to Proserpine' (1866)

13 Thou hast conquered, O pale Galilean; the
   world has grown grey from Thy breath;
   We have drunken of things Lethean, and
   fed on the fullness of death.
   'Hymn to Proserpine' (1866). Cf. 188:20

14 And the best and the worst of this is
   That neither is most to blame,
   If you have forgotten my kisses
   And I have forgotten your name.
   'An Interlude' (1866)

15 Swallow, my sister, O sister swallow,
   How can thine heart be full of the spring?
   A thousand summers are over and dead.
   What hast thou found in the spring to
   follow?
   'Itylus' (1864)

16 Till life forget and death remember,
   Till thou remember and I forget.
   'Itylus' (1864)

17 Blown fields or flowerful closes,
   Green pleasure or grey grief.
   'A Match' (1866)

18 I will go back to the great sweet mother,
   Mother and lover of men, the sea.
   'The Triumph of Time' (1866)

19 There lived a singer in France of old
   By the tideless dolorous midland sea.
   In a land of sand and ruin and gold
   There shone one woman, and none but
   she.
   'The Triumph of Time' (1866)

## John Addington Symonds
1840–93

20 These things shall be! A loftier race
   Than e'er the world hath known shall rise,
   With flame of freedom in their souls,
   And light of knowledge in their eyes.
   Hymn

## John Millington Synge 1871–1909

21 But we do be afraid of the sea, and we do
   only be drownded now and again.
   *The Aran Islands* (1907) pt. 2

22 Oh my grief, I've lost him surely. I've lost
   the only Playboy of the Western World.
   *The Playboy of the Western World* (1907) act 3 *ad
   fin.*

## Thomas Szasz 1920–

23 Happiness is an imaginary condition,
   formerly often attributed by the living to
   the dead, now usually attributed by adults
   to children, and by children to adults.
   *The Second Sin* (1973) 'Emotions'

24 The stupid neither forgive nor forget; the
   naïve forgive and forget; the wise forgive
   but do not forget.
   *The Second Sin* (1973) 'Personal Conduct'

25 If you talk to God, you are praying; if God
   talks to you, you have schizophrenia. If the
   dead talk to you, you are a spiritualist; if
   God talks to you, you are a schizophrenic.
   *The Second Sin* (1973) 'Schizophrenia'

1 Formerly, when religion was strong and science weak, men mistook magic for medicine; now, when science is strong and religion weak, men mistake medicine for magic.
   *The Second Sin* (1973) 'Science and Scientism'

2 Two wrongs don't make a right, but they make a good excuse.
   *The Second Sin* (1973) 'Social Relations'

## Albert von Szent-Györgyi
### 1893–1986

3 Discovery consists of seeing what everybody has seen and thinking what nobody has thought.
   In I. Good (ed.) *The Scientist Speculates* (1962) p. 15

## Tacitus AD c.56–after 117

4 They make a wilderness and call it peace.
   *Agricola* ch. 30

5 It is part of human nature to hate the man you have hurt.
   *Agricola* ch. 42

6 *Sine ira et studio.*
   With neither anger nor partiality.
   *Annals* bk. 1, ch. 1

7 *Elegantiae arbiter.*
   The arbiter of taste.
   *Annals* bk. 16, ch. 18 (of Petronius)

8 *Deos fortioribus adesse.*
   The gods are on the side of the stronger.
   *Histories* bk. 4, ch. 17. Cf. 83:19

## Sir Rabindranath Tagore
### 1861–1941

9 Bigotry tries to keep truth safe in its hand With a grip that kills it.
   *Fireflies* (1928) p. 29

## Nellie Talbot

10 Jesus wants me for a sunbeam.
   Title of hymn (1921)

## Charles-Maurice de Talleyrand
### 1754–1838

11 *Surtout, Messieurs, point de zèle.*
   Above all, gentlemen, not the slightest zeal.
   In P. Chasles *Voyages d'un critique à travers la vie et les livres* (1868) vol. 2, p. 407

12 *Ils n'ont rien appris, ni rien oublié.*
   They have learnt nothing, and forgotten nothing.
   Oral tradition (attributed to Talleyrand by the Chevalier de Panat, January 1796). See A. Sayons (ed.) *Mémoires et correspondance de Mallet du Pan* (1851) vol. 2, p. 196. Cf. 129:6

13 This is the beginning of the end.
   On hearing the outcome of the battle at Borodino, 1812; in Sainte-Beuve *M. de Talleyrand* (1870) ch. 3 (attributed)

## Booth Tarkington 1869–1946

14 There are two things that will be believed of any man whatsoever, and one of them is that he has taken to drink.
   *Penrod* (1914) ch. 10

## Nahum Tate 1652–1715

15 When I am laid in earth my wrongs create. No trouble in thy breast, Remember me, but ah! forget my fate.
   *Dido and Aeneas* (1689) act 3 ('Dido's Lament')

16 As pants the hart for cooling streams When heated in the chase.
   *New Version of the Psalms* (1696) Psalm 42 (with Nicholas Brady). Cf. 67:3

17 Through all the changing scenes of life, In trouble and in joy, The praises of my God shall still My heart and tongue employ.
   *New Version of the Psalms* (1696) Psalm 34 (with Nicholas Brady)

## R. H. Tawney 1880–1962

18 Militarism ... is fetish worship. It is the prostration of men's souls and the laceration of their bodies to appease an idol.
   *The Acquisitive Society* (1921) ch. 4

19 Private property is a necessary institution, at least in a fallen world; men work more and dispute less when goods are private than when they are common.
   *Religion and the Rise of Capitalism* (1926) ch. 1, sect. 1

20 To take usury is contrary to Scripture; it is contrary to Aristotle; it is contrary to nature, for it is to live without labour; it is to sell time, which belongs to God, for the advantage of wicked men.
   *Religion and the Rise of Capitalism* (1926) ch. 1, sect. 2

21 What harm have I ever done to the Labour Party?
   On declining the offer of a peerage; in *Evening Standard* 18 January 1962, p. 6

## A. J. P. Taylor 1906–90

22 History gets thicker as it approaches recent times.
   *English History 1914–45* (1965) bibliography

23 The First World War had begun—imposed on the statesmen of Europe by railway timetables.
   *The First World War* (1963) ch. 1

1 Like most of those who study history, he [Napoleon III] learned from the mistakes of the past how to make new ones.
*Listener* 6 June 1963 'Mistaken Lessons from the Past'

2 Crimea: The War That Would Not Boil.
*Rumours of Wars* (1952) ch. 6 (originally the title of an essay in *History Today* 2 February 1951)

## Ann Taylor 1782–1866 and Jane Taylor 1783–1824

3 Twinkle, twinkle, little star,
How I wonder what you are!
Up above the world so high,
Like a diamond in the sky!
*Rhymes for the Nursery* (1806) 'The Star'

## Bayard Taylor 1825–78

4 Till the sun grows cold,
And the stars are old,
And the leaves of the Judgement Book unfold.
'Bedouin Song'

## Bishop Jeremy Taylor 1613–67

5 The union of hands and hearts.
*XXV Sermons Preached at Golden Grove* (1653) 'The Marriage Ring' pt. 1

## Norman Tebbit 1931–

6 I grew up in the Thirties with our unemployed father. He did not riot, he got on his bike and looked for work.
Speech, 15 October 1981, in *Daily Telegraph* 16 October 1981

7 The cricket test—which side do they cheer for? . . . Are you still looking back to where you came from or where you are?
On the loyalties of Britain's immigrant population; interview in *Los Angeles Times*, reported in *Daily Telegraph* 20 April 1990

## Archbishop William Temple 1881–1944

8 Personally, I have always looked on cricket as organized loafing.
Attributed

## Sir John Tenniel 1820–1914

9 Dropping the pilot.
Cartoon caption, and title of poem, on Bismarck's departure from office; in *Punch* 29 March 1890

## Alfred, Lord Tennyson 1809–92

10 Break, break, break,
On thy cold grey stones, O Sea!
'Break, Break, Break' (1842)

11 And the stately ships go on
To their haven under the hill;
But O for the touch of a vanished hand,
And the sound of a voice that is still!
'Break, Break, Break' (1842)

12 I come from haunts of coot and hern,
I make a sudden sally
And sparkle out among the fern,
To bicker down a valley.
'The Brook' (1855) l. 23

13 For men may come and men may go,
But I go on for ever.
'The Brook' (1855) l. 33

14 Half a league, half a league,
Half a league onward,
All in the valley of Death
Rode the six hundred.
'The Charge of the Light Brigade' (1854)

15 'Forward, the Light Brigade!'
Was there a man dismayed?
Not though the soldier knew
Some one had blundered:
Theirs not to make reply,
Theirs not to reason why,
Theirs but to do and die:
Into the valley of Death
Rode the six hundred.
'The Charge of the Light Brigade' (1854)

16 Cannon to right of them,
Cannon to left of them,
Cannon in front of them
Volleyed and thundered.
'The Charge of the Light Brigade' (1854)

17 Into the jaws of Death,
Into the mouth of Hell.
'The Charge of the Light Brigade' (1854)

18 Sunset and evening star,
And one clear call for me!
And may there be no moaning of the bar,
When I put out to sea.
'Crossing the Bar' (1889)

19 For though from out our bourne of time and place
The flood may bear me far,
I hope to see my pilot face to face
When I have crossed the bar.
'Crossing the Bar' (1889)

20 A daughter of the gods, divinely tall,
And most divinely fair.
'A Dream of Fair Women' (1832) l. 87

21 He clasps the crag with crookèd hands;
Close to the sun in lonely lands,
Ringed with the azure world, he stands.
The wrinkled sea beneath him crawls;
He watches from his mountain walls,
And like a thunderbolt he falls.
'The Eagle' (1851)

22 The mellow lin-lan-lone of evening bells.
'Far-Far-Away' (1889)

23 More black than ashbuds in the front of March.
'The Gardener's Daughter' (1842) l. 28

24 A sight to make an old man young.
'The Gardener's Daughter' (1842) l. 140

1 Wearing the white flower of a blameless
  life,
  Before a thousand peering littlenesses,
  In that fierce light which beats upon a
  throne,
  And blackens every blot.
  *Idylls of the King* Dedication (1862) l. 24

2 Man's word is God in man.
  *Idylls of the King* 'The Coming of Arthur'
  (1869) l. 132

3 Clothed in white samite, mystic,
  wonderful.
  *Idylls of the King* 'The Coming of Arthur'
  (1869) l. 284; 'The Passing of Arthur' (1869)
  l. 199

4 From the great deep to the great deep he
  goes.
  *Idylls of the King* 'The Coming of Arthur'
  (1869) l. 410

5 Live pure, speak true, right wrong, follow
  the King—
  Else, wherefore born?
  *Idylls of the King* 'Gareth and Lynette' (1872)
  l. 117

6 It was my duty to have loved the highest:
  It surely was my profit had I known:
  It would have been my pleasure had I seen.
  We needs must love the highest when we
  see it.
  *Idylls of the King* 'Guinevere' (1859) l. 652

7 Elaine the fair, Elaine the loveable,
  Elaine, the lily maid of Astolat.
  *Idylls of the King* 'Lancelot and Elaine' (1859)
  l. 1

8 He is all fault who hath no fault at all:
  For who loves me must have a touch of
  earth.
  *Idylls of the King* 'Lancelot and Elaine' (1859)
  l. 132

9 His honour rooted in dishonour stood,
  And faith unfaithful kept him falsely true.
  *Idylls of the King* 'Lancelot and Elaine' (1859)
  l. 871

10 He makes no friend who never made a foe.
  *Idylls of the King* 'Lancelot and Elaine' (1859)
  l. 1082

11 The greater man, the greater courtesy.
  *Idylls of the King* 'The Last Tournament' (1871)
  l. 628

12 Our hoard is little, but our hearts are
  great.
  *Idylls of the King* 'The Marriage of Geraint'
  (1859) l. 352

13 It is the little rift within the lute,
  That by and by will make the music mute,
  And ever widening slowly silence all.
  *Idylls of the King* 'Merlin and Vivien' (1859)
  l. 388

14 And trust me not at all or all in all.
  *Idylls of the King* 'Merlin and Vivien' (1859)
  l. 396

15 Man dreams of fame while woman wakes
  to love.
  *Idylls of the King* 'Merlin and Vivien' (1859)
  l. 458

16 I found Him in the shining of the stars,
  I marked Him in the flowering of His
  fields,
  But in His ways with men I find Him not.
  *Idylls of the King* 'The Passing of Arthur'
  (1869) l. 9

17 So all day long the noise of battle rolled
  Among the mountains by the winter sea.
  *Idylls of the King* 'The Passing of Arthur'
  (1869) l. 170

18 Authority forgets a dying king.
  *Idylls of the King* 'The Passing of Arthur'
  (1869) l. 289

19 And the days darken round me, and the
  years,
  Among new men, strange faces, other
  minds.
  *Idylls of the King* 'The Passing of Arthur'
  (1869) l. 405

20 The old order changeth, yielding place to
  new,
  And God fulfils himself in many ways,
  Lest one good custom should corrupt the
  world.
  *Idylls of the King* 'The Passing of Arthur'
  (1869) l. 408

21 If thou shouldst never see my face again,
  Pray for my soul. More things are wrought
  by prayer
  Than this world dreams of.
  *Idylls of the King* 'The Passing of Arthur'
  (1869) l. 414

22           I am going a long way
  With these thou seëst—if indeed I go
  (For all my mind is clouded with a
  doubt)—
  To the island-valley of Avilion;
  Where falls not hail, or rain, or any snow,
  Nor ever wind blows loudly.
  *Idylls of the King* 'The Passing of Arthur'
  (1869) l. 424

23 Our little systems have their day;
  They have their day and cease to be:
  They are but broken lights of thee,
  And thou, O Lord, art more than they.
  *In Memoriam A. H. H.* (1850) Prologue

24 I held it truth, with him who sings
  To one clear harp in divers tones,
  That men may rise on stepping-stones
  Of their dead selves to higher things.
  *In Memoriam A. H. H.* (1850) canto 1

25           Never morning wore
  To evening, but some heart did break.
  *In Memoriam A. H. H.* (1850) canto 6

26 Dark house, by which once more I stand
  Here in the long unlovely street,
  Doors, where my heart was used to beat
  So quickly, waiting for a hand.
  *In Memoriam A. H. H.* (1850) canto 7

1 And ghastly through the drizzling rain
  On the bald street breaks the blank day.
  *In Memoriam A. H. H.* (1850) canto 7

2 The last red leaf is whirled away,
  The rooks are blown about the skies.
  *In Memoriam A. H. H.* (1850) canto 15

3 I envy not in any moods
  The captive void of noble rage,
  The linnet born within the cage,
  That never knew the summer woods.
  *In Memoriam A. H. H.* (1850) canto 27

4 'Tis better to have loved and lost
  Than never to have loved at all.
  *In Memoriam A. H. H.* (1850) canto 27.
  Cf. 106:16

5 A solemn gladness even crowned
  The purple brows of Olivet.
  *In Memoriam A. H. H.* (1850) canto 31

6 Her eyes are homes of silent prayer.
  *In Memoriam A. H. H.* (1850) canto 32

7 Be near me when my light is low,
  When the blood creeps, and the nerves
  prick
  And tingle; and the heart is sick,
  And all the wheels of Being slow.
  *In Memoriam A. H. H.* (1850) canto 50

8 Oh yet we trust that somehow good
  Will be the final goal of ill.
  *In Memoriam A. H. H.* (1850) canto 54

9 So runs my dream: but what am I?
  An infant crying in the night:
  An infant crying for the light:
  And with no language but a cry.
  *In Memoriam A. H. H.* (1850) canto 54

10 So careful of the type she seems,
   So careless of the single life.
   *In Memoriam A. H. H.* (1850) canto 55 (of
   Nature)

11            The great world's altar-stairs
   That slope through darkness up to God.
   *In Memoriam A. H. H.* (1850) canto 55

12 Nature, red in tooth and claw.
   *In Memoriam A. H. H.* (1850) canto 56

13 O Sorrow, wilt thou live with me
   No casual mistress, but a wife.
   *In Memoriam A. H. H.* (1850) canto 59

14 So many worlds, so much to do,
   So little done, such things to be.
   *In Memoriam A. H. H.* (1850) canto 73

15 Laburnums, dropping-wells of fire.
   *In Memoriam A. H. H.* (1850) canto 83

16 God's finger touched him, and he slept.
   *In Memoriam A. H. H.* (1850) canto 85

17            Fresh from brawling courts
   And dusty purlieus of the law.
   *In Memoriam A. H. H.* (1850) canto 89.
   Cf. 137:18

18 You tell me, doubt is Devil-born.
   *In Memoriam A. H. H.* (1850) canto 96

19 There lives more faith in honest doubt,
   Believe me, than in half the creeds.
   *In Memoriam A. H. H.* (1850) canto 96

20 Their meetings made December June,
   Their every parting was to die.
   *In Memoriam A. H. H.* (1850) canto 97

21 He seems so near and yet so far.
   *In Memoriam A. H. H.* (1850) canto 97

22 Ring out, wild bells, to the wild sky.
   *In Memoriam A. H. H.* (1850) canto 106

23 Ring out the old, ring in the new,
   Ring, happy bells, across the snow:
   The year is going, let him go;
   Ring out the false, ring in the true.
   *In Memoriam A. H. H.* (1850) canto 106

24 Ring out the want, the care, the sin,
   The faithless coldness of the times.
   *In Memoriam A. H. H.* (1850) canto 106

25 Ring out false pride in place and blood,
   The civic slander and the spite.
   *In Memoriam A. H. H.* (1850) canto 106

26 Ring out the thousand wars of old,
   Ring in the thousand years of peace.
   *In Memoriam A. H. H.* (1850) canto 106

27 Ring in the valiant man and free,
   The larger heart, the kindlier hand;
   Ring out the darkness of the land;
   Ring in the Christ that is to be.
   *In Memoriam A. H. H.* (1850) canto 106

28            Not the schoolboy heat,
   The blind hysterics of the Celt.
   *In Memoriam A. H. H.* (1850) canto 109

29 Now fades the last long streak of snow,
   Now burgeons every maze of quick
   About the flowering squares, and thick
   By ashen roots the violets blow.
   *In Memoriam A. H. H.* (1850) canto 115

30 And drowned in yonder living blue
   The lark becomes a sightless song.
   *In Memoriam A. H. H.* (1850) canto 115

31            Wearing all that weight
   Of learning lightly like a flower.
   *In Memoriam A. H. H.* (1850) canto 131

32 There hath he lain for ages and will lie
   Battening upon huge seaworms in his
   sleep.
   'The Kraken' (1830)

33 Kind hearts are more than coronets,
   And simple faith than Norman blood.
   'Lady Clara Vere de Vere' (1842) st. 7

34 On either side the river lie
   Long fields of barley and of rye,
   That clothe the wold and meet the sky;
   And through the field the road runs by
   To many-towered Camelot.
   'The Lady of Shalott' (1832, revised 1842)
   pt. 1

35 Willows whiten, aspens quiver,
   Little breezes dusk and shiver.
   'The Lady of Shalott' (1832, revised 1842)
   pt. 1

36 Only reapers, reaping early
   In among the bearded barley.
   'The Lady of Shalott' (1832, revised 1842)
   pt. 1

1 'I am half sick of shadows,' said
The Lady of Shalott.
  'The Lady of Shalott' (1832, revised 1842)
  pt. 2

2 A red-cross knight for ever kneeled
To a lady in his shield.
  'The Lady of Shalott' (1832, revised 1842)
  pt. 3

3 She left the web, she left the loom,
She made three paces through the room,
She saw the water-lily bloom,
She saw the helmet and the plume,
She looked down to Camelot.
Out flew the web and floated wide;
The mirror cracked from side to side;
'The curse is come upon me,' cried
The Lady of Shalott.
  'The Lady of Shalott' (1832, revised 1842)
  pt. 3

4 Slander, meanest spawn of Hell.
  'The Letters' (1855)

5 Airy, fairy Lilian.
  'Lilian' (1830)

6 In the spring a young man's fancy lightly
turns to thoughts of love.
  'Locksley Hall' (1842) l. 20

7 He will hold thee, when his passion shall
have spent its novel force,
Something better than his dog, a little
dearer than his horse.
  'Locksley Hall' (1842) l. 49

8 But the jingling of the guinea helps the
hurt that Honour feels.
  'Locksley Hall' (1842) l. 105

9 Men, my brothers, men the workers, ever
reaping something new:
That which they have done but earnest of
the things that they shall do.
  'Locksley Hall' (1842) l. 117

10 Pilots of the purple twilight, dropping
down with costly bales.
  'Locksley Hall' (1842) l. 122

11 Heard the heavens fill with shouting, and
there rained a ghastly dew
From the nations' airy navies grappling in
the central blue.
  'Locksley Hall' (1842) l. 123

12 Till the war-drum throbbed no longer, and
the battle-flags were furled
In the Parliament of man, the Federation
of the world.
  'Locksley Hall' (1842) l. 127

13 Science moves, but slowly slowly, creeping
on from point to point.
  'Locksley Hall' (1842) l. 134

14 Knowledge comes, but wisdom lingers.
  'Locksley Hall' (1842) l. 141

15 I will take some savage woman, she shall
rear my dusky race.
  'Locksley Hall' (1842) l. 168

16 I the heir of all the ages, in the foremost
files of time.
  'Locksley Hall' (1842) l. 178

17 Let the great world spin for ever down the
ringing grooves of change.
  'Locksley Hall' (1842) l. 182

18 Better fifty years of Europe than a cycle of
Cathay.
  'Locksley Hall' (1842) l. 184

19 Music that gentlier on the spirit lies,
Than tired eyelids upon tired eyes.
  'The Lotos-Eaters' (1832) Choric Song, st. 1

20                And the clouds are lightly
curled
Round their golden houses, girdled with
the gleaming world.
  'The Lotos-Eaters' (1832) Choric Song, st. 8
  (1842 revision)

21                I saw the flaring atom-streams
And torrents of her myriad universe,
Ruining along the illimitable inane.
  'Lucretius' (1868) l. 38

22 Weeded and worn the ancient thatch
Upon the lonely moated grange.
She only said, 'My life is dreary,
He cometh not,' she said;
She said, 'I am aweary, aweary,
I would that I were dead!'
  'Mariana' (1830) st. 1. Cf. 288:22

23 Faultily faultless, icily regular, splendidly
null,
Dead perfection, no more.
  Maud (1855) pt. 1, sect. 2

24 She came to the village church,
And sat by a pillar alone;
An angel watching an urn
Wept over her, carved in stone.
  Maud (1855) pt. 1, sect. 8

25 The snowy-banded, dilettante,
Delicate-handed priest.
  Maud (1855) pt. 1, sect. 8

26 One still strong man in a blatant land,
Whatever they call him, what care I,
Aristocrat, democrat, autocrat—one
Who can rule and dare not lie.
  Maud (1855) pt. 1, sect. 10, st. 5

27 Gorgonised me from head to foot
With a stony British stare.
  Maud (1855) pt. 1, sect. 13, st. 2

28 Come into the garden, Maud,
For the black bat, night, has flown,
Come into the garden, Maud,
I am here at the gate alone;
And the woodbine spices are wafted
abroad,
And the musk of the rose is blown.

For a breeze of morning moves,
And the planet of Love is on high,
Beginning to faint in the light that she
loves
On a bed of daffodil sky.
  Maud (1855) pt. 1, sect. 22, st. 1

29 Queen rose of the rosebud garden of girls.
  Maud (1855) pt. 1, sect. 22, st. 9

1 There has fallen a splendid tear
From the passion-flower at the gate.
She is coming, my dove, my dear;
She is coming, my life, my fate;
The red rose cries, 'She is near, she is near;'
And the white rose weeps, 'She is late.'
   *Maud* (1855) pt. 1, sect. 22, st. 10

2 She is coming, my own, my sweet;
Were it ever so airy a tread,
My heart would hear her and beat,
Were it earth in an earthy bed.
   *Maud* (1855) pt. 1, sect. 22, st. 11

3 O that 'twere possible
After long grief and pain
To find the arms of my true love
Round me once again!
   *Maud* (1855) pt. 2, sect. 4, st. 1

4 But the churchmen fain would kill their church,
As the churches have killed their Christ.
   *Maud* (1855) pt. 2, sect. 5, st. 2

5 You must wake and call me early, call me early, mother dear;
Tomorrow 'ill be the happiest time of all the glad New-year;
Of all the glad New-year, mother, the maddest merriest day;
For I'm to be Queen o' the May, mother, I'm to be Queen o' the May.
   'The May Queen' (1832)

6 After it, follow it,
Follow The Gleam.
   'Merlin and The Gleam' (1889) st. 9

7 God-gifted organ-voice of England,
Milton, a name to resound for ages.
   'Milton: Alcaics' (1863)

8 The brooks of Eden mazily murmuring.
   'Milton: Alcaics' (1863)

9 Doänt thou marry for munny, but goä wheer munny is!
   'Northern Farmer. New Style' (1869) st. 5

10 The poor in a loomp is bad.
   'Northern Farmer. New Style' (1869) st. 12

11 The last great Englishman is low.
   'Ode on the Death of the Duke of Wellington' (1852) st. 3

12 That world-earthquake, Waterloo!
   'Ode on the Death of the Duke of Wellington' (1852) st. 6

13 Who never sold the truth to serve the hour,
Nor paltered with Eternal God for power.
   'Ode on the Death of the Duke of Wellington' (1852) st. 7

14 I built my soul a lordly pleasure-house,
Wherein at ease for aye to dwell.
   'The Palace of Art' (1832) st. 1

15 Vex not thou the poet's mind
With thy shallow wit:
Vex not thou the poet's mind;
For thou canst not fathom it.
   'The Poet's Mind' (1830)

16 With prudes for proctors, dowagers for deans,
And sweet girl-graduates in their golden hair.
   *The Princess* (1847) 'Prologue' l. 141

17 And blessings on the falling out
That all the more endears,
When we fall out with those we love
And kiss again with tears!
   *The Princess* (1847) pt. 2, song (added 1850)

18 A classic lecture, rich in sentiment,
With scraps of thundrous epic lilted out
By violet-hooded Doctors, elegies
And quoted odes, and jewels five-words-long,
That on the stretched forefinger of all Time
Sparkle for ever.
   *The Princess* (1847) pt. 2, l. 352

19 Sweet and low, sweet and low,
Wind of the western sea,
Low, low, breathe and blow,
Wind of the western sea!
   *The Princess* (1847) pt. 3, song (added 1850)

20 The splendour falls on castle walls
And snowy summits old in story:
The long light shakes across the lakes,
And the wild cataract leaps in glory.
Blow, bugle, blow, set the wild echoes flying,
Blow, bugle; answer, echoes, dying, dying, dying.
   *The Princess* (1847) pt. 4, song (added 1850)

21 O sweet and far from cliff and scar
The horns of Elfland faintly blowing!
   *The Princess* (1847) pt. 4, song (added 1850)

22 Tears, idle tears, I know not what they mean,
Tears from the depth of some divine despair
Rise in the heart, and gather to the eyes,
In looking on the happy autumn-fields,
And thinking of the days that are no more.
   *The Princess* (1847) pt. 4, l. 21, song (added 1850)

23 Dear as remembered kisses after death.
   *The Princess* (1847) pt. 4, l. 36, song (added 1850)

24 O tell her, Swallow, thou that knowest each,
That bright and fierce and fickle is the South,
And dark and true and tender is the North.
   *The Princess* (1847) pt. 4, l. 78, song (added 1850)

25 Man is the hunter; woman is his game.
   *The Princess* (1847) pt. 5, l. 147

26 Home they brought her warrior dead.
She nor swooned, nor uttered cry:
All her maidens, watching said,
'She must weep or she will die.'
   *The Princess* (1847) pt. 6, song (added 1850)

27 Like summer tempest came her tears.
   *The Princess* (1847) pt. 6, song (added 1850)

1    The woman is so hard
Upon the woman.
> *The Princess* (1847) pt. 6, l. 205

2 I love not hollow cheek or faded eye.
> *The Princess* (1847) pt. 7, song (added 1850)

3 Now sleeps the crimson petal, now the white;
Nor waves the cypress in the palace walk.
> *The Princess* (1847) pt. 7, l. 161, song (added 1850)

4 Now lies the Earth all Danaë to the stars.
> *The Princess* (1847) pt. 7, l. 167, song (added 1850)

5 Now folds the lily all her sweetness up,
And slips into the bosom of the lake:
So fold thyself, my dearest, thou, and slip
Into my bosom and be lost in me.
> *The Princess* (1847) pt. 7, l. 171, song (added 1850)

6 Come down, O maid, from yonder mountain height:
What pleasure lives in height?
> *The Princess* (1847) pt. 7, l. 177, song (added 1850)

7 For Love is of the valley, come thou down
And find him.
> *The Princess* (1847) pt. 7, l. 184, song (added 1850)

8 The moan of doves in immemorial elms,
And murmuring of innumerable bees.
> *The Princess* (1847) pt. 7, l. 206, song (added 1850)

9 No little lily-handed baronet he.
> *The Princess* (1847) 'Conclusion' l. 84

10 At Flores in the Azores Sir Richard Grenville lay.
> 'The Revenge' (1878) st. 1

11 I should count myself the coward if I left them, my Lord Howard,
To these Inquisition dogs and the devildoms of Spain.
> 'The Revenge' (1878) st. 2

12 Let us bang these dogs of Seville, the children of the devil,
For I never turned my back upon Don or devil yet.
> 'The Revenge' (1878) st. 4

13 Sink me the ship, Master Gunner—sink her, split her in twain!
Fall into the hands of God, not into the hands of Spain!
> 'The Revenge' (1878) st. 11

14 And they praised him to his face with their courtly foreign grace.
> 'The Revenge' (1878) st. 13

15 My strength is as the strength of ten,
Because my heart is pure.
> 'Sir Galahad' (1842)

16 Alone and warming his five wits,
The white owl in the belfry sits.
> 'Song—The Owl' (1830)

17 The woods decay, the woods decay and fall,
The vapours weep their burthen to the ground,
Man comes and tills the field and lies beneath,
And after many a summer dies the swan.
Me only cruel immortality
Consumes: I wither slowly in thine arms,
Here at the quiet limit of the world.
> 'Tithonus' (1860, revised 1864) l. 1

18 The gods themselves cannot recall their gifts.
> 'Tithonus' (1860, revised 1864) l. 49

19 It little profits that an idle king,
By this still hearth, among these barren crags,
Matched with an agèd wife, I mete and dole
Unequal laws unto a savage race.
> 'Ulysses' (1842) l. 1

20    I will drink
Life to the lees: all times I have enjoyed
Greatly, have suffered greatly, both with those
That loved me, and alone.
> 'Ulysses' (1842) l. 6

21 Much have I seen and known; cities of men
And manners, climates, councils, governments,
Myself not least, but honoured of them all;
And drunk delight of battle with my peers,
Far on the ringing plains of windy Troy.
I am a part of all that I have met;
Yet all experience is an arch wherethrough
Gleams that untravelled world, whose margin fades
For ever and for ever when I move.
How dull it is to pause, to make an end,
To rust unburnished, not to shine in use!
As though to breathe were life.
> 'Ulysses' (1842) l. 13

22 This is my son, mine own Telemachus.
> 'Ulysses' (1842) l. 33

23 Death closes all: but something ere the end,
Some work of noble note, may yet be done,
Not unbecoming men that strove with gods.
> 'Ulysses' (1842) l. 51

24 It may be we shall touch the Happy Isles,
And see the great Achilles, whom we knew.
> 'Ulysses' (1842) l. 63

25    That which we are, we are;
One equal temper of heroic hearts,
Made weak by time and fate, but strong in will
To strive, to seek, to find, and not to yield.
> 'Ulysses' (1842) l. 67

26 Every moment dies a man,
Every moment one is born.
> 'The Vision of Sin' (1842) pt. 4, st. 9. Cf. 23:19

1 A land of settled government,
A land of just and old renown,
Where Freedom slowly broadens down
From precedent to precedent.
'You ask me, why, though ill at ease' (1842)
st. 3

2 A louse in the locks of literature.
Of Churton Collins, in E. Charteris *Life and
Letters of Sir Edmund Gosse* (1931) ch. 14

## Terence *c.*190–159 BC

3 *Hinc illae lacrimae.*
Hence those tears.
*Andria* l. 126

4 I am a man, I count nothing human
foreign to me.
*Heauton Timorumenos* l. 77

5 *Fortis fortuna adiuvat.*
Fortune assists the brave.
*Phormio* l. 203. Cf. 339:20

6 There are as many opinions as there are
people: each has his own correct way.
*Phormio* l. 454

## St Teresa of Ávila 1512–82

7 O Lord, to what a state dost Thou bring
those who love Thee!
*Interior Castle* Mansion 6, ch. 11, para. 6 (tr.
Benedictines of Stanbrook, 1921)

## Tertullian AD *c.*160–*c.*225

8 As often as we are mown down by you, the
more we grow in numbers; the blood of
Christians is the seed.
*Apologeticus* ch. 50, sect. 13 (traditionally 'The
blood of the martyrs is the seed of the
Church')

9 *Certum est quia impossibile est.*
It is certain because it is impossible.
*De Carne Christi* ch. 5 (often quoted 'Credo quia
impossibile [I believe because it is
impossible]')

## A. S. J. Tessimond 1902–62

10 Cats, no less liquid than their shadows,
Offer no angles to the wind.
*Cats* (1934) p. 20

## William Makepeace Thackeray 1811–63

11 'Tis strange what a man may do, and a
woman yet think him an angel.
*The History of Henry Esmond* (1852) bk. 1, ch. 7

12 The *Pall Mall Gazette* is written by
gentlemen for gentlemen.
*Pendennis* (1848–50) ch. 32

13 Business first; pleasure afterwards.
*The Rose and the Ring* (1855) ch. 1

14 A woman with fair opportunities and
without a positive hump, may marry
whom she likes.
*Vanity Fair* (1847–8) ch. 4

15 Whenever he met a great man he grovelled
before him, and my-lorded him as only a
free-born Briton can do.
*Vanity Fair* (1847–8) ch. 13

16 If a man's character is to be abused, say
what you will, there's nobody like a
relation to do the business.
*Vanity Fair* (1847–8) ch. 19

17 Them's my sentiments!
*Vanity Fair* (1847–8) ch. 21 (Fred Bullock)

18 Darkness came down on the field and city:
and Amelia was praying for George, who
was lying on his face, dead, with a bullet
through his heart.
*Vanity Fair* (1847–8) ch. 32

19 Nothing like blood, sir, in hosses, dawgs,
and men.
*Vanity Fair* (1847–8) ch. 35 (James Crawley)

20 How to live well on nothing a year.
*Vanity Fair* (1847–8) ch. 36 (title)

21 I think I could be a good woman if I had
five thousand a year.
*Vanity Fair* (1847–8) ch. 36

22 Come, children, let us shut up the box and
the puppets, for our play is played out.
*Vanity Fair* (1847–8) ch. 67

23 Werther had a love for Charlotte
Such as words could never utter;
Would you know how first he met her?
She was cutting bread and butter.
'Sorrows of Werther' (1855)

## Margaret Thatcher 1925–

24 We must try to find ways to starve the
terrorist and the hijacker of the oxygen of
publicity on which they depend.
Speech, 15 July 1985, in *The Times* 16 July
1985

25 There is no such thing as Society. There
are individual men and women, and there
are families.
In *Woman's Own* 31 October 1987

26 We have become a grandmother.
In *The Times* 4 March 1989

## William Roscoe Thayer 1859–1923

27 Log-cabin to White House.
Title of biography (1910) of James Garfield
(1831–81)

## Thomas à Kempis *c.*1380–1471

28 *O quam cito transit gloria mundi.*
Oh how quickly the glory of the world
passes away!
*De Imitatione Christi* bk. 1, ch. 3, sect. 6.
Cf. 13:22

1 For man proposes, but God disposes.
   *De Imitatione Christi* bk. 1, ch. 19, sect. 2

2 Would that we had spent one whole day
   well in this world!
   *De Imitatione Christi* bk. 1, ch. 23, sect. 2

## St Thomas Aquinas *c.*1225–74

3 *Pange, lingua, gloriosi*
   *Corporis mysterium.*
   Now, my tongue, the mystery telling
   Of the glorious Body sing.
   'Pange Lingua Gloriosi' (Corpus Christi
   hymn, tr. J. M. Neale, E. Caswall, and others)

4 *Tantum ergo sacramentum*
   *Veneremur cernui;*
   *Et antiquum documentum*
   *Novo cedat ritui.*
   Therefore we, before him bending,
   This great Sacrament revere,
   Types and shadows have their ending,
   For the newer rite is here.
   'Pange Lingua Gloriosi'

## Brandon Thomas 1856–1914

5 I'm Charley's aunt from Brazil—where the
   nuts come from.
   *Charley's Aunt* (1892) act 1

## Dylan Thomas 1914–53

6 Though lovers be lost love shall not;
   And death shall have no dominion.
   'And death shall have no dominion' (1936).
   Cf. 54:35

7 Do not go gentle into that good night,
   Old age should burn and rave at close of
   day;
   Rage, rage against the dying of the light.
   'Do Not Go Gentle into that Good Night'
   (1952)

8 Now as I was young and easy under the
   apple boughs
   About the lilting house and happy as the
   grass was green.
   'Fern Hill' (1946)

9 Oh as I was young and easy in the mercy of
   his means,
   Time held me green and dying
   Though I sang in my chains like the sea.
   'Fern Hill' (1946)

10 The force that through the green fuse
   drives the flower
   Drives my green age.
   'The force that through the green fuse'
   (1934)

11 The hand that signed the treaty bred
   a fever,
   And famine grew, and locusts came;
   Great is the hand that holds dominion over
   Man by a scribbled name.
   'The hand that signed the paper felled a city'
   (1936)

12 Light breaks where no sun shines;
   Where no sea runs, the waters of the heart
   Push in their tides.
   'Light breaks where no sun shines' (1934)

13 It was my thirtieth year to heaven.
   'Poem in October' (1946)

14 There could I marvel
   My birthday
   Away but the weather turned around.
   'Poem in October' (1946)

15 After the first death, there is no other.
   'A Refusal to Mourn the Death, by Fire, of
   a Child in London' (1946)

16 To begin at the beginning: It is spring,
   moonless night in the small town, starless
   and bible-black.
   *Under Milk Wood* (1954) p. 1

17 Chasing the naughty couples down the
   grassgreen gooseberried double bed of the
   wood.
   *Under Milk Wood* (1954) p. 7

18 Before you let the sun in, mind it wipes its
   shoes.
   *Under Milk Wood* (1954) p. 16

19 Oh, isn't life a terrible thing, thank God?
   *Under Milk Wood* (1954) p. 30

20 The land of my fathers. My fathers can
   have it.
   Of Wales, in *Adam* December 1953

## Edward Thomas 1878–1917

21 Yes; I remember Adlestrop—
   The name, because one afternoon
   Of heat the express-train drew up there
   Unwontedly. It was late June.
   'Adlestrop' (1917)

22 The past is the only dead thing that smells
   sweet.
   'Early one morning in May I set out' (1917)

23 If I should ever by chance grow rich
   I'll buy Codham, Cockridden, and
   Childerditch,
   Roses, Pyrgo, and Lapwater,
   And let them all to my elder daughter.
   'Household Poems: Bronwen' (1917)

24 I have come to the borders of sleep,
   The unfathomable deep
   Forest where all must lose
   Their way.
   'Lights Out' (1917)

25          I see and hear nothing;
   Yet seem, too, to be listening, lying in wait
   For what I should, yet never can,
   remember.
   'Old Man' (1917)

26 Out in the dark over the snow
   The fallow fawns invisible go.
   'Out in the dark' (1917)

## Elizabeth Thomas 1675–1731

1 From marrying in haste, and repenting at
  leisure; ·
  Not liking the person, yet liking his
  treasure:
  *Libera nos.*
  'A New Litany, occasioned by an invitation to
  a wedding' (1722). Cf. 106:13

## Irene Thomas

2 Protestant women may take the pill.
  Roman Catholic women must keep taking
  The Tablet.
  In *Guardian* 28 December 1990, p. 27

## R. S. Thomas 1913–

3                    Doctors in verse
  Being scarce now, most poets
  Are their own patients.
  'The Cure' (1958)

4 There is no love
  For such, only a willed
  gentleness.
  'They' (1968)

5 There is no present in Wales,
  And no future;
  There is only the past,
  Brittle with relics . . .
  And an impotent people,
  Sick with inbreeding,
  Worrying the carcase of an old song.
  'Welsh Landscape' (1955)

## Francis Thompson 1859–1907

6 As the run-stealers flicker to and fro,
  To and fro: —
  O my Hornby and my Barlow long ago!
  'At Lord's' (1913)

7 Nothing begins, and nothing ends,
  That is not paid with moan;
  For we are born in other's pain,
  And perish in our own.
  'Daisy' (1913)

8 I fled Him, down the nights and down the
  days;
  I fled Him, down the arches of the years;
  I fled Him, down the labyrinthine ways
  Of my own mind; and in the mist of tears
  I hid from Him, and under running
  laughter.
  'The Hound of Heaven' (1913) pt. 1

9 All things betray thee, who betrayest Me.
  'The Hound of Heaven' (1913) pt. 1

10 I said to Dawn: Be sudden — to Eve:
  Be soon.
  'The Hound of Heaven' (1913) pt. 2

11 Such is: what is to be?
  The pulp so bitter, how shall taste the
  rind?
  'The Hound of Heaven' (1913) pt. 4

12 Lo, all things fly thee, for thou fliest Me!
  'The Hound of Heaven' (1913) pt. 5

13 There is no expeditious road
  To pack and label men for God,
  And save them by the barrel-load.
  Some may perchance, with strange
  surprise,
  Have blundered into Paradise.
  'A Judgement in Heaven' (1913) epilogue

14 O world invisible, we view thee,
  O world intangible, we touch thee,
  O world unknowable, we know thee,
  Inapprehensible, we clutch thee!
  'The Kingdom of God' (1913)

15 'Tis ye, 'tis your estrangèd faces,
  That miss the many-splendoured thing.
  'The Kingdom of God' (1913)

16                    And upon thy so sore loss
  Shall shine the traffic of Jacob's ladder
  Pitched betwixt Heaven and Charing Cross.
  'The Kingdom of God' (1913)

17 And lo, Christ walking on the water
  Not of Gennesareth, but Thames!
  'The Kingdom of God' (1913)

18 Look for me in the nurseries of heaven.
  'To My Godchild Francis M.W.M.' (1913)

19 Insculped and embossed,
  With His hammer of wind,
  And His graver of frost.
  'To a Snowflake' (1913)

## James Thomson 1700–48

20 When Britain first, at heaven's command,
  Arose from out the azure main,
  This was the charter of the land,
  And guardian angels sung this strain:
  'Rule, Britannia, rule the waves;
  Britons never will be slaves.'
  *Alfred: a Masque* (1740) act 2

21 A little round, fat, oily man of God.
  *The Castle of Indolence* (1748) canto 1, st. 69

22 Delightful task! to rear the tender thought,
  To teach the young idea how to shoot.
  *The Seasons* (1746) 'Spring' l. 1152

23 An elegant sufficiency, content,
  Retirement, rural quiet, friendship, books.
  *The Seasons* (1746) 'Spring' l. 1161

24 Sighed and looked unutterable things.
  *The Seasons* (1746) 'Summer' l. 1188

25                    For loveliness
  Needs not the foreign aid of ornament,
  But is when unadorned adorned the most.
  *The Seasons* (1746) 'Autumn' l. 204

26 Welcome, kindred glooms!
  Congenial horrors, hail!
  *The Seasons* (1746) 'Winter' l. 5

27 Studious let me sit,
  And hold high converse with the mighty
  dead.
  *The Seasons* (1746) 'Winter' l. 431

## James Thomson 1834–82

1 The City is of Night; perchance of Death,
But certainly of Night.
  'The City of Dreadful Night' (written 1870–3)

2 As we rush, as we rush in the train,
The trees and the houses go wheeling
back,
But the starry heavens above that plain
Come flying on our track.
  'Sunday at Hampstead' (written 1863–5)
  st. 10

3 Give a man a horse he can ride,
Give a man a boat he can sail.
  'Sunday up the River' (written 1865) st. 15

## Roy Thomson (Lord Thomson of Fleet) 1894–1976

4 Like having your own licence to print
money.
  On the profitability of commercial television
  in Britain; in R. Braddon *Roy Thomson* (1965)
  ch. 32

## Henry David Thoreau 1817–62

5 Some circumstantial evidence is very
strong, as when you find a trout in the
milk.
  *Journal* 11 November 1850, in *Writings* (1906
  ed.) vol. 8, p. 94

6 Not that the story need be long, but it will
take a long while to make it short.
  Letter to Harrison Blake, 16 November 1857,
  in *Writings* (1906 ed.) vol. 6, p. 320. Cf. 245:24

7 I have travelled a good deal in Concord.
  *Walden* (1854) 'Economy' in *Writings* (1906
  ed.) vol. 2, p. 4

8 As if you could kill time without injuring
eternity.
  *Walden* (1854) 'Economy' in *Writings* (1906
  ed.) vol. 2, p. 8

9 The mass of men lead lives of quiet
desperation.
  *Walden* (1854) 'Economy' in *Writings* (1906
  ed.) vol. 2, p. 8

10 The three-o'-clock in the morning courage,
which Bonaparte thought was the rarest.
  *Walden* (1854) 'Sounds' in *Writings* (1906 ed.)
  vol. 2, p. 131. Cf. 140:22, 237:4

11 Our life is frittered away by detail ...
Simplify, simplify.
  *Walden* (1854) 'Where I lived, and what I
  lived for' in *Writings* (1906 ed.) vol. 2, p. 101

12 If a man does not keep pace with his
companions, perhaps it is because he hears
a different drummer. Let him step to the
music which he hears, however measured
or far away.
  *Walden* (1854) 'Conclusion' in *Writings* (1906
  ed.) vol. 2, p. 358

## Jeremy Thorpe 1929–

13 Greater love hath no man than this, that
he lay down his friends for his life.
  On Harold Macmillan sacking seven of his
  Cabinet on 13 July 1962; in D. E. Butler and
  A. King *General Election of 1964* (1965) ch. 1

## James Thurber 1894–1961

14 Her own mother lived the latter years of
her life in the horrible suspicion that
electricity was dripping invisibly all over
the house.
  *My Life and Hard Times* (1933) ch. 2

15 Early to rise and early to bed makes a male
healthy and wealthy and dead.
  'The Shrike and the Chipmunks' in *New
  Yorker* 18 February 1939

16 The war between men and women.
  Cartoon series title in *New Yorker*
  20 January–28 April 1934

17 It's a naïve domestic Burgundy without any
breeding, but I think you'll be amused by
its presumption.
  Cartoon caption in *New Yorker* 27 March 1937

18 Well, if I called the wrong number, why did
you answer the phone?
  Cartoon caption in *New Yorker* 5 June 1937

## Edward, 1st Baron Thurlow 1731–1806

19 Corporations have neither bodies to be
punished, nor souls to be condemned, they
therefore do as they like.
  In J. Poynder *Literary Extracts* (1844) vol. 1,
  p. 268 (usually quoted 'Did you ever expect a
  corporation to have a conscience, when it
  has no soul to be damned, and no body to be
  kicked?'). Cf. 103:9

## Thomas Tickell 1686–1740

20 There taught us how to live; and (oh! too
high
The price for knowledge) taught us how to
die.
  'To the Earl of Warwick. On the Death of Mr
  Addison' (1721) l. 81

## Paul Tillich 1886–1965

21 Neurosis is the way of avoiding non-being
by avoiding being.
  *The Courage To Be* (1952) pt. 2, ch. 3

## Emperor Titus AD 39–81

22 Friends, I have lost a day.
  On reflecting that he had done nothing to
  help anybody all day; in Suetonius *Lives of the
  Caesars* 'Titus' ch. 8, sect. 1

## Alexis de Tocqueville 1805–59

1 History is a gallery of pictures in which there are few originals and many copies.
*L'Ancien régime* (1856, ed. J. P. Mayer, 1951) p. 133 (tr. M. W. Patterson, 1933)

2 Of all nations, those submit to civilization with the most difficulty which habitually live by the chase.
*De la Démocratie en Amérique* (1835–40, ed. J. P. Mayer, 1951) vol. 1, p. 342 (tr. H. Reeve, 1841)

3 What is understood by republican government in the United States is the slow and quiet action of society upon itself.
*De la Démocratie en Amérique* (1835–40, ed. J. P. Mayer, 1951) vol. 1, p. 412 (tr. H. Reeve, 1841)

4 The French want no-one to be their *superior*. The English want *inferiors*. The Frenchman constantly raises his eyes above him with anxiety. The Englishman lowers his beneath him with satisfaction.
*Voyage en Angleterre et en Irlande de 1835* (ed. J. P. Mayer, 1958) 8 May 1835

5 It is from the midst of this putrid sewer that the greatest river of human industry springs up and carries fertility to the whole world. From this foul drain pure gold flows forth.
*Voyage en Angleterre et en Irlande de 1835* (ed. J. P. Mayer, 1958) 2 July 1835 (of Manchester)

## Alvin Toffler 1928–

6 Future shock.
Title of book (1970); defined by Toffler as 'the dizzying disorientation brought on by the premature arrival of the future' in *Horizon* Summer 1965

7 Culture shock is what happens when a traveller suddenly finds himself in a place where yes may mean no, where a 'fixed price' is negotiable, where to be kept waiting in an outer office is no cause for insult, where laughter may signify anger.
*Future Shock* (1970) ch. 1 (the term 'culture shock' appears to have been already in use by the 1940s)

## J. R. R. Tolkien 1892–1973

8 In a hole in the ground there lived a hobbit.
*The Hobbit* (1937) ch. 1

9 Never laugh at live dragons.
*The Hobbit* (1937) ch. 12

10 One Ring to rule them all, One Ring to find them
One Ring to bring them all and in the darkness bind them.
*The Lord of the Rings* pt. 1 *The Fellowship of the Ring* (1954) epigraph

## Leo Tolstoy 1828–1910

11 All happy families resemble one another, but each unhappy family is unhappy in its own way.
*Anna Karenina* (1875–7) pt. 1, ch. 1 (tr. A. and L. Maude)

12 Our body is a machine for living. It is organized for that, it is its nature. Let life go on in it unhindered and let it defend itself.
*War and Peace* (1865–9) bk. 10, ch. 29 (tr. A. and L. Maude). Cf. 204:3

13 I sit on a man's back, choking him and making him carry me, and yet assure myself and others that I am very sorry for him and wish to ease his lot by all possible means—except by getting off his back.
*What Then Must We Do?* (1886) ch. 16 (tr. A. Maude)

## A. M. Toplady 1740–78

14 Rock of Ages, cleft for me,
Let me hide myself in Thee;
Let the water and the blood,
From Thy riven side which flowed,
Be of sin the double cure,
Cleanse me from its guilt and power.
'Rock of Ages, cleft for me' (1776 hymn)

## Cyril Tourneur

*See* THOMAS MIDDLETON

## A. Toussenel 1803–85

15 The more one gets to know of men, the more one values dogs.
*L'Esprit des bêtes* (1847) ch. 3 (attributed to Mme Roland in the form 'The more I see of men, the more I like dogs')

## Pete Townshend 1945–

16 Hope I die before I get old.
'My Generation' (1965 song)

## Thomas Traherne c.1637–74

17 An empty book is like an infant's soul, in which anything may be written. It is capable of all things, but containeth nothing.
*Centuries of Meditations* 'First Century' opening words

18 The corn was orient and immortal wheat, which never should be reaped, nor was ever sown.
*Centuries of Meditations* 'Third Century' sect. 3

19 O what venerable creatures did the aged seem! Immortal cherubims! And young men glittering and sparkling angels, and maids strange seraphic pieces of life and beauty!
*Centuries of Meditations* 'Third Century' sect. 3

1 I within did flow
With seas of life, like wine.
I nothing in this world did know,
But 'twas divine!
'Wonder'

## Henry Duff Traill 1842–1900

2 Look in my face. My name is Used-to-was;
I am also called Played-out and Done-to-
death,
And It-will-wash-no-more.
'After Dilettante Concetti' (i.e. Dante Gabriel
Rossetti) st. 8. Cf. 263:8

## Joseph Trapp 1679–1747

3 The King, observing with judicious eyes
The state of both his universities,
To Oxford sent a troop of horse, and why?
That learned body wanted loyalty;
To Cambridge books, as very well
discerning
How much that loyal body wanted
learning.
Lines written on George I's donation of the
Bishop of Ely's library to Cambridge
University; in J. Nichols *Literary Anecdotes*
(1812–16) vol. 3, p. 330. Cf. 74:25

## Merle Travis 1917–83

4 Sixteen tons, what do you get?
Another day older and deeper in debt.
Say brother, don't you call me 'cause I
can't go
I owe my soul to the company store.
'Sixteen Tons' (1947 song)

## Sir Herbert Beerbohm Tree
1852–1917

5 He is an old bore. Even the grave yawns for
him.
Of Israel Zangwill, in Max Beerbohm *Herbert
Beerbohm Tree* (1920) appendix 4

## Herbert Trench 1865–1923

6 Come, let us make love deathless.
Title of poem (1901)

## G. M. Trevelyan 1876–1962

7 Disinterested intellectual curiosity is the
life-blood of real civilization.
*English Social History* (1942) introduction

8 If the French noblesse had been capable of
playing cricket with their peasants, their
chateaux would never have been burnt.
*English Social History* (1942) ch. 8

9 [Education] has produced a vast population
able to read but unable to distinguish what
is worth reading, an easy prey to
sensations and cheap appeals.
*English Social History* (1942) ch. 18

## Calvin Trillin 1935–

10 The shelf life of the modern hardback
writer is somewhere between the milk and
the yoghurt.
In *Sunday Times* 9 June 1991 (attributed)

## Tommy Trinder 1909–89

11 Overpaid, overfed, oversexed, and over
here.
Of American troops in Britain during the
Second World War (associated with Trinder,
but probably not original)

## Anthony Trollope 1815–82

12 Three hours a day will produce as much as
a man ought to write.
*Autobiography* (1883) ch. 15

13 Those who have courage to love should
have courage to suffer.
*The Bertrams* (1859) ch. 27

14 There is no road to wealth so easy and
respectable as that of matrimony.
*Doctor Thorne* (1858) ch. 16

15 It's dogged as does it. It ain't thinking
about it.
*The Last Chronicle of Barset* (1867) ch. 61 (Giles
Hoggett)

16 It is because we put up with bad things
that hotel-keepers continue to give them to
us.
*Orley Farm* (1862) ch. 18

17 As for conceit, what man will do any good
who is not conceited? Nobody holds a good
opinion of a man who has a low opinion of
himself.
*Orley Farm* (1862) ch. 22

18 She knew how to allure by denying, and to
make the gift rich by delaying it.
*Phineas Finn* (1869) ch. 57

19 I doubt whether any girl would be satisfied
with her lover's mind if she knew the
whole of it.
*The Small House at Allington* (1864) ch. 4

20 The tenth Muse, who now governs the
periodical press.
*The Warden* (1855) ch. 14

21 Love is like any other luxury. You have no
right to it unless you can afford it.
*The Way We Live Now* (1875) ch. 84

## Leon Trotsky 1879–1940

22 Old age is the most unexpected of all
things that happen to a man.
*Diary in Exile* (1959) 8 May 1935

23 Civilization has made the peasantry its
pack animal. The bourgeoisie in the long
run only changed the form of the pack.
*History of the Russian Revolution* (1933) vol. 3,
ch. 1

1 You [the Mensheviks] are pitiful isolated individuals; you are bankrupts; your role is played out. Go where you belong from now on—into the dustbin of history!
  *History of the Russian Revolution* (1933) vol. 3, ch. 10

2 Where force is necessary, there it must be applied boldly, decisively and completely. But one must know the limitations of force; one must know when to blend force with a manoeuvre, a blow with an agreement.
  *What Next?* (1932) ch. 14

## Harry S. Truman 1884–1972

3 Wherever you have an efficient government you have a dictatorship.
  Lecture at Columbia University, 28 April 1959, in *Truman Speaks* (1960) p. 51

4 A statesman is a politician who's been dead 10 or 15 years.
  In *New York World Telegram and Sun* 12 April 1958

5 It's a recession when your neighbour loses his job; it's a depression when you lose yours.
  In *Observer* 13 April 1958

6 The buck stops here.
  Unattributed motto on Truman's desk
  *See also* HARRY VAUGHAN

## Barbara W. Tuchman 1912–89

7 Dead battles, like dead generals, hold the military mind in their dead grip and Germans, no less than other peoples, prepare for the last war.
  *August 1914* (1962) ch. 2

8 For one August in its history Paris was French—and silent.
  *August 1914* (1962) ch. 20

## Sophie Tucker 1884–1966

9 From birth to 18 a girl needs good parents. From 18 to 35, she needs good looks. From 35 to 55, good personality. From 55 on, she needs good cash.
  In M. Freedland *Sophie* (1978) p. 214

## Martin Tupper 1810–89

10 A good book is the best of friends, the same to-day and for ever.
  *Proverbial Philosophy* Series I (1838) 'Of Reading'

## Ivan Turgenev 1818–83

11 Superfluous, superfluous ... A supernumerary—that's all. Nature, obviously, hadn't counted on my showing up and consequently treated me as an unexpected and uninvited guest.
  *Diary of a Superfluous Man* (1850) 23 March (tr. F. Reeve)

12 Nature is not a temple, but a workshop, and man's the workman in it.
  *Fathers and Sons* (1862) ch. 9 (tr. R. Edmonds)

13 I share no one's ideas. I have my own.
  *Fathers and Sons* (1862) ch. 13 (tr. R. Edmonds)

14 Just try and set death aside. It sets you aside, and that's the end of it!
  *Fathers and Sons* (1862) ch. 27 (tr. R. Edmonds)

15 Whatever a man prays for, he prays for a miracle. Every prayer reduces itself to this: Great God, grant that twice two be not four.
  *Poems in Prose* (1881) 'Prayer'

## A. R. J. Turgot 1727–81

16 He snatched the lightning shaft from heaven, and the sceptre from tyrants.
  Inscription for a bust of Benjamin Franklin, inventor of the lightning conductor

## Walter James Redfern Turner 1889–1946

17 When I was but thirteen or so
  I went into a golden land,
  Chimborazo, Cotopaxi
  Took me by the hand.
  'Romance' (1916)

## Mark Twain 1835–1910

18 There was things which he stretched, but mainly he told the truth.
  *The Adventures of Huckleberry Finn* (1884) ch. 1

19 'Pilgrim's Progress', about a man that left his family it didn't say why ... The statements was interesting, but tough.
  *The Adventures of Huckleberry Finn* (1884) ch. 17

20 All kings is mostly rapscallions.
  *The Adventures of Huckleberry Finn* (1884) ch. 23

21 Hain't we got all the fools in town on our side? and ain't that a big enough majority in any town?
  *The Adventures of Huckleberry Finn* (1884) ch. 26

22 Soap and education are not as sudden as a massacre, but they are more deadly in the long run.
  *A Curious Dream* (1872) 'Facts concerning the Recent Resignation'

23 Truth is the most valuable thing we have. Let us economize it.
  *Following the Equator* (1897) ch. 7. Cf. 16:6

24 Man is the Only Animal that Blushes. Or needs to.
  *Following the Equator* (1897) ch. 27

25 It takes your enemy and your friend, working together, to hurt you to the heart: the one to slander you and the other to get the news to you.
  *Following the Equator* (1897) ch. 45

1 They spell it Vinci and pronounce it
Vinchy; foreigners always spell better than
they pronounce.
*The Innocents Abroad* (1869) ch. 19

2 Lump the whole thing! say that the Creator
made Italy from designs by Michael
Angelo!
*The Innocents Abroad* (1869) ch. 27. Cf. 336:17

3 Familiarity breeds contempt—and children.
*Notebooks* (1935) p. 237

4 Cauliflower is nothing but cabbage with
a college education.
*Pudd'nhead Wilson* (1894) ch. 5

5 When angry, count four; when very angry,
swear.
*Pudd'nhead Wilson* (1894) ch. 10

6 As to the Adjective: when in doubt, strike
it out.
*Pudd'nhead Wilson* (1894) ch. 11

7 The report of my death was an
exaggeration.
*New York Journal* 2 June 1897 (usually quoted
'Reports of my death have been greatly
exaggerated')

## Kenneth Tynan 1927–80

8 A critic is a man who knows the way but
can't drive the car.
In *New York Times Magazine* 9 January 1966,
p. 27

9 A neurosis is a secret you don't know
you're keeping.
In Kathleen Tynan *Life of Kenneth Tynan* (1987)
ch. 19

## Ulpian d. 228

10 *Nulla iniuria est, quae in volentem fiat.*
No injustice is done to someone who
wants that thing done.
In *Corpus Iuris Civilis* Digests bk. 47, ch. 10,
sect. 1, subsect. 5 (usually quoted '*Volenti non
fit iniuria*')

## Miguel de Unamuno 1864–1937

11 *La vida es duda,*
*y la fe sin la duda es sólo muerte.*
Life is doubt,
And faith without doubt is nothing but
death.
*Poesías* (1907) 'Salmo II'

## John Updike 1932–

12 A soggy little island huffing and puffing to
keep up with Western Europe.
Of England, in *Picked Up Pieces* (1976) 'London
Life' (written 1969)

13 America is a land whose centre is nowhere;
England one whose centre is everywhere.
*Picked Up Pieces* (1976) 'London Life' (written
1969)

14 America is a vast conspiracy to make you
happy.
*Problems* (1980) 'How to love America and
Leave it at the Same Time'

## Sir Peter Ustinov 1921–

15 Laughter ... the most civilized music in
the world.
*Dear Me* (1977) ch. 3

16 I do not believe that friends are necessarily
the people you like best, they are merely
the people who got there first.
*Dear Me* (1977) ch. 5. Cf. 1:12

17 If Botticelli were alive today he'd be
working for *Vogue.*
In *Observer* 21 October 1962 'Sayings of the
Week'. Cf. 336:2

18 At the age of four with paper hats and
wooden swords we're all Generals. Only
some of us never grow out of it.
*Romanoff and Juliet* (1956) act 1

19 A diplomat these days is nothing but
a head-waiter who's allowed to sit down
occasionally.
*Romanoff and Juliet* (1956) act 1

## Paul Valéry 1871–1945

20 Science means simply the aggregate of all
the recipes that are always successful. The
rest is literature.
*Moralités* (1932) p. 41. Cf. 337:20

21 God created man and, finding him not
sufficiently alone, gave him a companion to
make him feel his solitude more keenly.
*Tel Quel 1* (1941) 'Moralités'

22 Politics is the art of preventing people
from taking part in affairs which properly
concern them.
*Tel Quel 2* (1943) 'Rhumbs'

## Sir John Vanbrugh 1664–1726

23 BELINDA: Ay, but you know we must return
good for evil.
LADY BRUTE: That may be a mistake in the
translation.
*The Provoked Wife* (1697) act 1, sc. 1

24 When once a woman has given you her
heart, you can never get rid of the rest of
her body.
*The Relapse* (1696) act 3, sc. 1

## Vivian van Damm c.1889–1960

25 We never closed.
Of the Windmill Theatre, London, during the
Second World War; in *Tonight and Every Night*
(1952) ch. 18

## William Henry Vanderbilt
1821–85

1 The public be damned!
   On consulting the public about luxury
   trains; in letter from A. W. Cole to *New York
   Times* 25 August 1918

## Harry Vaughan

2 If you can't stand the heat, get out of the
   kitchen.
   In *Time* 28 April 1952 (associated with Harry
   S. Truman, but attributed by him to
   Vaughan, his 'military jester')

## Henry Vaughan 1622–95

3 Man is the shuttle, to whose winding quest
   And passage through these looms
   God ordered motion, but ordained no rest.
   *Silex Scintillans* (1650–5) 'Man'

4 Wise Nicodemus saw such light
   As made him know his God by night.
   *Silex Scintillans* (1650–5) 'The Night'

5 Dear Night! this world's defeat;
   The stop to busy fools; care's check and
   curb.
   *Silex Scintillans* (1650–5) 'The Night'

6 My soul, there is a country
   Far beyond the stars,
   Where stands a wingèd sentry
   All skilful in the wars;
   There, above noise and danger,
   Sweet Peace is crowned with smiles,
   And One born in a manger
   Commands the beauteous files.
   *Silex Scintillans* (1650–5) 'Peace'

7 Happy those early days, when I
   Shined in my angel-infancy.
   Before I understood this place
   Appointed for my second race,
   Or taught my soul to fancy aught
   But a white, celestial thought.
   *Silex Scintillans* (1650–5) 'The Retreat'

8 And in those weaker glories spy
   Some shadows of eternity.
   *Silex Scintillans* (1650–5) 'The Retreat'

9 But felt through all this fleshly dress
   Bright shoots of everlastingness.
   *Silex Scintillans* (1650–5) 'The Retreat'

10 Some men a forward motion love,
   But I by backward steps would move,
   And when this dust falls to the urn,
   In that state I came, return.
   *Silex Scintillans* (1650–5) 'The Retreat'

11 They are all gone into the world of light,
   And I alone sit lingering here.
   *Silex Scintillans* (1650–5) 'They are all gone'

12 Dear, beauteous death! the jewel of the
   just,
   Shining nowhere but in the dark.
   *Silex Scintillans* (1650–5) 'They are all gone'

13 Sure thou didst flourish once! and many
   springs,
   Many bright mornings, much dew, many
   showers
   Passed o'er thy head.
   *Silex Scintillans* (1650–5) 'The Timber'

14 I saw Eternity the other night,
   Like a great ring of pure and endless light,
   All calm, as it was bright;
   And round beneath it, Time in hours, days,
   years,
   Driv'n by the spheres
   Like a vast shadow moved; in which the
   world
   And all her train were hurled.
   *Silex Scintillans* (1650–5) 'The World'

## Thomas, Lord Vaux 1510–56

15 For age with stealing steps
   Hath clawed me with his clutch.
   'The Aged Lover Renounceth Love' (1557)

## Thorstein Veblen 1857–1929

16 Conspicuous consumption of valuable
   goods is a means of reputability to the
   gentleman of leisure.
   *Theory of the Leisure Class* (1899) ch. 4

17 Conspicuous leisure and consumption . . .
   In the one case it is a waste of time and
   effort, in the other it is a waste of goods.
   *Theory of the Leisure Class* (1899) ch. 4

## Vegetius 4th century

18 *Qui desiderat pacem, praeparet bellum.*
   Let him who desires peace, prepare for
   war.
   *Epitoma Rei Militaris* bk. 3, prologue (usually
   quoted '*Si vis pacem, para bellum* [If you want
   peace, prepare for war]'). Cf. 7:16, 15:14

## Pierre Vergniaud 1753–93

19 There was reason to fear that the
   Revolution, like Saturn, might devour in
   turn each one of her children.
   In A. de Lamartine *Histoire des Girondins*
   (1847) bk. 38, ch. 20

## Paul Verlaine 1844–96

20 *Et tout le reste est littérature.*
   All the rest is mere fine writing.
   'Art poétique' (1882). Cf. 336:20

21 *Les sanglots longs
   Des violons
   De l'automne
   Blessent mon cœur
   D'une langueur
   Monotone.*
   The drawn-out sobs of autumn's violins
   wound my heart with a monotonous
   languor.
   'Chanson d'Automne' (1866)

1 *Et, Ô ces voix d'enfants chantants dans la coupole!*
And oh those children's voices, singing beneath the dome!
'Parsifal' A Jules Tellier (1886)

2 *Il pleure dans mon coeur
Comme il pleut sur la ville.*
Tears are shed in my heart like the rain on the town.
*Romances sans paroles* (1874) 'Ariettes oubliées' no. 3

## Emperor Vespasian AD 9–79

3 *Pecunia non olet.*
Money has no smell.
Traditional summary of Suetonius *Lives of the Caesars* 'Vespasian' sect. 23, subsect. 3 (quashing an objection to tax on public lavatories)

4 Woe is me, I think I am becoming a god.
When fatally ill; in Suetonius *Lives of the Caesars* 'Vespasian' sect. 23, subsect. 4

## Queen Victoria 1819–1901

5 The danger to the country, to Europe, to her vast Empire, which is involved in having all these great interests entrusted to the shaking hand of an old, wild, and incomprehensible man of 82, is very great!
On Gladstone's last appointment as Prime Minister; letter to Lord Lansdowne, 12 August 1892, in T. Wodehouse Legh *Lord Lansdowne* (1929) p. 100

6 We are not interested in the possibilities of defeat; they do not exist.
On the Boer War during 'Black Week', December 1899; in Lady Gwendolen Cecil *Life of Robert, Marquis of Salisbury* (1931) vol. 3, ch. 6

7 We are not amused.
Attributed, in Caroline Holland *Notebooks of a Spinster Lady* (1919) ch. 21 (2 January 1900)

8 I will be good.
On being shown a chart of the line of succession, 11 March 1830; in Sir Theodore Martin *The Prince Consort* (1875) vol. 1, ch. 2

9 He speaks to Me as if I was a public meeting.
Of Gladstone, in G. W. E. Russell *Collections and Recollections* (1898) ch. 14

10 Dirty, dark, and undevotional.
Of St Paul's Cathedral; attributed in this form, but recorded in her Journal, 27 February 1872, as 'so cold, dreary and dingy'. See G. E. Buckle (ed.) *Letters of Queen Victoria: 2nd Series* vol. 2 (1926)

## Gore Vidal 1925–

11 [Commercialism is] doing well that which should not be done at all.
In *Listener* 7 August 1975, p. 168

12 A triumph of the embalmer's art.
Of Ronald Reagan, in *Observer* 26 April 1981

13 Whenever a friend succeeds, a little something in me dies.
In *Sunday Times Magazine* 16 September 1973

14 He will lie even when it is inconvenient: the sign of the true artist.
Attributed

## King Vidor 1895–1982

15 Marriage isn't a word ... it's a *sentence*!
*The Crowd* (1928 film)

## José Antonio Viera Gallo 1943–

16 Socialism can only arrive by bicycle.
In Ivan Illich *Energy and Equity* (1974) epigraph

## Alfred de Vigny 1797–1863

17 *J'aime le son du cor, le soir, au fond des bois.*
I love the sound of the horn, at night, in the depth of the woods.
'Le Cor' (1826)

18 *Seul le silence est grand; tout le reste est faiblesse.*
Silence alone is great; all else is feebleness.
'La mort du loup' (1843) pt. 3

## Philippe-Auguste Villiers de L'Isle-Adam 1838–89

19 Living? The servants will do that for us.
*Axël* (1890) pt. 4, sect. 2

## François Villon b. 1431

20 *Mais où sont les neiges d'antan?*
But where are the snows of yesteryear?
*Le Grand Testament* (1461) 'Ballade des dames du temps jadis' (tr. D. G. Rossetti)

21 *En cette foi je veux vivre et mourir.*
In this faith I wish to live and to die.
*Le Grand Testament* (1461) 'Ballade pour prier Nôtre Dame'

## St Vincent of Lerins d. AD c.450

22 *Quod ubique, quod semper, quod ab omnibus creditum est.*
What is everywhere, what is always, what is by all people believed.
*Commonitorium Primum* sect. 2

## Virgil 70–19 BC

23 *Arma virumque cano, Troiae qui primus ab oris
Italiam fato profugus Laviniaque venit
Litora, multum ille et terris iactatus et alto
Vi superum, saevae memorem Iunonis ob iram.*
I sing of arms and the man who first from the shores of Troy came destined an exile to Italy and the Lavinian beaches, a man much buffeted on land and on the deep by force of the gods because of fierce Juno's never-forgetting anger.
*Aeneid* bk. 1, l. 1

1 *O passi graviora, dabit deus his quoque finem.*
O you who have borne even heavier things,
God will grant an end to these too.
*Aeneid* bk. 1, l. 199

2 *Forsan et haec olim meminisse iuvabit.*
Maybe one day it will be cheering to
remember even these things.
*Aeneid* bk. 1, l. 203

3 *Et vera incessu patuit dea.*
And her true godhead was evident from
her walk.
*Aeneid* bk. 1, l. 405

4 *Sunt lacrimae rerum et mentem mortalia
tangunt.*
There are tears shed for things and
mortality touches the heart.
*Aeneid* bk. 1, l. 462

5         *Equo ne credite, Teucri.*
*Quidquid id est, timeo Danaos et dona ferentis.*
Do not trust the horse, Trojans. Whatever
it is, I fear the Greeks even when they
bring gifts.
*Aeneid* bk. 2, l. 48

6 *Una salus victis nullam sperare salutem.*
The only safe course for the defeated is to
expect no safety.
*Aeneid* bk. 2, l. 354

7 *Dis aliter visum.*
The gods thought otherwise.
*Aeneid* bk. 2, l. 428

8         *Quid non mortalia pectora cogis,*
*Auri sacra fames!*
To what do you not drive human hearts,
cursed craving for gold!
*Aeneid* bk. 3, l. 56

9         *Varium et mutabile semper*
*Femina.*
Fickle and changeable always is woman.
*Aeneid* bk. 4, l. 569

10 *Hos successus alit: possunt, quia posse videntur.*
These success encourages: they can
because they think they can.
*Aeneid* bk. 5, l. 231

11         *Bella, horrida bella,*
*Et Thybrim multo spumantem sanguine cerno.*
I see wars, horrible wars, and the Tiber
foaming with much blood.
*Aeneid* bk. 6, l. 86

12         *Facilis descensus Averno:*
*Noctes atque dies patet atri ianua Ditis;*
*Sed revocare gradum superasque evadere ad*
    *auras,*
*Hoc opus, hic labor est.*
Easy is the way down to the Underworld:
by night and by day dark Hades' door
stands open; but to retrace one's steps and
to make a way out to the upper air, that's
the task, that is the labour.
*Aeneid* bk. 6, l. 126

13 *Procul, o procul este, profani.*
Far off, Oh keep far off, you uninitiated
ones.
*Aeneid* bk. 6, l. 258

14 *Ibant obscuri sola sub nocte.*
Darkling they went under the lonely night.
*Aeneid* bk. 6, l. 268

15 *Stabant orantes primi transmittere cursum*
*Tendebantque manus ripae ulterioris amore.*
They stood begging to be the first to make
the voyage over and they reached out their
hands in longing for the further shore.
*Aeneid* bk. 6, l. 313

16 *Tu regere imperio populos, Romane, memento*
*(Hae tibi erunt artes), pacique imponere morem,*
*Parcere subiectis et debellare superbos.*
You, Roman, make your task to rule
nations by your government (these shall be
your skills), to impose ordered ways upon a
state of peace, to spare those who have
submitted and to subdue the arrogant.
*Aeneid* bk. 6, l. 851

17 *Manibus date lilia plenis.*
Give me lilies in armfuls.
*Aeneid* bk. 6, l. 883

18         *Geniumque loci primamque deorum*
*Tellurem Nymphasque et adhuc ignota precatur*
*Flumina.*
He prays to the spirit of the place and to
Earth, the first of the gods, and to the
Nymphs and as yet unknown rivers.
*Aeneid* bk. 7, l. 136

19 *Macte nova virtute, puer, sic itur ad astra.*
Blessings on your young courage, boy;
that's the way to the stars.
*Aeneid* bk. 9, l. 641

20 *Audentis Fortuna iuvat.*
Fortune assists the bold.
*Aeneid* bk. 10, l. 284 (often quoted 'Fortune
favours the brave'). Cf. 329:5

21 *Et dulcis moriens reminiscitur Argos.*
And dying remembers his sweet Argos.
*Aeneid* bk. 10, l. 782

22 *Experto credite.*
Trust one who has gone through it.
*Aeneid* bk. 11, l. 283

23 *Trahit sua quemque voluptas.*
Everyone is dragged on by their favourite
pleasure.
*Eclogues* no. 2, l. 65

24 *Latet anguis in herba.*
There's a snake hidden in the grass.
*Eclogues* no. 3, l. 93

25 *Ultima Cumaei venit iam carminis aetas;*
*Magnus ab integro saeclorum nascitur ordo.*
*Iam redit et virgo, redeunt Saturnia regna,*
*Iam nova progenies caelo demittitur alto.*
Now has come the last age according to
the oracle at Cumae; the great series of
lifetimes starts anew. Now too the virgin
goddess returns, the golden days of
Saturn's reign return, now a new race is
sent down from high heaven.
*Eclogues* no. 4, l. 4

1 *Ambo florentes aetatibus, Arcades ambo,*
  *Et cantare pares et respondere parati.*
  Both in the flower of their youth,
  Arcadians both, and matched and ready
  alike to start a song and to respond.
  *Eclogues* no. 7, l. 4

2 *Non omnia possumus omnes.*
  We can't all do everything.
  *Eclogues* no. 8, l. 63. Cf. 212:1

3 *Nam neque adhuc Vario videor nec dicere Cinna*
  *Digna, sed argutos inter strepere anser olores.*
  For I don't seem yet to write things as
  good either as Varius or as Cinna, but to
  be a goose honking amongst tuneful
  swans.
  *Eclogues* no. 9, l. 35

4 *Omnia vincit Amor: et nos cedamus Amori.*
  Love conquers all things: let us too give in
  to Love.
  *Eclogues* no. 10, l. 69

5 *Ultima Thule.*
  Farthest Thule.
  *Georgics* no. 1, l. 30

6 *Imponere Pelio Ossam*
  *Scilicet atque Ossae frondosum involvere*
  *Olympum.*
  To pile Ossa on Pelion, no less, and to roll
  leafy Olympus on top of Ossa.
  *Georgics* no. 1, l. 281

7 *O fortunatos nimium, sua si bona norint,*
  *Agricolas!*
  O farmers excessively fortunate if only
  they recognized their blessings!
  *Georgics* no. 2, l. 458

8 *Felix qui potuit rerum cognoscere causas.*
  Lucky is he who has been able to
  understand the causes of things.
  *Georgics* no. 2, l. 490

9 *Sed fugit interea, fugit inreparabile tempus.*
  But meanwhile it is flying, irretrievable
  time is flying.
  *Georgics* no. 3, l. 284 (usually quoted '*tempus*
  *fugit* [time flies]')

## Voltaire 1694–1778

10 *Dans ce meilleur des mondes possibles ... tout*
   *est au mieux.*
   In this best of possible worlds ... all is for
   the best.
   *Candide* (1759) ch. 1 (usually quoted 'All is for
   the best in the best of all possible worlds')

11 *Si nous ne trouvons pas des choses agréables,*
   *nous trouverons du moins des choses nouvelles.*
   If we do not find anything pleasant, at
   least we shall find something new.
   *Candide* (1759) ch. 17

12 *Dans ce pays-ci il est bon de tuer de temps en*
   *temps un amiral pour encourager les autres.*
   In this country [England] it is thought well
   to kill an admiral from time to time to
   encourage the others.
   *Candide* (1759) ch. 23

13 *Il faut cultiver notre jardin.*
   We must cultivate our garden.
   *Candide* (1759) ch. 30

14 [Men] use thought only to justify their
   injustices, and speech only to conceal their
   thoughts.
   *Dialogues* (1763) 'Le Chapon et la poularde'

15 *Le mieux est l'ennemi du bien.*
   The best is the enemy of the good.
   *Contes* (1772) 'La Begueule' l. 2 (deriving from
   an Italian proverb quoted in Voltaire's
   *Dictionnaire philosophique* (1770 ed.) 'Art
   Dramatique')

16 Superstition sets the whole world in
   flames; philosophy quenches them.
   *Dictionnaire philosophique* (1764) 'Superstition'

17 The secret of being a bore ... is to tell
   everything.
   *Discours en vers sur l'homme* (1737) 'De la
   nature de l'homme' l. 172

18 *Si Dieu n'existait pas, il faudrait l'inventer.*
   If God did not exist, it would be necessary
   to invent him.
   *Épîtres* no. 96 'A l'Auteur du livre des trois
   imposteurs'. Cf. 243:11

19 This agglomeration which was called and
   which still calls itself the Holy Roman
   Empire was neither holy, nor Roman, nor
   an empire.
   *Essai sur l'histoire générale et sur les moeurs et*
   *l'esprit des nations* (1756) ch. 70

20 History is nothing more than a tableau of
   crimes and misfortunes.
   *L'Ingénu* (1767) ch. 10. Cf. 150:11

21 Whatever you do, stamp out superstition,
   and love those who love you.
   Letter to M. d'Alembert, 28 November 1762;
   in Voltaire Foundation (ed.) *Complete Works*
   vol. 25 (1973)

22 *Le superflu, chose très nécessaire.*
   The superfluous, a very necessary thing.
   *Le Mondain* (1736) l. 22

23 God is on the side not of the big battalions,
   but of the best shots.
   'The Piccini Notebooks' (c.1735–50) in T.
   Besterman (ed.) *Voltaire's Notebooks* (2nd ed.,
   1968) vol. 2, p. 547. Cf. 14:4, 83:20

24 We owe respect to the living; to the dead
   we owe only truth.
   'Première Lettre sur Oedipe' in *Oeuvres* (1785)
   vol. 1, p. 15 n.

25 The composition of a tragedy requires
   *testicles.*
   On being asked why no woman had ever
   written 'a tolerable tragedy'; letter from
   Byron to John Murray, 2 April 1817, in L. A.
   Marchand (ed.) *Byron's Letters and Journals*
   vol. 5 (1976)

26 The English plays are like their English
   puddings: nobody has any taste for them
   but themselves.
   In Joseph Spence *Anecdotes* (ed. J. M. Osborn,
   1966) no. 1033

1 I disapprove of what you say, but I will
defend to the death your right to say it.
   Attributed to Voltaire, but actually S. G.
   Tallentyre's summary of Voltaire's attitude
   towards Helvétius following the burning of
   the latter's *De l'esprit* in 1759; in *The Friends of
   Voltaire* (1907) p. 199

2 What a fuss about an omelette!
   What Voltaire *apparently* said on the burning
   of *De l'esprit*; in J. Parton *Life of Voltaire* (1881)
   vol. 2, ch. 25

3 This is no time for making new enemies.
   On being asked to renounce the Devil, on his
   deathbed (attributed)

## Alice Walker 1944–

4 Expect nothing. Live frugally
on surprise.
   'Expect nothing' (1973)

5 The quietly pacifist peaceful
always die
to make room for men
who shout.
   'The QPP' (1973)

## Felix Walker fl. 1820

6 I'm talking to Buncombe ['bunkum'].
   Excusing a long, dull, irrelevant speech in
   the House of Representatives, *c.*1820
   (Buncombe being his constituency). See W.
   Safire *New Language of Politics* (2nd ed., 1972)
   p. 80. Cf. 90:17

## Edgar Wallace 1875–1932

7 Dreamin' of thee! Dreamin' of thee!
   'T. A. in Love' (1900); popularized by Cyril
   Fletcher in 1930s radio shows

## George Wallace 1919–

8 Segregation now, segregation tomorrow
and segregation forever!
   Inaugural speech as Governor of Alabama,
   January 1963; in *Birmingham World*
   19 January 1963

## Henry Wallace 1888–1965

9 The century on which we are
entering—the century which will come out
of this war—can be and must be the
century of the common man.
   *Vital Speeches* (1942) vol. 8, p. 483 (8 May 1942)

## William Ross Wallace d. 1881

10 The hand that rocks the cradle
Is the hand that rules the world.
   'What rules the world' (1865)

## Graham Wallas 1858–1932

11 The little girl had the making of a poet in
her who, being told to be sure of her
meaning before she spoke, said, 'How can
I know what I think till I see what I say?'
   *The Art of Thought* (1926) ch. 4

## Edmund Waller 1606–87

12 Go, lovely rose!
Tell her, that wastes her time and me,
That now she knows,
When I resemble her to thee,
How sweet and fair she seems to be.
   'Go, lovely rose!' (1645)

13 Poets that lasting marble seek
Must carve in Latin or in Greek.
   'Of English Verse' (1645)

14 Why came I so untimely forth
Into a world which, wanting thee,
Could entertain us with no worth,
Or shadow of felicity?
   'To My Young Lady Lucy Sidney' (1645)

15 So all we know
Of what they do above,
Is that they happy are, and that they love.
   'Upon the Death of My Lady Rich' (1645) l. 75

## Horace Walpole (4th Earl of Orford) 1717–97

16 Our supreme governors, the mob.
   Letter to Sir Horace Mann, 7 September
   1743, in *Correspondence* (Yale ed., 1937–83)
   vol. 18

17 Every drop of ink in my pen ran cold.
   Letter to George Montagu, 30 July 1752, in
   *Correspondence* (Yale ed.) vol. 9

18 One of the greatest geniuses that ever
existed, Shakespeare, undoubtedly wanted
taste.
   Letter to Christopher Wren, 9 August 1764,
   in *Correspondence* (Yale ed.) vol. 40

19 It is charming to totter into vogue.
   Letter to George Selwyn, 2 December 1765,
   in *Correspondence* (Yale ed.) vol. 30

20 The best sun we have is made of Newcastle
coal.
   Letter to George Montagu, 15 June 1768, in
   *Correspondence* (Yale ed.) vol. 10

21 It was easier to conquer it [the East] than
to know what to do with it.
   Letter to Sir Horace Mann, 27 March 1772, in
   *Correspondence* (Yale ed.) vol. 23

22 The way to ensure summer in England is
to have it framed and glazed in a
comfortable room.
   Letter to Revd William Cole, 28 May 1774, in
   *Correspondence* (Yale ed.) vol. 1

23 This world is a comedy to those that think,
a tragedy to those that feel.
   Letter to Anne, Countess of Upper Ossory,
   16 August 1776, in *Correspondence* (Yale ed.)
   vol. 32

24 It is the story of a mountebank and his
zany.
   Of Boswell's *Tour of the Hebrides*; letter to
   Hon. Henry Conway, 6 October 1785, in
   *Correspondence* (Yale ed.) vol. 39

1 All his own geese are swans, as the swans
of others are geese.
> Of Sir Joshua Reynolds; letter to Anne,
> Countess of Upper Ossory, 1 December 1786,
> in *Correspondence* (Yale ed.) vol. 33

2 That hyena in petticoats, Mrs
Wollstonecraft.
> Letter to Hannah More, 26 January 1795, in
> *Correspondence* (Yale ed.) vol. 31

3 Virtue knows to a farthing what it has lost
by not having been vice.
> In L. Kronenberger *The Extraordinary Mr
> Wilkes* (1974) pt. 3, ch. 2

## Sir Hugh Walpole 1884–1941

4 'Tisn't life that matters! 'Tis the courage
you bring to it.
> *Fortitude* (1913) bk. 1, ch. 1

## Sir Robert Walpole (1st Earl of Orford) 1676–1745

5 They now *ring* the bells, but they will soon
*wring* their hands.
> On the declaration of war with Spain, 1739;
> in W. Coxe *Memoirs of Sir Robert Walpole*
> (1798) vol. 1, p. 618

6 All those men have their price.
> Of fellow parliamentarians; in W. Coxe
> *Memoirs of Sir Robert Walpole* (1798) vol. 1,
> p. 757

7 [Gratitude of place-expectants] is a lively
sense of future favours.
> In W. Hazlitt *Lectures on the English Comic
> Writers* (1819) 'On Wit and Humour'.
> Cf. 201:25

## William Walsh 1663–1708

8 I can endure my own despair,
But not another's hope.
> 'Song: Of All the Torments'

## Izaak Walton 1593–1683

9 As no man is born an artist, so no man is
born an angler.
> *The Compleat Angler* (1653) 'Epistle to the
> Reader'

10 I am, Sir, a Brother of the Angle.
> *The Compleat Angler* (1653) pt. 1, ch. 1

11 An excellent angler, and now with God.
> *The Compleat Angler* (1653) pt. 1, ch. 4

12 A good, honest, wholesome, hungry
breakfast.
> *The Compleat Angler* (1653) pt. 1, ch. 5

13 In so doing, use him as though you loved
him.
> *The Compleat Angler* (1653) pt. 1, ch. 8 (on
> baiting a hook with a live frog)

14 Look to your health; and if you have it,
praise God, and value it next to a good
conscience; for health is the second
blessing that we mortals are capable of; a
blessing that money cannot buy.
> *The Compleat Angler* (1653) pt. 1, ch. 21

15 But God, who is able to prevail, wrestled
with him, as the Angel did with Jacob, and
marked him; marked him for his own.
> *Life of Donne* (1670 ed.) p. 35

16 The great Secretary of Nature and all
learning, Sir Francis Bacon.
> *Life of Herbert* (1670 ed.) p. 26

## Bishop William Warburton 1698–1779

17 Orthodoxy is my doxy; heterodoxy is
another man's doxy.
> To Lord Sandwich, in Joseph Priestley
> *Memoirs* (1807) vol. 1, p. 372

## Artemus Ward (Charles Farrar Browne) 1834–67

18 Let us all be happy, and live within our
means, even if we have to borrer the
money to do it with.
> *Artemus Ward in London* (1867) ch. 7

19 Why is this thus? What is the reason of
this thusness?
> *Artemus Ward's Lecture* (1869) 'Heber C.
> Kimball's Harem'

## Andy Warhol 1927–87

20 In the future everybody will be world
famous for fifteen minutes.
> In *Andy Warhol* (1968) [p. 12]

## George Washington 1732–99

21 Let me ... warn you in the most solemn
manner against the baneful effects of the
spirit of party.
> *President's Address ... retiring from Public Life*
> (17 September 1796)

22 I can't tell a lie, Pa; you know I can't tell a
lie. I did cut it with my hatchet.
> In M. L. Weems *Life of George Washington*
> (10th ed., 1810) ch. 2

## Ned Washington 1901–76

23 Hi diddle dee dee (an actor's life for me).
> Title of song from the film *Pinocchio* (1940)

24 The night is like a lovely tune,
Beware my foolish heart!
How white the ever-constant moon,
Take care, my foolish heart!
> 'My Foolish Heart' (1949 song)

## William Watson c.1559–1603

25 *Fiat justitia et ruant coeli.*
Let justice be done though the heavens fall.
> *A Decacordon of Ten Quodlibeticall Questions
> Concerning Religion and State* (1602). Cf. 138:24

## William Watson 1858–1936

26 April, April,
Laugh thy girlish laughter.
> 'April'

1 My hand will miss the insinuated nose,
Mine eyes the tail that wagged contempt at
Fate.
   'An Epitaph' (for his dog)

## Isaac Watts 1674–1748

2 We are a garden walled around,
Chosen and made peculiar ground;
A little spot enclosed by grace,
Out of the world's wide wilderness.
   'The Church the Garden of Christ' (1707)

3 Come, let us join our cheerful songs
With angels round the throne;
Ten thousand thousand are their tongues,
But all their joys are one.
   'Come, let us join our cheerful songs' (1707)

4 When I survey the wondrous cross
On which the prince of glory died,
My richest gain I count but loss,
And pour contempt on all my pride.
   'Crucifixion to the World, by the Cross of
   Christ' (1707)

5 How doth the little busy bee
Improve each shining hour,
And gather honey all the day
From every opening flower!
   Divine Songs for Children (1715) 'Against
   Idleness and Mischief'

6 For Satan finds some mischief still
For idle hands to do.
   Divine Songs for Children (1715) 'Against
   Idleness and Mischief'

7 Let dogs delight to bark and bite,
For God hath made them so.
   Divine Songs for Children (1715) 'Against
   Quarrelling'

8 Birds in their little nests agree.
   Divine Songs for Children (1715) 'Love between
   Brothers and Sisters'

9 'Tis the voice of the sluggard; I heard him
complain,
'You have waked me too soon, I must
slumber again'.
   Divine Songs for Children (1715) 'The Sluggard'

10 Hark! from the tombs a doleful sound.
   'Hark! from the Tombs' (1707)

11 There is a land of pure delight,
Where saints immortal reign.
   'A Prospect of Heaven makes Death easy'
   (1707)

12 Jesus shall reign where'er the sun
Does his successive journeys run;
His kingdom stretch from shore to shore,
Till moons shall wax and wane no more.
   Psalms of David Imitated (1719) Psalm 72

13 Our God, our help in ages past
Our hope for years to come,
Our shelter from the stormy blast,
And our eternal home.
   Psalms of David Imitated (1719) Psalm 90 ('Our
   God' altered to 'O God' by John Wesley, 1738)

14 A thousand ages in Thy sight
Are like an evening gone.
   Psalms of David Imitated (1719) Psalm 90

15 Time, like an ever-rolling stream,
Bears all its sons away.
   The Psalms of David Imitated (1719) Psalm 90

## Evelyn Waugh 1903–66

16 I am not I: thou art not he or she: they are
not they.
   Brideshead Revisited (1945) 'Author's Note'

17 Charm is the great English blight. It does
not exist outside these damp islands. It
spots and kills anything it touches. It kills
love, it kills art.
   Brideshead Revisited (1945) bk. 3, ch. 2

18 The sound of English county families
baying for broken glass.
   Decline and Fall (1928) 'Prelude'. Cf. 33:23

19 I expect you'll be becoming a schoolmaster,
sir. That's what most of the gentlemen
does, sir, that gets sent down for indecent
behaviour.
   Decline and Fall (1928) 'Prelude'

20 Any one who has been to an English public
school will always feel comparatively at
home in prison. It is the people brought
up in the gay intimacy of the slums, Paul
learned, who find prison so soul-
destroying.
   Decline and Fall (1928) pt. 3, ch. 4

21 You never find an Englishman among the
under-dogs—except in England, of course.
   The Loved One (1948) ch. 1

22 He abhorred plastics, Picasso, sunbathing
and jazz—everything in fact that had
happened in his own lifetime.
   The Ordeal of Gilbert Pinfold (1957) ch. 1

23 The Beast stands for strong mutually
antagonistic governments everywhere ...
Self-sufficiency at home, self-assertion
abroad.
   Scoop (1938) bk. 1, ch. 1

24 Up to a point, Lord Copper.
   Scoop (1938) bk. 1, ch. 1

25 Feather-footed through the plashy fen
passes the questing vole.
   Scoop (1938) bk. 1, ch. 1

26 News is what a chap who doesn't care
much about anything wants to read. And
it's only news until he's read it. After that
it's dead.
   Scoop (1938) bk. 1, ch. 5

27 I will not stand for being called a woman
in my own house.
   Scoop (1938) bk. 2, ch. 1

28 Other nations use 'force'; we Britons alone
use 'Might'.
   Scoop (1938) bk. 2, ch. 5

29 Punctuality is the virtue of the bored.
   M. Davie (ed.) Diaries of Evelyn Waugh (1976)
   'Irregular Notes 1960–65' (26 March 1962)

1 A typical triumph of modern science to
find the only part of Randolph that was
not malignant and remove it.
   On hearing that Randolph Churchill's lung,
   when removed, proved non-malignant; in M.
   Davie (ed.) *Diaries of Evelyn Waugh* (1976)
   'Irregular Notes 1960–65' (March 1964)

2 Impotence and sodomy are socially O.K.
but birth control is flagrantly middle-class.
   'An Open Letter' pt. 3 in Nancy Mitford (ed.)
   *Noblesse Oblige* (1956)

3 Manners are especially the need of the
plain. The pretty can get away with
anything.
   In *Observer* 15 April 1962

## Frederick Weatherly 1848–1929

4 Where are the boys of the old Brigade,
Who fought with us side by side?
   'The Old Brigade' (1886 song)

5 Roses are flowering in Picardy,
But there's never a rose like you.
   'Roses of Picardy' (1916 song)

## Sidney Webb (Baron Passfield) 1859–1947

6 The inevitability of gradualness.
   In *The Labour Party on the Threshold* (Fabian
   Tract no. 207, 1923) p. 11 (26 June 1923)

## Max Weber 1864–1920

7 The protestant ethic and the spirit of
capitalism.
   Title of article in *Archiv für Sozialwissenschaft
   Sozialpolitik* vol. 20 (1904–5)

8 The concept of the 'official secret' is its
[bureaucracy's] specific invention.
   'Politik als Beruf' (1919) in *Gesammelte
   politische Schriften* (1921) p. 672

## Daniel Webster 1782–1852

9 Liberty *and* Union, now and forever, one
and inseparable!
   Speech, 26 January 1830, in *Writings and
   Speeches* vol. 6 (1903)

10 Fearful concatenation of circumstances.
   Argument on the murder of Captain Joseph
   White, 6 April 1830; in *Writings and Speeches*
   vol. 11 (1903)

11 The Law: It has honoured us, may we
honour it.
   Speech at the Charleston Bar Dinner, 10 May
   1847, in *Writings and Speeches* vol. 4 (1903)

12 There is always room at the top.
   On being advised against joining the
   overcrowded legal profession (attributed)

## John Webster c.1580–c.1625

13 Vain the ambition of kings
Who seek by trophies and dead things,
To leave a living name behind,
And weave but nets to catch the wind.
   *The Devil's Law-Case* (1623) act 5, sc. 4

14          Why should only I . . .
Be cased up, like a holy relic? I have youth
And a little beauty.
   *The Duchess of Malfi* (1623) act 3, sc. 2

15 Raised by that curious engine, your white
hand.
   *The Duchess of Malfi* (1623) act 3, sc. 2

16          O, that it were possible,
We might but hold some two days'
conference
With the dead!
   *The Duchess of Malfi* (1623) act 4, sc. 2

17 Glories, like glow-worms, afar off shine
bright,
But looked to near, have neither heat nor
light.
   *The Duchess of Malfi* (1623) act 4, sc. 2

18 I know death hath ten thousand several
doors
For men to take their exits.
   *The Duchess of Malfi* (1623) act 4, sc. 2.
   Cf. 222:6, 270:8

19 Cover her face; mine eyes dazzle: she died
young.
   *The Duchess of Malfi* (1623) act 4, sc. 2

20 Physicians are like kings,—they brook no
contradiction.
   *The Duchess of Malfi* (1623) act 5, sc. 2

21 We are merely the stars' tennis-balls,
struck and bandied
Which way please them.
   *The Duchess of Malfi* (1623) act 5, sc. 4

22          Fortune's a right whore:
If she give aught, she deals it in small
parcels,
That she may take away all at one swoop.
   *The White Devil* (1612) act 1, sc. 1

23 'Tis just like a summer birdcage in a
garden; the birds that are without despair
to get in, and the birds that are within
despair, and are in a consumption, for fear
they shall never get out.
   *The White Devil* (1612) act 1, sc. 2

24 A rape! a rape! . . .
Yes, you have ravished justice;
Forced me to do your pleasure.
   *The White Devil* (1612) act 3, sc. 2

25 Call for the robin-red-breast and the wren,
Since o'er shady groves they hover,
And with leaves and flowers do cover
The friendless bodies of unburied men.
   *The White Devil* (1612) act 5, sc. 4

26 But keep the wolf far thence that's foe to
men,
For with his nails he'll dig them up again.
   *The White Devil* (1612) act 5, sc. 4

27 We think caged birds sing, when indeed
they cry.
   *The White Devil* (1612) act 5, sc. 4. Cf. 284:1

28          I have caught
An everlasting cold; I have lost my voice
Most irrecoverably.
   *The White Devil* (1612) act 5, sc. 6

## Josiah Wedgwood 1730–95

1 Am I not a man and a brother.
   Legend on Wedgwood cameo, depicting a
   kneeling Negro slave in chains; reproduced
   in facsimile in E. Darwin *The Botanic Garden*
   pt. 1 (1791) facing p. 87

## Simone Weil 1909–43

2 All sins are attempts to fill voids.
   *La Pesanteur et la grâce* (1948) p. 27

3 What a country calls its vital economic
   interests are not the things which enable
   its citizens to live, but the things which
   enable it to make war.
   In W. H. Auden *A Certain World* (1971) p. 384

## Johnny Weissmuller 1904–84

4 Me Tarzan, you Jane.
   Summing up his role in *Tarzan, the Ape Man*
   (1932 film). The words occur neither in the
   film nor the original, by Edgar Rice
   Burroughs. See *Photoplay Magazine* June 1932

## Orson Welles 1915–85

5 In Italy for thirty years under the Borgias
   they had warfare, terror, murder,
   bloodshed — they produced Michelangelo,
   Leonardo da Vinci and the Renaissance. In
   Switzerland they had brotherly love, five
   hundred years of democracy and peace and
   what did that produce ... ? The cuckoo
   clock.
   *The Third Man* (1949 film); words added by
   Welles to Graham Greene's screenplay

## Duke of Wellington 1769–1852

6 All the business of war, and indeed all the
   business of life, is to endeavour to find out
   what you don't know by what you do;
   that's what I called 'guessing what was at
   the other side of the hill'.
   *The Croker Papers* (1885) vol. 3 ch. 28

7 As Lord Chesterfield said of the generals of
   his day, 'I only hope that when the enemy
   reads the list of their names, he trembles
   as I do.'
   Letter, 29 August 1810, in *Supplementary
   Despatches ...* (1860) vol. 6, p. 582 (usually
   quoted 'I don't know what effect these men
   will have upon the enemy, but, by God, they
   frighten me')

8 Up Guards and at them!
   In *The Battle of Waterloo* by a Near Observer
   [J. Booth] (1815) p. 57 (later denied by
   Wellington)

9 I never saw so many shocking bad hats in
   my life.
   On seeing the first Reformed Parliament; in
   Sir William Fraser *Words on Wellington* (1889)
   p. 12

10 The battle of Waterloo was won on the
   playing fields of Eton.
   Oral tradition, but not found in this form of
   words. See C. F. R. Montalembert *De l'avenir
   politique de l'Angleterre* (1856) ch. 10

11 Hard pounding, this, gentlemen; let's see
   who will pound longest.
   At the Battle of Waterloo; in Sir Walter Scott
   *Paul's Letters* (1816) Letter 8

12 Next to a battle lost, the greatest misery is
   a battle gained.
   In *Diary of Frances, Lady Shelley 1787–1817*
   (ed. R. Edgcumbe) vol. 1, ch. 9, p. 102

13 I used to say of him [Napoleon] that his
   presence on the field made the difference
   of forty thousand men.
   In Philip Henry Stanhope *Notes of
   Conversations with the Duke of Wellington* (1888)
   2 November 1831

14 Ours [our army] is composed of the scum
   of the earth—the mere scum of the earth.
   In Philip Henry Stanhope *Notes of
   Conversations with the Duke of Wellington* (1888)
   4 November 1831

15 Publish and be damned.
   Replying to a blackmail threat (attributed).
   See Elizabeth Longford *Wellington: The Years
   of the Sword* (1969) ch. 10

## H. G. Wells 1866–1946

16 He had read Shakespeare and found him
   weak in chemistry.
   *Complete Short Stories* (1927) 'Lord of the
   Dynamos'

17 'Sesquippledan,' he would say.
   'Sesquippledan verboojuice.'
   *The History of Mr Polly* (1909) ch. 1, pt. 5

18 'I'm a Norfan, both sides,' he would
   explain, with the air of one who had seen
   trouble.
   *Kipps* (1905) bk. 1, ch. 6, pt. 1

19 I was thinking jest what a Rum Go
   everything is.
   *Kipps* (1905) bk. 3, ch. 3, pt. 8

20 The Social Contract is nothing more or less
   than a vast conspiracy of human beings to
   lie to and humbug themselves and one
   another for the general Good. Lies are the
   mortar that bind the savage individual
   man into the social masonry.
   *Love and Mr Lewisham* (1900) ch. 23

21 Human history becomes more and more
   a race between education and catastrophe.
   *The Outline of History* (1920) vol. 2, ch. 41, pt. 4

22 Bah! the thing is not a nose at all, but a bit
   of primordial chaos clapped on to my face.
   *Select Conversations with an Uncle* (1895) 'The
   Man with a Nose'

23 The shape of things to come.
   Title of book (1933)

24 The war that will end war.
   Title of book (1914). Cf. 208:10

**1** Moral indignation is jealousy with a halo.
*The Wife of Sir Isaac Harman* (1914) ch. 9,
sect. 2

## Arnold Wesker 1932–

**2** Chips with every damn thing. You breed
babies and you eat chips with everything.
*Chips with Everything* (1962) act 1, sc. 2

## Charles Wesley 1707–88

**3** Amazing love! How can it be
That thou, my God, shouldst die for me?
'And can it be' (1738 hymn)

**4** O for a thousand tongues to sing.
'For the Anniversary Day of one's
Conversion' (1740)

**5** Forth in thy name, O Lord, I go,
My daily labour to pursue;
Thee, only thee, resolved to know,
In all I think or speak or do.
'Forth in thy name, O Lord, I go' (1749)

**6** Gentle Jesus, meek and mild,
Look upon a little child;
Pity my simplicity,
Suffer me to come to thee.
'Gentle Jesus, Meek and Mild' (1742)

**7** Hark! how all the welkin rings,
Glory to the King of kings.
Peace on earth and mercy mild,
God and sinners reconciled.
'Hymn for Christmas' (1739); altered to
'Hark! the herald-angels sing / Glory to the
new born king' by George Whitefield, 1753

**8** Jesu, lover of my soul,
Let me to thy bosom fly.
'In Temptation' (1740)

**9** Lo! He comes with clouds descending,
Once for favoured sinners slain.
'Lo! He comes' (1758)

**10** Love divine, all loves excelling,
Joy of heav'n, to earth come down,
Fix in us thy humble dwelling,
All thy faithful mercies crown.
'Love divine' (1747)

## John Wesley 1703–91

**11** The Gospel of Christ knows of no religion
but social; no holiness but social holiness.
*Hymns and Sacred Poems* (1739) Preface

**12** I went to America to convert the Indians;
but oh, who shall convert me?
*Journal* (ed. N. Curnock) 24 January 1738

**13** I look upon all the world as my parish.
*Journal* (ed. N. Curnock) 11 June 1739

**14** I design plain truth for plain people.
*Sermons on Several Occasions* (1746) in *Works*
(Centenary ed.) vol. 1, p. 104

**15** Let it be observed, that slovenliness is no
part of religion; that neither this, nor any
text of Scripture, condemns neatness of
apparel. Certainly this is a duty, not a sin.
'Cleanliness is, indeed, next to godliness.'
*Sermons on Several Occasions* (1788) Sermon 88

**16** Though I am always in haste, I am never in
a hurry.
Letter to Miss March, 10 December 1777, in
*Letters* (ed. J. Telford, 1931) vol. 6

**17** Time has shaken me by the hand and
death is not far behind.
Letter to Ezekiel Cooper, 1 February 1791, in
*Letters* (ed. J. Telford, 1931) vol. 8

## Samuel Wesley 1662–1735

**18** Style is the dress of thought; a modest
dress,
Neat, but not gaudy, will true critics
please.
'An Epistle to a Friend concerning Poetry'
(1700). Cf. 252:2

## Mae West 1892–1980

**19** I always say, keep a diary and some day it'll
keep you.
*Every Day's a Holiday* (1937 film)

**20** Beulah, peel me a grape.
*I'm No Angel* (1933 film)

**21** It's not the men in my life that
counts—it's the life in my men.
*I'm No Angel* (1933 film)

**22** 'Goodness, what beautiful diamonds!'
'Goodness had nothing to do with it.'
*Night After Night* (1932 film)

**23** Is that a gun in your pocket, or are you
just glad to see me?
In J. Weintraub *Peel Me a Grape* (1975) p. 47
(usually quoted 'Is that a pistol in your
pocket ... ')

**24** Why don't you come up sometime, and see
me?
*She Done Him Wrong* (1933 film); usually
quoted 'Why don't you come up and see me
sometime?'

## Rebecca West 1892–1983

**25** The point is that nobody likes having salt
rubbed into their wounds, even if it is the
salt of the earth.
*The Salt of the Earth* (1935) ch. 2

**26** Every other inch a gentleman.
Of Michael Arlen, in Victoria Glendinning
*Rebecca West* (1987) pt. 3, ch. 5

## John Fane, 10th Earl of Westmorland 1759–1841

**27** *Merit*, indeed! ... We are come to a pretty
pass if they talk of *merit* for a bishopric.
Noted in Lady Salisbury's diary, 9 December
1835; in C. Oman *The Gascoyne Heiress* (1968)
pt. 5, p. 188

## R. P. Weston 1878–1936 and Bert Lee 1880–1947

1 Good-bye-ee! — Good-bye-ee!
Wipe the tear, baby dear, from your eye-ee.
Tho' it's hard to part, I know,
I'll be tickled to death to go.
Don't cry-ee — don't sigh-ee!
There's a silver lining in the sky-ee!
Bonsoir, old thing! cheerio! chin-chin!
Nahpoo! Toodle-oo! Good-bye-ee!
  'Good-bye-ee!' (c.1915 song)

## Sir Charles Wetherell 1770–1846

2 Then there is my noble and biographical
friend who has added a new terror to
death.
  Of Lord Campbell, in Lord St Leonards
  *Misrepresentations in Campbell's Lives of
  Lyndhurst and Brougham* (1869) p. 3. Cf. 14:24,
  212:19

## Edith Wharton 1862–1937

3 An unalterable and unquestioned law of
the musical world required that the
German text of French operas sung by
Swedish artists should be translated into
Italian for the clearer understanding of
English-speaking audiences.
  *The Age of Innocence* (1920) bk. 1, ch. 1

4 Mrs Ballinger is one of the ladies who
pursue Culture in bands, as though it were
dangerous to meet it alone.
  *Xingu and Other Stories* (1916) 'Xingu'

## Thomas, 1st Marquess of Wharton 1648–1715

5 Ho, Brother Teague, dost hear de Decree?
*Lilli Burlero Bullena-la.*
Dat we shall have a new Debity,
*Lilli Burlero Bullena-la.*
  'A New Song' (written 1687), in *Poems on
  Affairs of State* (1704) vol. 3, p. 231 (*debity*
  deputy)

## Richard Whately 1787–1863

6 Happiness is no laughing matter.
  *Apophthegms* (1854)

7 It is not that pearls fetch a high price
*because* men have dived for them; but on
the contrary, men dive for them because
they fetch a high price.
  *Introductory Lectures on Political Economy* (1832)
  p. 253

## William Whewell 1794–1866

8 Hence no force however great can stretch a
cord however fine into an horizontal line
which is accurately straight: there will
always be a bending downwards.
  *Elementary Treatise on Mechanics* (1819) ch. 4,
  problem 2 (often cited as an example of
  accidental metre and rhyme)

## James McNeill Whistler 1834–1903

9 I am not arguing with you—I am telling
you.
  *The Gentle Art of Making Enemies* (1890) p. 51

10 I maintain that two and two would
continue to make four, in spite of the
whine of the amateur for three, or the cry
of the critic for five.
  *Whistler v. Ruskin. Art and Art Critics* (1878) p. 6

11 OSCAR WILDE: How I wish I had said that.
WHISTLER: You will, Oscar, you will.
  In R. Ellmann *Oscar Wilde* (1987) pt. 2, ch. 5

12 Yes madam, Nature is creeping up.
  To a lady who had been reminded of his
  work by an 'exquisite haze in the
  atmosphere'; in D. C. Seitz *Whistler Stories*
  (1913) p. 9

13 No, I ask it for the knowledge of a lifetime.
  In his case against Ruskin, replying to the
  question: 'For two days' labour, you ask two
  hundred guineas?'; in D. C. Seitz *Whistler
  Stories* (1913) p. 40

## E. B. White 1899–1985

14 Commuter—one who spends his life
In riding to and from his wife;
A man who shaves and takes a train,
And then rides back to shave again.
  'The Commuter' (1982)

15 MOTHER: It's broccoli, dear.
CHILD: I say it's spinach, and I say the hell
with it.
  *New Yorker* 8 December 1928 (cartoon
  caption)

## H. Kirke White 1785–1806

16 Much in danger, oft in woe,
Onward, Christians, onward go;
Bear the toil, maintain the strife,
Strengthened with the Bread of Life.
  'Much in danger, oft in woe' (1812 hymn);
  altered to 'Oft in danger' by W. J. Hall, 1836

## Patrick White 1912–90

17 Conversation is imperative if gaps are to
be filled, and old age, it is the last gap but
one.
  *The Tree of Man* (1955) ch. 22

## T. H. White 1906–64

18 The once and future king.
  Title of novel (1958), taken from Sir Thomas
  Malory *Le Morte d'Arthur* bk. 21, ch. 7: 'Hic
  iacet Arthurus, rex quondam rexque futurus'

## Alfred North Whitehead
1861–1947

**1** There are no whole truths; all truths are half-truths. It is trying to treat them as whole truths that plays the devil.
*Dialogues* (1954) prologue

**2** Intelligence is quickness to apprehend as distinct from ability, which is capacity to act wisely on the thing apprehended.
*Dialogues* (1954) 15 December 1939

**3** What is morality in any given time or place? It is what the majority then and there happen to like, and immorality is what they dislike.
*Dialogues* (1954) 30 August 1941

**4** Art is the imposing of a pattern on experience, and our aesthetic enjoyment is recognition of the pattern.
*Dialogues* (1954) 10 June 1943

**5** Civilization advances by extending the number of important operations which we can perform without thinking about them.
*Introduction to Mathematics* (1911) ch. 5

**6** The safest general characterization of the European philosophical tradition is that it consists of a series of footnotes to Plato.
*Process and Reality* (1929) pt. 2, ch. 1

## Katharine Whitehorn 1928–

**7** I wouldn't say when you've seen one Western you've seen the lot; but when you've seen the lot you get ⸢he feeling you've seen one.
*Sunday Best* (1976) 'Decoding the West'

## George Whiting

**8** When you're all dressed up and have no place to go.
Title of song (1912)

## William Whiting 1825–78

**9** Eternal Father, strong to save,
Whose arm doth bind the restless wave,
Who bidd'st the mighty ocean deep
Its own appointed limits keep:
O hear us when we cry to thee,
For those in peril on the sea.
'Eternal Father, Strong to Save' (1869 hymn)

## Walt Whitman 1819–92

**10** I sing the body electric.
Title of poem (1855)

**11** O Captain! my Captain! our fearful trip is done,
The ship has weathered every rack, the prize we sought is won.
'O Captain! My Captain!' (1871)

**12** Out of the cradle endlessly rocking,
Out of the mocking-bird's throat, the musical shuttle.
'Out of the cradle endlessly rocking' (1881)

**13** Have you your pistols? have you your sharp-edged axes?
Pioneers! O pioneers!
'Pioneers! O Pioneers!' (1881)

**14** Camerado, this is no book,
Who touches this touches a man.
'So Long!' (1881)

**15** Where the populace rise at once against the never-ending audacity of elected persons.
'Song of the Broad Axe' (1881) pt. 5, l. 12

**16** I celebrate myself, and sing myself.
'Song of Myself' (written 1855) pt. 1

**17** Urge and urge and urge,
Always the procreant urge of the world.
'Song of Myself' (written 1855) pt. 3

**18** I believe a leaf of grass is no less than the journey-work of the stars.
'Song of Myself' (written 1855) pt. 31

**19** I think I could turn and live with animals, they are so placid and self-contained,
I stand and look at them long and long.
They do not sweat and whine about their condition,
They do not lie awake in the dark and weep for their sins,
They do not make me sick discussing their duty to God.
'Song of Myself' (written 1855) pt. 32

**20** Behold, I do not give lectures or a little charity,
When I give I give myself.
'Song of Myself' (written 1855) pt. 40

**21** Do I contradict myself?
Very well then I contradict myself,
(I am large, I contain multitudes.)
'Song of Myself' (written 1855) pt. 51

**22** I sound my barbaric yawp over the roofs of the world.
'Song of Myself' (written 1855) pt. 52

**23** The earth does not argue,
Is not pathetic, has no arrangements,
'A Song of the Rolling Earth' (1881) pt. 1

**24** When lilacs last in the dooryard bloomed,
And the great star early drooped in the western sky in the night,
I mourned, and yet shall mourn with ever-returning spring.
'When lilacs last in the dooryard bloomed' (1881) st. 1

**25** The United States themselves are essentially the greatest poem.
*Leaves of Grass* (1855) preface

## John Greenleaf Whittier 1807–92

**26** Shoot, if you must, this old grey head,
But spare your country's flag.
'Barbara Frietchie' (1863)

**27** Dear Lord and Father of mankind,
Forgive our foolish ways!
Re-clothe us in our rightful mind,
In purer lives thy service find,
In deeper reverence praise.
'The Brewing of Soma' (1872)

1 For of all sad words of tongue or pen,
   The saddest are these: 'It might have been!'
   'Maud Muller' (1854). Cf. 163:12

## Robert Whittington

2 As time requireth, a man of marvellous
   mirth and pastimes, and sometime of as
   sad gravity, as who say: a man for all
   seasons.
   Of Sir Thomas More, in *Vulgaria* (1521) pt. 2
   'De constructione nominum'. In his
   prefatory letter to *In Praise of Folly* (1509),
   Erasmus describes More as '*omnium horarum
   hominem* [a man of all hours]'

## Charlotte Whitton 1896–1975

3 Whatever women do they must do twice as
   well as men to be thought half as good.
   In *Canada Month* June 1963

## Cornelius Whur

4 While lasting joys the man attend
   Who has a faithful female friend.
   'The Female Friend' (1837)

## George John Whyte-Melville 1821–78

5 But I freely admit that the best of my fun
   I owe it to horse and hound.
   'The Good Grey Mare' (1933)

## Bishop Samuel Wilberforce 1805–73

6 If I were a cassowary
   On the plains of Timbuctoo,
   I would eat a missionary,
   Cassock, band, and hymn-book too.
   Impromptu verse (attributed)

7 Was it through his grandfather or his
   grandmother that he claimed his descent
   from a monkey?
   Addressed to T. H. Huxley in a debate on
   Darwin's theory of evolution at Oxford, June
   1860; in *Macmillan's Magazine* vol. 78 (October
   1898) p. 433. Cf. 177:21

## Richard Wilbur 1921–

8 Spare us all word of the weapons, their
   force and range,
   The long numbers that rocket the mind.
   'Advice to a Prophet' (1961)

9 There is a poignancy in all things clear,
   In the stare of the deer, in the ring of a
   hammer in the morning.
   'Clearness' (1950)

10 We milk the cow of the world, and as we
    do
    We whisper in her ear, 'You are not true.'
    'Epistemology' (1950)

11 Mind in its purest play is like some bat
    That beats about in caverns all alone,
    Contriving by a kind of senseless wit
    Not to conclude against a wall of stone.
    'Mind' (1956)

12 The good grey guardians of art
    Patrol the halls on spongy shoes.
    'Museum Piece' (1950)

13 Love is the greatest mercy,
    A volley of the sun
    That lashes all with shade,
    That the first day be mended.
    'Someone Talking to Himself' (1961)

## Ella Wheeler Wilcox 1855–1919

14 Laugh and the world laughs with you;
    Weep, and you weep alone;
    For the sad old earth must borrow its
    mirth,
    But has trouble enough of its own.
    'Solitude'

15 So many gods, so many creeds,
    So many paths that wind and wind,
    While just the art of being kind
    Is all the sad world needs.
    'The World's Need'

## Oscar Wilde 1854–1900

16 The truth is rarely pure, and never simple.
    *The Importance of Being Earnest* (1895) act 1

17 In married life three is company and two
    none.
    *The Importance of Being Earnest* (1895) act 1

18 To lose one parent, Mr Worthing, may be
    regarded as a misfortune; to lose both
    looks like carelessness.
    *The Importance of Being Earnest* (1895) act 1
    (1948 ed.)

19 All women become like their mothers. That
    is their tragedy. No man does. That's his.
    *The Importance of Being Earnest* (1895) act 1 (in
    dialogue form in *A Woman of No Importance*
    (1893) act 2)

20 The good ended happily, and the bad
    unhappily. That is what fiction means.
    *The Importance of Being Earnest* (1895) act 2.
    Cf. 318:5

21 Charity, dear Miss Prism, charity! None of
    us are perfect. I myself am peculiarly
    susceptible to draughts.
    *The Importance of Being Earnest* (1895) act 2

22 Meredith's a prose Browning, and so is
    Browning.
    *Intentions* (1891) 'The Critic as Artist' pt. 1

23 A little sincerity is a dangerous thing, and
    a great deal of it is absolutely fatal.
    *Intentions* (1891) 'The Critic as Artist' pt. 2

24 I can resist everything except temptation.
    *Lady Windermere's Fan* (1892) act 1

25 We are all in the gutter, but some of us
    are looking at the stars.
    *Lady Windermere's Fan* (1892) act 3

1 A man who knows the price of everything and the value of nothing.
   *Lady Windermere's Fan* (1892) act 3 (definition of a cynic)

2 Experience is the name everyone gives to their mistakes.
   *Lady Windermere's Fan* (1892) act 3

3 There is no such thing as a moral or an immoral book. Books are well written, or badly written.
   *The Picture of Dorian Gray* (1891) preface

4 There is only one thing in the world worse than being talked about, and that is not being talked about.
   *The Picture of Dorian Gray* (1891) ch. 1

5 A man cannot be too careful in the choice of his enemies.
   *The Picture of Dorian Gray* (1891) ch. 1

6 Anybody can be good in the country.
   *The Picture of Dorian Gray* (1891) ch. 19

7 A thing is not necessarily true because a man dies for it.
   *Sebastian Melmoth* (1904 ed.) p. 12

8 MRS ALLONBY: They say, Lady Hunstanton, that when good Americans die they go to Paris.
   LADY HUNSTANTON: Indeed? And when bad Americans die, where do they go to?
   LORD ILLINGWORTH: Oh, they go to America.
   *A Woman of No Importance* (1893) act 1. Cf. 14:15

9 The English country gentleman galloping after a fox—the unspeakable in full pursuit of the uneatable.
   *A Woman of No Importance* (1893) act 1

10 One should never trust a woman who tells one her real age. A woman who would tell one that, would tell one anything.
   *A Woman of No Importance* (1893) act 1

11 LORD ILLINGWORTH: The Book of Life begins with a man and a woman in a garden.
    MRS ALLONBY: It ends with Revelations.
    *A Woman of No Importance* (1893) act 1

12 Children begin by loving their parents; after a time they judge them; rarely, if ever, do they forgive them.
    *A Woman of No Importance* (1893) act 2

13 GERALD: I suppose society is wonderfully delightful!
    LORD ILLINGWORTH: To be in it is merely a bore. But to be out of it simply a tragedy.
    *A Woman of No Importance* (1893) act 3

14 You should study the Peerage, Gerald ... It is the best thing in fiction the English have ever done.
    *A Woman of No Importance* (1893) act 3

15 I never saw a man who looked
    With such a wistful eye
    Upon that little tent of blue
    Which prisoners call the sky.
    *The Ballad of Reading Gaol* (1898) pt. 1, st. 3

16 Yet each man kills the thing he loves,
    By each let this be heard,
    Some do it with a bitter look,
    Some with a flattering word.
    The coward does it with a kiss,
    The brave man with a sword!
    *The Ballad of Reading Gaol* (1898) pt. 1, st. 7

17 And the wild regrets, and the bloody sweats,
    None knew so well as I:
    For he who lives more lives than one
    More deaths than one must die.
    *The Ballad of Reading Gaol* (1898) pt. 3, st. 37

18 I have nothing to declare except my genius.
    At the New York Custom House; in Frank Harris *Oscar Wilde* (1918) p. 75

19 Chaos, illumined by flashes of lightning.
    On Robert Browning's 'style'; in Ada Leverson *Letters to the Sphinx* (1930) pt. 1 'The Importance of Being Oscar'

20 Work is the curse of the drinking classes.
    In H. Pearson *Life of Oscar Wilde* (1946) ch. 12

21 He [Bernard Shaw] hasn't an enemy in the world, and none of his friends like him.
    In Bernard Shaw *Sixteen Self Sketches* (1949) ch. 17

22 Ah, well, then, I suppose that I shall have to die beyond my means.
    At the mention of a huge fee for a surgical operation; in R. H. Sherard *Life of Oscar Wilde* (1906) ch. 18

## Billy Wilder 1906–

23 Hindsight is always twenty-twenty.
    In J. R. Columbo *Wit and Wisdom of the Moviemakers* (1979) ch. 7

## Thornton Wilder 1897–1975

24 Literature is the orchestration of platitudes.
    In *Time* 12 January 1953

## Emperor Wilhelm II 1859–1941

25 We have ... fought for our place in the sun and have won it.
    Speech in Hamburg, 18 June 1901; in *The Times* 20 June 1901. Cf. 78:8

## John Wilkes 1727–97

26 [EARL OF SANDWICH:] 'Pon my soul, Wilkes, I don't know whether you'll die upon the gallows or of the pox.
    [WILKES:] That depends, my Lord, whether I first embrace your Lordship's principles, or your Lordship's mistresses.
    In Sir Charles Petrie *The Four Georges* (1935)

## Emma Hart Willard 1787–1870

27 Rocked in the cradle of the deep.
    Title of song (1840)

## William III (William of Orange) 1650–1702

1 'Do you not see your country is lost?' asked the Duke of Buckingham. 'There is one way never to see it lost' replied William, 'and that is to die in the last ditch.'
   In Bishop Gilbert Burnet *History of My Own Time* (1838 ed.) p. 218

2 Every bullet has its billet.
   In John Wesley *Journal* (1827) 6 June 1765

## Isaac Williams 1802–65

3 Be thou my Guardian and my Guide.
   Title of hymn (1842)

## Tennessee Williams 1911–83

4 We're all of us guinea pigs in the laboratory of God. Humanity is just a work in progress.
   *Camino Real* (1953) block 12

5 Mendacity is a system that we live in. Liquor is one way out an' death's the other.
   *Cat on a Hot Tin Roof* (1955) act 2

6 I have always depended on the kindness of strangers.
   *A Streetcar Named Desire* (1947) sc. 11

## William Carlos Williams 1883–1963

7 Minds like beds always made up,
   (more stony than a shore)
   unwilling or unable.
   *Paterson* (1946) bk. 1, preface

8 so much depends
   upon
   a red wheel
   barrow
   glazed with rain
   water
   beside the white
   chickens.
   'The Red Wheelbarrow' (1923)

## Wendell Willkie 1892–1944

9 The constitution does not provide for first and second class citizens.
   *An American Programme* (1944) ch. 2

## Angus Wilson 1913–91

10 Once a Catholic always a Catholic.
   *The Wrong Set* (1949) p. 168

## Charles E. Wilson 1890–1961

11 For years I thought what was good for our country was good for General Motors and vice versa.
   Testimony to the Senate Armed Services Committee on his proposed nomination for Secretary of Defence, 15 January 1953; in *New York Times* 24 February 1953, p. 8

## Harold Wilson 1916–95

12 All these financiers, all the little gnomes in Zurich.
   Speech, *Hansard* 12 November 1956, col. 578

13 This party is a moral crusade or it is nothing.
   Speech at the Labour Party Conference, 1 October 1962; in *The Times* 2 October 1962

14 From now on the pound abroad is worth 14 per cent or so less in terms of other currencies. It does not mean, of course, that the pound here in Britain, in your pocket or purse or in your bank, has been devalued.
   Ministerial broadcast, 19 November 1967; in *The Times* 20 November 1967

15 A week is a long time in politics.
   Probably first said at the time of the 1964 sterling crisis. See Nigel Rees *Sayings of the Century* (1984) p. 149

## Harriette Wilson 1789–1846

16 I shall not say why and how I became, at the age of fifteen, the mistress of the Earl of Craven.
   *Memoirs* (1825) opening words

## John Wilson

*See* CHRISTOPHER NORTH

## Sandy Wilson 1924–

17 We've got to have
   We plot to have
   For it's so dreary not to have
   That certain thing called the Boy Friend.
   *The Boyfriend* (1954) title song

## Woodrow Wilson 1856–1924

18 There is such a thing as a man being too proud to fight.
   Speech in Philadelphia, 10 May 1915, in *Selected Addresses* (1918) p. 88

19 We have stood apart, studiously neutral.
   Speech to Congress, 7 December 1915, in *New York Times* 8 December 1915, p. 4

20 Armed neutrality is ineffectual enough at best.
   Speech to Congress, 2 April 1917, in *Selected Addresses* (1918) p. 190

21 The world must be made safe for democracy.
   Speech to Congress, 2 April 1917, in *Selected Addresses* (1918) p. 195

22 Open covenants of peace, openly arrived at.
   Speech to Congress, 8 January 1918, in *Selected Addresses* (1918) p. 247; first of Fourteen Points

## Robb Wilton 1881–1957

23 The day war broke out.
   Customary preamble to radio monologues in the role of a Home Guard, from *c.*1940

## Anne Finch, Lady Winchilsea
1661–1720

1 Poetry's the feverish fit,
Th' o'erflowing of unbounded wit.
'Enquiry after Peace' (1713) l. 38

2 Now the jonquil o'ercomes the feeble
brain;
We faint beneath the aromatic pain.
'The Spleen' (1701) l. 40

3 My hand delights to trace unusual things,
And deviates from the known and common
way;
Nor will in fading silks compose
Faintly the inimitable rose.
'The Spleen' (1701) l. 83

## Catherine Winkworth 1827–78

4 Now thank we all our God,
With heart and hands and voices.
'Now thank we all our God' (1858)
(translation of Martin Rinkart's 'Nun danket
alle Gott', c.1636)

## George Wither 1588–1667

5 I loved a lass, a fair one,
As fair as e'er was seen;
She was indeed a rare one,
Another Sheba queen.
*A Description of Love* (1620) 'I loved a lass, a
fair one'

## Ludwig Wittgenstein 1889–1951

6 Philosophy is a battle against the
bewitchment of our intelligence by means
of language.
*Philosophische Untersuchungen* (1953) pt. 1,
sect. 109

7 What is your aim in philosophy?—To show
the fly the way out of the fly-bottle.
*Philosophische Untersuchungen* (1953) pt. 1,
sect. 309

8 What can be said at all can be said clearly;
and whereof one cannot speak thereof one
must be silent.
*Tractatus Logico-Philosophicus* (1922) preface

9 The world is everything that is the case.
*Tractatus Logico-Philosophicus* (1922) p. 30

10 The limits of my language mean the limits
of my world.
*Tractatus Logico-Philosophicus* (1922) p. 148

## P. G. Wodehouse 1881–1975

11 Chumps always make the best husbands
... All the unhappy marriages come from
the husbands having brains.
*The Adventures of Sally* (1920) ch. 10

12 There was another ring at the front door.
Jeeves shimmered out and came back with
a telegram.
*Carry On, Jeeves!* (1925) 'Jeeves Takes Charge'

13 He spoke with a certain what-is-it in his
voice, and I could see that, if not actually
disgruntled, he was far from being
gruntled.
*The Code of the Woosters* (1938) ch. 1

14 Slice him where you like, a hellhound is
always a hellhound.
*The Code of the Woosters* (1938) ch. 1

15 It is no use telling me that there are bad
aunts and good aunts. At the core, they are
all alike. Sooner or later, out pops the
cloven hoof.
*The Code of the Woosters* (1938) ch. 2

16 Roderick Spode? Big chap with a small
moustache and the sort of eye that can
open an oyster at sixty paces?
*The Code of the Woosters* (1938) ch. 2

17 To my daughter Leonora without whose
never-failing sympathy and encouragement
this book would have been finished in half
the time.
*The Heart of a Goof* (1926) dedication

18 I turned to Aunt Agatha, whose
demeanour was now rather like that of
one who, picking daisies on the railway,
has just caught the down express in the
small of the back.
*The Inimitable Jeeves* (1923) ch. 4

19 When Aunt is calling to Aunt like
mastodons bellowing across primeval
swamps.
*The Inimitable Jeeves* (1923) ch. 16

20 It was my Uncle George who discovered
that alcohol was a food well in advance of
medical thought.
*The Inimitable Jeeves* (1923) ch. 16

21 It is a good rule in life never to apologize.
The right sort of people do not want
apologies, and the wrong sort take a mean
advantage of them.
*The Man Upstairs* (1914) title story. Cf. 175:13

22 She fitted into my biggest armchair as if it
had been built round her by someone who
knew they were wearing armchairs tight
about the hips that season.
*My Man Jeeves* (1919) 'Jeeves and the
Unbidden Guest'

23 Ice formed on the butler's upper slopes.
*Pigs Have Wings* (1952) ch. 5

24 The Right Hon. was a tubby little chap who
looked as if he had been poured into his
clothes and had forgotten to say 'When!'
*Very Good, Jeeves* (1930) 'Jeeves and the
Impending Doom'

## Charles Wolfe 1791–1823

25 Not a drum was heard, not a funeral note,
As his corse to the rampart we hurried.
'The Burial of Sir John Moore at Corunna'
(1817)

26 We buried him darkly at dead of night,
The sods with our bayonets turning.
'The Burial of Sir John Moore at Corunna'
(1817)

1 We carved not a line, and we raised not a
stone—
But we left him alone with his glory.
'The Burial of Sir John Moore at Corunna'
(1817)

## Humbert Wolfe 1886–1940

2 You cannot hope
to bribe or twist,
thank God! the
British journalist.
But, seeing what
the man will do
unbribed, there's
no occasion to.
'Over the Fire' (1930)

## James Wolfe 1727–59

3 The General ... repeated nearly the whole
of Gray's Elegy ... adding, as he concluded,
that he would prefer being the author of
that poem to the glory of beating the
French to-morrow.
J. Playfair *Biographical Account of J. Robinson* in
*Transactions of the Royal Society of Edinburgh*
vol. 7 (1815) p. 499

4 Now God be praised, I will die in peace.
Dying words, in J. Knox *Historical Journal of
the Campaigns in North America* (ed. A. G.
Doughty, 1914) vol. 2, p. 114

## Thomas Wolfe 1900–38

5 Most of the time we think we're sick, it's
all in the mind.
*Look Homeward, Angel* (1929) pt. 1, ch. 1

6 'Where they got you stationed now, Luke?'
... 'In Norfolk at the Navy base,' Luke
answered, 'm-m-making the world safe for
hypocrisy.'
*Look Homeward, Angel* (1929) pt. 3, ch. 36.
Cf. 351:21

## Tom Wolfe 1931–

7 The bonfire of the vanities.
Title of novel (1987); deriving from
Savonarola's 'burning of the vanities' in
Florence, 1497

8 Electric Kool-Aid Acid test.
Title of novel on hippy culture (1968)

9 Radical Chic ... is only radical in Style; in
its heart it is part of Society and its
tradition—Politics, like Rock, Pop, and
Camp, has its uses.
*New York* 8 June 1970, p. 56

## Mary Wollstonecraft 1759–97

10 To give a sex to mind was not very
consistent with the principles of a man
[Rousseau] who argued so warmly, and so
well, for the immortality of the soul.
*A Vindication of the Rights of Woman* (1792)
ch. 3 (often quoted 'Mind has no sex')

11 I do not wish them [women] to have power
over men; but over themselves.
*A Vindication of the Rights of Woman* (1792)
ch. 4

12 When a man seduces a woman, it should, I
think, be termed a *left-handed* marriage.
*A Vindication of the Rights of Woman* (1792)
ch. 4

13 A slavish bondage to parents cramps every
faculty of the mind.
*A Vindication of the Rights of Woman* (1792)
ch. 11

14 Was not the world a vast prison, and
women born slaves?
*The Wrongs of Woman: or, Maria* (1798, ed. G.
Kelly, 1976) p. 79

## Cardinal Wolsey *c.*1475–1530

15 Father Abbot, I am come to lay my bones
amongst you.
In George Cavendish *Negotiations of Thomas
Wolsey* (1641) p. 108

16 Had I but served God as diligently as I have
served the King, he would not have given
me over in my grey hairs.
In George Cavendish *Negotiations of Thomas
Wolsey* (1641) p. 113

## Mrs Henry Wood 1814–87

17 Dead! and ... never called me mother.
*East Lynne* (dramatized by T. A. Palmer, 1874;
the words do not occur in the novel of 1861)

## Woodbine Willie

See G. A. STUDDERT KENNEDY

## Thomas Woodroofe 1899–1978

18 The whole Fleet's lit up. When I say 'lit up',
I mean lit up by fairy lamps.
First live outside broadcast, Spithead Review,
20 May 1937. See Asa Briggs *History of
Broadcasting in the UK* vol. 2 (1965) pt. 2, ch. 2

## Harry Woods

19 Oh we ain't got a barrel of money,
Maybe we're ragged and funny,
But we'll travel along
Singin' a song,
Side by side.
'Side by Side' (1927 song)

## Virginia Woolf 1882–1941

20 Trivial personalities decomposing in the
eternity of print.
*The Common Reader* (1925) 'The Modern Essay'

21 Examine for a moment an ordinary mind
on an ordinary day.
*The Common Reader* (1925) 'Modern Fiction'

22 Life is not a series of gig lamps
symmetrically arranged; life is a luminous
halo, a semi-transparent envelope
surrounding us from the beginning of
consciousness to the end.
*The Common Reader* (1925) 'Modern Fiction'

**1** A woman must have money and a room of her own if she is to write fiction.

*A Room of One's Own* (1929) ch. 1

**2** Women have served all these centuries as looking-glasses possessing the magic and delicious power of reflecting the figure of a man at twice its natural size.

*A Room of One's Own* (1929) ch. 2

**3** This is an important book, the critic assumes, because it deals with war. This is an insignificant book because it deals with the feelings of women in a drawing-room.

*A Room of One's Own* (1929) ch. 4

**4** So that is marriage, Lily thought, a man and a woman looking at a girl throwing a ball.

*To the Lighthouse* (1927) pt. 1, ch. 13

**5** I have lost friends, some by death ... others through sheer inability to cross the street.

*The Waves* (1931) p. 202

**6** The scratching of pimples on the body of the bootboy at Claridges.

Of James Joyce's *Ulysses*; letter to Lytton Strachey, 24 April 1922, in *Letters* (ed. N. Nicolson and J. Trautmann, 1976) vol. 2

## Alexander Woollcott 1887–1943

**7** A broker is a man who takes your fortune and runs it into a shoestring.

In S. Hopkins Adams *Alexander Woollcott* (1945) ch. 15

**8** All the things I really like to do are either illegal, immoral, or fattening.

In R. E. Drennan *Wit's End* (1973)

## Dorothy Wordsworth 1771–1855

**9** A beautiful evening, very starry, the horned moon.

'Alfoxden Journal' 23 March 1798, in *Journals* (ed. E. de Selincourt, 1941)

**10** I never saw daffodils so beautiful. They grew among the mossy stones about and about them; some rested their heads upon these stones as on a pillow for weariness; and the rest tossed and reeled and danced, and seemed as if they verily laughed with the wind that blew upon them over the lake.

'Grasmere Journal' 15 April 1802, in *Journals* (ed. E. de Selincourt, 1941). Cf. 355:4

## Elizabeth Wordsworth 1840–1932

**11** If all the good people were clever,
And all clever people were good,
The world would be nicer than ever
We thought that it possibly could.
But somehow, 'tis seldom or never
The two hit it off as they should;
The good are so harsh to the clever,
The clever so rude to the good!

'Good and Clever'

## William Wordsworth 1770–1850

**12** And five times did I say to him
'Why, Edward, tell me why?'

'Anecdote for Fathers' (1798)

**13** Action is transitory,—a step, a blow,
The motion of a muscle—this way or that—
'Tis done, and in the after vacancy
We wonder at ourselves like men betrayed:
Suffering is permanent, obscure and dark,
And shares the nature of infinity.

*The Borderers* (1842) act 3, l. 1539

**14** Who is the happy Warrior? Who is he
Whom every man in arms should wish to be?

'Character of the Happy Warrior' (1807)

**15** Earth has not anything to show more fair:
Dull would he be of soul who could pass by
A sight so touching in its majesty:
This City now doth like a garment wear
The beauty of the morning; silent, bare,
Ships, towers, domes, theatres, and temples lie
Open unto the fields, and to the sky;
All bright and glittering in the smokeless air.

'Composed upon Westminster Bridge' (1807)

**16** Dear God! the very houses seem asleep;
And all that mighty heart is lying still!

'Composed upon Westminster Bridge' (1807)

**17** The light that never was, on sea or land,
The consecration, and the Poet's dream.

'Elegiac Stanzas' (on a picture of Peele Castle in a storm, 1807)

**18** Not in the lucid intervals of life
That come but as a curse to party-strife ...
Is Nature felt, or can be.

'Evening Voluntaries' (1835) no. 4

**19**              The good die first,
And they whose hearts are dry as summer dust
Burn to the socket.

*The Excursion* (1814) bk. 1, l. 500

**20** This dull product of a scoffer's pen.

*The Excursion* (1814) bk. 2, l. 484 (Voltaire's *Candide*)

**21** Society became my glittering bride,
And airy hopes my children.

*The Excursion* (1814) bk. 3, l. 735

**22** 'To every Form of being is assigned,'
Thus calmly spoke the venerable Sage,
'An *active* Principle.'

*The Excursion* (1814) bk. 9, l. 1

**23** How fast has brother followed brother,
From sunshine to the sunless land!

'Extempore Effusion upon the Death of James Hogg' (1835)

**24** Bliss was it in that dawn to be alive,
But to be young was very heaven!

'The French Revolution, as it Appeared to Enthusiasts' (1809); also *The Prelude* (1850) bk. 9, l. 108

1 The moving accident is not my trade;
To freeze the blood I have no ready arts.
'Hart-Leap Well' (1800) pt. 2, l. 1

2         All shod with steel
We hissed along the polished ice, in games
Confederate.
'Influence of Natural Objects' (1809); also *The Prelude* (1850) bk. 1, l. 414

3 I travelled among unknown men,
In lands beyond the sea;
Nor England! did I know till then
What love I bore to thee.
'I travelled among unknown men' (1807)

4 I wandered lonely as a cloud
That floats on high o'er vales and hills,
When all at once I saw a crowd,
A host, of golden daffodils;
Beside the lake, beneath the trees,
Fluttering and dancing in the breeze.
'I wandered lonely as a cloud' (1815 ed.).
Cf. 354:10

5 For oft, when on my couch I lie
In vacant or in pensive mood,
They flash upon that inward eye
Which is the bliss of solitude;
And then my heart with pleasure fills,
And dances with the daffodils.
'I wandered lonely as a cloud' (1815 ed.)

6         The gods approve
The depth, and not the tumult, of the soul.
'Laodamia' (1815) l. 74

7         More pellucid streams,
An ampler ether, a diviner air,
And fields invested with purpureal gleams.
'Laodamia' (1815) l. 104

8 That best portion of a good man's life,
His little, nameless, unremembered, acts
Of kindness and of love.
'Lines composed a few miles above Tintern Abbey' (1798) l. 35

9         The sounding cataract
Haunted me like a passion: the tall rock,
The mountain, and the deep and gloomy wood,
Their colours and their forms, were then to me
An appetite.
'Lines composed ... above Tintern Abbey' (1798) l. 72

10 The still, sad music of humanity,
Nor harsh nor grating, though of ample power
To chasten and subdue.
'Lines composed ... above Tintern Abbey' (1798) l. 91

11 Milton! thou shouldst be living at this hour:
England hath need of thee: she is a fen
Of stagnant waters.
'Milton! thou shouldst be living at this hour' (1807)

12         Some happy tone
Of meditation, slipping in between
The beauty coming and the beauty gone.
'Most sweet it is' (1835)

13 My heart leaps up when I behold
A rainbow in the sky.
So was it when my life began;
So is it now I am a man.
'My heart leaps up when I behold' (1807)

14 The Child is father of the Man.
'My heart leaps up when I behold' (1807)

15 The Sonnet's scanty plot of ground.
'Nuns fret not ... ' (1807)

16         With gentle hand
Touch—for there is a spirit in the woods.
'Nutting' (1800)

17 There was a time when meadow, grove, and stream,
The earth, and every common sight,
To me did seem
Apparelled in celestial light,
The glory and the freshness of a dream.
'Ode. Intimations of Immortality' (1807) st. 1

18 The rainbow comes and goes,
And lovely is the rose.
'Ode. Intimations of Immortality' (1807) st. 2

19 Whither is fled the visionary gleam?
Where is it now, the glory and the dream?
'Ode. Intimations of Immortality' (1807) st. 4

20 Our birth is but a sleep and a forgetting:
The Soul that rises with us, our life's Star,
Hath had elsewhere its setting,
And cometh from afar:
Not in entire forgetfulness,
And not in utter nakedness,
But trailing clouds of glory do we come
From God, who is our home:
Heaven lies about us in our infancy!
Shades of the prison-house begin to close
Upon the growing boy.
'Ode. Intimations of Immortality' (1807) st. 5

21 At length the man perceives it die away,
And fade into the light of common day.
'Ode. Intimations of Immortality' (1807) st. 5

22 But for those obstinate questionings
Of sense and outward things,
Fallings from us, vanishings;
Blank misgivings of a creature
Moving about in worlds not realised,
High instincts before which our mortal nature
Did tremble like a guilty thing surprised.
'Ode. Intimations of Immortality' (1807) st. 9

23 Though nothing can bring back the hour
Of splendour in the grass, of glory in the flower.
'Ode. Intimations of Immortality' (1807) st. 10

24 To me the meanest flower that blows can give
Thoughts that do often lie too deep for tears.
'Ode. Intimations of Immortality' (1807) st. 11

25 Stern daughter of the voice of God!
'Ode to Duty' (1807)

1 Plain living and high thinking are no
   more:
   The homely beauty of the good old cause
   Is gone.
     'O friend! I know not which way I must look'
     (1807)

2 Once did she hold the gorgeous East in fee,
   And was the safeguard of the West.
     'On the Extinction of the Venetian Republic'
     (1807)

3 There's something in a flying horse,
   There's something in a huge balloon;
   But through the clouds I'll never float
   Until I have a little Boat,
   Shaped like the crescent-moon.
     *Peter Bell* (1819) prologue, l. 1

4 Is it some party in a parlour,
   Crammed just as they on earth were
   crammed—
   Some sipping punch, some sipping tea,
   But as you by their faces see
   All silent, and all damned?
     *Peter Bell* pt. 1, l. 541 in 1819 MS
     (subsequently deleted so as 'not to offend
     the pious')

5 Physician art thou?—one, all eyes,
   Philosopher!—a fingering slave,
   One that would peep and botanize
   Upon his mother's grave?
     'A Poet's Epitaph' (1800)

6 A reasoning, self-sufficing thing,
   An intellectual All-in-all!
     'A Poet's Epitaph' (1800)

7 In common things that round us lie
   Some random truths he can impart,—
   The harvest of a quiet eye
   That broods and sleeps on his own heart.
     'A Poet's Epitaph' (1800)

8 Unprofitably travelling toward the grave.
     *The Prelude* (1850) bk. 1, l. 267

9 Made one long bathing of a summer's day.
     *The Prelude* (1850) bk. 1, l. 290

10         The statue stood
   Of Newton, with his prism, and silent face:
   The marble index of a mind for ever
   Voyaging through strange seas of Thought,
   alone.
     *The Prelude* (1850) bk. 3, l. 60

11         Spirits overwrought
   Were making night do penance for a day
   Spent in a round of strenuous idleness.
     *The Prelude* (1850) bk. 4, l. 376

12 And, through the turnings intricate of
   verse,
   Present themselves as objects recognised,
   In flashes, and with glory not their own.
     *The Prelude* (1850) bk. 5, l. 605

13         All things have second birth;
   The earthquake is not satisfied at once.
     *The Prelude* (1850) bk. 10, l. 83

14 Not in Utopia,—subterranean fields,—
   Or some secreted island, Heaven knows
   where!
   But in the very world, which is the world
   Of all of us,—the place where in the end
   We find our happiness, or not at all!
     *The Prelude* (1850) bk. 11, l. 140

15         There is
   One great society alone on earth,
   The noble Living, and the noble Dead.
     *The Prelude* (1850) bk. 11, l. 393

16 I thought of Chatterton, the marvellous
   boy.
     'Resolution and Independence' (1807) st. 7

17 We poets in our youth begin in gladness;
   But thereof comes in the end despondency
   and madness.
     'Resolution and Independence' (1807) st. 7

18 Still glides the Stream, and shall for ever
   glide;
   The Form remains, the Function never dies.
     'The River Duddon' (1820) no. 34 'After-
     Thought'

19 Enough, if something from our hands have
   power
   To live, and act, and serve the future hour.
     'The River Duddon' (1820) no. 34 'After-
     Thought'

20 We feel that we are greater than we know.
     'The River Duddon' (1820) no. 34 'After-
     Thought'

21 Scorn not the Sonnet; Critic, you have
   frowned,
   Mindless of its just honours; with this key
   Shakespeare unlocked his heart.
     'Scorn not the Sonnet' (1827)

22 She dwelt among the untrodden ways
   Beside the springs of Dove,
   A maid whom there were none to praise
   And very few to love.
     'She dwelt among the untrodden ways'
     (1800)

23 She lived unknown, and few could know
   When Lucy ceased to be;
   But she is in her grave, and, oh,
   The difference to me!
     'She dwelt among the untrodden ways'
     (1800)

24 And now I see with eye serene
   The very pulse of the machine;
   A being breathing thoughtful breath;
   A traveller betwixt life and death.
     'She was a phantom of delight' (1807)

25 A slumber did my spirit seal;
   I had no human fears:
   She seemed a thing that could not feel
   The touch of earthly years.

   No motion has she now, no force;
   She neither hears nor sees;
   Rolled round in earth's diurnal course,
   With rocks, and stones, and trees.
     'A slumber did my spirit seal' (1800)

1 Behold her, single in the field,
Yon solitary Highland lass!
'The Solitary Reaper' (1807)

2 Will no one tell me what she sings?
Perhaps the plaintive numbers flow
For old, unhappy, far-off things,
And battles long ago.
'The Solitary Reaper' (1807)

3 What, you are stepping westward?
'Stepping Westward' (1807)

4 Surprised by joy—impatient as the wind
I wished to share the transport.
'Surprised by joy—impatient as the wind'
(1815)

5 Our meddling intellect
Mis-shapes the beauteous forms of
things:—
We murder to dissect.

Enough of science and of art;
Close up those barren leaves.
'The Tables Turned' (1798)

6 Two Voices are there; one is of the sea,
One of the mountains; each a mighty
Voice:
In both from age to age thou didst rejoice,
They were thy chosen music, Liberty!
'Thought of a Briton on the Subjugation of
Switzerland' (1807)

7 O blithe new-comer! I have heard,
I hear thee and rejoice:
O Cuckoo! Shall I call thee bird,
Or but a wandering voice?
'To the Cuckoo' (1807)

8 Oft on the dappled turf at ease
I sit, and play with similes,
Loose types of things through all degrees.
'To the Daisy' ('With little here to do or see',
1820 ed.)

9 Type of the wise who soar, but never roam;
True to the kindred points of heaven and
home!
'To a Skylark' ('Ethereal minstrel! pilgrim of
the sky', 1827)

10 The world is too much with us; late and
soon,
Getting and spending, we lay waste our
powers.
'The world is too much with us' (1807)

11        Great God! I'd rather be
A Pagan suckled in a creed outworn;
So might I, standing on this pleasant lea,
Have glimpses that would make me less
forlorn;
Have sight of Proteus rising from the sea;
Or hear old Triton blow his wreathèd horn.
'The world is too much with us' (1807)

12 Poetry is the spontaneous overflow of
powerful feelings: it takes its origin from
emotion recollected in tranquillity.
*Lyrical Ballads* (2nd ed., 1802) Preface

13 Never forget what I believe was observed
to you by Coleridge, that every great and
original writer, in proportion as he is great
and original, must himself create the taste
by which he is to be relished.
Letter to Lady Beaumont, 21 May 1807, in E.
de Selincourt (ed.) *Letters of William and
Dorothy Wordsworth* vol. 2 (rev. M. Moorman,
1969)

## Sir Henry Wotton 1568–1639

14 And entertains the harmless day
With a religious book, or friend.
'The Character of a Happy Life' (1614)

15 This man is freed from servile bands,
Of hope to rise, or fear to fall:—
Lord of himself, though not of lands,
And having nothing, yet hath all.
'The Character of a Happy Life' (1614)

16 You meaner beauties of the night,
That poorly satisfy our eyes,
More by your number, than your light;
You common people of the skies,
What are you when the moon shall rise?
'On His Mistress, the Queen of Bohemia'
(1624); sometimes 'sun shall rise'

17 He first deceased; she for a little tried
To live without him: liked it not, and died.
'Upon the Death of Sir Albertus Moreton's
Wife' (1651)

18 No man marks the narrow space
'Twixt a prison and a smile.
'Upon the sudden restraint of the Earl of
Somerset' (1651)

19 Well building hath three conditions.
Commodity, firmness, and delight.
*Elements of Architecture* (1624) pt. 1

20 Critics are like brushers of noblemen's
clothes.
In Francis Bacon *Apophthegms New and Old*
(1625) no. 64

21 Take heed of thinking, *The farther you go
from the church of Rome, the nearer you are to
God.*
In Izaak Walton *Reliquiae Wottonianae* (1651)
'Life of Sir Henry Wotton'

22 An ambassador is an honest man sent to
lie abroad for the good of his country.
Written in the album of Christopher
Fleckmore in 1604. See Izaak Walton
*Reliquiae Wottonianae* (1651) 'Life of Sir Henry
Wotton'

## Frank Lloyd Wright 1867–1959

23 The physician can bury his mistakes, but
the architect can only advise his client to
plant vines—so they should go as far as
possible from home to build their first
buildings.
*New York Times* 4 October 1953, sect. 6, p. 47

## Lady Mary Wroth c.1586–c.1652

1 Love, a child, is ever crying:
Please him and he straight is flying,
Give him, he the more is craving,
Never satisfied with having.
'Love, a child, is ever crying' (1621)

## Sir Thomas Wyatt c.1503–42

2 They flee from me, that sometime did me
seek
With naked foot, stalking in my chamber.
'They flee from me' (1557)

3 Throughout the world, if it were sought,
Fair words enough a man shall find.
They be good cheap; they cost right
naught;
Their substance is but only wind.
But well to say and so to mean—
That sweet accord is seldom seen.
'Throughout the world, if it were sought'
(1557)

## William Wycherley c.1640–1716

4 A mistress should be like a little country
retreat near the town, not to dwell in
constantly, but only for a night and away.
*The Country Wife* (1675) act 1, sc. 1

5 Go to your business, I say, pleasure, whilst
I go to my pleasure, business.
*The Country Wife* (1675) act 2

6 You who scribble, yet hate all who write ...
And with faint praises one another damn.
*The Plain Dealer* (1677) Prologue (of critics).
Cf. 251:6

## William of Wykeham 1324–1404

7 Manners maketh man.
Motto (proverbial since the mid-14th
century)

## Xenophon c.428–c.354 BC

8 The sea! the sea!
*Anabasis* bk. 4, ch. 7, sect. 24

## Augustin, Marquis de Ximénèz 1726–1817

9 *Attaquons dans ses eaux*
*La perfide Albion!*

Let us attack in her own waters perfidious
Albion!
'L'Ère des Français' (October 1793) in *Poésies
Révolutionnaires et contre-révolutionnaires* (1821)
vol. 1, p. 160. Cf. 70:2

## Bishop John Yates 1925–

10 There is a lot to be said in the Decade of
Evangelism for believing more and more in
less and less.
*Gloucester Diocesan Gazette* August 1991

## Thomas Russell Ybarra b. 1880

11 A Christian is a man who feels
Repentance on a Sunday
For what he did on Saturday
And is going to do on Monday.
'The Christian' (1909)

## W. F. Yeames 1835–1918

12 And when did you last see your father?
Title of painting (1878) in the Walker Art
Gallery, Liverpool

## W. B. Yeats 1865–1939

13 I said 'a line will take us hours maybe,
Yet if it does not seem a moment's thought
Our stitching and unstitching has been
naught.'
'Adam's Curse' (1904)

14 O body swayed to music, O brightening
glance
How can we know the dancer from the
dance?
'Among School Children' (1928)

15 That dolphin-torn, that gong-tormented
sea.
'Byzantium' (1933)

16 Now that my ladder's gone
I must lie down where all ladders start
In the foul rag and bone shop of the heart.
'The Circus Animals' Desertion' (1939) pt. 3

17        There's more enterprise
In walking naked.
'A Coat' (1914)

18 We were the last romantics — chose for
theme
Traditional sanctity and loveliness.
'Coole and Ballylee, 1931' (1933)

19 The intellect of man is forced to choose
Perfection of the life, or of the work.
'Coole Park and Ballylee, 1932' (1933)

20 A woman can be proud and stiff
When on love intent;
But Love has pitched his mansion in
The place of excrement;
For nothing can be sole or whole
That has not been rent.
'Crazy Jane Talks with the Bishop' (1932)

21 Nor dread nor hope attend
A dying animal;
A man awaits his end
Dreading and hoping all.
'Death' (1933)

22 He knows death to the bone—
Man has created death.
'Death' (1933)

**1** Down by the salley gardens my love and
    I did meet;
    She passed the salley gardens with little
     snow-white feet.
    She bid me take love easy, as the leaves
     grow on the tree;
    But I, being young and foolish, with her
     would not agree.
    'Down by the Salley Gardens' (1889)

**2** Too long a sacrifice
    Can make a stone of the heart.
    'Easter, 1916' (1921)

**3** All changed, changed utterly:
    A terrible beauty is born.
    'Easter, 1916' (1921)

**4** The fascination of what's difficult
    Has dried the sap out of my veins, and rent
    Spontaneous joy and natural content
    Out of my heart.
    'The Fascination of What's Difficult' (1910)

**5** Never to have lived is best, ancient writers
    say;
    Never to have drawn the breath of life,
     never to have looked into the eye of day;
    The second best's a gay goodnight and
     quickly turn away.
    'From *Oedipus at Colonus*' (1928). Cf. 311:13

**6** The ghost of Roger Casement
    Is beating on the door.
    'The Ghost of Roger Casement' (1939)

**7** I have spread my dreams under your feet;
    Tread softly because you tread on my
     dreams.
    'He Wishes for the Cloths of Heaven' (1899)

**8** The innocent and the beautiful
    Have no enemy but time.
    'In Memory of Eva Gore Booth and Con
     Markiewicz' (1933)

**9** My country is Kiltartan Cross;
    My countrymen Kiltartan's poor!
    'An Irish Airman Foresees his Death' (1919)

**10** Nor law, nor duty bade me fight,
    Nor public man, nor angry crowds.
    'An Irish Airman Foresees his Death' (1919)

**11** The years to come seemed waste of breath,
    A waste of breath the years behind.
    'An Irish Airman Foresees his Death' (1919)

**12** I will arise and go now, and go to
    Innisfree,
    And a small cabin build there, of clay and
     wattles made;
    Nine bean rows will I have there, a hive for
     the honey bee,
    And live alone in the bee-loud glade.
    'The Lake Isle of Innisfree' (1893)

**13** I hear lake water lapping with low sounds
     by the shore . . .
    I hear it in the deep heart's core.
    'The Lake Isle of Innisfree' (1893)

**14** A shudder in the loins engenders there
    The broken wall, the burning roof and
     tower
    And Agamemnon dead.
    'Leda and the Swan' (1928)

**15** Like a long-legged fly upon the stream
    His mind moves upon silence.
    'Long-Legged Fly' (1939)

**16** We had fed the heart on fantasies,
    The hear`'s grown brutal from the fare.
    'Medita` ons in Time of Civil War' no. 6 'The
     Stare's Nest by my Window' (1928)

**17** Think where man's glory most begins and
    ends
    And say my glory was I had such friends.
    'The Municipal Gallery Re-visited' (1939)

**18** A pity beyond all telling,
    Is hid in the heart of love.
    'The Pity of Love' (1893)

**19** Out of Ireland have we come.
    Great hatred, little room,
    Maimed us at the start.
    'Remorse for Intemperate Speech' (1933)

**20** That is no country for old men. The young
    In one another's arms, birds in the trees
    Those dying generations    at their song.
    'Sailing to Byzantium' (1928)

**21** An aged man is but a paltry thing,
    A tattered coat upon a stick, unless
    Soul clap its hands and sing, and louder
     sing
    For every tatter in its mortal dress.
    'Sailing to Byzantium' (1928)

**22** And therefore I have sailed the seas and
    come
    To the holy city of Byzantium.
    'Sailing to Byzantium' (1928)

**23** All shuffle there; all cough in ink;
    All wear the carpet with their shoes.
    'The Scholars' (1919)

**24** Things fall apart; the centre cannot hold;
    Mere anarchy is loosed upon the world,
    The blood-dimmed tide is loosed, and
     everywhere
    The ceremony of innocence is drowned;
    The best lack all conviction, while the
     worst
    Are full of passionate intensity.
    'The Second Coming' (1921)

**25** And what rough beast, its hour come
    round at last,
    Slouches towards Bethlehem to be born?
    'The Second Coming' (1921)

**26** Far-off, most secret and inviolate Rose.
    'The Secret Rose' (1899)

**27** A woman of so shining loveliness
    That men threshed corn at midnight by
     a tress,
    A little stolen tress.
    'The Secret Rose' (1899)

**28** Romantic Ireland's dead and gone,
    It's with O'Leary in the grave.
    'September, 1913' (1914)

**29** Oh, who could have foretold
    That the heart grows old?
    'A Song' (1919)

1 And pluck till time and times are done,
The silver apples of the moon,
The golden apples of the sun.
'Song of Wandering Aengus' (1899)

2 Swift has sailed into his rest;
Savage indignation there
Cannot lacerate his breast.
'Swift's Epitaph' (1933). Cf. 320:27

3 But where's the wild dog that has praised
his fleas?
'To a Poet, Who would have Me Praise
certain bad Poets, Imitators of His and of
Mine' (1910)

4 Red Rose, proud Rose, sad Rose of all my
days!
Come near me, while I sing the ancient
ways.
'To the Rose upon the Rood of Time' (1893)

5 Michaelangelo left a proof
On the Sistine Chapel roof,
Where but half-awakened Adam
Can disturb globe-trotting Madam.
'Under Ben Bulben' (1939) pt. 4

6 Irish poets, learn your trade,
Sing whatever is well made.
'Under Ben Bulben' (1939) pt. 5

7 Cast your mind on other days
That we in coming days may be
Still the indomitable Irishry.
'Under Ben Bulben' (1939) pt. 5

8 Cast a cold eye
On life, on death.
Horseman pass by!
'Under Ben Bulben' (1939) pt. 6

9 When you are old and grey and full of
sleep,
And nodding by the fire, take down this
book
And slowly read and dream of the soft look
Your eyes had once, and of their shadows
deep.
'When You Are Old' (1893)

10 We make out of the quarrel with others,
rhetoric, but of the quarrel with ourselves,
poetry.
*Essays* (1924) 'Anima Hominis' sect. 5

11 In dreams begins responsibility.
*Responsibilities* (1914) epigraph

## Sergei Yesenin 1895–1925

12 It's always the good feel rotten.
Pleasure's for those who are bad.
'Pleasure's for the Bad' (1923) (tr. G. McVay)

## Edward Young 1683–1765

13 Some for renown on scraps of learning
dote,
And think they grow immortal as they
quote.
*The Love of Fame* (1725–8) Satire 1, l. 89

14        Be wise with speed;
A fool at forty is a fool indeed.
*The Love of Fame* (1725–8) Satire 2, l. 282

15 One to destroy, is murder by the law;
And gibbets keep the lifted hand in awe;
To murder thousands, takes a specious
name,
'War's glorious art', and gives immortal
fame.
*The Love of Fame* (1725–8) Satire 7, l. 55.
Cf. 263:12

16 How science dwindles, and how volumes
swell,
How commentators each dark passage
shun,
And hold their farthing candle to the sun.
*The Love of Fame* (1725–8) Satire 7, l. 96.
Cf. 83:12, 184:15, 306:14

17 Tired Nature's sweet restorer, balmy sleep!
*Night Thoughts* (1742–5) 'Night 1' l. 1

18 Death! Great proprietor of all!
*Night Thoughts* (1742–5) 'Night 1' l. 204

19 Procrastination is the thief of time.
*Night Thoughts* (1742–5) 'Night 1' l. 393

20 At thirty a man suspects himself a fool;
Knows it at forty, and reforms his plan.
*Night Thoughts* (1742–5) 'Night 1' l. 417

21 By night an atheist half believes a God.
*Night Thoughts* (1742–5) 'Night 5' l. 176

22 To know the world, not love her, is thy
point,
She gives but little, nor that little, long.
*Night Thoughts* (1742–5) 'Night 8' l. 1276.
Cf. 154:27

23 Life is the desert, life the solitude;
Death joins us to the great majority.
*The Revenge* (1721) act 4. Cf. 248:9

## George W. Young 1846–1919

24 The lips that touch liquor must never
touch mine.
Title of verse (*c*.1870)

## Yevgeny Zamyatin 1884–1937

25 Heretics are the only bitter remedy against
the entropy of human thought.
'Literature, Revolution and Entropy' quoted
in *The Dragon and other Stories* (1967, tr. M.
Ginsberg) introduction

## Israel Zangwill 1864–1926

26 Scratch the Christian and you find the
pagan—spoiled.
*Children of the Ghetto* (1892) bk. 2, ch. 6

27 America is God's Crucible, the great
Melting-Pot where all the races of Europe
are melting and re-forming!
*The Melting Pot* (1908) act 1

## Frank Zappa 1940–93

1 Rock journalism is people who can't write
interviewing people who can't talk for
people who can't read.

In L. Botts *Loose Talk* (1980) p. 177.
Cf. 89:16

## Robert Zemeckis and Bob Gale

2 Back to the future.
Title of film (1985)

## Ronald L. Ziegler 1939–

3 [Mr Nixon's latest statement] is the
Operative White House Position ... and all
previous statements are inoperative.

At the time of the Watergate Affair; in *Boston
Globe* 18 April 1973

## Émile Zola 1840–1902

4 J'accuse.
I accuse.

Title of an open letter to the President of the
French Republic, in connection with the
Dreyfus affair; in *L'Aurore* 13 January 1898

# Index

act (cont.):

within the meaning of the A. — ANON 10:3
acted: a. so tragic the house — HARG 162:21
acting: a. of a dreadful thing — SHAK 281:3
people in them, a. — LARK 201:16
action: A. is consolatory — CONR 107:8
A. is transitory — WORD 354:13
a. of society upon itself — TOCQ 333:3
and a. is a most dangerous thing — CLOU 102:8
can only be grasped by a. — BRON 72:9
If ever I do a mean a. — STER 315:9
imitate the a. of the tiger — SHAK 279:5
lust in a. — SHAK 300:10
Makes that and th' a. fine — HERB 166:26
man of a. forced into a state — GALS 147:18
Suit the a. to the word — SHAK 276:6
Thought is the child of A. — DISR 122:9
actions: A. receive their tincture — DEFOE 115:19
my a. are my ministers — CHAR 95:2
Only the a. of the just — SHIR 306:11
active: a. line on a walk — KLEE 198:11
a. Principle — WORD 354:22
actor: a.'s life for me — WASH 342:23
actors: These our a. — SHAK 296:10
acts: all your a. are queens — SHAK 298:34
first four a. already past — BERK 35:19
His a. being seven ages — SHAK 272:24
nameless, unremembered, a. — WORD 355:8
no second a. in American lives — FITZ 140:23
who desires but a. not — BLAKE 61:3
actualité: economical with the a. — CLARK 101:13
adage: Like the poor cat i' the a. — SHAK 286:4
Adam: A. ate the apple — HUGH 175:21
A. had 'em — ANON 5:19
A. was a gardener — SHAK 280:11
For as in A. all die — BIBLE 55:17
old A. in this Child — BOOK 65:19
past Eve and A.'s — JOYCE 188:3
When A. dalfe and Eve spane — ROLLE 262:4
Where but half-awakened A. — YEATS 360:5
whipped the offending A. — SHAK 278:35
adamant: a. for drift — CHUR 99:9
frame of a., a soul of fire — JOHN 183:13
adazzle: a., dim — HOPK 172:13
adder: a. that stoppeth her ears — BOOK 67:13
day that brings forth the a. — SHAK 281:2
golden beat, and an a. — MAND 217:10
stingeth like an a. — BIBLE 43:33
addiction: Every form of a. is bad — JUNG 188:24
prisoners of a. — ILL 178:9
Addison: Cato did, and A. approved — BUDG 78:4
addresses: A. are given to us to — SAKI 265:21
adeste: A., fideles — ANON 13:9
adieu: Bidding a. — KEATS 191:27
ad infinitum: so proceed a. — SWIFT 320:23
adjective: As to the a. — TWAIN 336:6
Adlestrop: Yes; I remember A. — THOM 330:21
administered: best a. is best — POPE 252:20
administration: criticism of a. — BAG 26:6
admiral: a. from time to time — VOLT 340:12
admirals: A. extolled for standing still — COWP 110:5
admiralty: blood be the price of a. — KIPL 197:9
admirari: Nil a. — HOR 173:10
admire: Let none a. — MILT 228:19
Not to a., is all the art — POPE 252:26
admittance: No a. till the week after next — CARR 92:5
adolescence: a. and obsolescence — LINK 207:18
Adonais: I weep for A. — SHEL 303:3
adopted: by roads 'not a.' — BETJ 37:12
adorable: a. tennis-girl's hand — BETJ 37:13
adored: I was a. once too — SHAK 297:28
adoremus: Venite, a. — ANON 13:10
adorings: a. from their loves — KEATS 190:17
adorn: none that he did not a. — JOHN 185:12
To point a moral, or a. a tale — JOHN 183:14

adorned: unadorned a. the most — THOM 331:25
adornings: made their bends a. — SHAK 271:15
adorns: a. my legs — HOUS 174:7
ads: He watched the a. — NASH 237:13
adulteration: not adultery, but a. — BYRON 86:24
adulteries: all the a. of art — JONS 187:6
adulterous: found in a. bed — BLAKE 60:13
adultery: a. than in provincialism — HUXL 177:3
die for a.! — SHAK 283:23
Do not a. commit — CLOU 102:18
gallantry, and gods a. — BYRON 85:24
Not quite a., but adulteration — BYRON 86:24
Thou shalt not commit a. — BIBLE 40:9
woman taken in a. — BIBLE 53:25
adults: attributed by a. to children — SZASZ 321:23
children produce a. — DE VR 117:12
advantage: a. of doing one's praising — BUTL 84:9
A. rarely comes of it — CLOU 102:18
French are with equal a. — CANN 89:10
take a mean a. of them — WOD 352:21
undertaking of Great A. — ANON 6:21
advent: Hark to the a. voice — OAKL 240:16
adventure: a. is only an inconvenience — CHES 98:8
most beautiful a. in life — FROH 146:6
out into a. and sunshine — FORS 143:19
to die will be an awfully big a. — BARR 29:13
adventures: a. of his soul — FRAN 145:3
a. were by the fire-side — GOLD 155:12
hard a. t' undertake — FITZ 140:3
adversity: a. doth best discover — BACON 24:11
A.'s sweet milk, philosophy — SHAK 295:16
bread of a. — BIBLE 46:1
For of fortunes sharpe a. — CHAU 96:18
Sweet are the uses of a. — SHAK 272:14
advertisement: soul of an a. — JOHN 182:13
advertisers: prejudices the a. don't object to — SWAF 319:16
advertising: A. is the rattling of a stick — ORW 242:16
advice: a. is good or bad only — AUST 23:1
A. is seldom welcome — CHES 97:9
advise: A. the prince — ELIOT 134:1
STREETS FLOODED. PLEASE A. — BENC 34:6
aere: a. perennius — HOR 173:28
aeroplanes: it wasn't the a. — ROSE 111:17
Aesculapius: we owe a cock to A. — SOCR 310:25
aesthetic: a. enjoyment — WHIT 348:4
shine in the high a. line — GILB 152:9
afar: devotion to something a. — SHEL 305:5
affairs: a. which properly concern — VALE 336:21
tide in the a. of men — SHAK 282:1
affection: A. beaming in one eye — DICK 119:2
affections: holiness of the heart's a. — KEATS 192:23
T'a., and to faculties — DONNE 124:4
affinities: Elective a. — GOET 154:2
affliction: A. is enamoured of thy parts — SHAK 295:15
bread of a. — BIBLE 42:6
Remembering mine a. — BIBLE 47:1
waters of a. — BIBLE 46:1
afflictions: out of all their a. — BOOK 64:19
affluent: A. Society — GALB 147:14
afford: can a. to be good to her — SHAW 302:11
unless you can a. it — TROL 334:21
afloat: A. We move — CLOU 102:12
afraid: a. of his enemy — PLUT 250:2
And in short, I was a. — ELIOT 133:29
And many are a. of God — LOCK 209:1
I, a stranger and a. — HOUS 174:11
it is I; be not a. — BIBLE 50:8
It's not that I'm a. to die — ALLEN 4:16
they were sore a. — BIBLE 51:32
we do be a. of the sea — SYNGE 321:21
Who's a. of Virginia Woolf — ALBEE 3:12
Afric: geographers, in A.-maps — SWIFT 320:21
Where A.'s sunny fountains — HEBER 164:15

Africa: A. and her prodigies | BROW 74:13
foot—sloggin' over A. | KIPL 196:6
something new out of A. | PLINY 249:23
Till China and A. meet | AUDEN 20:11
with A. than my own body | ORTON 241:19
African: [A.] national consciousness | MACM 215:17
after: A. long grief and pain | TENN 327:3
a. many a summer | TENN 328:17
A. the first death | THOM 330:15
Or just a. | STEV 316:13
afternoon: At five in the a. | GARC 148:2
Lovely and willing every a. | AUDEN 20:25
summer a. | JAMES 180:5
Afton: Flow gently, sweet A. | BURNS 81:23
again: I'll see you a. | COW 109:2
we'll conquer a. and again | GARR 148:8
against: all life is 6 to 5 a. | RUNY 264:7
hand will be a. every man | BIBLE 39:13
he that is not with me is a. | BIBLE 50:1
I always vote a. | FIEL 139:18
I have somewhat a. thee | BIBLE 57:20
who can be a. us | BIBLE 54:41
Agamemnon: And A. dead | YEATS 359:14
When A. cried aloud | ELIOT 134:17
agate-stone: no bigger than an a. | SHAK 294:24
age: a. according to the oracle | VIRG 339:25
A. cannot wither her | SHAK 271:17
a. demanded an image | POUND 254:16
a. going to the workhouse | PAINE 244:13
A., I do abhor thee | SHAK 299:6
a. in pilèd stones | MILT 227:21
a. is a dream that is dying | O'SH 243:2
a. is as a lusty winter | SHAK 272:16
a. is rocking the wave | MAND 217:10
a. is the most unexpected | TROT 334:22
a. of chivalry is gone | BURKE 80:14
a. of ease | GOLD 154:19
a. of pamphleteers | HOGB 170:6
A. shall not weary them | BINY 59:12
a., which forgives itself | SHAW 302:6
A. will not be defied | BACON 25:8
a. with stealing steps | VAUX 337:15
at your a., it is right | CARR 91:4
buried in a good old a. | BIBLE 39:12
cold a., narrow jealousy | ROCH 261:2
companions for middle a. | BACON 25:2
Crabbed a. and youth | SHAK 299:5
dawning of the a. of Aquarius | RADO 257:18
days of our a. are threescore | BOOK 67:26
fetch the a. of gold | MILT 227:27
hath not forgotten my a. | SOUT 312:2
He died in a good old a. | BIBLE 42:18
He was not of an a. | JONS 187:28
His wealth a well-spent a. | CAMP 89:3
If youth knew; if a. could | EST 137:17
master spirits of this a. | SHAK 281:12
my Father, my a. | LOW 211:15
Old-a., a second child | CHUR 98:24
Old a. should burn | THOM 330:7
serene, That men call a. | BROO 72:20
soon comes a. | SPEN 313:12
Soul of the A. | JONS 187:25
stricken in a. | BIBLE 39:14
then the only end of a. | LARK 201:14
this a. best pleaseth | HERR 167:21
Unregarded a. in corners | SHAK 272:15
who tells one her real a. | WILDE 350:10
with a. and dust | RAL 258:1
With leaden a. o'ercargoed | FLEC 141:18
wonder of our a. | DYER 129:15
worth an a. without a name | MORD 234:21
aged: a. man is but a paltry | YEATS 359:21
Certainly a. | BYRON 86:21
creatures did the a. seem | TRAH 333:19

agenda: a. will be in inverse proportion | PARK 245:22
ages: A. of hopeless end | MILT 228:25
heir of all the a. | TENN 326:16
His acts being seven a. | SHAK 272:24
Our God, our help in a. past | WATTS 343:13
aggravating: She was an a. child | BELL 33:11
Agincourt: affright the air at A. | SHAK 278:34
agnus: A. Dei, qui tollis | MISS 231:19
ago: Hornby and my Barlow long a. | THOM 331:6
agony: a. is abated | MAC 213:23
Beyond is a. | GREV 158:17
agree: sugar, and saltness a. | GOLD 155:1
agreement: blow with an a. | TROT 335:2
death and an a. with hell | GARR 148:13
with hell are we at a. | BIBLE 45:28
a-hold: always keep a. of Nurse | BELL 33:5
a-hunting: a. we will go | FIEL 139:5
We daren't go a. | ALL 4:18
aid: Apt Alliteration's artful a. | CHUR 98:27
ailments: our a. are the same | SWIFT 320:2
aim: at which all things a. | ARIS 15:12
have forgotten your a. | SANT 266:21
you must a. a little above | LONG 209:14
aims: its divided a. | ARN 17:11
ain't: a. a fit night out | FIEL 139:17
A. it all a bleedin' shame | ANON 10:11
A. We Got Fun | KAHN 189:19
It a. necessarily so | GERS 168:5
air: a., a chartered libertine | SHAK 278:36
a. a solemn stillness holds | GRAY 157:4
a. broke into a mist | BROW 76:25
ampler ether, a diviner a. | WORD 355:7
Clear the a. | ELIOT 134:8
conscience-stricken a. | HOUS 174:6
Germans that of—the a. | RICH 260:6
His happy good-night a. | HARDY 162:7
into air, into thin a. | SHAK 296:10
lands hatless from the a. | BETJ 36:21
nipping and an eager a. | SHAK 274:25
Nor do not saw the a. | SHAK 276:4
Now a. is hushed | COLL 105:10
path along the dusky a. | COL 104:21
There is music in the a. | ELGAR 131:18
'twixt and angels' purity | DONNE 123:21
with pinions skim the a. | FRERE 145:22
airline: a. ticket to romantic places | MARV 221:4
airly: An' you've got to git up a. | LOW 211:4
airs: Sounds and sweet a. | SHAK 296:9
airy: A., fairy Lilian | TENN 326:5
aitches: nothing to lose but our a. | ORW 242:14
alarm: little a. now and then | BURN 81:16
SPREAD A. AND DESPONDENCY | PEN 247:8
alarms: confused a. of struggle | ARN 16:12
alas: A., poor Yorick | SHAK 277:8
Hugo— | GIDE 151:2
may say A. but cannot help | AUDEN 21:15
Albert: take a message to A. | DISR 122:22
Went there with young A. | EDGAR 130:15
Albion: La perfide A. | XIMÉ 358:9
Alcestis: like A. from the grave | MILT 230:24
alcohol: a. doesn't thrill me | PORT 253:20
A. is a very necessary article | SHAW 301:12
a. or morphine or idealism | JUNG 188:24
a. was a food well in advance | WOD 352:20
taken more out of a. than a. | CHUR 100:11
aldermen: divides the wives of a. | SMITH 308:20
Aldershot: burnish'd by A. sun | BETJ 37:10
ale: no more cakes and a. | SHAK 297:26
Sees bliss in a. | CRAB 110:21
Then to the spicy nut-brown a. | MILT 227:5
Aleppo: husband's to A. gone | SHAK 285:3
Alexander: but A. women | LEE 204:10
If I were not A. | ALEX 4:1
Some talk of A. | ANON 10:13

alexandrine: needless A. — POPE 252:4
alibi: He always has an a. — ELIOT 134:9
Alice: Pass the sick bag, A. — JUNOR 188:27
alien: a. people clutching — ELIOT 133:23
aliter: *Dis a. visum* — VIRG 339:7
alive: a. and well and living — ANON 8:13
dead, and is a. again — BIBLE 52:32
Half dead and half a. — BETJ 36:19
if he gets out of it a. — JONES 116:24
if I am a. — HOLL 170:11
in Christ shall all be made a. — BIBLE 55:17
in that dawn to be a. — WORD 354:24
Life's not just being a. — MART 220:6
noise and tumult when a. — EDW 131:4
Officiously to keep a. — CLOU 102:17
one of those half-a. things — FORS 144:1
ways of being a. — DAWK 115:3
What still a. at twenty-two — KING 195:19
all: A. before my little room — BROO 73:3
A. by my own-alone self — HARR 163:3
a. for love, and nothing for — SPEN 313:11
A. for one, one for all — DUMAS 129:4
a. in all for prose — CAREW 89:18
A. passes. Art alone — DOBS 122:25
a. shall be well — ELIOT 133:13
a. shall be well — JUL 188:21
A.'s right with the world — BROW 76:28
A. that a man hath — BIBLE 42:23
A. that I am I give to you — BOOK 66:2
a. that's best of dark — BYRON 87:6
A. things bright and beautiful — ALEX 4:2
a. things to all men — BIBLE 55:8
A things were made — BIBLE 53:7
A. we like sheep — BIBLE 46:19
at a. times, and in a. places — BOOK 65:15
don't think twice, it's a. right — DYLAN 130:1
From a. that terror teaches — CHES 97:24
have his a. neglected — JOHN 183:25
having nothing, yet hath a. — WOTT 357:15
Her a. on earth, and more — BYRON 85:18
I'm a. right — BONE 63:10
I would that you were a. to me — BROW 77:20
man for a. seasons — WHIT 349:2
not at all or all in a. — TENN 324:14
1066 and A. That — SELL 269:23
allegory: headstrong as an a. — SHER 305:30
alley: And she lives in our a. — CAREY 90:2
I think we are in rats' a. — ELIOT 134:23
alliance: A., *n.* union of two thieves — BIER 59:2
alliances: a. with none — JEFF 180:19
allies: no a. to be polite to — GEOR 150:5
we have no eternal a. — PALM 244:18
all-in-all: intellectual A. — WORD 356:6
alliteration: Apt A.'s artful aid — CHUR 98:27
allons: A., *enfants de la patrie* — ROUG 263:16
allure: how to a. by denying — TROL 334:18
Alma mater: A. lie dissolved in port — POPE 250:16
almanac: Look in the a. — SHAK 290:30
pious fraud of the a. — LOW 211:10
Almighty: A. placed it there — LAB 199:12
A.'s orders to perform — ADD 2:11
almost: a. thou persuadest me — BIBLE 54:27
alms: a. and oblations — BOOK 65:8
a. for oblivion — SHAK 297:4
alone: a. against smiling enemies — BOWEN 71:1
A. and palely loitering — KEATS 191:7
a. with the quiet day — JAMES 180:3
dangerous to meet it a. — WHAR 347:4
fastest who travels a. — KIPL 196:20
I want to be a. — GARBO 148:1
left a. with our day — AUDEN 21:15
left him a. with his glory — WOLFE 353:1
less a. than when alone — ROG 261:18
less alone than when wholly a. — CIC 100:24

alone (*cont.*):
man should be a. — BIBLE 38:20
not sufficiently a. — VALÉ 336:21
One is one and all a. — ANON 8:6
along: All a., down along — BALL 28:11
alpha: I am A. and Omega — BIBLE 57:19
Alps: A. of green ice — PHIL 248:15
fading and archipelagoes — ALDR 3:17
passages through the A. — COLM 105:15
altar: great world's a.-stairs — TENN 325:11
high a. on the move — BOWEN 71:2
lays upon the a. the dearest — SPR 313:26
self-slain on his own strange a. — SWIN 321:10
altars: even thy a., O Lord — BOOK 67:20
alteram: *Audi partem a.* — AUG 22:1
alteration: A. though it be from worse — HOOK 171:15
Which alters when it a. finds — SHAK 300:8
alternatives: a. that are not their own — BONH 63:11
altitudo: reason to an *O a.* — BROW 74:11
altogether: A. elsewhere — AUDEN 20:19
suit of clothes is a. — LOES 209:6
alway: They a. must be with us — KEATS 190:12
will not a. be chiding — BOOK 68:6
always: But he is a. great — DRYD 128:28
sometimes a., by God — RICH 260:5
There'll a. be an England — CHAR 245:15
am: I think, therefore I a. — DESC 117:9
ama: *A. et fac quod vis* — AUG 22:2
Amaryllis: sport with A. in the shade — MILT 227:14
amateur: whine of the a. for three — WHIS 347:10
amateurs: Hell is full of musical a. — SHAW 301:19
amaze: men themselves a. — MARV 220:14
amazing: A. grace! — NEWT 239:7
A. love! — WESL 346:3
ambassador: a. is an honest man sent abroad — WOTT 357:22
ambiguities: clear these a. — SHAK 295:26
ambiguity: Seven types of a. — EMPS 137:7
ambition: a. can creep as well — BURKE 81:8
A. first sprung from — POPE 250:24
A., in a private man a vice — MASS 222:3
a. mock their useful toil — GRAY 157:7
A.'s debt is paid — SHAK 281:11
A. should be made of sterner — SHAK 281:20
Art not without a. — SHAK 285:15
avarice and a. — SMITH 308:20
fling away a. — SHAK 280:19
Vain the a. of kings — WEBS 344:13
Vaulting a., which o'erleaps — SHAK 286:1
wars that make a virtue — SHAK 292:19
Who doth a. shun — SHAK 272:21
ambitious: he was a., I slew him — SHAK 281:24
O sacred hunger of a. minds — SPEN 313:16
ambo: *Arcades a.* — VIRG 340:1
Ambree: foremost in battle was Mary A. — BALL 28:1
ambrosial: Phallic and a. — POUND 254:17
ambulance: With an a.? — SIMP 307:12
âme: *Quelle â. est sans défauts* — RIMB 260:10
Amelia: A. was praying for George — THAC 329:18
amen: Like the sound of a great A. — PROC 255:14
So goodbye dear, and A. — PORT 253:21
Will no man say, a. — SHAK 294:4
amens: few mumbled a. — HUNT 176:18
America: America the beautiful — BATES 30:2
A. is a country of young men — EMER 137:1
A. is a land whose centre — UPD 336:13
A. is a vast conspiracy — UPD 336:14
A. is God's Crucible — ZANG 360:27
A. is just ourselves — ARN 17:24
A. is the proof — MCC 214:10
A., thou half-brother — BAIL 26:19
A. to convert the Indians — WESL 346:12
A. was thus clearly top — SELL 270:5
A. will think tomorrow — KIPL 197:16
come back to A. to die — JAMES 179:21

America (cont.):

| | |
|---|---|
| England and A. are two | SHAW 302:27 |
| glorious morning for A. | ADAMS 2:6 |
| God bless A. | BERL 35:21 |
| I like to be in A. | SOND 311:8 |
| I, too, sing A. | HUGH 175:19 |
| It's morning again in A. | RINEY 260:12 |
| next to of course god a. | CUMM 112:17 |
| O my A., my new found land | DONNE 123:6 |
| American: A. as cherry pie | BROWN 73:15 |
| A. beauty rose | ROCK 261:11 |
| A. girls turn into A. women | HAMP 161:5 |
| A. women shoot the hippopotamus | FORS 143:14 |
| business of the A. people | COOL 107:19 |
| bye, bye, Miss A. Pie | MCL 215:8 |
| fallen in love with A. names | BENÉT 34:8 |
| foreign oil controlling A. soil | DYLAN 130:8 |
| I am a free man, an A. | JOHN 181:19 |
| I am A. bred | MILL 224:24 |
| imported, elderly A. | JENK 181:3 |
| justice and the A. way | ANON 7:5 |
| no second acts in A. lives | FITZ 140:23 |
| Americans: And so, my fellow A. | KENN 194:6 |
| Good A., when they die | APPL 14:15 |
| new generation of A. | KENN 194:2 |
| when bad A. die | WILDE 350:8 |
| worse than ignorant A. | MASS 222:4 |
| amiable: how a. are thy dwellings | BOOK 67:19 |
| amicably: a. if they can | QUIN 257:9 |
| amicus: A. Plato, sed magis | ARIS 15:22 |
| amiss: rams speed not, all is a. | BARN 29:8 |
| amitti: non a. sed praemitti | CYPR 113:13 |
| ammunition: and pass the a. | FORGY 143:13 |
| amo: A., amas, I love a lass | O'KEE 241:5 |
| Non a. te, Sabidi | MART 220:4 |
| Odi et a. | CAT 93:7 |
| amor: A. vincit omnia | CHAU 95:16 |
| L'a, che muove il sole | DANTE 113:24 |
| Omnia vincit A. | VIRG 340:4 |
| amorem: subito deponere a. | CAT 93:5 |
| amorous: As a. of their strokes | SHAK 271:14 |
| dire offence from a. causes | POPE 253:2 |
| excite my a. propensities | JOHN 183:24 |
| amour: beginning of an A. | BEHN 32:20 |
| Plaisir d'a. | FLOR 142:12 |
| amours: Et nos a., faut-il qu'il | APOL 14:12 |
| amphibii: These rational a. go | MARV 221:3 |
| Amurath: Not A. an A. succeeds | SHAK 278:29 |
| amuse: talent to a. | COW 109:1 |
| amused: a. by its presumption | THUR 332:17 |
| People mutht be a. | DICK 118:28 |
| We are not a. | VICT 338:7 |
| amusements: tolerable but for its a. | LEWIS 206:15 |
| anarchism: A. is a game | SHAW 302:10 |
| anarchist: small a. community | BENN 34:15 |
| anarchy: a. is loosed upon the world | YEATS 359:24 |
| anatomy: A. is destiny | FREUD 145:23 |
| ancestors: look backward to their a. | BURKE 80:12 |
| ancestral: A. voices prophesying war | COL 103:25 |
| ancestry: without pride of a. | POWER 255:4 |
| ancient: A. of Days | GRANT 156:8 |
| A. of days did sit | BIBLE 47:14 |
| A. person of my heart | ROCH 261:9 |
| A. times were the youth | BACON 24:5 |
| both so a. and so fresh | AUG 21:24 |
| It is an a. Mariner | COL 104:3 |
| while I sing the a. ways | YEATS 360:4 |
| and: including 'a.' and 'the' | MCC 214:12 |
| Andromache: kissed his sad A. | CORN 108:5 |
| angel: action how like an a. | SHAK 275:16 |
| A. did with Jacob | WALT 342:15 |
| a. is a man right fair | SHAK 300:13 |
| a. is the English child | BLAKE 61:24 |
| a. of death has been abroad | BRIG 72:2 |
| a. of the Lord came upon | BIBLE 51:32 |

angel (cont.):

| | |
|---|---|
| a. travelling incognito | QUEN 257:6 |
| a. watching an urn | TENN 326:24 |
| beautiful and ineffectual a. | ARN 18:4 |
| drive an a. from your door | BLAKE 61:22 |
| enough for an a. to pass | FIRB 139:20 |
| ministering a. shall | SHAK 277:10 |
| ministering a. thou | SCOTT 268:22 |
| Recording A. | STER 315:22 |
| Shined in my a.-infancy | VAUG 337:7 |
| Though an a. should write | MOORE 234:10 |
| Who wrote like an a. | GARR 148:9 |
| woman yet think him an a. | THAC 329:11 |
| angels: A. and ministers of grace | SHAK 274:27 |
| A. bending near the earth | SEARS 269:11 |
| a. of God ascending | BIBLE 39:21 |
| a. on the walls of heaven | MARL 219:11 |
| a. sing thee to thy rest | SHAK 277:19 |
| band of a. comin' after me | ANON 10:17 |
| By that sin fell the a. | SHAK 280:19 |
| entertained a. unawares | BIBLE 56:29 |
| Four a. to my bed | ANON 9:8 |
| glittering and sparkling a. | TRAH 333:19 |
| glorious fault of a. | POPE 250:24 |
| his a. charge over thee | BOOK 67:30 |
| If a. fight | SHAK 293:23 |
| Let A. prostrate fall | PERR 248:4 |
| Michael and his a. fought | BIBLE 57:31 |
| neglect God and his A. | DONNE 124:21 |
| nor a., nor principalities | BIBLE 54:42 |
| Not Angles but A. | GREG 158:12 |
| on the side of the a. | DISR 121:15 |
| Though women are a. | BYRON 87:12 |
| To thee all A. cry aloud | BOOK 63:18 |
| 'twixt air and a. | DONNE 123:21 |
| where a. fear to tread | POPE 252:10 |
| With a. round the throne | WATTS 343:3 |
| Ye holy a. bright | GURN 159:11 |
| anger: A. and jealousy | ELIOT 132:12 |
| A. is a short madness | HOR 173:9 |
| A. is one of the sinews | FULL 147:5 |
| A. makes dull men witty | BACON 25:29 |
| a. of men who have no opinions | CHES 98:10 |
| contempt and a. of his lip | SHAK 298:6 |
| Juno's never-forgetting a. | VIRG 338:23 |
| keepeth he his a. for ever | BOOK 68:6 |
| laughter may signify a. | TOFF 333:7 |
| more in sorrow than in a. | SHAK 274:19 |
| outer life of telegrams and a. | FORS 143:20 |
| strike it in a. | SHAW 301:32 |
| thy mistress some rich a. shows | KEATS 191:26 |
| With neither a. nor partiality | TAC 322:6 |
| angle: Brother of the A. | WALT 342:10 |
| Themselves in every a. greet | MARV 220:13 |
| angler: excellent a. | WALT 342:11 |
| so no man is born an a. | WALT 342:9 |
| angles: Not A. but Angels | GREG 158:12 |
| Offer no a. to the wind | TESS 329:10 |
| angling: a. or float fishing | JOHN 186:11 |
| Anglo-Irishman: He was an A. | BEHAN 32:16 |
| Anglo-Saxon: A. attitudes | CARR 92:3 |
| angry: Be ye a. and sin not | BIBLE 55:33 |
| when very a. swear | TWAIN 336:5 |
| anguis: Latet a. in herba | VIRG 339:24 |
| anguish: With a. moist | KEATS 191:8 |
| animal: After coition every a. is sad | ANON 13:19 |
| Be a good a. | LAWR 202:16 |
| Man is by nature a political a. | ARIS 15:18 |
| nor hope attend a dying a. | YEATS 358:21 |
| only a. in the world to fear | LAWR 202:20 |
| Only A. that Blushes | TWAIN 335:24 |
| success in life is to be a good a. | SPEN 312:16 |
| This a. is very bad | ANON 12:3 |
| vegetable, a., and mineral | GILB 152:23 |
| animals: All a. are equal | ORW 241:23 |

animals (cont.):
A., whom we have made our slaves · DARW 114:6
a. will not look · AUDEN 21:15
could turn and live with a. · WHIT 348:19
distinguish us from other a. · BEAU 30:16
animula: A. vagula blandula · HADR 159:14
Ann: A., Ann! · DE L 116:11
Annabel Lee: I and my A. · POE 250:3
annals: a. blank in history-books · MONT 233:22
simple a. of the poor · GRAY 157:7
War's a. will cloud into night · HARDY 162:12
annihilating: A. all that's made · MARV 220:16
anniversaries: secret a. of the heart · LONG 209:20
anno domini: only a. · HILT 168:18
annoy: He only does it to a. · CARR 91:5
annual: A. income twenty pounds · DICK 118:12
annuity: a. is a very serious business · AUST 23:7
annus: a. horribilis · ELIZ 135:17
anointed: a. my head with oil · BOOK 66:18
wash the balm from an a. king · SHAK 293:22
anointing: Thou the a. Spirit art · BOOK 69:16
another: A. fine mess · LAUR 202:8
taste of a. man's bread · DANTE 113:23
that was in a. country · MARL 219:2
We are members one of a. · BIBLE 55:32
answer: A. a fool according · BIBLE 43:38
a. is blowin' in the wind · DYLAN 129:19
a. to a difficult situation · BEVAN 37:20
A. to the Great Question · ADAMS 1:9
But a. came there none · SCOTT 268:6
But a. made it none · SHAK 274:18
more than the wisest man can a. · COLT 105:17
on the way to a pertinent a. · BRON 72:10
soft a. turneth away wrath · BIBLE 43:24
what a dusty a. gets the soul · MER 223:24
why did you a. the phone · THUR 332:18
would not stay for an a. · BACON 25:18
answerable: We are a. · NEWM 239:1
answered: I came, and no one a. · DE L 116:19
persistence till it must be a. · BROW 77:17
answering: a. that of God · FOX 144:18
ant: Go to the a. thou sluggard · BIBLE 43:11
antagonistic: a. governments · WAUGH 343:23
anti: savage a.-everythings · HOLM 170:16
antic: goat feet dance an a. hay · MARL 218:15
rusty curb of old father a. · SHAK 277:24
To put an a. disposition on · SHAK 275:4
anti-destin: L'art est un a. · MALR 217:4
antipathy: strong a. of good to bad · POPE 252:32
antipodes: like A. in shoes · MARV 221:3
sheer opposite, a. · KEATS 190:25
antique: group that's quite a. · BYRON 86:8
noble and nude and a. · SWIN 321:6
traveller from an a. land · SHEL 304:11
antiquities: A. are history defaced · BACON 23:21
Antony: And Brutus A. · SHAK 281:26
A. shall be brought · SHAK 272:5
bear the weight of A. · SHAK 271:10
O! my oblivion is a very A. · SHAK 271:9
anvil: Church is an a. · MACL 215:6
England's on the a. · KIPL 196:3
any: A. old iron, any old iron · COLL 105:6
Ready to be a. thing · BROW 74:8
anybody: Is there a. there · DE L 116:18
Then no one's a. · GILB 151:8
anything: A. for a quiet life · MIDD 224:5
A. goes · PORT 253:17
fall for a. · HAM 160:16
apart: of man's life a thing a. · BYRON 86:4
We have stood a., studiously · WILS 351:19
ape: a. for his grandfather · HUXL 177:21
devil always God's a. · LUTH 212:9
gorgeous buttocks of the a. · HUXL 177:13
Is man an a. or an angel · DISR 121:15
apes: And a. are apes · JONS 187:10

apes (cont.):
a., and peacocks · BIBLE 41:31
aphrodisiac: Power is the great a. · KISS 198:6
Apollo: harsh after the songs of A. · SHAK 284:24
Yea, is not even A. · SWIN 321:12
young A., golden-haired · CORN 108:7
Apollos: A. watered · BIBLE 55:3
Apollyon: his name is A. · BUNY 78:20
apologies: people do not want a. · WOD 352:21
apologize: Never a. · FISH 139:24
rule in life never to a. · WOD 352:21
apology: a. for the Devil · BUTL 84:15
a. before you be accused · CHAR 94:22
Apostles: A. would have done · BYRON 85:25
glorious company of the A. · BOOK 63:19
Twelve for the twelve a. · ANON 8:6
Apostolick: Catholick and A. Church · BOOK 65:6
apothecary: a. than a starved poet · LOCK 209:2
apparel: a. oft proclaims the man · SHAK 274:21
appear: Cecilia, a. in visions · AUDEN 20:10
appearance: outward a. · BIBLE 41:15
appearances: Keep up a. · CHUR 98:25
appetite: a.; a feeling and a love · WORD 355:9
a. grows by eating · RAB 257:10
a. may sicken, and so die · SHAK 297:13
Now good digestion wait on a. · SHAK 287:10
satisfying a voracious a. · FIEL 139:10
appetites: a. as apt to change · DRYD 127:25
cloy the a. they feed · SHAK 271:17
applause: A., n. echo of a platitude · BIER 59:3
sunshine and with a. · BUNY 79:2
apple: a. falling towards England · AUDEN 21:5
a. of his eye · BIBLE 40:23
millionaires love a baked a. · FIRB 139:21
young and easy under the a. · THOM 330:8
apple-pie: A was an a. · ANON 6:6
cabbage-leaf to make an a. · FOOTE 142:20
apples: golden a. of the sun · YEATS 360:1
Kent—a., cherries, hops · DICK 119:26
On moon-washed a. of wonder · DRIN 126:24
Ripe a. drop about my head · MARV 220:15
Stolen, stolen, be your a. · HUNT 176:16
apply: a. our hearts unto wisdom · BOOK 67:27
know my methods. A. them · DOYLE 126:2
appointed: Its own a. limits keep · WHIT 348:9
Like pilgrims to th'a. place · DRYD 128:12
appointment: a. at the end of the world · DIN 121:1
a. by the corrupt few · SHAW 301:27
Every time I create an a. · LOUI 210:14
apprehension: a. of the good · SHAK 293:14
approaching: To see the a. sacrifice · MILM 225:13
après: A. nous le déluge · POMP 250:11
apricot: blushing a. and woolly peach · JONS 187:30
April: A., April, laugh · WATS 342:26
A. is the cruellest month · ELIOT 134:18
A. of your youth adorns · HERB 166:19
A. with his shoures soote · CHAU 95:10
Men are A. when they woo · SHAK 273:9
Now that A.'s there · BROW 76:1
uncertain glory of an A. day · SHAK 298:18
aprons: made themselves a. · BIBLE 38:26
apt: A. Alliteration's artful aid · CHUR 98:27
find myself so a. to die · SHAK 281:12
aquarium: a. is gone · LOW 211:12
Aquarius: age of A. · RADO 257:18
Aquitaine: prince of A. · NERV 238:8
Arabia: with the spell of far A. · DE L 116:13
Arabs: fold their tents, like the A. · LONG 209:13
Arbeit: A. macht frei · ANON 13:1
arbiter: Elegantiae a. · TAC 322:7
arbitrate: Does a. the event · MILT 226:13
arbitrator: old common a., Time · SHAK 297:11
Arcades: A. ambo · VIRG 340:1
Arcadia: Et in A. ego · ANON 13:15
Arcadians: A. both · VIRG 340:1

arch: All experience is an a. | ADAMS 1:13
all experience is an a. | TENN 328:21
a.-flatterer with whom | BACON 24:32
wide a. of the ranged empire | SHAK 271:5
archangel: A. a little damaged | LAMB 200:8
archbishop: a. had come to see me | BURG 79:14
archer: mark the a. little meant | SCOTT 268:15
arches: down the a. of the years | THOM 331:8
Underneath the A. | FLAN 141:2
archipelagoes: fading alps and a. | ALDR 3:17
architect: a. can only advise | WRIG 357:23
A. of the Universe | JEANS 180:17
architecture: A. is frozen music | SCH 267:17
A. is the art of how to waste | JOHN 182:2
A., of all the arts | DIMN 120:25
fall of English a. | BETJ 37:16
frolic a. of the snow | EMER 136:16
New styles of a. | AUDEN 21:14
Arcturi: those pearled A. | SHEL 304:29
ardeur: a. dans mes veines cachée | RAC 257:16
ardua: Per a. ad astra | ANON 13:18
are: Let them be as they a. | CLEM 102:3
That which we a., we are | TENN 328:25
we know what we a. | SHAK 276:33
area: despondently at a. gates | ELIOT 134:4
Argos: remembers his sweet A. | VIRG 339:21
argue: a. with someone who denies | AUCT 20:4
earth does not a. | WHIT 348:23
arguing: I am not a. with you | WHIS 347:9
argument: a. of the broken window | PANK 245:2
height of this great a. | MILT 228:9
I have found you an a. | JOHN 186:5
it is the a. of tyrants | PITT 249:7
stir without great a. | SHAK 276:31
This is a rotten a. | ANON 11:3
Tories own no a. but force | BROW 74:25
when blood is their a. | SHAK 279:13
Whigs admit no force but a. | BROW 74:25
would be a. for a week | SHAK 277:28
Argus: A. were her eunuch | SHAK 284:14
Ariel: Caliban casts out A. | POUND 254:17
arise: A., shine | BIBLE 46:23
I will a. and go now | YEATS 359:12
Let us a. and go like men | STEV 317:15
aristocracy: absentee a. | DISR 121:7
a. in a republic | MITF 232:8
a. means government by | CHES 98:12
A. of the Moneybag | CARL 90:15
aristocrat: A., democrat, autocrat | TENN 326:26
aristocratic: a. class from the Philistines | ARN 17:26
Aristotle: it is contrary to A. | TAWN 322:20
arithmetical: in an a. ratio | MALT 217:5
ark: two unto Noah into the A. | BIBLE 39:8
arm: a. doth bind the restless wave | WHIT 348:9
seal upon thine a. | BIBLE 45:1
strength with his a. | BIBLE 51:29
Wi' the auld moon in her a. | BALL 28:5
arma: A. virumque cano | VIRG 338:23
armadas: till the great A. come | NEWB 238:11
Armageddon: Lincoln County Road or A. | DYLAN 130:7
armchair: Fortieth spare A. | BROW 75:26
armchairs: a. tight about the hips | WOD 352:22
armed: A. neutrality is ineffectual | WILS 351:20
a. with more than complete steel | ANON 8:7
Armenteers: Mademoiselle from A. | ANON 9:5
armes: Aux a., citoyens | ROUG 263:16
armies: ignorant a. clash by night | ARN 16:12
plenty of money and large a. | ANOU 14:4
with your land a. in China | MONT 233:23
armistice: a. for twenty years | FOCH 142:15
armour: put on the a. of light | BIBLE 55:1
Put on the whole a. of God | BIBLE 56:3
put upon us the a. of light | BOOK 64:21
whole a. of God | BIBLE 56:4

armoured: a. cars of dreams | BISH 59:16
arms: a. against a sea of troubles | SHAK 275:25
A., and the man | DRYD 128:25
a. and the man | VIRG 338:23
a. of a chambermaid | JOHN 185:21
a. went round her waist | MAS 221:20
But in my a. till break of day | AUDEN 20:28
Emparadised in one another's a. | MILT 229:10
everlasting a. | BIBLE 40:25
every man in a. | WORD 354:14
haughty nation proud in a. | MILT 226:6
if my love were in my a. | ANON 11:18
In one another's a. | YEATS 359:20
it hath very long a. | HAL 160:8
So he laid down his a. | HOOD 171:4
To find the a. of my true love | TENN 327:3
To war and a. I fly | LOV 210:20
army: a. marches on its stomach | NAP 237:5
a. of unalterable law | MER 223:22
backbone of the A. | KIPL 196:10
brought the A. home | GUED 159:6
contemptible little a. | ANON 7:4
noble a. of Martyrs | BOOK 63:19
[our a.] the scum of the earth | WELL 345:14
aroint: A. thee, witch! | SHAK 285:3
aroma: a. of performing seals | HART 163:8
aromatic: faint beneath the a. pain | WINC 352:2
a-roving: I'll go no more a. | ANON 6:5
arrangements: has no a. | WHIT 348:23
arrayed: a. like one of these | BIBLE 49:4
arrest: Is swift in his a. | SHAK 277:15
arrive: better thing than to a. | STEV 317:6
to a. where we started | ELIOT 133:10
arrogant: to subdue the a. | VIRG 339:16
arrow: Every a. that flies | LONG 209:14
I shot an a. into the air | LONG 209:10
nor for the a. that flieth | BOOK 67:29
time's a. | EDD 130:10
arrows: a. in the hand of the giant | BOOK 68:31
a. of outrageous fortune | SHAK 275:25
Bring me my a. of desire | BLAKE 61:12
ars: A. longa, vita brevis | HIPP 168:19
arse: politician is an a. | CUMM 112:18
sit on your a. for fifty years | MACN 216:2
arsenal: great a. of democracy | ROOS 262:5
art: All passes. A. alone | DOBS 122:25
all the adulteries of a. | JONS 187:6
a. can wash her guilt away | GOLD 155:13
a. constantly aspires | PATER 246:14
A. does not reproduce | KLEE 198:10
A. for art's sake | CONS 107:13
a. for art's sake | COUS 108:17
A. has no other end | FLAU 141:13
A. is a jealous mistress | EMER 136:19
A. is a revolt against fate | MALR 217:4
A. is born of humiliation | AUDEN 21:20
A. is meant to disturb | BRAQ 71:14
A. is pattern informed by | READ 258:9
A. is significant deformity | FRY 147:3
A. is the imposing | WHIT 348:4
A. is vice | DEGAS 116:2
a. lawful as eating | SHAK 284:4
A. most cherishes | BROW 76:21
a. of the possible | BISM 59:17
a.'s hid causes | JONS 187:5
Desiring this man's a. | SHAK 299:14
Drawing is the true test of a. | INGR 178:17
Dying is an a. | PLATH 249:15
enemy of good a. the pram | CONN 106:25
Enough of science and of a. | WORD 357:5
excellence of every a. | KEATS 193:1
glib and oily a. | SHAK 282:18
good grey guardians of a. | WILB 349:12
history of a. | BUTL 84:14

art (cont.):

| | |
|---|---|
| importance of a work of a. | FLAU 141:8 |
| In a. the best is good enough | GOET 154:9 |
| industry without a. is brutality | RUSK 264:11 |
| It's clever, but is it A. | KIPL 196:8 |
| kills love, it kills a. | WAUGH 343:17 |
| Life is short, the a. long | HIPP 168:19 |
| Living is my job and my a. | MONT 233:16 |
| Minister that meddles with a. | MELB 222:21 |
| More matter with less a. | SHAK 275:10 |
| nature is the a. of God | BROW 74:14 |
| next to Nature, A. | LAND 200:22 |
| only interested in a. | SHAW 302:25 |
| people start on all this A. | HERB 166:12 |
| rest is the madness of a. | JAMES 179:23 |
| resuscitate the dead a. | POUND 254:14 |
| revenge of intellect upon a. | SONT 311:9 |
| Rules destroy genius and a. | HAZL 164:5 |
| Shakespeare wanted a. | JONS 187:31 |
| strains of unpremeditated a. | SHEL 305:6 |
| triumph of the embalmer's a. | VIDAL 338:12 |
| when A. is too precise | HERR 167:15 |

| | |
|---|---|
| artful: Apt Alliteration's a. aid | CHUR 98:27 |
| Arthur: He's in A.'s bosom | SHAK 279:3 |
| articles: These a. subscribed | CONG 106:21 |
| artifex: Qualis a. pereo! | NERO 238:7 |
| artificer: great a. made | STEV 317:20 |
| lean unwashed a. | SHAK 282:11 |
| artificial: All things are a. | BROW 74:14 |
| said it was a. respiration | BURG 79:15 |
| artisan: employment to the a. | BELL 33:22 |
| artist: a., like the God | JOYCE 188:8 |
| a. man and the mother woman | SHAW 301:18 |
| a. must be in his work | FLAU 141:11 |
| a. will be judged | CONN 106:27 |
| God is really only another a. | PIC 248:18 |
| no man is born an a. | WALT 342:9 |
| Portrait of the A. | JOYCE 188:6 |
| sign of the true a. | VIDAL 338:14 |
| trust the a. | LAWR 202:15 |
| What an a. dies with me | NERO 238:7 |
| artistic: intellectual and a. | BERL 36:4 |
| arts: a. babbladive and scribblative | SOUT 312:3 |
| cry both a. and learning down | QUAR 257:5 |
| Dear nurse of a. | SHAK 280:2 |
| famed in all great a. | ARN 17:21 |
| France, mother of a. | DU B 128:32 |
| Greece, mother of a. | MILT 230:6 |
| had I but followed the a. | SHAK 297:16 |
| No a.; no letters | HOBB 169:10 |
| as: A. with gladness men of old | DIX 122:24 |
| ascend: a. the brightest heaven | SHAK 278:33 |
| ascending: angels of God a. | BIBLE 39:21 |
| ash: A. on an old man's sleeve | ELIOT 133:8 |
| laughter of an empty a. can | CRANE 110:32 |
| Oak, and A., and Thorn | KIPL 197:1 |
| ashamed: more things a man is a. of | SHAW 301:16 |
| something he is a. of | SHAW 300:25 |
| to feel a. of home | DICK 118:25 |
| ashbuds: More black than a. | TENN 323:23 |
| ashen: By a. roots the violets blow | TENN 325:29 |
| ashes: a. to ashes, dust to dust | BOOK 66:8 |
| a. under Uricon | HOUS 174:23 |
| burnt to a. | GRAH 156:4 |
| For the a. of his fathers | MAC 214:3 |
| past is a bucket of a. | SAND 266:15 |
| sour grapes and a. | ASHF 18:24 |
| splendid in a. | BROW 74:7 |
| turn the universe to a. | MISS 231:23 |
| aside: Just try and set death a. | TURG 335:14 |
| ask: A., and it shall be given | BIBLE 49:9 |
| a. faithfully we may obtain | BOOK 64:27 |
| A. me no more | CAREW 89:20 |
| a. not what your country | KENN 194:6 |
| a. the hard question | AUDEN 21:16 |

ask (cont.):

| | |
|---|---|
| a. why | AUDEN 20:17 |
| Don't a. me, ask the horse | FREUD 146:2 |
| I a. and cannot answer | SHAW 303:1 |
| Where a. is have | SMART 308:11 |
| asking: and a. too much | CANN 89:10 |
| [or third] time of a. | BOOK 65:25 |
| asleep: Half a. as they stalk | HARDY 162:11 |
| men were all a. the snow | BRID 72:1 |
| That sucks the nurse a. | SHAK 272:9 |
| very houses seem a. | WORD 354:16 |
| asp: on the hole of the a. | BIBLE 45:20 |
| asparagus: A. and it appeared | DICK 118:30 |
| aspens: Willows whiten, a. quiver | TENN 325:35 |
| aspes: a. leef she gan to quake | CHAU 96:17 |
| asphalt: only monument the a. road | ELIOT 134:13 |
| aspidistra: biggest a. in the world | HARP 163:2 |
| Keep the a. flying | ORW 242:2 |
| aspire: light, and will a. | SHAK 300:17 |
| ass: jaw of an a. | BIBLE 41:5 |
| kiss my a. in Macy's window | JOHN 181:20 |
| law is a a. | DICK 119:20 |
| law is such an a. | CHAP 94:18 |
| nor his ox, nor his a. | BIBLE 40:9 |
| assassin: you are an a. | ROST 263:12 |
| assassination: absolutism moderated by a. | ANON 6:30 |
| A. is the extreme form | SHAW 302:22 |
| A. is the quickest way | MOL 232:22 |
| if the a. could trammel | SHAK 285:22 |
| assaults: all a. of our enemies | BOOK 64:5 |
| assent: a. with civil leer | POPE 251:6 |
| asses: seeking a. found a kingdom | MILT 230:5 |
| assume: A. a virtue | SHAK 276:23 |
| assurance: make a. double sure | SHAK 287:21 |
| One of the low on whom a. sits | ELIOT 134:29 |
| Assyrian: A. came down | BYRON 85:22 |
| Astolat: lily maid of A. | TENN 324:7 |
| astonish: A. me | DIAG 117:15 |
| astonished: a. at my own moderation | CLIVE 102:6 |
| astonishment: Your a.'s odd | KNOX 198:18 |
| astra: Per ardua ad a. | ANON 13:18 |
| sic itur ad a. | VIRG 339:19 |
| astray: sheep have gone a. | BIBLE 46:19 |
| astronomers: Confounding her a. | HODG 169:14 |
| asunder: let no man put a. | BOOK 66:3 |
| let not man put a. | BIBLE 50:20 |
| asylum: a. run by lunatics | LLOY 208:12 |
| taken charge of the a. | ROWL 264:1 |
| atheism: inclineth man's mind to a. | BACON 24:12 |
| atheist: a. half believes a God | YOUNG 360:21 |
| a. is a man who has no | BUCH 77:27 |
| a.-laugh's a poor exchange | BURNS 82:6 |
| female a. talks you dead | JOHN 183:8 |
| atheists: no a. in the foxholes | CUMM 113:6 |
| Athens: A. arose | SHEL 303:17 |
| A., the eye of Greece | MILT 230:6 |
| athirst: a. of the fountain | BIBLE 58:6 |
| Atlantic: In the steep A. stream | MILT 226:7 |
| Atlas: disencumbered A. | COWP 110:4 |
| atom: mystery of the a. | BRAD 71:10 |
| only because the carbon a. | JEANS 180:16 |
| saw the flaring a.-streams | TENN 326:21 |
| stars leads through the a. | EDD 130:12 |
| atomic: primordial a. globule | GILB 151:18 |
| atomies: team of little a. | SHAK 294:24 |
| atoms: a. of Democritus | BLAKE 61:14 |
| fortuitous concurrence of a. | PALM 244:19 |
| attach: Where people wish to a. | AUST 22:23 |
| attachment: a. à la Plato | GILB 152:11 |
| attack: both by his plan of a. | SASS 267:13 |
| dared a. my Chesterton | BELL 33:16 |
| lead such dire a. | MAC 214:6 |
| attacked: when a. it defends itself | ANON 12:3 |
| attacking: situation excellent, I am a. | FOCH 142:14 |
| attempt: a. and not the deed | SHAK 286:13 |

# B

back (cont.):
B. to the future GALE 361:2
B. to the garden MITC 232:4
boys in the b. room LOES 209:5
boys in the b. rooms BEAV 31:4
I counted them all b. HANR 161:8
I sit on a man's b. TOLS 333:13
never turned his b. BROW 75:11
safe to go b. in the water ANON 8:15
those before cried 'B.!' MAC 214:6
backbone: b. of the Army KIPL 196:10
backhand: wonderful b. drive BETJ 37:8
backs: beast with two b. SHAK 291:30
backward: B. ran sentences GIBBS 150:18
But I by b. steps would move VAUG 337:10
look b. to their ancestors BURKE 80:12
bacon: b.'s not the only thing KING 195:20
bad: animal is very b. ANON 12:3
b. against the worse DAY-L 115:6
b. aunts and good aunts WOD 352:15
b. die late DEFOE 115:17
b. end unhappily STOP 318:5
b. things that hotel-keepers TROL 334:16
b. unhappily WILDE 349:20
B. women never take the blame BROO 73:11
brave b. man CLAR 101:12
can't be all b. ROST 263:13
For being a little b. SHAK 288:26
How sad and b. and mad BROW 75:21
Mad, b., and dangerous LAMB 199:22
no such thing as b. publicity BEHAN 32:19
our sad b. glad mad brother's SWIN 321:5
Pleasure's for those who are b. YES 360:12
poor in a loomp is b. TENN 327:10
She was not really b. at heart BELL 33:11
so much b. in the best of us ANON 10:20
This bold b. man SHAK 280:15
When b. men combine BURKE 81:4
when she was b. LONG 210:6
Where everything is b. BRAD 71:9
badge: b. of all our tribe SHAK 289:4
red b. of courage CRANE 111:3
badly: it is worth doing b. CHES 98:16
badness: All good and no b. SKEL 308:2
bag: b. and baggage GLAD 153:10
not with b. and baggage SHAK 273:3
baggage: bag and b. GLAD 153:10
bagman: Cobden is an inspired b. CARL 90:25
bah: 'B.,' said Scrooge DICK 118:6
bainters: I hate all Boets and B. GEOR 149:20
baker: b. rhymes for his pursuit BROW 77:11
Baker Street: B. irregulars DOYLE 126:3
balance: uncertain b. of proud time GREE 158:8
balances: weighed in the b. BIBLE 47:12
bald: b., and short of breath SASS 267:8
Go up, thou b. head BIBLE 42:8
otherwise b. and unconvincing GILB 152:5
two b. men over a comb BORG 69:24
baldness: far side of b. SMITH 309:10
bales: with costly b. TENN 326:10
Balkans: silly thing in the B. BISM 59:20
ball: at a girl throwing a b. WOOLF 354:4
b. no question makes FITZ 140:13
like a man yawning at a b. LERM 205:25
Only wind it into a b. BLAKE 60:20
real business of a b. SURT 319:14
sweetness, up into one b. MARV 221:1
ballad: And I met with a b. CALV 88:7
ballads: B. and babies MCC 214:13
Of b., songs and snatches GILB 151:17
permitted to make all the b. FLET 142:3
ball-floor: Dance on this b. BLUN 62:14
Balliol: B. made me BELL 34:2
balloon: something in a huge b. WORD 356:3
ballot: b. stronger than the bullet LINC 207:4

balls: B. will be lost always BERR 36:11
our rackets to these b. SHAK 279:1
two pitch b. SHAK 284:14
balm: b. from an anointed king SHAK 293:22
general b. th'hydroptic earth DONNE 124:8
Is there no b. in Gilead BIBLE 46:29
pours out out a b. upon the world KEATS 190:25
banality: b. of evil AREN 15:4
Banbury: To B. came I BRAT 71:16
band: importunate b. BETJ 37:13
wearied B. swoons HUXL 177:12
we b. of brothers SHAK 279:20
bandied: tennis-balls, struck and b. WEBS 344:21
bands: drew them with b. of love BIBLE 47:18
loose the b. of Orion BIBLE 43:4
who pursue Culture in b. WHAR 347:4
bandy: b. civilities JOHN 184:19
bane: Deserve the precious b. MILT 228:19
baneful: b. effects of the spirit WASH 342:21
bang: b. these dogs of Seville TENN 328:12
b.—went sixpence PUNCH 256:12
bigger b. for a buck ANON 6:12
Not with a b. but a whimper ELIOT 133:20
banish: b. plump Jack SHAK 278:1
banishment: bitter bread of b. SHAK 293:21
bank: b. whereon the wild thyme SHAK 290:26
I cry all the way to the b. LIB 206:22
pregnant b. swelled up DONNE 124:2
this b. and shoal of time SHAK 285:22
banknotes: fill old bottles with b. KEYN 194:16
bankrupt: B. of life DRYD 127:8
banks: bonnie b. o' Loch Lomon' ANON 10:2
Ye b. and braes o' bonny Doon BURNS 81:27
banner: b. with the strange device LONG 209:17
'Tis the star-spangled b. KEY 194:12
banners: Confusion on thy b. wait GRAY 157:1
royal b. forward go FORT 144:5
banquet: trifling foolish b. SHAK 294:27
baptism: Godmothers in my B. BOOK 65:20
bar: if met where any b. is HARDY 162:13
no moaning of the b. TENN 323:18
When I have crossed the b. TENN 323:19
Barabbas: Now B. was a publisher CAMP 89:1
Now B. was a robber BIBLE 54:2
barbarians: B., Philistines, and Populace ARN 17:24
become of us without the b. CAV 93:11
his young b. all at play BYRON 85:10
name the former the B. ARN 17:26
barbaric: b. yawp over the roofs WHIT 348:22
barbarous: b. dissonance MILT 226:17
invention of a b. age MILT 228:5
bard: Hear the voice of the B. BLAKE 61:26
bare: B. like nude, giant girls SPEN 313:3
B. ruined choirs SHAK 299:24
barefoot: I was born b. LONG 209:8
bargain: dateless b. to engrossing death SHAK 295:25
Necessity never made a good b. FRAN 145:10
bargains: Here's the rule for b. DICK 119:3
barge: b. she sat in SHAK 271:14
bark: come out as I do, and b. JOHN 186:1
Though his b. cannot be lost SHAK 285:4
Barkis: B. is willin' DICK 118:9
barks: Nicean b. of yore POE 250:8
barley: among the bearded b. TENN 325:36
Long fields of b. and of rye TENN 325:34
Barlow: Hornby and my B. THOM 331:6
barmaid: shocking the b. SITW 307:18
barmaids: Are B. Chaste MAS 221:20
baronet: No little lily-handed b. TENN 328:9
barrel: drowned in a butt of Malmesey FABY 138:8
handful of meal in a b. BIBLE 41:35
Oh we ain't got a b. of money WOODS 353:19
out of the b. of a gun MAO T 217:19
barrels: slurp into the b. FISH 139:26

barren: acre of b. ground | SHAK 295:32
b. sister all your life | SHAK 290:12
Close up those b. leaves | WORD 357:5
I am but a b. stock | ELIZ 135:12
barricade: At some disputed b. | SEEG 269:13
barrow: red wheel b. | WILL 351:8
base: b., common and popular | SHAK 279:9
Labour without joy is b. | RUSK 264:18
Things b. and vile | SHAK 290:16
Why bastard? wherefore b. | SHAK 282:20
baseless: b. fabric of this vision | SHAK 296:10
baseness: Detraction is but b.' varlet | JONS 187:10
baser: lewd fellows of the b. sort | BIBLE 54:18
bashful: maiden of b. fifteen | SHER 306:6
basil-pot: To steal my B. | KEATS 191:4
Basingstoke: hidden meaning—like B. | GILB 152:27
Bass: Guinness, Allsopp, B. | CALV 88:8
bastard: all my eggs in one b. | PARK 245:15
Well, we knocked the b. off | HILL 168:15
Why b.? wherefore base | SHAK 282:20
bastards: b. grind you down | ANON 9:15
gods, stand up for b. | SHAK 282:21
bastion: like a b.'s mole | SMART 308:10
bat: beetle and the b. | JOHN 184:21
black b., night, has flown | TENN 326:28
Ere the b. hath flown | SHAK 287:5
On the b.'s back I do fly | SHAK 296:14
purest play is like some b. | WILB 349:11
Twinkle, twinkle, little b. | CARR 91:7
weak-eyed b. | COLL 105:10
bath: I test my b. before I sit | NASH 237:16
bathe: b. those beauteous feet | FLET 142:8
bathing: caught the Whigs b. | DISR 121:9
large b. machine | GILB 151:16
long b. of a summer's day | WORD 356:9
bathroom: revolutionary in a b. | LINK 207:17
baths: Two walking b. | CRAS 111:14
baton: cartridge-pouch the marshal's b. | LOUI 210:16
bats: B. with baby faces | ELIOT 134:30
batsman: I am the b. and the bat | LANG 201:2
battalions: big b. | VOLT 340:23
not single spies, but in b. | SHAK 276:35
your dreams in pale b. go | SORL 311:16
battening: B. upon huge seaworms | TENN 325:32
batter: B. my heart | DONNE 123:10
battle: B. method of untying | BIER 59:4
b. to the strong | DAV 114:12
better in b. than in bed | STER 315:20
die well that die in a b. | SHAK 279:13
drunk delight of b. | TENN 328:21
foremost in b. was Mary Ambree | BALL 28:1
France has lost a b. | DE G 116:3
greatest misery is a b. gained | WELL 345:12
marriage a field of b. | STEV 317:8
my tongue, the glorious b. | FORT 144:4
noise of battle rolled | TENN 324:17
nor the b. to the strong | BIBLE 44:20
No war, or b.'s sound | MILT 227:26
out of b. I escaped | OWEN 244:2
smelleth the b. afar off | BIBLE 43:5
strife is o'er, the b. done | POTT 253:28
When the b.'s lost and won | SHAK 284:25
battledore: B. and shuttlecock | DICK 119:29
battlefield: b. is the heart of man | DOST 125:2
battle-flags: b. were furled | TENN 326:12
battlements: from the white b. | HEAT 164:13
battles: b. long ago | WORD 357:2
b. of all subsequent wars | ORW 242:4
Dead b., like dead generals | TUCH 335:7
mother of b. | HUSS 176:22
baubles: Take away these b. | CROM 112:5
bawcock: king's a b. | SHAK 279:10
bawling: b. what it likes | ARN 17:27
bay: like a green b.-tree | BOOK 66:28

bay (cont.):
steamer breaking from the b. | AUDEN 20:25
baying: b. for broken glass | WAUGH 343:18
bayonet: b. is a weapon with a worker | ANON 6:7
bayonets: sods with our b. turning | WOLFE 352:26
throne of b. | INGE 178:14
Bayonne: thy hams, B.! | POPE 250:21
bays: oak, or b. | MARV 220:14
sprig of b. in fifty years | SWIFT 320:19
bazaar: Fate's great b. | MACN 216:9
be: And can it b. | WESL 346:3
b.-all and the end-all | SHAK 285:22
b. as they are or not at all | CLEM 102:3
Cared not to b. at all | MILT 228:22
Let b. be finale of seem | STEV 316:6
lief not b. as live to be | SHAK 280:26
poem should not mean but b. | MACL 215:9
that which shall b. | BIBLE 44:8
To b., or not to be | SHAK 275:25
beachèd: b. verge of the salt flood | SHAK 296:24
beaches: We shall fight on the b. | CHUR 99:13
Beachy Head: by way of B. | CHES 98:2
beacons: b. of wise men | HUXL 177:20
beaded: b. bubbles winking | KEATS 191:30
beak: He takes in his b. | MERR 223:26
thy b. from out my heart | POE 250:7
beaker: b. full of the warm South | KEATS 191:30
Beale: Miss Buss and Miss B. | ANON 9:10
beam: B. me up, Scotty | RODD 261:13
b. that is in thine own eye | BIBLE 49:7
beaming: Leading onward, b. bright | DIX 122:24
beamish: b. nephew, beware | CARR 92:8
beams: And tricks his b. | MILT 227:18
bean: home of the b. and the cod | BOSS 70:1
Nine b. rows will I have | YEATS 359:12
not too French French b. | GILB 152:11
bear: B. of Very Little Brain | MILNE 225:15
b. thee in their hands | BOOK 67:30
b. the yoke in his youth | BIBLE 47:2
b. with a sore head | MARR 219:26
Cannot b. very much reality | ELIOT 132:27
Exit, pursued by a b. | SHAK 298:25
fire was furry as a b. | SITW 307:17
fitted by nature to b. | AUR 22:9
Grizzly B. is huge and wild | HOUS 174:8
Moppsikon Floppsikon b. | LEAR 203:18
still less the B. | FRERE 145:22
wounded spirit who can b.? | BIBLE 43:29
bear-baiting: Puritan hated b. | MAC 213:19
beard: grey b. and glittering eye | COL 104:3
husband with a b. on his face | SHAK 291:15
King of Spain's B. | DRAKE 126:11
was an Old Man with a b. | LEAR 203:17
bearded: b. like the pard | SHAK 272:26
beards: merry in hall when b. | SHAK 278:31
beareth: B. all things | BIBLE 55:12
that b. up things light | BACON 25:7
bears: And dancing dogs and b. | HODG 169:13
b. might come with buns | ISH 178:21
tap crude rhythms for b. | FLAU 141:7
beast: And what rough b. | YEATS 359:25
beast, but a just b. | ANON 6:8
B. stands for strong mutually | WAUGH 343:23
b., that wants discourse | SHAK 274:12
Beauty killed the B. | ROSE 111:17
be either a b. or a god | ARIS 15:19
count the number of the b. | BIBLE 57:33
fit night out for man or b. | FIEL 139:17
making the b. with two backs | SHAK 291:30
more subtil than any b. | BIBLE 38:24
or the name of the b. | BIBLE 57:32
regardeth the life of his b. | BIBLE 43:20
serpent subtlest b. | MILT 229:22
terrible marks of the b. | HARDY 161:23
beastie: cow'rin', tim'rous b. | BURNS 82:26

| | |
|---|---|
| **beasties:** and long-leggety b. | ANON 7:7 |
| **beastly:** b. to the Germans | COW 108:20 |
| How b. the bourgeois is | LAWR 202:18 |
| **beasts:** b. that have no understanding | BOOK 65:26 |
| **beat:** b. him when he sneezes | CARR 91:5 |
| b. the ground | MILT 226:9 |
| b. their swords into plowshares | BIBLE 45:5 |
| **beaten:** b. road | SHEL 303:16 |
| No Englishman is ever fairly b. | SHAW 302:20 |
| **beating:** b. in the void his luminous | ARN 18:4 |
| b. myself for spite | SIDN 306:17 |
| Charity and b. begins at home | FLET 142:7 |
| glory of b. the French | WOLFE 353:3 |
| Is b. on the door | YEATS 359:6 |
| than driven by b. | ASCH 18:18 |
| two hearts b. each to each | BROW 76:17 |
| **beatings:** dread of b. | BETJ 37:14 |
| **Beatles:** And the B.' first LP | LARK 201:12 |
| **beats:** light which b. upon a throne | TENN 324:1 |
| **beatus:** B. vir qui timet Dominum | BIBLE 58:11 |
| **beauté:** tout n'est qu'ordre et b. | BAUD 30:4 |
| **beauties:** unripened b. of the north | ADD 2:14 |
| You meaner b. of the night | WOTT 357:16 |
| **beautiful:** b. and death-struck year | HOUS 174:25 |
| b. and simple | HENRY 166:4 |
| b. and therefore to be wooed | SHAK 280:6 |
| b. cannot be the way to | COUS 108:17 |
| B. dreamer, wake unto me | FOST 144:9 |
| b. things in the world | RUSK 264:17 |
| b. upon the mountains | BIBLE 46:15 |
| Black is b. | ANON 6:13 |
| deal of scorn looks b. | SHAK 298:6 |
| entirely b. | AUDEN 20:28 |
| innocent and the b. | YEATS 359:8 |
| or believe to be b. | MORR 235:18 |
| Our love of what is b. | PER 248:1 |
| perpetual hunger to be b. | RHYS 259:14 |
| see, not feel, how b. they are | COL 103:14 |
| singing 'Oh, how b.!' | KIPL 196:16 |
| Small is b. | SCH 267:25 |
| When a woman isn't b. | CHEK 96:29 |
| **beauty:** all that b., all that wealth | GRAY 157:7 |
| be a b. without a fortune | FARQ 138:16 |
| b. and truth | KEATS 193:1 |
| B. both so ancient | AUG 21:24 |
| b. coming and the beauty | WORD 355:12 |
| b. draws us with a single | POPE 253:4 |
| b. faded has no second | PHIL 248:14 |
| B. for some provides escape | HUXL 177:13 |
| B. is all very well at first | SHAW 301:25 |
| B. is momentary in the mind | STEV 316:11 |
| B. is mysterious as well as | DOST 125:2 |
| B. is Nature's brag | MILT 226:20 |
| B. is no quality in things | HUME 176:9 |
| b. is only sin deep | SAKI 265:19 |
| B. is truth, truth beauty | KEATS 191:24 |
| B. itself doth of itself | SHAK 299:7 |
| B. killed the Beast | ROSE 111:17 |
| b. lives though lilies | FLEC 141:16 |
| b. making beautiful old rime | SHAK 300:4 |
| b. of inflections | STEV 316:13 |
| b. of Israel is slain upon | BIBLE 41:20 |
| b. of the good old cause | WORD 356:1 |
| b.'s empires, like to | SUCK 318:23 |
| B.'s ensign | SHAK 295:24 |
| b.'s rose might never die | SHAK 299:11 |
| b. that hath not some strangeness | BACON 24:14 |
| B. that must die | KEATS 191:27 |
| B. too rich for use | SHAK 294:26 |
| B. vanishes; beauty passes | DE L 116:14 |
| body's b. lives | STEV 316:11 |
| conscious stone to b. grew | EMER 136:15 |
| delves the parallels in b.'s | SHAK 299:22 |
| dreamed that life was b. | HOOP 171:16 |

| | |
|---|---|
| **beauty** (*cont.*): | |
| England, home and b. | ARN 18:14 |
| fatal gift of b. | BYRON 85:7 |
| Helen, thy b. is to me | POE 250:8 |
| her b. made the bright world | SHEL 305:17 |
| in the b. of holiness | BOOK 68:2 |
| in the b. of holiness | MONS 233:3 |
| Of its own b. is the mind diseased | BYRON 85:9 |
| principal b. in building | FULL 147:6 |
| seizes as b. must be truth | KEATS 192:23 |
| She walks in b., like the night | BYRON 87:6 |
| simple b. and naught else | BROW 75:30 |
| terrible b. is born | YEATS 359:3 |
| thick, bereft of b. | SHAK 295:30 |
| thing of b. is a joy for ever | KEATS 190:11 |
| we just b. see | JONS 187:24 |
| where B. was, nothing ever | GALS 147:17 |
| Where perhaps some b. lies | MILT 227:3 |
| whose b. is past change | HOPK 172:13 |
| with him is b. slain | SHAK 300:19 |
| witty b. is a power | MER 223:12 |
| youth and a little b. | WEBS 344:14 |
| **Beaverbrook:** mind that of Lord B. | ATTL 19:12 |
| **because:** B. I do not hope to turn again | ELIOT 132:18 |
| B. it's there | MALL 216:22 |
| B. it was he; b. it was me | MONT 233:12 |
| smashed it into b. | CUMM 113:2 |
| B. we're here | ANON 11:13 |
| **becks:** Nods, and b. | MILT 227:1 |
| **become:** B. themselves in her | SHAK 271:17 |
| do all that may b. a man | SHAK 286:5 |
| **becomes:** nothing so b. a man | SHAK 279:5 |
| **bed:** And I in my b. again | ANON 11:18 |
| and's newly gone to b. | MILT 228:4 |
| And so to b. | PEPYS 247:12 |
| b. be blest that I lie on | ANON 9:8 |
| better in battle than in b. | STER 315:20 |
| black passage up to b. | STEV 317:15 |
| found in adulterous b. | BLAKE 60:13 |
| get out of b. for it | AMIS 5:7 |
| gooseberried double b. | THOM 330:17 |
| grave as little as my b. | KEN 193:22 |
| Has found out thy b. | BLAKE 62:4 |
| I have to go to b. by day | STEV 317:12 |
| in b. with my catamite | BURG 79:14 |
| I should of stood in b. | JAC 179:2 |
| kneels at the foot of the b. | MILNE 226:1 |
| migrations from the blue b. | GOLD 155:12 |
| mother, make my b. soon | BALL 27:19 |
| mother, mother, make my b. | BALL 27:13 |
| My mind is not a b. | AGATE 3:6 |
| my second best b. | SHAK 300:21 |
| not a b. of roses | STEV 317:8 |
| On a b. of daffodil sky | TENN 326:28 |
| out of his wholesome b. | SHAK 281:6 |
| Out on the lawn I lie in b. | AUDEN 21:7 |
| take up thy b., and walk | BIBLE 53:21 |
| This b. thy centre | DONNE 124:13 |
| thy cold b. | KING 195:5 |
| To be to more than one a b. | DONNE 124:9 |
| Up to b. | DE L 116:17 |
| Were it earth in an earthy b. | TENN 327:2 |
| **bedfellows:** strange b. | SHAK 296:5 |
| **bedroom:** French widow in every b. | HOFF 170:5 |
| Stranger, unless with b. eyes | AUDEN 21:8 |
| **beds:** Minds like b. always made up | WILL 351:7 |
| Warm b.: warm full blooded | JOYCE 188:17 |
| **bee:** butterfly, sting like a b. | ALI 4:10 |
| honeysuckle, I am the b. | FITZ 140:2 |
| How doth the little busy b. | WATTS 343:5 |
| live alone in the b.-loud glade | YEATS 359:12 |
| Where the b. sucks | SHAK 296:14 |
| **beef:** I am a great eater of b. | SHAK 297:15 |
| Oh! The roast b. of England | FIEL 139:6 |
| **beefsteak:** English an article as a b. | HAWT 163:19 |

beefy: As b. ATS without their hats — BETJ 37:1
Beelzebub: B. called for his syllabub — SITW 307:18
beer: B. and Britannia — SMITH 310:13
b. and skittles — CALV 88:9
chronicle small b. — SHAK 292:4
I'm only a b. teetotaller — SHAW 300:28
like thine inspirer, B. — POPE 250:15
muddy ecstasies of b. — CRAB 110:21
O B.! O Hodgson — CALV 88:8
torrent of gin and b. — GLAD 153:9
bees: Birds do it, b. do it — PORT 253:22
murmuring of innumerable b. — TENN 328:8
beetle: b. and the bat detract — JOHN 184:21
b. wheels his droning flight — GRAY 157:4
b. with his drowsy hums — SHAK 287:5
beetles: special preference for b. — HALD 160:3
before: And those b. cried 'Back!' — MAC 214:6
Broad b. and broad behind — BETJ 37:15
Going on b. — BAR 29:1
have said our remarks b. us — DON 123:1
not lost but sent b. — CYPR 113:13
began: So was it when my life b. — WORD 355:13
begetter: To the onlie b. — SHAK 299:10
beggar: whiles I am a b. — SHAK 282:5
beggared: It b. all description — SHAK 271:14
beggars: Lords in ermine, b. freezing — ROB 260:22
Our basest b. — SHAK 283:4
When b. die — SHAK 281:8
beggary: b. in the love that can be reckoned — SHAK 271:1
there is no vice, but b. — SHAK 282:5
begging: his seed b. their bread — BOOK 66:27
begin: B. at the beginning — CARR 91:13
b. with certainties and end — BACON 23:20
But let us b. — KENN 194:5
Then I'll b. — LANG 201:4
To b. at the beginning — THOM 330:16
When they b. the Beguine — PORT 253:18
beginning: As it was in the b. — BOOK 63:17
Before the b. of years — SWIN 321:3
begin at the b. — THOM 330:16
b., a muddle, and an end — LARK 201:20
b. God created the heaven — BIBLE 38:13
b. of an Amour — BEHN 32:20
b. of any great matter — DRAKE 126:10
end is to make a b. — ELIOT 133:11
even the b. of the end — CHUR 99:18
From quiet homes and first b. — BELL 34:3
In my b. is my end — ELIOT 133:2
In my end is my b. — MARY 221:16
In the b. was the Word — BIBLE 53:6
Is a new b., a raid on — ELIOT 133:6
Lord is the b. of wisdom — BOOK 68:15
Movies should have a b. — GOD 153:19
sequel of an unnatural b. — AUST 22:26
That is the true b. of our end — SHAK 291:6
This is the b. of the end — TALL 322:13
told you from the b. — BIBLE 46:12
beginnings: our ends by our b. know — DENH 116:26
begins: man's glory most b. and ends — YEATS 359:17
world's great age b. anew — SHEL 303:18
begot: were about when they b. me — STER 315:12
what's a son? A thing b. — KYD 199:10
begotten: It was b. by Despair — MARV 220:12
very God, B., not made — BOOK 65:5
beguile: And so b. thy sorrow — SHAK 296:27
beguiled: The serpent b. me — BIBLE 38:27
Beguine: begin the B. — PORT 253:18
begun: have b. is half the job — HOR 173:8
I have not yet b. to fight — JONES 186:21
behaviour: human b. — ROBB 260:15
behind: B., before, above — DONNE 123:6
But those b. cried 'Forward!' — MAC 214:6
Get thee b. me, Satan — BIBLE 50:14

behind (cont.):
in a moment it will be b. me — REGER 259:2
Scratches its innocent b. — AUDEN 21:2
She has no bosom and no b. — SMITH 309:21
behold: B. the man — BIBLE 58:20
being: all the wheels of B. slow — TENN 325:7
always at the edge of B. — SPEN 313:1
darkness of mere b. — JUNG 188:23
move, and have our b. — BIBLE 54:21
non-being by avoiding b. — TILL 332:21
not be worried into b. — FROST 146:25
unbearable lightness of b. — KUND 199:8
Belbroughton: B. Road is bonny — BETJ 37:6
Belgium: B.'s capital — BYRON 85:2
Belgrave Square: May beat in B. — GILB 151:11
Belial: sons of B. — MILT 228:15
belief: that is b. — SART 267:5
beliefs: dust of exploded b. — MADAN 216:13
believe: B. me, you who come after — HOR 173:24
b. what one does not believe — PAINE 244:6
Do you b. in the life to come — BECK 31:9
Firmly I b. and truly — NEWM 238:19
God, b. also in me — BIBLE 53:36
he wouldn't b. it — CUMM 112:19
I b. because it is impossible — TERT 329:9
I b. to One does feel — KNOX 198:17
these little ones which b. — BIBLE 50:16
Though ye b. not me — BIBLE 53:31
We can b. what we choose — NEWM 239:1
believed: what is by all people b. — VINC 338:22
Who against hope b. in hope — BIBLE 54:32
believer: In a b.'s ear — NEWT 239:9
believers: half-b. in our casual creeds — ARN 17:10
believeth: b. all things, hopeth — BIBLE 55:12
b. on me hath everlasting — BIBLE 53:24
whosoever believeth in him — BIBLE 53:19
believing: b. more and more in less — YATES 358:10
Belinda: B. smiled — POPE 253:5
bell: B., book, and candle — SHAK 282:7
b. invites me — SHAK 286:11
for whom the b. tolls — DONNE 124:20
heart as sound as a b. — SHAK 291:21
hear the surly sullen b. — SHAK 299:23
Let's mock the midnight b. — SHAK 271:19
merry as a marriage b. — BYRON 85:2
sexton tolled the b. — HOOD 171:7
Silence that dreadful b. — SHAK 292:7
very word is like a b. — KEATS 192:6
Bellamy: B.'s veal pies — PITT 249:10
belle: du temps que j'étais b. — RONS 262:5
belli: Nervos b. — CIC 100:29
bells: b. of Hell — ANON 9:21
broke into a mist with b. — BROW 76:25
From the b., bells — POE 250:4
lin-lan-lone of evening b. — TENN 323:22
Ring out, wild b. — TENN 325:22
so floating many b. down — CUMM 112:16
They now ring the b. — WALP 342:5
'Twould ring the b. of Heaven — HODG 169:13
belly: O wombe! O b.! — CHAU 95:30
bellyful: Rumble thy b.! — SHAK 283:7
bellyfulls: we want b. — GASK 148:19
belong: DON'T WANT TO B. TO ANY CLUB — MARX 221:5
To betray, you must first b. — PHIL 248:12
belongs: in the mind where it b. — ALD 3:1
beloved: bourn how far to be b. — SHAK 271:4
Cry, the b. country — PATON 246:19
O Daniel, a man greatly b. — BIBLE 47:16
suspenders, Best B. — KIPL 197:23
This is my b. Son — BIBLE 48:15
below: above, between, b. — DONNE 123:6
belted: b. you and flayed you — KIPL 196:17
Ben: B. Battle was a soldier bold — HOOD 171:4
bend: I b. and I break not — LA F 199:17
Keep right on round the b. — LAUD 202:5

bending: always be a b. downwards WHEW 347:8
bends: made their b. adornings SHAK 271:15
beneath: But I b. a rougher sea COWP 109:20
benedictus: B. qui venit in nomine MISS 231:17
benighted: B. walks under the midday sun MILT 226:12
benign: under that b. sky BRON 72:18
benison: For a b. to fall HERR 167:11
bent: fool me to the top of my b. SHAK 276:14
bereaved: black as if b. of light BLAKE 61:24
Berliner: Ich bin ein B. KENN 194:8
Bermoothes: still-vexed B. SHAK 295:34
Bermudas: Where the remote B. ride MARV 220:9
berry: could have made a better b. BUTL 84:22
  O sweeter than the b. GAY 149:1
berth: which happened in his b. HOOD 171:7
beside: B. a field of grain CHAR 245:19
  thou art b. thyself BIBLE 54:26
best: best administered is b. POPE 252:20
  b. and the worst of this is SWIN 321:14
  b. cannot be expected JOHN 184:3
  b. ends by the best means HUTC 177:1
  b. in this kind SHAK 291:8
  b. is the best QUIL 257:7
  b. is the enemy of the good VOLT 340:15
  b. is yet to be BROW 77:3
  b. lack all conviction YEATS 359:24
  b. men are moulded out SHAK 288:26
  b. of all possible worlds CAB 87:23
  b. of all possible worlds VOLT 340:10
  b. portion of a good man's WORD 355:8
  b. thing God invents BROW 76:30
  b. way out is always through FROST 146:22
  Fear not to touch the b. RAL 257:21
  In art the b. is good enough GOET 154:9
  It was the b. of times DICK 120:6
  past all prizing, b. SOPH 311:13
  poetry = the b. words COL 104:26
  record of the b. SHEL 305:18
  Sat we two, one another's b. DONNE 124:2
  Send forth the b. ye breed KIPL 197:15
  so much bad in the b. of us ANON 10:20
  than any other person's b. HAZL 164:6
  Thou art tired; b. be still ARN 16:18
  virtuousest, discreetest, b. MILT 229:20
  where the b. is like the worst KIPL 196:23
  wisest and justest and b. PLATO 249:20
bestial: what remains is b. SHAK 292:8
bestride: b. the narrow world SHAK 280:27
best-seller: b. is the gilded tomb SMITH 309:12
bet: Somebody b. on de bay FOST 144:10
Bethlehem: B. Ephratah BIBLE 47:22
  Slouches towards B. YEATS 359:25
betray: All things b. thee THOM 331:9
  guts to b. my country FORS 144:2
  To b., you must first belong PHIL 248:12
betrayed: like men b. WORD 354:13
betrothèd: bright face of my b. MIDD 224:8
better: become much more the b. SHAK 288:26
  begin to make a b. life SHAK 272:1
  B. by far you should forget ROSS 263:4
  b. day, the worse deed HENRY 166:2
  b. mouse-trap EMER 137:3
  b. part of biography STR 318:15
  B. than a play CHAR 95:3
  b. than a thousand BOOK 67:22
  b. than light and safer than HASK 163:16
  b. to be in chains KAFKA 189:18
  b. to have fought and lost CLOU 102:21
  b. to have loved and lost BUTL 84:11
  b. to have loved and lost TENN 325:4
  b. world than this SHAK 272:13
  even from worse to b. JOHN 182:3
  far b. thing that I do now DICK 120:7
  for b. for worse BOOK 66:1

better (cont.):
  from b. hap to worse SOUT 312:9
  from worse to b. HOOK 171:15
  Gad! she'd b. CARL 90:23
  getting b. and better COUÉ 108:16
  have better spared a b. man SHAK 278:15
  He is not b.—he is much worse ANON 6:1
  if they had been any b. CHAN 94:10
  If way to the B. there be HARDY 162:8
  I see the b. things OVID 243:15
  I took thee for thy b. SHAK 276:20
  music is b. than it sounds NYE 240:15
  nae b. than he shou'd BURNS 82:4
  Something b. than his dog TENN 326:7
  things I'd been b. without PARK 245:5
  We have seen b. days SHAK 296:21
  where it's likely to go b. FROST 146:8
  will b. the instruction SHAK 289:18
  You're a b. man than I am KIPL 196:17
bettered: b. expectation SHAK 291:11
between: B. the idea and the reality ELIOT 133:19
  I would try to get b. them STR 318:14
  wasn't for the 'ouses in b. BAT 30:1
betwixt: B. the stirrup and the ground CAMD 88:12
Beulah: B., peel me a grape WEST 346:20
beware: And all should cry, B.! COL 104:1
  Better b. COW 109:6
  B. my foolish heart WASH 342:24
  B. of rudely crossing it AUDEN 21:8
  B. of the man who does not SHAW 302:8
  B. the ides of March SHAK 280:25
  Sisters, I bid you b. KIPL 196:27
bewildered: bothered, and b. HART 163:7
  unprincipled to the utterly b. CAPP 89:16
bewitch: Do more b. me HERR 167:15
bewitched: B., bothered, and bewildered HART 163:7
bewrapt: B. past knowing HARDY 162:14
beyond: But is there anything b.? BROO 73:2
biases: critic is a bundle of b. BALL 28:12
bibble-babble: Leave thy vain b. SHAK 298:13
Bible: English B. MAC 213:20
  starless and b.-black THOM 330:16
  To read in de B. GERS 168:5
  used the B. as if it was KING 195:18
Bibles: B. laid open HERB 167:7
bicker: b. down a valley TENN 323:12
bicycle: like a fish without a b. STEI 315:2
  poets b.-pump the human heart AMIS 5:5
  Socialism can only arrive by b. VIER 338:16
bid: She b. me take love easy YEATS 359:1
bien: Le mieux est l'ennemi du b. VOLT 340:15
bier: float upon his watery b. MILT 227:11
big: b. battalions VOLT 340:23
  b. enough to take away FORD 143:5
  b. squadrons BUSS 83:20
  By the shining B.-Sea-Water LONG 210:1
  I am b. It's the pictures BRAC 71:5
  Thy great b. one on me FROST 146:10
bigamy: And b., Sir, is a crime MONK 232:26
  B. is having one husband too ANON 6:11
bigger: b. bang for a buck ANON 6:12
  b. they are, the further FITZ 141:1
bigotry: B. roughly defined CHES 98:10
  B. tries to keep truth TAG 322:9
bike: got on his b. TEBB 323:6
bill: b. of my divorce to all DONNE 123:15
billboard: b. lovely as a tree NASH 237:17
billet: Every bullet has its b. WILL 351:2
billiard: elliptical b. balls GILB 152:2
billiards: To play b. well is a sign ROUP 263:17
billow: Fierce was the wild b. ANAT 5:10
billows: solid b. of enormous size PHIL 248:15
Billy: B., in one of his nice new sashes GRAH 156:4
  That's the way for B. and me HOGG 170:7
  waited till his 'B.' boiled PAT 246:16

bind: b. their kings in chains — BOOK 69:11
b. the sweet influences — BIBLE 43:4
b. up the brokenhearted — BIBLE 46:24
I b. unto myself to-day — ALEX 4:5
My mother bids me b. my hair — HUNT 176:19
To b. another to its delight — BLAKE 62:2
binds: He who b. to himself a joy — BLAKE 61:16
biographers: Boswell is the first of b. — MAC 213:5
biographies: essence of innumerable b. — CARL 90:6
biography: B. is about Chaps — BENT 35:5
not the better part of b. — STR 318:15
properly no history; only b. — EMER 136:22
Read nothing but b. — DISR 121:28
bird: b. of dawning — SHAK 274:2
b. that thinks two notes — DAV 114:17
B. thou never wert — SHEL 305:6
born for death, immortal b. — KEATS 192:4
Both man and b. and beast — COL 104:18
catch the b. of paradise — KHR 194:20
I know why the caged b. sings — DUNB 129:7
It's a b.! It's a plane — ANON 7:5
It was only the note of a b. — SIMP 307:10
like a b. on the wing — BOUL 70:10
O Cuckoo! Shall I call thee b. — WORD 357:7
rare b. on this earth — JUV 189:7
Stirred for a b.,—the achieve — HOPK 172:21
wet b.-haunted English lawn — ARN 16:21
What b. so sings — LYLY 212:17
widow b. sat mourning — SHEL 303:14
birdcage: And a b., sir — DICK 120:2
summer in a garden — WEBS 344:23
birds: B. build—but not I — HOPK 172:19
b. got to fly — HAMM 160:19
B. in their little nests agree — WATTS 343:8
b. in the trees — YEATS 359:20
b. of the air — BIBLE 49:19
B. on box and laurels listen — SMART 308:9
b. that are without — WEBS 344:23
b., wild flowers, and P.M.s — BALD 27:10
But what these unobservant b. — ISH 178:21
If b. confabulate or no — COWP 109:29
I see all the b. are flown — CHAR 94:23
late the sweet b. sang — SHAK 299:24
singing of b. is come — BIBLE 44:32
sing like b. i' the cage — SHAK 284:1
we are a nest of singing b. — JOHN 183:22
We think caged b. sing — WEBS 344:27
When b. do sing, hey ding — SHAK 273:10
bird-song: B. at morning and star-shine — STEV 317:19
Birmingham: B. by way of Beachy Head — CHES 98:2
no great hopes from B. — AUST 22:17
When Jesus came to B. — STUD 318:19
Birnam wood: Till B. remove to Dunsinane — SHAK 287:32
birth: All things have second b. — WORD 356:13
bewailed at their b. — MONT 233:20
B., and copulation, and death — ELIOT 134:14
b. commonly abateth industry — BACON 25:5
disqualified by the accident of b. — CHES 98:14
give b. astride of a grave — BECK 31:15
I had seen b. and death — ELIOT 133:22
not conscious of his b. — LA BR 199:14
Or one that is coming to b. — O'SH 243:2
Our b. is but a sleep — WORD 355:20
Rainbow gave thee b. — DAV 114:19
that have a different b. — SHEL 305:14
Wherein our Saviour's b. — SHAK 274:2
birth control: b. is flagrantly middle-class — WAUGH 344:2
birthday: afternoon of my eighty-first b. — BURG 79:14
Because the b. of my life — ROSS 262:21
marvel my b. away — THOM 330:14
birthplace: accent of one's b. — LA R 202:1
birthright: b. for a mess of potage — BIBLE 39:17

birthright (cont.):
sold his b. unto Jacob — BIBLE 39:18
births: b. that may be yours — RIMB 260:11
plenties, and joyful b. — SHAK 280:2
which are the b. of time — BACON 24:30
bis: B. dat qui cito dat — PUBL 256:1
biscuits: hyacinths and b. — SAND 266:17
bisexuality: b. doubles your chances — ALLEN 4:17
bishop: b. then must be blameless — BIBLE 56:16
make a b. kick a hole — CHAN 94:7
No b., no King — JAM 179:11
bishopric: merit for a b. — WEST 346:27
bishops: all B. and Curates — BOOK 65:10
b. like best in their clergy — SMITH 309:24
bit: b. by him that comes behind — SWIFT 320:23
Though he had b. me — SHAK 283:28
bitch: old b. gone in the teeth — POUND 254:19
bitch-goddess: b. success — JAMES 180:7
bite: b. some of my other generals — GEOR 149:22
b. the hand that fed them — BURKE 81:3
man recovered of the b. — GOLD 154:28
bites: dead woman b. not — GRAY 156:19
biteth: it b. like a serpent — BIBLE 43:33
bitter: b. God to follow — SWIN 321:12
be not b. against them — BIBLE 56:11
b. bread of banishment — SHAK 293:21
news to hear and b. tears — CORY 108:13
Some do it with a b. look — WILDE 350:16
with b. herbs they shall eat — BIBLE 39:36
bitterness: scorn in the b. of his soul — BIBLE 47:33
bivouac: B. of the Dead — O'HARA 241:4
Bizet: I like Chopin and B. — FISH 139:26
blabbing: b., and remorseful day — SHAK 280:9
black: Any colour—so long as it's b. — FORD 143:7
b. against may — BUNT 78:15
b. and merciless things — JAMES 179:20
b. as if bereaved of light — BLAKE 61:24
b. as our loss — SITW 307:19
b. chaos comes again — SHAK 300:19
b. dog — JOHN 182:17
B. is beautiful — ANON 6:13
b. majority rule in Rhodesia — SMITH 309:9
B. Widow, death — LOW 211:16
devil damn thee b. — SHAK 287:33
I am b. — SHAK 292:15
I am b., but comely — BIBLE 44:29
long b. passage up to bed — STEV 317:15
more b. than ashbuds — TENN 323:23
nothing so much as a b. swan — JUV 189:7
sober-suited matron, all in b. — SHAK 295:12
Tip me the b. spot — STEV 317:3
What sad, b. isle — BAUD 30:5
Who art as b. as hell — SHAK 300:16
Young, gifted and b. — IRV 178:18
you wear b. all the time — CHEK 96:25
blackbird: B. has spoken — FARJ 138:12
b. whistling or just after — STEV 316:13
O b., what a boy you are — BROWN 73:20
blackbirds: B. are the cellos — STEV 316:22
blackens: And b. every blot — TENN 324:1
black-eyed: b. Susan — GAY 149:17
blackguard: Sesquipedalian b. — CLOU 102:10
blackly: glides along the water looking b. — BYRON 84:26
Blackpool: seaside place called B. — EDGAR 130:15
blacks: poor are Europe's b. — CHAM 94:4
bladders: wanton boys that swim on b. — SHAK 280:18
blade: B. on the feather — CORY 108:11
Steel-true and b.-straight — STEV 317:20
with bloody blameful b. — SHAK 291:7
blame: bad women never take the b. — BROO 73:11
It's the poor wot gets the b. — ANON 10:11
That neither is most to b. — SWIN 321:14
what they b. at night — POPE 252:6
blameless: Fearless, b. knight — ANON 12:4
white flower of a b. life — TENN 324:1

bois (cont.):

| | |
|---|---|
| Nous n'irons plus aux b. | ANON 12:13 |

bold: be b. and be sensible | HOR 173:8
be b., and everywhere be b. | SPEN 313:14
b. bad man, that dared | SPEN 313:8
bloody, b., and resolute | SHAK 287:20
drunk hath made me b. | SHAK 286:12
This b. bad man | SHAK 280:15
boldly: b. go where no man | RODD 261:12
boldness: B., and again b. | DANT 114:1
B. be my friend | SHAK 273:23
Bolingbroke: this canker, B. | SHAK 277:26
bolt: b. is shot back | ARN 16:10
like the b., and the breech | REED 258:16
bolts: b. up change | SHAK 272:2
bomb: b. is a paper tiger | MAO T 217:20
b. them back into the Stone Age | LEMAY 204:20
bombazine: B. would have shown | GASK 148:17
bombed: glad we've been b. | ELIZ 135:18
bomber: b. will always get through | BALD 27:5
bombs: Come, friendly b. | BETJ 37:9
Ears like b. and teeth like | CAUS 93:9
bond: And take a b. of fate | SHAK 287:21
Let him look to his b. | SHAK 289:15
pieces that great b. | SHAK 287:6
bondage: b. to parents | WOLL 353:13
b. which is freedom's self | SHEL 304:27
modern b. of rhyming | MILT 228:6
out of the house of b. | BIBLE 40:2
bondman: so base that would be a b. | SHAK 281:17
bonds: b. in thee are all determinate | SHAK 299:27
bondsmen: Hereditary b.! | BYRON 85:1
bone: B. of my bones | BIBLE 38:22
B. of my bone thou art | MILT 229:28
bright hair about the b. | DONNE 124:9
He knows death to the b. | YEATS 358:22
rag and a b. and a hank | KIPL 197:12
boneless: b. wonder | CHUR 99:8
bones: be he that moves my b. | SHAK 300:20
Can these b. live | BIBLE 47:9
conjuring trick with b. | JENK 181:4
dead men lost their b. | ELIOT 134:23
England keep my b. | SHAK 282:13
lay my b. amongst you | WOLS 353:15
Of his b. are coral made | SHAK 296:1
O ye dry b. | BIBLE 47:1C
Rattle his b. over the stones | NOEL 240:5
tongs and the b. | SHAK 290:35
valley which was full of b. | BIBLE 47:8
bonfire: b. of the vanities | WOLFE 353:7
bong-tree: land where the B. grows | LEAR 203:12
bonjour: B. tristesse | ELUA 136:9
bonnets: b. are bound for the Border | SCOTT 269:2
b. of Bonny Dundee | SCOTT 268:7
bonnie: b. banks o' Loch Lomon' | ANON 10:2
bonny: Am I no a b. fighter | STEV 316:25
Belbroughton Road is b. | BETJ 37:6
bono: Cui b.? | CIC 100:31
bonum: Summum b. | CIC 100:22
Boojum: If your Snark be a B.! | CARR 92:8
book: Bell, b., and candle | SHAK 282:7
b. a devil's chaplain | DARW 114:5
b. is like an infant's | TRAH 333:17
b. is the best of friends | TUPP 335:10
b. is the precious life-blood | MILT 230:30
B. of Life begins | WILDE 350:11
b. where men may read | SHAK 285:20
b. would have been finished | WOD 352:17
b. you would wish your wife | GRIF 159:2
Camerado, this is no b. | WHIT 348:14
dainties that are bred in a b. | SHAK 284:15
do not throw this b. about | BELL 32:25
Farewell my b. and my devocioun | CHAU 96:9
Go, litel b. | CHAU 96:20
Go, little b. | STEV 317:17

book (cont.):

Great b., great evil | CALL 88:5
I'll drown my b. | SHAK 296:13
leaves of the Judgement B. | TAYL 323:4
library to make one b. | JOHN 185:3
little volume, but large b. | CRAS 111:12
mentioning a single b. | REED 258:21
Not on his picture, but his b. | JONS 187:21
novel is the one bright b. | LAWR 202:14
read a b. before reviewing | SMITH 310:9
reading or non-reading a b. | BYRON 87:20
substance of a b. directly | KNOW 198:15
take down this b. | YEATS 360:9
thick, square b. | GLOU 153:17
this b. I directe | CHAU 96:23
What is the use of a b. | CARR 91:1
when I wrote that b. | SWIFT 320:25
With a religious b., or friend | WOTT 357:14
woman who wrote the b. | LINC 207:13
bookful: b. blockhead, ignorantly read | POPE 252:9
books: b. are either dreams | LOW 211:3
B. are made not like children | FLAU 141:12
B. are well written or badly | WILDE 350:3
B. do furnish a room | POW 254:25
B. from Boots' | BETJ 37:4
b. in the running brooks | SHAK 272:14
b. of the hour | RUSK 264:14
B. say: she did this because | BARN 29:5
b., the academes | SHAK 284:16
b. were opened | BIBLE 47:15
B. will speak plain | BACON 24:17
cannot learn men from b. | DISR 122:9
collection of b. | CARL 90:16
Deep-versed in b. | MILT 230:8
do you read b. through? | JOHN 184:26
equal skill to Cambridge b. | BROW 74:25
friendship, b. | THOM 331:21
gentleman is not in your b. | SHAK 291:13
has written all the b. | BUTL 84:15
his b. were read | BELL 33:27
many b. there is no end | BIBLE 44:27
my b. had been any worse | CHAN 94:10
No furniture so charming as b. | SMITH 310:2
proper study of mankind is b. | HUXL 177:5
read all the b. there are | MALL 216:20
Some b. are to be tasted | BACON 25:14
Things in b.' clothing | LAMB 200:4
Wherever b. will be burned | HEINE 164:21
Your borrowers of b. | LAMB 200:2
boon: b. and a blessing to men | ANON 11:1
boot: b. in the face, the brute | PLATH 249:14
B., saddle, to horse | BROW 75:17
b. stamping on a human face | ORW 242:11
bootboy: b. at Clarides | WOOLF 354:6
booted: b. and spurred to ride | RUMB 264:5
Booth: B. led boldly | LIND 207:16
boots: always have one's b. on | MONT 233:8
Books from B'. | BETJ 37:4
b.—movin' up and down | KIPL 196:6
carries his heart in his b. | HERB 166:11
doormat in a world of b. | RHYS 259:15
pleasure me in his top-b. | MARL 218:5
see my legs when I take my b. | DICK 118:21
truth is pulling its b. on | SPUR 314:2
boozes: tell a man who b. | BURT 83:1
Border: Bonnets are bound for the B. | SCOTT 269:2
Night Mail crossing the B. | AUDEN 21:4
borders: I have come to the b. of sleep | THOM 330:24
bore: be in it is merely a b. | WILDE 350:13
Every hero becomes a b. at last | EMER 136:30
He is an old b. | TREE 334:5
He was not only a b. | MUGG 236:5
if I was a b. | STEV 316:2
secret of being a b. | VOLT 340:17
bored: Bores and B. | BYRON 86:27

**bored** (*cont.*):

| | |
|---|---|
| Ever to confess you're b. | BERR 36:13 |
| virtue of the b. | WAUGH 343:29 |
| **boredom**: B. is a vital problem | RUSS 264:21 |
| b. on a large scale | INGE 178:11 |
| Life is first b., then fear | LARK 201:14 |
| **bores**: *B. and Bored* | BYRON 86:27 |
| B. have succeeded to dragons | DISR 122:11 |
| **boring**: Life, friends, is b. | BERR 36:13 |
| **born**: already b. before my lips | MAND 217:11 |
| And to the manner b. | SHAK 274:26 |
| b. free and equal in dignity | ANON 5:20 |
| B. in a cellar | FOOTE 142:19 |
| b. in days when wits were | ARN 17:11 |
| b. King of the Jews | BIBLE 48:9 |
| B. of the sun they travelled | SPEN 312:24 |
| B. of the very sigh | KEATS 191:5 |
| B. on the fourth of July | COHAN 103:5 |
| b. out of my due time | MORR 235:15 |
| b. to set it right | SHAK 275:6 |
| b. to set it right | STR 318:12 |
| b. under a rhyming planet | SHAK 291:26 |
| b. we cry that we are come | SHAK 283:27 |
| b. with your legs apart | ORTON 241:21 |
| British Bourgeoise is not b. | SITW 307:21 |
| But I was free b. | BIBLE 54:24 |
| Else, wherefore b. | TENN 324:5 |
| Every moment one is b. | TENN 328:26 |
| Except a man be b. again | BIBLE 53:17 |
| For we are b. in other's pain | THOM 331:7 |
| house where I was b. | HOOD 171:8 |
| I am not yet b.; O fill me | MACN 216:6 |
| if he had not been b. | BIBLE 51:8 |
| I was b. barefoot | LONG 209:8 |
| I was b. in a cellar | CONG 106:8 |
| I was b. sneering | GILB 151:18 |
| Man is b. to live | PAST 246:9 |
| Man is b. unto trouble | BIBLE 42:29 |
| Man that is b. of a woman | BIBLE 42:33 |
| Man that is b. of a woman | BOOK 66:6 |
| Man was b. free, and everywhere | ROUS 263:24 |
| natural to die as to be b. | BACON 24:22 |
| Not to be b. is, past all | SOPH 311:13 |
| Not to be b. is the best for man | AUDEN 20:15 |
| Not to be b., or being born | BACON 25:31 |
| one b. out of due time | BIBLE 55:16 |
| One is not b. a woman | DE B 115:8 |
| other powerless to be b. | ARN 17:16 |
| perish wherein I was b. | BIBLE 42:25 |
| person b. who is so unlucky | MARQ 219:21 |
| some men are b. great | SHAK 298:3 |
| soon as we were b. | BIBLE 47:30 |
| sucker b. every minute | BARN 29:9 |
| they had never been b. | BIBLE 48:8 |
| those who are to be b. | BURKE 80:17 |
| Thou wast not b. for death | KEATS 192:4 |
| time to be b., and a time to die | BIBLE 44:11 |
| 'Tis less than to be b. | FLET 31:2 |
| took the trouble to be b. | BEAU 30:17 |
| under that was I b. | SHAK 291:18 |
| unto us a child is b. | BIBLE 45:16 |
| We all are b. mad | BECK 31:14 |
| We were not b. to sue | SHAK 293:9 |
| **borne**: b. even heavier things | VIRG 339:1 |
| **borogoves**: mimsy were the b. | CARR 91:15 |
| **boroughs**: bright b., the circle-citadels | HOPK 172:16 |
| **borrow**: b. the money to do it | WARD 342:18 |
| *men who b.* | LAMB 200:1 |
| **borrower**: b. of the night | SHAK 287:1 |
| Neither a b., nor a lender be | SHAK 274:22 |
| **borrowers**: Your *b. of books* | LAMB 200:2 |
| **borrowing**: b. only lingers | SHAK 278:19 |
| **bosom**: close b.-friend of the maturing sun | KEATS 192:14 |
| her b. and half her side | COL 103:12 |

**bosom** (*cont.*):

| | |
|---|---|
| He's in Arthur's b. | SHAK 279:3 |
| Into my b. and be lost in me | TENN 328:5 |
| into the b. of the sea | SHAK 280:9 |
| Let me to thy b. fly | WESL 346:8 |
| She has no b. and no behind | SMITH 309:21 |
| **bosoms**: hang and brush their b. | BROW 77:19 |
| stockings and white b. | JOHN 183:24 |
| **boss**: b. there is always | MARQ 219:20 |
| **bossing**: shorter hours and nobody b. | ORW 242:13 |
| **bossy**: by the b. for the bully | SELD 269:22 |
| **Boston**: And this is good old B. | BOSS 70:1 |
| B. man is the east wind | APPL 14:14 |
| **Boswell**: B. the first of biographers | MAC 213:5 |
| **botanize**: that would peep and b. | WORD 356:5 |
| **botch**: sundial, and I make a b. | BELL 33:26 |
| **botches**: Leave no rubs nor b. | SHAK 287:2 |
| **bother**: Though 'B. it' may | GILB 152:16 |
| **bothered**: bewitched, b. | HART 163:7 |
| **Botticelli**: B.'s a *cheese* | PUNCH 256:18 |
| if B. were alive today | UST 336:17 |
| **bottle**: little for the b. | DIBD 117:17 |
| nor a b. to give him | DICK 118:20 |
| way out of the fly-b. | WITT 352:7 |
| **bottles**: English have hot-water b. | MIKES 224:11 |
| fill old b. with banknotes | KEYN 194:16 |
| put new wine into old b. | BIBLE 49:24 |
| **bottom**: at the b. of our garden | FYL 147:9 |
| forgotten man at the b. | ROOS 262:7 |
| **bottomless**: Law is a b. pit | ARB 14:22 |
| smoke of the pit that is b. | JAM 179:9 |
| **bottoms**: b. of my trousers rolled | ELIOT 134:2 |
| **boue**: *La nostalgie de la b.* | AUG 21:21 |
| **bough**: blossom that hangs on the b. | SHAK 296:14 |
| bread beneath the b. | FITZ 140:6 |
| Petals on a wet, black b. | POUND 254:20 |
| with bloom along the b. | HOUS 174:16 |
| **boughs**: b. which shake against the cold | SHAK 299:24 |
| **bounded**: b. in a nut-shell | SHAK 275:15 |
| **bounden**: and our b. duty | BOOK 65:15 |
| our b. duty and service | BOOK 65:17 |
| **bounds**: living know no b. | SHIR 306:12 |
| wider shall thy b. be set | BENS 34:20 |
| **bouquet**: b. is better than the taste | POTT 254:6 |
| **bourgeois**: b. climb up on them | FLAU 141:12 |
| How beastly the b. | LAWR 202:18 |
| One must astonish the b. | BAUD 30:9 |
| **bourgeoise**: British B. is not born | SITW 307:21 |
| **bourgeoisie**: b. in the long run | TROT 334:23 |
| discreet charm of the b. | BUÑ 78:16 |
| **bourn**: b. how far to be beloved | SHAK 271:4 |
| country from whose b. | SHAK 275:26 |
| our b. of time and place | TENN 323:19 |
| see beyond our b. | KEATS 192:18 |
| **bow**: b. myself in the house | BIBLE 42:11 |
| B. themselves when he did sing | SHAK 280:16 |
| b., ye tradesmen | GILB 151:9 |
| Bring me my b. of burning gold | BLAKE 61:12 |
| drew a b. at a venture | BIBLE 42:7 |
| every knee should b. | BIBLE 56:5 |
| putting b.-windows to the house | DICK 118:11 |
| set my b. in the cloud | BIBLE 39:10 |
| **bowels**: of Christ | CROM 112:2 |
| Have molten b. | BOTT 70:6 |
| **bower**: b. we shrined to Tennyson | HARDY 162:3 |
| **bowl**: Fill the Flowing B. | ANON 6:16 |
| golden be broken | BIBLE 44:26 |
| inverted b. we call The Sky | FITZ 140:15 |
| Morning in the b. of night | FITZ 140:4 |
| **bowler**: *I* am the b. and the ball | LANG 201:2 |
| **bows**: b. down to wood and stone | HEBER 164:16 |
| **bow-wow**: B. strain I can do | SCOTT 269:6 |
| were it not for his b. way | PEMB 247:7 |
| **box**: b. where sweets compacted | HERB 167:8 |
| **boxing**: B.'s just showbusiness | BRUNO 77:25 |

boy: any b. may become President STEV 316:17
Being read to by a b. ELIOT 133:14
b. brought the white sheet GARC 148:2
b. playing on the sea-shore NEWT 239:6
b. stood on the burning deck HEM 165:9
b.'s will is the wind's will LONG 209:21
b. will ruin himself GEOR 150:1
Cleopatra b. my greatness SHAK 272:5
fifteen-year-old b. until *they die* ROTH 263:14
journeying b. HARDY 162:14
Let the b. win his spurs EDW 130:21
Mad about the b. COW 109:3
misfortunes can befall a b. MAUG 222:12
O blackbird, what a b. BROWN 73:20
purblind, wayward b. SHAK 284:13
schoolrooms for 'the b.' COOK 107:17
Smiling the b. fell dead BROW 76:8
Speak roughly to your little b. CARR 91:5
Take the thanks of a b. BEEC 32:5
to be b. eternal SHAK 298:21
Upon the growing b. WORD 355:20
was and a little tiny b. SHAK 298:15
You silly twisted b. MILL 225:10
boy friend: certain thing called the B. WILS 351:17
boyhood: In the lost b. of Judas Æ 3:4
boys: As flies to wanton b. SHAK 283:21
b. in the back room LOES 209:5
b. in the back rooms BEAV 31:4
b. of the old Brigade WEAT 344:4
b. that swim on bladders SHAK 280:18
By office boys for office b. SAL 266:6
Christian b. ARN 18:15
few b. late at their play ARN 17:3
lightfoot b. are laid HOUS 175:2
Mealy b., and beef-faced DICK 119:19
Till the b. come Home FORD 143:12
bracelet: b. of bright hair DONNE 124:9
braces: Damn b.: Bless relaxes BLAKE 61:9
Bradford: silk hat on a B. millionaire ELIOT 134:29
Bradshaw: 'B.' is nervous and terse DOYLE 126:7
braes: banks and b. o' bonny Doon BURNS 81:27
brag: Beauty is Nature's b. MILT 226:20
Is left this vault to b. SHAK 286:26
braids: twisted b. of lilies MILT 226:21
brain: Bear of Very Little B. MILNE 225:15
b. of feathers POPE 250:14
b. perplexes and retards KEATS 192:1
draughts intoxicate the b. POPE 251:28
dry b. in a dry season ELIOT 133:14
from the heat-oppressèd b. SHAK 286:10
harmful to the b. JAM 179:9
has gleaned my teeming b. KEATS 192:19
instrumental to the b. SHAK 274:4
Owl hasn't exactly got B. MILNE 225:18
petrifactions of a plodding b. BYRON 86:32
schoolmasters puzzle their b. GOLD 155:8
should possess a poet's b. DRAY 126:19
young wife and a good b. JONS 186:23
brained: large-b. woman BROW 75:6
brains: And dash'd the b. out SHAK 286:6
gentleman said a girl with b. LOOS 210:7
brambles: b. in the fortresses BIBLE 46:3
branch: b. shall grow out BIBLE 45:18
b. that might have grown MARL 218:14
branchy: Towery city and b. between HOPK 172:2
brandy: B. for the Parson KIPL 196:28
b. of the damned SHAW 301:19
must drink b. JOHN 185:22
brass: become as sounding b. BIBLE 55:11
men's evil manners live in b. SHAK 280:22
brat: spurious b., Tom Jones RICH 260:4
brave: b. bad man CLAR 101:12
b. man with a sword WILDE 350:16
b. new world SHAK 296:15

brave (cont.):
Fortune assists the b. TER 329:5
Fortune favours the b. VIRG 339:20
home of the b. KEY 194:12
How sleep the b., who sink COLL 105:11
None but the b. DRYD 127:19
Toll for the b. COWP 109:28
to-morrow to be b. ARMS 16:2
What's b., what's noble SHAK 271:26
brawler: not a b., not covetous BIBLE 56:16
Brazil: Charley's aunt from B. THOM 330:5
breach: More honoured in the b. SHAK 274:26
Once more unto the b. SHAK 279:5
bread: bitter b. of banishment SHAK 293:21
b. and circuses JUV 189:12
b. eaten in secret BIBLE 43:15
b. of adversity BIBLE 46:1
b. of affliction BIBLE 42:6
b. to this intolerable deal SHAK 278:2
Cast thy b. upon the waters BIBLE 44:24
crammed with distressful b. SHAK 279:16
Give us this day our daily b. BIBLE 48:27
I am the b. of life BIBLE 53:22
Jesus took b., and blessed BIBLE 51:9
living HOMER begged his b. ANON 10:10
looked to government for b. BURKE 81:3
Man shall not live by b. BIBLE 48:16
Royal slice of b. MILNE 225:2
shalt thou eat b. BIBLE 39:2
She was cutting b. and butter THAC 329:23
Strengthened with the B. of Life WHITE 347:16
taste of another man's b. DANTE 113:23
that b. should be so dear HOOD 171:13
To eat dusty b. BOGAN 62:18
unleavened b. BIBLE 39:36
when we did eat b. BIBLE 40:1
whom if his son ask b. BIBLE 49:10
break: at the b. of the day STR 318:17
b. a man's spirit is devil's SHAW 300:27
B., break, break TENN 323:10
b. the bloody glass MACN 216:3
But b., my heart SHAK 274:13
can b. them at pleasure EDG 130:18
I bend and I b. not LA F 199:17
I'll b. my staff SHAK 296:13
Never give a sucker an even b. FIEL 139:16
Thou thyself must b. at last ARN 16:18
breakfast: critical period in matrimony is b. HERB 166:18
embarrassment and b. BARN 29:4
impossible things before b. CARR 91:24
wholesome, hungry b. WALT 342:9
breakfasted: b. with you and shall sup BRUCE 77:22
breaking: b. what it likes ARN 17:27
breaks: something twangs and b. MACN 216:4
breast: boiling bloody b. SHAK 291:7
charms to sooth a savage b. CONG 106:11
eternal in the human b. POPE 252:12
Of thy chaste b. LOV 210:20
stood b. high amid the corn HOOD 171:11
with dauntless b. GRAY 157:9
breastie: what a panic's in thy b. BURNS 82:26
breastplate: b. of righteousness BIBLE 56:4
breasts: b. by which France is fed SULLY 319:3
Come to my woman's b. SHAK 285:18
division of prodigious b. SWIN 321:4
why then her b. are dun SHAK 300:11
breath: And thou no b. at all SHAK 284:6
b. can make them GOLD 154:18
breathing thoughtful b. WORD 356:24
B.'s a ware that will not keep HOUS 174:18
b. thou art SHAK 288:19
have drawn the b. of life YEATS 359:5
mansion call the fleeting b. GRAY 157:8
seemed waste of b. YEATS 359:11

**breath** (cont.):
world draw thy b. in pain — SHAK 277:17
**breathe:** As though to b. were life — TENN 328:21
like the hair we b. — SURT 319:8
Low, low, b. and blow — TENN 327:19
on a summer's morn to b. — MILT 229:23
**breathes:** B. there the man — SCOTT 268:12
**breathless:** b. hush in the Close — NEWB 238:13
**bred:** B. en bawn in a brier-patch — HARR 163:5
**Bredon:** In summertime on B. — HOUS 174:20
**breeches:** made themselves b. — BIBLE 38:26
**breed:** b. of their horses — PENN 247:10
Feared by their b. — SHAK 293:16
not b. one work — HOPK 172:19
This happy b. of men — SHAK 293:16
**breeding:** Burgundy without any b. — THUR 332:17
with ease, to show your b. — SHER 306:8
**breeds:** Chaos often b. life — ADAMS 1:15
Or lesser b. without the Law — KIPL 197:4
**breeks:** b. aff a wild Highlandman — SCOTT 268:26
**breeze:** Fluttering and dancing in the b. — WORD 355:4
For a b. of morning moves — TENN 326:28
volleying rain and tossing b. — ARN 17:18
**breezes:** Little b. dusk and shiver — TENN 325:35
**breezy:** B., Sneezy, Freezy — ELLIS 136:4
**brekekekex:** B. koax koax — ARIS 15:11
**brethren:** least of these my b. — BIBLE 51:6
**brevis:** *Ars longa, vita b.* — HIPP 168:19
**brevity:** B. is the sister of talent — CHEK 96:31
B. is the soul of wit — SHAK 275:8
Its body b., and wit its soul — COL 103:17
**brew:** b. that is true — FRANK 245:1
**brewery:** O take me to a b. — ANON 8:3
**bribe:** b. or twist — WOLFE 353:2
done without a b. I find — CENT 93:15
**bribes:** man open to b. — GREE 158:4
**brick:** 'Eave 'arf a b. at 'im — PUNCH 256:9
found it b. and left it marble — AUG 22:7
piece of b. in his pocket — SWIFT 319:20
They threw it a b. at a time — HARG 162:21
**bride:** all jealousy to the b. — BARR 29:15
became my glittering b. — WORD 354:21
b. adorned for her husband — BIBLE 58:4
encounter darkness as a b. — SHAK 288:20
*mourning b.* — DRYD 128:13
Never the blushing b. — LEIGH 204:18
unravished b. of quietness — KEATS 191:17
**bridegrooms:** Of b., brides — HERR 167:12
**brides:** Of bridegrooms, b. — HERR 167:12
**bridesmaid:** always the b. — LEIGH 204:18
**bridge:** And keep the b. with me — MAC 214:4
b. too far — BROW 75:7
Champagne, and B. — BELL 33:25
Come shooting through the b. — BETJ 37:1
Like a b. over troubled water — SIMON 307:5
Railway B. of the Silv'ry Tay — MCG 214:19
**brief:** B. as the lightning — SHAK 290:14
b. wherein all marvels — SOUT 312:7
Drest in a little b. authority — SHAK 288:14
I strive to be b. — HOR 172:24
tragical! tedious and b. — SHAK 291:5
**brier:** Bred en bawn in a b.-patch — HARR 163:5
Thorough bush, thorough b. — SHAK 290:19
**brigade:** boys of the old B. — WEAT 344:4
**bright:** All calm, as it was b. — VAUG 337:14
All things b. and beautiful — ALEX 4:2
Behold the b. original appear — GAY 149:14
b. and fierce and fickle — TENN 327:24
B. as the day — GRAN 156:10
b. day is done — SHAK 272:4
b. day that brings forth — SHAK 281:2
b. particular star — SHAK 270:23
B. the vision that delighted — MANT 217:17
b. things come to confusion — SHAK 290:15
Dark with excessive b. — MILT 229:4

**bright** (cont.):
Goddess, excellently b. — JONS 187:3
look, the land is b. — CLOU 102:24
northern climes, obscurely b. — BYRON 85:20
thought thee b. — SHAK 300:16
was a young lady named B. — BULL 78:7
**brightest:** B. and best of the sons — HEBER 164:14
B. in dungeons, Liberty — BYRON 87:7
**brightness:** B. falls from the air — NASHE 237:19
**brillig:** 'Twas b., and the slithy toves — CARR 91:15
**brim:** bubbles winking at the b. — KEATS 191:30
**bring:** B. me my arrows of desire — BLAKE 61:12
would b. home knowledge — JOHN 185:18
**bringing:** B. the cheque and the postal order — AUDEN 21:4
Her b. me up by hand — DICK 118:24
**brink:** we walked to the b. — DULL 129:2
**brinkmanship:** boasting of his b. — STEV 316:20
**brisking:** by b. about the life — SMART 308:8
**Britain:** B. a fit country for heroes — LLOY 208:11
Hail, happy B.! — SOM 311:3
Say, B., could you ever boast — SWIFT 320:19
When B. first, at heaven's — THOM 331:20
**Britannia:** Beer and B. — SMITH 310:13
Rule, B., rule the waves — THOM 331:20
you've shouted 'Rule B.' — KIPL 196:2
**British:** B. Grenadier — ANON 10:13
life for the B. female — CLOU 102:7
We are B., thank God — MONT 233:24
With a stony B. stare — TENN 326:27
**Briton:** glory in the name of B. — GEOR 149:23
only a free-born B. — THAC 329:15
**Britons:** B. never will be slaves — THOM 331:20
we B. alone use 'Might' — WAUGH 343:28
**broad:** b. is the way — BIBLE 49:12
B. of Church — BETJ 37:15
By brooks too b. for leaping — HOUS 175:2
She's the B. and I'm the High — SPR 314:1
**broccoli:** It's b., dear — WHITE 347:15
**broke:** If it ain't b., don't fix it — LANCE 200:21
**broken:** baying for b. glass — WAUGH 343:18
b. open on the most scientific — PEAC 246:23
cord is not quickly b. — BIBLE 44:14
He liked the Sound of B. Glass — BELL 33:23
Laws were made to be b. — NORTH 240:7
When the lute is b. — SHEL 303:24
**brokenhearted:** bind up the b. — BIBLE 46:24
**broker:** b. is a man who — WOOL 354:7
more that of an honest b. — BISM 59:18
**bronze:** more lasting than b. — HOR 173:28
**brooch:** b. of gold ful sheene — CHAU 95:16
**brooches:** b. and toys for your delight — STEV 317:19
**brood:** b. of folly without father — MILT 226:22
fond of no second b. — SHAK 273:22
**broods:** b. and sleeps on his own — WORD 356:7
**brook:** Fell in the weeping b. — SHAK 277:7
willow grows aslant a b. — SHAK 277:6
**brooks:** b. of Eden mazily murmuring — TENN 327:8
By b. too broad for leaping — HOUS 175:2
purling b. — POPE 251:24
**broom:** I am sent with b. before — SHAK 291:10
**broomstick:** mortal man is a b. — SWIFT 320:6
**brothel:** metaphysical b. for emotions — KOES 199:1
**brothels:** b. with bricks of Religion — BLAKE 61:7
Keep thy foot out of b. — SHAK 283:13
**brother:** Am I my b.'s keeper — BIBLE 39:4
Am I not a man and a b. — WEDG 345:1
Be my b., or I kill you — CHAM 94:5
BIG B. IS WATCHING YOU — ORW 242:6
B. can you spare a dime — HARB 161:11
B., thy tail hangs down — KIPL 197:18
b. to the ox — MARK 218:4
Death and his b. Sleep — SHEL 304:26
has brother followed b. — WORD 354:23
hateth his b. — BIBLE 57:17

**brother** (*cont*.):
I am a b. to dragons · BIBLE 43:3
I am, Sir, a B. of the Angle · WALT 342:10
our sad bad glad mad b.'s · SWIN 321:5
shall my b. sin against me · BIBLE 50:19
sticketh closer than a b. · BIBLE 43:30
Strong b. in God · BELL 33:14
white man's b. · KING 195:7
**brotherhood**: crown thy good with b. · BATES 30:2
Love the b. · BIBLE 57:9
together at the table of b. · KING 195:9
**brother-in-law**: brother, not his b. · KING 195:7
**brothers**: And all the b. too · SHAK 298:2
happy few, we band of b. · SHAK 279:20
together as b. or perish · KING 195:10
**brought**: b. forth her firstborn · BIBLE 51:32
darkness safely b. · KEBLE 193:16
**brow**: mighty Victor's b. · KELLY 193:19
wanton with a velvet b. · SHAK 284:14
Your bonny b. was brent · BURNS 82:11
**Brown**: John B.'s body · ANON 8:14
**brown**: Jeanie with the light b. hair · FOST 144:11
river is a strong b. god · ELIOT 133:7
**Browning**: B. knew what it meant · KLOP 198:12
B. some 'Pomegranate' · BROW 75:3
Hang it all, Robert B. · POUND 254:12
Meredith's a prose B. · WILDE 349:22
safety-catch of my B. · JOHST 186:18
Wordsworth, Tennyson and B. · BAG 26:17
**bruised**: be b. in a new place · IRV 178:20
staff of this b. reed · BIBLE 42:16
was b. for our iniquities · BIBLE 46:19
**bruit**: *Dont meurt le b. parmi le vent* · APOL 14:11
**brush**: with my b. that I make love · REN 259:6
**brushers**: Critics are like b. · WOTT 357:20
**brutal**: grown b. from the fare · YEATS 359:16
**brutality**: industry without art is b. · RUSK 264:11
**brute**: Brute heart of a b. like you · PLATH 249:14
*Et tu, B.?* · CAES 88:3
*Et tu, B.?* · SHAK 281:10
**brutes**: Exterminate all the b. · CONR 107:4
**brutish**: nasty, b., and short · HOBB 169:10
**Brutus**: B. is an honourable man · SHAK 281:19
What! is B. sick · SHAK 281:6
You too, B. · CAES 88:3
**bubble**: Honour but an empty b. · DRYD 127:21
Life is mostly froth and b. · GORD 155:21
Seeking the b. reputation · SHAK 272:26
What is fame? an empty b. · GRAI 156:7
world's b. · BACON 25:30
**bubbles**: beaded b. winking at the brim · KEATS 191:30
**buck**: bigger bang for a b. · ANON 6:12
b. stops here · TRUM 335:6
**bucket**: past is a b. of ashes · SAND 266:15
stick inside a swill b. · ORW 242:16
**Buckingham**: changing guard at B. Palace · MILNE 225:19
so much for B. · CIBB 100:15
**buckle**: b. which fastens · BAG 26:5
**bud**: be a b. again · KEATS 190:20
I'll nip him in the b. · ROCHE 261:1
**budge**: b. doctors of the Stoic · MILT 226:19
**buds**: darling b. of May · SHAK 299:12
**bug**: this b. with gilded wings · POPE 251:8
**bugger**: B. Bognor · GEOR 150:2
**buggers**: b. can't be choosers · BOWRA 71:4
**bugle**: Blow, b., blow · TENN 327:20
**bugles**: Blow out, you b. · BROO 72:20
b. calling for them from sad · OWEN 243:22
**build**: And easy to b., too · IBSEN 178:6
build—but not I b. · HOPK 172:19
b. the house of death · MONT 233:10
Except the Lord b. the house · BOOK 68:30
think that we b. for ever · RUSK 264:16
**builders**: stone which the b. refused · BOOK 68:22

**building**: b. hath three conditions · WOTT 357:19
it's a very old b. · OSB 242:18
principal beauty in b. · FULL 147:6
We have a b. of God · BIBLE 55:24
**builds**: B. in the weather · SHAK 289:13
people b. on mud · MACH 215:2
**built**: are b. with stones of Law · BLAKE 61:7
b. my soul a lordly pleasure-house · TENN 327:14
It is not what they b. · FENT 138:23
**bull**: are gone to milk the b. · JOHN 184:12
Cock and a B. · STER 315:26
Dance tiptoe, b. · BUNT 78:15
savage b. doth bear the yoke · SHAK 291:14
**bullet**: Ballot stronger than the b. · LINC 207:4
b. through his heart · THAC 329:18
Every b. has its billet · WILL 351:2
faster than a speeding b. · ANON 7:5
**bullets**: b. made of platinum · BELL 33:1
**bullocks**: whose talk is of b. · BIBLE 48:6
**bully**: by the bossy for the b. · SELD 269:22
I love the lovely b. · SHAK 279:10
**bum**: Indicat Motorem B. · GODL 153:20
**bump**: that go b. in the night · ANON 7:7
**bumpy**: going to be a b. night · MANK 217:12
**Buncombe**: talking to B. · WALK 341:6
through reporters to B. · CARL 90:17
**bungler**: arts of peace Man is a b. · SHAW 301:22
**bunk**: History is more or less b. · FORD 143:6
**buns**: bears might come with b. · ISH 178:21
**Bunyan**: genius in literature—B. · ARN 18:11
**burden**: any price, bear any b. · KENN 194:3
b. and heat of the day · BIBLE 50:25
b. of them is intolerable · BOOK 65:11
impossible to carry the heavy b. · EDW 131:2
Is the b. of my song · ANON 9:4
my b. is light · BIBLE 49:36
Take up the White Man's b. · KIPL 197:15
**bureaucracy**: [b.'s] specific invention · WEBER 344:8
**Burg**: *Eine feste B.* · LUTH 212:10
**burgundy**: naïve domestic B. · THUR 332:17
**buried**: be b. in a good old age · BIBLE 39:12
b. him darkly · WOLFE 352:26
b. in so sweet a place · SHEL 303:2
**Burlington**: I'm B. Bertie · HARG 162:20
**burn**: better to marry than to b. · BIBLE 55:5
b. always with this hard · PATER 246:15
B., baby, burn · ANON 6:14
b. its children to save · MEYER 224:4
B. to the socket · WORD 354:19
old age should b. and rave · THOM 330:7
**burned**: B. on the water · SHAK 271:14
men in the end, are b. · HEINE 164:21
**burning**: boy stood on the b. deck · HEM 165:9
b. of the leaves · BINY 59:13
b. roof and tower · YEATS 359:14
Is Paris b.? · HITL 169:4
Keep the Home-fires b. · FORD 143:12
midst of a b. fiery furnace · BIBLE 47:11
Tiger, Tiger, b. bright · BLAKE 62:5
**burnish'd**: b. by Aldershot sun · BETJ 37:10
**Burns**: B., Shelley, were with us · BROW 76:14
**burnt-out**: b. ends of smoky days · ELIOT 134:10
**burr**: I am a kind of b. · SHAK 288:25
**burthen**: vapours weep their b. · TENN 328:17
**Burton**: why was B. built on Trent · HOUS 175:3
**bury**: B. it certain fathoms · SHAK 296:13
B. my heart at Wounded Knee · BENÉT 34:9
I come to b. Caesar · SHAK 281:18
Let the dead to b. their dead · BIBLE 49:20
physician can b. mistakes · WRIG 357:23
We will b. you · KHR 194:19
**bus**: Can it be a Motor B. · GODL 153:20
[Hitler] missed the b. · CHAM 94:3
I'm not even a b., I'm a tram · HARE 162:19

| | |
|---|---|
| **buses:** Bloody men are like bloody b. | COPE 107:22 |
| **bush:** b. was not consumed | BIBLE 39:30 |
| Thorough b., thorough brier | SHAK 290:19 |
| **bushel:** neither under a b. | BIBLE 52:15 |
| **busier:** he seemed b. than he was | CHAU 95:19 |
| **business:** be about my Father's b. | BIBLE 52:4 |
| b. being just the terrible | BROW 77:10 |
| B. carried on as usual | CHUR 99:6 |
| B. first; pleasure afterwards | THAC 329:13 |
| b. is merely a survival | ROCK 261:11 |
| b. of nobody | MAC 213:3 |
| b. of the American people | COOL 107:19 |
| b. that we love we rise | SHAK 271:20 |
| B. was his aversion | EDG 130:17 |
| For it is your b. | HOR 173:14 |
| go to my pleasure, b. | WYCH 358:5 |
| how to succeed in b. | MEAD 222:17 |
| importunity of b. | LAMB 200:10 |
| It is the b. of the wealthy man | BELL 33:22 |
| it's b. of consequence | BARH 28:22 |
| Liberty is always unfinished b. | ANON 8:19 |
| make b. for itself | DICK 118:4 |
| no b. like show business | BERL 35:20 |
| No praying, it spoils b. | OTWAY 243:7 |
| Pleasure is a *thief* to b. | DEFOE 115:11 |
| requisite in b. than dispatch | ADD 2:20 |
| servants of b. | BACON 24:27 |
| That's the b. precept | DICK 119:3 |
| their b. in great waters | BOOK 68:12 |
| totter on in b. to the last | POPE 251:23 |
| Treasury is the spring of b. | BAG 26:4 |
| **Buss:** Miss B. and Miss Beale | ANON 9:10 |
| **bust:** B. outlasts the throne | DOBS 122:25 |
| Can storied urn or animated b. | GRAY 157:8 |
| Uncorseted, her friendly b. | ELIOT 134:33 |
| When you dance it b. to bust | GREN 158:15 |
| **bustle:** B. in a House | DICK 120:10 |
| **busy:** B. old fool, unruly sun | DONNE 124:11 |
| Government of the b. by the bossy | SELD 269:22 |
| how b. I must be this day | ASTL 19:8 |
| Little man, you've had a b. day | HOFF 307:2 |
| **butcher:** Hog B. for the World | SAND 266:12 |
| I want to know a b. paints | BROW 77:11 |
| **butchered:** B. to make a Roman holiday | BYRON 85:10 |
| **butchers:** gentle with these b. | SHAK 281:13 |
| **butler:** on the b.'s upper slopes | WOD 352:23 |
| **butlers:** B. ought to know their place | BELL 33:6 |
| **butt:** journey's end, here is my b. | SHAK 293:4 |
| knocks you down with the b. | GOLD 155:14 |
| **butter:** *B. and eggs and a pound of cheese* | CALV 88:7 |
| Could we have some b. | MILNE 225:22 |
| forth b. in a lordly dish | BIBLE 40:33 |
| guns not with b. | GOEB 153:21 |
| rather have b. or guns | GOER 153:21 |
| **buttercup:** I'm called Little B. | GILB 152:14 |
| **buttercups:** B. and daisies | HOW 175:10 |
| **buttered:** always on the b. side | PAYN 246:20 |
| **butterflies:** Frogs Eat B. | STEV 316:7 |
| **butterfly:** b. dreaming I am a man | CHUA 98:19 |
| b. upon the road | KIPL 196:26 |
| can a b.'s wings in Brazil | LOR 210:10 |
| Float like a b., sting like a bee | ALI 4:10 |
| Who breaks a b. upon a wheel | POPE 251:7 |
| **butting:** B. through the Channel | MAS 221:19 |
| **buttock:** by boiling his b. | AUBR 20:1 |
| **buttocks:** chair that fits all b. | SHAK 270:25 |
| gorgeous b. of the ape | HUXL 177:13 |
| **button:** By each b., hook, and lace | LOW 211:2 |
| little round b. at top | FOOTE 142:20 |
| Pray you, undo this b. | SHAK 284:6 |
| **buttoning:** All this b. and unbuttoning | ANON 5:22 |
| **buttons:** taken of his b. off | KIPL 196:9 |
| **butty:** He's an oul' b. o' mine | O'CAS 240:21 |
| **buxom:** b., blithe, and debonair | MILT 226:28 |

| | |
|---|---|
| **buy:** For money can't b. me love | MCC 205:11 |
| I'll b. Codham, Cockridden | THOM 330:23 |
| I will b. with you | SHAK 288:31 |
| no man might b. or sell | BIBLE 57:32 |
| shall b. it like an honest man | NORT 240:9 |
| **buyer:** if a b. can be found | SALL 266:8 |
| **buys:** b. a minute's mirth | SHAK 299:8 |
| Civility costs nothing and b. | MONT 233:5 |
| **by:** B. and by God caught his eye | MCC 214:15 |
| **bymatter:** if it had been a b. | BACON 24:19 |
| **byway:** And the b. nigh me | STEV 317:24 |
| goes his own b. to heaven | DEFOE 115:23 |
| **byword:** proverb and a b. | BIBLE 41:29 |
| **Byzantium:** holy city of B. | YEATS 359:22 |

# C

| | |
|---|---|
| **C:** C cut it | ANON 6:6 |
| C Major of this life | BROW 75:9 |
| **ça:** *Ç. ira.* | ANON 12:2 |
| **cabbage:** c. with a college education | TWAIN 336:4 |
| **cabbage-leaf:** c. to make an apple-pie | FOOTE 142:20 |
| **cabbages:** find me planting my c. | MONT 233:9 |
| Of c.—and kings | CARR 91:22 |
| **cabin:** Make me a willow c. | SHAK 297:21 |
| small c. build there | YEATS 359:12 |
| **cabined:** Her c. ample Spirit | ARN 17:1 |
| Now I am c., cribbed | SHAK 287:9 |
| **Cabinet:** another to mislead the C. | ASQ 19:4 |
| c. is a combining committee | BAG 26:5 |
| consequence of c. government | BAG 26:6 |
| **cable:** little c. cars climb | CROSS 112:10 |
| **Cabots:** Lowells talk to the C. | BOSS 70:1 |
| **cad:** Flopshus C. | KIPL 198:2 |
| **cadence:** harsh c. of a rugged line | DRYD 128:21 |
| **Cadiz Bay:** reeking into C. | BROW 76:3 |
| **Caesar:** *Aut C., aut nihil* | BORG 69:25 |
| C. had his Brutus | HENRY 166:5 |
| C. hath wept | SHAK 281:20 |
| C.'s wife must be above suspicion | CAES 87:25 |
| Came from C.'s laurel crown | BLAKE 60:8 |
| did in envy of great C. | SHAK 282:2 |
| Hail C., those who are | ANON 13:12 |
| Hast thou appealed unto C. | BIBLE 54:25 |
| Imperious C., dead | SHAK 277:9 |
| Not that I loved C. less | SHAK 281:15 |
| On blossoming C. | SHAK 271:22 |
| Render therefore unto C. | BIBLE 50:29 |
| that C. might be great | CAMP 88:20 |
| where some buried C. | FITZ 140:8 |
| yesterday the word of C. | SHAK 281:21 |
| **café:** heart in ev'ry street c. | HAMM 161:1 |
| **caftan:** Iffucan of Azcan in c. | STEV 316:4 |
| **cage:** linnet born within the c. | TENN 325:3 |
| Nor iron bars a c. | LOV 210:19 |
| We cannot c. the minute | MACN 216:10 |
| **caged:** know why the c. bird sings | DUNB 129:7 |
| We think c. birds sing | WEBS 344:27 |
| **Cain:** and the first city C. | COWL 109:13 |
| C. went out from the presence | BIBLE 39:6 |
| cruel sons of C. | LE G 204:12 |
| Lord set a mark upon C. | BIBLE 39:5 |
| **cake:** Let them eat c. | MAR 218:3 |
| **cakes:** no more c. and ale | SHAK 297:26 |
| their bridal-c. | HERR 167:12 |
| **Calais:** 'C.' lying in my heart | MARY 221:17 |
| shew light at C. | JOHN 184:15 |
| **calamity:** thou art wedded to c. | SHAK 295:15 |
| **calculation:** c. shining out | DICK 119:2 |
| **calculators:** economists, and c. | BURKE 80:14 |
| **Caledonia:** C.! stern and wild | SCOTT 268:14 |
| **calf:** Bring hither the fatted c. | BIBLE 52:31 |
| c. and the young lion | BIBLE 45:19 |

Caliban: C. casts out Ariel — POUND 254:17
calico: c. millenium — CARL 90:25
California: C. to the New York Island — GUTH 159:12
call: And one clear c. for me — TENN 323:18
c. back yesterday — SHAK 293:24
c. me early, mother dear — TENN 327:5
C. no man foe — BENS 34:21
c. of the running tide — MAS 222:1
c. of the wild — LOND 209:7
it's time to c. it a day — GREEN 106:2
they c. you, Shepherd — ARN 17:4
they come when you do c. — SHAK 278:3
through curtains c. on us — DONNE 124:11
you call to me, c. to me — HARDY 162:15
called: c. them by wrong names — BROW 75:16
Out of the deep have I c. — BOOK 68:33
callous: c. engraved upon her heart — SELL 270:1
calls: High on a hill it c. to me — CROSS 112:10
If anybody s — BENT 35:9
calm: All C., as it was bright — VAUG 337:14
And all our c. is in that balm — NORT 240:10
still c. of life — ADAMS 1:7
calme: Luxe, c. et volupté — BAUD 30:4
calumnies: C. are answered best — JONS 187:14
calumny: thou shalt not escape c. — SHAK 275:29
calves: peculiarly susceptible to c. — HUXL 177:10
Calvin: land of C., oat-cakes — SMITH 309:26
Cambridge: C. ladies — CUMM 113:5
For C. people rarely smile — BROO 73:7
to C. books — BROW 74:25
To C. books — TRAPP 334:3
came: He c. unto his own — BIBLE 53:10
I c., I saw, I conquered — CAES 88:2
I c. through and I shall return — MAC 213:1
Tell them I c., and no one — DE L 116:19
where you c. from or where — TEBB 323:7
camel: c. is a horse designed — ISS 178:23
c. to go through the eye — BIBLE 50:22
How the C. got his Hump — KIPL 197:22
swallow a c. — BIBLE 50:31
Take my c., dear — MAC 213:2
Camelot: many-towered C. — TENN 325:34
camera: I am a c. — ISH 178:22
Camerado: C., this is no book — WHIT 348:14
cammin: mezzo del c. di nostra vita — DANTE 113:17
camps: Courts and c. are the only places — CHES 97:6
can: And c. it be — WESL 346:3
because they think they c. — VIRG 339:10
C. something, hope — HOPK 171:25
He who c., does — SHAW 301:29
Pass me the c., lad — HOUS 174:9
Canalettos: Then the C. go — MACM 215:20
cancel: c. all our vows — DRAY 126:16
C. and tear to pieces — SHAK 287:6
c. half a line — FITZ 140:14
cancer: Silence like a c. grows — SIMON 307:7
candid: be c. where we can — POPE 252:11
from the c. friend — CANN 89:12
candle: c. by God's grace — LAT 202:4
c. in that great turnip — CHUR 100:10
c. of understanding — BIBLE 47:28
c. shall not drive — SHAK 282:7
c. than curse the darkness — STEV 316:21
farthing c. at Dover — JOHN 184:15
farthing c. to the sun — YOUNG 360:16
Fire and fleet and c.-lighte — BALL 27:20
hold a c. to my shames — SHAK 289:11
Is scarcely fit to hold a c. — BYROM 84:24
light a c. to the sun — SIDN 306:14
little c. throws his beams — SHAK 290:4
My c. burns at both ends — MILL 224:22
out, brief c. — SHAK 288:5
set a c. in the sun — BURT 83:12
when he hath lighted a c. — BIBLE 52:15

candle-light: dress by yellow c. — STEV 317:12
candles: carry c. and set chairs — HERV 168:1
c. burn their sockets — HOUS 174:12
extinguishes c. and kindles fire — LA R 201:24
Night's c. are burnt out — SHAK 295:18
Their c. are all out — SHAK 286:9
candy: C. is dandy — NASH 237:15
canker: this c., Bolingbroke — SHAK 277:26
cannibal: progress if c. uses knife — LEC 204:1
cannon: C. to right of them — TENN 323:16
Even in the c.'s mouth — SHAK 272:26
cannon-ball: But a c. took off his legs — HOOD 171:4
cano: Arma virumque c. — VIRG 338:23
canoe: coffin clapt in a c. — BYRON 84:26
canoes: their heads in their c. — MARV 221:3
cant: clear your mind of c. — JOHN 186:3
Let them c. about DECORUM — BURNS 82:13
we have nothing but c. — PEAC 246:22
cantons: loyal c. of contemnèd love — SHAK 297:21
cantos: c. of unvanquished space — CRANE 110:31
cap: riband in the c. of youth — SHAK 277:5
capability: Negative C. — KEATS 193:2
capacity: transcendent c. of taking trouble — CARL 90:10
caparisons: No c., Miss — SHER 306:1
cape: c. of a sudden came — BROW 76:23
nobly C. Saint Vincent — BROW 76:3
capital: Pandemonium, the high c. — MILT 228:21
they say it is a c. offence — MARL 218:7
To that high C., where kingly — SHEL 303:4
capitalism: definition of c. — HAMP 161:5
ethic and the spirit of c. — WEBER 344:7
monopoly stage of c. — LENIN 205:2
unacceptable face of c. — HEATH 164:12
War is c. with the gloves off — STOP 318:7
capitalist: slave of c. society — CONN 107:3
captain: train-band c. eke was — COWP 109:23
c.'s but a choleric word — SHAK 288:15
Fighting in the c.'s tower — DYLAN 129:20
I am the c. of my soul — HENL 165:18
O C.! my Captain — WHIT 348:11
Our great captain's c. — SHAK 292:3
captains: All my sad c. — SHAK 271:19
c. and the kings depart — KIPL 197:2
c. courageous — BALL 28:1
C. of industry — CARL 90:20
Star c. glow — FLEC 141:14
thunder of the c. — BIBLE 43:5
captive: hast led captivity c. — BOOK 67:17
captives: To serve your c.' need — KIPL 197:15
captivity: hast led c. captive — BOOK 67:17
car: And the gilded c. of day — MILT 226:7
expands to tinker with his c. — MACN 216:9
caravan: Put up your c. — HODG 169:15
carbon: c. atom possesses — JEANS 180:16
carborundum: Nil c. illegitimi — ANON 9:15
carbuncle: monstrous c. — CHAR 95:8
carbuncles: Monstrous c. — SPEN 312:27
carcase: c. fit for hounds — SHAK 281:4
Wheresoever the c. — BIBLE 50:36
Worrying the c. of an old song — THOM 331:5
card: having a c. up his sleeve — LAB 199:12
cardboard: Sailing over a c. sea — HARB 161:12
cards: At c. for kisses — LYLY 212:16
not learned to play at c. — JOHN 183:20
old age of c. — POPE 251:11
Patience, and shuffle the c. — CERV 93:19
care: age is full of c. — SHAK 299:5
And Heaven's peculiar c. — SOM 311:3
are now with me past c. — SHAK 293:20
c. and valour in this Welshman — SHAK 279:11
C. of his Mother — MILNE 225:20
c.'s check and curb — VAUG 337:5
C. sits behind the horseman — HOR 173:25
c. to stay than will to go — SHAK 295:19

care (cont.):
don't c. too much for money     MCC 205:11
I c. for nobody     BICK 58:24
Lord, with what c.     HERB 167:7
Nor c. beyond to-day     GRAY 157:12
ravelled sleeve of c.     SHAK 286:15
she don't c.     MCC 205:16
so wan with c.     SHAK 277:21
Sport that wrinkled C. derides     MILT 227:2
Take c., my foolish heart     WASH 342:24
take c. of minutes     CHES 97:8
taken better c. of myself     BLAKE 60:4
Teach us to c. and not to care     ELIOT 132:19
this life if, full of c.     DAV 114:20
career: c. open to the talents     CARL 90:8
c. open to the talents     NAP 237:6
East is a c.     DISR 122:8
careful: c. in the choice of his enemies     WILDE 350:5
So c. of the type she seems     TENN 325:10
carefully: most c. upon your hour     SHAK 273:29
careless: C. talk costs lives     ANON 6:15
first fine c. rapture     BROW 76:2
So c. of the single life     TENN 325:10
carelessness: lose both looks like c.     WILDE 349:18
With carefullest c.     BETJ 37:11
cares: c. that infest the day     LONG 209:13
No more c. to make me squeak     ANON 9:17
Professional men, they have no c.     NASH 237:12
Carew: grave of Mad C.     HAYES 163:21
carf: c. biforn his fader     CHAU 95:14
cargo: With a c. of ivory     MAS 221:18
Carlyle: C. and Mrs. C.     BUTL 84:12
carnal: satisfy men's c. lusts     BOOK 65:26
carnally: To be c. minded is death     BIBLE 54:39
carnations: Soon will the musk c. break     ARN 17:19
caro: Verbum c. factum est     MISS 231:21
carol: chimes ring out with a c.     BOND 63:9
Carolina: ham'n eggs in C.     GORD 155:22
carollings: So little cause for c.     HARDY 162:7
carpe: c. diem     HOR 173:20
carpenter: c. who has made you a bad table
    JOHN 184:7
Walrus and the C.     CARR 91:21
carpet: figure in the c.     JAMES 179:17
wear the c. with their shoes     YEATS 359:23
carpets: c. rose along the gusty     KEATS 190:22
carping: obnoxious to each c. tongue     BRAD 71:12
carriage: c. has not arrived yet     LERM 205:25
C. held but just Ourselves     DICK 120:9
very small second class c.     GILB 151:16
carrion: c. comfort, Despair     HOPK 171:25
carrots: Sowe C. in your Gardens     GARD 148:4
carry: c. within us the wonders     BROW 74:13
certain we can c. nothing out     BIBLE 56:18
making him c. me     TOLS 333:13
must c. knowledge with him     JOHN 185:18
Speak softly and c. a big stick     ROOS 262:16
cars: c. nose forward like fish     LOW 211:12
c. today     BART 29:19
Carthage: C. must be destroyed     CATO 92:22
To come again to C.     SHAK 289:32
carve: c. heads upon cherry-stones     JOHN 186:4
c. him as a dish fit for the gods     SHAK 281:4
c. on every tree the fair     SHAK 273:2
Must c. in Latin or in Greek     WALL 341:13
carved: Last-supper-c.-on-a-peach-stone     LANC 200:20
case: And when a lady's in the c.     GAY 149:10
c. is concluded     AUG 22:5
everything that is the c.     WITT 352:9
Have nothing to do with the c.     GILB 152:6
heard one side of the c.     BUTL 84:15
Here's a corpse in the c.     BARH 28:21
this c. is that case     ARAB 14:18
which in our c. we have not got     REED 258:16
would have passed in any c.     BECK 31:13

cased: c. up, like a holy relic     WEBS 344:14
casement: c. ope at night     KEATS 192:9
ghost of Roger C.     YEATS 359:6
casements: Charmed magic c.     KEATS 192:5
cash: c. in hand and waive the rest     FITZ 140:7
c. payment has become     CARL 90:4
she needs good c.     TUCK 335:9
casket: hushèd c. of my soul     KEATS 192:13
casse: tout c., tout lasse     ANON 12:17
Cassius: C. has a lean and hungry look     SHAK 281:1
cassock: C., band, and hymn-book     WILB 349:6
cassocked: c. huntsman     COWP 110:1
cassowary: If I were a c.     WILB 349:6
cast: C. a cold eye on life     YEATS 360:8
c. away the works of darkness     BOOK 64:21
c. off the works of darkness     BIBLE 55:1
c. pearls before swine     BIBLE 49:8
C. thy bread upon the waters     BIBLE 44:24
C. your mind on other days     YEATS 360:7
first c. a stone at her     BIBLE 53:26
pale c. of thought     SHAK 275:26
will I c. out my shoe     BOOK 67:14
will in no wise c. out     BIBLE 53:23
Castilian: as might an old C.     BYRON 87:13
castle: In the c. of my skin     LAMM 200:17
Look owre the C. Downe     BALL 27:15
man's house is his c.     COKE 103:8
rich man in his c.     ALEX 4:3
splendour falls on c. walls     TENN 327:20
Castlereagh: had a mask like C.     SHEL 304:4
castles: C. in the air     IBSEN 178:6
casualty: force and road of c.     SHAK 289:13
Truth is the first c.     JOHN 182:12
cat: C. on a Hot Tin Roof     WILL 351:5
C., the Rat, and Lovell the dog     COLL 105:3
C. with crimson whiskers     LEAR 203:15
endow a college, or a c.     POPE 251:13
For I will consider my C.     SMART 308:7
Had Tiberius been a c.     ARN 16:23
Hanging of his c. on Monday     BRAT 71:16
Like the poor c. i' the adage     SHAK 286:4
Oh I am a c. that likes     SMITH 309:17
part to tear a c. in     SHAK 290:18
Touch not the c.     SCOTT 268:25
umpire, the pavilion c.     LANG 201:2
When I play with my c.     MONT 233:17
cataclysm: c. but one poor Noah     HUXL 177:11
catalogue: lamentable c. of human crime     CHUR 99:12
catamite: in bed with my c.     BURG 79:14
cataract: sounding c.     WORD 355:9
wild c. leaps in glory     TENN 327:20
cataracts: c. and hurricanoes     SHAK 283:6
catastrophe: I'll tickle your c.     SHAK 278:20
race between education and c.     WELLS 345:21
catch: catch as c. can     FOOTE 142:20
c. him once upon the hip     SHAK 289:2
First c. your hare     GLAS 153:16
that was C.-22     HELL 165:5
catcher: c. in the rye     SAL 266:1
catching: poverty's c.     BEHN 32:22
categorical: imperative is C.     KANT 189:23
category-habits: c. by category-disciplines     RYLE 265:10
caterpillars: c. of the commonwealth     SHAK 293:19
Cathay: cycle of C.     TENN 326:18
cathedral: heft of C. Tunes     DICK 120:14
cathedrals: cars are like Gothic c.     BART 29:19
Catherine: child of Karl Marx and C. the Great
    ATTL 19:13
Catholic: holy C. Church     BOOK 64:3
Once a C. always a C.     WILS 351:10
Roman C. Church     MACM 215:19
Roman C. women     THOM 331:2
Catholick: C. and Apostolick Church     BOOK 65:6
Catholics: C. and Communists     GREE 158:2

**Catholics** (cont.):
Hitler attacked the C. — NIEM 239:15
**Cato:** C. did, and Addison approved — BUDG 78:4
losing one pleased C. — LUCAN 211:23
**cats:** C. and monkeys — JAMES 179:22
C., no less liquid — TESS 329:10
dogs and killed the c. — BROW 76:26
greater c. with golden eyes — SACK 265:12
melodious c. under the moon — HUXL 177:4
where c. are cats — MARQ 219:18
**cattle-shed:** Stood a lowly c. — ALEX 4:4
**cauldron:** Fire burn and c. bubble — SHAK 287:15
**cauliflower:** C. is nothing but cabbage — TWAIN 336:4
**causa:** c. finita est — AUG 22:5
**causas:** potuit rerum cognoscere c. — VIRG 340:8
**cause:** c. may be inconvenient — BENN 34:18
c. of dullness in others — FOOTE 143:1
c. or just impediment — BOOK 65:25
c. that wit is in other men — SHAK 278:16
effect was already in the c. — BERG 35:13
good old C. — MILT 231:6
good old c. — WORD 356:1
it is the c., my soul — SHAK 292:28
judge thou my c. — BIBLE 47:3
man can shew any just c. — BOOK 65:27
perseverance in a good c. — STER 315:14
Rebel without a c. — LIND 207:15
So little c. for carollings — HARDY 162:7
winning c. pleased — LUCAN 211:23
**causer:** Heart's renying, c. of this — BARN 29:8
**causes:** Home of lost c. — ARN 18:2
knowledge of c. — BACON 25:26
malice, to breed c. — JONS 187:17
understand the c. of things — VIRG 340:8
**cavaliero:** he was a perfect c. — BYRON 84:27
**Cavaliers:** C. (Wrong but Wromantic) — SELL 270:2
**cave:** her vacant interlunar c. — MILT 230:12
**caverns:** c. measureless to man — COL 103:22
in c. all alone — WILB 349:11
**caves:** Mendip's sunless c. — MAC 213:24
pleasure-dome with c. of ice — COL 103:24
unfathomed c. of ocean bear — GRAY 157:9
**caviare:** to the general — SHAK 275:18
**Cawdor:** Glamis thou art, and C. — SHAK 285:15
**cease:** C.! must men kill and die — SHEL 303:19
c. upon the midnight — KEATS 192:3
have fears that I may c. — KEATS 192:19
will not c. from mental fight — BLAKE 61:12
**ceased:** it c. to be with Sarah — BIBLE 39:14
**ceasing:** Remembering without c. — BIBLE 56:13
**Cecilia:** Blessed C., appear in visions — AUDEN 20:10
**celestial:** And lighten with c. fire — BOOK 69:16
Apparelled in c. light — WORD 355:17
**Celia:** Come, my C., let us prove — JONS 187:16
**celibacy:** c. has no pleasures — JOHN 183:5
c. is almost always a muddy pond — PEAC 246:24
**cell:** narrow c. for ever laid — GRAY 157:6
tight hot c. of their hearts — BOGAN 62:18
**cellar:** Born in a c. — FOOTE 142:19
I was born in a c. — CONG 106:8
**cellos:** c. of the deep farms — STEV 316:22
**cells:** Than c. and gibbets — COOK 107:17
**Celt:** blind hysterics of the C. — TENN 325:28
**cement:** same c., ever sure — POPE 250:19
**cemetery:** c. is an open space — SHEL 303:2
**censorship:** extreme form of c. — SHAW 302:22
**censure:** c. of a man's self — JOHN 185:20
**centre:** c. cannot hold — YEATS 359:24
c. is everywhere — ANON 9:13
May sit i' the c. — MILT 226:12
My c. is giving way — FOCH 142:14
real c. of the household — SHAW 301:5
This bed thy c. — DONNE 124:13
whose c. is everywhere — UPD 336:13
**centuries:** All c. but this — GILB 151:20

**centuries** (cont.):
forty c. look down — NAP 237:3
Through what wild c. — DE L 116:12
**century:** c. of the common man — WALL 341:9
So the 20th C. — CRANE 111:2
**Cerberus:** Of C., and blackest Midnight — MILT 226:27
You are not like C. — SHER 306:2
**ceremony:** C. is an invention — LAMB 199:23
c. of innocence is drowned — YEATS 359:24
Save c., save general c. — SHAK 279:15
thrice-gorgeous c. — SHAK 279:16
**Ceres:** laughing C. re-assume the land — POPE 251:17
**certain:** c. thing called the Boy Friend — WILS 351:17
dirge of her c. ending — SHAK 299:9
lady of a 'c. age' — BYRON 86:21
One thing is c. — FITZ 140:10
**certainties:** better than most people's c. — HARD 161:17
hot for c. in this our life — MER 223:24
man will begin with c. — BACON 23:20
**cesspool:** London, that great c. — DOYLE 126:4
**Ceylon:** Blow soft o'er C.'s isle — HEBER 164:16
**chaff:** see that the c. is printed — HUBB 175:15
**chagrin:** C. d'amour — FLOR 142:12
**chain:** c. that is round us now — CORY 108:12
**chainless:** Eternal spirit of the c. mind — BYRON 87:7
**chains:** better to be in c. than to be free — KAFKA 189:18
everywhere he is in c. — ROUS 263:18
kings in c. — BOOK 69:11
nothing to lose but their c. — ENG 221:15
only by the slightest c. — EDG 130:18
sang in my c. like the sea — THOM 330:9
**chair:** And tilts up his c. — HOFF 169:19
c. that fits all buttocks — SHAK 270:25
La c. est triste — MALL 216:20
Seated in thy silver c. — JONS 187:3
**chairs:** carry candles and set c. — HERV 168:1
**chaise-longue:** hurly-burly of the c. — CAMP 88:15
**chalice:** c. from the palace — FRANK 245:1
**chalices:** treen priests and golden c. — JEWEL 181:14
**Cham:** great C. of literature — SMOL 310:17
**chamber:** stalking in my c. — WYATT 358:2
**chamberers:** That c. have — SHAK 292:15
**Chamberlain:** speech by C. — BEVAN 38:3
**chambermaid:** c. as of a Duchess — JOHN 185:21
**chambers:** whisper softness in c. — MILT 231:1
**champagne:** c. and a chicken at last — MONT 233:4
C., and Bridge — BELL 33:25
C. socialist — MORT 235:22
I get no kick from c. — PORT 253:20
It's like c. or high heels — BENN 34:18
not a c. teetotaller — SHAW 300:28
**chance:** c. favours only the prepared — PAST 246:11
C. has appointed her home — BUNT 78:14
Give peace a c. — MCC 205:13
I missed my c. — LAWR 202:22
too good to leave to c. — SIMON 307:8
voice to come in as by c. — BACON 24:18
Which erring men call c. — MILT 226:18
**Chancellor:** C. of the Exchequer — LOWE 211:1
**chances:** c. change by course — SOUT 312:9
changes and c. of this mortal — BOOK 65:18
**change:** and bolts up c. — SHAK 272:2
architecture, a c. of heart — AUDEN 21:14
certain relief in c. — IRV 178:20
C. and decay in all around — LYTE 212:20
c. from Jane to Elizabeth — AUST 23:3
c. from major to minor — PORT 253:19
c. Kate into Nan — BLAKE 60:15
C. not made without inconvenience — JOHN 182:3
c. something at once sordid — BAUD 30:7
c. that state by forces — NEWT 239:3
c. we think we see in life — FROST 146:9
c. your mind and follow him — AUR 22:11
Even a god cannot c. the past — AGAT 3:7
more things c. — KARR 190:2

**change** (cont.):

| | |
|---|---|
| necessary not to c. | FALK 138:11 |
| point is to c. it | MARX 221:11 |
| ringing grooves of c. | TENN 326:17 |
| things will have to c. | LAMP 200:19 |
| we c. with them | ANON 14:2 |
| wind of c. | MACM 215:17 |
| with fear of c. | MILT 228:17 |
| without the means of some c. | BURKE 80:10 |

**changeable:** Fickle and c. always is woman  VIRG 339:9

**changed:** changed, c. utterly  YEATS 359:3

| | |
|---|---|
| c. upon the blue guitar | STEV 316:9 |
| That all things are c. | BACON 24:4 |
| that it be not c. | BIBLE 47:13 |
| we have c. all that | MOL 232:19 |
| we shall all be c. | BIBLE 55:21 |

**changes:** c. and chances of this mortal life  BOOK 65:18

| | |
|---|---|
| sundry and manifold c. | BOOK 64:23 |
| world's a scene of c. | COWL 109:15 |

**changest:** who c. not, abide with me  LYTE 212:20

**changing:** all the c. scenes of life  TATE 322:17

| | |
|---|---|
| fixed point in a c. world | DOYLE 125:18 |
| Times They Are A-C. | DYLAN 130:9 |

**Chankly Bore:** Hills of the C.  LEAR 203:9

**channel:** C. is a mere ditch  NAP 237:1

| | |
|---|---|
| drum them up the C. | NEWB 238:10 |
| you are crossing the C. | GILB 151:16 |

**chanting:** C. faint hymns  SHAK 290:12

**chaos:** bit of primordial c.  WELLS 345:22

| | |
|---|---|
| black c. comes again | SHAK 300:19 |
| C. and darkness heard | MARR 219:24 |
| C., illumined by flashes of | WILDE 350:19 |
| C. is come again | SHAK 292:10 |
| C. often breeds life | ADAMS 1:15 |
| reign of C. and old Night | MILT 228:16 |
| thy dread empire, C. | POPE 250:22 |

**chapel:** devil would also build a c.  LUTH 212:9

| | |
|---|---|
| will build a c. just | BECON 31:17 |
| will have his c. | BANC 28:14 |

**chapels:** c. had been churches  SHAK 288:29

Stolen looks are nice in c.  HUNT 176:16

**chaplain:** What a book a devil's c.  DARW 114:5

**chaps:** Biography is about C.  BENT 35:5

**chapter:** c. of accidents  CHES 97:17

**character:** c. dead at every word  SHER 306:4

| | |
|---|---|
| c. in the full current of | GOET 154:11 |
| C. is destiny | ELIOT 132:15 |
| C. is destiny | NOV 240:12 |
| habit and you reap a c. | READE 258:11 |
| I leave my c. behind me | SHER 306:5 |
| man's c. is his fate | HER 166:9 |
| man's c. is to be abused | THAC 329:16 |
| What is c. | JAMES 179:24 |

**characters:** c. of hell to trace  GRAY 157:2

| | |
|---|---|
| from high life high c. | POPE 251:20 |
| Six c. in search of an author | PIR 249:1 |
| Who have c. to lose | BURNS 82:13 |

**charge:** angels c. over thee  BOOK 67:30

Take thou in c. this day  MAC 214:7

**charged:** c. the troops of error  BROW 74:9

thought c. with emotion  GIDE 151:1

**charging:** marching, c. feet, boy  RICH 179:7

**Charing Cross:** betwixt Heaven and C.  THOM 331:16

human existence at C.  JOHN 185:1

**chariot:** Bring me my c. of fire  BLAKE 61:12

| | |
|---|---|
| slap-up gal in a bang-up c. | DICK 119:23 |
| Swing low, sweet c. | ANON 10:17 |
| Time's wingèd c. | MARV 220:24 |

**charioted:** c. by Bacchus and his pards  KEATS 192:1

**chariots:** tarry the wheels of his c.  BIBLE 40:34

**charities:** cold c. of man to man  CRAB 110:30

**charity:** and have not c.  BIBLE 55:11

| | |
|---|---|
| C. and beating begins at home | FLET 142:7 |
| C., dear Miss Prism | WILDE 349:21 |
| c. envieth not | BIBLE 55:12 |

**charity** (cont.):

| | |
|---|---|
| C. never faileth | BIBLE 55:12 |
| C. shall cover the multitude | BIBLE 57:11 |
| C. suffereth long | BIBLE 55:12 |
| C. vaunteth not itself | BIBLE 55:12 |
| faith, hope, c. | BIBLE 55:14 |
| greatest of these is c. | BIBLE 55:14 |
| lectures or a little c. | WHIT 348:20 |
| Let holy c. | LITT 208:2 |
| need c. more than the dead | ARN 16:8 |
| puffeth up, but c. edifieth | BIBLE 55:7 |
| with c. for all | LINC 207:7 |

**Charlotte:** Werther had a love for C.  THAC 329:23

**charm:** c. can soothe her melancholy  GOLD 155:13

| | |
|---|---|
| c. he never so wisely | BOOK 67:13 |
| C. is the great English blight | WAUGH 343:17 |
| C…it's a sort of bloom | BARR 29:16 |
| Completing the c. | ELIOT 132:24 |
| discreet c. of the bourgeoisie | BUÑ 78:16 |
| hard words like a c. | OSB 242:17 |
| Oozing c. from every pore | LERN 206:2 |
| What is c. then | LESS 206:4 |
| You know what c. is | CAMUS 89:5 |

**charmed:** c. it with smiles and soap  CARR 92:9

I bear a c. life  SHAK 288:6

**charmer:** voice of the c.  BOOK 67:13

Were t'other dear c. away  GAY 149:7

**charming:** How c. is divine philosophy  MILT 226:15

**charms:** all c. fly  KEATS 191:14

| | |
|---|---|
| c. to sooth a savage breast | CONG 106:11 |
| those endearing young c. | MOORE 234:11 |

**charter:** c. of thy worth  SHAK 299:27

This was the c. of the land  THOM 331:20

**chase:** habitually live by the c.  TOCQ 333:2

When heated in the c.  TATE 322:16

**chasing:** always c. Rimbauds  PARK 245:10

**chassis:** worl's in a state o' c.  O'CAS 240:22

**chaste:** Be thou as c. as ice  SHAK 275:29

| | |
|---|---|
| c., and twenty-three | BYRON 85:23 |
| huntress, c. and fair | JONS 187:3 |
| men ask, Are Barmaids C. | MAS 221:20 |
| Nor ever c.. except you ravish | DONNE 123:11 |
| Was Jesus c. | BLAKE 60:13 |

**chasten:** To c. and subdue  WORD 355:10

**chasteneth:** Whom the Lord loveth he c.  BIBLE 56:28

**chastised:** c. you with whips  BIBLE 41:34

**chastisement:** c. of our peace  BIBLE 46:19

**chastity:** C.—the most unnatural  HUXL 177:7

| | |
|---|---|
| Give any lessons of c. | BLAKE 60:13 |
| Give me c. and continency | AUG 21:22 |
| 'Tis c., my brother, chastity | MILT 226:14 |

**châteaux:** Ô saisons, ô c.  RIMB 260:10

**chats:** spoiled the women's c.  BROW 76:26

**Chattanooga:** C. Choo-choo  GORD 155:22

**chatter:** c. of a transcendental kind  GILB 152:10

**chattering:** Dumb swans, not c. pies  SIDN 306:22

**Chatterley:** end of the C. ban  LARK 201:12

**Chatterton:** C., the marvellous boy  WORD 356:16

**Chaucer:** [of C.] here is God's plenty  DRYD 128:30

old famous poet C.  SPEN 313:19

**cheap:** And flesh and blood so c.  HOOD 171:13

| | |
|---|---|
| done as c. as other men | PEPYS 247:15 |
| how potent c. music is | COW 109:10 |
| They be good c. | WYATT 358:3 |

**cheaper:** c. seats clap your hands  LENN 205:9

**cheat:** c. at cards genteelly  BOSW 70:5

| | |
|---|---|
| sweet c. gone | DE L 116:16 |
| When it's so lucrative to c. | CLOU 102:19 |

**cheated:** Old men who never c.  BETJ 36:21

**cheating:** c. between two periods  BIER 59:7

**cheats:** c. with an oath  PLUT 250:2

**checks:** moves, and c., and slays  FITZ 140:12

**cheek:** call a blush into the c.  DICK 119:22

| | |
|---|---|
| Feed on her damask c. | SHAK 298:1 |
| hangs upon the c. of night | SHAK 294:26 |

**cheek** (*cont.*):
hollow c. or faded eye — TENN 328:2
smite thee on thy right c. — BIBLE 48:23
**cheeks**: And on thy c. a fading rose — KEATS 191:8
crack your c. — SHAK 283:6
**cheer**: Be of good c. — BIBLE 50:8
c. but not inebriate — BERK 35:16
c. but not inebriate — COWP 110:11
Could scarce forbear to c. — MAC 214:8
Don't c., men — PHIL 248:13
Greet the unseen with a c. — BROW 75:12
**cheerful**: c. as any man could — PEPYS 247:13
Come, let us join our c. songs — WATTS 343:3
God loveth a c. giver — BIBLE 55:26
maketh a c. countenance — BIBLE 43:25
**cheerfulness**: C. gives elasticity — SMIL 308:19
c. keeps up a kind of day-light — ADD 2:24
c. was always breaking in — EDW 131:5
**cheeriness**: Chintzy, Chintzy c. — BETJ 36:19
**cheerio**: it s c. my deario — MARQ 219:17
**cheerioh**: And 'c.' or 'cheeri-bye' — BETJ 37:1
**cheers**: Two c. for Democracy — FORS 144:3
**cheese**: Botticelli's a *c.* — PUNCH 256:18
*eggs and a pound of c.* — CALV 88:7
has 246 varieties of c. — DE G 116:7
I'll fill hup the chinks wi' c. — SURT 319:9
like some valley c. — AUDEN 21:13
night I've dreamed of c. — STEV 317:4
**chemistry**: weak in c. — WELLS 345:16
**cheque**: blank c. to Lord Salisbury — GOSC 155:24
c. and the postal order — AUDEN 21:4
**chequer-board**: c. of nights and days — FITZ 140:12
**cherchez**: C. la femme — DUMAS 129:3
**cherish**: c. those hearts that hate — SHAK 280:20
love, c., and to obey — BOOK 66:1
**cherished**: My no longer c. — MILL 224:23
**cherries**: apples, c., hops — DICK 119:26
Life is just a bowl of c. — BROWN 73:17
**cherry**: as American as c. pie — BROWN 73:15
C.-ripe — HERR 167:13
Loveliest of trees, the c. now — HOUS 174:14
O ruddier than the c. — GAY 149:1
To see the c. hung with snow — HOUS 174:17
**cherry-stones**: carve heads upon c. — JOHN 186:4
**cherubim**: C. and Seraphim — HEBER 164:17
**cherubims**: Immortal c. — TRAH 333:19
**cherubs**: As so near the c. hymn — SMART 308:9
**Cheshire**: smile of a cosmic C. cat — HUXL 177:14
**chest**: His c. against his foes — SMART 308:10
men on the dead man's c. — STEV 317:2
**Chesterton**: dared attack my C. — BELL 33:16
**chestnut**: Under a spreading c. tree — LONG 210:4
**chevalier**: *C. sans peur et sans reproche* — ANON 12:4
**Chevy**: Drove my C. to the levee — MCL 215:8
**chew**: fart and c. gum — JOHN 181:22
**chewing gum**: c. for the eyes — ANON 10:14
**chic**: Radical C. — WOLFE 353:9
**chicken**: c. in his pot — HENR 165:20
republic is like a c. — MITF 232:8
Some c.! Some neck! — CHUR 99:17
with champagne and a c. — MONT 233:4
**chickens**: beside the white c. — WILL 351:8
Curses are like young c. — SOUT 311:21
pretty c. and their dam — SHAK 287:26
**chiding**: He will not alway be c. — BOOK 68:6
**chief**: Cromwell, our c. of men — MILT 230:26
What is the c. end of man — SHOR 306:13
**chieftain**: C. Iffucan of Azcan — STEV 316:4
Great c. o' the puddin'-race — BURNS 82:24
**child**: angel is the English c. — BLAKE 61:24
c. born therein shall — RUSK 264:19
C.! do not throw this book — BELL 32:25
c. for the first seven years — ANON 7:10
C. is father of the Man — WORD 355:14
c. is owed the greatest — JUV 189:15

**child** (*cont.*):
c. of dirt that stinks — POPE 251:8
c. of Karl Marx and Catherine — ATTL 19:13
c.'s a plaything for an hour — LAMB 200:14
c. shall play on the hole — BIBLE 45:20
c. should always say what's — STEV 317:16
c. take care that you strike — SHAW 301:32
Christ, the c. of God — BOOK 65:20
every formal visit a c. — AUST 23:8
father that knows his own c. — SHAK 289:7
find I am to have his c. — BURG 79:15
for a c. in the street I could — CLOU 102:7
For unto us a c. is born — BIBLE 45:16
Get with c. a mandrake root — DONNE 124:10
God bless the c. that's got — HOL 170:10
hare's own c. — HOFF 170:3
heard one calling, 'C.' — HERB 166:23
He has devoured the infant c. — HOUS 174:8
Here a little c. I stand — HERR 167:11
Is it well with the c. — BIBLE 42:9
I speak like a c. — NAB 236:20
It's only my c.-wife — DICK 118:17
I was a c. and she was a c. — POE 250:3
leave a c. alone — BROW 77:7
little c., a limber elf — COL 103:13
little c. shall lead them — BIBLE 45:19
Love, a c., is ever crying — WROTH 358:1
mid-May's eldest c. — KEATS 192:2
my absent c. — SHAK 282:8
On a cloud I saw a c. — BLAKE 61:18
Perfection is the c. of Time — HALL 160:13
right to a c. — SHAW 301:4
She was an aggravating c. — BELL 33:11
shocks the mind of a c. — PAINE 244:7
spoil the c. — BUTL 84:3
that's governed by a c. — SHAK 294:16
There is a man c. conceived — BIBLE 42:25
thou show'st thee in a c. — SHAK 282:24
To have a thankless c. — SHAK 282:25
use of a new-born c. — FRAN 145:17
was the mother for the c. — COL 104:20
When I was a c., I spake — BIBLE 55:14
when thy king is a c. — BIBLE 44:22
**childbirth**: Death and taxes and c. — MITC 232:5
**childhood**: And sleep as I in c. — CLARE 101:9
C. is the kingdom where — MILL 224:21
c. when the door opens — GREE 158:6
'tis the eye of c. — SHAK 286:17
Where c. had strayed — Æ 3:4
**childish**: are either knavish or c. — JOHN 185:23
c. valorous than manly wise — MARL 219:13
I put away c. things — BIBLE 55:14
**childishness**: Second c. — SHAK 272:28
**childlike**: Whose trust, ever c. — STR 318:17
**children**: And airy hopes my c. — WORD 354:21
And oh those c.'s voices — VERL 338:1
be called the c. of God — BIBLE 48:19
become as little c. — BIBLE 50:15
breeds contempt—and c. — TWAIN 336:3
by c. to adults — SZASZ 321:23
C. are dumb to say how — GRAV 156:13
c. are heard on the green — BLAKE 61:25
c. at play are not playing — MONT 233:11
C. begin by loving — WILDE 350:12
c. cried in the streets — MOTL 236:1
c. hath given hostages — BACON 25:1
c. in whom is no faith — BIBLE 40:24
c. like the olive-branches — BOOK 68:32
c. love their parents — AUCT 20:7
c. of a larger growth — CHES 97:11
c. of a larger growth — DRYD 127:25
c. of the devil — TENN 328:12
c. of the kingdom — BIBLE 49:18
c. produce adults — DE VR 117:12
C. sweeten labours — BACON 25:6

**children** (*cont.*):

| | |
|---|---|
| c. to be always and forever | DE S 265:15 |
| c. who were rough | SPEN 312:25 |
| Come, dear c., let us away | ARN 16:16 |
| dogs than of their c. | PENN 247:10 |
| even so are the young c. | BOOK 68:31 |
| fathers upon the c. | BIBLE 40:5 |
| from c. and from fools | DRYD 128:16 |
| its c. to save its pride | MEYER 224:4 |
| little c. died in the streets | AUDEN 20:18 |
| Men fear death as c. fear | BACON 24:20 |
| Myself and c. three | COWP 109:24 |
| not much about having c. | LODGE 209:4 |
| poor get c. | EGAN 189:19 |
| provoke not your c. | BIBLE 56:2 |
| Rachel weeping for her c. | BIBLE 48:11 |
| sleepless c.'s hearts are glad | BETJ 36:17 |
| stars are my c. | KEATS 193:9 |
| Suffer the little c. | BIBLE 51:25 |
| That is known as the C.'s Hour | LONG 209:12 |
| thou shalt bring forth c. | BIBLE 39:1 |
| Too easy for c. | SCHN 267:23 |
| To whom the lips of c. | NEALE 237:21 |
| turn each one of her c. | VERG 337:19 |
| violations committed by c. | BOWEN 70:17 |
| We are c., playing on the line | FORS 143:22 |
| which holdeth c. from play | SIDN 306:27 |
| wiser than the c. of light | BIBLE 52:33 |
| with which men play like c. | EDD 130:13 |
| young c., were sooner | ASCH 18:18 |
| Your c. are not your c. | GIBR 150:19 |

**Chile**: small earthquake in C. | COCK 103:1
**chill**: bitter c. it was | KEATS 190:14
**chilly**: By c. fingered spring | KEATS 190:13
I feel c. and grown old | BROW 77:19
our c. women | BYRON 84:29
room grows c. | GRAH 156:4
**Chimborazo**: C., Cotopaxi | TURN 335:17
**chime**: c. had stroked the air | JONS 187:18
**chimeras**: dire c. and enchanted isles | MILT 226:16
**chimes**: c. at midnight | SHAK 278:24
c. ring out with a carol | BOND 63:9
**chimney**: old men from the c. | SIDN 306:27
**chimneys**: c. I sweep | BLAKE 61:19
good grove of c. for me | MORR 235:11
**chimney-sweepers**: As c., come to dust | SHAK 273:27
**chin**: his c. upon an orient wave | MILT 227:29
**China**: from C. to Peru | JOHN 183:11
Till C. and Africa meet | AUDEN 20:11
up like thunder outer C. | KIPL 196:21
your land armies in C. | MONT 233:23
**chinks**: fill hup the c. wi' cheese | SURT 319:9
**chintzy**: C., C. cheeriness | BETJ 36:19
**chip**: c. of the old 'block' | BURKE 81:11
**chips**: c. with everything | WESK 346:2
**chivalry**: age of c. is gone | BURKE 80:14
age of c. is past | DISR 122:11
nine-tenths of the law of c. | SAY 267:15
**chocolate**: c. cream soldier | SHAW 300:24
**choice**: being just the terrible c. | BROW 77:10
c. and master spirits | SHAK 281:12
money and you takes your c. | PUNCH 256:6
**choices**: all the c. gone before | DID 120:21
**choir**: c. of saints for evermore | DONNE 123:16
c. the small gnats mourn | KEATS 192:16
may I join the c. invisible | ELIOT 132:17
virgin-c. to make delicious moan | KEATS 192:8
**choirs**: Bare ruined c. | SHAK 299:24
demented c. of wailing shells | OWEN 243:22
in C. and Places where they sing | BOOK 64:7
**choking**: c. him and making him carry me | TOLS 333:13
**choleric**: captain's but a c. | SHAK 288:15
**choose**: *believe what we c.* | NEWM 239:1
C. an author as you choose | DILL 120:22
c. perfection of the life | YEATS 358:19

**choose** (*cont.*):

| | |
|---|---|
| not c. not to be | HOPK 171:25 |
| To govern is to c. | LÉVIS 206:10 |
| woman can hardly ever c. | ELIOT 132:5 |
| **choosers**: buggers can't be c. | BOWRA 71:4 |
| **chopcherry**: c., c. ripe within | PEELE 247:2 |
| **Chopin**: I like C. and Bizet | FISH 139:26 |
| **chopper**: c. on a big black block | GILB 151:25 |
| **chord**: feel for the common c. | BROW 75:9 |
| I struck one c. of music | PROC 255:14 |
| **chorus**: c.-ending from Euripides | BROW 75:13 |
| **chosen**: but few are c. | BIBLE 50:28 |
| ye are a c. generation | BIBLE 57:8 |
| **Christ**: *And C. receive thy saule* | BALL 27:20 |
| C. erecteth his Church | BANC 28:14 |
| C. follows Dionysus | POUND 254:17 |
| C. is the path and Christ | MONS 233:7 |
| C. perish in torment | SHAW 302:21 |
| C. risen from the dead | BIBLE 55:17 |
| C.'s particular love's | BROW 77:7 |
| C. walking on the water | THOM 331:17 |
| C. was betrayed | Æ 3:4 |
| churches have killed their C. | TENN 327:4 |
| If Jesus C. were to come | CARL 90:26 |
| in C. shall all be made alive | BIBLE 55:17 |
| Jesus C. the same yesterday | BIBLE 56:30 |
| Ring in the C. | TENN 325:27 |
| shuts the spouse C. home | HOPK 172:17 |
| through C. which strengtheneth | BIBLE 56:10 |
| Vision of C. | BLAKE 60:11 |
| was made a member of C. | BOOK 65:20 |

**Christ-Church**: line of festal light in C. | ARN 17:9
**Christe**: *C. eleison* | MISS 231:12
**Christian**: C. boys | ARN 18:15
C. ideal has not been tried | CHES 98:15
C. is a man who feels | YBAR 358:11
C. kisses on an 'eathen | KIPL 196:22
Onward, C. soldiers | BAR 29:1
persuadest me to be a C. | BIBLE 54:27
Scratch the C. and you | ZANG 360:26
tiger that hadn't *got* a C. | PUNCH 256:14
**Christianity**: C. is part of the laws | HALE 160:5
C., of course, but why journalism | BALF 27:11
C. was the religion | SWIFT 320:9
His C. was muscular | DISR 121:29
local thing called C. | HARDY 161:19
loving C. better than Truth | COL 104:23
rock 'n' roll or C. | LENN 205:8
**Christians**: C., awake! | BYROM 84:3
C. have burnt each other | BYRON 85:25
forty generations of C. | MAC 213:18
**Christmas**: C. Day in the Workhouse | SIMS 307:14
C. I no more desire a rose | SHAK 284:11
C.-morning bells | BETJ 36:17
C. should fall out in the | ADD 2:23
I'm dreaming of a white C. | BERL 36:3
Twas the night before C. | MOORE 234:3
**Christopher Robin**: C. is saying his prayers | MILNE 226:1
C. went down with Alice | MILNE 225:19
**Christ's College**: called him *the lady of* C. | AUBR 19:20
**chronicle**: and c. small beer | SHAK 292:4
When in time of wasted time | SHAK 300:4
**chronicles**: brief c. of the time | SHAK 275:19
**chumps**: C. make the best husbands | WOD 352:11
**church**: aristocracy, and an alien C. | DISR 121:7
As some to c. repair | POPE 252:3
Broad of C. and 'broad of mind' | BETJ 37:15
Catholick and Apostolick C. | BOOK 65:6
Christ erecteth his C. | BANC 28:14
C. is an anvil | MACL 215:6
C. militant here in earth | BOOK 65:7
C. [of E.] Conservative Party at prayer | ROYD 264:2
C.'s one foundation | STONE 317:27
C.'s Restoration | BETJ 37:3

**church** (cont.):

| | |
|---|---|
| c. without pulling off his hat | JOHN 184:8 |
| fain would kill their c. | TENN 327:4 |
| figure in a country c. | SWIFT 320:3 |
| free c. in a free state | CAV 93:14 |
| if undressed at C. | FARQ 138:21 |
| I like a c.; I like a cowl | EMER 136:14 |
| mere c. furniture at best | COWP 110:15 |
| nearer the C. the further from God | ANDR 5:16 |
| nor so wide as a c. door | SHAK 295:7 |
| not the c. for his mother | CYPR 113:12 |
| salvation outside the c. | AUG 21:26 |
| She came to the village c. | TENN 326:24 |
| Stands the C. clock at | BROO 73:8 |
| there must be the C. | AMBR 4:19 |
| understands [the C. of Rome] | MAC 213:16 |
| upon this rock I will build my c. | BIBLE 50:13 |
| where God built a c. | LUTH 212:9 |
| wheresoever God buildeth a c. | BECON 31:17 |
| **churches:** chapels had been c. | SHAK 288:29 |
| **Churchill:** [C.] mobilized the language | MURR 236:13 |
| voice was that of C. | ATTL 19:12 |
| **churchyards:** Troop home to c. | SHAK 290:34 |
| **cigar:** really good 5-cent c. | MARS 220:3 |
| sweet post-prandial c. | BUCH 77:29 |
| **cigarette:** c. that bears a lipstick's traces | MARV 221:4 |
| **cigars:** Call the roller of big c. | STEV 316:5 |
| **Cinara:** when good C. was my queen | HOR 173:30 |
| **Cincinnatus:** C. of the West | BYRON 87:4 |
| **cinders:** c., ashes, dust | KEATS 191:11 |
| **cinema:** c. is truth 24 times per second | GOD 153:18 |
| **circle:** c. of which the centre | ANON 9:13 |
| Round and round the c. | ELIOT 132:24 |
| Weave a c. round him thrice | COL 104:1 |
| **circumference:** c. is nowhere | ANON 9:13 |
| **circumlocution:** C. Office | DICK 118:29 |
| **circumspectly:** See then that ye walk c. | BIBLE 56:1 |
| **circumspice:** *Si monumentum requiris, c.* | ANON 13:23 |
| **circumstance:** c. of glorious war | SHAK 292:20 |
| **circumstances:** Fearful concatenation of c. | WEBS 344:10 |
| **circus:** no right in the bloody c. | MAXT 222:14 |
| **circuses:** bread and c. | JUV 189:12 |
| **cistern:** Cold the seat and loud the c. | BENN 34:16 |
| **citadels:** circle-c. there | HOPK 172:16 |
| **cities:** c. for our best morality | AUST 22:19 |
| c. of men and manners | TENN 328:21 |
| scabbed here and there by c. | BUNT 78:14 |
| Seven c. warred for Homer | HEYW 168:9 |
| streets of a hundred c. | HOOV 171:18 |
| thou art the flower of c. | ANON 9:2 |
| **citizen:** c., first in war | LEE 204:7 |
| completely a c. of the world | BOSW 70:3 |
| John Gilpin was a c. | COWP 109:23 |
| relation is a zealous c. | BURKE 80:20 |
| To the c. or the police | AUDEN 21:11 |
| **citizens:** Before Man made us c. | LOW 211:6 |
| first and second class c. | WILL 351:9 |
| Soldiers are c. of death | SASS 267:10 |
| **citizenship:** c. in the kingdom of the well | SONT 311:10 |
| **city:** citizen of no mean c. | BIBLE 54:23 |
| c. is not a concrete jungle | MORR 235:12 |
| C. is of Night | THOM 332:1 |
| C. now doth like a garment | WORD 354:15 |
| C. of the Big Shoulders | SAND 266:12 |
| c. that is set on a hill | BIBLE 48:21 |
| c., thus I turn my back | SHAK 273:20 |
| C. with her dreaming spires | ARN 17:17 |
| c. with no more personality | CHAN 94:8 |
| each and every town or c. | HOLM 170:14 |
| fallen, that great c. | BIBLE 57:34 |
| first c. Cain | COWL 109:13 |
| Happy is that c. | ANON 7:16 |
| have we no continuing c. | BIBLE 57:1 |
| Hell is a c. much like London | SHEL 304:13 |

**city** (cont.):

| | |
|---|---|
| I John saw the holy c. | BIBLE 58:4 |
| keep the c. | BOOK 68:30 |
| live in a c. | COLT 105:18 |
| London: a nation, not a c. | DISR 122:5 |
| long in populous c. pent | MILT 229:23 |
| Lord guards the c. | BIBLE 58:13 |
| oppressing c. | BIBLE 47:25 |
| people went up into the c. | BIBLE 40:27 |
| rose-red c. half as old as | BURG 79:17 |
| Sun-girt c., thou hast been | SHEL 304:2 |
| thou c. of God | BOOK 67:24 |
| To the holy c. of Byzantium | YEATS 359:22 |
| Up and down the C. Road | MAND 217:8 |
| venal c. ripe to perish | SALL 266:8 |
| What is the c. but the people | SHAK 273:19 |
| Without a c. wall | ALEX 4:6 |
| Woe to the bloody c. | BIBLE 47:24 |
| **civil:** dire effects from c. discord | ADD 2:19 |
| Here lies a civil servant | SISS 307:15 |
| Too c. by half | SHER 305:31 |
| **civilian:** mushroom rich c. | BYRON 87:13 |
| **civilities:** bandy c. with my Sovereign | JOHN 184:19 |
| **civility:** C. costs nothing and buys | MONT 233:5 |
| I see a wild c. | HERR 167:15 |
| **civilization:** As c. advances, poetry | MAC 213:7 |
| can't say c. don't advance | ROG 262:2 |
| C. advances by extending | WHIT 348:5 |
| C. and profits go hand in hand | COOL 107:18 |
| c. has become a thin crust | ELLIS 136:6 |
| C. has made the peasantry | TROT 334:23 |
| c. with the most difficulty | TOCQ 333:2 |
| farmyard c. of the Fabians | INGE 178:11 |
| For a botched c. | POUND 254:19 |
| great elements of modern c. | CARL 90:9 |
| last product of c. | RUSS 264:22 |
| life-blood of real c. | TREV 334:7 |
| resources of c. against | GLAD 153:17 |
| **civilized:** last thing c. by Man | MER 223:16 |
| **Civil Service:** C. is profoundly deferential | CROS 112:12 |
| **civis:** C. Romanus sum | CIC 100:27 |
| **clair:** *pas c. n'est pas français* | RIV 260:14 |
| **clamavi:** De profundis c. | BIBLE 58:14 |
| **clanging:** C. from the Severn to the Tyne | KIPL 196:3 |
| **clap:** cheaper seats c. | LENN 205:9 |
| c. your hands | BARR 29:14 |
| Don't c. too hard | OSB 242:18 |
| **clapped-out:** c., post-imperial slag-heap | DRAB 126:9 |
| **clapper:** his tongue is the c. | SHAK 291:21 |
| **claret:** C. is the liquor for boys | JOHN 185:22 |
| **Claridges:** bootboy at C. | WOOLF 354:6 |
| **clasps:** c. the crag with crookèd | TENN 323:21 |
| **class:** c. struggle necessarily | MARX 221:12 |
| free passes, c. distinction | BETJ 37:4 |
| history of c. struggles | ENG 221:14 |
| I could have had c. | SCH 267:24 |
| second c. citizens | WILL 351:9 |
| While there is a lower c. | DEBS 115:9 |
| **classes:** c. which need sanctuary | BALD 27:10 |
| masses against the c. | GLAD 153:13 |
| **classic:** C. music is th'kind | HUBB 175:16 |
| **classical:** c. mind at work | PIRS 249:2 |
| C. quotation is the *parole* | JOHN 185:30 |
| tragedy of the c. languages | MADAN 216:12 |
| **classics:** man with a bellyful of the c. | MILL 225:7 |
| **claw:** Nature, red in tooth and c. | TENN 325:12 |
| **clawed:** Hath c. me with his clutch | VAUX 337:15 |
| **claws:** c. that catch | CARR 91:15 |
| Had I been a pair of ragged c. | ELIOT 133:28 |
| **clay:** associate of this c. | HADR 159:14 |
| c. and wattles made | YEATS 359:12 |
| C. lies still, but blood's | HOUS 174:18 |
| informed the tenement of c. | DRYD 127:6 |
| They're only made of c. | GERS 150:7 |
| **clean:** And keep their teeth c. | SHAK 273:16 |

clean (cont.):
c. and comfortable I sit — KEATS 193:13
c. & in-between-the-sheets — MCG 214:21
C-l-e-a-n, c., verb active — DICK 119:13
c. place to die — KAV 190:7
c. the sky — ELIOT 134:8
Make me a c. heart — BOOK 67:10
one more thing to keep c. — FRY 146:30
small and white and c. — MORR 235:16
cleanliness: C. is next to godliness — WESL 346:15
cleanly: thus so c., I myself can free — DRAY 126:16
cleanness: swimmers into c. leaping — BROO 73:9
cleanse: C. me from its guilt and power — TOPL 333:14
clear: c. in his great office — SHAK 285:24
C. the air — ELIOT 134:8
poignancy in all things c. — WILB 349:9
What is not French — RIV 260:14
clearing-house: c. of the world — CHAM 93:22
cleave: c. the general ear — SHAK 275:23
shall c. unto his wife — BIBLE 38:23
cleft: Rock of Ages, c. for me — TOPL 333:14
Clementine: And his daughter, C. — MONT 234:2
Cleopatra: squeaking C. boy my greatness — SHAK 272:5
clercs: La trahison des c. — BENDA 34:7
clergy: c. is a dropping-down-deadness — SMITH 309:24
c. were beloved — SWIFT 320:9
clergymen: men, women, and c. — SMITH 310:4
cleric: C. before, and Lay behind — BUTL 84:1
clerk: C. there was of Oxenford — CHAU 95:17
'twixt the Priest and C. — HERR 167:18
clerks: c. been noght wisest men — CHAU 96:2
government of statesmen or of c. — DISR 121:24
clever: c. so rude to the good — WORD 354:11
c. theft was praiseworthy — SPEN 312:20
It's c., but is it Art? — KIPL 196:8
let who will be c. — KING 195:13
manage a c. man — KIPL 197:28
Too c. by half — SAL 266:7
cliché: c. and an indiscretion — MACM 215:14
cliffs: chalk c. of Dover — BALD 27:6
c. I never more must see — MAC 214:1
c. of fall frightful — HOPK 172:10
white c. of Dover — BURT 83:3
climate: in love with a cold c. — SOUT 312:6
Our chilling c. hardly bears — SWIFT 320:19
Our cloudy c., and our chilly women — BYRON 84:29
whole c. of opinion — AUDEN 20:20
climb: fails thee, c. not at all — ELIZ 135:9
Fain would I c., yet fear — RAL 257:24
climbing: c. clear up to the sky — HAMM 161:2
c., shakes his dewy wings — D'AV 114:10
Of c. heaven, and gazing — SHEL 305:14
climes: cloudless c. and starry skies — BYRON 87:6
cling: c. to the old rugged cross — BENN 34:10
Clive: What I like about C. — BENT 35:6
cloak: with the knyf under the c. — CHAU 95:27
clock: Ah! the c. is always slow — SERV 270:10
Church c. at ten to three — BROO 73:8
c. will strike, the devil will come — MARL 218:13
Court the slow c., and dine — POPE 251:25
forgot to wind up the c. — STER 315:13
clocks: c. were striking thirteen — ORW 242:5
clockwork: c. orange — BURG 79:13
clod: kneaded c. — SHAK 288:21
clods: Only a man harrowing c. — HARDY 162:11
Cloe: Such C. is — GRAN 156:10
cloisters: quiet collegiate c. — CLOU 102:9
close: c. ebbs out life's latest day — LYTE 212:20
C. encounters of the third kind — SPIE 313:21
c. the wall up with our — SHAK 279:5
c. your eyes before you see — AYCK 23:14
Doth c. behind him tread — COL 104:15
fatter man trying to c. in — AMIS 5:4
peacefully towards its c. — DAWS 115:5
She'll c. and be herself — SHAK 287:3

closed: We never c. — VAN D 336:25
closer: Oh! for a c. walk with God — COWP 109:27
sticketh c. than a brother — BIBLE 43:30
closes: Blown fields or flowerful c. — SWIN 321:17
Satire is what c. Saturday night — KAUF 190:3
closet: one by one back in the c. — FITZ 140:12
They put me in the c. — DICK 120:15
closing: c. time in the gardens — CONN 106:27
cloth: On a c. untrue — GILB 152:2
clothed: c., fed and educated — RUSK 264:19
C. in white samite — TENN 324:3
woman c. with the sun — BIBLE 57:30
clothes: been poured into his c. — WOD 352:24
brushers of noblemen's c. — WOTT 357:20
c. that I have ever seen — LOES 209:6
Kindles in c. a wantonness — HERR 167:15
She wears her c., as if — SWIFT 320:7
That liquefaction of her c. — HERR 167:26
walked away with their c. — DISR 121:9
who wore torn c. — SPEN 312:25
clothing: become mine inner c. — LITT 208:2
sheep in sheep's c. — CHUR 100:7
sheep in sheep's c. — GOSSE 155:25
Things in books' c. — LAMB 200:4
cloud: c.-continents of sunset-seas — ALDR 3:17
c. in trousers — MAY 222:15
c. of unknowing — ANON 6:16
c. which had outwept — SHEL 303:6
day in a pillar of a c. — BIBLE 39:39
Don't you each c. — BURKE 81:14
do set my bow in the c. — BIBLE 39:10
Get off of my c. — JAGG 179:4
great a c. of witnesses — BIBLE 56:27
I wandered lonely as a c. — WORD 355:4
Like a fiend hid in a c. — BLAKE 62:3
little c. out of the sea — BIBLE 42:2
On a c. I saw a child — BLAKE 61:18
Turn the dark c. inside out — FORD 143:12
When the c. is scattered — SHEL 303:24
cloudcuckooland: How about 'C.' — ARIS 15:9
clouded: Shine forth upon our c. hills — BLAKE 61:12
clouds: comes with c. descending — WESL 346:9
Never doubted c. would break — BROW 75:11
O c., unfold — BLAKE 61:12
through the c. I'll never float — WORD 356:3
trailing c. of glory — WORD 355:20
clouts: stones and c. make martyrs — BROW 74:4
cloven: out pops the c. hoof — WOD 352:15
cloverleaf: flower is the concrete c. — MUMF 236:8
clownage: conceits as c. keeps in pay — MARL 219:4
clowns: Send in the C. — SOND 311:7
club: savage wields his c. — HUXL 177:16
DON'T WANT TO BELONG TO ANY C. — MARX 221:5
clucked: Has c. thee to the wars — SHAK 273:22
clue: almost invariably a c. — DOYLE 125:14
Clunton: C. and Clunbury — HOUS 175:1
clusters: luscious c. of the vine — MARV 220:15
clutch: clawed me with his c. — VAUX 337:15
Inapprehensible, we c. thee — THOM 331:14
clutching: alien people c. their gods — ELIOT 133:23
Still c. the inviolable shade — ARN 17:12
coach: c. and six horses through the Act — RICE 259:19
her silver c. to climb — SPEN 313:5
rattling of a c. — DONNE 124:21
coach and six: indifference and a c. — GARR 105:12
coal: c. and surrounded by fish — BEVAN 37:17
made of Newcastle c. — WALP 341:20
Strong is the lion—like a c. — SMART 308:10
With a cargo of Tyne c. — MAS 221:19
coalitions: England does not love c. — DISR 121:13
coals: And all eyes else dead c. — SHAK 299:3
c. of fire upon his head — BIBLE 43:36
I sleep on the c. — DICK 118:10
No more c. to Newcastle — GEOR 149:26

coarse: And one of them is rather c.                ROYD 264:3
coarseness: c., revealing something                 FORS 143:23
coast: On the c. of Coromandel                      LEAR 203:7
  On the c. of Coromandel                           SITW 308:1
coaster: Dirty British c.                           MAS 221:19
coat: c. of many colours                            BIBLE 39:24
  eternal Footman hold my c.                        ELIOT 133:29
  Grab your c., and get your hat                    FIEL 139:15
  John Peel with his c. so grey                     GRAV 156:12
  riband to stick in his c.                         BROW 76:13
  tattered c. upon a stick                          YEATS 359:21
  that loves a scarlet c.                           HOOD 171:6
coats: In c. of red                                 DE L 116:17
cobble-stones: On c. I lay                          FLAN 141:2
cobweb: Learning, that c. of the brain              BUTL 84:2
cobwebs: Laws are like c.                           SWIFT 319:19
Coca-Cola: wherever blue jeans and C.               GREER 158:10
cock: before the c. crow                            BIBLE 51:10
  C. and a Bull                                     STER 315:26
  Nationalism is a silly c.                         ALD 3:15
  Our c. won't fight                                BEAV 31:6
  owe a c. to Aesculapius                           SOCR 310:25
cockatoo: green freedom of a c.                     STEV 316:12
cockatrice: hand on the c.' den                     BIBLE 45:20
cockle: By his c. hat and staff                     SHAK 276:32
cockpit: Can this c. hold                           SHAK 278:34
cocks: drowned the c.                               SHAK 283:6
cocktail: weasel under the c. cabinet               PINT 248:22
cod: bean and the c.                                BOSS 70:1
  O bely! O stynkyng c.                             CHAU 95:30
code: trail has its own stern c.                    SERV 270:9
coeur: Il pleure dans mon c.                        VERL 338:2
coffee: C. (which makes the politician wise)        POPE 253:9
  C. and oranges in a sunny                         STEV 316:12
  if this is c., I want tea                         PUNCH 256:20
  measured out my life with c. spoons               ELIOT 133:27
  slavery of the tea and c.                         COBB 102:25
coffin: grave in a Y-shaped c.                      ORTON 241:21
  like a c. clapt in a canoe                        BYRON 84:26
  Like the silver plate on a c.                     CURR 113:9
cogito: C., ergo sum                                DESC 117:9
cognoscere: qui potuit rerum c. causas              VIRG 340:8
cohorts: c. were gleaming in purple                 BYRON 85:22
coin: The C., Tiberius                              DOBS 122:25
coition: trivial and vulgar way of c.               BROW 74:18
coitum: Post c. omne animal triste                  ANON 13:19
cold: Aching, shaking, crazy, c.                    ROCH 261:9
  blow in c. blood                                  SHAW 301:32
  Cast a c. eye on life                             YEATS 360:8
  C. as paddocks                                    HERR 167:11
  c. charities of man to man                        CRAB 110:30
  c. coming they had                                ANDR 5:15
  c. coming we had of it                            ELIOT 133:21
  c. hearts and muddy understandings                BURKE 80:15
  c. metal of economic theory                       SCH 267:26
  C. Pastoral                                       KEATS 191:23
  c. relation is a zealous citizen                  BURKE 80:20
  C. the seat and loud the cistern                  BENN 34:16
  everlasting c.                                     WEBS 344:28
  I beg c. comfort                                  SHAK 282:14
  ink in my pen ran c.                              WALP 341:17
  in love with a c. climate                         SOUT 312:6
  midst of a c. war                                 BAR 29:20
  Poor Tom's a-c.                                   SHAK 283:17
  spy who came in from the c.                       LE C 204:2
  straight past the common c.                       AYRES 23:15
  'tis bitter c.                                    SHAK 273:30
  To lie in c. obstruction                          SHAK 288:21
coldly: C., sadly descends                          ARN 17:3
coldness: faithless c. of the times                 TENN 325:24
Coliseum: While stands the C.                       BYRON 85:11
collapse: C. of Stout Party                         ANON 6:17
collateral: c. security                             CHES 97:14
collections: those mutilators of c.                 LAMB 200:2

collects: c. which had soothed                      MAC 213:18
college: cabbage with a c. education                TWAIN 336:4
  Die, and endow a c., or a cat                     POPE 251:13
collegiate: faces in quiet c. cloisters             CLOU 102:9
colonel: C.'s Lady an' Judy O'Grady                 KIPL 196:19
colonnade: whispering sound of the cool c.
                                                    COWP 109:30
Colonus: Singer of sweet C.                         ARN 17:20
Colossus: Like a C.                                 SHAK 280:27
colour: And Life is C. and Warmth                   GREN 158:16
  Any c.—so long as it's black                      FORD 143:7
  giveth his c. in the cup                          BIBLE 43:33
  horse of that c.                                  SHAK 297:27
  I know the c. rose                                ABSE 1:1
  prison for the c. of his hair                     HOUS 174:6
  coloured: no 'c.' signs on the foxholes           KENN 194:7
colourless: C. green ideas                          CHOM 98:18
colours: All c. will agree in the dark              BACON 25:19
  Their c. and their forms                          WORD 355:9
  your c. dont quite match                          ASHF 18:21
comb: two bald men over a c.                        BORG 69:24
combination: You may call it c.                     PALM 244:19
combine: When bad men c.                            BURKE 81:4
come: And cannot c. again                           HOUS 174:24
  believe in the life to c.                         BECK 31:9
  C., and he cometh                                 BIBLE 49:17
  C. away, come away, death                         SHAK 297:32
  C., dear children, let us away                    ARN 16:16
  C. down, O Love divine                            LITT 208:2
  C., friendly bombs                                BETJ 37:9
  C. hither, come hither                            SHAK 272:19
  C., Holy Spirit                                   LANG 201:10
  C. in the speaking silence                        ROSS 263:1
  C. into the garden, Maud                          TENN 326:28
  C., let us join our cheerful songs                WATTS 343:3
  C., lovely Morning                                DAV 114:21
  C., my Celia, let us prove                        JONS 187:16
  c. out, thou bloody man                           BIBLE 41:25
  C. over into Macedonia                            BIBLE 54:16
  c. to the end of a perfect day                    BOND 63:9
  C. unto me, all ye                                BIBLE 49:35
  C. unto these yellow sands                        SHAK 295:36
  c. when you do call                               SHAK 278:3
  C. you back to Mandalay                           KIPL 196:21
  Even so, c., Lord Jesus                           BIBLE 58:8
  had better not c. at all                          KEATS 193:4
  if it be now, 'tis not to come                    SHAK 298:3
  leave to c. unto my love                          SPEN 313:6
  let him c. out as I do                            JOHN 186:1
  men may c. and men may go                         TENN 323:13
  O c., all ye faithful                             ANON 13:9
  O c. to my heart, Lord Jesus                      ELL 136:1
  Of things to c. at large                          SHAK 296:32
  or c. without warning                             DAVIS 115:1
  Out of Ireland have we c.                         YEATS 359:19
  Softly c. and softly go                           ORRED 241:18
  Suffer me to c. to thee                           WESL 346:6
  therefore I cannot c.                             BIBLE 52:23
  war and nobody will c.                            SAND 266:16
  What's to c. is still unsure                      SHAK 297:23
  what's to c. is strewed                           SHAK 297:10
  where do they all c. from                         MCC 205:12
  whistle, an' I'll come to you                     BURNS 82:19
  Why don't you c. up and see me                    WEST 346:24
  world's at an end, and we c.                      D'AV 114:9
comedies: All c. ended by a marriage                BYRON 86:12
comedy: All I need to make a c.                     CHAP 94:12
  C. is an imitation                                SIDN 306:28
  c. to those that think                            WALP 341:23
comely: I am black, but c.                          BIBLE 44:29
comes: Nothing happens, nobody c.                   BECK 31:12
cometh: c. in the Name of the Lord                  BOOK 68:23
  Him that c. to me                                 BIBLE 53:23
  no man c. unto the Father                         BIBLE 53:38

concealing: hazard of c.     BURNS 82:5
concealment: c., like a worm i' the bud     SHAK 298:1
conceit: wise in his own c.     BIBLE 43:38
conceited: any good who is not c.     TROL 334:17
conceits: Be not wise in your own c.     BIBLE 54:44
  current and accepted for c.     BACON 23:23
conceive: virgin shall c.     BIBLE 45:14
concentrates: c. his mind wonderfully     JOHN 185:14
conception: dad is present at the c.     ORTON 241:20
concerned: nobody left to be c.     NIEM 239:15
concessions: c. of the weak     BURKE 79:27
concluded: Rome has spoken; the case is c.     AUG 22:5
conclusions: pursued c. infinite     SHAK 272:11
concord: lover of c.     BOOK 64:5
  oft in pleasing c. end     MILT 230:15
  travelled a good deal in C.     THOR 332:7
  truth, unity, and c.     BOOK 65:9
  with c. of sweet sounds     SHAK 290:3
concordia: C. discors     HOR 173:12
concrete: city is not a c. jungle     MORR 235:12
  flower is the c. cloverleaf     MUMF 236:8
concupiscent: c. curds     STEV 316:5
concurrence: sweet c. of the heart     HERR 167:17
condemn: does some delights c.     MOL 232:23
  needs to c. a little more     MAJOR 216:19
  Neither do I c. thee     BIBLE 53:27
condemned: c. to have an itching palm     SHAK 281:29
  I am c. to be free     SART 267:2
condition: O wearisome c. of humanity     GREV 158:19
conditions: all sorts and c. of men     BOOK 64:18
conduct: C. is three-fourths     ARN 18:9
  c. of a losing party     BURKE 79:18
  C. to the prejudice     ANON 6:22
  c. unbecoming     ANON 6:2
cone: despot is an inverted c.     JOHN 185:17
cones: c. under his pines     FROST 146:16
confabulate: If birds c. or no     COWP 109:29
confederate: in games C.     WORD 355:2
conference: c. a ready man     BACON 25:15
  hold some two days' c.     WEBS 344:16
  naked into the c. chamber     BEVAN 38:1
confident: Never glad c. morning     BROW 76:15
confine: verge of her c.     SHAK 283:3
conflict: field of human c.     CHUR 99:15
  We are in an armed c.     EDEN 130:14
confound: C. their politics     ANON 7:14
confounded: Confusion worse c.     MILT 229:1
  let me never be c.     BOOK 63:22
confounding: C. her astronomers     HODG 169:14
confused: c. doesn't really understand     MURR 236:14
confusion: bright things come to c.     SHAK 290:15
  C. now hath made his masterpiece     SHAK 286:23
  C. on thy banners wait     GRAY 157:1
  C. worse confounded     MILT 229:1
congeals: When love c.     HART 163:8
congratulatory: series of c. regrets     DISR 121:19
congregation: largest c.     DEFOE 115:22
congress: C. makes no progress     LIGNE 207:2
conjecture: entertain c. of a time     SHAK 279:7
conjunction: c. of the mind     MARV 220:13
conjuring: c. trick with bones     JENK 181:4
connect: Only c.     FORS 143:21
conquer: die here, and we will c.     BEE 31:22
  easier to c. it than to know     WALP 341:21
  hard to catch and c.     MER 223:20
  In this sign shalt thou c.     CONS 107:14
conquered: c. and peopled     SEEL 269:15
  I came, I saw, I c.     CAES 88:2
  perpetually to be c.     BURKE 80:1
  Thou hast c., O pale Galilean     SWIN 321:13
conquering: C. kings their titles     CHAN 94:6
  See, the c. hero comes     MOR 235:5
conqueror: proud foot of a c.     SHAK 282:15
  you are a c.     ROST 263:12

conquest: C.'s crimson wing     GRAY 157:1
conscience: catch the c. of the king     SHAK 275:24
  C. avaunt, Richard's himself     CIBB 100:17
  c. doth make cowards     SHAK 275:26
  C. first, the Pope afterwards     NEWM 238:18
  C. is thoroughly well-bred     BUTL 84:20
  C.: the inner voice     MENC 223:8
  corporation to have a c.     THUR 332:19
  good c. on the proceeds     SMITH 309:14
  happiness or a quiet c.     BERL 36:6
  however strict their social c.     SMITH 309:15
  value it next to a good c.     WALT 342:14
  will not cut my c.     HELL 165:7
conscious: c. stone to beauty grew     EMER 136:15
consciousness: beginning of c.     WOOLF 353:22
  C. is the phenomenon     PENR 247:11
consecration: c., and the Poet's dream     WORD 354:17
consent: inferior without your c.     ROOS 262:6
  like enough to c.     SHAK 273:8
  Rome is the c. of heaven     JONS 187:1
  whispering 'I will ne'er c.'     BYRON 86:1
consented: ne'er consent'—c.     BYRON 86:1
consequence: If it's business of c.     BARH 28:22
  trammel up the c.     SHAK 285:22
consequences: damn the c.     MILN 226:2
  nor punishments—there are c.     ING 178:16
conservatism: barren thing this C.     DISR 121:27
conservative: C. Government is     DISR 121:11
  C., n. A statesman     BIER 59:5
  C. Party at prayer     ROYD 264:2
  most c. man in this world     BEVIN 38:8
  Or else a little C.     GILB 151:12
  revolutionary will become a c.     AREN 15:5
  sound C. government     DISR 121:26
  which makes a man more c.     KEYN 194:15
  would make me c. when old     FROST 146:18
consider: c. her ways     BIBLE 43:11
  c. how my light is spent     MILT 230:22
  C. the lilies of the field     BIBLE 49:4
  For I will c. my Cat Jeoffry     SMART 308:7
consideration: C. like an angel     SHAK 278:35
consistency: C. is contrary to nature     HUXL 177:6
  c. is the hobgoblin of little minds     EMER 136:24
consistent: c. people are the dead     HUXL 177:6
consoles: Anything that c. is fake     MURD 236:11
conspicuous: C. consumption     VEBL 337:16
  Vega c. overhead     AUDEN 21:7
conspiracies: c. against the laity     SHAW 301:3
conspiracy: America is a vast c.     UPD 336:14
  c. against the public     SMITH 308:21
  Indecency's c. of silence     SHAW 302:3
conspiring: C. with him how to     KEATS 192:14
constabulary: c. duty's to be done     GILB 152:24
constancy: is but c. in a good     BROW 74:15
  Tell me no more of c.     ROCH 261:2
constant: But c., he were perfect     SHAK 298:20
  c. as the northern star     SHAK 281:9
  C., in Nature were inconstancy     COWL 109:15
  Friendship is c. in all     SHAK 291:17
  One here will c. be     BUNY 79:9
constitution: c. does not provide     WILL 351:9
  country has its own c.     ANON 6:30
  I invoke the genius of the C.     PITT 249:5
constitutional: no eyes but c. eyes     LINC 207:14
construction: mind's c. in the face     SHAK 285:14
consul: born when I was c.     CIC 101:2
consulted: right to be c.     BAG 26:14
consume: more history than they can c.     SAKI 265:17
consumer: c. isn't a moron     OGIL 241:2
  c. is the king     SAM 266:11
  In a c. society     ILL 178:9
consummation: c. devoutly to be wished     SHAK 275:25
  Quiet c. have     SHAK 273:28
consummatum: C. est     BIBLE 58:21

| | |
|---|---|
| consumption: Conspicuous c. | VEBL 337:16 |
| C. is the sole end and purpose | SMITH 308:24 |
| c. of the purse | SHAK 278:19 |
| contact: Fly hence, our c. fear | ARN 17:11 |
| contagion: of the world's slow stain | SHEL 303:11 |
| vile c. of the night | SHAK 281:6 |
| contemplates: thing it c. | SHEL 304:25 |
| contemplation: Beneath thy c. | NEALE 237:22 |
| by action, not by c. | BRON 72:9 |
| Has left for c. not what | BETJ 37:3 |
| mind serene for c. | GAY 149:13 |
| contempt: Familiarity breeds c. | TWAIN 336:3 |
| In the c. and anger of his lip | SHAK 298:6 |
| pour c. on all my pride | WATTS 343:4 |
| religion when in rags and c. | BUNY 79:2 |
| tail that wagged c. at Fate | WATS 343:1 |
| contemptible: c. little army | ANON 7:4 |
| contender: could have been a c. | SCH 267:24 |
| contending: fierce c. nations | ADD 2:19 |
| content: land of lost c. | HOUS 174:24 |
| Spontaneous joy and natural c. | YEATS 359:4 |
| contented: most enjoy c. least | SHAK 299:14 |
| contention: Let the long c. cease | ARN 16:18 |
| contentment: Preaches c. to that toad | KIPL 196:26 |
| contest: not the victory but the c. | COUB 108:15 |
| continency: chastity and c. | AUG 21:22 |
| continent: C. people have good food | MIKES 224:10 |
| C. will [not] suffer England | DISR 121:6 |
| Thou knowest of no strange c. | DAV 114:22 |
| continental: C. people have sex life | MIKES 224:11 |
| kiss on the hand may be quite c. | ROBIN 260:18 |
| continual: c. dew of thy blessing | BOOK 64:9 |
| continually: I think c. of those | SPEN 312:24 |
| continuance: Patient c. in well doing | BIBLE 54:28 |
| continuation: c. of politics by other | CLAU 101:16 |
| continuing: no c. city | BIBLE 57:1 |
| contract: C. into a span | HERB 167:5 |
| nature is tugging at every c. | EMER 136:18 |
| Society is indeed a c. | BURKE 80:17 |
| Social C. a vast conspiracy | WELLS 345:20 |
| verbal c. isn't worth the paper | GOLD 155:17 |
| contradict: Do I c. myself | WHIT 348:21 |
| Never c. Never explain | FISH 139:24 |
| truth which you cannot c. | SOCR 310:24 |
| contradiction: c. in terms | SIMP 307:12 |
| they brook no c. | WEBS 344:20 |
| Woman's at best a c. still | POPE 251:12 |
| contradictions: one chain of c. | CLARE 101:4 |
| paradox, a bundle of c. | COLT 106:1 |
| contrary: everythink goes c. | DICK 118:8 |
| trial is by what is c. | MILT 230:31 |
| control: his c. stops | BYRON 85:13 |
| wrong members in c. | ORW 242:3 |
| controls: Who c. the past c. the future | ORW 242:8 |
| convenient: c. that there be gods | OVID 243:11 |
| convent: C. of the Sacred Heart | ELIOT 134:17 |
| conventional: merely c. signs | CARR 92:7 |
| conversation: C. is imperative if | WHITE 347:17 |
| c. without one single pause | PLOM 250:1 |
| different name for c. | STER 315:17 |
| half-gathered, c.-scraps | CRAB 110:19 |
| make his c. perfectly delightful | SMITH 310:6 |
| subject of c. in mixed company | CHES 97:3 |
| those soft parts of c. | SHAK 292:15 |
| conversations: without pictures or c. | CARR 91:1 |
| converse: c. with the mighty dead | THOM 331:27 |
| conversion: Till the c. of the Jews | MARV 220:23 |
| convert: oh, who shall c. me | WESL 346:12 |
| converted: Except ye be c. | BIBLE 50:15 |
| You have not c. a man | MORL 235:9 |
| conviction: best lack all c. | YEATS 359:24 |
| convince: To teach, c., subdue | AUBER 19:15 |
| we c. ourselves | JUN 188:26 |
| convinces: man who c. the world | DARW 114:7 |

| | |
|---|---|
| convincing: two excuses always less c. | HUXL 177:9 |
| Oh! too c.—dangerously dear | BYRON 85:17 |
| convoy: crowns for c. | SHAK 279:18 |
| cook: C. is a little unnerved | BETJ 37:2 |
| cookery: Kissing don't last: c. do | MER 223:17 |
| cooks: as good c. go, she went | SAKI 265:18 |
| Devil sends c. | GARR 148:11 |
| entrusted to 'plain' c. | MORP 235:10 |
| cool: c. gales shall fan | POPE 253:1 |
| c. web of language | GRAV 156:14 |
| garden in the c. of the day | BIBLE 38:26 |
| sound of the c. colonnade | COWP 109:30 |
| cooled: C. a long age | KEATS 191:29 |
| Coolidge: admiration for Mr C. | ANON 11:4 |
| cooling: for c. the blood | FLAN 141:4 |
| coot: haunts of c. and hern | TENN 323:12 |
| copier: c. of nature can never | REYN 259:9 |
| copies: few originals and many c. | TOCQ 333:1 |
| coppers: like the old time 'c.' | COLL 105:7 |
| copulating: skeletons c. | BEEC 32:1 |
| copulation: Birth, and c., and death | ELIOT 134:14 |
| Let c. thrive | SHAK 283:23 |
| cor: J'aime le son du c. | VIGNY 338:17 |
| coral: C. is far more red | SHAK 300:11 |
| From India's c. strand | HEBER 164:15 |
| Of his bones are c. made | SHAK 296:1 |
| cord: silver c. be loosed | BIBLE 44:26 |
| threefold c. | BIBLE 44:14 |
| triple c. | BURKE 79:21 |
| corkscrews: as crooked as c. | AUDEN 20:15 |
| cormorant: common c. or shag | ISH 178:21 |
| C. devouring Time | SHAK 284:9 |
| corn: amid the alien c. | KEATS 192:5 |
| breast high amid the c. | HOOD 171:11 |
| c. is as high as an elephant's eye | HAMM 161:2 |
| c. was orient | TRAH 333:18 |
| could make two ears of c. grow | SWIFT 319:21 |
| stop raising c. | LEASE 203:20 |
| threshed c. at midnight | YEATS 359:27 |
| Corneille: C. is to Shakespeare | JOHN 186:12 |
| corner: At every c. I meet my father | LOW 211:15 |
| c. in the thing I love | SHAK 292:17 |
| head-stone in the c. | BOOK 68:22 |
| in a c., some untidy spot | AUDEN 21:2 |
| lew c. of airth to lie in | PHIL 248:17 |
| Sits the wind in that c. | SHAK 291:20 |
| some c. of a foreign field | BROO 73:10 |
| corners: c. of the world in arms | SHAK 282:15 |
| round earth's imagined c. | DONNE 123:7 |
| Unregarded age in c. thrown | SHAK 272:15 |
| Cornish: twenty thousand C. men | HAWK 163:17 |
| corns: shower your shooting c. | SWIFT 320:14 |
| corny: c. as Kansas in August | HAMM 161:4 |
| Coromandel: On the coast of C. | LEAR 203:7 |
| coronets: Kind hearts are more than c. | TENN 325:33 |
| corporation: c. to have a conscience | THUR 332:19 |
| corporations: [c.] cannot commit treason | COKE 103:9 |
| corpse: carry one's father's c. | APOL 14:13 |
| c. in the case | BARH 28:21 |
| good wishes to the c. | BARR 29:15 |
| He'd make a lovely c. | DICK 119:5 |
| corpus: Ave verum c. | ANON 13:14 |
| correct: All present and c. | ANON 5:21 |
| than be c. with those men | CIC 101:1 |
| correcteth: whom the Lord loveth he c. | BIBLE 43:7 |
| correctly: problems c. presented | CHEK 97:1 |
| correlative: objective c. | ELIOT 135:1 |
| correspondent: like a special c. | BAG 26:16 |
| corridors: c. of power | SNOW 310:18 |
| corrugated: copulating on a c. tin roof | BEEC 32:1 |
| corrupt: moth and rust doth c. | BIBLE 49:1 |
| one good custom should c. | TENN 324:20 |
| Unlimited power is apt to c. | PITT 249:4 |
| corrupted: c. by sentiment | GREE 158:4 |

corruptible: magistrate c. — ROB 260:17
corruption: be turned into c. — BOOK 69:15
  C. wins not more than honesty — SHAK 280:20
  Fulfilled of dong and of c. — CHAU 95:30
corrupts: absolute power c. — ACTON 1:5
cors: Les souvenirs sont c. de chasse — APOL 14:11
corse: c. to the rampart we hurried — WOLFE 352:25
Cortez: like stout C. — KEATS 192:11
coruscations: c. of summer lightning — GOUL 155:26
cosmopolitan: C. critics — DISR 121:17
cost: But at what c. — BECK 31:8
  they c. right naught — WYATT 358:3
  Why so large c. — SHAK 300:14
costs: C. merely register — KNIG 198:14
  c. more than it is worth — MAC 213:12
cot: c. with a pot of pink geraniums — MACN 216:2
Cotopaxi: Chimborazo, C. — TURN 335:17
cottage: he before his c. door — SOUT 311:18
  left as a c. in a vineyard — BIBLE 45:3
  Love and a c.! — GARR 105:12
  Wherever there's a c. small — CHAR 245:19
cotton: an' the c. is high — GERS 168:6
couch: flinty and steel c. of war — SHAK 292:1
  For oft, when on my c. I lie — WORD 355:5
  There I c. when owls do cry — SHAK 296:14
cough: all c. in ink — YEATS 359:23
  Keep a c. by them ready made — CHUR 98:22
coughs: C. and sneezes spread — ANON 6:23
counsel: princely c. in his face — MILT 228:27
  sometimes c. take — POPE 253:6
  spirit of c. and might — BIBLE 45:18
counsellor: Wonderful, C. — BIBLE 45:16
counsellors: Kings and c. of the earth — BIBLE 42:26
  speak plain when c. blanch — BACON 24:17
counsels: all good c. — BOOK 64:11
count: the number of the beast — BIBLE 57:33
  I c. it not an inn — BROW 74:20
  I won the c. — SOM 311:4
  Let me c. the ways — BROW 75:5
  let us c. our spoons — JOHN 184:11
  To give and not to c. the cost — IGN 178:8
  when angry, c. four — TWAIN 336:5
counted: c. them all out — HANR 161:8
  faster we c. our spoons — EMER 136:20
countenance: damned disinheriting c. — SHER 306:7
  did the C. Divine — BLAKE 61:12
  Knight of the Doleful C. — CERV 93:18
  Lord lift up his c. — BIBLE 40:15
  maketh a cheerful c. — BIBLE 43:25
  Till grim, grim grew his c. — BALL 27:16
  withal of a beautiful c. — BIBLE 41:16
counter: All things c., original — HOPK 172:13
countercheck: c. quarrelsome — SHAK 273:12
counterfeit: Teach light to c. a gloom — MILT 226:25
counterpane: pleasant land of c. — STEV 317:14
counterpoint: Too much c. — BEEC 32:3
counters: Words are wise men's c. — HOBB 169:6
counties: see the coloured c. — HOUS 174:20
  six c. overhung with smoke — MORR 235:16
counting: democracy, it's the c. — STOP 317:28
countries: all c. before his own — OVER 243:8
country: America is a c. of young men — EMER 137:1
  another c. — MARL 219:2
  Anybody can be good in the c. — WILDE 350:6
  ask not what your c. can do — KENN 194:6
  best c. ever is, at home — GOLD 155:4
  betraying my c. — FORS 144:2
  Britain a fit c. for heroes — LLOY 208:11
  By all their c.'s wishes blest — COLL 105:11
  c. continually under hatches — KEATS 193:6
  country for his c.'s sake — FITZ 140:3
  country for our c.'s good — CART 92:12
  c. governed by a despot — JOHN 185:17
  c. has its own constitution — ANON 6:30

country (cont.):
  c. has the government it deserves — MAIS 216:18
  C. in the town — MART 220:8
  c. of the blind the one-eyed — ERAS 137:14
  c. retreat near the town — WYCH 358:4
  c. which has 246 varieties — DE G 116:7
  Cry, the beloved c. — PATON 246:19
  die but once to serve our c. — ADD 2:16
  died to save their c. — CHES 97:23
  die for one's c. — HOR 173:26
  every c. but his own — GILB 151:20
  fight for its King and C. — GRAH 156:2
  For your King and your C. — RUB 264:4
  friend of every c. but his own — CANN 89:11
  friends of every c. — DISR 121:17
  God made the c., and man — COWP 110:6
  good for our c. good for General — WILS 351:11
  good news from a far c. — BIBLE 43:37
  good to be had in the c. — HAZL 164:3
  great deal of unmapped c. — ELIOT 132:2
  grow up with the c. — GREE 157:20
  how I leave my c. — PITT 249:10
  I love thee still—My c. — COWP 110:8
  Indeed I tremble for my c. — JEFF 180:24
  in the c. places — STEV 317:18
  In this frozen whited c. — HUGH 175:22
  I pray for the c. — HALE 160:4
  Isn't this a billion dollar c. — FOST 144:6
  lie abroad for the good of his c. — WOTT 357:22
  may our c. be always successful — ADAMS 2:5
  My c. is Kiltartan Cross — YEATS 359:9
  My c. is the world — PAINE 244:14
  My c., right or wrong — SCH 268:1
  My c., 'tis of thee — SMITH 309:16
  My soul, there is a c. — VAUG 337:6
  no relish for the c. — SMITH 309:25
  one life to lose for my c. — HALE 160:6
  our c., right or wrong — DEC 115:10
  past is a foreign c. — HART 163:14
  quarrel in a far away c. — CHAM 94:1
  she is my c. still — CHUR 98:21
  sucked on c. pleasures — DONNE 124:5
  That is no c. for old men — YEATS 359:20
  this c. of ours where nobody is well — AUDEN 21:19
  While there's a c. lane — CHAR 245:19
countrymen: friends, Romans, c. — SHAK 281:18
county: c. families baying — WAUGH 343:18
couple: Just like a young c. — PLOM 250:1
couples: c. down the grassgreen — THOM 330:17
courage: Blessings on your young c. — VIRG 339:19
  C. in your own — GORD 155:21
  C. is not simply one of the virtues — LEWIS 206:13
  C., mon ami, le diable — READE 258:10
  c. the greater — ANON 11:5
  c. to suffer — TROL 334:13
  c. you bring to it — WALP 342:4
  piety, c.—they exist — FORS 143:25
  red badge of c. — CRANE 111:3
  screw your c. to the sticking-place — SHAK 286:6
  strong and of a good c. — BIBLE 40:26
  three-o'-clock in the morning c. — THOR 332:10
  two o'clock in the morning c. — NAP 237:4
  unto him with a good c. — BOOK 66:24
courageous: captains c. — BALL 28:1
couriers: Vaunt-c. to oak-cleaving — SHAK 283:6
course: betake myself to that c. — PEPYS 247:22
  c. of true love never did run — SHAK 290:13
  I have finished my c. — BIBLE 56:21
  Of c., of course — JAMES 180:4
court: C. him, elude him — BLUN 62:14
  c. in beauty and decay — SHEL 303:4
  c. is obliged to submit — CHEK 97:1
  Let her alone, she will c. you — JONS 187:22
courtesy: greater man, the greater c. — TENN 324:11
  I am the very pink of c. — SHAK 295:6

courtesy (cont.):
Showed thy dear mother any c.    SHAK 273:22
courtmartialled: c. in my absence    BEHAN 32:18
courts: Approach with joy his c.    KETHE 194:11
C. and camps are the only places    CHES 97:6
Fresh from brawling c.    TENN 325:17
one day in thy c.    BOOK 67:22
still before the c.    HOR 172:25
courtship: C. to marriage    CONG 106:14
cousins: his c. and his aunts    GILB 152:17
covenant: c. with death    BIBLE 45:28
c. with death    GARR 148:13
token of a c.    BIBLE 39:10
covenants: Open c. of peace    WILS 351:22
cover: C. her face    WEBS 344:19
I am the grass; I c. all    SAND 266:14
covered: with twain he c. his face    BIBLE 45:10
covet: c. thy neighbour's house    BIBLE 40:9
Thou shalt not c.; but tradition    CLOU 102:20
covetous: not a brawler, not c.    BIBLE 56:16
cow: c. is of the bovine ilk    NASH 237:10
I never saw a Purple C.    BURG 79:16
isn't grass to graze a c.    BETJ 37:9
Three acres and a c.    ANON 11:6
Truth Sir, is a c.    JOHN 184:12
Two wise acres and a c.    COW 109:12
We milk the c. of the world    WILB 349:10
coward: count myself the c.    TENN 328:11
c. does it with a kiss    WILDE 350:16
c.'s weapon, poison    FLET 142:11
May c. shame distain his name    BURNS 82:15
No c. soul is mine    BRON 72:16
sea hates a c.    O'NEI 241:11
cowards: conscience doth make c.    SHAK 275:26
C. die many times before    SHAK 281:8
C. in scarlet pass    GRAN 156:11
such c. in reasoning    SHAF 270:21
would be c. if they durst    ROCH 261:7
cowl: I like a church; I like a c.    EMER 136:14
cowslip: In a c.'s bell I lie    SHAK 296:14
pearl in every c.'s ear    SHAK 290:20
coy: Then be not c.    HERR 167:25
coyness: c., lady, were no crime    MARV 220:22
crabbed: C. age and youth    SHAK 299:5
Not harsh and c.    MILT 226:15
crack: and c. it too    JONS 186:23
C. and sometimes break    ELIOT 133:1
c. in the tea-cup opens    AUDEN 20:12
c. in your upper storey    SMOL 310:16
heaven's vaults should c.    SHAK 284:4
cracked: bloody noses and c. crowns    SHAK 277:31
crackling: c. of thorns under a pot    BIBLE 44:16
cracks: Now c. a noble heart    SHAK 277:19
cradle: c. and the grave    DYER 129:17
c. endlessly rocking    WHIT 348:12
c. rocks above an abyss    NAB 236:19
from the c. to the grave    CHUR 99:20
from the c. to the grave    SHEL 304:24
hand that rocks the c.    WALL 341:10
Rocked in the c. of the deep    WILL 350:27
craft: c. so long to lerne    CHAU 96:12
crag: c. with crooked hands    TENN 323:21
crags: among these barren c.    TENN 328:19
crammed: C. just as they on earth    WORD 356:4
crane: Tall as a c.    SITW 307:16
cranks: Quips and c.    MILT 227:1
crankum: crinkum c.    AUBR 19:18
crave: still my mind forbids to c.    DYER 129:16
craving: And full as c. too    DRYD 127:25
c. of the rich for titles    PEAR 246:26
cursed c. for gold    VIRG 339:8
Give him, he the more is c.    WROTH 358:1
crazed: c. with the spell    DE L 116:13
crazy: Aching, shaking, c., cold    ROCH 261:9
C. like a fox    PER 247:23

crazy (cont.):
Just two c. people together    HART 163:10
creaks: morning light c. down    SITW 307:16
cream-faced: thou c. loon    SHAK 287:33
created: all men are c. equal    ANON 11:12
c. him in his own image    DOST 125:3
Nothing c. out of nothing    LUCR 212:3
creation: been present at the C.    ALF 4:8
not got your niche in c.    HALL 160:14
Now I hold C. in my foot    HUGH 175:20
pilf'ring from the first c.    LLOYD 208:7
She is his new c.    STONE 317:27
woman is a blind fury of c.    SHAW 301:17
creative: destruction is also a c.    BAK 26:22
creator: C. and Preserver of all    BOOK 64:18
C. made Italy from designs    TWAIN 336:2
Remember now thy C.    BIBLE 44:25
creature: I am a lone lorn c.    DICK 118:8
Let the living c. lie    AUDEN 20:28
Y'are the deed's c.    MIDD 224:7
creatures: All c. great and small    ALEX 4:2
credit: c. in this world much wrong    FITZ 140:17
give thee c. for the rest    CHUR 98:25
In science the c. goes    DARW 114:7
let the c. go    FITZ 140:7
Of c. and renown    COWP 109:23
credite: C. posteri    HOR 173:24
Experto c.    VIRG 339:22
credo: C. in unum Deum    MISS 231:15
C. quia impossibile    TERT 329:9
creed: it is the c. of slaves    PITT 249:7
Pagan suckled in a c. outworn    WORD 357:11
solemn c. with solemn sneer    BYRON 85:6
You mustn't monkey with the C.    BELL 33:15
creeds: dust of c. outworn    SHEL 304:19
half-believers in our casual c.    ARN 17:10
So many gods, so many c.    WILC 349:15
than in half the c.    TENN 325:19
creep: ambition can c.    BURKE 81:8
C. in our ears    SHAK 290:1
C. into thy narrow bed    ARN 16:18
creeps: C. in this petty pace    SHAK 288:5
c. rustling to her knees    KEATS 190:18
crème: c. de la crème    SPARK 312:11
Cressid: Where C. lay that night    SHAK 289:31
crew: We were a ghastly c.    COL 104:14
cribbed: cabined, c., confined    SHAK 287:9
cricket: C.—a game which    MANC 217:7
c. as organized loafing    TEMP 323:8
c. test—which side    TEBB 323:7
playing c. with their peasants    TREV 334:8
Save the c. on the hearth    MILT 226:25
cried: c. the little children died    AUDEN 20:18
from the depths I have c.    BIBLE 58:14
little children c.    MOTL 236:1
when that the poor have c.    SHAK 281:20
crieth: that c. in the wilderness    BIBLE 46:8
crime: catalogue of human c.    CHUR 99:12
commonplace a c.    DOYLE 125:14
coyness, lady, were no c.    MARV 220:22
c. of being a young man    PITT 249:3
c. so shameful as poverty    FARQ 138:15
c.'s so great as daring to excel    CHUR 98:20
c. you haven't committed    POW 255:1
first impulse was never a c.    CORN 108:3
Napoleon of c.    DOYLE 125:20
punishment fit the c.    GILB 152:1
worse than a c., it is a blunder    BOUL 70:9
crimes: C. their own rewards    FARQ 138:17
free of c.    HOR 173:17
liberty! what c. are committed    ROL 262:3
one virtue, and a thousand c.    BYRON 85:19
register of the c.    GIBB 150:11
Successful c. alone    DRYD 128:8
virtues made or c.    DEFOE 115:19

crimes (cont.):
worst of c. is poverty — SHAW 301:8
criminal: for ends I think c. — KEYN 194:13
while there is a c. element — DEBS 115:9
crimson: c. in thy lips — SHAK 295:24
cringe: cultural c. you came from — KEAT 190:8
cripple: comfort's a c. — DRAY 126:15
crisis: C.? What Crisis? — ANON 6:24
Crispian: called the feast of C. — SHAK 279:18
Crispin: C. Crispian shall ne'er — SHAK 279:20
criterion: c. of wisdom to vulgar — BURKE 79:18
critic: c. is a bundle of biases — BALL 28:12
c. is a man who knows — TYNAN 336:8
c. is he who relates — FRAN 145:3
C., you have frowned — WORD 356:21
cry of the c. for five — WHIS 347:10
important book, the c. assumes — WOOLF 354:3
critical: c. period in matrimony — HERB 166:18
criticism: at bottom a c. of life — ARN 18:6
c. of administration — BAG 26:6
father of English c. — JOHN 182:20
wreathed the rod of c. — D'ISR 122:23
criticize: And don't c. — DYLAN 130:9
critics: c. all are ready made — BYRON 86:31
C. are like brushers — WOTT 357:20
Turned c. next, and proved — POPE 251:27
croaks: c. the fatal entrance — SHAK 285:16
crocodile: How doth the little c. — CARR 91:3
Cromwell: Charles the First, his C. — HENRY 166:5
C. guiltless — GRAY 157:9
C., I charge thee — SHAK 280:19
C., our chief of men — MILT 230:26
genius in politics—C. — ARN 18:11
ruin that C. knocked about — SULL 31:21
crook: their President is a c. — NIXON 240:3
crooked: as c. as corkscrews — AUDEN 20:15
c. be made straight — ELIOT 132:24
c. shall be made straight — BIBLE 46:9
C. things may be as stiff — LOCKE 208:17
c. timber of humanity — KANT 189:25
set the c. straight — MORR 235:15
croon: Wanna cry, wanna c. — HARB 161:13
croppy: Hoppy, C., Droppy — ELLIS 136:4
cross: At the c. her station keeping — JAC 179:3
cling to the old rugged c. — BENN 34:10
inability to c. the street — WOOLF 354:5
marble c. below the town — HAYES 163:21
mystery of the c. — FORT 144:5
no c., no crown — PENN 247:9
With the c. of Jesus — BAR 29:1
crossed: oyster may be c. in love — SHER 305:25
When I have c. the bar — TENN 323:19
crosses: Between the c., row on row — MCCR 214:17
cross-gartered: see thee ever c. — SHAK 298:4
crossing: C. the stripling Thames — ARN 17:7
crossness: c. and dirt succeed — FORS 143:18
crow: c.'s feet be growe — CHAU 96:15
crowd: c. flowed over London Bridge — ELIOT 134:21
c. is not company — BACON 24:23
Far from the madding c. — GRAY 157:10
try to c. out real life — FORS 144:1
Will she pass in a c. — SWIFT 320:3
crowds: C. without company — GIBB 150:15
If you can talk with c. — KIPL 197:7
Nor public man, nor angry c. — YEATS 359:10
crown: All thy faithful mercies c. — WESL 346:10
c. Him Lord of all — PERR 248:4
c. imperial — SHAK 279:16
C. is the fountain of honour — BAG 26:4
c. of thorns and the thirty — BEVAN 38:4
c. o' the earth doth melt — SHAK 271:25
c. the wat'ry glade — GRAY 157:11
c. thy good with brotherhood — BATES 30:2
exchange it some day for a c. — BENN 34:10
father's c. into the hazard — SHAK 279:1

crown (cont.):
give thee a c. of life — BIBLE 57:21
glory of my c. — ELIZ 135:7
head a c. of twelve stars — BIBLE 57:30
head that wears a c. — SHAK 278:23
influence of the C. — DUNN 129:10
no cross, no c. — PENN 247:9
sweet fruition of an earthly c. — MARL 219:8
throne and thy kingly c. — ELL 136:1
Within the hollow c. — SHAK 293:28
woman is a c. to her husband — BIBLE 43:19
crowned: c. with thorns — KELLY 193:19
crowner: Medical C.'s — BARH 28:21
crowning: c. mercy — CROM 112:3
crowns: c. are empty things — DEFOE 116:1
c. for convoy — SHAK 279:18
end that c. us — HERR 167:16
golden c. around the glassy sea — HEBER 164:17
crucible: America is God's C. — ZANG 360:27
crucified: when they c. my Lord — ANON 11:14
crucify: people would not even c. him — CARL 90:26
cruel: C., but composed and bland — ARN 16:23
C. necessity — CROM 112:1
I must be c. only to be kind — SHAK 276:24
That comfort c. men — CHES 97:24
you c. men of Rome — SHAK 280:24
cruellest: April is the c. month — ELIOT 134:18
cruelty: C. has a human heart — BLAKE 52:7
topfull of direst c. — SHAK 285:17
cruise: all on our last c. — STEV 317:5
crumbling: C. between the fingers — MACN 216:4
crumbs: bags to hold the c. — ISH 178:21
c. which fall — BIBLE 50:11
c. which fell — BIBLE 52:34
crusade: This party is a moral c. — WILS 351:13
cruse: c. best fits my little wine — HERR 167:22
little oil in a c. — BIBLE 41:35
crust: c. over a volcano of revolution — ELLIS 136:6
cry: c. of his hounds — GRAV 156:12
c. of the Little Peoples — LE G 204:12
C., the beloved country — PATON 246:19
cuckoo's parting c. — ARN 17:18
his little son should c. — CORN 108:5
I c. all the way to the bank — LIB 206:22
I hear a sudden c. of pain — STEP 315:7
let our c. come unto thee — BOOK 65:24
Some must c. so that others — RHYS 259:13
that we still should c. — BACON 25:31
Truth is the c. of all — BERK 35:17
when indeed they c. — WEBS 344:27
When we are born we c. — SHAK 283:27
with no language but a c. — TENN 325:9
crying: Love, a child, is ever c. — WROTH 358:1
one c. in the wilderness — BIBLE 48:13
crystal: golden sands and c. brooks — DONNE 123:23
cuckoo: as the c. is in June — SHAK 278:6
c. clock — WELL 345:5
c. then, on every tree — SHAK 284:21
heard the c.'s parting cry — ARN 17:18
hear the pleasant c. — DAV 114:17
Lhude sing c. — ANON 10:16
O C.! Shall I call thee bird — WORD 357:7
rainbow and a c.'s song — DAV 114:18
weather the c. likes — HARDY 162:16
cucumber: c. should be well sliced — JOHN 183:19
cucumbers: lodge in a garden of c. — BIBLE 45:3
sun-beams out of c. — SWIFT 319:22
they are but c. after all — JOHN 185:27
cue: With a twisted c. — GILB 152:2
cui: C. bono? — CIC 100:31
culpa: mea c., mea culpa — MISS 231:11
cultivate: We must c. our garden — VOLT 340:13
cultural: c. cringe you came from — KEAT 190:8
culture: as a man of c. rare — GILB 152:9
c. shock is what happens — TOFF 333:7

cultures (cont.):
Whenever I hear the word c. — JOHST 186:18
who pursue C. in bands — WHAR 347:4
cultures: two c. — SNOW 310:19
cumbered: c. about much serving — BIBLE 52:14
cunning: C. is the dark sanctuary — CHES 97:4
right hand forget her c. — BOOK 69:4
silence, exile, and c. — JOYCE 188:9
cunningly: little world made c. — DONNE 123:12
cup: Ah, fill the c. — FITZ 140:11
giveth his colour in the c. — BIBLE 43:33
let this c. pass from me — BIBLE 51:11
my c. overflows — SCOT 269:9
my c. shall be full — BOOK 66:18
There's death in the c. — BURNS 82:10
We'll tak a c. o' kindness yet — BURNS 81:25
Cupid: C. and my Campaspe — LYLY 212:16
C.'s darts do not feel — ANON 9:10
giant-dwarf, Dan C. — SHAK 284:13
winged C. painted blind — SHAK 290:16
Cupidinesque: Veneres C. — CAT 93:1
cups: c. that cheer — COWP 110:11
curate: c. something between a eunuch — FIRB 139:19
c. who has strayed by mistake — AUDEN 21:18
I was a pale young c. then — GILB 152:29
very name of a C. — SMITH 309:23
curates: abundant shower of c. — BRON 72:13
all Bishops and C. — BOOK 65:10
C., long dust, will come and go — BROO 73:5
preached to death by wild c. — SMITH 310:8
curb: care's check and c. — VAUG 337:5
snaffle and the c. — CAMP 88:16
cure: Be of sin the double c. — TOPL 333:14
c. for this ill is not to sit still — KIPL 197:22
c. of all diseases — BROW 74:19
C. the disease and kill the patient — BACON 24:25
love's a malady without a c. — DRYD 128:9
there is no C. for this Disease — BELL 33:4
cured: c. by hanging from a string — KING 195:20
C. yesterday of my disease — PRIOR 255:11
cures: If a lot of c. are suggested — CHEK 96:24
curfew: c. tolls the knell of parting — GRAY 157:4
curiosities: c. would be quite forgot — AUBR 19:16
curiosity: Disinterested intellectual c. — TREV 334:7
Love, c., freckles, and doubt — PARK 245:5
was full of 'satiable c. — KIPL 197:21
curious: nectarine, and c. peach — MARV 220:15
Raised by that c. engine — WEBS 344:15
curiouser: C. and curiouser! — CARR 91:2
curl: Who had a little c. — LONG 210:6
curlèd: c. darlings of our nation — SHAK 291:32
curls: And Frocks and C. — DICK 120:17
currency: Debasing the moral c. — ELIOT 132:7
debauch the c. — KEYN 194:14
curse: And the c. be ended — ELIOT 132:24
C. God, and die — BIBLE 42:24
c. is come upon me — TENN 326:3
c. of the drinking classes — WILDE 350:20
c. to party-strife — WORD 354:18
heard such a terrible c. — BARH 28:19
I know how to c. — SHAK 295:35
open foe may prove a c. — GAY 149:11
real c. of Eve — RHYS 259:14
cursed: c. be he that moves — SHAK 300:20
to all succeeding ages c. — DRYD 127:5
whom thou cursest is c. — BIBLE 40:17
curses: C. are like young chickens — SOUT 311:21
c. heaped on each gashed head — SORL 311:16
curtain: Bring down the c. — RAB 257:13
iron c. — CHUR 100:1
lets the c. fall — POPE 250:22
Spread thy close c. — SHAK 295:11
curtained: C. with cloudy red — MILT 227:29
curtains: fringèd c. of thine eye — SHAK 296:2
curteis: C. he was, lowely — CHAU 95:14

curiosity: full of 'satiable c. — KIPL 197:21
curtsey: C. while you're thinking — CARR 91:17
Curzon: George Nathaniel C. — ANON 9:12
cushion: c. and soft Dean invite — POPE 251:16
custodiet: Quis c. ipsos custodes? — JUV 189:9
custody: Wragg is in c. — ARN 18:3
custom: c. loathsome to the eye — JAM 179:9
C. reconciles us to everything — BURKE 80:8
c. should corrupt the world — TENN 324:20
C., that unwritten law — D'AV 114:8
C., then, is the great guide — HUME 176:3
nor c. stale her infinite variety — SHAK 271:17
customer: c. is never wrong — RITZ 260:13
cut: c. him out in little stars — SHAK 295:14
c. my conscience to fit — HELL 165:7
c. off Israel out of the land — BIBLE 41:29
c. off out of the land of the — BIBLE 46:21
c., the style, the line — LOES 209:6
flower, and is c. down — BIBLE 42:33
guardsman's c. and thrust — HUXL 177:16
most unkindest c. of all — SHAK 281:23
cutting: c. edge of the mind — BRON 72:9
cycle: c. of Cathay — TENN 326:18
cymbal: or a tinkling c. — BIBLE 55:11
cymbals: upon the well-tuned c. — BOOK 69:12
cynicism: C. is intellectual dandyism — MER 223:14
cynosure: c. of neighbouring eyes — MILT 227:3
cypress: c. in the palace walk — TENN 328:3
in sad c. let me be laid — SHAK 297:32
Cyprus: rings black C. with a lake — FLEC 141:18
Cythère: C'est C. — BAUD 30:5

# D

D: I never use a big, big D — GILB 152:16
dad: d. is present at the conception — ORTON 241:20
girls in slacks remember D. — BETJ 36:17
dada: mama of D. — FAD 138:10
daddy: My heart belongs to D. — PORT 253:24
daffodil: On a bed of d. sky — TENN 326:28
daffodils: D. that come before the swallow — SHAK 298:32
Fair d., we weep to see — HERR 167:23
host, of golden d. — WORD 355:4
never saw d. so beautiful — WORD 354:10
When d. begin to peer — SHAK 298:26
dagger: d. which I see before me — SHAK 286:10
daggers: Give me the d. — SHAK 286:17
There's d. in men's smiles — SHAK 286:27
daily: Give us this day our d. bread — BIBLE 48:27
My d. labour to pursue — WESL 346:5
dainties: hath not fed of the d. — SHAK 284:15
We donnot want d. — GASK 148:19
daintily: D. alights Elaine — BETJ 37:7
must have things d. served — BETJ 37:2
dairy: doth nightly rob the d. — JONS 187:4
dairymaid: Queen asked the D. — MILNE 225:22
daisies: Buttercups and d. — HOW 175:10
D., those pearled Arcturi — SHEL 304:29
When d. pied and violets blue — SHAK 284:21
daisy: D. and Lily — SITW 307:20
'd.,' or elles the 'ye of day' — CHAU 96:10
dalliance: d. in the wardrobe lies — SHAK 279:2
primrose path of d. — SHAK 274:20
dam: pretty chickens and their d. — SHAK 287:26
damaged: Archangel a little d. — LAMB 200:8
damages: He first d. his mind — ANON 13:8
dame: La belle d. sans merci — KEATS 191:10
damn: D. braces: Bless relaxes — BLAKE 61:9
d. the consequences — MILN 226:2
D. with faint praise — POPE 251:6
faint praises one another d. — WYCH 358:6
I don't give a d. — MITC 232:6

**damn** (cont.):
old man who said, 'D.' — HARE 162:19
with a spot I d. him — SHAK 281:28
**damnation**: deep d. of his taking-off — SHAK 285:24
From sleep and from d. — CHES 97:24
**damnations**: Twenty-nine distinct d. — BROW 77:12
**damned**: All silent, and all d. — WORD 356:4
brandy of the d. — SHAW 301:19
D. from here to Eternity — KIPL 196:15
d. lies and statistics — DISR 122:21
Faustus must be d. — MARL 218:13
have written a d. play — REYN 259:7
Life is just one d. thing — HUBB 175:14
must be d. perpetually — MARL 218:12
Out, d. spot — SHAK 287:27
public be d. — VAND 337:1
Publish and be d. — WELL 345:15
will be d. if you don't — DOW 125:11
**damning**: d. those they have no mind — BUTL 83:24
**damnosa**: D. hereditas — GAIUS 147:13
**damozel**: blessed d. leaned out — ROSS 263:6
**damp**: d. souls of housemaids — ELIOT 134:4
**Danaë**: Now lies the Earth all D. — TENN 328:4
**Danaos**: timeo D. et dona ferentis — VIRG 339:5
**dance**: D., d., d., little lady — COW 108:19
d. is a measured pace — BACON 23:24
D. on this ball-floor — BLUN 62:14
dancer from the d. — YEATS 358:14
d. round in a ring — FROST 146:30
departs too far from the d. — POUND 254:22
I am the Lord of the D. — CART 92:13
Let's face the music and d. — BERL 35:22
On with the d.! — BYRON 85:3
will you join the d. — CARR 91:12
**danced**: d. by the light of the moon — LEAR 203:13
his didn't he d. his did — CUMM 112:16
**dancer**: know the d. from the dance — YEATS 358:14
**dancers**: d. are all gone under the hill — ELIOT 133:4
nation of d., singers — EQUI 137:13
**dances**: And d. with the daffodils — WORD 355:5
makes no progress; it d. — LIGNE 207:2
**danceth**: hope d. without music — HERB 167:10
**dancing**: And d. dogs and bears — HODG 169:13
D. in the chequered shade — MILT 227:4
[D.] a perpendicular expression — SHAW 302:26
d. is love's proper exercise — DAV 114:15
Fluttering and d. in the breeze — WORD 355:4
manners of a d. master — JOHN 184:1
Singing, d. to itself — COL 103:13
You and I are past our d. days — SHAK 294:25
**dandy**: I'm a Yankee Doodle D. — COHAN 103:5
**dandyism**: Cynicism is intellectual d. — MER 223:14
**Dane**: antique Roman than a D. — SHAK 277:16
**danger**: But only when in d. — OWEN 243:17
d. chiefly lies in acting — CHUR 98:20
d. of her former tooth — SHAK 287:3
D., the spur of all great — CHAP 94:20
d., we pluck this flower — SHAK 277:30
everything is in d. — NIET 239:19
five-and-twenty per cent of its d. — SURT 319:8
oft in d., oft in woe — WHITE 347:16
One would be in less d. — NASH 237:11
run into any kind of d. — BOOK 64:6
**dangerous**: action is a most d. thing — CLOU 102:8
delays are d. in war — DRYD 128:22
interest's on the d. edge — BROW 75:15
little knowledge is d. — HUXL 177:17
Mad, bad, and d. to know — LAMB 199:22
Nothing more d. than an idea — ALAIN 3:1
so many a d. thing — BISH 59:16
such men are d. — SHAK 281:1
were d. to meet it alone — WHAR 347:4
**dangerously**: live d. — NIET 239:21
**dangers**: D. by being despised — BURKE 81:2
No d. fright him — JOHN 183:13

**dangers** (cont.):
On the d. of the seas — PARK 245:17
perils and d. of this night — BOOK 64:12
She loved me for the d. — SHAK 291:35
**Daniel**: D. come to judgement — SHAK 289:29
desolation, spoken of by D. — BIBLE 50:35
O D., a man greatly beloved — BIBLE 47:16
**danket**: Nun d. alle Gott — WINK 352:4
**Dan McGrew**: Dangerous D. — SERV 270:13
**Danny**: they're hangin' D. Deever — KIPL 196:9
**dapper**: d. from your napper — COLL 105:6
**dappled**: Glory be to God for d. things — HOPK 172:12
**dapples**: D. the drowsy east — SHAK 291:27
**dare**: Do I d. to eat a peach — ELIOT 134:3
Letting 'I d. not' wait — SHAK 286:4
menace heaven and d. the gods — MARL 219:6
none d. call it treason — HAR 162:22
**dared**: Determined, d., and done — SMART 308:14
**dares**: that d. love attempt — SHAK 294:32
Who d. do more is none — SHAK 286:5
Who d. wins — ANON 11:20
**Darien**: upon a peak in D. — KEATS 192:11
**daring**: d. young man on the flying — LEYB 206:21
**dark**: And we are for the d. — SHAK 272:4
At one stride comes the d. — COL 104:9
blind man in a d. room — BOWEN 70:13
children fear to go in the d. — BACON 24:20
colours will agree in the d. — BACON 25:19
d., amid the blaze — MILT 230:11
d. and go into the dark — MANN 217:13
d. and true and tender — TENN 327:24
D. as the world of man — SITW 307:19
d. is light enough — FRY 146:29
d. night of the soul — FITZ 140:22
d. Satanic mills — BLAKE 61:12
D. with excessive bright — MILT 229:4
d. world where gods have — ROET 261:15
day of his death was a d. — AUDEN 20:21
Dirty, d., and undevotional — VICT 338:10
great leap in the d. — HOBB 169:11
hell, as d. as night — SHAK 300:16
I knew you in this d. — OWEN 244:3
Lady is as good i' th' d. — HERR 167:18
murmur and the poring d. — SHAK 279:7
Out in the d. over the snow — THOM 330:26
Shining nowhere but in the d. — VAUG 337:12
Sons of the d. and bloody — O'HARA 241:4
this d. world of sin — BICK 58:25
We work in the d. — JAMES 179:23
What in me is d. — MILT 228:9
**darkies**: d., how my heart grows — FOST 144:13
**darkling**: as on a d. plain — ARN 16:12
D. I listen — KEATS 192:3
D. they went under the lonely — VIRG 339:14
**darkly**: through a glass, d. — BIBLE 55:14
**darkness**: against the rulers of the d. — BIBLE 56:4
And universal d. buries all — POPE 250:22
between two eternities of d. — NAB 236:19
candle than curse the d. — STEV 316:21
cast off the works of d. — BIBLE 55:1
cast out into outer d. — BIBLE 49:18
Chaos and d. heard — MARR 219:24
D. at Noon — KOES 199:1
d. bind them — TOLK 333:10
D. came down on the field — SMART 308:8
d. by his electrical skin — THAC 329:18
d. comprehended it not — BIBLE 53:8
d. falls at Thy behest — ELL 135:21
d. I wretch lay wrestling — HOPK 172:1
d. of mere being — JUNG 188:23
d. visible — MILT 228:10
d. was upon the face — BIBLE 38:13
Dawn on our d. and lend — HEBER 164:14
even d. which may be felt — BIBLE 39:35
Go out into the d. — HASK 163:16

**darkness** (cont.):

| | |
|---|---|
| Heart of D. | CONR 107:4 |
| I will encounter d. as a bride | SHAK 288:20 |
| leaves the world to d. | GRAY 157:4 |
| Lighten our d., we beseech | BOOK 64:12 |
| lump bred up in d. | KYD 199:10 |
| people that walked in d. | BIBLE 45:15 |
| pestilence that walketh in d. | BOOK 67:29 |
| Prince of d. and dead night | SPEN 313:8 |
| prince of d. is a gentleman | SHAK 283:16 |
| race that long in d. pined | SCOT 269:10 |
| Ring out the d. of the land | TENN 325:27 |
| silent d. born | DAN 113:15 |
| slope through d. up to God | TENN 325:11 |
| them that sit in d. | BIBLE 51:30 |
| then d. again and a silence | LONG 210:3 |
| there was an ocean of d. | FOX 144:17 |
| To sit in d. here | MILT 228:28 |
| When awful d. and silence | LEAR 203:8 |
| works of d. | BOOK 64:21 |

**darlin':** oh, he's a d. man — O'CAS 240:21

**darling:** d. buds of May — SHAK 299:12

| | |
|---|---|
| d. of our crew | DIBD 117:19 |
| D. of the music halls | SMITH 309:8 |
| green lap was Nature's d. | GRAY 157:16 |
| She is the d. of my heart | CAREY 90:2 |

**darlings:** wealthy curlèd d. — SHAK 291:32

**dart:** Time shall throw a d. at thee — BROW 74:24

**dastard:** and a d. in war — SCOTT 268:20

**date:** d. which will live in infamy — ROOS 262:14

| | |
|---|---|
| doubles your chances for a d. | ALLEN 4:17 |
| Standards are always out of d. | BENN 34:14 |

**dateless:** d. bargain to engrossing — SHAK 295:25

**daughter:** As is the mother, so is her d. — BIBLE 47:4

| | |
|---|---|
| D. am I in my mother's house | KIPL 196:25 |
| d. hath soft brown hair | CALV 88:7 |
| d. of debate | ELIZ 135:13 |
| d. of the gods, divinely | TENN 323:20 |
| D. of the Moon, Nokomis | LONG 210:1 |
| Don't put your d. on the stage | COW 109:5 |
| Elderly ugly d. | GILB 152:30 |
| let them all to my elder d. | THOM 330:23 |
| O my ducats! O my d. | SHAK 289:12 |
| Sole of his voice | MILT 229:25 |
| Stern of the voice of God | WORD 355:25 |

**daughters:** d. of my father's house — SHAK 298:2

| | |
|---|---|
| thunder, fire, are my d. | SHAK 283:7 |
| Words are men's d. | MADD 216:14 |
| words are the d. of earth | JOHN 182:4 |

**dauntless:** and so d. in war — SCOTT 268:19

with d. breast — GRAY 157:9

**dauphin:** kingdom of daylight's d. — HOPK 172:20

**David:** D. wrote the Psalms — NAYL 237:20

Once in royal D.'s city — ALEX 4:4

**Davy:** Sir Humphrey D. — BENT 35:8

**dawn:** d. comes up like thunder — KIPL 196:21

| | |
|---|---|
| d. of the morning after | ADE 3:1 |
| D. on our darkness | HEBER 164:14 |
| Hail, redemption's happy d. | CASW 92:18 |
| in that d. to be alive | WORD 354:24 |
| I said to D.: Be sudden | THOM 331:10 |
| music of its trees at d. | ARN 16:21 |
| Rosy-fingered d. | HOMER 171:2 |

**dawning:** bird of d. singeth all — SHAK 274:2

d. of the age of Aquarius — RADO 257:18

**day:** All d. long from 10 till 4 — BELL 33:24

| | |
|---|---|
| And d.'s at the morn | BROW 76:28 |
| And every dog his d. | KING 195:17 |
| Another d. older and deeper | TRAV 334:4 |
| arrow that flieth by d. | BOOK 67:29 |
| breaks the blank d. | TENN 325:1 |
| bright cold d. in April | ORW 242:5 |
| bright d. is done | SHAK 272:4 |
| burden and heat of the d. | BIBLE 50:25 |
| compare thee to a summer's d. | SHAK 299:12 |

**day** (cont.):

| | |
|---|---|
| d. brought back my night | MILT 230:25 |
| D. by day: we magnify thee | BOOK 63:21 |
| d. in a pillar of a cloud | BIBLE 39:39 |
| d. of his death was a dark | AUDEN 20:21 |
| d. of salvation | BIBLE 55:25 |
| d. of small nations | CHAM 93:23 |
| d. of wrath | MISS 231:23 |
| d. once or twice in a man's | PEPYS 247:21 |
| d. o' the Oppressor | KIPL 197:16 |
| d. perish wherein I was born | BIBLE 42:25 |
| d. the music died | MCL 215:7 |
| d. Thou gavest | ELL 135:21 |
| d. war broke out | WILT 351:23 |
| each d. dies with sleep | HOPK 172:11 |
| ebbs out life's little d. | LYTE 212:20 |
| end of a perfect d. | BOND 63:9 |
| Friends, I have lost a d. | TITUS 332:22 |
| Go ahead, make my d. | STIN 317:26 |
| have their d. and cease to be | TENN 324:23 |
| Hide me from d.'s garish eye | MILT 226:26 |
| knell of parting d. | GRAY 157:4 |
| last, everlasting d. | DONNE 123:22 |
| left alone with our d. | AUDEN 21:15 |
| live this d. as if thy last | KEN 193:21 |
| long d.'s journey into night | O'NEI 241:11 |
| long weary d. have end | SPEN 313:6 |
| mansions to the peering d. | MILT 227:28 |
| mind on an ordinary d. | WOOLF 353:21 |
| morning were the first d. | BIBLE 38:14 |
| murmur of a summer's d. | ARN 17:5 |
| night do penance for a d. | WORD 356:11 |
| night of this immortal d. | SHEL 304:24 |
| not a second on the d. | COOK 107:15 |
| one d. in thy courts | BOOK 67:22 |
| remorseful d. | SHAK 280:9 |
| seize the d. | HOR 173:20 |
| So foul and fair a d. | SHAK 285:6 |
| spent one whole d. well | THOM 330:2 |
| This'll be the d. that I die | MCL 215:8 |
| thou d. in night | SHAK 295:13 |
| tomorrow is another d. | MITC 232:7 |
| Underneath D.'s azure eyes | SHEL 304:1 |
| unto the d. is the evil | BIBLE 49:5 |
| upon every d. to be lost | JOHN 186:7 |
| wish d. come, not choose | HOPK 171:25 |
| Without all hope of d. | MILT 230:11 |

**daylight:** cheerfulness keeps up a kind of d. — ADD 2:24

| | |
|---|---|
| kingdom of d.'s dauphin | HOPK 172:20 |
| methinks is but the d. sick | SHAK 290:6 |
| must not let in d. upon magic | BAG 26:13 |

**days:** all the d. of my life — BOOK 66:18

| | |
|---|---|
| And the d. grow short | AND 5:12 |
| because the d. are evil | BIBLE 56:1 |
| behold these present d. | SHAK 300:5 |
| burnt-out ends of smoky d. | ELIOT 134:10 |
| Cast your mind on other d. | YEATS 360:7 |
| d. are swifter than a weaver's | BIBLE 42:30 |
| D. are where we live | LARK 201:13 |
| d. darken round me | TENN 324:19 |
| d. of our youth | BYRON 87:10 |
| d. of wine and roses | DOWS 125:13 |
| d. that are no more | TENN 327:22 |
| finished in the first 1,000 d. | KENN 194:5 |
| Length of d. is in her right | BIBLE 43:8 |
| number of my d. | BOOK 67:1 |
| number our d. | BOOK 67:27 |
| of few d. and full of trouble | BIBLE 42:33 |
| our d. on the earth | BIBLE 42:17 |
| seemed unto him but a few d. | BIBLE 39:22 |
| We have seen better d. | SHAK 296:21 |

**day-star:** d. in the ocean bed — MILT 227:18

**day-to-day:** what a d. business life is — LAF 199:20

**dazzle:** d. for an hour — MORE 234:22

mine eyes d. — WEBS 344:19

**dea:** *Et vera incessu patuit d.* — VIRG 339:3

**dead:** After that it's d. — WAUGH 343:26
And he is d., who will not fight — GREN 158:16
And simplify me when I'm d. — DOUG 125:9
Beautiful Evelyn Hope is d. — BROW 75:28
besides, the wench is d. — MARL 219:2
Bivouac of the D. — O'HARA 241:4
blooming well d. — SAR 267:1
character d. at every word — SHER 306:4
charity more than the d. — ARN 16:8
cold and pure and very d. — LEWIS 206:18
converse with the mighty d. — THOM 331:27
D.! and never called me mother — WOOD 353:17
D. battles, like dead generals — TUCH 335:7
d., but in the Elysian fields — DISR 122:18
d. donkey — DICK 120:4
d. don't die — LAWR 202:26
D., for a ducat — SHAK 276:19
d. he would like to see me — HOLL 170:11
d. Indian — SHAK 296:4
d. Indian — SHER 305:22
d. level of provincial — ELIOT 132:13
d. men lost their bones — ELIOT 134:23
d. selves to higher things — TENN 324:24
d. shall be raised — BIBLE 55:21
d. shall not have died in vain — LINC 207:8
d. sinner revised — BIER 59:9
d. we owe only truth — VOLT 340:24
d. woman bites not — GRAY 156:19
d. YESTERDAY — FITZ 140:11
democracy of the d. — CHES 98:13
Down among the d. men — DYER 129:18
Either he's d., or my watch — MARX 221:6
fairy that falls down d. — BARR 29:12
Faith without works is d. — BIBLE 57:3
Fame is a food that d. men — DOBS 122:26
female atheist talks you d. — JOHN 183:8
For being d. — BENT 35:6
For y'er a lang time d. — ANON 6:9
*God is d.* — FROMM 146:7
healthy and wealthy and d. — THUR 332:15
If the d. talk to you — SZASZ 321:25
*In the long run* we are all d. — KEYN 194:17
I would that I were d. — TENN 326:22
King of all these the d. — HOMER 171:3
kissed by the English d. — OWEN 244:1
lasting mansions of the d. — CRAB 110:22
Let the d. bury their dead — BIBLE 49:20
Lilacs out of the d. land — ELIOT 134:18
maid is not d. — BIBLE 49:26
millions of the mouthless d. — SORL 311:16
Mistah Kurtz—he d. — CONR 107:6
more to say when I am d. — ROB 260:20
more ways of being d. — DAWK 115:3
noble D. — WORD 356:15
not d.—but gone before — ROG 261:18
Not many d. — COCK 103:1
only consistent people are the d. — HUXL 177:6
our English d. — SHAK 279:5
over the rich D. — BROO 72:20
past is the only d. thing — THOM 330:22
quick, and the d. — DEWAR 117:14
renown and grace is d. — SHAK 286:26
sculptured d. — KEATS 190:15
sea gave up the d. — BIBLE 58:3
Sea shall give up her d. — BOOK 69:15
sheeted d. did squeak — SHAK 274:1
sleeping and the d. — SHAK 286:17
Smiling the boy fell d. — BROW 76:8
their home among the d. — SHEL 303:16
There are no d. — MAET 216:15
They must be d. — DICK 118:19
they told me you were d. — CORY 108:13
This my son was d. — BIBLE 52:32

**dead** (*cont.*):
those who are d. — BURKE 80:17
two days' conference with the d. — WEBS 344:16
very d. of Winter — ANDR 5:15
very d. of winter — ELIOT 133:21
Weep me not d. — DONNE 124:16
When I am d. — BELL 33:27
Where d. men meet — BUTL 84:21
**dead-born:** *d. from the press* — HUME 176:10
**deadener:** Habit is a great d. — BECK 31:16
**deadlock:** Holy d. — HERB 166:16
**deadly:** more d. in the long run — TWAIN 335:22
more d. than the male — KIPL 196:12
**deaf:** For, d., how should they — SORL 311:16
**deal:** be given a square d. — ROOS 262:17
new d. for the American — ROOS 262:8
**dean:** cushion and soft D. — POPE 251:16
D. of Christ Church — SPR 314:1
no dogma, no D. — DISR 122:16
sly shade of a Rural D. — BROO 73:5
**deans:** dowagers for d. — TENN 327:16
**dear:** After all, my erstwhile d. — MILL 224:23
dangerously d. — BYRON 85:17
D. as remembered kisses — TENN 327:23
D. Lord and Father of mankind — WHIT 348:27
D. One is mine as mirrors — AUDEN 21:9
d. to me as are the ruddy — SHAK 281:7
Farewell d., deluding woman — BURNS 82:28
Plato is d. to me — ARIS 15:22
that bread should be so d. — HOOD 171:13
too d. for my possessing — SHAK 299:27
**dearer:** d. still is truth — ARIS 15:22
D. than self — BYRON 84:30
d. was the mother — COL 104:20
little d. than his horse — TENN 326:7
**death:** abolish the d. penalty — KARR 190:1
added a new terror to d. — WETH 347:2
added another terror to d. — LYND 212:19
afraid of d. — CHUR 98:24
After the first d. — THOM 330:15
All in the valley of D. — TENN 323:14
And D. once dead — SHAK 300:15
And d. shall have no dominion — THOM 330:6
And D., who had the soldier — DOUG 125:10
And make d. proud to take us — SHAK 271:26
bargain to engrossing d. — SHAK 295:25
Be absolute for d. — SHAK 288:18
Be thou faithful unto d. — BIBLE 57:21
Birth, and copulation, and d. — ELIOT 134:14
Black Widow, d. — LOW 211:16
blaze forth the d. of princes — SHAK 281:8
Brother to D. — DAN 113:15
Brother to D. — FLET 142:5
Brought d. into the world — MILT 228:7
build the house of d. — MONT 233:10
captains courageous whom d. — BALL 28:1
citizens of d.'s grey land — SASS 267:10
Come away, come away, d. — SHAK 297:32
day of our Jubilee is d. — BROW 74:17
Dear, beauteous d. — VAUG 337:12
d. after life does greatly — SPEN 313:9
D. and his brother Sleep — SHEL 304:26
d. and taxes — FRAN 145:15
D. and taxes and childbirth — MITC 232:5
D. be not proud — DONNE 123:8
D. closes all — TENN 328:23
D. cometh soon or late — MAC 214:3
d. does end and each day — HOPK 172:11
D., ere thou hast slain — BROW 74:24
D.! Great proprietor of all — YOUNG 360:18
d. had undone so many — ELIOT 134:21
D. has a thousand doors — MASS 222:6
D. has got something to be said — AMIS 5:7
D. hath no more dominion — BIBLE 54:35
D. hath so many doors — FLET 142:4

death (cont.):

| | |
|---|---|
| d. hath ten thousand doors | WEBS 344:18 |
| d. in a blizzard | CHER 19:11 |
| D. is a fearful thing | SHAK 288:21 |
| d. is but a groom | DONNE 123:19 |
| [D. is] nature's way | ANON 6:25 |
| d. is not far behind | WESL 346:17 |
| D. is nothing at all | HOLL 170:12 |
| d. is the cure of all diseases | BROW 74:19 |
| D. joins us to the great majority | YOUNG 360:23 |
| D. lies dead | SWIN 321:10 |
| D. lies on her like | SHAK 295:21 |
| D. never takes the wise | LA F 199:13 |
| d. obscured that eye | KEATS 192:17 |
| d.'s counterfeit | SHAK 286:24 |
| d.'s pale flag | SHAK 295:24 |
| D.'s shadow at the door | BLUN 62:12 |
| D. the journey's end | DRYD 128:12 |
| D.! the poor man's | BURNS 82:17 |
| D. thou shalt die | DONNE 123:9 |
| D. tramples it to fragments | SHEL 303:13 |
| d., where is thy sting | BIBLE 55:22 |
| D., where is thy sting-a-ling | ANON 9:21 |
| D. will come when thou | SHEL 305:13 |
| d. will have his day | SHAK 293:25 |
| disappointed by that stroke of d. | JOHN 182:23 |
| disqualified by the accident of d. | CHES 98:14 |
| doubt is nothing but d. | UNAM 336:11 |
| dread of something after d. | SHAK 275:26 |
| dull cold ear of d. | GRAY 157:8 |
| enormously improved by d. | SAKI 265:16 |
| Ev'ry day a little d. | SOND 311:6 |
| fear d. as children fear | BACON 24:20 |
| Fear d.?—to feel the fog | BROW 77:2 |
| fear of d. disquiets me | DUNB 129:8 |
| fed on the fullness of d. | SWIN 321:13 |
| Finality is d. | STEP 315:6 |
| For since by man came d. | BIBLE 55:17 |
| half in love with easeful D. | KEATS 192:3 |
| heroes up the line to d. | SASS 267:8 |
| His d., which happened | HOOD 171:7 |
| I could not stop for D. | DICK 120:9 |
| If there wasn't d. | SMITH 309:22 |
| I had seen birth and d. | ELIOT 133:22 |
| I have a rendezvous with D. | SEEG 269:13 |
| in d. they were not divided | BIBLE 41:22 |
| In the hour of d. | BOOK 64:16 |
| Into the jaws of D. | TENN 323:17 |
| It is but D. who comes at last | SCOTT 268:17 |
| just, and mighty D. | RAL 258:2 |
| Just try and set d. aside | TURG 335:14 |
| Keeps D. his court | SHAK 293:28 |
| killed than frightened to d. | SURT 319:12 |
| kingly D. keeps his pale court | SHEL 303:4 |
| land of the shadow of d. | BIBLE 45:15 |
| Let me die a youngman's d. | MCG 214:21 |
| life forget and d. remember | SWIN 321:16 |
| life half dead, a living d. | MILT 230:13 |
| lightning before d. | SHAK 295:23 |
| little room do we take up in d. | SHIR 306:12 |
| made a covenant with d. | BIBLE 45:28 |
| make one in love with d. | SHEL 303:2 |
| Man has created d. | YEATS 358:22 |
| man's d. diminishes me | DONNE 124:20 |
| Meetest for d. | SHAK 289:24 |
| midst of life we are in d. | BOOK 66:7 |
| much possessed by d. | ELIOT 134:32 |
| must hate and d. return | SHEL 303:19 |
| My name is D. | SOUT 311:23 |
| nearest d. in life | ANON 9:14 |
| neither d. nor life | BIBLE 54:42 |
| nervousness or d. | LEB 203:24 |
| new terrors of D. | ARB 14:24 |
| no mean of d. | SHAK 281:12 |
| none blessed before his d. | BIBLE 48:1 |

death (cont.):

| | |
|---|---|
| no one knew my d. | ROET 261:16 |
| no one [stop] his d. | SEN 270:8 |
| not at their d. | MONT 233:20 |
| one life and one d. | BROW 76:6 |
| On life, on d. | YEATS 360:8 |
| or give me d. | HENRY 166:6 |
| overcome the sharpness of d. | BOOK 63:20 |
| perchance of D. | THOM 332:1 |
| prepare as though for d. | MANS 217:15 |
| remembered kisses after d. | TENN 327:23 |
| Reports of my d. | TWAIN 336:7 |
| shadow of d. | BROW 74:2 |
| shall be destroyed is d. | BIBLE 55:18 |
| signed my d. warrant | COLL 105:8 |
| sleep of d. what dreams | SHAK 275:25 |
| sleep the sleep of d. | BLAKE 60:21 |
| snares of d. compassed | BOOK 68:19 |
| some one's d. | BROW 75:13 |
| So shalt thou feed on D. | SHAK 300:15 |
| steps that led assuredly to d. | GUIB 159:8 |
| stories of the d. of kings | SHAK 293:27 |
| suffers at his d. | LA BR 199:14 |
| suicide 25 years after his d. | BEAV 31:5 |
| swallow up d. in victory | BIBLE 45:25 |
| Swarm over, D. | BETJ 37:9 |
| talks of Arthur's d. | SHAK 282:11 |
| that sat on him was D. | BIBLE 57:25 |
| there is an image of d. | ELIOT 132:16 |
| There is d. in the pot | BIBLE 42:10 |
| There's d. in the cup | BURNS 82:10 |
| there shall be no more d. | BIBLE 58:5 |
| This fell sergeant, d. | SHAK 277:15 |
| till d. us do part | BOOK 66:1 |
| To be carnally minded is d. | BIBLE 54:39 |
| tragedies are finished by a d. | BYRON 86:12 |
| traveller betwixt life and d. | WORD 356:24 |
| valiant never taste of d. | SHAK 281:8 |
| vasty hall of d. | ARN 17:1 |
| wast not born for d. | KEATS 192:4 |
| way out an' d.'s the other | WILL 351:5 |
| way to dusty d. | SHAK 288:5 |
| we owe God a d. | SHAK 278:25 |
| Why fear d.? | FROH 146:6 |
| Will keep a league till d. | SHAK 294:6 |
| with d. and an agreement | GARR 148:13 |
| **deathless**: let us make love d. | TREN 334:6 |
| **deaths**: More d. than one must die | WILDE 350:17 |
| **death-sentence**: d. without a whimper | LAWR 202:27 |
| **death-struck**: beautiful and d. year | HOUS 174:25 |
| **debars**: Fate so enviously d. | MARV 220:13 |
| **debasing**: D. the moral currency | ELIOT 132:7 |
| **debate**: daughter of d. | ELIZ 135:13 |
| Rupert of D. | BULW 78:9 |
| **debellare**: subiectis et d. superbos | VIRG 339:16 |
| **debonair**: buxom, blithe, and d. | MILT 226:28 |
| **deboshed**: Thou d. fish | SHAK 296:6 |
| **debt**: Ambition's d. is paid | SHAK 281:11 |
| he paid the d. of nature | FABY 138:6 |
| midst of life we are in d. | MUMF 236:7 |
| National D. is a very Good | SELL 270:4 |
| older and deeper in d. | TRAV 334:4 |
| pay a d. to pleasure too | ROCH 261:3 |
| promise made is a d. | SERV 270:9 |
| **debtor**: d. to his profession | BACON 24:9 |
| **debts**: And forgive us our d. | BIBLE 48:27 |
| He that dies pays all d. | SHAK 296:8 |
| **decay**: Change and d. in all around | LYTE 212:20 |
| D. with imprecision | ELIOT 133:1 |
| Only our love hath no d. | DONNE 123:22 |
| things are subject to d. | DRYD 128:4 |
| **decayed**: you are sufficiently d. | GILB 152:8 |
| **deceitful**: heart is d. | BIBLE 46:31 |
| **deceits**: all the d. of the world | BOOK 64:15 |
| prophesy d. | BIBLE 45:29 |

| | |
|---|---|
| deceive: don't d. me | ANON 6:27 |
| we d. ourselves | BIBLE 57:14 |
| When first we practise to d. | SCOTT 268:21 |
| deceived: d. with ornament | SHAK 289:21 |
| deceiver: I'm a gay d. | COLM 105:1.4 |
| deceivers: Men were d. ever | SHAK 291:19 |
| December: D.'s bareness | SHAK 300:3 |
| D. when they wed | SHAK 273:9 |
| From May to D. | AND 5:12 |
| Their meetings made D. June | TENN 325:20 |
| decencies: dwell in d. for ever | POPE 251:10 |
| decency: D. is Indecency's conspiracy | SHAW 302:3 |
| Terrible that old life of d. | LOW 211:11 |
| want of d. is want of sense | DILL 120:23 |
| decently: done d. and in order | BIBLE 55:15 |
| decent: d. obscurity | GIBB 150:16 |
| decide: comes the moment to d. | LOW 211:7 |
| decided: d. only to be undecided | CHUR 99:9 |
| decision: in the valley of d. | BIBLE 47:21 |
| deck: boy stood on the burning d. | HEM 165:9 |
| declaration: no d. of war | EDEN 130:14 |
| declare: And then, I d. | HOFF 169:19 |
| nothing to d. except my genius | WILDE 350:18 |
| decomposing: d. in the eternity of print | WOOLF 353:20 |
| decorum: Dulce et d. est | HOR 173:26 |
| hunt D. down | BYRON 86:33 |
| Let them cant about D. | BURNS 82:13 |
| decoyed: these poor fools d. | PEPYS 247:18 |
| decree: d. from Caesar Augustus | BIBLE 51:31 |
| establish the d. | BIBLE 47:13 |
| deed: attempt and not the d. | SHAK 286:13 |
| d. is all, the glory | GOET 154:7 |
| d. of dreadful note | SHAK 287:5 |
| d. without a name | SHAK 287:19 |
| good d. in a naughty world | SHAK 290:4 |
| leff woord and tak the d. | LYDG 212:15 |
| one that will do the d. | SHAK 284:14 |
| right d. for the wrong reason | ELIOT 134:7 |
| water clears us of this d. | SHAK 286:19 |
| Y'are the d.'s creature | MIDD 224:7 |
| deeds: Makes ill d. done | SHAK 282:12 |
| sight of means to do ill d. | SHAK 282:12 |
| though the sager sort our d. | CAMP 89:2 |
| deemed: Some d. him wondrous wise | BEAT 30:13 |
| deep: commit his body to the d. | BOOK 69:15 |
| D. is the silence | DRIN 126:24 |
| d. sleep of England | ORW 242:1 |
| d. upon her peerless eyes | KEATS 191:26 |
| D.-versed in books | MILT 230:8 |
| face of the d. | BIBLE 38:13 |
| From the great d. | TENN 324:4 |
| gentle motion with the d. | DAV 114:22 |
| Not d. the Poet sees, but wide | ARN 17:2 |
| often lie too d. for tears | WORD 355:24 |
| One d. calleth another | BOOK 67:4 |
| one is of the d. | STEP 315:4 |
| Out of the d. have I called | BOOK 68:33 |
| Rocked in the cradle of the d. | WILL 350:27 |
| 'tis not so d. as a well | SHAK 295:7 |
| deepens: d. like a coastal shelf | LARK 201:18 |
| deeper: and d. in debt | TRAV 334:4 |
| d. than did ever plummet | SHAK 296:13 |
| deer: Around the dying d. | AYT 23:16 |
| In the stare of the d. | WILB 349:9 |
| let the stricken d. go | SHAK 276:12 |
| defeat: Dear Night! this world's d. | VAUG 337:5 |
| d. is an orphan | CIANO 100:12 |
| In d.: defiance | CHUR 100:4 |
| In d. unbeatable | CHUR 100:9 |
| possibilities of d. | VICT 338:6 |
| defeated: Down with the d. | LIVY 208:5 |
| History to the d. | AUDEN 21:15 |
| safe course for the d. | VIRG 339:6 |
| defect: did make d. perfection | SHAK 271:16 |

| | |
|---|---|
| defect (cont.): | |
| this fair d. of Nature | MILT 229:30 |
| defence: d. of England | BALD 27:6 |
| Never make d. or apology | CHAR 94:22 |
| only d. is in offence | BALD 27:5 |
| defend: d. ourselves with guns | GOEB 153:21 |
| d. to the death your right | VOLT 341:1 |
| d. us from all perils | BOOK 64:12 |
| D. us thy humble servants | BOOK 64:5 |
| defended: God abandoned, these d. | HOUS 174:13 |
| defends: when attacked it d. itself | ANON 12:3 |
| defiance: In defeat: d. | CHUR 100:4 |
| defiled: toucheth pitch shall be d. | BIBLE 48:2 |
| definition: d. is the enclosing a wilderness | BUTL 84:16 |
| deflower: that will her pride d. | SPEN 313:12 |
| deformity: time's d. | JONS 187:7 |
| defy: d. the foul fiend | SHAK 283:13 |
| degree: exalted them of low d. | BIBLE 51:29 |
| Take but d. away | SHAK 296:30 |
| degrees: things through all d. | WORD 357:8 |
| Dei: Ad majorem D. gloriam | ANON 13:11 |
| Vox populi, vox D. | ALC 3:14 |
| deities: some other new d. | PLATO 249:18 |
| deity: D. and the Drains | STR 318:13 |
| For D. offended | BURNS 82:6 |
| delay: In d. there lies no plenty | SHAK 297:23 |
| In me is no d. | MILT 230:1 |
| Nothing was ever lost by d. | GREE 158:3 |
| delaying: make the gift rich by d. | TROL 334:18 |
| delays: All d. are dangerous in war | DRYD 128:22 |
| delenda: D. est Carthago | CATO 92:22 |
| deleted: Expletive d. | ANON 7:3 |
| Delia: While D. is away | JAGO 179:8 |
| deliberate: Where both d., the love | MARL 218:18 |
| deliberation: D. sat | MILT 228:27 |
| delight: And go to 't with d. | SHAK 271:20 |
| And turn d. into a sacrifice | HERB 166:21 |
| best gift, my ever new d. | MILT 229:15 |
| Commodity, firmness, and d. | WOTT 357:19 |
| d. and ends in wisdom | FROST 146:24 |
| D. hath a joy in it either | SIDN 306:29 |
| d. is in proper young men | BURNS 82:12 |
| d. of battle with my peers | TENN 328:21 |
| D. of lust is gross and brief | PETR 248:10 |
| each thing met conceives d. | MILT 229:23 |
| Energy is Eternal D. | BLAKE 60:24 |
| Let dogs d. to bark and bite | WATTS 343:7 |
| phantom of d. | WORD 356:24 |
| source of little visible d. | BRON 72:17 |
| Spirit of D. | SHEL 304:32 |
| Studies serve for d. | BACON 25:13 |
| sweet airs, that give d. | SHAK 296:9 |
| There is a land of pure d. | WATTS 343:11 |
| To bind another to its d. | BLAKE 62:2 |
| top-gallant d. is to him | MELV 223:2 |
| unrest which men miscall d. | SHEL 303:11 |
| yet I hear thy shrill d. | SHEL 305:8 |
| delighteth: king d. to honour | BIBLE 42:20 |
| neither d. he in any man's | BOOK 69:10 |
| delightful: And almost as d. | LOCK 208:22 |
| marriages, but no d. ones | LA R 201:22 |
| delighting: But, O! d. me | HODG 169:14 |
| delights: does some d. condemn | MOL 232:23 |
| king of intimate d. | COWP 110:12 |
| scorn d., and live laborious | MILT 227:14 |
| delinquent: condemns a less d. for't | BUTL 84:8 |
| delitabill: Storys to rede ar d. | BARB 28:15 |
| deliver: d. us from evil | BIBLE 48:27 |
| D. us, good Lord | CHES 97:24 |
| Good Lord, d. us | BOOK 64:14 |
| delivered: d. them into the hands | BIBLE 40:30 |
| d. my soul from death | BOOK 68:20 |
| delphiniums: d. blue and geraniums red | MILNE 225:21 |
| deluding: Fareweel dear, d. woman | BURNS 82:28 |
| déluge: Après nous le d. | POMP 250:11 |

destruction (cont.):
d. of the poor BIBLE 43:17
d. of the whole world HUME 176:11
Pride goeth before d. BIBLE 43:28
that leadeth to d. BIBLE 49:12
to their d. draw DONNE 123:22
destructive: to the d. element submit CONR 107:7
detail: frittered away by d. THOR 332:11
Merely corroborative d. GILB 152:5
details: mind which reveres d. LEWIS 206:19
detect: lose it in the moment you d. POPE 251:19
determinate: My bonds in thee are all d. SHAK 299:27
determination: character but the d. of incident
JAMES 179:24
determined: D., dared, and done SMART 308:14
detest: they d. at leisure BYRON 86:25
detraction: D. is but baseness' varlet JONS 187:10
Deutschland: D. über alles HOFF 169:16
deviates: Shadwell never d. into sense DRYD 128:5
device: banner with the strange d. LONG 209:17
devices: d. and desires of our own hearts BOOK 63:13
devil: apology for the D. BUTL 84:15
book a d.'s chaplain might write DARW 114:5
D. always builds a chapel DEFOE 115:22
d. a monk would be MOTT 236:3
d. and all his works BOOK 65:21
d. can cite Scripture SHAK 289:3
d. damn thee black SHAK 287:33
D. howling 'Ho!' SQUI 314:4
d. in the same churchyard BANC 28:14
d. is dead READE 258:10
D. knows Latin KNOX 198:19
D. sends cooks GARR 148:11
d. have all the good tunes HILL 168:14
d.'s most devilish when BROW 74:26
D.'s party BLAKE 60:25
d. understands Welsh SHAK 278:5
d. will come, and Faustus MARL 218:13
doubt is D.-born TENN 325:18
Drink and the d. had done STEV 317:2
For he counteracts the D. SMART 308:8
If the d. doesn't exist DOST 125:3
man's spirit is d.'s work SHAW 300:27
my back upon Don or d. TENN 328:12
Old D. Moon HARB 161:13
Or who cleft the D.'s foot DONNE 124:10
that d.'s madness—War SERV 270:12
That fears a painted d. SHAK 286:17
d. would also build a chapel LUTH 212:9
What! can the d. speak true SHAK 285:9
world, the flesh, and the d. BOOK 64:15
your adversary the d. BIBLE 57:12
devildoms: d. of Spain TENN 328:11
devilish: d. thing is 8 times 8 FLEM 141:22
devils: still 'tis d. must print MOORE 234:10
devoid: D. of sense and motion MILT 228:24
Devon: If the Dons sight D. NEWB 238:10
devotion: Farewell my bok and my d. CHAU 96:9
d. to something afar SHEL 305:5
devour: seeking whom he may d. BIBLE 57:12
devourer: Time the d. of everything OVID 243:16
devout: cannot be d. in dishabilly FARQ 138:21
devoutly: D. to be wished SHAK 275:25
dew: continual d. of thy blessing BOOK 64:9
d. of heaven drops now FORD 143:9
d. of yon high eastern hill SHAK 274:3
d. will rust them SHAK 291:31
drenched with d. DE L 116:21
fades awa' like morning d. BALL 28:10
resolve itself into a d. SHAK 274:9
there rained a ghastly d. TENN 326:11
dewdrop: Starlight and d. FOST 144:9
dewy: from noon to d. eve MILT 228:20
shakes his d. wings D'AV 114:10
diable: le d. est mort READE 258:10

diadem: A royal d. adorns KELLY 193:19
Bring forth the royal d. PERR 248:4
diagnostician: makes a good d. OSLER 243:3
diagonally: lie d. in his bed STER 315:23
dialect: D. words HARDY 161:23
To purify the d. of the tribe ELIOT 133:9
diamond: Like a d. in the sky TAYL 323:3
rough than polished d. CHES 97:12
diamonds: d. are a girl's best friend ROBIN 260:18
Goodness, what beautiful d. WEST 346:22
Diana: Let us be D.'s foresters SHAK 277:22
diary: d. and some day it'll keep you WEST 346:19
dibble: d. in earth to set one SHAK 298:30
dice: [God] does not play d. EINS 131:9
Dick: D. the shepherd SHAK 284:23
dictates: d. to me slumbering MILT 229:21
woman d. before marriage ELIOT 132:8
dictation: at d. speed what he knew AMIS 5:3
dictatorship: of the proletariat MARX 221:12
government you have a d. TRUM 335:3
dictionaries: D. are like watches JOHN 184:3
To make d. is dull work JOHN 182:6
writer of d., a harmless drudge JOHN 182:8
dictionary: He will be but a walking d. CHAP 94:21
did: And d. it very well GILB 151:14
d. for them both with his plan SASS 267:13
didn't he danced his d. CUMM 112:16
Dido: D. with a willow SHAK 289:32
die: about to d. salute you ANON 13:12
Americans, when they d. APPL 14:15
And how can man d. better MAC 214:3
And yet I love her till I d. ANON 10:18
back to America to d. JAMES 179:21
clean place to d. KAV 190:7
Cowards d. many times SHAK 281:8
Curse God, and d. BIBLE 42:24
determine to d. here BEE 31:22
D., and endow a college POPE 251:13
d., and go we know not SHAK 288:21
d. before we have explained ADAMS 2:3
d. beyond my means WILDE 350:22
d. but do not surrender CAMB 88:11
d. but once to serve our ADD 2:16
d. by famine die by inches HENRY 166:3
d. for adultery! SHAK 283:23
d. for one's country HOR 173:26
D. he or justice must MILT 229:3
d. in that man's company SHAK 279:18
d. in the last ditch WILL 351:1
d. is cast CAES 88:1
d. like a true-blue rebel HILL 168:13
D., my dear Doctor PALM 244:22
d. of that roar which lies ELIOT 132:10
d. on your feet IBAR 178:1
d. well that die in a battle SHAK 279:13
d. when the trees were CLARE 101:3
d. will be an awfully big BARR 29:13
d. with kissing of my Lord MARL 219:12
Easy live and quiet d. SCOTT 268:24
Few d. and none resign JEFF 180:22
find myself so apt to d. SHAK 281:12
For as in Adam all d. BIBLE 55:17
greatly think, or bravely d. POPE 250:23
harder lesson! how to d. PORT 253:27
He shall not d. STER 315:22
He will, he must d. NICH 239:10
Hope I d. before I get old TOWN 333:16
I am sick, I must d. NASHE 237:19
I die because I do not d. JOHN 181:10
If I should d. before I wake ANON 9:20
If I should d., think only BROO 73:10
If it were now to d. SHAK 292:5
If we are marked to d. SHAK 279:17
I'll d. for him to-morrow BALL 27:13

die (cont.):

| | |
|---|---|
| I shall d. at the top | SWIFT 320:26 |
| I shall not altogether d. | HOR 173:29 |
| it was sure to d. | MOORE 234:19 |
| I will d. in peace | WOLFE 353:4 |
| Let me d. a youngman's death | MCG 214:21 |
| Let us do—or d. | BURNS 82:22 |
| man can d. but once | SHAK 278:25 |
| must be with us, or we d. | KEATS 190:12 |
| myself to d. upon a kiss | SHAK 293:6 |
| natural to d. as to be born | BACON 24:22 |
| Not d. here in a rage | SWIFT 320:5 |
| not so difficult to d. | BYRON 87:2 |
| not that I'm afraid to d. | ALLEN 4:16 |
| not to live, but to d. in | BROW 74:20 |
| Of easy ways to d. | SHAK 272:11 |
| Old soldiers never d. | FOLEY 142:16 |
| or being born, to d. | BACON 25:31 |
| or like Douglas d. | HOME 170:19 |
| passing-bells for these who d. | OWEN 243:21 |
| pie in the sky when you d. | HILL 168:12 |
| poison us, do we not d. | SHAK 289:17 |
| seems it rich to d. | KEATS 192:3 |
| She must weep or she will d. | TENN 327:26 |
| should d. for the people | BIBLE 53:34 |
| something he will d. for | KING 195:8 |
| taught us how to d. | TICK 332:20 |
| Their every parting was to d. | TENN 325:20 |
| Theirs but to do and d. | TENN 323:15 |
| thereof thou shalt surely d. | BIBLE 38:19 |
| they only let Him d. | STUD 318:19 |
| This'll be the day that I d. | MCL 215:8 |
| time to d. | BIBLE 44:11 |
| To d. and know it | LOW 211:16 |
| To d., to sleep | SHAK 275:25 |
| To go away is to d. a little | HAR 161:9 |
| To-morrow let us do or d. | CAMP 88:18 |
| to morrow we shall d. | BIBLE 45:24 |
| We d. in earnest | RAL 257:22 |
| We must love one another or d. | AUDEN 21:11 |
| We shall d. alone | PASC 246:4 |
| What 'tis to d. | FLET 31:2 |
| When beggars d. | SHAK 281:8 |
| Who did not wish to d. | SHAW 303:1 |
| wish to live and to d. | VILL 338:21 |
| wretch that dares not d. | BURNS 82:15 |
| you asked this man to d. | AUDEN 20:17 |
| died: d. by the hand of the Lord | BIBLE 40:1 |
| d. last night of my physician | PRIOR 255:11 |
| D. some, pro patria | POUND 254:18 |
| d. to save their country | CHES 97:23 |
| He d. in a good old age | BIBLE 42:18 |
| He that d. o' Wednesday | SHAK 278:12 |
| If any question why we d. | KIPL 196:7 |
| liked it not, and d. | WOTT 357:17 |
| Mithridates, he d. old | HOUS 175:5 |
| she d. young | WEBS 344:19 |
| She should have d. hereafter | SHAK 288:5 |
| thought it d. of grieving | KEATS 191:3 |
| Who d. to save us all | ALEX 4:6 |
| would God I had d. for thee | BIBLE 41:27 |
| diem: carpe d. | HOR 173:20 |
| dies: d. rich dies disgraced | CARN 90:27 |
| D. irae, dies illa | MISS 231:23 |
| Every moment d. a man | BABB 23:19 |
| Every moment d. a man | TENN 328:26 |
| hath blown for ever all | FITZ 140:10 |
| He that d. pays all debts | SHAK 296:8 |
| kingdom where nobody d. | MILL 224:21 |
| little something in me d. | VIDAL 338:13 |
| man happy before he d. | SOLON 310:27 |
| One d. only once | MOL 232:17 |
| true because a man d. for it | WILDE 350:7 |
| Who d. if England live | KIPL 196:13 |
| Whom the gods love d. young | MEN 223:5 |

| | |
|---|---|
| diesel: D.-engined | FLAN 141:6 |
| diet: d. unparalleled | DICK 119:10 |
| difference: and, oh, the d. to me | WORD 356:23 |
| And that has made all the d. | FROST 146:19 |
| d. of forty thousand men | WELL 345:13 |
| Divines, and d. of texts | SPEN 313:16 |
| silk makes the d. | FULL 147:7 |
| wear your rue with a d. | SHAK 277:3 |
| different: because he hears a d. drummer | THOR 332:12 |
| But had thought they were d. | ELIOT 133:22 |
| clean d. things | CHAR 94:25 |
| d. from the home life of our | ANON 8:1 |
| How d. from us | ANON 9:10 |
| rich are d. | FITZ 140:20 |
| We boil at d. degrees | EMER 136:32 |
| differently: one who thinks d. | LUX 212:12 |
| difficile: D. est longum subito deponere | CAT 93:5 |
| difficult: D. do you call it | JOHN 186:16 |
| difficult we do immediately | CAL 88:6 |
| fascination of what's d. | YEATS 359:4 |
| first step that is d. | DU D 129:1 |
| It has been found d. | CHES 98:15 |
| Poets must be d. | ELIOT 135:3 |
| 'tis not so d. to die | BYRON 87:2 |
| too d. for artists | SCHN 267:23 |
| upon which it is d. to speak | BURKE 80:26 |
| difficulties: d. do not make one doubt | NEWM 238:16 |
| little local d. | MACM 215:16 |
| difficulty: with d. and labour | MILT 229:2 |
| diffidence: her name was D. | BUNY 79:3 |
| dig: D. for victory | DORM 124:24 |
| d. till you gently perspire | KIPL 197:22 |
| with his nails he'll d. | WEBS 344:26 |
| digest: inwardly d. them | BOOK 64:22 |
| digestion: good d. wait on appetite | SHAK 287:10 |
| sweet to taste prove in d. | SHAK 293:11 |
| dignified: d. parts | BAG 26:3 |
| dignitate: Cum d. otium | CIC 100:32 |
| dignity: equal in d. and rights | ANON 5:20 |
| left the room with silent d. | GROS 159:4 |
| digressions: D. are the sunshine | STER 315:15 |
| dilectione: d. hominum et odio vitiorum | AUG 22:4 |
| dilettante: snowy-banded, d. | TENN 326:25 |
| dilige: D. et quod vis fac | AUG 22:2 |
| dillied: But I d. and dallied | COLL 105:7 |
| dilly-dally: Don't d. on the way | COLL 105:7 |
| dim: bright world d. | SHEL 305:17 |
| d. in the intense inane | SHEL 304:23 |
| dime: Brother can you spare a d. | HARB 161:11 |
| dimensions: When my d. are | SHAK 282:20 |
| diminished: and ought to be d. | DUNN 129:10 |
| dine: d. exact at noon | POPE 251:25 |
| going to d. with some men | BENT 35:9 |
| hang that jury-men may d. | POPE 253:8 |
| dined: d. against than dining | BOWRA 71:3 |
| I have d. to-day | SMITH 310:7 |
| dining: more dined against than d. | BOWRA 71:3 |
| dinner: D. in the diner | GORD 155:22 |
| d. of herbs | BIBLE 43:26 |
| I get too hungry for d. at eight | HART 163:9 |
| They would ask him to d. | CARL 90:26 |
| three hours' march to d. | HAZL 164:8 |
| tocsin of the soul—the d. bell | BYRON 86:20 |
| Diogenes: I would be D. | ALEX 4:1 |
| diplomacy: D. is to do and say | GOLD 154:16 |
| diplomat: d. these days is | UST 336:19 |
| diplomatic: d. boathook | SAL 266:2 |
| dipping: age o'ercargoed, d. deep | FLEC 141:18 |
| directions: By indirections find d. out | SHAK 275:7 |
| rode madly off in all d. | LEAC 203:5 |
| direful: something d. in the sound | AUST 22:17 |
| dirge: d. of her certain ending | SHAK 299:9 |
| dirt: d. doesn't get any worse | CRISP 111:20 |
| D. is matter out of place | GRAY 156:18 |

**dirt** (cont.):
d. succeed where sweetness — FORS 143:18
In poverty, hunger, and d. — HOOD 171:12
thicker will be the d. — GALB 147:15
**dirty:** D. British coaster — MAS 221:19
D., dark, and undevotional — VICT 338:10
d. work for the rest — RUSK 264:15
'Jug Jug' to d. ears — ELIOT 134:22
Is sex d.? — ALLEN 4:15
**dis:** D. aliter visum — VIRG 339:7
**disagreeables:** making all d. evaporate — KEATS 193:1
**disappointed:** d. by that stroke of death — JOHN 182:23
Sir! you have d. us — BELL 33:7
**disappointing:** he'll be the least d. — BAR 29:21
**disappointment:** D. all I endeavour end — HOPK 172:18
**disapprove:** it's no d. of what you say — VOLT 341:1
**disaster:** meet with triumph and d. — KIPL 197:6
**disasters:** d. in his morning face — GOLD 154:23
guilty of our own d. the sun — SHAK 282:22
**disbelief:** willing suspension of d. — COL 104:24
**discandy:** do d., melt their sweets — SHAK 271:22
**discerning:** Gives genius a better d. — GOLD 155:8
**discharge:** no d. in that war — BIBLE 44:17
**discipline:** good order and military d. — ANON 6:22
**disciplines:** category-d. — RYLE 265:10
**discommendeth:** He who d. others — BROW 74:1
**discontent:** In pale contented sort of d. — KEATS 191:13
Now is the winter of our d. — SHAK 294:13
**discord:** dire effects from civil d. flow — ADD 2:19
that eke d. doth sow — ELIZ 135:13
what d. follows — SHAK 296:30
**discors:** Concordia d. — HOR 173:12
**discouragement:** There's no d. — BUNY 79:9
**discourse:** d. and nearest prose — DRYD 128:14
that wants d. of reason — SHAK 274:22
**discoverers:** ill d. that think — BACON 23:22
**discovery:** D. consists of — SZEN 322:3
Medicinal is — AYRES 23:15
**discreet:** d. charm of the bourgeoisie — BUÑ 78:16
**discretion:** D. is not the better part — STR 318:15
**discunt:** Homines dum docent d. — SEN 270:6
**discussion:** government by d. — ATTL 19:14
**disdain:** little d. is not amiss — CONG 106:19
**disease:** Cured yesterday of my d. — PRIOR 255:11
Cure the d. and kill — BACON 24:25
D., Ignorance, Squalor — BEV 38:7
d. is incurable — SHAK 278:19
d. of not listening — SHAK 278:17
D., or sorrows strike him — CLOU 102:15
d. requires a dangerous — FAWK 138:22
d. that gave death time — GUIB 159:8
incurable d. of writing — JUV 189:10
Life is an incurable d. — COWL 109:17
Progress is a comfortable d. — CUMM 112:20
remedy is worse than the d. — BACON 25:11
sexually transmitted d. — ANON 8:20
strange d. of modern life — ARN 17:11
that the d. is incurable — CHEK 96:24
There is no Cure for this D. — BELL 33:4
this long d., my life — POPE 251:4
**diseased:** minister to a mind d. — SHAK 288:2
Of its own beauty is the mind d. — BYRON 85:9
**diseases:** Coughs and sneezes spread d. — ANON 6:23
death is the cure of all d. — BROW 74:19
D. desperate grown — SHAK 276:27
**disgrace:** It's no d. t'be poor — HUBB 175:17
Its private life is a d. — ANON 10:8
**disgraced:** dies rich dies d. — CARN 90:27
**disgraceful:** something d. in mind — JUV 189:15
**disgruntled:** if not actually d. — WOD 352:13
**disguise:** D. fair nature with hard-favoured — SHAK 279:5
**dish:** butter in a lordly d. — BIBLE 40:33
Let's carve him as a d. fit — SHAK 281:4
**dishabilly:** cannot be devout in d. — FARQ 138:21
**dishes:** no washing of d. — ANON 7:17

**disinheriting:** damned d. countenance — SHER 306:7
**disinterested:** D. intellectual curiosity — TREV 334:7
**dismal:** D. Science — CARL 90:18
With d. stories — BUNY 79:9
**dismayed:** neither be thou d. — BIBLE 40:26
Was there a man d. — TENN 323:15
**dismiss:** Lord, d. us with Thy blessing — BUCK 78:3
**disobedience:** man's first d. — MILT 228:7
**disorder:** green ice, in wild d. rise — PHIL 248:15
sweet d. in the dress — HERR 167:15
**disparity:** Just such d. 'twixt — DONNE 123:21
**dispatch:** requisite in business than d. — ADD 2:20
**disposes:** man proposes, God d. — THOM 330:1
**disposition:** Foul d., thoughts unnatural — SHAK 292:13
To put an antic d. on — SHAK 275:4
truant d., good my lord — SHAK 274:14
**dispraised:** d. were no small praise — MILT 230:3
**dispute:** work more and d. less — TAWN 322:19
**disquieted:** Never to be d. — KING 195:5
**dissect:** thro' creatures you d. — POPE 251:19
We murder to d. — WORD 357:5
**dissipation:** d. without pleasure — GIBB 150:15
**dissolution:** A lingering d. — BECK 31:7
**dissolve:** Fade far away, d. — KEATS 191:31
**dissonance:** with barbarous d. — MILT 226:17
**distance:** d. between Russia and British — SAL 266:3
d. is nothing — DU D 129:1
d. lends enchantment — CAMP 88:19
or prestige without d. — DE G 116:5
seconds' worth of d. run — KIPL 197:7
**distant:** d. from Heaven alike — BURT 83:11
d. scene, one step enough — NEWM 238:21
prospect of a d. good — DRYD 127:32
**distempered:** That questions the d. part — ELIOT 133:5
**distillation:** History is a d. of rumour — CARL 90:12
**distinguished:** d. thing — JAMES 180:6
**distraction:** Into a fine d. — HERR 167:15
**distress:** All pray in their d. — BLAKE 61:20
**distressed:** afflicted, or d., in mind — BOOK 64:19
**distribute:** d. as fairly as he can — LOWE 211:1
**ditch:** Channel is a mere d. — NAP 237:1
die in the last d. — WILL 351:1
he wasn't as dull as d. water — DICK 119:24
**ditches:** of Dutchmen and of d. — BYRON 86:22
**dive:** Heav'n's great lamps do d. — CAMP 89:2
search for pearls must d. — DRYD 127:23
**divers:** sundry times and in d. places — BIBLE 56:25
**diversity:** arise d. of sects — SPEN 313:16
them and servants some d. — BARC 28:17
**divided:** d. by a common language — SHAW 302:27
I do perceive here a d. duty — SHAK 291:36
If a house be d. — BIBLE 51:19
in their death they were not d. — BIBLE 41:22
sick hurry, its d. aims — ARN 17:11
whole is d. into three — CAES 87:24
**dividend:** d. from time's tomorrows — SASS 267:10
**dividing:** by d. we fall — DICK 120:18
days d. lover and lover — SWIN 321:2
**divine:** Ah, what the form d. — LAND 200:23
All things, by a law d. — SHEL 304:3
And Love, the human form d. — BLAKE 61:21
But 'twas d. — TRAH 334:1
depth of some d. despair — TENN 327:22
hand that made us is d. — ADD 2:26
little heavy, but no less d. — BYRON 86:15
Right D. of Kings to govern — POPE 250:18
To err is human; to forgive, d. — POPE 252:7
You look d. as you advance — NASH 237:18
**divinely:** And most d. fair — TENN 323:20
**divines:** Doubts 'mongst D. — SPEN 313:16
**divinest:** d. things this world has — HUNT 176:17
**divinity:** d. that shapes our ends — SHAK 277:12
such d. doth hedge a king — SHAK 277:1
surely a piece of d. in us — BROW 74:21

**divinity** (*cont.*):
There is d. in odd numbers — SHAK 290:11
those wingy mysteries in d. — BROW 74:10
**division**: D. is as bad — ANON 9:11
**divisions**: How many d. has *he* got? — STAL 314:8
**divorce**: d. of steel falls on me — SHAK 280:14
this bill of my d. to all — DONNE 123:15
**do**: Diplomacy is to d. and say — GOLD 154:16
d. a girl — ELIOT 134:15
D. not fold, spindle — ANON 6:26
d. only one thing at once — SMIL 308:18
D. other men, for they would — DICK 119:3
D. this, and he doeth — BIBLE 49:17
d. were as easy as to know — SHAK 288:29
D. what thou wilt shall be — CROW 112:14
D. what you like — RAB 257:12
d. ye even so to them — BIBLE 49:11
HOW NOT TO D. IT — DICK 118:29
I am to d. what I please — FRED 145:19
I can d. no other — LUTH 212:8
I'll do, I'll do, and I'll d. — SHAK 285:3
Let's d. it, let's fall in love — PORT 253:22
Let us d.—or die — BURNS 82:22
Love and d. what you will — AUG 22:2
So little done, so much to d. — RHOD 259:12
so much to d., so little done — TENN 325:14
Theirs but to d. and die — TENN 323:15
To d. it as for Thee — HERB 166:25
To-morrow let us d. or die — CAMP 88:18
Whatever you d., do cautiously — ANON 13:20
**docent**: *Homines dum d. discunt* — SEN 270:6
**doctor**: God and the d. we alike adore — OWEN 243:17
Knocked down a d. — SIMP 307:12
**doctors**: budge a d. of the Stoic fur — MILT 226:19
By violet-hooded D. — TENN 327:18
D. in verse — THOM 331:3
We d. know — CUMM 113:1
**doctrine**: d. of ignoble ease — ROOS 262:15
d. set forth thy true — BOOK 65:10
loved the d. for the teacher — DEFOE 115:18
Not for the d. — POPE 252:3
**doctrines**: all d. plain and clear — BUTL 84:5
**doers**: Be ye d. of the word — BIBLE 57:2
**doffed**: fogies who d. their lids — KEAT 190:9
**dog**: beaten d. beneath the hail — POUND 254:21
been working like a d. — MCC 205:14
black d. waits — JOHN 182:17
But if a man bites a d. — BOG 62:19
d. is turned to his own — BIBLE 57:13
d. it was that died — GOLD 154:28
d. that has praised his fleas — YEATS 360:3
engine of pollution, the d. — SPAR 312:14
every d. has his day — BORR 69:27
every d. his day — KING 195:17
giving your heart to a d. — KIPL 196:27
If you call a d. *Hervey* — JOHN 183:23
incident of the d. in the night — DOYLE 125:21
Is thy servant a d. — BIBLE 42:12
jumps over the lazy d. — ANON 10:7
Lovell our d. — COLL 105:3
Mine enemy's d. — SHAK 283:28
misbeliever, cut-throat d. — SHAK 289:5
Something better than his d. — TENN 326:7
very d. to the commonalty — SHAK 273:15
whose d. are you? — POPE 251:1
woman's preaching is like a d.'s — JOHN 184:16
**dogged**: It's d. as does it — TROL 334:15
**dogma**: no d., no Dean — DISR 122:16
will serve to beat a d. — GUED 159:5
**dogs**: bang these d. of Seville — TENN 328:12
d. and killed the cats — BROW 76:26
d. delight to bark — WATTS 343:7
d. go on with their doggy — AUDEN 21:2
d. than of their children — PENN 247:10
hates d. and babies — ROST 263:13

**dogs** (*cont.*):
Lame d. over stiles — KING 195:14
let slip the d. of war — SHAK 281:14
Mad d. and Englishmen — COW 109:4
more I like d. — TOUS 333:15
Things are but as straw d. — LAO-T 201:11
Throw physic to the d. — SHAK 288:3
**doing**: joy's soul lies in the d. — SHAK 296:29
next to fine d. the top thing — KEATS 193:12
Patient continuance in well d. — BIBLE 54:28
put me to d. — METH 223:28
see what she's d. — PUNCH 256:13
What was he d., the great — BROW 75:4
**doleful**: Knight of the D. Countenance — CERV 93:16
**doll**: doll in the d.'s house — DICK 119:25
**dollar**: d. is the only object — ANON 5:23
Isn't this a billion d. country — FOST 144:6
**Dolores**: splendid and sterile D. — SWIN 321:8
**dolorous**: d. mansions to the peering day — MILT 227:28
**dolour**: d. of pad and paper-weight — ROET 261:14
**dolphin-torn**: d., that gong-tormented sea — YEATS 358:15
**dome**: d. of many-coloured glass — SHEL 303:13
singing beneath the d. — VERL 338:1
**domestic**: d. business is no less — MONT 233:13
Milk-soup men call d. bliss — PATM 246:18
respectable d. establishment — BENN 34:12
**dominant**: d.'s persistence — BROW 77:17
**dominion**: death hath no more d. — BIBLE 54:35
death shall have no d. — THOM 330:6
hand that holds d. over Man — THOM 330:11
**dominions**: His Majesty's d. — NORTH 240:6
sun does not set in my d. — SCH 267:19
**domino**: 'falling d.' principle — EIS 131:15
**dominus**: *D. illuminatio mea* — BIBLE 58:9
*D. vobiscum* — MISS 231:9
*Nisi D. custodierit civitatem* — BIBLE 58:13
**don**: my back upon D. or devil — TENN 328:12
Remote and ineffectual D. — BELL 33:16
**dona**: *timeo Danaos et d. ferentis* — VIRG 339:5
**done**: decide that nothing can be d. — ALLEN 4:12
Determined, dared, and d. — SMART 308:14
D. because we are too menny — HARDY 161:22
d. the state some service — SHAK 293:5
d. those things which we — BOOK 63:14
d. very well out of the war — BALD 27:9
he d. her wrong — ANON 7:6
Inasmuch as ye have d. it — BIBLE 51:6
much is to be d. and little — JOHN 182:27
must be seen to be d. — OSB 242:25
Nay, I have d. — DRAY 126:16
Nothing to be d. — BECK 31:10
Played-out and D.-to-death — TRAI 334:2
should not be d. at all — VIDAL 338:11
so I order it d. — JUV 189:8
surprised to find it d. at all — JOHN 184:16
that which is d. is that which — BIBLE 44:8
Think nothing d. — LUCAN 211:25
though it were d. before — DONNE 123:17
were d. when 'tis done — SHAK 285:22
What is to be d. — LENIN 205:3
What's d. cannot be undone — SHAK 287:31
what's d. is done — SHAK 287:3
won are d. — SHAK 296:29
**dong**: D. with a Luminous Nose — LEAR 203:8
**donkey**: that's a dead d. — DICK 120:4
**donkeys**: Lions led by d. — HOFF 169:17
**Donne**: another Newton, a new D. — HUXL 177:11
D., for not keeping of accent — JONS 187:31
D.'s verses are like — JAM 179:13
D., whose muse on dromedary — COL 104:2
**dons**: D. admirable! D. of Might — BELL 33:17
If the D. sight Devon — NEWB 238:10
**don't**: persons about to marry.—'D.' — PUNCH 256:5
**doom**: even to the edge of d. — SHAK 300:9

**doom** (*cont.*):

| | |
|---|---|
| regardless of their d. | GRAY 157:12 |
| **Doon:** banks and braes o' bonny D. | BURNS 81:27 |
| **door:** coming in at one d. | BEDE 31:20 |
| Death's shadow at the d. | BLUN 62:12 |
| d. flew open, in he ran | HOFF 169:21 |
| d. opens and lets the future in | GREE 158:6 |
| d. we never opened | ELIOT 132:26 |
| drive an angel from your d. | BLAKE 61:22 |
| I am the d. | BIBLE 53:29 |
| instrument here at the d. | DONNE 123:16 |
| interest a knock at the d. | LAMB 200:3 |
| Is beating on the d. | YEATS 359:6 |
| I stand at the d. | BIBLE 57:23 |
| knocking at Preferment's d. | ARN 17:6 |
| On the wrong side of the d. | CHES 97:21 |
| prejudices through the d. | FRED 145:18 |
| whining of a d. | DONNE 124:21 |
| **door-keeper:** d. in the house of my God | BOOK 67:22 |
| **doormat:** d. in a world of boots | RHYS 259:15 |
| **doors:** d. of perception | BLAKE 61:11 |
| D., where my heart was used | TENN 324:26 |
| In Little Girls is slamming D. | BELL 33:10 |
| many to let out life | FLET 142:4 |
| ten thousand several d. | WEBS 344:18 |
| their d. against a setting sun | SHAK 296:19 |
| thousand d. open on to it | SEN 270:8 |
| thousand d. to let out life | MASS 222:6 |
| ye everlasting | BOOK 66:20 |
| **doorstep:** Leave your worry on the d. | FIEL 139:15 |
| **dooryard:** When lilacs last in the d. | WHIT 348:24 |
| **Dorcas:** D.: this woman was | BIBLE 54:14 |
| **dorma:** *Nessun d.* | ADAMI 1:6 |
| **dotage:** Pedantry is the d. of knowledge | JACK 178:24 |
| **Dotheboys Hall:** Squeer's Academy, D. | DICK 119:10 |
| **dotting:** D. the shoreless watery wild | ARN 17:22 |
| **double:** Double, d. toil and trouble | SHAK 287:15 |
| so d. be his praise | SPEN 313:10 |
| **double-bed:** d. after the hurly-burly | CAMP 88:15 |
| **doubles:** d. your chances of a date | ALLEN 4:17 |
| **doublet:** tailor make thy d. | SHAK 297:33 |
| **doublethink:** *D.* means | ORW 242:10 |
| **doubt:** do not make one d. | NEWM 238:16 |
| d. is our passion | JAMES 179:23 |
| freckles, and d. | PARK 245:5 |
| Humility is only d. | BLAKE 60:12 |
| Life is d. | UNAM 336:11 |
| mind is clouded with a d. | TENN 324:22 |
| more faith in honest d. | TENN 325:19 |
| night of d. and sorrow | BAR 29:2 |
| No possible d. whatever | GILB 151:5 |
| Oh! let us never, never d. | BELL 33:21 |
| when in d., strike it out | TWAIN 336:6 |
| When in d., win the trick | HOYLE 175:12 |
| wherefore didst thou d. | BIBLE 50:9 |
| You tell me, d. is Devil-born | TENN 325:18 |
| **doubter:** I am the d. and the doubt | EMER 136:11 |
| **doubtless:** d. God never did | BUTL 84:22 |
| **doubts:** D. 'mongst Divines | SPEN 313:16 |
| he shall end in d. | BACON 23:20 |
| His d. are better than | HARD 161:17 |
| To saucy d. and fears | SHAK 287:9 |
| **Douglas:** Like D. conquer | HOME 170:19 |
| **Dove:** all the eagle in thee, all the d. | CRAS 111:8 |
| and the sweet d. died | KEATS 191:3 |
| Beside the springs of D. | WORD 356:22 |
| hawk at eagles with a d. | HERB 167:6 |
| that I had wings like a d. | BOOK 67:11 |
| **Dover:** farthing candle at D. | JOHN 184:15 |
| white cliffs of D. | BURT 83:3 |
| **doves:** harmless as d. | BIBLE 49:29 |
| **dowagers:** d. for deans | TENN 327:16 |
| **down:** D. among the dead men | DYER 129:18 |
| D. and away below | ARN 16:16 |
| D. by the salley gardens | YEATS 359:1 |

**down** (*cont.*):

| | |
|---|---|
| d. express in the small | WOD 352:18 |
| D. in the forest something | SIMP 307:10 |
| d. needs fear no fall | BUNY 79:7 |
| d. the nights and down | THOM 331:8 |
| D. these mean streets | CHAN 94:9 |
| D. to Gehenna or up to | KIPL 196:20 |
| go d. to the sea again | MAS 221:21 |
| meet 'em on your way d. | MIZN 232:11 |
| quite, quite, d. | SHAK 276:2 |
| thou knowest my d.-sitting | BOOK 69:5 |
| valley, come thou d. | TENN 328:7 |
| **downhearted:** Are we d.? | KNIG 198:13 |
| Are we d.? | ANON 6:4 |
| We are not d. | CHAM 93:24 |
| **downs:** All in the D. the fleet | GAY 149:17 |
| **downwards:** could look no way but d. | BUNY 79:6 |
| **dozens:** Mother to d. | HERB 166:13 |
| Whom he reckons up by d. | GILB 152:17 |
| **dragon:** angels fought against the d. | BIBLE 57:31 |
| d.-green, the luminous, the dark | FLEC 141:15 |
| **dragons:** be an habitation of d. | BIBLE 46:3 |
| Bores have succeeded to d. | DISR 122:11 |
| D. in their pleasant palaces | BIBLE 45:21 |
| I am a brother to d. | BIBLE 43:3 |
| Never laugh at live d. | TOLK 333:9 |
| **drain:** d. pure gold flows forth | TOCQ 333:5 |
| **drains:** Deity and the D. | STR 318:13 |
| Democracy and proper d. | BETJ 37:4 |
| some dull opiate to the d. | KEATS 191:28 |
| **Drake:** D. he's in his hammock | NEWB 238:11 |
| **drama:** close the d. with the day | BERK 35:19 |
| d.'s laws the drama's patrons | JOHN 183:10 |
| general d. of pain | HARDY 161:24 |
| **dramatist:** d. only wants more liberties | JAMES 179:15 |
| **Drang:** *Sturm und D.* | KAUF 190:6 |
| **draughts:** peculiarly susceptible to d. | WILDE 349:21 |
| **draw:** began to d. to our end | BIBLE 47:30 |
| d. but twenty miles a day | MARL 219:14 |
| D. not up seas to drown | DONNE 124:16 |
| d. you to her *with a single* hair | DRYD 128:24 |
| **drawers:** and d. of water | BIBLE 40:28 |
| **drawing:** D. is the true test of art | INGR 178:17 |
| Mrs Gaskell! no d. back | BRON 72:19 |
| **drawing-room:** feelings of women in a d. | WOOLF 354:3 |
| **drawn:** D. with a team of little atomies | SHAK 294:24 |
| **dread:** d. of beatings | BETJ 37:14 |
| Nor d. nor hope attend | YEATS 358:17 |
| **dreadful:** acting of a d. thing | SHAK 281:3 |
| City of D. Night | THOM 332:1 |
| deed of d. note | SHAK 287:5 |
| **dreading:** D. and hoping all | YEATS 358:21 |
| **Dreadnoughts:** Duke costs as much as two D. | LLOY 208:9 |
| **dream:** And slowly read and d. | YEATS 360:9 |
| Because thou must not d. | ARN 16:15 |
| behold it was a d. | BUNY 79:5 |
| d. but of a shadow | CHAP 94:15 |
| d. doth flatter | SHAK 299:28 |
| D. of Fair Women | TENN 323:20 |
| d. of money-bags to-night | SHAK 289:9 |
| d. of reason produces monsters | GOYA 156:1 |
| D. the impossible dream | DAR 114:2 |
| d. within a dream | POE 250:5 |
| d. you are crossing the Channel | GILB 151:16 |
| For each age is a d. | O'SH 243:2 |
| freshness of a d. | WORD 355:17 |
| from a deep d. of peace | HUNT 176:12 |
| glory and the d. | WORD 355:19 |
| I d. my dreams away | FLAN 141:2 |
| I have a d. | KING 195:9 |
| In a d. you are never eighty | SEXT 270:15 |
| love's young d. | MOORE 234:15 |
| perchance to d. | SHAK 275:25 |
| phantasma, or a hideous d. | SHAK 281:3 |

**dream** (cont.):

| | |
|---|---|
| quiet sleep and a sweet d. | MAS 222:2 |
| salesman is got to d. | MILL 225:4 |
| short as any d. | SHAK 290:14 |
| So runs my d. | TENN 325:9 |
| speaking silence of a d. | ROSS 263:1 |
| traveller's d. under the hill | BLAKE 60:15 |
| True to the d. I am dreaming | COW 109:7 |
| vision, or a waking d. | KEATS 192:7 |
| Where we used to sit and d. | ARMS 15:24 |

**dreamed:** d. that Greece

| | |
|---|---|
| d. that I dwelt in marble | BYRON 86:14 |
| night I've d. of cheese | BUNN 78:13 |

**dreamer:** Beautiful d., wake unto me

| | |
|---|---|
| Behold, this d. cometh | FOST 144:9 |
| D. of dreams, born out of | BIBLE 39:25 |
| or a d. of dreams | MORR 235:15 |
| poet and the d. | BIBLE 40:22 |
| | KEATS 190:25 |

**dreamers:** We are the d. of dreams

| | |
|---|---|
| | O'SH 243:1 |

**dreamin':** D. of thee!

| | |
|---|---|
| little d., a little dyin' | WALL 341:7 |
| | PHIL 248:17 |

**dreaming:** City within her d. spires

| | |
|---|---|
| d. on the verge of strife | ARN 17:17 |
| I'm d. of a white Christmas | CORN 108:7 |
| man I. I was a butterfly | BERL 36:3 |
| | CHUA 98:19 |

**dreams:** armoured cars of d.

| | |
|---|---|
| As d. are made on | BISH 59:16 |
| awoke from uneasy d. | SHAK 296:10 |
| because you tread on my d. | KAFKA 189:16 |
| beyond the d. of avarice | YEATS 359:7 |
| beyond the d. of avarice | JOHN 185:29 |
| books are either d. or swords | MOORE 234:5 |
| D. are the royal road | LOW 211:3 |
| d. happy as her day | FREUD 146:1 |
| d. out of the ivory gate | BROO 73:10 |
| Fanatics have their d. | BROW 74:23 |
| forgotten scream for help in d. | KEATS 190:24 |
| If there were d. to sell | CAN 89:9 |
| Inaudible as d. | BEDD 31:19 |
| In d. begins responsibility | COL 103:19 |
| Into the land of my d. | YEATS 360:11 |
| Made holy by their d. | KING 195:12 |
| not that I have bad d. | GIBS 150:22 |
| old men shall dream d. | SHAK 275:15 |
| quick D., the passion-wingèd | BIBLE 47:20 |
| we who lived by honest d. | SHEL 303:5 |
| | DAY-L 115:6 |

**dreamt:** d. I went to Manderley

| | |
|---|---|
| d. of in your philosophy | DU M 129:5 |
| | SHAK 275:3 |

**dreary:** d. length before the Court

| | |
|---|---|
| She only said, 'My life is d. | DICK 118:1 |
| | TENN 326:22 |

**dress:** And Peace, the human d.

| | |
|---|---|
| d. by yellow candle-light | BLAKE 61:21 |
| Expression is the d. of thought | STEV 317:12 |
| Full evening d. is a must | POPE 252:2 |
| Style is the d. of thought | GREN 158:15 |
| sweet disorder in the d. | WESL 346:18 |
| through all this fleshly d. | HERR 167:15 |
| You will put on a d. of guilt | VAUG 337:9 |

**dressed:** D. in style, brand new tile

| | |
|---|---|
| d. up and have no place | MCG 214:20 |
| d. up and no place to go | COLL 105:6 |
| | WHIT 348:8 |
| | BURT 83:2 |

**dressing:** best is d. old words new

| | |
|---|---|
| | SHAK 299:25 |

**drew:** d. them...with bands of love

| | |
|---|---|
| | BIBLE 47:18 |

**Dr Fell:** I do not love thee, D.

| | |
|---|---|
| | BROWN 73:18 |

**drift:** adamant for d.

| | |
|---|---|
| | CHUR 99:9 |

**drifts:** Strewn with its dank yellow d.

| | |
|---|---|
| | ARN 17:3 |

**drink:** d., and be merry

| | |
|---|---|
| D. and the devil had done | BIBLE 52:18 |
| d., and to be merry | STEV 317:2 |
| D. deep, or taste not | BIBLE 44:18 |
| D., sir, is a great provoker | POPE 251:28 |
| D. to me only with thine eyes | SHAK 286:21 |
| eat and d.; for tomorrow | JONS 187:23 |
| eat with you, d. with you | BIBLE 45:24 |
| Give strong d. unto him | SHAK 288:31 |
| | BIBLE 44:5 |

**drink** (cont.):

| | |
|---|---|
| I will d. life to the lees | TENN 328:20 |
| Man wants but little d. below | HOLM 170:17 |
| Nor any drop to d. | COL 104:7 |
| strong d. is raging | BIBLE 43:31 |
| that he has taken to d. | TARK 322:14 |
| We'll teach you to d. deep | SHAK 274:15 |

**drinking:** curse of the d. classes

| | |
|---|---|
| d. at somebody else's expense | WILDE 350:20 |
| d. largely sobers us again | LEIGH 204:19 |
| D. when we are not thirsty | POPE 251:28 |
| very merry, dancing, d. | BEAU 30:16 |
| | DRYD 128:15 |

**dripping:** electricity was d.

| | |
|---|---|
| | THUR 332:14 |

**drive:** but can't d. the car

| | |
|---|---|
| | TYNAN 336:8 |

**driveth:** he d. furiously

| | |
|---|---|
| | BIBLE 42:13 |

**driving:** d. briskly in a post-chaise

| | |
|---|---|
| like the driving of Jehu | JOHN 185:13 |
| | BIBLE 42:13 |

**dromedary:** muse on d. trots

| | |
|---|---|
| | COL 104:2 |

**droning:** beetle wheels his d.

| | |
|---|---|
| | GRAY 157:4 |

**droop:** D. in a hundred A.B.C.'s

| | |
|---|---|
| | ELIOT 132:22 |

**droopingly:** Lady Jane, a little d.

| | |
|---|---|
| | LAWR 202:10 |

**droops:** D. on the little hands

| | |
|---|---|
| | MILNE 226:1 |

**drop:** Drop, d., slow tears

| | |
|---|---|
| Nor any d. to drink | FLET 142:8 |
| One d. would save my soul | COL 104:7 |
| Turn on, tune in and d. out | MARL 218:13 |
| | LEARY 203:19 |

**dropping:** clergy is a d.-down-deadness

| | |
|---|---|
| d. down with costly bales | SMITH 309:24 |
| d. in a very rainy day | TENN 326:10 |
| D. the pilot | BIBLE 44:1 |
| | TENN 323:9 |

**drops:** D. earliest to the ground

| | |
|---|---|
| d. on gate-bars hang | SHAK 289:24 |
| ruddy d. that visit my sad heart | HARDY 162:17 |
| | SHAK 281:7 |

**drought:** d. is destroying his roots

| | |
|---|---|
| d. of March hath perced | HERB 166:11 |
| | CHAU 95:10 |

**drown:** I'll d. my book

| | |
|---|---|
| | SHAK 296:13 |

**drownded:** we do only be d. now and then

| | |
|---|---|
| | SYNGE 321:21 |

**drowned:** And d. in yonder living blue

| | |
|---|---|
| BETTER D. THAN DUFFERS | TENN 325:30 |
| d. in a barrel of Malmesey | RANS 258:7 |
| d. in the depth of the sea | FABY 138:8 |
| d. with us in endless sleep | BIBLE 50:16 |
| | HERR 167:14 |

**drowning:** By d. their speaking

| | |
|---|---|
| hath no d. mark upon him | BROW 76:26 |
| not waving but d. | SHAK 295:31 |
| | SMITH 309:19 |

**drowns:** d. things weighty and solid

| | |
|---|---|
| | BACON 25:7 |

**drowsy:** Dapples the d. east

| | |
|---|---|
| d. numbness pains | SHAK 291:27 |
| Vexing the dull ear of a d. | KEATS 191:28 |
| | SHAK 282:9 |

**drudge:** dictionaries, a harmless d.

| | |
|---|---|
| | JOHN 182:8 |

**drudgery:** Makes d. divine

| | |
|---|---|
| vocation is the love of the d. | HERB 166:2 |
| | SMITH 309:11 |

**drug:** literature is a d.

| | |
|---|---|
| or you can d., with words | BORR 69:26 |
| Poetry's a mere d., Sir | LOW 211:3 |
| | FARQ 138:19 |

**drugs:** Sex and d. and rock and roll

| | |
|---|---|
| | DURY 129:14 |

**drum:** brave music of a *distant* d.

| | |
|---|---|
| d. them up the Channel | FITZ 140:7 |
| Dumb as a d. vith a hole | NEWB 238:10 |
| Not a d. was heard | DICK 119:31 |
| pulse, like a soft d. | WOLFE 352:25 |
| still the most effective d. | KING 195:6 |
| Take my d. to England | GIR 153:5 |
| | NEWB 238:10 |

**drummer:** hears a different d.

| | |
|---|---|
| | THOR 332:12 |

**drums:** trumpets, beat the d.

| | |
|---|---|
| when the d. begin to roll | MOR 235:5 |
| | KIPL 197:11 |

**drunk:** being reasonable, must get d.

| | |
|---|---|
| d. deep of the Pierian spring | BYRON 86:7 |
| d. hath made me bold | DRAY 126:20 |
| I have d., and seen the spider | SHAK 286:12 |
| I'm not so think as you d. I am | SHAK 298:23 |
| Philip d. to Philip sober | SQUI 314:3 |
| Was the hope d. wherein | ANON 6:3 |
| Wordsworth d. and Porson | SHAK 286:3 |
| | HOUS 175:6 |

**dying** (*cont.*):
I am d., Egypt, dying                         SHAK 271:24
If this is d., I don't think much             STR 318:16
it had a d. fall                              SHAK 297:14
living indisposeth us for d.                  BROW 74:5
mouth of the d. day                           AUDEN 20:21
rage against the d. of the light              THOM 330:7
sunsets exquisitely d.                        HUXL 177:13
there's no more d. then                       SHAK 300:15
Those d. generations                          YEATS 359:20
those poor devils are d.                      PHIL 248:13
Turkey is a d. man                            NICH 239:10
unconscionable time d.                        CHAR 95:6
**dyke**: last d. of prevarication            BURKE 80:27

# E

**each**: e. according to his needs           MARX 221:9
**eagle**: By all the e. in thee             CRAS 111:8
e. among blinking owls                        SHEL 303:23
E. has landed                                 ALDR 3:18
e. know what is in the pit                    BLAKE 60:10
Fate is not an e.                             BOWEN 70:18
In and out the E.                             MAND 217:8
stout Cortez when with e.                     KEATS 192:11
way of an e. in the air                       BIBLE 44:4
**eagles**: hawk at e. with a dove            HERB 167:6
mount up with wings as e.                     BIBLE 46:13
there will the e. be gathered                 BIBLE 50:36
were swifter than e.                          BIBLE 41:22
**ear**: beat upon my whorlèd e.              HOPK 172:5
cleave the general e.                         SHAK 275:23
close at the e. of Eve                        MILT 229:13
dull cold e. of death                         GRAY 157:8
dull e. of a drowsy man                       SHAK 282:9
fearful hollow of thine e.                    SHAK 295:17
In Reason's e. they all                       ADD 2:6
jewel in an Ethiop's e.                       SHAK 294:26
Oon e. it herde                               CHAU 96:19
pierced through the e.                        SHAK 291:38
Unpleasing to a married e.                    SHAK 284:22
**early**: E. one morning                     ANON 6:27
E. to rise and early to bed                   THUR 332:15
Vote e. and vote often                        ANON 11:9
you've got to get up e.                       LOW 211:4
**earn**: And there's little to e.            KING 195:16
**earnest**: e. of the things that they shall do   TENN 326:9
I am in e.—I will not equivocate              GARR 148:12
Life is real! Life is e.                      LONG 209:22
**earnings**: division of unequal e.          ELL 136:3
**ears**: adder that stoppeth her e.          BOOK 67:13
Creep in our e.                               SHAK 290:1
e. are listening to you                       ANON 12:15
E. like bombs and teeth like                  CAUS 93:9
He that hath e. to hear                       BIBLE 51:20
lend me your e.                               SHAK 281:18
They have e., and hear not                    BOOK 68:18
**earth**: did thee feel the e. move          HEM 165:12
dust return to the e.                         BIBLE 44:26
E. all Danaë to the stars                     TENN 328:4
e. a richer dust concealed                    BROO 73:10
e. does not argue                             WHIT 348:23
E. felt the wound                             MILT 229:26
E. has not anything to show                   WORD 354:15
e. his sober inn                              CAMP 89:3
e. in fast thick pants                        COL 103:23
e. is all the home I have                     AYT 23:18
e. is full of his glory                       BIBLE 45:10
e. is the Lord's                              BIBLE 55:9
e. is the Lord's                              BOOK 66:19
e. must borrow its mirth                      WILC 349:14
E., receive an honoured guest                 AUDEN 20:24
e.'s diurnal course                           WORD 356:25
e. shall be filled                            AING 3:9

**earth** (*cont.*):
e. shall be full                              BIBLE 45:20
E.'s shadows fly                              SHEL 303:13
E.'s the right place for love                 FROST 146:8
E. stood hard as iron                         ROSS 263:2
e. to earth, ashes to ashes                   BOOK 66:8
e. was without form                           BIBLE 38:13
for e. too dear                               SHAK 294:26
general balm th'hydroptic e.                  DONNE 124:8
girdle round about the e.                     SHAK 290:25
going the way of all the e.                   BIBLE 40:29
going to and fro in the e.                    BIBLE 42:21
Her all on e., and more                       BYRON 85:18
in the deep-delvèd e.                         KEATS 191:29
It fell to e., I knew not where               LONG 209:10
I will move the e.                            ARCH 15:3
lards the lean e. as he walks                 SHAK 277:29
let the whole e. stand                        BOOK 68:2
Lie heavy on him, E.                          EVANS 137:23
must have a touch of e.                       TENN 324:8
new heaven and a new e.                       BIBLE 58:4
new heaven, new e.                            SHAK 271:4
new heavens and a new e.                      BIBLE 46:26
On the cool flowery lap of e.                 ARN 16:19
round e.'s human shores                       KEATS 190:10
round e.'s imagined corners                   DONNE 123:7
round e.'s shore                              ARN 16:11
sleepers in that quiet e.                     BRON 72:18
Than anywhere else on e.                      GURN 159:10
There were giants in the e.                   BIBLE 39:7
they shall inherit the e.                     BIBLE 48:19
This e. of majesty                            SHAK 293:16
this e., this realm                           SHAK 293:16
This litel spot of e.                         CHAU 96:21
thou bleeding piece of e.                     SHAK 281:13
Were it e. in an earthy bed                   TENN 327:2
What if e. be but the shadow                  MILT 229:18
When I am laid in e.                          TATE 322:15
Which men call e.                             MILT 226:5
whole e. as their memorial                    PER 248:2
Ye are the salt of the e.                     BIBLE 48:20
Yours is the E.                               KIPL 197:7
**earthquake**: e. is not satisfied           WORD 356:13
Lord was not in the e.                        BIBLE 42:3
Small e. in Chile                             COCK 103:1
that's an e.                                  MILL 225:4
That world-e., Waterloo                       TENN 327:12
**earthy**: man is of the earth, e.           BIBLE 55:20
**ease**: But for another gives its e.        BLAKE 62:1
doctrine of ignoble e.                        ROOS 262:15
E. after war, death after                     SPEN 313:9
Joys in another's loss of e.                  BLAKE 62:2
labour with an age of e.                      GOLD 154:19
Some come to take their e.                    SHAK 280:23
Studious of elegance and e.                   GAY 149:12
Studious of laborious e.                      COWP 110:10
take thine e., eat                            BIBLE 52:18
Wherein at e. for aye to dwell                TENN 327:14
**easeful**: half in love with e. Death       KEATS 192:3
**easer**: thou e. of all woes                FLET 142:5
**easier**: e. to make war                    CLEM 102:2
**easing**: call it e. the Spring             REED 258:16
**east**: Boston man is the e. wind           APPL 14:14
cometh neither from the e.                    BOOK 67:18
Dapples the drowsy e.                         SHAK 291:27
easier to conquer it [the E.]                 WALP 341:21
E. is a career                                DISR 122:8
E. is East, and West is West                  KIPL 196:4
fiery portal of the e.                        SHAK 293:29
hold the gorgeous E. in fee                   WORD 356:2
It is the e., and Juliet                      SHAK 294:29
look the E. End in the face                   ELIZ 135:18
on the e. of Eden                             BIBLE 39:6
somewheres e. of Suez                         KIPL 196:23
tried to hustle the E.                        KIPL 196:24

Eastertide: Wearing white for E. — HOUS 174:16
eastward: for a garden e. in Eden — BIBLE 38:18
easy: do were as e. as to know — SHAK 288:29
E. is the way down — VIRG 339:12
E. live and quiet die — SCOTT 268:24
e. to shake a man's faith — SHAW 300:27
e. writing's vile hard — SHER 306:8
Of e. ways to die — SHAK 272:11
on the rack of a too e. chair — POPE 250:20
She bid me take love e. — YEATS 359:1
so e. to take refuge — IBSEN 178:6
Summer time an' the livin' is e. — GERS 168:6
Too e. for children — SCHN 267:23
type of the normal and e. — JAMES 180:1
eat: e., drink, and be merry — BIBLE 52:18
e. one of Bellamy's veal pies — PITT 249:10
e. the fat of the land — BIBLE 39:27
I see what I e. — CARR 91:6
I will not e. with you — SHAK 288:31
Let us e. and drink — BIBLE 45:24
neither should he e. — BIBLE 56:15
One should e. to live — MOL 232:14
shalt thou e. bread — BIBLE 39:2
So I did sit and e. — HERB 167:3
Some have meat and cannot e. — BURNS 82:14
Take, e.; this is my body — BIBLE 51:9
Tell me what you e. — BRIL 72:7
than to e., and to drink — BIBLE 44:18
thou shalt not e. of it — BIBLE 38:19
ye shall e. it in haste — BIBLE 39:37
eaten: He has been e. by the bear — HOUS 174:8
eater: Out of the e. came forth meat — BIBLE 41:3
eating: appetite grows by e. — RAB 257:10
E. people is wrong — FLAN 141:5
eats: Man is what he e. — FEUE 139:1
ebbing: steady than an e. sea — FORD 143:11
Ebenezer: E. thought it wrong — BELL 33:28
ecce: E. homo — BIBLE 58:20
ecclesiastic: E. tyranny's the worst — DEFOE 115:25
ecclesiologist: A keen e. — BETJ 37:15
echo: E. beyond the Mexique Bay — MARV 220:11
e. of a platitude — BIER 59:3
Footfalls e. in the memory — ELIOT 132:26
Still left an e. in the sense — JONS 187:18
Sweet E., sweetest nymph — MILT 226:10
waiting for the e. — MARQ 219:22
echoes: answer, e., dying — TENN 327:20
e. back the public voice — JOHN 183:10
set the wild e. flying — TENN 327:20
echoing: e. straits between us thrown — ARN 17:22
eclipse: e. disastrous twilight — MILT 228:17
E. first, the rest nowhere — O'KEL 241:7
Irrecoverably dark, total e. — MILT 230:11
eclipsed: e. the gaiety of nations — JOHN 182:23
economic: calls its vital e. interests — WEIL 345:3
cold metal of e. theory — SCH 267:26
economical: e. with the actualité — CLARK 101:13
e. with the truth — ARMS 16:6
economics: E. is the science — ROBB 260:15
economists: e., and calculators — BURKE 80:14
economy: E. is going without something — HOPE 171:19
fear of Political E. — SELL 270:4
ecstasy: e. of being ever — BROW 74:8
maintain this e. — PATER 246:15
not e. but it was comfort — DICK 118:30
ecstatic: Of such e. sound — HARDY 162:7
Eden: E.'s dread probationary — COWP 110:3
E. took their solitary way — MILT 230:2
garden eastward in E. — BIBLE 38:18
on the east of E. — BIBLE 39:6
happier E. — MILT 229:10
This other E., demi-paradise — SHAK 293:16
voice that breathed o'er E. — KEBLE 193:18
With loss of E. — MILT 228:7

edge: always at the e. of Being — SPEN 313:1
e. of the abyss — STEV 316:20
interest's on the dangerous e. — BROW 75:15
my teeth nothing on e. — SHAK 278:4
edges: down the vast e. drear — ARN 16:11
editor: E.: a person employed — HUBB 175:15
Edom: over E. will I cast out — BOOK 67:14
educated: clothed, fed and e. — RUSK 264:19
government by the badly e. — CHES 98:12
education: between e. and catastrophe — WELLS 345:21
cabbage with a college e. — TWAIN 336:4
E.—At Mr Wackford Squeers's — DICK 119:10
E. has been theirs — AUST 22:27
[E.] has produced a vast — TREV 334:9
e. I have received has — BOTT 70:7
e. is a little too pedantic — CONG 106:10
E. is what survives when — SKIN 308:6
Nothing in e. is so astonishing — ADAMS 1:20
Soap and e. — TWAIN 335:22
thank your e. — JONS 187:17
To love her is a liberal e. — STEE 314:16
travel . . . is a part of e. — BACON 25:17
educe: e. the man — BROW 76:7
Edward: Why, E., tell me why — WORD 354:12
eels: I gat e. boil'd in broo — BALL 27:19
effect: e. was already in the cause — BERG 35:13
little e. after much labour — AUST 23:10
effects: dire e. from civil discord flow — ADD 2:19
effectually: we may obtain e. — BOOK 64:27
efficient: dignified parts and e. parts — BAG 26:3
e. and the inefficient — SHAW 301:7
e. government you have dictatorship — TRUM 335:3
effort: e. nor the failure tires — EMPS 137:6
redoubling your e. when — SANT 266:21
What is written without e. — JOHN 186:15
egg: afraid you've got a bad e. — PUNCH 256:19
e. boiled very soft — AUST 22:13
e. of a North African Empire — GLAD 153:11
fatal e. by pleasure laid — COWP 110:2
like eating an e. without salt — KIPL 198:3
Wall St. lays an e. — ANON 11:10
white and hairless as an e. — HERR 167:20
eggs: all my e. in one bastard — PARK 245:15
Lays e. inside a paper bag — ISH 178:21
as a weasel sucks e. — SHAK 272:20
To boil e. in your shoes — LEAR 203:16
eglantine: musk-roses, and with e. — SHAK 290:26
ego: Et in Arcadia e. — ANON 13:15
egotistical: e. sublime — KEATS 193:8
Egypt: darkness over the land of E. — BIBLE 39:35
Our first site in E. — GLAD 153:11
out of the land of E. — BIBLE 40:2
Egyptians: And they spoiled the E. — BIBLE 39:38
Eheu: E. fugaces, Postume — HOR 173:23
eight: We want e., and we won't wait — ANON 11:17
eighty: In a dream you are never e. — SEXT 270:15
ein: E. Reich, ein Volk, ein Führer — ANON 13:2
Einstein: Let E. be — SQUI 314:4
either: How happy could I be with e. — GAY 149:7
Elaine: E., the lily maid of Astolat — TENN 324:7
élan: L'é. vital — BERG 35:14
elbow: e. has a fascination — GILB 152:3
elder: An e. than herself — SHAK 297:30
e. man not at all — BACON 25:3
elderly: imported, e. American — JENK 181:3
Mr Salteena was an e. man of 42 — ASHF 18:20
eldest: Sable-vested Night, e. of things — MILT 228:32
eldorado: E. banal de tous les vieux — BAUD 30:5
elected: audacity of e. persons — WHIT 348:15
election: An e. is coming — ELIOT 132:4
e. by the incompetent — SHAW 301:2
elections: E. are won by — ADAMS 1:10
it's no go the e. — MACN 216:2
won the e., but I won the count — SOM 311:4

English (cont.):

| | |
|---|---|
| E. talk is a quadrille | JAMES 179:16 |
| E. that of the sea | RICH 260:6 |
| E. tongue a gallimaufry | SPEN 313:20 |
| E. unofficial rose | BROO 73:4 |
| E. up with which I will not put | CHUR 100:5 |
| E. want *inferiors* | TOCQ 333:4 |
| game which the E. invented | MANC 217:7 |
| Johnson's morality was as E. | HAWT 163:19 |
| really nice E. people | SHAW 301:5 |
| rolling E. drunkard | CHES 98:1 |
| Roman-Saxon-Danish-Norman E. | DEFOE 115:24 |
| shed one E. tear | MAC 214:1 |
| stones kissed by the E. dead | OWEN 244:1 |
| Student of our sweet E. tongue | FLEC 141:20 |
| This is the E., not the Turkish | SHAK 278:29 |
| white as an angel is the E. child | BLAKE 61:24 |
| words in the E. language | JAMES 180:5 |
| Englishman: Either for E. or Jew | BLAKE 60:14 |
| E. a combination of qualities | DICK 119:22 |
| E. among the under-dogs | WAUGH 343:21 |
| E., being flattered | CHAP 94:14 |
| E., even if he is alone | MIKES 224:12 |
| E. hate or despise him | SHAW 302:16 |
| E. thinks he is moral | SHAW 301:21 |
| find an E. in the wrong | SHAW 302:9 |
| He remains an E. | GILB 152:21 |
| last great E. is low | TENN 327:11 |
| No E. is ever fairly beaten | SHAW 302:20 |
| religious rights of an E. | JUN 188:25 |
| Englishmen: E. never will be slaves | SHAW 301:20 |
| first to his E. | MILT 231:2 |
| Mad dogs and E. | COW 109:4 |
| When two E. meet | JOHN 182:11 |
| Englishwoman: E. is so refined | SMITH 309:21 |
| enigma: e. of the fever chart | ELIOT 133:5 |
| mystery inside an e. | CHUR 99:10 |
| enjoy: I can e. while she's kind | DRYD 128:23 |
| to e. him forever | SHOR 306:13 |
| enjoyed: all times I have e. | TENN 328:20 |
| little to be e. | JOHN 183:4 |
| warm and still to be e. | KEATS 191:21 |
| enjoying: Think, oh think, it worth e. | DRYD 127:21 |
| enjoyment: e. as the greatest orator | HUME 176:7 |
| e. of riches consists | SMITH 308:22 |
| enjoyments: Fire-side e. | COWP 110:12 |
| if it were not for its e. | SURT 319:13 |
| enlargement: e. of the language | JOHN 182:5 |
| enmities: e. of twenty generations | MAC 213:14 |
| enormity: womb and bed of e. | JONS 186:24 |
| enough: e. in the world | BUCH 77:30 |
| E. that he heard it once | BROW 75:8 |
| enskyed: thing e. and sainted | SHAK 288:10 |
| ensue: seek peace, and e. it | BOOK 66:25 |
| entbehren: E. sollt Du! | GOET 154:4 |
| enter: Abandon all hope, you who e. | DANTE 113:18 |
| e. into the kingdom | BIBLE 50:15 |
| e. into the kingdom | BIBLE 50:22 |
| e. who does not know geometry | ANON 13:6 |
| entered: iron e. into his soul | BOOK 68:9 |
| enterprise: There's more e. | YEATS 358:17 |
| voyages of the starship *E.* | RODD 261:12 |
| enterprised: Not by any to be e. | BOOK 65:26 |
| entertain: better to e. an idea | JARR 180:13 |
| e. us with no worth | WALL 341:14 |
| To e. divine Zenocrate | MARL 219:11 |
| To e. this starry stranger | CRAS 111:10 |
| entertained: e. angels unawares | BIBLE 56:29 |
| entertainment: exotic and irrational e. | JOHN 182:22 |
| mere gossiping e. | HUNT 176:18 |
| entertains: e. the harmless day | WOTT 357:14 |
| enthral: Except you e. me | DONNE 123:11 |
| enthralled: unjust force, but not e. | MILT 226:18 |
| enthusiasts: how to deal with e. | MAC 213:16 |
| entire: E. and whole and perfect | SPR 313:26 |

| | |
|---|---|
| entirely: e. beautiful | AUDEN 20:28 |
| entrance: To e. the prophet's ear | MANT 217:17 |
| entrances: their exits and their e. | SHAK 272:24 |
| entropy: e. of human thought | ZAMY 360:25 |
| envelope: semi-transparent e. | WOOLF 353:22 |
| envious: e. fever | SHAK 296:31 |
| envy: did in e. of great Caesar | SHAK 282:2 |
| E. and calumny and hate | SHEL 303:11 |
| e. of less happier lands | SHAK 293:16 |
| from e., hatred, and malice | BOOK 64:14 |
| I e. not in any moods | TENN 325:3 |
| prisoners of e. | ILL 178:9 |
| Toil, e., want | JOHN 183:12 |
| épater: Il faut é. le bourgeois | BAUD 30:9 |
| epic: thundrous e. lilted out | TENN 327:18 |
| epicure: Serenely full, the e. would say | SMITH 310:7 |
| epigram: purrs like an e. | MARQ 219:23 |
| What is an E.? | COL 103:17 |
| epigrams: despotism tempered by e. | CARL 90:14 |
| epiphany: By an e. he meant | JOYCE 188:10 |
| episode: e. in a general drama | HARDY 161:24 |
| To the end of a brief e. | MERC 223:11 |
| epitaph: Wit is the e. of an emotion | NIET 239:23 |
| epitaphs: nice derangement of e. | SHER 305:29 |
| worms, and e. | SHAK 293:26 |
| epithet: Fair is too foul an e. | MARL 219:10 |
| epitome: all mankind's e. | DRYD 127:12 |
| eppur: E. si muove | GAL 147:16 |
| equal: all men are created e. | JEFF 180:18 |
| all men are created e. | LINC 207:8 |
| e. division of unequal earnings | ELL 136:3 |
| E., unclassed, tribeless | SHEL 304:22 |
| faith shines e. | BRON 72:16 |
| free and e. in dignity | ANON 5:20 |
| some animals are more e. | ORW 241:23 |
| equality: e. in the servants' hall | BARR 29:10 |
| Freedom! E.! Brotherhood | ANON 12:11 |
| not e. or fairness | BERL 36:6 |
| equals: live together as e. | MILL 224:20 |
| equanimity: No man can face with e. | GILB 151:13 |
| equation: e. is something for eternity | EINS 131:12 |
| equators: North Poles and E. | CARR 92:7 |
| equipment: e. always deteriorating | ELIOT 133:6 |
| equity: judge people with e. | BOOK 68:4 |
| equivocate: I will not e. | GARR 148:12 |
| erect: e. and manly foe | CANN 89:12 |
| err: e. as grossly as the few | DRYD 127:15 |
| e. while yet he strives | GOET 154:3 |
| To e. is human but to really | ANON 11:7 |
| To e. is human, to forgive | POPE 252:7 |
| errands: e. for the Ministers | GILB 151:6 |
| erred: We have e., and strayed | BOOK 63:13 |
| error: All men are liable to e. | LOCKE 208:18 |
| charged the troops of e. | BROW 74:9 |
| E. has never approached | METT 224:2 |
| e. is immense | BOL 63:5 |
| in endless e. hurled | POPE 252:18 |
| positive in e. as in truth | LOCKE 208:17 |
| show a man that he is in e. | LOCKE 208:15 |
| stalking-horse to e. | BOL 63:3 |
| errors: common e. of our life | SIDN 306:28 |
| E., like straws | DRYD 127:23 |
| e. of those who think | BID 59:1 |
| more harmful than reasoned e. | HUXL 177:19 |
| erstwhile: e. dear | MILL 224:23 |
| Esau: E. is a hairy man | BIBLE 39:19 |
| E. selleth his birthright | BIBLE 39:17 |
| hands are the hands of E. | BIBLE 39:20 |
| escalier: L'esprit de l'e. | DID 120:20 |
| escape: Beauty for some provides e. | HUXL 177:13 |
| What struggle to e. | KEATS 191:18 |
| escaped: e. with the skin of my teeth | BIBLE 42:35 |
| eschew: E. evil, and do good | BOOK 66:25 |
| escutcheon: blot on the e. | GRAY 156:18 |

| | |
|---|---|
| **Eskdale**: E. and Liddesdale | SCOTT 269:2 |
| **espoused**: my e., my latest found | MILT 229:15 |
| my late e. saint | MILT 230:24 |
| **esprit**: *L'e. de l'escalier* | DID 120:20 |
| **essence**: e. of innumerable biographies | CARL 90:6 |
| **establishment**: British e. | KEAT 190:9 |
| **estate**: become a fourth e. | MAC 213:4 |
| low e. of his handmaiden | BIBLE 51:28 |
| mind, body, or e. | BOOK 64:19 |
| ordered their e. | ALEX 4:3 |
| **estimate**: know'st thy e. | SHAK 299:27 |
| **estranging**: unplumbed, salt, e. sea | ARN 17:23 |
| **état**: *L'É. c'est moi* | LOUI 210:12 |
| **eternal**: E. Father, strong to save | WHIT 348:9 |
| e. Footman hold my coat | ELIOT 133:29 |
| e. in the heavens | BIBLE 55:24 |
| E. Passion | ARN 16:22 |
| Grant them e. rest | MISS 231:22 |
| himself and her of an e. tie | AUDEN 21:5 |
| Hope springs e. | POPE 252:12 |
| lay hold on e. life | BIBLE 56:20 |
| our e. home | WATTS 343:13 |
| resembles the e. rocks beneath | BRON 72:17 |
| Thou, whose e. Word | MARR 219:24 |
| thy e. summer shall not fade | SHAK 299:13 |
| to be boy e. | SHAK 298:21 |
| **eternities**: for Seasons; not E. | MER 223:23 |
| **eternity**: candidates for e. | MORE 234:22 |
| Damned from here to E. | KIPL 196:15 |
| decomposing in the e. of print | WOOLF 353:20 |
| Deserts of vast e. | MARV 220:24 |
| equation is something for e. | EINS 131:12 |
| e. in an hour | BLAKE 60:5 |
| E. is in love with the productions | BLAKE 61:5 |
| E.'s a terrible thought | STOP 318:4 |
| E. shut in a span | CRAS 111:11 |
| E.! thou pleasing, dreadful thought | ADD 2:18 |
| I saw E. the other night | VAUG 337:14 |
| kill time without injuring e. | THOR 332:8 |
| sells e. to get a toy | SHAK 299:8 |
| some conception of e. | MANC 217:7 |
| Some shadows of e. | VAUG 337:8 |
| teacher affects e. | ADAMS 1:16 |
| time is a pinprick of e. | AUR 22:10 |
| Time's thievish progress to e. | SHAK 299:26 |
| white radiance of E. | SHEL 303:13 |
| **ether**: ampler e., a diviner air | WORD 355:7 |
| **etherized**: patient e. upon a table | ELIOT 133:24 |
| **Eton**: playing fields of E. | WELL 345:10 |
| **étonne**: *É.-moi* | DIAG 117:15 |
| **eunuch**: between a e. and a snigger | FIRB 139:19 |
| Female E. | GREER 158:10 |
| prerogative of the e. | STOP 318:1 |
| Though Argus were her e. | SHAK 284:14 |
| Time's e. | HOPK 172:19 |
| To be a kind of moral e. | SHEL 304:14 |
| **eunuchs**: seraglio of e. | FOOT 142:17 |
| **eureka**: E.! | ARCH 15:2 |
| **Europe**: better fifty years of E. | TENN 326:18 |
| community of E. | SAL 266:4 |
| E. a continent of energetic mongrels | FISH 139:22 |
| E. is the unfinished negative | MCC 214:10 |
| E. of the ancient parapets | RIMB 260:9 |
| glory of E. is extinguished | BURKE 80:14 |
| keep up with Western E. | UPD 336:12 |
| lamps are going out all over E. | GREY 159:1 |
| last gentleman in E. | LEV 206:6 |
| poor are E.'s blacks | CHAM 94:4 |
| save E. by her example | PITT 249:8 |
| **Europeans**: You are learned E. | MASS 222:4 |
| **Euston**: in E. waiting-room | CORN 108:5 |
| **Eve**: E. ate Adam | HUGH 175:21 |
| fallen sons of E. | CHES 98:5 |
| past E. and Adam's | JOYCE 188:3 |

| | |
|---|---|
| **Eve** (*cont.*): | |
| real curse of E. | RHYS 259:14 |
| When Adam dalfe and E. spane | ROLLE 262:4 |
| **Evelyn**: E. Hope is dead | BROW 75:28 |
| **even**: E. so, come, Lord Jesus | BIBLE 58:8 |
| **evening**: beautiful e., very starry | WORD 354:9 |
| bright exhalation in the e. | SHAK 280:17 |
| e. and the morning | BIBLE 38:14 |
| e. is spread out | ELIOT 133:24 |
| e. star, love's harbinger | MILT 229:32 |
| hands be an e. sacrifice | BOOK 69:8 |
| It was a summer e. | SOUT 311:18 |
| like an e. gone | WATTS 343:14 |
| Of grateful e. mild | MILT 229:11 |
| sadly descends the autumn e. | ARN 17:3 |
| Softly along the road of e. | DE L 116:21 |
| welcome peaceful e. in | COWP 110:11 |
| winter e. settles down | ELIOT 134:10 |
| **event**: How much the greatest e. | FOX 144:16 |
| hurries to the main e. | HOR 173:1 |
| only as the e. decides | AUST 23:1 |
| **eventide**: fast falls the e. | LYTE 212:20 |
| **events**: e. have controlled me | LINC 207:9 |
| e., mostly unimportant | BIER 59:6 |
| **ever**: Hardly e. | GILB 152:15 |
| Round the world for e. and aye | ARN 16:17 |
| **everlasting**: caught an e. cold | WEBS 344:28 |
| hath e. life | BIBLE 53:24 |
| have e. life | BIBLE 53:19 |
| Timon hath made his e. mansion | SHAK 296:24 |
| underneath are the e. arms | BIBLE 40:25 |
| **everlastingness**: Bright shoots of e. | VAUG 337:9 |
| **evermore**: and e. shalt be | HEBER 164:17 |
| this time forth for e. | BOOK 68:27 |
| **every**: E. Day a Little Death | SOND 311:6 |
| E. day, in every way | COUÉ 108:16 |
| e. thing there is a season | BIBLE 44:11 |
| E. time we say goodbye | PORT 253:19 |
| E. which way but loose | KRON 199:6 |
| **everyman**: E., I will go with thee | ANON 7:1 |
| **everyone**: E. suddenly burst out singing | SASS 267:11 |
| When e. is wrong | LA CH 199:15 |
| **everything**: chips with e. | WESK 346:2 |
| e. in its place | BEET 32:15 |
| e. in its place and nothing | BEVAN 38:3 |
| Life, the Universe and E. | ADAMS 1:9 |
| robbed a man of e. | SOLZ 310:28 |
| sans taste, sans e. | SHAK 272:28 |
| smattering of e. | DICK 120:5 |
| we cannot all do e. | LUC 212:1 |
| We can't all do e. | VIRG 340:2 |
| world is e. that is the case | WITT 352:9 |
| **everywhere**: Out of the e. into here | MACD 214:18 |
| Water, water, e. | COL 104:7 |
| What is e., what is always | VINC 338:22 |
| **evidence**: before you have all the e. | DOYLE 126:5 |
| circumstantial e. is very strong | THOR 332:5 |
| clearer e. than this | ARAB 14:18 |
| e. of things not seen | BIBLE 56:26 |
| it's not e. | DICK 119:34 |
| **evil**: all e. shed away | BROO 73:10 |
| banality of e. | AREN 15:4 |
| because the days are e. | BIBLE 56:1 |
| defend ourselves by doing e. | SOCR 310:23 |
| deliver us from e. | BIBLE 48:27 |
| doeth e. hath not seen God | BIBLE 57:18 |
| Do e. in return | AUDEN 21:10 |
| do e., that good may come | BIBLE 54:30 |
| do nothing for e. to triumph | BURKE 81:13 |
| Eschew e., and do good | BOOK 66:25 |
| everything is a necessary e. | BRAD 71:8 |
| E., be thou my good | MILT 229:7 |
| E. be to him who evil thinks | ANON 12:5 |
| E. communications corrupt | BIBLE 55:19 |
| e. is simply ignorance | FORD 143:8 |

evil (cont.):
e. that men do lives after — SHAK 281:18
e. which I would not — BIBLE 54:38
face of 'e.' — BURR 82:31
Government is a necessary e. — PAINE 244:9
Great book, great e. — CALL 88:5
knowing good and e. — BIBLE 38:25
money is the root of all e. — BIBLE 56:19
only e. that walks invisible — MILT 229:5
on the e. and on the good — BIBLE 48:24
open and notorious e. liver — BOOK 64:29
punishment in itself is e. — BENT 35:2
Resist not e. — BIBLE 48:23
return good for e. — VANB 336:23
sometimes meet e.-willers — ELIZ 135:5
still to find means of e. — MILT 228:11
sufficient unto the day is the e. — BIBLE 49:5
them that call e. good — BIBLE 45:9
Whenever God prepares e. — ANON 13:8
withstand in the e. day — BIBLE 56:4
evils: enamoured of existing e. — BIER 59:5
greater e. than the first — CHUR 98:24
greatest of e....poverty — SHAW 301:8
must expect new e. — BACON 24:31
evolution: Some call it e. — CARR 92:10
ewe: tupping your white e. — SHAK 291:29
ewes: my e. breed not — BARN 29:8
exact: greatness not to be e. — BURKE 79:24
writing an e. man — BACON 25:15
exactitude: L'e. est la politesse — LOUI 210:17
exaggerated: have been greatly e. — TWAIN 336:7
exaggeration: e. is a truth that has lost its temper — GIBR 150:21
exalted: Every valley shall be e. — BIBLE 46:9
e. them of low degree — BIBLE 51:29
exalteth: e. himself shall be abased — BIBLE 52:22
examinations: E. are formidable — COLT 105:17
In e. those who do not wish to know — RAL 258:5
examine: E. for a moment — WOOLF 353:21
example: E. is always more efficacious — JOHN 183:6
save Europe by her e. — PITT 249:8
examples: philosophy from e. — DION 121:4
exceed: reach should e. his grasp — BROW 75:10
excel: so great as daring to e. — CHUR 98:20
excellent: e. thing in woman — SHAK 284:5
e. things are spoken — BOOK 67:24
O! it is e. — SHAK 288:13
Parts of it are e. — PUNCH 256:19
excellently: Goddess, e. bright — JONS 187:3
I see them all so e. fair — COL 103:14
excelling: Love divine, all loves e. — WESL 346:10
Excelsior: banner with the strange device, E. — LONG 209:17
excelsis: Gloria in e. Deo — MISS 231:13
Hosanna in e. — MISS 231:17
except: E. the Lord build the house — BOOK 68:30
exception: I'll be glad to make an e. — MARX 221:7
excess: Give me e. of it — SHAK 297:13
Nothing in e. — ANON 13:7
road of e. leads to the — BLAKE 61:1
Such an e. of stupidity — JOHN 184:14
wasteful and ridiculous e. — SHAK 282:10
excessit: Abiit, e., evasit, erupit — CIC 100:26
excessive: Dark with e. bright — MILT 229:4
right of an e. wrong — BROW 77:8
exchange: by just e. one for the other — SIDN 306:15
excise: E. A hateful tax — JOHN 182:7
excite: e. my amorous propensities — JOHN 183:24
exciting: films. They are too e. — BERR 36:14
too e. to be pleasant — DICK 119:29
excrement: place of e. — YEATS 358:20
excursion: poem, called the 'E.' — BYRON 86:16
steamers made an e. to hell — PRIE 255:8
excuse: e. every man will plead — SELD 269:17
I will not e. — GARR 148:12

excuse (cont.):
they make a good e. — SZASZ 322:2
excuses: two e. less convincing than one — HUXL 177:9
execution: and the e. confined — SHAK 297:2
their stringent e. — GRANT 156:9
executioner: I am mine own E. — DONNE 124:18
executioners: victims who respect their e. — SART 267:7
executive: weakest e. in the world — DISR 121:7
executives: e. would never want to tamper — AUDEN 20:23
executors: Let's choose e. — SHAK 293:26
exercise: dancing is love's proper e. — DAV 114:15
mind what e. is to the body — STEE 314:17
exhalation: bright e. in the evening — SHAK 280:17
exhausted: enemies are not yet e. — GLAD 153:12
exile: destined an e. — VIRG 338:23
Go, bind your sons to e. — KIPL 197:15
silence, e., and cunning — JOYCE 188:9
therefore I die in e. — GREG 158:13
exiles: Thou Paradise of e., Italy — SHEL 303:21
Which none save e. feel — AYT 23:17
exist: they e., but are identical — FORS 143:25
existence: e. is but a brief crack — NAB 236:19
paint on the face of E. — BYRON 87:16
Struggle for E. — DARW 114:4
'Tis woman's whole e. — BYRON 86:4
when e. or when hope is gone — AUST 22:28
exists: And no one is e. alone — AUDEN 21:1
exit: E., pursued by a bear — SHAK 298:25
exits: For men to take their e. — WEBS 344:18
their e. and their entrances — SHAK 272:24
exorciser: No e. harm thee — SHAK 273:28
exordium: E. of our woes — DRAY 126:18
exotic: e. follies o'er the town — BYRON 86:33
expect: E. nothing. Live frugally — WALK 341:4
people e. most from others — AUST 22:19
expectancy: e. and rose of the fair state — SHAK 276:2
expectation: better bettered e. — SHAK 291:11
e. whirls me round — SHAK 297:1
Singing songs of e. — BAR 29:2
expediency: sacrificed to e. — MAUG 222:8
expedient: as may be most e. for them — BOOK 64:10
e. that one man should die — BIBLE 53:34
not a principle, but an e. — DISR 121:10
expedition: abandoning the e. — DOUG 125:8
expeditious: There is no e. road — THOM 331:13
expenditure: annual e. — DICK 118:12
E. rises to meet income — PARK 245:20
expense: drinking at somebody else's e. — LEIGH 204:19
e. damnable — CHES 97:18
e. of spirit in a waste of shame — SHAK 300:10
repay the trouble and e. — BELL 33:2
use alone that sanctifies e. — POPE 251:18
Would be at the e. of two — CLOU 102:16
expenses: facts are on e. — STOP 318:3
expensive: extremely e. to be poor — BALD 27:2
experience: e. is an arch — ADAMS 1:13
e. is an arch — TENN 328:21
E. is the child of Thought — DISR 122:9
E. is the name everyone gives — WILDE 350:2
E., though noon auctoritee — CHAU 96:5
I know it from e. — ARAB 14:19
in the elder, a part of e. — BACON 25:17
knowledge can go beyond his e. — LOCKE 208:14
never had much e. — MARQ 219:16
triumph of hope over e. — JOHN 184:24
we need not e. it — FRIS 146:5
experiences: in between lie the e. of our life — MANN 217:13
experimental: any e. reasoning — HUME 176:4
expert: e. is one who knows more — BUTL 83:21
e. is someone who knows — HEIS 165:4
experto: E. credite — VIRG 339:22
expiate: I have something to e. — LAWR 202:22
explain: Never complain and never e. — DISR 122:19

explain (cont.):

| | |
|---|---|
| Never e. Never apologise | FISH 139:24 |
| Never e.—your friends do not | HUBB 175:13 |
| explained: die before we have e. | ADAMS 2:3 |
| explaining: forever e. things | DE S 265:15 |
| expletive: E. deleted | ANON 7:3 |
| explorers: endeavours are unlucky e. | DOUG 125:8 |
| exploring: 'end of all our e. | ELIOT 133:10 |
| explosive: 'philosopher': a terrible e. | NIET 239:19 |
| exposed: intellect is improperly e. | SMITH 310:3 |
| exposition: e. of sleep | SHAK 291:1 |
| express: down e. in the small of the back | WOD 352:18 |
| expressed: ne'er so well e. | POPE 252:1 |
| expression: E. is the dress of thought | POPE 252:2 |
| exquisite: e. touch | SCOTT 269:6 |
| exquisitely: Autumn sunsets e. dying | HUXL 177:13 |
| extenuate: nothing e. | SHAK 293:5 |
| extenuates: e. not wrong | SHAK 296:33 |
| exterminate: E. all the brutes | CONR 107:4 |
| extol: How shall we e. thee | BENS 34:20 |
| extra: add some e., just for you | LARK 201:17 |
| extras: No e., no vacations | DICK 119:10 |
| extravagance: beautiful does not lead to e. | PER 248:1 |
| extremes: toil in other men's e. | KYD 199:9 |
| extremism: e. in the defence of liberty | GOLD 155:15 |
| eye: Affection beaming in one e. | DICK 119:2 |
| apple of his e. | BIBLE 40:23 |
| beam that is in thine own e. | BIBLE 49:7 |
| bright e. of peninsulas | CAT 93:3 |
| Cast a cold e. on life | YEATS 360:8 |
| custom loathsome to the e. | JAM 179:9 |
| death obscured that e. | KEATS 192:17 |
| E. for eye, tooth for tooth | BIBLE 40:10 |
| e. of heaven to garnish | SHAK 282:10 |
| e. sinks inward | ARN 16:10 |
| e. that can open an oyster | WOD 352:16 |
| fringèd curtains of thine e. | SHAK 296:2 |
| God caught his e. | MCC 214:15 |
| harvest of a quiet e. | WORD 356:7 |
| He had but one e. | DICK 119:11 |
| Hide me from day's garish e. | MILT 226:26 |
| If thine e. offend thee | BIBLE 50:17 |
| I have neither e. to see | LENT 205:20 |
| language in her e. | SHAK 297:9 |
| long grey beard and glittering e. | COL 104:3 |
| looked into the e. of day | YEATS 359:5 |
| mild and magnificent e. | BROW 76:14 |
| My tiny watching e. | DE L 116:23 |
| Sail and sail, with unshut e. | ARN 16:17 |
| tender e. of pitiful day | SHAK 287:6 |
| they shall see e. to eye | BIBLE 46:16 |
| through the e. of a needle | BIBLE 50:22 |
| twinkling of an e. | BIBLE 55:21 |
| unforgiving e. | SHER 306:7 |
| with its soft black e. | MOORE 234:19 |
| with not through the e. | BLAKE 60:12 |
| eyeball: His e.—like a bastion's mole | SMART 308:10 |
| We're e. to eyeball | RUSK 264:9 |
| eyebrows: e. made of platinum | FORS 143:14 |
| eyeless: E. in Gaza | MILT 230:10 |
| eyelids: tired e. upon tired eyes | TENN 326:19 |
| eyes: all e. else dead coals | SHAK 299:3 |
| bodily hunger in his e. | SHAW 301:10 |
| Closed his e. in endless night | GRAY 157:17 |
| close my e., open my legs | HILL 168:17 |
| close your e. before you see | AYCK 23:14 |
| Crumbling behind the e. | MACN 216:4 |
| cynosure of neighbouring e. | MILT 227:3 |
| deep upon her peerless e. | KEATS 191:26 |
| Drink to me only with thine e. | JONS 187:23 |
| electrical skin and glaring e. | SMART 308:8 |
| e. are homes of silent prayer | TENN 325:6 |
| e. are nothing like the sun | SHAK 300:11 |
| e. as wide as a football-pool | CAUS 93:9 |
| e. have they, and see not | BOOK 68:18 |

eyes (cont.):

| | |
|---|---|
| e. of gold and bramble-dew | STEV 317:20 |
| E. of most unholy blue | MOORE 234:12 |
| e. to wonder, but lack tongues | SHAK 300:5 |
| e. were deeper than the depth | ROSS 263:6 |
| her e. were wild | KEATS 191:9 |
| Foolish e., thy streams | SANS 266:20 |
| frightened look in its e. | SITW 307:21 |
| From women's e. | SHAK 284:16 |
| gather to the e. | TENN 327:22 |
| Get thee glass e. | SHAK 283:26 |
| God be in my e. | ANON 7:11 |
| good Lord made your e. | LEHR 204:14 |
| Hath not a Jew e. | SHAK 289:16 |
| lift up thine e. | MONS 233:2 |
| lightened are our e. | SORL 311:15 |
| Love looks not with the e. | SHAK 290:16 |
| Love's tongue is in the e. | FLET 142:9 |
| Mine e. have seen the glory | HOWE 175:7 |
| night has a thousand e. | BOUR 70:12 |
| Night hath a thousand e. | LYLY 212:18 |
| no eyes but constitutional e. | LINC 207:14 |
| one, all e., Philosopher! | WORD 356:5 |
| Or was it his bees-winged e. | BETJ 36:16 |
| our e. the frosty sagas | CRANE 110:31 |
| pearls that were his e. | SHAK 296:1 |
| see the white of their e. | PUTN 256:24 |
| Smoke gets in your e. | HARB 161:10 |
| soft look your e. had once | YEATS 360:9 |
| So much chewing gum for the e. | ANON 10:14 |
| stuck in her face for e. | SHAK 284:14 |
| Take a pair of sparkling e. | GILB 151:7 |
| tempts your wand'ring e. | GRAY 157:15 |
| tended her i' the e. | SHAK 271:15 |
| these e. to behold felicity | BROW 74:17 |
| They strike mine e. | JONS 187:6 |
| with cold commemorative e. | ROSS 263:9 |
| with his half-shut e. | POPE 253:9 |
| with sad and wond'ring e. | MILM 225:13 |
| your e. with holy dread | COL 104:1 |

# F

| | |
|---|---|
| Fabians: civilization of the F. | INGE 178:11 |
| good man fallen among F. | LENIN 205:5 |
| fable: f., song, or fleeting shade | HERR 167:14 |
| that thai be nocht bot f. | BARB 28:15 |
| fables: profane and old wives' f. | BIBLE 56:17 |
| fabric: baseless f. of this vision | SHAK 296:10 |
| face: Cover her f. | WEBS 344:19 |
| day's disasters in his morning f. | GOLD 154:23 |
| dew on the f. of the dead | BEERS 32:14 |
| dont quite match your f. | ASHF 18:21 |
| f. is a mute recommendation | PUBL 255:22 |
| f. of 'evil' | BURR 82:31 |
| f. of my betrothèd lady | MIDD 224:8 |
| f. of the world would have | PASC 246:2 |
| f. that launched a thousand ships | MARL 218:11 |
| f. the index of a feeling mind | CRAB 110:29 |
| False f. must hide | SHAK 286:8 |
| Fanny Kelly's divine plain f. | LAMB 200:9 |
| garden of your f. | HERB 166:19 |
| has the f. he deserves | ORW 241:24 |
| He hides a smiling f. | COWP 109:26 |
| Her f., at first … just ghostly | REID 259:3 |
| his listless form and f. | HARDY 162:14 |
| his prism, and silent f. | WORD 356:10 |
| huge massy f. | MAC 213:6 |
| I am the family f. | HARDY 162:10 |
| I never forget a f. | MARX 221:7 |
| I wish I loved its silly f. | RAL 258:6 |
| labour bears a lovely f. | DEKK 116:9 |
| Lift up thine eyes and seek his f. | MONS 233:2 |
| Look in my f. | TRAI 334:2 |

face (cont.):

| | |
|---|---|
| Lord make his f. shine | BIBLE 40:15 |
| mind's construction in the f. | SHAK 285:14 |
| mist in my f. | BROW 77:2 |
| never f. so pleased my mind | ANON 10:18 |
| never see my f. again | TENN 324:21 |
| night's starred f. | KEATS 192:20 |
| paint in the public's f. | RUSK 264:10 |
| Pity a human f. | BLAKE 61:21 |
| rabbit has a charming f. | ANON 10:8 |
| see my pilot face to f. | TENN 323:19 |
| sing in the robber's f. | JUV 189:11 |
| smile on the f. of the tiger | ANON 10:22 |
| socialism would not lose its human f. | DUBC 128:31 |
| spirit passed before my f. | BIBLE 42:28 |
| stamping on a human f. | ORW 242:11 |
| then f. to face | BIBLE 55:14 |
| they praised him to his f. | TENN 328:14 |
| turning your f. to the light | SASS 267:9 |
| unacceptable f. of capitalism | HEATH 164:12 |
| upon the f. of the deep | BIBLE 38:13 |
| upon the f. of the waters | BIBLE 38:13 |
| with how wan a f. | SIDN 306:18 |
| with twain he covered his f. | BIBLE 45:10 |
| Your f., my thane, is as a book | SHAK 285:20 |
| your honest, sonsie f. | BURNS 82:24 |

faces: accuse 'em of not having any f.

| | |
|---|---|
| | PRIE 255:7 |
| baby f. in the violet light | ELIOT 134:30 |
| Bid them wash their f. | SHAK 273:16 |
| cantan', grace-proud f. | BURNS 82:29 |
| f. are but a gallery of pictures | BACON 24:23 |
| grind the f. of the poor | BIBLE 45:6 |
| In nice clean f. | BARH 28:18 |
| monastic f. in quiet collegiate | CLOU 102:9 |
| old familiar f. | LAMB 200:13 |
| public f. in private places | AUDEN 21:6 |
| these f. in the crowd | POUND 254:20 |

facilis: F. descensus Averno

| | |
|---|---|
| | VIRG 339:12 |

fact: fatal futility of F.

| | |
|---|---|
| | JAMES 180:2 |
| hypothesis by an ugly f. | HUXL 177:15 |
| irritable reaching after f. | KEATS 193:2 |
| judges of f. | PULT 256:4 |

faction: it made them a f.

| | |
|---|---|
| | MAC 213:17 |
| whisper of a f. | RUSS 265:5 |

factions: religious f. are volcanoes

| | |
|---|---|
| | BURKE 81:1 |

facts: alone are wanted

| | |
|---|---|
| | DICK 118:27 |
| f. are on expenses | STOP 318:3 |
| f. are sacred | SCOTT 268:3 |
| f. when you come to brass tacks | ELIOT 134:14 |
| form of inert f. | ADAMS 1:20 |
| give you all the f. | AUDEN 21:12 |
| politics consists in ignoring f. | ADAMS 1:19 |
| Science is built up of f. | POIN 250:10 |

faculties: each according to his f.

| | |
|---|---|
| | BAK 27:1 |
| Hath borne his f. so meek | SHAK 285:24 |
| Taffections, and to f. | DONNE 124:8 |
| very f. of eyes and ears | SHAK 275:23 |

fade: F. far away, dissolve

| | |
|---|---|
| | KEATS 191:31 |
| f. into the light of common day | WORD 355:21 |
| They simply f. away | FOLEY 142:16 |

faded: not hollow cheek or f. eye

| | |
|---|---|
| | TENN 328:2 |

fades: f. awa' like morning dew

| | |
|---|---|
| | BALL 28:10 |
| Now f. the glimmering landscape | GRAY 157:4 |

fading: in f. silks compose

| | |
|---|---|
| | WINC 352:3 |

faery: f. lands forlorn

| | |
|---|---|
| | KEATS 192:5 |
| Full metall, a f.'s child | KEATS 191:9 |

faiblesse: tout le reste est f.

| | |
|---|---|
| | VIGNY 338:18 |

fail: F. not our feast

| | |
|---|---|
| | SHAK 287:1 |
| we'll not f. | SHAK 286:6 |
| We shall not flag or f. | CHUR 99:13 |

failed: fluttered and f. for breath

| | |
|---|---|
| | ARN 17:1 |

fails: One sure, if another f.

| | |
|---|---|
| | BROW 77:12 |

failure: f.'s no success at all

| | |
|---|---|
| | DYLAN 130:4 |
| not the effort nor the f. | EMPS 137:6 |
| Women can't forgive f. | CHEK 96:26 |

faint: beginning to f. in the light

| | |
|---|---|
| | TENN 326:28 |
| Damn with f. praise | POPE 251:6 |
| f. praises one another damn | WYCH 358:5 |
| F., yet pursuing | BIBLE 41:1 |
| walk, and not f. | BIBLE 46:13 |

fair: all so excellently f.

| | |
|---|---|
| | COL 103:14 |
| anything to show more f. | WORD 354:15 |
| days when I was f. | RONS 262:5 |
| Dream of F. Women | TENN 323:20 |
| f. as is the rose in May | CHAU 96:11 |
| F. is foul, and foul is fair | SHAK 285:1 |
| F. is too foul an epithet | MARL 219:10 |
| F. shares for all | JAY 180:14 |
| F. stood the wind for France | DRAY 126:22 |
| Fat, f. and forty | O'KEE 241:6 |
| How sweet and f. she seems | WALL 341:12 |
| I have sworn thee f. | SHAK 300:16 |
| noble, historically f. | LERN 205:26 |
| None but the brave deserves the f. | DRYD 127:19 |
| Outward be f. | CHUR 98:25 |
| Sabrina f. | MILT 226:21 |
| She f., divinely fair | MILT 229:24 |
| so foul and f. a day | SHAK 285:6 |
| this f. defect of nature | MILT 229:30 |
| Thou art all f., my love | BIBLE 44:35 |
| thou art f., my love | BIBLE 44:34 |
| With you f. maid | ANON 6:5 |

fairer: surely the f. way

| | |
|---|---|
| | BACON 24:3 |

fairest: f. creatures we desire

| | |
|---|---|
| | SHAK 299:11 |
| F. Isle, all isles excelling | DRYD 128:2 |
| O f. of creation, last and best | MILT 229:27 |

fairies: beginning of f.

| | |
|---|---|
| | BARR 29:11 |
| Do you believe in f. | BARR 29:14 |
| f. at the bottom of our garden | FYL 147:9 |
| Farewell, rewards and F. | CORB 107:23 |
| She is the f.' midwife | SHAK 294:24 |
| since the f. left off dancing | SELD 269:19 |

fairness: equality or f. or justice

| | |
|---|---|
| | BERL 36:6 |

fairy: f. somewhere that falls

| | |
|---|---|
| | BARR 29:12 |
| Like f. gifts fading away | MOORE 234:11 |
| loves a f. when she's forty | HENL 165:16 |
| of F. me thoghte | LANG 201:6 |
| wide enough to wrap a f. in | SHAK 290:27 |

fais: F. ce que voudras

| | |
|---|---|
| | RAB 257:12 |

faith: author and finisher of our f.

| | |
|---|---|
| | BIBLE 56:27 |
| children in whom is no f. | BIBLE 40:24 |
| easy to shake a man's f. | SHAW 300:27 |
| f, hope, charity | BIBLE 55:14 |
| f. shines equal | BRON 72:16 |
| f. that stands on authority | EMER 136:23 |
| F. the substance of things hoped for | BIBLE 56:26 |
| f. unfaithful kept him falsely | TENN 324:9 |
| f. without doubt is nothing | UNAM 336:11 |
| F. without works is dead | BIBLE 57:3 |
| Fight the good fight of f. | BIBLE 56:20 |
| future states of both are left to f. | BYRON 86:12 |
| I have kept the f. | BIBLE 56:21 |
| in the seat to f. assigned | SMART 308:11 |
| In this f. I wish to live | VILL 338:21 |
| Love in dying, F. is defying | BARN 29:8 |
| more f. in honest doubt | TENN 325:19 |
| My staff of f. to walk upon | RAL 257:23 |
| O thou of little f. | BIBLE 50:9 |
| scientific f.'s absurd | BROW 75:27 |
| Sea of F. | ARN 16:11 |
| simple f. than Norman blood | TENN 325:33 |
| though I have all f. | BIBLE 55:11 |
| Thy f. hath made thee whole | BIBLE 49:25 |
| you have kept f. | HARDY 162:9 |
| your work of f. and labour | BIBLE 56:13 |

faithful: Be thou f. unto death

| | |
|---|---|
| | BIBLE 57:21 |
| Ever f., ever sure | MILT 227:9 |
| good and f. servant | BIBLE 51:1 |
| I have been f. to thee, Cynara | DOWS 125:12 |

faithful (cont.):

| | |
|---|---|
| mentally f. to himself | PAINE 244:6 |
| O come, all ye f. | ANON 13:9 |
| So f. in love, and so dauntless | SCOTT 268:19 |
| faithfully: ask f. we may obtain | BOOK 64:27 |
| faithless: f. coldness of the times | TENN 325:24 |
| Human on my f. arm | AUDEN 20:27 |
| fake: Anything that consoles us is f. | MURD 236:11 |
| falcon: dapple-dawn-drawn F. | HOPK 172:20 |
| f., towering in her pride | SHAK 286:28 |
| Gentle as f. | SKEL 308:3 |
| Falklands: F. thing was a fight | BORG 69:24 |
| fall: by dividing we f. | DICK 120:18 |
| diggeth a pit shall f. into it | BIBLE 44:21 |
| f. for anything | HAM 160:16 |
| F. into the hands of God | TENN 328:13 |
| f. into the hands of the living God | BIBLE 56:25 |
| f. into the hands of the Lord | BIBLE 47:32 |
| f. not out by the way | BIBLE 39:28 |
| f. out with those we love | TENN 327:17 |
| further they have to f. | FITZ 141:1 |
| hard rain's a gonna f. | DYLAN 130:2 |
| haughty spirit before a f. | BIBLE 43:28 |
| I shall f. like a bright exhalation | SHAK 280:17 |
| it had a dying f. | SHAK 297:14 |
| Life is a horizontal f. | COCT 103:2 |
| needs fear no f. | BUNY 79:7 |
| Things f. apart | YEATS 359:24 |
| Weak men must f. | SHAK 293:23 |
| we f. to rise | BROW 75:11 |
| what a f. was there | SHAK 281:24 |
| yet fear I to f. | RAL 257:24 |
| fallacy: Pathetic F. | RUSK 264:12 |
| fallen: art thou f. from heaven | BIBLE 45:22 |
| Babylon is f. | BIBLE 57:34 |
| good man f. among Fabians | LENIN 205:5 |
| lot is f. unto me | BOOK 66:15 |
| Ye are f. from grace | BIBLE 55:29 |
| falling: apple f. towards England | AUDEN 21:5 |
| 'f. domino' principle | EIS 131:15 |
| Go, and catch a f. star | DONNE 124:10 |
| my feet from f. | BOOK 68:20 |
| fallings: F. from us, vanishings | WORD 355:22 |
| falls: And then he f., as I do | SHAK 280:18 |
| F. the Shadow | ELIOT 133:19 |
| false: all was f. and hollow | MILT 228:23 |
| Beware of f. prophets | BIBLE 49:14 |
| by the philosopher, as equally f. | GIBB 150:10 |
| F. face must hide | SHAK 286:8 |
| f. sincere | POPE 251:21 |
| f. witness against thy neighbour | BIBLE 40:9 |
| Followed f. lights | DRYD 127:29 |
| not then be f. to any man | SHAK 274:23 |
| Ring out the f. | TENN 325:23 |
| thou be not f. to others | BACON 25:21 |
| wouldst not play f. | SHAK 285:15 |
| falsehood: express lying or f. | SWIFT 320:1 |
| F. has a perennial spring | BURKE 79:25 |
| neither Truth nor F. | HOBB 169:5 |
| falsehoods: f. which interest | JOHN 182:12 |
| falsely: kept him f. true | TENN 324:9 |
| Falstaff: F. sweats to death | SHAK 277:29 |
| falter: hesitate and f. life away | ARN 17:10 |
| falters: love that never f. | SPR 313:26 |
| Famagusta: F. and the hidden sun | FLEC 141:18 |
| fame: blush to find it f. | POPE 252:31 |
| call the Temple of F. | LICH 207:1 |
| F. is a food that dead men eat | DOBS 122:26 |
| F. is like a river | BACON 25:7 |
| F. is the spur | MILT 227:14 |
| his f. the ocean sea | BARN 29:7 |
| love and f. to nothingness | KEATS 192:21 |
| Man dreams of f. | TENN 324:15 |
| Physicians of the Utmost F. | BELL 33:4 |
| servants of f. | BACON 24:27 |

fame (cont.):

| | |
|---|---|
| We came here for f. | DISR 122:12 |
| What is f.? an empty bubble | GRAI 156:7 |
| famed: f. in all great arts | ARN 17:21 |
| fames: Auri sacra f. | VIRG 339:8 |
| familiar: Mine own f. friend | BOOK 67:2 |
| mine own f. friend | BOOK 67:12 |
| old f. faces | LAMB 200:13 |
| familiarity: F. breeds contempt | TWAIN 336:3 |
| families: All happy f. resemble | TOLS 333:11 |
| f. in a country village | AUST 23:9 |
| mothers of large f. | BELL 33:2 |
| occur in the best-regulated f. | DICK 118:16 |
| old f. last not three oaks | BROW 74:6 |
| family: f.—that dear octopus | SMITH 309:9 |
| f. that prays together | SCAL 267:16 |
| f. with the wrong members | ORW 242:3 |
| I am the f. face | HARDY 162:10 |
| left his f. it didn't say why | TWAIN 335:19 |
| running of a f. | MONT 233:13 |
| famine: die by f. die by inches | HENRY 166:3 |
| famous: become f. without ability | SHAW 300:29 |
| f. by their birth | SHAK 293:16 |
| f. for fifteen minutes | WARH 342:20 |
| F. men have the whole earth | PER 248:2 |
| found myself f. | BYRON 87:21 |
| Let us now praise f. men | BIBLE 48:7 |
| fan: F.-vaulting | LANC 200:20 |
| with her f. spread | CONG 106:17 |
| fanaticism: F. consists in redoubling | SANT 266:21 |
| fanatics: F. have their dreams | KEATS 190:24 |
| fancies: F. that broke through | BROW 77:4 |
| With a heart of furious f. | ANON 11:23 |
| fancy: Ever let the f. roam | KEATS 190:26 |
| f. is the sails | KEATS 192:22 |
| In the spring a young man's f. | TENN 326:8 |
| of most excellent f. | SHAK 277:8 |
| sweetest Shakespeare f.'s child | MILT 227:8 |
| Tell me where is f. bred | SHAK 289:20 |
| fancy-free: In maiden meditation, f. | SHAK 290:24 |
| fantasies: fed the heart on f. | YEATS 359:16 |
| fantastic: In a light f. round | MILT 226:9 |
| On the light f. toe | MILT 227:2 |
| fantasy: much too strong for f. | DONNE 124:1 |
| far: audacity is knowing how f. | COCT 103:4 |
| bridge too f. | BROW 75:7 |
| f. above the great | GRAY 157:19 |
| F. and wide, far and few | LEAR 203:10 |
| F. from the madding crowd | GRAY 157:10 |
| f. gone from original righteousness | BOOK 69:17 |
| f. side of despair | SART 267:6 |
| It is a f., far better thing | DICK 120:7 |
| keep f. from me, you grim women | OVID 243:9 |
| Mexico, so f. from God | DIAZ 117:16 |
| much too f. out all my life | SMITH 309:19 |
| news from a f. country | BIBLE 43:37 |
| Oh keep f. off, you uninitiated | VIRG 339:13 |
| old, unhappy, f.-off things | WORD 357:2 |
| Over the hills and f. away | GAY 149:5 |
| quarrel in a f. away country | CHAM 94:1 |
| so near and yet so f. | TENN 325:21 |
| farce: f. is played out | RAB 257:13 |
| longest running f. | SMITH 309:3 |
| second as f. | MARX 221:10 |
| second time as f. | BARN 29:6 |
| farewell: Ae f., and then for ever | BURNS 81:22 |
| f. content | SHAK 292:19 |
| f., he is gon | CHAU 95:25 |
| f. my bok and my devocioun | CHAU 96:9 |
| F.! thou art too dear | SHAK 299:27 |
| f. to the snade | COWP 109:30 |
| hail, and f. evermore | CAT 93:8 |
| long f., to all my greatness | SHAK 280:18 |
| Too-late, F. | ROSS 263:8 |

farm: keep 'em down on the f. — YOUNG 206:17
farmer: f. that hanged himself — SHAK 286:20
  F. will never be happy — HERB 166:11
farmers: embattled f. stood — EMER 136:12
  f. excessively fortunate — VIRG 340:7
farms: cellos of the deep f. — STEV 316:22
  What spires, what f. are those — HOUS 174:24
farrow: old sow that eats her f. — JOYCE 188:7
fart: can't f. and chew gum — JOHN 181:22
  Love is the f. — SUCK 318:22
farther: f. you go from the church — WOTT 357:21
farthing: Virtue knows to a f. — WALP 342:3
farthings: sparrows sold for two f. — BIBLE 52:17
fascination: f. of what's difficult — YEATS 359:4
  There's a f. frantic — GILB 152:8
Fascist: Every woman adores a F. — PLATH 249:14
fashion: faithful to thee, Cynara! in my f. — DOWS 125:12
  f. of this world passeth — BIBLE 55:6
  glass of f. — SHAK 276:2
  not for the f. of these times — SHAK 272:17
  out of the world, as out of the f. — CIBB 100:14
fashions: conscience to fit this year's f. — HELL 165:7
fast: but none so f. as stroke — COKE 103:6
  come he slow, or come he f. — SCOTT 268:17
  earth in f. thick pants — COL 103:23
  F. by their native shore — COWP 109:28
  fun grew f. and furious — BURNS 82:23
  Silently and very f. — AUDEN 20:19
  Snip! Snap! Snip! They go so f. — HOFF 169:22
  who will not f. in peace — CRAB 110:24
fasten: F. your seat-belts — MANK 217:12
  if they think, they f. — HOUS 174:10
faster: F. than a speeding bullet — ANON 7:5
fastest: f. who travels alone — KIPL 196:20
fasting: lives upon hope will die f. — FRAN 145:11
  thank heaven, f. — SHAK 273:6
fat: Butter merely makes us f. — GOER 153:22
  eat the f. of the land — BIBLE 39:27
  F., fair and forty — O'KEE 241:6
  f. gentleman in such a passion — SHAW 302:29
  F. is a feminist issue — ORB 241:15
  f., oily man of God — THOM 331:21
  f. white woman whom nobody — CORN 108:6
  Imprisoned in every f. man — CONN 106:28
  men about me that are f. — SHAK 281:1
  opera ain't over 'til the f. lady — COOK 107:16
  Outside every f. man — AMIS 5:4
  thin man inside every f. man — ORW 241:25
fatal: fair and f. king — JOHN 181:17
  f. futility of Fact — JAMES 180:2
  f. gift of beauty — BYRON 85:7
  great deal of it is absolutely f. — WILDE 349:23
  most f. complaint of all — HILT 168:18
  So sweet was ne'er so f. — SHAK 293:1
  strange and f. interview — DONNE 123:5
fate: Art is a revolt against f. — MALR 217:4
  become the makers of our f. — POPP 253:15
  cannot suspend their f. — DEFOE 115:17
  Character is f. — NOV 240:12
  down the torrent of his f. — JOHN 183:16
  F. cannot harm me — SMITH 310:7
  F. is not an eagle — BOWEN 70:18
  F.'s great bazaar — MACN 216:9
  F. so enviously debars — MARV 220:13
  F. wrote her a most tremendous — BEER 32:13
  forget my f. — TATE 322:15
  I am the master of my f. — HENL 165:18
  I hold f. clasped in my fist — FORD 143:11
  limits of a vulgar f. — GRAY 157:19
  man's character is his f. — HER 166:9
  over-ruled by f. — MARL 218:17
  take a bond of f. — SHAK 287:21
  Till I thy f. shall overtake — KING 195:5
  transient is the smile of f. — DYER 129:17

fate (cont.):
  wagged contempt at F. — WATS 343:1
  when f. summons — DRYD 128:4
fates: masters of their f. — SHAK 280:27
  periods set, and hidden f. — SUCK 318:23
father: about my F.'s business — BIBLE 52:4
  brood of folly without f. bred — MILT 226:22
  cannot have God for his f. — CYPR 113:12
  Child is f. of the Man — WORD 355:14
  Dear Lord and F. of mankind — WHIT 348:27
  either my f. or my mother — STER 315:12
  F., I have sinned against heaven — BIBLE 52:30
  f is gone wild into his grave — SHAK 278:30
  F. is rather vulgar — DICK 119:1
  f. of English criticism — JOHN 182:20
  f.'s corpse — APOL 14:13
  Glory be to the F. — BOOK 63:12
  Honour thy f. and thy mother — BIBLE 40:8
  I meet my F., my age — LOW 211:15
  limp f. of thousands — JOYCE 188:16
  Lloyd George knew my f. — ANON 9:1
  My f. feeds his flocks — HOME 170:18
  My mother groaned! my f. wept — BLAKE 62:3
  no man cometh unto the F. — BIBLE 53:38
  one God the F. Almighty — BOOK 65:5
  Our F. which art in heaven — BIBLE 48:27
  polite f. of his people — JAM 179:10
  rather have a turnip than his f. — JOHN 186:13
  resembled my f. as he slept — SHAK 286:14
  shall a man leave his f. — BIBLE 38:23
  She gave her f. forty-one — ANON 8:22
  thicker than my f.'s loins — BIBLE 41:33
  When did you last see your f. — YEAM 358:12
  wise f. that knows his own child — SHAK 289:7
  wise son maketh a glad f. — BIBLE 43:16
  wish was f., Harry, to that thought — SHAK 278:27
  You are old, F. William — CARR 91:4
  your F. which is in heaven — BIBLE 48:25
fatherhood: Mirrors and f. — BORG 69:23
fatherless: f. children, and widows — BOOK 64:17
fatherly: thy f. goodness — BOOK 64:19
fathers: f.-forth whose beauty is past — HOPK 172:13
  f., provoke not your children — BIBLE 56:2
  iniquity of the f. upon the children — BIBLE 40:5
  My f. can have it — THOM 330:20
  our f. brought forth upon this — LINC 207:8
  sojourners, as were all our f. — BIBLE 42:17
  spake in time past unto the f. — BIBLE 56:23
  Tell them, because our f. lied — KIPL 196:7
  Victory has a hundred f. — CIANO 100:12
fathom: f.-line could never touch — SHAK 277:27
  For thou canst not f. it — TENN 322:13
  Full f. five thy father lies — SHAK 296:1
fathomed: sheer, no-man-f. — HOPK 172:10
fathoms: 'Tis fifty f. deep — BALL 28:6
fatling: young lion and the f. — BIBLE 45:19
fatted: Bring hither the f. calf — BIBLE 52:31
fattening: illegal, immoral, or f. — WOOL 354:8
fault: all f. who hath no fault — TENN 324:8
  f., dear Brutus — SHAK 280:27
  f. of angels and of gods — POPE 250:24
  Good women think it is their f. — BROO 73:11
  happy f. — MISS 232:1
  It has no kind of f. or flaw — GILB 151:10
  through my most grievous f. — MISS 231:11
  What soul is without f. — RIMB 260:10
faultless: Faultily f., icily regular — TENN 324:8
  F. to a fault — BROW 77:9
  thinks a f. piece to see — POPE 251:29
faults: Be to her f. a little blind — PRIOR 255:9
  England, with all thy f. — COWP 110:8
  Jesus! with all thy f. — BUTL 84:19
  men are moulded out of f. — SHAK 288:26
  Some f. to make us men — SHAK 271:27
  their f. confessing — BUCK 278:3

**faults** (cont.):

| | |
|---|---|
| They fill you with the f. | LARK 201:17 |
| vile ill-favoured f. | SHAK 290:10 |
| With all her f., she is my country | CHUR 98:21 |
| **Faustus**: F. must be damned | MARL 218:13 |
| **favour**: being in and out of f. | FROST 146:9 |
| out of f. grudge at knaves | DEFOE 115:21 |
| **favoured**: thou that art highly f. | BIBLE 51:27 |
| **favours**: lively sense of future f. | WALP 342:7 |
| middle of her f. | SHAK 275:13 |
| secret hope for greater f. | LA R 201:25 |
| **fawning**: How like a f. publican | SHAK 289:1 |
| **fawns**: fallow f. invisible go | THOM 330:26 |
| **fear**: acting and reasoning as f. | BURKE 80:7 |
| by means of pity and f. | ARIS 15:15 |
| concessions of f. | BURKE 79:27 |
| equal poise of hope and f. | MILT 226:13 |
| f. first in the world made gods | JONS 187:11 |
| F. God. Honour the King | BIBLE 57:9 |
| F. God. Honour the King | KITC 198:8 |
| F. God, and keep his commandments | BIBLE 44:28 |
| f. in a handful of dust | ELIOT 134:20 |
| F. is the foundation | ADAMS 2:2 |
| f. no more the heat o' the sun | SHAK 273:27 |
| f. of finding something worse | BELL 33:5 |
| f. of the Law | JOYCE 188:4 |
| f. of the Lord | BIBLE 45:18 |
| f. of the Lord | BOOK 68:15 |
| f. usually ends in folly | COL 104:28 |
| Fly hence, our contact f. | ARN 17:11 |
| For f. of little men | ALL 4:18 |
| freedom from f. | ROOS 262:13 |
| hate, so long as they f. | ACC 1:2 |
| hate that which we often f. | SHAK 271:8 |
| hope that never had a f. | COWP 110:17 |
| hope to rise, or f. to fall | WOTT 357:15 |
| I cannot taint with f. | SHAK 287:32 |
| I f. thee, ancient Mariner | COL 104:11 |
| I f. those big words | JOYCE 188:13 |
| I will f. no evil | BOOK 66:18 |
| Life is first boredom, then f. | LARK 201:14 |
| natural f. in children | BACON 24:20 |
| needs f. no fall | BUNY 79:7 |
| never f. to negotiate | KENN 194:4 |
| Perfect f. casteth out love | CONN 107:2 |
| perfect love casteth out f. | BIBLE 57:16 |
| salvation with f. and trembling | BIBLE 56:6 |
| so whom shall I f. | BIBLE 58:9 |
| their one f., Death's shadow | BLUN 62:12 |
| to f. is fear itself | ROOS 262:9 |
| too much joy or too much f. | GRAV 156:14 |
| travel in the direction of our f. | BERR 36:12 |
| without f. the lawless roads | MUIR 236:6 |
| word of f. unpleasing to a married ear | SHAK 284:22 |
| **feared**: f. nor flattered any flesh | DOUG 125:7 |
| prince to be f. than loved | MACH 215:1 |
| **fearful**: f. thing to fall | BIBLE 56:25 |
| frame thy f. symmetry | BLAKE 62:5 |
| our f. trip is done | WHIT 348:11 |
| **fearfully**: f. and wonderfully made | BOOK 69:7 |
| **fearless**: F., blameless knight | ANON 12:4 |
| **fears**: f. his fellowship to die | SHAK 279:18 |
| f. may be liars | CLOU 102:23 |
| f. that I may cease to be | KEATS 192:19 |
| grown from sudden f. | BYRON 87:5 |
| I had no human f. | WORD 356:25 |
| man who f. the Lord | BIBLE 58:11 |
| Our f. do make us traitors | SHAK 287:22 |
| Present f. are less | SHAK 285:11 |
| To saucy doubts and f. | SHAK 287:9 |
| **feast**: Fail not our f. | SHAK 287:1 |
| great f. of languages | SHAK 284:17 |
| Paris is a movable f. | HEM 165:13 |
| **feather**: Blade on the f. | CORY 108:11 |
| F.-footed through the plashy | WAUGH 343:25 |

**feather** (cont.):

| | |
|---|---|
| f. to tickle the intellect | LAMB 200:6 |
| my foot, my each f. | HUGH 175:20 |
| Stuck a f. in his cap | ANON 11:24 |
| **feathered**: f. race with pinions | FRERE 145:22 |
| **feats**: What f. he did that day | SHAK 279:19 |
| **fed**: But it is f. and watered | CAMP 88:13 |
| every child f. and educated | RUSK 264:19 |
| f. of the dainties | SHAK 284:15 |
| f. on the fullness of death | SWIN 321:13 |
| **federation**: F. of the world | TENN 326:12 |
| **fee**: For a small f. in America | SOND 311:8 |
| gorgeous East in f. | WORD 356:2 |
| set my life at a pin's f. | SHAK 274:28 |
| **feeble**: confirm the f. knees | BIBLE 46:5 |
| jonquil o'ercomes the f. brain | WINC 352:2 |
| not enough to help the f. | SHAK 296:16 |
| Superstition is the religion of f. | BURKE 80:18 |
| **feed**: f. deep, deep upon her | KEATS 191:26 |
| f. his flock like a shepherd | BIBLE 46:11 |
| f. me in a green pasture | BOOK 66:17 |
| F. my sheep | BIBLE 54:7 |
| shalt thou f. on Death | SHAK 300:15 |
| will you still f. me | LENN 205:17 |
| **feel**: *believe* to One *does* f. | KNOX 198:17 |
| f. for the common chord | BROW 75:9 |
| f. what wretches feel | SHAK 283:12 |
| see and hear and f. | JOYCE 188:17 |
| thing that could not f. | WORD 356:25 |
| tragedy to those that f. | WALP 341:23 |
| **feeling**: formal f. comes | DICK 120:8 |
| mess of imprecision of f. | ELIOT 133:6 |
| Music is f., then, not sound | STEV 316:10 |
| petrifies the f. | BURNS 82:5 |
| To f. as to sight | SHAK 286:10 |
| without f. gay | CHUR 98:26 |
| **fees**: accompanied by a few f. | HUNT 176:18 |
| they took their F. | BELL 33:4 |
| **feet**: And did those f. | BLAKE 61:12 |
| bathe those beauteous f. | FLET 142:8 |
| die on your f. than to live | IBAR 178:1 |
| f. are always in the water | AMES 4:22 |
| f. have they, and walk not | BOOK 68:18 |
| f. into the way of peace | BIBLE 51:30 |
| f. of him that bringeth good tidings | BIBLE 46:15 |
| Her f. beneath her petticoat | SUCK 318:21 |
| Its f. were tied | KEATS 191:3 |
| Just direct your f. | FIEL 139:15 |
| lantern unto my f. | BOOK 68:24 |
| marching, charging f. | JAGG 179:7 |
| moon under her f. | BIBLE 57:30 |
| my f. from falling | BOOK 68:20 |
| off the dust of your f. | BIBLE 49:28 |
| on little cat f. | SAND 266:13 |
| our f. when we want shoes | SWIFT 320:12 |
| palms before my f. | CHES 97:22 |
| slipping underneath our f. | FITZ 140:11 |
| stranger's f. may find the meadow | HOUS 174:14 |
| Til crowes f. be growe under | CHAU 96:15 |
| To his f. thy tribute bring | LYTE 212:21 |
| wash their f. in soda water | ELIOT 134:26 |
| Wi' the Scots lords at his f. | BALL 28:4 |
| with twain he covered his f. | BIBLE 45:10 |
| **felicity**: Absent thee from f. | SHAK 277:17 |
| Or shadow of f. | WALL 341:14 |
| these eyes to behold f. | BROW 74:17 |
| **felix**: F. *qui potuit rerum* | VIRG 340:8 |
| O f. culpa | MISS 232:1 |
| **fell**: f. among thieves | BIBLE 52:11 |
| To noon he f., from noon | MILT 228:20 |
| **fellow**: one that loves his f.-men | HUNT 176:13 |
| Sweetes' li'l' f. | STAN 314:11 |
| testy, pleasant f. | ADD 2:22 |
| **fellow-feeling**: f. makes one | GARR 148:10 |
| **fellowship**: F. is heaven | MORR 235:17 |

female: f. atheist talks you dead     JOHN 183:8
F. Eunuch     GREER 158:10
f. of the species is more deadly     KIPL 196:12
f. worker is the slave     CONN 107:3
flaming racket of the f.     OSB 242:22
into the Ark, the male and the f.     BIBLE 39:8
life for the British f.     CLOU 102:7
Male and f. created he them     BIBLE 38:16
Who has a faithful f. friend     WHUR 349:4
feminine: Taste is the f. of genius     FITZ 140:19
feminist: Fat is a f. issue     ORB 241:15
femme: Cherchez la f.     DUMAS 129:3
fen: f. of stagnant water     WORD 355:11
plashy f. passes the questing     WAUGH 343:25
fence: o'er the f. leaps Sunny Jim     HANFF 161:6
fences: f. make good neighbours     FROST 146:16
Fermanagh: steeples of F.     CHUR 99:7
fern: sparkle out among the f.     TENN 323:12
fertile: In such a fix to be so f.     NASH 237:9
twice five miles of f. ground     COL 103:22
fertilize: f. a problem with a solution     SIMP 307:13
festal: f. light in Christ-Church     ARN 17:9
fester: Lilies that f.     SHAK 300:2
limbs that f. are not springlike     ABSE 1:1
festina: F. lente     AUG 22:6
fetch: f. the age of gold     MILT 227:27
fetish: Militarism is f. worship     TAWN 322:18
fetters: reason Milton wrote in f.     BLAKE 60:25
feuds: Forget all f.     MAC 214:1
fever: after life's fitful f.     SHAK 287:4
enigma of the f. chart     ELIOT 133:5
f., and the fret     KEATS 191:31
f. called 'Living'     POE 250:6
grows to an envious f.     SHAK 296:31
signed the treaty bred a f.     THOM 330:11
feverish: Poetry's the f. fit     WINC 352:1
few: Far and f., far and few     LEAR 203:10
f. are chosen     BIBLE 50:28
f. child's squalls     HUNT 176:18
fit audience find, though f.     MILT 229:19
Gey f., and they're a' deid     ANON 7:18
many for the gain of a f.     POPE 253:11
owed by so many to so f.     CHUR 99:15
rather hated the ruling f.     BENT 35:4
we happy f., we band     SHAK 279:20
fiat: F. justitia et pereat mundus     FERD 138:24
F. justitia et ruant coeli     WATS 342:25
fickle: fierce and f. is the South     TENN 327:24
Whatever is f., freckled     HOPK 172:13
fiction: condemn it as an improbable f.     SHAK 298:10
f. is a necessity     CHES 98:9
house of f.     JAMES 179:25
if she is to write f.     WOOLF 354:1
It is sometimes f.     MAC 213:22
one form of continuous f.     BEVAN 38:6
Peerage. . .best thing in f.     WILDE 350:14
Poetry is the supreme f.     STEV 316:8
Stranger than f.     BYRON 86:29
That is what f. means     WILDE 349:20
fictions: f. only and false hair     HERB 167:1
fiddle: and I the second f.     SPR 314:1
fiddling: huntsman and a f. priest     COWP 110:1
fide: Punica f.     SALL 266:9
Fidele: To fair F.'s grassy tomb     COLL 105:9
fideles: Adeste, f.     ANON 13:9
fidgety: f. Phil, he won't sit still     HOFF 169:19
field: Consider the lilies of the f.     BIBLE 49:4
corner of a foreign f.     BROO 73:10
f. ful of folk fond I ther     LANG 201:7
F. strewn with its dank yellow     ARN 17:3
For Vaguery in the F.     OSB 242:21
From the wet f.     ARN 17:18
lay f. to field     BIBLE 45:8
Man comes and tills the f.     TENN 328:17

field (cont.):
Never in the f. of human conflict     CHUR 99:15
simple as to cross a f.     PAST 246:10
Till the f. ring again     BOWEN 70:16
fields: Blown f. or flowerful closes     SWIN 321:17
f. invested with purpureal     WORD 355:7
flowering of His f.     TENN 324:16
flowerless f. of heaven     SWIN 320:28
Open unto the f.     WORD 354:15
To f. where flies no sharp     HOPK 172:7
walk through the f. in gloves     CORN 108:6
We plough the f., and scatter     CAMP 88:13
whispering of f. half-sown     OWEN 243:24
fiend: dark dominion swung the f.     MER 223:21
defy the foul f.     SHAK 283:13
foul F. coming over     BUNY 78:20
frightful f. doth close behind     COL 104:15
Like a f. hid in a cloud     BLAKE 62:3
fiends: foreigners are f.     MITF 232:10
fierce: bright and f. and fickle     TENN 327:24
f. light which beats upon     TENN 324:1
F. was the wild billow     ANAT 5:10
though she be but little, she is f.     SHAK 290:33
fiery: burning f. furnace     BIBLE 47:11
f. portal of the east     SHAK 293:29
f. soul, which working     DRYD 127:6
fifteen: famous for f. minutes     WARH 342:20
F. men on the dead man's chest     STEV 317:2
fifth: F. of November     ANON 10:5
fifties: tranquillized F.     LOW 211:14
fig: sewed f. leaves together     BIBLE 38:26
fight: bade me f. had told me so     EWER 138:1
dead, who will not f.     GREN 158:16
end that crowns us, not the f.     HERR 167:16
f. and fight and fight again     GAIT 147:11
f. and not to heed the wounds     IGN 178:8
f. for freedom and truth     IBSEN 178:3
f. for its King and Country     GRAH 156:2
F. on, my men, sayes Sir     BALL 28:3
f. on the beaches     CHUR 99:13
F. the good fight     MONS 233:2
F. the good fight of faith     BIBLE 56:20
fought a good f.     BIBLE 56:21
I have not yet begun to f.     JONES 186:21
Ile rise and f. againe     BALL 28:3
man being too proud to f.     WILS 351:18
must f. on to the end     HAIG 159:17
Never give up the f.     MARL 218:6
no peril in the f.     CORN 108:1
Nor law, nor duty bade me f.     YEATS 359:10
no stomach to this f.     SHAK 279:18
Quit yourselves like men, and f.     BIBLE 41:10
thought it wrong to f.     BELL 33:28
Ulster will f.     CHUR 99:2
when men refuse to f.     ANON 11:11
fighter: Am I no a bonny f.     STEV 316:25
fighting: between two periods of f.     BIER 59:7
consisteth not in actual f.     HOBB 169:9
f. Blenheim all over again     BEVAN 37:20
f. for this woman's honour     KALM 189:20
F. in the captain's tower     DYLAN 129:20
F. still, and still destroying     DRYD 127:21
She's the F. Téméraire     NEWB 238:12
Street F. Man     JAGG 179:7
What are WE f. for?     SERV 270:12
who dies f. has increase     GREN 158:16
fights: knows what he f. for     CROM 111:24
figure: f. a poem makes     FROST 146:24
f. in a country church     SWIFT 320:3
f. in the carpet     JAMES 179:17
f. that thou here seest     JONS 187:20
filches: f. from me my good name     SHAK 292:11
files: Commands the beauteous f.     VAUG 337:6
foremost f. of time     TENN 326:16
fill: Come f. up my cup     SCOTT 268:7

**fill** (*cont.*):

| | |
|---|---|
| f. hup the chinks wi' cheese | SURT 319:9 |
| f. the cup | FITZ 140:11 |
| I am not yet born; O f. me | MACN 216:6 |
| To f. the hour | EMER 136:26 |
| **filled**: they shall be f. | BIBLE 48:19 |
| **film**: f. of death obscured | KEATS 192:17 |
| Only that f., which fluttered | COL 103:20 |
| **films**: I seldom go to f. | BERR 36:14 |
| **filth**: identical, and so is f. | FORS 143:25 |
| **filthy**: greedy of f. lucre | BIBLE 56:16 |
| that is f. and polluted | BIBLE 47:25 |
| **finale**: Let be be f. of seem | STEV 316:6 |
| **finality**: Perfection is f. | STEP 315:6 |
| **finance**: F. is the stomach of the country | GLAD 153:7 |
| **financiers**: f., the little gnomes | WILS 351:12 |
| **Finchley**: Lord F. tried | BELL 33:22 |
| **find**: do not f. anything pleasant | VOLT 340:11 |
| returns home to f. it | MOORE 234:7 |
| searching f. out God | BIBLE 42:32 |
| Someday I'll f. you | COW 109:7 |
| to f., and not to yield | TENN 328:25 |
| with men I f. Him not | TENN 324:16 |
| **findeth**: f. his life shall lose it | BIBLE 49:33 |
| **finds**: Who f. himself, loses | ARN 17:13 |
| **fine**: Another F. Mess | LAUR 202:8 |
| f. madness | DRAY 126:19 |
| f. romance with no kisses | FIEL 139:14 |
| F. writing is next to fine | KEATS 193:12 |
| first f. careless rapture | BROW 76:2 |
| **finer**: nothing could be f. | GORD 155:22 |
| **fines**: interest and f. on sorrow | MAY 222:16 |
| **finest**: This was their f. hour | CHUR 99:14 |
| Yes, this is our f. shower | OSB 242:19 |
| **finger**: chills the f. not a bit | NASH 237:16 |
| f. do you want on the trigger | ANON 11:21 |
| f. in the throat | OSLER 243:3 |
| God's f. touched him | TENN 325:16 |
| his slow and moving f. | SHAK 292:24 |
| little f. shall be thicker | BIBLE 41:33 |
| measured by the f. and thumb | SAL 266:3 |
| moving f. writes | FITZ 140:14 |
| ring without the f. | MIDD 224:6 |
| scratching of my f. | HUME 176:11 |
| **fingernails**: paring his f. | JOYCE 188:8 |
| **fingers**: Crumbling between the f. | MACN 216:4 |
| cut their own f. | EDD 130:13 |
| Stop twisting in your yellow f. | HEAT 164:13 |
| **finger-stalls**: in fitless f. | GILB 152:2 |
| **finish**: Nice guys. F. last | DUR 129:13 |
| start together and f. | BEEC 31:23 |
| tools and we will f. the job | CHUR 99:16 |
| **finished**: f. in half the time | WOD 352:17 |
| f. in the first 100 days | KENN 194:5 |
| I have f. my course | BIBLE 56:21 |
| It is f. | BIBLE 54:5 |
| world where England is f. | MILL 224:24 |
| **finisher**: author and f. of our faith | BIBLE 56:27 |
| **fire**: C'mon, baby, light my f. | MORR 235:19 |
| done while Mrs Bennet was stirring the f. | AUST 23:3 |
| don't one of you f. until you see | PUTN 256:24 |
| dropping-wells of f. | TENN 325:15 |
| every time She shouted 'F.!' | BELL 33:9 |
| extinguishes candles and kindles f. | LA R 201:24 |
| Fell in the f. and was burnt | GRAH 156:4 |
| F. and fleet and candle-lighte | BALL 27:20 |
| f. and the rose are one | ELIOT 133:13 |
| F. burn and cauldron bubble | SHAK 287:15 |
| f. next time | ANON 7:12 |
| f. of my loins | NAB 236:18 |
| f. was furry as a bear | SITW 307:17 |
| frame of adamant, a soul of f. | JOHN 183:13 |
| frighted with false f. | SHAK 276:11 |
| heap coals of f. | BIBLE 43:36 |
| Lord was not in the f. | BIBLE 42:3 |

**fire** (*cont.*):

| | |
|---|---|
| Muse of f. | SHAK 278:33 |
| neighbour's house is on f. | BURKE 80:9 |
| night in a pillar of f. | BIBLE 39:39 |
| nodding by the f. | YEATS 360:9 |
| Now stir the f. | COWP 110:11 |
| pale f. | SHAK 296:23 |
| spirit all compact of f. | SHAK 300:17 |
| Thorough flood, thorough f. | SHAK 290:19 |
| world will end in f. | FROST 146:12 |
| youth of England are on f. | SHAK 279:2 |
| **fire-folk**: f. sitting in the air | HOPK 172:16 |
| **fires**: Big f. flare up in a wind | FRAN 145:5 |
| thought-executing f. | SHAK 283:6 |
| **fireside**: adventures were by the f. | GOLD 155:12 |
| F. enjoyments | COWP 110:12 |
| **firewood**: F., ironware | MAS 221:19 |
| **firm**: old f., is selling out | OSB 242:23 |
| **firmament**: blood streams in the f. | MARL 218:13 |
| no fellow in the f. | SHAK 281:3 |
| spacious f. on high | ADD 2:25 |
| **firmly**: F. I believe and truly | NEWM 238:19 |
| **firmness**: Commodity, f., and delight | WOTT 357:19 |
| **first**: Eclipse f., the rest nowhere | O'KEL 241:7 |
| f. day be mended | WILB 349:13 |
| f. fine careless rapture | BROW 76:2 |
| f. fruits of them | BIBLE 55:17 |
| f. in a village than second | CAES 87:26 |
| f. in the hearts of his | LEE 204:7 |
| f., last, everlasting day | DONNE 123:22 |
| f. man is of the earth | BIBLE 55:20 |
| f. step that is difficult | DU D 129:1 |
| know the place for the f. time | ELIOT 133:10 |
| last shall be f. | BIBLE 50:24 |
| nothing be done for the f. time | CORN 108:8 |
| no truck with f. impulses | MONT 234:1 |
| people who got there f. | UST 336:16 |
| there is no last nor f. | BROW 77:1 |
| We were the f. that ever burst | COL 104:5 |
| **firstborn**: her f. son | BIBLE 51:32 |
| **first-class**: f. fightin' man | KIPL 196:14 |
| **fish**: cars nose forward like f. | LOW 211:12 |
| coal and surrounded by f. | BEVAN 37:17 |
| F. are jumpin' | GERS 168:6 |
| F. got to swim and birds | HAMM 160:19 |
| F. say, they have their stream | BROO 73:2 |
| He replied, — 'F. fiddle de-dee!' | LEAR 203:14 |
| like a f. without a bicycle | STEI 315:2 |
| Phone for the f.-knives, Norman | BETJ 37:9 |
| There's a f. that *talks* | DE L 116:11 |
| Thou deboshed f. thou | SHAK 296:6 |
| **fishbone**: monument sticks like a f. | LOW 211:13 |
| **fished**: He f. by obstinate isles | POUND 254:15 |
| **fishers**: will make you f. of men | BIBLE 48:18 |
| **fishes**: notes like little f. | MACN 216:9 |
| Where the flyin'-f. play | KIPL 196:21 |
| **fishified**: flesh, how art thou f. | SHAK 295:5 |
| **fishing**: angling or float f. | JOHN 186:11 |
| **fishpond**: That great f. | DEKK 116:8 |
| **fist**: f. most valiant | SHAK 279:10 |
| **fit**: f. audience find | MILT 229:19 |
| for nothing but to carry | HERV 168:1 |
| It isn't f. for humans now | BETJ 37:9 |
| only the F. survive | SERV 270:11 |
| **fittest**: survival of the f. | ROCK 261:11 |
| Survival of the f. | SPEN 312:17 |
| **five**: At f. in the afternoon | GARC 148:2 |
| chirche dore she hadde f. | CHAU 95:20 |
| f. miles of fertile ground | COL 103:22 |
| f. minutes too late | COWL 109:18 |
| Full fathom f. thy father lies | SHAK 296:1 |
| Wrapped up in a f.-pound note | LEAR 203:11 |
| **fix**: F. in us thy humble dwelling | WESL 346:10 |
| If it ain't broke, don't f. it | LANCE 200:21 |
| **fixed**: f. point in a changing world | DOYLE 125:18 |

fixèd: f. figure for the time — SHAK 292:24
flag: death's pale f. — SHAK 295:24
High as a f. on the Fourth of July — HAMM 161:4
Jelly-bellied F.-flapper — KIPL 198:2
spare your country's f. — WHIT 348:26
We'll keep the red f. flying — CONN 106:23
We shall not f. or fail — CHUR 99:13
flame: Both moth and f. — ROET 261:16
hard, gemlike f. — PATER 246:15
Still plays about the f. — GAY 149:2
tongues of f. are in-folded — ELIOT 133:13
tongues of living f. — AUBER 19:15
When a lovely f. dies — HARB 161:10
Flanders: brought him a F. mare — HENR 166:1
In F. fields the poppies blow — MCCR 214:17
flashes: recognised, in f. — WORD 356:12
occasional f. of silence — SMITH 310:6
flashing: His f. eyes — COL 104:1
flat: divide characters into f. and round — FORS 143:17
Very f., Norfolk — COW 109:9
flats: different sharps and f. — BROW 76:26
flatten: His hide is sure to f. 'em — BELL 33:1
flatter: F. the mountain-tops — SHAK 299:17
flattered: Being f., is a lamb — CHAP 94:14
being then most f. — SHAK 281:5
feared nor f. any flesh — DOUG 125:7
flatterers: f. have intelligence — BACON 24:32
flattering: f. unction to your soul — SHAK 276:22
Some with a f. word — WILDE 350:16
flattery: Everyone likes f. — DISR 122:20
f. soothe the dull cold ear — GRAY 157:8
paid with f. — JOHN 182:10
suppose f. hurts no one — STEV 316:14
Flaubert: true Penelope was F. — POUND 254:15
flea: between a louse and a f. — JOHN 186:2
f. hath smaller fleas — SWIFT 320:23
literature's performing f. — O'CAS 240:23
fleas: dog that has praised his f. — YEATS 360:3
Even educated f. do it — PORT 253:22
F. know not whether — LAND 200:25
f. that tease in the High — BELL 34:1
fled: F. is that music — KEATS 192:7
f. from this vile world — SHAK 299:23
I f. Him, down the nights — THOM 331:8
flee: f. from the wrath to come — BIBLE 48:14
then would I f. away — BOOK 67:11
They f. from me, that sometime — WYATT 358:2
fleece: Its f. was white as snow — HALE 160:7
fleet: All in the Downs the f. — GAY 149:17
Fire and f. and candle-lighte — BALL 27:20
F. in which we serve — BOOK 69:13
f. of stars is anchored — FLEC 141:14
F. the time carelessly — SHAK 272:12
whole F.'s lit up — WOOD 353:18
fleeting: fable, song, or f. shade — HERR 167:14
fleets: f. sweep over thee in vain — BYRON 85:13
Fleet Street: who can be dull in F. — LAMB 200:7
flesh: All f. is as grass — BIBLE 57:6
All f. is grass — BIBLE 46:10
all f. shall see it — BIBLE 46:9
delicate white human f. — FIEL 139:10
east wind made f. — APPL 14:14
eat the f. in that night — BIBLE 39:36
feared nor flattered any f. — DOUG 125:7
f., alas, is wearied — MALL 216:20
f. and blood so cheap — HOOD 171:13
f., how art thou fishified — SHAK 295:5
f. is heir to — SHAK 275:25
F. of flesh — MILT 229:28
f. of my flesh — BIBLE 38:22
F. perishes, I live — HARDY 162:10
Frail f. and die — CROS 112:13
in the f. it is immortal — STEV 316:11
I wants to make your f. creep — DICK 119:27

flesh (cont.):
more f. than another man — SHAK 278:9
not against f. and blood — BIBLE 56:4
spirit willing but the f. is weak — BIBLE 51:13
they shall be one f. — BIBLE 38:23
thorn in the f. — BIBLE 55:28
too solid f. would melt — SHAK 274:9
world, f., and the devil — BOOK 64:15
Word was made f. — BIBLE 53:11
word was made f. — MISS 231:21
fleshly: through all this f. dress — VAUG 337:9
flesh pots: when we sat by the f. — BIBLE 40:1
flicker: moment of my greatness f. — ELIOT 133:29
flies: As f. to wanton boys — SHAK 283:21
murmurous haunt of f. — KEATS 192:2
fliest: fly thee, for thou f. Me — THOM 331:12
flight: alarms of struggle and f. — ARN 16:12
And took their f. — MARR 219:24
His cloistered f. — SHAK 287:5
His f. was madness — SHAK 287:22
fling: f. the ringleaders — ARN 18:16
flirtation: Merely innocent f. — BYRON 86:24
float: English policy is to f. — SAL 266:2
F. like a butterfly — ALI 4:10
f. upon his watery bier — MILT 227:11
through the clouds I'll never f. — WORD 356:3
floating: his f. hair — COL 104:1
floats: f. on high o'er vales — WORD 355:4
She f., she hesitates — RAC 257:15
flock: feed his f. like a shepherd — BIBLE 46:11
keeping watch over their f. — BIBLE 51:32
silent was the f. in woolly fold — KEATS 190:14
tainted wether of the f. — SHAK 289:24
flocks: father feeds his f. — HOME 170:18
My f. feed not — BARN 29:8
Flodden: Of F.'s fatal field — SCOTT 268:23
flog: f. the rank and file — ARN 18:16
flood: beachèd verge of the salt f. — SHAK 296:24
taken at the f. — SHAK 282:1
ten years before the f. — MARV 220:23
Thorough f., thorough fire — SHAK 290:19
vapour and return it as a f. — GLAD 153:15
flooded: STREETS F. PLEASE ADVISE — BENC 34:6
floods: neither can the f. drown — BIBLE 45:2
floor: curled up on the f. — HARTE 163:13
He oiled his way around the f. — LERN 206:2
Look, how the f. of heaven — SHAK 290:2
rose along the gusty f. — KEATS 190:22
floors: across the f. of silent seas — ELIOT 133:28
Flopshus: F. Cad — KIPL 198:2
Flora: F. and the country green — KEATS 191:29
floraisons: O mois des f. — ARAG 14:21
Flores: At F. in the Azores — TENN 328:10
flotilla: Where the old f. lay — KIPL 196:21
flourish: Princes and lords may f. — GOLD 154:18
Sure thou didst f. once — VAUG 337:13
transfix the f. set on youth — SHAK 299:22
flourishing: f. like a green bay-tree — BOOK 66:28
flout: scout 'em, and f. 'em — SHAK 296:7
flow: f. gently, sweet Afton — BURNS 81:23
I within did f. — TRAH 334:1
flower: cometh forth like a f. — BIBLE 42:33
constellated f. that never sets — SHEL 304:29
flourisheth as a f. of a field — BOOK 68:7
f. fadeth — BIBLE 46:10
f. is born to blush unseen — GRAY 157:9
f. no sooner blown — MILT 227:22
f. of a blameless life — TENN 324:1
f. of cities all — ANON 9:2
f. that once hath blown — FITZ 140:10
f. thereof falleth away — BIBLE 57:6
From every opening f. — WATTS 343:5
glory in the f. — WORD 355:23
goodliness thereof is as the f. — BIBLE 46:10
green fuse drives the f. — THOM 330:10

**flower** (cont.):
| | |
|---|---|
| meanest f. that blows can give | WORD 355:24 |
| Of learning lightly like a f. | TENN 325:31 |
| same f. that smiles to-day | HERR 167:24 |
| sweetest f. for scent | SHEL 304:31 |
| This midsummer f. | SKEL 308:3 |
| we pluck this f., safety | SHAK 277:30 |

**flowering**: About the f. squares — TENN 325:29
f. of His fields — TENN 324:16
**flowers**: bunch of other men's f. — MONT 233:19
emperice and flour of f. — CHAU 96:10
Ensnared with f., I fall — MARV 220:15
F. in the garden — STEV 317:17
F. of all hue — MILT 229:8
f. of the forest — COCK 102:27
f. that bloom in the spring — GILB 152:6
f. the tenderness of patient minds — OWEN 243:23
frosts are slain and f. begotten — SWIN 321:2
her f. to love — BROO 73:10
hundred f. blossom — MAO T 218:1
I got me f. to strew Thy way — HERB 166:24
of June, and July-f. — HERR 167:12
No f., by request — AING 3:8
Too many f. . . . too little fruit — SCOTT 269:7
Where have all the f. gone — SEEG 269:14
wild f., and Prime Ministers — BALD 27:10
**flowery**: cool f. lap of earth — ARN 16:19
**flowing**: land f. with milk and honey — BIBLE 39:32
**flown**: I see all the birds are f. — CHAR 94:23
**fluidity**: solid for f. — CHUR 99:9
**flung**: f. himself from the room — LEAC 203:5
**flush**: roses for the f. of youth — ROSS 263:3
**flute**: soft complaining f. — DRYD 128:18
**flutes**: tune of f. kept stroke — SHAK 271:14
**flutter**: f. and bear him up — BETJ 36:20
**fluttered**: f. and failed for breath — ARN 17:1
**fluttering**: F. and dancing — WORD 355:4
**flutters**: Still f. there, the sole unquiet — COL 103:20
**fly**: all things f. thee — THOM 331:12
F. envious Time — MILT 228:3
F. fishing — JOHN 186:11
f. from, need not to hate — BYRON 85:5
F. hence, our contact fear — ARN 17:11
f. may sting a stately horse — JOHN 183:27
f. out through another — BEDE 31:20
f. sat upon the axletree — BACON 25:20
f. the way out of the fly-bottle — WITT 352:7
f. to India for gold — MARL 218:8
He wouldn't hurt a f. — LEAC 203:4
I will f. to thee — KEATS 192:1
long-legged f. upon the stream — YEATS 359:15
man is not a f. — POPE 252:14
noise of a f. — DONNE 124:21
said a spider to a f. — HOW 175:11
seen spiders f. — EDW 131:3
small gilded f. does lecher — SHAK 283:23
Which way I f. is hell — MILT 229:6
with twain he did f. — BIBLE 45:10
**fly-blown**: f. phylacteries — ROS 262:20
**flying**: asleep the snow came f. — BRID 72:1
he straight is f. — WROTH 358:1
Keep the aspidistra f. — ORW 242:2
**foam**: F. glimmered white — ANAT 5:10
opening on the f. — KEATS 192:5
**foaming**: Tiber f. with much blood — POW 255:3
Tiber f. with much blood — VIRG 339:11
**foe**: Call no man f. — BENS 34:21
erect and manly f. — CANN 89:12
f. was folly and his weapon wit — HOPE 171:20
friend who never made a f. — TENN 324:10
my dearest f. in heaven — SHAK 274:16
open f. may prove a curse — GAY 149:11
perhaps a jealous f. — SHEL 303:16
willing f. and sea room — ANON 11:22
wolf far thence that's f. to men — WEBS 344:26

**foes**: man's f. shall be they — BIBLE 49:32
**fog**: feel the f. in my throat — BROW 77:2
f. comes on little cat feet — SAND 266:13
London particular . . . A f. — DICK 118:2
morning f. may chill the air — CROSS 112:10
through the f. and filthy air — SHAK 285:1
yellow f. that rubs its back — ELIOT 133:26
**fogies**: f. who doffed their lids — KEAT 190:9
**fogs**: f. prevail upon the day — DRYD 128:5
**fold**: f., spindle or mutilate — ANON 6:26
like the wolf on the f. — BYRON 85:22
So f. thyself, my dearest — TENN 328:5
**folded**: To undo the f. lie — AUDEN 21:11
**folders**: misery of manilla f. — ROET 261:14
**folding**: little f. of the hands — BIBLE 43:12
**folds**: spring has kept in its f. — ARAG 14:21
tinklings lull the distant f. — GRAY 157:4
**folk**: All music is f. music — ARMS 16:3
f. to goon on pilgrimages — CHAU 95:11
**folk-dancing**: incest and f. — ANON 12:1
**folks**: Far from the old f. at home — FOST 144:13
O yonge, fresshe f. — CHAU 96:22
**follies**: f., and misfortunes — GIBB 150:11
Pour her exotic f. o'er — BYRON 86:33
**follow**: F. me, and I will make — BIBLE 48:18
F. The Gleam — TENN 327:6
F. the yellow brick road — BAUM 30:10
F. up — BOWEN 70:16
I f. the worse — OVID 243:15
I really had to f. them — LEDR 204:4
My old man said, 'F. the van — COLL 105:7
Pay, pack, and f. — BURT 83:4
**folly**: begins in fear ends in f. — COL 104:28
brood of f. without father — MILT 226:22
foe was f. and his weapon wit — HOPE 171:20
f. he hath committed — BROW 74:1
f. like a stalking-horse — SHAK 273:14
F.'s at full length — BRER 71:22
fool according to his f. — BIBLE 43:38
fool would persist in his f. — BLAKE 61:6
Love the f. of the wise — JOHN 186:9
Public schools 'tis public f. — COWP 110:13
shoot F. as it flies — POPE 252:11
'Tis f. to be wise — GRAY 157:14
When lovely woman stoops to f. — GOLD 155:13
**fond**: au f. des bois — VIGNY 338:2
reason to be f. of grief — SHAK 282:8
should grow too f. of it — LEE 204:11
so f. of one another — SWIFT 320:2
When men were f., I smiled — SHAK 288:16
**fons**: Salva me, f. pietatis — MISS 231:24
**food**: chief of Scotia's f. — BURNS 82:2
Continent people have good f. — MIKES 224:10
discovered that alcohol was a f. — WOD 352:20
Fame is a f. that dead — DOBS 122:26
finds its f. in music — LILLO 207:3
F. comes first, then morals — BREC 71:19
F. enough for a week — MERR 223:26
f. that raises him — HANFF 161:6
homely was their f. — GARTH 148:14
music be the f. of love — SHAK 297:13
problem is f. — DONL 123:2
struggle for room and f. — MALT 217:6
**fool**: and life time's f. — SHAK 278:14
Behold, I have played the f. — BIBLE 41:19
Busy old f., unruly sun — DONNE 124:11
clever woman to manage a f. — KIPL 197:28
every f. is not a poet — POPE 251:2
f. according to his folly — BIBLE 43:38
f. all the people some of the — LINC 207:10
f. and his words soon parted — SHEN 305:20
f. at forty is a fool indeed — YOUNG 360:14
f. at least in every married — FIEL 139:4
f. consistent and the false — POPE 251:21

**fool** (*cont.*):

| | |
|---|---|
| f. hath said in his heart | BOOK 66:12 |
| f. his whole life long | LUTH 212:11 |
| f. lies here who tried | KIPL 196:24 |
| f. may ask more | COLT 105:17 |
| f. me to the top of my bent | SHAK 276:14 |
| 'F.,' said my Muse to me | SIDN 306:17 |
| f. sees not the same tree | BLAKE 61:4 |
| f. uttereth all his mind | BIBLE 44:2 |
| f. would persist in his folly | BLAKE 61:6 |
| he is a wise man or a f. | BLAKE 60:22 |
| how ill white hairs become a f. | SHAK 278:32 |
| I am Fortune's f. | SHAK 295:9 |
| knowledgeable f. is a greater f. | MOL 232:18 |
| laughter of a f. | BIBLE 44:16 |
| man suspects himself a f. | YOUNG 360:20 |
| smarts so little as a f. | POPE 251:3 |
| So true a f. is love | SHAK 299:20 |
| Thou f., this night thy soul | BIBLE 52:19 |
| wisest f. in Christendom | HENR 165:22 |
| worm at one end and a f. | JOHN 186:11 |

| | |
|---|---|
| **foolery**: little f. governs the world | OXEN 244:5 |
| **foolish**: being young and f. | YEATS 359:1 |
| Beware my f. heart | WASH 342:24 |
| f. son is the heaviness | BIBLE 43:16 |
| f. thing was but a toy | SHAK 298:15 |
| f. thing well done | JOHN 184:25 |
| Forgive our f. ways | WHIT 348:21 |
| from saying a f. thing | STER 315:25 |
| He never said a f. thing | ROCH 261:4 |
| I am a very f., fond old man | SHAK 283:29 |
| These F. Things | MARV 221:4 |
| **foolishest**: it is the f. act | BROW 74:18 |
| **foolishness**: Mix a little f. | HOR 174:1 |
| **fools**: flannelled f. at the wicket | KIPL 196:14 |
| f. by heavenly compulsion | SHAK 282:22 |
| f. decoyed into our condition | PEPYS 247:18 |
| F.! For I also had my hour | CHES 97:22 |
| f. in town on our side | TWAIN 335:21 |
| F. out of favour grudge | DEFOE 115:21 |
| F. rush in where angels | POPE 252:10 |
| f., who came to scoff | GOLD 154:22 |
| from children and from f. | DRYD 128:16 |
| I am two f., I know | DONNE 124:14 |
| lighted f. the way to dusty death | SHAK 288:5 |
| Lord, what f. these mortals be | SHAK 290:32 |
| perish together as f. | KING 195:10 |
| proved plain f. at last | POPE 251:27 |
| scarecrows of f. | HUXL 177:20 |
| shoal of f. for tenders | CONG 106:17 |
| Silence is the virtue of f. | BACON 24:8 |
| suffer f. gladly | BIBLE 55:27 |
| To this great stage of f. | SHAK 283:27 |
| world made up of f. and knaves | BUCK 78:1 |
| **foot**: caught my f. in the mat | GROS 159:4 |
| f. already in the stirrup | CERV 93:21 |
| F.-in-the-grave young man | GILB 152:13 |
| f.—sloggin' over Africa | KIPL 196:6 |
| Forty-second F. | HOOD 171:5 |
| her f. speaks | SHAK 297:9 |
| her f. was light | KEATS 191:9 |
| Now I hold Creation in my f. | HUGH 175:20 |
| on an 'eathen idol's f. | KIPL 196:22 |
| proud f. of a conqueror | SHAK 282:15 |
| thy f. against a stone | BOOK 67:30 |
| **football**: f. is a matter of life | SHAN 300:22 |
| he's f. crazy, he's f. mad | MCGR 214:22 |
| **footfalls**: F. echo in the memory | ELIOT 132:26 |
| **footman**: eternal F. hold my coat | ELIOT 133:29 |
| **footmen**: lowest class is *literary* f. | HAZL 164:4 |
| **footnotes**: series of f. to Plato | WHIT 348:6 |
| **foot-path**: jog on the f. way | SHAK 298:28 |
| **footprints**: F. on the sands of time | LONG 209:23 |
| **footsteps**: plants his f. in the sea | COWP 109:25 |
| **footstool**: make thine enemies thy f. | BOOK 68:14 |

| | |
|---|---|
| **foppery**: excellent f. of the world | SHAK 282:22 |
| sound of shallow f. | SHAK 289:10 |
| **for**: f. whom the bell tolls | DONNE 124:20 |
| F. you but not for me | ANON 9:21 |
| F. your tomorrows | EDM 130:20 |
| **forasmuch**: f. as without thee | BOOK 64:26 |
| **forbid**: He shall live a man f. | SHAK 285:4 |
| **forbidden**: Of that f. tree | MILT 228:7 |
| **force**: blend f. with a manoeuvre | TROT 335:2 |
| f. alone is but *temporary* | BURKE 80:1 |
| f. and road of casualty | SHAK 289:13 |
| F. is not a remedy | BRIG 72:6 |
| 'F.' is the food that raises | HANFF 161:6 |
| f. maintaining the life | DOST 125:1 |
| f. that through the green fuse | THOM 330:10 |
| may the f. be with you | LUCAS 211:28 |
| No motion has she now, no f. | WORD 356:25 |
| other nations use 'f' | WAUGH 343:28 |
| own no argument but f. | BROW 74:25 |
| Surprised by unjust f. | MILT 226:18 |
| Who overcomes by f. | MILT 228:18 |
| **forced**: F. her to do your pleasure | WEBS 344:24 |
| **forces**: change that state by f. | NEWT 239:3 |
| **forcibly**: f. if we must | CLAY 101:17 |
| **Ford**: I am a F., not a Lincoln | FORD 143:3 |
| **forefathers**: f. of the hamlet sleep | GRAY 157:6 |
| Think of your f.! | ADAMS 2:4 |
| **forefinger**: stretched f. of all Time | TENN 327:18 |
| **forehead**: f. of the morning sky | MILT 227:18 |
| **foreign**: attacking the F. Secretary | BEVAN 37:21 |
| F. Secretary naked into | BEVAN 38:1 |
| Life is a f. language | MORL 235:7 |
| my f. policy: I wage war | CLEM 102:1 |
| past is a f. country | HART 163:14 |
| some corner of a f. field | BROO 73:10 |
| Thracian ships and the f. faces | SWIN 321:1 |
| with their courtly f. grace | TENN 328:14 |
| **foreigners**: f. always spell better | TWAIN 336:1 |
| f. are fiends | MITF 232:10 |
| more f. I saw | BELL 34:5 |
| **forelock**: f. to the British establishment | KEAT 190:9 |
| **foremost**: none who would be f. | MAC 214:6 |
| **forepangs**: schooled at f. | HOPK 172:9 |
| **foreplay**: No f. No afterplay | BENN 34:11 |
| **forest**: clipped hedge is to a f. | JOHN 186:12 |
| Down in the f. something | SIMP 307:10 |
| flowers of the f. | COCK 102:27 |
| f. laments in order | CHUR 99:1 |
| F. where all must lose | THOM 330:24 |
| This is the f. primeval | LONG 209:15 |
| **forests**: In the f. of the night | BLAKE 62:5 |
| **foretold**: f. that the heart grows old | YEATS 359:29 |
| **forever**: Man has F. | BROW 75:32 |
| picket's off duty f. | BEERS 32:14 |
| **forge**: f. and working-house | SHAK 280:1 |
| **forget**: but do not quite f. | CHES 98:4 |
| do not thou f. me | ASTL 19:8 |
| F. all feuds | MAC 214:1 |
| F. six counties | MORR 235:16 |
| honour both f. men's names | SHAK 282:3 |
| If I f. thee, O Jerusalem | BOOK 69:4 |
| I never f. a face | MARX 221:7 |
| In violence, we f. who we | MCC 214:11 |
| Lest we f.—lest we forget | KIPL 197:2 |
| nor worms f. | DICK 119:9 |
| *not* f. the suspenders | KIPL 197:23 |
| Old men f. | SHAK 279:19 |
| Till thou remember and I f. | SWIN 321:16 |
| we f. because we must | ARN 16:9 |
| wise forgive but do not f. | SZASZ 321:24 |
| you should f. and smile | ROSS 263:4 |
| **forgetfulness**: Not in entire f. | WORD 355:20 |
| **forgetting**: grand memory for f. | STEV 316:26 |
| sleep and a f. | WORD 355:20 |

**forgetting** (*cont.*):
world f., by the world forgot — POPE 250:26
**forgive**: allows you to f. yourself — SHAW 302:8
Father, f. them — BIBLE 53:2
F., O Lord, my little jokes — FROST 146:10
F. our foolish ways — WHIT 348:27
f. that sin where I begun — DONNE 123:17
f. us our debts — BIBLE 48:27
f. us our trespasses — BOOK 63:16
good Lord will f. me — CATH 92:21
lambs could not f. — DICK 119:9
rarely, if ever, do they f. them — WILDE 360:12
sin against me, and I f. him — BIBLE 50:19
To err is human; to f., divine — POPE 252:7
wise f. but do not forget — SZASZ 321:24
woman can f. a man the harm — MAUG 222:10
Women can't f. failure — CHEK 96:26
**forgiven**: ransomed, healed, restored, f. — LYTE 212:21
sins, which are many, are f. — BIBLE 52:8
Youth, which is f. everything — SHAW 302:6
**forgiveness**: ask of thee f. — SHAK 284:1
F. of sins — BOOK 64:3
such knowledge, what f. — ELIOT 133:15
**forgot**: by the world f. — POPE 250:26
curiosities would be quite f. — AUBR 19:16
Honey, I just f. to duck — DEMP 116:25
unknown proposed as things f. — POPE 252:8
**forgotten**: always a f. thing — CHES 97:21
been learned has been f. — SKIN 308:6
f. before God — BIBLE 52:17
f. man — ROOS 262:7
f. nothing and learnt nothing — DUM 129:6
f. scream for help in dreams — CAN 89:9
He hath not f. my age — SOUT 312:2
I am all f. — SHAK 271:9
I have f. your name — SWIN 321:14
injury sooner f. than an insult — CHES 97:5
learned nothing, and f. nothing — TALL 322:11
ruins of f. times — BROW 74:3
**forked**: f. animal as thou art — SHAK 283:14
**forks**: pursued it with f. and hope — CARR 92:9
**forlorn**: F.! the very word — KEATS 192:6
that would make me less f. — WORD 357:11
**form**: earth was without f. — BIBLE 38:13
F. follows function — SULL 319:1
F. of being is assigned — WORD 354:22
F. remains — WORD 356:18
mould of f. — SHAK 276:2
silent f., dost tease us — KEATS 191:23
take thy f. from off my door — POE 250:7
Terror the human f. divine — BLAKE 62:7
**formal**: f. feeling comes — DICK 120:8
**formed**: small, but perfectly f. — COOP 107:21
**former**: f. and the latter rain — BOOK 64:20
f. things are passed — BIBLE 58:5
**formerly**: what we were f. told — BLUN 62:15
**forms**: f. of things unknown — SHAK 291:4
**forsaken**: never the righteous f. — BOOK 66:27
why hast thou f. me — BIBLE 51:16
**forsaking**: f. all other — BOOK 65:28
**forsan**: F. et haec olim — VIRG 339:2
**forsythia**: Of prunus and f. — BETJ 37:6
**fort**: Hold the f. — BLISS 62:10
**forth**: F. in thy name — WESL 346:5
Man goeth f. to his work — BOOK 68:8
**fortis**: F. fortuna adiuvat — TER 329:5
**fortress**: f. built by Nature — SHAK 293:16
**fortresses**: brambles in the f. — BIBLE 46:3
**fortunate**: farmers excessively f. — VIRG 340:7
he is at best but f. — SOLON 310:27
**fortune**: arrows of outrageous f. — SHAK 275:25
Base F., now I see — MARL 218:16
beauty without a f. — FARQ 138:16
Blind F. still bestows — JONS 187:8
F. assists the brave — TER 329:5

**fortune** (*cont.*):
F. favours the brave — VIRG 339:20
F.'s a right whore — WEBS 344:22
f.'s sharpe adversitee — CHAU 96:18
F., that favours fools — JONS 186:22
hostages to f. — BACON 25:1
how does f. banter us — BOL 63:6
I am F.'s fool — SHAK 295:9
leads on to f. — SHAK 282:1
little value of f. — STEE 314:18
man who takes your f. — WOOL 354:7
O fickle F. — COCK 102:27
possession of a good f. — AUST 23:2
You fools of f. — SHAK 296:20
**forty**: Fat, fair and f. — O'KEE 241:6
fool at f. is a fool indeed — YOUNG 360:14
F. years on — BOWEN 70:15
Knows it at f. — YOUNG 360:20
loves a fairy when she's f. — HENL 165:16
man over f. is a scoundrel — SHAW 302:5
**forty-five**: At f. what next? — LOW 211:15
**forty-three**: very well pass for f. — GILB 152:31
**forward**: hold from this day f. — BOOK 66:1
looking f. to the past — OSB 242:24
marched breast f. — BROW 75:11
not look f. to posterity — BURKE 80:12
Some men a f. motion love — VAUG 337:10
those behind cried 'F.!' — MAC 214:6
**fossil**: Language is f. poetry — EMER 136:28
**foster-child**: f. of silence — KEATS 191:17
**fou**: I wasna f. — BURNS 82:3
**fought**: f. against Sisera — BIBLE 40:32
f. against the dragon — BIBLE 57:31
f. the dogs and killed the cats — BROW 76:26
f. with us upon Saint Crispin's — SHAK 279:20
I have f. a good fight — BIBLE 56:21
not to have won but to have f. — COUB 108:15
Than never to have f. at all — CLOU 102:21
they f. each other — SOUT 311:19
**foul**: Fair is foul, and f. is fair — SHAK 285:1
Fair is too f. an epithet — MARL 219:10
f. and fair a day — SHAK 285:6
f. Fiend coming over — BUNY 78:20
f. things up requires a computer — ANON 11:7
however f. within — CHUR 98:25
Murder most f. — SHAK 274:31
**foulest**: shortest way the f. — BACON 24:3
**found**: f. Him in the shining — TENN 324:16
f. myself famous — BYRON 87:21
f. my sheep which was lost — BIBLE 52:27
Hast thou f. me, O mine enemy — BIBLE 42:5
he was lost, and is f. — BIBLE 52:32
man who has f. himself out — BARR 29:18
When f., make a note of — DICK 118:20
**foundation**: f. of most governments — ADAMS 2:2
Good order is the f. — BURKE 80:21
**fount**: f. whence honour — MARL 219:9
slow, fresh f. — JONS 187:2
**fountain**: f. momently was forced — COL 103:23
f. of all goodness — BOOK 64:8
f. of honour — BACON 24:10
f. of honour — BAG 26:4
f. of the water of life — BIBLE 58:6
Thou f., at which drink — COWP 110:3
woman moved is like a f. — SHAK 295:30
**fountains**: from little f. flow — EVER 137:24
Where Afric's sunny f. — HEBER 164:15
**four**: F. legs good, two legs bad — ORW 241:22
two plus two make f. — ORW 242:9
**fourscore**: F. and seven years ago — LINC 207:8
strong that they come to f. — BOOK 67:26
**fourth**: f. estate of the realm — MAC 213:4
**fowls**: smale f. maken melodye — CHAU 95:11
**fox**: ar'n't that I loves the f. less — SURT 319:10
Crazy like a f. — PER 247:23

fox (*cont.*):

| | |
|---|---|
| f. from his lair | GRAV 156:12 |
| f. jumps over the lazy dog | ANON 10:7 |
| f. knows many things | ARCH 15:1 |
| gentleman galloping after a f. | WILDE 350:9 |
| mentality of a f. at large | LEVIN 206:7 |
| My God! They've shot our f. | BIRCH 59:14 |
| prince must be a f. | MACH 215:3 |

foxes: f. have a sincere interest | ELIOT 132:4

| | |
|---|---|
| f. have holes | BIBLE 49:19 |
| little f., that spoil the vines | BIBLE 44:33 |
| portion for f. | BOOK 67:15 |
| second to the f. | BERL 36:4 |

foxholes: on the f. or graveyards | KENN 194:7
There are no atheists in the f. | CUMM 113:6
fox-hunters: people that think, and f. | SHEN 305:21
frabjous: O f. day! | CARR 91:16
fragments: f. I have shored | ELIOT 134:31
frailty: F., thy name is woman | SHAK 274:12

| | |
|---|---|
| love's the noblest f. | DRYD 127:33 |
| noblest f. of the mind | SHAD 270:18 |
| therefore more f. | SHAK 278:9 |

frame: f. of adamant | JOHN 183:13
framed: to have it f. and glazed | WALP 341:22
français: *pas clair n'est pas f.* | RIV 260:14
France: best thing between F. and England | JERR 181:11

| | |
|---|---|
| Fair stood the wind for F. | DRAY 126:22 |
| F., famed in all great arts | ARN 17:21 |
| F. has lost a battle | DE G 116:3 |
| F., mother of arts | DU B 128:32 |
| F. was long a despotism | CARL 90:14 |
| order this matter better in F. | STER 315:8 |
| sweet enemy, F. | SIDN 306:21 |
| There lived a singer in F. | SWIN 321:19 |
| two breasts by which F. | SULLY 319:3 |
| vasty fields of F. | SHAK 278:34 |
| will in F., by God's grace | SHAK 279:1 |

Francesca di Rimini: F., miminy | GILB 152:12
Frankie: F. and Albert were lovers | ANON 7:6
frankincense: f., and myrrh | BIBLE 48:10
frankly: F., my dear | MITC 232:6
frantic: There's a fascination f. | GILB 152:8
fraternité: *Liberté! Égalité! F.!* | ANON 12:11
fraternize: I beckon you to f. | AUDEN 21:8
fraud: pious f. of the almanac | LOW 211:10
freckled: Whatever is fickle, f. | HOPK 172:13
freckles: curiosity, f., and doubt | PARK 245:5
free: better to be in chains than to be f. | KAFKA 189:18

| | |
|---|---|
| born f. and equal in dignity | ANON 5:20 |
| Comment is f. | SCOTT 268:3 |
| Ev'rything f. in America | SOND 311:8 |
| f. agent that you were | AUR 22:11 |
| f. as nature first made man | DRYD 127:26 |
| f. society … safe to be unpopular | STEV 316:18 |
| F. speech, free passes | BETJ 37:4 |
| f. themselves must strike | BYRON 85:1 |
| Greece might still be f. | BYRON 86:14 |
| half slave and half f. | LINC 207:5 |
| he's f. again | SOLZ 310:28 |
| I am a f. man, an American | JOHN 181:19 |
| I am condemned to be f. | SART 267:2 |
| I was f. born | BIBLE 54:24 |
| Man was born f., and everywhere | ROUS 263:18 |
| Mother of the F. | BENS 34:20 |
| nominally f., but enslaved | BOOTH 69:21 |
| no such thing as a f. lunch | ANON 10:21 |
| O'er the land of the f. | KEY 194:12 |
| perfectly f. till all are free | SPEN 312:21 |
| Ring in the valiant man and f. | TENN 325:27 |
| soul in prison, I am not f. | DEBS 115:9 |
| that moment they are f. | COWP 110:7 |
| they are f. to do whatever | SHAW 301:20 |
| Thou art f. | ARN 17:14 |
| Thought is f. | SHAK 296:7 |
| truth shall make you f. | BIBLE 53:28 |

free (*cont.*):

| | |
|---|---|
| truth which makes men f. | AGAR 3:5 |
| Was he f.? Was he happy? | AUDEN 21:17 |
| We *know* our will is f. | JOHN 184:20 |
| wholly slaves or wholly f. | DRYD 127:30 |
| worth nothin', but it's f. | KRIS 199:5 |
| yearning to breathe f. | LAZ 203:2 |

freedom: better organised than f. | PÉGUY 247:4

| | |
|---|---|
| bondage which is f.'s self | SHEL 304:27 |
| enemies of F. do not argue | INGE 178:10 |
| establishes his true f. | MONT 233:14 |
| fight for f. and truth | IBSEN 178:3 |
| flame of f. in their souls | SYM 321:20 |
| F. and Whisky gang thegither | BURNS 81:26 |
| f. for the one who thinks | LUX 212:12 |
| f. is a noble thing | BARB 28:16 |
| F. is slavery | ORW 242:7 |
| F. is the freedom to say | ORW 242:9 |
| F. of the press in Britain | SWAF 319:16 |
| F.'s just another word | KRIS 199:5 |
| giving f. to the slave | LINC 207:6 |
| green f. of a cockatoo | STEV 316:12 |
| I gave my life for f. | EWER 138:1 |
| O F., what liberties | GEOR 150:6 |
| Perfect f. is reserved | COLL 105:5 |
| preserve and enlarge f. | LOCKE 208:20 |
| rest love not f. | MILT 231:7 |
| what is F.? | COL 103:11 |
| What stands if f. fall | KIPL 196:13 |
| Where F. slowly broadens down | TENN 329:1 |
| with a great sum obtained I this f. | BIBLE 54:24 |
| whose service is perfect f. | BOOK 64:5 |

freedoms: four essential human f. | ROOS 262:13
Natural f. are but just | ROCH 261:5
freehold: life is given to none f. | LUCR 212:6
freely: F. ye have received | BIBLE 49:27
freemasonry: kind of bitter f. | BEER 32:11
freeze: f. my humanity | MACN 216:6

| | |
|---|---|
| f. thy young blood | SHAK 274:30 |
| To f. the blood | WORD 355:1 |

freezes: Yours till Hell f. | FISH 139:25
freezings: What f. have I felt | SHAK 300:3
frei: *Arbeit macht f.* | ANON 13:1
French: F. are wiser than they seem | BACON 25:12

| | |
|---|---|
| F. are with equal advantage | CANN 89:10 |
| F. noblesse had been capable | TREV 334:8 |
| F. of Parys was to hire | CHAU 95:15 |
| F., or Turk, or Proosian | GILB 152:21 |
| F. the empire of the land | RICH 260:6 |
| F. want no-one to be their | TOCQ 333:4 |
| F. widow in every bedroom | HOFF 170:5 |
| glory of beating the F. | WOLFE 353:3 |
| No more Latin, no more F. | ANON 9:17 |
| not too F. French bean | GILB 152:11 |
| Paris was F.—and silent | TUCH 335:8 |
| Speak in F. when you can't | CARR 91:19 |
| to women Italian, men F. | CHAR 95:7 |
| We are not F. | MONT 233:24 |
| What is not clear is not F. | RIV 260:14 |

Frenchmen: Fifty million F. | GUIN 159:9
frenzy: Demoniac f. | MILT 229:31
fine f. rolling | SHAK 291:4
frequency: very fact of f. | ELIOT 132:11
frère: *mon semblable,—mon f.* | BAUD 30:3
fresh: both so ancient and so f. | AUG 21:24

| | |
|---|---|
| f. as is the month of May | CHAU 95:13 |
| f. lap of the crimson rose | SHAK 290:23 |
| noted for f. air and fun | EDGAR 130:15 |
| O yonge, f. folkes | CHAU 96:22 |
| Tomorrow to f. woods | MILT 227:20 |
| women of that ever-f. terrain | AMIS 5:8 |

fret: fever, and the f. | KEATS 191:31
F. not thyself | BOOK 66:26
frets: struts and f. his hour | SHAK 288:5
fretted: F. the pigmy body | DRYD 127:6

Freud: trouble with F. DODD 122:29
Freude: F., schöner Götterfunken SCH 267:18
Freudian: her F. papa and maids LOW 211:11
Friday: My man F. DEFOE 115:15
friend: At luncheon with a city f. BELL 33:24
author as you choose a f. DILL 120:22
betraying my f. FORS 144:2
Boldness be my f. SHAK 273:23
diamonds are a girl's best f. ROBIN 260:18
faithful female f. WHUR 349:4
F. and associate of this clay HADR 159:14
F., go up higher BIBLE 52:21
f. in power is a friend lost ADAMS 1:14
f. of every country but his own CANN 89:11
f. of flattering illusions CONR 107:8
f. sincere enough to tell BULW 78:12
f. that sticketh closer BIBLE 43:30
f. unseen, unborn, unknown FLEC 141:20
from the candid f. CANN 89:12
goodnatured f. or another SHER 305:23
have a f. is to be one EMER 136:21
homes without a f. CLARE 101:5
last best f. am I SOUT 311:23
lay down his wife for his f. JOYCE 188:18
Little F. of all the World KIPL 197:25
loss of a dear f. SOUT 312:5
Mine own familiar f. BOOK 67:2
mine own familiar f. BOOK 67:12
mistress or a f. SHEL 303:15
much-loved and elegant f. CHAR 95:8
never want a f. in need DICK 118:20
no f. who never made a foe TENN 324:10
Nor a f. to know me STEV 317:25
paint a portrait I lose a f. SARG 266:23
plain, blunt man that love my f. SHAK 281:25
pretended f. is worse GAY 149:11
What is a f. ARIS 15:21
Whenever a f. succeeds VIDAL 338:13
With a religious book, or f. WOTT 357:14
With one chained f. SHEL 303:16
woman can become a man's f. CHEK 96:28
your enemy and your f. TWAIN 335:25
friendless: f. bodies of unburied WEBS 344:25
friends: book is the best of f. TUPP 335:10
dear f. have to part BOND 63:9
f. of every country save DISR 121:17
f. . . . people who got there first UST 336:16
F., Romans, countrymen SHAK 281:18
glory was I had such f. YEATS 359:17
Good thoughts his only f. CAMP 89:3
How to win f. CARN 90:28
I have lost f. WOOLF 354:5
laughter and the love of f. BELL 34:3
lay down his f. for his life THOR 332:13
little help from my f. MCC 205:18
Money couldn't buy f. MILL 225:11
none of his f. like him WILDE 350:21
Of two close f., one is LERM 205:24
Our f., the enemy BÉR 35:11
something left to treat my f. MALL 216:21
Soul and body part like f. CRAS 111:15
To my f. pictured within ELGAR 131:17
want of f., and empty purse BRET 71:23
friendship: F. is a disinterested commerce GOLD 155:6
F. is constant in all other SHAK 291:17
F. is Love without his wings BYRON 87:1
f. recognised by the police STEV 317:7
his f. in constant repair JOHN 184:4
honest f. with all nations JEFF 180:19
frieze: striped f. STR 318:11
frighted: f. with false fire SHAK 276:11
frighten: by God, they f. me WELL 345:7
don't f. the horses CAMP 88:14
frightened: f. look in its eyes SITW 307:21

frightened (cont.):
killed than f. to death SURT 319:12
fringèd: f. curtains of thine eye SHAK 296:2
frocks: F. and Curls DICK 120:17
frog: Eye of newt, and toe of f. SHAK 287:16
frogs: F. Eat Butterflies STEV 316:7
frolics: youth of f. POPE 251:11
frontier: f. of my Person goes AUDEN 21:8
on the edge of a new f. KENN 194:1
frontiers: old f. are gone BALD 27:6
frost: F. at Midnight COL 103:18
f. performs its secret ministry COL 103:18
f. which binds so dear SHEL 303:3
His graver of f. THOM 331:19
like an untimely f. SHAK 295:21
lovely Morning, rich in f. DAV 114:21
third day comes a f. SHAK 280:18
frosts: f. are slain SWIN 321:2
hoary-headed f. SHAK 290:23
frosty: F., but kindly SHAK 272:16
froth: Life is mostly f. GORD 155:21
froward: very f. generation BIBLE 40:24
frown: Convey a libel in a f. SWIFT 320:16
Phyllis, without f. or smile SEDL 269:12
frowning: Behind a f. providence COWP 109:26
frowst: f. with a book by the fire KIPL 197:22
frozen: Architecture is f. music SCH 267:17
f. wind crept on above SHEL 303:14
trembling through the f. grass KEATS 190:14
Your tiny hand is f. ILL 150:9
fruit: disobedience, and the f. MILT 228:7
humid nightblue f. JOYCE 188:19
Too many flowers, too little f. SCOTT 269:7
veranda, and the f. AUDEN 20:25
weakest kind of f. SHAK 289:24
fruitful: Be f., and multiply BIBLE 38:17
f. ground, the quiet mind SURR 319:6
shall be as the f. vine BOOK 68:32
vineyard in a very f. hill BIBLE 45:7
fruitfulness: mists and mellow f. KEATS 192:14
fruition: f. of an earthly crown MARL 219:8
fruits: By their f. ye shall know them BIBLE 49:15
first f. of them that slept BIBLE 55:17
frustra: f. vigilat qui custodit BIBLE 58:13
frustrate: F. their knavish tricks ANON 7:14
frying-pan: fish that talks in the f. DE L 116:11
fuck: f. all in between BENN 34:11
They f. you up, your mum LARK 201:17
fugaces: Eheu f., Postume HOR 173:23
fugit: f. inreparabile tempus VIRG 340:9
fugitive: f. from th' law of averages MAUL 222:13
Führer: Ein Reich, ein Volk, ein F. ANON 13:2
fulfil: F. now, O Lord, the desires BOOK 64:10
full: F. fathom five thy father SHAK 296:1
f. of passionate intensity YEATS 359:24
f. tide of human existence JOHN 185:1
Reading maketh a f. man BACON 25:15
Sea of faith was once, too, at the f. ARN 16:11
Serenely f., the epicure SMITH 310:7
fulness: and the f. thereof BIBLE 55:9
fume: stinking f. thereof JAM 179:9
fun: Ain't We Got F. KAHN 189:19
f. in any Act of Parliament HERB 166:17
F. is fun but no girl wants LOOS 210:9
f. is nine-tenths of the law SAY 267:15
It was great f. PORT 253:21
more f. to be with NASH 237:11
most f. without laughing ALLEN 4:13
function: Form follows f. SULL 319:1
F. never dies WORD 356:18
fundament: frigid upon the f. NASH 237:16
fundamental: f. things apply HUPF 176:20
funeral: f. baked meats SHAK 274:16
not a f. note WOLFE 352:25
No war, nor prince's f. MARV 220:21

**funeral** (*cont.*):
present is the f. of the past — CLARE 101:8
**funk**: poor world in a blue f. — CRANE 111:1
**funny**: f. as long as it is happening — ROG 261:22
Funny-peculiar or f. ha-ha — HAY 163:20
It's a f. old world — JONES 116:24
**furious**: fun grew fast and f. — BURNS 82:23
**furiously**: green ideas sleep f. — CHOM 98:18
heathen so f. rage together — BOOK 66:9
he driveth f. — BIBLE 42:13
**furnace**: burning fiery f. — BIBLE 47:11
**furnaces**: Your worship is your f. — BOTT 70:6
**furnish**: Books do f. a room — POW 254:25
Would f. all we ought to ask — KEBLE 193:17
**furnished**: F. and burnish'd — BETJ 37:10
ladies who live in f. souls — CUMM 113:5
large upper room f. — BIBLE 52:40
**furniture**: No f. so charming as books — SMITH 310:2
piece of mere church f. — COWP 110:15
**furry**: fire was f. as a bear — SITW 307:17
**further**: f. from God — ANDR 5:16
**fury**: blind f. of creation — SHAW 301:17
full of sound and f. — SHAK 288:5
f. of a patient man — DRYD 127:17
no f. like a non-combatant — MONT 233:7
Nor Hell a f., like a woman — CONG 106:12
**fuse**: green f. drives the flower — THOM 330:10
**fuss**: What a f. about an omelette — VOLT 341:2
**fustian**: f.'s so sublimely bad — POPE 251:5
**futility**: fatal f. of Fact — JAMES 180:2
**future**: Back to the f. — GALE 361:2
cannot fight against the f. — GLAD 153:8
door opens and lets the f. in — GREE 158:6
F. as a promised land — LEWIS 206:11
f. everybody will be famous — WARH 342:20
F. shock — TOFF 333:6
f. states of both are left to faith — BYRON 86:12
I never think of the f. — EINS 131:13
lively sense of f. favours — WALP 342:7
once and f. king — WHITE 347:18
past controls the f. — ORW 242:8
picture of the f. — ORW 242:11
plan the f. by the past — BURKE 79:20
present in time f. — ELIOT 132:25
put no trust in the f. — HOR 173:20
seen the f. and it works — STEF 314:19
serve the f. hour — WORD 356:19
**Fuzzy-Wuzzy**: 'ere's to you, F. — KIPL 196:14
**Fyfe**: David Patrick Maxwell F. — ANON 9:14

# G

**gabardine**: spit upon my Jewish g. — SHAK 289:5
**gadding**: thyme and the g. vine — MILT 227:13
**Gaels**: great G. of Ireland — CHES 97:20
**gag**: tight g. of place — HEAN 164:11
**gaiety**: eclipsed the g. of nations — JOHN 182:23
Take me back to the G. hotel — ASHF 18:25
**gaily**: G. into Ruislip Gardens — BETJ 37:7
**gain**: g. the whole world — BIBLE 51:23
richest g. I count but loss — WATTS 343:4
**gains**: no g. without pains — STEV 316:16
**gait**: forced g. of a shuffling nag — SHAK 278:4
**gaiters**: All is gas and g. — DICK 119:17
**Galatians**: great text in G. — BROW 77:12
**Galilean**: You have won, G. — JUL 188:20
**Galilee**: rolls nightly on deep G. — BYRON 85:22
**gall**: take my milk for g. — SHAK 285:18
wormwood and the g. — BIBLE 47:1
**gallant**: died a very g. gentleman — CHER 19:11
g. trim the gilded vessel — GRAY 157:3
**gallantry**: What men call g. — BYRON 85:24
**galleon**: Stately as a G. — GREN 158:15
**gallery**: faces are but a g. — BACON 24:23

**gallery** (*cont.*):
History is a g. of pictures — TOCQ 333:1
**Gallia**: G. est omnis divisa — CAES 87:24
**gallimaufry**: g. or hodgepodge — SPEN 313:20
**gallop**: G. about doing good — SMITH 309:17
G. apace, you fiery-footed — SHAK 295:10
**galloped**: we g. all three — BROW 76:5
**gallows**: complexion is perfect g. — SHAK 295:31
upon the g. or of the pox — WILK 350:26
**gamble**: Life is a g. at terrible odds — STOP 318:6
**gambler**: whore and g. — BLAKE 60:9
**game**: Anarchism is a g. — SHAW 302:10
g. at which two can play — BEER 32:12
g. is never lost till won — CRAB 110:28
g.'s afoot — SHAK 279:6
giving over of a g. — FLET 31:2
hard if I cannot start some g. — HAZL 164:8
helpless pieces of the g. — FITZ 140:12
how you played the G. — RICE 259:17
more than a g. — HUGH 175:23
play up! and play the g. — NEWB 238:13
time to win this g. — DRAKE 126:13
Truth the g. of the few — BERK 35:17
woman is his g. — TENN 327:25
**games**: dread of g. — BETJ 37:14
G. people play — BERNE 36:10
their g. should be seen as — MONT 233:11
**gamesmanship**: g. or The art of — POTT 254:7
**gamut**: g. of the emotions — PARK 245:16
**gang**: may g. a kennin wrang — BURNS 81:21
**gangsters**: always acted like g. — KUBR 199:7
**gap**: it is the last g. but one — WHITE 347:17
**garde**: La G. meurt — CAMB 88:11
**garden**: Almighty first planted a g. — BACON 24:26
Back to the g. — MITC 232:4
Come into the g., Maud — TENN 326:28
cultivate our g. — VOLT 340:13
fairies at the bottom of our g. — FYL 147:9
g. is a lovesome thing — BROWN 73:19
g. of your face — HERB 166:19
g.'s umbrage mild — SMART 308:12
g. walled around — WATTS 343:2
Glory of the G. — KIPL 196:16
God the first g. made — COWL 109:13
image walking in the g. — SHEL 304:15
imperfections of my g. — MONT 233:9
land where a g. should be — HOR 174:4
lodge in a g. of cucumbers — BIBLE 45:3
man and a woman in a g. — WILDE 350:11
Mr McGregor's g. — POTT 254:3
nearer God's Heart in a g. — GURN 159:10
Our England is a g. — KIPL 196:16
planted a g. eastward in Eden — BIBLE 38:18
rosebud of girls — TENN 326:29
sunlight on the g. — MACN 216:10
through the vext g.-trees — ARN 17:18
unweeded g. — SHAK 274:10
walking in the g. in the cool — BIBLE 38:26
**gardener**: Adam was a g. — SHAK 280:11
**gardens**: closing time in the g. of the West — CONN 106:27
g. with real toads in them — MOORE 234:8
Sowe Carrets in your G. — GARD 148:4
**garish**: Hide me from day's g. eye — MILT 226:26
I loved the g. day — NEWM 238:22
no worship to the g. sun — SHAK 295:14
**garland**: green willow is my g. — HEYW 168:8
withered is the g. of the war — SHAK 271:25
**garlands**: not shackles ... they are g. — BENN 34:13
**garment**: g. was white as snow — BIBLE 47:14
know the g. from the man — BLAKE 60:15
**garmented**: g. in light — SHEL 305:16
**garments**: Reasons are not like g. — ESSEX 137:16
Stuffs out his vacant g. — SHAK 282:8
They part my g. among them — BOOK 66:16

garnished: swept, and g. — BIBLE 50:3
garret: Genius in a g. starving — ROB 260:22
living in a g. — FOOTE 142:19
Garrick: Our G.'s a salad — GOLD 155:1
gas: All is g. and gaiters — DICK 119:17
G. smells awful — PARK 245:8
gate: hear November at the g. — PUSH 256:22
I am here at the g. alone — TENN 326:28
poor man at his g. — ALEX 4:3
sings hymns at heaven's g. — SHAK 299:15
stood at the g. of the year — HASK 163:16
watchful at his g. — DODD 122:30
Wide is the g., and broad — BIBLE 49:12
gates: despondently at area g. — ELIOT 134:4
enter then his g. with praise — KETHE 194:11
g. to the glorious — FORS 143:19
go to the g. of Hell — PIUS 249:11
Lift up your heads, O ye g. — BOOK 66:20
Gath: Tell it not in G. — BIBLE 41:21
gather: G. therefore the rose — SPEN 313:12
G. ye rosebuds while ye may — HERR 167:24
gathered: when two or three are g. — BOOK 64:10
where two or three are g. — BIBLE 50:18
gathering: g. where thou hast — BIBLE 51:2
gat-tothed: G. I was — CHAU 96:7
gaudeamus: G. igitur — ANON 13:16
gaudy: doffed her g. trim — MILT 227:25
g., blabbing, and remorseful day — SHAK 280:9
one other g. night — SHAK 271:19
Gaul: G. as a whole is divided — CAES 87:24
gay: and without feeling g. — CHUR 98:26
g. Lothario — ROWE 263:20
Her heart was warm and g. — HAMM 161:1
I'm a g. deceiver — COLM 105:14
impiously g. — CRAB 110:23
second best's a g. goodnight — YEATS 359:5
So g. the band — GREN 158:15
Gaza: Eyeless in G. — MILT 230:10
gazelle: I never nursed a dear g. — MOORE 234:19
geese: G. are swans — ARN 16:18
Like g. about the sky — AUDEN 20:11
swans of others are g. — WALP 342:1
Gehenna: Down to G. — KIPL 196:20
gem: g. of purest ray serene — GRAY 157:9
gems: prow-promoted g. again — BETJ 37:1
Rich and rare were the g. — MOORE 234:17
these the g. of heaven — MILT 229:11
gender: she's of the feminine g. — O'KEE 241:5
general: caviare to the g. — SHAK 275:18
civil war, a g. must know — REED 258:18
generalities: glittering and sounding g. — CHOA 98:17
Glittering g. — EMER 137:2
General Motors: good for G. — WILS 351:11
generals: bite some of my other g. — GEOR 149:22
dead battles, like dead g. — TUCH 335:7
Russia has two g. — NICH 239:11
wooden swords we're all G. — UST 336:18
generation: g. destroyed by madness — GINS 153:3
g. of them that hate me — BIBLE 40:5
leaves is a g. of men — HOMER 170:21
O g. of vipers — BIBLE 48:14
very froward g. — BIBLE 40:24
ye are a chosen g. — BIBLE 57:8
You are all a lost g. — STEIN 314:23
generations: all g. shall call me blessed — BIBLE 51:28
G. pass while some trees — BROW 74:6
shirtsleeves in three g. — ANON 7:8
Those dying g.—at their song — YEATS 359:20
generous: first impulses ... always g. — MONT 234:1
My mind as g., and my shape — SHAK 282:20
something g. in mere lust — ROCH 261:5
Geneva: grim G. ministers — AYT 23:16
geniumque: G. loci — VIRG 339:18
genius: believe yourself a great g. — BEAU 30:17

genius (cont.):
G. a greater aptitude for patience — BUFF 78:6
g. a mind of large general power — JOHN 182:18
G. ... capacity of taking trouble — CARL 90:10
G. does what it must — MER 223:25
g. I had when I wrote — SWIFT 320:25
G. in a garret starving — ROB 260:22
G. is one per cent inspiration — EDIS 130:19
G. is the child of imitation — REYN 259:10
g. of Einstein leads — PIC 248:19
g. of its scientists — EIS 131:14
g. of the Constitution — PITT 249:5
g. of the place — POPE 251:15
g. that could cut a Colossus — JOHN 186:4
Gives g. a better discerning — GOLD 155:8
I think like a g. — NAB 236:20
models destroy g. and art — HAZL 164:5
nothing to declare except my g. — WILDE 350:18
Philistine of g. in religion — ARN 18:11
Ramp up my g. — JONS 187:9
talent instantly recognizes g. — DOYLE 126:8
Taste is the feminine of g. — FITZ 140:19
times in which a g. would — ADAMS 1:7
true g. appears in the world — SWIFT 320:11
Whence g. wildly flashed — KEATS 192:17
genteelly: committed very g. — BOSW 70:5
gentle: G. as falcon — SKEL 308:3
G. Child of gentle Mother — DEAR 115:7
g. into that good night — THOM 330:7
G. Jesus, meek and mild — WESL 346:6
g. motion with the deep — DAV 114:22
g. rain from heaven — SHAK 289:26
His life was g. — SHAK 282:2
parfit g. knyght — CHAU 95:12
shall g. his condition — SHAK 279:20
gentleman: died a very gallant g. — CHER 19:11
Every other inch a g. — WEST 346:26
'g.' and is nothing else — CROM 111:24
g. having nothing-a-year — SURT 319:15
g. in Whitehall does know better — JAY 180:15
g. is not in your books — SHAK 291:13
g. never inflicts pain — NEWM 238:17
last g. in Europe — LEV 206:6
little too pedantic for a g. — CONG 106:10
mariner with the g. — DRAKE 126:12
officer and a g. — ANON 6:2
prince of darkness is a g. — SHAK 283:16
talking about being a g. — SURT 319:17
who was then the gentleman — ROLLE 262:4
gentlemen: Dust was G. and Ladies — DICK 120:17
G. do not take soup at luncheon — CURZ 113:11
g. in England, now a-bed — SHAK 279:20
G. Prefer Blondes — LOOS 210:7
G.-rankers out on a spree — KIPL 196:15
not to forget we are g. — BURKE 81:5
Three jolly g. — DE L 116:17
what most of the g. does — WAUGH 343:19
while the G. go by — KIPL 196:28
written by gentlemen for g. — THAC 329:12
You g. of England — PARK 245:17
gentleness: only a willed g. — THOM 331:4
ways are ways of g. — SPR 313:27
gently: dig till you g. perspire — KIPL 197:22
g., in Afric-maps — SWIFT 320:21
geographers: g., in Afric-maps — SWIFT 320:21
geographical: Italy is a g. expression — METT 224:3
geography: G. is about Maps — BENT 35:5
geometrical: in a g. ratio — MALT 217:5
geometry: no-one enter who does not know g. — ANON 13:6
no 'royal road' to g. — EUCL 137:21
poetry a subject as precise as g. — FLAU 141:9
George: Amelia was praying for G. — THAC 329:18
G. the Third ought never — BENT 35:7
Harry! England and Saint G. — SHAK 279:6
if his name be G. — SHAK 282:3

**George** (*cont.*):
Vile, but viler G. the Second — LAND 200:24
**Georges:** G. ended — LAND 200:24
**Georgia:** G. on my mind — GORR 155:23
on the red hills of G. — KING 195:9
**Georgian:** all the G. silver goes — MACM 215:20
**geranium:** madman shakes a dead g. — ELIOT 134:11
**geraniums:** and g. (red) — MILNE 225:21
pot of pink g. — MACN 216:2
**German:** G. soldier trying to violate — STR 318:14
to my horse—G. — CHAR 95:7
**Germans:** beastly to the G. — COW 108:20
G. are going to be squeezed — GEDD 149:19
to the G.—the air — RICH 260:6
**Germany:** G. above all — HOFF 169:16
Offering G. too little — NEV 238:9
**germs:** g. in your handkerchief — ANON 6:23
**Gert:** G.'s writings are punk — ANON 8:2
**Gesang:** *Das ist der ewige G.* — GOET 154:4
**gestures:** In the g., in the sighs — SOND 311:6
**get:** forced to like what you g. — SHAW 302:7
g. anywhere in a marriage — MURD 236:10
G. out as early as you can — LARK 201:18
g. out of these wet clothes — ANON 8:18
G. thee behind me, Satan — BIBLE 50:14
G. up, stand up — MARL 218:6
governments better g. out of the way — EIS 131:16
you've got to g. up airly — LOW 211:4
**getting:** G. and spending — WORD 357:10
Gospel of G. On — SHAW 302:12
**ghastly:** G. good taste — BETJ 37:16
g. through the drizzling rain — TENN 325:1
We were a g. crew — COL 104:14
**ghost:** G. in the Machine — RYLE 265:11
g. of a great name — LUCAN 211:24
g. of Roger Casement — YEATS 359:6
G. unlaid forbear thee — SHAK 273:28
Vex not his g. — SHAK 284:7
**ghosties:** From ghoulies and g. — ANON 7:7
**ghostly:** Her face, at first just g. — REID 259:3
**ghosts:** g. from an enchanter fleeing — SHEL 304:6
g. of departed quantities — BERK 35:15
G., wandering here and there — SHAK 290:34
**ghoulies:** g. and ghosties — ANON 7:7
**giant:** arrows in the hand of the g. — BOOK 68:31
baby figure of the g. mass — SHAK 296:32
G. Despair had a wife — BUNY 79:3
I was the g. great and still — STEV 317:14
one g. leap for mankind — ARMS 16:5
To have a g.'s strength — SHAK 288:13
upon the body of a g. or — LAND 200:25
**giants:** g. in the earth in those days — BIBLE 39:7
on the shoulders of g. — BERN 36:9
on the shoulders of g. — NEWT 239:2
Want is one only of five g. — BEV 38:7
**gibber:** Did squeak and g. — SHAK 274:1
**gibbets:** cells and g. for 'the man' — COOK 107:17
g. keep the lifted hand in awe — YOUNG 360:15
**Gibbon:** scribble! Eh! Mr G. — GLOU 153:17
while G. levelled walks — COLM 105:15
**Gibraltar:** G. may tumble — GERS 150:7
**giddy:** I am g., expectation whirls — SHAK 297:1
So g. the sight — GREN 158:15
**giddy-pacèd:** brisk and g. times — SHAK 297:29
**gift:** g. of oneself — ANOU 14:8
g. rich by delaying it — TROL 334:18
Heaven's last best g. — MILT 229:15
You have a g., sir — JONS 187:17
your g. survived it all — AUDEN 20:22
**gifted:** Young, g. and black — IRV 178:18
**giftie:** some Pow'r the g. gie us — BURNS 82:25
**gifts:** cannot recall their g. — TENN 328:18
even when they bring g. — VIRG 339:5
g. of God are strown — HEBER 164:16
g. on such as cannot use — JONS 187:8

**gifts** (*cont.*):
They presented unto him g. — BIBLE 48:10
**gig:** Life is not a series of g. lamps — WOOLF 353:22
**gigantic:** g. body, huge massy face — MAC 213:6
**gilded:** g. loam or painted clay — SHAK 293:7
**gilding:** G. pale streams — SHAK 299:17
**Gilead:** Is there no balm in G. — BIBLE 46:29
**Gilpin:** John G. was a citizen — COWP 109:23
**gin:** g. joints in all the towns — EPST 137:9
G. was mother's milk to her — SHAW 302:18
proper union of g. and vermouth — DE V 117:11
sooner we can get out the g. — REED 258:19
torrent of g. and beer — GLAD 153:9
**Gioconda:** one isn't the real G. — CRANE 111:1
**Giotto:** G.'s tower — LONG 209:18
**Gipper:** Win just one for the G. — GIPP 153:4
**gipsy:** Time, you old g. man — HODG 169:15
**girded:** g. with praise — GRANT 156:8
**girdle:** folds of a bright g. furled — ARN 16:11
g. round about the earth — SHAK 290:25
**girdled:** g. with the gleaming world — TENN 326:20
**girl:** diamonds are a g.'s best friend — ROBIN 260:18
g. at an impressionable age — SPARK 312:12
g. needs good parents — TUCK 335:9
g. next door — AUDEN 21:4
g. throwing a ball — WOOLF 354:4
g. with brains ought to do — LOOS 210:7
I can't get no g. reaction — RICH 179:6
no g. wants to laugh all the time — LOOS 210:9
Once in a lifetime, do a g. in — ELIOT 134:15
Poor little rich g. — COW 109:6
pretty g. is like a melody — BERL 36:1
There was a little g. — LONG 210:6
unlessoned g., unschooled — SHAK 289:22
zephyr and khaki shorts g. — BETJ 37:8
**girlish:** Laugh thy g. laughter — WATS 342:26
**girls:** At g. who wear glasses — PARK 245:6
G. aren't like that — AMIS 5:5
g. in slacks remember Dad — BETJ 36:17
g. turn into American women — HAMP 161:5
In Little G. is slamming Doors — BELL 33:10
nude, giant g. that have no secret — SPEN 313:3
rosebud garden of g. — TENN 326:29
Treaties are like g. and roses — DE G 116:4
**give:** freely g. — BIBLE 49:27
G., and it shall be given — BIBLE 52:7
g. and not to count the cost — IGN 178:8
G. him, he the more is craving — WROTH 358:1
G. me your tired, your poor — LAZ 203:2
G. to me the life I love — STEV 317:24
g. to the poor — BIBLE 50:21
G. us this day our daily bread — BIBLE 48:27
g. what you command — AUG 21:25
more blessed to g. than to receive — BIBLE 54:22
never g. up their liberties — BURKE 80:25
such as I have g. I thee — BIBLE 54:9
**given:** g. me over in my grey hairs — WOLS 353:16
one that hath shall be g. — BIBLE 51:3
**giver:** author and g. of all good — BOOK 64:25
God loveth a cheerful g. — BIBLE 55:26
**gives:** gives twice who g. soon — PUBL 256:1
who ever g. takes liberty — DONNE 123:14
**giving:** not in the g. vein to-day — SHAK 294:18
**glacier:** g. knocks in the cupboard — AUDEN 20:12
**glad:** g. me with its soft black eye — MOORE 234:19
I'm g. we've been bombed — ELIZ 135:18
I was g. when they said — BOOK 68:28
Never g. confident morning — BROW 76:15
or are you just g. to see me — WEST 346:23
shew ourselves g. — BOOK 67:31
wise sun maketh a g. father — BIBLE 43:16
**glade:** alone in the bee-loud g. — YEATS 359:12
That crown the wat'ry g. — GRAY 157:11
**gladly:** g. wolde he lerne — CHAU 95:18
**gladness:** As with g. men of old — DIX 122:24

gladness *(cont.)*:
serve the Lord with g.                      BIBLE 58:10
serve the Lord with g.                      BOOK 68:5
solemn g. even crowned                      TENN 325:5
Teach me half the g.                        SHEL 305:11
gladsome: Let us with a g. mind             MILT 227:9
Gladstone: Mr G. may perspire               CHUR 99:1
Glamis: G. hath murdered sleep              SHAK 286:16
G. thou art, and Cawdor                     SHAK 285:15
glance: g. from heaven to earth             SHAK 291:4
O brightening g.                            YEATS 358:14
Glasgow: play the old G. Empire             DODD 122:29
glass: baying for broken g.                 WAUGH 343:18
double g. o' the inwariable                 DICK 119:32
Get thee g. eyes                            SHAK 283:26
g. of blessings                             HERB 167:5
Grief with a g. that ran                    SWIN 321:3
hate you through the g.                     BLUN 62:14
Satire is a sort of g.                      SWIFT 319:17
she made mouths in a g.                     SHAK 283:8
Sound of Broken G.                          BELL 33:23
through a g. darkly                         BIBLE 55:14
you break the bloody g.                     MACN 216:3
glasses: At girls who wear g.               PARK 245:6
Wiv a ladder and some g.                    BAT 30:1
glassy: crowns around the g. sea            HEBER 164:17
g., cool, translucent wave                  MILT 226:21
gleam: Follow The G.                        TENN 327:6
gleaming: girdled with the g. world         TENN 326:20
glee: Piping songs of pleasant g.           BLAKE 61:18
glen: Down the rushy g.                     ALL 4:18
glib: I want that g. and oily art           SHAK 282:18
gliding: But g. like a queen                SPEN 312:23
glimmering: fades the g. landscape          GRAY 157:4
glimpses: g. that would make me             WORD 357:11
glittering: g. and sounding generalities    CHOA 98:17
g. in the smokeless air                     WORD 354:15
g. prizes                                   SMITH 309:6
grey beard and g. eye                       COL 104:3
gloaming: In the g.                         ORRED 241:18
Roamin' in the g.                           LAUD 202:7
global: g. village                          MCL 215:11
Were g. from the start                      REED 258:17
globe: great g. itself                      SHAK 296:10
globe-trotting: disturb g. Madam            YEATS 360:5
globule: primordial atomic g.               GILB 151:18
gloom: inspissated g.                       JOHN 184:21
light to counterfeit a g.                   MILT 226:25
glooms: Welcome, kindred g.                 THOM 331:26
gloria: G. in excelsis Deo                  MISS 231:13
Sic transit g. mundi                        ANON 13:22
gloriam: Ad majorem Dei g.                  ANON 13:11
glories: G., like glow-worms                WEBS 344:17
g. of our blood and state                   SHIR 306:10
in those weaker g. spy                      VAUG 337:8
its g. pass away                            LYTE 212:20
my g. and my state depose                   SHAK 294:5
glorious: g. and the unknown                FORS 143:19
g. morning for America                      ADAMS 2:6
G. the northern lights astream              SMART 308:13
G. things of thee are spoken                NEWT 239:8
worship the King, all-g. above             GRANT 156:8
Mud! Mud! G. mud                            SWANN 141:4
Sheds not its g. ray                        MARR 219:24
glory: All g., laud, and honour             NEALE 237:21
all the g. of man                           BIBLE 57:6
count the g. of my crown                    ELIZ 135:7
crowned with g. now                         KELLY 193:19
day of g. has arrived                       ROUG 263:16
days of our g.                              BYRON 87:10
deed is all, the g. nothing                 GOET 154:7
drowned my g. in a shallow cup              FITZ 140:17
earth is full of his g.                     BIBLE 45:10
finished yields the true g.                 DRAKE 126:10
g. and the dream                            WORD 355:19

glory *(cont.)*:
g. and the freshness of a dream             WORD 355:17
g. and the nothing of a name                BYRON 85:15
G. be to God for dappled things             HOPK 172:12
G. be to the Father                         BOOK 63:17
g. in the name of Briton                    GEOR 149:23
g. is departed from Israel                  BIBLE 41:11
g. of Europe is extinguished                BURKE 80:14
G. of the Garden                            KIPL 196:16
g. of the Lord is risen                     BIBLE 46:23
g. of the Lord shall be revealed            BIBLE 46:9
g. of the Lord shone round                  BIBLE 51:32
g. of the winning                           MER 223:20
g. of the world passes                      THOM 329:28
g. shall not be blotted out                 BIBLE 48:8
g. that was Greece                          POE 250:9
G. to God in the highest                    BIBLE 52:2
G. to Man in the highest                    SWIN 321:11
G. to the new born king                     WESL 346:5
g. was I had such friends                   YEATS 359:17
Heaven and earth are full of thy g.         MISS 231:17
I felt it was g.                            BYRON 87:11
I g. more in the cunning                    JONS 187:12
King of g. shall come in                    BOOK 66:20
Land of Hope and G.                         BENS 34:20
left him alone with his g.                  WOLFE 353:1
long hair, it is a g. to her                BIBLE 55:10
looks on war as all g.                      SHER 306:9
madness is the g. of this life              SHAK 296:18
mellow g. of the Attic stage                ARN 17:20
Mine eyes have seen the g.                  HOWE 175:7
My gown of g.                               RAL 257:23
no g. in the triumph                        CORN 108:1
paths of g. lead but to the grave           GRAY 157:7
Solomon in all his g.                       BIBLE 49:4
Thus passes the g. of the world             ANON 13:22
To the greater g. of God                    ANON 13:11
to thy name give g.                         BIBLE 58:12
trailing clouds of g.                       WORD 355:20
What price g.                               STAL 5:13
When gout and g. seat me there              BROW 75:26
with g. not their own                       WORD 356:12
Gloucestershire: stranger here in G.        SHAK 293:17
gloves: capitalism with the g. off          STOP 318:7
through the fields in g.                    CORN 108:6
with my g. on my hand                       HARG 162:20
glow: her g. has warmed                     STEV 316:21
glow-worms: Glories, like g.                WEBS 344:17
glut: g. thy sorrow on a morning            KEATS 191:26
gluttons: Titled g.                         ROB 260:22
gnashing: weeping and g. of teeth           BIBLE 49:18
gnat: which strain at a g.                  BIBLE 50:31
gnats: small g. mourn                       KEATS 192:16
gnomes: little g. in Zurich                 WILS 351:12
go: better 'ole, g. to it                   BAIR 26:20
boldly g. where no man                      RODD 261:12
G. ahead, make my day                       STIN 317:26
G., and catch a falling star                DONNE 124:10
G., and do thou likewise                    BIBLE 52:13
G., and he goeth                            BIBLE 49:17
g., and sin no more                         BIBLE 53:27
g. anywhere I please                        BEVIN 38:9
g. away is to die a little                  HAR 161:9
G. down, Moses                              ANON 11:19
G., for they call you                       ARN 17:4
g. into the house of the Lord               BOOK 68:28
G., litel bok                               CHAU 96:20
G., little book                             STEV 317:17
G., lovely rose                             WALL 341:12
G. out into the highways                    BIBLE 52:25
G. to the ant thou sluggard                 BIBLE 43:11
g. we know not where                        SHAK 288:21
G. West, young man                          GREE 157:20
G. ye into all the world                    BIBLE 51:26
G., you are dismissed                       MISS 231:20

**go** (cont.):

| | |
|---|---|
| How you do g. it | BROWN 73:20 |
| I g. on for ever | TENN 323:13 |
| I have a g., lady | OSB 242:20 |
| In the name of God, g. | CROM 112:4 |
| I will arise and g. now | YEATS 359:12 |
| Let my people g. | BIBLE 39:34 |
| Let us g. then | ELIOT 133:24 |
| no place to g. | WHIT 348:8 |
| shalt thou g. and no further | PARN 245:23 |
| Time stays, we g. | DOBS 122:28 |
| we'll g. no more a-roving | BYRON 87:8 |
| we think you ought to g. | RUB 264:4 |
| with thee to g. is to stay | MILT 230:1 |
| **goal**: moving freely without a g. | KLEE 198:11 |
| Will be the final g. of ill | TENN 325:8 |
| **goals**: muddied oafs at the g. | KIPL 196:18 |
| **goat**: Gall of g., and slips of yew | SHAK 287:17 |
| g. feet dance an antic hay | MARL 218:15 |
| sort of fleecy hairy g. | BELL 33:19 |
| **goats**: g. on the left | BIBLE 51:4 |
| **god**: angler, and now with G. | WALT 342:11 |
| attracted by G. | INGE 178:13 |
| best of all G.'s works | MILT 229:27 |
| best thing G. invents | BROW 75:30 |
| bitter G. to follow | SWIN 321:12 |
| bogus G. | MACN 215:21 |
| bring us, daily, nearer G. | KEBLE 193:17 |
| burial-ground G.'s Acre | LONG 209:19 |
| By G.'s almighty hand | CAMP 88:13 |
| by searching find out G. | BIBLE 42:32 |
| Cabots talk only to G. | BOSS 70:1 |
| called the children of G. | BIBLE 48:19 |
| cannot have G. for his father | CYPR 113:12 |
| cannot serve G. and mammon | BIBLE 49:3 |
| charged with the grandeur of G. | HOPK 172:3 |
| closer walk with G. | COWP 109:27 |
| conscious water saw its G. | CRAS 111:6 |
| daughter of the voice of G. | WORD 355:25 |
| discussing their duty to G. | WHIT 348:19 |
| door-keeper in the house of my G. | BOOK 67:22 |
| Ef you want to take in G. | LOW 211:4 |
| either a beast or a g. | ARIS 15:19 |
| even G. was born too late | LOW 211:19 |
| Fear G., and keep his commandments | BIBLE 44:28 |
| Fear G. Honour the King | BIBLE 57:19 |
| For G.'s sake look after our people | SCOTT 268:5 |
| From G., who is our home | WORD 355:20 |
| further from G. | ANDR 5:16 |
| G. Almighty first planted | BACON 24:26 |
| G. and angels to be lookers on | BACON 24:1 |
| G. and devil are fighting | DOST 125:2 |
| G. and I both knew | KLOP 198:12 |
| G. and nature do nothing | AUCT 20:5 |
| G. and the doctor we alike | OWEN 243:17 |
| G. be in my head | ANON 7:11 |
| G. be merciful to me a sinner | BIBLE 52:39 |
| G. be thanked Who has matched | BROO 73:9 |
| G. be with you, Balliol men | BELL 34:2 |
| G. bless America | BERL 35:21 |
| G. bless the child | HOL 170:10 |
| G. bless the Prince of Wales | LINL 208:1 |
| G. bless us every one | DICK 118:7 |
| g. cannot change the past | AGAT 3:7 |
| G. caught his eye | MCC 214:15 |
| G. created man | VALÉ 336:21 |
| [G.] does not play dice | EINS 131:9 |
| G. does some delights condemn | MOL 232:23 |
| G. disposes | THOM 330:1 |
| G. erects a house of prayer | DEFOE 115:22 |
| G. fulfils himself | TENN 324:20 |
| G. gave Noah the rainbow sign | ANON 7:12 |
| G. has given you good abilities | ARAB 14:20 |
| G. has written all the books | BUTL 84:15 |
| G. hath joined together | BIBLE 50:20 |

**god** (cont.):

| | |
|---|---|
| G. hath joined together | BOOK 66:3 |
| G. hath made them so | WATTS 343:7 |
| G. hath numbered thy kingdom | BIBLE 47:12 |
| G. help me | LUTH 212:8 |
| G. help the Minister | MELB 222:21 |
| G.-intoxicated man | NOV 240:13 |
| G. is beginning to resemble | HUXL 177:14 |
| G. is dead | FROMM 146:7 |
| G. is just | JEFF 180:24 |
| G. is love | BIBLE 57:15 |
| G. is love, but get it in writing | LEE 204:5 |
| G. is no respecter of persons | BIBLE 54:15 |
| G. is not a man | BIBLE 40:18 |
| G. is not mocked | BIBLE 55:30 |
| G. is on everyone's side | ANOU 14:4 |
| G. is on the side of the best shots | VOLT 340:23 |
| G. is on the side of the big squadrons | BUSS 83:20 |
| G. is our hope and strength | BOOK 67:6 |
| G. is really only another artist | PIC 248:18 |
| G. is subtle but he is not malicious | EINS 131:8 |
| G. is Three, and God is One | NEWM 238:19 |
| G. is working his purpose out | AING 3:9 |
| G. made me to know Him | CAT 92:20 |
| G. made the country | COWP 110:6 |
| G. moves in a mysterious way | COWP 109:25 |
| G. must think it exceedingly odd | KNOX 198:18 |
| G. of Things as They are | KIPL 197:13 |
| G., or in other words, Nature | SPIN 313:22 |
| G. prepares evil for a man | ANON 13:8 |
| G. punish England | FUNKE 147:8 |
| G. reigns, and the Government | GARF 148:6 |
| G. save our gracious king | ANON 7:13 |
| G. save the king | BIBLE 41:12 |
| G. save the king | HOGG 170:8 |
| G. save the king | SHAK 294:4 |
| G. save the Queen | KIPL 196:2 |
| G. saw that it was good | BIBLE 38:15 |
| g. self-slain on his own altar | SWIN 321:10 |
| G. shall wipe away all tears | BIBLE 57:28 |
| G. shall wipe away all tears | BIBLE 58:5 |
| G.'s in his heaven | BROW 76:28 |
| G. so loved the world | BIBLE 53:19 |
| G. the first garden made | COWL 109:13 |
| G., to me, it seems, is a verb | FULL 147:4 |
| G. was certainly not orthodox | STR 318:13 |
| G. who made thee mighty | BENS 34:20 |
| G. whom he hath not seen | BIBLE 57:17 |
| G. will pardon me | HEINE 165:3 |
| G. won't, and we can't mend it | CLOU 102:13 |
| good G. prepare me | PEPYS 246:7 |
| good of G. to let Carlyle | BUTL 84:12 |
| hands of the living G. | BIBLE 56:25 |
| hath not seen G. | BIBLE 57:19 |
| Have G. to be his guide | BUNY 79:7 |
| he thinks little of G. | PLUT 250:2 |
| honest G. is the noblest work | ING 178:15 |
| Honest to G. | ROB 260:21 |
| How odd of G. | EWER 138:2 |
| I am a G. and cannot find it | SHEL 304:18 |
| I am becoming a g. | VESP 338:4 |
| If G. be for us | BIBLE 54:41 |
| If G. did not exist | VOLT 340:18 |
| if G. talks to thee | SZASZ 321:25 |
| if there be a G. | ANON 9:22 |
| in apprehension how like a g. | SHAK 275:16 |
| Inclines think there is a G. | CLOU 102:15 |
| I remembered my G. | SOUT 312:2 |
| Jewish G., and spurn the Jews | BROW 73:21 |
| justify G.'s ways to man | HOUS 175:4 |
| justify the ways of G. | MILT 228:9 |
| know his G. by night | VAUG 337:4 |
| Knowledge enormous makes a g. | KEATS 191:2 |
| know the mind of G. | HAWK 163:18 |
| leaping, and praising G. | BIBLE 54:10 |

**god** (*cont.*):

| | |
|---|---|
| Let G. be true | BIBLE 54:29 |
| Lord G. will wipe | BIBLE 45:25 |
| Man's word is G. in man | TENN 324:2 |
| many are afraid of G. | LOCK 209:1 |
| May G. us keep | BLAKE 60:23 |
| My G. and King | HERB 166:20 |
| my G., why hast thou forsaken me | BIBLE 51:16 |
| nature of G. is a circle | ANON 9:13 |
| *nearer you are to G.* | WOTT 357:21 |
| neglect G. and his Angels | DONNE 124:21 |
| next to of course g. america | CUMM 112:17 |
| not G. that I don't accept | DOST 125:4 |
| Now G. be praised | WOLFE 353:4 |
| O G., our help in ages past | WATTS 343:13 |
| one G. only | CLOU 102:16 |
| only G. can make a tree | KILM 195:1 |
| others call it G. | CARR 92:10 |
| Our G.'s forgotten | QUAR 256:27 |
| paltered with Eternal G. | TENN 327:13 |
| presume not G. to scan | POPE 252:17 |
| Put on the whole armour of G. | BIBLE 56:3 |
| Put your trust in G. | BLAC 59:22 |
| ranks the same with G. | BROW 77:1 |
| Read G. aright | QUAR 257:4 |
| safe stronghold our G. | LUTH 212:10 |
| served G. as diligently | WOLS 353:16 |
| she for G. in him | MILT 229:9 |
| spirit shall return unto G. | BIBLE 44:26 |
| Strong brother in G. | BELL 33:14 |
| strong brown g. | ELIOT 133:7 |
| Teach me, my G. and King | HERB 166:25 |
| that of G. in every one | FOX 144:18 |
| There but for the grace of G. | BRAD 71:6 |
| There is no G. | BOOK 66:12 |
| they shall see G. | BIBLE 48:19 |
| thou city of G. | BOOK 67:24 |
| three-personed G. | DONNE 123:10 |
| through darkness up to G. | TENN 325:11 |
| thy God is a jealous G. | BIBLE 40:21 |
| thy God my G. | BIBLE 41:8 |
| To glorify G. | SHOR 306:13 |
| To G. I speak Spanish | CHAR 95:7 |
| To the greater glory of G. | ANON 13:11 |
| TO THE UNKNOWN G. | BIBLE 54:20 |
| triangles were to make a G. | MONT 233:21 |
| Verb is G. | HUGO 175:24 |
| Very God of very G. | BOOK 65:5 |
| voice of the people is the voice of G. | ALC 3:14 |
| What G. abandoned | HOUS 174:13 |
| What hath G. wrought | BIBLE 40:19 |
| When G. at first made man | HERB 167:5 |
| when G.'s the theme | SMART 308:13 |
| Where G. paints the scenery | HART 163:10 |
| whom G. would destroy | DUP 129:11 |
| whose g. is in the skies | SHAW 301:33 |
| who think not G. at all | MILT 230:14 |
| will of G. prevail | ARN 17:25 |
| with G. all things are possible | BIBLE 50:23 |
| Woman was G.'s second blunder | NIET 239:18 |
| Word was with G. | BIBLE 53:6 |
| wrestling with my G. | HOPK 172:1 |
| ye believe in G. | BIBLE 53:36 |
| you are a g. | ROST 263:12 |
| **Goddamm:** Lhude sing G. | POUND 254:8 |
| **goddess:** G., excellently bright | JONS 187:3 |
| **godfathers:** G. and Godmothers | BOOK 65:20 |
| **godhead:** g. was evident | VIRG 339:3 |
| **godless:** Here were decent g. people | ELIOT 134:13 |
| **godliness:** cleanliness is next to g. | WESL 346:15 |
| **godly:** g., righteous, and sober life | BOOK 63:15 |
| **godmothers:** Godfathers and G. | BOOK 65:20 |
| **Godot:** Waiting for G. | BECK 31:10 |
| **gods:** By the nine g. he swore | MAC 214:2 |
| convenient that there be g. | OVID 243:11 |

**gods** (*cont.*):

| | |
|---|---|
| daughter of the g., divinely tall | TENN 323:20 |
| dish fit for the g. | SHAK 281:4 |
| divinely fair, fit love for g. | MILT 229:24 |
| first in the world made g. | JONS 187:11 |
| g. are on the side of | TAC 322:8 |
| g. that the city recognizes | PLATO 249:18 |
| g. themselves cannot recall | TENN 328:18 |
| g. themselves struggle | SCH 267:20 |
| g. thought otherwise | VIRG 339:7 |
| g. wish to destroy they | CONN 106:24 |
| It lies in the lap of the g. | HOMER 170:23 |
| leave the outcome to the G. | CORN 108:2 |
| loved by the g. because | PLATO 249:19 |
| men that strove with g. | TENN 328:23 |
| nature gave birth to the G. | HOLB 170:9 |
| people clutching their g. | ELIOT 133:23 |
| shalt have no other g. | BIBLE 40:3 |
| So many g., so many creeds | WILC 349:15 |
| they first make g. | LEVIN 206:8 |
| What men or g. are these | KEATS 191:18 |
| where g. have lost their way | ROET 261:15 |
| Whom the g. love dies young | MEN 223:5 |
| Ye shall be as g. | BIBLE 38:25 |
| **goest:** whithersoever thou g. | BIBLE 40:26 |
| whither thou g. | BIBLE 41:8 |
| **goeth:** g. after her straightway | BIBLE 43:13 |
| **going:** g. down of the sun | BINY 59:12 |
| g. the way of all the earth | BIBLE 40:29 |
| g. to and fro in the earth | BIBLE 42:21 |
| He is gone, and we are g. | JOHN 182:16 |
| knowing to what he was g. | HARDY 162:14 |
| Than greatness g. off | SHAK 271:23 |
| Their g. hence | SHAK 283:30 |
| upon the order of your g. | SHAK 287:12 |
| When the g. gets tough | KENN 194:10 |
| **goings-on:** numberless g. of life | COL 103:19 |
| **gold:** apples of g. in pictures of silver | BIBLE 43:35 |
| blue of the night meets the g. | CROS 112:9 |
| builded over with pillars of g. | BLAKE 60:17 |
| cursed craving for g. | VIRG 339:8 |
| fetch the age of g. | MILT 227:27 |
| fly to India for g. | MARL 218:8 |
| From the g. bar of Heaven | ROSS 263:6 |
| gleaming in purple and g. | BYRON 85:22 |
| g., and frankincense | BIBLE 48:10 |
| G.?, a transient shining trouble | GRAI 156:7 |
| g. of obedience and incense | MONS 233:3 |
| harpstring of g. | SWIN 321:2 |
| If g. ruste, what shall iren do | CHAU 95:22 |
| I stuffed their mouths with g. | BEVAN 38:2 |
| little g. head | MILNE 226:1 |
| Nor all, that glisters, g. | GRAY 157:15 |
| rarer gifts than g. | BROO 72:20 |
| Royalty is the g. filling | OSB 242:26 |
| sand and ruin and g. | SWIN 321:19 |
| streets are paved with g. | COLM 105:13 |
| this foul drain pure g. | TOCQ 333:5 |
| This g., my dearest | LEAP 203:6 |
| To gild refinèd g. | SHAK 282:10 |
| travelled in the realms of g. | KEATS 192:10 |
| what's become of all the g. | BROW 77:19 |
| Within its net of g. | MACN 216:10 |
| with patines of bright g. | SHAK 290:2 |
| **golden:** as they did in the g. world | SHAK 272:12 |
| Casting down their g. crowns | HEBER 164:17 |
| chalices and g. priests | JEWEL 181:14 |
| girl-graduates in their g. hair | TENN 327:16 |
| G. lads and girls all must | SHAK 273:27 |
| g. locks time hath to silver | PEELE 247:3 |
| G. opinions from all sorts | SHAK 286:2 |
| G. Road to Samarkand | FLEC 141:17 |
| g. years return | SHEL 303:18 |
| I went into a g. land | TURN 335:17 |
| Jerusalem the g. | NEALE 237:22 |

**golden** (*cont.*):

| | |
|---|---|
| Like g. lamps in a green night | MARV 220:10 |
| Miles and miles of g. moss | AUDEN 20:19 |
| Of g. sands, and crystal | DONNE 123:23 |
| Or love in a g. bowl | BLAKE 60:10 |
| or the g. bowl be broken | BIBLE 44:26 |
| perturbation! g. care | SHAK 278:26 |
| Roll down their g. sand | HEBER 164:15 |
| Someone who loves the g. mean | HOR 173:22 |
| We are stardust, we are g. | MITC 232:4 |
| **Goldengrove:** Over G. unleaving | HOPK 172:14 |
| **Goldsmith:** Here lies Nolly G. | GARR 148:9 |
| To Oliver G., A Poet | JOHN 185:12 |
| **golf:** made more liars than G. | ROG 261:21 |
| thousand lost g. balls | ELIOT 134:13 |
| **gondola:** What else is like the g. | CLOU 102:12 |
| **gone:** far g. from original righteousness | BOOK 69:17 |
| g.: aye ages long ago | KEATS 190:23 |
| G. before to that unknown | LAMB 200:13 |
| g. into the world of light | VAUG 337:11 |
| g., the old familiar faces | LAMB 200:13 |
| g. up with a merry noise | BOOK 67:8 |
| g. with the wind | DOWS 125:12 |
| He is g., and we are going | JOHN 182:16 |
| not dead—but g. before | ROG 261:18 |
| Not lost but g. before | NORT 240:10 |
| She's g. for ever | SHAK 284:4 |
| welcomest when they are g. | SHAK 280:4 |
| what haste I can to be g. | CROM 112:8 |
| What's g. and what's past help | SHAK 298:24 |
| **gongs:** g. groaning as the guns | CHES 97:25 |
| struck regularly, like g. | COW 109:11 |
| **gong-tormented:** that g. sea | YEATS 358:15 |
| **good:** And common g. to all | SHAK 282:2 |
| And God saw that it was g. | BIBLE 38:15 |
| apprehension of the g. | SHAK 293:14 |
| be a g. animal | SPEN 312:16 |
| Be g., sweet maid | KING 195:13 |
| Beneath the g. how far | GRAY 157:19 |
| best is the enemy of the g. | VOLT 340:15 |
| be thought half as g. | WHIT 349:3 |
| can be g. in the country | WILDE 350:6 |
| corrupt g. manners | BIBLE 55:19 |
| crown thy g. with brotherhood | BATES 30:2 |
| do evil, that g. may come | BIBLE 54:30 |
| Do g. by stealth, and blush | POPE 252:31 |
| do g. to them which hate | BIBLE 52:6 |
| evil and on the g. | BIBLE 48:24 |
| Evil, be thou my g. | MILT 229:7 |
| evil good, and g. evil | BIBLE 45:9 |
| for the public g. | LOCKE 208:21 |
| Gallop about doing g. | SMITH 309:17 |
| giver of all g. things | BOOK 64:25 |
| g. action by stealth | LAMB 200:11 |
| g. and bad of every land | BAIL 26:19 |
| g. are so harsh to the clever | WORD 354:11 |
| G., but not religious-good | HARDY 162:1 |
| g. deed in a naughty world | SHAK 290:4 |
| g. die early | DEFOE 115:17 |
| g. die first | WORD 354:19 |
| g. ended happily | WILDE 349:20 |
| g. [end] unluckily | STOP 318:5 |
| G. fences make g. neighbours | FROST 146:16 |
| g. for America | WILS 351:11 |
| g. for that man if he had | BIBLE 51:8 |
| g. in everything | SHAK 272:14 |
| G. is best when soonest | SOUT 312:8 |
| g. is oft interrèd | SHAK 281:18 |
| G. is That at which all | ARIS 15:12 |
| g. man to do nothing | BURKE 81:13 |
| g. minute goes | BROW 77:21 |
| g. must associate | BURKE 81:4 |
| g. of man must be the end | ARIS 15:13 |
| g. of subjects is the end | DEFOE 116:1 |
| g. of the people | CIC 100:20 |

**good** (*cont.*):

| | |
|---|---|
| g. old Cause | MILT 231:6 |
| g. still to find means of evil | MILT 228:11 |
| g. that I would I do not | BIBLE 54:38 |
| G. Thing | SELL 269:24 |
| g. thing come out of Nazareth | BIBLE 53:14 |
| g. thing left to me | MUSS 236:16 |
| g. time was had by all | SMITH 309:18 |
| g. to be had in the country | HAZL 164:3 |
| g. will be the final goal of ill | TENN 325:8 |
| g. will toward men | BIBLE 52:2 |
| g. woman if I had five thousand | THAC 329:21 |
| G. women always think it | BROO 73:11 |
| Hanging is too g. for him | BUNY 78:22 |
| He was a g. man, and a just | BIBLE 53:5 |
| highest g. | CIC 100:22 |
| His own g., either physical | MILL 224:15 |
| hold fast that which is g. | BIBLE 56:14 |
| In art the best is g. enough | GOET 154:9 |
| It's always the g. feel rotten | YES 360:12 |
| I will be g. | VICT 338:8 |
| know better what is g. for people | JAY 180:15 |
| knowing g. and evil | BIBLE 38:25 |
| Knowledge of g. and evil | COWP 110:3 |
| Lady is as g. i' th' dark | HERR 167:18 |
| luxury of doing g. | CRAB 110:27 |
| much g. in the worst of us | ANON 10:20 |
| must return g. for evil | VANB 336:23 |
| Never Had It So G. | MACM 215:15 |
| nor g. compensate bad in men | BROW 77:10 |
| nor it cannot come to g. | SHAK 274:13 |
| nothing either g. or bad but | SHAK 275:14 |
| policy of the g. neighbour | ROOS 262:10 |
| prospect of a distant g. | DRYD 127:32 |
| she needs g. cash | TUCK 335:9 |
| strong antipathy of g. to bad | POPE 252:32 |
| that can afford to be g. | SHAW 302:11 |
| that doeth g. is of God | BIBLE 57:18 |
| their luxury was doing g. | GARTH 148:14 |
| things work together for g. | BIBLE 54:40 |
| those who go about doing g. | CREI 111:18 |
| thou g. and faithful servant | BIBLE 51:1 |
| Time makes ancient g. | LOW 211:9 |
| to be obscurely g. | ADD 2:17 |
| universal licence to be g. | COL 103:11 |
| what g. came of it at last | SOUT 311:20 |
| When she was g. | LONG 210:6 |
| would do g. to another | BLAKE 60:19 |
| **goodbye:** Every time we say g. | PORT 253:19 |
| G., moralitee | HERB 166:12 |
| G. to all that | GRAV 156:17 |
| **good-bye-ee:** G.! — Good-bye-ee! | LEE 347:1 |
| **goodliness:** g. thereof is as the flower | BIBLE 46:10 |
| **goodly:** g. fellowship of the Prophets | BOOK 63:19 |
| g. to look to | BIBLE 41:16 |
| I have a g. heritage | BOOK 66:15 |
| **goodness:** And g. only knowes | CHES 98:6 |
| fountain of all g. | BOOK 64:8 |
| G. had nothing to do with it | WEST 346:22 |
| long-suffering, and of great g. | BOOK 68:6 |
| powerful g. want | SHEL 304:17 |
| **good-night:** gay g. and quickly turn away | YEATS 359:5 |
| g., sweet ladies | SHAK 276:34 |
| G., sweet prince | SHAK 277:19 |
| My last G.! | KING 195:5 |
| **goods:** when g. are private | TAWN 322:19 |
| with all my worldly g. | BOOK 66:2 |
| **goodwill:** In peace: g. | CHUR 100:4 |
| **goose:** And every g. a swan | KING 195:17 |
| g. honking amongst tuneful | VIRG 340:3 |
| gott'st thou that g. look | SHAK 287:33 |
| **gooseberried:** g. double bed of the wood | THOM 330:17 |
| **Gorgon:** Great G., Prince of darkness | SPEN 313:8 |
| **gorgonised:** G. me from head to foot | TENN 326:27 |
| **gormed:** I'm G. | DICK 118:18 |

gory: shake thy g. locks at me SHAK 287:11
Welcome to your g. bed BURNS 82:21
gosling: such a g. to obey instinct SHAK 273:21
gospel: Four for the G. makers ANON 8:6
G. of Christ knows of no WESL 346:11
G. of Getting On SHAW 302:12
music of the G. FABER 138:4
preach the G. BIBLE 51:26
gossip: babbling g. of the air SHAK 297:21
G. is a sort of smoke ELIOT 131:20
Like all g.—it's merely FORS 144:1
got: which in our case we have not g. REED 258:16
Gothic: cars are like great G. cathedrals BART 29:19
gotta: g. use words when I talk to you ELIOT 134:16
gout: g. and glory seat me there BROW 75:26
I say give them the g. MONT 233:6
govern: Go out and g. New South Wales BELL 33:7
g. according to the common JAM 179:12
To g. is to choose LÉVIS 206:10
governed: nation is not g. BURKE 80:1
governess: Be a g.! Better be a slave BRON 72:14
governing: g. was not property FOX 144:15
government: art of g. is the organization SHAW 301:26
best g. is that which O'SUL 243:4
cabinet g. BAG 26:6
efficient g. you have a dictatorship TRUM 335:3
forms of g. let fools contest POPE 252:20
G. and public opinion allow SHAW 301:20
G. at Washington GARF 148:6
g. by discussion ATTL 19:14
g. by the uneducated CHES 98:12
G., even in its best state PAINE 244:9
G. is big enough to take FORD 143:5
g. it deserves MAIS 216:18
g. of laws, and not of men ADAMS 1:22
g. of statesmen or of clerks DISR 121:24
G. of the busy by the bossy SELD 269:22
g. of the people LINC 208:8
g. shall be upon his shoulder BIBLE 45:16
g. to protect all conscientious PAINE 244:10
It's no go the G. grants MACN 216:2
land of settled g. TENN 329:1
No G. secure without DISR 121:23
representative g. DISR 122:7
republican g. TOCQ 333:3
rule nations by your g. VIRG 339:16
society is the end of g. ADAMS 2:1
work for a G. I despise for ends KEYN 194:13
worst form of G. CHUR 100:2
governments: foundation of most g. ADAMS 2:2
g. had better get out of the way EIS 131:16
nations and g. have never learned HEGEL 164:18
governors: Our supreme g., the mob WALP 341:16
governs: that which g. least O'SUL 243:4
gowd: man's the g. for a' that BURNS 82:7
Gower: O moral G. CHAU 96:23
grace: Amazing g.! NEWT 239:7
Angels and ministers of g. SHAK 274:27
be the new light of g. SMOL 310:16
By the g. of God there goes BRAD 71:6
does it with a better g. SHAK 297:24
Give us g. to persevere DEAR 115:7
G. is given of God CLOU 102:11
G. me no grace, nor uncle SHAK 293:18
g. of a boy BETJ 37:11
g.-proud faces BURNS 82:29
G. under pressure HEM 165:15
inward and spiritual g. BOOK 65:23
speech be alway with g. BIBLE 56:12
that g. may abound BIBLE 54:33
their courtly foreign g. TENN 328:14
through God's good g. MONS 233:2
Ye are fallen from g. BIBLE 55:29
graces: G. do not seem to be natives CHES 97:12

graces (cont.):
half-mile g. BURNS 82:29
gracious: be g. unto thee BIBLE 40:15
Lord, for he is g. BOOK 69:1
Lord is g. BIBLE 57:7
Remembers me of all his g. parts SHAK 282:8
gradualness: inevitability of g. WEBB 344:6
graduates: And sweet girl-g. TENN 327:16
graft: G. in our hearts the love BOOK 64:25
grail: g. of laughter of an empty CRANE 110:32
grain: like to a g. of mustard BIBLE 50:5
rain is destroying his g. HERB 166:11
Rot half a g. a day SHAK 293:3
see a world in a g. of sand BLAKE 60:5
which g. will grow SHAK 285:7
grains: Little g. of sand CARN 90:29
grammar: G., the ground of al LANG 201:8
Heedless of g. BARH 28:20
I don't want to talk g. SHAW 302:12
posterity talking bad g. DISR 122:14
With g., and nonsense GOLD 155:8
grand: Dumb, inscrutable and g. ARN 16:23
g. Perhaps BROW 75:14
g. to be blooming well dead SAR 267:1
Grand Canyon: rose petal down the G. MARQ 219:22
grandeur: And the g. that was Rome POE 250:9
charged with the g. of God HOPK 172:3
g. hear with a disdainful smile GRAY 157:7
grandfather: ape for his g. HUXL 177:21
through his g. or his WILB 349:7
grandmother: We have become a g. THAT 329:26
grange: at the moated g. SHAK 288:22
Upon the lonely moated g. TENN 326:22
granites: g. which titanic wars OWEN 244:2
grape: Beulah, peel me a g. WEST 346:20
G. is my mulatto mother HUGH 175:22
g. who will the vine destroy SHAK 299:8
grapes: fathers have eaten sour g. BIBLE 47:5
sour g. and ashes without you ASHF 18:24
vintage where the g. of wrath HOWE 175:7
grapeshot: whiff of g. CARL 90:11
grasp: G. it like a man of mettle HILL 168:11
reach should exceed his g. BROW 75:10
grass: All flesh is as g. BIBLE 57:6
days of man are but as g. BOOK 68:7
g. below, above the vaulted CLARE 101:7
g. will grow in the streets HOOV 171:18
g. withereth, the flower BIBLE 46:10
happy as the g. was green THOM 330:8
I am the g.; I cover all SAND 266:14
I fall on g. MARV 220:15
If we could hear the g. grow ELIOT 132:10
I know the g. beyond the door ROSS 263:10
leaf of g. is no less WHIT 348:18
Pigeons on the g. alas STEIN 314:21
snake hidden in the g. VIRG 339:24
splendour in the g. WORD 355:23
two blades of g. to grow SWIFT 319:21
uninterrupted by a g. and a hare LAWR 202:17
grassy: fair Fidele's g. tomb COLL 105:9
grate: G. on their scrannel pipes MILT 227:15
grateful: g. thought raised to heaven LESS 206:5
gratefully: O g. sing his power GRANT 156:8
gratias: Deo g. MISS 231:14
gratified: lineaments of g. desire BLAKE 61:17
grating: Nor harsh nor g. WORD 355:10
gratitude: g. is merely a secret hope LA R 201:25
grave: And renowned be thy g. SHAK 273:28
And the g. is not its goal LONG 209:22
Between the cradle and the g. DYER 129:17
birth astride of a g. BECK 31:15
But she is in her g., and, oh WORD 356:23
Dig the g. and let me lie STEV 317:21
Duncan is in his g. SHAK 287:4
Even the g. yawns for him TREE 334:5

grave (cont.):

| | |
|---|---|
| from the cradle to the g. | CHUR 99:20 |
| from the cradle to the g. | SHEL 304:24 |
| glory lead but to the g. | GRAY 157:7 |
| gone wild into his g. | SHAK 278:30 |
| g. as little as my bed | KEN 193:22 |
| g. hides all things beautiful | SHEL 304:18 |
| g. in a Y-shaped coffin | ORTON 241:21 |
| g. of Mad Carew | HAYES 163:21 |
| g.'s a fine and private place | MARV 220:25 |
| g., whither thou goest | BIBLE 44:19 |
| G. without thought | CHUR 98:26 |
| In every g. make room | D'AV 114:9 |
| It's with O'Leary in the g. | YEATS 359:28 |
| kind of healthy g. | SMITH 309:25 |
| kingdom for a little g. | SHAK 294:2 |
| like Alcestis from the g. | MILT 230:24 |
| Marriage is the g. or tomb | CAV 93:13 |
| O g., where is thy victory | BIBLE 55:22 |
| pompous in the g. | BROW 74:7 |
| receive no letters in the g. | JOHN 186:8 |
| see myself go into my g. | PEPYS 247:22 |
| shown Longfellow's g. | MOORE 234:9 |
| travelling toward the g. | WORD 356:8 |
| Upon his mother's g. | WORD 356:5 |
| When my g. is broke up again | DONNE 124:9 |
| Without a g., unknelled | BYRON 85:14 |
| with sorrow to the g. | BIBLE 39:26 |
| graved: G. inside of it, 'Italy' | BROW 75:24 |
| graven: unto thee any g. image | BIBLE 40:4 |
| graver: Wherein the g. had a strife | JONS 187:20 |
| graves: dig our g. with our teeth | SMIL 308:16 |
| g. of little magazines | PRES 255:5 |
| g. stood tenantless | SHAK 274:1 |
| Let's talk of g., of worms | SHAK 293:26 |
| ourselves dishonourable g. | SHAK 280:27 |
| quietly among the g. | EDW 131:4 |
| they watch from their g. | BROW 76:14 |
| graveyards: signs on the foxholes or g. | KENN 194:7 |
| gravy: Abominated g. | BENT 35:8 |
| It's the rich wot gets the g. | ANON 10:11 |
| Gray: whole of G.'s Elegy | WOLFE 353:3 |
| grazing: Tilling and g. | SULLY 319:3 |
| grease: slides by on g. | LOW 211:12 |
| greasy: top of the g. pole | DISR 122:17 |
| great: All creatures g. and small | ALEX 4:2 |
| All things both g. and small | COL 104:18 |
| between the small and g. | COWP 110:16 |
| But he is always g. | DRYD 128:28 |
| far above the g. | GRAY 157:19 |
| g. deep to the great deep | TENN 324:4 |
| G. hatred, little room | YEATS 359:19 |
| g. illusion | ANG 5:17 |
| G. is the hand that holds | THOM 330:11 |
| G. is Truth, and mighty | BIBLE 47:27 |
| g. is truth, and shall | BROO 73:14 |
| g. life if you don't weaken | BUCH 77:26 |
| g. man he grovelled before | THAC 329:15 |
| g. no heart | LA BR 199:13 |
| it kindles the g. | BUSS 83:19 |
| many people think him g. | JOHN 184:28 |
| our hearts are g. | TENN 324:12 |
| Rightly to be g. | SHAK 276:31 |
| some men are born g. | SHAK 298:3 |
| there is nothing g. but man | HAM 160:18 |
| There's a g. spirit gone | SHAK 271:7 |
| those who were truly g. | SPEN 312:24 |
| thou wouldst be g. | SHAK 285:15 |
| To be g. is to be misunderstood | EMER 136:25 |
| Great Britain: G. has lost an empire | ACH 1:3 |
| greater: G. love hath no man | BIBLE 53:40 |
| G. love than this | JOYCE 188:18 |
| g. man, the greater courtesy | TENN 324:11 |
| g. than Solomon is here | BIBLE 50:2 |
| necessity is yet g. than mine | SIDN 306:30 |

greater (cont.):

| | |
|---|---|
| we are g. than we know | WORD 356:20 |
| greatest: g. event it is that ever | FOX 144:16 |
| g. happiness for the greatest | HUTC 177:2 |
| g. happiness of the greatest | BENT 35:1 |
| g. thing in the world | MONT 233:15 |
| hath a life to live as the g. he | RAIN 257:19 |
| greatly: who would g. win | BYRON 87:3 |
| greatness: farewell, to all my g. | SHAK 280:18 |
| G. knows itself | SHAK 278:10 |
| have g. thrust upon them | SHAK 298:3 |
| moment of my g. flicker | ELIOT 133:29 |
| nature of g. not to be exact | BURKE 79:24 |
| squeaking Cleopatra boy my g. | SHAK 272:5 |
| Tell out my soul, the g. | BIBLE 51:28 |
| Than g. going off | SHAK 271:23 |
| Greece: G. might still be free | BYRON 86:13 |
| isles of G.! | BYRON 86:14 |
| greed: enough for everyone's g. | BUCH 77:30 |
| greedy: not g. of filthy lucre | BIBLE 56:16 |
| Greek: loving, natural, and G. | BYRON 86:8 |
| Must carve in Latin or in G. | WALL 341:13 |
| ne of G. that breed doubts | SPEN 313:16 |
| No more Latin, no more G. | ANON 9:17 |
| small Latin, and less G. | JONS 187:27 |
| Greeks: fear G. when they bring gifts | VIRG 339:5 |
| G. had a word for it | AKINS 3:10 |
| When G. joined Greeks | LEE 204:9 |
| green: a' babbled of g. fields | SHAK 279:4 |
| actual life springs ever g. | GOET 154:5 |
| And hae laid him on the g. | BALL 27:14 |
| As g. as emerald | COL 104:4 |
| bordered by its gardens g. | MORR 235:16 |
| By slow Meander's margent g. | MILT 226:10 |
| children are heard on the g. | BLAKE 61:25 |
| Colourless g. ideas sleep | CHOM 98:18 |
| Drives my g. age | THOM 330:10 |
| England's g. and pleasant land | BLAKE 61:12 |
| feed me in a g. pasture | BOOK 66:17 |
| Flora and the country g. | KEATS 191:29 |
| g. days telling with a quiet beat | QUIL 257:8 |
| g.-eyed monster | SHAK 292:12 |
| G. grow the rashes, O | BURNS 82:9 |
| *G. grow the rushes O* | ANON 8:6 |
| G. how I love you green | GARC 148:3 |
| g. lap was Nature's darling | GRAY 157:16 |
| g. mantle of the standing pool | SHAK 283:15 |
| G. pleasure or grey grief | SWIN 321:17 |
| G. Things upon the Earth | BOOK 64:1 |
| g. thought in a green shade | MARV 220:16 |
| How g. was my valley | LLEW 208:6 |
| laughs to see the g. man pass | HOFF 170:1 |
| Like golden lamps in a g. night | MARV 220:10 |
| Making the g. one red | SHAK 286:18 |
| Praise the g. earth | BUNT 78:14 |
| shoot the sleepy, g.-coat man | HOFF 170:2 |
| There is a g. hill far away | ALEX 4:6 |
| Time held me g. and dying | THOM 330:9 |
| wearin' o' the G. | ANON 8:9 |
| When I was g. in judgement | SHAK 271:12 |
| when the trees were g. | CLARE 101:3 |
| greenery: In a mountain g. | HART 163:10 |
| greenery-yallery: g., Grosvenor Gallery | GILB 152:13 |
| Greenland: From G.'s icy mountains | HEBER 164:15 |
| greens: And healing g. | ABSE 1:1 |
| Greensleeves: G. was all my joy | ANON 7:15 |
| greenwood: Under the g. tree | SHAK 272:19 |
| greet: G. the unseen with a cheer | BROW 75:12 |
| grenadier: British G. | ANON 10:13 |
| grenadiers: talk of Pensions and G. | STER 315:19 |
| Grenville: Sir Richard G. | TENN 328:10 |
| grey: all theory is g. | GOET 154:5 |
| given me over in my g. hairs | WOLS 353:16 |
| Green pleasure or g. grief | SWIN 321:17 |
| g. and full of sleep | YEATS 360:9 |

grey (cont.):
| | |
|---|---|
| g. hairs with sorrow | BIBLE 39:26 |
| lend me your g. mare | BALL 28:11 |
| philosophy paints its g. | HEGEL 164:20 |
| this old g. head | WHIT 348:26 |
| world has grown g. | SWIN 321:13 |
| **greyhounds**: like g. in the slips | SHAK 279:6 |
| **grief**: acquainted with g. | BIBLE 46:17 |
| After long g. and pain | TENN 327:3 |
| And g. itself be mortal | SHEL 303:8 |
| Every one can master a g. | SHAK 291:22 |
| Green pleasure or grey g. | SWIN 321:17 |
| G. fills the room up | SHAK 282:8 |
| g. flieth to it | BACON 24:21 |
| G. for awhile is blind | SHEL 304:16 |
| G. is a species of idleness | JOHN 182:15 |
| g. returns with the revolving | SHEL 303:7 |
| g. that does not speak | SHAK 287:25 |
| G. with a glass that ran | SWIN 321:3 |
| hopeless g. is passionless | BROW 75:2 |
| journeyman to g. | SHAK 293:12 |
| Of g. I died | ROET 261:16 |
| past help should be past g. | SHAK 298:24 |
| Patch g. with proverbs | SHAK 291:25 |
| Pitched past pitch of g. | HOPK 172:9 |
| Silence augmenteth g. | DYER 129:15 |
| silent manliness of g. | GOLD 154:26 |
| Smiling at g. | SHAK 298:1 |
| time remembered is g. forgotten | SWIN 321:2 |
| **griefs**: cutteth g. in halves | BACON 24:24 |
| g. of forty generations | MAC 213:18 |
| I know you: solitary g. | JOHN 181:18 |
| my state depose, but not my g. | SHAK 294:5 |
| Surely he hath borne our g. | BIBLE 46:18 |
| **grievance**: Comparisouns doon offte gret g. | |
| | LYDG 212:14 |
| **grieve**: what could it g. for | KEATS 191:3 |
| **grieves**: thing that g. not | MARK 218:4 |
| **grieving**: Márgarét, áre you ag | HOPK 172:14 |
| **grievous**: remembrance of them is g. | BOOK 65:11 |
| through my most g. fault | MISS 231:11 |
| **grim**: g. grew his countenance | BALL 27:16 |
| **grimace**: Of its accelerated g. | POUND 254:16 |
| **grin**: wears one universal g. | FIEL 139:13 |
| **grind**: bastards g. you down | ANON 9:15 |
| g. the faces of the poor | BIBLE 45:6 |
| He did g. in the prison house | BIBLE 41:6 |
| mills of God g. slowly | LONG 209:24 |
| **grinders**: incisors and g. | BAG 26:15 |
| **groan**: Condemned alike to g. | GRAY 157:13 |
| **groans**: How alike are the g. of love | LOWRY 211:22 |
| **groined**: which titanic wars had g. | OWEN 244:2 |
| **Gromboolian**: great G. plain | LEAR 203:8 |
| **groom**: death is but a g. | DONNE 123:19 |
| **grooves**: In determinate g. | HARE 162:19 |
| ringing of change | TENN 326:17 |
| **grope**: Whose buildings g. the sky | AUDEN 21:11 |
| **gross**: Not g. to sink, but light | SHAK 300:17 |
| things rank and g. | SHAK 274:10 |
| **Groucho**: G. tendency | ANON 12:7 |
| **ground**: acre of barren g. | SHAK 295:32 |
| Betwixt the stirrup and the g. | CAMD 88:12 |
| Chosen and made peculiar g. | WATTS 343:2 |
| fallen unto me in a fair g. | BOOK 66:15 |
| gain a little patch of g. | SHAK 276:28 |
| Grammer, the g. of al | LANG 201:8 |
| here at last on the g. | SOND 311:7 |
| let us sit upon the g. | SHAK 293:27 |
| lose to-morrow the g. won | ARN 17:10 |
| They are the g., the books | SHAK 284:16 |
| whereon thou standest is holy g. | BIBLE 39:31 |
| **grouse**: g. against life | ELIOT 135:4 |
| **grove**: good g. of chimneys for me | MORR 235:11 |
| olive g. of Academe | MILT 230:6 |
| **grovelled**: met a great man he g. | THAC 329:15 |

| | |
|---|---|
| **groves**: forsake her Cyprian g. | DRYD 128:2 |
| g. of Academe | HOR 173:17 |
| **grow**: They shall g. not old | BINY 59:12 |
| **growed**: I s'pect I g. | STOWE 318:8 |
| **growl**: does nothing but sit and g. | JOHN 186:1 |
| **growth**: children of a larger g. | CHES 97:11 |
| children of a larger g. | DRYD 127:25 |
| genuine g. in the individual | SMIL 308:17 |
| **grudge**: ancient g. I bear him | SHAK 289:2 |
| **grumbling**: piece of rhythmical g. | ELIOT 135:4 |
| **Grundy**: And more of Mrs G. | LOCK 209:1 |
| What will Mrs G. think | MORT 235:23 |
| **gruntled**: far from being g. | WOD 352:13 |
| **guardian**: Be thou my G. and my Guide | WILL 351:3 |
| **guardians**: good grey g. of art | WILB 349:12 |
| **guards**: Brigade of G. | MACM 215:19 |
| guard the g. themselves | JUV 189:9 |
| G. die but do not surrender | CAMB 88:11 |
| Up G. and at them | WELL 345:8 |
| **guardsman**: g.'s cut and thrust | HUXL 177:16 |
| **guerre**: *mais ce n'est pas la g.* | BOSQ 69:28 |
| **guest**: Earth, receive an honoured g. | AUDEN 20:24 |
| Go, Soul, the body's g. | RAL 257:21 |
| g. that tarrieth | BIBLE 47:31 |
| Some second g. to entertain | DONNE 124:9 |
| speed the parting g. | POPE 252:24 |
| This g. of summer | SHAK 285:21 |
| unexpected and uninvited. | TURG 335:11 |
| **guests**: Unbidden g. | SHAK 280:4 |
| **guide**: Have God to be his g. | BUNY 79:7 |
| Providence their g. | MILT 230:2 |
| **guides**: Ye blind g., which strain | BIBLE 50:31 |
| **guiding**: Did the g. star behold | DIX 122:24 |
| **Guildenstern**: Rosencrantz and G. are dead | |
| | SHAK 277:20 |
| **guile**: in whom is no g. | BIBLE 53:15 |
| packed with g. | BROO 73:7 |
| that they speak no g. | BOOK 66:25 |
| **guilt**: Cleanse me from its g. | TOPL 333:14 |
| Image of war, without its g. | SOM 311:2 |
| Life without industry is g. | RUSK 264:11 |
| pens dwell on g. and misery | AUST 22:21 |
| unfortunate circumstance of g. | STEV 317:10 |
| What art can wash her g. away | GOLD 155:13 |
| You will put on a dress of g. | MCG 214:20 |
| **guilty**: g. man is acquitted if | JUV 189:14 |
| G. of dust and sin | HERB 167:2 |
| g. of our own disasters | SHAK 282:22 |
| g. persons escape | BLAC 60:3 |
| like a g. thing surprised | WORD 355:22 |
| Make mad the g., and appal | SHAK 275:23 |
| Mortal, g., but to me | AUDEN 20:28 |
| **guinea**: g. helps the hurt | TENN 326:8 |
| g. pigs in the laboratory | WILL 351:4 |
| rank is but the g.'s stamp | BURNS 82:7 |
| **Guinness**: Hodgson, G., Allsopp | CALV 88:8 |
| **guitar**: changed upon the blue g. | STEV 316:9 |
| **gulf**: redwood forest to the G. | GUTH 159:12 |
| there is a great g. fixed | BIBLE 52:35 |
| **gulfs**: whelmed in deeper g. | COWP 109:20 |
| **gullet**: g. of New York swallowing | MILL 225:5 |
| **gum**: can't fart and chew g. | JOHN 181:22 |
| **gun**: barrel of a g. | MAO 217:19 |
| I have no g., but I can spit | AUDEN 21:8 |
| we have got the Maxim G. | BELL 33:18 |
| **gun-boat**: send a g. | BEVAN 37:20 |
| **Gunga Din**: better man than I am, G. | KIPL 196:17 |
| **gunpowder**: g., and the magnet | BACON 25:28 |
| G., Printing, and the Protestant | CARL 90:9 |
| G. Treason and Plot | ANON 10:5 |
| till the g. ran out | FOOTE 142:20 |
| **guns**: butter or g. | GOER 153:22 |
| gongs groaning as the g. boom | CHES 97:25 |
| G. aren't lawful | PARK 245:8 |

guns (cont.):

| | |
|---|---|
| monstrous anger of the g. | OWEN 243:21 |
| than a hundred men with g. | PUZO 256:26 |
| with g. not with butter | GOEB 153:21 |
| gurly: And g. grew the sea | BALL 27:16 |
| gusts: explanation of our g. and storms | ELIOT 132:2 |
| guts: lug the g. into the neighbour room | SHAK 276:26 |
| strangled with the g. of priests | MESL 223:27 |
| gutta: G. cavat lapidem | OVID 243:12 |
| gutter: We are all in the g. | WILDE 349:25 |
| guys: Nice g. Finish last | DUR 129:13 |
| gypsy: vagrant g. life | MAS 222:2 |
| gyre: g. and gimble in the wabe | CARR 91:15 |

# H

| | |
|---|---|
| ha: among the trumpets, H., ha | BIBLE 43:5 |
| habit: H. is a great deadener | BECK 31:16 |
| H. is second nature | AUCT 20:3 |
| h. of living indisposeth | BROW 74:5 |
| H. with him was all the test | CRAB 110:20 |
| sow a h. and you reap | READE 258:11 |
| when order breeds h. | ADAMS 1:15 |
| habitation: local h. and a name | SHAK 291:4 |
| habitual: nothing is h. but indecision | JAMES 180:8 |
| hack: do not h. me as you did | MONM 233:1 |
| Hackney: see to H. Marshes | BAT 30:1 |
| Hades: dark H.' door stands open | VIRG 339:12 |
| haggard: If I do prove her h. | SHAK 292:14 |
| Haggards: And the H. ride no more | STEP 315:5 |
| hags: and midnight h. | SHAK 287:19 |
| hail: All h. the power of Jesus' name | PERR 248:4 |
| beaten dog beneath the h. | POUND 254:21 |
| flies no sharp and sided h. | HOPK 172:7 |
| h., and farewell evermore | CAT 93:8 |
| H., fellow, well met | SWIFT 320:17 |
| H. holy queen, mother | ANON 13:21 |
| H. Mary, full of grace | ANON 13:13 |
| H., thou ever-blessèd morn | CASW 92:18 |
| H., thou that art highly | BIBLE 51:27 |
| H. to thee, blithe Spirit | SHEL 305:6 |
| Where falls not h. | TENN 324:22 |
| hair: And the stars in her h. | ROSS 263:6 |
| bright h. about the bone | DONNE 124:9 |
| colour of his h. | HOUS 174:6 |
| draws us with a single h. | POPE 253:4 |
| draw you to her with a single h. | DRYD 128:24 |
| h. has become very white | CARR 91:4 |
| h. of a woman can draw | HOW 175:9 |
| h. of his head | BIBLE 47:14 |
| h. of my flesh | BIBLE 42:28 |
| Her h. was long, her foot | KEATS 191:9 |
| like the h. we breathe | SURT 319:8 |
| My h. is grey, but not | BYRON 87:5 |
| My mother bids me bind my h. | HUNT 176:19 |
| never hurt a h. of Him | STUD 318:19 |
| part my h. behind | ELIOT 134:3 |
| pin up my h. with prose | CONG 106:18 |
| She has brown h., and speaks | SHAK 290:8 |
| thy amber-dropping h. | MILT 226:21 |
| with such h., too | BROW 77:19 |
| woman have long h. | BIBLE 55:10 |
| you have lovely h. | CHEK 96:29 |
| hairless: white and h. as an egg | HERR 167:20 |
| hairs: grey h. with sorrow | BIBLE 39:26 |
| h. of your head are numbered | BIBLE 49:30 |
| If h. be wires, black wires | SHAK 300:11 |
| hairy: my brother is a h. man | BIBLE 39:19 |
| halcyon: Martin's summer, h. days | SHAK 280:3 |
| hale: You are h., Father William | SOUT 312:1 |
| half: finished in h. the time | WOD 352:17 |
| h.-angel and half-bird | BROW 77:5 |
| h. as old as Time | BURG 79:17 |
| H. dead and half alive | BETJ 36:19 |

half (cont.):

| | |
|---|---|
| h. in love with easeful death | KEATS 192:3 |
| h. is greater than the whole | HES 168:2 |
| h. slave and half free | LINC 207:5 |
| h. that's got my keys | GRAH 156:3 |
| h. to rise, and h. to fall | POPE 252:18 |
| h. was not told me | BIBLE 41:30 |
| hath overcome but h. his foe | MILT 228:18 |
| myself and dearer h. | MILT 229:16 |
| One h. of the world cannot | AUST 22:14 |
| one of those h.-alive things | FORS 144:1 |
| temple h. as old as Time | ROG 261:19 |
| three years old is h. his height | LEON 205:23 |
| Too clever by h. | SAL 266:7 |
| half-a-crown: Or help to h. | HARDY 162:13 |
| half-brother: America, h. of the world | BAIL 26:19 |
| half-way: H. House to Rome, Oxford | PUNCH 256:7 |
| hall: fly swiftly into the h. | BEDE 31:20 |
| vasty H. of death | ARN 17:1 |
| hallowed: H. be thy name | BIBLE 48:27 |
| hallows: his mother and all his h. | HOPK 172:17 |
| halls: Amphitrite's destined h. | SHEL 304:1 |
| I dwelt in marble h. | BUNN 78:13 |
| halo: h.? one more thing to keep clean | FRY 146:30 |
| indignation is jealousy with a h. | WELLS 346:1 |
| life is a luminous h. | WOOLF 353:22 |
| halt: h., and the blind | BIBLE 52:24 |
| h. ye between two opinions | BIBLE 41:36 |
| Of tan with henna hackles, h. | STEV 316:4 |
| halting: Words came h. forth | SIDN 306:16 |
| ham: h.'n eggs in Carolina | GORD 155:22 |
| hame: Hame's h., be it never so | ARB 14:23 |
| Hamlet: H. without the Prince | SCOTT 269:5 |
| I am not Prince H. | ELIOT 134:1 |
| hammer: h. along the 'ard 'igh road | PUNCH 256:11 |
| ring of a h. | WILB 349:9 |
| hammers: anvil which has worn out many h. | |
| | MACL 215:6 |
| hammock: Drake he's in his h. | NEWB 238:11 |
| Hampshire: Hertford, Hereford, and H. | LERN 206:1 |
| hams: thy h., Bayonne | POPE 250:21 |
| hand: adorable tennis-girl's h. | BETJ 37:13 |
| bite the h. that fed them | BURKE 81:3 |
| bloody and invisible h. | SHAK 287:6 |
| by Time's devouring h. | BRAM 71:13 |
| cloud, like a man's h. | BIBLE 42:2 |
| curious engine, your white h. | WEBS 344:15 |
| died by the h. of the Lord | BIBLE 40:1 |
| dyer's h. | SHAK 300:7 |
| Emprison her soft h. | KEATS 191:26 |
| every man's h. against him | BIBLE 39:13 |
| h. a needle better fits | BRAD 71:12 |
| h. delights to trace unusual | WINC 352:3 |
| h. in hand, on the edge of the sand | LEAR 203:13 |
| h. in hand, with wandering steps | MILT 230:2 |
| h. is the cutting edge of the mind | BRON 72:9 |
| h. more instrumental | SHAK 274:4 |
| h. of Rousseau | HEINE 165:2 |
| h. of the physician | BIBLE 48:5 |
| h. on the cockatrice' den | BIBLE 45:20 |
| h. that made us is divine | ADD 2:26 |
| h. that rocks the cradle | WALL 341:10 |
| h. that signed the treaty | THOM 330:11 |
| h. to execute | GIBB 150:12 |
| h. to execute any mischief | CLAR 101:10 |
| h. will miss the insinuated nose | WATS 343:1 |
| Have still the upper h. | COW 108:8 |
| Heaving up my either h. | HERR 167:11 |
| Her h. on her bosom | SHAK 292:26 |
| His mind and h. | COND 165:11 |
| infection and the h. of war | SHAK 293:16 |
| it will go into his h. | BIBLE 42:16 |
| kingdom of heaven is at h. | BIBLE 48:12 |
| kiss on the h. may be quite | ROBIN 260:18 |
| larger heart, the kindlier h. | TENN 325:27 |

**hand** (cont.):

| | |
|---|---|
| my sword sleep in my h. | BLAKE 61:12 |
| O! let me kiss that h. | SHAK 283:24 |
| put your h. into the h. of God | HASK 163:16 |
| right h. forget her cunning | BOOK 69:4 |
| shaking h. of an old, wild | VICT 338:5 |
| sweeten this little h. | SHAK 287:30 |
| there also shall thy h. lead me | BOOK 69:6 |
| thine h. toward heaven | BIBLE 39:35 |
| Took me by the h. | TURN 335:17 |
| touch of a vanished h. | TENN 323:11 |
| waiting for a h. | TENN 324:26 |
| wash this blood clean from my h. | SHAK 286:18 |
| was the h. that wrote it | CRAN 111:4 |
| Whatsoever thy h. findeth to do | BIBLE 44:19 |
| what thy right h. doeth | BIBLE 48:26 |
| Wouldst hold my h.? | HART 163:11 |
| Your tiny h. is frozen | ILL 150:9 |
| **handclasp:** Out where the h.'s | CHAP 94:13 |
| **Handel:** Compared to H.'s a mere ninny | BYROM 84:24 |
| Dance they to the tunes of H. | SITW 308:1 |
| **handful:** fear in a h. of dust | ELIOT 134:20 |
| h. of meal in a barrel | BIBLE 41:35 |
| **handkerchief:** Trap the germs in your h. | ANON 6:23 |
| **handle:** h. of the big front door | GILB 152:18 |
| **handmaid:** Riches are a good h. | BACON 24:6 |
| **handmaiden:** low estate of his h. | BIBLE 51:28 |
| **hands:** Beneath the bleeding h. | ELIOT 133:5 |
| by joining of h. | BOOK 66:4 |
| caught the world's great h. | HUNT 176:14 |
| clasps the crag with crookèd h. | TENN 323:21 |
| h. are the hands of Esau | BIBLE 39:20 |
| h. from picking and stealing | BOOK 65:22 |
| h. I commend my spirit | BIBLE 53:4 |
| h. I commend my spirit | BOOK 66:23 |
| h. I loved beside the Shalimar | HOPE 171:22 |
| h. that hold the aces | BETJ 36:22 |
| has such small h. | CUMM 113:3 |
| He hath shook h. with time | FORD 143:10 |
| Holding h. at midnight | GERS 150:8 |
| horny h. of toil | LOW 211:5 |
| house not made with h. | BIBLE 55:24 |
| into the h. of spoilers | BIBLE 40:30 |
| into the h. of the living | BIBLE 56:25 |
| knit h., and beat the ground | MILT 226:9 |
| Let the lifting up of my h. | BOOK 69:8 |
| Licence my roving h. | DONNE 123:6 |
| little folding of the h. | BIBLE 43:12 |
| not into the h. of men | BIBLE 47:32 |
| not into the h. of Spain | TENN 328:13 |
| or have laid violent h. | BOOK 66:5 |
| reached out their h. in longing | VIRG 339:15 |
| Shake h. for ever, cancel | DRAY 126:16 |
| Soul clap its h. and sing | YEATS 359:21 |
| spits on its h. and goes to work | SAND 266:18 |
| Strengthen ye the weak h. | BIBLE 46:5 |
| their h. are blue | LEAR 203:10 |
| Their h. upon their hearts | HOUS 174:10 |
| these h. ne'er be clean | SHAK 287:29 |
| They have h., and handle | BOOK 68:18 |
| union of h. and hearts | TAYL 323:5 |
| **handsaw:** know a hawk from a h. | SHAK 275:17 |
| **handsome:** h. in three hundred pounds | SHAK 290:10 |
| **hang:** all h. together | FRAN 145:13 |
| h. a pearl in every cowslip's | SHAK 290:20 |
| H. it all, Robert Browning | POUND 254:12 |
| h. my hat is home sweet home | JER 181:9 |
| h. that jury-men may dine | POPE 253:8 |
| Here they h. a man first | MOL 232:21 |
| let him h. there | EHRL 131:7 |
| on gate-bars h. in a row | HARDY 162:17 |
| **hanged:** And my poor fool is h. | SHAK 284:6 |
| be h. in a fortnight | JOHN 185:14 |
| h. for stealing horses | HAL 160:11 |
| h. himself | BIBLE 41:26 |

**hanged** (cont.):

| | |
|---|---|
| Here's a farmer that h. | SHAK 286:20 |
| Major-general Harrison h. | PEPYS 247:13 |
| **hanging:** H. and marriage | FARQ 138:20 |
| h. Danny Deever | KIPL 196:9 |
| H. is too good for him | BUNY 78:22 |
| h. men an' women | ANON 8:9 |
| H. of his cat on Monday | BRAT 71:16 |
| h. prevents a bad marriage | SHAK 297:18 |
| **hangs:** And thereby h. a tale | SHAK 272:22 |
| H. in the uncertain balance | GREE 158:8 |
| What h. people | STEV 317:10 |
| **hank:** rag and a bone and a h. of hair | KIPL 197:12 |
| **happen:** accidents which started to h. | MARQ 219:21 |
| **happens:** dependent on what h. to her | ELIOT 132:5 |
| Nothing h., nobody comes | BECK 31:12 |
| something, h. anywhere | LARK 201:15 |
| **happier:** happiest if ye seek no h. state | MILT 229:12 |
| **happiest:** h. and best minds | SHEL 305:18 |
| h. if ye seek no happier state | MILT 229:12 |
| h. time of all the glad New-year | TENN 327:5 |
| h. women, like h. nations | ELIOT 132:14 |
| **happiness:** best recipe for h. | AUST 22:20 |
| consume h. without producing | SHAW 300:26 |
| flaw in h., to see beyond | KEATS 192:18 |
| For all the h. mankind can gain | DRYD 127:35 |
| great enemy to human h. | JOHN 185:31 |
| h. for the greatest numbers | HUTC 177:2 |
| H. is an imaginary condition | SZASZ 321:23 |
| H. is no laughing matter | WHAT 347:6 |
| H. is not an ideal of reason | KANT 189:24 |
| H. makes up in height | FROST 146:14 |
| h. of society | ADAMS 2:1 |
| h. of the greatest number | BENT 35:1 |
| h. of the human race | BURKE 80:6 |
| h. or a quiet conscience | BERL 36:6 |
| h. produced by a good tavern | JOHN 185:8 |
| H. the occasional episode | HARDY 161:24 |
| home-born h. | COWP 110:12 |
| liberty and the pursuit of h. | ANON 11:12 |
| lifetime of h. would be hell on earth | SHAW 301:15 |
| most suited to human h. | DEFOE 115:14 |
| pursuit of h. | JEFF 180:18 |
| result h. | DICK 118:12 |
| somebody else's h. | HUXL 177:8 |
| To fill the hour—that is h. | EMER 136:26 |
| uncertain of giving h. | AUST 23:4 |
| We find our h., or not at all | WORD 356:14 |
| Who gain a h. in eyeing | HUXL 177:13 |
| you take away his h. | IBSEN 178:7 |
| **happy:** all h. families resemble | TOLS 333:11 |
| Be h. while y'er leevin | ANON 6:9 |
| call no man h. before he dies | SOLON 310:27 |
| conspiracy to make you h. | UPD 336:14 |
| Farmer will never be h. | HERB 166:11 |
| Hail, redemption's h. dawn | CASW 92:18 |
| h. and keep him that way | HOR 173:10 |
| h. as the grass was green | THOM 330:8 |
| H. field or mossy cavern | KEATS 191:16 |
| h. he who crowns in shades | GOLD 154:19 |
| H. he who like Ulysses | DU B 128:33 |
| h. highways where I went | HOUS 174:24 |
| h. in the arms of a chambermaid | JOHN 185:21 |
| H. in this, she is not yet so old | SHAK 289:22 |
| h. issue out of all their | BOOK 64:19 |
| H. is that city | ANON 7:16 |
| H. is the man who fears | BIBLE 58:11 |
| h. noise to hear | HOUS 174:20 |
| H. the hare at morning | AUDEN 20:16 |
| H. the people whose annals | MONT 233:22 |
| H. those early days | VAUG 337:7 |
| His h. good-night air | HARDY 162:7 |
| How h. could I be with either | GAY 149:7 |
| Is that they h. are | WALL 341:15 |
| Lucid intervals and h. pauses | BACON 25:22 |

**happy** (cont.):
needed one thing to make me h. — HAZL 164:2
O h. Rome, born when — CIC 101:2
one who has been h. — BOET 62:17
pain than to remember a h. time — DANTE 113:21
perfectly happy till all are h. — SPEN 312:21
remote from the h. — AUDEN 20:9
should all be as h. as kings — STEV 317:13
someone somewhere, may be h. — MENC 223:7
splendid and a h. land — GOLD 154:25
stayed me in a h. hour — SHAK 291:24
This h. breed of men — SHAK 293:16
to attain the h. life — SURR 319:6
To make men h., and to keep — POPE 252:26
touch the H. Isles — TENN 328:24
'Twere now to be most h. — SHAK 292:5
Was he free? Was he h.? — AUDEN 21:17
We can't all be h. — RHYS 259:13
Well, I've had a h. life — HAZL 164:9
you cease to be h. — MILL 224:13
**harbinger:** evening star, Love's h. — MILT 229:32
**harbour:** Though the h. bar be moaning — KING 195:16
**hard:** ask the h. question — AUDEN 21:16
Between a rock and a h. place — ANON 6:10
Breeds h. English men — KING 195:15
h. rain's a gonna fall — DYLAN 130:2
h. words like a charm — OSB 242:17
It's been a h. day's night — MCC 205:14
Long is the way and h. — MILT 228:30
soldier's life is terrible h. — MILNE 225:19
thou art an h. man — BIBLE 51:2
woman is so h. upon the man — TENN 328:1
**hard-faced:** lot of h. men — BALD 27:9
**hardly:** Johnny, I h. knew ye — BALL 27:18
**hare:** Happy the h. at morning — AUDEN 20:16
h. limped trembling through — KEATS 190:14
h. sits snug in leaves — HOFF 170:1
h. sitting up — LAWR 202:17
h.'s own child, the little hare — HOFF 170:3
Take your h. when it is cased — GLAS 153:16
that Caught the Pubic H. — BEHAN 32:17
**hares:** And little hunted h. — HODG 169:13
**hark:** H.! hark! the lark — SHAK 273:25
H.! the herald-angels — WESL 346:7
**harlot:** Every h. was a virgin once — BLAKE 60:15
h.'s cry from street to street — BLAKE 60:9
h. we have got hold of — BYRON 87:16
Portia is Brutus' h. — SHAK 281:7
prerogative of the h. — KIPL 198:5
**harlots:** MOTHER OF H. — BIBLE 58:2
**harm:** do so much h. as those who — CREI 111:18
forgive a man for the h. — MAUG 222:10
I fear we'll come to h. — BALL 28:5
meaning no h. — GREE 158:7
prevent h. to others — MILL 224:15
that does h. to my wit — SHAK 297:15
**harmless:** entertains the h. day — WOTT 357:14
h. as doves — BIBLE 49:29
only h. great thing — DONNE 123:20
**harmonical:** h. and ingenious soul — AUBR 19:19
**harmonious:** Such h. madness — SHEL 305:11
**harmony:** Discordant h. — HOR 173:12
price is asked for h. — DOST 125:4
touches of sweet h. — SHAK 290:1
**harness:** between the joints of the h. — BIBLE 42:7
h. and not the horses — CANN 89:13
**harp:** clear h. in divers tones — TENN 324:24
H. not on that string — SHAK 294:19
h. on a weeping willow-tree — ANON 8:5
h. that once through Tara's — MOORE 234:14
wild h. slung behind him — MOORE 234:16
**Harpic:** As I read the H. tin — BENN 34:16
**harps:** To touch their h. of gold — SEARS 269:11
**harrow:** H. the house of the dead — AUDEN 21:14
Would h. up thy soul — SHAK 274:30

**harrowing:** Only a man h. clods — HARDY 162:11
**Harry:** banish not him thy H.'s company — SHAK 278:1
But H., Harry — SHAK 278:29
Cry 'God for H.! — SHAK 279:6
touch of H. in the night — SHAK 279:8
**harsh:** Nor h. nor grating — WORD 355:10
**hart:** h. desireth the water-brooks — BOOK 67:3
h. ungallèd play — SHAK 276:12
pants the h. for cooling streams — TATE 322:16
**Harvard:** glass flowers at H. — MOORE 234:9
Yale College and my H. — MELV 223:3
**harvest:** h. of a quiet eye — WORD 356:7
shine on, h. moon — NORW 240:11
she laughs with a h. — JERR 181:12
**harvests:** Deep h. bury all his pride — POPE 251:17
**Harwich:** in a steamer from H. — GILB 151:16
**haste:** I said in my h. — BOOK 68:21
Make h. slowly — AUG 22:6
Men love in h. — BYRON 86:25
they repent in h. — CONG 106:13
Though I am always in h. — WESL 346:16
what h. I can to be gone — CROM 112:8
**hasten:** So do our minutes h. — SHAK 299:21
**hat:** hang my h. is home sweet — JER 181:9
hang your h. on a pension — MACN 216:2
looking for a black h. — BOWEN 70:13
without pulling off his h. — JOHN 184:8
**hatches:** continually under h. — KEATS 193:6
**hatchet:** I did cut it with my h. — WASH 342:22
**hatching:** H. vain empires — MILT 228:28
**hate:** cherish those hearts that h. — SHAK 280:20
do good to them which h. — BIBLE 52:6
enough religion to make us h. — SWIFT 320:10
Envy and calumny and h. — SHEL 303:11
generation of them that h. — BIBLE 40:5
h. a fellow whom more light — JOHN 186:1
h. any one that we know — HAZL 164:7
h. something in him — HESSE 168:3
h. that which we often — SHAK 271:8
h. the man you have hurt — TAC 322:5
h. you through the glass — BLUN 62:14
have seen much to h. here — MILL 224:24
I h. all Boets and Bainters — GEOR 149:20
I h. and I love — CAT 93:7
Let them h., so long as they fear — ACC 1:2
man you love to h. — ANON 9:7
must h. and death return — SHEL 303:19
need not be to h. mankind — BYRON 85:5
never bother with people I h. — HART 163:9
sprung from my only h. — SHAK 294:28
time to love, and a time to h. — BIBLE 44:13
**hated:** h. the ruling few — BENT 35:4
**hateful:** And shamed life a h. — SHAK 288:21
**hates:** h. dogs and babies — ROST 263:13
man who h. his mother — BENN 34:19
**hateth:** h. his brother — BIBLE 57:17
**hath:** that h. shall be given — BIBLE 51:3
**hating:** h. all other nations — GASK 148:20
**hatless:** lands h. from the air — BETJ 36:21
**hatred:** feel any h. for him — RAC 257:14
from envy, h., and malice — BOOK 64:14
Great h., little room — YEATS 359:19
h. for the Tory Party — BEVAN 37:18
h. is by far the longest — BYRON 86:25
like love to h. turned — CONG 106:12
no h. or bitterness — CAV 93:12
Regulated h. — HARD 161:16
stalled ox and h. — BIBLE 43:26
**hatreds:** systematic organization of h. — ADAMS 1:11
**hats:** so many shocking bad h. — WELL 345:9
**haughty:** h. spirit before — BIBLE 43:28
**haunches:** on silent h. — SAND 266:13
**haunt:** h. of flies on summer eves — KEATS 192:2
**haunted:** h. town it is to me — LANG 201:1

| | |
|---|---|
| **haunts:** from h. of coot and hern | TENN 323:12 |
| That h. you night and day | BERL 36:1 |
| **have:** I h. thee not, and yet | SHAK 286:10 |
| They h. to take you in | FROST 146:11 |
| to h. and to hold | BOOK 66:1 |
| they will not let you h. it | HAZL 164:3 |
| **have-his-carcase:** h., next to the perpetual | DICK 120:3 |
| **haven:** their h. under the hill | TENN 323:11 |
| **haves:** h. and the have-nots | CERV 93:18 |
| **having:** Never satisfied with h. | WROTH 358:1 |
| **havoc:** Cry, 'H.!' and let slip | SHAK 281:14 |
| Strokes of h. únselve | HOPK 171:24 |
| **hawk:** But his h., his hound | BALL 28:9 |
| h. at eagles with a dove | HERB 167:6 |
| know a h. from a handsaw | SHAK 275:17 |
| Or h. of the tower | SKEL 308:3 |
| **hay:** Work and pray, live on h. | HILL 168:12 |
| **hazard:** father's crown into the h. | SHAK 279:1 |
| **he:** H. that is without six | BIBLE 53:26 |
| H. would, wouldn't he | RIC 259:20 |
| **head:** bear with a sore h. | MARR 219:26 |
| God be in my h. | ANON 7:11 |
| Go up, thou bald h. | BIBLE 42:8 |
| hairs of your h. are numbered | BIBLE 49:30 |
| hath not where to lay his h. | BIBLE 49:19 |
| h. could carry all he knew | GOLD 154:24 |
| h. grown grey in vain | SHEL 303:11 |
| h. is not more native | SHAK 274:4 |
| h. that once was crowned | KELLY 193:19 |
| h. thou dost with oil anoint | SCOT 269:9 |
| h. to contrive | CLAR 101:10 |
| h. to contrive | GIBB 150:12 |
| heaped on each gashed h. | SORL 311:16 |
| her h. on her knee | SHAK 292:26 |
| If sex ever rears its ugly h. | AYCK 23.14 |
| If you can keep your h. | KIPL 197:5 |
| ignorance bumping its h. | FORD 143:8 |
| incessantly stand on your h. | CARR 91:4 |
| Lay your sleeping h., my love | AUDEN 20:27 |
| learned lumber in his h. | POPE 252:9 |
| make you shorter by the h. | ELIZ 135:8 |
| no matter which way the h. lies | RAL 258:4 |
| Off with his h. | CIBB 100:15 |
| Or in the head or in the h. | SHAK 289:20 |
| repairs his drooping h. | MILT 227:18 |
| shew his glorious h. | SPEN 313:5 |
| so young a body with so old a h. | SHAK 289:25 |
| Uneasy lies the h. | SHAK 278:23 |
| which binds so dear a h. | SHEL 303:3 |
| **headache:** awake with a dismal h. | GILB 151:15 |
| **headin':** you know where we're h. | DYLAN 130:7 |
| **head-in-air:** Little Johnny H. | HOFF 169:20 |
| **headpiece:** H. filled with straw | ELIOT 133:17 |
| **heads:** Its h. o'ertaxed, its palsied | ARN 17:11 |
| Lift up your h. | BOOK 66:20 |
| Their h. are green | LEAR 203:10 |
| **head-stone:** become the h. in the corner | BOOK 68:22 |
| **headstrong:** h. as an allegory | SHER 305:30 |
| **head-waiter:** diplomat nothing but a h. | UST 336:19 |
| **heady:** H., not strong | POPE 250:15 |
| **heal:** Physician, h. thyself | BIBLE 52:5 |
| healed: h. also the hurt | BIBLE 46:28 |
| Ransomed, h., restored | LYTE 212:21 |
| with his stripes we are h. | BIBLE 46:19 |
| **healer:** compassion of the h.'s art | ELIOT 133:5 |
| **healing:** h. of the nations | BIBLE 58:7 |
| with h. in his wings | BIBLE 47:26 |
| **health:** And there is no h. in us | BOOK 63:14 |
| h. of his wife | CONN 106:29 |
| His h., his honour | BLUN 62:15 |
| Look to your h. | WALT 342:14 |
| saving h. among all nations | BOOK 67:16 |
| when you have both, it's h. | DONL 123:2 |
| **healthy:** h. and wealthy and dead | THUR 332:15 |

| | |
|---|---|
| **heap:** rude h. together hurled | MARV 221:2 |
| **hear:** h. it in the deep heart's core | YEATS 359:13 |
| H. the other side | AUG 22:1 |
| h. the pleasant cuckoo | DAV 114:17 |
| h. the word of the Lord | BIBLE 47:10 |
| H. us, we humbly pray | MARR 219:24 |
| He that hath ears to h. | BIBLE 51:20 |
| I h. a smile | CROSS 112:11 |
| I h. a sudden cry of pain | STEP 315:7 |
| I h. thy shrill delight | SHEL 305:8 |
| Lord, h. our prayers | BOOK 65:24 |
| may in such wise h. them | BOOK 64:22 |
| O h. us when we cry to thee | WHIT 348:9 |
| O let me h. thee speaking | BODE 62:16 |
| see and h. and feel yet | JOYCE 188:17 |
| time will come when you will h. me | DISR 121:5 |
| we shall h. it by-and-by | BROW 75:8 |
| which men prefer not to h. | AGAR 3:5 |
| who do not wish to h. it | BUTL 84:20 |
| **heard:** And then is h. no more | SHAK 288:5 |
| have ye not h.? | BIBLE 46:12 |
| H., not regarded | SHAK 278:6 |
| h. one side of the case | BUTL 84:15 |
| I will be h.! | GARR 148:12 |
| Oon ere it h., at tother | CHAU 96:19 |
| should certainly have h. | AUDEN 21:17 |
| voice of the turtle is h. | BIBLE 44:32 |
| You Ain't H. Nothing Yet | JOLS 186:19 |
| **hearers:** not h. only | BIBLE 57:2 |
| **hearing:** passionate my sense of h. | SHAK 284:12 |
| People h. without listening | SIMON 307:7 |
| **hears:** She neither h. nor sees | WORD 356:25 |
| **hearse:** Underneath this sable h. | BROW 74:24 |
| **heart:** Ancient person of my h. | ROCH 261:9 |
| And I am sick at h. | SHAK 273:30 |
| and the h. is sick | TENN 325:7 |
| And with a well-tuned h. | GURN 159:11 |
| anniversaries of the h. | LONG 209:20 |
| autumn's violins wound my h. | VERL 337:21 |
| Batter my h., three-personed | DONNE 123:10 |
| battlefield is the h. of man | DOST 125:2 |
| Because my h. is pure | TENN 328:15 |
| Beware my foolish h. | WASH 342:24 |
| bicycle-pump the human h. | AMIS 5:5 |
| blind side of the h. | CHES 97:21 |
| broken h. lies here | MAC 214:1 |
| Brute h. of a brute like you | PLATH 249:14 |
| Bury my h. at Wounded Knee | BENÉT 34:9 |
| But break, my h. | SHAK 274:13 |
| 'Calais' lying in my h. | MARY 221:17 |
| 'CALLOUS' engraved on her h. | SELL 270:1 |
| Can make a stone of the h. | YEATS 359:2 |
| can no longer tear his h. | SWIFT 320:27 |
| corrupt the h. | BYRON 86:33 |
| count time by h.-throbs | BAIL 26:18 |
| cracks a noble h. | SHAK 277:19 |
| desires of the h. as crooked | AUDEN 20:15 |
| false h. doth know | SHAK 286:8 |
| For Mercy has a human h. | BLAKE 61:21 |
| from hell's h. I stab at thee | MELV 223:4 |
| God be in my h. | ANON 7:11 |
| great [have] no h. | LA BR 199:13 |
| hear it in the deep h.'s core | YEATS 359:13 |
| h. and stomach of a king | ELIZ 135:6 |
| h. as sound as a bell | SHAK 291:21 |
| h. be full of the spring | SWIN 321:15 |
| h. expands to tinker | MACN 216:9 |
| h. grown cold, a head | SHEL 303:11 |
| h. grows old | YEATS 359:29 |
| h. has its reasons | PASC 246:5 |
| h. hath 'scaped this sorrow | SHAK 300:1 |
| h. is a lonely hunter | MCL 215:10 |
| h. is deceitful above all | BIBLE 46:31 |
| h. is Highland | GALT 147:19 |

heart (cont.):

| | |
|---|---|
| h. is inditing | BOOK 67:5 |
| h. is on the left | MOL 232:19 |
| h. is strong and the human | BAG 26:12 |
| h. lies plain | ARN 16:10 |
| H. of Darkness | CONR 107:4 |
| H. of England | DRAY 126:17 |
| h. of kings is unsearchable | BIBLE 43:34 |
| h. of lead | POPE 250:14 |
| H. of oak are our ships | GARR 148:8 |
| h. speaks to heart | FRAN 145:6 |
| H.'s renying, causer of this | BARN 29:8 |
| h. the keener, courage | ANON 11:5 |
| heart to h., and mind to mind | SCOTT 268:11 |
| h. too soon made glad | BROW 76:19 |
| h. to poke poor Billy | GRAH 156:4 |
| h. was piercèd through | SHAK 291:38 |
| h. was to thy rudder tied | SHAK 271:18 |
| h. within blood-tinctured | BROW 75:3 |
| He carries his h. in his boots | HERB 166:11 |
| he had a h. to resolve | GIBB 150:12 |
| Her h. was warm and gay | HAMM 161:1 |
| his little h., dispossessed | JAMES 180:3 |
| holiness of the h.'s affections | KEATS 192:23 |
| Hope deferred maketh the h. sick | BIBLE 43:21 |
| If thy h. fails thee | ELIZ 135:9 |
| I left my h. in San Francisco | CROSS 112:10 |
| In my h.'s core | SHAK 276:7 |
| I said to H. 'How goes it?' | BELL 33:12 |
| larger h., the kindlier hand | TENN 325:27 |
| laughter of her h. | HAMM 161:1 |
| let not your h. be troubled | BIBLE 53:36 |
| let your h. be strong | LAUD 202:5 |
| look in thy h. and write | SIDN 306:17 |
| loosed our h. in tears | ARN 16:19 |
| Lord looketh on the h. | BIBLE 41:15 |
| Make me a clean h. | BOOK 67:10 |
| man after his own h. | BIBLE 41:13 |
| merry h. maketh a cheerful | BIBLE 43:25 |
| mighty h. is lying still | WORD 354:16 |
| mine eyes, but not my h. | JONS 187:6 |
| My h. aches, and a drowsy | KEATS 191:28 |
| My h. and tongue employ | TATE 322:17 |
| My h. belongs to Daddy | PORT 253:24 |
| My h. in hiding stirred | HOPK 172:21 |
| My h. is heavy | GOET 154:6 |
| My h. leaps up when I behold | WORD 355:13 |
| My h.'s in the Highlands | BURNS 82:18 |
| My h. would hear her and beat | TENN 327:2 |
| My true love hath my h. | SIDN 306:15 |
| natural language of the h. | SHAD 270:17 |
| naughtiness of thine h. | BIBLE 41:17 |
| nearer God's H. in a garden | GURN 159:10 |
| no matter from the h. | SHAK 297:12 |
| not more native to the h. | SHAK 274:4 |
| Open my h. and you will see | BROW 75:24 |
| Or in the h. or in the head | SHAK 289:20 |
| pastoral h. of England | QUIL 257:8 |
| plotting h. in the world | RICH 260:2 |
| rag and bone shop of the h. | YEATS 358:16 |
| Religion's in the h. | JERR 181:10 |
| revolting and a rebellious h. | BIBLE 46:27 |
| Rise in the h., and gather | TENN 327:22 |
| seal upon thine h. | BIBLE 45:1 |
| Sink h. and voice oppressed | NEALE 237:22 |
| softer pillow than my h. | BYRON 87:22 |
| some h. did break | TENN 324:25 |
| So the h. be right | RAL 258:4 |
| squirrel's h. beat | ELIOT 132:10 |
| Sweeping up the H. | DICK 120:10 |
| sweet concurrence of the h. | HERR 167:17 |
| tears out the h. of it | KNOW 198:15 |
| That visit my sad h. | SHAK 281:7 |
| There is room in my h. for thee | ELL 136:1 |
| there will your h. be also | BIBLE 49:2 |

heart (cont.):

| | |
|---|---|
| this h., all evil shed | BROO 73:10 |
| thy beak from out my h. | POE 250:7 |
| tiger's h. wrapped in a woman | SHAK 280:13 |
| waters of the h. | THOM 330:12 |
| wear my h. upon my sleeve | SHAK 291:28 |
| We had fed the h. on fantasies | YEATS 359:16 |
| where my h. is turning ever | FOST 144:12 |
| Whispers the o'er-fraught h. | SHAK 287:25 |
| With a h. of furious fancies | ANON 11:23 |
| With h. and hands and voices | WINK 352:4 |
| woman has given you her h. | VANB 336:24 |
| wound a h. that's broken | SCOTT 268:15 |
| wounded is the wounding h. | CRAS 111:7 |
| your h. to a dog to tear | KIPL 196:27 |

heartache: h. and the thousand natural shocks

| | |
|---|---|
| | SHAK 275:25 |
| heartbeat: just a h. away | STEV 316:19 |
| heartbreak: h. in the heart of things | GIBS 150:22 |
| heart-easing: tell the most h. things | KEATS 192:12 |
| hearth: By this still h. | TENN 328:19 |
| Save the cricket on the h. | MILT 226:25 |

hearts: cold h. and muddy understandings

| | |
|---|---|
| | BURKE 80:15 |
| first in the h. of his countrymen | LEE 204:7 |
| harden not your h. | BOOK 68:1 |
| h. are dry as summer dust | WORD 354:19 |
| H. just as pure and fair | GILB 151:11 |
| h. that spanieled me | SHAK 271:22 |
| H. wound up with love | SPEN 313:2 |
| heedless h. | GRAY 157:15 |
| hidden in each other's h. | DICK 119:6 |
| Incline our h. to keep this law | BOOK 65:3 |
| In h. at peace, under | BROO 73:10 |
| Lift up your h. | BOOK 65:13 |
| our h. are great | TENN 324:12 |
| O you hard h., you cruel | SHAK 280:24 |
| shall keep your h. and minds | BIBLE 56:8 |
| Their hands upon their h. | HOUS 174:10 |
| those that be of heavy h. | BIBLE 44:5 |
| thousand h. beat happily | BYRON 85:2 |
| two h. beating each to each | BROW 76:1 |
| Two h. that beat as one | HALM 160:15 |
| undeveloped h. | FORS 143:15 |
| union of hands and h. | TAYL 323:5 |
| unto whom all h. be open | BOOK 65:2 |
| with Splendid H. may go | BROO 73:6 |

heartstrings: jesses were my dear h. SHAK 292:14

| | |
|---|---|
| heat: burden and h. of the day | BIBLE 50:25 |
| Fear no more the h. o' the sun | SHAK 273:27 |
| if you can't stand the h. | VAUG 337:2 |
| have neither h. nor light | WEBS 344:17 |
| not without dust and h. | MILT 230:31 |
| heated: When h. in the chase | TATE 322:16 |
| heath: Upon this blasted h. | SHAK 285:8 |
| heathen: h. in his blindness | HEBER 164:16 |
| h. in 'is blindness | KIPL 196:10 |
| pore benighted h. | KIPL 196:14 |
| Why do the h. so furiously rage | BOOK 66:9 |
| heather: bonnie bloomin' h. | LAUD 202:6 |
| heaths: some game on these lone h. | HAZL 164:8 |
| heaven: All I seek, the h. above | STEV 317:25 |
| All this, and h. too | HENRY 166:7 |
| And a h. in a wild flower | BLAKE 60:5 |
| And H.'s peculiar care | SOM 311:3 |
| and more than all in h. | BYRON 85:18 |
| betwixt H. and Charing Cross | THOM 331:16 |
| But to be young was very h. | WORD 354:24 |
| call it the Road to H. | BALL 28:7 |
| Can make a h. of hell | MILT 228:12 |
| consent of h. | JONS 187:1 |
| distant from H. alike | BURT 83:11 |
| eleven who went to h. | ANON 8:6 |
| Fellowship is h., and lack of | MORR 235:17 |
| flowerless fields of h. | SWIN 320:28 |

**heaven** (*cont.*):

| | |
|---|---|
| Give the jolly h. above | STEV 317:24 |
| God created the h. | BIBLE 38:13 |
| God's in his h. | BROW 76:28 |
| goes his own by-way to h. | DEFOE 115:23 |
| h. above me and moral law | KANT 189:22 |
| H. and Earth are not ruthful | LAO-T 201:11 |
| H. and earth shall pass away | BIBLE 50:37 |
| h. by sea as by land | GILB 151:3 |
| H. has no rage, like love | CONG 106:12 |
| H. in Hell's despair | BLAKE 62:1 |
| H. lies abou us in our infancy | WORD 355:20 |
| H. sends us good meat | GARR 148:11 |
| H.'s great lamps do dive | CAMP 89:2 |
| H.'s light forever shines | SHEL 303:13 |
| h. still guards the right | SHAK 293:23 |
| H. stops the nose at it | SHAK 292:25 |
| h.'s vaults should crack | SHAK 284:4 |
| H. take my soul, and England | SHAK 282:13 |
| h. will help you | LA F 199:16 |
| H. will protect a working-girl | SMITH 309:5 |
| hell that are not h. | MARL 218:10 |
| house as nigh h. as my own | MORE 235:2 |
| How art thou fallen from h. | BIBLE 45:22 |
| hymns at h.'s gate | SHAK 299:15 |
| Imagine there's no h. | LENN 205:7 |
| Is he in h.?—Is he in hell? | ORCZY 241:17 |
| It was my thirtieth year to h. | THOM 330:13 |
| kindred points of h. and home | WORD 357:9 |
| lead you in at H.'s gate | BLAKE 60:20 |
| Look, how the floor of h. | SHAK 290:2 |
| may merrily meet in h. | MORE 235:4 |
| met my dearest foe in h. | SHAK 274:16 |
| more things in h. and earth | SHAK 275:3 |
| My idea of h. is, eating | SMITH 310:11 |
| new h. and a new earth | BIBLE 58:4 |
| new h., new earth | SHAK 271:4 |
| nurseries of h. | THOM 331:18 |
| One h., one hell | BROW 76:6 |
| only a patriot to h. | MELV 223:2 |
| On whom the dew of h. drops | FORD 143:9 |
| Or what's a h. for? | BROW 75:10 |
| Parting is all we know of h. | DICK 120:12 |
| Pennies from h. | BURKE 81:14 |
| Puts all H. in a rage | BLAKE 60:6 |
| reign in hell, than serve in h. | MILT 228:13 |
| silence in h. | BIBLE 57:29 |
| steep and thorny way to h. | SHAK 274:20 |
| summons thee to h. or to hell | SHAK 286:11 |
| things are the sons of h. | JOHN 182:4 |
| top of it reached to h. | BIBLE 39:21 |
| 'Twould ring the bells of H. | HODG 169:13 |
| under an English h. | BROO 73:10 |
| waiting for the spark from h. | ARN 17:8 |
| war in h. | BIBLE 57:31 |
| watered h. with their tears | BLAKE 62:6 |
| way to h. as ready by water | ELST 136:7 |
| We are all going to H. | GAIN 147:10 |
| weariness of climbing h. | SHEL 305:14 |
| Which we ascribe to h. | SHAK 270:24 |
| wonder in h. | BIBLE 57:30 |
| **heavenly:** Observant of his h. word | DODD 122:30 |
| **heavens:** H., and all the Powers | BOOK 63:18 |
| h. fill with shouting | TENN 326:11 |
| h. from pole to pole | BLAKE 60:12 |
| h. my wide roof-tree | AYT 23:18 |
| h. themselves blaze forth | SHAK 281:8 |
| new h. and a new earth | BIBLE 46:26 |
| starry h. above that plain | THOM 332:2 |
| **heaviness:** h. may endure for a night | BOOK 66:22 |
| h. of his mother | BIBLE 43:16 |
| **heavy:** But makes it much more h. | SHAK 296:33 |
| little h., but no less divine | BYRON 86:15 |
| Sob, h. world | AUDEN 20:9 |
| ugly, h. and complex | FLAU 141:13 |

| | |
|---|---|
| **Hebraism:** H. and Hellenism | ARN 18:1 |
| **Hebrides:** in dreams behold the H. | GALT 147:19 |
| seas colder than the H. | FLEC 141:14 |
| **Hecate:** black H.'s summons | SHAK 287:5 |
| **hectic:** pale, and h. red | SHEL 304:6 |
| **Hector:** H. took off his plume | CORN 108:5 |
| **Hecuba:** H. to him or he to H. | SHAK 275:22 |
| **hedge:** clipped h. is to a forest | JOHN 186:12 |
| divinity doth h. a king | SHAK 277:1 |
| **hedgehog:** h. one *big* one | ARCH 15:1 |
| **hedgehogs:** h., the second to foxes | BERL 36:4 |
| start throwing h. under me | KHR 194:21 |
| Thorny h., be not seen | SHAK 290:28 |
| **hedges:** into the highways and h. | BIBLE 52:25 |
| Unkempt about those h. blows | BROO 73:4 |
| Where a few surviving h. | BETJ 37:7 |
| **heedless:** H. of grammar | BARH 28:20 |
| **heft:** like the H. of Cathedral tunes | DICK 120:14 |
| **height:** Happiness makes up in h. | FROST 146:14 |
| Nor h., nor depth | BIBLE 54:42 |
| three years old is half his h. | LEON 205:23 |
| What pleasure lives in h. | TENN 328:6 |
| **heights:** let's suffer on the h. | HUGO 176:1 |
| **heir:** h. of all the ages | TENN 326:16 |
| So, Pietro craved an h. | BROW 77:6 |
| **Helicon:** watered our horses in H. | CHAP 94:17 |
| **hell:** agreement with h. | GARR 148:13 |
| all h. broke loose | MILT 229:14 |
| And all we need of h. | DICK 120:12 |
| And h. itself will pass away | MILT 227:28 |
| begin raising h. | LEASE 203:20 |
| bells of H. go ting-a-ling | ANON 9:21 |
| boys, it is all h. | SHER 306:9 |
| characters of h. to trace | GRAY 157:2 |
| dunnest smoke of h. | SHAK 285:19 |
| from h.'s heart I stab at thee | MELV 223:4 |
| go to the gates of H. | PIUS 249:11 |
| h. for horses | BURT 83:13 |
| H. in Heaven's despite | BLAKE 62:2 |
| H. is a city much like London | SHEL 304:13 |
| H. is full of musical amateurs | SHAW 301:19 |
| H. is oneself | ELIOT 132:21 |
| H. is other people | SART 267:4 |
| H. is to love no more | BERN 36:8 |
| h. of heaven | MILT 228:12 |
| h. of horses | FLOR 142:13 |
| h. on earth | SHAW 301:15 |
| h. that are not heaven | MARL 218:10 |
| injured lover's h. | MILT 229:17 |
| Into the mouth of H. | TENN 323:17 |
| I say the h. with it | WHITE 347:15 |
| lack of fellowship is h. | MORR 235:17 |
| made an excursion to h. | PRIE 255:8 |
| mentions H. to ears polite | POPE 251:16 |
| myself am h. | MILT 229:6 |
| Nor H. a fury, like a woman | CONG 106:12 |
| pains of h. gat hold | BOOK 68:19 |
| Quiet to quick bosoms is a h. | BYRON 85:4 |
| reign in h., than serve in heaven | MILT 228:13 |
| riches grow in h. | MILT 228:19 |
| shout that tore h.'s concave | MILT 228:16 |
| Slander, meanest spawn of H. | TENN 326:4 |
| society would be a h. | MILL 224:19 |
| summons thee to heaven or to h. | SHAK 286:11 |
| that out of h. leads up | MILT 228:30 |
| this is h., nor am I out of it | MARL 218:9 |
| though h. should bar the way | NOYES 240:14 |
| walked eye-deep in h. | POUND 254:18 |
| where we are is H. | MARL 218:10 |
| whose entrance leads to h. | MILT 226:16 |
| with h. are we at agreement | BIBLE 45:28 |
| working definition of h. | SHAW 302:14 |
| Yours till H. freezes | FISH 139:25 |
| **Hellenism:** Hebraism and H. | ARN 18:1 |

**hellhound:** h. is always a h. — WOD 352:14
**helmet:** She saw the h. and the plume — TENN 326:3
**help:** cannot h. or pardon — AUDEN 21:15
  can't h. lovin' dat man of mine — HAMM 160:19
  encumbers him with h. — JOHN 183:26
  enough to h. the feeble up — SHAK 296:16
  from whence cometh my h. — BOOK 68:25
  h. and support of the woman — EDW 131:2
  H. of the helpless — LYTE 212:20
  h. thou mine unbelief — BIBLE 51:24
  H. yourself, and heaven — LA F 199:16
  how can I h. England — BROW 76:4
  place where h. wasn't hired — ANON 7:17
  present h. in time of trouble — ANON 5:18
  present h. in trouble — BOOK 67:6
  scream for h. in dreams — CAN 89:9
  Since there's no h. — DRAY 126:16
  They look on and h. — LAWR 202:26
  will make him an h. meet — BIBLE 38:20
  with a little h. from my friends — MCC 205:18
  you can't h. it — SMITH 309:7
  your countrymen cannot h. — JOHN 184:6
**helper:** mother's little h. — RICH 179:5
**helpers:** When other h. fail — LYTE 212:20
**helping:** H., when we meet them — KING 195:14
**helpless:** H., naked, piping loud — BLAKE 62:3
  Help of the h., O abide with me — LYTE 212:20
**hem:** of h. of Nature's shift — SHEL 304:14
**hemlock:** though of h. I had drunk — KEATS 191:28
**hempen:** h. home-spuns — SHAK 290:31
**hen:** better take a wet h. — KHR 194:20
**hence:** H., loathèd Melancholy — MILT 226:27
  H., vain deluding joys — MILT 226:22
**henna:** Of tan with h. hackles — STEV 316:4
**Heraclitus:** They told me, H. — CORY 108:13
**herald:** Hark! the h.-angels — WESL 346:7
**heraldry:** boast of h., the pomp — GRAY 157:7
**herb:** h. of grace o' Sundays — SHAK 277:3
**herbs:** dinner of h. — BIBLE 43:26
  with bitter h. they shall eat — BIBLE 39:36
**Hercules:** and some of H. — ANON 10:13
**herd:** lowing h. wind slowly — GRAY 157:4
  Morality is the h.-instinct — NIET 239:20
**here:** H. am I; send me — BIBLE 45:12
  H. and here did England — BROW 76:4
  H. I am, and here I stay — MACM 215:13
  H.'s a how-de-doo — GILB 151:26
  H.'s looking at you, kid — EPST 137:11
  H.'s tae us; wha's like us — ANON 7:18
  H.'s to the widow of fifty — SHER 306:6
  h.'s to you, Mrs Robinson — SIMON 307:6
  H. today—in next week — GRAH 156:6
  I have been h. before — ROSS 263:10
  We're h. because we're here — ANON 11:13
**hereditary:** H. bondsmen! — BYRON 85:1
**hereditas:** Damnosa h. — GAIUS 147:13
**Hereford:** Hertford, H., and Hampshire — LERN 206:1
**heresies:** And hateful h. — SPEN 313:16
  new truths to begin as h. — HUXL 177:18
**heresy:** h. signifies no more — HOBB 169:7
**heretics:** H. are the only bitter remedy — ZAMY 360:25
**heritage:** I have a goodly h. — BOOK 66:15
  we have come into our h. — BROO 72:21
**hermitage:** palace for a h. — SHAK 294:2
**hern:** haunts of coot and h. — TENN 323:12
**hero:** Every h. becomes a bore — EMER 136:30
  Millions a h. — PORT 253:26
  No man is a h. to his valet — CORN 108:9
  See, the conquering h. comes — MOR 235:5
  very valet seemed a h. — BYRON 84:27
  who aspires to be a h. — JOHN 185:22
**Herod:** it out-herods H. — SHAK 276:5
  Oh, for an hour of H. — HOPE 171:21
**heroes:** all the world's brave h. — ANON 10:13

**heroes** (cont.):
  And its h. were made — Æ 3:4
  Britain a fit country for h. — LLOY 208:11
  glum h. up the line to death — SASS 267:8
  thin red line of h. — KIPL 197:11
**heroic:** finished a life h. — MILT 230:17
  h. for earth too hard — BROW 75:8
  H. womanhood — LONG 209:25
  One equal temper of h. hearts — TENN 328:25
**heroically:** in one word, h. mad — DRYD 127:18
**heroine:** when a h. goes mad — SHER 305:24
**herring:** plague o' these pickle h. — SHAK 297:19
**Hertford:** H., Hereford, and Hampshire — LERN 206:1
**Hervey:** If you call a dog H. — JOHN 183:23
**hesitate:** h. and falter life away — ARN 17:10
**hesitates:** She floats, she h. — RAC 257:15
**Hesperus:** H. entreats thy light — JONS 187:3
  Wreck of the H. — LONG 210:5
**heterodoxy:** h. is another man's doxy — WARB 342:17
**heures:** h. propices — LAM 199:21
**hew:** h. him as a carcass fit — SHAK 281:4
**hewers:** h. of wood and drawers — BIBLE 40:28
**hey:** Then h. for boot and horse — KING 195:17
**hi:** H. diddle dee dee — WASH 342:23
**hic:** H. jacet — RAL 258:2
**hick:** Sticks nix h. pix — ANON 10:15
**hid:** I h. from Him — THOM 331:8
**hidden:** h. in each other's hearts — DICK 119:6
**hide:** H. me from day's garish eye — MILT 226:26
  Is it a world to h. virtues — SHAK 297:17
  Let me h. myself in Thee — TOPL 333:14
  wrapped in a woman's h. — SHAK 280:13
**hideous:** h. notes of woe — BYRON 86:28
**hides:** he that h. a dark soul — MILT 226:12
  H. from himself his state — JOHN 183:15
**Hierusalem:** H., my happy home — ANON 7:19
**high:** get h. with a little help — MCC 205:18
  h. as an elephant's eye — HAMM 161:2
  h. life high characters — POPE 251:20
  h. that proved too high — BROW 75:8
  like champagne or h. heels — BENN 34:18
  She's the Broad and I'm the H. — SPR 314:1
  This h. man, with a great — BROW 75:33
  upon the h. horse — BROWN 73:16
  wickedness in h. places — BIBLE 56:4
  ye'll tak' the h. road — ANON 10:2
**higher:** Can Stuart or Nassau go h. — PRIOR 255:10
  Friend, go up h. — BIBLE 52:21
  their dead selves to h. things — TENN 324:24
**highest:** h. good — CIC 100:22
  needs must love the h. — TENN 324:6
**highland:** heart is H. — GALT 147:19
  Yon solitary H. lass — WORD 357:1
**Highlandman:** breeks aff a wild H. — SCOTT 268:26
**highlands:** In the h., in the country — STEV 317:18
  My heart's in the H. — BURNS 82:18
  Ye H. and ye Lawlands — BALL 27:14
**highly:** what thou wouldst h. — SHAK 285:15
**highway:** broad h. of the world — SHEL 303:16
  H., since you my chief — SIDN 306:24
**highways:** happy h. where I went — HOUS 174:24
  out into the h. and hedges — BIBLE 52:25
**hill:** all gone under the h. — ELIOT 133:4
  city that is set on an h. — BIBLE 48:21
  every mountain and h. — BIBLE 46:9
  High on an h. it calls to me — CROSS 112:10
  hunter home from the h. — STEV 317:22
  laughing is heard on the h. — BLAKE 61:25
  Mahomet will go to the h. — BACON 24:16
  nursed upon the self-same h. — MILT 227:12
  other side of the h. — WELL 345:6
  rest upon thy holy h. — BOOK 66:13
  To their haven under the h. — TENN 323:11
  traveller's dream under the h. — BLAKE 60:15
**hills:** Along Morea's h. — BYRON 85:20

**hills** (cont.):

| | |
|---|---|
| blue remembered h. | HOUS 174:24 |
| high wild h. | SHAK 293:17 |
| h. of Georgia | KING 195:9 |
| H. of the Chankly Bore | LEAR 203:9 |
| H. of the North, rejoice | OAKL 240:16 |
| lift up mine eyes unto the h. | BOOK 68:25 |
| little h. like young sheep | BOOK 68:16 |
| Over the h. and far away | GAY 149:5 |
| to the reverberate h. | SHAK 297:21 |

**hill-side**: h.'s dew-pearled — BROW 76:28
**him**: they all cried 'That's h.!' — BARH 28:20
**himself**: He h. said it — CIC 100:21
**hindsight**: H. is always twenty-twenty — WILD 350:23
**hinky**: H., dinky, parley-voo — ANON 9:5
**hip**: catch him once upon the h. — SHAK 289:2
He smote them h. and thigh — BIBLE 41:4
**Hippocrene**: blushful H. — KEATS 191:30
**hippopotamus**: I shoot the H. — BELL 33:1
shoot the h. with eyebrows — FORS 143:14
**hips**: armchairs tight about the h. — WOD 352:22
We swing ungirded h. — SORL 311:15
**hire**: labourer is worthy of his h. — BIBLE 52:10
**hired**: They h. the money — COOL 107:20
**Hiroshima**: Einstein leads to H. — PIC 248:19
**hissed**: h. along the polished ice — WORD 355:2
**historian**: h. wants more documents — JAMES 179:15
**historians**: h. left blanks — POUND 254:13
**historically**: Eternally noble, h. fair — LERN 205:26
**histories**: H. make men wise — BACON 25:16
**history**: annals are blank in h.-books — MONT 233:22
Antiquities are h. defaced — BACON 23:21
dustbin of h. — TROT 335:1
dust-heap called 'h.' — BIRR 59:15
great deal of h. to produce — JAMES 179:18
happiest nations, have no h. — ELIOT 132:14
h. becomes a race — WELLS 345:21
H. came to a . — SELL 270:5
H. gets thicker — TAYL 322:22
[h.] is a debatable line — MAC 213:22
H. [is] a distillation of rumour — CARL 90:12
H. is a gallery of pictures — TOCQ 333:1
H. is a nightmare — JOYCE 188:14
H. is . . . a tableau of crimes — VOLT 340:20
H. is littered with the wars — POW 255:2
H. is more or less bunk — FORD 143:6
H. is not what you thought — SELL 269:23
H. is now and England — ELIOT 133:12
h. is on our side — KHR 194:19
H. is past politics — FREE 145:21
H. is philosophy from examples — DION 121:4
H. is the essence of — CARL 90:6
h. is the world's judgement — SCH 267:21
H. just burps — BARN 29:6
H. is little more than the register — GIBB 150:11
H., n. An account — BIER 59:6
h. of art is the history of revivals — BUTL 84:14
h. of class struggles — MARX 221:14
H. to the defeated — AUDEN 21:15
H. will absolve me — CAST 92:16
more h. than they can consume — SAKI 265:17
never learned anything from h. — HEGEL 164:18
no h.; only biography — EMER 136:22
Read no h. — DISR 121:28
Thames is liquid h. — BURNS 81:20
thousand years of h. — GAIT 147:12
War makes rattling good h. — HARDY 161:20
worthy of serious attention than h. — ARIS 15:16
**hit**: hit, a very palpable h. — SHAK 277:14
h. it off as they should — WORD 354:11
**hitch**: H. your wagon to a star — EMER 136:31
**Hitler**: H. attacked the Jews — NIEM 239:15
[H.] missed the bus — CHAM 94:3
H. swept out — ANON 8:12
kidding, Mister H. — PERRY 248:5

| | |
|---|---|
| **hive**: h. for the honey bee | YEATS 359:12 |
| **hoard**: Our h. is little | TENN 324:12 |
| **Hoares**: no more H. to Paris | GEOR 149:26 |
| **hoarse**: raven himself is h. | SHAK 285:16 |
| **Hobbes**: H. clearly proves | SWIFT 320:22 |
| **hobbit**: there lived a h. | TOLK 333:8 |
| **hobgoblin**: h. of little minds | EMER 136:24 |
| **hock**: weak h. and seltzer | BETJ 36:16 |
| **hodgepodge**: gallimaufry or h. | SPEN 313:20 |
| **hoe**: Man with the H. | MARK 218:4 |
| tickle her with a h. | JERR 181:12 |
| **hog**: Rule all England under a h. | COLL 105:3 |
| **hogamus**: H., higamous | JAMES 180:11 |
| **hogs**: Men Eat H. | STEV 316:7 |
| **hoist**: H. with his own petar | SHAK 276:25 |
| **hold**: always keep a-h. of Nurse | BELL 33:5 |
| first cries, 'H., enough' | SHAK 288:8 |
| hereafter for ever h. his peace | BOOK 65:27 |
| h. fast blessed hope | BIBLE 56:14 |
| H. the fort | BLISS 62:10 |
| h. the gorgeous East | WORD 356:2 |
| **hole**: drop of rain maketh a h. | LAT 202:3 |
| h. in the ground | TOLK 333:8 |
| kick a h. in a stained glass | CHAN 94:7 |
| knows of a better h. | BAIR 26:20 |
| play on the h. of the asp | BIBLE 45:20 |
| poisoned rat in a h. | SWIFT 320:5 |
| **holes**: foxes have h. | BIBLE 49:19 |
| **holiday**: Butchered to make a Roman h. | BYRON 85:10 |
| h. is a good working definition | SHAW 302:14 |
| now I am in a h. humour | SHAK 273:8 |
| **holidays**: all the year were playing h. | SHAK 277:25 |
| holiest of all h. | LONG 209:20 |
| **holier**: I am h. than thou | BIBLE 46:25 |
| **holiest**: Praise to the H. | NEWM 238:20 |
| **holily**: That thou wouldst h. | SHAK 285:15 |
| **holiness**: beauty of h. | BOOK 68:2 |
| Go! put off h. | BLAKE 60:22 |
| h. of the heart's affections | KEATS 192:23 |
| no holiness but social h. | WESL 346:11 |
| **hollow**: fearful h. of thine ear | SHAK 295:17 |
| We are the h. men | ELIOT 133:17 |
| Within the h. crown | SHAK 293:28 |
| **Hollywood**: invited to H. | CHAN 94:10 |
| **holy**: As proofs of h. writ | SHAK 292:18 |
| coming to that h. room | DONNE 123:16 |
| H. deadlock | HERB 166:16 |
| h. ground | BIBLE 39:31 |
| H., holy, holy | BIBLE 57:24 |
| Holy, Holy, H. | HEBER 164:17 |
| H., holy, holy | MISS 231:17 |
| h. hush of ancient sacrifice | STEV 316:12 |
| h., is the Lord of hosts | BIBLE 45:10 |
| h. loved by the gods | PLATO 249:19 |
| h. nation | BIBLE 57:8 |
| h. simplicity | JER 181:6 |
| h.-water dealt | MCG 214:21 |
| Made h. by their dreams | GIBS 150:22 |
| nothing is h. | BOOK 64:24 |
| Roman Empire was neither h. | VOLT 340:19 |
| sabbath day, to keep it h. | BIBLE 40:7 |
| with an h. kiss | BIBLE 55:2 |
| **Holy Ghost**: Come, H. | BOOK 69:16 |
| I believe in the H. | BOOK 64:3 |
| temple of the H. | BIBLE 55:6 |
| **homage**: claims the h. of a tear | BYRON 84:30 |
| **home**: ashamed of h. | DICK 118:25 |
| beating begins at h. | FLET 142:7 |
| can't find your way h. | COLL 105:7 |
| comes safe h. | SHAK 279:18 |
| Comin' for to carry me h. | ANON 10:17 |
| difficult is it to bring it h. | DOYLE 125:14 |
| earth is all the h. I have | AYT 23:18 |
| England, h. and beauty | ARN 18:14 |

**home** (cont.):

| | |
|---|---|
| first, best country is at h. | GOLD 155:4 |
| H. art gone and ta'en thy wages | SHAK 273:27 |
| H. is home | CLAR 101:15 |
| H. is the girl's prison | SHAW 302:4 |
| H. is the place where | FROST 146:11 |
| H. is the sailor | STEV 317:22 |
| H. James, and don't spare | HILL 168:16 |
| h. life of our own dear Queen | ANON 8:1 |
| H. of lost causes | ARN 18:2 |
| h. of the bean and the cod | BOSS 70:1 |
| h. of the brave | KEY 194:12 |
| h., rejoicing, brought me | BAKER 26:21 |
| H., Sweet Home | PAYNE 246:21 |
| H. they brought her warrior | TENN 327:26 |
| house is not a h. | ADLER 3:3 |
| hunter h. from the hill | STEV 317:22 |
| I can hang my hat is h. | JER 181:9 |
| it never is at h. | COWP 109:22 |
| Keep the H.-fires burning | FORD 143:12 |
| Look as much like h. as we can | FRY 147:2 |
| man goeth to his long h. | BIBLE 44:26 |
| My h. it is the Sule Skerry | BALL 27:17 |
| points of heaven and h. | WORD 357:9 |
| refuge from h. | SHAW 302:23 |
| their h. among the dead | SHEL 303:16 |
| there's nobody at h. | POPE 250:27 |
| there's no place like h. | PAYNE 246:21 |
| Till the boys come H. | FORD 143:12 |
| what is it to be at h. | BECK 31:7 |
| What's the good of a h. | GROS 159:3 |

**homeland**: more I loved my h. — BELL 34:5

**homely**: h. beauty — WORD 356:1

| though it be never so h. | CLAR 101:15 |
| youth have ever h. wits | SHAK 298:16 |

**Homer**: even excellent H. nods — HOR 173:3

| H. smote 'is bloomin' lyre | KIPL 197:14 |
| H. sometimes sleeps | BYRON 86:17 |
| In Homer more than H. knew | SWIFT 320:20 |
| Seven cities warred for H. | HEYW 168:9 |
| towns contend for H. | ANON 10:10 |

**homes**: h. without a friend — CLARE 101:5

| quiet h. and first beginning | BELL 34:3 |
| Stately H. of England | COW 108:8 |
| stately h. of England | HEM 165:10 |

**home-spuns**: hempen h. — SHAK 290:31

**homeward**: Look h. angel now — MILT 227:17

**rooks** in families h. go — HARDY 162:17

**homo**: Ecce h. — BIBLE 58:20

| Et h. factus est | MISS 231:16 |

**honest**: buy it like an h. man — NORT 240:9

| general h. thought | SHAK 282:2 |
| h. broker | BISM 59:18 |
| h. God is the noblest work | ING 178:15 |
| H. labour bears a lovely face | DEKK 116:9 |
| h. man's the noblest work | POPE 252:22 |
| h., sonsie face | BURNS 82:24 |
| H. to God | ROB 260:21 |
| least h. themselves | AUST 22:18 |
| She was poor but she was h. | ANON 10:11 |
| Though I am not naturally h. | SHAK 299:2 |
| we who lived by h. dreams | DAY-L 115:6 |
| whatsoever things are h. | BIBLE 56:9 |

**honestly**: If possible h. — HOR 173:6

**honesty**: H. is praised and left — JUV 189:1

| wins not more than h. | SHAK 280:20 |

**honey**: did but taste a little h. — BIBLE 41:14

| flowing with milk and h. | BIBLE 39:32 |
| gather h. all the day | WATTS 343:5 |
| hive for the h. bee | YEATS 359:12 |
| H., your silk stocking's | SELL 269:25 |
| is there h. still for tea | BROO 73:8 |
| They took some h. | LEAR 203:11 |
| With milk and h. blessed | NEALE 237:22 |

**honey-dew**: he on h. hath fed — COL 104:1

| | |
|---|---|
| **honeyed**: h. middle of the night | KEATS 190:17 |
| **honeysuckle**: h., I am the bee | FITZ 140:2 |
| **honi**: H. soie qui mal y pense | SELL 269:25 |
| *H. soit qui mal y pense* | ANON 12:5 |
| **honour**: air signed with their h. | SPEN 312:24 |
| All is lost save h. | FRAN 145:4 |
| as he was valiant, I h. him | SHAK 281:16 |
| cannot be maintained with h. | RUSS 265:6 |
| drownèd h. by the locks | SHAK 277:27 |
| Fear God. H. the King | KITC 198:8 |
| fighting for this woman's h. | KALM 189:20 |
| fountain of h. | BACON 24:10 |
| fountain of h. | BAG 26:4 |
| fount whence h. springs | MARL 219:9 |
| Giving h. unto the wife | BIBLE 57:10 |
| greater share of h. | SHAK 279:17 |
| helps the hurt that H. feels | TENN 326:8 |
| H. all men | BIBLE 57:9 |
| h., and keep her | BOOK 65:28 |
| h., and welfare of this realm | CHAR 95:1 |
| h. aspireth to it | BACON 24:21 |
| H. but an empty bubble | DRYD 127:21 |
| H. has come back | BROO 72:21 |
| h. is the subject of my story | SHAK 280:26 |
| h. rooted in dishonour | TENN 324:9 |
| h.'s voice provoke | GRAY 157:8 |
| H. thy father and thy mother | BIBLE 40:8 |
| Keeps h. bright | SHAK 297:5 |
| king delighteth to h. | BIBLE 42:20 |
| left hand riches and h. | BIBLE 43:8 |
| Leisure with h. | CIC 100:32 |
| louder he talked of his h. | EMER 136:20 |
| Loved I not h. more | LOV 210:21 |
| may we h. it | WEBS 344:11 |
| Mine h. is my life | SHAK 293:8 |
| new-made h. doth forget | SHAK 282:3 |
| Of h. and the sword | CHES 97:24 |
| peace I hope with h. | DISR 121:18 |
| peace with h. | CHAM 94:2 |
| pension list a roll of h. | CLEV 102:4 |
| plains of h. and reputation | JONS 187:13 |
| pluck bright h. | SHAK 277:27 |
| post of h. is a private station | ADD 2:17 |
| prophet is not without h. | BIBLE 50:7 |
| What is h.? A word | SHAK 278:12 |
| When h.'s at the stake | SHAK 276:31 |
| **honourable**: designs were strictly h. | FIEL 139:11 |
| For Brutus is an h. man | SHAK 281:19 |
| h. provision for well-educated | AUST 23:4 |
| Let us make an h. retreat | SHAK 273:3 |
| **honoured**: He hath h. me of late | SHAK 286:2 |
| h. in the breach | SHAK 274:26 |
| h. of them all | TENN 328:21 |
| **honours**: bears his blushing h. | SHAK 280:18 |
| **hoofs**: plunging h. were gone | DE L 116:20 |
| **hook**: leviathan with an h. | BIBLE 43:6 |
| **hoot**: literary mornings with its h. | AUDEN 20:25 |
| **hooting**: shunting and h. | BURR 82:32 |
| **Hoover**: onto the board of H. | GREER 158:11 |
| **hop**: H. forty paces | SHAK 271:16 |
| **hope**: Abandon all h. | DANTE 113:18 |
| against hope believed in h. | BIBLE 54:32 |
| All my h. on God is founded | BRID 71:24 |
| Beautiful Evelyn H. is dead | BROW 75:28 |
| best h. of earth | LINC 207:6 |
| equal poise of h. and fear | MILT 226:13 |
| faith, h., charity | BIBLE 55:14 |
| H. could ne'er have flown | MARV 220:12 |
| h. danceth without music | HERB 167:10 |
| H. deferred | BIBLE 43:21 |
| h. for greater favours | LA R 201:25 |
| h. for the best | SMITH 310:1 |
| Hopeless h. hopes | CLARE 101:5 |
| h. of the Resurrection | BOOK 66:8 |

# I

idle (cont.):
idle than when wholly i.     CIC 100:24
mock the air with i. state     GRAY 157:1
would all be i. if we could     JOHN 185:9
idleness: Grief is a species of i.     JOHN 182:15
I. is only the refuge     CHES 97:13
round of strenuous i.     WORD 356:11
idlers: loungers and i. of the Empire     DOYLE 126:4
progress is a doctrine of i.     BAUD 30:8
idling: enjoy i. thoroughly     JER 181:7
idol: one-eyed yellow i.     HAYES 163:21
idolatry: organization of i.     SHAW 301:26
idols: i. I have loved so long     FITZ 140:17
old i., lost obscene     BOTT 70:6
if: I. it moves, salute it     ANON 8:4
I. you can keep your head     KIPL 197:5
much virtue in 'i.'     SHAK 273:13
ignis: i. fatuus of the mind     ROCH 261:6
ignoble: doctrine of i. ease     ROOS 262:15
ignorance: except the fact of my i.     SOCR 310:21
helpless man, in i. sedate     JOHN 183:16
I. is not innocence but sin     BROW 76:9
I. is strength     ORW 242:7
i. it accumulates     ADAMS 1:20
Ignorance, madam, pure i.     JOHN 184:2
I. of the law excuses no     SELD 269:17
there is no sin but i.     MARL 218:19
What we call evil is simply i.     FORD 143:8
Where i. is bliss     GRAY 157:14
women in a state of i.     KNOX 198:21
ignorant: Confound the i.     SHAK 275:23
i. armies clash by night     ARN 16:12
i. have prescribed     DUPPA 129:12
they should always be i.     AUST 22:23
île: cette i. triste et noire     BAUD 30:5
ill: he thinks no i.     SHAK 299:20
I. fares the land     GOLD 154:18
i.-favoured thing     SHAK 273:11
I. met by moonlight     SHAK 290:22
Looking i. prevail     SUCK 318:20
means to do i. deeds     SHAK 282:12
Nothing i. come near thee     SHAK 273:28
one-third of a nation i.-housed     ROOS 262:11
though she's not really i.     JAGG 179:5
warn you not to fall i.     KINN 196:1
Will be the final goal of i.     TENN 325:8
illegal: i., immoral, or fattening     WOOL 354:8
illegitimate: strangled i. child     ARN 18:3
illegitimi: Nil carborundum i.     ANON 9:15
illimitable: i. inane     TENN 326:21
illiterate: I. him, I say     SHER 305:26
illness: i. in stages     GUIB 159:8
I. is the night-side     SONT 311:10
i. should attend it     SHAK 285:15
ills: i. of democracy     SMITH 309:2
no sense have they of i. to come     GRAY 157:12
rather bear those i. we have     SHAK 275:26
illuminatio: Dominus i. mea     BIBLE 58:9
illusion: great i.     ANG 5:17
nothing but sophistry and i.     HUME 176:4
illusions: It's life's i. I recall     MITC 232:3
image: age demanded an i.     POUND 254:16
fleeting i. of a shade     SHEL 305:17
graven i.     BIBLE 40:4
i. of death     ELIOT 132:16
i. of myself and dearer     MILT 229:16
i. walking in the garden     SHEL 304:15
Scattered his Maker's i.     DRYD 127:3
imagination: as i. bodies forth     SHAK 291:4
ideal of reason but of i.     KANT 189:24
if i. amend them     SHAK 291:8
i. droops her pinion     BYRON 86:19
i. resembled the wings     MAC 213:21
i. the rudder     KEATS 192:22
My shaping spirit of i.     COL 103:15

imagination (cont.):
no i. there is no horror     DOYLE 126:6
of i. all compact     SHAK 291:3
poetic i.     ELIOT 132:9
save those that have no i.     SHAW 302:21
scattered the proud in the i.     BIBLE 51:29
truth of i.     KEATS 192:23
whispering chambers of I.     DICK 119:7
imagine: I. there's no heaven     LENN 205:7
people i. a vain thing     BOOK 66:9
imaginings: less than horrible i.     SHAK 285:11
imitate: i. the action of the tiger     SHAK 279:5
Immature poets i.     ELIOT 135:2
imitation: All the art of I.     LLOYD 208:7
Genius is the child of i.     REYN 259:10
imitators: O i., you slavish herd     HOR 173:15
immanent: I. Will that stirs     HARDY 162:5
Immanuel: call his name I.     BIBLE 45:14
immemorial: doves in i. elms     TENN 328:8
immense: but error is i.     BOL 63:5
immensity: i. cloistered in thy dear womb
    DONNE 123:18
immoral: illegal, i., or fattening     WOOL 354:8
moral or an i. book     WILDE 350:3
immorality: i. is what they dislike     WHIT 348:3
nurseries of all vice and i.     FIEL 139:8
immortal: But in the flesh it is i.     STEV 316:11
I have lost the i. part     SHAK 292:8
I., invisible, God only wise     SMITH 310:15
I. longings in me     SHAK 272:7
make me i. with a kiss     MARL 218:11
they grow i. as they quote     YOUNG 360:13
What i. hand or eye     BLAKE 62:5
immortality: belief in i.     DOST 125:1
If I. unveil     DICK 120:11
just ourselves—and I.     DICK 120:9
Me only cruel i. consumes     TENN 328:17
Milk's leap toward i.     FAD 138:9
Millions long for i.     ERTZ 137:15
Their sons, they gave, their i.     BROO 72:20
immortalize: mortal thing so to i.     SPEN 313:4
imp: lad of life, an i. of fame     SHAK 279:10
impartial: neutrality of an i. judge     BURKE 81:12
impediment: cause, or just i.     BOOK 65:25
impediments: admit i.     SHAK 300:8
imperative: i. is Categorical     KANT 189:23
imperial: Of the i. theme     SHAK 285:19
imperialism: I. is the monopoly stage     LENIN 206:2
imperium: I. et Libertas     DISR 121:21
impertinent: ask an i. question     BRON 72:10
impious: i. men bear sway     ADD 2:17
imponere: I. Pelio Ossam     VIRG 340:6
important: i. thing is not the victory     COUB 108:15
importunate for being less i.     MONT 233:13
This is an i. book because     WOOLF 354:3
imported: i., elderly American     JENK 181:3
importunate: i. for being less important     MONT 233:13
importunity: ever-haunting i.     LAMB 200:10
impossibilities: i. enough in religion     BROW 74:10
Probable i. are to be preferred     ARIS 15:17
impossibility: by Despair upon I.     MARV 220:12
impossible: believe because it is i.     TERT 329:9
Dream the i. dream     DAR 114:2
have eliminated the i.     DOYLE 126:1
if he says that it is i.     CLAR 101:14
i. takes a little longer     CAL 88:6
i. things before breakfast     CARR 91:24
i. to be silent     BURKE 80:26
i. to carry the heavy burden     EDW 131:2
I wish it were i.     JOHN 186:16
That not i. she     CRAS 111:16
imposters: two i. just the same     KIPL 197:6
impotence: I. and sodomy     WAUGH 344:2
impotent: And an i. people     THOM 331:5
imprecision: Decay with i.     ELIOT 133:1

imprecision (*cont.*):
general mess of i. of feeling | ELIOT 133:6
impressionable: girl at an i. age | SPARK 312:12
impressive: few more i. sights | BARR 29:17
imprison: Take me to you, i. me | DONNE 123:11
imprisonment: leaves his well-beloved i. | DONNE 123:18
improbability: life is statistical i. | DAWK 115:4
improbable: preferred to i. possibilities | ARIS 15:17
improper: not a noun, proper or i. | FULL 147:4
impropriety: I. is the soul of wit | MAUG 222:9
indulge in, without i. | GILB 151:15
improve: I. each shining hour | WATTS 343:5
improved: enormously i. by death | SAKI 265:16
improvement: schemes of political i. | JOHN 184:22
improvisation: I. is too good to leave | SIMON 307:8
impudence: men starve for want of i. | DRYD 127:28
impulse: first i. was never a crime | CORN 108:3
impulses: no truck with first i. | MONT 234:1
impune: *Nemo me i. lacessit* | ANON 13:17
impunity: No one provokes me with i. | ANON 13:17
impure: Puritan all things are i. | LAWR 202:9
in: thy coming i. | BOOK 68:27
inability: i. to put on your socks | GONC 155:20
inactivity: wise and masterly i. | MACK 215:5
inane: along the illimitable i. | TENN 326:21
Pinnacled dim in the intense i. | SHEL 304:23
inapprehensible: I., we clutch thee | THOM 331:14
inarticulate: raid on the i. | ELIOT 133:6
inasmuch: I. as ye have done it | BIBLE 51:6
inaudible: I. as dreams | COL 103:19
in-between: Don't mess with Mister I. | MERC 223:9
inbreeding: Sick with i. | THOM 331:5
incapacity: dark sanctuary of i. | CHES 97:4
old maid courted by I. | BLAKE 61:2
incense: and i. of lowliness | MONS 233:3
incest: i. and folk-dancing | ANON 12:1
inch: Ay, every i. a king | SHAK 283:22
Every other i. a gentleman | WEST 346:26
inches: die by famine die by i. | HENRY 166:3
Some thirty i. from my nose | AUDEN 21:8
incident: determination of i. | JAMES 179:24
i. of the dog in the night-time | DOYLE 125:21
incisors: i. and grinders | BAG 26:15
inclination: not at the door of i. | DEFOE 115:12
ought to read just as i. | JOHN 184:10
incline: I. our hearts | BOOK 65:3
include: i. me out | GOLD 155:16
incognito: fallen angel travelling i. | QUEN 257:6
income: Annual i. twenty pounds | DICK 118:12
Expenditure rises to meet i. | PARK 245:20
£40,000 a year a moderate i. | LAMB 200:16
large i. is the best recipe | AUST 22:20
income tax: I. made more Liars than Golf | ROG 261:21
incomparable: i. Max | SHAW 302:24
incompetence: rise to his level of i. | PETER 248:8
incompetent: election by the i. many | SHAW 301:27
incomprehensible: i. man of 82 | VICT 338:5
inconnu: l'*I. pour trouver du nouveau* | BAUD 30:6
inconstancy: in Nature were i. | COWL 109:15
inconstant: i. woman | GAY 149:16
inconvenience: i. is often considerable | AUST 22:16
i. is only an adventure | CHES 98:8
not made without i. | JOHN 182:3
inconvenient: cause may be i. | BENN 34:18
incorruptible: dead shall be raised i. | BIBLE 55:21
seagreen I. | CARL 90:13
increase: creatures we desire i. | SHAK 299:11
God gave the i. | BIBLE 55:3
who dies fighting has i. | GREN 158:16
increasing: i., and ought to be diminished | DUNN 129:10
increment: unearned i. of rent | MILL 224:14
indecency: Decency is I.'s conspiracy | SHAW 302:3
indecent: sent down for i. behaviour | WAUGH 343:19

indecision: nothing habitual but i. | JAMES 180:8
index: i. of a feeling mind | CRAB 110:29
India: between Russia and British I. | SAL 266:3
From I.'s coral strand | HEBER 164:15
key of I. is London | DISR 121:22
Indian: lay out ten to see a dead I. | SHAK 296:4
Like the base I. | SHAK 293:5
only good Indian is a dead I. | SHER 305:22
poor I., whose untutored | POPE 252:13
Indians: America to convert the I. | WESL 346:12
indictment: I. against an whole people | BURKE 80:2
indifference: i. and a coach and six | GARR 105:12
indignation: i. can no longer tear | SWIFT 320:27
i. makes me write verse | JUV 189:2
Moral i. is jealousy | WELLS 346:1
Savage i. there | YEATS 360:2
indirections: By i. find directions out | SHAK 275:7
indiscretion: between a cliché and an i. | MACM 215:14
lover without i. | HARDY 161:21
inditing: My heart is i. | BOOK 67:5
individual: liberty of the i. | MILL 224:16
No i. could resent | SWIFT 320:24
not the i., but the species | JOHN 183:2
There are i. men and women | THAT 329:25
individualism: American system of rugged i. | HOOV 171:17
indolent: i. expression and an undulating | BELL 33:19
indomitable: Still the i. Irishry | YEATS 360:7
indubitably: They so very i. *are* | BEER 32:7
indulgent: makes one very i. | STAËL 314:5
industries: solemnest of i. | DICK 120:10
industry: Avarice, the spur of i. | HUME 176:5
Captains of i. | CARL 90:20
greatest river of human i. | TOCQ 333:5
i. will supply their deficiency | REYN 259:8
i. without art | RUSK 264:11
national i. of Prussia | MIR 231:8
Nobility of birth abateth i. | BACON 25:5
not his i. only | BURKE 80:22
inebriate: cheer but not i. | BERK 35:16
cheer but not i. | COWP 110:11
ineffectual: Remote and i. Don | BELL 33:16
inefficient: efficient and the i. | SHAW 301:7
inevitability: i. of gradualness | WEBB 344:6
inexactitude: terminological i. | CHUR 99:4
infallible: only i. rule we know | SURT 319:7
infamy: date which will live in i. | ROOS 262:14
infancy: Heaven lies about us in our i. | WORD 355:20
Nations, like men, have their i. | BOL 63:4
infant: At first the i., mewling | SHAK 272:25
describe the i. phenomenon | DICK 119:16
i. crying in the night | TENN 325:9
Sooner murder an i. | BLAKE 61:10
infection: i. and the hand of war | SHAK 293:16
it's the i. of things gone | LOW 211:20
inferior: are disgraced by the i. | SHAW 301:31
i. without your consent | ROOS 262:6
inferiors: The English want i. | TOCQ 333:4
inferno: i. of his passions | JUNG 188:22
infidelity: i. and household removals | BAUD 30:7
I. does not consist | PAINE 244:6
infinite: i.-resource-and-sagacity | KIPL 197:24
I. riches in a little room | MARL 219:1
I. wrath, and infinite despair | MILT 229:6
silence of these i. spaces | PASC 246:3
Though i., can never meet | MARV 220:13
infinities: you numberless i. | DONNE 123:7
infinitive: When I split an i. | CHAN 94:11
infinity: i. in the palm of your hand | BLAKE 60:5
i. torments me | MUSS 236:15
shares the nature of i. | WORD 354:13
infirmity: last i. of noble mind | MILT 227:14
inflation: to get i. down | LAM 200:18
inflections: beauty of i. | STEV 316:13

| | |
|---|---|
| influence: tell where his i. stops | ADAMS 1:16 |
| win friends and i. people | CARN 90:28 |
| influences: bind the sweet i. | BIBLE 43:4 |
| in-folded: tongues of flame are i. | ELIOT 133:13 |
| inform: How all occasions do i. | SHAK 276:29 |
| information: I only ask for i. | DICK 118:15 |
| knowledge we have lost in i. | ELIOT 134:12 |
| ingratitude: As man's i. | SHAK 273:1 |
| I., thou marble-hearted fiend | SHAK 282:24 |
| inhale: and I didn't i. | CLIN 102:5 |
| if he doesn't i. | STEV 316:14 |
| inherit: i. the vasty hall of death | ARN 17:1 |
| they shall i. the earth | BIBLE 48:19 |
| inheritance: Ruinous i. | GAIUS 147:13 |
| inherited: i. it brick and left it marble | AUG 22:7 |
| inhumanity: Man's i. to man | BURNS 82:16 |
| inimitable: Faintly the i. rose | WINC 352:3 |
| iniquities: bruised for our i. | BIBLE 46:19 |
| iniquity: i. of the fathers | BIBLE 40:5 |
| loved justice and hated i. | GREG 158:13 |
| injuries: adding insult to i. | MOORE 234:4 |
| take revenge for slight i. | MACH 214:23 |
| injury: i. much sooner forgotten | CHES 97:5 |
| injustice: all the rapine and i. | SMITH 308:20 |
| i. is done to someone | ULP 336:10 |
| i. makes democracy necessary | NIEB 239:14 |
| justice or i. of the cause | JOHN 183:17 |
| so finely felt, as i. | DICK 118:23 |
| injustices: only to justify their i. | VOLT 340:14 |
| ink: all cough in i. | YEATS 359:23 |
| he hath not drunk i. | SHAK 284:15 |
| i. in my pen ran cold | WALP 341:17 |
| inlaid: i. with patines of bright | SHAK 290:2 |
| inn: by a good tavern or i. | JOHN 185:8 |
| Do you remember an I. | BELL 34:1 |
| earth his sober i. | CAMP 89:3 |
| I count it not an i. | BROW 74:20 |
| room for them in the i. | BIBLE 51:32 |
| To gain the timely i. | SHAK 287:7 |
| world's an i. | DRYD 128:12 |
| inner: I. Resources | BERR 36:13 |
| Innisfree: and go to I. | YEATS 359:12 |
| innocence: badge of lost i. | PAINE 244:9 |
| ceremony of i. is drowned | YEATS 359:24 |
| Ignorance is not i. but sin | BROW 76:9 |
| i. is like a dumb leper | GREE 158:7 |
| innocent: i. and the beautiful | YEATS 359:8 |
| reward against the i. | BOOK 66:14 |
| than one i. suffer | BLAC 60:3 |
| innocents: I. Abroad | TWAIN 336:1 |
| innocuous: lambent but i. | GOUL 155:26 |
| innovations: i. are the births of time | BACON 24:30 |
| innovator: time is the greatest i. | BACON 24:31 |
| innuendoes: i. will serve him no longer | PULT 256:4 |
| Or the beauty of i. | STEV 316:13 |
| inoperative: previous statements are i. | ZIEG 361:3 |
| Inquisition: I. dogs | TENN 328:11 |
| inscriptions: in lapidary i. | JOHN 185:6 |
| inscrutable: Dumb, i. and grand | ARN 16:23 |
| insculped: I. and embossed | THOM 331:19 |
| insect: one is but an i. | JOHN 183:27 |
| transformed into a gigantic i. | KAFKA 189:16 |
| insensibility: No, Sir; stark i. | JOHN 183:21 |
| inside: i. the tent pissing out | JOHN 181:21 |
| insincerity: i. possible between | BAUM 30:11 |
| insolence: flown with i. and wine | MILT 228:15 |
| i. of wealth will creep | JOHN 185:19 |
| wretch who supports with i. | JOHN 182:10 |
| inspiration: Genius one per cent i. | EDIS 130:19 |
| inspire: Holy Ghost, our souls i. | BOOK 69:16 |
| inspissated: i. gloom | JOHN 184:21 |
| instinct: all healthy i. for it | BUTL 84:17 |
| such a gosling to obey i. | SHAK 273:21 |
| what we believe upon i. | BRAD 71:7 |

| | |
|---|---|
| instincts: animal, true to your i. | LAWR 202:16 |
| i. before which our mortal | WORD 355:22 |
| institute: I., Legion and Social | BETJ 36:22 |
| institution: more than a game. It's an i. | HUGH 175:23 |
| instruct: i. them or endure them | AUR 22:12 |
| instruction: I will better the i. | SHAK 289:18 |
| wiser than the horses of i. | BLAKE 61:8 |
| instrument: between your legs an i. | BEEC 32:4 |
| I tune the i. here at the door | DONNE 123:16 |
| make me an i. of Your peace | FRAN 145:7 |
| only the i. of science | JOHN 182:4 |
| instrumental: hand more i. to the brain | SHAK 274:4 |
| instruments: i. to plague us | SHAK 284:2 |
| What i. we have agree | AUDEN 20:21 |
| insufferable: Oxford made me i. | BEER 32:8 |
| insufficiency: i. of human enjoyments | JOHN 183:7 |
| insult: sooner forgotten than an i. | CHES 97:5 |
| This is adding i. to injuries | MOORE 234:4 |
| insulted: could never hope to get i. | DAVIS 114:23 |
| insurance: i. for all classes | CHUR 99:20 |
| intangible: O world i. | THOM 331:14 |
| integer: I. vitae scelerisque purus | HOR 173:21 |
| intellect: And put on I. | BLAKE 60:22 |
| feather to tickle the i. | LAMB 200:6 |
| i. is improperly exposed | SMITH 310:3 |
| i. of man is forced to choose | YEATS 358:19 |
| march of i. | SOUT 312:4 |
| Our meddling i. | WORD 357:5 |
| revenge of the i. upon art | SONT 311:9 |
| intellectual: An i. All-in-all | WORD 356:6 |
| For a tear is an i. thing | BLAKE 60:18 |
| i. and artistic personality | BERL 36:4 |
| i. is someone whose mind | CAMUS 89:4 |
| North-west passage to the i. | STER 315:21 |
| word 'l.' suggests straight away | AUDEN 21:3 |
| intellectuals: treachery of the i. | BENDA 34:7 |
| intelligence: i. by means of language | WITT 352:6 |
| I. is quickness to apprehend | WHIT 348:2 |
| Men started at the i. | SOUT 312:5 |
| people have little i. | LA BR 199:13 |
| intelligencies: we the i. | DONNE 124:3 |
| intelligent: Most i., very elegant | RUBY 77:31 |
| so elegant, so i. | ELIOT 134:24 |
| intensity: full of passionate i. | YEATS 359:24 |
| intent: His first avowed i. | BUNY 79:9 |
| prick the sides of my i. | SHAK 286:1 |
| truth that's told with bad i. | BLAKE 60:7 |
| interest: i. and fines on sorrow | MAY 222:16 |
| i.'s on the dangerous edge | BROW 75:15 |
| natural i. of money | MAC 213:10 |
| interested: I am only i. in money | SHAW 302:25 |
| proceedings i. him no more | HARTE 163:13 |
| interesting: person doing i. actions | BAG 26:12 |
| statements was i. | TWAIN 335:19 |
| interests: Our i. are eternal | PALM 244:18 |
| interim: i. is like a phantasma | SHAK 281:3 |
| intermission: but the i. of pain | SELD 269:20 |
| interpose: I should i. my body | STR 318:14 |
| interpretation: I. is the revenge of the intellect | SONT 311:9 |
| what is lost in i. | FROST 146:28 |
| interpreted: i. the world | MARX 221:11 |
| interrèd: good is oft i. | SHAK 281:18 |
| interval: make a lucid i. | DRYD 128:5 |
| intervals: Lucid i. and happy | BACON 25:22 |
| Not in the lucid i. of life | WORD 354:18 |
| interview: first strange and fatal i. | DONNE 123:5 |
| intestine: This is the dark i. | HUGH 175:21 |
| intimacy: without unseemly i. | LOW 211:11 |
| intolerable: burden of them is i. | BOOK 65:11 |
| I., not to be endured | SHAK 295:29 |
| intoxicated: A God-i. man | NOV 240:13 |
| intoxication: best of life is but i. | BYRON 86:7 |
| intricated: Poor i. soul | DONNE 124:22 |

intrigues: I. half-gathered — CRAB 110:19
intrinsicate: this knot i. — SHAK 272:8
invasion: against i. by an idea — HUGO 176:2
invent: necessary to i. him — VOLT 340:18
invented: only lies are i. — BRAQ 71:15
invention: i. is but the talent — BYRON 87:18
i. of a barbarous age — MILT 228:5
brightest heaven of i. — SHAK 278:33
wanting I.'s stay — SIDN 306:16
inventions: in her i. nothing is lacking — LEON 205:22
whoring with their own i. — BOOK 68:11
inventor: To plague her — SHAK 285:23
inverse: agenda will be in i. — PARK 245:22
inviolable: clutching the i. shade — ARN 17:12
inviolate: secret and i. Rose — YEATS 359:26
invisible: all things visible and i. — BOOK 65:5
Immortal, i., God only wise — SMITH 310:15
I., except to God alone — MILT 229:5
no i. means of support — BUCH 77:27
Oh may I join the choir i. — ELIOT 132:17
O world i., we view thee — THOM 331:14
priest of the i. — STEV 316:3
thy bloody and i. hand — SHAK 287:6
invocation: By i. of the same — ALEX 4:5
invulnerable: I. nothings — SHEL 303:10
inward: i. and spiritual grace — BOOK 65:23
They flash upon that i. eye — WORD 355:5
inwariable: double glass o' the i. — DICK 119:32
ipse: I. dixit — CIC 100:21
ira: Ça i. — ANON 12:2
Sine i. et studio — TAC 322:6
irae: Dies i., dies illa — MISS 231:23
Ireland: great Gaels of I. — CHES 97:20
How's poor ould I. — ANON 8:9
I. gives England her soldiers — MER 223:13
I. hurt you into poetry — AUDEN 20:22
I. is the old sow that eats her — JOYCE 188:7
Out of I. have we come — YEATS 359:19
Romantic I.'s dead and gone — YEATS 359:28
Irish: I. poets, learn your trade — YEATS 360:6
It is a symbol of I. art — JOYCE 188:12
Let the I. vessel lie — AUDEN 20:24
That is the I. Question — DISR 121:7
Irishry: Still the indomitable I. — YEATS 360:7
iron: Any old i., any old iron — COLL 105:6
beat the i. while it is hot — DRYD 128:26
blood and i. — BISM 59:19
i. curtain has descended — CHUR 100:1
i. entered into his soul — BOOK 68:9
nobles with links of i. — BOOK 69:11
Nor i. bars a cage — LOV 210:19
On i., wood and glass — DAV 114:21
painted to look like i. — BISM 59:21
Thorough the i. gates of life — MARV 221:1
what shall i. do — CHAU 95:22
irrational: exotic and i. entertainment — JOHN 182:22
irregulars: Baker Street i. — DOYLE 126:3
Ishmael: Call me I. — MELV 223:1
Isis: 'Till I.' elders reel — POPE 250:16
island: i. is made mainly of coal — BEVAN 37:17
i., the veranda, and the fruit — AUDEN 20:25
Look, stranger, at this i. now — AUDEN 20:26
No man is an I. — DONNE 124:19
Or some secreted i. — WORD 356:14
right little, tight little I. — DIBD 117:20
soggy little i. — UPD 336:12
islands: eye of peninsulas and i. — CAT 93:3
their favourite i. — AUDEN 20:14
isle: Fairest I., all isles excelling — DRYD 128:2
highly favoured i. — SOM 311:3
i. is full of noises — SHAK 296:9
it frights the i. — SHAK 292:7
ship, an i., a sickle moon — FLEC 141:19
this sceptered i. — SHAK 293:16

isles: i. of Greece! — BYRON 86:13
Islington: from I. to Marybone — BLAKE 60:17
isn't: but as it i., it ain't — CARR 91:20
isolation: Splendid I. — FOST 144:7
Israel: glory is departed from I. — BIBLE 41:11
I arose a mother in I. — BIBLE 40:31
I. loved Joseph more — BIBLE 39:24
I. shall be a proverb — BIBLE 41:29
I.'s monarch, after Heaven's own — DRYD 127:3
sweet psalmist of I. — BIBLE 41:28
Israelite: Behold an I. — BIBLE 53:15
issue: i. out of all their afflictions — BOOK 64:19
it: It's just I. — KIPL 198:4
Italia: I.! oh Italia! — BYRON 85:7
Italian: Or perhaps I. — GILB 152:21
to women I., to men French — CHAR 95:7
Italy: Graved inside of it, 'I.' — BROW 75:24
I. a paradise for horses — BURT 83:13
I. is a geographical expression — METT 224:3
made I. from designs by — TWAIN 336:2
Thou Paradise of exiles, I. — SHEL 303:21
itch: i. of literature — LOVER 210:22
itching: condemned to have an i. palm — SHAK 281:29
ite: I. missa est — MISS 231:20
Ithaka: When you set out for I. — CAV 93:10
iubeo: Hoc volo, sic i. — JUV 189:8
ivory: if in his i. tower — SAIN 265:14
i. on which I work — AUST 23:10
silver, i., and apes — BIBLE 41:31
With a cargo of i. — MASE 221:18
ivy: pluck an i. branch for me — ROSS 263:3
with i. never sere — MILT 227:10

# J

Jabberwock: Beware the J. — CARR 91:15
Jack: banish plump J. — SHAK 278:1
It's 'Damn you, J. — BONE 63:10
jackals: J. piss at their foot — FLAU 141:12
jacket: short j. is always worn — EDW 130:22
jack-knife: Just a j. has Macheath — BREC 71:18
Jacks: He calls the knaves, J. — DICK 118:22
Jackson: J. with his Virginians — BEE 31:22
Jacob: Angel did with J. — WALT 342:15
J. served seven years — BIBLE 39:22
traffic of J.'s ladder — THOM 331:16
voice is J.'s voice — BIBLE 39:20
jade: Let the galled j. wince — SHAK 276:10
jades: Go spin, you j. — PEMB 247:5
pampered j. of Asia — MARL 219:14
pampered j. of Asia — SHAK 278:21
jail: being in a ship is being in a j. — JOHN 184:5
patron, and the j. — JOHN 183:12
stealin' dey gits you in j. — O'NEI 241:9
jam: j. to-morrow — CARR 91:23
jamais: j. triste archy — MARQ 219:19
James: J. James Morrison — MILNE 225:20
J. the old Pretender — GUED 159:7
Jane: J., Jane, tall as a crane — SITW 307:16
Me Tarzan, you J. — WEIS 345:4
January: Generals Janvier [J.] — NICH 239:11
Jarndyce: J. and Jarndyce — DICK 118:1
jasper: j. of jocunditie — ANON 9:2
jaw: j. of an ass have I slain — BIBLE 41:5
jaw-jaw: j. better than to war-war — CHUR 100:3
jaws: Into the j. of Death — TENN 323:17
j. that bite, the claws — CARR 91:15
jazz: sunbathing and j. — WAUGH 343:22
jealous: Art is a j. mistress — EMER 136:19
as thou art j., Lord — DONNE 123:14
But jealous for they are j. — SHAK 292:22
j. confirmations strong — SHAK 292:18
J. in honour, sudden — SHAK 272:26

jealous (cont.):

| | |
|---|---|
| Lord thy God am a j. God | BIBLE 40:5 |
| Lord thy God is a j. God | BIBLE 40:21 |
| Not over-j., yet an eager husband | PHIL 248:16 |
| Of one not easily j. | SHAK 293:5 |
| jealousy: And J. a human face | BLAKE 62:7 |
| Anger and j. can no more | ELIOT 132:12 |
| indignation is j. with a halo | WELLS 346:1 |
| J. is no more than | BOWEN 71:1 |
| j. to the bride | BARR 29:15 |
| Nor j. was understood | MILT 229:17 |
| O! beware, my lord, of j. | SHAK 292:12 |
| Of cold age, narrow j. | ROCH 261:2 |
| quiet resting from all j. | FLET 31:2 |
| To j., nothing is more | SAGAN 265:13 |
| Jeanie: J. with the light brown | FOST 144:11 |
| jeans: j. and Coca-Cola | GREER 158:10 |
| jeepers: J. Creepers | MERC 223:10 |
| Jeeves: J. shimmered out | WOD 352:12 |
| jelly: Out, vile j. | SHAK 283:19 |
| jellybeans: way of eating j. | REAG 258:12 |
| je-ne-sais-quoi: J. young man | GILB 152:12 |
| Jenny: J. kissed me when we met | HUNT 176:15 |
| jerks: right to bring me up by j. | DICK 118:24 |
| Jerusalem: Built in J.'s wall | BLAKE 60:20 |
| holy city, new J. | BIBLE 58:4 |
| J. builded here | BLAKE 61:12 |
| J., my happy home | ANON 7:19 |
| J. the golden | NEALE 237:22 |
| J. thy sister calls | BLAKE 60:21 |
| there J.'s pillars stood | BLAKE 60:17 |
| jessamine: And the j. faint | SHEL 304:31 |
| Jesse: out of the stem of J. | BIBLE 45:18 |
| jesses: j. were my dear heart-strings | SHAK 292:14 |
| jest: die in earnest, that's no j. | RAL 257:22 |
| fellow of infinite j. | SHAK 277:8 |
| good j. for ever | SHAK 277:28 |
| J. and youthful jollity | MILT 227:1 |
| j.'s prosperity lies | SHAK 284:20 |
| Life is a j. | GAY 149:15 |
| jests: He j. at scars, that never | SHAK 294:29 |
| Jesu: J., good above all other | DEAR 115:7 |
| J., lover of my soul | WESL 346:8 |
| J., the very thought of Thee | CASW 92:17 |
| Jesus: At the name of J. | BIBLE 56:5 |
| Even so, come, Lord J. | BIBLE 58:8 |
| Gentle J., meek and mild | WESL 346:6 |
| How sweet the name of J. sounds | NEWT 239:9 |
| I am sure this J. will not do | BLAKE 60:14 |
| j. told him; he wouldn't believe | CUMM 112:19 |
| J. came to Birmingham | STUD 318:19 |
| J. Christ the same yesterday | BIBLE 56:30 |
| J. Christ were to come | CARL 90:26 |
| J. loves you more than | SIMON 307:6 |
| J. shall reign where'er the sun | WATTS 343:12 |
| J. the author and finisher | BIBLE 56:27 |
| J. wants me for a sunbeam | TALB 322:10 |
| J. wept | BIBLE 53:33 |
| J.! with all thy faults | BUTL 84:19 |
| more popular than J. now | LENN 205:8 |
| O J., I have promised | BODE 62:16 |
| Was J. chaste | BLAKE 60:13 |
| jeunesse: Si j. savait | EST 137:17 |
| Jew: for Englishman or J. | BLAKE 60:14 |
| Hath not a J. eyes | SHAK 289:16 |
| J.-ish. Not the whole hog | MILL 225:8 |
| Liver of blaspheming J. | SHAK 287:17 |
| which am a J. of Tarsus | BIBLE 54:23 |
| jewel: immediate j. of their souls | SHAK 292:11 |
| j. in the crown | GRAY 156:18 |
| j. of the just | VAUG 337:12 |
| precious j. in his head | SHAK 272:14 |
| rich j. in an Ethiop's ear | SHAK 294:26 |
| jewellery: just rattle your j. | LENN 205:9 |
| jewels: j. five-words-long | TENN 327:18 |

jewels (cont.):

| | |
|---|---|
| my j. for a set of beads | SHAK 294:2 |
| Jewish: J. man with parents | ROTH 263:14 |
| spit upon my J. gabardine | SHAK 289:5 |
| total solution of the J. question | GOER 154:1 |
| Jews: born King of the J. | BIBLE 48:9 |
| But spurn the J. | BROW 73:21 |
| Hitler attacked the J. | NIEM 239:15 |
| odd of God to choose the J. | EWER 138:2 |
| Till the conversion of the J. | MARV 220:23 |
| Joan: greasy J. doth keel the pot | SHAK 284:23 |
| Job: heard of the patience of J. | BIBLE 57:4 |
| I am as poor as J. | SHAK 278:18 |
| job: Living is my j. and my art | MONT 233:16 |
| neighbour loses his j. | TRUM 335:5 |
| we will finish the j. | CHUR 99:16 |
| Jock: J. became a member | MCGR 214:22 |
| jog: j. on the foot-path way | SHAK 298:28 |
| man might j. on with | LAMB 200:16 |
| John: J. Anderson my jo | BURNS 82:11 |
| J. Peel with his coat so grey | GRAV 156:12 |
| J. Thomas says good-night | LAWR 202:10 |
| Land's End to J. of Gaunt | SPOO 313:24 |
| Johnny: J.-head-in-air | PUDN 256:3 |
| Little J. Head-In-Air | HOFF 169:20 |
| Och, J., I hardly knew ye | BALL 27:18 |
| Johnson: J. hewed passages | COLM 105:15 |
| J.'s morality was as English | HAWT 163:19 |
| There is no arguing with J. | GOLD 155:14 |
| join: j. the choir invisible | ELIOT 132:17 |
| that j. house to house | BIBLE 45:8 |
| joined: j. together in holy Matrimony | BOOK 65:25 |
| What therefore God hath j. | BIBLE 50:20 |
| joint: j. and motive of her body | SHAK 297:9 |
| time is out of j. | SHAK 275:6 |
| joints: Of all the gin j. in all | EPST 137:9 |
| tough j. more than somewhat | RUNY 264:6 |
| joke: Dullness ever loves a j. | POPE 250:13 |
| Life is a j. that's just begun | GILB 151:22 |
| jokes: difference of taste in j. | ELIOT 132:1 |
| hackneyed j. from Miller | BYRON 86:31 |
| my little j. on Thee | FROST 146:10 |
| jollity: Jest and youthful j. | MILT 227:1 |
| jolly: J. boating weather | CORY 108:11 |
| wish I thought What J. Fun! | RAL 258:6 |
| Jonathan: Saul and J. were lovely | BIBLE 41:22 |
| jonquil: j. o'ercomes the feeble | WINC 352:2 |
| Jonson: If J.'s learnèd sock be on | MILT 227:8 |
| J. his best piece of poetry | JONS 187:19 |
| learn'd J., in this list I bring | DRAY 126:20 |
| Jordan: over J. and what did I see | ANON 10:17 |
| Joseph: Now Israel loved J. more | BIBLE 39:24 |
| Josephine: Not tonight, J. | NAP 237:8 |
| jostling: not done by j. in the street | BLAKE 61:15 |
| jot: one j. of former love retain | DRAY 126:16 |
| journal: J. is like a cake of portable | BOSW 70:4 |
| journalism: but why j.? | BALF 27:11 |
| journalist: British j. | WOLFE 353:2 |
| journalists: j. have constructed | LICH 207:1 |
| journey: begin a j. on Sundays | SWIFT 320:8 |
| death the j.'s end | DRYD 128:12 |
| dreariest and the longest j. go | SHEL 303:16 |
| Here is my j.'s end | SHAK 293:4 |
| j. I prepare as for death | MANS 217:15 |
| j. take the whole long day | ROSS 263:5 |
| j.-work of the stars | WHIT 348:18 |
| long day's j. into night | O'NEI 241:11 |
| Ulysses has made a great j. | DU B 128:33 |
| Up, lad: when the j.'s over | HOUS 174:18 |
| worst time of year for a j. | ANDR 5:15 |
| worst time of year for a j. | ELIOT 133:21 |
| journeying: sat the j. boy | HARDY 162:14 |
| journeyman: I was a j. to grief | SHAK 293:12 |
| journeys: J. end in lovers meeting | SHAK 297:23 |
| Jowett: First come I; my name is J. | BEEC 32:6 |

**joy:** And J., whose hand is ever | KEATS 191:27
Break forth into j. | BIBLE 46:16
good tidings of great j. | BIBLE 52:1
He who binds to himself a j. | BLAKE 61:16
I wish you all j. of the worm | SHAK 272:6
J. always came after pain | APOL 14:12
J., beautiful radiance of the gods | SCH 267:18
j. cometh in the morning | BOOK 66:22
j. is ever on the wing | MILT 230:9
J. of heav'n, to earth | WESL 346:10
j. of love is too short | MAL 217:2
j. of the working | KIPL 197:13
J. shall be in heaven over | BIBLE 52:28
j.'s soul lies in the doing | SHAK 296:29
j. that the day has brought | BOND 63:9
j. the world can give like | BYRON 87:9
kisses the j. as it flies | BLAKE 61:16
Labour without j. is base | RUSK 264:18
let j. be unconfined | BYRON 85:3
Lord of all j. | STR 318:17
much j. or too much fear | GRAV 156:14
My scrip of j., immortal diet | RAL 257:23
Of crimson j. | BLAKE 62:4
shall reap in j. | BOOK 68:29
stern j. which warriors feel | SCOTT 268:9
Strength through j. | LEY 206:20
Such perfect j. therein I find | DYER 129:16
Surprised by j. | WORD 357:4
thing of beauty is a j. for ever | KEATS 190:11
Where there is sadness, j. | FRAN 145:7
**joyful:** O be j. in the Lord | BOOK 68:5
**joyfully:** Sing j. to God | BIBLE 58:10
**joys:** All my j. to this are folly | BURT 83:5
But all their j. are one | WATTS 343:3
Earth's j. grow dim | LYTE 212:20
Hence, vain deluding j. | MILT 226:22
It redoubleth j. | BACON 24:24
j. are more to flesh | DRYD 127:32
J. in another's loss of ease | BLAKE 62:2
Their homely j., and destiny | GRAY 157:7
Thou minds me o' departed j. | BURNS 81:28
Thy j. when shall I see | ANON 7:19
While lasting j. the man attend | WHUR 349:4
Youth's the season made for j. | GAY 149:6
**jubilate:** J. Deo | BIBLE 58:10
**jubilee:** day of our J. is death | BROW 74:17
**Judah:** Once the sight of J.'s seer | MANT 217:17
**Judas:** In the lost boyhood of J. | Æ 3:4
**judge:** after a time they j. them | WILDE 350:12
be decided by the j. | JOHN 183:17
J. none blessed before | BIBLE 48:1
J. not, that ye be not judged | BIBLE 49:6
j. thou my cause | BIBLE 47:3
neutrality of an impartial j. | BURKE 81:12
righteousness shall he j. | BOOK 68:4
Sole j. of truth, in endless | POPE 252:18
**judged:** if j. by himself | JUV 189:14
**judgement:** Daniel come to j. | SHAK 289:29
day of j. | BOOK 64:16
Don't wait for the last j. | CAMUS 89:6
God's great J. Seat | KIPL 196:4
history is the world's j. | SCH 267:21
It biases the j. | DOYLE 126:5
j. of his peers | MAGN 216:16
j. was set | BIBLE 47:15
j. will probably be right | MANS 217:16
leaves of thy J. Book unfold | TAYL 323:4
not his industry only, but his j. | BURKE 80:22
people's j. always true | DRYD 127:15
will replace reasoned j. | JUV 189:8
**judges:** And were j. of fact | PULT 256:4
hundred j. have declared it so | QUIL 257:7
hungry j. soon the sentence sign | POPE 253:8
**judicious:** little j. levity | STEV 317:11

**Judy O'Grady:** Colonel's Lady an' J. | KIPL 196:19
**jug:** J., jug, jug | LYLY 212:17
'J. Jug' to dirty ears | ELIOT 134:22
j. of wine, a loaf of bread | FITZ 140:6
**Julia:** kiss my J.'s dainty leg | HERR 167:20
Whenas in silks my J. goes | HERR 167:26
Where my J.'s lips do smile | HERR 167:13
**Juliet:** J. is the sun | SHAK 294:29
**July:** Born on the fourth of J. | COHAN 103:5
High as a flag on the Fourth of J. | HAMM 161:4
**Jumblies:** lands where the J. live | LEAR 203:10
**jump:** We'd j. the life to come | SHAK 285:22
**June:** January, J., or July | NORW 240:11
J. that was stabbed | ARAG 14:21
meetings made December J. | TENN 325:20
Unwontedly. It was late J. | THOM 330:21
When J. is past, the fading | CAREW 89:20
**jungle:** not a concrete j. | MORR 235:12
this is the Law of the J. | KIPL 198:1
**juniper:** sat under a j.-tree | ELIOT 132:20
**junk:** Ep's statues are j. | ANON 8:2
**Juno:** J.'s never-forgetting anger | VIRG 338:23
**Jupiter:** J. from on high laughs | OVID 243:10
**jury:** j. do the deciding | CHEK 97:1
**just:** all j. works do proceed | BOOK 64:11
gods are j. | SHAK 284:2
He was a good man, and a j. | BIBLE 53:5
jewel of the j. | VAUG 337:12
j. and on the unjust | BIBLE 48:24
J. are the ways of God | MILT 230:14
J. as I am, without one plea | ELL 136:2
j. one of those things | PORT 253:21
'j.' or 'right' means | PLATO 249:21
j. representations of general | JOHN 182:24
J. when we are safest | BROW 75:13
J. when you thought it was safe | ANON 8:15
land of j. and old renown | TENN 329:1
ninety and nine j. persons | BIBLE 52:28
Only the actions of the j. | SHIR 306:11
rain, it raineth on the j. | BOWEN 70:14
reflect that God is j. | JEFF 180:24
that hath his quarrel j. | SHAK 280:8
Thou art indeed j. | HOPK 172:18
whatsoever things are j. | BIBLE 56:9
**justest:** wisest and j. and best | PLATO 249:20
**justice:** Die he or j. must | MILT 229:3
For J., though she's painted | BUTL 84:7
j. be done though the heavens | WATS 342:25
J. is in one scale | JEFF 180:25
j. is open to all | MATH 222:7
J. is truth in action | DISR 121:12
j. makes democracy possible | NIEB 239:14
j. of my quarrel | ANON 8:7
J. or injustice | JOHN 183:17
J. should not only be done | HEW 168:4
'J.' was done | HARDY 161:25
J. with mercy | MILT 229:29
Let j. be done | FERD 138:24
liberty plucks j. by the nose | SHAK 288:9
like the old line about j. | OSB 242:25
loved j. and hated iniquity | GREG 158:13
or j. or human happiness | BERL 36:6
price of j. is eternal publicity | BENN 34:17
pursuit of j. is no virtue | GOLD 155:15
Revenge is a kind of wild j. | BACON 25:9
sell, or deny, or delay, right or j. | MAGN 216:17
Though j. be thy plea | SHAK 289:27
truth, j. and the American way | ANON 7:5
what you think j. requires | MANS 217:16
Yes, you have ravished j. | WEBS 344:24
**justifiable:** j. to men | MILT 230:14
**justifies:** end j. the means | BUS 83:16
**justify:** j. the ways of God to men | MILT 228:9

**justify** (cont.):
| | |
|---|---|
| To j. God's ways to man | HOUS 175:4 |
| **justitia:** Fiat j. et pereat mundus | FERD 138:24 |
| **justly:** to do j., and to love mercy | BIBLE 47:23 |

# K

| | |
|---|---|
| **Kaiser:** kibosh on the K. | ELL 135:20 |
| **Kansas:** corny as K. in August | HAMM 161:4 |
| K. had better stop raising corn | LEASE 203:20 |
| What the horses o' K. think | KIPL 197:16 |
| **Kaspar:** Old K.'s work was done | SOUT 311:18 |
| **Keats:** K.'s vulgarity | LEAV 203:22 |
| out-glittering K. | BULW 78:10 |
| **keel:** greasy Joan doth k. the pot | SHAK 284:23 |
| **keener:** edged tool that grows k. | IRV 178:19 |
| **keep:** Except the Lord k. the city | BOOK 68:30 |
| If you can k. your head | KIPL 197:5 |
| k. 'em down on the farm | YOUNG 206:17 |
| k. her in sickness | BOOK 65:28 |
| K. right on to the end | LAUD 202:5 |
| K. the aspidistra flying | ORW 242:2 |
| k. the bridge with me | MAC 214:4 |
| k. thee in all thy ways | BOOK 67:30 |
| k. thee only unto her | BOOK 65:28 |
| K. the Home-fires burning | FORD 143:12 |
| K. up your bright swords | SHAK 291:31 |
| K. violence in the mind | ALD 3:16 |
| k. your hearts and minds | BIBLE 56:8 |
| little to earn, and many to k. | KING 195:16 |
| mercy k. us in the same | BOOK 64:25 |
| some day it'll k. you | WEST 346:19 |
| ware that will not k. | HOUS 174:18 |
| **keeper:** Am I my brother's k. | BIBLE 39:4 |
| **keeping:** k. up with yesterday | MARQ 219:15 |
| **keeps:** gave it us for k. | AYRES 23:15 |
| He jus' k. rollin' along | HAMM 161:3 |
| **Kelly:** K. from the Isle of Man | LETT 236:12 |
| **Kensal Green:** by way of K. | CHES 98:3 |
| **Kent:** K.—apples, cherries, hops | DICK 119:26 |
| **kept:** I have k. the faith | BIBLE 56:11 |
| I k. my word,' he said | DE L 116:19 |
| **kersey:** honest k. noes | SHAK 284:19 |
| **kettle:** speech is like a cracked k. | FLAU 141:7 |
| **key:** half that's got my k. | KEATS 192:13 |
| k. of India is London | DISR 121:22 |
| k. of knowledge | BIBLE 52:16 |
| out of k. with his time | POUND 254:14 |
| with this k. Shakespeare | WORD 356:21 |
| **keys:** half that's got my k. | GRAH 156:3 |
| **khaki:** gentleman in K. | KIPL 196:2 |
| **Khatmandu:** idol to the north of K. | HAYES 163:21 |
| **kibosh:** k. on the Kaiser | ELL 135:20 |
| **kick:** great k. at misery | LAWR 202:25 |
| k. against the pricks | BIBLE 54:12 |
| under water I would scarcely k. | KEATS 193:7 |
| **kicked:** and no body to be k. | THUR 332:19 |
| k. up stairs | HAL 160:12 |
| **kid:** Here's looking at you, k. | EPST 137:11 |
| lie down with the k. | BIBLE 45:19 |
| **kiddies:** k. have crumpled | BETJ 37:2 |
| **kidding:** k., Mr Hitler | PERRY 248:5 |
| **kids:** don't have any k. yourself | LARK 201:18 |
| **kill:** Be my brother, or I k. you | CHAM 94:5 |
| get out and k. something | LEAC 203:4 |
| k. a good book | MILT 230:29 |
| k. animals and stick in stamps | NIC 239:13 |
| k. a wife with kindness | SHAK 295:28 |
| K. millions of men | ROST 263:12 |
| k. more women and children | BALD 27:5 |
| k. one another if it is not done | SHAW 301:14 |
| k. the patient | BACON 24:25 |
| k. us for their sport | SHAK 283:21 |
| k. you in a new way | ROG 262:2 |

**kill** (cont.):
| | |
|---|---|
| let's k. all the lawyers | SHAK 280:10 |
| Otherwise k. me | MACN 216:7 |
| poor half-kisses k. me | DRAY 126:21 |
| sin to k. a mockingbird | LEE 204:6 |
| Thou shalt not k. | BIBLE 40:9 |
| Thou shalt not k.; but need'st | CLOU 102:17 |
| **killed:** don't mind your being k. | KITC 198:9 |
| I am the enemy you k. | OWEN 244:3 |
| I kissed thee ere I k. thee | SHAK 293:6 |
| k. than frightened to death | SURT 319:12 |
| Roaring Bill (who k. him) | BELL 33:28 |
| **killer:** lover and k. are mingled | DOUG 125:10 |
| **killeth:** letter k. | BIBLE 55:23 |
| **killing:** k. frost | SHAK 280:18 |
| K. no murder briefly discourst | SEXBY 270:14 |
| k. of a mouse on Sunday | BRAT 71:16 |
| k. time is only the name | SITW 307:22 |
| Men talk of k. time | BOUC 70:8 |
| **kills:** It spots and k. anything | WAUGH 343:17 |
| man k. the thing he loves | WILDE 350:16 |
| With a grip that k. it | TAG 322:9 |
| **Kiltartan:** My country is K. Cross | YEATS 359:9 |
| **kin:** little more than k. | SHAK 274:5 |
| makes the whole world k. | SHAK 297:6 |
| **kind:** enjoy her while she's k. | DRYD 128:23 |
| I must be cruel only to be k. | SHAK 276:24 |
| just the art of being k. | WILC 349:15 |
| K. hearts are more than coronets | TENN 325:33 |
| makes one wond'rous k. | GARR 148:10 |
| more than kin, and less than k. | SHAK 274:5 |
| not k. sir quite usual | ASHF 18:22 |
| people will always be k. | SASS 267:9 |
| Too kind, too k. | NIGH 240:1 |
| **kindest:** k. and the best | BURNS 82:17 |
| **kindle:** k. a light in the darkness | JUNG 188:23 |
| **kindliness:** cool k. of sheets | BROO 73:1 |
| **kindness:** it generates k. | JOHN 183:20 |
| kill a wife with k. | SHAK 295:28 |
| K. in another's trouble | GORD 155:21 |
| k. of strangers | WILL 351:6 |
| milk of human k. | SHAK 285:15 |
| We'll tak a cup o' k. yet | BURNS 81:25 |
| **king:** Authority forgets a dying k. | TENN 324:18 |
| banners of the k. advance | FORT 144:5 |
| born K. of the Jews | BIBLE 48:9 |
| despised, and dying k. | SHEL 305:3 |
| divinity doth hedge a k. | SHAK 277:1 |
| every inch a k. | SHAK 283:22 |
| fair and fatal k. | JOHN 181:17 |
| Fear God. Honour the k. | BIBLE 57:9 |
| fight for its K. and Country | GRAH 156:2 |
| follow the K. | TENN 324:5 |
| God save our gracious k. | ANON 7:13 |
| God save the k. | BIBLE 41:12 |
| God save the k. | HOGG 170:8 |
| God save the k. | SHAK 294:4 |
| heart and stomach of a k. | ELIZ 135:6 |
| Here lies a great and mighty k. | ROCH 261:4 |
| I have made unto the K. | BOOK 67:5 |
| I have served the K. | WOLS 353:16 |
| I served my k. | SHAK 280:21 |
| K. asked the Queen | MILNE 225:22 |
| K. born of all England | MAL 216:23 |
| k. can do no wrong | BLAC 60:2 |
| K. David and K. Solomon | NAYL 237:20 |
| k. delighteth to honour | BIBLE 42:20 |
| K. enjoys his own again | PARK 245:18 |
| k. indeed | CHAP 94:16 |
| k. is but a man | SHAK 279:12 |
| k. is truly parens patriae | JAM 179:10 |
| k. never dies | BLAC 60:1 |
| K., observing with judicious eyes | TRAPP 334:3 |
| K. of all these the dead | HOMER 171:3 |
| K. of glory shall come in | BOOK 66:20 |

**king** (cont.):

| | |
|---|---|
| K. of heaven | LYTE 212:21 |
| k. of infinite space | SHAK 275:15 |
| k. of intimate delights | COWP 110:12 |
| K. of love my shepherd is | BAKER 26:1 |
| k. of shreds and patches | SHAK 276:21 |
| K. of tremendous majesty | MISS 231:24 |
| K. over the Water | ANON 8:16 |
| k.'s a bawcock | SHAK 279:10 |
| k.'s head on republican | SHAW 302:9 |
| K.'s life is moving peacefully | DAWS 115:5 |
| K.'s Moll Reno'd | ANON 8:17 |
| k.'s name is a tower | SHAK 294:20 |
| k. sits in Dunfermline town | BALL 28:4 |
| K. to have things done as cheap | PEPYS 247:15 |
| K. to Oxford sent a troop | BROW 74:25 |
| K. will never leave | ELIZ 135:19 |
| little profits that an idle k. | TENN 328:19 |
| man who would be k. | KIPL 197:27 |
| *more royalist than the k.* | ANON 12:8 |
| No bishop, no K. | JAM 179:11 |
| *not offended the k.* | MORE 235:1 |
| once and future k. | WHITE 347:18 |
| one-eyed man is k. | ERAS 137:14 |
| passing brave to be a k. | MARL 219:7 |
| played the K. | FIELD 139:3 |
| Ruin seize thee, ruthless K. | GRAY 157:1 |
| still am I k. of those | SHAK 294:5 |
| subject's duty is the k.'s | SHAK 279:14 |
| What must the k. do now | SHAK 294:2 |
| when thy k. is a child | BIBLE 44:22 |
| your K. and your Country both | RUB 264:4 |

**kingdom**: In this k. by the sea POE 250:3

| | |
|---|---|
| k. against kingdom | BIBLE 50:34 |
| k. of the well | SONT 311:10 |
| k. stretch from shore | WATTS 343:12 |
| k. where nobody dies | MILL 224:21 |
| large k. for a little grave | SHAK 294:2 |
| my k. for a horse | SHAK 294:21 |
| My k., safeliest when | DONNE 123:6 |
| My mind to me a k. is | DYER 129:16 |
| seeking asses found a k. | MILT 230:5 |
| Thy k. come | BIBLE 48:27 |
| Thy k. is divided | BIBLE 47:12 |

**kingdom of God**: fit for the k. BIBLE 52:9

| | |
|---|---|
| he cannot see the k. | BIBLE 53:17 |
| k. is within you | BIBLE 52:36 |
| rich man to enter into the k. | BIBLE 50:22 |
| such is the k. | BIBLE 51:25 |

**kingdom of heaven**: inheritor of the k. BOOK 65:20

| | |
|---|---|
| k. is at hand | BIBLE 48:12 |
| k. is like to a grain | BIBLE 50:5 |
| shall not enter into the k. | BIBLE 50:15 |
| theirs is the k. | BIBLE 48:19 |
| thou didst open the K. | BOOK 63:20 |

**kingdoms**: goodly states and k. KEATS 192:10

**kingly**: k. crop DAV 114:11

**kings**: accounted poet k. KEATS 192:12

| | |
|---|---|
| be as happy as k. | STEV 317:13 |
| bind their k. in chains | BOOK 69:11 |
| cabbages—and k. | CARR 91:22 |
| captains and the k. depart | KIPL 197:2 |
| Conquering k. their titles | CHAN 94:6 |
| five K. left | FAR 138:14 |
| good of subjects is the end of k. | DEFOE 116:1 |
| heart of k. is unsearchable | BIBLE 43:34 |
| keep even k. in awe | D'AV 114:8 |
| K. and counsellors | BIBLE 42:26 |
| k. crept out again | BROW 74:27 |
| k. is mostly rapscallions | TWAIN 335:20 |
| k. that privates have not too | SHAK 279:15 |
| K. will be tyrants | BURKE 80:16 |
| mad k.! mad composition! | SHAK 282:4 |
| Physicians are like k. | WEBS 344:20 |
| politeness of k. | LOUI 210:17 |

**kings** (cont.):

| | |
|---|---|
| ruin k. | DRYD 127:4 |
| sport of k. | SOM 311:2 |
| sport of k. | SURT 319:8 |
| stories of the death of k. | SHAK 293:27 |
| Vain the ambition of k. | WEBS 344:13 |
| walk with K. | KIPL 197:7 |
| War is the trade of k. | DRYD 128:1 |
| Kipling: Rudyards cease from k. | STEP 315:5 |

**kiss**: Ae fond k. BURNS 81:22

| | |
|---|---|
| Colder than k. | BYRON 87:14 |
| come k. me, sweet and twenty | SHAK 297:23 |
| come let us k. and part | DRAY 126:16 |
| coward does it with a k. | WILDE 350:16 |
| die upon a k. | SHAK 293:6 |
| I k. his dirty shoe | SHAK 279:10 |
| I saw you take his k. | PATM 246:17 |
| k. again with tears | TENN 327:17 |
| k., a sigh, and so away | CRAS 111:15 |
| k. is still a kiss | HUPF 176:20 |
| K. me, Hardy | NELS 238:6 |
| K. me Kate | SHAK 295:27 |
| k. my ass in Macy's window | JOHN 181:20 |
| k. my Julia's dainty leg | HERR 167:20 |
| k. of the sun for pardon | GURN 159:10 |
| k. on the hand | ROBIN 260:18 |
| k. the rod | SHAK 298:17 |
| leave a k. but in the cup | JONS 187:23 |
| let me k. that hand | SHAK 283:24 |
| make me immortal with a k. | MARL 218:11 |
| rough male k. | BROO 73:1 |
| with an holy k. | BIBLE 55:2 |
| Wouldst k. me pretty | HART 163:11 |

**kissed**: Hasn't been k. for forty years ANON 9:5

| | |
|---|---|
| k. by a man who *didn't* wax | KIPL 198:3 |
| k. his sad Andromache | CORN 108:5 |
| k. thee ere I killed thee | SHAK 293:6 |
| righteousness and peace have k. | BOOK 67:23 |

**kisses**: At cards for k. LYLY 212:16

| | |
|---|---|
| fine romance with no k. | FIEL 139:14 |
| half-k. kill me | DRAY 126:21 |
| If you have forgotten my k. | SWIN 321:14 |
| more than k., letters mingle | DONNE 124:17 |
| remembered k. after death | TENN 327:23 |
| Stolen k. much completer | HUNT 176:16 |
| wastin' Christian k. | KIPL 196:22 |

**kissing**: die with k. of my Lord MARL 219:12

| | |
|---|---|
| K. don't last: cookery do | MER 223:17 |
| K. with golden face | SHAK 299:17 |
| when the k. had to stop | BROW 77:18 |

**kit-bag**: troubles in your old k. ASAF 18:17

**kitchen**: get out of the k. VAUG 337:2

| | |
|---|---|
| In k. cups concupiscent curds | STEV 316:5 |
| K.-cabals, and nursery-mishaps | CRAB 110:19 |

**Kitchener**: K. is a great poster ASQ 19:5

**kith**: If one's own kin and k. NASH 237:11

**knave**: makes an honest man a k. DEFOE 115:16

| | |
|---|---|
| slipper and subtle k. | SHAK 292:6 |

**knaves**: grudge at k. in place DEFOE 115:21

| | |
|---|---|
| He calls the k., Jacks | DICK 118:22 |
| most part of fools and k. | BUCK 78:1 |

**knavish**: either k. or childish JOHN 185:23

**knee**: every k. should bow BIBLE 56:5

**kneel**: K. and adore him MONS 233:3

**kneeled**: red-cross knight for ever k. TENN 326:2

**knees**: confirm the feeble k. BIBLE 46:5

| | |
|---|---|
| creeps rustling to her k. | KEATS 190:18 |
| in the heart, not in the k. | JERR 181:10 |
| than to live on your k. | IBAR 178:1 |
| With your body between your k. | CORY 108:11 |

**knell**: curfew tolls the k. GRAY 157:4

| | |
|---|---|
| k. that summons thee | SHAK 286:11 |
| strikes like a rising k. | BYRON 85:2 |

**knew**: He said it that k. it best BACON 24:15

| | |
|---|---|
| Johnny, I hardly k. ye | BALL 27:18 |

**knife**: k. see not the wound SHAK 285:19
progress if a cannibal uses k. LEC 204:1
smylere with the k. CHAU 95:27
War to the k. PAL 244:16
wind's like a whetted k. MAS 222:2
**knight**: Fearless, blameless k. ANON 12:4
K. of the Doleful Countenance CERV 93:16
k. was pricking on the plain SPEN 313:7
red-cross k. for ever kneeled TENN 326:2
verray, parfit gentil k. CHAU 95:12
**knighthoods**: looking for your k. KEAT 190:8
**knights**: ladies dead and lovely k. SHAK 300:4
**knits**: k. up the ravelled sleeve SHAK 286:15
**knitters**: k. in the sun SHAK 297:31
**knitting**: braids of lilies k. MILT 226:21
**knives**: night of the long k. HITL 168:21
**knock**: As yet but k., breathe DONNE 123:10
k., and it shall be opened BIBLE 49:9
K. as you please POPE 250:27
k. at the door LAMB 200:3
k. it never is at home COWP 109:22
right to k. him down for it JOHN 185:26
stand at the door, and k. BIBLE 57:23
Where k. is open wide SMART 308:11
**knocked**: K. down a doctor? SIMP 307:12
ruin that Cromwell k. about SULL 31:21
we k. the bastard off HILL 168:15
what they k. down FENT 138:23
**knocking**: k. at Preferment's door ARN 17:6
K. on the moonlit door DE L 116:18
**knocks**: k. you down with the butt GOLD 155:14
**knot**: certain k. of peace SIDN 306:20
crowned k. of fire ELIOT 133:13
political k. BIER 59:4
So the k. be unknotted ELIOT 132:24
this k. intrinsicate SHAK 272:8
**knots**: pokers into true-love k. COL 104:2
**knotted**: Sat and k. all the while SEDL 269:12
**knotty**: k. as a root of heath BRON 72:15
**know**: all ye need to k. KEATS 191:24
By their fruits ye shall k. them BIBLE 49:15
do not k. what they have said CHUR 99:5
do not wish to k. ask questions RAL 258:5
do were as easy as to k. SHAK 288:29
God made me to k. Him CAT 92:20
hate any one that we k. HAZL 164:7
He must k. sumpin' HAMM 161:3
How do they k. PARK 245:12
I do not k. myself GOET 154:14
k., and not be known COLT 105:18
k. enough who know how ADAMS 1:17
k. how to be oneself MONT 233:18
k. is what I read in the papers ROG 262:1
k. nothing except the fact SOCR 310:21
k. that I am God BOOK 67:7
k. that which we are BYRON 86:30
K. then thyself POPE 252:17
k. the place for the first time ELIOT 133:10
K. thyself ANON 13:5
k. to know no more MILT 229:12
k. what I think till I see what WALL 341:11
men naturally desire to k. AUCT 20:6
neither shall his place k. him BIBLE 42:31
no one to k. what it is ANON 6:21
now I k. it GAY 149:15
only thee, resolved to k. WESL 346:5
others that we k. not SHAK 275:26
place thereof shall k. it no more BOOK 68:7
So all we k. of what they do WALL 341:15
they k. not what they do BIBLE 53:2
things they didn't k. POUND 254:13
To k. the world, not love YOUNG 360:22
To k. this only MILT 230:7
We k. our will is free JOHN 184:20

**know** (cont.):
What do I k. MONT 233:18
what we would, we k. ARN 16:10
when it came to k. me well MOORE 234:19
Whitehall really does k. better JAY 180:15
**knoweth**: loveth not k. not God BIBLE 57:15
**knowing**: k. to what he was going HARDY 162:14
k. what should not be known FLEC 141:17
misfortune of k. any thing AUST 22:23
**knowledge**: After such k. ELIOT 133:15
all k. to be my province BACON 25:23
all mysteries, and all k. BIBLE 55:11
All our k. is, ourselves to know POPE 252:23
ask it for the k. of a lifetime WHIS 347:13
desire more love and k. SHAK 272:13
full of k. of the Lord BIBLE 45:20
he would bring home k. JOHN 185:18
increaseth k. increaseth sorrow BIBLE 44:10
in k. of whom standeth BOOK 64:5
K. comes, but wisdom lingers TENN 326:14
K. enormous makes a god of me KEATS 191:2
k. is bought in the market CLOU 102:11
K. is of two kinds JOHN 185:5
k. itself is power BACON 25:25
K. may give weight CHES 97:16
k. of causes BACON 25:26
K. of good and evil COWP 110:3
k. of nothing DICK 120:5
K. puffeth up BIBLE 55:7
k. we have lost in information ELIOT 134:12
k. which they cannot lose OPP 241:14
light of k. in their eyes SYM 321:20
little k. is dangerous HUXL 177:17
No man's k. here can go beyond LOCKE 208:14
Opinion in good men is but k. MILT 231:4
Out-topping k. ARN 17:14
Pedantry is the dotage of k. JACK 178:24
province of k. to speak HOLM 170:15
Science is organized k. SPEN 312:15
spirit of k. BIBLE 45:18
taken away the key of k. BIBLE 52:16
There's no k. but I know it BEEC 32:6
thorough k. of human nature AUST 22:22
too high the price for k. TICK 332:20
tree of the k. of good and evil BIBLE 38:19
**known**: Have ye not k.? BIBLE 46:12
If you would be k. COLT 105:18
know even as also I am k. BIBLE 55:14
k. and common way WINC 352:3
k. and the unknown PINT 248:21
k. no more than other men AUBR 19:17
k. too late SHAK 294:28
much to be done and little to be k. JOHN 182:27
safer than a k. way HASK 163:16
thy way may be k. upon earth BOOK 67:16
**knows**: HE k.—HE knows FITZ 140:13
He k. nothing SHAW 301:13
he K. Things MILNE 225:18
if you k. of a better 'ole BAIR 26:20
sits in the middle and k. FROST 146:20
**knuckle-end**: That k. of England SMITH 309:26
**Kruger**: killing K. KIPL 196:2
**Kubla**: In Xanadu did K. Khan COL 103:22
**Kurtz**: Mistah K.—he dead CONR 107:6
**kyrie**: K. eleison MISS 231:12

# L

**labor**: Hoc opus, hic l. est VIRG 339:12
**laboratory**: l. of God WILL 351:4
**laborious**: Studious of l. ease COWP 110:10
**labour**: done to the L. Party TAWN 322:21
fair shares for all, is L.'s call JAY 180:14
Honest l. bears a lovely face DEKK 116:9

**labour** (*cont.*):

| | |
|---|---|
| I have had my l. for my travail | SHAK 296:28 |
| insupportable l. of doing nothing | STEE 314:14 |
| l. and are heavy laden | BIBLE 49:35 |
| l. and not to ask for any reward | IGN 178:8 |
| l. of love | BIBLE 56:13 |
| l. we delight in physics pain | SHAK 286:22 |
| L. without joy is base | RUSK 264:18 |
| mixed his l. with | LOCKE 208:19 |
| My daily l. to pursue | WESL 346:5 |
| strength then but l. and sorrow | BOOK 67:26 |
| that's the task, that is the l. | VIRG 339:12 |
| their l. is but lost | BOOK 68:30 |
| to his work, and to his l. | BOOK 68:8 |
| true success is to l. | STEV 317:6 |
| usury ... to live without l. | TAWN 322:20 |
| with difficulty and l. | MILT 229:2 |
| youth of l. with an age of ease | GOLD 154:19 |

**labourage**: *L. et pâturage* — SULLY 319:3

**labourer**: l. is worthy of his hire — BIBLE 52:10

**labouring**: Sleep is sweet to the l. man — BUNY 79:4

| sleep of a l. man is sweet | BIBLE 44:15 |
|---|---|

**labours**: and no l. tire — JOHN 183:13

| Children sweeten l. | BACON 25:6 |
|---|---|
| Lingered l. come to naught | SOUT 312:8 |

**laburnums**: L., dropping-wells — TENN 325:15

**labyrinth**: peopled l. of walls — SHEL 304:1

**labyrinthical**: l. soul — DONNE 124:22

**labyrinthine**: down the l. ways — THOM 331:8

| Still more l. buds the rose | BROW 77:14 |
|---|---|

**lace**: Nottingham l. of the curtains — BETJ 36:16

**lacerate**: Cannot l. his breast — YEATS 360:2

**lack**: therefore can I l. nothing — BOOK 66:17

**lacrimae**: *Hinc illae l.* — TER 329:3

| l. rerum | VIRG 339:4 |
|---|---|

**lad**: l. that's born to be king — BOUL 70:10

| Sing me a song of a l. | STEV 317:23 |
|---|---|

**ladder**: l. set up on the earth — BIBLE 39:21

| Now that my l.'s gone | YEATS 358:16 |
|---|---|
| Wiv a l. and some glasses | BAT 30:1 |

**ladders**: where all l. start — YEATS 358:16

**laden**: labour and are heavy l. — BIBLE 49:35

**ladies**: Come from a l.' seminary — GILB 151:23

| Dust was Gentlemen and L. | DICK 120:17 |
|---|---|
| l. apparently rolled along | HUXL 177:10 |
| l. dead and lovely knights | SHAK 300:4 |
| l. of St James's | DOBS 122:27 |
| l. should ever sit down | MORE 234:22 |

**lads**: Come lasses and l. — ANON 6:19

| Golden l. and girls all must | SHAK 273:27 |
|---|---|
| l. that will never be old | HOUS 174:21 |

**lady**: certain little l. comes by — GAY 149:18

| dying l., lean and pale | SHEL 305:15 |
|---|---|
| full-blown l. | CLOU 102:7 |
| hound, and his l. fair | BALL 28:9 |
| I met a l. in the meads | KEATS 191:9 |
| kneeled to a l. in his shield | TENN 326:2 |
| Laces for a l. | KIPL 196:28 |
| lang will his L. look owre | BALL 27:15 |
| l. doth protest too much | SHAK 276:9 |
| l. is a tramp | HART 163:9 |
| L., it is to be presumed | JONS 187:5 |
| l. of a 'certain age' | BYRON 86:21 |
| l. *of* Christ's College | AUBR 19:20 |
| L. of Shalott | TENN 326:1 |
| L. of Spain, I adore you | REAV 258:13 |
| L.'s not for Burning | FRY 146:30 |
| l. sweet and kind | ANON 10:18 |
| l. that's known as Lou | SERV 270:13 |
| L. with a Lamp shall stand | LONG 209:25 |
| lovely l., garmented in light | SHEL 305:16 |
| Our L. of Pain | SWIN 321:8 |
| want to talk like a l. | SHAW 302:17 |
| when a l.'s in the case | GAY 149:10 |
| young l. named Bright | BULL 78:7 |

**Lady Jane**: good-night to L. — LAWR 202:10

**lady-smocks**: l. all silver-white — SHAK 284:21

**Lafayette**: L., *nous voilà!* — STAN 314:10

**laggard**: For a l. in love — SCOTT 268:20

**laid**: He l. us as we lay at birth — ARN 16:19

| When I am l. in earth | TATE 322:15 |
|---|---|

**lain**: l. for ages and will lie — TENN 325:32

**laisser-faire**: *L.* — ARG 15:6

**laissez-nous-faire**: *L.* — ANON 12:9

**laity**: conspiracies against the l. — SHAW 301:1

| To tell the l. our love | DONNE 124:15 |
|---|---|

**lake**: Cyprus with a l. of fire — FLEC 141:18

| into the bosom of the l. | TENN 328:5 |
|---|---|
| l. water lapping | YEATS 359:13 |

**lakes**: light shakes across the l. — TENN 327:20

**lamb**: Behold the L. of God — BIBLE 53:13

| blood of the L. | BIBLE 57:26 |
|---|---|
| Did he who made the L. | BLAKE 62:6 |
| holy L. of God | BLAKE 61:12 |
| L. of God, who takest away | MISS 231:19 |
| l. to the slaughter | BIBLE 46:20 |
| leads me to the L. | COWP 109:27 |
| Little L. who made thee | BLAKE 61:23 |
| Mary had a little l. | HALE 160:5 |
| save one little ewe l. | BIBLE 41:24 |
| tempers the wind to the shorn l. | STER 315:11 |
| wolf shall dwell with the l. | BIBLE 45:19 |

**lambent**: l. but innocuous — GOUL 155:26

**lambs**: he shall gather the l. — BIBLE 46:11

| l. could not forgive | DICK 119:9 |
|---|---|
| little l. eat ivy | DRAKE 126:14 |

**lamentable**: l. catalogue — CHUR 99:12

**lamentation**: l., and weeping — BIBLE 48:11

**lamp**: Lady with a L. — LONG 209:25

| leaning on a l.-post | GAY 149:18 |
|---|---|
| Slaves of the L. | ARN 16:7 |
| smell too strong of the l. | STER 315:16 |
| unlit l. and the ungirt loin | BROW 77:16 |
| When the l. is shattered | SHEL 303:24 |

**lampada**: *vitai l.* — LUCR 212:5

**lamprey**: surfeit by eating of a l. — FABY 138:7

**lamps**: Heav'n's great l. do dive — CAMP 89:2

| l. are going out all over | GREY 159:1 |
|---|---|
| old l. for new ones | ARAB 14:16 |
| Ye living l. | MARV 220:20 |

**land**: Ceres re-assume the l. — POPE 251:17

| England's green and pleasant l. | BLAKE 61:12 |
|---|---|
| French the empire of the l. | RICH 260:6 |
| good and bad of every l. | BAIL 26:19 |
| Ill fares the l., to hast'ning ills | GOLD 154:18 |
| l. flowing with milk and honey | BIBLE 39:32 |
| l. of embarrassment | BARN 29:4 |
| L. of Hope and Glory | BENS 34:20 |
| l. of lost content | HOUS 174:24 |
| l. of meanness, sophistry | BYRON 85:21 |
| l. of my fathers | THOM 330:20 |
| l. of poverty | BAUD 30:5 |
| l. of pure delight | WATTS 343:11 |
| l. of sand and ruin | SWIN 321:19 |
| l. of the living | BIBLE 46:20 |
| l. of the shadow of death | BIBLE 45:15 |
| L. that I love | BERL 35:21 |
| l. was ours before we were | FROST 146:13 |
| l. where the lemon-trees | GOET 154:13 |
| lane to the l. of the dead | AUDEN 20:12 |
| like night, from l. to land | COL 104:17 |
| O'er the l. of the free | KEY 194:12 |
| piece of l. not so very large | HOR 174:4 |
| pleasant l. of counterpane | STEV 317:14 |
| ready by water as by l. | ELST 136:7 |
| splendid and a happy l. | GOLD 154:25 |
| that think there is no l. | BACON 23:22 |
| There's the l., or cherry-isle | HERR 167:13 |
| This l. is your land | GUTH 159:12 |

land (cont.):
  Woe to the l. that's governed — SHAK 294:16
landing: fight on the l. grounds — CHUR 99:13
landlord: L., Fill the Flowing Bowl — ANON 6:18
lands: envy of less happier l. — SHAK 293:16
  Lord of himself, though not of l. — WOTT 357:15
landscape: Claude's l. — CONS 107:12
landscapes: If l. were sold — STEV 317:1
Land's End: L. to John of Gaunt — SPOO 313:24
lane: l. to the land of the dead — AUDEN 20:12
lang: y'er a l. time deid — ANON 6:9
language: best chosen l. — AUST 22:22
  cool web of l. — GRAV 156:14
  divided by a common l. — SHAW 302:27
  enlargement of the l. — JOHN 182:5
  Fancies that broke through l. — BROW 77:4
  In l., the ignorant have — DUPPA 129:12
  In such lovely l. — LAWR 202:24
  intelligence by means of l. — WITT 352:6
  l. he was the lodesterre — LYDG 212:13
  L. is fossil poetry — EMER 136:28
  L. is only the instrument — JOHN 182:4
  L. is the dress of thought — JOHN 182:19
  l. of priorities — BEVAN 37:19
  l. of the heart — POPE 251:9
  l. of the unheard — KING 195:11
  L. was not powerful enough — DICK 119:16
  l. which I spake unto thee — MAC 214:1
  Learned his great l. — BROW 76:14
  Life is a foreign l. — MORL 235:7
  limits of my l. mean — WITT 352:10
  mobilised the English l. — MURR 236:13
  Money speaks sense in a l. — BEHN 32:23
  natural l. of the heart — SHAD 270:17
  obscurity of a learned l. — GIBB 150:16
  our l. should perish — MAC 213:20
  Political l. — ORW 242:15
  some entrance into the l. — BACON 25:17
  Speech happens not to be his l. — STAËL 314:7
  There's l. in her eye — SHAK 297:9
  use any l. you choose — GILB 151:15
  with no l. but a cry — TENN 325:9
  You taught me l. — SHAK 295:35
languages: all l. living and dead — DICK 119:10
  great feast of l. — SHAK 284:17
  l. are the pedigree of nations — JOHN 183:18
  live l. for Miss Blimber — DICK 118:19
  wit in all l. — DRYD 128:27
languor: monotonous l. — VERL 337:21
languors: lilies and l. of virtue — SWIN 321:7
lantern: word is a l. unto my feet — BOOK 68:24
lap: flowery l. of earth — ARN 16:19
  fresh l. of the crimson rose — SHAK 290:23
  It lies in the l. of the gods — HOMER 170:23
  l. of the new come spring — SHAK 294:8
lapdogs: when l. breathe — POPE 253:10
lapidary: l. inscriptions — JOHN 185:6
lapidem: Gutta cavat l. — OVID 243:12
lapping: lake water l. — YEATS 359:13
lards: l. the lean earth — SHAK 277:29
large: It's as l. as life — CARR 92:4
  l.-brained woman — BROW 75:6
  l.-hearted man — BROW 75:6
  too l. to hang on a watch-chain — ANON 11:8
lark: bisy l., messager of day — CHAU 95:26
  l. ascending — MER 223:19
  l. at break of day — SHAK 299:15
  l. at heaven's gate — SHAK 273:25
  l. becomes a sightless song — TENN 325:30
  l. now leaves his wat'ry nest — D'AV 114:10
  l.'s on the wing — BROW 76:28
  nightingale, and not the l. — SHAK 295:17
larks: Four L. and a Wren — LEAR 203:17
  hear the l. so high — HOUS 174:20
Lars Porsena: L. of Clusium — MAC 214:2

lasciate: L. OGNI SPERANZA — DANTE 113:18
lash: dost thou l. that whore — SHAK 283:25
  rum, sodomy, and the l. — CHUR 100:6
lashes: That l. all with shade — WILB 349:13
lass: Amo, amas, I love a l. — O'KEE 241:5
  every l. a queen — KING 195:17
  It came with a l. — JAM 179:14
  It was a lover and his l. — SHAK 273:10
  l. unparalleled — SHAK 272:10
lasse: tout casse, tout l. — ANON 12:17
lasses: Come l. and lads — ANON 6:19
lassie: I love a l. — LAUD 202:6
last: Heaven's l. best gift — MILT 229:15
  It will l. my time — CARL 90:5
  l. and best of all God's works — MILT 229:27
  l. great Englishman is low — TENN 327:11
  l. person who has sat on him — HAIG 159:16
  l. red leaf is whirled — TENN 325:2
  l. romantics — YEATS 358:18
  l. shall be first — BIBLE 50:24
  l. thing I shall do — PALM 244:22
  l. time I saw Paris — HAMM 161:1
  live this day as if thy l. — KEN 193:21
  Look thy l. on all things lovely — DE L 116:15
  Nice guys. Finish l. — DUR 129:13
  there is no l. nor first — BROW 77:1
  they l. while they last — DE G 116:4
  unto this l. — BIBLE 50:26
  wait for the l. judgement — CAMUS 89:6
latchet: shoe's l. I am not worthy — BIBLE 53:12
late: Dread of being l. — BETJ 37:14
  five minutes too l. all my life — COWL 109:18
  offering even that too l. — NEV 238:9
  So l. into the night — BYRON 87:8
  Too l. came I to love thee — AUG 21:24
  too l. into a world too old — MUSS 236:17
  Which was rather l. for me — LARK 201:12
  white rose weeps, 'She is l.' — TENN 327:1
later: It is l. than you think — SERV 270:10
Latin: carve in L. or in Greek — WALL 341:13
  Devil knows L. — KNOX 198:19
  he speaks L. — SHAK 280:12
  L. for a whopping — ANST 14:10
  Ne yet of L., ne of Greek — SPEN 313:16
  No more L., no more French — ANON 9:17
  small L., and less Greek — JONS 187:27
latrine: mouth used as a l. — AMIS 5:2
latter: former and the l. rain — BOOK 64:20
  he shall stand at the l. day — BIBLE 42:36
laudamus: Te Deum l. — ANON 14:1
laudator: l. temporis acti — HOR 173:2
laugh: atheist-l.'s a poor exchange — BURNS 82:6
  L. and the world laughs — WILC 349:14
  l. at human actions — SPIN 313:23
  l. at them in our turn — AUST 23:6
  l. broke into a thousand pieces — BARR 29:11
  L. no man to scorn — BIBLE 47:33
  l. that spoke the vacant mind — GOLD 154:20
  l. the more heartily — RHYS 259:13
  L. where we must — POPE 252:11
  Never l. at live dragons — TOLK 333:9
  no girl wants to l. all the time — LOOS 210:9
  nothing sillier than a silly l. — CAT 93:4
  tickle us, do we not l. — SHAK 289:17
  time to weep, and a time to l. — BIBLE 44:12
  Wanna l. like a loon — HARB 161:13
laughed: When he l., respectable — AUDEN 20:18
laughing: Happiness is no l. matter — WHAT 347:6
  l. is heard on the hill — BLAKE 61:25
  Minnehaha, L. Water — LONG 210:2
  most fun I ever had without l. — ALLEN 4:13
laughs: l. to see the green man — HOFF 170:1
  she l. with a harvest — JERR 181:12
laughter: faculty of l. — ADD 2:27

**laughter** (*cont.*):

| | |
|---|---|
| grail of l. of an empty ash can | CRANE 110:32 |
| l. and ability and Sighing | DICK 120:17 |
| l. and the love of friends | BELL 34:3 |
| l. for a month | SHAK 277:28 |
| L. holding both his sides | MILT 227:2 |
| L. is pleasant | PEAC 246:25 |
| l., learnt of friends | BROO 73:10 |
| l. of her heart | HAMM 161:1 |
| L. only a scornful tickling | SIDN 306:29 |
| L. ... the most civilized music | UST 336:15 |
| Laugh thy girlish l. | WATS 342:26 |
| more frightful than l. | SAGAN 265:13 |
| Our sincerest l. | SHEL 305:10 |
| Present mirth hath present l. | SHAK 297:23 |
| so is the l. of a fool | BIBLE 44:16 |
| under running l. | THOM 331:8 |
| where l. may signify anger | TOFF 333:7 |
| **laurel:** Apollo's l. bough | MARL 218:14 |
| l. for the perfect prime | ROSS 263:3 |
| **laurels:** Birds on box and l. | SMART 308:9 |
| l. all are cut | ANON 12:13 |
| l. to paeans | CIC 100:23 |
| worth all your l. | BYRON 87:10 |
| Yet once more, O ye l. | MILT 227:10 |
| **lave:** Let the l. go by me | STEV 317:24 |
| **law:** army of unalterable l. | MER 223:22 |
| Born under one l. | GREV 158:19 |
| breaks the l. by corrupting | PLATO 249:18 |
| Custom, that unwritten l. | D'AV 114:8 |
| dusty purlieus of the l. | TENN 325:17 |
| end of l. is, not to abolish | LOCKE 208:20 |
| fugitive from th' l. of averages | MAUL 222:13 |
| good of the people is the chief l. | CIC 100:20 |
| Ignorance of the l. excuses | SELD 269:17 |
| I, my Lords, embody the L. | GILB 151:10 |
| Just to the windward of the l. | CHUR 98:23 |
| l. and the prophets | BIBLE 49:11 |
| l. can take a purse | BUTL 84:8 |
| l. is a ass | DICK 119:20 |
| L. is a bottomless pit | ARB 14:22 |
| l. is such an ass | CHAP 94:18 |
| L.: It has honoured us | WEBS 344:11 |
| L. of the Jungle | KIPL 198:1 |
| l. of the Medes and Persians | BIBLE 47:13 |
| l. of the Yukon | SERV 270:11 |
| L. to our selves | MILT 229:25 |
| lesser breeds without the L. | KIPL 197:4 |
| majestic equality of the l. | FRAN 145:2 |
| make a scarecrow of the l. | SHAK 288:12 |
| moral l. within me | KANT 189:22 |
| more ought l. to weed it out | BACON 25:9 |
| Necessity has no l. | PUBL 256:2 |
| Necessity hath no l. | CROM 112:6 |
| No brilliance is needed in the l. | MORT 235:21 |
| Nor l., nor duty bade me fight | YEATS 359:10 |
| not a l. at all | ROB 260:16 |
| not known sin, but by the l. | BIBLE 54:37 |
| of no force in l. | COKE 103:7 |
| old father antick, the l. | SHAK 277:24 |
| People crushed by l. | BURKE 81:9 |
| perfection of our l. | ANON 7:9 |
| prescription of the l. | LOCKE 208:21 |
| principle of the English l. | DICK 118:4 |
| Prisons built with stones of L. | BLAKE 61:7 |
| purlieus of the L. | ETH 137:18 |
| rich men rule the l. | GOLD 155:5 |
| royal L., lively Oracles | COR 108:10 |
| till the fear of the L. | JOYCE 188:4 |
| Where no l. is | BIBLE 54:31 |
| Who to himself is l. | CHAP 94:16 |
| whole of the L. | CROW 112:14 |
| windy side of the l. | SHAK 298:12 |
| Wrest once the l. | SHAK 289:28 |
| **lawful:** L. as eating | SHAK 299:4 |

**lawful** (*cont.*):

| | |
|---|---|
| that which is l. and right | BIBLE 47:6 |
| upon their l. occasions | BOOK 69:14 |
| **lawn:** bird-haunted English l. | ARN 16:21 |
| l. about the shoulders thrown | HERR 167:15 |
| Out on the l. I lie in bed | AUDEN 21:7 |
| twice a saint in l. | POPE 251:20 |
| **lawns:** house with l. enclosing it | STEV 317:17 |
| **laws:** Bad l. are the worst sort | BURKE 80:24 |
| Christianity is part of the l. | HALE 160:5 |
| government of L., and not of men | ADAMS 1:22 |
| If l. are their enemies | BURKE 81:9 |
| L. are like cobwebs | SWIFT 319:19 |
| l. are like spider's webs | ANAC 5:9 |
| L. are silent in time of war | CIC 100:30 |
| L. grind the poor | GOLD 155:5 |
| L., like houses, lean | BURKE 81:6 |
| l. of God and man and metre | LOCK 209:3 |
| l. of most countries | MILL 224:19 |
| L. were made to be broken | NORTH 240:7 |
| make the l. of a nation | FLET 142:3 |
| not judges of l. | PULT 256:4 |
| obedient to their l. | SIM 307:9 |
| prescribed l. to the learned | DUPPA 129:12 |
| repeal of bad or obnoxious l. | GRANT 156:9 |
| to do with l. but to obey them | HORS 174:5 |
| Unequal l. unto a savage race | TENN 328:19 |
| warfare, and of l. | DU B 128:32 |
| Who sweeps a room as for Thy l. | HERB 166:26 |
| **lawyer:** l. has no business | JOHN 183:17 |
| l. interprets the truth | GIR 153:6 |
| l. with his briefcase can steal | PUZO 256:26 |
| **lawyers:** let's kill all the l. | SHAK 280:10 |
| two l. the battledores | DICK 119:29 |
| Woe unto you, l.! | BIBLE 52:16 |
| **lay:** Cleric before, and L. behind | BUTL 84:1 |
| l. down his friends for his life | THOR 332:13 |
| l. down his life for his friends | BIBLE 53:40 |
| l. down his wife for his friend | JOYCE 188:18 |
| l. hold on eternal life | BIBLE 56:20 |
| l. mee downe and bleed | BALL 28:3 |
| l. not up for yourselves | BIBLE 49:1 |
| L. on, Macduff | SHAK 288:8 |
| L. your sleeping head, my love | AUDEN 20:27 |
| **lazy:** L. and silly | SITW 307:20 |
| l. leaden-stepping hours | MILT 228:3 |
| **lead:** L., kindly Light | NEWM 238:21 |
| l. them the way | BIBLE 39:39 |
| l. those that are with young | BIBLE 46:11 |
| l. us not into temptation | BIBLE 48:27 |
| You can l. a horticulture | PARK 245:14 |
| **leaden:** With l. foot time creeps | JAGO 179:8 |
| **leading:** L. onward, beaming bright | DIX 122:24 |
| **leaf:** last red l. is whirled | TENN 325:2 |
| Right as an aspes l. | CHAU 96:17 |
| sear, the yellow l. | SHAK 288:1 |
| **leafmeal:** worlds of wanwood l. | HOPK 172:15 |
| **league:** Half a l. onward | TENN 323:14 |
| She hadna sailed a l. | BALL 27:16 |
| Will keep a l. till death | SHAK 294:6 |
| **lean:** dying lady, l. and pale | SHEL 305:15 |
| Laws, like houses, l. | BURKE 81:6 |
| l. and hungry look | SHAK 281:1 |
| **leap:** great l. in the dark | HOBB 169:11 |
| methinks it were an easy l. | SHAK 277:27 |
| one giant l. for mankind | ARMS 16:5 |
| **leaping:** brooks too broad for l. | HOUS 175:2 |
| l., and praising God | BIBLE 54:10 |
| l. from place to place | HARDY 162:10 |
| swimmers into cleanness l. | BROO 73:9 |
| **leaps:** It moves in mighty l. | AYRES 23:15 |
| **learn:** cannot l. men from books | DISR 122:9 |
| craft so long to l. | CHAU 96:12 |
| enough who know how to l. | ADAMS 1:17 |
| Even while they teach, men l. | SEN 270:6 |

**learn** (cont.):

| | |
|---|---|
| gladly wolde he l. | CHAU 95:18 |
| l. in suffering | SHEL 303:22 |
| mark, l., and inwardly digest | BOOK 64:22 |
| not yet so old but she may l. | SHAK 289:22 |
| places to l. the world in | CHES 97:6 |
| so dull but she can l. | SHAK 289:22 |

**learned:** been l. has been forgotten

| | |
|---|---|
| grew within this l. man | SKIN 308:6 |
| l. lumber in his head | MARL 218:14 |
| L. without sense | POPE 252:9 |
| prescribed laws to the l. | CHUR 98:29 |
| Things l. on earth | DUPPA 129:12 |
| | BROW 76:21 |

**learning:** attain good l.

| | |
|---|---|
| deep l. little had he need | ASCH 18:18 |
| encourage a will to l. | SPEN 313:16 |
| enough of l. to misquote | ASCH 18:19 |
| grammar, and nonsense, and l. | BYRON 86:31 |
| grow old ever l. many things | GOLD 155:8 |
| L., that cobweb of the brain | SOLON 310:26 |
| little l. is a dangerous thing | BUTL 84:2 |
| loyal body wanted l. | POPE 251:28 |
| much l. doth make thee mad | TRAPP 334:3 |
| on scraps of l. dote | BIBLE 54:26 |
| sleep—and l. of a sort | YOUNG 360:13 |
| wearing all that weight of l. | BELL 33:17 |
| Wear your l., like your watch | TENN 325:31 |
| We'll cry both arts and l. down | CHES 97:10 |
| written for our l. | QUAR 257:5 |
| | BOOK 64:22 |

**learnt:** forgotten nothing and l.

| | |
|---|---|
| They have l. nothing | DUM 129:6 |

**lease:** having so short a l.

| | |
|---|---|
| summer's l. hath all too short | TALL 322:12 |

**leasehold:** it is l. for all

| | |
|---|---|
| | SHAK 300:14 |
| | SHAK 299:12 |
| | LUCR 212:6 |

**least:** l. of these my brethren

| | |
|---|---|
| man who promises l. | BIBLE 51:6 |
| | BAR 29:21 |

**leathern:** Their l. boats

| | |
|---|---|
| | MARV 221:3 |

**leave:** be ready to l.

| | |
|---|---|
| couldn't l. without the King | MONT 233:8 |
| for ever taking l. | ELIZ 135:19 |
| Intreat me not to l. thee | RILKE 260:7 |
| l. him for religion | BIBLE 41:8 |
| l. his father and his mother | SPARK 312:10 |
| l. in a minute and a huff | BIBLE 38:23 |
| l. me there to die | KALM 189:21 |
| L. not a rack behind | ANON 8:3 |
| L. off first for manners' sake | SHAK 296:10 |
| L. them while you're looking | BIBLE 48:4 |
| l. the outcome to the Gods | LOOS 210:8 |
| Oh, never l. me | CORN 108:2 |
| | ANON 6:27 |

**leaves:** among the l. hast never known

| | |
|---|---|
| burning of the l. | KEATS 191:31 |
| Close up those barren l. | BINY 59:13 |
| glad green l. like wings | WORD 357:5 |
| l. dead are driven | HARDY 162:2 |
| l. is a generation of men | SHEL 304:6 |
| l. of the tree for the healing | HOMER 170:21 |
| naturally as the l. to a tree | BIBLE 58:7 |
| noiseless noise among the l. | KEATS 193:4 |
| tender l. of hope | KEATS 191:5 |
| Thick as autumnal l. | SHAK 280:18 |
| yellow drifts of withered l. | MILT 228:14 |
| yellow l., or none | ARN 17:3 |
| | SHAK 299:24 |

**leaving:** Became him like the l. it

| | |
|---|---|
| L. his country for his country's | SHAK 285:13 |
| | FITZ 140:3 |

**lecher:** Does l. in my sight

| | |
|---|---|
| | SHAK 283:23 |

**lecherous:** l. mouth

| | |
|---|---|
| | CHAU 96:6 |

**lechery:** L., sir, it provokes

| | |
|---|---|
| | SHAK 286:21 |

**lecture:** classic l., rich in sentiment

| | |
|---|---|
| | TENN 327:18 |

**lectures:** l. or a little charity

| | |
|---|---|
| | WHIT 348:20 |

**lees:** drink life to the l.

| | |
|---|---|
| mere l. is left | TENN 328:20 |
| | SHAK 286:26 |

**left:** better to be l. than never

| | |
|---|---|
| heart is on the l. | CONG 106:16 |
| l. hand know what thy right | MOL 232:19 |
| | BIBLE 48:26 |

**left** (cont.):

| | |
|---|---|
| l. her husband because | MURD 236:9 |
| l. thee all her lovely hues | DAV 114:19 |
| l. thy first love | BIBLE 57:20 |
| let them be l., wildness and wet | HOPK 172:8 |
| something l. to treat my friends | MALL 216:21 |

**left-handed:** l. marriage

| | |
|---|---|
| | WOLL 353:12 |

**leg:** here I leave my second l.

| | |
|---|---|
| kiss my Julia's dainty l. | HOOD 171:5 |
| | HERR 167:20 |

**lege:** *Tolle l., tolle lege*

| | |
|---|---|
| | AUG 21:23 |

**legion:** L. and Social Club

| | |
|---|---|
| My name is L. | BETJ 36:22 |
| | BIBLE 51:21 |

**legislator:** l. of mankind

| | |
|---|---|
| | JOHN 183:3 |

**legislators:** l. of the world

| | |
|---|---|
| | SHEL 305:19 |

**legs:** adorns my l.

| | |
|---|---|
| between your l. an instrument | HOUS 174:7 |
| born with your l. apart | BEEC 32:4 |
| cannon-ball took off his l. | ORTON 241:21 |
| delighteth he in any man's l. | HOOD 171:4 |
| fold his l. and have out his talk | BOOK 69:10 |
| Four legs good, two l. bad | JOHN 185:16 |
| l. when I take my boots off | ORW 241:22 |
| open my l., and think of | DICK 118:21 |
| trunkless l. of stone | HILL 168:17 |
| Walk under his huge l. | SHEL 304:13 |
| | SHAK 280:27 |

**leisure:** At l. married, they repent

| | |
|---|---|
| Conspicuous l. and consumption | CONG 106:13 |
| fill l. intelligently | VEBL 337:17 |
| he is never at l. | RUSS 264:22 |
| L. with honour | JOHN 185:16 |
| they detest at l. | CIC 100:32 |
| we may polish it at l. | BYRON 86:25 |
| | DRYD 128:26 |

**lemon:** squeezed as a l. is

| | |
|---|---|
| where the l.-trees bloom | GEDD 149:19 |
| | GOET 154:13 |

**lend:** l. me your ears

| | |
|---|---|
| men who l. | SHAK 281:18 |
| | LAMB 200:1 |

**lender:** borrower, nor a l. be

| | |
|---|---|
| | SHAK 274:22 |

**lenders:** thy pen from l.' books

| | |
|---|---|
| | SHAK 283:13 |

**lends:** Three things I never l.

| | |
|---|---|
| | SURT 319:11 |

**length:** drags its slow l. along

| | |
|---|---|
| L. of days is in her right hand | POPE 252:4 |
| still drags its dreary l. | BIBLE 43:8 |
| what it lacks in l. | DICK 118:1 |
| | FROST 146:14 |

**Lenin:** L. was right

| | |
|---|---|
| | KEYN 194:14 |

**lente:** *Festina l.*

| | |
|---|---|
| *O lente l. currite noctis equi* | AUG 22:6 |
| | MARL 218:13 |

**leopard:** l. shall lie down

| | |
|---|---|
| or the l. his spots | BIBLE 45:19 |
| | BIBLE 46:30 |

**leopards:** l. sat under a juniper-tree

| | |
|---|---|
| | ELIOT 132:20 |

**leper:** innocence is like a dumb l.

| | |
|---|---|
| | GREE 158:7 |

**Lesbia:** L. let us live and love

| | |
|---|---|
| *Vivamus, mea L., atque amemus* | CAMP 89:2 |
| | CAT 93:2 |

**less:** believing more and more in l.

| | |
|---|---|
| had he pleased us l. | YATES 358:10 |
| How l. what we may be | ADD 2:10 |
| knows more about less and l. | BYRON 86:30 |
| little l., and what worlds away | BUTL 83:21 |
| L. than the dust, beneath | BROW 75:19 |
| nothing l. than thee | HOPE 171:23 |
| rather than be l. | DONNE 124:1 |
| You mean you can't take l. | MILT 228:22 |
| | CARR 91:8 |

**lessen:** they l. from day to day

| | |
|---|---|
| | CARR 91:10 |

**lesser:** l. breeds without the Law

| | |
|---|---|
| | KIPL 197:4 |

**lessons:** reason they're called l.

| | |
|---|---|
| | CARR 91:10 |

**lest:** L. we forget

| | |
|---|---|
| | KIPL 197:2 |

**let:** L. my people go

| | |
|---|---|
| L. my people go | ANON 11:19 |
| l. them all to my elder daughter | BIBLE 39:34 |
| L. there be light | THOM 330:23 |
| L. us with a gladsome mind | BIBLE 38:13 |
| | MILT 227:9 |

**Lethe:** go not to L.

| | |
|---|---|
| | KEATS 191:25 |

**letter:** l. killeth

| | |
|---|---|
| [L.] longer than usual | BIBLE 55:23 |
| This is my l. to the world | PASC 245:24 |
| thou unnecessary l. | DICK 120:16 |
| | SHAK 283:2 |

letters: L. for the rich — AUDEN 21:4
l. get in the wrong places — MILNE 225:17
l. mingle souls — DONNE 124:17
l. should be free and easy — OSB 242:17
No arts; no l.; no society — HOBB 169:10
receive no l. in the grave — JOHN 186:8
than a man of l. — STER 315:25
lettuce: too much l. is 'soporific' — POTT 254:2
levee: Drove my Chevy to the l. — MCL 215:8
level: dead l. of provincial — ELIOT 132:13
one dead l. ev'ry mind — POPE 250:19
levellers: l. wish to level *down* — JOHN 184:13
levelling: l. *up* to themselves — JOHN 184:13
leviathan: draw out l. with an hook — BIBLE 43:6
levity: little judicious l. — STEV 317:11
levy: Malice domestic, foreign l. — SHAK 287:4
lewd: l. fellows of the baser sort — BIBLE 54:18
lex: *Salus populi suprema est* l. — CIC 100:20
lexicographer: L. A writer of — JOHN 182:8
liar: best l. is he who makes — BUTL 84:10
easy virtue and a proved l. — HAIL 160:1
every man a l. — BIBLE 54:29
They only answered 'Little L.!' — BELL 33:9
liars: All men are l. — BOOK 68:21
fears may be l. — CLOU 102:23
Income Tax has made more L. — ROG 261:21
libel: Convey a l. in a frown — SWIFT 320:16
Liberal: distinguished from the L. — BIER 59:5
Is either a little L. — GILB 151:12
libertas: *Imperium et L.* — DISR 121:21
liberté: *L.! Égalité! Fraternité!* — ANON 12:11
liberties: dramatist wants more l. — JAMES 179:15
people never give up their l. — BURKE 80:25
what l. are taken in thy name — GEOR 150:6
libertine: puffed and reckless l. — SHAK 274:20
air, a chartered l. — SHAK 278:36
liberty: at l. when of Devils and Hell — BLAKE 60:25
Brightest in dungeons, L. — BYRON 87:7
defence of l. is no vice — GOLD 155:15
end to a woman's l. — BURN 81:19
give me l., or give me death — HENRY 166:6
Let there be light! said l. — SHEL 303:17
l. and the pursuit of happiness — ANON 11:12
l., and the pursuit of happiness — JEFF 180:18
L. *and* Union, now and forever — WEBS 344:9
L. consists in doing what — MILL 224:17
L. is always unfinished — ANON 8:19
L. is liberty, not equality — BERL 36:6
L. is precious — LENIN 205:6
L. means responsibility — SHAW 301:28
l. of the individual — MILL 224:16
l. plucks justice by the nose — SHAK 288:9
L.'s in every blow — BURNS 82:22
L. to be saucy — HAL 160:10
l. to man is eternal vigilance — CURR 113:8
L. too must be limited — BURKE 79:23
l.! what crimes are committed — ROL 262:3
mansion-house of l. — MILT 231:3
men are to wait for l. — MAC 213:8
Money is coined l. — DOST 125:5
people contend for their l. — HAL 160:9
priests have been enemies of l. — HUME 176:8
proclaim l. to the captives — BIBLE 46:24
seek power and to lose l. — BACON 24:28
survival and the success of l. — KENN 194:3
Sweet land of l. — SMITH 309:16
they mean when they cry l. — MILT 230:21
This is L.-Hall — GOLD 155:10
thy chosen music, L. — WORD 357:6
tree of l. must be refreshed — JEFF 180:21
who ever gives, takes l. — DONNE 123:14
library: half a l. to make one book — JOHN 185:3
l. is thought in cold storage — SAM 266:10
take choice of all my l. — SHAK 296:27

library (cont.):
than a public l. — JOHN 183:1
licence: L. my roving hands — DONNE 123:6
L. they mean when they cry — MILT 230:21
l. to print money — THOM 332:4
love not freedom, but l. — MILT 231:7
universal l. to be good — COL 103:11
licensed: based upon l. premises — O'BR 240:19
licorice: l. fields at Pontefract — BETJ 37:5
Liddell: this is Mrs L. — SPR 314:1
Liddesdale: Eskdale and L. — SCOTT 269:2
lids: fogies who doffed their l. — KEAT 190:9
lie: compulsion doth in music l. — MILT 226:3
corner of airth to l. in — PHIL 248:17
every word she writes is a l. — MCC 214:12
fain wald l. down — BALL 27:19
fall victim to a big l. — HITL 169:3
give the world the l. — RAL 257:21
He makes me down to l. — SCOT 269:8
home to a l. — POUND 254:18
I can't tell a l. — WASH 342:22
leads you to believe a l. — BLAKE 60:12
l. abroad for the good — WOTT 357:22
l. as quietly among the graves — EDW 131:4
l. circumstantial — SHAK 273:12
l. *diagonally* in his bed — STER 315:23
l. direct — SHAK 273:12
l. even when it is inconvenient — VIDAL 338:14
L. follows by post — BER 35:12
L. heavy on him, Earth — EVANS 137:23
l. in cold obstruction — SHAK 288:21
l. in the soul is a true lie — JOW 188:2
l. of Authority — AUDEN 21:11
l. than a truth misunderstood — JAMES 180:10
l. usefully should lie seldom — HERV 167:27
l. will go round the world — SPUR 314:2
not a man, that he should l. — BIBLE 40:18
possible to l. for the truth — ADLER 3:2
To undo the folded l. — AUDEN 21:11
what is a l.? — BYRON 86:23
Who can rule and dare not l. — TENN 326:26
Who loves to l. with me — SHAK 272:19
lied: because our fathers l. — KIPL 196:7
lies: all the l. you can invent — BLAKE 60:7
damned l. and statistics — DISR 122:21
From l. of tongue and pen — CHES 97:24
l. about the Democrats — STEV 316:15
cruellest l. often told in silence — STEV 317:9
L. are the mortar — WELLS 345:20
l. poor Tom Bowling — DIBD 117:19
l. sound truthful — ORW 242:15
Matilda told such Dreadful L. — BELL 33:8
only l. are invented — BRAQ 71:15
produces l. like sand — ANON 13:3
rest is l. — FITZ 140:10
spring of endless l. — COWP 110:3
life: actor's l. for me — WASH 342:23
all human l. is there — JAMES 179:22
all l. death does end — HOPK 172:11
all l. is 6 to 5 against — RUNY 264:7
Anyone can stop a man's l. — SEN 270:8
As though to breathe were l. — TENN 328:21
at bottom a criticism of l. — ARN 18:6
believe in the l. to come — BECK 31:9
biography is l. without theory — DISR 121:28
Book of L. begins — WILDE 350:11
changing scenes of l. — TATE 322:17
crowd out real l. — FORS 144:1
day-to-day business l. is — LAF 199:20
disease of modern l. — ARN 17:11
doctrine of the strenuous l. — ROOS 262:15
drink l. to the lees — TENN 328:20
evidence of l. after death — SOPER 311:11
findeth his l. shall lose it — BIBLE 49:33
following l. thro' creatures — POPE 251:19

life (cont.):

| | |
|---|---|
| football a matter of l. and death | SHAN 300:22 |
| force maintaining the l. | DOST 125:1 |
| former naughty l. | BOOK 65:1 |
| found that l. was duty | HOOP 171:16 |
| gave my l. for freedom | EWER 138:1 |
| give thee a crown of l. | BIBLE 57:21 |
| giveth his l. for the sheep | BIBLE 53:30 |
| glory of this l. | SHAK 296:18 |
| great l. if you don't weaken | BUCH 77:26 |
| His l. was gentle | SHAK 282:2 |
| Human l. is a sad show | FLAU 141:13 |
| I bear a charmèd l. | SHAK 288:6 |
| I count l. just a stuff | BROW 76:7 |
| in his pleasure is l. | BOOK 66:22 |
| in the sea of l. enisled | ARN 17:22 |
| I really don't know l. at all | MITC 232:3 |
| iron gates of l. | MARV 221:1 |
| Is it not l. | BYRON 87:19 |
| isn't l. a terrible thing | THOM 330:19 |
| I've had a happy l. | HAZL 164:9 |
| jump the l. to come | SHAK 285:22 |
| lad of l., an imp of fame | SHAK 279:10 |
| lay down his friends for his l. | THOR 332:13 |
| lay down his l. for his friends | BIBLE 53:40 |
| l. began by flickering out | GONC 155:19 |
| l. closed twice before its close | DICK 120:11 |
| l. everlasting | BOOK 64:3 |
| L. exists in the universe | JEANS 180:16 |
| l. forget and death remember | SWIN 321:16 |
| L. for life | BIBLE 40:10 |
| l. for the British female | CLOU 102:7 |
| L., friends, is boring | BERR 36:13 |
| l. had been ruined by literature | BROO 73:13 |
| l. hath been one chain | CLARE 101:4 |
| l. heroic | MILT 230:17 |
| l. in my men | WEST 346:21 |
| L. is a foreign language | MORL 235:7 |
| L. is a gamble at terrible odds | STOP 318:6 |
| l. is a glorious cycle | PARK 245:4 |
| L. is a horizontal fall | COCT 103:2 |
| L. is a jest | GAY 149:15 |
| L. is a joke that's just begun | GILB 151:22 |
| L. is all a VARIORUM | BURNS 82:13 |
| L. is an incurable disease | COWL 109:17 |
| L. is a sexually transmitted | ANON 8:20 |
| L. is as tedious as a twice-told | SHAK 282:9 |
| L. is a top | GREV 158:18 |
| L. is but the shadow of death | BROW 74:2 |
| L. is Colour and Warmth | GREN 158:16 |
| L. is doubt | UNAM 336:11 |
| l. is everywhere a state | JOHN 183:4 |
| L. is first boredom, then fear | LARK 201:14 |
| l. is given to none freehold | LUCR 212:6 |
| L. is just a bowl of cherries | BROWN 73:17 |
| L. is just one damned thing | HUBB 175:14 |
| L. is mostly froth and bubble | GORD 155:21 |
| L. is not a series of gig lamps | WOOLF 353:22 |
| L. is one long process | BUTL 84:13 |
| L. is real! Life is earnest | LONG 209:22 |
| L. is short, the art long | HIPP 168:19 |
| L. is the desert | YOUNG 360:23 |
| L. is the other way round | LODGE 209:4 |
| l. is the thing, but I prefer | SMITH 309:13 |
| L. is too short to stuff | CONR 107:10 |
| l. is washed in the speechless real | BARZ 29:22 |
| l., it's enemy | ANOU 14:7 |
| l., liberty, and the pursuit | ANON 11:12 |
| L., like a dome of many-coloured | SHEL 303:13 |
| l. may perfect be | JONS 187:24 |
| l. of man less than a span | BACON 25:30 |
| l. of sensations | KEATS 192:24 |
| l. protracted is protracted woe | JOHN 183:15 |
| l. ran gaily as the sparkling | ARN 17:11 |
| l.'s a pain and but a span | DAV 114:14 |

life (cont.):

| | |
|---|---|
| L. says: she did this | BARN 29:5 |
| L.'s but a walking shadow | SHAK 288:5 |
| l.'s dim windows | BLAKE 60:12 |
| L.'s longing for itself | GIBR 150:19 |
| L.'s not just being alive | MART 220:6 |
| l. so short, the craft so long | CHAU 96:12 |
| L.'s rich pageant | MARS 220:2 |
| L., the Universe and Everything | ADAMS 1:9 |
| l. time's fool | SHAK 278:14 |
| l. well spent is long | LEON 205:21 |
| l. will be sour grapes | ASHF 18:24 |
| L. with its way before us lies | MONS 233:2 |
| L. without industry is guilt | RUSK 264:11 |
| L. would be tolerable | LEWIS 206:15 |
| L. would be very pleasant | SURT 319:13 |
| long disease, my l. | POPE 251:4 |
| looked at l. from both sides | MITC 232:3 |
| many doors to let out l. | FLET 142:4 |
| married my husband for l. | ANON 8:8 |
| measured out my l. with coffee | ELIOT 133:27 |
| midst of l. we are in death | BOOK 66:7 |
| midst of l. we are in debt | MUMF 236:7 |
| Midway along the path of our l. | DANTE 113:17 |
| Mine honour is my l. | SHAK 293:8 |
| more a way of l. | ANON 9:19 |
| mourning for my l. | CHEK 96:25 |
| My l. is dreary | TENN 326:22 |
| nearest thing to death in l. | ANON 9:14 |
| No, no, no l.! | SHAK 284:6 |
| Nothing in his l. became him | SHAK 285:13 |
| Nothing in l. shall sever | CORY 108:12 |
| no wealth but l. | RUSK 264:20 |
| of man's l. a thing apart | BYRON 86:4 |
| One crowded hour of glorious l. | MORD 234:21 |
| one l. and one death | BROW 76:6 |
| one l. to lose for my country | HALE 160:6 |
| On l., on death | YEATS 360:8 |
| Our end is L. Put out to sea | MACN 216:11 |
| our little l. is rounded | SHAK 296:10 |
| out-do the l. | JONS 187:20 |
| outer l. of telegrams and anger | FORS 143:20 |
| Perfection of the l. | YEATS 358:19 |
| present l. of men on earth | BEDE 31:20 |
| preservation of l. | JEFF 180:18 |
| resurrection, and the l. | BIBLE 53:32 |
| seas of l., like wine | TRAH 334:1 |
| secret love does thy l. destroy | BLAKE 62:4 |
| set my l. at a pin's fee | SHAK 274:28 |
| shilling l. will give you | AUDEN 21:12 |
| sketchy understanding of l. | CRICK 111:9 |
| So careless of the single l. | TENN 325:10 |
| spirit giveth l. | BIBLE 55:23 |
| studied from the l. | ARMS 16:1 |
| Style is l.! | FLAU 141:10 |
| such is l. | DICK 118:26 |
| taking l. by the throat | FROST 146:27 |
| thousand doors to let out l. | MASS 222:6 |
| tired of London ... tired of l. | JOHN 185:15 |
| 'Tisn't l. that matters | WALP 342:4 |
| To live a l. half dead | MILT 230:13 |
| traveller betwixt l. and death | WORD 356:24 |
| tree of l. | BIBLE 43:21 |
| University of L. | BOTT 70:7 |
| Variety's the very spice of l. | COWP 110:9 |
| walk in newness of l. | BIBLE 54:34 |
| warm full blooded l. | JOYCE 188:17 |
| way, the truth, and the l. | BIBLE 53:38 |
| way which leadeth unto l. | BIBLE 49:13 |
| well-written L. as rare | CARL 90:7 |
| What is this l. if full of care | DAV 114:20 |
| Wholesome of l. | HOR 173:21 |
| Who saw l. steadily | ARN 17:20 |
| will he give for his l. | BIBLE 42:23 |
| **life-blood**: book is the precious l. | MILT 230:30 |

life-lie: Take the l. away — IBSEN 178:7
life-sentence: l. which fate carries — LAWR 202:27
lifetime: knowledge of a l. — WHIS 347:13
l. of happiness — SHAW 301:15
lifetimes: series of l. starts anew — VIRG 339:25
lift: l. me as a wave, a leaf — SHEL 304:8
l. up his countenance — BIBLE 40:15
l. up mine eyes — BOOK 68:25
L. up your heads — BOOK 66:20
L. up your hearts — BOOK 65:13
lifting: l. up of my hands — BOOK 69:8
light: against the dying of the l. — THOM 330:7
all *know* what l. is — JOHN 185:11
armour of l. — BOOK 64:21
As if they feared the l. — SUCK 318:21
bear witness of that L. — BIBLE 53:9
Be near me when my l. is low — TENN 325:7
black as if bereaved of l. — BLAKE 61:24
blasted with excess of l. — GRAY 157:17
certain Slant of l. — DICK 120:14
children of l. — BIBLE 52:33
C'mon, baby, l. my fire — MORR 235:19
dark is l. enough — FRY 146:29
festal l. in Christ-Church — ARN 17:9
fire, to give them l. — BIBLE 39:39
garmented in l. — SHEL 305:16
gone into the world of l. — VAUG 337:11
how my l. is spent — MILT 230:22
infant crying for the l. — TENN 325:9
infinite ocean of l. and love — FOX 144:17
In the dusk with a l. behind her — GILB 152:31
Jeanie with the l. brown hair — FOST 144:11
kindle a l. in the darkness — JUNG 188:23
Lead, kindly L. — NEWM 238:21
let perpetual l. shine on them — MISS 231:22
Let there be l. — BIBLE 38:13
Let there be l. — MARR 219:24
Let there be l.! said Liberty — SHEL 303:17
l., and will aspire — SHAK 300:17
l. at the end of the tunnel — DICK 120:19
l. at the end of the tunnel — LOW 211:18
l. between two eternities — NAB 236:19
L. breaks where no sun shines — THOM 330:12
l. fantastic round — MILT 226:9
l. fantastic toe — MILT 227:2
l. gleams an instant — BECK 31:15
L. God's eldest daughter — FULL 147:6
l. in the dust lies dead — SHEL 303:24
l. of common day — WORD 355:21
l. of Terewth — DICK 118:3
l. of the world — BIBLE 48:21
l. shineth in darkness — BIBLE 53:8
l. so shine before men — BIBLE 48:22
l. that I may tread safely — HASK 163:16
l. that loses, the night that — SWIN 321:2
l. that never was — WORD 354:17
l. through yonder window — SHAK 294:29
l. to counterfeit a gloom — MILT 226:25
l. to shine upon the road — COWP 109:27
l. to them that sit in darkness — BIBLE 51:30
l. unto my paths — BOOK 68:24
l. within his own clear breast — MILT 226:12
mend the Electric L. — BELL 33:22
More l. — GOET 154:15
neither heat nor l. — WEBS 344:17
new l. of grace — SMOL 310:16
Newton's particles of l. — BLAKE 61:14
once set is our little l. — CAMP 89:2
put on the armour of l. — BIBLE 55:1
Put out the l. — SHAK 292:29
ring of pure and endless l. — VAUG 337:14
seen a glorious l. — SCOT 269:10
seen a great l. — BIBLE 45:15
Servants of L. — ARN 16:7

light (cont.):
shew l. at Calais — JOHN 184:15
source of my l. and my safety — BIBLE 58:9
sweetness and l. — ARN 17:25
sweetness and l. — SWIFT 319:18
thy l. is come — BIBLE 46:23
turning your face to the l. — SASS 267:9
turret in a noose of l. — FITZ 140:4
unclouded blaze of living l. — BYRON 85:20
upon them hath the l. shined — BIBLE 45:15
while the l. fails — ELIOT 133:12
Light Brigade: Forward, the L. — TENN 323:15
lighten: L. our darkness — BOOK 64:12
l. with celestial fire — BOOK 69:16
lightly: l. as it comth — CHAU 96:1
l. skims the midge — BETJ 37:1
unadvisedly, l., or wantonly — BOOK 65:26
lightness: unbearable l. of being — KUND 199:8
lightning: Brief as the l. in the collied night — SHAK 290:14
coruscations of summer l. — GOUL 155:26
illumined by flashes of l. — WILDE 350:19
l. before death — SHAK 295:23
l. of his terrible swift sword — HOWE 175:7
Shakespeare by flashes of l. — COL 104:25
snatched the l. shaft — TURG 335:16
to keep the l. out — ISH 178:21
lights: all-the-l.-on man — REED 258:20
broken l. of thee — TENN 324:23
Followed false l. — DRYD 127:29
Glorious the northern l. — SMART 308:13
l. around the shore — ROSS 263:10
tail l. wizen and converge — CRANE 111:2
Truth may bear all l. — SHAF 270:22
When the l. are dim and low — ORRED 241:18
your l. burning — BIBLE 52:20
like: Do what you l. — RAB 257:12
forced to l. what you get — SHAW 302:7
l. this sort of thing — LINC 207:12
none of his friends l. him — WILDE 350:21
No wonder we l. them — AMIS 5:6
shall not look upon his l. again — SHAK 274:17
want it the most l. it least — CHES 97:9
liked: L. it not, and died — WOTT 357:17
l. whate'er she looked on — BROW 76:19
likely: Walk! Not bloody l. — SHAW 302:19
likerous: l. mouth moste han — CHAU 96:6
likewise: go and do thou l. — BIBLE 52:13
liking: mayse man to haiff l. — BARB 28:16
Not l. the person — THOM 331:1
lilac: forget the l. and the roses — ARAG 14:21
Just now the l. is in bloom — BROO 73:3
lilacs: l. last in the dooryard — WHIT 348:24
L. out of the dead land — ELIOT 134:18
Lilian: Airy, fairy L. — TENN 326:5
lilies: And a few l. blow — HOPK 172:7
beauty lives though l. die — FLEC 141:16
Consider the l. of the field — BIBLE 49:4
Give me l. in armfuls — VIRG 339:17
l. and languors of virtue — SWIN 321:7
L. that fester smell far worse — SHAK 300:2
pale, lost l. out of mind — DOWS 125:12
peacocks and l. — RUSK 264:17
She had three l. in her hand — ROSS 263:6
Lilli Burlero: L. *Bullena-la* — WHAR 347:5
lilting: About the l. house — THOM 330:8
lily: Elaine, the l. maid of Astolat — TENN 324:7
folds the l. all her sweetness up — TENN 328:5
gold, to paint the l. — SHAK 282:10
I see a l. on thy brow — KEATS 191:8
lies across the l. leven — BALL 28:7
l. of Florence blossoming — LONG 209:18
l. of the valleys — BIBLE 44:31
She's as pure as the l. — LAUD 202:6
lily-white: Two, two, the l. boys — ANON 8:6

| | |
|---|---|
| limbs: l. of a poet | HOR 174:3 |
| l. that fester | ABSE 1:1 |
| slope of mighty l. asleep | SWIN 321:4 |
| Yours are the l., my sweeting | NASH 237:18 |
| lime-tree: This L. Bower my Prison | COL 104:21 |
| limit: act a slave to l. | SHAK 297:2 |
| quiet l. of the world | TENN 328:17 |
| limited: Liberty too must be l. | BURKE 79:23 |
| nervous and terse, but l. | DOYLE 126:7 |
| so whizzed the L. | CRANE 111:2 |
| limits: l. of my language | WITT 352:10 |
| stony l. cannot hold love out | SHAK 294:32 |
| limousine: l. and a ticket | MACN 216:1 |
| One perfect l. | PARK 245:7 |
| limp: l. father of thousands | JOYCE 188:16 |
| Lincoln: I am a Ford, not a L. | FORD 143:3 |
| L. County Road or Armageddon | DYLAN 130:7 |
| line: active l. on a walk | KLEE 198:11 |
| cancel half a l. | FITZ 140:14 |
| cut, the style, the l. | LOES 209:6 |
| horizontal l. | WHEW 347:8 |
| l. is length without breadth | EUCL 137:20 |
| l. upon line | BIBLE 45:27 |
| l. will take us hours maybe | YEATS 358:13 |
| lives along the l. | POPE 252:15 |
| Marlowe's mighty l. | JONS 187:26 |
| quarrelling on the l. | FORS 143:22 |
| Thin red l. of 'eroes | KIPL 197:11 |
| thin red l. tipped with steel | RUSS 265:7 |
| We carved not a l. | WOLFE 353:1 |
| lineaments: l. of gratified desire | BLAKE 61:17 |
| linen: In blanchèd l. | KEATS 190:21 |
| Love is like l. often changed | FLET 142:10 |
| very fine l. | BRUM 77:24 |
| lines: As l. (so loves) | MARV 220:13 |
| consisted of l. like these | CALV 88:7 |
| l. are fallen unto me | BOOK 66:15 |
| Prose is when all the l. | BENT 35:3 |
| town-crier spoke my l. | SHAK 276:4 |
| linger: l. out a purposed overthrow | SHAK 300:1 |
| lingered: I l. round them | BRON 72:18 |
| lingering: I alone sit l. here | VAUG 337:11 |
| l. dissolution | BECK 31:7 |
| Something l., with boiling oil | GILB 152:4 |
| lingua: Pange, l. | THOM 330:3 |
| lin-lan-lone: mellow l. | TENN 323:22 |
| linnet: l. born within the cage | TENN 325:3 |
| linsy-woolsy: lawless l. brother | BUTL 84:1 |
| lion: devil, as a roaring l. | BIBLE 57:12 |
| l. and the fatling together | BIBLE 45:19 |
| l. to frighten the wolves | MACH 215:3 |
| Strong is the l.—like a coal | SMART 308:10 |
| threatened, a l. | CHAP 94:14 |
| lions: L. led by donkeys | HOFF 169:17 |
| they were stronger than l. | BIBLE 41:22 |
| lips: already born before my l. | MAND 217:11 |
| hand is ever at his l. | KEATS 191:27 |
| l. ne'er act the winning part | HERR 167:17 |
| l. of living men | BUTL 84:21 |
| l., that they speak no guile | BOOK 66:25 |
| l. that touch liquor | YOUNG 360:24 |
| My l. are sealed | BALD 27:7 |
| people of unclean l. | BIBLE 45:11 |
| Read my l.: no new taxes | BUSH 83:18 |
| Red l. are not so red | OWEN 244:1 |
| Truth sits upon the l. of dying | ARN 17:15 |
| very good words for the l. | DICK 119:1 |
| When the l. have spoken | SHEL 303:24 |
| lipstick: l.'s traces | MARV 221:4 |
| liquefaction: l. of her clothes | HERR 167:26 |
| liquid: less l. than their shadows | TESS 329:10 |
| let their l. siftings fall | ELIOT 134:17 |
| Thames is l. history | BURNS 81:20 |
| liquor: But l. is quicker | NASH 237:15 |

| | |
|---|---|
| liquor (cont.): | |
| Good l., I stoutly maintain | GOLD 155:8 |
| lips that touch l. | YOUNG 360:24 |
| L. is one way out | WILL 351:5 |
| lisp: l. of leaves | SWIN 321:1 |
| list: I've got a little l. | GILB 151:19 |
| listen: Darkling I l. | KEATS 192:3 |
| privilege of wisdom to l. | HOLM 170:15 |
| world should l. then | SHEL 305:11 |
| listening: disease of not l. | SHAK 278:17 |
| l., lying in wait | THOM 330:25 |
| People hearing without l. | SIMON 307:7 |
| listeth: wind bloweth where it l. | BIBLE 53:18 |
| lit: whole Fleet's l. up | WOOD 353:18 |
| literary: beloved by l. pundits | CONN 106:26 |
| l. man—with a wooden leg | DICK 119:21 |
| l. mornings with its hoot | AUDEN 20:25 |
| lowest class is l. footmen | HAZL 164:4 |
| Of all the l. scenes | PRES 255:5 |
| quotation is the parole of l. men | JOHN 185:30 |
| uncorrupted with l. prejudices | JOHN 182:21 |
| unsuccessful l. man | BELL 33:19 |
| literature: English l.'s performing flea | O'CAS 240:23 |
| great Cham of l. | SMOL 310:17 |
| history to produce a little l. | JAMES 179:18 |
| itch of l. | LOVER 210:22 |
| life had been ruined by l. | BROO 73:13 |
| l. clear and cold and pure | LEWIS 206:18 |
| l. is a drug | BORR 69:26 |
| L. is a luxury | CHES 98:9 |
| L. is mostly about having sex | LODGE 209:4 |
| l. is my mistress | CHEK 96:30 |
| L. is news that STAYS news | POUND 254:23 |
| L. is the orchestration | WILD 350:24 |
| louse in the locks of l. | TENN 329:2 |
| Philistine of genius in l. | ARN 18:11 |
| Remarks are not l. | STEIN 314:20 |
| rest is l. | VALE 336:20 |
| littérature: tout le reste est l. | VERL 337:20 |
| little: But wants that l. strong | HOLM 170:17 |
| cry of the L. Peoples | LE G 204:12 |
| either a l. Liberal | GILB 151:12 |
| Ev'ry day a l. death | SOND 311:6 |
| Go, l. bok | CHAU 96:20 |
| hare's own child, the l. hare | HOFF 170:3 |
| here a l., and there a little | BIBLE 46:25 |
| hobgoblin of l. minds | EMER 136:24 |
| L. boxes on the hillside | REYN 259:11 |
| L. Boy kneels at the foot | MILNE 226:1 |
| L. drops of water | CARN 90:29 |
| L. Englanders | ANON 8:21 |
| l. finger shall be thicker | BIBLE 41:33 |
| L. Friend of all the World | KIPL 197:25 |
| little l. grave | SHAK 294:2 |
| Little man, l. man | ELIZ 135:10 |
| L. man, you've had a busy day | HOFF 307:2 |
| l. may be diffused into | BOSW 70:4 |
| l. more, and how much it is | BROW 75:19 |
| L. one! Oh, little one | STEP 315:7 |
| l. saint best fits a l. shrine | HERR 167:22 |
| l. ships of England | GUED 159:6 |
| L. subject, little wit | CAREY 90:1 |
| l. volume but large book | CRAS 111:12 |
| Man wants but l. here below | GOLD 154:27 |
| mother's l. helper | RICH 179:5 |
| much to be done and l. to be known | JOHN 182:27 |
| nor that l., long | YOUNG 360:22 |
| nothing as much as too l. | COMP 106:4 |
| offend one of these l. ones | BIBLE 50:16 |
| Only the l. people pay taxes | HELM 165:8 |
| our l. life is rounded | SHAK 296:10 |
| snug l. Island | DIBD 117:20 |
| So l. done, so much to do | RHOD 259:12 |
| So l. done, such things to be | TENN 325:14 |
| this l. world | SHAK 293:16 |

**little** (*cont.*):

| | |
|---|---|
| though she be but l. | SHAK 290:33 |
| too l., too late | NEV 238:9 |
| turn to l. things | GIBS 150:22 |
| very l. one | MARR 219:27 |
| **littleness:** long l. of life | CORN 108:7 |
| **littlenesses:** thousand peering l. | TENN 324:1 |
| **live:** Come l. with me | DONNE 123:23 |
| Come l.w ith me | MARL 219:3 |
| Days are where we l. | LARK 201:13 |
| do never l. long | SHAK 294:17 |
| Easy l. and quiet die | SCOTT 268:24 |
| enable its citizens to l. | WEIL 345:3 |
| ended by your inability to l. | GONC 155:20 |
| end for which we l. | PEPYS 247:21 |
| forgets to l. | LA BR 199:14 |
| he isn't fit to l. | KING 195:8 |
| He shall not l. | SHAK 281:28 |
| I cannot l. with you | MART 220:7 |
| I must l. | ARG 15:7 |
| in him we l., and move | BIBLE 54:21 |
| In this faith I wish to l. | VILL 338:21 |
| known I was gonna l. this long | BLAKE 60:4 |
| Let us l., my Lesbia | CAT 93:2 |
| l. alone and smash his mirror | ANON 12:10 |
| l. alone in the bee-loud glade | YEATS 359:12 |
| L. a thousand years | SHAK 281:12 |
| l. *dangerously* | NIET 239:21 |
| L. frugally | WALK 341:4 |
| l. together as brothers | KING 195:10 |
| l. well on nothing a year | THAC 329:20 |
| l. without labour | TAWN 322:20 |
| man desires to l. long | SWIFT 320:13 |
| Man is born to l. | PAST 246:9 |
| mortal millions l. *alone* | ARN 17:22 |
| My self now l. | HERR 167:21 |
| nor l. so long | SHAK 284:8 |
| not l. to eat | MOL 232:14 |
| not to l., but to die | BROW 74:20 |
| Rascals, would you l. for ever | FRED 145:20 |
| shall no man see me and l. | BIBLE 40:12 |
| short time to l. | BOOK 66:6 |
| So longe mote ye l. | CHAU 96:15 |
| taught us how to l. | TICK 332:20 |
| teaching nations how to l. | MILT 231:5 |
| Teach me to l. | KEN 193:22 |
| they sometimes l. apart | SAKI 265:22 |
| To l. is like to love | BUTL 84:17 |
| to l. on your knees | IBAR 178:1 |
| To l. without him | WOTT 357:17 |
| To l. with thee | RAL 257:20 |
| to l. your life is not as simple | PAST 246:10 |
| too small to l. in | ANON 11:8 |
| turn and l. with animals | WHIT 348:19 |
| We l. our lives, for ever | RILKE 260:7 |
| we that l. to please | JOHN 183:10 |
| wouldn't l. under Niagara | CARL 90:24 |
| write too much, and l. too long | DAN 113:16 |
| You might as well l. | PARK 245:8 |
| **lived:** I have l. long enough | SHAK 288:1 |
| L. in his mild and magnificent | BROW 76:14 |
| never loved, has never l. | GAY 149:8 |
| Never to have l. is best | YEATS 359:5 |
| To have l. light in the spring | ARN 16:14 |
| your mother and I should have l. | GAY 149:3 |
| **lively:** these are the l. Oracles | COR 108:10 |
| thy true and l. Word | BOOK 65:10 |
| **liver:** L. of blaspheming Jew | SHAK 287:17 |
| open and notorious evil l. | BOOK 64:29 |
| **livery:** l. of the burnished sun | SHAK 289:6 |
| **lives:** Careless talk costs l. | ANON 6:15 |
| ends marked than their l. | SHAK 293:15 |
| l. along the line | POPE 252:15 |
| L. in Eternity's sunrise | BLAKE 61:16 |
| L. of great men all remind us | LONG 209:23 |

**lives** (*cont.*):

| | |
|---|---|
| l. of quiet desperation | THOR 332:9 |
| l. upon hope will die fasting | FRAN 145:11 |
| who lives more l. than one | WILDE 350:17 |
| woman who l. for others | LEWIS 206:12 |
| **living:** alive and well and l. | ANON 8:13 |
| between those who are l. | BURKE 80:17 |
| bodies a l. sacrifice | BIBLE 54:43 |
| body is a machine for l. | TOLS 333:12 |
| Earned a precarious l. | ANON 6:28 |
| fever called 'L.' | POE 250:6 |
| hands of the l. God | BIBLE 56:25 |
| L. and partly living | ELIOT 134:6 |
| l., had no roof to shroud | HEYW 168:9 |
| L. is my job and my art | MONT 233:16 |
| l. know no bounds | SHIR 306:12 |
| l. need charity more | ARN 16:8 |
| L.? The servants will do that | VILL 338:19 |
| long habit of l. indisposeth | BROW 74:5 |
| noble L., and the noble Dead | WORD 356:15 |
| no l. with thee | ADD 2:22 |
| out of the land of the l. | BIBLE 46:21 |
| Plain l. and high thinking | WORD 356:1 |
| respect to the l. | VOLT 340:24 |
| revolutions is l. to some purpose | PAINE 244:15 |
| shadows of the l. | BROW 74:2 |
| start by l. | ANOU 14:9 |
| Summer time an' the l. is easy | GERS 168:6 |
| thou shouldst be l. at this hour | WORD 355:11 |
| unexamined life is not worth l. | SOCR 310:22 |
| wouldn't be l. with me | STEV 316:2 |
| **Livingstone:** Dr L., I presume | STAN 314:9 |
| **Lizzie Borden:** L. took an axe | ANON 8:22 |
| **llama:** L. is a woolly sort | BELL 33:19 |
| **Lloyd George:** L. knew my father | ANON 9:1 |
| **lo:** L.! He comes with clouds | WESL 346:9 |
| L.! the poor Indian | POPE 252:14 |
| **load:** how to l. and bless | KEATS 192:14 |
| L. every rift with ore | KEATS 193:14 |
| **loaf:** l. of bread beneath | FITZ 140:6 |
| **loafing:** cricket as organized l. | TEMP 323:8 |
| **local:** little l. difficulties | MACM 215:16 |
| l., but prized elsewhere | AUDEN 21:13 |
| l. thing called Christianity | HARDY 161:19 |
| **loch:** bonnie banks o' L. Lomon' | ANON 10:2 |
| **Lochinvar:** knight like the young L. | SCOTT 268:19 |
| L. is come out of the west | SCOTT 268:18 |
| **loci:** *Geniumque l.* | VIRG 339:18 |
| **locks:** louse in the l. of literature | TENN 329:2 |
| l. which are left you | SOUT 312:1 |
| shake thy gory l. at me | SHAK 287:11 |
| Your l. were like the raven | BURNS 82:11 |
| **loco:** *Dulce est desipere in l.* | HOR 174:1 |
| **locust:** years that the l. hath eaten | BIBLE 47:19 |
| **locusts:** famine grew, and l. came | THOM 330:11 |
| **locuta:** *Roma l. est* | AUG 22:5 |
| **lodesterre:** language he was the l. | LYDG 212:13 |
| **lodge:** Is best to l. | SHAK 298:8 |
| l. in a garden of cucumbers | BIBLE 45:3 |
| thou lodgest, I will l. | BIBLE 41:8 |
| **lodged:** L. with me useless | MILT 230:22 |
| **lodging:** Hard was their l. | GARTH 148:14 |
| **loftier:** l. race | SYM 321:20 |
| **log-cabin:** L. to White House | THAY 329:27 |
| **logic:** It is the l. of our times | DAY-L 115:6 |
| l. and rhetoric | BACON 25:16 |
| That's l. | CARR 91:20 |
| This Second L. | ARIS 15:10 |
| **logical:** L. consequences | HUXL 177:20 |
| **logs:** Tom bears l. into the hall | SHAK 284:23 |
| **loin:** unlit lamp and the ungirt l. | BROW 77:16 |
| **loins:** l. girt about with truth | BIBLE 56:4 |
| shudder in the l. engenders | YEATS 359:14 |
| thicker than my father's l. | BIBLE 41:33 |
| With your l. girded | BIBLE 39:37 |

loins (cont.):

| | |
|---|---|
| your l. be girded about | BIBLE 52:20 |

loitering: Alone and palely l. KEATS 191:7
Lolita: L., light of my life NAB 236:18
London: And dream of L. MORR 235:16
crowd flowed over L. Bridge ELIOT 134:21
gazed at the L. skies BETJ 36:16
Hell is a city much like L. SHEL 304:13
key of India is L. DISR 121:22
L.: a nation, not a city DISR 122:5
L. Bridge to sketch the ruins MAC 213:15
L. doth pour out her citizens SHAK 280:1
L. is a fine town COLM 105:13
L. like a special correspondent BAG 26:16
L. particular DICK 118:2
L., that great cesspool DOYLE 126:4
L., thou art the flower ANON 9:2
L. Transport diesel-engined FLAN 141:6
parks are the lungs of L. PITT 249:6
rainy Sunday in L. DE Q 117:4
tired of L., he is tired of life JOHN 185:15
lone: I am a l. lorn creetur DICK 118:8
l. shieling of the misty island GALT 147:19
loneliness: l. of the long-distance SILL 307:3
Well of L. HALL 160:14
lonely: All the l. people MCC 205:12
as mirrors are l. AUDEN 21:9
heart is a l. hunter MCL 215:10
l. sea and the sky MAS 221:21
Only the l. MELS 241:16
rapture on the l. shore BYRON 85:12
troubled with her l. life PEPYS 247:16
lonesome: one, that on a l. road COL 104:15
lonesomeness: starlight lit my l. HARDY 162:18
long: Ask that your way be l. CAV 93:10
as l. as ye both shall live BOOK 65:28
certified how l. I have to live BOOK 67:1
gonna live this l. BLAKE 60:4
I am going a l. way TENN 324:22
if a man have l. hair BIBLE 55:10
In the l. run we are all dead KEYN 194:17
it's for such a l. time MOL 232:17
l., and lank, and brown COL 104:11
l. and the short and the tall HUGH 175:18
l. a time lies in one little word SHAK 293:10
l. for scenes where man CLARE 101:7
L. is the way and hard MILT 228:30
l. littleness of life CORN 108:7
Long, l. thoughts LONG 209:21
l., long while AND 5:12
l. awinding KING 195:12
l., withdrawing roar ARN 16:11
Lord, how l. BIBLE 45:13
Love me little, love me l. ANON 9:4
man goeth to his l. home BIBLE 44:26
night of the l. knives HITL 168:21
Nor wants that little l. GOLD 154:27
Not that the story need be l. THOR 332:6
So l. mote ye lyve CHAU 96:15
week is a l. time in politics WILS 351:15
witty and it sha'n't be l. CHES 97:2
longa: Ars l., vita brevis HIPP 168:19
long-distance: l. runner SILL 307:3
longen: l. folk to goon on pilgrimages CHAU 95:11
longer: I am no l. my own METH 223:28
less fun and it lasts l. ANOU 14:9
longings: Immortal l. in me SHAK 272:7
longitude: l. with no platitude FRY 147:1
long-suffering: L., and of great goodness BOOK 68:6
look: all l. just the same REYN 259:11
full l. at the worst HARDY 162:8
know not which way I must l. WORD 356:1
Let him l. to his bond SHAK 289:15
l. after our people SCOTT 268:5
l., and pass on DANTE 113:19

look (cont.):

L. as much like home as we can FRY 147:2
L. at the stars HOPK 172:16
l. at things in bloom HOUS 174:17
L. for me by moonlight NOYES 240:14
L. for me in the nurseries THOM 331:18
l. in my face TRAI 334:2
l. in thy heart and write SIDN 306:17
l. no way but downwards BUNY 79:6
l. shining at new styles AUDEN 21:14
L., stranger, at this island AUDEN 20:26
l. the East End in the face ELIZ 135:18
L. thy last on all things lovely DE L 116:15
L.! Up in the sky! ANON 7:5
l. upon his like again SHAK 274:17
Only a l. and a voice LONG 210:3
row one way and l. another BURT 83:7
They l. on and help LAWR 202:26
looked: more he l. inside MILNE 225:14
lookers on: God and angels to be l. BACON 24:1
looketh: l. on the outward BIBLE 41:15
looking: Here's l. at you, kid EPST 137:11
Leave them while you're l. good LOOS 210:8
l. one way, and rowing another BUNY 79:1
plough, and l. back BIBLE 52:9
someone may be l. MENC 223:8
looking-glass: cracked l. JOYCE 188:12
looks: her l. went everywhere BROW 76:19
His l. do menace heaven MARL 219:6
she needs good l. TUCK 335:9
Stolen l. are nice in chapels HUNT 176:16
loom: she left the l. TENN 326:3
looms: passage through these l. VAUG 337:3
loon: thou cream-faced l. SHAK 287:33
Wanna laugh like a l. HARB 161:13
loose: Every which way but l. KRON 199:6
l. the bands of Orion BIBLE 43:4
L. types of things WORD 357:8
man who should l. me LOW 211:2
loosed: l. our heart in tears ARN 16:19
lord: come, L. Jesus BIBLE 58:8
cometh in the Name of the L. BOOK 68:23
coming of the L. HOWE 175:7
dear L. was crucified ALEX 4:6
die with kissing of my L. MARL 219:12
earth is the L.'s BOOK 66:19
glory of the L. BIBLE 46:9
Great l. of all things POPE 252:18
I am the L. thy God BIBLE 40:2
I replied, 'My L.' HERB 166:23
let the L. be thankit BURNS 82:14
L. be with you MISS 231:9
L., dismiss us BUCK 78:3
L. gave, and the L. hath taken BIBLE 42:22
L. God made them all ALEX 4:2
L. guards the city BIBLE 58:13
L. how it talk't FLET 31:3
L., how long BIBLE 45:13
L. is his name MONS 233:3
L. is my shepherd BOOK 66:17
L. is the source of my light BIBLE 58:9
L. looketh on the heart BIBLE 41:15
L. loveth he chasteneth BIBLE 56:28
L. make his face shine BIBLE 40:15
L., now lettest thou thy servant BIBLE 52:3
L. of all hopefulness STR 318:17
L. of himself, though not WOTT 357:15
L. of the Dance CART 92:13
L. once own the happy lines POPE 252:5
L. Randal, my Son BALL 27:19
L. require of thee BIBLE 47:23
L. shall raise me up RAL 258:1
L.'s my shepherd SCOT 269:8
L. survives the rainbow LOW 211:17

**lord** (*cont.*):
L. thy God is with thee | BIBLE 40:26
L. watch between me | BIBLE 39:23
L., what fools these mortals be | SHAK 290:32
L., with what care | HERB 167:7
Love, thou art absolute sole L. | CRAS 111:9
mouth of the L. hath spoken | BIBLE 46:9
My L. should take frail flesh | CROS 112:13
O L., to what a state dost | TER 329:7
Prepare ye the way of the L. | BIBLE 46:8
sing the L.'s song | BOOK 69:3
sought the L. aright | BURNS 82:1
thou, O L., art more than they | TENN 324:23
Up to a point, L. Copper | WAUGH 343:24
we own thee L. | ANON 14:1
when they crucified my L. | ANON 11:14
**lordliest:** Lords are l. in their wine | MILT 230:16
**lordly:** butter in a l. dish | BIBLE 40:33
**lords:** For the l. who lay ye low | SHEL 305:1
L. are lordliest in their wine | MILT 230:16
L. in ermine, beggars freezing | ROB 260:22
l. will alway that people note | BARC 28:17
one of the L. of life | LAWR 202:22
only a wit among L. | JOHN 183:28
Wi' the Scots l. at his feet | BALL 28:6
**lordships:** l. on a hot afternoon | ANON 11:3
**lose:** findeth his life shall l. it | BIBLE 49:33
l. his own soul | BIBLE 51:23
l. itself in the sky | BROW 75:8
lose thee, I do l. a thing | SHAK 288:18
l. to-morrow the ground won | ARN 17:10
nobly save, or meanly l. | LINC 207:6
nothing to l. but our aitches | ORW 242:14
nothing to l. but their chains | MARX 221:15
To l. one parent | WILDE 349:18
we don't want to l. you | RUB 264:4
**losers:** all are l. | CHAM 93:25
**loses:** l. his misery | ARN 17:13
**losing:** conduct of a l. party | BURKE 79:18
Does it matter?—l. your sight | SASS 267:9
l. one pleased Cato | LUCAN 211:23
**loss:** deeper sense of her l. | GASK 148:17
My richest gain I count but l. | WATTS 343:4
To do our country l. | SHAK 279:17
**lost:** All is l. save honour | FRAN 145:4
all was l. | MILT 229:26
Balls will be l. always | BERR 36:11
be l. in me | TENN 328:5
better to have fought and l. | CLOU 102:21
better to have loved and l. | BUTL 84:11
better to have loved and l. | TENN 325:4
Britain has l. an empire | ACH 1:3
found my sheep which was l. | BIBLE 52:27
France has not l. the war | DE G 116:3
Friends, I have l. a day | TITUS 332:22
he was l., and is found | BIBLE 52:32
Home of l. causes | ARN 18:2
In search of l. time | PROU 255:17
land of l. content | HOUS 174:24
l. boyhood of Judas | Æ 3:4
L. Chord | PROC 255:13
l. generation | STEIN 314:23
l. in translation | FROST 146:28
l., that is unsought | CHAU 96:14
l. the only Playboy | SYNGE 321:22
make wherever we're l. in | FRY 147:2
never l. till won | CRAB 110:28
never to have l. | BUTL 84:11
Not l. but gone before | NORT 240:10
not l. but sent before | CYPR 113:13
not that you won or l. | RICE 259:17
paradises that we have l. | PROU 255:21
want of a horse the rider was l. | FRAN 145:12
woman that deliberates is l. | ADD 2:15
**lot:** l. is fallen unto me | BOOK 66:15

**lot** (*cont.*):
policeman's l. is not | GILB 152:24
Remember L.'s wife | BIBLE 52:37
**Lothario:** gallant, gay L. | ROWE 263:20
**lots:** cast l. upon my vesture | BOOK 66:16
**Lou:** lady that's known as L. | SERV 270:13
**loungers:** l. and idlers | DOYLE 126:4
**louse:** between a l. and a flea | JOHN 186:2
l. in the locks of literature | TENN 329:2
**lousy:** L. but loyal | ANON 9:3
l. skin scabbed here | BUNT 78:14
**love:** Absence is to l. | BUSS 83:19
all for l. | SPEN 313:11
all for l., and a little for the bottle | DIBD 117:17
All l., all liking, all delight | HERR 167:14
all she loves is l. | BYRON 86:9
All that matters is l. and work | FREUD 146:4
Amazing l.! | WESL 346:3
america i l. you | CUMM 112:17
As great in l. as in religion | COWL 109:16
aside a long-cherished l. | CAT 93:5
bring those who l. Thee | TER 329:7
call a dog *Hervey*, I shall l. him | JOHN 183:23
cantons of contemnèd l. | SHAK 297:21
Christ's particular L.'s sake | BROW 77:7
Come down, O L. divine | LITT 208:2
constant l. deemed there | SIDN 306:19
corner in the thing I l. | SHAK 292:17
course of true l. | SHAK 290:13
dark secret l. | BLAKE 62:4
Dear l., for nothing less | DONNE 124:1
dinner of herbs where l. is | BIBLE 43:26
doesn't l. a wall | FROST 146:15
fit l. for gods | MILT 229:24
God is L., but get it in writing | LEE 204:5
good man's l. | SHAK 273:6
Greater l. hath no man | BIBLE 53:40
greater l. hath no man | THOR 332:13
Greater l. than this | JOYCE 188:18
groans of l. to those of the dying | LOWRY 211:22
half in l. with easeful death | KEATS 192:3
Hearts wound up with l. | SPEN 313:2
Hell, madam, is to l. no more | BERN 36:8
hid in the heart of l. | YEATS 359:18
hir housbond as hir l. | CHAU 96:8
hold your tongue, and let me l. | DONNE 123:24
hour of l. | BYRON 86:18
How do I l. thee | BROW 75:5
How I l. my country | PITT 249:10
How should I your true l. know | SHAK 276:32
I could not l. thee | LOV 210:21
I do not l. thee, Dr Fell | BROWN 73:18
I don't l. you, Sabidius | MART 220:4
I drew them ... with bands of l. | BIBLE 47:18
If music be the food of l. | SHAK 297:13
if my l. were in my arms | ANON 11:18
I got to l. one man till I die | HAMM 160:19
I hate and I l. | CAT 93:7
I knew it was l. | BYRON 87:11
I'll l. you, dear | AUDEN 20:11
I l. all waste and solitary | SHEL 303:20
I l. her till I die | ANON 10:18
I l. not man the less | BYRON 85:12
I l. thee still | COWP 110:8
I l. you, Nellie Dean | ARMS 15:24
I'm tired of L. | BELL 33:13
in l. with a cold climate | SOUT 312:6
in l. with the productions of time | BLAKE 61:5
It kills l., it kills art | WAUGH 343:17
joy of l. is too short | MAL 217:2
labour of l. | BIBLE 56:13
Land that I l. | BERL 35:21
laughter and the l. of friends | BELL 34:3
leave to come unto my l. | SPEN 313:6
left thy first l. | BIBLE 57:20

love (cont.):

| | |
|---|---|
| less the object of l. | LAMB 199:23 |
| let me sow l. | FRAN 145:7 |
| Let's do it, let's fall in l. | PORT 253:22 |
| little duty and less l. | SHAK 280:5 |
| live is like to l. | BUTL 84:17 |
| live with me, and be my l. | DONNE 123:23 |
| live with me, and be my l. | MARL 219:3 |
| live with thee, and be thy l. | RAL 257:20 |
| lost the world for l. | DRYD 128:10 |
| L., a child, is ever crying | WROTH 358:1 |
| L., all alike, no season | DONNE 124:12 |
| L. alters not | SHAK 300:9 |
| l., an abject intercourse | GOLD 155:6 |
| L. and a cottage | GARR 105:12 |
| L. and do what you will | AUG 22:2 |
| l. and fame to nothingness | KEATS 192:21 |
| l., and life, it's enemy | ANOU 14:7 |
| L. and marriage rarely can | BYRON 86:10 |
| l. and murder will out | CONG 106:7 |
| L. and scandal are the best | FIEL 139:9 |
| l. a womman that she woot | CHAU 96:14 |
| L. bade me welcome | HERB 167:2 |
| L. built on beauty | DONNE 123:3 |
| l. can do that dares l. attempt | SHAK 294:32 |
| L. ceases to be a pleasure | BEHN 32:21 |
| L. comforteth like sunshine | SHAK 300:18 |
| L. conquers all things | VIRG 340:4 |
| L., curiosity, freckles | PARK 245:5 |
| L. divine, all loves excelling | WESL 346:10 |
| l. for Heathcliff resembles | BRON 72:17 |
| l. God whom he hath not seen | BIBLE 57:17 |
| L. goes toward love | SHAK 295:2 |
| L. has pitched his mansion | YEATS 358:20 |
| l. her, comfort her | BOOK 65:28 |
| l. him, and serve Him | CAT 92:20 |
| l. in a golden bowl | BLAKE 60:10 |
| l. in a hut, with water | KEATS 191:11 |
| l. indeed who quake to say | SIDN 306:22 |
| L. in dying, Faith is defying | BARN 29:8 |
| L. in this part of the world | BYRON 87:17 |
| L. is a boy, by poets styled | BUTL 84:3 |
| L. is a growing or full | DONNE 124:6 |
| L. is a spirit all compact | SHAK 300:17 |
| l. is a thing. It is a prick | PEELE 247:1 |
| l. is a thing that can never | PARK 245:4 |
| l. is hard to catch | MER 223:20 |
| L. is like any other luxury | TROL 334:21 |
| l. is like linen | FLET 142:10 |
| l. is more cruel than lust | SWIN 321:9 |
| L. is not love which alters | SHAK 300:8 |
| l. is not secure | CHES 97:21 |
| l. is of man's life a thing apart | BYRON 86:4 |
| L. is of the valley | TENN 328:7 |
| L. is only one of many passions | JOHN 182:25 |
| l. is slight | MARL 218:18 |
| L. is the delusion | MENC 223:6 |
| l. is the fart | SUCK 318:22 |
| l. is the gift of oneself | ANOU 14:8 |
| L. is the greatest mercy | WILB 349:13 |
| L. is then our duty | GAY 149:6 |
| L. is the wisdom | JOHN 186:9 |
| L. iz like the meazles | BILL 59:10 |
| L. looks not with the eyes | SHAK 290:16 |
| L. me little, love me long | ANON 9:4 |
| l. men too little | BURKE 80:19 |
| L. of money is the root | BIBLE 56:19 |
| l. of what is beautiful | PER 248:1 |
| L.-quarrels oft in pleasing | MILT 230:15 |
| l.'s a malady without a cure | DRYD 128:9 |
| l. Scotland better than truth | JOHN 182:14 |
| L. seeketh not itself to please | BLAKE 62:1 |
| L. seeketh only Self to please | BLAKE 62:2 |
| L. set you going | PLATH 249:16 |
| l. should have courage | TROL 334:13 |

love (cont.):

| | |
|---|---|
| l. slights it | BACON 24:21 |
| L.'s like the measles | JERR 181:13 |
| L. sought is good | SHAK 298:7 |
| L.'s passives are his activ'st | CRAS 111:7 |
| L.'s pleasure lasts | FLOR 142:12 |
| l.'s the noblest frailty | DRYD 127:33 |
| L.'s young dream | MOORE 234:15 |
| l. that asks no question | SPR 313:26 |
| l. that can be reckoned | SHAK 271:4 |
| L. that dare not speak its name | DOUG 125:6 |
| l. that loves a scarlet coat | HOOD 171:6 |
| l. that moves the sun | DANTE 113:24 |
| L. the Beloved Republic | FORS 144:3 |
| L. the brotherhood | BIBLE 57:9 |
| l. the highest when we see it | TENN 324:6 |
| L., the human form divine | BLAKE 61:21 |
| L. the sinner but hate | AUG 22:4 |
| L.-thirty, love-forty | BETJ 37:11 |
| l. those who love you | VOLT 340:21 |
| L., thou art absolute sole Lord | CRAS 111:9 |
| l. thy neighbour as thyself | BIBLE 40:14 |
| L. thyself last | SHAK 280:20 |
| l. to hatred turned | CONG 106:12 |
| l. up groweth with youre age | CHAU 96:22 |
| L. without his wings | BYRON 87:1 |
| L. wol nat been constreyned | CHAU 95:25 |
| L. you ten years before | MARV 220:23 |
| L. your enemies | BIBLE 52:6 |
| make l. deathless | TREN 334:6 |
| make us l. one another | SWIFT 320:10 |
| making l. all year round | BEAU 30:16 |
| man you l. to hate | ANON 9:7 |
| many waters cannot quench l. | BIBLE 45:2 |
| Men l. in haste | BYRON 86:25 |
| more l. and knowledge of you | SHAK 272:13 |
| my Lesbia, and let us l. | CAT 93:2 |
| My l. and I did meet | BETJ 37:5 |
| my l. and I did meet | YEATS 359:1 |
| My l. and I would lie | HOUS 174:20 |
| My l. has died for me to-day | BALL 27:13 |
| my l. is come to me | ROSS 262:21 |
| My l. is of a birth as rare | MARV 220:12 |
| My L.'s a noble madness | DRYD 127:24 |
| my L.'s like a red, red rose | BURNS 82:20 |
| my only l. sprung from | SHAK 294:28 |
| My song is l. unknown | CROS 112:13 |
| My vegetable l. should grow | MARV 220:23 |
| Need we say it was not l. | MILL 224:23 |
| never l. a stranger | BENS 34:21 |
| office and affairs of l. | SHAK 291:17 |
| O lyric L., half-angel | BROW 77:5 |
| one jot of former l. retain | DRAY 126:16 |
| Only our l. hath no decay | DONNE 123:22 |
| our l. is here to stay | GERS 150:7 |
| outward parts L.'s always seen | COWL 109:14 |
| passing the l. of women | BIBLE 41:23 |
| Perfect fear casteth out l. | CONN 107:2 |
| perfect l. casteth out fear | BIBLE 57:16 |
| planet of L. is on high | TENN 326:28 |
| putting L. away | DICK 120:10 |
| right place for l. | FROST 146:8 |
| right true end of l. | DONNE 123:4 |
| says L. | HERB 167:3 |
| separate us from the l. of God | BIBLE 54:42 |
| She bid me take l. easy | YEATS 359:1 |
| So faithful in l. | SCOTT 268:19 |
| soft philosopher of l. | DRYD 128:3 |
| some l. but little policy | SHAK 294:7 |
| sooner allured by l. | ASCH 18:18 |
| so simple, l. | PRÉV 255:6 |
| So true a fool is l. | SHAK 299:20 |
| sports of l. | JONS 187:16 |
| spring of l. resembleth | SHAK 298:18 |
| that they l. | WALL 341:15 |

Magdalen: fourteen months at M. College   GIBB 150:13
magic: house rose like m.   HARG 162:21
If this be m.   SHAK 299:4
let in daylight upon m.   BAG 26:13
m. in a pint bottle   DICK 118:30
mistake medicine for m.   SZASZ 322:1
secret m. of numbers   BROW 74:12
this rough m.   SHAK 296:12
magical: purely m. object   BART 29:19
magistrate: m. corruptible   ROB 260:17
shocks the m.   RUSS 265:4
magna: M. est veritas   BIBLE 58:23
Magna Charta: M. is such a fellow   COKE 103:10
magnanimity: In victory: m.   CHUR 100:4
M. in politics   BURKE 80:5
magnet: gunpowder, and the m.   BACON 25:28
magnificat: M. anima mea   BIBLE 58:16
magnificent: his mild and m. eye   BROW 76:14
Mute and m., without a tear   DRYD 128:20
magnifique: C'est m., mais ce n'est pas   BOSQ 69:28
magnify: Day by day: we m. thee   BOOK 63:21
My soul doth m. the Lord   BIBLE 51:28
My soul doth m. the Lord   BIBLE 58:16
magpie: swollen m. in a fitful sun   POUND 254:21
magus: M. Zoroaster   SHEL 304:15
Mahomet: M. will go to the hill   BACON 24:16
maid: Be good, sweet m.   KING 195:13
I once was a m.   BURNS 82:12
lugger and the m. is mine   JOHN 186:17
m. is not dead   BIBLE 49:26
m. sing in the valley below   ANON 6:27
m. whom there were none   WORD 356:22
many a youth, and many a m.   MILT 227:4
She could not live a m.   PEELE 247:2
way of a man with a m.   BIBLE 44:4
Yonder a m. and her wight   HARDY 162:12
maiden: In m. meditation   SHAK 290:24
M., and mistress   SWIN 320:28
m. of bashful fifteen   SHER 306:6
maidenly: So m., womanly   SKEL 308:2
maidens: all the m. pretty   COLM 105:13
What m. loth   KEATS 191:18
maids: m. are May   SHAK 273:9
m. strange seraphic pieces   TRAH 333:19
malady most incident to m.   SHAK 298:33
seven m. with seven mops   CARR 91:21
Three little m. from school   GILB 151:21
maimed: m., and the halt   BIBLE 52:24
M. us at the start   YEATS 359:19
maintenance: Art of Motorcycle M.   PIRS 249:2
maior: M. erat natu   LUC 212:1
Maisie: Proud M. is in the wood   SCOTT 269:1
majestic: M. though in ruin   MILT 228:27
majestical: laid in bed m.   SHAK 279:16
majesty: as his m., so is his mercy   BIBLE 47:32
Ride on! ride on in m.   MILM 225:13
sight so touching in its m.   WORD 354:15
This earth of m.   SHAK 293:16
Thy M. how bright   FABER 138:3
major: change from m. to minor   PORT 253:19
M. Major   HELL 165:6
major-general: modern M.   GILB 152:23
majority: big enough m.   TWAIN 335:21
Death joins us to the great m.   YOUNG 360:23
join the m. [the dead]   PETR 248:9
what the m. happen to like   WHIT 348:3
majors: scarlet M. at the Base   SASS 267:8
make: Go ahead, m. my day   STIN 317:26
he who made the Lamb m. thee   BLAKE 62:6
I m. on the one day   SKEL 308:4
M. me a willow cabin   SHAK 297:21
no mistakes does not usually m.   PHEL 248:11
Scotsman on the m.   BARR 29:17
M. IT NEW   POUND 254:10

maker: M. of heaven and earth   BOOK 65:5
that sinneth before his M.   BIBLE 48:5
makes: m. me or fordoes me quite   SHAK 292:27
making: came to the m. of man   SWIN 321:3
m. of not marking   SHAK 278:17
malady: love's a m. without a cure   DRYD 128:9
m. of not marking   SHAK 278:17
m. most incident to maids   SHAK 298:33
male: M. and female created he   BIBLE 38:16
m. and the female   BIBLE 39:8
m. of the species   LAWR 202:18
more deadly than the m.   KIPL 196:12
malice: envy, hatred, and m.   BOOK 64:14
M. domestic   SHAK 287:4
M. is of a low stature   HAL 160:8
m. mingled with a little wit   DRYD 127:31
m., to breed causes   JONS 187:17
Nor set down aught in m.   SHAK 293:5
our poor m. remains   SHAK 287:3
With m. toward none   LINC 207:7
Yet m. never was his aim   SWIFT 320:24
malicious: God is subtle but not m.   EINS 131:8
malignant: not m. and remove it   WAUGH 344:1
malmesey: barrel of M. wine   FABY 138:8
malt: m. does more than Milton   HOUS 175:4
Malverne: on M. hilles   LANG 201:6
Malvernian: That old M. brother   BETJ 37:8
mama: M. may have   HOL 170:10
m. of dada   FAD 138:10
mammon: authentic m.   MACN 215:21
cannot serve God and m.   BIBLE 49:3
man: all that may become a m.   SHAK 286:5
Am I not a m. and a brother   WEDG 345:1
And was made m.   MISS 231:16
Any m. has to, needs to   ELIOT 134:15
apparel oft proclaims the m.   SHAK 274:21
Arms and the m.   DRYD 128:25
arms and the m.   VIRG 338:23
bold bad m.   SHAK 280:15
bold bad m., that dared   SPEN 313:8
Both m. and bird and beast   COL 104:18
but be a m.   ARN 16:13
by m. shall his blood be shed   BIBLE 39:9
came to the making of m.   SWIN 321:3
Can't help lovin' dat m.   HAMM 160:19
century of the common m.   WALL 341:9
Child is father of the M.   WORD 355:14
every m. against every man   HOBB 169:8
Every m. is surrounded by   AUST 22:25
everyone has sat except a m.   CUMM 112:18
fat, oily m. of God   THOM 331:21
fit night out for m. or beast   FIEL 139:17
garment from the m.   BLAKE 60:15
gibbets for 'the m.'   COOK 107:17
God created m.   VALE 336:21
God is not a m.   BIBLE 40:18
handsome, well-shaped m.   AUBR 20:2
helpless m., in ignorance   JOHN 183:16
He was a m., take him for all   SHAK 274:17
He was her m., but he done   ANON 7:6
hour is come, but not the m.   SCOTT 268:27
I am a m. upon the land   BALL 27:17
if a m. bites a dog   BOG 62:19
I know myself a m.   DAV 114:14
I met a m. who wasn't there   MEAR 222:18
incomprehensible m. of 82   VICT 338:5
in m. there is nothing great   HAM 160:18
I saw a m. this morning   SHAW 303:1
It's that m. again   ANON 8:12
large-hearted m.   BROW 75:6
last thing civilized by M.   MER 223:16
let him pass for a m.   SHAK 288:30
let no m. put asunder   BOOK 66:3
make a m. a woman   PEMB 247:6
m. after his own heart   BIBLE 41:13

**man** (*cont.*):

| | |
|---|---|
| m. delights not me | SHAK 275:16 |
| m. dreaming I was a butterfly | CHUA 98:19 |
| M. dreams of fame while | TENN 324:15 |
| m. for all seasons | WHIT 349:2 |
| M. goeth forth to his work | BOOK 68:8 |
| m. goeth to his long home | BIBLE 44:26 |
| M. hands on misery to man | LARK 201:18 |
| m. has a right to utter | JOHN 185:26 |
| M. has created death | YEATS 358:22 |
| m. has Forever | BROW 75:32 |
| m.-in-the-street, who, I'm sorry to say | AUDEN 21:3 |
| M. is a nasty creature | MOL 232:25 |
| M. is a noble animal | BROW 74:7 |
| M. is a tool-using animal | CARL 90:21 |
| M. is a useless passion | SART 267:3 |
| M. is born unto trouble | BIBLE 42:29 |
| M. is man's ABC | QUAR 257:4 |
| M. is Nature's sole mistake | GILB 152:25 |
| m. is *so* in the way in the house | GASK 148:16 |
| M. is something to be surpassed | NIET 239:16 |
| M. is the hunter | TENN 327:25 |
| M. is the master of things | SWIN 321:11 |
| M. is the measure of all things | PROT 255:15 |
| M. is the Only Animal that Blushes | TWAIN 335:24 |
| M. is the shuttle | VAUG 337:3 |
| M. is to be held only | EDG 130:18 |
| m. made the town | COWP 110:6 |
| M. marks the earth | BYRON 85:13 |
| m. not old, but mellow | PHIL 248:16 |
| m. of many devices | HOMER 171:1 |
| m. of restless and versatile | HUXL 177:21 |
| m. over forty is a scoundrel | SHAW 302:5 |
| m. owes his entire existence | HEGEL 164:19 |
| M. partly is and wholly hopes | BROW 75:23 |
| m. proposes, but God disposes | THOM 330:1 |
| M., proud man | SHAK 288:14 |
| m. recovered of the bite | GOLD 154:28 |
| m. remains sceptreless | SHEL 304:22 |
| m.'s a man for a' that | BURNS 82:8 |
| m.'s desire is for the woman | COL 104:27 |
| m.'s first disobedience | MILT 228:7 |
| M. shall not live by bread | BIBLE 48:16 |
| m. should be alone | BIBLE 38:20 |
| M.'s inhumanity to man | BURNS 82:16 |
| m.'s the gowd for a' that | BURNS 82:7 |
| M.'s word is God in man | TENN 324:2 |
| m. that hath no music | SHAK 290:3 |
| M. that is born of a woman | BIBLE 42:33 |
| M. that is born of a woman | BOOK 66:6 |
| M. wants but little here below | GOLD 154:27 |
| m. who has found himself out | BARR 29:18 |
| m. who has no office | SHAW 301:6 |
| m. who should loose me | LOW 211:2 |
| m. who stood at the gate | HASK 163:16 |
| m. who's untrue to his wife | AUDEN 21:3 |
| m. who used to notice such | HARDY 162:2 |
| m. who would be king | KIPL 197:27 |
| M. will err while yet | GOET 154:3 |
| m. write a better book | EMER 137:3 |
| m. you love to hate | ANON 9:7 |
| mortal m. is a broomstick | SWIFT 320:6 |
| my m. and I ain't together | KOEH 198:22 |
| No m., having put his hand | BIBLE 52:9 |
| no m. is wanted much | EMER 136:27 |
| number of a m. | BIBLE 57:33 |
| Once to every m. and nation | LOW 211:7 |
| one small step for a m. | ARMS 16:5 |
| only m. is vile | HEBER 164:16 |
| people arose as one m. | BIBLE 41:7 |
| problem is that *m. is dead* | FROMM 146:7 |
| reflecting the figure of a m. | WOOLF 354:2 |
| repelled by m. | INGE 178:13 |
| science and study of m. | CHAR 95:9 |
| sensual m.-in-the-street | AUDEN 21:11 |

**man** (*cont.*):

| | |
|---|---|
| She knows her m. | DRYD 128:24 |
| since by m. came death | BIBLE 55:17 |
| strange what a m. may do | THAC 329:11 |
| This is the state of m. | SHAK 280:18 |
| This was a m. | SHAK 282:2 |
| way of a m. with a maid | BIBLE 44:4 |
| What a piece of work is a m. | SHAK 275:16 |
| what is m., that thou hast | CRAS 111:5 |
| what is m.? Wherefore | LENO 205:19 |
| What is the chief end of m. | SHOR 306:13 |
| when a m. should marry | BACON 25:3 |
| When God at first made m. | HERB 167:5 |
| when I became a m. | BIBLE 55:14 |
| Who's master, who's m. | SWIFT 320:17 |
| Why, m., he doth bestride | SHAK 280:27 |
| woman make more like a m. | LERN 205:26 |
| woman without a m. is like | STEI 315:2 |
| Women who love the same m. | BEER 32:11 |
| Would this m., could he see | AUDEN 20:17 |
| you'll be a M., my son | KIPL 197:7 |
| **Manchester:** school of M. | DISR 122:13 |
| **Mandalay:** Come you back to M. | KIPL 196:21 |
| **mandarin:** M. style | CONN 106:26 |
| **Manderley:** I dreamt I went to M. | DU M 129:5 |
| **mandrake:** m. root | DONNE 124:10 |
| **manger:** In a m. for his bed | ALEX 4:4 |
| laid him in a m. | BIBLE 51:32 |
| One born in a m. | VAUG 337:6 |
| wrapped in the rude m. | MILT 227:25 |
| **manhood:** M. a struggle | DISR 121:26 |
| M. taken by the Son | NEWM 238:19 |
| My m., long misled by wandering | DRYD 127:29 |
| **manhoods:** m. cheap | SHAK 279:20 |
| **manibus:** M. *date lilia plenis* | VIRG 339:17 |
| **manifesto:** first powerful plain m. | SPEN 312:23 |
| **manifold:** m. sins and wickedness | BOOK 63:12 |
| sundry and m. changes | BOOK 64:23 |
| **mankind:** beauteous m. | SHAK 296:15 |
| in th'original perused m. | ARMS 16:1 |
| legislator of m. | JOHN 183:3 |
| M. have been created | AUR 22:12 |
| need not be to hate, m. | BYRON 85:5 |
| proper study of m. is books | HUXL 177:5 |
| proper study of m. is man | POPE 252:17 |
| ride m. | EMER 136:13 |
| **manliness:** silent m. of grief | GOLD 154:26 |
| **manly:** valorous than m. wise | MARL 219:13 |
| **manna:** Dropped m. | MILT 228:23 |
| **manned:** with one man m. | DONNE 123:6 |
| **manner:** All m. of thing | ELIOT 133:13 |
| all m. of thing | JUL 188:21 |
| m. of his speech | SHAK 271:13 |
| m. which is my aversion | BYRON 86:16 |
| to the m. born | SHAK 274:26 |
| **manners:** catch the M. living | POPE 252:11 |
| corrupt good m. | BIBLE 55:19 |
| English m. more frightening | JARR 180:12 |
| good table m. | MIKES 224:10 |
| Leave off first for m.' sake | BIBLE 48:4 |
| M. maketh man | WYK 358:7 |
| m. of a dancing master | JOHN 184:1 |
| m. of a Marquess | GILB 152:26 |
| M. the need of the plain | WAUGH 344:3 |
| Men's evil m. live in brass | SHAK 280:22 |
| Oh, the times! Oh, the m. | CIC 100:25 |
| thereby to rectify m. | MILT 230:32 |
| To soften m., but corrupt | BYRON 86:33 |
| **manoeuvre:** blend force with a m. | TROT 335:2 |
| **mansion:** Love has pitched his m. | YEATS 358:20 |
| made his everlasting m. | SHAK 296:24 |
| m. call the fleeting breath | GRAY 157:8 |
| upon thy fading m. spend | SHAK 300:14 |
| **mansion-house:** m. of liberty | MILT 231:3 |
| **mansions:** dolorous m. | MILT 227:28 |

**mansions** (*cont.*):
  Father's house are many m.      BIBLE 53:37
  lasting m. of the dead      CRAB 110:22
**mantle**: cast his m. upon him      BIBLE 42:4
  green m. of the standing pool      SHAK 283:15
  russet m. clad      SHAK 274:3
**mantled**: M. in mist      AUDEN 20:9
**manunkind**: busy monster, m.      CUMM 112:20
**manure**: It is its natural m.      JEFF 180:21
**many**: Done because we are too m.      HARDY 161:22
  How m. things I can do without      SOCR 310:20
  Legion: for we are m.      BIBLE 51:21
  loved the suffering m.      BENT 35:4
  makes so m. of them      LINC 207:11
  m. are called, but few      BIBLE 50:28
  m. change and pass      SHEL 303:13
  m.-splendoured thing      THOM 331:15
  owed by so m. to so few      CHUR 99:15
  So m. worlds, so much to do      TENN 325:14
**map**: Roll up that m.      PITT 249:9
**maps**: geographers, in Afric-m.      SWIFT 320:21
  Geography is about M.      BENT 35:5
  m. on a small scale      SAL 266:3
**mar**: I m. on the other      SKEL 308:4
  m. all with this starting      SHAK 287:29
**Marathon**: M. looks on the sea      BYRON 86:14
  skirmish fought near M.      GRAV 156:15
**marble**: dwelt in m. halls      BUNN 78:13
  left it m.      AUG 22:7
  m. index of a mind      WORD 356:10
  m. to retain      BYRON 84:28
  Not m., nor the gilded      SHAK 299:19
  Poets that lasting m. seek      WALL 341:13
**March**: ashbuds in the front of M.      TENN 323:23
  Beware the ides of M.      SHAK 280:25
  droghte of M. hath perced      CHAU 95:10
  winds of M. with beauty      SHAK 298:32
**march**: Do not m. on Moscow      MONT 233:23
  m. of a nation      PARN 245:23
  m. of intellect      SOUT 312:4
  three hours' m. to dinner      HAZL 164:8
**marche**: *Le congrès ne m. pas*      LIGNE 207:2
**marched**: m. breast forward      BROW 75:11
**marching**: His soul is m. on      ANON 8:14
  His truth is m. on      HOWE 175:7
  I hear the sound of m.      RICH 179:7
  M. as to war      BAR 29:1
  M. to the Promised Land      BAR 29:2
  M. where it likes      ARN 17:27
**mare**: brought him a Flanders m.      HENR 166:1
  lend me your grey m.      BALL 28:11
**mares**: M. eat oats      DRAKE 126:14
**Margaret**: M., áre you grieving      HOPK 172:14
  Merry M.      SKEL 308:3
**margin**: meadow of m.      SHER 306:3
  world, whose m. fades      TENN 328:21
**Mariana**: dejected M.      SHAK 288:22
**Marie**: I am M. of Roumania      PARK 245:4
**Maries**: Queen had four M.      BALL 28:2
**marigold**: m., that goes to bed      SHAK 298:31
**marijuana**: experimented with m.      CLIN 102:5
**mariner**: haul and draw with the m.      DRAKE 126:12
  It is an ancient M.      COL 104:3
**mark**: If you would hit the m.      LONG 209:14
  Lord set a m. upon Cain      BIBLE 39:5
  man's distinctive m. alone      BROW 75:23
  m., or the name of the beast      BIBLE 57:32
  read, m., learn      BOOK 64:22
**marked**: m. him for his own      WALT 342:15
  m. Him in the flowering      TENN 324:16
**market**: bought in the m.      CLOU 102:11
**marking**: malady of not m.      SHAK 278:17
**marks**: bears the m. of the last      HAIG 159:16
  m. of the beast      HARDY 161:23
**Marlowe**: M.'s mighty line      JONS 187:26

**Marquess**: manners of a M.      GILB 152:26
**marred**: man that's m.      SHAK 271:1
**marriage**: comedies ended by a m.      BYRON 86:12
  companionship as in m.      ADAMS 1:12
  Courtship to m.      CONG 106:14
  furnish forth the m. tables      SHAK 274:16
  get anywhere in a m.      MURD 236:10
  Hanging and m.      FARQ 138:20
  hanging prevents a bad m.      SHAK 297:18
  her fortune by way of m.      FIEL 139:11
  *left-handed* m.      WOLL 353:12
  Love and m. rarely can      BYRON 86:10
  M. always demands the finest      BAUM 30:11
  M. had always been her object      AUST 23:4
  M. has many pains      JOHN 183:5
  M. is like life in this      STEV 317:8
  m. is not that adults produce      DE VR 117:12
  M. isn't a word, it's a *sentence*      VIDOR 338:15
  M. is popular because      SHAW 301:30
  M. is the grave or tomb of wit      CAV 93:13
  M. may be a stormy lake      PEAC 246:24
  m. of true minds      SHAK 300:8
  m. than a ministry      BAG 26:11
  My definition of m.      SMITH 310:5
  nor are given in m.      BIBLE 50:30
  retrieve his fortunes by m.      DICK 118:31
  So that is m., Lily thought      WOOLF 354:4
  To speke of wo that is in m.      CHAU 96:5
  woman dictates before m.      ELIOT 132:8
**marriages**: happiest m. on earth      DE V 117:11
  There are good m.      LA R 201:22
  unhappy m. come from      WOD 352:11
  we will have no more m.      SHAK 276:1
**married**: if ever we had been m.      GAY 149:3
  if m. life were all      MILL 224:19
  I m. beneath me      ASTOR 19:9
  imprudently m. the barber      FOOTE 142:20
  in m. life three is company      WILDE 349:17
  I would be m. to a single life      CRAS 111:13
  like other m. couples      SAKI 265:22
  M., charming, chaste      BYRON 85:23
  M. in haste, we may repent      CONG 106:13
  m. is a man that's married      SHAK 271:1
  m. past redemption      DRYD 128:7
  m. people have to see these      PEPYS 247:18
  m. to a poem      KEATS 193:11
  Mocks m. men      SHAK 284:21
  one fool at least in every m.      FIEL 139:4
  Reader, I m. him      BRON 72:12
  Trade Unionism of the m.      SHAW 301:24
  well-bred as if we were not m.      CONG 106:20
**marries**: signify whom one m.      ROG 261:20
**marry**: better to m. than to burn      BIBLE 55:5
  Can't get away to m. you today      LEIGH 204:17
  Carlyle and Mrs Carlyle m.      BUTL 84:12
  Doänt thou m. for munny      TENN 327:9
  Man may not m. his Mother      BOOK 69:19
  m. a man who hates his      BENN 34:19
  M. my body to that dust      KING 195:5
  m. whom she likes      THAC 329:14
  men we wanted to m.      STEI 314:25
  not taken in when they m.      AUST 22:18
  persons about to m.      PUNCH 256:6
  resurrection they neither m.      BIBLE 50:30
  when a man should m.      BACON 25:3
  while ye may, go m.      HERR 167:25
**marrying**: From m. in haste      THOM 331:1
**marshal**: m.'s baton      LOUI 210:16
**Martha**: M. was cumbered about      BIBLE 52:14
**martial**: M., the things for to attain      SURR 319:6
**Martini**: into a dry M.      ANON 8:18
**martlet**: Like the m.      SHAK 289:13
  temple-haunting m.      SHAK 285:21
**martyrdom**: dreadful m. must run      AUDEN 21:2

martyrdom (*cont.*):
M. is the test
M. ... only way to become famous | JOHN 185:26 | | SHAW 300:29
martyrs: blood of the m. | TERT 329:8
noble army of M. | BOOK 63:19
stones and clouts make m. | BROW 74:4
marvel: There could I m. | THOM 330:14
marvellous: done m. things | BOOK 68:3
m. boy | WORD 356:16
marvels: wherein all m. summèd | SOUT 312:7
Marx: Karl M. and Catherine | ATTL 19:13
Marxist: M.—of the Groucho | ANON 12:7
Mary: Hail M., full of grace | ANON 13:13
M. Ambree | BALL 28:1
M. had a little lamb | HALE 160:7
M. was found in adulterous bed | BLAKE 60:13
*What* is the matter with M. Jane | MILNE 225:23
mask: loathsome m. has fallen | SHEL 304:22
m. like Castlereagh | SHEL 304:4
masonry: man into the social m. | WELLS 345:20
masquerade: truth in m. | BYRON 86:23
mass: Paris is well worth a m. | HENR 165:21
two thousand years of m. | HARDY 162:4
massacre: not as sudden as a m. | TWAIN 335:22
masses: bow, ye m. | GILB 151:9
calling 'em the m. | PRIE 255:7
m. against the classes | GLAD 153:13
m. yearning to breathe free | LAZ 203:2
massy: huge m. face | MAC 213:6
mast: bends the gallant m. | CUNN 113:7
master: eateth your M. with publicans | BIBLE 49:21
great m. so to sympathize | MILT 227:25
mad and savage m. | SOPH 311:14
Man is the m. of things | SWIN 321:11
m. a grief | SHAK 291:22
M.-morality and slave-morality | NIET 239:22
m. of my fate | HENL 165:18
M. of this college | BEEC 32:6
swear allegiance to any m. | HOR 173:5
which is to be m. | CARR 92:1
Who's m., who's man | SWIFT 320:17
masterpieces: in the midst of m. | FRAN 145:3
masters: m. of their fates | SHAK 280:27
never wrong, the Old M. | AUDEN 21:1
people are the m. | BURKE 80:23
serve two m. | BIBLE 49:3
their victory but new m. | HAL 160:9
We are the m. now | SHAW 302:28
mastery: constreyned by m. | CHAU 95:25
m. of the thing | HOPK 172:21
mastodons: calling to Aunt like m. | WOD 352:19
masturbation: Don't knock m. | ALLEN 4:14
match: blue spurt of a lighted m. | BROW 76:17
colors dont quite m. your face | ASHF 18:21
m. with shedding tears | SHAK 294:3
Ten to make and the m. to win | NEWB 238:13
matched: m. us with His hour | BROO 73:9
matches: he plays extravagant m. | GILB 152:2
With that stick of m. | MAND 217:9
matchless: m. deed's achieved | SMART 308:14
mate: Made my m. | STEV 317:20
mater: *Stabat M. dolorosa* | JAC 179:3
mathematician: pure m. | JEANS 180:17
mathematics: M. may be defined | RUSS 265:2
M. possesses not only truth | RUSS 265:3
m., subtle | BACON 25:16
no place for ugly m. | HARDY 161:18
Matilda: M. told such Dreadful Lies | BELL 33:8
matrimony: argument in favour of m. | AUST 23:11
critical period in m. | HERB 166:18
joined together in holy M. | BOOK 65:25
respectable as that of m. | TROL 334:14
safest in m. to begin | SHER 305:27
take m. at its lowest | STEV 317:7
matron: Thou sober-suited m. | SHAK 295:12

matter: altering the position of m. | RUSS 265:1
beginning of any great m. | DRAKE 126:10
Dirt is only m. out of place | GRAY 156:18
Does it m.?—losing your sight | SASS 267:9
if it is it doesn't m. | GILB 152:28
m. enough to save one's own | BROW 76:12
More m. for a May morning | SHAK 298:11
More m. with less art | SHAK 275:10
not much dislike the m. | SHAK 271:13
order this m. better in France | STER 315:8
sum of m. remains | BACON 24:4
What is M.?—Never mind | PUNCH 256:10
*What* is the m. with Mary Jane | MILNE 225:23
wretched m. and lame metre | MILT 228:5
matters: Nobody that m. | MILL 224:21
Matthew: M., Mark | ANON 9:8
mattress: crack it open on a m. | MILL 225:2
maturing: my mind is m. | NASH 237:14
Maud: Come into the garden, M. | TENN 326:28
mausoleum: then as its m. | AMIS 5:2
mawkish: So sweetly m. | POPE 250:15
Max: incomparable M. | SHAW 302:24
maxim: we have got the M. Gun | BELL 33:18
maxima: *mea m. culpa* | MISS 231:11
maximum: m. of temptation | SHAW 301:30
May: darling buds of M. | SHAK 299:12
fayr as is the rose in M. | CHAU 96:11
fressh as is the month of M. | CHAU 95:13
From M. to December | AND 5:12
I'm to be Queen o' the M. | TENN 327:5
maids are M. | SHAK 273:9
M. is a pious fraud | LOW 211:10
M. month flaps | HARDY 162:2
M. mornyng on Maluerne hulles | LANG 201:6
M. without cloud | ARAG 14:21
More matter for a M. morning | SHAK 298:11
snow in M.'s new-fangled | SHAK 284:11
there's an end of M. | HOUS 174:9
may: know not what we m. | SHAK 276:33
maypole: away to the M. hie | ANON 6:19
where's the M. in the Strand | BRAM 71:13
maypoles: I sing of M. | HERR 167:12
maze: Now burgeons every m. | TENN 325:29
mazily: m. murmuring | TENN 327:8
MBE: M.s and your knighthoods | KEAT 190:8
McGregor: Mr M.'s garden | POTT 254:3
me: For you but not for m. | ANON 9:21
queer save thee and m. | OWEN 243:18
meadow: painted m. | ADD 2:21
through a m. of margin | SHER 306:3
meadows: m. green | SHAK 299:17
meal: handful of m. in a barrel | BIBLE 41:35
mean: Down these m. streets | CHAN 94:9
*He* nothing common did or m. | MARV 220:18
It all depends what you m. by | JOAD 181:15
loves the golden m. | HOR 173:22
no m. city | BIBLE 54:23
no m. of death | SHAK 281:12
poem should not m. but be | MACL 215:9
say what you m. | CARR 91:6
They may not m. to | LARK 201:17
what we m., we say | ARN 16:10
meander: M.'s margent green | MILT 226:10
meaner: m. things are within her | ELIOT 132:5
meaning: faint m. make pretence | DRYD 128:5
Free from all m. | DRYD 127:18
m. doesn't matter | GILB 152:10
plain man in his plain m. | SHAK 289:23
teems with hidden m. | GILB 152:27
within the m. of the Act | ANON 10:3
meanings: two m. packed | CARR 92:2
With words and m. | ELIOT 133:3
meanly: m. wrapped | MILT 227:25
means: best ends by the best m. | HUTC 177:1

means (cont.):

| | |
|---|---|
| between ends and scarce m. | ROBB 260:15 |
| die beyond my m. | WILDE 350:22 |
| end justifies the m. | BUS 83:16 |
| invisible m. of support | BUCH 77:27 |
| live within our m. | WARD 342:18 |
| m. intensely, and m. good | BROW 75:31 |
| m. just what I choose | CARR 91:26 |
| m. to do ill deeds | SHAK 282:12 |
| mercy of his m. | THOM 330:9 |
| No one m. all he says | ADAMS 1:21 |
| politics by other m. | CLAU 101:16 |
| Private M. is dead | SMITH 309:20 |
| without m. of some change | BURKE 80:10 |

| | |
|---|---|
| meant: knew what it m. once | KLOP 198:12 |
| measles: Love iz like the m. | BILL 59:10 |
| Love's like the m. | JERR 181:13 |
| measure: good m., pressed down | BIBLE 52:7 |
| Man is the m. of all things | PROT 255:15 |
| m. of the universe | SHEL 304:20 |
| M. your mind's height | BROW 76:22 |
| Time is the m. of movement | AUCT 20:8 |
| measured: dance is a m. pace | BACON 23:24 |
| m. out my life with coffee | ELIOT 133:27 |
| measures: in short m. | JONS 187:24 |
| M. not men | CANN 89:13 |
| meat: eater came forth m. | BIBLE 41:3 |
| m. in the hall | STEV 317:17 |
| Heaven sends us good m. | GARR 148:11 |
| I have no stomach for such m. | DOBS 122:26 |
| On our m., and on us all | HERR 167:11 |
| Some have m. and cannot eat | BURNS 82:14 |
| taste my m. | HERB 167:3 |
| meats: funeral baked m. | SHAK 274:16 |
| méchant: un m. animal | MOL 232:25 |
| meddle: M. and muddle | DERBY 117:7 |
| medias: in m. res | HOR 173:1 |
| medical: in advance of m. thought | WOD 352:20 |
| M. Crowner's a queer sort | BARH 28:21 |
| medicinal: M. discovery | AYRES 23:15 |
| medicine: M. is my lawful wife | CHEK 96:30 |
| men mistake m. for magic | SZASZ 322:1 |
| miserable have no other m. | SHAK 288:17 |
| mediocre: Some men are born m. | HELL 165:6 |
| Titles distinguish the m. | SHAW 301:31 |
| mediocrity: M. knows nothing higher | DOYLE 126:8 |
| m. thrust upon them | HELL 165:6 |
| meditation: In maiden m. | SHAK 290:24 |
| some happy tone of m. | WORD 355:12 |
| medium: m. is the message | MCL 215:12 |
| medley: of extemporanea | PARK 245:4 |
| meed: m. of some melodious tear | MILT 227:11 |
| meek: Blessed are the m. | BIBLE 48:19 |
| meet: hoping we m. now and then | PORT 253:21 |
| make him an help m. | BIBLE 38:20 |
| m. and fight so to do | BOOK 65:14 |
| m. 'em on your way down | MIZN 232:11 |
| m., right, and our bounden | BOOK 65:15 |
| merrily m. in heaven | MORE 235:4 |
| never the twain shall m. | KIPL 196:4 |
| Though infinite, can never m. | MARV 220:13 |
| To m. thee in that hollow vale | KING 195:5 |
| We loved, sir—used to m. | BROW 75:21 |
| Yet m. we shall, and part | BUTL 84:21 |
| meeting: Journeys end in lovers m. | SHAK 297:23 |
| m. where it likes | ARN 17:27 |
| méfiez-vous: M.! Les oreilles | ANON 12:15 |
| melancholy: green and yellow m. | SHAK 298:1 |
| Hence, loathèd M. | MILT 226:27 |
| m. god protect thee | SHAK 297:33 |
| m., long, withdrawing roar | ARN 16:11 |
| m. out of a song as a weasel | SHAK 272:20 |
| m. sold a goodly manor | SHAK 271:2 |
| moping m. | MILT 229:31 |
| Naught so sweet as M. | BURT 83:5 |

melancholy (cont.):

| | |
|---|---|
| rare recipe for m. | LAMB 200:7 |
| What charm can soothe her m. | GOLD 155:13 |
| meliora: Video m. | OVID 243:15 |
| melodies: Heard m. are sweet | KEATS 191:19 |
| melody: m. lingers on | BERL 36:2 |
| my Luve's like the m. | BURNS 82:20 |
| pretty girl is like a m. | BERL 36:1 |
| smale foweles maken m. | CHAU 95:11 |
| melons: Stumbling on m. | MARV 220:15 |
| Melrose: view fair M. aright | SCOTT 268:10 |
| melt: crown o' the earth doth m. | SHAK 271:25 |
| m. with ruth | MILT 227:17 |
| So let us m. | DONNE 124:15 |
| too solid flesh would m. | SHAK 274:9 |
| melted: m. into air | SHAK 296:10 |
| melting-pot: great M. [America] | ZANG 360:27 |
| member: ACCEPT ME AS A M. | MARX 221:5 |
| members: m. one of another | BIBLE 55:32 |
| membra: Etiam disiecti m. | HOR 174:3 |
| même: plus c'est la m. chose | KARR 190:2 |
| meminisse: haec olim m. iuvabit | VIRG 339:2 |
| memoirs: To write one's m. | PÉT 248:7 |
| memorable: Upon that m. scene | MARV 220:18 |
| memorandum: m. is written to | ACH 1:4 |
| memorial: which have no m. | BIBLE 48:8 |
| whole earth as their m. | PER 248:2 |
| memories: m. are card-indexes | CONN 107:1 |
| M. are hunting horns | APOL 14:11 |
| M. are not shackles | BENN 34:13 |
| memory: brings back a m. ever green | PORT 253:18 |
| Fond M. brings the light | MOORE 234:20 |
| Footfalls echo in the m. | ELIOT 132:26 |
| grand m. for forgetting | STEV 316:26 |
| Illiterate him from your m. | SHER 305:26 |
| m. revealed itself | PROU 255:18 |
| Midnight shakes the m. | ELIOT 134:11 |
| Quick, thy tablets, M. | ARN 16:20 |
| Thanks for the m. | ROBIN 260:19 |
| Vibrates in the m. | SHEL 305:4 |
| women'll stay in a man's m. | KIPL 198:4 |
| men: all m. are created equal | ANON 11:12 |
| bloody m. are like bloody buses | COPE 107:22 |
| boon and a blessing to m. | ANON 11:1 |
| Bring forth m.-children only | SHAK 286:7 |
| fishers of m. | BIBLE 48:18 |
| For fear of little m. | ALL 4:18 |
| great Nature made us m. | LOW 211:6 |
| I see m. as trees, walking | BIBLE 51:22 |
| leaves is a generation of m. | HOMER 170:21 |
| life in my men | WEST 346:21 |
| Measures not m. | CANN 89:13 |
| m. also are burned | HEINE 164:21 |
| m. and malice to breed causes | JONS 187:17 |
| M. are April when they woo | SHAK 273:9 |
| M. are but children of a larger | DRYD 127:25 |
| M. are but gilded loam | SHAK 293:7 |
| m. are created equal | JEFF 180:18 |
| M. are so honest | LERN 205:26 |
| m. at whiles are sober | HOUS 174:10 |
| m. decay | GOLD 154:18 |
| M. Eat Hogs | STEV 316:7 |
| M. have had every advantage | AUST 22:27 |
| M. in great place | BACON 24:27 |
| m. in women do require | BLAKE 61:17 |
| m. may be as positive in error | LOCKE 208:17 |
| m. may come and m. may go | TENN 323:13 |
| M. must be taught | POPE 252:8 |
| M. must endure their going | SHAK 283:30 |
| m. must work, and women | KING 195:16 |
| M., my brothers, men | TENN 326:9 |
| m. of stones | SHAK 284:4 |
| M. seldom make passes | PARK 245:6 |
| M.! The only animal | LAWR 202:20 |
| m. were all asleep | BRID 72:1 |

**midnight** (cont.):

| | |
|---|---|
| cease upon the m. with no pain | KEATS 192:3 |
| chimes at m. | SHAK 278:24 |
| Frost at M. | COL 103:18 |
| Holding hands at m. | GERS 150:8 |
| iron tongue of m. | SHAK 291:9 |
| m. never come | MARL 218:12 |
| m. oil | QUAR 257:2 |
| M. shakes the memory | ELIOT 134:11 |
| mock the m. bell | SHAK 271:19 |
| sighed upon a m. pillow | SHAK 272:18 |
| still her woes at m. rise | LYLY 212:17 |
| 'Tis the year's m. | DONNE 124:7 |
| Upon the m. hours | KEATS 192:8 |
| visions before m. | BROW 74:23 |

**midst**: m. of life we are in death  BOOK 66:7
there am I in the m. of them  BIBLE 50:18

**midsummer**: high M. pomps  ARN 17:19
Why, this is very m. madness  SHAK 298:9

**midway**: M. along the path of our life  DANTE 113:17

**midwife**: She is the fairies' m.  SHAK 294:24

**mid-winter**: In the bleak m.  ROSS 263:2

**mieux**: Le m. est l'ennemi du bien  VOLT 340:15
tout est au m.  VOLT 340:10

**might**: Britons alone use 'M.'  WAUGH 343:28
do it with thy m.  BIBLE 44:19
Exceeds man's m.  SHAK 297:3
It m. have been  HARTE 163:12
It m. have been  WHIT 349:1
Lord of all power and m.  BOOK 64:25
our m. lessens  ANON 11:5
spirit of counsel and m.  BIBLE 45:18

**might-have-been**: my name is M.  ROSS 263:8

**mightier**: make thee m. yet  BENS 34:20
pen is m. than the sword  BULW 78:11

**mightiest**: 'Tis m. in the mightiest  SHAK 289:26

**mighty**: how are the m. fallen  BIBLE 41:20
Marlowe's m. line  JONS 187:26
M. and dreadful  DONNE 123:8
m. from their seats  BIBLE 51:29
m. lak' a rose  STAN 314:11
m. roar of London's traffic  ANON 9:23
m. Victor's brow  KELLY 193:19
rushing m. wind  BIBLE 54:8
thou m. man of valour  BIBLE 40:35

**migrations**: all our m.  GOLD 155:12

**mild**: draw'd m.  DICK 119:4
his m. and magnificent eye  BROW 76:14

**miles**: draw but twenty m. a day  MARL 219:14
Draw out our m.  SHAK 293:17
go but thirty m. a day  SHAK 278:21
m. to go before I sleep  FROST 146:23

**militant**: first m. lowbrow  BERL 36:5
state of Christ's Church m.  BOOK 65:7

**militarism**: M. is fetish worship  TAWN 322:18

**military**: hold the m. mind  TUCH 335:7
matter to entrust to m. men  CLEM 101:21
order and m. discipline  ANON 6:22
When the m. man approaches  SHAW 301:23

**milk**: drunk the m. of Paradise  COL 104:1
find a trout in the m.  THOR 332:5
flowing with m. and honey  BIBLE 39:32
Gin was mother's m. to her  SHAW 302:18
gone to m. the bull  JOHN 184:12
m. and the yoghurt  TRIL 334:10
m. comes frozen home  SHAK 284:23
m. my ewes and weep  SHAK 299:1
m. of human kindness  SHAK 285:15
M.'s leap toward immortality  FAD 138:9
m. the cow of the world  WILB 349:10
m. were scarce out of him  SHAK 297:20
One end is moo, the other, m.  NASH 237:10
putting m. into babies  CHUR 99:21
sincere m. of the word  BIBLE 57:7
take my m. for gall  SHAK 285:18

**milk** (cont.):

With m. and honey blessed  NEALE 237:22

**milk-soup**: M. men call  PATM 246:18

**mill**: at the m. with slaves  MILT 230:10
More water glideth by the m.  SHAK 296:26
old m. by the stream  ARMS 15:24

**millenium**: calico m.  CARL 90:25

**miller**: hackneyed jokes from M.  BYRON 86:31
M. of Dee  BICK 58:24
Than wots the m.  SHAK 296:26

**million**: Fifty m. Frenchmen  GUIN 159:9
m. million spermatozoa  HUXL 177:11

**millionaire**: M. That is my religion  SHAW 301:9
old-fashioned m.  FISH 140:1
silk hat on a Bradford m.  ELIOT 134:29

**millionaires**: m. love a baked apple  FIRB 139:21

**millions**: M. long for immortality  ERTZ 137:15
m. of strange shadows  SHAK 299:18
m. of surprises  HERB 167:7
m. of the mouthless dead  SORL 311:16

**mills**: dark Satanic m.  BLAKE 61:12
m. of God grind slowly  LONG 209:24

**millstone**: m. were hanged about  BIBLE 50:16

**millstones**: Turned to m.  SHEL 304:5

**Milton**: malt does more than M.  HOUS 175:4
M., a name to resound for ages  TENN 327:7
M., Madam, was a genius  JOHN 186:4
M.'s the prince of poets  BYRON 86:15
M.! thou shouldst be living  WORD 355:11
M. was for us  BROW 76:14
M. wrote in fetters  BLAKE 60:25
mute inglorious M.  GRAY 157:9

**mimsy**: m. were the borogoves  CARR 91:15

**mince**: They dined on m.  LEAR 203:13

**mind**: beauty is the m. diseased  BYRON 85:9
body filled and vacant m.  SHAK 279:16
Cast your m. on other days  YEATS 360:7
concentrates his m.  JOHN 185:14
conjunction of the m.  MARV 220:13
could not make up his m.  OLIV 241:8
cutting edge of the m.  BRON 72:9
dagger of the m.  SHAK 286:10
distressed, in m., body  BOOK 64:19
fool uttereth all his m.  BIBLE 44:2
Georgia on my m.  GORR 155:23
He first damages his m.  ANON 13:8
His m. moves upon silence  YEATS 359:15
how little the m. is actually  JOHN 185:2
human m. in ruins  DAV 114:16
If I am out of my m.  BELL 34:4
index of a feeling m.  CRAB 110:29
it's all in the m.  WOLFE 353:5
Keep violence in the m.  ALD 3:16
know the m. of God  HAWK 163:18
many men and knew their m.  HOMER 171:1
marble index of a m.  WORD 356:10
Measure your m.'s height  BROW 76:22
m. a mirror is of heavenly  SOUT 312:7
m. and hand went together  COND 165:11
m. does not make us soft  PER 248:1
m. has mountains  HOPK 172:10
M. has no sex  WOLL 353:10
M. in its purest play  WILB 349:11
m. is a very opal  SHAK 297:33
m. is clouded with a doubt  TENN 324:22
m. is its own place  MILT 228:12
m. is not a bed to be made  AGATE 3:6
m.'s construction in the face  SHAK 285:14
m. serene for contemplation  GAY 149:13
m. that of Lord Beaverbrook  ATTL 19:12
m. watches itself  CAMUS 89:4
m. which contemplates them  HUME 176:9

mind (cont.):
m. which reveres details | LEWIS 206:19
minister to a m. diseased | SHAK 288:2
my m. forbids to crave | DYER 129:16
my m. is maturing late | NASH 237:14
my m.'s unsworn | EUR 137:22
My m. to me a kingdom is | DYER 129:16
noblest frailty of the m. | SHAD 270:18
nothing great but m. | HAM 160:18
not in my perfect m. | SHAK 283:29
no way out of the m. | PLATH 249:13
one dead level ev'ry m. | POPE 250:19
ordinary m. on an ordinary day | WOOLF 353:21
padlock—on her m. | PRIOR 255:9
Reading is to the m. | STEE 314:17
robs the m. of all its powers | BURKE 80:7
satisfied with her lover's m. | TROL 334:19
sentences until reeled the m. | GIBBS 150:18
sex in the m. | LAWR 202:19
shocks the m. of a child | PAINE 244:7
sound m. in a sound body | JUV 189:13
To change your m. | AUR 22:11
true genius is a m. of large | JOHN 182:18
what a noble m. is here | SHAK 276:2
What is M.?—No matter | PUNCH 256:10
minds: comfortable m. | CUMM 113:5
fairly developed m. | FORS 143:15
great empire and little m. | BURKE 80:5
marriage of true m. | SHAK 300:8
M. are like parachutes | DEWAR 117:13
M. like beds always made up | WILL 351:7
m. made better by their | ELIOT 132:17
m. of my generation destroyed | GINS 153:3
pervert climbs into the m. | BRON 72:11
spur of all great m. | CHAP 94:20
Thou m. me o' departed joys | BURNS 81:28
mine: but m. own | SHAK 273:11
If they are m. or no | HOUS 174:14
m. own familiar friend | BOOK 67:12
she is m. for life | SPARK 312:12
'Twas m., 'tis his | SHAK 292:11
miner: Dwelt a m., Forty-niner | MONT 234:2
mineral: animal, and m. | GILB 152:23
miners: m. poured to war | MAC 213:24
Mineworkers: Union of M. | MACM 215:19
mingle: In one spirit meet and m. | SHEL 304:3
minion: morning's m. | HOPK 172:20
minister: help the M. that meddles | MELB 222:21
m. to a mind diseased | SHAK 288:2
Yes, M. | CROS 112:12
ministering: m. angel shall my sister | SHAK 277:10
m. angel thou | SCOTT 268:22
ministers: Angels and m. of grace | SHAK 274:27
grim Geneva m. | AYT 23:16
little errands for the M. | GILB 151:6
my actions are my m. | CHAR 95:2
passion-wingèd M. of thought | SHEL 303:5
you murdering m. | SHAK 285:18
ministries: made many m. | BAG 26:7
ministry: marriage than a m. | BAG 26:11
m. of all the talents | ANON 9:9
performs its secret m. | COL 103:18
Minnehaha: M., Laughing Water | LONG 210:2
minnows: Triton of the m. | SHAK 273:18
minor: change from major to m. | PORT 253:19
minorities: M. are almost always in the right
 | SMITH 310:10
minstrel: M. Boy to the war is gone | MOORE 234:16
wandering m. I | GILB 151:17
minute: do it in m. particulars | BLAKE 60:19
his first m., after noon | DONNE 124:6
leave in a m. and a huff | KALM 189:21
Then the good m. goes | BROW 77:21
We cannot cage the m. | MACN 216:10
minutes: famous for fifteen m. | WARH 342:20

minutes (cont.):
five m. too late all my life | COWL 109:18
m. hasten to their end | SHAK 299:21
round the earth in forty m. | SHAK 290:25
take care of m. | CHES 97:8
Mirabeau: Sous le pont M. | APOL 14:12
miracle: he prays for a m. | TURG 335:15
m. of our age | CAREW 89:18
m. of rare device | COL 103:24
Miranda: remember an inn, M. | BELL 34:1
mirk: It was m., mirk night | BALL 28:8
mirror: courteous eyes oppose a m. | JONS 187:7
live alone and smash his m. | ANON 21:9
Man's mind a m. is | SOUT 312:7
m. cracked from side | TENN 326:3
novel is a m. which passes | STEN 315:3
mirrored: Lie m. on her sea | HODG 169:14
mirrors: as m. are lonely | AUDEN 21:9
M. and fatherhood | BORG 69:23
m. of the sea are strewn | FLEC 141:19
mirth: buys a minute's m. | SHAK 299:8
earth must borrow its m. | WILC 349:14
Far from all resort of m. | MILT 226:25
m. hath present laughter | SHAK 297:23
time for m. and laughter | ADE 3:1
misbeliever: You call me m. | SHAK 289:5
mischief: All punishment is m. | BENT 35:2
For Satan finds some m. still | WATTS 343:6
hand to execute any m. | CLAR 101:10
misdoings: sorry for these our m. | BOOK 65:11
miserable: Me m.! which way shall I fly | MILT 229:6
mercy upon us m. sinners | BOOK 64:13
M. comforters are ye all | BIBLE 42:19
m. have no other medicine | SHAK 288:17
no more m. human being | JAMES 180:8
miserere: m. nobis | MISS 231:19
miseries: in shallows and in m. | SHAK 282:1
misery: certain amount of m. | LOWE 211:1
dwell on guilt and m. | AUST 22:21
fatal dumb-show of our m. | DRAY 126:18
finds himself, loses his m. | ARN 17:13
full of m. | BOOK 66:6
great kick at m. | LAWR 202:25
Man hands on m. to man | LARK 201:18
mine affliction and my m. | BIBLE 47:1
M. acquaints a man | SHAK 296:5
m. of manilla folders | ROET 261:14
result in m. | DICK 118:12
vale of m. | BOOK 67:21
misfortune: m. of our best friends | LA R 202:2
misfortunes: m. can befall a boy | MAUG 222:12
m. of mankind | GIBB 150:11
strong enough to bear the m. | LA R 201:21
tableau of crimes and m. | VOLT 340:20
they make m. more bitter | BACON 25:6
misgivings: Blank m. of a creature | WORD 355:22
mislead: one to m. the public | ASQ 19:4
mislike: M. me not | SHAK 289:6
misquote: enough of learning to m. | BYRON 86:31
miss: little m., dressed | HUME 176:7
missa: Ite m. est | MISS 231:20
missed: [Hitler] m. the bus | CHAM 94:3
who never would be m. | GILB 151:19
Woman much m. | HARDY 162:15
missing: M. so much and so much | CORN 108:6
missionary: I would eat a m. | WILB 349:6
mis-spent: Redeem thy m. time | KEN 193:21
mist: broke into a m. with bells | BROW 76:25
sophistry, and m. | BYRON 85:21
m. in my face | BROW 77:2
mistake: Man is Nature's sole m. | GILB 152:25
m. in the translation | VANB 336:23
mistaken: possible you may be m. | CROM 112:2
mistakes: everyone gives to their m. | WILDE 350:2
learned from the m. of the past | TAYL 323:1

mistakes (cont.):

| | |
|---|---|
| man who makes no m. | PHEL 248:11 |
| worst m. that can be made | HEIS 165:4 |
| mistress: acquaintance, next a m. | CHEK 96:28 |
| Art is a jealous m. | EMER 136:19 |
| crowd a m. or a friend | SHEL 303:15 |
| literature is my m. | CHEK 96:30 |
| m. in my own | KIPL 196:25 |
| m. of the Earl of Craven | WILS 351:16 |
| m. of the months | SWIN 320:28 |
| m. should be like | WYCH 358:4 |
| m. some rich anger shows | KEATS 191:26 |
| No casual m., but a wife | TENN 325:13 |
| O m. mine | SHAK 297:23 |
| Riches, the worst m. | BACON 24:6 |
| So court a m., she denies you | JONS 187:22 |
| mistresses: No, I shall have m. | GEOR 149:21 |
| or your Lordship's m. | WILK 350:26 |
| Wives are young men's m. | BACON 25:2 |
| mists: low the m. of evening lie | BETJ 37:1 |
| season of m. and mellow | KEATS 192:14 |
| misty: seyn of a ful m. morwe | CHAU 96:16 |
| misunderstood: To be great is to be m. | EMER 136:25 |
| worse lie than a truth m. | JAMES 180:10 |
| misused: m. words | SPEN 312:18 |
| Mithridates: M., he died old | HOUS 175:5 |
| mix: M. a little foolishness | HOR 174:1 |
| Moab: M. is my wash-pot | BOOK 67:14 |
| moan: m. of doves | TENN 328:8 |
| not paid with m. | THOM 331:7 |
| virgin-choir to make delicious m. | KEATS 192:8 |
| moanday: m., tearsday, wailsday | JOYCE 188:4 |
| moaning: no m. of the bar | TENN 323:18 |
| Though the harbour bar be m. | KING 195:16 |
| moat: m. defensive to a house | SHAK 293:16 |
| moated: at the m. grange | SHAK 288:22 |
| Upon the lonely m. grange | TENN 326:22 |
| mob: do what the m. do | DICK 119:28 |
| Our supreme governors, the m. | WALP 341:16 |
| mock: How my achievements m. me | SHAK 297:7 |
| m. on Voltaire Rousseau | BLAKE 61:13 |
| m. the air with idle state | GRAY 157:1 |
| mocked: God is not m. | BIBLE 55:30 |
| mocker: Wine is a m. | BIBLE 43:31 |
| mockingbird: Out of the m.'s throat | WHIT 348:12 |
| to kill a m. | LEE 204:6 |
| mocks: M. married men | SHAK 284:21 |
| model: m. of a modern Major-General | GILB 152:23 |
| models: Rules and m. destroy | HAZL 164:5 |
| moderation: astonished at my own m. | CLIVE 102:6 |
| easier than perfect m. | AUG 22:3 |
| m. in everything | HOR 174:2 |
| m. in the pursuit of justice | GOLD 155:15 |
| m. is a sort of treason | BURKE 79:22 |
| No term of m. takes place | BACON 24:7 |
| modern: m. Major-General | GILB 152:23 |
| strange disease of m. life | ARN 17:11 |
| modest: M.? My word, no | REED 258:20 |
| modesty: Enough for m. | BUCH 77:28 |
| modified: M. rapture | GILB 151:24 |
| mois: m. des floraisons | ARAG 14:21 |
| mole: like a bastion's m. | SMART 308:10 |
| molecules: without understanding m. | CRICK 111:19 |
| moll: King's M. Reno'd | ANON 8:17 |
| Molly Stark: or M.'s a widow | STARK 314:12 |
| Moloch: right of that great M. | MEYER 224:4 |
| mome: m. raths outgrabe | CARR 91:15 |
| moment: Every m. dies a man | BABB 23:19 |
| Every m. dies a man | TENN 328:26 |
| m. of my greatness flicker | ELIOT 133:29 |
| momentary: Beauty is m. | STEV 316:11 |
| pleasure is m. | CHES 97:18 |
| moments: O m. big as years | KEATS 191:1 |
| Wagner has lovely m. | ROSS 263:11 |
| monarch: hereditary m. was insane | BAG 26:8 |

monarch (cont.):

| | |
|---|---|
| merry m., scandalous | ROCH 261:8 |
| m. better than his crown | SHAK 289:26 |
| m. of all I survey | COWP 110:18 |
| m. of the road | SWANN 141:6 |
| monarchs: m. must obey | DRYD 128:4 |
| Perplexes m. | MILT 228:17 |
| monarchy: m. is a merchantman | AMES 4:22 |
| universal m. of wit | CAREW 89:19 |
| monastic: m. faces | CLOU 102:9 |
| Monday: going to do on M. | YBAR 358:11 |
| money: barrel of m. | WOODS 353:19 |
| blessing that m. cannot buy | WALT 342:14 |
| corrupted by m. | GREE 158:4 |
| draining m. from the pockets | SMITH 309:1 |
| given his m. upon usury | BOOK 66:14 |
| goä wheer m. is | TENN 327:9 |
| her voice is full of m. | FITZ 140:21 |
| hired the m. | COOL 107:20 |
| licence to print m. | THOM 332:4 |
| love of m. is the root of all evil | BIBLE 56:19 |
| m. and a room of her own | WOOLF 354:1 |
| m. and large armies | ANOU 14:4 |
| m. answereth all things | BIBLE 44:23 |
| m. can't buy me love | LENN 205:11 |
| M. couldn't buy friends | MILL 225:11 |
| M. doesn't talk, it swears | DYLAN 130:3 |
| M. gives me pleasure all | BELL 33:13 |
| M. has no smell | VESP 338:3 |
| M. is coined liberty | DOST 125:5 |
| M. is like a sixth sense | MAUG 222:11 |
| M. is like muck | BACON 25:10 |
| M. is none of the wheels | HUME 176:6 |
| M. is the sinews of love | FARQ 138:18 |
| M. speaks sense in a language | BEHN 32:23 |
| M. was exactly like sex | BALD 27:3 |
| natural interest of m. | MAC 213:10 |
| No m., no service | RAC 257:17 |
| not spending m. alone | EIS 131:14 |
| only interested in m. | SHAW 302:25 |
| pleasant it is to have m. | CLOU 102:14 |
| pretty to see what m. | PEPYS 247:20 |
| private parts, his m. | BUTL 84:18 |
| rub up against m. | RUNY 264:8 |
| sinews of war, unlimited m. | CIC 100:29 |
| somehow, make m. | HOR 173:6 |
| time is m. | FRAN 145:8 |
| uses his m. as votes | SAM 266:11 |
| way the m. goes | MAND 217:8 |
| We haven't got the m. | RUTH 265:9 |
| we have to borrer the m. | WARD 342:18 |
| When you have m., it's sex | DONL 123:2 |
| wrote, except for m. | JOHN 185:10 |
| Yes, they have more m. | FITZ 140:20 |
| You pays your m. | PUNCH 256:6 |
| moneybag: Aristocracy of the M. | CARL 90:15 |
| moneybags: dream of m. | SHAK 289:9 |
| moneys: m. are for values | BACON 23:23 |
| mongrels: continent of energetic m. | FISH 139:22 |
| monk: devil a m. he'd be | MOTT 236:3 |
| m. who shook the world | MONT 233:26 |
| monkey: descent from a m. | WILB 349:7 |
| m. when the organ grinder | BEVAN 37:21 |
| You mustn't m. with the Creed | BELL 33:15 |
| monkeys: Cats and m. | JAMES 179:22 |
| monogamous: Woman m. | JAMES 180:11 |
| monogamy: M. is the same | ANON 6:11 |
| monopoly: m. profits is a quiet life | HICKS 168:10 |
| m. stage of capitalism | LENIN 205:2 |
| monotony: bleats articulate m. | STEP 315:4 |
| monster: green-eyed m. | SHAK 292:12 |
| pity this busy m., manunkind | CUMM 112:20 |
| monsters: dream of reason produces m. | GOYA 156:1 |
| monstrous: m. anger of the guns | OWEN 243:21 |
| m. animal, a husband | FIEL 139:12 |

**monstrous** (*cont.*):
m. carbuncle — CHAR 95:8
M. carbuncles — SPEN 312:22
M. Regiment of Women — KNOX 198:16
**monstruosity:** m. in love — SHAK 297:2
**Montezuma:** who imprisoned M. — MAC 213:13
**month:** A little m. — SHAK 274:12
April is the cruellest m. — ELIOT 134:18
August is a wicked m. — O'BR 240:18
fressh as is the m. of May — CHAU 95:13
m. of tension — LESS 206:3
**months:** fourteen m. the most idle — GIBB 150:13
mother of m. in meadow — SWIN 321:1
**monument:** If you seek a m. — ANON 13:23
m. more lasting than bronze — HOR 173:28
m. of the insufficiency — JOHN 183:7
m. sticks like a fishbone — LOW 211:13
only m. the asphalt road — ELIOT 134:13
patience on a m. — SHAK 298:1
sonnet is a moment's m. — ROSS 263:7
**monuments:** nor the gilded m. — SHAK 299:19
**moo:** One end is m. — NASH 237:10
**moocow:** there was a m. — JOYCE 188:6
**moon:** Beneath the visiting m. — SHAK 271:25
by the light of the m. — LEAR 203:13
cold fruitless m. — SHAK 290:12
Daughter of the M., Nokomis — LONG 210:1
from the pale-faced m. — SHAK 277:27
hornèd M. — COL 104:10
How white the ever-constant m. — WASH 342:24
melodious cats under the m. — HUXL 177:4
minions of the m. — SHAK 277:22
m. be still as bright — BYRON 87:8
m. in lonely alleys — CRANE 110:32
m. is in the seventh house — RADO 257:18
m.'s an arrant thief — SHAK 296:23
m. shines bright — SHAK 289:31
m. shone bright on Mrs Porter — ELIOT 134:26
m. under her feet — BIBLE 57:30
m. winks — SHAK 292:25
neither the m. by night — BOOK 68:26
Old Devil M. — HARB 161:13
O more than m. — DONNE 124:16
only a paper m. — HARB 161:12
Only you beneath the m. — PORT 253:25
owl does to the m. complain — GRAY 157:5
Shaped like the crescent-m. — WORD 356:3
ship, an isle, a sickle m. — FLEC 141:19
silent as the m. — MILT 230:12
silver apples of the m. — YEATS 360:1
Slowly, silently, now the m. — DE L 116:22
swear not by the m. — SHAK 294:33
waning m. was haunted — COL 103:23
when the m. shall rise — WOTT 357:16
Wi' the auld m. in her arm — BALL 28:5
With how sad steps, O M. — SIDN 306:18
**moonlight:** How sweet the m. sleeps — SHAK 290:1
Ill met by m. — SHAK 290:22
m. and music and love — BERL 35:22
M. behind you — COW 109:7
visit it by the pale m. — SCOTT 268:10
Watch for me by m. — NOYES 240:14
**moonlit:** Knocking on the m. door — DE L 116:18
**moons:** m. shall wax and wane — WATTS 343:12
Reason has m. — HODG 169:14
**moonshine:** find out m. — SHAK 290:30
Transcendental m. — CARL 90:19
**moon-struck:** m. madness — MILT 229:31
**moorish:** It is m., and wild — BRON 72:15
**moppsikon:** M. Floppsikon bear — LEAR 203:18
**mops:** seven maids with seven m. — CARR 91:21
**moral:** Debasing the m. currency — ELIOT 132:7
Englishman thinks he is m. — SHAW 301:21
kind of m. eunuch — SHEL 304:14
m. as soon as one is unhappy — PROU 255:19

**moral** (*cont.*):
m. crusade or it is nothing — WILS 351:13
m. Gower — CHAU 96:23
m., grave — BACON 25:16
M. indignation is jealousy — WELLS 346:1
m. is (it is indeed!) — BELL 33:15
m. law within me — KANT 189:22
m. or an immoral book — WILDE 350:3
m. virtues at the highest — CHES 97:14
perfectly moral till all are m. — SPEN 312:21
point a m., or adorn a tale — JOHN 183:14
**moralist:** vital problem for the m. — RUSS 264:21
**morality:** cities for our best m. — AUST 22:19
Goodbye, m. — HERB 166:12
Johnson's m. was as English — HAWT 163:19
imperative may be called M. — KANT 189:23
Master-m. and slave-m. — NIET 239:22
m. for morality's sake — COUS 108:17
m. in any given time — WHIT 348:3
M. in the novel — LAWR 202:12
M. is a private luxury — ADAMS 1:18
M. is the herd-instinct — NIET 239:20
m. touched by emotion — ARN 18:8
periodical fits of m. — MAC 213:9
some people talk of m. — EDG 130:16
**morals:** Food comes first, then m. — BREC 71:19
teach the m. of a whore — JOHN 184:1
with the m. of a Methodist — GILB 152:26
**more:** art m. than they — TENN 324:23
believing m. and more in less — YATES 358:10
condemn a little m. — MAJOR 216:19
days that are no m. — TENN 327:22
For, I have m. — DONNE 123:17
knows m. and m. about less — BUTL 83:21
m. equal than others — ORW 241:23
m. Piglet wasn't there — MILNE 225:14
m. than she ever did — KALM 189:20
m. than somewhat — RUNY 264:6
m. things in heaven and earth — SHAK 275:3
M. will mean worse — AMIS 5:1
No m. I will abroad — HERB 166:22
No m. o' that, my lord — SHAK 287:29
O m. than moon — DONNE 124:16
Please, sir, I want some m. — DICK 119:18
take m. than nothing — CARR 91:8
you get no m. of me — DRAY 126:16
**mores:** O tempora, O m.! — CIC 100:25
**mori:** pro patria m. — HOR 173:26
**moriar:** Non omnis m. — HOR 173:29
**Moriarty:** M. of mathematical — DOYLE 125:20
**morituri:** m. te salutant — ANON 13:12
**morn:** From m. to night — ROSS 263:5
m., in russet mantle — SHAK 274:3
still m. went out with sandals — MILT 227:19
Son of M. in weary Night — BLAKE 60:15
**morning:** beauty of the m. — WORD 354:15
Come, lovely M. — DAV 114:21
disasters in his m. face — GOLD 154:23
Early one m. — ANON 6:27
evening and the m. — BIBLE 38:14
Full many a glorious m. — SHAK 299:17
glorious m. for America — ADAMS 2:6
glut thy sorrow on a m. rose — KEATS 191:26
grey dawn of the m. after — ADE 3:1
joy cometh in the m. — BOOK 66:22
Lucifer, son of the m. — BIBLE 45:22
methinks I scent the m. — SHAK 275:1
m. again in America — RINEY 260:12
m. cometh — BIBLE 45:23
M. has broken — FARJ 138:12
M. in the bowl of night — FITZ 140:4
m. light creaks down again — SITW 307:16
M.'s at seven — BROW 76:28
m.'s minion — HOPK 172:20
m. well-aired — BRUM 77:23

**morning** (*cont.*):

| | |
|---|---|
| Never glad confident m. | BROW 76:15 |
| Never m. wore to evening | TENN 324:25 |
| New every m. | KEBLE 193:16 |
| they take you in the m. | BALD 27:4 |
| thy princes eat in the m. | BIBLE 44:22 |
| To pay thy m. sacrifice | KEN 193:20 |
| When m. gilds the skies | CASW 92:19 |
| wings of the m. | BOOK 69:6 |

**mornings**: literary m. with its hoot AUDEN 20:25

| | |
|---|---|
| Many bright m. | VAUG 337:13 |

**Mornington**: present of M. Crescent HARG 162:21
**Morocco**: we're M. bound BURKE 81:15
**moron**: consumer isn't a m. OGIL 241:2

| | |
|---|---|
| See the happy m. | ANON 10:9 |

**morrow**: no thought for the m. BIBLE 49:5
**mortal**: m. thing so to immortalize SPEN 313:4

| | |
|---|---|
| grief itself be m. | SHEL 303:8 |
| chances of this m. life | BOOK 65:18 |
| desperately m. | SHAK 288:24 |
| every tatter in its m. dress | YEATS 359:21 |
| shuffled off this m. coil | SHAK 275:25 |
| M., guilty, but to me | AUDEN 20:28 |
| We m. millions live *alone* | ARN 17:22 |

**mortality**: Insensible of m. SHAK 288:24

| | |
|---|---|
| it smells of m. | SHAK 283:24 |
| m. touches the heart | VIRG 339:4 |
| nothing serious in m. | SHAK 286:26 |
| Old m. | BROW 74:3 |

**mortals**: Composing m. AUDEN 20:10

| | |
|---|---|
| Lord, what fools these m. be | SHAK 290:32 |
| not in m. to command success | ADD 2:13 |

**mortar**: Lies are the m. WELLS 345:20
**mortis**: *Timor m. conturbat me* DUNB 129:8
**morts**: *Il n'y a pas de m.* MAET 216:15
**mortuus**: *Passer m. est* CAT 93:1
**Moscow**: Do not march on M. MONT 233:23

| | |
|---|---|
| M.: those syllables can start | PUSH 256:23 |

**Moses**: *Go down, M.* ANON 11:19

| | |
|---|---|
| M. sent to spy out | BIBLE 40:16 |

**moss**: miles of golden m. AUDEN 20:19
**mossy**: Happy field or m. cavern KEATS 191:16

| | |
|---|---|
| m. stones about and about | WORD 354:10 |

**mote**: m. that is in thy brother's BIBLE 49:7
**motes**: m. that people the sunbeams MILT 226:23
**moth**: Both m. and flame ROET 261:16

| | |
|---|---|
| desire of the m. for the star | SHEL 305:5 |
| How, like a m., the simple maid | GAY 149:2 |
| m. and rust doth corrupt | BIBLE 49:1 |
| m. of peace | SHAK 292:2 |

**mother**: artist man and m. woman SHAW 301:18

| | |
|---|---|
| As is the m., so is her daughter | BIBLE 47:4 |
| Behold thy m. | BIBLE 54:4 |
| Care of his M. | MILNE 225:20 |
| church for his m. | CYPR 113:12 |
| Dead! and never called me m. | WOOD 353:17 |
| either my father or my m. | STER 315:12 |
| gave her m. forty whacks | ANON 8:22 |
| Gentle Child of gentle M. | DEAR 115:7 |
| heaviness of his m. | BIBLE 43:16 |
| Honour thy father and thy m. | BIBLE 40:8 |
| I arose a m. in Israel | BIBLE 40:31 |
| I have no pain, dear m., now | FARM 138:13 |
| Man may not marry his M. | BOOK 69:19 |
| man who hates his m. | BENN 34:19 |
| m. and I should have lived | GAY 149:3 |
| M. and lover of men, the sea | SWIN 321:18 |
| m. bore me in the southern | BLAKE 61:24 |
| M., give me the sun | IBSEN 178:4 |
| m., make my bed | BALL 27:13 |
| m. of arts, of warfare | DU B 128:32 |
| m. of battles | HUSS 176:22 |
| M. OF HARLOTS | BIBLE 58:2 |
| m. of months | SWIN 321:1 |
| m. of Parliaments | BRIG 72:5 |

**mother** (*cont.*):

| | |
|---|---|
| m. of sciences | BACON 25:27 |
| M. of the Free | BENS 34:20 |
| m.'s little helper | RICH 179:5 |
| m.'s sake the child was dear | COL 104:20 |
| M. to dozens | HERB 166:13 |
| My m. bids me bind my hair | HUNT 176:19 |
| My m. groaned | BLAKE 62:3 |
| my m. taught me as a boy | BERR 36:13 |
| really affectionate m. | MAUG 222:12 |
| *There* was their Dacian m. | BYRON 85:10 |
| thou hast murdered thy m. | MAL 217:1 |
| thy dear m. any courtesy | SHAK 273:22 |
| Where a m. laid her baby | ALEX 4:4 |

**mothers**: Come m. and fathers DYLAN 130:9

| | |
|---|---|
| m. of large families | BELL 33:2 |
| women become like their m. | WILDE 349:19 |

**mother-wits**: rhyming m. MARL 219:4
**motion**: Between the m. and the act ELIOT 133:19

| | |
|---|---|
| Devoid of sense and m. | MILT 228:24 |
| dreadful thing and the first m. | SHAK 281:3 |
| gentle m. with the deep | DAV 114:22 |
| God ordered m. | VAUG 337:3 |
| next to the perpetual m. | DICK 120:3 |
| No m. has she now | WORD 356:25 |
| oil which renders the m. | HUME 176:6 |
| Poetry in m. | ANTH 190:5 |
| poetry of m. | GRAH 156:6 |
| their m. in one sphere | SHAK 278:13 |
| This sensible warm m. | SHAK 288:21 |
| time's eternal m. | FORD 143:11 |
| uniform m. in a right line | NEWT 239:3 |

**motions**: two weeping m. CRAS 111:14

| | |
|---|---|
| secret m. of things | BACON 25:26 |
| stings and m. of the sense | SHAK 288:11 |

**motive**: joint and m. of her body SHAK 297:9
**motley**: M.'s the only wear SHAK 272:23

| | |
|---|---|
| m. to the view | SHAK 300:6 |

**motorcycle**: Art of M. Maintenance PIRS 249:2
**motto**: that is my m. MARQ 219:19
**mottoes**: m. on sundials POUND 254:15
**mould**: broke the m. ARIO 15:8
**moulded**: men are m. out of faults SHAK 288:26
**mouldering**: in many a m. heap GRAY 157:6
**mount**: m. up with wings as eagles BIBLE 46:13

| | |
|---|---|
| rejected the Sermon on the M. | BRAD 71:10 |

**mountain**: every m. and hill BIBLE 46:9

| | |
|---|---|
| from yonder m. height | TENN 328:6 |
| He watches from his m. walls | TENN 323:21 |
| If the m. will not come | BACON 24:16 |
| in all my holy m. | BIBLE 45:20 |
| In a m. greenery | HART 163:10 |
| Over all the m. tops is peace | GOET 154:12 |
| river jumps over the m. | AUDEN 20:11 |
| sun looked over the m.'s rim | BROW 76:23 |
| tiptoe on the misty m. tops | SHAK 295:18 |
| Up the airy m. | ALL 4:18 |

**mountains**: Among the m. by the winter sea TENN 324:17

| | |
|---|---|
| From the m. to the prairies | BERL 35:21 |
| M. are the beginning and the end | RUSK 264:13 |
| m. look on Marathon | BYRON 86:14 |
| m. skipped like rams | BOOK 68:16 |
| M. will go into labour | HOR 172:27 |
| one is of the sea, one of the m. | WORD 357:6 |
| that I could remove m. | BIBLE 55:11 |
| when men and m. meet | BLAKE 61:15 |

**mountain-tops**: m. that freeze SHAK 280:16

| | |
|---|---|
| Flatter the m. | SHAK 299:17 |

**mountebank**: m. and his zany WALP 341:24
**mourir**: *Partir c'est m. un peu* HAR 161:9
**mourn**: Blessed are they that m. BIBLE 48:19

| | |
|---|---|
| don't m. for me never | ANON 7:17 |
| Makes countless thousands m. | BURNS 82:16 |
| m. for me when I am dead | SHAK 299:23 |

**mourn** (cont.):

| | |
|---|---|
| m. with ever-returning spring | WHIT 348:24 |
| M., you powers of Charm | CAT 93:1 |
| now can never m. | SHEL 303:11 |
| time to m., and a time to dance | BIBLE 44:12 |
| **mourned:** Would have m. longer | SHAK 274:12 |
| **mournful:** M. ever weeping | BLAKE 60:16 |
| **mourning:** Don't waste any time in m. | HILL 168:13 |
| great m., Rachel weeping | BIBLE 48:11 |
| I'm in m. for my life | CHEK 96:25 |
| M. becomes Electra | O'NEI 241:12 |
| widow bird sat m. | SHEL 303:14 |
| **mouse:** killing of a m. on Sunday | BRAT 71:16 |
| little m. will be born | HOR 172:27 |
| Not a m. shall disturb | SHAK 291:10 |
| not even a m. | MOORE 234:3 |
| **mouse-trap:** or make a better m. | EMER 137:3 |
| **moustache:** didn't wax his m. | KIPL 198:3 |
| **mouth:** Englishman to open his m. | SHAW 302:16 |
| God be in my m. | ANON 7:11 |
| in the cannon's m. | SHAK 272:26 |
| keeping your m. shut | EINS 131:10 |
| Keep your m. shut | ANON 12:15 |
| m. had been used as a latrine | AMIS 5:2 |
| m. of the Lord hath spoken | BIBLE 46:9 |
| m. of very babes and sucklings | BOOK 66:10 |
| proceedeth out of the m. of God | BIBLE 48:16 |
| purple-stainèd m. | KEATS 191:30 |
| sank in the m. of the dying | AUDEN 20:21 |
| spew thee out of my m. | BIBLE 57:22 |
| **mouthful:** gold filling in a m. | OSB 242:26 |
| **mouths:** she made m. in a glass | SHAK 283:8 |
| stuffed their m. with gold | BEVAN 38:2 |
| They have m., and speak not | BOOK 68:18 |
| **movable:** Paris is a m. feast | HEM 165:13 |
| **move:** Afloat. We m. | CLOU 102:12 |
| But it does m. | GAL 147:12 |
| feel the earth m. | HEM 165:12 |
| great affair is to m. | STEV 316:27 |
| I will m. the earth | ARCH 15:3 |
| m., and have our being | BIBLE 54:21 |
| M. him into the sun | OWEN 243:24 |
| **moved:** I do not like being m. | CLOU 102:8 |
| m. by what is not unusual | ELIOT 132:11 |
| m. to folly by a noise | LAWR 202:28 |
| We shall not be m. | ANON 11:15 |
| **movement:** measure of m. | AUCT 20:8 |
| **movers:** m. and shakers | O'SH 243:1 |
| **moves:** If it m., salute it | ANON 8:4 |
| **movies:** M. should have a beginning | GOD 153:19 |
| **moving:** m. accident is not my trade | WORD 355:1 |
| m. finger writes | FITZ 140:14 |
| m. toyshop of their heart | POPE 253:3 |
| **Mozart:** Children are given M. | SCHN 267:23 |
| **MPs:** dull M. in close proximity | GILB 151:13 |
| **much:** doesn't seem m. for them to be | COMP 106:3 |
| Missing so m. and so much | CORN 108:6 |
| M. as you said you were | HARDY 162:9 |
| M. have I seen and known | TENN 328:21 |
| m. to be done, little to be known | JOHN 182:27 |
| So little done, so m. to do | RHOD 259:12 |
| So many worlds, so m. to do | TENN 325:14 |
| so m. owed by so many | CHUR 99:15 |
| You that are just so m. | BROW 77:20 |
| **muck:** Money is like m. | BACON 25:10 |
| Sing 'em m. | MELBA 222:19 |
| **muckrake:** with a m. in his hand | BUNY 79:6 |
| **muckrakes:** men with the m. | ROOS 262:18 |
| **mud:** cover the universe with m. | FORS 143:18 |
| Longing to be back in the m. | AUG 21:21 |
| M.! Mud! Glorious mud | SWANN 141:4 |
| M.'s sister, not himself | HOUS 174:7 |
| on the people builds on m. | MACH 215:2 |
| **muddle:** beginning, a m. | LARK 201:20 |
| manage somehow to m. through | BRIG 72:4 |

**muddle** (cont.):

| | |
|---|---|
| Meddle and m. | DERBY 117:7 |
| **muddy:** celibacy a m. horsepond | PEAC 246:24 |
| m. ecstasies of beer | CRAB 110:21 |
| M., ill-seeming, thick | SHAK 295:30 |
| m. understandings | BURKE 80:15 |
| **muero:** *Muero porque no m.* | JOHN 181:16 |
| **mulatto:** Grape is my m. mother | HUGH 175:22 |
| **mule:** m. of politics | DISR 121:27 |
| **mules:** m. of politics | POWER 255:4 |
| **multiplication:** M. is vexation | ANON 9:11 |
| **multiply:** Be fruitful, and m. | BIBLE 38:17 |
| **multitude:** cover the m. of sins | BIBLE 57:11 |
| m. is always in the wrong | DILL 120:24 |
| **multitudes:** I contain m. | WHIT 348:21 |
| m. in the valley of decision | BIBLE 47:21 |
| Pestilence-stricken m. | SHEL 304:6 |
| Weeping, weeping m. | ELIOT 132:22 |
| **mum:** fuck you up, your m. and dad | LARK 201:17 |
| oafish louts remember M. | BETJ 36:17 |
| **mumbled:** few m. cakes | HUNT 176:18 |
| **munch:** So m. on | BROW 76:27 |
| **mundi:** *cito transit gloria m.* | THOM 329:28 |
| *Sic transit gloria m.* | ANON 13:22 |
| **muove:** *Eppur si m.* | GAL 147:16 |
| **murder:** I met M. on the way | SHEL 304:4 |
| Killing no m. briefly discourst | SEXBY 270:14 |
| love and m. will out | CONG 106:17 |
| Macbeth does m. sleep | SHAK 286:15 |
| m. an infant in its cradle | BLAKE 61:10 |
| m. by the law | YOUNG 360:15 |
| m. cannot be hid long | SHAK 289:8 |
| m. for the truth | ADLER 3:2 |
| M. most foul | SHAK 274:31 |
| M. one of the fine arts | DE Q 117:5 |
| m. respectable | ORW 242:15 |
| M.'s out of tune | SHAK 293:2 |
| M. wol out | CHAU 95:29 |
| One m. made a villain | PORT 253:26 |
| Television has brought back m. | HITC 168:20 |
| Thou shalt do no m. | BOOK 65:4 |
| To m. thousands | YOUNG 360:15 |
| Vanity, like m., will out | COWL 109:19 |
| We m. to dissect | WORD 357:5 |
| **murdered:** m. reputations | CONG 106:15 |
| thou hast m. thy mother | MAL 217:1 |
| **murderers:** m. take the first step | KARR 190:1 |
| **murdering:** you m. ministers | SHAK 285:18 |
| **murmur:** creeping m. | SHAK 279:7 |
| live m. of a summer's day | ARN 17:5 |
| Seem to m. sweet and low | ARMS 15:24 |
| **murmuring:** brooks of Eden mazily m. | TENN 327:8 |
| m. of innumerable bees | TENN 328:8 |
| **murmurs:** In the m., in the pauses | SOND 311:6 |
| m. of self-will | BODE 62:16 |
| **Murray:** slain the Earl of M. | BALL 27:14 |
| **muscle:** motion of a m. | WORD 354:13 |
| **muscles:** M. better and nerves more | CUMM 113:4 |
| **muscular:** His Christianity was m. | DISR 121:29 |
| **muse:** M. of fire | SHAK 278:33 |
| tenth M., who now governs | TROL 334:20 |
| whose m. on dromedary trots | COL 104:2 |
| **mushroom:** I am . . . a m. | FORD 143:9 |
| Life is too short to stuff a m. | CONR 107:10 |
| meet a m. rich civilian | BYRON 87:13 |
| **music:** All m. is folk music | ARMS 16:3 |
| Architecture is frozen m. | SCH 267:17 |
| brave m. of a *distant* drum | FITZ 140:7 |
| Classic m. is th'kind | HUBB 175:16 |
| danceth without m. | HERB 167:10 |
| Darling of the m. halls | SMITH 309:8 |
| day the m. died | MCL 215:7 |
| Fading in m. | SHAK 289:19 |
| finds its food in m. | LILLO 207:3 |
| Fled is that m. | KEATS 192:7 |

music (cont.):

| | |
|---|---|
| how potent cheap m. is | COW 109:10 |
| If m. be the food of love | SHAK 297:13 |
| I shall be made thy m. | DONNE 123:16 |
| Let's face the m. and dance | BERL 35:22 |
| let the sounds of m. creep | SHAK 290:1 |
| Like m. on my heart | COL 104:16 |
| make the m. mute | TENN 324:13 |
| man that hath no m. | SHAK 290:3 |
| most civilized m. | UST 336:15 |
| M. and women I cannot | PEPYS 247:19 |
| M. begins to atrophy when | POUND 254:22 |
| M. has charms to soothe | CONG 106:11 |
| m. in its roar | BYRON 85:12 |
| m. in the air | ELGAR 131:18 |
| M. is feeling, then, not sound | STEV 316:10 |
| m. is the brandy of the damned | SHAW 301:19 |
| m. of its trees at dawn | ARN 16:21 |
| m. of men's lives | SHAK 294:11 |
| m. of the Gospel leads | FABER 138:4 |
| m. sent up to God | BROW 75:8 |
| m. that excels the sound | FISH 139:26 |
| M. that gentlier on the spirit | TENN 326:19 |
| m. the only sensual pleasure | JOHN 186:10 |
| M., when soft voices die | SHEL 305:4 |
| not for the doctrine, but the m. | POPE 252:3 |
| O body swayed to m. | YEATS 358:14 |
| seduction of martial m. | BURN 81:18 |
| softest m. to attending ears | SHAK 295:3 |
| step to the m. which he hears | THOR 332:12 |
| still, sad m. of humanity | WORD 355:10 |
| thou hast thy m. too | KEATS 192:15 |
| thy chosen m., Liberty | WORD 357:6 |
| towards the condition of m. | PATER 246:14 |
| uproar's your only m. | KEATS 193:3 |
| We are the m. makers | O'SH 243:1 |
| What passion cannot M. raise | DRYD 128:17 |
| musical: m. Malcolm Sargent | BEEC 32:2 |
| m. as is Apollo's lute | MILT 226:15 |
| So m. a discord | SHAK 291:2 |
| musk: m. carnations break | ARN 17:19 |
| m. of the rose is blown | TENN 326:28 |
| musk-rose: coming m. | KEATS 192:2 |
| musk-roses: With sweet m. | SHAK 290:26 |
| must: m. a word to be addressed | ELIZ 135:10 |
| we forget because we m. | ARN 16:9 |
| mustard: like to a grain of m. | BIBLE 50:5 |
| mutabile: Varium et m. semper | VIRG 339:9 |
| mute: M. and magnificent | DRYD 128:20 |
| mutilate: Do not fold, spindle or m. | ANON 6:26 |
| mutiny: Rome to rise and m. | SHAK 281:26 |
| my-lorded: m. him | THAC 329:15 |
| myriad: There died a m. | POUND 254:19 |
| myrrh: frankincense, and m. | BIBLE 48:10 |
| m. is my wellbeloved | BIBLE 44:30 |
| myrtle: m. and ivy | BYRON 87:10 |
| m. and turkey part of it | AUST 22:20 |
| myrtles: Ye m. brown | MILT 227:10 |
| myself: I celebrate m. | WHIT 348:16 |
| I do not know m. | GOET 154:14 |
| In awe of such a thing as I m. | SHAK 280:26 |
| When I give I give m. | WHIT 348:20 |
| mysteries: m. in divinity | BROW 74:10 |
| mysterious: God moves in a m. way | COWP 109:25 |
| mystery: Behold, I shew you a m. | BIBLE 55:21 |
| lose myself in a m. | BROW 74:11 |
| M., BABYLON THE GREAT | BIBLE 58:2 |
| m. inside an enigma | CHUR 99:10 |
| m. of the cross shines | FORT 144:5 |
| Now, my tongue, the m. telling | THOM 330:3 |
| pluck out the heart of my m. | SHAK 276:13 |
| mystic: m., wonderful | TENN 324:3 |
| myths: Science must begin with m. | POPP 253:16 |

# N

| | |
|---|---|
| nag: gait of a shuffling n. | SHAK 278:4 |
| nagging: N. is the repetition | SUMM 319:5 |
| nail: for want of a n. | FRAN 145:12 |
| n. my pictures together | SCHW 268:2 |
| walks away with the n. | LAWR 202:11 |
| nails: n. he'll dig them up again | WEBS 344:26 |
| nineteen hundred and forty n. | SITW 307:19 |
| relatively clean finger n. | MORT 235:21 |
| naïve: n. domestic Burgundy | THUR 332:17 |
| n. forgive and forget | SZASZ 321:24 |
| naked: Half n., loving, natural | BYRON 86:8 |
| In walking n. | YEATS 358:17 |
| left me n. to mine enemies | SHAK 280:21 |
| n. into the conference chamber | BEVAN 38:1 |
| stark n. truth | CLEL 101:20 |
| starving hysterical n. | GINS 153:3 |
| With n. foot, stalking | WYATT 358:2 |
| nakedness: not in utter n. | WORD 355:20 |
| name: at the n. of Jesus | BIBLE 56:5 |
| cometh in the N. of the Lord | BOOK 68:23 |
| Corsair's n. to other times | BYRON 85:19 |
| coward shame distain his n. | BURNS 82:15 |
| deed without a n. | SHAK 287:19 |
| Democracy is the n. | CAIL 142:2 |
| gathered together in my n. | BIBLE 50:18 |
| ghost of a great n. | LUCAN 211:24 |
| glory in the n. of Briton | GEOR 149:23 |
| Good n. in man and woman | SHAK 292:11 |
| his n. shall be called | BIBLE 45:16 |
| I have forgotten your n. | SWIN 321:14 |
| In the n. of God | CROM 112:4 |
| In the N. of the Father | MISS 231:10 |
| leave a living n. behind | WEBS 344:13 |
| Let me not n. it to you | SHAK 292:28 |
| local habitation and a n. | SHAK 291:4 |
| love that dare not speak its n. | DOUG 125:6 |
| my n. is Jowett | BEEC 32:6 |
| my wife, and my n. | SURT 319:11 |
| n. great in story | BYRON 87:10 |
| n. liveth for evermore | BIBLE 48:8 |
| n. of the Lord thy God | BIBLE 40:6 |
| n. to all succeeding ages | DRYD 127:5 |
| n. to the reverberate hills | SHAK 297:21 |
| n. was writ in water | KEATS 193:15 |
| nothing of a n. | BYRON 85:15 |
| number of his n. | BIBLE 57:32 |
| provides us with n. and nation | BUNT 78:14 |
| spared the n. | SWIFT 320:24 |
| thy n. give glory | BIBLE 58:12 |
| thy N. give the praise | BOOK 68:17 |
| What's in a n. | SHAK 294:31 |
| worth an age without a n. | MORD 234:21 |
| yet can't quite n. | LARK 201:16 |
| nameless: n. unremembered | WORD 355:8 |
| names: confused things with their n. | SART 267:5 |
| gaunt n. that never get fat | BENÉT 34:8 |
| honour doth forget men's n. | SHAK 282:3 |
| n. in many a musèd rhyme | KEATS 192:3 |
| N. that should be on every | CALV 88:8 |
| naming: n. of parts | REED 258:15 |
| Nan: change Kate into N. | BLAKE 60:15 |
| Napoleon: N. of crime | DOYLE 125:20 |
| narrative: unconvincing n. | GILB 152:5 |
| narrow: n. is the way | BIBLE 49:13 |
| O make it saft and n. | BALL 27:13 |
| Nassau: Can Stuart or N. go | PRIOR 255:10 |
| nastiest: n. thing in the nicest way | GOLD 154:16 |
| nasty: Man is a n. creature | MOL 232:25 |
| n., brutish, and short | HOBB 169:10 |
| Something n. in the woodshed | GIBB 150:17 |
| nation: against the voice of a n. | RUSS 265:5 |

**nation** (*cont.*):

| | |
|---|---|
| boundary of the march of a n. | PARN 245:23 |
| haughty n. proud in arms | MILT 226:6 |
| holy n., a peculiar people | BIBLE 57:8 |
| Licensed build that n.'s fate | BLAKE 60:9 |
| London: a n., not a city | DISR 122:5 |
| n. is not governed | BURKE 80:1 |
| n. of dancers, singers | EQUI 137:13 |
| n. of shopkeepers | ADAMS 2:7 |
| n. of shopkeepers | NAP 237:7 |
| n. of shopkeepers | SMITH 308:23 |
| n. shall not lift up sword | BIBLE 45:5 |
| n. shall rise against nation | BIBLE 50:34 |
| N. shall speak peace unto | REND 259:5 |
| N. spoke to a Nation | KIPL 196:25 |
| n. talking to itself | MILL 225:6 |
| Once to every man and n. | LOW 211:7 |
| one-third of a n. ill-housed | ROOS 262:11 |
| places the n. at his service | POMP 250:12 |
| provides us with name and n. | BUNT 78:14 |
| this continent a new n. | LINC 207:8 |
| top n. | SELL 270:5 |
| what our N. stands for | BETJ 37:4 |
| whole n. perish not | BIBLE 53:34 |
| **national**: N. Debt is a very Good | SELL 270:4 |
| **nationalism**: N. is a silly cock | ALD 3:15 |
| **nationless**: tribeless, and n. | SHEL 304:22 |
| **nations**: day of small n. | CHAM 93:23 |
| fierce contending n. | ADD 2:19 |
| friendship with all n. | JEFF 180:19 |
| great n. have always acted | KUBR 199:7 |
| happiest n. have no history | ELIOT 132:14 |
| hating all other n. | GASK 148:20 |
| healing of the n. | BIBLE 58:7 |
| languages are the pedigree of n. | JOHN 183:18 |
| n. have never learned | HEGEL 164:18 |
| N. have their infancy | BOL 63:4 |
| N. touch at their summits | BAG 26:9 |
| Other n. use 'force' | WAUGH 343:28 |
| task to rule n. | VIRG 339:16 |
| teaching n. how to live | MILT 231:5 |
| To belong to other n. | GILB 152:21 |
| two different n. | FOST 144:8 |
| Two n. | DISR 122:6 |
| **native**: Fast by their n. shore | COWP 109:28 |
| not more n. to the heart | SHAK 274:4 |
| This is my own, my n. land | SCOTT 268:12 |
| **natural**: He wants the n. touch | SHAK 287:23 |
| I do it more n. | SHAK 297:24 |
| N. rights is simple nonsense | BENT 34:22 |
| N. Selection | DARW 114:3 |
| N. selection has no vision | DAWK 115:2 |
| n. to die as to be born | BACON 24:22 |
| twice as n. | CARR 92:4 |
| **nature**: Beauty is N.'s brag | MILT 226:20 |
| drive out n. with a pitchfork | HOR 173:11 |
| Eye N.'s walks | POPE 252:11 |
| heartless, witless n. | HOUS 174:14 |
| God and n. do nothing in vain | AUCT 20:5 |
| God, or in other words, N. | SPIN 313:22 |
| Good painters imitate n. | CERV 93:20 |
| great N. made us men | LOW 211:6 |
| great Secretary of N. | WALT 342:16 |
| horridly cruel works of n. | DARW 114:5 |
| I do fear thy n. | SHAK 285:15 |
| in N. were inconstancy | COWL 109:15 |
| interpreter of n. | JOHN 183:3 |
| Is N. felt | WORD 354:18 |
| knowledge of n. is destined | HOLB 170:9 |
| Man is N.'s sole mistake | GILB 152:25 |
| man the less, but n. more | BYRON 85:12 |
| mere copier of n. | REYN 259:9 |
| My n. is subdued | SHAK 300:7 |
| N. abhors a vacuum | RAB 257:11 |
| N. does nothing without purpose | ARIS 15:20 |

| | |
|---|---|
| N. from her seat | MILT 229:26 |
| n. gave me at my birth | COL 103:15 |
| N. hadn't counted on | TURG 335:11 |
| N. in awe to him | MILT 227:25 |
| N. in you stands | SHAK 283:3 |
| N. is creeping up | WHIS 347:12 |
| N. is not a temple | TURG 335:12 |
| n. is the art of God | BROW 74:14 |
| n. is tugging at every | EMER 136:18 |
| n. itselfe cant endure | FLEM 141:22 |
| N. made him, and then broke | ARIO 15:8 |
| N. never makes enny blunders | BILL 59:11 |
| n. of God is a circle | ANON 9:13 |
| N., red in tooth and claw | TENN 325:12 |
| N.'s decorations glisten | SMART 308:9 |
| N.'s laws lay hid in night | POPE 251:26 |
| n.'s way of telling you to slow | ANON 6:25 |
| n. there are neither rewards | ING 178:16 |
| N. wears one universal grin | FIEL 139:13 |
| next to N., Art | LAND 200:22 |
| one touch of n. | SHAK 297:6 |
| paid the debt of n. | FABY 138:6 |
| poet interpreted n. | GIR 153:6 |
| priketh hem n. in hir corages | CHAU 95:11 |
| Progress...a part of n. | SPEN 312:19 |
| ruined piece of n. | SHAK 283:24 |
| state that n. hath provided | LOCKE 208:19 |
| Tired N.'s sweet restorer | YOUNG 360:17 |
| True wit is N. to advantage | POPE 252:1 |
| With N., to out-do the life | JONS 187:20 |
| **naught**: n. for your comfort | CHES 97:19 |
| Say not the struggle n. | CLOU 102:22 |
| **naughtiness**: n. of thine heart | BIBLE 41:17 |
| **naughty**: good deed in a n. world | SHAK 290:4 |
| His former n. life | BOOK 65:1 |
| **naval**: n. tradition | CHUR 100:6 |
| **navies**: n. grappling | TENN 326:11 |
| **navy**: n. under the good Providence | CHAR 95:1 |
| put at the head of the N. | CARS 92:11 |
| Ruler of the Queen's N. | GILB 152:18 |
| **nay**: your n., nay | BIBLE 57:5 |
| **Nazareth**: good thing come out of N. | BIBLE 53:14 |
| **Neaera**: tangles of N.'s hair | MILT 227:14 |
| **near**: come not n. to me | BIBLE 46:25 |
| He seems so n. and yet so far | TENN 325:21 |
| n. me when my light is low | TENN 325:7 |
| She is n., she is near | TENN 327:1 |
| **nearer**: N. and nearer draws | AING 3:9 |
| n. bloody | SHAK 286:27 |
| n. God's Heart in a garden | GURN 159:10 |
| N., my God, to thee | ADAMS 2:8 |
| n. the Church the further | ANDR 5:16 |
| *n. you are to God* | WOTT 357:21 |
| **nearest**: those who are n. to him | MILL 224:18 |
| To catch the n. way | SHAK 285:15 |
| **nearly**: I was n. kept waiting | LOUI 210:13 |
| **neat**: You look n. | COLL 105:6 |
| **necessarily**: It ain't n. so | GERS 168:5 |
| **necessary**: government is a n. evil | PAINE 244:9 |
| little visible delight, but n. | BRON 72:17 |
| Make yourself n. to someone | EMER 136:17 |
| n. evil | BRAD 71:8 |
| n. not to change | FALK 138:11 |
| superfluous, a very n. thing | VOLT 340:22 |
| **necessities**: n. call out great virtues | ADAMS 1:7 |
| will dispense with its n. | MOTL 236:2 |
| **necessity**: always at the door of n. | DEFOE 115:12 |
| Cruel n. | CROM 111:3 |
| grim N. | SHAK 294:6 |
| I do not see the n. | ARG 15:7 |
| N. has no law | PUBL 256:2 |
| N. hath no law | CROM 112:6 |
| N. is the plea | PITT 249:7 |
| N. makes an honest man a knave | DEFOE 115:16 |

necessity (cont.):

| | |
|---|---|
| N. never made a good bargain | FRAN 145:10 |
| no virtue like n. | SHAK 293:13 |
| Progress not an accident, but a n. | SPEN 312:19 |

neck: n. God made for other use — HOUS 174:19

Some chicken! Some n.! — CHUR 99:17

necklace: matches, with our n. — MAND 217:9

nectar: To comprehend a n. — DICK 120:13

Work without hope draws n. — COL 104:22

nectarine: n., and curious peach — MARV 220:15

need: and all ye n. to know — KEATS 191:24

| | |
|---|---|
| enough for everyone's n. | BUCH 77:30 |
| face of total n. | BURR 82:31 |
| n. of a world of men | BROW 76:23 |
| people whenever we n. them | CAIL 142:2 |
| Requires sorest n. | DICK 120:13 |
| thy n. is greater than mine | SIDN 306:30 |
| Will you still n. me | MCC 205:17 |

needle: my hand a n. better fits — BRAD 71:12

through the eye of a n. — BIBLE 50:22

Why are the n. and the pen — LEWIS 206:14

needs: each according to his n. — BAK 27:1

each according to his n. — MARX 221:9

negative: Elim-my-nate the n. — MERC 223:9

| | |
|---|---|
| N. Capability | KEATS 193:2 |
| n. of which America is the | MCC 214:10 |

neglect: n. may breed mischief — FRAN 145:12

Such sweet n. more taketh me — JONS 187:6

neglected: to have his all n. — JOHN 183:25

negotiate: never n. out of fear — KENN 194:4

Negro: N. could never hope — DAVIS 114:23

neiges: où sont les n. d'antan? — VILL 338:20

neighbour: I am a n. — SHAK 289:6

| | |
|---|---|
| love thy n. as thyself | BIBLE 40:14 |
| our n.'s house is on fire | BURKE 80:9 |
| policy of the good n. | ROOS 262:10 |
| shalt not covet thy n.'s wife | BIBLE 40:9 |

neighbourhood: n. of voluntary spies — AUST 22:25

neighbours: Good fences make good n. — FROST 146:16

| | |
|---|---|
| make sport for our n. | AUST 23:6 |
| to have good n. | ELIZ 135:5 |
| upon his n. to do his work | BAUD 30:8 |
| what is happening to our n. | CHAM 93:24 |
| will the n. say, 'He was a man | HARDY 162:2 |

neither: n. death, nor life — BIBLE 54:42

Nell: Pretty witty N. — PEPYS 247:17

Nellie Dean: I love you, N. — ARMS 15:24

Nelly: Let not poor N. starve — CHAR 95:4

Nelson: N. touch — NELS 238:2

nemo: N. me impune lacessit — ANON 13:17

nerve: after the n. has been — ROWL 263:21

Anatomised in every n. — JONS 187:7

nerves: and the n. prick — TENN 325:7

Muscles better and n. more — CUMM 113:4

nervos: N. belli — CIC 100:29

nervous: n. and terse, but limited — DOYLE 126:7

nervousness: only n. or death — LEB 203:24

nessun: N. dorma — ADAMI 1:6

nest: n. of singing birds — JOHN 183:22

| | |
|---|---|
| her soft and chilly n. | KEATS 190:19 |
| now leaves his wat'ry n. | D'AV 114:10 |
| swallow a n. | BOOK 67:20 |

nests: Birds in their little n. agree — WATTS 343:8

| | |
|---|---|
| birds of the air have n. | BIBLE 49:19 |
| built their n. in my beard | LEAR 203:17 |

nets: n. to catch the wind — WEBS 344:13

nettle: Out of this n., danger — SHAK 277:30

Tender-handed stroke a n. — HILL 168:11

nettles: n. and brambles — BIBLE 46:3

neurosis: n. is a secret — TYNAN 336:9

N. is the way of avoiding — TILL 332:21

neutral: stood apart, studiously n. — WILS 351:19

neutrality: Armed n. — WILS 351:20

Just for a word 'n.' — BETH 36:15

n. of an impartial judge — BURKE 81:12

never: always, by God, n. — RICH 260:5

| | |
|---|---|
| I n. use a big, big D | GILB 152:16 |
| N. do to-day what you can | PUNCH 256:8 |
| N. explain | FISH 139:24 |
| N. explain | HUBB 175:13 |
| N. glad confident morning | BROW 76:15 |
| N. Had It So Good | MACM 215:15 |
| N. in the field of human conflict | CHUR 99:15 |
| N. in the way | CHAR 95:5 |
| N. knowingly undersold | LEWIS 206:16 |
| N., never, never, never, never | SHAK 284:6 |
| N. the time and the place | BROW 76:20 |
| N. to have lived is best | YEATS 359:5 |
| She who has n. loved | GAY 149:8 |
| than n. to have been loved | CONG 106:16 |
| Than n. to have fought at all | CLOU 102:21 |
| This will n. do | JEFF 181:2 |
| We n. closed | VAN D 336:25 |
| What, n.? No, never! | GILB 152:15 |

nevermore: Quoth the Raven, 'N.' — POE 250:7

new: dull in a n. way — JOHN 184:28

| | |
|---|---|
| find something n. | VOLT 340:11 |
| make all things n. | BIBLE 58:5 |
| make a n. acquaintance | JOHN 186:7 |
| MAKE IT N. | POUND 254:10 |
| my n. found land | DONNE 123:6 |
| n. deal for the American | ROOS 262:8 |
| N. every morning is the love | KEBLE 193:16 |
| n. heaven and a new earth | BIBLE 58:4 |
| n. heaven, new earth | SHAK 271:4 |
| new heavens and a n. earth | BIBLE 46:26 |
| n. man may be raised up | BOOK 65:19 |
| n. men, strange faces | TENN 324:19 |
| n. thing under the sun | BIBLE 44:8 |
| n. wine into old bottles | BIBLE 49:24 |
| old lamps for n. | ARAB 14:16 |
| piping songs for ever n. | KEATS 191:20 |
| ring in the n. | TENN 325:23 |
| shock of the n. | DUNL 129:9 |
| sing unto the Lord a n. song | BOOK 68:3 |
| something n. out of Africa | PLINY 249:23 |
| so quite n. a thing | CUMM 113:4 |
| time for making n. enemies | VOLT 341:3 |
| we'll find the n. | BAUD 30:6 |

new-born: use of a n. child — FRAN 145:17

Newcastle: No more coals to N. — GEOR 149:26

newcomer: O blithe n. — WORD 357:7

newest: oldest sins the n. kind — SHAK 278:28

newness: walk in n. of life — BIBLE 54:34

news: All the n. that's fit to print — OCHS 241:1

| | |
|---|---|
| bitter n. to hear | CORY 108:13 |
| good n. from a far country | BIBLE 43:37 |
| good n. yet to hear | CHES 98:3 |
| Ill n. hath wings | DRAY 126:15 |
| Literature is n. that STAYS n. | POUND 254:23 |
| man bites a dog, that is n. | BOG 62:19 |
| n. and Prince of Peace | FLET 142:8 |
| only n. until he's read it | WAUGH 343:26 |
| other to get the n. to you | TWAIN 335:25 |
| passion is the love of n. | CRAB 110:25 |
| What n. on the Rialto | SHAK 288:31 |

New South Wales: govern N. — BELL 33:7

newspaper: good n. is a nation — MILL 225:6

newspapers: I read the n. avidly — BEVAN 38:6

It's the n. I can't stand — STOP 318:2

newt: Eye of n., and toe of frog — SHAK 287:16

Newton: another N., a new Donne — HUXL 177:11

| | |
|---|---|
| Let N. be | POPE 251:26 |
| make us as N. was | AUDEN 21:5 |
| N.'s particles of light | BLAKE 61:14 |
| Single vision and N.'s sleep | BLAKE 60:23 |
| statue stood of N. | WORD 356:10 |

New World: N. into existence — CANN 89:14

New York: California to the N. Island — GUTH 159:12

**New York** (cont.):
N. swallowing the tonnage — MILL 225:5
**New Zealand**: traveller from N. — MAC 213:15
**next**: n. to Nature, Art — LAND 200:22
n. to of course god america i — CUMM 112:17
What n., what next — LOW 211:15
**nexus**: sole n. of man to man — CARL 90:4
**Niagara**: wouldn't live under N. — CARL 90:24
**nice**: In n. clean faces — BARH 28:18
N. guys. Finish last — DUR 129:13
n. to people on your way up — MIZN 232:11
N. work if you can get it — GERS 150:8
Too n. for a statesman — GOLD 155:2
**nicens**: n. little boy named baby — JOYCE 188:6
**nicest**: nastiest thing in the n. — GOLD 154:16
**niche**: got your n. in creation — HALL 160:14
**Nicodemus**: Wise N. saw — VAUG 337:4
**nigger**: Woman is the n. of the world — ONO 241:13
**night**: ain't a fit n. out for man — FIEL 139:17
as a watch in the n. — BOOK 67:25
black bat, n. — TENN 326:28
blue of the n. meets the gold — CROS 112:9
borrower of the n. — SHAK 287:1
breath of the n.-wind — ARN 16:11
City is of N. — THOM 332:1
Closed his eyes in endless n. — GRAY 157:17
Come, civil n. — SHAK 295:12
Come, seeling n. — SHAK 287:6
Come, thick n. — SHAK 285:19
come, thou day in n. — SHAK 295:13
dangers of this n. — BOOK 64:12
dark n. of the soul — FITZ 140:22
day brought back my n. — MILT 230:25
Dear N.! this world's defeat — VAUG 337:5
dog in the n.-time — DOYLE 125:21
drowned with us in endless n. — HERR 167:14
dusky n. rides down the sky — FIEL 139:5
evening mild, then silent n. — MILT 229:11
Every n. and alle — BALL 27:20
first minute, after noon, is n. — DONNE 124:6
gentle into that good n. — THOM 330:7
genuine n. admits no ray — DRYD 128:5
go bump in the n. — ANON 7:7
hangs upon the cheek of n. — SHAK 294:26
hard day's n. — LENN 205:14
haunts you n. and day — BERL 36:1
honeyed middle of the n. — KEATS 190:17
ignorant armies clash by n. — ARN 16:12
Illness is the n.-side of life — SONT 311:10
infant crying in the n. — TENN 325:9
in weary N.'s decline — BLAKE 60:15
I pass, like n., from land — COL 104:17
know his God by n. — VAUG 337:4
lightning in the collied n. — SHAK 290:14
long day's journey into n. — O'NEI 241:11
love-performing n. — SHAK 295:11
mirk, mirk n. — BALL 28:8
moonless n. in the small town — THOM 330:16
Morning in the bowl of n. — FITZ 140:4
n. after tonight — AMIS 5:8
N. and day, you are the one — PORT 253:25
n. before Christmas — MOORE 234:3
n. do penance for a day — WORD 356:11
n. has a thousand eyes — BOUR 70:12
N. hath a thousand eyes — LYLY 212:18
n. in a pillar of fire — BIBLE 39:39
n. in her silver shoon — DE L 116:22
n. is like a lovely n. — WASH 342:24
N. Mail crossing the Border — AUDEN 21:4
N. makes no difference — HERR 167:18
n. methinks is but the daylight — SHAK 290:6
n. of the long knives — HITL 168:21
n. of this immortal day — SHEL 304:24
n. of tropical splendour — PORT 253:18
n. of tyranny had descended — MURR 236:13

**night** (cont.):
N.'s candles are burnt — SHAK 295:18
n. that wins — SWIN 321:2
n. we went to Birmingham — CHES 98:2
only for a n. and away — WYCH 358:4
reign of Chaos and old N. — MILT 228:16
returned on the previous n. — BULL 78:7
rung n.'s yawning peal — SHAK 287:5
Sable-vested N. — MILT 228:32
Ships that pass in the n. — LONG 210:3
sleep one ever-during n. — CAMP 89:2
So late into the n. — BYRON 87:8
sound of revelry by n. — BYRON 85:2
Spirit of N. — SHEL 305:12
such a n. as this — SHAK 289:31
tender is the n. — KEATS 192:1
terror by n. — BOOK 67:29
then it's n. once more — BECK 31:15
This is the n. — SHAK 292:27
Through the n. of doubt — BAR 29:2
tire the n. in thought — QUAR 257:2
'Tis with us perpetual n. — JONS 187:15
touch of Harry in the n. — SHAK 279:8
under the lonely n. — VIRG 339:14
upon the n.'s starred face — KEATS 192:20
very witching time of n. — SHAK 276:15
vile contagion of the n. — SHAK 281:6
Watchman, what of the n. — BIBLE 45:23
world's last n. — DONNE 123:13
What hath n. to do with sleep — MILT 226:8
When n. darkens the streets — MILT 228:15
wide womb of uncreated n. — MILT 228:24
You meaner beauties of the n. — WOTT 357:16
**night-gown**: down stairs in his n. — MILL 225:9
**nightingale**: brown bright n. — SWIN 321:1
n., and not the lark — SHAK 295:17
n. does sit so late — MARV 220:20
O 'tis the ravished n. — LYLY 212:17
**nightingales**: n. are singing — ELIOT 134:17
**nightmare**: History is a n. — JOYCE 188:14
Our long national n. is over — FORD 143:4
**nights**: chequer-board of n. and days — FITZ 140:12
down the n. and down the days — THOM 331:8
**nihil**: Aut Caesar, aut n. — BORG 69:25
N. est sine ratione — LEIB 204:15
Vox et praeterea n. — ANON 14:3
**nil**: N. admirari — HOR 173:10
N. carborundum illegitimi — ANON 9:15
N. desperandum — HOR 173:19
N. posse creari — LUCR 212:3
**Nile**: allegory on the banks of the N. — SHER 305:30
pour the waters of the N. — CARR 91:3
Where's my serpent of old N. — SHAK 271:11
**Nimrod**: N. the mighty hunter — BIBLE 39:11
**nine**: N. bean rows will I have — YEATS 359:12
**ninety**: heave the n. and nine — BIBLE 52:26
**Nineveh**: one with N., and Tyre — KIPL 197:3
**ninny**: compared to Handel's a mere n. — BYROM 84:24
**Niobe**: Like N., all tears — SHAK 274:12
**nip**: I'll n. him in the bud — ROCHE 261:1
**nipping**: n. and an eager air — SHAK 274:25
**nipple**: plucked my n. — SHAK 286:6
**nisi**: N. Dominus custodierit — BIBLE 58:13
**nix**: Sticks n. hick pix — ANON 10:15
**no**: citizen of n. mean city — BIBLE 54:23
everlasting N. — CARL 90:22
I am also called N.-more — ROSS 263:8
land of the omnipotent N. — BOLD 63:2
man who says n. — CAMUS 89:7
n. go the merrygoround — MACN 216:1
N.! I am not Prince Hamlet — ELIOT 134:1
N. money, no service — RAC 257:17
N. sun—no moon — HOOD 171:9
**Noah**: but one poor N. — HUXL 177:11
God gave N. the rainbow sign — ANON 7:12

**Noah** (*cont.*):
N. he often said — CHES 98:7

**nobility:** ancient n. — BACON 25:4
N. of birth commonly abateth — BACON 25:5

**nobis:** *Non n., Domine* — BIBLE 58:12

**noble:** Eternally n., historically fair — LERN 205:26
fredome is a n. thing — BARB 28:16
My love's a n. madness — DRYD 127:24
n. and nude and antique — SWIN 321:6
n. Living, and the n. Dead — WORD 356:15
n. mind is here o'erthrown — SHAK 276:2
n. savage — DRYD 127:26
Some work of n. note — TENN 328:23
What's brave, what's n. — SHAK 271:26

**nobleman:** underrated N. — GILB 151:4

**nobleness:** N. walks in our ways — BROO 72:21

**nobler:** n. in the mind to suffer — SHAK 275:25

**nobles:** their n. with links of iron — BOOK 69:11

**noblesse:** *N. oblige* — LEVIS 206:9

**noblest:** honest God is the n. work — ING 178:15
honest man's the n. work — POPE 252:22
n. Roman of them all — SHAK 282:2

**nobly:** n. Cape Saint Vincent — BROW 76:3

**nobody:** business of n. — MAC 213:3
gave a war & N. came — GINS 153:2
give a war and n. will come — SAND 266:16
n. comes, nobody goes — BECK 31:12

**noctis:** *lente currite n. equi* — MARL 218:13

**Nod:** dwelt in the land of N. — BIBLE 39:6
Old N., the shepherd, goes — DE L 116:21

**nods:** even excellent Homer n. — HOR 173:3
N., and becks — MILT 227:1

**noise:** gone up with a merry n. — BOOK 67:8
happy n. to hear — HOUS 174:20
melt, and make no n. — DONNE 124:15
moved to folly by a n. — LAWR 202:28
n. at one end and no sense — KNOX 198:20
noiseless n. among the leaves — KEATS 191:5
n., my dear! And the people — ANON 9:16
n. of battle rolled — TENN 324:17

**noiseless:** n. tenor of their way — GRAY 157:10

**noises:** isle is full of n. — SHAK 296:9

**noli:** *N. me tangere* — BIBLE 58:22

**nominative:** her n. case — O'KEE 241:5

**nomine:** *In N. Patris* — MISS 231:10

**non:** *N. nobis, Domine* — BIBLE 58:12

**non-being:** avoiding n. — TILL 332:21

**non-combatant:** no fury like a n. — MONT 233:7

**non-commissioned:** n. man — KIPL 196:10

**none:** answer came there n. — SCOTT 268:6
answer made it n. — SHAK 274:18
malice toward n. — LINC 207:7
N. but the brave — DRYD 127:19
N. shall sleep — ADAMI 1:6

**nonsense:** damned n. will I put — RICH 260:5
n., and learning — GOLD 155:8
n. upon stilts — BENT 34:22

**noon:** amid the blaze of n. — MILT 230:11
first minute, after n., is night — DONNE 124:6
returned before n. — SAIN 265:14

**noon-day:** destroyeth in the n. — BOOK 67:29

**noose:** turret in a n. of light — FITZ 140:4

**Norfan:** I'm a N., both sides — WELLS 345:18

**Norfolk:** bear him up the N. sky — BETJ 36:20
Very flat, N. — COW 109:9

**normal:** N. is the good smile — SHAF 270:19
Thank God we're n. — OSB 242:19
type of the n. and easy — JAMES 180:1

**Norman:** simple faith than N. blood — TENN 325:33

**north:** triumph from the n. — MAC 213:25
true and tender is the N. — TENN 327:24
unripened beauties of the n. — ADD 2:14

**North African:** egg of a N. Empire — GLAD 153:11

**northern:** constant as the n. star — SHAK 281:9
Glorious the n. lights astream — SMART 308:13

**northern** (*cont.*):
Lucasta that bright n. star — LOV 210:18
N. reticence — HEAN 164:11
prim prater of the n. race — CHUR 98:28

**north-west:** N. passage — STER 315:21

**Norval:** My name is N. — HOME 170:18

**nose:** Any n. may ravage — BROW 77:15
Cleopatra's n. been shorter — PASC 246:2
great hook n. like thine — BLAKE 60:11
hateful to the n. — JAM 179:9
Heaven stops the n. at it — SHAK 292:25
His n.'s cast is of the roman — FLEM 142:1
miss the insinuated n. — WATS 343:1
n. dead against the Pope — BALD 27:8
n. was as sharp as a pen — SHAK 279:4
plucks justice by the n. — SHAK 288:9
ring at the end of his n. — LEAR 203:12
Some thirty inches from my n. — AUDEN 21:8
thing is not a n. at all — WELLS 345:22

**noselessness:** N. of Man — CHES 98:6

**noses:** men's n. as they lie asleep — SHAK 294:24
n. have they, and smell not — BOOK 68:18
They haven't got no n. — CHES 98:5

**nostalgia:** N. isn't what it used — ANON 9:18

**nostalgie:** *La n. de la boue* — AUG 21:21

**noster:** *Pater n., qui es in coelis* — MISS 231:18

**not:** n. I, but the wind — LAWR 202:23
N. so much a programme — ANON 9:19
N. unto us, O Lord — BOOK 68:17
thing which was n. — SWIFT 320:1

**note:** only the n. of a bird — SIMP 307:10
When found, make a n. of — DICK 118:20

**notes:** n. like little fishes — MACN 216:9
thick-warbled n. — MILT 230:6

**nothing:** brought n. into this world — BIBLE 56:18
Did n. in particular — GILB 151:14
doing n. with a deal of skill — COWP 110:5
do n. for ever and ever — ANON 7:17
do n. for evil to triumph — BURKE 81:13
don't resent having n. — COMP 106:4
easy to take *more* than n. — CARR 91:8
everything by starts, and n. long — DRYD 127:12
forgotten n. and learnt nothing — DUM 129:6
gives to airy n. — SHAK 291:4
glory and the n. of a name — BYRON 85:15
have not charity, I am n. — BIBLE 55:11
having n., yet hath all — WOTT 357:15
How to live well on n. a year — THAC 329:20
I have n. to say — CAGE 88:4
individually can do n. — ALLEN 4:12
insupportable labour of doing n. — STEE 314:14
Is it n. to you — BIBLE 46:32
I will say n. — SHAK 283:9
know this only, that he n. knew — MILT 230:7
learnt n., and forgotten n. — TALL 322:12
marvel at n. — HOR 173:10
N. ain't worth nothin' — KRIS 199:5
n. a-year, paid quarterly — SURT 319:15
N. begins, and nothing ends — THOM 331:7
N. can be created out of — LUCR 212:3
n. can be sole or whole — YEATS 358:20
n. could be finer — GORD 155:22
n. done for the first time — CORN 108:8
n. ever ran quite straight — GALS 147:17
n. extenuate — SHAK 293:5
N. happens, nobody comes — BECK 31:12
N. happens to anybody — AUR 22:9
N. in excess — ANON 13:7
N. is ever done in this world — SHAW 301:14
N. is here for tears — MILT 230:18
N. is wasted — HERB 166:15
n. left remarkable — SHAK 271:25
N., like something — LARK 201:15
n. something straight begot — ROCH 261:10
N. to be done — BECK 31:10

**nothing** (*cont.*):

| | |
|---|---|
| N. to do but work | KING 195:4 |
| n. to do with the case | GILB 152:6 |
| N. will come of nothing | SHAK 282:16 |
| Signifying n. | SHAK 288:5 |
| stand for n. fall for anything | HAM 160:16 |
| Tar-baby ain't sayin' n. | HARR 163:6 |
| Thinking n. done while | LUCAN 211:25 |
| Think n. done while aught | ROG 261:17 |
| 'tis something, that | SHAK 292:11 |
| When you have n. to say | COLT 105:16 |
| without whom n. is strong | BOOK 64:24 |
| You Ain't Heard N. Yet | JOLS 186:19 |

**nothingness**: Pass into n. | KEATS 190:11
Till love and fame to n. | KEATS 192:21
**nothings**: Invulnerable n. | SHEL 303:10
**notice**: man who used to n. | HARDY 162:2
**notorious**: n. evil liver | BOOK 64:29
**nought**: N. but vast Sorrow | DE L 116:16
So much a thing of n. | CRAS 111:5
**noun**: verb not a n. | FULL 147:4
**nourish**: n. us with all goodness | BOOK 64:25
**nouveau**: *pour trouver du n.* | BAUD 30:6
**nouvelles**: *du moins des choses n.* | VOLT 340:11
**novel**: given away by a n. | KEATS 193:11
it is only a n. | AUST 22:22
Morality in the n. | LAWR 202:12
n. gets up and walks away | LAWR 202:11
n. is a mirror which passes | STEN 315:3
n. is the one bright book | LAWR 202:14
yes, then it tells a story | FORS 143:16
**novelty**: This n. on earth | MILT 229:30
**November**: no birds, | HOOD 171:10
remember the Fifth of N. | ANON 10:5
Who hear N. at the gate | PUSH 256:22
**now**: If it be n., 'tis not to come | SHAK 277:13
Leave N. for dogs and apes | BROW 75:32
N. I lay me down to sleep | ANON 9:20
N. is the accepted time | BIBLE 55:25
N. more than ever seems | KEATS 192:3
N. thank we all our God | WINK 352:4
**nowhere**: Eclipse first, the rest n. | O'KEL 241:7
**noxious**: most n. is a tourist | KILV 195:3
**nuclear**: n. arms race | MOUN 236:4
**nude**: noble and n. and antique | SWIN 321:6
To keep one from going n. | KING 195:4
**nuisance**: n. to other people | MILL 224:16
n. for another nuisance | ELLIS 136:5
**null**: splendidly n. | TENN 326:23
**nullius**: *N. in verba* | HOR 173:5
**NUM**: against the Pope or the N. | BALD 27:8
**number**: count the n. of the beast | BIBLE 57:33
happiness of the greatest n. | BENT 35:1
n. of his name | BIBLE 57:32
teach us to n. our days | BOOK 67:27
world is so full of a n. of things | STEV 317:13
**numbered**: God hath n. thy kingdom | BIBLE 47:12
hairs of your head are all n. | BIBLE 49:30
**numberless**: As thick and n. | MILT 226:23
n. goings-on of life | COL 103:19
you n. infinities | DONNE 123:7
**numbers**: divinity in odd n. | SHAK 290:11
happiness for the greatest n. | HUTC 177:2
n. that rocket the mind | WILB 349:8
secret magic of n. | BROW 74:12
**numbness**: drowsy n. pains | KEATS 191:28
**nun**: *N. danket alle Gott* | WINK 352:4
pensive n., devout | MILT 226:24
**nunc dimittis**: *N. servum tuum* | BIBLE 58:17
**nunnery**: Get thee to a n. | SHAK 275:28
n. of thy chaste breast | LOV 210:20
**nurse**: always keep a-hold of N. | BELL 33:5
Dear n. of arts | SHAK 280:2
Meet n. for a poetic child | SCOTT 268:14
n. unacted desires | BLAKE 61:10

**nurse** (*cont.*):

| | |
|---|---|
| sucks the n. asleep | SHAK 272:9 |
| This n., this teeming womb | SHAK 293:16 |
| will scratch the n. | SHAK 298:17 |

**nursed**: I never n. a dear gazelle | MOORE 234:19
n. upon the self-same hill | MILT 227:12
**nurseries**: in the n. of heaven | THOM 331:18
public schools the n. of all vice | FIEL 139:8
**nursery**: n.-mishaps | CRAB 110:19
n. of future revolutions | BURKE 80:11
**nurses**: old men's n. | BACON 25:2
**nursing**: n. the unconquerable hope | ARN 17:12
**nuts**: N.! | MCAU 214:9
where the n. come from | THOM 330:5
**nut-shell**: bounded in a n. | SHAK 275:15
**nymph**: N., in thy orisons | SHAK 275:27

# O

| | |
|---|---|
| O: O Death, where is thy sting | ANON 9:21 |
| O that Shakespeherian Rag | ELIOT 134:24 |

**oafish**: o. louts remember Mum | BETJ 36:17
**oafs**: muddied o. at the goals | KIPL 196:16
**oak**: Heart of o. are our ships | GARR 148:8
O., and Ash, and Thorn | KIPL 197:1
**oaks**: families last not three o. | BROW 74:6
o. from little acorns grow | EVER 137:24
**oars**: O. laboured heavily | ANAT 5:10
**oat-cakes**: Calvin, o., and sulphur | SMITH 309:26
**oath**: He who cheats with an o. | PLUT 250:2
man is not upon o. | JOHN 185:6
**oaths**: Full of strange o. | SHAK 272:26
O. are but words | BUTL 84:4
**oats**: Mares eat o. | DRAKE 126:14
O. A grain, which in England | JOHN 182:9
**obedience**: gold of o. and incense | MONS 233:3
o. of distant provinces | MAC 213:12
o. of planetary influence | SHAK 282:22
Rebellion to tyrants is o. to God | BRAD 71:11
**obedient**: o. to their laws we lie | SIM 307:9
**obey**: robot must o. the orders | ASIM 19:1
to love, cherish, and to o. | BOOK 66:1
with the laws but to o. | HORS 174:5
**obeyed**: I o. as a son | GIBB 150:14
She who must be o. | HAGG 159:15
**obituary**: o. in serial form | CRISP 111:21
publicity except your own o. | BEHAN 32:19
**object**: My o. all sublime | GILB 152:1
see the o. as in itself | ARN 18:12
**objective**: o. correlative | ELIOT 135:1
**oblation**: o. of himself | BOOK 65:16
**oblations**: accept our alms and o. | BOOK 65:8
**oblige**: *Noblesse o.* | LÉVIS 206:9
**oblivion**: alms for o. | SHAK 297:4
childishness, and mere o. | SHAK 272:28
commend to cold o. | SHEL 303:15
formless ruin of o. | SHAK 297:10
my o. is a very Antony | SHAK 271:9
place to place over o. | HARDY 162:10
**obnoxious**: o. to each carping tongue | BRAD 71:12
**obscenes**: old idols, lost o. | BOTT 70:6
**obscenity**: 'o.' is not a term | RUSS 265:4
**obscure**: and I become o. | HOR 172:24
palpable o. | MILT 228:29
**obscurely**: o. bright | BYRON 85:20
o. good | ADD 2:17
**obscuri**: *Ibant o. sola sub nocte* | VIRG 339:14
**obscurity**: not easily rise out of o. | JUV 189:5
o. of a learned language | GIBB 150:16
snatches a man from o. | REYN 259:7
**observation**: Let o. with extensive view | JOHN 183:11
Where o. is concerned | PAST 246:11
**observe**: see, but you do not o. | DOYLE 125:16
**observed**: o. of all observers | SHAK 276:2

observer: keen o. of life | AUDEN 21:3
obsolescence: adolescence and o. | LINK 207:18
based on planned o. | STEV 316:1
obstinacy: O. in a bad cause | BROW 74:15
o. in a bad one | STER 315:14
obstruct: circumstances o. at home | JUV 189:5
obtain: we may o. effectually | BOOK 64:27
occasion: on o.'s forelock | MILT 230:4
occasions: o. do inform against me | SHAK 276:29
upon their lawful o. | BOOK 69:14
occidental: that bright O. Star | BIBLE 38:12
occupation: Othello's o.'s gone | SHAK 292:21
occupations: let us love our o. | DICK 118:5
occurred: Ought never to have o. | BENT 35:7
ocean: day-star in the o. bed | MILT 227:18
In the o.'s bosom unespied | MARV 220:9
like o. on a western beach | LANG 201:3
Neptune's o. wash this blood | SHAK 286:18
o. of darkness and death | FOX 144:17
o. of life we pass | LONG 210:3
O.'s child, and then his queen | SHEL 304:2
O.'s nursling, Venice lies | SHEL 304:1
Ransack the o. for orient pearl | MARL 218:8
sapless foliage of the o. | SHEL 304:7
thou deep and dark blue O. | BYRON 85:13
till the o. is folded | AUDEN 20:11
Upon a painted o. | COL 104:6
Who bidd'st the mighty o. deep | WHIT 348:9
Yet for his fame the o. | BARN 29:7
oceans: compendious o. | CRAS 111:14
To the o. white with foam | BERL 35:21
October: What of O. | LESS 206:3
octopus: dear o. | SMITH 309:4
odd: divinity in o. numbers | SHAK 290:11
How o. of God | EWER 138:2
Must think it exceedingly o. | KNOX 198:18
Nothing o. will do long | JOHN 185:7
not so o. as those who choose | BROW 73:21
odds: facing fearful o. | MAC 214:3
o. is gone | SHAK 271:25
odes: quoted o. | TENN 327:18
odi: O. et amo | CAT 93:7
odious: O.! in woollen | POPE 251:22
odium: He lived in the o. | BENT 35:8
odorous: Comparisons are o. | SHAK 291:23
odours: O., when sweet violets | SHEL 305:4
star-led wizards haste with o. | MILT 227:24
Odyssey: thunder of the O. | LANG 201:3
o'erflowing: o. of unbounded wit | WINC 352:1
off: O. with his head | CIBB 100:15
walk down again with them o. | HARG 162:20
offence: my o. is rank | SHAK 276:16
o. from am'rous causes | POPE 253:2
only defence is in o. | BALD 27:5
where the o. is let the great axe | SHAK 277:4
whom I was like to give o. | FROST 146:17
yet detest th'o. | POPE 250:25
offences: pardoning our o. | BOOK 65:17
sins and o. of my youth | BOOK 66:21
offend: o. one of these little ones | BIBLE 50:16
others doth o. | SUCK 318:22
offended: him have I o. | SHAK 281:17
This hath not o. the king | MORE 235:1
offender: love th'o. | POPE 250:25
offenders: society o. | GILB 151:19
offensive: You are extremely o. | SMITH 309:7
offer: o. he can't refuse | PUZO 256:25
offering: o. too little and asking | CANN 89:10
office: By office boys for o. boys | SAL 266:6
Each in his o. wait | DODD 122:30
in the o. of a wall | SHAK 293:16
man who has no o. | SHAW 301:6
officer: art thou o. | SHAK 279:9
o. and a gentleman shall | ANON 6:2

official: concept of the 'o. secret' | WEBER 344:8
This high o., all allow | HERB 166:14
officialism: where there is o. | FORS 143:26
officiously: O. to keep alive | CLOU 102:17
offspring: Time's noblest o. | BERK 35:19
oft: O. in danger, oft in woe | WHITE 347:16
O., in the stilly night | MOORE 234:20
What o. was thought | POPE 252:1
often: But not so o. | STER 315:25
Vote early and vote o. | ANON 11:9
oil: anointed my head with o. | BOOK 66:18
foreign o. controlling | DYLAN 130:8
head thou dost with o. anoint | SCOT 269:9
little o. in a cruse | BIBLE 41:35
midnight o. | QUAR 257:2
o. which renders the motion | HUME 176:6
sound of o. wells | FISH 139:26
with boiling o. in it | GILB 152:4
oiled: key deftly in the o. words | KEATS 192:13
o. his way around the floor | LERN 206:2
oily: I want that glib and o. art | SHAK 282:18
round, fat, o. man of God | THOM 331:21
Okie: O. means you're scum | STEI 314:24
old: Any o. iron | COLL 105:6
boys of the o. Brigade | WEAT 344:4
buried in a good o. age | BIBLE 39:12
chilly and grown o. | BROW 77:19
conservative when o. | FROST 146:18
country for o. men | YEATS 359:20
died in a good o. age | BIBLE 42:18
Grown o. before my time | ROSS 263:3
Grow o. along with me | BROW 77:3
heart grows o. | YEATS 359:29
Hope I die before I get o. | TOWN 333:16
I grow o. . . . I grow old | ELIOT 134:2
lads that will never be o. | HOUS 174:21
make an o. man young | TENN 323:24
Mithridates, he died o. | HOUS 175:5
no man would be o. | SWIFT 320:13
not yet so o. but she may learn | SHAK 289:22
now am not too o. | BLUN 62:15
O. Age a regret | DISR 121:26
O.-age, a second child | CHUR 98:24
O. age is the most unexpected | TROT 334:22
o. age, it is the last gasp but one | WHITE 347:17
o. age of cards | POPE 251:11
O. age should burn | THOM 330:7
o. and grey and full of sleep | YEATS 360:9
O. and young, we are all | STEV 317:5
o. ever learning many things | SOLON 310:26
o. familiar faces | LAMB 200:13
o. folks at home | FOST 144:13
o. heads on your young | SPARK 312:11
o. is having lighted rooms | LARK 201:16
o. is like being increasingly | POW 255:1
o. lamps for new ones | ARAB 14:16
o., mad, blind, despised | SHEL 305:3
o. man in a dry month | ELIOT 133:14
o. man in a hurry | CHUR 99:3
O. Masters | AUDEN 21:1
O. men forget | SHAK 279:19
o. men from the chimney | SIDN 306:27
o. order changeth | TENN 324:20
o. plain men have rosy faces | STEV 317:18
O. soldiers never die | FOLEY 142:16
O, sir! you are o. | SHAK 283:3
Ring out the o. | TENN 325:23
shaking hand of an o. man | VICT 338:5
Tell me the o., old story | HANK 161:7
They shall grow not o. | BINY 59:12
too late into a world too o. | MUSS 236:17
very foolish, fond o. man | SHAK 283:29
warn you not to grow o. | KINN 196:1
wars are planned by o. men | RICE 259:18

old (cont.):
When you are very o.                        RONS 262:5
You are o., Father William                  CARR 91:4
You are o., Father William                  SOUT 312:1
young a body with so o. a head              SHAK 289:25
young, and now am o.                        BOOK 66:27
your o. men shall dream                     BIBLE 47:20
older: I was so much o. then                DYLAN 130:6
o. than the rocks among                     PATER 246:13
o. we do not get any younger                REED 258:14
oldest: o. hath borne most                  SHAK 284:8
o. sins the newest kind                     SHAK 278:28
old-fashioned: I want an o. house           FISH 140:1
olive-branches: children like the o.        BOOK 68:32
Olivet: purple brows of O.                  TENN 325:5
Olivia: Cry out, 'O.!'                      SHAK 297:21
Olympus: leafy O. on top of Ossa            VIRG 340:6
Omega: I am Alpha and O.                     BIBLE 57:19
omelette: What a fuss about an o.           VOLT 341:2
omen: Quod di o. avertant                   CIC 100:28
omitted: O., all the voyage                 SHAK 282:1
omnia: Non o. possumus omnes                VIRG 340:2
O. vincit Amor                              VIRG 340:2
omnibus: horse power O.                     FLAN 141:6
omnipotent: land of the o. No               BOLD 63:2
once: himself o. offered                    BOOK 65:16
o. and future king                          WHITE 347:18
o. in a great while                         PEPYS 247:21
O. in royal David's city                    ALEX 4:4
O. more unto the breach                     SHAK 279:5
O. to every man and nation                  LOW 211:7
through this world but o.                    GREL 158:14
one: All for one, o. for all                DUMAS 129:4
But the O. was Me                           HUXL 177:11
Dear O. is mine as mirrors                  AUDEN 21:9
do only o. thing at once                    SMIL 308:18
How to be o. up                             POTT 254:4
Make it o. for my baby                      MERC 223:11
o. by one back in the closet                FITZ 140:12
o. day in thy courts                        BOOK 67:22
O. man shall have one vote                  CART 92:14
O. remains, the many                        SHEL 303:13
O. who never turned                         BROW 75:11
she who but trifles with o.                 GAY 149:9
Win just o. for the Gipper                  GIPP 153:4
one-eyed: o. man is king                    ERAS 137:14
o. yellow idol to the north                 HAYES 163:21
only: It's the o. thing                     SAND 266:19
o. begetter of these                        SHAK 299:10
O. connect                                  FORS 143:21
O. the lonely                               MELS 241:16
pint of plain is your o. man                O'BR 240:20
only-begotten: o. Son of God                BOOK 65:5
onset: Vain thy o.                          ARN 16:18
onward: O., Christian soldiers              BAR 29:1
O. goes the pilgrim band                    BAR 29:2
'O.,' the sailors cry                       BOUL 70:10
upward still, and o.                        LOW 211:9
oozing: O. charm from every pore            LERN 206:2
oozy: o. woods which wear                   SHEL 304:7
opal: thy mind is a very o.                 SHAK 297:33
open: great o. spaces                       MARQ 219:18
o. and notorious evil liver                 BOOK 64:29
O. covenants of peace                       WILS 351:22
O. Sesame                                   ARAB 14:17
o. to the poor and the rich                 ANON 7:9
O. unto the fields                          WORD 354:15
Secret thoughts and o.                      ALB 3:13
slepen al the nyght with o. ye              CHAU 95:11
Where knock is o. wide                      SMART 308:11
opened: o. the seventh seal                 BIBLE 57:29
opera: o. ain't over 'til                   COOK 107:16
O. is when a guy gets stabbed               GARD 148:5
operas: o. sung by Swedish artists          WHAR 347:3
operatic: so romantic, so o.                PROU 255:20

operations: number of o.                    WHIT 348:5
opiate: dull o. to the drains               KEATS 191:28
opinion: common o. and uncommon             BAG 26:2
low o. of himself                           TROL 334:17
man can brave o.                            STAËL 314:6
no more than private o.                     HOBB 169:7
of his own o. still                         BUTL 84:6
O. in good men                              MILT 231:4
o. one man entertains                       PALM 244:20
Party is organized o.                       DISR 121:14
sacrifices it to your o.                    BURKE 80:22
think the last o. right                     POPE 252:6
vagrant o. without visible                  BIER 59:8
whole climate of o.                         AUDEN 20:20
opinions: anger of men who have no o.       CHES 98:10
as many o. as there are people              TER 329:6
Golden o. from all sorts                    SHAK 286:2
halt ye between two o.                      BIBLE 41:36
New o. are always suspected                 LOCKE 208:13
Stiff in o.                                 DRYD 127:12
opium: o.-dose for keeping                  KING 195:18
o. of the people                           MARX 221:8
opponents: o. eventually die                PLAN 249:12
opportunity: O. makes a thief               BACON 25:24
Thou strong seducer, o.                     DRYD 127:27
with the maximum of o.                      SHAW 301:30
oppose: everything, and propose             DERBY 117:6
opposing: by o. end them                    SHAK 275:25
opposites: o. are obviously absurd          BOHR 63:1
opposition: duty of an O.                    DERBY 117:6
Her Majesty's O.                            BAG 26:6
His Majesty's O.                            HOBH 169:12
o. of the stars                             MARV 220:13
without a formidable O.                     DISR 121:23
oppressed: Sink heart and voice o.          NEALE 237:22
oppressing: o. city                         BIBLE 47:25
oppression: O. makes the wise               BROW 76:16
oppressor: day o' the O. is ended           KIPL 197:16
oppugnancy: In mere o.                      SHAK 296:30
optimist: o. is a guy                       MARQ 219:16
o. proclaims that we live                   CAB 87:23
opus: Hoc o., hic labor est                 VIRG 339:12
oracles: these are the lively O.            COR 108:10
oracular: use of my o. tongue               SHER 305:29
orange: clockwork o.                        BURG 79:13
shades the o. bright                        MARV 220:10
oranges: Coffee and o.                      STEV 316:12
orantes: Stabant o.                         VIRG 339:15
oration: not studied as an o.               OSB 242:17
orator: enjoyment as the greatest o.        HUME 176:7
eyes of men without an o.                   SHAK 299:7
I am no o.                                  SHAK 281:25
orators: swords shall play the o.           MARL 219:5
orchestra: o. is playing to the rich        AUDEN 20:13
rules for an o.                             BEEC 31:23
orchestration: o. of platitudes            WILD 350:24
order: all is in o.                         MANS 217:15
Democrat, in that o.                        JOHN 181:19
done decently and in o.                     BIBLE 55:15
good o. and military                        ANON 6:22
Good o. is the foundation                   BURKE 80:21
Half of one o., half another                BUTL 84:1
not necessarily in that o.                  GOD 153:19
old o. changeth                             TENN 324:20
only war creates o.                         BREC 71:20
o. of the acts is planned                   PAST 246:10
O. reigns in Warsaw                         ANON 12:12
put his household in o.                     BIBLE 41:26
Set thine house in o.                       BIBLE 46:6
They o. this matter better                  STER 315:8
upon the o. of your going                   SHAK 287:12
when o. breeds habit                        ADAMS 1:15
ordered: o. their estate                    ALEX 4:3
ordering: better o. of the universe         ALF 4:8

| | |
|---|---|
| **pacifist**: quietly p. peaceful | WALK 341:5 |
| **pack**: changed the form of the p. | TROT 334:23 |
| I will p., and take a train | BROO 73:6 |
| p. up your troubles | ASAF 18:17 |
| Pay, p., and follow | BURT 83:4 |
| To p. and label men for God | THOM 331:13 |
| **pack-horse**: p. on the down | MORR 235:16 |
| **pack-horses**: P. and hollow pampered jades | |
| | SHAK 278:21 |
| **Paddington**: ever weeping P. | BLAKE 60:16 |
| **paddles**: p. chunkin' | KIPL 196:21 |
| **paddocks**: Cold as p. | HERR 167:11 |
| **padlock**: clap your p.—on her mind | PRIOR 255:9 |
| **paeans**: laurels to p. | CIC 100:23 |
| **pagan**: find the p.—spoiled | ZANG 360:26 |
| P. suckled in a creed outworn | WORD 357:11 |
| **page**: I turn the p. | BROW 75:18 |
| **pageant**: insubstantial p. faded | SHAK 296:10 |
| part of life's rich p. | MARS 220:2 |
| **pagus**: private p. or demesne | AUDEN 21:8 |
| **paid**: Lord God, we ha' p. in full | KIPL 197:9 |
| So attention must be p. | MILL 225:3 |
| well p. that is well satisfied | SHAK 289:30 |
| **pain**: After great p. | DICK 120:8 |
| After long grief and p. | TENN 327:3 |
| beneath the aromatic p. | WINC 352:2 |
| born in other's p. | THOM 331:7 |
| Eternal P. | ARN 16:22 |
| general drama of p. | HARDY 161:24 |
| I feel no p. dear mother now | ANON 8:3 |
| I have no p., dear mother, now | FARM 138:13 |
| intermission of p. | SELD 269:20 |
| Joy always came after p. | APOL 14:12 |
| labour we delight in physics p. | SHAK 286:22 |
| life's a p. and but a span | DAV 114:14 |
| midnight with no p. | KEATS 192:3 |
| momentary intoxication with p. | BRON 72:11 |
| not because it gave p. | MAC 213:19 |
| one who never inflicts p. | NEWM 238:17 |
| Our Lady of P. | SWIN 321:8 |
| p. and anguish wring | SCOTT 268:22 |
| pleasure turns to pleasing p. | SPEN 313:13 |
| rest from p. | DRYD 127:35 |
| shall there be any more p. | BIBLE 58:5 |
| she hasn't a p. | MILNE 225:23 |
| Sweet is pleasure after p. | DRYD 127:20 |
| tender for another's p. | GRAY 157:13 |
| tongueless vigil and all the p. | SWIN 321:1 |
| With some p. is fraught | SHEL 305:10 |
| **painful**: p. pleasure turns | SPEN 313:13 |
| **pains**: let our p. be less | BROME 72:8 |
| Marriage has many p. | JOHN 183:5 |
| no gains without p. | STEV 316:16 |
| p. a man when 'tis kept close | SUCK 318:22 |
| p. of hell gat hold upon me | BOOK 68:19 |
| So double was his p. | SPEN 313:10 |
| sympathize with people's p. | HUXL 177:8 |
| **paint**: can't pick it up, p. it | ANON 8:4 |
| flinging a pot of p. | RUSK 264:10 |
| I p. with my prick | REN 259:6 |
| p. 'em truest praise 'em | ADD 2:12 |
| p. on the face of Existence | BYRON 87:16 |
| p. the meadows with delight | SHAK 284:21 |
| refinèd gold, to p. the lily | SHAK 282:10 |
| **painted**: As idle as a p. ship | COL 104:6 |
| fears a p. devil | SHAK 286:17 |
| gilded loam or p. clay | SHAK 293:7 |
| Lift not the p. veil | SHEL 305:2 |
| p. meadow, or a purling stream | ADD 2:21 |
| She p. her face | BIBLE 42:14 |
| They're p. to the eyes | DOBS 122:27 |
| wood p. to look like iron | BISM 59:21 |
| **painter**: p. and I nail my pictures | SCHW 268:2 |
| **painters**: Good p. imitate nature | CERV 93:20 |

| | |
|---|---|
| **painters** (cont.): | |
| I hate all Poets and P. | GEOR 149:20 |
| **painting**: poem is like a p. | HOR 173:4 |
| **paint-pots**: throws aside his p. | HOR 172:26 |
| **paints**: I want to know a butcher p. | BROW 77:11 |
| Where God p. the scenery | HART 163:10 |
| **pair**: Blest p. of Sirens | MILT 226:4 |
| p. of ragged claws | ELIOT 133:28 |
| Sleep on, blest p. | MILT 229:12 |
| Take a p. of sparkling eyes | GILB 151:7 |
| **palace**: chalice from the p. | FRANK 245:1 |
| leads to the p. of wisdom | BLAKE 61:1 |
| My gorgeous p. for a hermitage | SHAK 294:2 |
| purple-linèd p. of sweet sin | KEATS 191:12 |
| **palaces**: Dragons in their pleasant p. | BIBLE 45:21 |
| fair, frail p. | ALDR 3:17 |
| gorgeous p. | SHAK 296:10 |
| Mid pleasures and p. | PAYNE 246:21 |
| **paladin**: Sidney's self, the starry p. | BROW 77:13 |
| **palate**: P., the hutch of tasty lust | HOPK 172:6 |
| **pale**: behold a p. horse | BIBLE 57:25 |
| p. and bloodless emulation | SHAK 296:31 |
| p. cast of thought | SHAK 275:26 |
| p. contented sort of discontent | KEATS 191:13 |
| p. fire she snatches | SHAK 296:23 |
| P. grew thy cheek and cold | BYRON 87:14 |
| P. hands I loved | HOPE 171:22 |
| P. prime-roses | SHAK 298:33 |
| p., unripened beauties | ADD 2:14 |
| p. young curate | GILB 152:29 |
| started at the intelligence, and turned p. | SOUT 312:5 |
| whiter shade of p. | REID 259:3 |
| Which keeps me p. | SHAK 287:6 |
| Why so p. and wan | SUCK 318:20 |
| **palely**: Alone and p. loitering | KEATS 191:7 |
| **paling**: piece-bright p. | HOPK 172:17 |
| **Palladium**: press is the P. | JUN 188:25 |
| **pallor**: p. of girls' brows | OWEN 243:23 |
| **palm**: has won it bear the p. | JORT 188:1 |
| Hold infinity in the p. | BLAKE 60:5 |
| itching p. | SHAK 281:29 |
| Quietly sweating p. to palm | HUXL 177:12 |
| To win the p., the oak | MARV 220:14 |
| **palms**: p. before my feet | CHES 97:22 |
| **palmy**: high and p. state of Rome | SHAK 274:1 |
| **palpable**: very p. hit | SHAK 277:14 |
| **palsied**: o'ertaxed, its p. hearts | ARN 17:11 |
| **paltered**: p. with Eternal God | TENN 327:13 |
| **paltry**: aged man is but a p. thing | YEATS 359:21 |
| **Pam**: P., I adore you | BETJ 37:8 |
| **pampered**: Holla, ye p. jades of Asia | MARL 219:14 |
| hollow p. jades of Asia | SHAK 278:21 |
| **Pan**: great god P. | BROW 75:4 |
| **pandemonium**: P., the high capital | MILT 228:21 |
| **Pandora**: open that P.'s Box | BEVIN 38:10 |
| **pane**: tap at the p. | BROW 76:17 |
| **pange**: P., lingua, gloriosi | FORT 144:4 |
| P., lingua, gloriosi | THOM 330:3 |
| **panic**: what a p.'s in thy breastie | BURNS 82:26 |
| **panjandrum**: grand P. himself | FOOTE 142:20 |
| **pansies**: p., that's for thoughts | SHAK 277:2 |
| **pantaloon**: lean and slippered p. | SHAK 272:27 |
| **panting**: For ever p. | KEATS 191:21 |
| **pants**: earth in fast thick p. | COL 103:23 |
| p. the hart for cooling | TATE 322:16 |
| your lower limbs in p. | NASH 237:18 |
| **papa**: P., potatoes, poultry | DICK 119:1 |
| **paper**: age of four with p. hats | UST 336:18 |
| All reactionaries are p. tigers | MAO T 217:20 |
| he hath not eat p. | SHAK 284:15 |
| just for a scrap of p. | BETH 36:15 |
| Make dust our p. | SHAK 293:26 |
| more personality than a p. cup | CHAN 94:8 |
| only a p. moon | HARB 161:12 |
| verbal contract isn't worth the p. | GOLD 155:17 |

papers: He's got my p., this man    PINT 248:20
   what I read in the p.    ROG 262:1
parachutes: Minds are like p.    DEWAR 117:13
parade: p. of riches    SMITH 308:22
paradise: blundered into P.    THOM 331:13
   cannot catch the bird of p.    KHR 194:20
   drunk the milk of P.    COL 104:1
   England is a p. for women    BURT 83:13
   England is the p. of women    FLOR 142:13
   P. by way of Kensal Green    CHES 98:3
   p. for a sect    KEATS 190:24
   shalt thou be with me in p.    BIBLE 53:3
   Thou P. of exiles, Italy    SHEL 303:21
   wilderness is p. enow    FITZ 140:6
paradises: p. we have lost    PROU 255:21
   Two p. 'twere in one    MARV 220:17
paradox: Man is an embodied p.    COLT 106:1
parallel: But ours so truly p.    MARV 220:13
parallelograms: Princess of P.    BYRON 87:15
parallels: p. in beauty's brow    SHAK 299:22
parapets: Europe of the ancient p.    RIMB 260:9
parcels: she deals it in small p.    WEBS 344:22
parcere: P. subiectis    VIRG 339:16
pardlike: p. Spirit    SHEL 303:9
pardon: Bretful of p.    CHAU 95:23
   but cannot help or p.    AUDEN 21:15
   God may p. you, but I never can    ELIZ 135:11
   God will p. me, it is His trade    HEINE 165:3
   kiss of the sun for p.    GURN 159:10
   P. all, their faults confessing    BUCK 78:3
   With a thousand Ta's and P.'s    BETJ 37:7
pards: by Bacchus and his p.    KEATS 192:1
parens: king is truly p. patriae    JAM 179:10
parent: p. of settlement    BURKE 80:11
   To lose one p., Mr Worthing    WILDE 349:18
parents: At 18 a girl needs good p.    TUCK 335:9
   begin by loving their p.    WILDE 350:12
   Jewish man with p. alive    ROTH 263:14
   Of p. good    SHAK 279:10
   p. kept me from children    SPEN 312:25
   P. love their children more    AUCT 20:7
   slavish bondage to p.    WOLL 353:13
parfit: verray p. gentil knyght    CHAU 95:12
Paris: Americans die they go to P.    WILDE 350:8
   Is P. burning    HITL 169:4
   last time I saw P.    HAMM 161:1
   no more Hoares to P.    GEOR 149:26
   P. is a movable feast    HEM 165:13
   P. is well worth a mass    HENR 165:21
   P. was French—and silent    TUCH 335:8
   when they die, go to P.    APPL 14:15
parish: ail the world as my p.    WESL 346:13
   p. of rich women    AUDEN 20:22
park: p., a policeman and a pretty girl    CHAP 94:12
parks: p. are the lungs of London    PITT 249:6
parley-voo: Hinky, dinky, p.    ANON 9:5
parliament: In the P. of man    TENN 326:12
   [p.] are a lot of hard-faced men    BALD 27:9
   p. can do any thing    PEMB 247:6
   P. speaking through reporters    CARL 90:17
   P. to do things at eleven    SHAW 301:12
parliamentarian: only safe pleasure for a p.    CRIT 111:22
parliaments: mother of P.    BRIG 72:5
parlour: some party in a p.    WORD 356:4
   Will you walk into my p.    HOW 175:11
Parnassus: my chief P.    SIDN 306:24
parochial: he was p.    JAMES 179:19
parole: p. of literary men    JOHN 185:30
parson: If P. lost his senses    HODG 169:13
   p. knows enough who knows    COWP 110:14
   P. left conjuring    SELD 269:19
parsons: This merriment of p.    JOHN 185:28
part: come let us kiss and p.    DRAY 126:16

part (cont.):
   every man must play a p. .    SHAK 288:27
   My soul, bear thou thy p.    GURN 159:11
   p. to tear a cat in    SHAK 290:18
   p. my garments among them    BOOK 66:16
   p. of all that I have met    TENN 328:21
   Shall I p. my hair behind    ELIOT 134:3
   we know in p.    BIBLE 55:13
   What isn't p. of ourselves    HESSE 168:3
   Yet meet we shall, and p.    BUTL 84:21
parted: fool and his words are soon p.    SHEN 305:20
   P. are those who are singing    BOWEN 70:15
   When we two p.    BYRON 87:14
partiality: neither anger nor p.    TAC 322:6
particles: Newton's p. of light    BLAKE 61:14
particular: bright p. star    SHAK 270:23
   London p. . . . . A fog    DICK 118:2
particulars: do it in minute p.    BLAKE 60:19
parting: P. is all we know of heaven    DICK 120:12
   p. is such sweet sorrow    SHAK 295:4
   p. there is an image of death    ELIOT 132:16
   rive not more in p.    SHAK 271:23
   speed the p. guest    POPE 252:24
   stood at the p. of the ways    BIBLE 47:7
   Their every p. was to die    TENN 325:20
partir: P. c'est mourir un peu    HAR 161:9
partly: Living and p. living    ELIOT 134:6
partridge: Always p.    ANON 12:16
parts: dignified and efficient p.    BAG 26:3
   in his time plays many p.    SHAK 272:24
   P. of it are excellent    PUNCH 256:19
   secret p. of Fortune    SHAK 275:13
   Today we have naming of p.    REED 258:15
parturient: P. montes    HOR 172:27
party: Collapse of Stout P.    ANON 6:17
   conduct of a losing p.    BURKE 79:18
   effects of the spirit of p.    WASH 342:21
   I always voted at my p.'s call    GILB 152:19
   none was for a p.    MAC 214:5
   p. is not to be brought down    HAIL 160:1
   P. is organized opinion    DISR 121:14
   p.'s over    GREEN 106:2
   save the P. we love    GAIT 147:11
   some p. in a parlour    WORD 356:4
   sooner every p. breaks up    AUST 22:15
   Stick to your p.    DISR 122:15
party-spirit: P., which at best    POPE 253:11
pasarán: No p.    IBAR 178:2
pass: I keep, and p., and turn again    EMER 136:10
   I p., like night, from land    COL 104:17
   let him p.    SHAK 284:7
   let him p. for a man    SHAK 288:30
   look, and p. on    DANTE 113:19
   my words shall not p.    BIBLE 50:37
   p. for forty-three    GILB 152:31
   p. into nothingness    KEATS 190:11
   P. me the can, lad    HOUS 174:9
   p. the ammunition    FORGY 143:13
   p. the sick bag, Alice    JUNOR 188:27
   p. through this world    GREL 158:14
   p. with a lass    JAM 179:14
   pay us, p. us    CHES 98:4
   Ships that p. in the night    LONG 210:3
   they p. all understanding    JAM 179:13
   They shall not p.    ANON 12:6
   They shall not p.    IBAR 178:2
   Will she p. in a crowd    SWIFT 320:3
passage: long black p. up to bed    STEV 317:15
   North-west p.    STER 315:21
   p. which we did not take    ELIOT 132:26
   p. you think is particularly fine    JOHN 184:27
passageways: smell of steaks in p.    ELIOT 134:10
passe: Tout p., tout casse    ANON 12:17
passed: former things are p.    BIBLE 58:5
   He p. by on the other side    BIBLE 52:12

**pay** (*cont.*):

| | |
|---|---|
| We shall p. any price | KENN 194:3 |
| wonders what's to p. | HOUS 174:12 |
| **paying**: price well worth p. | LAM 200:18 |
| **pays**: p. your money | PUNCH 256:6 |
| **peace**: all her paths are p. | BIBLE 43:9 |
| all her paths are P. | SPR 313:27 |
| author of p. and lover of | BOOK 64:5 |
| certain knot of p. | SIDN 306:20 |
| chastisement of our p. | BIBLE 46:19 |
| deep dream of p. | HUNT 176:12 |
| for ever hold his p. | BOOK 65:27 |
| Give p. a chance | MCC 205:13 |
| Give p. in our time, O Lord | BOOK 64:4 |
| good war makes a good p. | HERB 167:9 |
| good war, or a bad p. | FRAN 145:14 |
| hard and bitter p. | KENN 194:2 |
| I came not to send p. | BIBLE 49:31 |
| In His will is our p. | DANTE 113:22 |
| In p.: goodwill | CHUR 100:4 |
| in p. there's nothing so becomes | SHAK 279:5 |
| instrument of Your p. | FRAN 145:7 |
| into the way of p. | BIBLE 51:30 |
| Let war yield to p. | CIC 100:23 |
| like the p. of God | JAM 179:13 |
| make war than to make p. | CLEM 102:2 |
| May they rest in p. | MISS 231:25 |
| moth of p. | SHAK 292:2 |
| mountain tops is p. | GOET 154:12 |
| My p. is gone | GOET 154:6 |
| Nation shall speak p. unto | REND 259:5 |
| news and Prince of P. | FLET 142:8 |
| no such thing as inner p. | LEB 203:24 |
| on earth p., good will | BIBLE 52:2 |
| Open covenants of p. | WILS 351:22 |
| P. be unto you | BIBLE 58:18 |
| p. cannot be maintained | RUSS 265:6 |
| P., commerce, and honest | JEFF 180:19 |
| p. for our time | CHAM 94:2 |
| p. has broken out | BREC 71:21 |
| P. hath her victories | MILT 230:27 |
| P. I leave with you | BIBLE 53:39 |
| P. is crowned with smiles | VAUG 337:6 |
| P. is indivisible | LITV 208:4 |
| P. is in the grave | SHEL 304:18 |
| P. is nothing but slovenliness | BREC 71:20 |
| P. is poor reading | HARDY 161:20 |
| P.! it is I | ANAT 5:10 |
| p. Man is a bungler | SHAW 301:22 |
| P., *n.* In international | BIER 59:7 |
| p. of God, which passeth | BIBLE 56:8 |
| p. of the double-bed | CAMP 88:15 |
| P. on earth and mercy mild | WESL 346:7 |
| P., perfect peace | BICK 58:25 |
| P., retrenchment and reform | BRIG 72:3 |
| P., the human dress | BLAKE 61:21 |
| p. which the world cannot give | BOOK 64:11 |
| p. with honour | CHAM 94:2 |
| p. with honour | DISR 121:18 |
| people want p. so much | EIS 131:16 |
| poor, and manglèd P. | SHAK 280:2 |
| publisheth p. | BIBLE 46:15 |
| righteousness and p. have kissed | BOOK 67:23 |
| seek p., and ensue it | BOOK 66:25 |
| So enamoured on p. | CLAR 101:11 |
| soft phrase of p. | SHAK 291:33 |
| state of p. | VIRG 339:16 |
| that we may live in p. | ARIS 15:14 |
| There is no p., saith the Lord | BIBLE 46:14 |
| This is not a p. treaty | FOCH 142:15 |
| thousand years of p. | TENN 325:26 |
| thy servant depart in p. | BIBLE 52:3 |
| time of p. | BIBLE 44:13 |
| time of p. thinks of war | ANON 7:16 |
| want p., prepare for war | VEG 337:18 |

**peace** (*cont.*):

| | |
|---|---|
| War is p. | ORW 242:7 |
| weak piping time of p. | SHAK 294:14 |
| when there is no p. | BIBLE 46:28 |
| wilderness and call it p. | TAC 322:4 |
| **peaceably**: p. if we can | CLAY 101:17 |
| **peacefully**: King's life is moving p. | DAWS 115:5 |
| **peacemakers**: Blessed are the p. | BIBLE 48:19 |
| **peach**: apricot and woolly p. | JONS 187:30 |
| Do I dare to eat a p. | ELIOT 134:3 |
| nectarine, and curious p. | MARV 220:15 |
| **peacocks**: apes and p. | MAS 221:18 |
| apes, and p. | BIBLE 41:31 |
| p. and lilies | RUSK 264:17 |
| **peal**: rung night's yawning p. | SHAK 287:5 |
| **pear**: round the prickly p. | ELIOT 133:18 |
| **pearl**: one p. of great price | BIBLE 50:6 |
| p. in every cowslip's ear | SHAK 290:20 |
| ransack the ocean for orient p. | MARL 218:8 |
| threw a p. away | SHAK 293:5 |
| **pearls**: p. before swine | BIBLE 49:8 |
| p. fetch a high price *because* | WHAT 347:7 |
| p. that were his eyes | SHAK 296:1 |
| search for p. must dive below | DRYD 127:23 |
| string the p. were strung on | JAMES 179:17 |
| **pearly**: shows them p. white | BREC 71:18 |
| **peasant**: rogue and p. slave | SHAK 275:21 |
| **peasantry**: But a bold p. | GOLD 154:18 |
| Civilization has made the p. | TROT 334:23 |
| **peasants**: cricket with their p. | TREV 334:8 |
| **pebble**: p. or a prettier shell | NEWT 239:6 |
| **peccavi**: P. *nimis cogitatione* | MISS 231:11 |
| **pécher**: *p. que p. en silence* | MOL 232:24 |
| **peck**: For daws to p. at | SHAK 291:28 |
| **pecker**: want his p. in my pocket | JOHN 181:20 |
| **peculiar**: holy nation, a p. people | BIBLE 57:8 |
| **pecunia**: P. *non olet* | VESP 338:3 |
| **pedantic**: too p. for a gentleman | CONG 106:10 |
| **pedantry**: P. the dotage of knowledge | JACK 178:24 |
| **pedestrians**: two classes of p. | DEWAR 117:14 |
| **pedigree**: languages the p. of nations | JOHN 183:18 |
| **peel**: Beulah, p. me a grape | WEST 346:20 |
| **peep**: p. and botanize | WORD 356:5 |
| **peepers**: where you get them p. | MERC 223:10 |
| **peepshow**: ticket for the p. | MACN 216:1 |
| **peer**: paper p. Lord Peter | LOCK 209:3 |
| **peerage**: p. or Westminster Abbey | NELS 237:23 |
| want a p., I shall buy one | NORT 240:9 |
| You should study the P. | WILDE 350:14 |
| **peering**: mansions to the p. day | MILT 227:28 |
| **peers**: House of P. | GILB 151:14 |
| **peignoir**: Complacencies of the p. | STEV 316:12 |
| **pelican**: wondrous bird is the p. | MERR 223:26 |
| **Pelion**: To pile Ossa on P. | VIRG 340:6 |
| **pellet**: p. with the poison's | FRANK 245:1 |
| **pellucid**: More p. streams | WORD 355:7 |
| **Pemberley**: P. to be thus polluted | AUST 23:5 |
| **pen**: Biting my truant p. | SIDN 306:17 |
| From lies of tongue and p. | CHES 97:24 |
| nose was as sharp as a p. | SHAK 279:4 |
| p. has been in their hands | AUST 22:27 |
| p. has gleaned my teeming | KEATS 192:19 |
| p. is mightier than the sword | BULW 78:11 |
| p. is worse than the sword | BURT 83:9 |
| poet's p. | SHAK 291:4 |
| product of a scoffer's p. | WORD 354:20 |
| scratching of a p. | LOVER 210:22 |
| spark-gap mightier than the p. | HOGB 170:6 |
| tongue is the p. | BOOK 67:5 |
| Waverley p. | ANON 11:1 |
| Why is the needle and the p. | LEWIS 206:14 |
| **penance**: night do p. for a day | WORD 356:11 |
| **pence**: Take care of the p. | LOWN 211:21 |
| **pencils**: inexorable sadness of p. | ROET 261:14 |
| **Penelope**: true P. was Flaubert | POUND 254:15 |

pervert: p. climbs into the minds — BRON 72:11
pessimist: p. fears this — CAB 87:23
pestilence: acts not, breeds p. — BLAKE 61:3
p. that walketh in darkness — BOOK 67:29
petal: Now sleeps the crimson p. — TENN 328:3
p. down the Grand Canyon — MARQ 219:22
petals: P. on a wet, black bough — POUND 254:20
petar: Hoist with his own p. — SHAK 276:25
Peter: first 'twas P.'s drift — SHEL 304:14
I'll call him P. — SHAK 282:3
raree-show of P.'s successor — BROW 75:20
Shock-headed P. — HOFF 170:4
Thou art P., and upon this rock — BIBLE 50:13
Where P. is, there must — AMBR 4:19
petitions: desires and p. — BOOK 64:10
Petrarch: P.'s wife — BYRON 86:11
petrifactions: p. of a plodding brain — BYRON 86:32
petrifies: p. the feeling — BURNS 82:5
petticoat: Her feet beneath her p. — SUCK 318:21
never keep down a single p. — BYRON 87:20
petticoats: hyena in p. — WALP 342:2
pettiness: to expiate a p. — LAWR 202:22
petty: Creeps in this p. pace — SHAK 288:5
we p. men walk under his huge legs — SHAK 280:27
phagocytes: Stimulate the p. — SHAW 301:2
phallic: P. and ambrosial — POUND 254:17
phantom: She was a p. of delight — WORD 356:24
twin realities of this p. world — COL 105:1
Pharisees: P.' hypocrisy — PAST 246:10
phenomenon: infant p. — DICK 119:16
Phil: fidgety P. — HOFF 169:19
Philip: P. drunk to P. sober — ANON 6:3
P. fought men, but Alexander — LEE 204:10
Philistine: P. of genius — ARN 18:11
Philistines: P., and Populace — ARN 17:24
P. proper, or middle class — ARN 17:26
philosopher: P.!—a fingering slave — WORD 356:5
some p. has said it — CIC 100:19
soft p. of love — DRYD 128:3
tried too in my time to be a p. — EDW 131:5
What I understand by 'p.' — NIET 239:19
philosophical: poetry is something more p. — ARIS 15:16
philosophy: Adversity's sweet milk, p. — SHAK 295:16
barbarous p. — BURKE 80:15
dreamt of in your p. — SHAK 275:3
History is p. from examples — DION 121:4
How charming is divine p. — MILT 226:15
little p. inclineth man's mind — BACON 24:12
mere touch of cold p. — KEATS 191:14
natural p., deep — BACON 25:16
P. is a battle against — WITT 352:6
p. is but an handmaid — BACON 24:2
p. is the replacement — RYLE 265:10
p. paints its grey on grey — HEGEL 164:20
p. quenches them — VOLT 340:16
P.! the lumber of the schools — SWIFT 320:18
P. will clip an Angel's wings — KEATS 191:15
superstition to enslave a p. — INGE 178:12
Phoebus: P., arise — DRUM 127:1
P. gins to shew his glorious — SPEN 313:5
phone: P. for the fish-knives — BETJ 37:2
why did you answer the p. — THUR 332:18
photography: P. is truth — GOD 153:18
phrases: Taffeta p., silken terms — SHAK 284:18
phylacteries: fly-blown p. — ROS 262:20
Phyllis: P., without frown — SEDL 269:12
physic: Take p., pomp — SHAK 283:12
Throw p. to the dogs — SHAK 288:3
physician: I died last night of my p. — PRIOR 255:11
into the hand of the p. — BIBLE 48:5
need not a p. — BIBLE 49:22
P. art thou?—one, all eyes — WORD 356:5
p. can bury his mistakes — WRIG 357:23
P., heal thyself — BIBLE 52:5

physician (cont.):
Time is the great p. — DISR 122:3
physicians: P. are like kings — WEBS 344:20
P. of the Utmost Fame — BELL 33:4
physicists: p. have known sin — OPP 241:14
physics: p. or stamp collecting — RUTH 265:8
pianist: do not shoot the p. — ANON 10:4
Picardy: Roses are flowering in P. — WEAT 344:5
Picasso: P., sunbathing and jazz — WAUGH 343:22
picket: p.'s off duty forever — BEERS 32:14
picking: p. and stealing — BOOK 65:22
pickle: weaned on a p. — ANON 11:4
pick-purse: no p. of another's wit — SIDN 306:23
Pickwick: P., the Owl — ANON 11:1
pictura: Ut p. poesis — HOR 173:4
picture: Earth's Last P. — KIPL 197:13
Every p. tells a story — ANON 7:2
It's no go the p. palace — MACN 216:2
Not on his p., but his book — JONS 187:21
p. is worth ten thousand words — BARN 29:3
Poetry [is] a speaking p. — SIDN 306:26
pictured: my friends p. within — ELGAR 131:17
pictures: Are but as p. — SHAK 286:17
History is a gallery of p. — TOCQ 333:1
It's the p. that got small — WILD 71:5
painter and I nail my p. — SCHW 268:2
P. are for entertainment — GOLD 155:18
P. of perfection — AUST 23:12
without p. or conversations — CARR 91:1
pie: into a p. by Mrs McGregor — POTT 254:3
p. in the sky when you die — HILL 168:12
So, bye, bye, Miss American P. — MCL 215:8
pieces: thirty p. of silver — BIBLE 51:7
pierce: into his hand, and p. it — BIBLE 42:16
pies: Bellamy's veal p. — PITT 249:10
piety: Pathos, p., courage — FORS 143:25
to p. more prone — ALEX 4:7
piffle: p. before the wind — ASHF 18:23
pig: p. got up and slowly walked — BURT 83:1
pigeons: P. on the grass alas — STEIN 314:21
piggy-wig: P. stood — LEAR 203:12
pigmy: Fretted the p. body — DRYD 127:6
pigs: whether p. have wings — CARR 91:22
Pilate: hands than water like P. — GREE 158:2
P. saith unto him — BIBLE 54:1
pile: P. the bodies high — SAND 266:14
To p. Ossa on Pelion — VIRG 340:6
pilfering: p., unprotected race — CLARE 101:6
pilgrim: Onward goes the p. band — BAR 29:2
'P.'s Progress', about a man — TWAIN 335:19
To be a p. — BUNY 79:6
pilgrimage: quiet p. — CAMP 89:3
succeed me in my p. — BUNY 79:10
thus I'll take my p. — RAL 257:23
pilgrimages: to go on p. — CHAU 95:11
pilgrims: love your land of the p. — CUMM 112:17
p. to th'appointed place — DRYD 128:12
pill: little yellow p. — RICH 179:5
Protestant women may take the p. — THOM 331:2
pillar: day in a p. of a cloud — BIBLE 39:39
p. of state — MILT 228:27
p. of the world transformed — SHAK 271:3
she became a p. of salt — BIBLE 39:15
pillars: hewn out her seven p. — BIBLE 43:14
p. of gold — BLAKE 60:17
Pylons, those p. bare — SPEN 313:3
pillow: like the feather p. — HAIG 159:16
on a p. for weariness — WORD 354:10
sighed upon a midnight p. — SHAK 272:18
sits upon the p.-hill — STEV 317:14
softer p. than my heart — BYRON 87:22
Where, like a p. on a bed — DONNE 124:2
pillows: P. his chin — MILT 227:29
pills: back to 'plasters, p. — LOCK 209:2
pilot: Dropping the p. — TENN 323:9

pilot (cont.):
see my p. face to face | TENN 323:19
pilots: P. of the purple twilight | TENN 326:10
pimpernel: demmed, elusive P. | ORCZY 241:17
pimples: scratching of p. | WOOLF 354:6
pin: life at a p.'s fee | SHAK 274:28
p. up my hair with prose | CONG 106:18
pineapple: very p. of politeness | SHER 305:28
pinion: imagination droops her p. | BYRON 86:19
pinions: with p. skim the air | FRERE 145:22
pink: very p. of courtesy | SHAK 295:6
very p. of perfection | GOLD 155:9
pinkly: p. bursts the spray | BETJ 37:6
pinko-grey: white races are really p. | FORS 143:24
pinnacled: P. dim in the intense inane | SHEL 304:23
pinprick: time is a p. of eternity | AUR 22:10
pint: like magic in a p. bottle | DICK 118:30
p. of plain is your only man | O'BR 240:20
pioneers: P.! O pioneers | WHIT 348:13
pipes: Grate on their scrannel p. | MILT 227:15
piping: For ever p. songs | KEATS 191:20
Helpless, naked, p. loud | BLAKE 62:3
P. songs of pleasant glee | BLAKE 61:18
weak p. time of peace | SHAK 294:14
Pippa: P. passes | BEER 32:9
Pippin: Right as a Ribstone P. | BELL 33:12
pips: until the p. squeak | GEDD 149:19
pirate: To be a P. King | GILB 152:22
piss: worth a pitcher of warm p. | GARN 148:7
pissing: inside the tent p. out | JOHN 181:21
pistol: I reach for my p. | JOHST 186:18
Is that a p. in your pocket | WEST 346:23
[pun] is a p. let off at the ear | LAMB 200:6
when his p. misses | GOLD 155:14
pistols: Have you your p.? | WHIT 348:13
piston: steam and p. stroke | MORR 235:16
pistons: black statement of p. | SPEN 312:23
pit: know what is in the p. | BLAKE 60:10
Law is a bottomless p. | ARB 14:22
diggeth a p. shall fall | BIBLE 44:21
pitch: Pitched past p. of grief | HOPK 172:9
toucheth p. shall be defiled | BIBLE 48:2
pitched: Love has p. his mansion | YEATS 358:20
pitcher: or the p. be broken | BIBLE 44:26
worth a p. of warm piss | GARN 148:7
pitchfork: drive out nature with a p. | HOR 173:11
thrown on her with a p. | SWIFT 320:7
use my wit as a p. | LARK 201:19
pith: p. is in the postscript | HAZL 163:22
pitiful: lips say, 'God be p.' | BROW 75:1
pity: cherish p., lest you | BLAKE 61:22
loved her that she did p. them | SHAK 291:35
P. a human face | BLAKE 61:21
p. and fear bringing about | ARIS 15:15
p. beyond all telling | YEATS 359:18
p. never ceases to be shown | DRYD 127:14
p. of it | SHAK 292:23
p. of War | OWEN 243:19
save me, O source of p. | MISS 231:24
'Tis P. She's a Whore | FORD 143:11
pix: Sticks nix hick p. | ANON 10:15
place: all other things give p. | GAY 149:10
bourne of time and p. | TENN 323:19
genius of the p. | POPE 251:15
Get p. and wealth | POPE 252:25
great p. is by a winding stair | BACON 24:29
I go to prepare a p. | BIBLE 53:37
In p. of strife | CAST 92:15
keep in the same p. | CARR 91:18
know the p. for the first time | ELIOT 133:10
Men in great p. are thrice | BACON 24:27
neither shall his p. know him | BIBLE 42:31
Never the time and the p. | BROW 76:20
no p. to go | WHIT 348:8
p. for everything | BEET 32:15

place (cont.):
p. in the sun | BULOW 78:8
p. in the sun | WILH 350:25
p. of understanding | BIBLE 43:1
P., that great object | SMITH 308:20
p. thereof shall know it no more | BOOK 68:7
spirit of the p. | VIRG 339:18
till there be no p. | BIBLE 45:8
time and p. were not | ROCH 261:10
To know their p. | BELL 33:6
places: all p. were alike to him | KIPL 197:20
Proper words in proper p. | SWIFT 320:4
quietest p. under the sun | HOUS 175:1
Quires and P. where they sing | BOOK 64:7
which built desolate p. | BIBLE 42:29
plackets: thy hand out of p. | SHAK 283:13
plagiarism: one author, it's p. | MIZN 232:12
plagiarize: P.! Let no one else's | LEHR 204:14
plague: Make instruments to p. us | SHAK 284:2
p. o' both your houses | SHAK 295:8
To p. the inventor | SHAK 285:23
plagues: p. with which mankind | DEFOE 115:25
plain: best p. set | BACON 24:13
especially the need of the p. | WAUGH 344:3
great Gromboolian p. | LEAR 203:8
on a darkling p. | ARN 16:12
pint of p. is your only man | O'BR 240:20
p., blunt man | SHAK 281:25
'p.' cooking | MORP 235:10
P. living and high thinking | WORD 356:1
p. man in his plain meaning | SHAK 289:23
plain truth for p. people | WESL 346:14
pricking on the p. | SPEN 313:7
rough places p. | BIBLE 46:9
plains: p. of honour and reputation | JONS 187:13
ringing p. of windy Troy | TENN 328:21
plaintive: p. numbers flow | WORD 357:2
plaisir: P. d'amour | FLOR 142:12
plan: by his p. of attack | SASS 267:13
plane: It's a bird! It's a p.! | ANON 7:5
planet: born under a rhyming p. | SHAK 291:26
new p. swims into his ken | KEATS 192:11
p. of Love is on high | TENN 326:28
planetary: p. influence | SHAK 282:22
planned: p. obsolescence | STEV 316:1
Yet the order of the acts is p. | PAST 246:10
plant: Sensitive P. in a garden grew | SHEL 304:30
time to p., and a time to pluck | BIBLE 44:11
weed is a p. whose virtues | EMER 136:29
planted: I have p., Apollos | BIBLE 55:3
planting: p. my cabbages | MONT 233:9
plants: They are forced p. | JOHN 185:27
plashy: through the p. fen | WAUGH 343:25
plasters: back to 'p., pills | LOCK 209:2
plastics: abhorred p., Picasso | WAUGH 343:22
plate: silver p. on a coffin | CURR 113:9
platinum: bullets made of p. | BELL 33:1
eyebrows made of p. | FORS 143:14
platitude: echo of a p. | BIER 59:3
longitude with no p. | FRY 147:1
stroke a p. until it purrs | MARQ 219:23
platitudes: orchestration of p. | WILD 350:24
Plato: attachment à la P. | GILB 152:11
P. is dear to me, but dearer | ARIS 15:22
P.'s retirement | MILT 230:6
p. told him | CUMM 112:19
rather be wrong with P. | CIC 101:1
series of footnotes to P. | WHIT 348:6
play: Better than a p. | CHAR 95:3
children at p. are not playing | MONT 233:11
damned p. than no play at all | REYN 259:7
do not p. things as they are | STEV 316:9
game at which two can p. | BEER 32:12
Games people p. | BERNE 36:10
holdeth children from p. | SIDN 306:27

**play** (*cont.*):

| | |
|---|---|
| *House Beautiful* is p. lousy | PARK 245:13 |
| It'll p. in Peoria | ANON 8:11 |
| our p. is played out | THAC 329:22 |
| p. before the play is done | QUAR 257:1 |
| p. Ercles rarely | SHAK 290:18 |
| P. it again, Sam | EPST 137:10 |
| p.'s the thing | SHAK 275:24 |
| play up! and p. the game | NEWB 238:13 |
| p. without a woman in it | KYD 199:11 |
| prologue to a very dull p. | CONG 106:14 |
| to p. with souls | BROW 76:12 |
| When I p. with my cat | MONT 233:17 |
| Work is *x*; *y* is p. | EINS 131:10 |
| You would p. upon me | SHAK 276:13 |
| **playboy**: P. of the Western World | SYNGE 321:22 |
| **played**: I have p. the fool | BIBLE 41:9 |
| P.-out and Done-to-Death | TRAI 334:2 |
| p. the King as though under | FIELD 139:3 |
| **player**: as strikes the p. | FITZ 140:13 |
| poor p., that struts | SHAK 288:5 |
| **players**: men and women merely p. | SHAK 272:24 |
| see the p. well bestowed | SHAK 275:19 |
| **playing**: on the p. fields of Eton | WELL 345:10 |
| p. or quarrelling on the line | FORS 143:22 |
| **plays**: English p. are like | VOLT 340:26 |
| **plaything**: child's a p. for an hour | LAMB 200:14 |
| **plea**: Just as I am, without one p. | ELL 136:2 |
| Though justice be thy p. | SHAK 289:27 |
| **pleasance**: Youth is full of p. | SHAK 299:5 |
| **pleasant**: abridgement of all that was p. | GOLD 155:3 |
| fallen unto me in p. places | BOOK 66:15 |
| hear the p. cuckoo | DAV 114:17 |
| if we do not find anything p. | VOLT 340:11 |
| Jonathan were lovely and p. | BIBLE 41:22 |
| Life would be very p. if | SURT 319:13 |
| p. it is to have money | CLOU 102:14 |
| too excitin' to be p. | DICK 119:29 |
| Who is to do the p. work? | RUSK 264:15 |
| **pleasantness**: ways are ways of p. | BIBLE 43:9 |
| **please**: death after life does greatly p. | SPEN 313:9 |
| I am to do what I p. | FRED 145:19 |
| Love seeketh only Self to p. | BLAKE 62:2 |
| must p. to live | JOHN 183:10 |
| Myself alone I seek to p. | GAY 149:12 |
| Nothing can p. many | JOHN 182:24 |
| P. him and he straight is | WROTH 358:1 |
| p. the touchy breed of poets | HOR 173:18 |
| To tax and to p. | BURKE 79:26 |
| Towered cities p. us then | MILT 227:6 |
| Uncertain, coy, and hard to p. | SCOTT 268:22 |
| we are not able to p. thee | BOOK 64:26 |
| **pleased**: And p. with what he gets | SHAK 272:21 |
| had he p. us less | ADD 2:10 |
| in whom I am well p. | BIBLE 48:15 |
| P. with a rattle, tickled | POPE 252:19 |
| **pleases**: Though every prospect p. | HEBER 164:16 |
| **pleaseth**: this age best p. me | HERR 167:21 |
| **pleasing**: pleasure turns to pain | SPEN 313:13 |
| **pleasure**: Business first; p. afterwards | THAC 329:13 |
| But the privilege and p. | GILB 151:6 |
| dragged on by their favourite p. | VIRG 339:23 |
| fatal egg by p. laid | COWP 110:2 |
| Forced her to do your p. | WEBS 344:24 |
| gave p. to the spectators | MAC 213:19 |
| greatest p. I know | LAMB 200:11 |
| Green p. or grey grief | SWIN 321:17 |
| his p. is life | BOOK 66:22 |
| If they have p., the servant | BARC 28:17 |
| in general read without p. | JOHN 186:15 |
| Love ceases to be a p. | BEHN 32:21 |
| Love's p. lasts but a moment | FLOR 142:12 |
| must we not pay a debt to p. | ROCH 261:3 |
| my heart with p. fills | WORD 355:5 |
| not in p., but in rest from pain | DRYD 127:35 |

**pleasure** (*cont.*):

| | |
|---|---|
| painful p. turns to pleasing | SPEN 313:13 |
| P. at the helm | GRAY 157:3 |
| p. in the pathless woods | BYRON 85:12 |
| p. in the strength of an horse | BOOK 69:10 |
| P. is a *thief* to business | DEFOE 115:11 |
| p. is momentary | CHES 97:18 |
| p. is not enhanced | AUST 22:16 |
| P. is nothing else but | SELD 269:20 |
| p. me in his top-boots | MARL 218:5 |
| P. never is at home | KEATS 190:26 |
| p. of drinking at somebody else's | LEIGH 204:19 |
| P.'s a sin, and sometimes sin's | BYRON 86:3 |
| P.'s for those who are bad | YES 360:12 |
| p. was his business | EDG 130:17 |
| public stock of harmless p. | JOHN 182:23 |
| suburbs of your good p. | SHAK 281:7 |
| Sweet is p. after pain | DRYD 127:20 |
| There is a p. sure | DRYD 128:19 |
| What p. lives in height | TENN 328:6 |
| when Youth and P. meet | BYRON 85:3 |
| whilst I go to my p. | WYCH 358:5 |
| would have been my p. | TENN 324:6 |
| **pleasure-dome**: stately p. | COL 103:22 |
| sunny p. with caves of ice | COL 103:24 |
| **pleasure-house**: I built my soul a lordly p. | TENN 327:14 |
| **pleasures**: And we will all the p. prove | MARL 219:3 |
| And we will some new p. prove | DONNE 123:23 |
| celibacy has no p. | JOHN 183:5 |
| English take their p. sadly | SULLY 319:4 |
| Mid p. and palaces | PAYNE 246:21 |
| No man is a hypocrite in his p. | JOHN 186:6 |
| purest of human p. | BACON 24:26 |
| understand the p. of the other | AUST 22:14 |
| **pledge**: And I will p. with mine | JONS 187:23 |
| **pledged**: p. their troth either | BOOK 66:4 |
| **Pleiads**: rainy P. wester | HOUS 174:15 |
| **plenty**: here is God's p. | DRYD 128:30 |
| In delay there lies no p. | SHAK 297:23 |
| I wasna fou, but just had p. | BURNS 82:3 |
| on the expectation of p. | SHAK 286:20 |
| P. has made me poor | OVID 243:14 |
| **pleuré**: *Est d'avoir quelquefois p.* | MUSS 236:16 |
| **pleut**: *Comme il p. sur la ville* | VERL 338:2 |
| **plot**: Her p. hath many changes | QUAR 257:1 |
| p. for a short story | CHEK 96:27 |
| p. thickens very much upon | BUCK 78:2 |
| Sonnet's scanty p. | WORD 355:15 |
| This blessèd p., this earth | SHAK 293:16 |
| **plots**: P., true or false | DRYD 127:4 |
| **plough**: Men of England, wherefore p. | SHEL 305:1 |
| put his hand to the p. | BIBLE 52:9 |
| this morning held the p. | BETJ 36:22 |
| We p. the fields, and scatter | CAMP 88:13 |
| **ploughman**: p. homeward plods | GRAY 157:4 |
| wrong even the poorest p. | CHAR 94:24 |
| **ploughshares**: swords into p. | BIBLE 45:5 |
| **pluck**: offend thee, p. it out | BIBLE 50:17 |
| p. bright honour from | SHAK 277:27 |
| p. till time and times | YEATS 360:1 |
| **plucked**: p. my nipple from | SHAK 286:6 |
| **plume**: In blast-beruffled p. | HARDY 162:6 |
| **plunder**: separately p. a third | BIER 59:2 |
| What a place to p.! | BLÜCH 62:11 |
| **plunging**: When the p. hoofs were gone | DE L 116:20 |
| **plures**: *Abiit ad p.* | PETR 248:9 |
| **plus**: *P. ça change* | KARR 190:2 |
| **pneumatic**: promise of p. bliss | ELIOT 134:33 |
| **Pobble**: P. who has no toes | LEAR 203:14 |
| **pocket**: Is that a pistol in your p. | WEST 346:23 |
| not scruple to pick a p. | DENN 117:1 |
| pound in your p. | WILS 351:14 |
| want his pecker in my p. | JOHN 181:20 |
| **pockets**: young man feels his p. | HOUS 174:12 |
| **poem**: bathed in the P. of the Sea | RIMB 260:8 |

**poem** (*cont.*):

| | |
|---|---|
| drowsy frowzy p. | BYRON 86:16 |
| figure a p. makes | FROST 146:24 |
| ice on a hot stove the p. | FROST 146:25 |
| like to be married to a p. | KEATS 193:11 |
| ought himself to be a true p. | MILT 230:28 |
| p. is like a painting | HOR 173:4 |
| p. is a test of invention | KEATS 192:22 |
| p. lovely as a tree | KILM 194:22 |
| p. should not mean but be | MACL 215:9 |
| p. to the glory of beating | WOLFE 353:3 |
| p., whose subject is not truth | CHAP 94:19 |
| United States ... the greatest p. | WHIT 348:25 |
| **poems**: P. are made by fools like | KILM 195:1 |
| we all scribble p. | HOR 173:16 |
| **poesis**: *Ut pictura p.* | HOR 173:4 |
| **poesy**: viewless wings of P. | KEATS 192:1 |
| **poet**: All a p. can do today is warn | OWEN 243:20 |
| apothecary than a starved p. | LOCK 209:2 |
| because he was a true P. | BLAKE 60:25 |
| better p. than Porson | HOUS 175:6 |
| business of a p. | JOHN 183:2 |
| every fool is not a p. | POPE 251:2 |
| Like a P. hidden | SHEL 305:9 |
| limbs of a p. | HOR 174:3 |
| lover, and the p. | SHAK 291:3 |
| Not deep the P. sees, but wide | ARN 17:2 |
| p. and the dreamer | KEATS 190:25 |
| [p.] cometh unto you with a tale | SIDN 306:27 |
| p. ever interpreted nature | GIR 153:6 |
| p. is always indebted | MAY 222:16 |
| p. is the priest | STEV 316:3 |
| P.'s dream | WORD 354:17 |
| p.'s eye, in a fine frenzy | SHAK 291:4 |
| p.'s hope: to be like some | AUDEN 21:13 |
| shall be accounted p. kings | KEATS 192:12 |
| should possess a p.'s brain | DRAY 126:19 |
| Thus every p., in his kind | SWIFT 320:23 |
| Vex not thou the p.'s mind | TENN 327:15 |
| **poetic**: Meet nurse for a p. child | SCOTT 268:14 |
| which constitutes p. faith | COL 104:24 |
| **poetical**: claim to p. honours | JOHN 182:21 |
| **poetry**: and that is p. | CAGE 88:4 |
| cradled into p. by wrong | SHEL 303:22 |
| Emptied of its p. | AUDEN 20:24 |
| geniune p. is conceived | ARN 18:5 |
| grotesque art in English p. | BAG 26:17 |
| In p., no less than in life | ARN 18:4 |
| In whining p. | DONNE 124:14 |
| Ireland hurt you into p. | AUDEN 20:22 |
| It is not p., but prose | POPE 251:5 |
| Jonson his best piece of p. | JONS 187:19 |
| Language is fossil p. | EMER 136:28 |
| most p. ignores most people | MITC 232:2 |
| Nothing so much as mincing p. | SHAK 278:4 |
| p. begins to atrophy when | POUND 254:22 |
| p. comes not as naturally | KEATS 193:4 |
| P. in motion | ANTH 190:5 |
| P. [is] a speaking picture | SIDN 306:26 |
| P. is a subject as precise | FLAU 141:9 |
| P. is at bottom a criticism | ARN 18:6 |
| P. is a way of taking life | FROST 146:27 |
| p. is conceived and composed | ARN 18:5 |
| P. is in the pity | OWEN 243:19 |
| p. is like dropping a rose | MARQ 219:22 |
| p. is more philosophical | ARIS 15:16 |
| P. is the record | SHEL 305:18 |
| P. is the spontaneous overflow | WORD 357:12 |
| P. is the supreme fiction | STEV 316:8 |
| P. is the synthesis of hyacinths | SAND 266:17 |
| P. is what is lost in translation | FROST 146:28 |
| P. is when all the lines | BENT 35:3 |
| p. makes nothing happen | AUDEN 20:23 |
| P. must be *as well written* | POUND 254:24 |
| p. necessarily declines | MAC 213:7 |

**poetry** (*cont.*):

| | |
|---|---|
| p. of motion | GRAH 156:6 |
| P.'s a mere drug, Sir | FARQ 138:19 |
| P.'s the feverish fit | WINC 352:1 |
| p. = the *best* words | COL 104:26 |
| polar star of p. | KEATS 192:22 |
| quarrel with ourselves, p. | YEATS 360:10 |
| resuscitate the dead art of p. | POUND 254:14 |
| Sir, what is p. | JOHN 185:11 |
| Superstition is the p. of life | GOET 154:10 |
| **poets**: All p. are mad | BURT 83:8 |
| first for wits, then p. passed | POPE 251:27 |
| impossible to hold the p. back | GIR 153:5 |
| Irish p., learn your trade | YEATS 360:6 |
| mature p. steal | ELIOT 135:2 |
| Milton's the prince of p. | BYRON 86:15 |
| most p. are their own patients | THOM 331:3 |
| p. bicycle-pump the human | AMIS 5:5 |
| P. in our civilization | ELIOT 135:3 |
| p. in our youth begin | WORD 356:17 |
| P. that lasting marble seek | WALL 341:13 |
| p., witty | BACON 25:16 |
| Souls of p. dead and gone | KEATS 191:16 |
| spite of all romantic p. | LEAP 203:6 |
| Such sights as youthful p. dream | MILT 227:7 |
| theft in other p. | DRYD 128:29 |
| Three p. in an age at most | SWIFT 320:19 |
| touchy breed of p. | HOR 173:18 |
| **point**: creeping on from p. to point | TENN 326:13 |
| in thy wheel there is a p. | MARL 218:16 |
| p. his slow and moving finger | SHAK 292:24 |
| still p. of the turning world | ELIOT 132:28 |
| *Surtout, Messieurs, p. de zèle* | TALL 322:11 |
| To p. a moral, or adorn a tale | JOHN 183:14 |
| Up to a p., Lord Copper | WAUGH 343:24 |
| **poison**: coward's weapon, p. | FLET 142:11 |
| if you p. us, do we not die | SHAK 289:17 |
| *p. the wells* | NEWM 238:15 |
| p. the whole blood stream | EMPS 137:6 |
| strongest p. ever known | BLAKE 60:8 |
| We've got as far as p.-gas | HARDY 162:4 |
| **poisonous**: for its p. wine | KEATS 191:25 |
| **poke**: heart to p. poor Billy | GRAH 156:4 |
| **pokers**: p. into true-love knots | COL 104:2 |
| **pole**: Beloved from pole to p. | COL 104:13 |
| returning from the P. | CHER 19:11 |
| top of the greasy p. | DISR 122:17 |
| **polecat**: semi-house-trained p. | FOOT 142:18 |
| **police**: friendship recognised by the p. | STEV 317:7 |
| game at which the p. can beat you | SHAW 302:10 |
| To the citizen or the p. | AUDEN 21:11 |
| **policeman**: park, a p. and a pretty girl | CHAP 94:12 |
| p.'s lot is not a happy one | GILB 152:24 |
| terrorist and the p. | CONR 107:9 |
| **policy**: My home p.: I wage war | CLEM 102:1 |
| my p. is to be able to take | BEVIN 38:9 |
| p. is to float lazily downstream | SAL 266:2 |
| p. of the good neighbour | ROOS 262:10 |
| some love but little p. | SHAK 294:7 |
| will be tyrants from p. | BURKE 80:16 |
| **polish**: we may p. it at leisure | DRYD 128:27 |
| **polished**: O p. perturbation! | SHAK 278:26 |
| p. up that handle so carefullee | GILB 152:18 |
| **polite**: have no allies to be p. to | GEOR 150:5 |
| **politeness**: pineapple of p. | SHER 305:28 |
| Punctuality is the p. of kings | LOUI 210:17 |
| When suave p., tempering | KNOX 198:17 |
| **political**: fear of P. Economy | SELL 270:4 |
| Man is by nature a p. animal | ARIS 15:18 |
| points clearly to a p. career | SHAW 301:13 |
| P. language | ORW 242:15 |
| schemes of p. improvement | JOHN 184:22 |
| **politician**: like a scurvy p. | SHAK 283:26 |
| p. is a statesman who | POMP 250:12 |
| p. is an arse upon | CUMM 112:18 |

politician (cont.):
| | |
|---|---|
| p. is to render vice serviceable | BOL 63:7 |
| statesman is a p. who's been dead | TRUM 335:4 |
| which makes the p. wise | POPE 253:9 |
| politicians: Old p. chew on wisdom past | POPE 251:23 |
| whole race of p. put together | SWIFT 319:21 |
| politics: Confound their p. | ANON 7:14 |
| continuation of p. by other means | CLAU 101:16 |
| From p., it was an easy step | AUST 22:24 |
| In p., what begins in fear | COL 104:28 |
| Magnanimity in p. is not | BURKE 80:5 |
| mule of p. that engenders | DISR 121:27 |
| mules of p. | POWER 255:4 |
| Philistine of genius in p. | ARN 18:11 |
| p. as well as in religion | JUN 188:26 |
| p. consists in ignoring | ADAMS 1:19 |
| p. is for the present | EINS 131:12 |
| p. is present history | FREE 145:21 |
| P. is the art of preventing | VALÉ 336:22 |
| P. is war without bloodshed | MAO T 217:18 |
| P., like Rock, Pop | WOLFE 353:9 |
| p. the middle way is none | ADAMS 1:23 |
| P. the only profession for which no | STEV 316:24 |
| P. the organization of hatreds | ADAMS 1:11 |
| science of p. | ARIS 15:13 |
| week is a long time in p. | WILS 351:15 |
| polluted: Pemberley to be thus p. | AUST 23:5 |
| that is filthy and p. | BIBLE 47:25 |
| pollution: unsavoury engine of p. | SPAR 312:14 |
| polygamous: Man is p. | JAMES 180:11 |
| polygamy: Before p. was made a sin | DRYD 127:2 |
| pomegranate: from Browning some P. | BROW 75:3 |
| pomp: heraldry, the p. of pow'r | GRAY 157:7 |
| Lo, all our p. of yesterday | KIPL 197:3 |
| nor the tide of p. | SHAK 279:16 |
| p., and circumstance | SHAK 292:20 |
| Take physic, p. | SHAK 283:12 |
| Pompey: Knew you not P. | SHAK 280:24 |
| pompous: p. in the grave | BROW 74:7 |
| pomps: high Midsummer p. | ARN 17:19 |
| p. and vanity of this wicked | BOOK 65:21 |
| pond: have their stream and p. | BROO 73:2 |
| ponies: Five and twenty p. | KIPL 196:28 |
| wretched, blind, pit p. | HODG 169:13 |
| Pontefract: licorice fields at P. | BETJ 37:5 |
| poodle: right hon. Gentleman's p. | LLOY 208:8 |
| pools: p. are bright and deep | HOGG 170:7 |
| p. are filled with water | BOOK 67:21 |
| poop: p. was beaten gold | SHAK 271:14 |
| poor: And makes me p. indeed | SHAK 292:11 |
| Blessed are the p. in spirit | BIBLE 48:19 |
| Bring in hither the p. | BIBLE 52:24 |
| expensive it is to be p. | BALD 27:2 |
| Give me your tired, your p. | LAZ 203:2 |
| give to the p. | BIBLE 50:21 |
| grind the faces of the p. | BIBLE 45:6 |
| have in common being so p. | BLUN 62:12 |
| It's no disgrace t'be p. | HUBB 175:17 |
| It's the p. wot gets the blame | ANON 10:11 |
| Laws grind the p. | GOLD 155:5 |
| murmuring p. | CRAB 110:24 |
| My countrymen Kiltartan's p. | YEATS 359:9 |
| open to the p. and the rich | ANON 7:9 |
| Plenty has made me p. | OVID 243:14 |
| p. always ye have with you | BIBLE 53:35 |
| p. are Europe's blacks | CHAM 94:4 |
| p. are to be proud | SHAK 298:5 |
| p. get children | EGAN 189:19 |
| p. have cried, Caesar hath wept | SHAK 281:20 |
| p. in a loomp is bad | TENN 327:10 |
| p. is their poverty | BIBLE 43:17 |
| P. little rich girl | COW 109:6 |
| p. man at his gate | ALEX 4:3 |
| p. man had nothing | BIBLE 41:24 |
| p. man's dearest friend | BURNS 82:17 |

poor (cont.):
| | |
|---|---|
| p. relation is the most irrelevant | LAMB 200:5 |
| p. soul sat sighing | SHAK 292:26 |
| p. to do him reverence | SHAK 281:21 |
| propensity for being p. | AUST 23:11 |
| Resolve not to be p. | JOHN 185:31 |
| RICH AND THE P. | DISR 122:6 |
| rich as well as the p. | FRAN 145:2 |
| She was p. but she was honest | ANON 10:11 |
| simple annals of the p. | GRAY 157:7 |
| poorest: p. he that is in England | RAIN 257:19 |
| wrong even the p. ploughman | CHAR 94:24 |
| pop: P. goes the weasel | MAND 217:8 |
| Pope: against the P. or the NUM | BALD 27:8 |
| Conscience first, the P. afterwards | NEWM 238:18 |
| poetry of Dryden, P. | ARN 18:5 |
| P.! How many divisions | STAL 314:8 |
| poplars: p. are felled, farewell | COWP 109:30 |
| poppies: In Flanders fields the p. | MCCR 214:17 |
| populace: Philistines, and P. | ARN 17:24 |
| propriety give the name of P. | ARN 17:27 |
| popular: base, common and p. | SHAK 279:9 |
| population: P., when unchecked | MALT 217:5 |
| you have a starving p. | DISR 121:7 |
| populi: Salus p. suprema est lex | CIC 100:20 |
| Vox p., vox Dei | ALC 3:14 |
| porcupines: couple of p. under you | KHR 194:21 |
| Porlock: person on business from P. | COL 103:21 |
| pornography: P. is the attempt to insult sex | |
| | LAWR 202:13 |
| porpoise: p. close behind us | CARR 91:11 |
| porridge: healsome p. | BURNS 82:2 |
| Porson: better poet than P. | HOUS 175:6 |
| port: alma mater lie dissolved in p. | POPE 250:16 |
| ancient tales, and p. | BELL 33:17 |
| I'll quit the p. o' Heaven | NEWB 238:10 |
| In every p. a wife | DIBD 117:18 |
| It would be p. if it could | BENT 35:10 |
| p. after stormy seas | SPEN 313:9 |
| p., for men | JOHN 185:22 |
| to which p. one is sailing | SEN 270:7 |
| portable: P., and compendious oceans | CRAS 111:14 |
| portal: fiery p. of the east | SHAK 293:29 |
| fitful tracing of a p. | STEV 316:11 |
| Porter: moon shone bright on Mrs P. | ELIOT 134:26 |
| portion: p. for foxes | BOOK 67:15 |
| portmanteau: it's like a p. | CARR 92:2 |
| portrait: paint a p. I lose a friend | SARG 266:23 |
| p. of a blinking idiot | SHAK 289:14 |
| P. of the Artist | JOYCE 188:6 |
| two styles of p. painting | DICK 119:15 |
| position: p. must be held | HAIG 159:17 |
| p. of matter at or near | RUSS 265:1 |
| p. ridiculous | CHES 97:18 |
| positive: ac-cent-tchu-ate the p. | MERC 223:9 |
| p. value has its price | PIC 248:19 |
| possessed: limited in order to be p. | BURKE 79:23 |
| Webster was much p. by death | ELIOT 134:32 |
| possessing: too dear for my p. | SHAK 299:27 |
| possession: p. of a good fortune | AUST 23:2 |
| Than in the glad p. | JONS 187:12 |
| possessions: p. for a moment of time | ELIZ 135:15 |
| that are behind the great p. | JAMES 179:20 |
| possibilities: preferred to improbable p. | ARIS 15:17 |
| possibility: deny the p. of anything | HUXL 177:22 |
| possible: effecting of all things p. | BACON 25:26 |
| if a thing is p. | CAL 88:6 |
| Politics is the art of the p. | BISM 59:17 |
| p. you may be mistaken | CROM 112:2 |
| says that something is p. | CLAR 101:14 |
| With God all things are p. | BIBLE 50:23 |
| world is the best of all p. | BRAD 71:8 |
| Possum: said the Honourable P. | BERR 36:14 |
| possumus: Non omnia p. omnes | VIRG 340:2 |
| possunt: p., quia posse videntur | VIRG 339:10 |

| | |
|---|---|
| **post:** Lie follows by p. | BER 35:12 |
| *P. coitum omne animal triste* | ANON 13:19 |
| p. of honour is a private station | ADD 2:17 |
| **postal:** cheque and the p. order | AUDEN 21:4 |
| **postboy:** Never see a dead p. | DICK 120:4 |
| **post-chaise:** driving briskly in a p. | JOHN 185:13 |
| **posted:** p. presence of the watcher | JAMES 179:25 |
| **poster:** Kitchener is a great p. | ASQ 19:5 |
| **posterity:** ancestry, or hope of p. | POWER 255:4 |
| not look forward to p. | BURKE 80:12 |
| P. do something for us | ADD 2:28 |
| p. talking bad grammar | DISR 122:14 |
| Think of your p. | ADAMS 2:4 |
| **postern:** Present has latched its p. | HARDY 162:2 |
| **posters:** P. of the sea and land | SHAK 285:5 |
| **postscript:** all the pith is in the p. | HAZL 163:22 |
| her mind but in her p. | STEE 314:13 |
| most material in the p. | BACON 24:19 |
| **pot:** greasy Joan doth keel the p. | SHAK 284:23 |
| have a chicken in his p. | HENR 165:20 |
| potter pray, and who the p. | FITZ 140:16 |
| There is death in the p. | BIBLE 42:10 |
| thorns under a p. | BIBLE 44:16 |
| **potage:** birthright for a mess of p. | BIBLE 39:17 |
| **potato:** bashful young p. | GILB 152:11 |
| **potent:** how p. cheap music is | COW 109:10 |
| **Potomac:** All quiet along the P. | MCCL 214:14 |
| All quiet along the P. | BEERS 32:14 |
| **potter:** Who *is* the p., pray | FITZ 140:16 |
| **poultry:** prolonging the lives of the p. | ELIOT 132:4 |
| **Pound:** And Ezra P. and T. S. Eliot | DYLAN 129:20 |
| **pound:** p. here in Britain | WILS 351:14 |
| **pounding:** Hard p. this | WELL 345:11 |
| **pounds:** handsome in three hundred p. | SHAK 290:10 |
| passing rich with forty p. | GOLD 154:21 |
| p. will take care | LOWN 211:21 |
| two hundred p. a year | BUTL 84:5 |
| **poured:** p. into his clothes | WOD 352:24 |
| **poverty:** by p. depressed | JOHN 183:9 |
| Come away; p.'s catching | BEHN 32:22 |
| crime so shameful as p. | FARQ 138:15 |
| destruction of the poor is their p. | BIBLE 43:17 |
| Give me not p. lest I steal | DEFOE 115:13 |
| In p., hunger, and dirt | HOOD 171:12 |
| misfortunes of p. | JUV 189:4 |
| P. and oysters always seem | DICK 119:30 |
| P. is a great enemy | JOHN 185:31 |
| p. knows how extremely | BALD 27:2 |
| she scorns our p. | SHAK 280:7 |
| worst of crimes is p. | SHAW 301:8 |
| **powder:** keep your p. dry | BLAC 59:22 |
| when your p.'s runnin' low | NEWB 238:10 |
| **power:** absolute p. corrupts | ACTON 1:5 |
| All hail the p. of Jesus' Name | PERR 248:4 |
| All p. is a trust | DISR 122:10 |
| corridors of p. | SNOW 310:18 |
| Everyone who desires p. | MILL 224:18 |
| friend in p. is a friend lost | ADAMS 1:14 |
| good want p. | SHEL 304:17 |
| gratefully sing his p. | GRANT 156:8 |
| have p. over men | WOLL 353:11 |
| Horses and P. and War | KIPL 196:5 |
| knowledge itself is p. | BACON 25:25 |
| lies not in our p. to love or hate | MARL 218:17 |
| Lord of all p. and might | BOOK 64:25 |
| more contracted that p. is | JOHN 185:17 |
| nobility is but the act of p. | BACON 25:4 |
| no hopes but from p. | BURKE 81:9 |
| no more than p. in trust | DRYD 127:10 |
| only have p. over people as long | SOLZ 310:28 |
| O wad some P. the giftie gie us | BURNS 82:25 |
| pains be less, or p. more | BROME 72:8 |
| p., and the glory | BIBLE 48:27 |
| p. breathe forth | SHAK 271:16 |

| | |
|---|---|
| **power** *(cont.):* | |
| p. can be rightfully exercised | MILL 224:15 |
| p. grows out of the barrel | MAO 217:19 |
| p. is apt to corrupt | PITT 249:4 |
| P. is so apt to be insolent | HAL 160:10 |
| P. is the great aphrodisiac | KISS 198:6 |
| p. of suppress | NORT 240:8 |
| p. thrown away | LESS 206:4 |
| p. to act according | LOCKE 208:21 |
| p. to hurt us that we love | FLET 31:1 |
| p. to live, and act | WORD 356:19 |
| P. to the people | ANON 10:6 |
| p. which erring men call chance | MILT 226:18 |
| p. which stands on Privilege | BELL 33:25 |
| P. without responsibility | KIPL 198:5 |
| responsibility without p. | STOP 38:1 |
| Restored to life, and p., and | KEBLE 193:16 |
| seek p. and to lose liberty | BACON 24:28 |
| though stripped of p. | SCOTT 268:16 |
| with Eternal God for p. | TENN 327:13 |
| witty beauty is a p. | MER 223:12 |
| world desires to have—P. | BOUL 70:11 |
| **powerful:** All-p. as the wind | AUBER 19:15 |
| p. goodness want | SHEL 304:17 |
| **powerless:** p. to be born | ARN 17:16 |
| **powers:** nor p., nor things present | BIBLE 54:42 |
| principalities, against p. | BIBLE 56:4 |
| we lay waste our p. | WORD 357:10 |
| **pox:** die upon the gallows or of the p. | WILK 350:26 |
| **practice:** And P. drives me mad | ANON 9:11 |
| **practise:** Go p. if you please | BROW 77:7 |
| we shall p. in heaven | BROW 76:21 |
| **praemitti:** *sciamus non amitti sed p.* | CYPR 113:13 |
| **praeterea:** *Vox et p. nihil* | ANON 14:3 |
| **prairies:** From the mountains to the p. | BERL 35:21 |
| **praise:** all other p. is shame | SIDN 306:25 |
| Damn with faint p. | POPE 251:6 |
| dispraised were no small p. | MILT 230:3 |
| girded with p. | GRANT 156:8 |
| Give them not p. | SORL 311:16 |
| if there be any p. | BIBLE 56:9 |
| lack tongues to p. | SHAK 300:5 |
| Let us now p. famous men | BIBLE 48:7 |
| no such whetstone as p. | ASCH 18:19 |
| oblique p. | JOHN 185:20 |
| paint 'em truest p. 'em most | ADD 2:12 |
| p. a fugitive and cloistered | MILT 230:31 |
| p. and true perfection | SHAK 290:5 |
| p. at morning what they | POPE 252:6 |
| P. him upon the well-tuned | BOOK 69:12 |
| P. my soul, the King of heaven | LYTE 212:21 |
| P. the green earth | BUNT 78:14 |
| P. the Lord and pass the | FORGY 143:13 |
| P. the Lord, for he is kind | MILT 227:9 |
| P. they that will times past | HERR 167:21 |
| P. to the Holiest | NEWM 238:20 |
| so double be his p. | SPEN 313:10 |
| They p. those works | MART 220:5 |
| unto thy Name give the p. | BOOK 68:17 |
| We p. thee, God | ANON 14:1 |
| We p. thee, O God | BOOK 63:18 |
| Who like me his p. should sing | LYTE 212:21 |
| whom there were none to p. | WORD 356:22 |
| **praised:** everybody p. the Duke | SOUT 311:20 |
| p. him to his face | TENN 328:14 |
| Who ne'er said, 'God be p.' | BROW 75:1 |
| **praiser:** p. of past times | HOR 173:2 |
| **praises:** faint p. one another damn | WYCH 358:6 |
| sing p. lustily unto him | BOOK 66:24 |
| **praising:** doing one's p. for oneself | BUTL 84:9 |
| **pram:** p. in the hall | CONN 106:25 |
| **prater:** p. of the northern race | CHUR 98:28 |
| **pray:** All p. in their distress | BLAKE 61:20 |
| came to scoff, remained to p. | GOLD 154:22 |
| I p. for the country | HALE 160:4 |

pray (cont.):

| | |
|---|---|
| More things are wrought by p. | TENN 324:21 |
| nor p. with you | SHAK 288:31 |
| p. for you at St Paul's | SMITH 310:14 |
| Watch and p., that ye enter | BIBLE 51:13 |
| we do p. for mercy | SHAK 289:27 |
| Work and p., live on hay | HILL 168:12 |
| prayer: are homes of silent p. | TENN 325:6 |
| Ave Maria! 'tis the hour of p. | BYRON 86:18 |
| called the house of p. | BIBLE 50:27 |
| Comin' in on a wing and a p. | ADAM 2:9 |
| Conservative Party at p. | ROYD 264:2 |
| Every p. reduces itself | TURG 335:15 |
| More things are wrought by p. | TENN 324:21 |
| most perfect p. | LESS 206:5 |
| p. the lips ne'er act | HERR 167:17 |
| P. the Church's banquet | HERB 167:4 |
| publick P. in the Church | BOOK 69:18 |
| wish for p. is a p. in itself | BERN 36:7 |
| prayers: Christopher Robin is saying his p. | |
| | MILNE 226:1 |
| have the p. of the church | SWIFT 320:8 |
| Knelt down with angry p. | HODG 169:13 |
| Lord, hear our p. | BOOK 65:24 |
| Their three-mile p. | BURNS 82:29 |
| This was among my p. | HOR 174:4 |
| prayeth: p. well, who loveth well | COL 104:18 |
| praying: Amelia was p. for George | THAC 329:18 |
| do it pat, now he is p. | SHAK 276:17 |
| Nay that's past p. | SHAK 277:33 |
| No p., it spoils business | OTWAY 243:7 |
| prays: family that p. together | SCAL 267:16 |
| p. but faintly and would be | SHAK 294:9 |
| preach: p. the gospel | BIBLE 51:26 |
| preached: p. to death by wild curates | SMITH 310:8 |
| preaching: woman's p. is like | JOHN 184:16 |
| precedency: p. between a louse and a flea | JOHN 186:2 |
| precedent: dangerous p. | CORN 108:8 |
| From precedent to p. | TENN 329:1 |
| p. embalms a principle | STOW 318:10 |
| precept: more efficacious than p. | JOHN 183:6 |
| p. must be upon precept | BIBLE 45:27 |
| precepts: icy p. of respect | SHAK 296:22 |
| precious: Deserve the p. bane | MILT 228:19 |
| Liberty is p. | LENIN 205:6 |
| p. stone set in the silver sea | SHAK 293:16 |
| precise: Is too p. in every part | HERR 167:15 |
| precisely: thinking too p. on the event | SHAK 276:30 |
| preference: special p. for beetles | HALD 160:3 |
| preferment: knocking at P.'s door | ARN 17:6 |
| preferred: after me is p. before me | BIBLE 53:12 |
| pregnant: p. bank swelled up | DONNE 124:2 |
| prejudice: popular p. runs in favour | DICK 119:11 |
| P., n. A vagrant opinion | BIER 59:8 |
| p. of good order | ANON 6:22 |
| result of PRIDE AND P. | BURN 81:17 |
| prejudices: Drive out p. through the door | FRED 145:18 |
| p. as the advertisers don't | SWAF 319:16 |
| reviewing it; it p. a man so | SMITH 310:9 |
| premises: based upon licensed p. | O'BR 240:19 |
| prepare: I go to p. a place | BIBLE 53:37 |
| not to p. for life | PAST 246:9 |
| p. to shed them now | SHAK 281:22 |
| P. ye the way of the Lord | BIBLE 46:8 |
| P. ye the way of the Lord | BIBLE 48:13 |
| prepared: BE P. | BAD 26:1 |
| chance favours only the p. | PAST 246:11 |
| world is not yet p. | DOYLE 125:17 |
| prerogative: p. of the eunuch | STOP 318:1 |
| p. of the harlot | KIPL 198:5 |
| that which is called p. | LOCKE 208:21 |
| presbyter: P. is but old Priest | MILT 228:2 |
| presence: before his p. with a song | BOOK 68:5 |
| his p. with thanksgiving | BOOK 67:31 |
| posted p. of the watcher | JAMES 179:25 |

| | |
|---|---|
| present: All p. and correct | ANON 5:21 |
| know nothing but the p. | KEYN 194:15 |
| nor things p., nor things | BIBLE 54:42 |
| p. at the conception | ORTON 241:20 |
| p. contains nothing more | BERG 35:13 |
| P. has latched its postern | HARDY 162:2 |
| p. help in time of trouble | ANON 5:18 |
| p. is the funeral | CLARE 101:8 |
| Present mirth hath p. laughter | SHAK 297:23 |
| p. of Mornington Crescent | HARG 162:21 |
| p. were the world's last night | DONNE 123:13 |
| p., yes, we are in it | LOW 211:20 |
| There is no p. in Wales | THOM 331:5 |
| Time p. and time past | ELIOT 132:25 |
| un-birthday p. | CARR 91:25 |
| very p. help in trouble | BOOK 67:6 |
| Who p., past, and future, sees | BLAKE 61:26 |
| presents: P. endear Absents | LAMB 199:24 |
| preservative: pleasantest p. from want | AUST 23:4 |
| preserve: shall p. thy going out | BOOK 68:27 |
| preserver: Creator and P. | BOOK 64:18 |
| presidency: P. of the United States | STEV 316:19 |
| president: any boy may become P. | STEV 316:17 |
| As P., I have no eyes | LINC 207:14 |
| P. of the Immortals | HARDY 161:25 |
| rather be right than be P. | CLAY 101:18 |
| their P. is a crook | NIXON 240:3 |
| We are the P.'s men | KISS 198:7 |
| press: fell dead-born from the p. | HUME 176:10 |
| Freedom of the p. in Britain | SWAF 319:16 |
| god of our idolatry, the p. | COWP 110:3 |
| governs the periodical p. | TROL 334:20 |
| power of the p. | NORT 240:8 |
| p. is the Palladium | JUN 188:25 |
| P.-men; Slaves of the Lamp | ARN 16:7 |
| with you on the free p. | STOP 318:2 |
| pressed: p. into service means | FROST 146:21 |
| pressure: Grace under p. | HEM 165:15 |
| prestige: p. without distance | DE G 116:5 |
| presumed: Lady, it is to be p. | JONS 187:5 |
| presumption: Of surquidrie and foul p. | CHAU 96:13 |
| you'll be amused by its p. | THUR 332:17 |
| pretence: some faint meaning make p. | DRYD 128:5 |
| pretender: James II, and the Old P. | GUED 159:7 |
| pretexts: Tyrants seldom want p. | BURKE 79:19 |
| pretio: Cum p. | JUV 189:6 |
| pretty: He is a very p. weoman | FLEM 142:1 |
| It is a p., pretty thing | PEELE 247:1 |
| It is a p. thing | GREE 158:9 |
| policeman and a p. girl | CHAP 94:12 |
| p. can get away with | WAUGH 344:3 |
| p. chickens and their dam | SHAK 287:26 |
| p. girl is like a melody | BERL 36:1 |
| p. to see what money will do | PEPYS 247:20 |
| Puts on his p. looks | SHAK 282:8 |
| prevail: great is truth, and shall p. | BROO 73:14 |
| prevails: Great is truth, and it p. | BIBLE 58:23 |
| prevarication: last dyke of p. | BURKE 80:27 |
| prevent: duty to try to p. it | MILN 226:2 |
| preventing: Politics is the art of p. | VALE 336:22 |
| prey: hast'ning ills a p. | GOLD 154:18 |
| thou soon must be his p. | SHEL 304:2 |
| Venus entire latched onto her p. | RAC 257:16 |
| yet a p. to all | POPE 252:18 |
| price: All those men have their p. | WALP 342:6 |
| because they fetch a high p. | WHAT 347:7 |
| blood be the p. of admiralty | KIPL 197:9 |
| Everything in Rome has its p. | JUV 189:6 |
| 'fixed p.' is negotiable | TOFF 333:7 |
| have bought it at any p. | CLAR 101:11 |
| her p. is far above rubies | BIBLE 44:6 |
| knows the p. of everything | WILDE 350:1 |
| love that pays the p. | SPR 313:26 |
| one pearl of great p. | BIBLE 50:6 |

price (cont.):

| | |
|---|---|
| positive value has its p. | PIC 248:19 |
| p. is asked for harmony | DOST 125:4 |
| p. of justice is eternal | BENN 34:17 |
| p. of wisdom is above rubies | BIBLE 43:2 |
| p. well worth paying | LAM 200:18 |
| What p. glory | STAL 5:13 |
| Wot p. Selvytion nah | SHAW 301:11 |

prices: contrivance to raise p. — SMITH 308:21

prick: If you p. us, do we not bleed — SHAK 289:17

| | |
|---|---|
| I paint with my p. | REN 259:6 |
| It is a p., it is a sting | PEELE 247:1 |
| p. the sides of my intent | SHAK 286:1 |

pricking: By the p. of my thumbs — SHAK 287:18

knight was p. on the plain — SPEN 313:7

prickly: Here we go round the p. pear — ELIOT 133:18

pricks: kick against the p. — BIBLE 54:12

| | |
|---|---|
| pride: And pour contempt on all my p. | WATTS 343:4 |
| burn its children to save its p. | MEYER 224:4 |
| false p. in place and blood | TENN 325:25 |
| from p., vain-glory | BOOK 64:14 |
| He that is low no p. | BUNY 79:7 |
| I know thy p. | BIBLE 41:17 |
| Is p. that apes humility | COL 103:16 |
| P. goeth before destruction | BIBLE 43:28 |
| p. is something in-conceivable | GILB 151:18 |
| P. ruled my will | NEWM 238:22 |
| result of P. AND PREJUDICE | BURN 81:17 |
| that will her p. deflower | SPEN 313:12 |

priest: Am I both p. and clerk — SHAK 294:4

| | |
|---|---|
| Delicate-handed p. | TENN 326:25 |
| huntsman and a fiddling p. | COWP 110:1 |
| Presbyter is but old P. writ | MILT 228:2 |
| p., a piece of mere church | COWP 110:15 |
| p. of the invisible | STEV 316:3 |
| rid me of this turbulent p. | HENR 165:23 |
| 'twixt the P. and Clerk | HERR 167:18 |

priestcraft: ere p. did begin — DRYD 127:2

priesthood: royal p., an holy nation — BIBLE 57:8

priestlike: moving waters at their p. task — KEATS 190:10

priests: p. have been enemies — HUME 176:8

| | |
|---|---|
| strangled with the guts of p. | MESL 223:27 |
| treen p. and golden chalices | JEWEL 181:14 |
| with women nor with p. | SOUT 311:24 |

prime: having lost but once your p. — HERR 167:25

| | |
|---|---|
| laurel for the perfect p. | ROSS 263:3 |
| One's p. is elusive | SPARK 312:13 |

Prime Minister: buried the Unknown P. — ASQ 19:3

next P. but three — BELL 33:7

Prime Ministers: P. wedded to the truth — SAKI 265:22

wild flowers, and P. — BALD 27:10

prime-roses: Pale p. — SHAK 298:33

primeval: This is the forest p. — LONG 209:15

primordial: p. atoms clapped — WELLS 345:22

protoplasmal p. atomic — GILB 151:18

primrose: p. path of dalliance — SHAK 274:20

To P. Hill and Saint John's Wood — BLAKE 60:17

primroses: Wan as p. — KEATS 190:13

prince: Advise the p. — ELIOT 134:1

| | |
|---|---|
| Else a great p. in prison lies | DONNE 124:4 |
| God bless the P. of Wales | LINL 208:1 |
| Good-night, sweet p. | SHAK 277:19 |
| Is in a p. the virtue | MASS 222:3 |
| news and P. of Peace | FLET 142:8 |
| On which the p. of glory died | WATTS 343:4 |
| P. of darkness and dead night | SPEN 313:8 |
| p. of darkness is a gentleman | SHAK 283:16 |
| P. of Peace | BIBLE 45:16 |

princes: blaze forth the death of a p. — SHAK 281:8

| | |
|---|---|
| O put not your trust in p. | BOOK 69:9 |
| P. and lords may flourish | GOLD 154:8 |
| p. are come home again | SHAK 282:15 |
| thy p. eat in the morning | BIBLE 44:22 |
| word to be addressed to p. | ELIZ 135:10 |

princess: P. of Parallelograms — BYRON 87:15

principalities: against p. — BIBLE 56:4

nor p., nor powers — BIBLE 54:42

principle: An active P. — WORD 354:22

| | |
|---|---|
| 'falling domino' p. | EIS 131:15 |
| good men to rise above p. | LONG 209:9 |
| He does everything on p. | SHAW 302:9 |
| precedent embalms a p. | STOW 318:10 |
| p. can be sacrificed to expediency | MAUG 222:8 |
| Protection is not a p. | DISR 121:10 |
| subjects are rebels from p. | BURKE 80:16 |

principles: Damn your p.! — DISR 122:15

| | |
|---|---|
| Lordship's p. or your mistress | WILK 350:26 |
| shows that he has good p. | JOHN 184:8 |
| who denies the first p. | AUCT 20:4 |

print: All the news that's fit to p. — OCHS 241:1

decomposing in the eternity of p. — WOOLF 353:20

licence to p. money — THOM 332:4

p. such of the proprietor's — SWAF 319:16

still 'tis devils must p. — MOORE 234:10

printemps: p. dans ses plis a gardé — ARAG 14:21

printing: Gunpowder, P. — CARL 90:9

| | |
|---|---|
| P., gunpowder | BACON 25:28 |
| we think to regulate p. | MILT 230:32 |

printless: lissom, clerical, p. toe — BROO 73:5

priorities: language of p. — BEVAN 37:19

prism: Of Newton, with his p. — WORD 356:10

prison: Come, let's away to p. — SHAK 284:1

| | |
|---|---|
| comparatively at home in p. | WAUGH 343:20 |
| Else a great prince in p. lies | DONNE 124:4 |
| He did grind in the p. house | BIBLE 41:6 |
| Lime-Tree Bower my P. | COL 104:21 |
| p. and the woman's workhouse | SHAW 302:4 |
| p. for the colour of his hair | HOUS 174:6 |
| prison in a p. | DICK 120:2 |
| p. to them that are bound | BIBLE 46:24 |
| p. where I live unto the world | SHAK 294:10 |
| Shades of the p.-house | WORD 355:20 |
| Stone walls do not a p. make | LOV 210:19 |
| 'Twixt a p. and a smile | WOTT 357:18 |
| was not the world a vast p. | WOLL 353:14 |
| What is a ship but a p. | BURT 83:10 |
| while there is a soul in p. | DEBS 115:9 |

prisoner: thoughts of a p. — SOLZ 311:1

your being taken p. — KITC 198:9

prisoners: p. of addiction — ILL 178:9

Which p. call the sky — WILDE 350:15

prisons: Madhouses, p. — CLARE 101:4

P. are built with stones — BLAKE 61:7

private: grave's a fine and p. place — MARV 220:25

| | |
|---|---|
| his p. parts, his money | BUTL 84:18 |
| invade the sphere of p. life | MELB 222:23 |
| Its p. life is a disgrace | ANON 10:8 |
| kind heaven, a p. station | GAY 149:13 |
| post of honour is a p. station | ADD 2:17 |
| P. faces in public places | AUDEN 21:6 |
| P. Means is dead | SMITH 309:20 |
| P. property is a necessary | TAWN 322:19 |
| silk hat at a p. view | EDW 130:22 |

privates: Faith, her p., we — SHAK 275:13

what have kings that p. — SHAK 279:15

privilege: But the p. and pleasure — GILB 151:6

| | |
|---|---|
| power which stands on P. | BELL 33:25 |
| p. I claim for my own sex | AUST 22:28 |

prize: heedless hearts, is lawful p. — GRAY 157:15

| | |
|---|---|
| is the path and Christ the p. | MONS 233:2 |
| p. we sought is won | WHIT 348:11 |
| We do not run for p. | SORL 311:15 |

prized: local, but p. elsewhere — AUDEN 21:13

prizes: offer glittering p. — SMITH 309:6

probable: P. impossibilities — ARIS 15:17

probationary: Eden's dread p. tree — COWP 110:3

problem: It is quite a three-pipe p. — DOYLE 125:15

| | |
|---|---|
| not a single p. is solved | CHEK 97:1 |
| or you're part of the p. | CLEA 101:19 |

problem (cont.):
p. left to itself dries up — SIMP 307:13
proceed: all just works do p. — BOOK 64:11
proceedings: p. interested him no more — HARTE 163:13
proceeds: good conscience on the p. — SMITH 309:14
procession: torchlight p. — O'SUL 243:5
proclaims: apparel oft p. the man — SHAK 274:21
procrastination: p. is the art of — MARQ 219:15
P. is the thief of time — YOUNG 360:19
procreant: p. urge of the world — WHIT 348:17
proctors: With prudes for p. — TENN 327:16
procul: P. hinc, procul este — OVID 243:9
Procul, o p. este, profani — VIRG 339:13
prodigal: yet p. of ease — DRYD 127:8
production: sole end and purpose of p. — SMITH 308:24
productions: in love with the p. of time — BLAKE 61:5
profanation: From sale and p. — CHES 97:24
'Twere p. of our joys — DONNE 124:15
profane: Coldly p. and impiously gay — CRAB 110:23
P., erroneous, and vain — BUTL 84:2
To Banbury came I, O p. one — BRAT 71:16
profaned: word is too often p. — SHEL 305:5
profani: Procul, o procul este, p. — VIRG 339:13
profession: ancient p. in the world — KIPL 197:17
discharge of any p. — JOHN 185:2
man a debtor to his p. — BACON 24:9
ornament to her p. — BUNY 79:8
professional: P. men, they have no cares — NASH 237:12
professions: p. are conspiracies — SHAW 301:3
professor: called a p. emeritus — LEAC 203:3
professors: protect all conscientious p. — PAINE 244:10
profit: no p. but the name — SHAK 276:28
surely was my p. had I known — TENN 324:6
To whose p.? — CIC 100:31
what shall it p. a man — BIBLE 51:23
profits: Civilization and p. — COOL 107:18
It little p. that an idle king — TENN 328:19
monopoly p. is a quiet life — HICKS 168:10
profound: p. truths recognized — BOHR 63:1
profundis: De p. clamavi ad te — BIBLE 58:14
programme: Not so much a p. — ANON 9:19
progress: Congress makes no p. — LIGNE 207:2
Humanity is just a work in p. — WILL 351:4
It was no summer p. — ANDR 5:15
principle of all social p. — FOUR 144:14
p. depends on the unreasonable — SHAW 302:1
p. if a cannibal uses knife — LEC 204:1
P. is a comfortable disease — CUMM 112:20
p. is a doctrine of idlers — BAUD 30:8
P. is not an accident — SPEN 312:19
p. is the exchange of one nuisance — ELLIS 136:5
P., man's distinctive mark — BROW 75:23
P. through technology — ANON 13:4
Reason and P., the old firm — OSB 242:23
swell a p., start a scene or two — ELIOT 134:1
Time's thievish p. to eternity — SHAK 299:26
projections: Merely p. — ELIOT 132:21
proletariat: dictatorship of the p. — MARX 221:12
prologue: p. to a very dull play — CONG 106:14
What's past is p. — SHAK 296:3
prologues: happy p. to the swelling act — SHAK 285:10
Promethean: true P. fire — SHAK 284:16
promise: P., large promise — JOHN 182:13
p. made is a debt unpaid — SERV 270:9
Whose p. none relies — ROCH 261:4
promised: Jesus, I have p. — BODE 62:16
Marching to the P. Land — BAR 29:2
never p. you a rose garden — GREEN 158:1
think of the Future as a p. land — LEWIS 206:11
promises: But I have p. to keep — FROST 146:23
he is a young man of p. — BALF 27:12
man who p. least — BAR 29:21
promising: destroy they first call p. — CONN 106:24
promotion: none will sweat but for p. — SHAK 272:17
p. cometh neither from — BOOK 67:18

prone: Orion plunges p. — HOUS 174:15
to piety more p. — ALEX 4:7
pronounce: not frame to p. it right — BIBLE 41:2
spell better than they p. — TWAIN 336:1
pronounced: He p. the letter R — AUBR 19:21
proof: of which America is the p. — MCC 214:10
proofs: As p. of holy writ — SHAK 292:18
Proosian: French, or Turk, or P. — GILB 152:21
propensities: ruined on the side of their
  natural p. — BURKE 81:7
proper: know our p. stations — DICK 118:5
my delight is in p. young men — BURNS 82:12
no p. time of day — HOOD 171:9
noun, p. or improper — FULL 147:4
p. study of mankind is books — HUXL 177:5
p. study of mankind is man — POPE 252:17
P. words in proper places — SWIFT 320:4
properly: never did anything p. — LEAR 203:16
property: consider himself public p. — JEFF 181:1
give me a little snug p. — EDG 130:16
governing not p. but a trust — FOX 144:15
Private p. is a necessary — TAWN 322:19
P. has its duties as well as — DRUM 126:25
P. is theft — PROU 255:16
thereby makes it his p. — LOCKE 208:19
Thieves respect p. — CHES 98:11
prophecy: though I have the gift of p. — BIBLE 55:11
prophesy: p. deceits — BIBLE 45:29
we p. in part — BIBLE 55:13
your daughters shall p. — BIBLE 47:20
prophet: I love a p. of the soul — EMER 136:14
p. is not without honour — BIBLE 50:7
there arise among you a p. — BIBLE 40:22
To entrance the p.'s ear — MANT 217:17
prophetic: O my p. soul — SHAK 274:32
With such p. greeting — SHAK 285:8
prophets: Beware of false p. — BIBLE 49:14
ceased to pose as its p. — POPP 253:15
goodly fellowship of the P. — BOOK 63:19
this is the law and the p. — BIBLE 49:11
unto the fathers by the p. — BIBLE 56:23
proportion: broke, and no p. kept — SHAK 294:11
some strangeness in the p. — BACON 24:14
propose: oppose everything, and p. nothing — DERBY 117:6
Whoever loves, if he do not p. — DONNE 123:4
proposes: man p. but God disposes — THOM 330:1
proposition: p. is the method — SCHL 267:22
proprietor: Death! Great p. of all — YOUNG 360:19
propriety: From her p. — SHAK 292:7
prose: all for p. and verse — CAREW 89:18
All that is not p. is verse — MOL 232:15
as well written as p. — POUND 254:24
discourse and nearest p. — DRYD 128:14
Not verse now, only p. — BROW 75:18
pin up my hair with p. — CONG 106:18
p. and the passion — FORS 143:21
P. is when all the lines — BENT 35:3
p. run mad — POPE 251:5
P. = words in their best order — COL 104:26
speaking p. without knowing it — MOL 232:16
They shut me up in p. — DICK 120:15
unattempted yet in p. or rhyme — MILT 228:8
prospect: dull p. of a distant good — DRYD 127:32
Though every p. pleases — HEBER 164:16
prosper: I grow, I p. — SHAK 282:21
Treason doth never p. — HAR 162:22
Why do sinners' ways p. — HOPK 172:18
prosperity: jest's p. lies in the ear — SHAK 284:20
man to han ben in p. — CHAU 96:18
P. doth best discover vice — BACON 24:11
prostitute: I puff the p. away — DRYD 128:23
prostitutes: small nations like p. — KUBR 199:7
protect: Heaven will p. a working girl — SMITH 309:5

protection: Innocence calls mutely for p.  GREE 158:7
P. is not a principle                          DISR 121:10
protector: p. of all that trust in thee        BOOK 64:24
protest: lady doth p. too much                 SHAK 276:9
Protestant: attacked me and the P. church     NIEM 239:15
Gunpowder, Printing and the P.                 CARL 90:9
I am the P. whore                              GWYN 159:13
p. ethic and the spirit of                     WEBER 344:7
P. with a horse                                BEHAN 32:16
worse, P. counterpoint                         BEEC 32:3
Proteus: P. rising from the sea                WORD 357:11
protoplasmal: p. primordial                    GILB 151:18
protracted: life p. is p. woe                  JOHN 183:15
proud: Death be not p.                         DONNE 123:8
how apt the poor are to be p.                  SHAK 298:5
make death p. to take us                       SHAK 271:26
man being too p. to fight                      WILS 351:18
nation p. in arms                              MILT 226:6
p. and yet a wretched thing                    DAV 114:14
p. in the imagination                          BIBLE 51:29
p. me no prouds                                SHAK 295:20
So longe mote ye lyve, and alle p.             CHAU 96:15
too p. for a wit                               GOLD 155:2
woman can be p. and stiff                      YEATS 358:20
prove: I could p. everything                   PINT 248:20
P. all things                                  BIBLE 56:14
proved: p. to be much as you said              HARDY 162:9
proverb: shall be a p. and a byword            BIBLE 41:29
proverbs: King Solomon wrote the P.            NAYL 237:20
Patch grief with p.                            SHAK 291:25
providence: Behind a frowning p.               COWP 109:26
I go the way that P. dictates                  HITL 169:1
I may assert eternal p.                        MILT 228:9
P. had sent a few men                          RUMB 264:5
p. in the fall of a sparrow                    SHAK 277:13
P. their guide                                 MILT 230:2
provident: They are p. instead                 BOGAN 62:18
province: all knowledge my p.                  BACON 25:23
provinces: p. generally costs more             MAC 213:12
provincial: dead level of p. existence         ELIOT 132:13
worse than p.—he was parochial                 JAMES 179:19
provincialism: adultery than in p.             HUXL 177:3
provocation: as in the p.                      BOOK 68:1
Ask you what p. I have had                     POPE 252:32
provoker: Drink, sir, is a great p.            SHAK 286:21
provokes: No one p. me with impunity           ANON 13:17
proxy: p. for risk and a dummy                 MACH 215:4
prudence: effect of p. on rascality            SHAW 301:34
forced into p. in her youth                    AUST 22:26
P. is a rich, ugly, old maid                   BLAKE 61:2
prudenter: p. agas                             ANON 13:20
prudes: With p. for proctors                   TENN 327:11
prunes: especially p. and prism                DICK 119:1
pruninghooks: spears into p.                   BIBLE 45:5
prunus: p. and forsythia                       BETJ 37:6
Prussia: national industry of P.               MIR 231:8
Prussian: French, or Turk, or P.               GILB 152:21
psalm: like a p. of green days                 QUIL 257:8
psalmist: sweet p. of Israel                   BIBLE 41:28
psalms: glad in him with p.                    BOOK 67:31
King David wrote the P.                        NAYL 237:20
pubic: that Caught the P. Hare                 BEHAN 32:17
public: as if I was a p. meeting               VICT 338:9
Desolation in immaculate p.                    ROET 261:14
forsythia across the p. way                    BETJ 37:6
I and the p. know                              AUDEN 21:10
man assumes a p. trust                         JEFF 181:1
Nor p. man, nor angry crowds                   YEATS 359:10
one to mislead the p.                          ASQ 19:4
Private faces in p. places                     AUDEN 21:6
p. be damned                                   VAND 337:1
p. doesn't give a damn                         BEEC 31:23
publican: How like a fawning p.                SHAK 289:1
publicans: Master with p. and sinners          BIBLE 49:21

publicity: oxygen of p.                        THAT 329:24
price of justice is eternal p.                 BENN 34:17
p. except your own obituary                    BEHAN 32:19
public school: been at an English p.           WAUGH 343:20
Keats's vulgarity with a P. accent             LEAV 203:22
public schools: P. the nurseries of all vice   FIEL 139:8
P. 'tis public folly feeds                     COWP 110:13
publish: P. and be damned                      WELL 345:15
p. it not in the streets                       BIBLE 41:21
publisher: Barabbas was a p.                   CAMP 89:1
pudding: p.—it has no theme                    CHUR 100:8
puddings: are like their English p.            VOLT 340:26
puddin'-race: Great chieftain o' the p.        BURNS 82:24
puff: I p. the prostitute away                 DRYD 128:23
puking: Mewling and p.                         SHAK 272:25
pull: P. down thy vanity                       POUND 254:21
pulls: p. a lady through                       MARQ 219:17
pulp: p. so bitter, how shall taste            THOM 331:11
pulse: My p., like a soft drum                 KING 195:6
p. in the eternal mind                         BROO 73:10
p. of feeling stirs again                      ARN 16:10
than feeling a woman's p.                      STER 315:10
two people with the one p.                     MACN 216:5
very p. of the machine                         WORD 356:24
pumpkins: Where the early p. blow              LEAR 203:7
pun: man who could make so vile a p.           DENN 117:1
p. is a pistol let off at the ear              LAMB 200:6
punch: Some sipping p.                         WORD 356:4
punctilio: None of your dam p.                 MER 223:15
punctuality: P. is the politeness of kings     LOUI 210:17
P. is the virtue of the bored                  WAUGH 343:29
punica: P. fide                                SALL 266:9
punishment: All p. is mischief                 BENT 35:2
it shall suffer first p.                       CRAN 111:4
To let the p. fit the crime                    GILB 152:1
punk: Gert's writings are p.                   ANON 8:2
punt: p. than to be punted                     SAY 267:15
puppets: shut up the box and the p.            THAC 329:22
whose p., best and worst                       BROW 77:1
purchase: cunning p. of my wealth              JONS 187:12
pure: Because my heart is p.                   TENN 328:15
Blessed are the p. in heart                    BIBLE 48:19
chaste as ice, as p. as snow                   SHAK 275:29
If I have led a p. life                        CAT 93:6
Live p., speak true                            TENN 324:5
p. as the lily in the dell                     LAUD 202:6
too p. an Air For Slaves                       ANON 10:1
truth is rarely p. and never simple            WILDE 349:16
Unto the p. all things are pure                BIBLE 56:22
whatsoever things are p.                       BIBLE 56:9
purer: In p. lives thy service find            WHIT 348:27
purest: p. of human pleasures                  BACON 24:26
purgatorial: black, p. rails                   KEATS 190:15
purge: shalt p. me with hyssop                 BOOK 67:9
purify: p. the dialect of the tribe            ELIOT 133:9
puritan: P. hated bear-baiting                 MAC 213:19
To the P. all things are impure                LAWR 202:9
Where I saw a P.-one                            BRAT 71:16
puritanism: P. The haunting fear               MENC 223:7
purlieus: dusty p. of the law                  TENN 325:17
I walk within the p. of the Law                ETH 137:18
purling: painted meadow, or a p. stream        ADD 2:1
to plain work, and to p. brooks                POPE 251:24
purple: And p.-stainèd mouth                   KEATS 191:30
deep p. falls over sleepy                      PAR 245:3
gleaming in p. and gold                        BYRON 85:22
I never saw a P. Cow                           BURG 79:16
Pilots of the p. twilight                      TENN 326:10
p. brows of Olivet                             TENN 325:5
p.-linèd palace of sweet sin                   KEATS 191:12
p. patch or two                                HOR 172:23
p. testament of bleeding                       SHAK 294:1
P. the sails, and so perfumed                  SHAK 271:14
purpose: any p. perverts art                   CONS 107:13

**purpose** (*cont.*):
does nothing without p. ARIS 15:20
God is working his p. out AING 3:9
Infirm of p. SHAK 286:17
living to some p. PAINE 244:15
My p. is, indeed, a horse SHAK 297:27
p. of human existence JUNG 188:23
Shake my fell p. SHAK 285:17
To speak and p. not SHAK 282:18
**purpureal**: invested with p. gleams WORD 355:7
**purrs**: p. like an epigram MARQ 219:23
**purse**: consumption of the p. SHAK 278:19
law can take a p. BUTL 84:8
steals my p. steals trash SHAK 292:11
want of friends, and empty p. BRET 71:23
**pursuing**: Faint, yet p. BIBLE 41:1
**pursuit**: common p. LEAV 203:21
p. of happiness ANON 11:12
p. of happiness JEFF 180:18
p. of the uneatable WILDE 350:9
What mad p. KEATS 191:18
**pussy-cat**: Owl and the P. LEAR 203:11
**put**: I p. away childish things BIBLE 55:14
Our end is Life. P. out to sea MACN 216:11
P. me to what you will METH 223:28
P. on the whole armour of God BIBLE 56:3
P. out the light, and then SHAK 292:29
p. upon us the armour of light BOOK 64:21
up with which I will not p. CHUR 100:5
what p. me up to it BEVIN 38:11
**puzzle**: Don't p. me, said I STER 315:24
Rule of Three doth p. me ANON 9:11
**pylons**: P., those pillars SPEN 313:3
**pyramid**: bottom of the economic p. ROOS 262:7
**pyramids**: books made like p. FLAU 141:12
p. a monument of the insufficiency JOHN 183:7
summit of these p. NAP 237:3
**Pyrenees**: P. are no more LOUI 210:15
tease in the High P. BELL 34:1
**Pythagoras**: mystical way of P. BROW 74:12
this 'himself' was P. CIC 100:21

# Q

**quad**: no one about in the Q. KNOX 198:18
**quadrille**: q. in a sentry-box JAMES 179:16
**quaffing**: q., and unthinking time DRYD 128:15
**quailing**: No q., Mrs Gaskell BRON 72:19
**quaint**: q. and curious war HARDY 162:13
**quake**: aspes leef she gan to q. CHAU 96:17
They love indeed who q. SIDN 306:22
**qualis**: *Non sum q. eram bonae* HOR 173:30
**qualities**: q. as would wear well GOLD 155:11
**quality**: his honour and his q. BLUN 62:15
q. of mercy is not strained SHAK 289:26
**quantities**: ghosts of departed q. BERK 35:15
**quantity**: vile, holding no q. SHAK 290:16
**quantum**: I waive the q. o'the sin BURNS 82:5
**quarks**: Three q. for Muster Mark JOYCE 188:5
**quarrel**: find q. in a straw SHAK 276:31
justice of my q. ANON 8:7
q. in a far away country CHAM 94:1
q. with ourselves, poetry YEATS 360:10
that hath his q. just SHAK 280:8
therefore a perpetual q. BURKE 80:3
**quarrels**: unseemly intimacy or q. LOW 211:11
**quarterly**: nothing a-year, paid q. SURT 319:15
**quarto**: q. page where a neat rivulet SHER 306:3
q. volumes against. q. SHER 306:6
**quean**: flaunting, extravagant q. ANON 13:21
**queen**: Hail holy q. ANON 8:1
home life of our own dear Q. ANON 8:1
I'll q. it no inch further SHAK 299:1

**queen** (*cont.*):
I'm to be Q. o' the May TENN 327:5
Ocean's child, and then his q. SHEL 304:2
Q. and huntress, chaste JONS 187:3
Q. had four Maries BALL 28:2
Q. Mab hath been with you SHAK 294:24
q. of Scots is this day ELIZ 135:12
Q. rose of the rosebud TENN 326:29
q. that caught the world's HUNT 176:14
Ruler of the Q.'s Navee GILB 152:18
when good Cinara was my q. HOR 173:30
**queens**: Q. have died young and fair NASHE 237:19
That all your acts are q. SHAK 298:34
**queer**: q. save thee and me OWEN 243:18
q. sort of thing BARH 28:21
**queerer**: q. than we *can* suppose HALD 160:2
**quest**: winding q. and passage VAUG 337:3
**questing**: passes the q. vole WAUGH 343:25
**question**: ask an impertinent q. BRON 72:10
having asked any clear q. CAMUS 89:5
If any q. why we died KIPL 196:7
Others abide our q. ARN 17:14
q. is absurd AUDEN 21:17
such a silly q. STER 315:13
To ask the hard q. is simple AUDEN 21:16
To be or not to be: that is the q. SHAK 275:25
**questionings**: those obstinate q. WORD 355:22
**questions**: ask q. of those who cannot tell RAL 258:5
That q. the distempered part ELIOT 133:5
**queue**: forms an orderly q. of one MIKES 224:12
**quick**: Come! q. as you can DE L 116:11
Now burgeons every maze of q. TENN 325:29
q., and the dead DEWAR 117:14
Q., thy tablets, Memory ARN 16:20
So q. bright things come to SHAK 290:15
Touched to the q., he said BROW 76:8
**quickly**: It were done q. SHAK 285:22
**quiddities**: in thy quips and thy q. SHAK 277:23
**quidquid**: *Q. agis, prudenter agas* ANON 13:20
**quiet**: All q. along the Potomac BEERS 32:14
All q. along the Potomac MCCL 214:14
All q. on the western front REM 259:4
alone with the q. day JAMES 180:3
Anything for a q. life MIDD 224:5
Easy live and q. die SCOTT 268:24
Fie upon this q. life SHAK 277:32
fruitful ground, the q. mind SURR 319:6
Give me my scallop-shell of q. RAL 257:23
lives of q. desperation THOR 332:9
monopoly profits is a q. life HICKS 168:10
never have a q. world till SHAW 302:13
q. limit of the world TENN 328:17
q., pilfering, unprotected race CLARE 101:6
Q. to quick bosoms is a hell BYRON 85:4
telling with a q. beat QUIL 257:8
**quietest**: q. places under the sun HOUS 175:1
**quietness**: unravished bride of q. KEATS 191:17
**quince**: slices of q. LEAR 203:13
**quinquireme**: Q. of Nineveh MAS 221:18
**quip**: q. modest SHAK 273:12
**quips**: thy q. and thy quiddities SHAK 277:23
**quires**: Q. and Places where they sing BOOK 64:7
**quis**: *Q. custodiet ipsos custodes?* JUV 189:9
**quit**: I q. such odious subjects AUST 22:21
Q. yourselves like men BIBLE 41:10
**quiver**: hath his q. full of them BOOK 68:31
**quo**: *vadis?* BIBLE 58:19
**quod**: *Q. erat demonstrandum* EUCL 137:19
**quotation**: every q. contributes JOHN 182:5
**quote**: grow immortal as they q. YOUNG 360:13
**quotidienne**: *Ah! que la vie est q.* LAF 199:20

# R

rabbit: r. has a charming face — ANON 10:8
There is a r. in a snare — STEP 315:7
race: avails the sceptred r. — LAND 200:23
loftier r. — SYM 321:20
lovely ere his r. be run — BYRON 85:20
pilfering, unprotected r. — CLARE 101:6
r. between education — WELLS 345:21
r. is not to the swift — BIBLE 44:20
r. is sent down from high — VIRG 339:25
r. is to the swift — DAV 114:12
r. that is set before us — BIBLE 56:27
r. that long in darkness — SCOT 269:10
r. through God's good grace — MONS 233:2
shall rear my dusky r. — TENN 326:15
slinks out of the r. — MILT 230:31
till thou run out thy r. — MILT 228:3
races: white r. are really pinko-grey — FORS 143:24
Rachel: R. weeping for her children — BIBLE 48:11
served seven years for R. — BIBLE 39:22
rack: Leave not a r. behind — SHAK 296:10
r. of a too easy chair — POPE 250:20
r. of this tough world — SHAK 284:7
racket: flaming r. of the female — OSB 242:22
rackets: matched our r. to these balls — SHAK 279:1
radiance: white r. of Eternity — SHEL 303:13
radical: dared be r. when young — FROST 146:18
R. Chic — WOLFE 353:9
r. revolutionary will become — AREN 15:5
raft: republic is a r. — AMES 4:22
rag: O that Shakespeherian R. — ELIOT 134:24
r. and a bone and a hank — KIPL 197:12
r. and bone shop of the heart — YEATS 358:16
rage: captive void of noble r. — TENN 325:3
heathen so furiously r. — BOOK 66:9
Heaven has no r. — CONG 106:12
nature with hard-favoured r. — SHAK 279:5
Not die here in a r. — SWIFT 320:5
Puts all Heaven in a r. — BLAKE 60:6
r. against the dying of the light — THOM 330:7
writing increaseth r. — DYER 129:15
rages: weight of r. — SPOO 313:25
ragged: been a pair of r. claws — ELIOT 133:28
rags: when in r. and contempt — BUNY 79:2
which are the r. of time — DONNE 124:12
raid: r. on the inarticulate — ELIOT 133:6
rail: her six young on the r. — BROW 76:10
railing: R. at life, and yet afraid — CHUR 98:24
rails: black, purgatorial r. — KEATS 190:15
railway: imposed by r. timetables — TAYL 322:23
R. Bridge of the Silv'ry Tay — MCG 214:19
R. termini are our gates — FORS 143:19
threatened its life with a r. share — CARR 92:9
rain: droppeth as the gentle r. — SHAK 289:26
former and the latter r. — BOOK 64:20
glazed with r. — WILL 351:8
hard r.'s a gonna fall — DYLAN 130:2
like sunshine after r. — SHAK 300:18
not even the r., has such small — CUMM 113:3
R. in Spain — LERN 206:1
r. is destroying his grain — HERB 166:11
r. is on our lips — SORL 311:15
r. it raineth every day — SHAK 298:15
r., it raineth on the just — BOWEN 70:14
r. maketh a hole — LAT 202:3
Rain! R.! — KEATS 193:6
sendeth r. on the just — BIBLE 48:24
small rain down can r. — ANON 11:18
sound of abundance of r. — BIBLE 42:1
Spout, r. — SHAK 283:7
Still falls the R. — SITW 307:19
through the drizzling r. — TENN 325:1

rain (cont.):
waiting for r. — ELIOT 133:14
which had outwept its r. — SHEL 303:6
rainbow: God gave Noah the r. sign — ANON 7:12
It was the R. gave thee birth — DAV 114:19
Lord survives the r. — LOW 211:17
r. and a cuckoo's song — DAV 114:18
r. comes and goes — WORD 355:18
r. in the sky — WORD 355:13
r.'s glory is shed — SHEL 303:24
Somewhere over the r. — HARB 161:14
raineth: R. drop and staineth slop — POUND 254:8
rains: r. pennies from heaven — BURKE 81:14
rainy: r. day and a contentious woman — BIBLE 44:1
r. Pleiads wester — HOUS 174:15
windy night a r. morrow — SHAK 300:1
raise: The Lord shall r. me up — RAL 258:1
raising: corn and begin r. hell — LEASE 203:20
ram: r. caught in a thicket — BIBLE 39:16
r. is tupping your white ewe — SHAK 291:29
Rama: In R. was there a voice — BIBLE 48:11
rampage: On the R., Pip, and off — DICK 118:26
rampart: As his corse to the r. — WOLFE 352:25
rams: mountains skipped like r. — BOOK 68:16
My r. speed not, all is amiss — BARN 29:8
Ramsbottom: Mr and Mrs R. — EDGAR 130:15
Randal: your dinner, Lord R. — BALL 27:19
random: many a word, at r. spoken — SCOTT 268:15
rangers: Eight for the eight bold r. — ANON 8:6
Rangoon: from R. to Mandalay — KIPL 196:21
rank: flog the r. and file — ARN 18:16
my offence is r. — SHAK 276:16
r. is but the guinea's stamp — BURNS 82:7
r. me with whom you will — METH 223:28
things r. and gross — SHAK 274:10
track marched, r. on rank — MER 223:22
ranks: even the r. of Tuscany — MAC 214:8
r. of death you'll find him — MOORE 234:16
ransack: R. the ocean for orient pearl — MARL 218:8
ransomed: R., healed, restored — LYTE 212:21
rape: A r.! a rape — WEBS 344:24
you don't marry it, you r. it — DEGAS 116:2
rapscallions: All kings is mostly r. — TWAIN 335:20
rapture: first fine careless r. — BROW 76:2
Modified r. — GILB 151:24
r. on the lonely shore — BYRON 85:12
raptures: r. and roses of vice — SWIN 321:7
rara: R. avis in terris nigroque — JUV 189:7
rare: Rich and r. were the gems — MOORE 234:17
She was indeed a r. one — WITH 352:5
raree-show: r. of Peter's successor — BROW 76:9
rarely: Rarely, r., comest thou — SHEL 304:32
rarer: r. spirit never did steer — SHAK 271:27
rascality: effect of prudence on r. — SHAW 301:34
rascals: R., would you live for ever — FRED 145:20
rash: It is too r., too unadvised — SHAK 295:1
You look rather r. my dear — ASHF 18:21
rashes: Green grow the r., O — BURNS 82:9
rat: And, like a r. without a tail — SHAK 285:3
Cat, the R., and Lovell our dog — COLL 105:3
giant r. of Sumatra — DOYLE 125:17
How now! a r.? — SHAK 276:19
it creeps like a r. — BOWEN 70:18
Mr Speaker, I smell a r. — ROCHE 261:1
poisoned r. in a hole — SWIFT 320:5
rational: These r. amphibii go — MARV 221:3
rats: I think we are in r.' alley — ELIOT 134:23
R.! They fought the dogs — BROW 76:26
rattle: Pleased with a r. — POPE 252:19
R. his bones over the stones — NOEL 240:5
rattling: Advertising is the r. of a stick — ORW 242:16
ravage: r. with impunity a rose — BROW 77:15
rave: and let her r. — KEATS 191:26
old age should burn and r. — THOM 330:7
raved: r. and grew more fierce — HERB 166:23

ravelling: I am worn to a r.     POTT 254:1
raven: Quoth the R., 'Nevermore'     POE 250:7
r. himself is hoarse     SHAK 285:16
ravens: As you have seen the r. flock     AYT 23:16
ravish: except you r. me     DONNE 123:11
ravished: would have r. her     FIEL 139:7
Yes, you have r. justice     WEBS 344:24
ravishing: what a dear r. thing     BEHN 32:20
ray: genuine night admits no r.     DRYD 128:5
many a gem of purest r.     GRAY 157:9
razor: hew blocks with a r.     POPE 253:12
reach: culture, I r. for my pistol     JOHST 186:18
r. should exceed his grasp     BROW 75:10
reaching: r. after fact and reason     KEATS 193:2
reaction: I can't get no girl r.     RICH 179:6
opposed an equal r.     NEWT 239:4
third r. of man upon     HOLM 170:13
reactionaries: All r. are paper tigers     MAO 217:20
read: Being t. to by a boy     ELIOT 133:14
but his books were r.     BELL 33:27
do you r. books through?     JOHN 184:26
in general r. without pleasure     JOHN 186:15
I r., much of the night     ELIOT 134:19
May r. strange matters     SHAK 285:20
Much had he r.     ARMS 16:1
only news until he's r. it     WAUGH 343:26
people that r., people that write     SHEN 305:21
people who can't r.     ZAPPA 361:1
praise those works, but r. these     MART 220:5
r. and dream of the soft     YEATS 360:9
r. as much as other men     AUBR 19:17
r. but unable to distinguish     TREV 334:9
r. just as inclination     JOHN 184:10
r., mark, learn, and inwardly     BOOK 64:22
R. my lips: no new taxes     BUSH 83:18
R. out my words at night     FLEC 141:20
r. the hunter's waking thoughts     AUDEN 20:16
Take up and r., take up     AUG 21:23
what I r. in the papers     ROG 262:1
reader: common r.     JOHN 182:21
one r. in a hundred years     KOES 199:3
R., I married him     BRON 72:12
written not to inform the r. but to     ACH 1:4
readiness: r. is all     SHAK 277:13
reading: but I prefer r.     SMITH 309:13
Digressions ... the life, the soul of r.     STER 315:15
distinguish what is worth r.     TREV 334:9
easy writing's vile hard r.     SHER 306:8
Peace is poor r.     HARDY 161:20
r. is right which requires     JOHN 182:26
R. is to the mind what exercise     STEE 314:17
R. maketh a full man     BACON 25:15
r. or non-reading a book     BYRON 87:20
reads: R. verse and thinks she     BROW 75:25
ready: conference r. a man     BACON 25:15
he is always r. to go     LA F 199:19
R. to be any thing     BROW 74:8
real: Life is r.! Life is earnest     LONG 209:22
washed in the speechless r.     BARZ 29:22
realities: twin r. of this phantom world     COL 105:1
reality: between the idea and the r.     ELIOT 133:19
Cannot bear very much r.     ELIOT 132:27
really: R. Useful Engine     AWDRY 23:13
realm: this r., this England     SHAK 293:16
realms: travelled in the r. of gold     KEATS 192:10
reap: and you r. a character     READE 258:11
sow in tears shall r. in joy     BOOK 68:29
that shall he also r.     BIBLE 55:30
they shall r. the whirlwind     BIBLE 47:17
reaped: which never should be r.     TRAH 333:18
reapers: Only r., reaping early     TENN 325:36
reaping: ever r. something new     TENN 326:9
r. where thou hast not sown     BIBLE 51:2
rear: r. the tender thought     THOM 331:22

rear (cont.):
she shall r. my dusky race     TENN 326:15
rearward: r. of a conquered woe     SHAK 300:1
reason: all r. is against it     BUTL 84:17
erring R.'s spite     POPE 252:16
For r., much too strong     DONNE 124:1
Happiness is not an ideal of r.     KANT 189:24
How noble in r.     SHAK 275:16
human r. weak     BAG 26:12
if it be against r.     COKE 103:7
In R.'s ear they all rejoice     ADD 2:26
kills r. itself     MILT 230:29
O r. not the need     SHAK 283:4
our r. is our law     MILT 229:25
pursue my r. to an O altitudo     BROW 74:11
R. and Progress, the old firm     OSB 242:23
r. and the will of God     ARN 17:25
R., an ignis fatuus     ROCH 261:6
R. has moons     HODG 169:14
R. is natural revelation     LOCKE 208:16
R. means what someone else     GASK 148:18
r. of the strongest     LA F 199:18
r. produces monsters     GOYA 156:1
R. thus with life     SHAK 288:18
right deed for the wrong r.     ELIOT 134:7
ruling passion conquers r.     POPE 251:14
that wants discourse of r.     SHAK 274:12
Theirs not to r. why     TENN 323:15
There is nothing without a r.     LEIB 204:15
ultimate triumph of human r.     HAWK 163:18
who listens to R. is lost     SHAW 302:2
worse appear the better r.     MILT 228:23
reasonable: r. man adapts himself     SHAW 302:1
They never r. people     BROO 73:12
reasonableness: sweet r.     ARN 18:10
reasoning: contain any abstract r.     HUME 176:4
cowards in r.     SHAF 270:21
r., self-sufficing thing     WORD 356:6
reasons: heart has its r.     PASC 246:5
R. are not like garments     ESSEX 137:16
r. for what we believe     BRAD 71:7
your r. will certainly be wrong     MANS 217:16
rebecks: And the jocund r. sound     MILT 227:4
rebel: die like a true-blue r.     HILL 168:13
R. without a cause     LIND 207:15
What is a r.? A man who says no     CAMUS 89:7
rebellion: R. lay in his way     SHAK 278:11
r. now and then is a good     JEFF 180:20
R. to tyrants is obedience     BRAD 71:11
Romanism, and r.     BURC 79:12
rebellions: and everyday r.     STEI 315:1
rebellious: revolting and a r. heart     BIBLE 46:27
rebels: r. from principle     BURKE 80:16
recall: cannot r. their gifts     TENN 328:18
word takes wing beyond r.     HOR 173:13
receive: blessed to give than to r.     BIBLE 54:22
received: Freely ye have r.     BIBLE 49:27
receiver: left the r. off the hook     KOES 199:2
recession: It's a r. when     TRUM 335:5
recherche: A la r. du temps perdu     PROU 255:17
recipes: aggregate of successful r.     VALÉ 336:20
recirculation: vicus of r.     JOYCE 188:3
reckoned: love that can be r.     SHAK 271:4
recks: And r. not his own rede     SHAK 274:20
re-clothe: R. us in our rightful mind     WHIT 348:27
recognised: objects r., in flashes     WORD 356:12
recommendation: beautiful face is a mute r.
    PUBL 255:22
reconciliation: silence and r.     MAC 213:14
recte: Si possis r.     HOR 173:6
rectum: and one in the r.     OSLER 243:3
red: Making the green one r.     SHAK 286:18
more red than her lips' r.     SHAK 300:11
my Luve's like a r. red rose     BURNS 82:20
Nature, r. in tooth and claw     TENN 325:12

red (cont.):
| | |
|---|---|
| r. flag flying here | CONN 106:23 |
| R. lips are not so red | OWEN 244:1 |
| r. wheel barrow | WILL 351:8 |
| rose-r. city half as old as time | BURG 79:17 |
| that never blows so r. | FITZ 140:8 |
| Their r. it never dies | DOBS 122:27 |
| Thin r. line of 'eroes | KIPL 197:11 |
| thin r. line tipped with steel | RUSS 265:7 |
| your raiment all r. | MAC 213:25 |

rede: And recks not his own r. | SHAK 274:20
redeem: R. thy mis-spent time | KEN 193:21
redeemer: I know that my r. liveth | BIBLE 42:36
Our blest R. | AUBER 19:15
To thee, R., King | NEALE 237:21
redeeming: R. the time | BIBLE 56:1
redemption: Hail, r.'s happy dawn | CASW 92:18
married past r. | DRYD 128:7
redress: Things past r. | SHAK 293:20
redwood: r. forest to the Gulf Stream | GUTH 159:12
reed: Man is only a r. | PASC 246:6
r. shaken with the wind | BIBLE 49:34
staff of this bruised r. | BIBLE 42:16
reeds: Down in the r. by the river | BROW 75:4
reeking: r. into Cadiz Bay | BROW 76:3
reel: I've gotten a r. | BLAM 62:8
They r. to and fro | BOOK 68:13
reeled: until r. the mind | GIBBS 150:18
references: verify your r. | ROUTH 263:19
refined: r. out of existence | JOYCE 188:3
This Englishwoman is so r. | SMITH 309:21
reflecting: r. the figure of a man | WOOLF 354:2
reform: retrenchment, and r. | BRIG 72:3
reformers: All r. are bachelors | MOORE 234:6
All R., however strict | SMITH 309:15
refuge: eternal God is thy r. | BIBLE 40:25
last r. of a scoundrel | JOHN 185:4
r. from home life | SHAW 302:23
r. of weak minds | CHES 97:13
so easy to take r. in | IBSEN 178:6
refusal: great r. | DANTE 113:20
refuse: offer he can't r. | PUZO 256:25
r. till the conversion of the Jews | MARV 220:23
refused: stone which the builders r. | BOOK 68:22
refute: I r. it thus | JOHN 184:17
Who can r. a sneer | PALEY 244:17
regalia: r. that comes with it | KEAT 190:8
regard: Should be without r. | SHAK 287:3
regardless: r. of their doom | GRAY 157:12
regiment: Monstrous R. of Women | KNOX 198:16
regina: Salve, r. | ANON 13:21
region: r. of thick-ribbèd ice | SHAK 288:21
register: r. of the crimes | GIBB 150:11
regret: Old Age a r. | DISR 121:26
regrets: Miss Otis r. | PORT 253:23
series of congratulatory r. | DISR 121:19
wild r. | WILDE 350:17
regular: Brought r. and draw'd mild | DICK 119:4
icily r., splendidly null | TENN 326:23
regulate: r. all recreations | MILT 230:32
regulated: R. hatred | HARD 161:16
Reich: Ein R., ein Volk | ANON 13:2
reign: Better to r. in hell | MILT 228:13
Long to r. over us | HOGG 170:8
r. of Chaos and old Night | MILT 228:16
reigned: r. with your loves | ELIZ 135:7
reindeer: Herds of r. move across | AUDEN 20:19
rejected: despised and r. of men | BIBLE 46:17
rejoice: desert shall r. | BIBLE 46:4
Let us then r. | ANON 13:16
R. in the Lord alway | BIBLE 56:7
rejoicing: home, r., brought me | BAKER 26:21
relation: nobody like a r. to do | THAC 329:16
No cold r. is a zealous citizen | BURKE 80:20
poor r.—is the most irrelevant | LAMB 200:5

| | |
|---|---|
| relations: Personal r. | FORS 143:20 |
| relationship: every human r. | FORS 143:26 |
| relative: In a r. way | BULL 78:7 |
| Success is r. | ELIOT 132:23 |
| relaxes: Damn braces: Bless r. | BLAKE 61:9 |
| relent: Shall make him once r. | BUNY 79:9 |
| relic: cased up, like a holy r. | WEBS 344:14 |
| relief: For this r. much thanks | SHAK 273:30 |
| relieve: comfort and r. them | BOOK 64:19 |
| religio: Tantum r. potuit suadere | LUCR 212:2 |
| religion: all of the same r. | DISR 122:1 |
| As great in love as in r. | COWL 109:16 |
| As to r., I hold it to be | PAINE 244:10 |
| bringeth men's minds to r. | BACON 24:12 |
| brothels with bricks of R. | BLAKE 61:7 |
| enough r. to make us hate | SWIFT 320:10 |
| handmaid to r. | BACON 24:2 |
| increase in us true r. | BOOK 64:25 |
| indirect way to plant r. | BROW 74:16 |
| In their r. they are so uneven | DEFOE 115:23 |
| leave him for r. | SPARK 312:10 |
| men of sense are really but of one r. | SHAF 270:20 |
| Millionaire. That is my r. | SHAW 301:9 |
| my r. is to do good | PAINE 244:14 |
| no amusements but vice and r. | SMITH 310:12 |
| no r. but social | WESL 346:11 |
| not impossibilities enough in r. | BROW 74:10 |
| One r. is as true as another | BURT 83:14 |
| only one r. | SHAW 302:15 |
| Philistine of genius in r. | ARN 18:11 |
| r. allowed to invade the sphere | MELB 222:23 |
| r. at the lowest | CHES 97:14 |
| r. but a childish toy | MARL 218:19 |
| R. by no means a proper subject | CHES 97:3 |
| r. for religion's sake | COUS 108:17 |
| r. into after-dinner toasts | NEWM 238:18 |
| r. is powerless to bestow | FORB 143:2 |
| R. is the frozen thought | KRIS 199:3 |
| R. is the opium of the people | MARX 221:8 |
| r. is thus not simply morality | ARN 18:8 |
| r. of Socialism | BEVAN 37:19 |
| R.'s in the heart | JERR 181:10 |
| r. that has any thing in it | PAINE 244:7 |
| r. to a man without bodily hunger | SHAW 301:10 |
| r. when in rags and contempt | BUNY 79:2 |
| r. without science is blind | EINS 131:11 |
| rum and true r. | BYRON 86:5 |
| science is strong and r. weak | SZASZ 322:1 |
| slovenliness is no part of r. | WESL 346:15 |
| some of r. | EDG 130:16 |
| So much wrong could r. induce | LUCR 212:2 |
| Superstition is the r. of feeble | BURKE 80:18 |
| To become a popular r. | INGE 178:12 |
| too late to trust the old r. | LOW 211:19 |
| zeal in politics as well as in r. | JUN 188:26 |
| religions: sixty different r. | CAR 89:17 |
| religious: even r. concord | GIBB 150:10 |
| his r. opinions | BUTL 84:18 |
| r. factions are volcanoes | BURKE 81:1 |
| With a r. book, or friend | WOTT 357:14 |
| religious-good: Good, but not r. | HARDY 162:1 |
| rem: R. tene; verba sequentur | CATO 92:23 |
| remain: things r. | CLOU 102:22 |
| remains: r., however improbable | DOYLE 126:1 |
| while aught r. to do | ROG 261:17 |
| remarkable: nothing left r. | SHAK 271:25 |
| remarks: R. are not literature | STEIN 314:20 |
| said our r. before us | DON 123:1 |
| remedies: not apply new r. | BACON 24:31 |
| Our r. oft in ourselves do lie | SHAK 270:24 |
| remedy: Force is not a r. | BRIG 72:6 |
| know not how to r. our own | KYD 199:9 |
| r. against the entropy | ZAMY 360:25 |
| r. is worse than the disease | BACON 25:11 |

| | |
|---|---|
| remedy (*cont.*): | |
| requires a dangerous r. | FAWK 138:22 |
| Things without all r. | SHAK 287:3 |
| 'Tis a sharp r. | RAL 258:3 |
| remember: Do you r. an Inn | BELL 34:1 |
| I r., I remember | HOOD 171:8 |
| no greater pain than to r. | DANTE 113:21 |
| r. and be sad | ROSS 263:4 |
| r. even these things | VIRG 339:2 |
| R. me, but ah! forget my fate | TATE 322:15 |
| R. me when I am dead | DOUG 125:9 |
| r. not past years | NEWM 238:22 |
| R. now thy Creator | BIBLE 44:25 |
| r. the Fifth of November | ANON 10:5 |
| R. the sabbath day | BIBLE 40:7 |
| r. with advantages | SHAK 279:19 |
| should, yet never can, r. | THOM 330:25 |
| Till thou r. and I forget | SWIN 321:16 |
| wake, and r., and understand | BROW 75:29 |
| We will r. them | BINY 59:12 |
| *what you can* r. | SELL 269:23 |
| Yes; I r. Adlestrop | THOM 330:21 |
| You must r. this, a kiss | HUPF 176:20 |
| remembered: blue r. hills | HOUS 174:24 |
| my youth I r. my God | SOUT 312:2 |
| r. for a very long time | MCG 214:19 |
| we in it shall be r. | SHAK 279:20 |
| remembering: R. without ceasing | BIBLE 56:13 |
| remembers: R. me of all his gracious | SHAK 282:8 |
| remembrance: R. of things past | PROU 255:17 |
| r. of things past | SHAK 299:16 |
| r. of a guest that tarrieth | BIBLE 47:31 |
| r. of them is grievous | BOOK 65:11 |
| rosemary, that's for r. | SHAK 277:2 |
| remembren: it r., whan it passed | CHAU 96:18 |
| remind: Foolish Things R. Me | MARV 221:4 |
| remission: shedding of blood is no r. | BIBLE 56:24 |
| remorse: access and passage to r. | SHAK 285:17 |
| Farewell r.! | MILT 229:7 |
| R., the fatal egg | COWP 110:2 |
| remote: R. and ineffectual Don | BELL 33:16 |
| removals: household r. | BAUD 30:7 |
| remove: fat greedy owl of the R. | RICH 260:1 |
| not malignant and r. it | WAUGH 344:1 |
| render: doth teach us all to r. | SHAK 289:27 |
| R. therefore unto Caesar | BIBLE 50:29 |
| rendezvous: r. with Death | SEEG 269:13 |
| renew: r. a right spirit | BOOK 67:10 |
| Reno'd: King's Moll R. | ANON 8:17 |
| renown: land of just and old r. | TENN 329:1 |
| r. on scraps of learning | YOUNG 360:13 |
| rent: R. is that portion | RIC 259:16 |
| That has not been r. | YEATS 358:20 |
| unearned increment of r. | MILL 224:14 |
| why? for r. | BYRON 84:25 |
| repair: friendship in constant r. | JOHN 184:4 |
| repay: I will r., saith the Lord | BIBLE 54:45 |
| Will find a Tiger well r. | BELL 33:2 |
| repeat: past are condemned to r. | SANT 266:22 |
| repeats: r. his words | SHAK 282:8 |
| repelled: only r. by man | INGE 178:13 |
| repent: r. at leisure | CONG 106:11 |
| R. ye | BIBLE 48:12 |
| weak alone r. | BYRON 85:16 |
| repentance: R. is but want of power | DRYD 128:11 |
| R. is the virtue of weak minds | DRYD 127:34 |
| R. on a Sunday | YBAR 358:11 |
| sinners to r. | BIBLE 49:23 |
| with the morning cool r. came | SCOTT 269:3 |
| repented: she strove, and much r. | BYRON 86:1 |
| repenting: r. at leisure | THOM 331:1 |
| repetition: r. of unpalatable truths | SUMM 319:5 |
| reply: the r. churlish | SHAK 273:12 |
| report: are of good r. | BIBLE 56:9 |
| reporter: mild-mannered r. | ANON 7:5 |

| | |
|---|---|
| reports: Bring me no more r. | SHAK 287:32 |
| R. of my death | TWAIN 336:7 |
| repose: r. is taboo'd by anxiety | GILB 151:15 |
| r. of a pacific station | ADAMS 1:7 |
| representation: Taxation without r. | OTIS 243:6 |
| representations: just r. of a general | JOHN 182:24 |
| representative: r. government | DISR 122:7 |
| Your r. owes you | BURKE 80:22 |
| repress: r. the speech they know | ELIOT 132:3 |
| reproof: r. valiant | SHAK 273:12 |
| republic: England is a disguised r. | BAG 26:10 |
| Love the Beloved R. | FORS 144:3 |
| r. is a raft | AMES 4:22 |
| r. is like a chicken | MITF 232:8 |
| republican: on r. principles | SHAW 302:9 |
| r. government in the United | TOCQ 333:3 |
| Republicans: We are R. | BURC 79:12 |
| republics: R. weak because | BAG 26:12 |
| repugnant: r. to the Word of God | BOOK 69:18 |
| repulsive: Right but R. | SELL 270:2 |
| reputation: At ev'ry word a r. dies | POPE 253:7 |
| I have lost my r. | SHAK 292:8 |
| plains of honour and r. | JONS 187:13 |
| Seeking the bubble r. | SHAK 272:26 |
| sold my r. for a song | FITZ 140:17 |
| spotless r. | SHAK 293:7 |
| wink a r. down | SWIFT 320:16 |
| reputations: home of ruined r. | ELIOT 132:6 |
| sit upon the murdered r. | CONG 106:15 |
| request: No flowers, by r. | AING 3:8 |
| requiem: R. aeternam dona eis | MISS 231:22 |
| requiescat: R. in pace | MISS 231:25 |
| require: doth the Lord r. of thee | BIBLE 47:23 |
| he thought 'e might r. | KIPL 197:14 |
| What is it men in women do r. | BLAKE 61:17 |
| required: thy soul shall be r. | BIBLE 52:19 |
| requisite: r. in business | ADD 2:20 |
| res: *in medias* r. | HOR 173:1 |
| research: steal from many, it's r. | MIZN 232:12 |
| resent: don't r. having nothing | COMP 106:4 |
| resign: Few die and none r. | JEFF 180:22 |
| resist: r. everything except temptation | WILDE 349:24 |
| R. not evil | BIBLE 48:23 |
| resistentialism: R. is concerned with | JENN 181:5 |
| resistible: r. rise of Arturo Ui | BREC 71:17 |
| resolute: Be bloody, bold, and r. | SHAK 287:20 |
| resolution: In war: r. | CHUR 100:4 |
| native hue of r. | SHAK 275:26 |
| resolve: R. to be thyself | ARN 17:13 |
| resolved: speech they r. not to make | ELIOT 132:3 |
| resource: infinite-r.-and-sagacity | KIPL 197:24 |
| resources: born to consume r. | HOR 173:7 |
| Inner R. | BERR 36:13 |
| r. of civilization | GLAD 153:12 |
| respect: child is owed the greatest r. | JUV 189:15 |
| icy precepts of r. | SHAK 296:22 |
| no r. of place, persons | SHAK 297:25 |
| R. was mingled with surprise | SCOTT 268:9 |
| We owe r. to the living | VOLT 340:24 |
| respectable: more r. he is | SHAW 301:16 |
| most devilish when r. | BROW 74:26 |
| respecter: God is no r. of persons | BIBLE 54:15 |
| respice: r. *finem* | ANON 13:20 |
| respiration: artificial r. | BURG 79:15 |
| responsibility: In dreams begins r. | YEATS 360:17 |
| Liberty means r. | SHAW 301:28 |
| no sense of r. | KNOX 198:20 |
| Power without r. | KIPL 198:5 |
| r. without power | STOP 318:1 |
| rest: far, far better r. that I go to | DICK 120:7 |
| flee away, and be at r. | BOOK 67:11 |
| Grant them eternal r. | MISS 231:22 |
| I will give you r. | BIBLE 49:35 |
| ordained no r. | VAUG 337:3 |

rest (cont.):
R. in soft peace                                    JONS 187:19
r. is literature                                    VALE 336:20
r. is mere fine writing                             VERL 337:20
r. is silence                                       SHAK 277:18
R., rest, perturbèd spirit                          SHAK 275:5
r. upon thy holy hill                               BOOK 66:13
Swift has sailed into his r.                        YEATS 360:2
talk about the r. of us                             ANON 10:20
Their place of r.                                   MILT 230:2
weary be at r.                                      BIBLE 42:27
restless: bind the r. wave                          WHIT 348:9
restoration: Church's R.                            BETJ 37:3
restored: Ransomed, healed, r.                      LYTE 212:21
R. to life, and power                               KEBLE 193:16
restorer: Tired Nature's sweet r.                   YOUNG 360:17
restraint: r. with which they write                 CAMP 88:16
result: r. happiness                                DICK 118:12
resurrection: certain hope of the R.                BOOK 66:8
I am the r., and the life                           BIBLE 53:32
R. of the body                                      BOOK 64:3
r. of the dead                                      BIBLE 55:17
r. they neither marry                               BIBLE 50:30
resuscitate: r. the dead art                        POUND 254:14
retainer: Old R. night and day                      BELL 33:6
reticence: Northern r.                              HEAN 164:11
R., in three volumes                                GLAD 153:14
retirement: there must be no r.                     HAIG 159:17
retort: r. courteous                                SHAK 273:12
retreat: honourable r.                              SHAK 273:3
I will not r. a single inch                         GARR 148:12
retreating: seen yourself r.                        NASH 237:18
retrenchment: r., and reform                        BRIG 72:3
retrograde: be not r.                               JONS 187:9
return: came through and I shall r.                 MAC 213:1
In that state I came, r.                            VAUG 337:10
r. into my house                                    BIBLE 50:3
r. no more to his house                             BIBLE 42:31
Should I never r.                                   MANS 217:15
spirit shall r. unto God                            BIBLE 44:26
unto dust shalt thou r.                             BIBLE 39:3
who does not r. your blow                           SHAW 302:8
returned: r. on the previous night                  BULL 78:7
returning: R. were as tedious                       SHAK 287:14
reveal: r. Himself to his servants                  MILT 231:2
revealed: Lord shall be r.                          BIBLE 46:9
revelation: Reason is natural r.                    LOCKE 208:16
revelations: It ends with R.                        WILDE 350:11
offers stupendous r.                                HOFF 170:5
revelry: sound of r. by night                       BYRON 85:2
revels: Our r. now are ended                        SHAK 296:10
revenge: r. for slight injuries                     MACH 214:23
R. is a kind of wild justice                        BACON 25:9
r. of the intellect                                 SONT 311:9
R. triumphs over death                              BACON 24:21
Sweet is r.                                         BYRON 86:2
sweet r. grows harsh                                SHAK 293:2
wrong us, shall we not r.                           SHAK 289:17
revenges: time brings in his r.                     SHAK 298:14
revenons: R. à ces moutons                          ANON 12:14
revenue: Instead of a standing r.                   BURKE 80:3
revenues: She bears a duke's r.                     SHAK 280:7
reverence: In deeper r. praise                      WHIT 348:27
none so poor to do him r.                           SHAK 281:21
reversion: no bright r. in the sky                  POPE 250:23
review: have your r. before me                      REGER 259:2
reviewing: book before r. it                        SMITH 310:9
revivals: art is the history of r.                  BUTL 84:14
revolting: r. and a rebellious heart                BIBLE 46:27
revolution: crust over a volcano of r.              ELLIS 136:6
explain the French R.                               BAUD 30:7
on the day after the r.                             AREN 15:5
R., like Satan, might devour                        VERG 337:19
revolutionary: r. in a bathroom                     LINK 207:17
r. will become a conservative                       AREN 15:5

revolutions: main cause of r.                       INGE 178:11
nursery of future r.                                BURKE 80:11
r. have ended in a reinforcement                    CAMUS 89:8
share in two r.                                     PAINE 244:15
revolving: returns with the r. year                 SHEL 303:7
reward: nothing for r.                              SPEN 313:11
r. against the innocent                             BOOK 66:14
rewards: Crimes are their own r.                    FARQ 138:17
Farewell, r. and Fairies                            CORB 107:23
rex: caecorum r. est luscus                         ERAS 137:14
R. tremendae maiestatis                             MISS 231:24
rhetoric: logic and r., able                        BACON 25:16
quarrel with others, r.                             YEATS 360:10
rhetorician: sophistical r.                         DISR 121:20
Rhine: king-like rolls the R.                       CALV 88:10
you think of the R.                                 BALD 27:6
rhyme: could not get a r. for roman                 FLEM 142:1
making beautiful old r.                             SHAK 300:4
names in many a musèd r.                            KEATS 192:3
outlive this powerful r.                            SHAK 299:19
R. being no necessary adjunct                       MILT 228:5
R. is still the most effective                      GIR 153:5
r. the rudder is of verses                          BUTL 83:25
still more tired of R.                              BELL 33:13
unattempted yet in prose or r.                      MILT 228:8
rhyming: born under a r. planet                     SHAK 291:26
modern bondage of r.                                MILT 228:6
r. is nat worth a toord                             CHAU 96:4
rhythmical: piece of r. grumbling                   ELIOT 135:4
rhythms: r. for bears to dance                      FLAU 141:7
Rialto: What news on the R.                         SHAK 288:31
rib: r., which the Lord                             BIBLE 38:21
riband: r. in the cap of youth                      SHAK 277:5
r. to stick in his coat                             BROW 76:13
ribbon: blue r. of the turf                         DISR 122:4
ribboned: sake of a r. coat                         NEWB 238:13
Ribstone: Right as a R. Pippin                      BELL 33:9
rice: r. pudding for dinner again                   MILNE 225:23
rich: dies r. dies disgraced                        CARN 90:27
Do you sincerely want to be r.                      CORN 108:4
ever by chance grow r.                              THOM 330:23
forbids the r. as well as the poor                  FRAN 145:2
from the r. man's table                             BIBLE 52:34
Isn't it r.                                         SOND 311:7
most r., being poor                                 SHAK 282:19
no sin, but to be r.                                SHAK 282:5
open to the poor and the r.                         ANON 7:9
orchestra is playing to the r.                      AUDEN 20:13
parish of r. women                                  AUDEN 20:22
passing r. with forty pounds                        GOLD 154:21
Poor little r. girl                                 COW 109:6
R. and rare were the gems                           MOORE 234:17
R. AND THE POOR                                     DISR 122:6
r. are different from you and me                    FITZ 140:20
r. beyond the dreams of                             JOHN 185:29
r. beyond the dreams of                             MOORE 234:5
r. get rich and the poor get                        KAHN 189:19
r. he hath sent empty away                          BIBLE 51:29
r. man in his castle                                ALEX 4:3
r. man to enter into                                BIBLE 50:22
r. men rule the law                                 GOLD 155:5
r. wot gets the gravy                               ANON 10:11
seems it r. to die                                  KEATS 192:3
something r. and strange                            SHAK 296:1
Richard: R.'s himself again                         CIBB 100:17
To put down R.                                      SHAK 277:26
richer: for r. for poorer                           BOOK 66:1
R. than all his tribe                               SHAK 293:5
riches: craving of the titled for r.                PEAR 246:26
embarrassment of r.                                 ALL 4:11
Infinite r. in a little room                        MARL 219:1
left hand r. and honour                             BIBLE 43:8
Let the world's r.                                  HERB 167:5
parade of r.                                        SMITH 308:22

road (cont.):

| | |
|---|---|
| Dreams are the royal r. | FREUD 146:1 |
| Golden R. to Samarkand | FLEC 141:17 |
| keep right on to the end of the r. | LAUD 202:5 |
| light to shine upon the r. | COWP 109:27 |
| Like one, that on a lonesome r. | COL 104:15 |
| merry r., a mazy road | CHES 98:2 |
| middle of the r. | BEVAN 38:5 |
| one more for the r. | MERC 223:11 |
| r. below me | STEV 317:25 |
| r. of excess leads | BLAKE 61:1 |
| r. that leads him to England | JOHN 184:9 |
| r. through the woods | KIPL 197:8 |
| r. to bring us daily nearer | KEBLE 193:17 |
| R. to Heaven | BALL 28:7 |
| r. to the City of Emeralds | BAUM 30:10 |
| r. to wealth so easy | TROL 334:14 |
| r. up and the road down | HER 166:10 |
| r. wind up-hill all the way | ROSS 263:5 |
| rolling English r. | CHES 98:1 |
| Softly along the r. of evening | DE L 116:21 |
| watched the ads, and not the r. | NASH 237:13 |
| winding r. before me | HAZL 164:8 |
| ye'll tak' the high r. | ANON 10:2 |
| yon braid, braid r. | BALL 28:7 |
| roads: By r. 'not adopted' | BETJ 37:12 |
| How many r. must a man | DYLAN 129:19 |
| lawless r. ran wrong | MUIR 236:6 |
| Two r. diverged in a wood | FROST 146:19 |
| roam: don't know where to r. | COLL 105:7 |
| Everywhere I r. | FOST 144:13 |
| who soar, but never r. | WORD 357:9 |
| roaming: R. in the gloamin' | LAUD 202:7 |
| where are you r. | SHAK 297:23 |
| roar: long, withdrawing r. | ARN 16:11 |
| mighty r. of London's traffic | ANON 9:23 |
| we should die of that r. | ELIOT 132:10 |
| roareth: What is this that r. thus | GODL 153:20 |
| roaring: But R. Bill | BELL 33:28 |
| r. of the wind is my wife | KEATS 193:9 |
| rob: r. a lady of her fortune | FIEL 139:11 |
| robbed: We was r. | JAC 179:1 |
| robber: Now Barabbas was a r. | BIBLE 54:2 |
| robe: intertissued r. | SHAK 279:16 |
| robes: washed their r. | BIBLE 57:26 |
| Robespierre: R. was nothing | HEINE 165:2 |
| Robey: R. is the Darling | SMITH 309:8 |
| robin: Call for the r.-red-breast | WEBS 344:25 |
| r. red breast in a cage | BLAKE 60:6 |
| Sweet R. sits in the bush | SCOTT 269:1 |
| Robinson: here's to you, Mrs R. | SIMON 307:6 |
| robot: r. may not injure | ASIM 19:1 |
| rock: I've gotten a r. | BLAM 62:8 |
| Politics, like R., Pop | WOLFE 353:9 |
| r. and a hard place | ANON 6:10 |
| R. journalism | ZAPPA 361:1 |
| R. of Ages, cleft for me | TOPL 333:14 |
| serpent upon a r. | BIBLE 44:4 |
| Sex and drugs and r. and roll | DURY 129:14 |
| tall r., the mountain | WORD 355:9 |
| upon this r. I will build | BIBLE 50:13 |
| rocked: R. in the cradle of the deep | WILL 350:27 |
| rocket: As he rose like a r. | PAINE 244:12 |
| long numbers that r. the mind | WILB 349:8 |
| Rockies: R. may crumble | GERS 150:7 |
| rocking: endlessly r. | WHIT 348:12 |
| R. and shocking the barmaid | SITW 307:18 |
| rocks: eternal r. beneath | BRON 72:17 |
| hand that r. the cradle | WALL 341:10 |
| older than the r. | PATER 246:13 |
| rifted r. whose entrance leads | MILT 226:16 |
| r. remain | HERB 166:15 |
| With r., and stones, and trees | WORD 356:25 |
| rod: all humbled kiss the r. | SHAK 298:17 |
| r. and thy staff comfort | BOOK 66:18 |

rod (cont.):

| | |
|---|---|
| r. out of the stem of Jesse | BIBLE 45:18 |
| spare the r., and spoil the child | BUTL 84:3 |
| spareth his r. hateth his son | BIBLE 43:23 |
| rode: r. madly off in all directions | LEAC 203:5 |
| R. the six hundred | TENN 323:15 |
| rogue: r. and peasant slave am I | SHAK 275:21 |
| Roland: R. to the dark tower | SHAK 283:18 |
| role: and not yet found a r. | ACH 1:3 |
| roll: r. all our strength | MARV 221:1 |
| R. on, thou deep and dark | BYRON 85:13 |
| R. up that map | PITT 249:9 |
| Sex and drugs and rock and r. | DURY 129:14 |
| rolled: r. along on wheels | HUXL 177:10 |
| bottoms of my trousers r. | ELIOT 134:2 |
| roller: r., pitch, and stumps | LANG 201:2 |
| rolling: Go r. down to Rio | KIPL 197:19 |
| jus' keeps r. along | HAMM 161:3 |
| r. English drunkard | CHES 98:1 |
| Roman: after the high R. fashion | SHAK 271:26 |
| antique R. than a Dane | SHAK 277:16 |
| Before the R. came to Rye | CHES 98:1 |
| Butchered to make a R. holiday | BYRON 85:10 |
| His noses cast is of the r. | FLEM 141:7 |
| I am a R. citizen | CIC 100:27 |
| nor R., nor an empire | VOLT 340:19 |
| noblest R. of them all | SHAK 282:2 |
| R.'s life, a Roman's arms | MAC 214:7 |
| R. thought hath struck him | SHAK 271:6 |
| To-day the R. and his trouble | HOUS 174:23 |
| Roman Catholic: [R. Church] | MAC 213:15 |
| romance: fine r. with no kisses | FIEL 139:14 |
| learned r. as she grew older | AUST 22:26 |
| music and love and r. | BERL 35:22 |
| symbols of a high r. | KEATS 192:20 |
| Romanism: R., and rebellion | BURC 79:12 |
| Romans: Friends, R., countrymen | SHAK 281:18 |
| romantic: airline ticket to r. places | MARV 221:4 |
| In a ruin that's r. | GILB 152:8 |
| In spite of all r. poets sing | LEAP 203:6 |
| R. Ireland's dead and gone | YEATS 359:28 |
| r. lie in the brain | AUDEN 21:11 |
| Wrong but R. | SELL 270:2 |
| romantics: We were the last r. | YEATS 358:18 |
| Romanus: Civis R. sum | CIC 100:27 |
| Rome: comen from R. al hoot | CHAU 95:23 |
| Everything in R. has its price | JUV 189:6 |
| go from the church of R. | WOTT 357:21 |
| grandeur that was R. | POE 250:9 |
| high and palmy state of R. | SHAK 274:1 |
| I loved R. more | SHAK 281:15 |
| Let R. in Tiber melt | SHAK 271:5 |
| O happy R., born when | CIC 101:2 |
| Oh R.! my country | BYRON 85:8 |
| R. has spoken | AUG 22:5 |
| second at R. | CAES 87:26 |
| voice of R. is the consent | JONS 187:1 |
| When in R. | AMBR 4:20 |
| when R. falls—the World | BYRON 85:11 |
| you cruel men of R. | SHAK 280:24 |
| Romeo: Come night! come, R.! | SHAK 295:13 |
| Give me my R. | SHAK 295:14 |
| wherefore art thou R. | SHAK 294:30 |
| Ronsard: R. sang of me | RONS 262:5 |
| roof: no r. to shroud | HEYW 168:9 |
| on a corrugated tin r. | BEEC 32:1 |
| shouldest come under my r. | BIBLE 49:16 |
| roofs: barbaric yawp over the r. | WHIT 348:22 |
| roof-tree: heavens my wide r. | AYT 23:18 |
| roof-wrecked: Is r. | HARDY 162:3 |
| rook: When the last r. | COL 104:21 |
| rooks: dull aunts, and croaking r. | POPE 251:24 |
| r. are blown about | TENN 325:2 |
| r. in families homeward go | HARDY 162:17 |
| room: All before my little r. | BROO 73:3 |

room (cont.):
boys in the back r. — LOES 209:5
end of the enormous r. — AUDEN 20:13
Fifty springs are little r. — HOUS 174:17
fill the r. my heart keeps empty — KING 195:5
Great hatred, little r. — YEATS 359:19
How little r. do we take up — SHIR 306:12
In every grave make r. — D'AV 114:9
Infinite riches in a little r. — MARL 219:1
make r. for men who shout — WALK 341:5
no r. for them in the inn — BIBLE 51:32
ocean sea, was not sufficient r. — BARN 29:7
r. at the top — WEBS 344:12
r. grows chilly — GRAH 156:4
r. in my heart for thee — ELL 136:1
r. of her own — WOOLF 354:1
R. to deny ourselves — KEBLE 193:17
sitting in the smallest r. — REGER 259:2
slipped away into the next r. — HOLL 170:12
smoke-filled r. — SIMP 307:11
struggle for r. and food — MALT 217:6
taper to the outward r. — DONNE 123:19
upper r. furnished — BIBLE 52:40
rooms: boys in the back r. — BEAV 31:4
In council r. apart — RICE 259:18
lighted r. inside your head — LARK 201:16
Other voices, other r. — CAP 89:15
roost: always come home to r. — SOUT 311:21
root: knotty as a r. — BRON 72:15
March hath perced to the r. — CHAU 95:10
money is the r. of all evil — BIBLE 56:19
nips his r. — SHAK 280:18
roots: drought is destroying his r. — HERB 166:11
shall grow out of his r. — BIBLE 45:18
rope: fourfold r. of nerves — HEAT 164:13
set his hand to a r. — DRAKE 126:12
Rose: R., were you not extremely — PRIOR 255:12
rose: American beauty r. — ROCK 261:11
As though a r. should shut — KEATS 190:20
beauty's r. might never die — SHAK 299:11
blossom as the r. — BIBLE 46:4
Christmas I no more desire a r. — SHAK 284:11
English unofficial r. — BROO 73:4
fading r. — CAREW 89:20
Faintly the inimitable r. — WINC 352:3
fayr as is the r. in May — CHAU 96:11
fire and the r. — ELIOT 133:13
fresh lap of the crimson r. — SHAK 290:13
Gather therefore the r. — SPEN 313:12
glut thy sorrow on a morning r. — KEATS 191:26
Go, lovely r. — WALL 341:12
I know the colour r. — ABSE 1:1
Into the r.-garden — ELIOT 132:26
labyrinthine buds the r. — BROW 77:14
last r. of summer — MOORE 234:18
lovely is the r. — WORD 355:18
mighty lak' a r. — STAN 314:11
musk of the r. — TENN 326:28
never blows so red the r. — FITZ 140:8
never promised you a r. garden — GREEN 158:1
No thorns go as deep as a r.'s — SWIN 321:9
O, my Luve's like a red, red r. — BURNS 82:20
One perfect r. — PARK 245:7
O R., thou art sick — BLAKE 62:4
ravage with impunity a r. — BROW 77:15
r. by any other name — SHAK 294:31
R. is a rose is a rose — STEIN 314:22
r. of Sharon — BIBLE 44:31
r. of the fair state — SHAK 276:2
r. of yesterday — FITZ 140:5
r.-red city half as old as Time — BURG 79:17
Roves back the r. — DE L 116:12
sad R. of all my days — YEATS 360:4
scent is of the summer r. — GRAV 156:13
secret and inviolate R. — YEATS 359:26

rose (cont.):
vanish with the r. — FITZ 140:18
white r. weeps — TENN 327:1
without thorn the r. — MILT 229:8
rosebud: Queen rose of the r. garden — TENN 326:29
rosebuds: Gather ye r. — HERR 167:24
rosemary: r. and rue — SHAK 298:29
r., that's for remembrance — SHAK 277:2
Rosencrantz: R. and Guildenstern — SHAK 277:20
roses: ash the burnt r. leave — ELIOT 133:8
days of wine and r. — DOWS 125:13
Everything's coming up r. — SOND 311:5
Flung r., roses, riotously — DOWS 125:12
forget the lilac and the r. — ARAG 14:21
not a bed of r. — STEV 317:8
raptures and r. of vice — SWIN 321:7
R. are flowering in Picardy — WEAT 344:5
r. for the flush of youth — ROSS 263:3
roses, r., all the way — BROW 76:24
scent of the r. — MOORE 234:13
Treaties are like girls and r. — DE G 116:4
rosy: old plain men have r. faces — STEV 317:18
r. morn long since left — SPEN 313:5
rosy-fingered: R. dawn — HOMER 171:2
rot: cold obstruction and to r. — SHAK 288:21
R. half a grain a day — SHAK 293:3
we r. and rot — SHAK 272:22
rotted: Or simply r. early — NASH 237:14
rotten: It's always the good feel r. — YES 360:1
r. in the state of Denmark — SHAK 274:29
rotundity: thick r. o' the world — SHAK 283:6
rough: from children who were r. — SPEN 312:25
r. places plain — BIBLE 46:9
r. than polished diamond — CHES 97:12
this r. magic — SHAK 296:12
winter and r. weather — SHAK 272:19
rough-hew: R. them how we will — SHAK 277:12
round: little r., fat, oily man — THOM 331:21
R. and round the circle — ELIOT 132:24
r. earth's imagined corners — DONNE 123:7
R. the world for ever and aye — ARN 16:17
R. up the usual suspects — EPST 137:12
test of a r. character — FORS 143:17
rounded: r. with a sleep — SHAK 296:10
Roundheads: R. (Right but — SELL 270:2
Rousseau: mock on Voltaire R. — BLAKE 61:13
not ask Jean Jacques R. — COWP 109:29
[R.] is the first militant — BERL 36:5
whose soul R. had created — HEINE 165:2
rover: blood's a r. — HOUS 174:14
roves: R. back the rose — DE L 116:12
roving: we'll go no more a-r. — BYRON 87:8
row: gate-bars hang in a r. — HARDY 162:17
r. one way and look another — BURT 83:7
rowed: All r. fast, but none so fast — COKE 103:6
rowing: one way, and r. another — BUNY 79:1
royal: Dreams are the r. road — FREUD 146:1
no 'r. road' to geometry — EUCL 137:21
r. banners forward go — FORT 144:5
r. priesthood — BIBLE 57:8
r. throne of kings — SHAK 293:16
subjects with a r. wage — BROO 72:21
this is the r. Law — COR 108:10
royalist: more of a r. than the king — ANON 12:8
royalty: R. is the gold filling — OSB 242:26
R. . . . lay it on with a trowel — DISR 122:20
R. will be strong — BAG 26:12
rub: there's the r. — SHAK 275:25
r. up against money — RUNY 264:8
rubbish: What r.! — BLÜC 62:11
rubies: her price is far above r. — BIBLE 44:6
price of wisdom is above r. — BIBLE 43:2
R. unparagoned — SHAK 273:24
rubs: r. nor botches in the work — SHAK 287:2
rudder: My heart was to thy r. tied — SHAK 271:18

rudder (*cont.*):
 rhyme the r. is of verses | BUTL 83:25
ruddier: O r. than the cherry | GAY 149:1
ruddy: Now he was r. | BIBLE 41:16
rude: only rather r. and wild | BELL 33:11
 R. am I in my speech | SHAK 291:33
 r. heap together hurled | MARV 221:2
Rudyards: R. cease from kipling | STEP 315:5
rue: nought shall make us r. | SHAK 282:15
 there's rosemary and r. | SHAK 298:29
 There's r. for you | SHAK 277:3
ruffle: Would r. up your spirits | SHAK 281:26
rug: cockatoo upon a r. | STEV 316:12
rugged: cling to the old r. cross | BENN 34:10
 harsh cadence of a r. line | DRYD 128:21
 system of r. individualism | HOOV 171:17
Ruh: *Meine R.' ist hin* | GOET 154:6
ruin: boy will r. himself | GEOR 150:1
 formless r. of oblivion | SHAK 297:10
 Majestic though in r. | MILT 228:27
 R. seize thee, ruthless King! | GRAY 157:1
 r. that Cromwell knocked about | SULL 31:21
 r. that's romantic | GILB 152:8
 sand and r. and gold | SWIN 321:19
 With ruin upon r. | MILT 229:1
ru-i-n: Since roving's been my r. | ANON 6:5
ruined: home of r. reputations | ELIOT 132:6
 O r. piece of nature | SHAK 283:24
 r. on the side of their natural | BURKE 81:7
ruining: R. along the illimitable inane | TENN 326:21
ruinous: R. inheritance | GAIUS 147:13
ruins: shored against my r. | ELIOT 134:31
 human mind in r. | DAV 114:16
Ruislip: Gaily into R. Gardens | BETJ 37:7
rule: little r., a little sway | DYER 129:17
 only infallible r. | SURT 319:7
 Rowe's R. | DICK 120:19
 R. 1, on page 1, of the book of war | MONT 233:23
 R., Britannia, rule the waves | THOM 331:20
 R. of Three doth puzzle me | ANON 9:11
 Who can r. and dare not lie | TENN 326:26
ruler: R. of the Queen's Navee | GILB 152:18
 r. in Israel | BIBLE 47:22
rulers: brought about by r. | BIER 59:6
 r. of the darkness | BIBLE 56:4
 R. of the Queen's Navee | GILB 152:20
rules: fundamental R. of Robotics | ASIM 19:1
 golden r. for an orchestra | BEEC 31:23
 hand that r. the world | WALL 341:10
 people wouldn't obey the r. | BENN 34:15
 R. and models destroy genius | HAZL 164:5
rulest: thou r. in might | SMITH 310:15
ruling: r. passion conquers reason | POPE 251:14
 Search then the R. Passion | POPE 251:21
rum: r. and true religion | BYRON 86:5
 r., Romanism, and rebellion | BURC 79:12
 r., sodomy, and the lash | CHUR 100:6
 what a R. Go everything is | WELLS 345:19
 Yo-ho-ho, and a bottle of r. | STEV 317:2
rumble: r. of a distant drum | FITZ 140:7
 R. thy bellyful | SHAK 283:7
rumour: distillation of r. | CARL 90:12
rumours: r. of wars | BIBLE 50:33
rump: R. Parliament | SELL 270:3
run: Gwine to r. all day | FOST 144:10
 r., though not to soar | MAC 213:21
 R., run, Orlando | SHAK 273:2
 r. to and fro like sparks | BIBLE 47:29
 They get r. down | BEVAN 38:5
 till thou r. out thy race | MILT 228:3
 true love never did r. smooth | SHAK 290:13
 yet we will make him r. | MARV 221:1
runcible: ate with a r. spoon | LEAR 203:13
 R. Cat with crimson whiskers | LEAR 203:15
runic: In a sort of R. rhyme | POE 250:4

runnable: r. stag, a kingly crop | DAV 114:11
runners: Song of the Ungirt R. | SORL 311:15
running: R. it never runs from us | DONNE 123:22
 shaken together, and r. over | BIBLE 52:7
 she'll be constantly r. back | HOR 173:11
 takes all the r. *you* can do | CARR 91:18
Rupert: R. of Debate | BULW 78:9
 R. of Parliamentary discussion | DISR 121:8
rural: lovely woman in a r. spot | HUNT 176:17
 r. quiet, friendship | THOM 331:23
rus: *R. in urbe* | MART 220:8
rushes: *Green grow the r. O* | ANON 8:6
 Green grow the r. O | BURNS 82:9
rushing: r. mighty wind | BIBLE 54:8
russet: r. yeas | SHAK 284:19
russet-coated: r. captain | CROM 111:24
Russia: between R. and British India | SAL 266:3
 forecast to you the action of R. | CHUR 99:10
 R. has two generals | NICH 239:11
Russian: might have been a R. | GILB 152:21
 tumult in the R. heart | PUSH 256:23
rust: moth and r. doth corrupt | BIBLE 49:1
 To r. unburnished | TENN 328:21
 wear out than to r. out | CUMB 112:15
rusty: r. curb of old father antick | SHAK 277:24
Ruth: Through the sad heart of R. | KEATS 192:5
Rye: Before the Roman came to R. | CHES 98:1
rye: catcher in the r. | SAL 266:1
 Comin thro' the r. | BURNS 81:29
 fields of barley and of r. | TENN 325:34
 r. reach to the chin | PEELE 247:2

# S

sabbath: Remember the s. day | BIBLE 40:7
 s. was made for man | BIBLE 51:18
sable: paint the s. skies | DRUM 127:1
 son of the s. Night | DAN 113:15
sable-vested: S. Night | MILT 228:32
Sabrina: S. fair | MILT 226:21
sack: intolerable deal of s. | SHAK 278:2
 S. the lot | FISH 139:23
sacrament: by this word S. | BOOK 65:23
 This great S. revere | THOM 330:4
sacraments: S. in a tongue not | BOOK 69:18
sacred: only s. thing | FRAN 145:1
sacrifice: be an evening s. | BOOK 69:8
 final s. | SPR 313:26
 full, perfect, and sufficient s. | BOOK 65:16
 holy hush of ancient s. | STEV 316:12
 s. in a contemptible struggle | BURKE 81:4
 Still stands Thine ancient S. | KIPL 197:2
 Too long a s. | YEATS 359:2
 To pay thy morning s. | KEN 193:20
 To see the approaching s. | MILM 225:13
 turn delight into a s. | HERB 166:21
 your bodies a living s. | BIBLE 54:43
 your prayers one sweet s. | SHAK 280:14
sacrificed: s. to expediency | MAUG 222:8
sacrifices: forgive him for the s. | MAUG 222:10
sad: All my s. captains | SHAK 271:19
 all their songs are s. | CHES 97:20
 How s. and bad and mad it was | BROW 75:21
 mine a s. one | SHAK 288:27
 remember and be s. | ROSS 263:4
 s., black isle | BAUD 30:5
 s. stories of the death of kings | SHAK 293:27
 s. tale's best for winter | SHAK 298:22
 s. vicissitude of things | STER 315:27
 s. words of tongue or pen | WHIT 349:1
 With how s. steps | SIDN 306:18
 Your s. tires in a mile-a | SHAK 298:28
sadder: s. and a wiser man | COL 104:19

| | |
|---|---|
| saddest: tell of s. thought | SHEL 305:10 |
| wisest aunt telling the s. tale | SHAK 290:21 |
| saddle: Boot, s., to horse | BROW 75:17 |
| Come s. your horses | SCOTT 268:7 |
| Things are in the s. | EMER 136:13 |
| saddled: he s. his ass, and arose | BIBLE 41:26 |
| s. and bridled to be ridden | RUMB 264:5 |
| sadly: take their pleasures s. | SULLY 319:4 |
| saeclorum: integro s. nascitur | VIRG 339:25 |
| safe: s. course for the defeated | VIRG 339:6 |
| s. for democracy | WILS 351:21 |
| s. to be unpopular | STEV 316:18 |
| s. to go back in the water | ANON 8:15 |
| We are none of us s. | FORS 143:22 |
| world s. for hypocrisy | WOLFE 353:6 |
| safeguard: s. of the West | WORD 356:2 |
| safeliest: s. when with one man manned | DONNE 123:6 |
| safely: most s. by the middle way | OVID 243:13 |
| safer: s. for a prince to be feared | MACH 215:1 |
| s. than a known way | HASK 163:16 |
| safest: Just when we are s. | BROW 75:13 |
| safety: pluck this flower, s. | SHAK 277:30 |
| s., honour, and welfare | CHAR 95:1 |
| source of my light and my s. | BIBLE 58:9 |
| sagacity: infinite-resource-and-s. | KIPL 197:24 |
| sagas: our eyes the frosty s. | CRANE 110:31 |
| sager: s. sort our deeds reprove | CAMP 89:2 |
| said: fool hath s. in his heart | BOOK 66:12 |
| s. the thing which was not | SWIFT 320:1 |
| sail: comes i' faith full s. | CONG 106:17 |
| in a sieve I'll thither s. | SHAK 285:3 |
| S. and sail, with unshut eye | ARN 16:17 |
| s. on, O Ship of State | LONG 209:11 |
| sea-mark of my utmost s. | SHAK 293:4 |
| white and rustling s. | CUNN 113:7 |
| sailed: s. away for a year | LEAR 203:12 |
| s. the seas and come to | YEATS 359:22 |
| She hadna s. a league | BALL 27:16 |
| sailing: which port one is s. | SEN 270:7 |
| sailor: Home is the s. | STEV 317:22 |
| saint: England and S. George | SHAK 279:6 |
| little s. best fits a little shrine | HERR 167:22 |
| neither s. nor sophist-led | ARN 16:13 |
| s. in crape is twice | POPE 251:20 |
| S., n. A dead sinner | BIER 59:9 |
| saw my late espousèd s. | MILT 230:24 |
| worst of madmen is a s. | POPE 252:27 |
| sainted: thing enskyed and s. | SHAK 288:10 |
| saints: Communion of S. | BOOK 64:3 |
| pair of carved s. | SHAK 294:2 |
| Where s. immortal reign | WATTS 343:11 |
| with thy choir of s. | DONNE 123:16 |
| sais: Que s.-je? | MONT 233:18 |
| saisons: Ô s., ô châteaux | RIMB 260:10 |
| sake: Christ's particular love's s. | BROW 77:7 |
| country for his country's s. | FITZ 140:3 |
| loseth his life for my s. | BIBLE 49:33 |
| O, who am I, that for my s. | CROS 112:13 |
| salad: My s. days | SHAK 271:12 |
| Our Garrick's a s. | GOLD 155:1 |
| sale: From s. and profanation | CHES 97:24 |
| salesman: Death of a S. | MILL 225:22 |
| s. is got to dream | MILL 225:4 |
| salley: Down by the s. gardens | YEATS 359:1 |
| Sally: S. in our Alley | CAREY 90:2 |
| sally: I make a sudden s. | TENN 323:12 |
| salmon: s. sing in the street | AUDEN 20:11 |
| salt: pillar of s. | BIBLE 39:15 |
| s., estranging sea | ARN 17:23 |
| s. is the taste of another's bread | DANTE 113:23 |
| s. of the earth | BIBLE 48:20 |
| s. of the earth | WEST 346:25 |
| seasoned with s. | BIBLE 56:12 |
| verge of the s. flood | SHAK 296:24 |

| | |
|---|---|
| Salteena: Mr S. was an elderly man | ASHF 18:20 |
| salus: S. populi suprema est lex | CIC 100:20 |
| s. victis nullam sperare | VIRG 339:6 |
| salute: If it moves, s. it | ANON 8:4 |
| S. one another | BIBLE 55:2 |
| S. the happy morn | BYROM 84:23 |
| who are about to die s. you | ANON 13:12 |
| salva: S. me, fons pietatis | MISS 231:24 |
| salvation: My bottle of s. | RAL 257:23 |
| none of us should see s. | SHAK 289:27 |
| no s. outside the church | AUG 21:26 |
| now is the day of s. | BIBLE 55:25 |
| publisheth s. | BIBLE 46:15 |
| s. with fear and trembling | BIBLE 56:6 |
| There cannot be s. | CYPR 113:14 |
| Wot prawce S. nah | SHAW 301:11 |
| salve: S., regina | ANON 13:21 |
| Sam: nephew of my Uncle S.'s | COHAN 103:5 |
| Play it again, S. | EPST 137:10 |
| Samarkand: Golden Road to S. | FLEC 141:19 |
| same: the s. yesterday | BIBLE 56:30 |
| he is much the s. | ANON 6:1 |
| I'm having the s. | LOES 209:5 |
| more they are the s. | KARR 190:2 |
| s. a hundred years hence | DICK 119:14 |
| s. the whole world over | ANON 10:11 |
| we must all say the s. | MELB 222:20 |
| you are the s. you | MART 220:7 |
| samite: Clothed in white s. | TENN 324:3 |
| Samson: S. hath quit himself | MILT 230:17 |
| sancta: O s. simplicitas! | HUSS 176:21 |
| sed s. simplicitas | JER 181:8 |
| sanctuary: dark s. of incapacity | CHES 97:4 |
| three classes which need s. | BALD 27:10 |
| sanctus: S., sanctus, sanctus | MISS 231:17 |
| sand: land of s. and ruin | SWIN 321:19 |
| on the edge of his s. | LEAR 203:13 |
| s. against the wind | BLAKE 61:13 |
| Such quantities of s. | CARR 91:21 |
| To see a world in a grain of s. | BLAKE 60:5 |
| sandal: And his s. shoon | SHAK 276:32 |
| sandals: morn went out with s. | MILT 227:19 |
| sandalwood: S., cedarwood | MAS 221:18 |
| sands: Come unto these yellow s. | SHAK 295:36 |
| Footprints on the s. of time | LONG 209:23 |
| s. upon the Red sea shore | BLAKE 61:14 |
| sandwich: raw-onion s. | BARN 29:6 |
| San Francisco: left my heart in S. | CROSS 112:10 |
| sang: s. his didn't he danced | CUMM 112:16 |
| s. in my chains | THOM 330:9 |
| s. within the bloody wood | ELIOT 134:17 |
| sanglots: Les s. longs | VERL 337:21 |
| sanitary: glorified s. engineer | STR 318:13 |
| sans: s. End | FITZ 140:9 |
| s. everything | SHAK 272:28 |
| sap: dried the s. out of my veins | YEATS 359:4 |
| world's whole s. is sunk | DONNE 124:8 |
| sapere: s. aude | HOR 173:8 |
| sapient: s. sutlers of the Lord | ELIOT 134:5 |
| sapless: s. foliage of the ocean | SHEL 304:7 |
| Sappho: burning S. loved | BYRON 86:13 |
| Sarah: it ceased to be with S. | BIBLE 39:14 |
| Sargent: musical Malcolm S. | BEEC 32:2 |
| sashes: one of his nice new s. | GRAH 156:4 |
| sassy: I'm sickly but s. | HARR 163:4 |
| sat: I s. down and wept | SMART 308:15 |
| S. and knotted all the while | SEDL 269:12 |
| s. too long here | CROM 112:4 |
| upon which everyone has s. | CUMM 112:18 |
| we s. down and wept | BOOK 69:2 |
| when they have s. down | CHUR 99:5 |
| Satan: capital of S. and his peers | MILT 228:21 |
| Get thee behind me, S. | BIBLE 50:14 |
| Lord said unto S. | BIBLE 42:21 |

| | |
|---|---|
| **Satan** (*cont.*): | |
| messenger of S. | BIBLE 55:28 |
| my S., thou art but a dunce | BLAKE 60:15 |
| S. finds some mischief | WATTS 343:6 |
| S. met his ancient friend | BYRON 87:13 |
| **Satanic:** dark S. mills | BLAKE 61:12 |
| **'satiable:** full of s. curtiosity | KIPL 197:21 |
| **satin:** always goes into white s. | SHER 305:24 |
| **satire:** S. is a sort of glass | SWIFT 319:17 |
| S. is what closes Saturday | KAUF 190:3 |
| S. or sense, alas | POPE 251:7 |
| **satirical:** certain sign of a s. wit | AUBR 19:21 |
| **satisfaction:** I can't get no s. | RICH 179:6 |
| **satisfied:** Never s. with having | WROTH 358:1 |
| well paid that is well s. | SHAK 289:30 |
| **satisfies:** Where most she s. | SHAK 271:17 |
| **satisfy:** That poorly s. our eyes | WOTT 357:16 |
| **satisfying:** s. a voracious appetite | FIEL 139:10 |
| **Saturday:** For what he did on S. | YBAR 358:11 |
| Glasgow Empire on a S. night | DODD 122:29 |
| Satire is what closes S. night | KAUF 190:3 |
| **Saturn:** days of S.'s reign return | VIRG 339:25 |
| **Saturnia:** *redeunt S. regna* | VIRG 339:25 |
| **satyr:** Hyperion to a s. | SHAK 274:11 |
| **satyrs:** My men, like s. grazing | MARL 218:15 |
| **sauce:** Hunger is the best s. | CERV 93:17 |
| religions, and only one s. | CAR 89:17 |
| **saucy:** with s. looks | SHAK 284:10 |
| **Saul:** S. and Jonathan were lovely | BIBLE 41:22 |
| S., why persecutest thou me | BIBLE 54:11 |
| **savage:** noble s. | DRYD 127:26 |
| s. place | COL 103:23 |
| s. wields his club | HUXL 177:16 |
| soothe a s. breast | CONG 106:11 |
| take some s. woman | TENN 326:15 |
| Unequal laws unto a s. race | TENN 328:19 |
| **savaged:** s. by a dead sheep | HEAL 164:10 |
| **save:** destroy the town to s. it | ANON 8:10 |
| God s. the king | HOGG 170:8 |
| he shall s. his soul alive | BIBLE 47:6 |
| himself he cannot s. | BIBLE 51:15 |
| little less democracy to s. | ATK 19:10 |
| matter enough to s. | BROW 76:12 |
| s. Europe by her example | PITT 249:8 |
| s. me, from the candid friend | CANN 89:12 |
| s. me, O source of pity | MISS 231:24 |
| s. my soul | ANON 9:22 |
| s. them by the barrel-load | THOM 331:13 |
| s. those that have no imagination | SHAW 302:21 |
| To s. your world you asked | AUDEN 20:17 |
| We shall nobly s. | LINC 207:6 |
| **saved:** could have s. sixpence | BECK 31:8 |
| He s. others | BIBLE 51:15 |
| they only s. the world | CHES 97:23 |
| What must I do to be s. | BIBLE 54:17 |
| **saving:** thy s. health among all | BOOK 67:16 |
| **saviour:** S. of the world was born | BYROM 84:23 |
| S.'s birth is celebrated | SHAK 274:2 |
| **savour:** salt have lost his s. | BIBLE 48:20 |
| Seeming and s. all the winter | SHAK 298:29 |
| **saw:** Nor do not s. the air | SHAK 276:4 |
| **say:** all s. *the same* | MELB 222:20 |
| don't s. nothin' | HAMM 161:3 |
| easier to s. what it is not | JOHN 185:11 |
| Have something to s. | ARN 18:13 |
| I have nothing to s. | CAGE 88:4 |
| I s. the hell with it | WHITE 347:15 |
| know what they are going to s. | CHUR 99:5 |
| more to s. when I am dead | ROB 260:20 |
| Need we s. it was not love | MILL 224:23 |
| nothing to say, s. nothing | COLT 105:16 |
| s. what they please | FRED 145:19 |
| s. what you mean | CARR 91:6 |
| s. why and how I became | WILS 351:16 |
| someone else has got to s. | GASK 148:18 |

| | |
|---|---|
| **say** (*cont.*): | |
| think till I see what I s. | WALL 341:11 |
| We must not s. so | BERR 36:13 |
| Whatever you s., s. nothing | HEAN 164:11 |
| **saying:** and I am s. it | CAGE 88:4 |
| For loving, and for s. so | DONNE 124:14 |
| not know what they are s. | CHUR 99:5 |
| something is not worth s. | BEAU 30:15 |
| We were s. yesterday | LUIS 212:7 |
| **scabbard:** he threw away the s. | CLAR 101:9 |
| **scaffold:** Truth forever on the s. | LOW 211:8 |
| **scale:** puts his thumb in the s. | LAWR 202:12 |
| **scales:** someone is practising s. | MACN 216:9 |
| **scallop-shell:** s. of quiet | RAL 257:23 |
| **scan:** gently s. your brother man | BURNS 81:21 |
| **scandal:** love and s. are the best | FIEL 139:9 |
| no s. like rags | FARQ 138:15 |
| Retired to their tea and s. | CONG 106:6 |
| s. by a woman of easy virtue | HAIL 160:1 |
| s. that constitutes offence | MOL 232:24 |
| **scandalous:** s. and poor | ROCH 261:8 |
| **scapegoat:** s. into the wilderness | BIBLE 40:13 |
| **scarecrow:** s. of the law | SHAK 288:12 |
| **scarecrows:** s. of fools | HUXL 177:20 |
| **scarf:** S. up the tender eye | SHAK 287:6 |
| **scarlet:** Cowards in s. | GRAN 156:11 |
| His sins were s. | BELL 33:27 |
| love that loves a s. coat | HOOD 171:6 |
| raise the s. standard high | CONN 106:23 |
| though clothed in s. | JONS 187:10 |
| Though your sins be as s. | BIBLE 45:4 |
| **scars:** He jests at s. | SHAK 294:29 |
| **scattered:** he hath s. the proud | BIBLE 51:29 |
| S. his Maker's image | DRYD 127:3 |
| **scene:** Speaks a new s. | QUAR 257:1 |
| start a s. or two | ELIOT 134:1 |
| **scenery:** end of all natural s. | RUSK 264:13 |
| S. is fine | KEATS 193:5 |
| s.'s divine | CALV 88:10 |
| Standing among savage s. | HOFF 170:5 |
| Where God paints the s. | HART 163:10 |
| **scenes:** I long for s. where man | CLARE 101:7 |
| no more behind your s. | JOHN 183:24 |
| **scent:** I s. the morning air | SHAK 275:1 |
| s. is of the summer rose | GRAV 156:13 |
| s. of the roses | MOORE 234:13 |
| sweetest flower for s. | SHEL 304:31 |
| whose is the s. the fair annoys | COWP 109:21 |
| **sceptic:** to much of a s. to deny | HUXL 177:22 |
| What ever s. could inquire | BUTL 83:22 |
| **sceptre:** s. and the ball | SHAK 279:16 |
| s. for a palmer's walking staff | SHAK 294:2 |
| s. from tyrants | TURG 335:16 |
| **sceptred:** this s. isle | SHAK 293:16 |
| what avails the s. race | LAND 200:23 |
| **sceptreless:** S., free | SHEL 304:22 |
| **schemes:** best laid s. o' mice an' men | BURNS 82:27 |
| s. of political improvement | JOHN 184:22 |
| **schizophrenic:** you are a s. | SZASZ 321:25 |
| **Schleswig-Holstein:** S. question | PALM 244:21 |
| **scholar:** better s. than Wordsworth | HOUS 175:6 |
| ills the s.'s life assail | JOHN 183:12 |
| s. all Earth's volumes carry | CHAP 94:21 |
| **scholars:** S. dispute | HOR 172:25 |
| **school:** language, goeth to s. | BACON 25:17 |
| s. of Manchester | DISR 122:13 |
| Three little maids from s. | GILB 151:21 |
| till he's been to a good s. | SAKI 265:20 |
| Unwillingly to s. | SHAK 272:25 |
| vixen when she went to s. | SHAK 290:33 |
| **schoolboy:** every s. knows | MAC 213:13 |
| Not the s. heat | TENN 325:28 |
| tell what every s. knows | SWIFT 320:15 |
| whining s. | SHAK 272:25 |
| **schoolboys:** s. from their books | SHAK 295:2 |

schoolboys (cont.):
s. playing in the stream — PEELE 247:2
schoolchildren: What all s. learn — AUDEN 21:10
schoolman: knew no s.'s subtle art — POPE 251:9
schoolmaster: becoming a s. — WAUGH 343:19
schoolmasters: Let s. puzzle — GOLD 155:8
schoolrooms: build s. for 'the boy' — COOK 107:17
schools: hundred s. of thought — MAO 218:1
lumber of the s. — SWIFT 320:18
schooner: It was the s. Hesperus — LONG 210:5
sciatica: S.: he cured it — AUBR 20:1
science: Dismal S. — CARL 90:18
Enough of s. and of art — WORD 357:5
essence of s. — BRON 72:10
How s. dwindles — YOUNG 360:16
Language the instrument of s. — JOHN 182:4
only applications of s. — PAST 246:12
s. and study of man — CHAR 95:9
S. is an edged tool — EDD 130:13
S. is built up of facts — POIN 250:10
s. is either physics or stamp — RUTH 265:8
s. is nothing but trained — HUXL 177:16
S. is organized knowledge — SPEN 312:15
s. is strong and religion weak — SZASZ 322:1
S. means simply the aggregate — VALÉ 336:20
S. moves, but slowly slowly — TENN 326:13
s. must begin with myths — POPP 253:16
s. of politics — ARIS 15:13
s. reassures — BRAQ 71:14
s. the credit goes to the man — DARW 114:7
S. without religion is lame — EINS 131:11
tragedy of S. — HUXL 177:15
typical triumph of modern s. — WAUGH 344:1
sciences: That great mother of s. — BACON 25:27
scientific: broken open on s. principles — PEAC 246:23
judgement of our s. age — HOLM 170:13
s. faith's absurd — BROW 75:27
s. truth does not triumph — PLAN 249:12
scientist: distinguished s. says — CLAR 101:14
research s. to discard — LOR 210:11
scientists: in the company of s. — AUDEN 21:18
scintillations: s. of your wit — GOUL 155:26
scissor-man: long, red-legged s. — HOFF 169:21
scoff: who came to s. — GOLD 154:22
scoffer: dull product of a s.'s pen — WORD 354:20
scones: Over buttered s. — ELIOT 132:22
scope: and that man's s. — SHAK 299:14
scorer: One Great S. comes — RICE 259:17
scorn: deal of s. looks beautiful — SHAK 298:6
fixed figure for the time of s. — SHAK 292:24
laugh no man to s. — BIBLE 47:33
little s. is alluring — CONG 106:19
S. not the Sonnet — WORD 356:21
scorned: fury, like a woman s. — CONG 106:12
scorpions: chastise you with s. — BIBLE 41:34
Scotch: Mary, ma S. Bluebell — LAUD 202:6
scotched: We have s. the snake — SHAK 287:3
Scotchman: noblest prospect which a S. — JOHN 184:9
Scotia: chief of S.'s food — BURNS 82:2
Scotland: from S. but I cannot help it — JOHN 184:6
I'll be in S. afore ye — ANON 10:2
in S. supports the people — JOHN 182:9
love S. better than truth — JOHN 182:14
S., land of the omnipotent No — BOLD 63:2
shivered was fair S.'s spear — SCOTT 268:23
Stands S. where it did — SHAK 287:24
Scots: S., wha hae — BURNS 82:21
Scotsman: S. on the make — BARR 29:17
Scotty: Beam me up, S. — RODD 261:13
scoundrel: last refuge of a s. — JOHN 185:4
man over forty is a s. — SHAW 302:5
scout: s. 'em, and flout 'em — SHAK 296:7
scouts: s.' motto is founded — BAD 26:1
scowl: With anxious s. drew near — AYT 23:16
scrap: just for a s. of paper — BETH 36:15

scraps: stolen the s. — SHAK 284:17
scratch: all you can do is s. it — BEEC 32:4
quick sharp s. — BROW 76:17
S. the Christian — ZANG 360:26
s. the nurse — SHAK 298:17
scratches: S. its innocent behind — AUDEN 21:2
scratching: s. of a pen — LOVER 210:22
s. of pimples on the body — WOOLF 354:6
world to the s. of my finger — HUME 176:11
scream: s. and s. till I'm thick — CROM 111:23
screw: s. your courage — SHAK 286:6
Turn of the S. — JAMES 180:3
scribblative: arts babblative and s. — SOUT 312:3
scribble: Always s., scribble — GLOU 153:17
s., to a man — POPE 252:29
we all s. poems — HOR 173:16
scribbled: Man by a s. name — THOM 330:11
scrip: yet with s. and scrippage — SHAK 273:3
scripture: devil can cite S. — SHAK 289:3
S. moveth us in sundry places — BOOK 63:12
usury is contrary to S. — TAWN 322:20
scriptures: caused all Holy S. — BOOK 64:22
Let us look at the s. — SELD 269:16
scruple: Some craven s. — SHAK 276:30
scrutamini: S. scripturas — SELD 269:16
scullion: Away, you s.! — SHAK 278:20
sculpture: austere, like that of s. — RUSS 265:3
sculptured: s. dead — KEATS 190:15
scum: mere s. of the earth — WELL 345:14
Okie means you're s. — STEI 314:24
scuttling: S. across the floors — ELIOT 133:28
sea: afraid of the s. — SYNGE 321:21
against a s. of troubles — SHAK 275:25
all gone under the s. — ELIOT 133:4
As is the ribbed s.-sand — COL 104:11
as near to heaven by s. — GILB 151:3
bathed in the Poem of the S. — RIMB 260:8
boy playing on the s.-shore — NEWT 239:6
But I beneath a rougher s. — COWP 109:20
cold grey stones, O S. — TENN 323:10
crowns around the glassy s. — HEBER 164:17
dominion of the s. — COV 108:18
Down to a sunless s. — COL 103:22
down to the s. again — MAS 221:21
down to the s. in ships — BOOK 68:12
English that of the s. — RICH 260:6
forbear to teach the s. — DONNE 124:16
From s. to shining sea — BATES 30:2
goes to s. for nothing — DONNE 123:4
gong-tormented s. — YEATS 358:15
gurly grew the s. — BALL 27:16
home from s. — STEV 317:22
if we gang to s. master — BALL 28:5
in peril on the s. — WHIT 348:9
in the flat s. sunk — MILT 226:11
in the s. of life enisled — ARN 17:22
Into a s. of dew — FIELD 139:2
Into that silent s. — COL 104:5
Lie mirrored on her s. — HODG 169:14
little cloud out of the s. — BIBLE 42:2
lover of men, the s. — SWIN 321:18
my chains like the s. — THOM 330:9
never go to s. — GILB 152:20
no more s. — BIBLE 58:4
one is of the s. — WORD 357:6
Put out to s. — MACN 216:11
sailed the wintry s. — LONG 210:5
salt, estranging s. — ARN 17:23
scrotumtightening s. — JOYCE 188:11
s.-blooms and the oozy woods — SHEL 304:7
s. gave up the dead — BIBLE 58:3
s. hates a coward — O'NEI 241:12
s.-mark of my utmost sail — SHAK 293:4
S. of Faith — ARN 16:11

sea (cont.):

| | |
|---|---|
| S. shall give up her dead | BOOK 69:15 |
| s.! the sea! | XEN 358:8 |
| s. was made his tomb | BARN 29:7 |
| see nothing but s. | BACON 23:22 |
| serpent-haunted s. | FLEC 141:15 |
| She sells s.-shells | SULL 319:2 |
| ship in the midst of the s. | BIBLE 44:4 |
| shore of the wan grassy s. | SITW 307:20 |
| steady than an ebbing s. | FORD 143:11 |
| sudden came the s. | BROW 76:23 |
| suffer a s.-change | SHAK 296:1 |
| summers in a s. of glory | SHAK 280:18 |
| tideless dolorous midland s. | SWIN 321:19 |
| uttermost parts of the s. | BOOK 69:6 |
| very much at s. | CARS 92:11 |
| water in the rough rude s. | SHAK 293:22 |
| waves on the great s. | LUCR 212:4 |
| wet sheet and a flowing s. | CUNN 113:7 |
| When I put out to s. | TENN 323:18 |
| Where no s. runs | THOM 330:12 |
| why the s. is boiling hot | CARR 91:22 |
| willing foe and s. room | ANON 11:22 |
| with the s. embraced | CHAU 96:21 |
| wrinkled s. beneath him crawls | TENN 323:21 |
| seagreen: s. Incorruptible | CARL 90:13 |
| seagull: I'm a s. | CHEK 96:27 |
| seal: opened the seventh s. | BIBLE 57:29 |
| s. upon thine heart | BIBLE 45:1 |
| S. up the mouth of outrage | SHAK 295:26 |
| sealed: My lips are s. | BALD 27:7 |
| sealing wax: ships—and s. | CARR 91:22 |
| sear: fall'n into the s. | SHAK 288:1 |
| search: characters in s. of an author | PIR 249:1 |
| In s. of lost time | PROU 255:17 |
| in s. of what he needs | MOORE 234:7 |
| searched: deep-s. with saucy looks | SHAK 284:10 |
| thou hast s. me out | BOOK 69:5 |
| searching: by s. find out God | BIBLE 42:32 |
| I am s. everywhere | STEP 315:7 |
| seas: dangers of the s. | PARK 245:17 |
| Draw not up s. to drown | DONNE 124:16 |
| floors of silent s. | ELIOT 133:28 |
| multitudinous s. incarnadine | SHAK 286:18 |
| perilous s., in faery lands | KEATS 192:5 |
| s. colder than the Hebrides | FLEC 141:14 |
| s. roll over but the rocks | HERB 166:15 |
| s. upon their lawful occasions | BOOK 69:14 |
| therefore I have sailed the s. | YEATS 359:22 |
| through strange s. of Thought | WORD 356:10 |
| season: all alike, no s. knows | DONNE 124:12 |
| by s. seasoned | SHAK 290:5 |
| dry brain in a dry s. | ELIOT 133:14 |
| every thing there is a s. | BIBLE 44:11 |
| In a somer s. | LANG 201:5 |
| S. of mists and mellow | KEATS 192:14 |
| s. of snows and sins | SWIN 321:2 |
| selfish hope of a s.'s fame | NEWB 238:13 |
| that in s. grows | SHAK 284:11 |
| word spoken in due s. | BIBLE 43:27 |
| Youth's the s. made for joys | GAY 149:6 |
| seasoned: s. with salt | BIBLE 56:12 |
| seasons: I play for S. | MER 223:23 |
| man for all s. | WHIT 349:2 |
| O s., O castles! | RIMB 260:10 |
| we see the s. alter | SHAK 290:23 |
| seat: s. to faith assigned | SMART 308:11 |
| this s. of Mars | SHAK 293:16 |
| seat-belts: Fasten your s. | MANK 217:12 |
| seated: S. one day at the organ | PROC 255:13 |
| seaworms: Battening upon huge s. | TENN 325:32 |
| second: All things have s. birth | WORD 356:13 |
| Appointed for my s. race | VAUG 337:7 |
| beauty faded has no s. spring | PHIL 248:14 |
| Habit is s. nature | AUCT 20:3 |

second (cont.):

| | |
|---|---|
| not a s. on the day | COOK 107:15 |
| s. at Rome | CAES 87:26 |
| s. best bed | SHAK 300:21 |
| s. best's a gay goodnight | YEATS 359:5 |
| S. childishness | SHAK 272:28 |
| secrecy: S. the human dress | BLAKE 62:7 |
| secret: bread eaten in s. | BIBLE 43:15 |
| Et Vigny plus s. | SAIN 265:14 |
| giant girls that have no s. | SPEN 313:3 |
| I know that's a s. | CONG 106:9 |
| in s. sin | CHUR 98:25 |
| most s. and inviolate Rose | YEATS 359:26 |
| neurosis is a s. | TYNAN 336:9 |
| official s. | WEBER 344:8 |
| s. anniversaries | LONG 209:20 |
| s., black, and midnight hags | SHAK 287:19 |
| S. sits in the middle | FROST 146:20 |
| S. thoughts and open countenance | ALB 3:13 |
| Vereker's s. | JAMES 179:17 |
| when it ceases to be a s. | BEHN 32:21 |
| secretary: S. of Nature | WALT 342:16 |
| secrets: from whom no s. are hid | BOOK 65:2 |
| s. are edged tools | DRYD 128:16 |
| sect: attached to that great s. | SHEL 303:15 |
| found them a s. | MAC 213:17 |
| loving his own s. | COL 104:23 |
| paradise for a s. | KEATS 190:24 |
| serious, sad-coloured s. | HOOD 171:14 |
| sects: diversity of s. | SPEN 313:16 |
| secure: He is s. | SHEL 303:11 |
| securities: trust to two s. | CHES 97:14 |
| security: best s. of the land | COV 108:18 |
| sedate: s., sober, silent sect | HOOD 171:14 |
| seducer: Thou strong s. | DRYD 127:27 |
| seduction: s. of martial music | BURN 81:18 |
| see: All that we s. or seem | POE 250:5 |
| come up and s. me sometime | WEST 346:24 |
| complain we cannot s. | BERK 35:18 |
| do not s. the signal | NELS 238:1 |
| everywhere but never s. him | FLAU 141:11 |
| I'd rather s. than be one | BURG 79:16 |
| I eat what I s. | CARR 91:6 |
| I'll s. you again | COW 109:2 |
| In all things Thee to s. | HERB 166:25 |
| I s. and hear nothing | THOM 330:25 |
| I s., not feel, how beautiful | COL 103:14 |
| I think that I shall never s. | NASH 237:17 |
| last I s. your father | YEAM 358:12 |
| more people s. than weigh | CHES 97:16 |
| no man s. me more | SHAK 280:17 |
| not worth going to s. | JOHN 185:24 |
| S., amid the winter's snow | CASW 92:18 |
| s. and hear and feel yet | JOYCE 188:17 |
| s. beyond our bourn | KEATS 192:18 |
| s. it often | AUDEN 20:25 |
| s. the object as in itself | ARN 18:12 |
| s. with not through | BLAKE 60:12 |
| seem to s. the things | SHAK 283:26 |
| Shall never s. so much | SHAK 284:8 |
| shall no man s. me and live | BIBLE 40:12 |
| they shall s. God | BIBLE 48:19 |
| till I s. what I say | WALL 341:14 |
| To s. oursels as others see us | BURNS 82:25 |
| yet I s. thee still | SHAK 286:10 |
| You s., but you do not observe | DOYLE 125:16 |
| seed: s. shall remain for ever | BIBLE 48:8 |
| garden, that grows to s. | SHAK 274:10 |
| good s. on the land | CAMP 88:13 |
| s. of the Church | TERT 329:8 |
| seeds: look into the s. of time | SHAK 285:7 |
| s. fell by the wayside | BIBLE 50:4 |
| seeing: Discovery consists of s. | SZEN 322:3 |
| seek: All I s., the heaven above | STEV 317:25 |
| s., and ye shall find | BIBLE 49:9 |

seek (cont.):

| | |
|---|---|
| s. me if you had not found me | PASC 246:8 |
| that sometime did me s. | WYATT 358:2 |
| To strive, to s., to find | TENN 328:25 |
| We s. him here | ORCZY 241:17 |
| where s. is find | SMART 308:11 |
| seem: Let be be finale of s. | STEV 316:6 |
| seeming: S. and savour | SHAK 298:29 |
| seems: it is; I know not 's.' | SHAK 274:7 |
| seen: evidence of things not s. | BIBLE 56:26 |
| God whom he hath not s. | BIBLE 57:17 |
| Has anybody here s. Kelly | MURP 236:12 |
| Much more had s. | ARMS 16:1 |
| s. further it is by standing | NEWT 239:2 |
| s. one Western you've seen | WHIT 348:7 |
| s. to be done | HEW 168:4 |
| seen what I have s. | SHAK 276:3 |
| Too early s. unknown | SHAK 294:28 |
| What things have we s. | BEAU 30:18 |
| seeth: Lord s. not as man seeth | BIBLE 41:15 |
| segregation: S. now, s. tomorrow | WALL 341:8 |
| seize: s. the day | HOR 173:20 |
| seldom: s. come, they wished for come | SHAK 277:25 |
| selection: Natural S. | DARW 114:3 |
| self: Love seeketh only S. to please | BLAKE 62:2 |
| s. is hateful | PASC 246:7 |
| to thine own s. be true | SHAK 274:23 |
| self-assertion: s. abroad | WAUGH 343:23 |
| self-contempt: S., well-grounded | LEAV 203:23 |
| self-defence: I swear it was in s. | MARL 218:7 |
| self-denial: S. is not a virtue | SHAW 301:34 |
| self-evident: hold these truths to be s. | ANON 11:12 |
| self-help: s. the root of all growth | SMIL 308:17 |
| selfish: sensible people are s. | EMER 136:18 |
| self-love: s. and social are the same | POPE 252:21 |
| self-made: s. man is one who | STEAD 314:13 |
| self-preservation: s. in the other | JEFF 180:25 |
| self-slain: As a god s. | SWIN 321:10 |
| self-sufficiency: S. at home | WAUGH 343:23 |
| self-sufficing: reasoning, s. thing | WORD 356:6 |
| self-will: murmurs of s. | BODE 62:16 |
| selkie: I am a s. in the sea | BALL 27:17 |
| sell: go and s. that thou hast | BIBLE 50:21 |
| If there were dreams to s. | BEDD 31:19 |
| I s. what all the world desires | BOUL 70:11 |
| s. with you, talk with you | SHAK 288:31 |
| that no man might buy or s. | BIBLE 57:32 |
| who had a mind to s. his house | SWIFT 319:20 |
| selling: Every one lives by s. | STEV 316:23 |
| old firm, it's. is out | OSB 242:23 |
| sells: Or s. eternity to get a toy | SHAK 299:8 |
| seltzer: weak hock and s. | BETJ 36:16 |
| semblable: mon s.,—mon frère | BAUD 30:3 |
| seminary: Come from a ladies' s. | GILB 151:23 |
| semper: Quod ubique, quod s. | VINC 338:22 |
| Sic s. tyrannis | BOOTH 69:20 |
| Sempronius: we'll do more, S. | ADD 2:13 |
| senator: S., and a Democrat | JOHN 181:19 |
| senators: look at the s. and pray for | HALE 160:4 |
| respectable s. burst with | AUDEN 20:18 |
| teach his s. wisdom | BOOK 68:10 |
| send: Here am I; s. me | BIBLE 45:12 |
| S. in the Clowns | SOND 311:7 |
| se'nnights: s. nine times nine | SHAK 285:4 |
| sensations: easy prey to s. | TREV 334:9 |
| s. rather than of thoughts | KEATS 192:24 |
| sense: borrows all her rays from s. | POPE 251:18 |
| decency is want of s. | DILL 120:23 |
| Devoid of s. and motion | MILT 228:24 |
| disease and want of s. | ROCH 261:2 |
| Learned without s. | CHUR 98:29 |
| light of nature, s. | ROCH 261:6 |
| men of s. never tell | SHAF 270:20 |
| Money is like a sixth s. | MAUG 222:11 |
| never deviates into s. | DRYD 128:5 |

sense (cont.):

| | |
|---|---|
| Not when the s. is dim | BEEC 32:5 |
| Of s. and outward things | WORD 355:22 |
| Satire or s., alas | POPE 251:7 |
| s. to the American people | STEV 316:16 |
| stings and motions of the s. | SHAK 288:11 |
| Take care of the s. | CARR 91:9 |
| within the s. they quicken | SHEL 305:4 |
| without one grain of s. | DRYD 127:28 |
| senseless: by a kind of s. wit | WILB 349:11 |
| you worse than s. things | SHAK 280:24 |
| senses: If Parson lost his s. | HODG 169:13 |
| sensibility: pattern informed by s. | READ 258:9 |
| sensible: All s. people are selfish | EMER 136:18 |
| be bold and be s. | HOR 173:8 |
| S. men never tell | DISR 122:1 |
| sensitive: S. Plant in a garden grew | SHEL 304:30 |
| sensual: s. pleasure without vice | JOHN 186:10 |
| sentence: Marriage isn't a word, it's a s. | VIDOR 338:15 |
| S. first—verdict afterwards | CARR 91:14 |
| sentenced: s. to death in my absence | BEHAN 32:18 |
| sentences: Backward ran s. | GIBBS 150:18 |
| sentiment: classic lecture, rich in s. | TENN 327:18 |
| s. might uncoil in the heart | GREE 158:4 |
| sentiments: Them's my s. | THAC 329:17 |
| sentinels: s. to warn th' immortal | MARL 219:11 |
| sentry: Where stands a wingèd s. | VAUG 337:6 |
| sentry-box: quadrille in a s. | JAMES 179:16 |
| separate: s. us from the love | BIBLE 54:42 |
| separately: we shall all hang s. | FRAN 145:13 |
| separation: prepare for a s. | QUIN 257:9 |
| September: Thirty days hath S. | ANON 11:2 |
| When you reach S. | AND 5:12 |
| sepulchre: man the living s. of life | CLARE 101:8 |
| sepulchres: like unto whited s. | BIBLE 50:32 |
| sequel: natural s. of an unnatural | AUST 22:26 |
| seraglio: s. of eunuchs | FOOT 142:17 |
| seraphic: maids strange s. pieces | TRAH 333:19 |
| seraphims: Above it stood the s. | BIBLE 45:10 |
| sere: Now my s. fancy | BYRON 86:19 |
| serene: that unhoped s. | BROO 72:20 |
| serf: soil as another man's s. | HOMER 171:3 |
| sergeant: This fell s., death | SHAK 277:15 |
| serial: obituary in s. form | CRISP 111:21 |
| serious: annuity is a very s. business | AUST 23:7 |
| nothing s. in mortality | SHAK 286:26 |
| s. and the smirk | DICK 119:15 |
| their most s.-minded activity | MONT 233:11 |
| War is too s. a matter | CLEM 101:24 |
| sermon: find him, who a s. flies | HERB 166:21 |
| good honest and painful s. | PEPYS 247:14 |
| rejected the S. on the Mount | BRAD 71:10 |
| sermons: S. and soda-water | BYRON 86:6 |
| S. in stones | SHAK 272:14 |
| serpent: it biteth like a s. | BIBLE 43:33 |
| s. ate Eve | HUGH 175:21 |
| s. beguiled me | BIBLE 38:27 |
| s. subtlest beast of all | MILT 229:22 |
| s. was more subtil | BIBLE 38:24 |
| sharper than a s.'s tooth | DICK 119:24 |
| sharper than a s.'s tooth | SHAK 282:25 |
| way of a s. upon a rock | BIBLE 44:4 |
| Where's my s. of old Nile | SHAK 271:11 |
| serpent-haunted: s. sea | FLEC 141:15 |
| serpents: therefore wise as s. | BIBLE 49:29 |
| servant: become the s. of a man | SHAW 301:4 |
| cracked lookingglass of a s. | JOYCE 188:12 |
| Is thy s. a dog | BIBLE 42:12 |
| Our ugly comic s. | AUDEN 20:25 |
| s. of the Living God | SMART 308:7 |
| s. shall have small | BARC 28:17 |
| s.'s too often a negligent elf | BARH 28:22 |
| s. to be bred at an University | CONG 106:10 |
| s. to the devil | SISS 307:10 |
| s. with this clause | HERB 166:26 |

servant (cont.):
| | |
|---|---|
| thou good and faithful s. | BIBLE 51:1 |
| thy s. depart in peace | BIBLE 52:3 |
| thy s. depart in peace | BIBLE 58:17 |
| thy s. heareth | BIBLE 41:9 |
| Your s.'s cut in half | GRAH 156:3 |

servants: equality in the s.' hall — BARR 29:10
one of them hired s. — BIBLE 52:30
S. of Light — ARN 16:7
s. of the sovereign — BACON 24:27
s. will do that for us — VILL 338:19
wish your wife or your s. to read — GRIF 159:2
Ye s. of the Lord — DODD 122:30
serve: And s. him right — BELL 33:22
Fleet in which we s. — BOOK 69:13
no man can s. two masters — BIBLE 49:3
once to s. our country — ADD 2:16
reign in hell than s. in heaven — MILT 228:13
s. Him in this world — CAT 92:20
s. the future hour — WORD 356:19
s. the Lord with gladness — BIBLE 58:10
s. the Lord with gladness — BOOK 68:5
s. who only stand and wait — MILT 230:23
'tis enough, 'twill s. — SHAK 295:7
served: s. my God with half the zeal — SHAK 280:21
service: All s. ranks the same with God — BROW 77:1
done the state some s. — SHAK 293:5
In purer lives thy s. find — WHIT 348:21
No money, no s. — RAC 257:17
our bounden duty and s. — BOOK 65:17
places the nation at his s. — POMP 250:12
pressed into s. means — FROST 146:21
s. of my love — SPR 313:26
whose s. is perfect freedom — BOOK 64:5
serviettes: kiddies have crumpled the s. — BETJ 37:2
servile: to all the skyey influences — SHAK 288:19
servility: savage s. — LOW 211:12
serving: cumbered about much s. — BIBLE 52:14
sesame: Open S. — ARAB 14:17
sesquipedalia: Proicit ampullas et s. verba — HOR 172:26
sesquipedalian: S. blackguard — CLOU 102:10
sesquippledan: S. verboojuice — WELLS 345:17
sessions: s. of sweet silent thought — SHAK 299:16
set: by God's grace, play a s. — SHAK 279:1
s. one slip of them — SHAK 298:30
S. thine house in order — BIBLE 46:6
setting: doors against a s. sun — SHAK 296:19
Hath had elsewhere its s. — WORD 355:20
settlement: Revolution a parent of s. — BURKE 80:11
seven: child for the first s. years — ANON 7:10
hewn out her s. pillars — BIBLE 43:14
His acts being s. ages — SHAK 272:24
If s. maids with seven mops — CARR 91:21
S. types of ambiguity — EMPS 137:7
S. wealthy towns contend — ANON 10:10
thy s.-fold gifts impart — BOOK 69:16
Until seventy times s. — BIBLE 50:19
Seven Dials: lowly air of S. — GILB 151:11
seventh: opened the s. seal — BIBLE 57:29
When the moon is in the s. house — RADO 257:18
seventy: Until s. times seven — BIBLE 50:19
sever: Ae fond kiss, and then we s. — BURNS 81:22
Nothing in life shall s. — CORY 108:12
To s. for years — BYRON 87:14
severae: procul este, s. — OVID 243:9
severity: set in with its usual s. — COL 105:2
Severn: from the S. to the Tyne — KIPL 196:3
Seville: bang these dogs of S. — TENN 328:12
sewer: midst of this putrid s. — TOCQ 333:5
s. in a glass-bottomed boat — MIZN 232:13
sewers: s. annoy the air — MILT 229:23
sex: attempt to insult s. — LAWR 202:13
Continental people have s. life — MIKES 224:11
How is your s.-life now? — SOPH 311:14
If S. ever rears its ugly head — AYCK 23:14

sex (cont.):
Is s. dirty? — ALLEN 4:15
Literature mostly about having s. — LODGE 209:4
Mind has no s. — WOLL 353:10
Money was exactly like s. — BALD 27:3
practically conceal its s. — NASH 237:9
privilege I claim for my own s. — AUST 22:28
proxy for risk and a dummy for s. — MACH 215:4
S. and drugs and rock and roll — DURY 129:14
[S.] the most fun without laughing — ALLEN 4:13
s. with someone I love — ALLEN 4:14
soft, unhappy s. — BEHN 32:24
weaker s., to piety more prone — ALEX 4:7
we have s. in the mind — LAWR 202:19
When you have money, it's s. — DONL 123:2
sexes: there are three s. — SMITH 310:4
sexophones: s. wailed — HUXL 177:4
sexton: that bald s., Time — SHAK 282:6
s. tolled the bell — HOOD 171:7
sexual: most unnatural of s. perversions — HUXL 177:7
S. intercourse began — LARK 201:12
sexually: s. transmitted disease — ANON 8:20
shackles: Memories are not s. — BENN 34:13
their s. fall — COWP 110:7
shade: clutching the inviolable s. — ARN 17:12
Dancing in the chequered s. — MILT 227:4
farewell to the s. — COWP 109:30
fleeting image of a s. — SHEL 305:17
gentlemen of the s. — SHAK 277:22
green thought in a green s. — MARV 220:16
shall crowd into a s. — POPE 253:1
sly s. of a Rural Dean — BROO 73:5
That lashes all with s. — WILB 349:13
whiter s. of pale — REID 259:3
Within its s. we'll live or die — CONN 106:23
shades: S. of the prison-house — WORD 355:20
where the Etrurian s. — MILT 228:14
shadow: Be but the s. of heaven — MILT 229:18
days on the earth are as a s. — BIBLE 42:17
dream but of a s. — CHAP 94:15
Falls the S. — ELIOT 133:19
he fleeth also as a s. — BIBLE 42:33
land of the s. of death — BIBLE 45:15
Life's but a walking s. — SHAK 288:5
Like a vast s. moved — VAUG 337:14
Or s. of felicity — WALL 341:14
out-soared the s. of our night — SHEL 303:11
s. of death — BIBLE 51:30
Swift as a s., short as any dream — SHAK 290:14
valley of the s. of death — BOOK 66:18
shadows: Cats, no less liquid than their s. — TESS 329:10
I am half sick of s. — TENN 326:1
In ancient s. and twilights — Æ 3:4
millions of strange s. — SHAK 299:18
of their s. deep — YEATS 360:9
s., not substantial things — SHIR 306:10
Styled but the s. of us men — JONS 187:22
this kind are but s. — SHAK 291:8
Types and s. have their ending — THOM 330:4
Shadwell: S. never deviates into sense — DRYD 128:5
shaft: many a s., at random sent — SCOTT 268:15
shag: common cormorant (or s.) — ISH 178:21
shake: S. off dull sloth — KEN 193:20
s. off the dust — BIBLE 49:28
those boughs which s. against — SHAK 299:24
shaken: S. and not stirred — FLEM 141:21
So s. as we are, so wan — SHAK 277:21
Time has s. me by the hand — WESL 346:17
shakers: We are the movers and s. — O'SH 243:1
Shakespeare: Corneille is to S. — JOHN 186:12
It was for gentle S. cut — JONS 187:20
Or sweetest S. fancy's child — MILT 227:8
read in S. and found him weak — WELLS 345:16
S., another Newton — HUXL 177:11
S. by flashes of lightning — COL 104:25

Shakespeare (*cont.*):
S. for his honoured bones — MILT 227:21
S. I am struck with wonder — LAWR 202:24
S., undoubtedly wanted taste — WALP 341:18
S. unlocked his heart — WORD 356:21
S. wanted art — JONS 187:31
S. was of us, Milton was — BROW 76:14
such stuff as great part of S. — GEOR 149:24
Shakespearian: That S. rag — RUBY 77:31
Shakespeherian: that S. Rag — ELIOT 134:24
shaking: Aching, s., crazy, cold — ROCH 261:9
Shalimar: loved beside the S. — HOPE 171:22
shall: His absolute 's.' — SHAK 273:18
s. and finding only why — CUMM 113:2
shallow: Deep-versed in books and s. — MILT 230:8
shallows: bound in s. and in miseries — SHAK 282:1
Shalott: Lady of S. — TENN 326:3
shame: Ain't it all a bleedin' s. — ANON 10:11
expense of spirit in a waste of s. — SHAK 300:10
if you still have to ask ... s. on you — ARMS 16:4
shamed: And s. life a hateful — SHAK 288:21
shames: hold a candle to my s. — SHAK 289:11
shape: means pressed out of s. — FROST 146:21
s. of things to come — WELLS 345:23
share: All that I have I s. with you — BOOK 66:2
greater s. of honour — SHAK 279:17
I s. no one's ideas — TURG 335:13
I wished to s. the transport — WORD 357:4
shares: Fair s. for all — JAY 180:14
shark: s. has pretty teeth — BREC 71:18
Sharon: I am the rose of S. — BIBLE 44:31
sharp: 'Tis a s. remedy — RAL 258:3
sharper: s. than a serpent's tooth — DICK 119:24
s. than a serpent's tooth — SHAK 282:25
sharpness: overcome the s. of death — BOOK 63:20
sharps: different s. and flats — BROW 76:26
shatter: you may s. the vase — MOORE 234:13
shaves: man who s. and takes a train — WHITE 347:14
Shaw: S. hasn't an enemy — WILDE 350:21
she: S. must weep or she will die — TENN 327:26
S. sells sea-shells — SULL 319:2
S. went, to plain-work — POPE 251:24
S. who must be obeyed — HAGG 159:15
That not impossible s. — CRAS 111:16
unexpressive s. — SHAK 273:2
shears: resembles a pair of s. — SMITH 310:5
Sheba: Another S. queen — WITH 352:5
shed: prepare to s. them now — SHAK 281:22
shedding: s. of blood is no remission — BIBLE 56:24
sheep: come you in s.'s clothing — BIBLE 49:14
Feed my s. — BIBLE 54:7
found my s. which was lost — BIBLE 52:27
from thy ways like lost s. — BOOK 63:13
get back for these s. — ANON 12:14
giveth his life for the s. — BIBLE 53:30
like s. have gone astray — BIBLE 46:19
little hills like young s. — BOOK 68:16
noble ensample to his s. — CHAU 95:21
old half-witted s. — STEP 315:4
savaged by a dead s. — HEAL 164:10
s. in sheep's clothing — CHUR 100:7
s. in sheep's clothing — GOSSE 155:25
s. on his right hand — BIBLE 51:4
sheet: boy brought the white s. — GARC 148:2
old England's winding s. — BLAKE 60:9
waters were his winding s. — BARN 29:7
sheets: cool kindliness of s. — BROO 73:1
shelf-life: s. of the modern hardback — TRIL 334:10
shell: pebble or a prettier s. — NEWT 239:6
thou s. of death — MIDD 224:8
underneath that gloomy s. — ANON 9:14
Within thy airy s. — MILT 226:10
Shelley: Burns, S., were with us — BROW 76:14
did you once see S. plain — BROW 76:18
shells: choirs of wailing s. — OWEN 243:22

shelter: s. from the stormy blast — WATTS 343:13
shelves: symmetry of s. — LAMB 200:2
shene: most s. is the sonne — LANG 201:9
shepherd: As sweet unto a s. as a king — GREE 158:9
feed his flock like a s. — BIBLE 46:11
I am the good s. — BIBLE 53:30
King of love my s. is — BAKER 26:21
Lord is my s. — BOOK 66:17
Old Nod, the s., goes — DE L 116:21
they call you, S., from the hill — ARN 17:4
shepherds: s. abiding in the field — BIBLE 51:32
sheriff: I shot the s. — MARL 218:7
sherry: s. flowing into second-rate — PLOM 250:1
Shibboleth: Say now S. — BIBLE 41:2
shield: And broken was her s. — SCOTT 268:23
Our S. and Defender — GRANT 156:8
To a lady in his s. — TENN 326:2
trusty s. and weapon — LUTH 212:10
shieling: From the lone s. — GALT 147:19
shift: let me s. for myself — MORE 235:3
shilling: s. in my little tambourine — KIPL 196:2
s. life will give you all — AUDEN 21:12
shimmered: Jeeves s. out — WOD 352:12
shine: Arise, s. — BIBLE 46:23
Let your light so s. before men — BIBLE 48:22
Lord make his face s. upon thee — BIBLE 40:15
not to s. in use — TENN 328:21
s. in the high aesthetic line — GILB 152:9
s. on, harvest moon — NORW 240:11
shiners: Nine for the nine bright s. — ANON 8:6
shingles: naked s. of the world — ARN 16:11
shining: I see it plain — HOUS 174:24
s. morning face — SHAK 272:25
S. nowhere but in the dark — VAUG 337:12
woman of so s. loveliness — YEATS 359:27
ship: As idle as a painted s. — COL 104:6
being in a s. is being in a jail — JOHN 184:5
O S. of State — LONG 209:11
s., an isle, a sickle moon — FLEC 141:19
s. has weathered every rack — WHIT 348:11
S. me somewheres east of Suez — KIPL 196:23
s. on the sea and the horse — GARC 148:3
s. was still as she could be — SOUT 311:22
way of a s. — BIBLE 44:4
What is 83 but a prison — BURT 83:10
ships: go down to the sea in s. — BOOK 68:12
launched a thousand s. — MARL 218:11
little s. of England — GUED 159:6
shoes—and s.—and sealing wax — CARR 91:22
s. sail like swans asleep — FLEC 141:18
S. that pass in the night — LONG 210:3
S., towers, domes — WORD 354:15
stately s. go to their haven — TENN 323:11
Thracian s. and the foreign faces — SWIN 321:1
wrong with our bloody s. — BEAT 30:14
shipwreck: escaped the s. of time — BACON 23:21
Shiraz: wine of S. into urine — DIN 121:20
shires: both the s. they ring them — HOUS 174:20
calling for them from sad s. — OWEN 243:22
shirt: sang the 'Song of the S.' — HOOD 171:12
shirtsleeves: s. to s. in three — ANON 7:8
shiver: Little breezes dusk and s. — TENN 325:35
praised and left to s. — JUV 189:1
shoal: this bank and s. of time — SHAK 285:22
shock: And we shall s. them — SHAK 282:15
Future s. — TOFF 333:6
sensation of a short, sharp s. — GILB 151:25
s. of the new — DUNL 129:9
shock-headed: S. Peter — HOFF 170:4
shocking: and s. the barmaid — SITW 307:18
looked on as something s. — PORT 253:17
shocks: s. the mind of a child — PAINE 244:7
s. the magistrate — RUSS 265:4
thousand natural s. — SHAK 275:25

shod: All s. with steel — WORD 355:2
s. their heads in their canoes — MARV 221:3
shoe: cast out my s. — BOOK 67:14
I kiss his dirty s. — SHAK 279:10
Sailed off in a wooden s. — FIELD 139:2
whose s.'s latchet I am — BIBLE 53:12
shoes: mind it wipes its s. — THOM 330:18
Of s.—and ships — CARR 91:22
or ere those s. were old — SHAK 274:12
s. with broken high ideals — MCG 214:20
thy s. from off thy feet — BIBLE 39:31
To boil eggs in your s. — LEAR 203:16
your s. on your feet — BIBLE 39:37
shoeshine: on a smile and a s. — MILL 225:4
shoestring: careless s. — HERR 167:15
fortune and runs it into a s. — WOOL 354:7
shone: There s. one woman — SWIN 321:19
shook: He hath s. hands with time — FORD 143:10
monk who s. the world — MONT 233:25
more it's s. it shines — HAM 160:17
Ten days that s. the world — REED 259:1
shoot: could s. me in my absence — BEHAN 32:18
Please go on you the pianist — ANON 10:4
S., if you must, this old — WHIT 348:26
s. the Hippopotamus — BELL 33:1
s. the hippopotamus — FORS 143:14
teach the young idea how to s. — THOM 331:22
They s. horses don't they — MCCOY 214:16
they shout and they s. — INGE 178:10
To s. the sleepy, green-coat — HOFF 170:2
You s. a fellow down — HARDY 162:13
shooting: than to hunting and s. — BURR 82:32
shop: little back s., all his own — MONT 233:14
rag and bone s. of the heart — YEATS 358:16
s. at the corner — AUDEN 21:4
shopkeepers: nation of s. — ADAMS 2:7
nation of s. — NAP 237:7
nation of s. — SMITH 308:23
shore: By the s. of Gitche Gumee — LONG 210:1
high s. of this world — SHAK 279:16
kingdom stretch from s. to s. — WATTS 343:12
lights around the s. — ROSS 263:10
longing for the further s. — VIRG 339:15
rapture on the lonely s. — BYRON 85:12
s. of the wan grassy sea — SITW 307:20
Stops with the s. — BYRON 85:13
Then on the s. of the wide world — KEATS 192:21
To that unknown and silent s. — LAMB 200:12
with low sounds by the s. — YEATS 359:13
shored: have s. against my ruins — ELIOT 134:31
shores: wilder s. of love — BLAN 62:9
short: be but a s. time tonight — BALD 27:7
hath but a s. time to live — BOOK 66:6
long and the s. and the tall — HUGH 175:18
long while to make it s. — THOR 332:6
lyf so s., the craft so long — CHAU 96:12
nasty, brutish, and s. — HOBB 169:10
s., sharp shock — GILB 151:25
Take s. views, hope for the best — SMITH 310:1
shortage: s. of coal and fish — BEVAN 37:17
shorter: make you s. by the head — ELIZ 135:8
not had the time to make it s. — PASC 245:24
shortest: s. way is commonly — BACON 24:3
shot: he was s. silk — STR 318:11
I s. the sheriff — MARL 218:7
My God! They've s. our fox — BIRCH 59:14
Remember you s. a seagull — CHEK 96:27
s. heard round the world — EMER 136:12
shoulder: And on his s. gently laid — BAKER 26:21
government shall be upon his s. — BIBLE 45:16
shoulder-blade: s. that is a miracle — GILB 152:3
shoulders: City of the Big S. — SAND 266:12
dwarfs on the s. of giants — BERN 36:9
lawn about the s. of the thrown — HERR 167:15

shoulders (cont.):
old heads on your young s. — SPARK 312:11
s. held the sky suspended — HOUS 174:13
standing on the s. of giants — NEWT 239:2
shout: hardly a s. from a few boys — ARN 17:3
men who s. — WALK 341:5
shouted with a great s. — BIBLE 40:27
s. that tore hell's concave — MILT 228:16
S. with the largest — DICK 119:28
There was a s. about my ears — CHES 97:22
they s. and they shoot — INGE 178:10
shouting: captains, and the s. — BIBLE 43:5
heavens fill with s. — TENN 326:11
tumult and the s. dies — KIPL 197:2
shovel: S. them under — SAND 266:14
show: s. ourselves glad in him — BOOK 67:31
s. you fear in a handful of dust — ELIOT 134:20
to s. that you have one — CHES 97:10
showbusiness: no business like s. — BERL 35:20
s. with blood — BRUNO 77:25
shower: s. of curates — BRON 72:13
s. your shooting corns — SWIFT 320:14
showers: After sharpest s. — LANG 201:9
Aprill with his s. soute — CHAU 95:10
much dew, many s. — VAUG 337:13
showery: S., Flowery, Bowery — ELLIS 136:4
shreds: king of s. and patches — SHAK 276:21
thing of s. and patches — GILB 151:17
shrewishly: he speaks very s. — SHAK 297:20
shriek: s. flits by on leathern — COLL 105:10
shrieking: With s. and squeaking — BROW 76:26
shrieks: s. to pitying heav'n — POPE 253:10
shrimp: s. learns to whistle — KHR 194:18
shrine: little saint best fits a little s. — HERR 167:22
shrined: bower we s. to Tennyson — HARDY 162:3
shroud: stiff dishonoured s. — ELIOT 134:17
shudder: s. in the loins — YEATS 359:14
shuffle: All s. there — YEATS 359:23
Patience, and s. the cards — CERV 93:19
shuffled: s. off this mortal coil — SHAK 275:25
shunting: s. and hooting — BURR 82:32
shut: s. their doors against — SHAK 296:19
shutters: close the s. fast — COWP 110:11
we'd need keep the s. up — DICK 119:6
shuttle: Man is the s. — VAUG 337:3
musical s. — WHIT 348:12
swifter than a weaver's s. — BIBLE 42:30
shuttlecock: Battledore and s. — DICK 119:29
sick: And I am s. at heart — SHAK 273:30
Created s., commanded to be — GREV 158:19
I am half s. of shadows — TENN 326:1
I am s., I must die — NASHE 237:19
kingdom of the s. — SONT 311:10
make me s. and wicked — AUST 23:12
night … is but the daylight s. — SHAK 290:6
nothing but to make him s. — DONNE 123:4
O Rose, thou art s. — BLAKE 62:4
Pass the s. bag, Alice — JUNOR 188:27
Ruth, when, s. for home — KEATS 192:5
s. discussing their duty — WHIT 348:19
s. hurry, its divided aims — ARN 17:11
s. of an old passion — DOWS 125:12
s. that surfeit with too much — SHAK 288:28
S. with inbreeding — THOM 331:5
thcream till I'm s. — CROM 111:23
they that are s. — BIBLE 49:22
were you not extremely s. — PRIOR 255:12
sickle: ship, an isle, a s. moon — FLEC 141:19
sicklied: s. o'er with the pale cast — SHAK 275:26
sickly: I'm s. but sassy — HARR 163:4
smiled a s. smile — HARTE 163:13
sickness: in s. and in health — BOOK 65:28
in s. and in health — BOOK 66:1
s. that destroyeth — BOOK 67:29
Till age, or grief, or s. must — KING 195:5

Sidcup: I could get down to S.     PINT 248:20
side: God is on everyone's s.     ANOU 14:4
   Hear the other s.     AUG 22:1
   her bosom and half her s.     COL 103:12
   move over to the other s.     REED 258:18
   on the s. of the angels     DISR 121:15
   S. by side     WOODS 353:19
   This s. the tomb     DAV 114:18
   trumpets sounded on the other s.     BUNY 79:11
   which s. do they cheer     TEBB 323:7
   Who is on my s.     BIBLE 42:15
sides: I'm a Norfan, both s.     WELLS 345:18
   looked at life from both s.     MITC 232:3
Sidney: miracle of our age, Sir Philip S.     CAREW 89:18
   S.'s self, the starry paladin     BROW 77:13
siege: s. of the city of Gaunt     BALL 28:1
Siegfried: washing on the S. line     KENN 193:23
siesta: Englishmen detest a s.     COW 109:4
sieve: in a s. I'll thither sail     SHAK 285:3
   they went to sea in a S.     LEAR 203:10
siftings: let their liquid s. fall     ELIOT 134:17
sigh: nor s.-tempests move     DONNE 124:15
   s. is just a sigh     HUPF 176:20
   s. is the sword of an Angel     BLAKE 60:18
   S. no more, ladies     SHAK 291:19
   very s. that silence heaves     KEATS 191:5
sighed: I s. as a lover     GIBB 150:14
   S. and looked, and sighed     DRYD 127:22
   S. and looked unutterable     THOM 331:24
   s. his soul toward     SHAK 289:31
sighing: soul sat s. by a sycamore     SHAK 292:26
   Was laughter and ability and S.     DICK 120:17
sighs: In the gestures, in the s.     SOND 311:6
   S. are the natural language     SHAD 270:17
sight: And he keeps it out of s.     BREC 71:18
   does it matter?—losing your s.     SASS 267:9
   gimleted and neatly out of s.     CRANE 111:2
   sensible to feeling as to s.     SHAK 286:10
   s. so touching in its majesty     WORD 354:15
   s. to dream of, not to tell     COL 103:12
   s. to make an old man young     TENN 323:24
sights: Her s. and sounds     BROO 73:10
   impressive s. in the world     BARR 29:17
   Such s. as youthful poets dream     MILT 227:7
sign: In this s. shalt thou conquer     CONS 107:14
   s. of inward and spiritual grace     BOOK 65:23
   s. of the true artist     VIDAL 338:14
signal: Only a s. shown     LONG 210:3
signed: s. my death warrant     COLL 105:8
signo: In hoc s. vinces     CONS 107:14
signs: discern the s. of the times     BIBLE 50:12
   Except ye see s. and wonders     BIBLE 53:20
   merely conventional s.     CARR 92:7
   words are but the s. of ideas     JOHN 182:4
silence: answered best with s.     JONS 187:14
   darkness again and a s.     LONG 210:3
   Deep is the s., deep on     DRIN 126:24
   easy step to s.     AUST 22:24
   Elected S., sing to me     HOPK 172:5
   His mind moves upon s.     YEATS 359:15
   Indecency's conspiracy of s.     SHAW 302:3
   In s. and tears     BYRON 87:14
   lies are often told in s.     STEV 317:9
   My gracious s., hail     SHAK 273:17
   occasional flashes of s.     SMITH 310:6
   on the other side of s.     ELIOT 132:10
   rest is s.     SHAK 277:18
   Seul le s. est grand     VIGNY 338:18
   s. all the airs and madrigals     MILT 231:1
   S. augmenteth grief     DYER 129:15
   s., exile, and cunning     JOYCE 188:9
   s. in heaven     BIBLE 57:29
   S. is become his mother tongue     GOLD 155:7
   S. is effectively compressed     MORL 235:8

silence (cont.):
   S. is the virtue of fools     BACON 24:8
   S. like a cancer grows     SIMON 307:7
   s. of these infinite spaces     PASC 246:3
   s. sank like music     COL 104:16
   s. surged softly backward     DE L 116:20
   S. that dreadful bell     SHAK 292:7
   slowly s. all     TENN 324:13
   small change of s.     MER 223:18
   Sorrow and s. are strong     LONG 209:16
   speaking s. of a dream     ROSS 263:1
   Thou foster-child of s.     KEATS 191:17
   very sigh that s. heaves     KEATS 191:5
   When awful darkness and s.     LEAR 203:8
silenced: because you have s. him     MORL 235:9
silent: All s., and all damned     WORD 356:4
   impossible to be s.     BURKE 80:26
   Laws are s. in time of war     CIC 100:30
   Paris was French—and s.     TUCH 335:8
   s. manliness of grief     GOLD 154:26
   s. touches of time     BURKE 81:2
   S., upon a peak in Darien     KEATS 192:11
   that strong, s. man     MORL 235:8
   thereof one must be s.     WITT 352:8
   t is s., as in Harlow     ASQ 19:6
   unhasting, and s. as light     SMITH 310:15
silently: How s., and with how wan     SIDN 306:18
   S. and very fast     AUDEN 20:19
silk: And it soft as s. remains     HILL 168:15
   he was shot s.     STR 318:11
   s. hat at a private view     EDW 130:22
   s. hat on a Bradford millionaire     ELIOT 134:29
   s. makes the difference     FULL 147:7
silken: s. terms precise     SHAK 284:18
   silver link, the s. tie     SCOTT 268:11
   With s. lines, and silver hooks     DONNE 123:23
silks: in fading s. compose     WINC 352:3
   Whenas in s. my Julia goes     HERR 167:26
silk-worm: s. expend her yellow labours     MIDD 224:9
silliest: s. woman can manage a clever     KIPL 197:28
silly: sillier than a s. laugh     CAT 93:4
   s. at the right moment     HOR 174:1
   with such a s. question     STER 315:13
   You were s. like us     AUDEN 20:22
silver: all the Georgian s. goes     MACM 215:20
   apples of gold in pictures of s.     BIBLE 43:35
   Between their s. bars     FLEC 141:19
   Can wisdom be put in a s. rod     BLAKE 60:10
   ever the s. cord be loosed     BIBLE 44:26
   golden locks time hath to s.     PEELE 247:3
   handful of s. he left us     BROW 76:13
   precious stone set in the s. sea     SHAK 293:16
   silken lines, and s. hooks     DONNE 123:23
   S. and gold have I none     BIBLE 54:9
   s. apples of the moon     YEATS 360:1
   s. lining in the sky-ee     LEE 347:1
   s. link, the silken tie     SCOTT 268:11
   s., snarling trumpets     KEATS 190:16
   There's a s. lining     FORD 143:12
   thirty pieces of s.     BEVAN 38:4
   thirty pieces of s.     BIBLE 51:7
   Walks the night in her s. shoon     DE L 116:22
silver-sweet: s. sound lovers' tongues     SHAK 295:3
Silvia: Who is S.? what is she     SHAK 298:19
similes: I sit, and play with s.     WORD 357:8
simple: C'est tellement s., l'amour     PRÉV 255:6
   It was beautiful and s.     HENRY 166:4
   rarely pure, and never s.     WILDE 349:16
   To ask the hard question is s.     AUDEN 21:16
simplicity: holy s.     HUSS 176:21
   holy s.     JER 181:6
   Pity my s.     WESL 346:6
   s. of the three per cents     DISR 122:2
   s. of the three per cents     STOW 318:9
simplify: s. me when I'm dead     DOUG 125:9

**simplify** (cont.):

| | |
|---|---|
| S., simplify | THOR 332:11 |

**sin**: And say there is no s. | SHAK 282:5
beauty is only s. deep | SAKI 265:19
Be of s. the double cure | TOPL 333:14
Be ye angry and s. not | BIBLE 55:33
brother s. against me | BIBLE 50:19
By that s. fell the angels | SHAK 280:19
fall into no s., neither run | BOOK 64:6
go, and s. no more | BIBLE 53:27
hate the s. | AUG 22:4
He that is without s. | BIBLE 53:26
How shall I lose the s. | POPE 250:25
If we say that we have no s. | BIBLE 57:14
I had not known s. | BIBLE 54:37
in secret s. | CHUR 98:25
I waive the quantum o'the s. | BURNS 82:5
Lukewarmness I account a s. | COWL 109:16
My s., my soul. Lo-lee-ta | NAB 236:18
no s. but ignorance | MARL 218:19
not innocence but s. | BROW 76:9
physicists have known s. | OPP 241:14
purple-linèd palace of sweet s. | KEATS 191:12
Shall we continue in s. | BIBLE 54:33
S. is behovely | JUL 188:21
s. ye do by two and two | KIPL 197:10
sometimes s.'s a pleasure | BYRON 86:3
this dark world of s. | BICK 58:25
to s. in secret is not to sin | MOL 232:24
wages of s. is death | BIBLE 54:36
want of power to s. | DRYD 128:11
want, the care, the s. | TENN 325:24
Which is my s., though it were | DONNE 123:17
which taketh away the s. | BIBLE 53:13
your s. will find you out | BIBLE 40:20

**sincerely**: s. want to be rich | CORN 108:4
**sincerity**: s. is a dangerous thing | WILDE 349:23
**sinecure**: Love … is no s. | BYRON 87:17
**sinew**: every nerve, and s. | JONS 187:7
**sinews**: Money is the s. of love | FARQ 138:18
s. of war, unlimited money | CIC 100:29
Stiffen the s., summon up | SHAK 279:5
**sinewy**: With large and s. hands | LONG 210:4

**sing**: And I will s. of the sun | POUND 254:11
Elected Silence, s. to me | HOPK 172:5
I'll s. you twelve O | ANON 8:6
I s. of brooks, of blossoms | HERR 167:12
I s. the body electric | WHIT 348:16
I, too, s. America | HUGH 175:19
Let all the world in ev'ry corner s. | HERB 166:20
never heard no horse s. | ARMS 16:3
O for a thousand tongues to s. | WESL 346:4
Of the glorious Body s. | THOM 330:3
Quires and Places where they s. | BOOK 64:7
S. 'em muck | MELBA 222:19
s. in the robber's face | JUV 189:11
s. like birds i' the cage | SHAK 284:1
S. me a song of a lad | STEV 317:23
s. myself | WHIT 348:16
S., my tongue | FORT 144:4
S. thou the songs of love | GURN 159:11
S. unto the Lord a new song | BOOK 66:2a
s. unto the Lord a new song | BOOK 68:3
S. whatever is well made | YEATS 360:6
Soul clap its hands and s. | YEATS 359:21
That can s. both high and low | SHAK 297:23
while I s. the ancient ways | YEATS 360:4
worth saying, people s. it | BEAU 30:15
**singe**: S. my white head | SHAK 283:6
**singeing**: s. of the King of Spain's | DRAKE 126:11
**singer**: idle s. of an empty day | MORR 235:14
lived a s. in France of old | SWIN 321:19
s. not the song | ANON 10:12
S. of sweet Colonus | ARN 17:20
**singing**: s. still dost soar | SHEL 305:7

**singing** (cont.):

six little S-boys | BARH 28:18
Beside me s. in the wilderness | FITZ 140:6
Everyone suddenly burst out s. | SASS 267:11
silver waves of thy sweet s. | SHEL 304:21
S., dancing to itself | COL 103:13
S. so rarely | SCOTT 269:1
s. will never be done | SASS 267:12
time of the s. of birds | BIBLE 44:32
we are a nest of s. birds | JOHN 183:22

**single**: Behold her, s. in the field | WORD 357:1
married to a s. life | CRAS 111:13
Nor grew it white in a s. night | BYRON 87:5
Nothing in the world is s. | SHEL 304:3
s. man in possession of a fortune | AUST 23:2
S. vision and Newton's | BLAKE 60:23
S. women have a dreadful | AUST 23:11
they came not s. spies | SHAK 276:35
Two souls with but a s. | HALM 160:15
**sings**: he s. each song twice | BROW 76:2
instead of bleeding, he s. | GARD 148:5
tell me what she s. | WORD 357:2
**singular**: So s. in each particular | SHAK 298:34
**singularity**: S. is almost invariably | DOYLE 125:14
**sinister**: strange and s. | JAMES 180:1
**sink**: Not gross to s., but light | SHAK 300:17
raft which would never s. | AMES 4:22
S. me the ship, Master | TENN 328:13
**sinned**: I have s. against heaven | BIBLE 52:30
More s. against than sinning | SHAK 283:10
people s. against are not | COMP 106:5
s. exceedingly in thought | MISS 231:11
**sinner**: dead s. revised | BIER 59:9
God be merciful to me a s. | BIBLE 52:39
Love the s., but hate the sin | AUG 22:4
over one s. that repenteth | BIBLE 52:28
**sinners**: God and s. reconciled | WESL 346:7
Master with publicans and s. | BIBLE 49:21
mercy upon us miserable s. | BOOK 64:13
Once for favoured s. slain | WESL 346:9
s. to repentance | BIBLE 49:23
Why do s.' ways prosper | HOPK 172:18
**sinning**: sinned against than s. | SHAK 283:10
**sins**: Be all my s. remembered | SHAK 275:27
Compound for s. | BUTL 83:24
half the s. of mankind | RUSS 264:21
Her s., which are many | BIBLE 52:8
His s. were scarlet | BELL 33:27
multitude of s. | BIBLE 57:11
oldest s. the newest kind | SHAK 278:28
s. and offences of my youth | BOOK 66:21
s. are attempts to fill voids | WEIL 345:2
takest away the s. of the world | MISS 231:19
Though your s. be as scarlet | BIBLE 45:4
weep for their s. | WHIT 348:19
**sint**: S. ut sunt aut non sint | CLEM 102:3
**Sion**: remembered thee, O S. | BOOK 69:2
**sir**: S., no man's enemy | AUDEN 21:14
**sirens**: Blest pair of S. | MILT 226:4
**Sirmio**: S., bright eye of peninsulas | CAT 93:3
**Sisera**: fought against S. | BIBLE 40:32
**sister**: barren s. all your life | SHAK 290:12
My s. and my sister's child | COWP 109:24
trying to violate your s. | STR 318:14
**sisterhood**: S. is powerful | MORG 235:6
**sisters**: And so do his s. | GILB 152:17
Are s. under their skins | KIPL 196:19
Sphere-born harmonious s. | MILT 226:4
weird s., hand in hand | SHAK 285:5
**Sistine**: On the S. Chapel roof | YEATS 360:5
**sit**: allowed to s. down | UST 336:19
Here I s., alone and sixty | BENN 34:16
let us s. upon the ground | SHAK 293:27
May s. i' the centre | MILT 226:12
S. thou on my right hand | BOOK 68:14

sit (cont.):
| | |
|---|---|
| So I did s. and eat | HERB 167:3 |
| Teach us to s. still | ELIOT 132:19 |
| that s. in darkness | BIBLE 51:30 |
| Though I s. down now | DISR 121:5 |
| we used to s. and dream | ARMS 15:24 |

sits: Sometimes I s. and thinks — PUNCH 256:21

sitting: Are you s. comfortably
| | |
|---|---|
| Lord s. upon a throne | BIBLE 45:10 |
| s. in the smallest room | REGER 259:2 |

situation: retreating, s. excellent — FOCH 142:14

six: Rode the s. hundred — TENN 323:14

s. little Singing-boys — BARH 28:18

sixpence: and nothing above s. — BEVAN 38:3

bang—went s. — PUNCH 256:12

We could have saved s. — BECK 31:8

sixteen: S. tons, what do you get — TRAV 334:4

sixth: s. age shifts into the lean — SHAK 272:27

sixty: Here I sit, alone and s. — BENN 34:16

rate of s. minutes an hour — LEWIS 206:11

When I'm s.-four — MCC 205:17

skeletons: s. copulating — BEEC 32:1

skies: And paint the sable s. — DRUM 127:1
| | |
|---|---|
| some watcher of the s. | KEATS 192:11 |
| whose god is in the s. | SHAW 301:33 |
| You common people of the s. | WOTT 357:16 |

skill: nothing with a deal of s. — COWP 110:5

To show our simple s. — SHAK 291:6

skin: Ethiopian change his s. — BIBLE 46:30
| | |
|---|---|
| In the castle of my s. | LAMM 200:17 |
| skull beneath the s. | ELIOT 134:32 |
| throws her enamelled s. | SHAK 290:27 |
| with the s. of my teeth | BIBLE 42:35 |

skinny: I fear thy s. hand — COL 104:11

skins: Are sisters under their s. — KIPL 196:19

skipped: mountains s. like rams — BOOK 68:16

skirmish: s. fought near Marathon — GRAV 156:15

skittles: all beer and s. — CALV 88:9

skivvies: it would take a dozen s. — MCGR 214:22

skull: s. beneath the skin — ELIOT 134:32

sky: above, the vaulted s. — CLARE 101:7
| | |
|---|---|
| Above us only s. | LENN 205:7 |
| clean the s. | ELIOT 134:8 |
| clear blue s. over my head | HAZL 164:8 |
| climbin' clear up to the s. | HAMM 161:2 |
| clothe the wold and meet the s. | TENN 325:34 |
| inverted bowl we call The S. | FITZ 140:15 |
| lonely sea and the s. | MAS 221:21 |
| lose itself in the s. | BROW 75:8 |
| On a bed of daffodil s. | TENN 326:28 |
| Open unto the fields, and to the s. | WORD 354:15 |
| pie in the s. when you die | HILL 168:12 |
| sent him down the s. | CORY 108:13 |
| s. changes when they are wives | SHAK 273:9 |
| spread out against the s. | ELIOT 133:24 |
| Their shoulders held the s. | HOUS 174:13 |
| Under the wide and starry s. | STEV 317:21 |
| Which prisoners call the s. | WILDE 350:15 |
| With all the blue ethereal s. | ADD 2:25 |
| wrote my will across the s. | LAWR 203:1 |

Skye: Over the sea to S. — BOUL 70:10

Over the sea to S. — STEV 317:23

skyey: Servile to all the s. influences — SHAK 288:19

slab: Beneath this s. — NASH 237:13

slacks: girls in s. remember Dad — BETJ 36:17

slag-heap: post-industrial s. — DRAB 126:9

slain: ere thou hast s. another — BROW 74:24
| | |
|---|---|
| I am hurt but I am not s. | BALL 28:3 |
| jaw of an ass have I s. | BIBLE 41:5 |
| Or if the s. think he is slain | EMER 136:10 |

slamming: s. Doors — BELL 33:10

S. their doors, stamping — OSB 242:22

slander: civic s. and the spite — TENN 325:25

one to s. you and the other — TWAIN 335:25

S., meanest spawn of Hell — TENN 326:4

slang: S. is a language that rolls — SAND 266:18

slant: certain S. of light — DICK 120:14

slap-up: s. gal in a bang-up chariot — DICK 119:23

slaughter: as a lamb to the s. — BIBLE 46:20

ox goeth to the s. — BIBLE 43:13

slave: act a s. to limit — SHAK 297:2
| | |
|---|---|
| Better be a s. at once | BRON 72:14 |
| giving freedom to the s. | LINC 207:6 |
| half s. and half free | LINC 207:5 |
| has been s. to thousands | SHAK 292:11 |
| one is always the s. | LERM 205:24 |
| Philosopher!—a fingering s. | WORD 356:5 |
| rogue and peasant s. | SHAK 275:21 |
| s.-morality | NIET 239:22 |
| slave of that s. | CONN 107:3 |
| soundly as the wretched s. | SHAK 279:16 |

slavery: wise and good in s. — MAC 213:8
| | |
|---|---|
| s. in which a man does | GILL 153:1 |
| s. of the tea and coffee | COBB 102:25 |
| S. they can have anywhere | BURKE 80:4 |

slaves: all women are born s. — AST 19:7
| | |
|---|---|
| at the mill with s. | MILT 230:10 |
| Britons never will be s. | THOM 331:20 |
| Englishmen never will be s. | SHAW 301:20 |
| it is the creed of s. | PITT 249:7 |
| S. cannot breathe in England | COWP 110:7 |
| S. of the Lamp | ARN 16:7 |
| s. with weary footsteps | SHEL 303:16 |
| sons of former s. | KING 195:9 |
| too pure an Air for S. | ANON 10:1 |
| wholly s. or wholly free | DRYD 127:30 |
| whom we have made our s. | DARW 114:6 |
| women born s. | WOLL 353:14 |

slavish: O imitators, you s. herd — HOR 173:15

slayer: If the red s. think he slays — EMER 136:10

sleave: knits up the ravelled s. of care — SHAK 286:15

sleek-headed: S. men — SHAK 281:1

sleekit: Wee, s., cow'rin' — BURNS 82:7

sleep: And miles to go before I s. — FROST 146:23
| | |
|---|---|
| And s. an act or two | SHAK 280:23 |
| azure-lidded s. | KEATS 190:21 |
| Care-charmer S. | DAN 113:15 |
| Care-charming S. | FLET 142:5 |
| come to the borders of s. | THOM 330:24 |
| Death and his brother S. | SHEL 304:26 |
| deep, deep s. of England | ORW 242:1 |
| do I wake or s. | KEATS 192:7 |
| each day dies with s. | HOPK 172:11 |
| Entice the dewy-feathered S. | MILT 229:12 |
| From s. and from damnation | CHES 97:24 |
| Glamis hath murdered s. | SHAK 286:16 |
| green ideas s. furiously | CHOM 98:18 |
| grey and full of s. | YEATS 360:9 |
| have an exposition of s. | SHAK 291:1 |
| How s. the brave, who sink | COLL 105:11 |
| In s. a king, but, waking | SHAK 299:28 |
| in soot I s. | BLAKE 61:19 |
| Is rounded with a s. | SHAK 296:10 |
| lasting s.; a quiet resting | BEAU 31:2 |
| Let us s. now | OWEN 244:4 |
| Macbeth does murder s. | SHAK 286:15 |
| Macbeth shall s. no more | SHAK 286:16 |
| Me biful for to s. | LANG 201:6 |
| None shall s. | ADAMI 1:9 |
| Now I lay me down to s. | ANON 9:20 |
| Oh S.! it is a gentle thing | COL 104:13 |
| One short s. past, we wake | DONNE 123:9 |
| quiet s. and a sweet dream | MAS 222:2 |
| Shake off this downy s. | SHAK 286:24 |
| single vision and Newton's s. | BLAKE 60:23 |
| Sleek-headed men and such as s. | SHAK 281:1 |
| S. on (my Love!) | KING 195:5 |
| S. after toil, port after stormy | SPEN 313:9 |
| s. and a forgetting | WORD 355:20 |

sleep (cont.):

| | |
|---|---|
| s. and darkness safely brought | KEBLE 193:16 |
| s. as I in childhood sweetly | CLARE 101:7 |
| S. is sweet to the labouring | BUNY 79:4 |
| s. of a labouring man | BIBLE 44:15 |
| s. one ever-during night | CAMP 89:2 |
| S. shall neither night nor day | SHAK 285:4 |
| s. so soundly as the wretched | SHAK 279:16 |
| s., the certain knot of peace | SIDN 306:20 |
| s. the sleep of death | BLAKE 60:21 |
| S. to wake | BROW 75:11 |
| sweet restorer, balmy s. | YOUNG 360:17 |
| There'll be time enough to s. | HOUS 174:18 |
| To s.: perchance to dream | SHAK 275:25 |
| We shall not all s. | BIBLE 55:21 |
| We term s. a death | BROW 74:22 |
| What hath night to do with s. | MILT 226:8 |
| while some must s. | SHAK 276:12 |
| sleepers: in the seven s. den | DONNE 124:5 |
| unquiet slumbers for the s. | BRON 72:18 |
| sleepeth: maid is not dead, but s. | BIBLE 49:26 |
| sleeping: art tha s. there below | NEWB 238:11 |
| Lay your s. head, my love | AUDEN 20:27 |
| s. and the dead are but as pictures | SHAK 286:17 |
| sleepless: S. with cold commemorative | ROSS 263:9 |
| sleeps: and s. on his own heart | WORD 356:7 |
| Homer sometimes s. | BYRON 86:17 |
| Now s. the crimson petal | TENN 328:3 |
| softly s. the calm Ideal | DICK 119:7 |
| sleepwalker: assurance of a s. | HITL 169:1 |
| sleepy: not s. and there is no place | DYLAN 130:5 |
| sleeve: Ash on an old man's s. | ELIOT 133:8 |
| wear my heart upon my s. | SHAK 291:28 |
| sleeves: language that rolls up its s. | SAND 266:18 |
| Tie up my s. with ribbons rare | HUNT 176:19 |
| slepen: s. al the nyght with open | CHAU 95:11 |
| slept: fruits of them that s. | BIBLE 55:17 |
| thought he thought I s. | PATM 246:17 |
| slew: he was ambitious, I s. him | SHAK 281:16 |
| slice: S. him where you like | WOD 352:14 |
| slight: Away, s. man | SHAK 281:30 |
| slimy: thousand thousand s. things | COL 104:12 |
| slings: s. and arrows of outrageous | SHAK 275:25 |
| slip: catch no s. | BUNY 78:19 |
| let s. the dogs of war | SHAK 281:14 |
| s. into my bosom | TENN 328:5 |
| s., slide, perish | ELIOT 133:1 |
| to set one s. of them | SHAK 298:30 |
| slipped: s. away into the next room | HOLL 170:12 |
| slipper: s. and subtle knave | SHAK 292:6 |
| slippers: walks in his golden s. | BUNY 79:2 |
| slipping: s. gimleted | CRANE 111:2 |
| slips: like greyhounds in the s. | SHAK 279:6 |
| slit: S. your girl's, and swing | KING 195:19 |
| sliver: envious s. broke | SHAK 277:7 |
| slogged: s. up to Arras with rifle | SASS 267:13 |
| slopes: on the butler's upper s. | WOD 352:23 |
| slop-kettle: coffee and other s. | COBB 102:25 |
| slop-pail: woman with a s. | HOPK 172:22 |
| sloth: Shake off dull s. | KEN 193:20 |
| slouches: S. towards Bethlehem | YEATS 359:25 |
| Slough: bombs, and fall on S. | BETJ 37:9 |
| slough: s. was Despond | BUNY 78:18 |
| slovenliness: Peace is nothing but s. | BREC 71:20 |
| s. is no part of religion | WESL 346:15 |
| slow: come he s., or come he fast | SCOTT 268:17 |
| cripple and comes ever s. | DRAY 126:15 |
| Slow, s., fresh fount | JONS 187:2 |
| telling you to s. down | ANON 6:25 |
| slowly: angel to pass, flying s. | FIRB 139:20 |
| let him twist s. in the wind | EHRL 131:7 |
| Science moves, but s. slowly | TENN 326:13 |
| sluggard: Go to the ant thou s. | BIBLE 43:11 |
| foul s.'s comfort | CARL 90:5 |
| 'Tis the voice of the s. | WATTS 343:9 |

| | |
|---|---|
| slumber: Ere S.'s chain has bound | MOORE 234:20 |
| little sleep, a little s. | BIBLE 43:12 |
| s. did my spirit seal | WORD 356:25 |
| slumbers: Golden s. kiss your eyes | DEKK 116:10 |
| unquiet s. for the sleepers | BRON 72:18 |
| slums: gay intimacy of the s. | WAUGH 343:20 |
| slurp: As they s., slurp, slurp | FISH 139:26 |
| sluts: For now foul s. in dairies | CORB 107:23 |
| sly: s. shade of a Rural Dean | BROO 73:5 |
| smack: Just a s. at Auden | EMPS 137:4 |
| small: All things both great and s. | COL 104:18 |
| between the s. and great | COWP 110:16 |
| big squadrons against the s. | BUSS 83:20 |
| day of s. nations | CHAM 93:23 |
| deals it in s. parcels | WEBS 344:22 |
| down express in the s. of the back | WOD 352:18 |
| In s. proportions we just | JONS 187:24 |
| Is it so s. a thing | ARN 16:14 |
| It extinguishes the s. | BUSS 83:19 |
| Microbe is so very s. | BELL 33:20 |
| pictures that got s. | WILD 71:5 |
| s., but perfectly formed | COOP 107:21 |
| s. change of silence | MER 223:18 |
| S. is beautiful | SCH 267:25 |
| s. nations like prostitutes | KUBR 199:7 |
| s. talk flows from lip to lip | CRAB 110:19 |
| speaks s. like a woman | SHAK 290:8 |
| still s. voice | BIBLE 42:3 |
| That's one s. step for a man | ARMS 16:5 |
| Too s. to live in | ANON 11:8 |
| smallest: s. amount of lying | BUTL 84:10 |
| small-talking: this s. world | FRY 147:1 |
| smart: stranger shall s. | BIBLE 43:18 |
| smashed: s. it into because | CUMM 113:2 |
| smattering: s. of everything | DICK 120:5 |
| smell: I s. a rat | ROCHE 261:1 |
| Money has no s. | VESP 338:3 |
| shares man's s. | HOPK 172:4 |
| s. and hideous hum | GODL 153:20 |
| s. of the blood | SHAK 287:30 |
| s. the blood of a British | SHAK 283:18 |
| s. too strong of the lamp | STER 315:16 |
| Sweet s. of success | LEHM 204:13 |
| sweet keen s. | ROSS 263:10 |
| smelleth: he s. the battle afar | BIBLE 43:5 |
| smells: it s. of mortality | SHAK 283:24 |
| rank, it s. to heaven | SHAK 276:16 |
| smile: And s., smile, smile | ASAF 18:17 |
| Cambridge people rarely s. | BROO 73:7 |
| Did he s. his work to see | BLAKE 62:6 |
| I hear a s. | CROSS 112:11 |
| Normal is the good s. | SHAF 270:19 |
| on a s. and a shoeshine | MILL 225:4 |
| S. at us, pay us, pass us | CHES 98:4 |
| smiled a kind of sickly s. | HARTE 163:13 |
| s. dwells a little longer | CHAP 94:13 |
| s. of a cosmic Cheshire | HUXL 177:14 |
| s. on the face of the tiger | ANON 10:22 |
| transient is the s. of fate | DYER 129:17 |
| 'Twixt a prison and a s. | WOTT 357:18 |
| Where my Julia's lips do s. | HERR 167:13 |
| you should forget and s. | ROSS 263:4 |
| smiler: s. with the knyf | CHAU 95:27 |
| smiles: becks, and wreathèd s. | MILT 227:1 |
| charmed it with s. and soap | CARR 92:9 |
| Nae mair your s. can cheer me | COCK 102:27 |
| robbed that s. steals something | SHAK 291:37 |
| S. awake you when you rise | DEKK 116:10 |
| Their s., wan as primroses | KEATS 190:13 |
| There's daggers in men's s. | SHAK 286:27 |
| smilest: Thou s. and art still | ARN 17:14 |
| smiling: He hides a s. face | COWP 109:26 |
| S. at grief | SHAK 298:1 |
| S. the boy fell dead | BROW 76:8 |

solace: With s. and gladness SKEL 308:2
sold: s. his birthright BIBLE 39:18
 s. my reputation FITZ 140:17
 s. the truth to serve the hour TENN 327:13
 went and s. all BIBLE 50:6
soldier: Ben Battle was a s. bold HOOD 171:4
 chocolate cream s. SHAW 300:24
 death, who had the s. singled DOUG 125:10
 in the s. is flat blasphemy SHAK 288:15
 not tell us what the s. said DICK 119:34
 s. full of strange oaths SHAK 272:26
 s. is no more exempt STER 315:25
 s.'s life is terrible hard MILNE 225:19
 s.'s pole is fall'n SHAK 271:25
 s. stand up to anything except SHAW 301:1
 summer s. and the sunshine PAINE 244:11
soldiers: having s. under me BIBLE 49:17
 Ireland gives England her s. MER 223:13
 Old s. never die FOLEY 142:16
 our s. slighted QUAR 256:27
 S. are citizens of death's SASS 267:10
 s. by two and by three BALL 28:1
 s., mostly fools BIER 59:6
sole: nothing can be s. or whole YEATS 358:20
solemn: s. bird and this fair moon MILT 229:11
 s. creed with solemn sneer BYRON 85:6
solid: s. for fluidity CHUR 99:9
 too too s. flesh would melt SHAK 274:9
solidity: appearance of s. to pure wind ORW 242:15
solitary: Be not s., be not idle BURT 83:15
 if you are s., be not idle JOHN 185:25
 Through Eden took their s. way MILT 230:2
 waste and s. places SHEL 303:20
 Yon s. Highland lass WORD 357:1
solitude: Life is the desert, life the s. YOUNG 360:23
 make him feel his s. VALE 336:21
 place of seclusion and s. MONT 233:14
 resonance of his s. CONN 106:27
 Which is the bliss of s. WORD 355:5
Solomon: greater than S. is here BIBLE 50:2
 King S. wrote the Proverbs NAYL 237:20
 S. in all his glory BIBLE 49:4
 S. loved many strange women BIBLE 41:32
solution: fertilize a problem with a s. SIMP 307:13
 part of the s. or you're part CLEA 101:19
 Those people were a kind of s. CAV 93:11
 total s. of the Jewish question GOER 154:1
somebody: When every one is s. GILB 151:8
someday: S. I'll find you COW 109:7
someone: s. somewhere may be happy MENC 223:7
something: S. must be done EDW 131:1
 S. you somehow haven't FROST 146:11
 Time for a little s. MILNE 225:16
sometime: that s. did me seek WYATT 358:2
 woman is a s. thing GERS 168:7
sometimes: s. always, by God RICH 260:5
somewhat: I have s. against thee BIBLE 57:20
 tough joints more than s. RUNY 264:6
somewhere: want to get s. else CARR 91:18
 S. over the rainbow HARB 161:14
son: conceive, and bear a s. BIBLE 45:14
 gave his only begotten S. BIBLE 53:19
 keep his only s., myself HOME 170:18
 leichter of a fair s. ELIZ 135:12
 my s., mine own Telemachus TENN 327:13
 O Absalom, my s. BIBLE 41:27
 s. of Adam and of Eve PRIOR 255:10
 s. of his old age BIBLE 39:24
 S. of man hath not where BIBLE 49:19
 S. of Morn in weary Night's BLAKE 60:15
 spareth his rod hateth his s. BIBLE 43:23
 This is my beloved S. BIBLE 48:15
 two-legged thing, a s. DRYD 127:9
 unto us a s. is given BIBLE 45:16

son (cont.):
 what's a s.? A thing begot KYD 199:10
 whom if his s. ask bread BIBLE 49:10
 wise s. maketh a glad father BIBLE 43:16
 Woman, behold thy s. BIBLE 54:4
 worthy to be called thy s. BIBLE 52:30
 your s.'s tender years JUV 189:15
song: becomes a sightless s. TENN 325:30
 before his presence with a s. BOOK 68:5
 burden of my s. ANON 9:4
 burthen of his s. BICK 58:24
 carcase of an old s. THOM 331:5
 Glorious the s. SMART 308:13
 goodly manor for a s. SHAK 271:2
 my reputation for a s. FITZ 140:17
 My s. is love unknown CROS 112:13
 On wings of s. HEINE 165:1
 play a s. for me DYLAN 130:5
 self-same s. that found a path KEATS 192:5
 Singin' a s., side by side WOODS 353:19
 Sing unto the Lord a new s. BOOK 66:24
 sing unto the Lord a new s. BOOK 68:3
 s. charms the sense MILT 228:31
 s. is ended (but the melody BERL 36:2
 S. of the Shirt HOOD 171:12
 s. that never ends GOET 154:4
 s. was wordless SASS 267:12
 start a s. and to respond VIRG 340:1
 suck melancholy out of a s. SHAK 272:20
 suffering what they teach in s. SHEL 303:22
 That glorious s. of old SEARS 269:11
 that thinks two notes a s. DAV 114:17
 there's ane end of ane old s. OGIL 241:3
 There's no love s. finer PORT 253:19
 till I end my s. SPEN 313:18
 Time is our tedious s. should MILT 228:1
 Unlike my subject will I frame my s. CHES 97:2
 woman, wine, and s. LUTH 212:11
songs: after the s. of Apollo SHAK 284:24
 And all their s. are sad CHES 97:20
 piping s. for ever new KEATS 191:20
 Piping s. of pleasant glee BLAKE 61:18
 Sing thou the s. of love GURN 159:11
 s. beguile your pilgrimage FLEC 141:16
 sweetest s. are those that tell SHEL 305:10
 Their lean and flashy s. MILT 227:15
 Where are the s. of Spring KEATS 192:15
sonnet: Scorn not the S. WORD 356:21
 s. is a moment's monument ROSS 263:7
 S.'s scanty plot of ground WORD 355:15
sonnets: written s. all his life BYRON 86:11
sons: Bears all its s. away WATTS 343:15
 Brightest and best of the s. HEBER 164:14
 cruel s. of Cain LE G 204:12
 fallen s. of Eve CHES 98:5
 Go, bind your s. to exile KIPL 197:15
 God's s. are things MADD 216:14
 s. and daughters of Life's GIBR 150:19
 s. and your daughters shall BIBLE 47:20
 S. of the dark and bloody O'HARA 241:4
 then wander forth the s. MILT 228:15
soon: to Eve: Be s. THOM 331:10
sooner: s. every party breaks up AUST 22:15
soonest: Good is best when s. wrought SOUT 312:8
soot: and in s. I sleep BLAKE 61:19
sophist: neither saint nor s.-led ARN 16:13
sophistry: s. and illusion HUME 176:4
soporific: too much lettuce is 's.' POTT 254:2
Sordello: can be but the one 'S.' POUND 254:12
sore: bear with a s. head MARR 219:26
sorrow: And so beguile thy s. SHAK 296:27
 and the s. thereof MAL 217:2
 From the sphere of our s. SHEL 305:5
 Give s. words SHAK 287:25
 glut thy s. on a morning rose KEATS 191:26

**sorrow** (*cont.*):

| | |
|---|---|
| hairs with s. to the grave | BIBLE 39:26 |
| heart hath 'scaped this s. | SHAK 300:1 |
| in s. thou shalt bring forth | BIBLE 39:1 |
| interest and fines on s. | MAY 222:16 |
| knowledge increaseth s. | BIBLE 44:10 |
| labour and s. | BOOK 67:26 |
| Labour without s. is base | RUSK 264:18 |
| more in s. than in anger | SHAK 274:19 |
| night of doubt and s. | BAR 29:2 |
| Nought but vast S. was there | DE L 116:16 |
| O S., wilt thou live with me | TENN 325:13 |
| parting is such sweet s. | SHAK 295:4 |
| S. and silence are strong | LONG 209:16 |
| S. is tranquillity remembered | PARK 245:11 |
| s. lasts all through life | FLOR 142:12 |
| sorrow like unto my s. | BIBLE 46:32 |
| top whom whipping S. | GREV 158:18 |
| Write s. on the bosom | SHAK 293:26 |
| **sorrowful:** s. birth | MAL 217:1 |
| **sorrows:** carried our s. | BIBLE 46:18 |
| Disease, or s. strike him | CLOU 102:15 |
| man of s., and acquainted | BIBLE 46:17 |
| s. of women would be averted | ELIOT 132:3 |
| When shall my s. have an end | ANON 7:19 |
| When s. come, they come | SHAK 276:35 |
| world's great s. were born | Æ 3:4 |
| **sorry:** saw a wild thing s. for itself | LAWR 202:21 |
| s. for these our misdoings | BOOK 65:11 |
| **sorts:** s. and conditions of men | BOOK 64:18 |
| **sought:** s. in vain that sought | BURNS 82:1 |
| They s. it with thimbles | CARR 92:9 |
| **soul:** adventures of his s. | FRAN 145:3 |
| As if that s. were fled | MOORE 234:14 |
| bitterness of his s. | BIBLE 47:33 |
| buried s. and all its gems | BLAKE 60:12 |
| city of the s. | BYRON 85:8 |
| dark night of the s. | FITZ 140:22 |
| depth, and not the tumult, of the s. | WORD 355:6 |
| empty book is like an infant's s. | TRAH 333:17 |
| frame of adamant, a s. of fire | JOHN 183:13 |
| God rest his s., officers | SMITH 309:20 |
| Go, S., the body's guest | RAL 257:21 |
| harmonical and ingenious s. | AUBR 19:19 |
| Heaven take my s. | SHAK 282:13 |
| he shall save his s. alive | BIBLE 47:6 |
| he that hides a dark s. | MILT 226:12 |
| His s. is marching on | ANON 8:14 |
| hushèd casket of my s. | KEATS 192:13 |
| I am the captain of my s. | HENL 165:18 |
| I pray the Lord my s. to keep | ANON 9:20 |
| I pray the Lord my s. to take | ANON 9:20 |
| iron entered into his s. | BOOK 68:9 |
| Jesu, lover of my s. | WESL 346:8 |
| lie in the s. is a true lie | JOW 188:2 |
| life's dim windows of the s. | BLAKE 60:12 |
| lift my s. to heaven | SHAK 280:14 |
| lose his own s. | BIBLE 51:23 |
| man, with s. so dead | SCOTT 268:12 |
| Memorial from the S.'s eternity | ROSS 263:7 |
| Merry of s. he sailed on a day | STEV 317:23 |
| My s., bear thou thy part | GURN 159:11 |
| My s. doth magnify the Lord | BIBLE 51:28 |
| My s. doth magnify the Lord | BIBLE 58:16 |
| my soul, if I have a s. | ANON 9:22 |
| My s. is an enchanted boat | SHEL 304:21 |
| my s. is white | BLAKE 61:24 |
| My s., sit thou a patient | QUAR 257:1 |
| My s., there is a country | VAUG 337:6 |
| my s. within the house | SHAK 297:21 |
| No coward s. is mine | BRON 72:16 |
| no s. to be damned | THUR 332:19 |
| Or taught my s. to fancy aught | VAUG 337:7 |
| Perdition catch my s. | SHAK 292:10 |
| poetry ... composed in the s. | ARN 18:5 |

**soul** (*cont.*):

| | |
|---|---|
| Poor intricated s. | DONNE 124:22 |
| sighed his s. toward | SHAK 289:31 |
| sinews of the s. | FULL 147:5 |
| so longeth my s. after thee | BOOK 67:3 |
| s. a lordly pleasure-house | TENN 327:14 |
| S. and body part like friends | CRAS 111:15 |
| S. clap its hands and sing | YEATS 359:21 |
| s. inhabiting two bodies | ARIS 15:21 |
| s. of our dear brother | BOOK 66:8 |
| S. of the Age | JONS 187:25 |
| s. shall be required | BIBLE 52:19 |
| S., thou hast much goods | BIBLE 52:18 |
| s. to the company store | TRAV 334:4 |
| S. that rises with us | WORD 355:20 |
| subject's s. is his own | SHAK 279:14 |
| Thou hast delivered my s. | BOOK 68:20 |
| try the s.'s strength | BROW 76:7 |
| two to bear my s. away | ANON 9:8 |
| vale of s.-making | KEATS 193:10 |
| yet my s. drew back | HERB 167:2 |
| **souls:** damp s. of housemaids | ELIOT 134:4 |
| letters mingle s. | DONNE 124:4 |
| Most people sell their s. | SMITH 309:14 |
| open windows into men's s. | ELIZ 135:14 |
| play with s. | BROW 76:12 |
| prostration of men's s. | TAWN 322:18 |
| So must pure lovers' s. | DONNE 124:4 |
| S. of poets dead and gone | KEATS 191:16 |
| they have no s. | COKE 103:9 |
| times that try men's s. | PAINE 244:11 |
| Two s. with but a single | HALM 160:15 |
| **sound:** all is not sweet, all is not s. | JONS 187:5 |
| commanded to be s. | GREV 158:19 |
| full of s. and fury | SHAK 288:5 |
| Like the s. of a great Amen | PROC 255:14 |
| Music is feeling, then, not s. | STEV 316:10 |
| sighing s., the lights around | ROSS 263:10 |
| s. me from my lowest note | SHAK 276:13 |
| sound mind in a s. body | JUV 189:13 |
| s. of abundance of rain | BIBLE 42:1 |
| s. of shallow foppery | SHAK 289:10 |
| s. of surprise | BALL 28:13 |
| s. strikes like a rising knell | BYRON 85:2 |
| s. were parted thence | JONS 187:18 |
| Whose s. dies on the wind | APOL 14:11 |
| **sounding:** Come s. through the town | BALL 27:15 |
| **sounds:** S. and sweet airs | SHAK 296:9 |
| s. of music | SHAK 290:1 |
| s. will take care | CARR 91:9 |
| Wagner's music better than it s. | NYE 240:15 |
| with concord of sweet s. | SHAK 290:3 |
| **soup:** I won't have any s. today | HOFF 169:18 |
| like a cake of portable s. | BOSW 70:4 |
| not take s. at luncheon | CURZ 113:11 |
| **sour:** fathers have eaten s. grapes | BIBLE 47:5 |
| How s. sweet music | SHAK 294:11 |
| life will be s. grapes | ASHF 18:24 |
| **source:** Lord is the s. of my light | BIBLE 58:9 |
| s. of little visible delight | BRON 72:17 |
| **sourest:** sweetest things turn s. | SHAK 300:2 |
| **south:** beaker full of the warm S. | KEATS 191:30 |
| fierce and fickle is the S. | TENN 327:24 |
| gentleman in *Kharki* ordered S. | KIPL 196:2 |
| go s. in the winter | ELIOT 134:19 |
| nor yet from the s. | BOOK 67:18 |
| S. is avenged | BOOTH 69:20 |
| Yes, but not in the S. | POTT 254:5 |
| **Southampton:** weekly from S. | KIPL 197:19 |
| **southern:** bore me in the s. wild | BLAKE 61:24 |
| **souvenirs:** *Les s. sont cors de chasse* | APOL 14:11 |
| **sovereign:** bandy civilities with my S. | JOHN 184:19 |
| Here lies our s. lord | ROCH 261:4 |
| servants of the s. or state | BACON 24:27 |
| S. has three rights | BAG 26:14 |

| | |
|---|---|
| **sovereign** (*cont.*): | |
| subject and a s. are | CHAR 94:25 |
| that he will have no s. | COKE 103:10 |
| to be a S. | ELIZ 135:5 |
| **sovereignty**: Wommen desiren to have s. | CHAU 96:8 |
| **Soviet**: S. power plus | LENIN 205:1 |
| **sow**: Ireland is the old s. | JOYCE 188:7 |
| sower went forth to s. | BIBLE 50:4 |
| They that s. in tears | BOOK 68:29 |
| **sower**: s. went forth to sow | BIBLE 50:4 |
| **soweth**: whatsoever a man s. | BIBLE 55:30 |
| **sown**: reaped, nor was ever s. | TRAH 333:18 |
| They have s. the wind | BIBLE 47:17 |
| where thou hast not s. | BIBLE 51:2 |
| **space**: art of how to waste s. | JOHN 182:2 |
| cantos of unvanquished s. | CRANE 110:31 |
| Here is my s. | SHAK 271:5 |
| myself a king of infinite s. | SHAK 275:15 |
| **spaces**: It is the s. between | FENT 138:23 |
| **spacious**: s. firmament on high | ADD 2:25 |
| **spade**: I call a s. a spade | BURT 83:6 |
| nominate a s. a spade | JONS 187:9 |
| **Spain**: Lady of S., I adore you | REAV 258:13 |
| not into the hands of S. | TENN 328:13 |
| Rain in S. | LERN 206:1 |
| **span**: Contract into a s. | HERB 167:5 |
| Eternity shut in a s. | CRAS 111:11 |
| Less than a s. | BACON 25:30 |
| life's a pain and but a s. | DAV 114:14 |
| **spangled**: s. heavens | ADD 2:25 |
| **Spaniards**: S. seem wiser | BACON 25:12 |
| thrash the S. too | DRAKE 126:13 |
| **spanieled**: That s. me at heels | SHAK 271:22 |
| **Spanish**: To God I speak S. | CHAR 95:7 |
| **spare**: Brother can you s. a dime | HARB 161:11 |
| He was a s. man | AUBR 19:19 |
| likes to do in his s. time | GILL 153:1 |
| s. those who have submitted | VIRG 339:16 |
| S. us all word of the weapons | WILB 349:8 |
| s. your country's flag | WHIT 348:26 |
| Woodman, s. that tree | MORR 235:13 |
| woodman, s. the beechen tree | CAMP 88:17 |
| **spared**: better s. a better man | SHAK 278:15 |
| **spares**: man that s. these stones | SHAK 300:20 |
| **spareth**: s. his rod hateth his son | BIBLE 43:23 |
| **spark**: s. from heaven | ARN 17:10 |
| s. from heaven to fall | ARN 17:8 |
| **spark-gap**: s. is mightier | HOGB 170:6 |
| **sparkle**: s. out among the fern | TENN 323:12 |
| S. for ever | TENN 327:18 |
| **sparks**: like s. among the stubble | BIBLE 47:29 |
| s. fly upward | BIBLE 42:29 |
| **sparrow**: My lady's s. is dead | CAT 93:1 |
| providence in the fall of a s. | SHAK 277:13 |
| s. hath found her an house | BOOK 67:20 |
| s. should fly swiftly | BEDE 31:20 |
| **sparrows**: s. sold for two farthings | BIBLE 52:17 |
| **Spartans**: Go, tell the S. | SIM 307:9 |
| **spawn**: meanest s. of Hell | TENN 326:4 |
| **speak**: dare not s. its name | DOUG 125:6 |
| did you s. to him again | BROW 76:18 |
| difficult to s., and impossible to be | BURKE 80:26 |
| In all I think or s. or do | WESL 346:5 |
| let him now s., or else | BOOK 65:27 |
| Let us not s. of them | DANTE 113:19 |
| province of knowledge to s. | HOLM 170:15 |
| S. for England | AMERY 4:21 |
| s. ill of everybody | PÉT 248:7 |
| S., Lord; for thy servant | BIBLE 41:9 |
| S. low, if you speak love | SHAK 291:16 |
| S. roughly to your little boy | CARR 91:5 |
| S. softly and carry a big stick | ROOS 262:16 |
| S. the speech, I pray you | SHAK 276:4 |
| s. they through their throat | BOOK 68:18 |
| S. unto us smooth things | BIBLE 45:29 |

| | |
|---|---|
| **speak** (*cont.*): | |
| s. when he is spoken to | STEV 317:16 |
| S. ye comfortably to Jerusalem | BIBLE 46:7 |
| Though I s. with the tongues | BIBLE 55:11 |
| To s. and purpose not | SHAK 282:18 |
| whereof one cannot s. | WITT 352:8 |
| **speaking**: adepts in the s. trade | CHUR 98:22 |
| By drowning their s. | BROW 76:26 |
| Parliament s. through | CARL 90:17 |
| People talking without s. | SIMON 307:7 |
| Poetry [is] a s. picture | SIDN 306:26 |
| **speaks**: Gladstone s. to Me | VICT 338:9 |
| her foot s. | SHAK 297:9 |
| s. small like a woman | SHAK 290:8 |
| When he s., the air | SHAK 278:36 |
| **spear**: Bring me my s. | BLAKE 61:12 |
| With a burning s. | ANON 11:23 |
| **spears**: sheen of their s. | BYRON 85:22 |
| stars threw down their s. | BLAKE 62:6 |
| their s. into pruninghooks | BIBLE 45:5 |
| **specials**: 's.' like the old time | COLL 105:7 |
| **species**: individual, but the s. | JOHN 183:2 |
| **spectacle**: s. so ridiculous | MAC 213:9 |
| **spectacles**: s. on nose | SHAK 272:27 |
| What a pair of s. is here | SHAK 297:8 |
| **spectre**: s. of Communism | ENG 221:13 |
| **spectres**: S. fly before it | SMIL 308:19 |
| **spectre-thin**: youth grows pale, and s. | KEATS 191:32 |
| **speech**: freedom of s. | ROOS 262:13 |
| I have strange power of s. | COL 104:17 |
| manner of his s. | SHAK 271:13 |
| Rude am I in my s. | SHAK 291:33 |
| Speak the s., I pray you | SHAK 276:4 |
| s. be alway with grace | BIBLE 56:12 |
| s. by Chamberlain is like | BEVAN 38:3 |
| s. created thought | SHEL 304:20 |
| S. impelled us | ELIOT 133:9 |
| s. is like a cracked kettle | FLAU 141:7 |
| S. is the small change | MER 223:18 |
| S [is] not his language | STAËL 314:7 |
| s. only to conceal | VOLT 340:14 |
| s. they have resolved not | ELIOT 132:3 |
| verse is a measured s. | BACON 23:24 |
| where s. is not, there is | HOBB 169:5 |
| **speeches**: From all the easy s. | CHES 97:24 |
| **speechless**: washed in the s. real | BARZ 29:22 |
| **speed**: S., bonnie boat | BOUL 70:10 |
| s. glum heroes up the line | SASS 267:8 |
| s. the parting guest | POPE 252:24 |
| s. was far faster than light | BULL 78:7 |
| Unsafe at any s. | NADER 236:21 |
| **speeding**: Faster than a s. bullet | ANON 7:5 |
| **spell**: foreigners always s. better | TWAIN 336:1 |
| unless he first s. Man | QUAR 257:4 |
| Who lies beneath your s. | HOPE 171:22 |
| **speller**: taste and fancy of the s. | DICK 119:33 |
| **spelling**: My s. is Wobbly | MILNE 225:17 |
| **spend**: so wol we s. | CHAU 96:1 |
| whatever you have, s. less | JOHN 185:31 |
| **spending**: Getting and s. | WORD 357:10 |
| S. again what is already spent | SHAK 299:25 |
| **speranza**: LASCIATE OGNI S. | DANTE 113:18 |
| **sperare**: salus victis nullam s. | VIRG 339:6 |
| **spermatozoa**: million million s. | HUXL 177:11 |
| **spew**: bad ones s. it up | CERV 93:20 |
| s. thee out of my mouth | BIBLE 57:22 |
| **sphere**: their motion in one s. | SHAK 278:13 |
| these walls thy s. | DONNE 124:13 |
| they the s. | DONNE 124:3 |
| **spheres**: Driv'n by the s. | VAUG 337:14 |
| **spice**: Variety's the very s. of life | COWP 110:9 |
| **spices**: land of s. | HERB 167:4 |
| **spicy**: s. nut-brown ale | MILT 227:5 |
| What though the s. breezes | HEBER 164:16 |
| **spider**: drunk, and seen the s. | SHAK 298:23 |

**spider** (*cont.*):

| | |
|---|---|
| laws are like s.'s webs | ANAC 5:9 |
| said a s. to a fly | HOW 175:11 |
| s. is sole denizen | HARDY 162:3 |
| s.'s touch, how exquisitely | POPE 252:15 |
| **spiders:** No more s. in my bath | ANON 9:17 |
| often have seen s. fly | EDW 131:3 |
| Weaving s. come not here | SHAK 290:29 |
| **spies:** neighbourhood of voluntary s. | AUST 22:25 |
| **spill:** let them not s. me | MACN 216:7 |
| **spin:** Go s., you jades | PEMB 247:5 |
| Let the great world s. | TENN 326:17 |
| neither do they s. | BIBLE 49:4 |
| Sob as you s. | AUDEN 20:9 |
| **spinach:** I say it's s. | WHITE 347:15 |
| **spindle:** fold, s. or mutilate | ANON 6:26 |
| **spinners:** long-legged s. | SHAK 290:29 |
| **spinning:** evening s. by the fire | RONS 262:5 |
| **spinning-wheel:** wee bit s. | BLAM 62:8 |
| **spinsters:** s. and the knitters | SHAK 297:31 |
| **spires:** dreaming s. | ARN 17:17 |
| What s., what farms are those | HOUS 174:24 |
| Ye distant s. | GRAY 157:11 |
| **spirit:** And with thy s. | MISS 231:9 |
| Blessed are the poor in s. | BIBLE 48:19 |
| break a man's s. | SHAW 300:27 |
| Come, Holy S. | LANG 201:10 |
| elasticity to the s. | SMIL 308:19 |
| Hail to thee, blithe S. | SHEL 305:6 |
| haughty s. before a fall | BIBLE 43:28 |
| Her cabined ample S. | ARN 17:1 |
| I commend my s. | BIBLE 53:4 |
| I commend my s. | BOOK 66:23 |
| My shaping s. of imagination | COL 103:15 |
| never approached my s. | METT 224:2 |
| no s. can walk abroad | SHAK 274:2 |
| pardlike S. | SHEL 303:9 |
| renew a right s. within me | BOOK 67:10 |
| Rest, rest, perturbèd s. | SHAK 275:5 |
| slumber did my s. seal | WORD 356:25 |
| s. all compact of fire | SHAK 300:17 |
| s. burning but unbent | BYRON 85:16 |
| s. giveth life | BIBLE 55:23 |
| s. hath rejoiced in God | BIBLE 51:28 |
| s. indeed is willing | BIBLE 51:13 |
| S. of Delight | SHEL 304:32 |
| S. of God moved | BIBLE 38:13 |
| s. of party | WASH 342:21 |
| s. of the chainless mind | BYRON 87:7 |
| s. of the Lord shall rest | BIBLE 45:18 |
| s. of the place | VIRG 339:18 |
| s. of truth, unity, and concord | BOOK 65:9 |
| s. passed before my face | BIBLE 42:28 |
| s. shall return unto God | BIBLE 44:26 |
| s. in the woods | WORD 355:16 |
| There's a great s. gone | SHAK 271:7 |
| wounded s. who can bear | BIBLE 43:29 |
| **spirits:** her wanton s. look out | SHAK 297:9 |
| master s. of this age | SHAK 281:12 |
| ruffle up your s. | SHAK 281:26 |
| s. from the vasty deep | SHAK 278:3 |
| S. of well-shot woodcock | BETJ 36:20 |
| S. overwrought | WORD 356:11 |
| s. which are the house of life | BROW 74:22 |
| **spiritu:** Et cum s. tuo | MISS 231:9 |
| **spiritual:** inward and s. grace | BOOK 65:23 |
| not being a s. people | MANC 217:7 |
| **spiritualist:** you are a s. | SZASZ 321:25 |
| **spiritus:** Veni, Sancte S. | LANG 201:10 |
| **spit:** I have no gun, but I can s. | AUDEN 21:8 |
| s. upon my Jewish gabardine | SHAK 289:5 |
| **spite:** civic slander and the s. | TENN 325:25 |
| **splendid:** s. and a happy land | GOLD 154:25 |
| S. Isolation | FOST 144:7 |
| **splendide:** S. mendax | HOR 173:27 |

| | |
|---|---|
| **splendour:** Pavilioned in s. | GRANT 156:8 |
| s. borrows all her rays | POPE 251:18 |
| s. falls on castle walls | TENN 327:20 |
| s. in the grass | WORD 355:23 |
| Stung by the s. of a sudden | BROW 75:22 |
| **splendoured:** many-s. thing | THOM 331:15 |
| **split:** to make all s. | SHAK 290:18 |
| s. her in twain | TENN 328:13 |
| When I s. an infinitive | CHAN 94:11 |
| **spoil:** hath been the s. of me | SHAK 278:8 |
| **spoiled:** they s. the Egyptians | BIBLE 39:38 |
| **spoilers:** into the hands of s. | BIBLE 40:30 |
| **spoils:** victor belong the s. | MARCY 218:2 |
| **spoken:** Excellent things are s. | BOOK 67:24 |
| mouth of the Lord hath s. | BIBLE 46:9 |
| Rome has s. | AUG 22:5 |
| that never have s. yet | CHES 98:4 |
| When the lips have s. | SHEL 303:24 |
| **spongy:** on s. shoes | WILB 349:12 |
| **spontaneous:** S. joy | YEATS 359:4 |
| **spoon:** ate with a runcible s. | LEAR 203:13 |
| **spoons:** faster we counted our s. | EMER 136:20 |
| let us count our s. | JOHN 184:11 |
| world locks up its s. | SHAW 301:23 |
| **sport:** ended his s. with Tess | HARDY 161:5 |
| make s. for our neighbours | AUST 23:6 |
| s. of kings | SOM 311:2 |
| s. of kings | SURT 319:8 |
| S. that wrinkled Care derides | MILT 227:2 |
| To s. with Amaryllis | MILT 227:14 |
| To s. would be as tedious | SHAK 277:25 |
| They kill us for their s. | SHAK 283:21 |
| **sporting:** why this cruel s. | COCK 102:27 |
| **sports:** mountainous s. girl | BETJ 37:8 |
| While we can, the s. of love | JONS 187:16 |
| **sportsman:** s. is a man who | LEAC 203:4 |
| **spot:** little s. enclosed by grace | WATTS 343:2 |
| Out, damned s. | SHAK 287:27 |
| some untidy s. | AUDEN 21:2 |
| there is no s. in thee | BIBLE 44:35 |
| Tip me the black s. | STEV 317:3 |
| with a s. I damn him | SHAK 281:28 |
| **spots:** or the leopard his s. | BIBLE 46:30 |
| s. and kills anything | WAUGH 343:17 |
| **spotted:** s. snakes | SHAK 290:28 |
| **spouse:** shuts the s. Christ | HOPK 172:17 |
| **spout:** hurricanoes, s. | SHAK 283:6 |
| **sprang:** I s. to the stirrup | BROW 76:5 |
| **spray:** pinkly bursts the s. | BETJ 37:6 |
| rime was on the s. | HARDY 162:18 |
| thy hand a withered s. | ARN 17:8 |
| **spread:** Masters, s. yourselves | SHAK 290:17 |
| S. ALARM AND DESPONDENCY | PEN 247:8 |
| s. my dreams | YEATS 359:7 |
| **spree:** out on the s. | KIPL 196:15 |
| **spring:** Blossom by blossom the s. | SWIN 321:2 |
| can S. be far behind | SHEL 304:10 |
| chilly fingered s. | KEATS 190:13 |
| drunk deep of the Pierian s. | DRAY 126:2 |
| easing the S. | REED 258:16 |
| ever-bubbling s. of endless lies | COWP 110:3 |
| Falsehood has a perennial s. | BURKE 79:25 |
| found in the s. to follow | SWIN 321:15 |
| hounds of s. | SWIN 321:1 |
| In the s. a young man's fancy | TENN 326:6 |
| It is s., moonless night | THOM 330:16 |
| lap of the new come s. | SHAK 294:8 |
| rifle all the breathing s. | COLL 105:9 |
| s. breaks through again | COW 109:2 |
| s. has kept in its folds | ARAG 14:21 |
| s. is wound up tight | ANOU 14:5 |
| s. should vanish | FITZ 140:18 |
| s. summer autumn winter | CUMM 112:16 |
| suddenly was changed to S. | SHEL 304:28 |

spring (cont.):
| | |
|---|---|
| Sweet lovers love the s. | SHAK 273:10 |
| Sweet s., full of sweet days | HERB 167:8 |
| this s. of love resembleth | SHAK 298:18 |
| To have lived light in the s. | ARN 16:14 |
| Treasury is the s. of business | BAG 26:4 |
| Where are the songs of S. | KEATS 192:15 |
| with ever-returning s. | WHIT 348:24 |
| springes: s. to catch woodcocks | SHAK 274:24 |
| springlike: that fester are not s. | ABSE 1:1 |
| springs: Fifty s. are little room | HOUS 174:17 |
| many s., many bright | VAUG 337:13 |
| s. o' that countrie | BALL 28:8 |
| Wastes without s. | CLARE 101:5 |
| Where s. not fail | HOPK 172:7 |
| sprite: fleeting, wav'ring s. | HADR 159:14 |
| sprouting: S. despondently | ELIOT 134:4 |
| spur: Fame is the s. | MILT 227:14 |
| I have no s. | SHAK 286:1 |
| s. of all great minds | CHAP 94:20 |
| spurious: s. brat, Tom Jones | RICH 260:4 |
| spurs: Let the boy win his s. | EDW 130:21 |
| spy: letters for a s. | KIPL 196:28 |
| sent to s. out the land | BIBLE 40:16 |
| s. who came in from the cold | LE C 204:2 |
| squad: awkward s. fire over me | BURNS 82:30 |
| squadrons: side of the big s. | BUSS 83:20 |
| wingèd s. of the sky | MILM 225:13 |
| square: so thoroughly s. | LERN 205:26 |
| s. deal | ROOS 262:17 |
| squat: s., and packed with guile | BROO 73:7 |
| S. like a toad | MILT 229:13 |
| squawking: seven stars go s. | AUDEN 20:11 |
| squeak: s. and gibber | SHAK 274:1 |
| squeaking: With shrieking and s. | BROW 76:26 |
| squeezed: s. as a lemon is s. | GEDD 149:19 |
| squint: banish s. suspicion | MILT 226:13 |
| squire: Bless the s. | DICK 118:5 |
| stab: from hell's heart I s. | MELV 223:4 |
| stabant: S. orantes | VIRG 339:15 |
| stabat: S. Mater dolorosa | JAC 179:3 |
| stability: s. or enlargement | JOHN 182:5 |
| stable: In a s. born our Brother | DEAR 115:7 |
| stables: s. are the real centre | SHAW 301:5 |
| staff: By his cockle hat and s. | SHAK 276:32 |
| I'll break my s. | SHAK 296:13 |
| s. of this bruised reed | BIBLE 42:16 |
| thy rod and thy s. comfort me | BOOK 66:18 |
| your s. in your hand | BIBLE 39:37 |
| stag: runnable s., a kingly crop | DAV 114:11 |
| S. at Bay with the mentality | LEVIN 206:7 |
| stage: All the world's a s. | SHAK 272:24 |
| daughter on the s. | COW 109:5 |
| drown the s. with tears | SHAK 275:23 |
| played upon a s. now | SHAK 298:10 |
| Something for the modern s. | POUND 254:16 |
| s. where every man must play | SHAK 288:27 |
| this great s. of fools | SHAK 283:27 |
| to the well-trod s. anon | MILT 227:8 |
| two hours' traffick of our s. | SHAK 294:23 |
| wonder of our s. | JONS 187:25 |
| stagger: s. like a drunken man | BOOK 68:13 |
| stagnant: Of s. waters | WORD 355:11 |
| stagnation: keeps life from s. | BURN 81:16 |
| St Agnes: S.' Eve | KEATS 190:14 |
| stain: s. the stiff dishonoured | ELIOT 134:17 |
| world's slow s. | SHEL 303:11 |
| stained: hole in a s. glass window | CHAN 94:7 |
| stains: S. the white radiance | SHEL 303:13 |
| stair: place is by a winding s. | BACON 24:29 |
| structure in a winding s. | HERB 167:1 |
| staircase: S. wit | DID 120:20 |
| stairs: any that was kicked up s. | HAL 160:12 |
| down another man's s. | DANTE 113:23 |
| stale: How weary, s., flat | SHAK 274:10 |

stale (cont.):
| | |
|---|---|
| Tho' s., not ripe | POPE 250:15 |
| staled: S. are my thoughts | DYER 129:15 |
| stalk: Half asleep as they s. | HARDY 162:11 |
| stalking: s. in my chamber | WYATT 358:2 |
| stalking-horse: s. to error | BOL 63:3 |
| uses his folly like a s. | SHAK 273:14 |
| stall: Baby in an ox's s. | BETJ 36:18 |
| stalled: than a s. ox and hatred | BIBLE 43:26 |
| stamp: physics or s. collecting | RUTH 265:8 |
| rank is but the guinea's s. | BURNS 82:7 |
| stampa: e poi roppe la s. | ARIO 15:8 |
| stamps: kill animals and stick in s. | NIC 239:13 |
| stand: British soldier can s. up to | SHAW 301:1 |
| By uniting we s. | DICK 120:18 |
| firm spot on which to s. | ARCH 15:3 |
| Get up, s. up | MARL 218:6 |
| Here s. I. I can do no other | LUTH 212:8 |
| I s. at the door | BIBLE 57:23 |
| serve who only s. and wait | MILT 230:23 |
| s. and look at them long | WHIT 348:19 |
| s. at the latter day | BIBLE 42:36 |
| S. by thyself | BIBLE 46:25 |
| s. for nothing fall for anything | HAM 160:16 |
| S. not upon the order | SHAK 287:12 |
| s. out of my sun a little | DIOG 121:3 |
| S. still, you ever-moving spheres | MARL 218:12 |
| S. therefore | BIBLE 56:4 |
| s. up for bastards | SHAK 282:21 |
| time to s. and stare | DAV 114:20 |
| who will s. on either hand | MAC 214:4 |
| standard: raise the scarlet s. high | CONN 106:23 |
| standards: S. are always out of date | BENN 34:14 |
| St Andrews: S. by the Northern sea | LANG 201:1 |
| stands: s. about the woodland ride | HOUS 174:16 |
| S. the Church clock | BROO 73:8 |
| star: bright northern s. | LOV 210:18 |
| bright Occidental S. | BIBLE 38:12 |
| bright particular s. | SHAK 270:23 |
| Bright s., would I were | KEATS 190:10 |
| By a high s. our course is set | MACN 216:11 |
| catch a falling s. | DONNE 124:10 |
| constant as the northern s. | SHAK 281:9 |
| each, in his separate s. | KIPL 197:13 |
| great s. early drooped | WHIT 348:24 |
| Hitch your wagon to a s. | EMER 136:31 |
| like a falling s. | MILT 228:20 |
| moth for the s. | SHEL 305:5 |
| one bright s. | COL 104:10 |
| our life's S. | WORD 355:20 |
| seen his s. in the east | BIBLE 48:9 |
| S. captains glow | FLEC 141:14 |
| Sunset and evening s. | TENN 323:18 |
| tall ship and a s. to steer her | MAS 221:21 |
| There was a s. danced | SHAK 291:18 |
| Twinkle, twinkle, little s. | TAYL 323:3 |
| Westward the s. of empire | BERK 35:19 |
| you've got to come back a s. | JAMES 270:16 |
| Star-Chamber: S. matter | SHAK 290:7 |
| star-crossed: s. lovers | SHAK 294:22 |
| stardust: We are s. | MITC 232:4 |
| stare: dead s. in a million adults | SHAF 270:19 |
| In the s. of the deer | WILB 349:9 |
| no time to stand and s. | DAV 114:20 |
| With a stony British s. | TENN 326:27 |
| staring: Truth is s. at the sun | BELL 33:3 |
| stark: No, Sir; s. insensibility | JOHN 183:21 |
| starless: s. and bible-black | THOM 330:16 |
| starlight: S. and dewdrop | FOST 144:9 |
| s. lit my lonesomeness | HARDY 162:18 |
| there was nae s. | BALL 28:8 |
| starred: s. night Prince Lucifer | MER 223:21 |
| starry: heaven, her s. train | MILT 229:11 |
| Sidney's self, the s. paladin | BROW 77:13 |
| To entertain this s. stranger | CRAS 111:10 |

starry (cont.):
| | |
|---|---|
| very s., the horned moon | WORD 354:9 |

stars: climb half-way to the s.
| | |
|---|---|
| stars: climb half-way to the s. | CROSS 112:10 |
| crown of twelve s. | BIBLE 57:30 |
| cut him out in little s. | SHAK 295:14 |
| Far beyond the s. | VAUG 337:6 |
| journey-work of the s. | WHIT 348:18 |
| Look at the s.! | HOPK 172:16 |
| looking at the s. | WILDE 349:25 |
| not in our s. | SHAK 280:27 |
| opposition of the s. | MARV 220:13 |
| puts the s. to flight | FITZ 140:4 |
| seven s. go squawking | AUDEN 20:11 |
| seven s. in the sky | ANON 8:6 |
| shining of the s. | TENN 324:16 |
| s. are dead | AUDEN 21:15 |
| s. are my children | KEATS 193:9 |
| s. are old | TAYL 323:4 |
| s. hung with humid nightblue | JOYCE 188:19 |
| s. in her hair were seven | ROSS 263:6 |
| s. in their courses fought | BIBLE 40:32 |
| s. keep not their motion | SHAK 278:13 |
| s. leads through the atom | EDD 130:12 |
| s. move still | MARL 218:13 |
| s. rush out | COL 104:9 |
| S. scribble on our eyes | CRANE 110:31 |
| Stars, s.! and all eyes else | SHAK 299:3 |
| s. threw down their spears | BLAKE 62:6 |
| sun and the other s. | DANTE 113:24 |
| that's the way to the s. | VIRG 339:19 |
| Through struggle to the s. | ANON 13:18 |
| with how splendid s. | FLEC 141:19 |
| you chaste s. | SHAK 292:28 |
| Your chilly s. I can forgo | CORY 108:14 |

star-shine: s. at night
| | |
|---|---|
| star-shine: s. at night | STEV 317:19 |

starship: s. Enterprise
| | |
|---|---|
| starship: s. Enterprise | RODD 261:12 |

start: end is where we s. from
| | |
|---|---|
| start: end is where we s. from | ELIOT 133:11 |
| s. a scene or two | ELIOT 134:1 |
| s. from their spheres | SHAK 274:30 |
| s. together and finish | BEEC 31:23 |

started: to arrive where we s.
| | |
|---|---|
| started: to arrive where we s. | ELIOT 133:10 |

starting: you mar all with this s.
| | |
|---|---|
| starting: you mar all with this s. | SHAK 287:29 |

startle: come down and s.
| | |
|---|---|
| startle: come down and s. | AUDEN 20:10 |

starts: Was everything by s.
| | |
|---|---|
| starts: Was everything by s. | DRYD 127:12 |

starve: Let not poor Nelly s.
| | |
|---|---|
| starve: Let not poor Nelly s. | CHAR 95:4 |
| s. for want of impudence | DRYD 127:28 |

starved: apothecary than a s. poet
| | |
|---|---|
| starved: apothecary than a s. poet | LOCK 209:2 |

state: all were for the s.
| | |
|---|---|
| state: all were for the s. | MAC 214:5 |
| done the s. some service | SHAK 293:5 |
| free church in a free s. | CAV 93:14 |
| from thy s. mine never shall | MILT 229:28 |
| glories and my s. depose | SHAK 294:5 |
| glories of our blood and s. | SHIR 306:10 |
| Here's a s. of things | GILB 151:27 |
| I am the S. | LOUI 210:12 |
| In that s. I came, return | VAUG 337:10 |
| life is everywhere a s. | JOHN 183:4 |
| mine was the middle s. | DEFOE 115:14 |
| no such thing as the S. | AUDEN 21:11 |
| Only in the s. | HEGEL 164:19 |
| reinforcement of the S. | CAMUS 89:8 |
| sail on, O Ship of S. | LONG 209:11 |
| servants of the sovereign or s. | BACON 24:27 |
| S. in wonted manner keep | JONS 187:3 |
| S. is not 'abolished' | ENG 137:8 |
| s. without the means of change | BURKE 80:10 |
| to what a s. dost Thou bring | TER 329:7 |
| worl's in a s. o' chassis | O'CAS 240:22 |

stately: S. as a galleon
| | |
|---|---|
| stately: S. as a galleon | GREN 158:15 |
| s. tents of war | MARL 219:4 |
| S. Homes of England | COW 109:8 |
| s. homes of England | HEM 165:10 |

statement: black s. of pistons
| | |
|---|---|
| statement: black s. of pistons | SPEN 312:23 |

statements: previous s. are inoperative
| | |
|---|---|
| statements: previous s. are inoperative | ZIEG 361:3 |
| s. was interesting | TWAIN 335:19 |

states: goodly s. and kingdoms
| | |
|---|---|
| states: goodly s. and kingdoms | KEATS 192:10 |
| like to greater s. | SUCK 318:23 |

statesman: constitutional s.
| | |
|---|---|
| statesman: constitutional s. | BAG 26:2 |
| s. is a politician | POMP 250:12 |
| s. is a politician | TRUM 335:4 |
| s. who is enamoured | BIER 59:5 |
| Too nice for a s. | GOLD 155:2 |

statesmen: government of s.
| | |
|---|---|
| statesmen: government of s. | DISR 121:24 |

station: At the cross her s.
| | |
|---|---|
| station: At the cross her s. | JAC 179:3 |
| By Grand Central S. I sat down | SMART 308:15 |
| Hurries down the concrete s. | BETJ 37:7 |
| private s. | GAY 149:13 |
| she leaves the s. | SPEN 312:23 |
| walls of that antique s. | BEER 32:10 |

stations: know our proper s.
| | |
|---|---|
| stations: know our proper s. | DICK 118:5 |

statistical: s. improbability
| | |
|---|---|
| statistical: s. improbability | DAWK 115:4 |

statistics: damned lies and s.
| | |
|---|---|
| statistics: damned lies and s. | DISR 122:21 |
| We are just s., born | HOR 173:7 |

statues: Ep's s. are junk
| | |
|---|---|
| statues: Ep's s. are junk | ANON 8:2 |

status quo: restored the s.
| | |
|---|---|
| status quo: restored the s. | SQUI 314:4 |

stay: care to s. than will to go
| | |
|---|---|
| stay: care to s. than will to go | SHAK 295:19 |
| Here I am, and here I s. | MACM 215:13 |
| our love is here to s. | GERS 150:7 |
| S. for me there | KING 195:5 |
| want things to s. as they are | LAMP 200:19 |
| will not s. in place | ELIOT 133:1 |
| without thee here to s. | MILT 230:1 |

stay-at-home: Sweet S.
| | |
|---|---|
| stay-at-home: Sweet S. | DAV 114:22 |

stayed: s. me in a happy hour
| | |
|---|---|
| stayed: s. me in a happy hour | SHAK 291:24 |

stays: prays together s. together
| | |
|---|---|
| stays: prays together s. together | SCAL 267:16 |

steadfast: would I were s. as thou art
| | |
|---|---|
| steadfast: would I were s. as thou art | KEATS 190:10 |

steady: S., boys, steady
| | |
|---|---|
| steady: S., boys, steady | GARR 148:8 |
| thought more s. than an ebbing | FORD 143:11 |

steaks: smell of s. in passageways
| | |
|---|---|
| steaks: smell of s. in passageways | ELIOT 134:3 |

steal: Give me not poverty lest I s.
| | |
|---|---|
| steal: Give me not poverty lest I s. | DEFOE 115:13 |
| if you s. from many | MIZN 232:12 |
| lawyer can s. more | PUZO 256:26 |
| silently s. away | LONG 209:13 |
| s. my Basil-pot | KEATS 191:4 |
| s. the very teeth | ARAB 14:19 |
| they s. my thunder | DENN 117:2 |
| thieves break through and s. | BIBLE 49:1 |
| Thou shalt not s. | BIBLE 40:9 |
| Thou shalt not s. | CLOU 102:19 |

stealing: hands from picking and s.
| | |
|---|---|
| stealing: hands from picking and s. | BOOK 65:22 |
| Men are not hanged for s. | HAL 160:11 |
| s. dey gits you in jail | O'NEI 241:9 |
| s. ducks | ARAB 14:20 |

steals: s. my purse steals trash
| | |
|---|---|
| steals: s. my purse steals trash | SHAK 292:11 |
| s. something from the thief | SHAK 291:37 |

stealth: do a good action by s.
| | |
|---|---|
| stealth: do a good action by s. | LAMB 200:11 |
| Do good by s., and blush | POPE 252:31 |

steamer: in a s. from Harwich
| | |
|---|---|
| steamer: in a s. from Harwich | GILB 151:16 |
| s. breaking from the bay | AUDEN 20:25 |

steamers: Great s., white and gold
| | |
|---|---|
| steamers: Great s., white and gold | KIPL 197:19 |
| s. made an excursion to hell | PRIE 255:8 |

steaming: s. phrases
| | |
|---|---|
| steaming: s. phrases | SCH 267:26 |

steamy: Throws up a s. column
| | |
|---|---|
| steamy: Throws up a s. column | COWP 110:11 |

steed: his s. was the best
| | |
|---|---|
| steed: his s. was the best | SCOTT 268:18 |

steel: All shod with s.
| | |
|---|---|
| steel: All shod with s. | WORD 355:2 |
| clad in complete s. | MILT 226:14 |
| foemen worthy of their s. | SCOTT 268:9 |
| Give them the cold s., boys | ARM 15:23 |
| long divorce of s. | SHAK 280:14 |
| more than complete s. | ANON 8:7 |
| S.-true and blade-straight | STEV 317:20 |
| thin red line tipped with s. | RUSS 265:7 |
| wounded surgeon plies the s. | ELIOT 133:5 |

steeples: In s. far and near
| | |
|---|---|
| steeples: In s. far and near | HOUS 174:20 |
| s. of Fermanagh and Tyrone | CHUR 99:7 |
| you have drenched our s. | SHAK 283:6 |

steer: they s. their courses
| | |
|---|---|
| steer: they s. their courses | BUTL 83:25 |

Stein: I don't like the family S.
| | |
|---|---|
| Stein: I don't like the family S. | ANON 8:2 |

stem: rod out of the s. of Jesse
| | |
|---|---|
| stem: rod out of the s. of Jesse | BIBLE 45:18 |

strain: not I build; no, but s. — HOPK 172:19
That s. again — SHAK 297:14
which s. at a gnat — BIBLE 50:31
Words s. — ELIOT 133:1
strains: s. of unpremeditated art — SHEL 305:6
strait: S. is the gate, and narrow — BIBLE 49:13
straits: With echoing s. between — ARN 17:22
Strand: I walk down the S. — HARG 162:20
where's the Maypole in the S. — BRAM 71:13
strands: these last s. of man — HOPK 171:25
strange: foul, s., and unnatural — SHAK 274:31
Into something rich and s. — SHAK 296:1
Let us be very s. and well-bred — CONG 106:20
Lord's song: in a s. land — BOOK 69:3
millions of s. shadows — SHAK 299:18
s. and sinister embroidered — JAMES 180:1
s. faces, other minds — TENN 324:19
stranger in a s. land — BIBLE 39:29
s. the change from major — PORT 253:19
strangeness: some s. in the proportion — BACON 24:14
stranger: From the wiles of the s. — NASH 237:11
I, a s. and afraid — HOUS 174:11
I was a s., and ye took me in — BIBLE 51:5
Look, s., at this island now — AUDEN 20:26
never love a s. — BENS 34:21
s.! 'Eave 'arf a brick at 'im — PUNCH 256:9
s. here in Gloucestershire — SHAK 293:17
s. in a strange land — BIBLE 39:29
S. than fiction — BYRON 86:29
S., unless with bedroom eyes — AUDEN 21:8
surety for a s. shall smart — BIBLE 43:18
To entertain this starry s. — CRAS 111:10
strangers: kindness of s. — WILL 351:6
forgetful to entertain s. — BIBLE 56:29
For we are s. before thee — BIBLE 42:17
I do desire we may be better s. — SHAK 273:5
strangled: s. with the guts of priests — MESL 223:27
strangling: Than s. in a string — HOUS 174:19
Stratford atte Bowe: scole of S. — CHAU 95:15
straw: Take a s. and throw it up — SELD 269:18
Things are but as s. dogs — LAO-T 201:11
strawberries: S. swimming in the cream — PEELE 247:2
strawberry: S. fields forever — MCC 205:15
strawed: where thou hast not s. — BIBLE 51:2
strayed: s. from thy ways like — BOOK 63:13
stream: have their s. and pond — BROO 73:2
leaves in the glassy s. — SHAK 277:6
long-legged fly upon the s. — YEATS 359:15
On summer eves by haunted s. — MILT 227:7
painted meadow, or a purling s. — ADD 2:21
Still glides the S. — WORD 356:18
There's an old mill by the s. — ARMS 15:24
Time, like an ever-rolling s. — WATTS 343:15
streamers: s. waving in the wind — GAY 149:17
streams: Gilding pale s. — SHAK 299:17
More pellucid s. — WORD 355:7
pants the hart for cooling s. — TATE 322:16
street: breaks at the end of the s. — MACN 216:4
bald s. breaks the blank day — TENN 325:1
done by jostling in the s. — BLAKE 61:15
Here in the long unlovely s. — TENN 324:26
inability to cross the s. — WOOLF 354:5
s. fighting man — JAGG 179:7
s. which is called Straight — BIBLE 54:13
sunny side of the s. — FIEL 139:15
streets: children died in the s. — AUDEN 20:18
Down these mean s. — CHAN 94:9
s. are paved with gold — COLM 105:13
S. FLOODED. PLEASE ADVISE — BENC 34:6
s. of a hundred cities — HOOV 171:18
s. that no longer exist — FENT 138:23
when night darkens the s. — MILT 228:15
strength: full of the s. of five — BETJ 37:8
His s. the more is — BUNY 79:9

strength (cont.):
king's name is a tower of s. — SHAK 294:20
Let us roll all our s. — MARV 221:1
pleasure in the s. of an horse — BOOK 69:10
shewed s. with his arm — BIBLE 51:29
strength is as the s. of ten — TENN 328:15
s. then but labour and sorrow — BOOK 67:26
S. through joy — LEY 206:20
sucklings hast thou ordained s. — BOOK 66:10
To have a giant's s. — SHAK 288:13
strengthen: S. ye the weak hands — BIBLE 46:5
strengtheneth: Christ which s. — BIBLE 56:10
strenuous: doctrine of the s. life — ROOS 262:15
round of s. idleness — WORD 356:11
stress: Storm and s. — KAUF 190:6
stretch: S. him out longer — SHAK 284:7
stretched: things which he s. — TWAIN 335:18
stricken: old and well s. in age — BIBLE 39:14
Why, let the s. deer go weep — SHAK 276:12
stride: At one s. comes the dark — COL 104:9
strife: Bear the toil, maintain the s. — WHITE 347:16
curse to party-s. — WORD 354:18
In place of s. — CAST 92:15
stern s., and carnage dear — SCOTT 268:23
s. is o'er, the battle done — POTT 253:28
Wherein the graver had a s. — JONS 187:20
strike: S. flat the thick rotundity — SHAK 283:6
s. his father's crown — SHAK 279:1
s. it out — JOHN 184:27
that you s. it in anger — SHAW 301:32
when in doubt, s. it out — TWAIN 336:6
striker: no s., not greedy of filthy — BIBLE 56:16
string: end of a golden s. — BLAKE 60:20
Harp not on that s. — SHAK 294:19
s. that ties them together — MONT 233:19
Than strangling in a s. — HOUS 174:19
untune that s. — SHAK 296:30
strings: s. in the human heart — DICK 117:21
strip: S. thine own back — SHAK 283:25
striped: He was no s. frieze — STR 318:11
stripes: with his s. we are healed — BIBLE 46:19
strive: s. officiously to keep alive — CLOU 102:17
To s., to seek, to find — TENN 328:25
strives: Man will err while yet he s. — GOET 154:3
stroke: none so fast as s. — COKE 103:6
s. a platitude until it purrs — MARQ 219:23
strokes: As amorous of their s. — SHAK 271:14
strong: advantage of s. people — BONH 63:11
battle to the s. — DAV 114:12
but s. in will — TENN 328:25
But wants that little s. — HOLM 170:17
Eternal Father, s. to save — WHIT 348:9
nor the battle to the s. — BIBLE 44:20
only the S. shall thrive — SERV 270:11
river is a s. brown god — ELIOT 133:7
Sorrow and silence are s. — LONG 209:16
s. and of a good courage — BIBLE 40:26
S. brother in God — BELL 33:14
s. came forth sweetness — BIBLE 41:3
s. drink unto him — BIBLE 44:5
S. is the lion—like a coal — SMART 308:10
s. man in a blatant land — TENN 326:26
s. name of the Trinity — ALEX 4:5
s. that they come to fourscore — BOOK 67:26
that s., silent man — MORL 235:8
those who think they are s. — BID 59:1
without whom nothing is s. — BOOK 64:24
stronger: are on the side of the s. — TAC 322:8
interest of the s. party — PLATO 249:21
s. by every thing you see — STER 315:18
they were s. than lions — BIBLE 41:22
strongest: reason of the s. — LA F 199:18
stronghold: safe is our God is still — LUTH 212:10
strove: A little still she s. — BYRON 86:1
unbecoming men that s. with — TENN 328:23

| | | | |
|---|---|---|---|
| struck: I s. the board, and cried | HERB 166:22 | sublime: audience yelled 'You're s.' | HARG 162:21 |
| s. regularly like gongs | COW 109:11 | Howls the s. | DICK 119:7 |
| struggle: alarms of s. and flight | ARN 16:12 | My object all s. | GILB 152:1 |
| gods themselves s. in vain | SCH 267:20 | Of poetry; to maintain 'the s.' | POUND 254:14 |
| perpetual s. for room and food | MALT 217:6 | One step above the s. | PAINE 244:8 |
| Say not the s. naught availeth | CLOU 102:22 | s. to the ridiculous | NAP 237:2 |
| s. between the artist man | SHAW 301:18 | Wordsworthian or egotistical s. | KEATS 193:8 |
| S. for Existence | DARW 114:4 | submerged: The S. Tenth | BOOTH 69:21 |
| What s. to escape | KEATS 191:18 | submission: appetite for s. | ELIOT 132:8 |
| struggles: history of class s. | ENG 221:14 | submit: to the destructive element s. | CONR 107:7 |
| strumpet: Into a s.'s fool | SHAK 271:3 | Must he s.? | SHAK 294:2 |
| she is a s. | SHAK 275:13 | subsistence: S. only increases | MALT 217:5 |
| struts: s. and frets his hour upon | SHAK 288:5 | substance: summed with all his s. | CHAP 94:15 |
| Stuart: S. or Nassau go higher | PRIOR 255:10 | Wasted his s. with riotous | BIBLE 52:29 |
| stubble: like sparks among the s. | BIBLE 47:29 | subterranean: s. fields | WORD 356:14 |
| studied: he s. from the life | ARMS 16:1 | subtle: God is s. but not malicious | EINS 131:8 |
| studies: S. serve for delight | BACON 25:13 | more s. than any beast | BIBLE 38:24 |
| studio: Sine ira et s. | TAC 322:6 | slipper and s. knave | SHAK 292:6 |
| studious: S. let me sit | THOM 331:27 | suburb: s. stretched beyond | BETJ 36:21 |
| S. of elegance and ease | GAY 149:12 | suburbs: In the south s. | SHAK 298:8 |
| S. of laborious ease | COWP 110:10 | s. of your good pleasure | SHAK 281:7 |
| studiously: stood apart, s. neutral | WILS 351:19 | succeed: How to s. in business | MEAD 222:17 |
| study: craggy paths of s. | JONS 187:13 | succeeds: Whenever a friend s. | VIDAL 338:13 |
| My s.'s ornament, thou shell | MIDD 224:8 | success: bitch-goddess s. | JAMES 180:7 |
| proper s. of mankind is books | HUXL 177:5 | ecstasy, is s. in life | PATER 246:15 |
| proper s. of mankind is man | POPE 252:17 | If A is a s. in life | EINS 131:10 |
| science and s. of man | CHAR 95:9 | mortals to command s. | ADD 2:13 |
| s. is a weariness | BIBLE 44:27 | s. in life is to be a good | SPEN 312:16 |
| S. is like the heaven's | SHAK 284:10 | S. is counted sweetest | DICK 120:13 |
| studying: s. how I may compare | SHAK 294:10 | S. is relative | ELIOT 132:23 |
| stuff: I count life just a s. | BROW 76:7 | Sweet smell of s. | LEHM 204:13 |
| should be made of sterner s. | SHAK 281:20 | there's no s. like failure | DYLAN 130:4 |
| s. as great part of Shakespeare | GEOR 149:24 | These s. encourages | VIRG 339:10 |
| such s. as dreams are made on | SHAK 296:10 | true s. is to labour | STEV 317:6 |
| too short to s. a mushroom | CONR 107:10 | very lively hope of s. | SMITH 310:14 |
| stuffed: s. their mouths with gold | BEVAN 38:2 | vulgar judgements—s. | BURKE 79:18 |
| We are the s. men | ELIOT 133:17 | With his surcease s. | SHAK 285:22 |
| stuffs: S. out his vacant garments | SHAK 282:8 | successful: S. crimes alone | DRYD 128:8 |
| stumbling: S. on melons, as I pass | MARV 220:15 | successive: his s. journeys run | WATTS 343:12 |
| stumps: pitch, and s., and all | LANG 201:2 | suck: I have given s., and know | SHAK 286:6 |
| stung: S. by the splendour | BROW 75:22 | sucked: s. on country pleasures | DONNE 124:5 |
| stupid: s. man is doing something | SHAW 300:25 | sucker: give a s. an even break | FIEL 139:16 |
| s. neither forgive nor forget | SZASZ 321:24 | There's a s. born every minute | BARN 29:9 |
| stupidity: Such an excess of s. | JOHN 184:14 | sucking: s. child shall play | BIBLE 45:20 |
| With s. the gods struggle in vain | SCH 267:20 | suckle: s. fools and chronicle | SHAK 292:4 |
| Sturm: S. und Drang | KAUF 190:6 | sucklings: babes and s. | BOOK 66:10 |
| Stygian: In S. cave forlorn | MILT 226:27 | sudden: I said to Dawn: Be s. | THOM 331:10 |
| S. smoke of the pit | JAM 179:9 | splendour of a s. thought | BROW 75:22 |
| style: cut, the s., the line | LOES 209:6 | too unadvised, too s. | SHAK 295:1 |
| He has no real s. | PIC 248:18 | suddenly: s. became depraved | JUV 189:3 |
| how the s. refines | POPE 252:5 | sue: used to s. than to command | SCOTT 268:8 |
| only secret of s. | ARN 18:13 | Suez: somewheres east of S. | KIPL 196:23 |
| S. is life | FLAU 141:10 | suffer: For ye s. fools gladly | BIBLE 55:27 |
| S. is the dress of thought | WESL 346:18 | let's on the heights | HUGO 176:1 |
| S. is the man | BUFF 78:5 | should have courage to s. | TROL 334:13 |
| true definition of a s. | SWIFT 320:4 | S. the little children | BIBLE 51:25 |
| When we see a natural s. | PASC 246:1 | sufferance: s. is the badge of all | SHAK 289:4 |
| suave: S., mari magno turbantibus | LUCR 212:4 | suffering: About s. they were never wrong | AUDEN 21:1 |
| subdue: It may s. for a moment | BURKE 80:1 | learn in s. what they teach | SHEL 303:22 |
| replenish the earth, and s. it | BIBLE 38:17 | put me to s. | METH 223:28 |
| s. the arrogant | VIRG 339:16 | S. is permanent, obscure | WORD 354:13 |
| To chasten and s. | WORD 355:10 | sufferings: patience under their s. | BOOK 64:19 |
| To teach, convince, s. | AUBER 19:15 | To each his s. | GRAY 157:13 |
| subdued: My nature is s. | SHAK 300:7 | sufficiency: An elegant s. | THOM 331:23 |
| subiectis: Parcere s. et debellare | VIRG 339:16 | sufficient: perfect and s. sacrifice | BOOK 65:16 |
| subject: Grasp the s., the words | CATO 92:23 | S. unto the day | BIBLE 49:5 |
| honour is the s. | SHAK 280:26 | suicide: longest s. note in history | KAUF 190:4 |
| I know what it is to be a s. | ELIZ 135:5 | It is s. to be abroad | BECK 31:7 |
| Lies the s. of all verse | BROW 74:24 | s. 25 years after his death | BEAV 31:5 |
| Little s., little wit | CAREY 90:1 | s. kills two people | MILL 225:1 |
| s. and a sovereign | CHAR 94:25 | suis: J'y s., j'y reste | MACM 215:13 |
| s.'s duty is the king's | SHAK 279:14 | Suisse: point de S. | RAC 257:17 |
| We know a s. ourselves | JOHN 185:5 | suits: trappings and the s. of woe | SHAK 274:8 |
| subjects: policy when s. are rebels | BURKE 80:16 | suivre: il fallait bien les s. | LEDR 204:4 |

Sule Skerry: My home it is the S. — BALL 27:17
sulphur: oat-cakes, and s. — SMITH 309:26
sulphurous: s. and thought-executing fires — SHAK 283:6
sultry: where the climate's s. — BYRON 85:24
sum: Cogito, ergo s. — DESC 117:9
s. obtained I this freedom — BIBLE 54:24
s. of matter remains exactly — BACON 24:4
s. of things for pay — HOUS 174:13
Sumatra: giant rat of S. — DOYLE 125:17
summer: after many a s. dies the swan — TENN 328:17
compare thee to a s.'s day — SHAK 299:12
Eternal s. gilds them yet — BYRON 86:13
Expect Saint Martin's s. — SHAK 280:3
ful ofte a myrie s.'s day — CHAU 96:16
In a s. seson, whan softe — LANG 201:5
In s., quite the other way — STEV 317:12
It was a s. evening — SOUT 311:18
long bathing of a s.'s day — WORD 356:9
lordships on a hot s. afternoon — ANON 11:3
murmur of a s.'s day — ARN 17:5
On s. eves by haunted stream — MILT 227:7
s. afternoon — JAMES 180:5
s. birdcage in a garden — WEBS 344:23
s. by this sun of York — SHAK 294:13
S. has set in with its usual — COL 105:2
s. in England — WALP 341:22
S. is icumen in — ANON 10:16
s.'s lease hath all too short — SHAK 299:12
S. time an' the livin' is easy — GERS 168:6
That never knew the s. woods — TENN 325:3
This guest of s. — SHAK 285:21
thy eternal s. shall not fade — SHAK 299:13
'Tis the last rose of s. — MOORE 234:18
summers: s. in a sea of glory — SHAK 280:18
thousand s. are over and dead — SWIN 321:15
summertime: In s. on Bredon — HOUS 174:20
summits: Nations touch at their s. — BAG 26:9
summons: s. thee to heaven — SHAK 286:11
summum: S. bonum — CIC 100:22
sun: all, except their s., is set — BYRON 86:13
And I will sing of the s. — POUND 254:11
And loves to live i' the s. — SHAK 272:21
Before you let the s. in — THOM 330:18
blushing discontented s. — SHAK 293:29
bosom-friend of the maturing s. — KEATS 192:14
Busy old fool, unruly s. — DONNE 124:11
crept out again to feel the s. — BROW 74:27
doors against a setting s. — SHAK 296:19
farthing candle to the s. — YOUNG 360:16
glorious summer by this s. of York — SHAK 294:13
going down of the s. — BINY 59:12
golden apples of the s. — YEATS 360:1
Go out in the midday s. — COW 109:4
heaven's glorious s. — SHAK 284:10
hidden s. that rings black Cyprus — FLEC 141:18
I am too much i' the s. — SHAK 274:6
Juliet is the s. — SHAK 294:29
knitters in the s. — SHAK 297:31
light a candle to the s. — SIDN 306:14
Light breaks where no s. — THOM 330:12
little window where the s. — HOOD 171:8
livery of the burnished s. — SHAK 289:6
love that moves the s. — DANTE 113:24
more the heat o' the s. — SHAK 273:27
most shene in the s. — LANG 201:9
Mother, give me the s. — IBSEN 178:4
Move him into the s. — OWEN 243:24
new thing under the s. — BIBLE 44:8
nothing like the s. — SHAK 300:11
Now the s. is laid to sleep — JONS 187:3
on which the s. never sets — NORTH 240:6
our own disasters the s. — SHAK 282:22
owes no homage unto the s. — BROW 74:21
place in the s. — BÜLOW 78:8

sun (cont.):
place in the s. — WILH 350:25
short while towards the s. — SPEN 312:24
So when the s. in bed — MILT 227:29
stand out of my s. a little — DIOG 121:3
s. also rises — HEM 165:14
s. does not set in my dominions — SCH 267:19
s. go down upon your wrath — BIBLE 55:33
s. goes down with a flaming — BOND 63:9
s. in lonely lands — TENN 323:21
s. looked over the mountain's — BROW 76:23
S. of righteousness arise — BIBLE 47:26
s. shall not burn thee — BOOK 68:26
s. shall rise — WOTT 357:16
S.'s rim dips — COL 104:9
s. to me is dark — MILT 230:12
s. to rise on the evil — BIBLE 48:24
s. we have is made of Newcastle — WALP 341:20
though we cannot make our s. — MARV 221:1
Till the s. grows cold — TAYL 323:4
tired the s. with talking — CORY 108:13
To have enjoyed the s. — ARN 16:14
Truth is staring at the s. — BELL 33:3
Under the s. — HOUS 175:1
volley of the s. — WILB 349:13
walks under the midday s. — MILT 226:12
Was sitting in the s. — SOUT 311:18
whan softe was the s. — LANG 201:5
what are you when the s. shall rise — WOTT 357:16
woman clothed with the s. — BIBLE 57:30
worship to the garish s. — SHAK 295:14
sunbathing: s. and jazz — WAUGH 343:22
sunbeam: Jesus wants me for a s. — TALB 322:10
s. in a winter's day — DYER 129:17
sunbeams: motes that people the s. — MILT 226:23
s. out of cucumbers — SWIFT 319:22
Sunday: For this is S. morning — MACN 216:9
Here of a S. morning — HOUS 174:20
on a rainy S. afternoon — ERTZ 137:15
Repentance on a S. — YBAR 358:11
than a rainy S. in London — DE Q 117:4
Sundays: begin a journey on S. — SWIFT 320:8
sundial: s., and I make a botch — BELL 33:26
sundry: s. and manifold changes — BOOK 64:23
s. times and in divers manners — BIBLE 56:23
sunk: All s. beneath the wave — COWP 109:28
sunless: Down to a s. sea — COL 103:22
From sunshine to the s. land — WORD 354:23
sunlight: s. on the garden — MACN 216:10
sunny: leaps St Jim — HANFF 161:6
To the s. side of the street — FIEL 139:15
sunrise: Lives in Eternity's s. — BLAKE 61:16
suns: blest by s. of home — BROO 73:10
S., that set, may rise again — JONS 187:15
sunset: beliefs may make a fine s. — MADAN 216:13
cloud-continents of s.-seas — ALDR 3:17
Now the s. breezes shiver — NEWB 238:12
S. and evening star — TENN 323:18
there's a s.-touch — BROW 75:13
sunsets: I have a horror of s. — PROU 255:20
Or Autumn s. exquisitely dying — HUXL 177:13
sunshine: calm s. of the heart — CONS 107:12
comforteth like s. after rain — SHAK 300:18
digressions are the s. — STER 315:15
From s. to the sunless land — WORD 354:23
out into adventure and s. — FORS 143:19
s. and with applause — BUNY 79:2
sunt: Sint ut s. aut non sint — CLEM 102:3
sup: shall s. with my Lord — BRUCE 77:22
superbos: subiectis et debellare s. — VIRG 339:16
superfluity: barren s. of words — GARTH 148:15
superfluous: in the poorest thing s. — SHAK 283:4
nothing is s. — LEON 205:22
s. . . . A supernumerary—that's all — TURG 335:11
s., a very necessary thing — VOLT 340:22

**superfluous** (cont.):
s. in me to point out ADAMS 1:8
**superior:** embarrass the s. SHAW 301:31
I am a most s. person ANON 9:12
S. people never make long MOORE 234:9
want no-one to be their s. TOCQ 333:4
**superman:** I teach you the s. NIET 239:16
It's a plane! It's S. ANON 7:5
**superstition:** stamp out s. VOLT 340:21
S. is the poetry of life GOET 154:10
S. is the religion of feeble BURKE 80:18
S. sets the whole world VOLT 340:16
s. to enslave a philosophy INGE 178:12
**superstitions:** to end as s. HUXL 177:18
**supped:** Hobson has s. MILT 228:4
I have s. full with horrors SHAK 288:4
**supper:** Last-s.-carved-on-a-peach-stone LANC 200:20
consider s. as a turnpike EDW 131:6
**supplications:** make our common s. BOOK 64:10
**supplied:** once destroyed, can never be s. GOLD 154:18
**supplies:** I've just bought fresh s. BREC 71:21
**support:** But to s. him after SHAK 296:16
help and s. of the woman EDW 131:2
no invisible means of s. BUCH 77:27
s. me when I am in the wrong MELB 222:22
without visible means of s. BIER 59:8
**supports:** s. with insolence JOHN 182:10
**suppress:** power of s. NORT 240:8
**supreme:** great arts, in none s. ARN 17:21
**sure:** Ever faithful, ever s. MILT 227:9
Most s. in all His ways NEWM 238:20
What nobody is s. about BELL 33:21
**surety:** s. for a stranger BIBLE 43:18
**surface:** looks dingy on the s. PIRS 249:2
**surfeit:** s. by eating of a lamprey FABY 138:7
They are as sick that s. SHAK 288:28
**surge:** s. and thunder of the Odyssey LANG 201:3
**surgeon:** wounded s. plies the steel ELIOT 133:5
**surmise:** with a wild s. KEATS 192:11
**surprise:** Live frugally on s. WALK 341:4
Respect was mingled with s. SCOTT 268:9
sound of s. BALL 28:13
what gave rise to no little s. BARH 28:19
**surprised:** like a guilty thing s. WORD 355:22
S. by joy—impatient as the wind WORD 357:4
S. by unjust force MILT 226:18
**surprises:** millions of s. HERB 167:7
S. are foolish things AUST 22:16
**surquidrie:** Of s. and foul presumpcioun CHAU 96:13
**surrender:** Guards die but do not s. CAMB 88:11
we shall never s. CHUR 99:13
**survey:** I am monarch of all I s. COWP 110:18
time that takes s. of all SHAK 278:14
When I s. the wondrous cross WATTS 343:4
**survival:** s. of the fittest ROCK 261:11
S. of the fittest SPEN 312:17
**survive:** Noah dare hope to s. HUXL 177:11
**survived:** I s. SIEY 307:1
**survives:** s. in the valley of its AUDEN 20:23
**survivors:** dying is more the s.' affair MANN 217:14
**Susan:** black-eyed S. GAY 149:17
**susceptible:** peculiarly s. to calves HUXL 177:10
peculiarly s. to draughts WILDE 349:21
**suspects:** Round up the usual s. EPST 137:12
**suspenders:** must not forget the s. KIPL 197:23
**suspension:** willing s. of disbelief COL 104:24
**suspicion:** banish squint s. MILT 226:13
Caesar's wife must be above s. CAES 87:25
**sutlers:** sapient s. of the Lord ELIOT 134:5
**swaddling:** in s. clothes BIBLE 51:32
**swagman:** Once a jolly s. PAT 246:16
**swain:** a frugal s. HOME 170:18
**swains:** all our s. commend her SHAK 298:19
**swallow:** and the s. a nest BOOK 67:20
come before the s. dares SHAK 298:32

**swallow** (cont.):
O tell her, S. TENN 327:24
speed of a s., the grace of a boy BETJ 37:11
s. a camel BIBLE 50:31
s. has set her six young BROW 76:10
S., my sister, O sister SWIN 321:15
**swamps:** bellowing across primeval s. WOD 352:19
**swan:** He makes a s.-like end SHAK 289:19
like a sleeping s. SHEL 304:21
many a summer dies the s. TENN 328:17
nothing so much as a black s. JUV 189:7
pale s. in her watery nest SHAK 299:9
Sweet S. of Avon JONS 187:29
**Swanee:** down upon the S. River FOST 144:12
**swans:** Dumb s., not chattering SIDN 306:22
honking amongst tuneful s. VIRG 340:5
old ships sail like s. FLEC 141:18
saw two s. of goodly hue SPEN 313:17
s. are geese ARN 16:18
s. of others are geese WALP 342:1
**swarm:** S. over, Death BETJ 37:9
**sway:** A little rule, a little s. DYER 129:17
**sways:** the level in her husband's SHAK 297:30
**swear:** s. not by the moon SHAK 294:33
when very angry, s. TWAIN 336:5
**swears:** Money doesn't talk, it s. DYLAN 130:3
**sweat:** blood, toil, tears and s. CHUR 99:11
s. of its labourers EIS 131:14
s. of thy face shalt thou BIBLE 39:2
They do not s. and whine WHIT 348:19
We spend our midday s. QUAR 257:2
will s. but for promotion SHAK 272:17
**sweating:** Quietly s. palm to palm HUXL 177:12
**sweats:** regrets, and the bloody s. WILDE 350:17
**sweep:** chimneys I s. and in soot BLAKE 61:19
To s. the dust behind the door SHAK 291:10
**sweeping:** The S. up the Heart DICK 120:10
**sweeps:** Who s. a room HERB 166:26
**sweet:** All is not s., all is not JONS 187:5
Amazing grace! how s. the sound NEWT 239:7
buried in so s. a place SHEL 303:2
But then, how it was s. BROW 75:21
come kiss me, s. and twenty SHAK 297:23
comes in the s. o' the year SHAK 298:26
dead thing that smells s. THOM 330:22
full of s. days and roses HERB 167:8
How s. the name of Jesus NEWT 239:9
parting is such s. sorrow SHAK 295:4
Sleep is s. to the labouring BUNY 79:4
sleep of a labouring man is s. BIBLE 44:15
So s. was ne'er so fatal SHAK 293:1
Stolen waters are s. BIBLE 43:15
s. and fair she seems WALL 341:12
s. and low ARMS 15:24
S. and low, sweet and low TENN 327:19
S. are the uses of adversity SHAK 272:14
S. is pleasure after pain DRYD 127:20
S. is revenge BYRON 86:2
S. reasonableness of Jesus ARN 18:10
S. smell of success LEHM 204:13
S. Stay-at-Home DAV 114:22
S. the countless tongues MANT 217:17
s. the moonlight sleeps SHAK 290:1
s. to taste prove in digestion SHAK 293:11
would smell as s. SHAK 294:31
**sweeten:** not s. this little hand SHAK 287:30
**sweeteners:** Love and scandal are the best s. FIEL 139:9
**sweeter:** O s. than the berry GAY 149:1
those unheard are s. KEATS 191:19
**sweetest:** Success is counted s. DICK 120:13
s. things turn sourest SHAK 300:2
**sweetness:** its s. on the desert air GRAY 157:9
Our s., up into one ball MARV 221:1
strong came forth s. BIBLE 41:3
s. and light ARN 17:25

sweetness (cont.):

| | |
|---|---|
| where s. and light failed | FORS 143:18 |
| which are s. and light | SWIFT 319:18 |
| With s. fills the breast | CASW 92:17 |
| sweet peas: s., on tip-toe | KEATS 191:6 |
| sweets: bag of boiled s. | CRIT 111:22 |
| box where s. compacted lie | HERB 167:8 |
| discandy, melt their s. | SHAK 271:22 |
| Stolen s. are always sweeter | HUNT 176:16 |
| Stolen s. are best | CIBB 100:18 |
| S. into your list | HUNT 176:15 |
| S. to the sweet | SHAK 277:11 |
| swell: Thou s.! Thou witty | HART 163:1 |
| To s. a progress, start a scene | ELIOT 134:1 |
| swelling: prologues to the s. act | SHAK 285:10 |
| swept: s., and garnished | BIBLE 50:3 |
| S. it for half a year | CARR 91:21 |
| S. with confused alarms | ARN 16:12 |
| Swift: S. has sailed into his rest | YEATS 360:2 |
| swift: race is not to the s. | BIBLE 44:20 |
| race is to the s. | DAV 114:12 |
| swifter: s. than a weaver's shuttle | BIBLE 42:30 |
| they were s. than eagles | BIBLE 41:22 |
| swiftness: O s. never ceasing | PEELE 247:3 |
| swim: boys that s. on bladders | SHAK 280:18 |
| swimmers: s. into cleanness leaping | BROO 73:9 |
| swimming: surprise s. in the air | EDW 131:3 |
| s. down along the Lee | SPEN 313:17 |
| swindles: all truly great s. | HENRY 166:4 |
| swine: pearls before s. | BIBLE 49:8 |
| swing: and s. for it | KING 195:19 |
| S. low, sweet chariot | ANON 10:17 |
| Swing, s. together | CORY 108:11 |
| We s. ungirded hips | SORL 311:15 |
| Switzerland: S. they had brotherly love | WELL 345:5 |
| swoons: S. to a waltz | HUXL 177:12 |
| swoop: At one fell s. | SHAK 287:26 |
| take away all at one s. | WEBS 344:22 |
| sword: brave man with a s. | WILDE 350:16 |
| father's s. he has girded on | MOORE 234:16 |
| his terrible swift s. | HOWE 175:7 |
| I gave them a s. | NIXON 240:4 |
| mightier than the s. | BULW 78:11 |
| My s., I give to him | BUNY 79:10 |
| my s. sleep in my hand | BLAKE 61:12 |
| nation shall not lift up s. | BIBLE 45:5 |
| pen is worse than the s. | BURT 83:9 |
| Of honour and the s. | CHES 97:24 |
| not to send peace, but a s. | BIBLE 49:31 |
| shall perish with the s. | BIBLE 51:14 |
| sigh is the s. of an angel | BLAKE 60:18 |
| s. is the axis of the world | DE G 116:6 |
| s. of this stone and anvil | MAL 216:23 |
| upon the edge of the s. | BOOK 67:15 |
| when he first drew the s. | CLAR 101:9 |
| swords: either dreams or s. | LOW 211:3 |
| Keep up your bright s. | SHAK 291:31 |
| s. into plowshares | BIBLE 45:5 |
| s. shall play the orators | MARL 219:5 |
| swore: My tongue s. | EUR 137:22 |
| sworn: had I so s. as you | SHAK 286:6 |
| sycamore: soul sat sighing by a s. | SHAK 292:26 |
| syllable: last s. of recorded time | SHAK 288:5 |
| syllables: S. govern the world | SELD 269:21 |
| syllabub: s. in the hotel in Hell | SITW 307:18 |
| syllogism: conclusion of your s. | O'BR 240:19 |
| symbol: for the s. at your door | ANON 8:6 |
| symbols: s. of a high romance | KEATS 192:20 |
| symmetry: frame thy fearful s. | BLAKE 62:5 |
| sympathize: s. with people's pains | HUXL 177:8 |
| With her great master so to s. | MILT 227:25 |
| sympathy: It is the secret s. | SCOTT 268:11 |
| Tea and s. | AND 5:14 |
| symptoms: dying of a hundred good s. | POPE 253:14 |
| systems: Our little s. have their day | TENN 324:23 |

# T

| | |
|---|---|
| T: t. is silent, as in Harlow | ASQ 19:6 |
| tabernacle: who shall dwell in thy t. | BOOK 66:13 |
| table: behave mannerly at t. | STEV 317:16 |
| carf biforn his fader at the t. | CHAU 95:14 |
| from their masters' t. | BIBLE 50:11 |
| from the rich man's t. | BIBLE 52:34 |
| patient etherized upon a t. | ELIOT 133:24 |
| prepare a t. before me | BOOK 66:18 |
| though you cannot make a t. | JOHN 184:7 |
| tableau: history nothing more than a t. | VOLT 340:20 |
| Tablet: keep taking The T. | THOM 331:2 |
| tablets: Quick, thy t., Memory | ARN 16:20 |
| tactful: t. in audacity is knowing | COCT 103:4 |
| taffeta: doublet of changeable t. | SHAK 297:33 |
| T. phrases, silken terms | SHAK 284:18 |
| tail: And, like a rat without a t. | SHAK 285:3 |
| he's treading on my t. | CARR 91:11 |
| Improve his shining t. | CARR 91:3 |
| moste han a likerous t. | CHAU 96:6 |
| O! thereby hangs a t. | SHAK 292:9 |
| t. that wagged contempt | WATS 343:1 |
| thy t. hangs down behind | KIPL 197:18 |
| tailor: t. make thy doublet | SHAK 297:33 |
| taint: I cannot t. with fear | SHAK 287:32 |
| tainted: t. wether of the flock | SHAK 289:24 |
| taisez-vous: T.! Méfiez-vous | ANON 12:15 |
| take: big enough to t. away | FORD 143:5 |
| O t. the nasty soup away | HOFF 169:18 |
| T. a pair of sparkling eyes | GILB 151:7 |
| t. away all at one swoop | WEBS 344:22 |
| T. away these baubles | CROM 112:5 |
| T., eat , this is my Body | BIBLE 51:9 |
| T. the thanks of a boy | BEEC 32:5 |
| T. up the White Man's burden | KIPL 197:15 |
| they t. you in the morning | BALD 27:4 |
| taken: Lord hath t. away | BIBLE 42:22 |
| not t. in when they marry | AUST 22:18 |
| t. away even that which | BIBLE 51:3 |
| takes: like that it t. away | BYRON 87:9 |
| taketh: t. away the sin | BIBLE 53:13 |
| taking-off: deep damnation of his t. | SHAK 285:24 |
| tale: And thereby hangs a t. | SHAK 272:22 |
| Cuts off his t. and talks of | SHAK 282:11 |
| I could a t. unfold | SHAK 274:30 |
| point a moral, or adorn a t. | JOHN 183:14 |
| sad t.'s best for winter | SHAK 298:22 |
| t. told by an idiot | SHAK 288:5 |
| t. which holdeth children | SIDN 306:27 |
| tedious as a twice-told t. | SHAK 282:9 |
| telling the saddest t. | SHAK 290:21 |
| This most tremendous t. of all | BETJ 36:18 |
| Trust the t. | LAWR 202:15 |
| unvarnished t. deliver | SHAK 291:34 |
| talent: t. to amuse | COW 109:1 |
| Brevity is the sister of t. | CHEK 96:31 |
| gilded tomb of a mediocre t. | SMITH 309:12 |
| invention the t. of a liar | BYRON 87:18 |
| T. develops in quiet places | GOET 154:11 |
| T. does what it can | MER 223:25 |
| t. instantly recognizes | DOYLE 126:8 |
| t. which is death to hide | MILT 230:22 |
| talents: career open to the t. | NAP 237:6 |
| If you have great t. | REYN 259:8 |
| ministry of all the t. | ANON 9:9 |
| talk: Careless t. costs lives | ANON 6:15 |
| English t. is a quadrille | JAMES 179:16 |
| fold his legs and have out his t. | JOHN 185:16 |
| gotta use words when I t. to you | ELIOT 134:16 |
| If you can t. with crowds | KIPL 197:7 |
| If you t. to God | SZASZ 321:25 |
| interviewing people who can't t. | ZAPPA 361:1 |

talk (cont.):
I want to t. like a lady | SHAW 302:17
Money doesn't t., it swears | DYLAN 130:3
t. but a tinkling cymbal | BACON 24:23
t. not to me of a name | BYRON 87:10
t. with you, walk with you | SHAK 288:31
Then he will t., Good Gods | LEE 204:8
think too little and who t. too | DRYD 127:11
To t. about the rest of us | ANON 10:20
To t. of many things | CARR 91:22
world may t. of hereafter | COLL 105:4
wished him to t. on for ever | HAZL 164:1
talked: least t. about by men | PER 248:3
Lord how it t. | BEAU 31:3
not being t. about | WILDE 350:4
t. like poor Poll | GARR 148:9
talking: Had tired the sun with t. | CORY 108:13
nation t. to itself | MILL 225:6
never know what we are t. | RUSS 265:2
People t. without speaking | SIMON 307:7
soon leaves off t. | BUTL 84:20
you can stop people t. | ATTL 19:14
tall: gods, divinely t. | TENN 323:20
Jane, Jane, t. as a crane | SITW 307:16
long and the short and the t. | HUGH 175:18
t. ship and a star to steer | MAS 221:21
tambourine: Hey! Mr T. Man | DYLAN 130:5
tamper: Would never want to t. | AUDEN 20:23
Tandy: I met wid Napper T. | ANON 8:9
tangere: Noli me t. | BIBLE 58:22
tangles: t. of Neaera's hair | MILT 227:14
tantum: T. ergo sacramentum | THOM 330:4
T. religio potuit suadere | LUCR 212:2
taper: rainbow, or with t. light | SHAK 282:10
t. to the outward room | DONNE 123:19
tapestry: wrong side of a Turkey t. | HOW 175:8
tar: T.-baby ain't sayin' nuthin' | HARR 163:6
[T. water] is of a nature | BERK 35:16
wine that tasted of the t. | BELL 34:1
Tara: harp that once through T.'s | MOORE 234:14
tarnished: neither t. nor afraid | CHAN 94:9
Tarpeian: ringleaders from the T. | ARN 18:16
tarrieth: guest that t. but a day | BIBLE 47:31
tarry: t. the wheels of his chariots | BIBLE 40:34
You may for ever t. | HERR 167:25
tart: t. who has finally married | BAXT 30:12
tarts: by the action of two t. | MACM 215:18
Tarzan: Me T., you Jane | WEIS 345:4
task: that's the t., that is the labour | VIRG 339:12
Thou thy worldly t. hast done | SHAK 273:27
what he reads as a t. | JOHN 184:10
taste: arbiter of t. | TAC 322:7
bad t. of the smoker | ELIOT 131:20
bouquet is better than the t. | POTT 254:6
difference of t. in jokes | ELIOT 132:1
Ghastly good t. | BETJ 37:16
held together by a sense of t. | BALL 28:12
himself create the t. by which | WORD 357:13
Shakespeare wanted t. | WALP 341:18
t. a little honey | BIBLE 41:14
T. is the feminine of genius | FITZ 140:19
t. my meat | HERB 167:3
Things sweet to t. prove | SHAK 293:11
tasted: Some books are to be t. | BACON 25:14
t. that the Lord is gracious | BIBLE 57:7
tasting: T. of Flora | KEATS 191:29
Tat: Die T. ist alles | GOET 154:7
tatter: t. in its mortal dress | YEATS 359:21
taught: afterward he t. | CHAU 95:21
taught as if you t. them not | POPE 252:8
You t. me language | SHAK 295:35
tavern: by a good t. or inn | JOHN 185:8
So is the London T. | ANON 7:9
T. in the Town | ANON 8:5
tax: Excise. A hateful t. | JOHN 182:7

tax (cont.):
I t. not you, you elements | SHAK 283:7
To t. and to please | BURKE 79:26
taxation: T. without representation | OTIS 243:6
taxed: world should be t. | BIBLE 51:31
taxes: Death and t. | MITC 232:5
except death and t. | FRAN 145:15
Only the little people pay t. | HELM 165:8
Read my lips: no new t. | BUSH 83:18
taxi: If you can't leave in a t. | KALM 189:21
Like a t. throbbing waiting | ELIOT 134:27
taxing: t. machine | LOWE 211:1
Tay: Bridge of the Silv'ry T. | MCG 214:19
te: T. Deum laudamus | ANON 14:1
tea: And is there honey still for t. | BROO 73:8
best sweeteners of t. | FIEL 139:9
counsel take and sometimes t. | POPE 253:6
if this is t., then I want coffee | PUNCH 256:20
Retired to their t. and scandal | CONG 106:6
slavery of the t. and coffee | COBB 102:25
some sipping t. | WORD 356:4
Take some more t. | CARR 91:8
T. and sympathy | AND 5:14
t.'s out of the way | REED 258:19
teach: and gladly t. | CHAU 95:18
apt to t. | BIBLE 56:16
Even while they t., men learn | SEN 270:6
suffering what they t. in song | SHEL 303:22
t. and delight | SIDN 306:26
T. him how to live | PORT 253:27
t. his senators wisdom | BOOK 68:10
T. me, my God and King | HERB 166:25
T. me to live, that I may dread | KEN 193:22
t. the young idea how to | THOM 331:22
T. us to care and not to care | ELIOT 132:19
t. you to drink deep | SHAK 274:15
To t., convince, subdue | AUBER 19:15
teacher: A t. affects eternity | ADAMS 1:16
doctrine for the t.'s sake | DEFOE 115:18
teaches: From all that terror t. | CHES 97:24
He who cannot, t. | SHAW 301:29
teaching: t. nations how to live | MILT 231:5
teacup: crack in the t. opens | AUDEN 20:12
tear: claims the homage of a t. | BYRON 84:30
dropped a t. upon the word | STER 315:22
magnificent, without a t. | DRYD 128:20
meed of some melodious t. | MILT 227:11
shed one English t. | MAC 214:1
t.-floods, nor sigh-tempests | DONNE 124:15
T. him for his bad verses | SHAK 281:27
t. is an intellectual thing | BLAKE 60:18
t. our pleasures with rough | MARV 221:1
There has fallen a splendid t. | TENN 327:1
unanswerable t. | BYRON 85:17
Wipe the t., baby dear | LEE 347:1
tears: And kiss again with t. | TENN 327:17
blood, toil, t. and sweat | CHUR 99:11
Drop, drop, slow t. | FLET 142:8
Hence those t. | TER 329:3
His big t., for he wept well | SHEL 304:5
If you have t., prepare | SHAK 281:22
In silence and t. | BYRON 87:14
keep time with my salt t. | JONS 187:2
Like Niobe, all t. | SHAK 274:12
loosed our heart in t. | ARN 16:19
Lord God will wipe away t. | BIBLE 45:25
match with shedding t. | SHAK 294:3
mine eyes from t. | BOOK 68:20
mist of t. | THOM 331:8
news to hear and bitter t. | CORY 108:13
Nothing is here for t. | MILT 230:18
often lie too deep for t. | WORD 355:24
shall wipe away all t. | BIBLE 57:28
shall wipe away all t. | BIBLE 58:5
Smiling through her t. | HOMER 170:22

tears (cont.):
| | |
|---|---|
| sow in t. | BOOK 68:29 |
| summer tempest came her t. | TENN 327:27 |
| t. I cannot hide | HARB 161:10 |
| T., idle tears, I know | TENN 327:22 |
| t. shed for things | VIRG 339:4 |
| Time with a gift of t. | SWIN 321:3 |
| watered heaven with their t. | BLAKE 62:6 |
| tease: dost t. us out of thought | KEATS 191:23 |
| t. in the High Pyrenees | BELL 34:1 |
| teases: Because he knows it t. | CARR 91:5 |
| teatray: Like a t. in the sky | CARR 91:7 |
| Technik: *Vorsprung durch T.* | ANON 13:4 |
| technology: Progress through t. | ANON 13:4 |
| T. ... the knack of so arranging | FRIS 146:5 |
| tedious: Returning were as t. | SHAK 287:14 |
| t. and brief | SHAK 291:5 |
| teeming: has gleaned my t. brain | KEATS 192:19 |
| teeth: And keep their t. clean | SHAK 273:16 |
| children's t. are set on edge | BIBLE 47:5 |
| dig our graves with our t. | SMIL 308:16 |
| Ears like bombs and t. like | CAUS 93:9 |
| old bitch gone in the t. | POUND 254:19 |
| set my t. nothing on edge | SHAK 278:4 |
| shark has pretty t. | BREC 71:18 |
| steal the very t. out of your | ARAB 14:19 |
| untying with t. a political knot | BIER 59:4 |
| weeping and gnashing of t. | BIBLE 49:18 |
| with the skin of my t. | BIBLE 42:36 |
| teetotaller: I'm only a beer t. | SHAW 300:28 |
| tekel: T.; Thou art weighed | BIBLE 47:12 |
| telegrams: life of t. and anger | FORS 143:20 |
| Telemachus: mine own T. | TENN 328:22 |
| television: T. brought back murder | HITC 168:20 |
| tell: Go, t. the Spartans | SIM 307:9 |
| men of sense never t. it | SHAF 270:20 |
| t. her she mustn't | PUNCH 256:13 |
| T. it not in Gath | BIBLE 41:21 |
| T. me not, Sweet, I am unkind | LOV 210:20 |
| T. me the old, old story | HANK 161:7 |
| T. me what you eat | BRIL 72:7 |
| T. out my soul | BIBLE 51:28 |
| t. sad stories of the death | SHAK 293:27 |
| T. them I came, and no one | DE L 116:19 |
| t. them of us and say | EDM 130:20 |
| telling: not arguing, I am t. you | WHIS 347:9 |
| pity beyond all t. | YEATS 359:18 |
| Téméraire: Fighting T. | NEWB 238:12 |
| temper: Keep me in t. | SHAK 283:1 |
| One equal t. of heroic hearts | TENN 328:25 |
| t. justice with mercy | MILT 229:29 |
| truth that has lost its t. | GIBR 150:21 |
| temperance: t. would be difficult | JOHN 186:14 |
| temperate: more lovely and more t. | SHAK 299:12 |
| temperature: t. not naturally its own | SCH 267:26 |
| tempered: t. by war, disciplined | KENN 194:2 |
| tempest: Like summer t. came her tears | TENN 327:27 |
| Yet it shall be t.-tost | SHAK 285:4 |
| tempests: nor sigh-t. move | DONNE 124:15 |
| temple: his train filled the t. | BIBLE 45:10 |
| t. of silence and reconciliation | MAC 213:14 |
| t. of the Holy Ghost | BIBLE 55:4 |
| temples: And the t. of his Gods | MAC 214:3 |
| solemn t., the great globe | SHAK 296:10 |
| theatres, and t. lie | WORD 354:15 |
| out of which they build t. | KRIS 199:4 |
| tempora: *O t., O mores!* | CIC 100:25 |
| T. *mutantur, et nos mutamur* | ANON 14:2 |
| temps: *A la recherche du t. perdu* | PROU 255:17 |
| *Ô t.! suspend ton vol* | LAM 199:21 |
| tempt: not t. the Lord thy God | BIBLE 48:17 |
| T. not a desperate man | SHAK 295:22 |
| temptation: And lead us not into t. | BIBLE 48:27 |
| combines the maximum of t. | SHAW 301:30 |
| insist on their resisting t. | KNOX 198:21 |

temptation (cont.):
| | |
|---|---|
| resist everything except t. | WILDE 349:24 |
| t. in the wilderness | BOOK 68:1 |
| t. is the greatest treason | ELIOT 134:7 |
| that ye enter not into t. | BIBLE 51:13 |
| temptations: But in spite of all t. | GILB 152:21 |
| tempus: *T. edax rerum* | OVID 243:16 |
| *t. fugit* | VIRG 340:9 |
| ten: Church clock at t. to three | BROO 73:8 |
| t. or twelve strokes of havoc | HOPK 171:24 |
| 1066 and All That | SELL 269:23 |
| T. thousand times t. thousand | BIBLE 47:15 |
| tenants: graves stood t. | SHAK 274:1 |
| tenants: T. of life's middle state | COWP 110:16 |
| T. of the house | ELIOT 133:16 |
| tendebantque: *T. manus* | VIRG 339:15 |
| tendency: Groucho t. | ANON 12:7 |
| tender: I'll be irreproachably t. | MAY 222:15 |
| t. for another's pain | GRAY 157:13 |
| t. is the night | KEATS 192:1 |
| true and t. is the North | TENN 327:24 |
| tenders: shoal of fools for t. | CONG 106:17 |
| ténébreux: *Je suis le t.* | NERV 238:8 |
| tenement: informed the t. of clay | DRYD 127:6 |
| tennis: t. with the net down | FROST 146:26 |
| tennis-balls: merely the stars' t. | WEBS 344:21 |
| Tennyson: bower we shrined to T. | HARDY 162:3 |
| Lawn T., gentleman poet | JOYCE 188:15 |
| T. and Browning | BAG 26:17 |
| tenor: They kept the noiseless t. | GRAY 157:10 |
| tent: inside the t. pissing out | JOHN 181:21 |
| Upon that little t. of blue | WILDE 350:15 |
| tenth: The Submerged T. | BOOTH 69:21 |
| tents: Israel's t. do shine | BLAKE 61:14 |
| Shall fold their t. | LONG 209:13 |
| stately t. of war | MARL 219:4 |
| t. of ungodliness | BOOK 67:22 |
| termagant: whipped for o'erdoing T. | SHAK 276:5 |
| terminological: t. inexactitude | CHUR 99:4 |
| terms: hard to come to t. with Him | MOL 232:23 |
| terrible: being just the t. choice | BROW 77:10 |
| isn't life a t. thing | THOM 330:19 |
| t. beauty is born | YEATS 359:3 |
| T. that old life of decency | LOW 211:11 |
| that t. football club | MCGR 214:22 |
| Then lend the eye a t. aspect | SHAK 279:5 |
| territorial: last t. claim | HITL 169:2 |
| territory: It comes with the t. | MILL 225:4 |
| terror: added a new t. to death | WETH 347:2 |
| added another t. to death | LYND 212:19 |
| afraid for any t. by night | BOOK 67:29 |
| From all that t. teaches | CHES 97:24 |
| T. the human form divine | BLAKE 62:7 |
| terrorist: t. and the policeman | CONR 107:9 |
| terrors: little t. | GAV 148:21 |
| new t. of Death | ARB 14:24 |
| t. of the earth | SHAK 283:5 |
| terse: nervous and t. | DOYLE 126:7 |
| Tess: ended his sport with T. | HARDY 161:25 |
| test: t. of a vocation | SMITH 309:11 |
| testament: purple t. of bleeding war | SHAK 294:1 |
| testicles: tragedy requires t. | VOLT 340:25 |
| testing: every virtue at the t. point | LEWIS 206:13 |
| text: great t. in Galatians | BROW 77:12 |
| where a neat rivulet of t. | SHER 306:3 |
| Thames: Not of Gennesareth, but T. | THOM 331:17 |
| Oh shall I see the T. again | BETJ 37:1 |
| stripling T. at Bab-lock-hithe | ARN 17:7 |
| Sweet T., run softly | SPEN 313:18 |
| T. bordered by its gardens | MORR 235:16 |
| T. is liquid history | BURNS 81:20 |
| thank: And t. heaven, fasting | SHAK 273:6 |
| Now t. we all our God | WINK 352:4 |
| T. me no thankings | SHAK 295:20 |
| t. thee, that I am not as other men | BIBLE 52:38 |

| | |
|---|---|
| thankless: To have a t. child | SHAK 282:25 |
| Upon a t. arrant | RAL 257:21 |
| thanks: for this relief much t. | SHAK 273:30 |
| give t. unto thee | BOOK 65:15 |
| I will give t. unto thee | BOOK 69:7 |
| O give t. unto the Lord | BOOK 69:1 |
| Take the t. of a boy | BEEC 32:5 |
| T. be to God | MISS 231:14 |
| T. for mercies past receive | BUCK 78:3 |
| T. for the memory | ROBIN 260:19 |
| thanksgiving: presence with t. | BOOK 67:31 |
| that: man's a man for a' t. | BURNS 82:8 |
| thatch: vines that round the t.-eaves | KEATS 192:14 |
| Weeded and worn the ancient t. | TENN 326:22 |
| thcream: t. till I'm thick | CROM 111:23 |
| theatre: I like the t., but never | HART 163:9 |
| t. of man's life | BACON 24:1 |
| theatres: t., and temples lie | WORD 354:15 |
| thee: Dreamin' of t.! | WALL 341:7 |
| queer save t. and me | OWEN 243:18 |
| theft: clever t. was praiseworthy | SPEN 312:20 |
| Property is t. | PROU 255:16 |
| would be t. in other poets | DRYD 128:29 |
| theme: It was a t. for reason | DONNE 124:1 |
| pudding — it has no t. | CHUR 100:8 |
| theorize: mistake to t. before | DOYLE 126:5 |
| theory: All t. is grey | GOET 154:5 |
| [biography] is life without t. | DISR 121:28 |
| sometimes fiction, sometimes t. | MAC 213:22 |
| t. is found to be against | EDD 130:11 |
| there: Because it's t. | MALL 216:22 |
| I met a man who wasn't t. | MEAR 222:18 |
| T. but for the grace of God | BRAD 71:6 |
| t. when they crucified | ANON 11:14 |
| thereby: O! t. hangs a tail | SHAK 292:9 |
| therein: and all that t. is | BOOK 66:19 |
| thermodynamics: second law of t. | EDD 130:11 |
| Thermopylae: old man of T. | LEAR 203:16 |
| they: t. are not they | WAUGH 343:16 |
| thick: one can lay it on so t. | BUTL 84:9 |
| thcream till I'm t. | CROM 111:23 |
| t. and numberless as the gay | MILT 226:23 |
| T. as autumnal leaves | MILT 228:14 |
| thicker: History gets t. as | TAYL 322:22 |
| shall be t. than my father | BIBLE 41:33 |
| thicket: ram caught in a t. | BIBLE 39:16 |
| thief: Behold, I come as a t. | BIBLE 58:1 |
| Opportunity makes a t. | BACON 25:24 |
| Pleasure is a t. to business | DEFOE 115:11 |
| Procrastination is the t. of time | YOUNG 360:19 |
| steals something from the t. | SHAK 291:37 |
| Time the subtle t. of youth | MILT 230:20 |
| thieves: fell among t. | BIBLE 52:11 |
| have made it a den of t. | BIBLE 50:27 |
| One of the t. was saved | BECK 31:11 |
| T. respect property | CHES 98:11 |
| union of two t. | BIER 59:2 |
| where t. break through | BIBLE 49:1 |
| thievish: Time's t. progress | SHAK 299:26 |
| thigh: smote them hip and t. | BIBLE 41:4 |
| thimbles: They sought it with t. | CARR 92:9 |
| thin: in every fat man a t. one | CONN 106:28 |
| t. man inside every fat man | ORW 241:25 |
| t. red line of 'eroes | KIPL 197:11 |
| t. red line tipped with steel | RUSS 265:7 |
| tho' t., yet never clear | POPE 250:15 |
| thine: For t. is the kingdom | BIBLE 48:27 |
| thing: do that t. that ends all other | SHAK 272:2 |
| is it not the t. | BYRON 87:19 |
| National Debt a *Good* T. | SELL 269:24 |
| play's the t. | SHAK 275:24 |
| sort of t. they like | LINC 207:12 |
| T. as he sees It | KIPL 197:13 |
| t. enskyed and sainted | SHAK 288:10 |

| | |
|---|---|
| thing (cont.): | |
| Thou art the t. itself | SHAK 283:14 |
| thingish: thing which seemed T. | MILNE 225:15 |
| things: all t. to all men | BIBLE 55:8 |
| as t. have been, t. remain | CLOU 102:22 |
| confused t. with their names | SART 267:5 |
| do all t. through Christ | BIBLE 56:10 |
| earnest of the t. that they | TENN 326:9 |
| excellent t. are spoken | BOOK 67:24 |
| for t. they didn't know | POUND 254:13 |
| God's sons are t. | MADD 216:14 |
| infection of t. gone | LOW 211:20 |
| I will do such t. | SHAK 283:5 |
| just one of those t. | PORT 253:21 |
| More t. are wrought by prayer | TENN 324:21 |
| nor t. to come | BIBLE 54:42 |
| O all ye Green T. | BOOK 64:1 |
| people don't do such t. | IBSEN 178:5 |
| shape of t. to come | WELLS 345:23 |
| So little done, such t. to be | TENN 325:14 |
| tears shed for t. and mortality | VIRG 339:4 |
| These t. shall be! | SYM 321:20 |
| T. ain't what they used to be | PERS 248:6 |
| T. are but as straw dogs | LAO-T 201:11 |
| T. are in the saddle | EMER 136:13 |
| t. are the sons of heaven | JOHN 182:4 |
| T. fall apart | YEATS 359:24 |
| t. to come | SHAK 296:32 |
| t. unknown proposed | POPE 252:8 |
| what T. think about men | JENN 181:5 |
| think: And t. by fits and starts | HOUS 174:10 |
| And t., this heart | BROO 73:10 |
| comedy to those that t. | WALP 341:23 |
| don't t. foolishly | JOHN 186:3 |
| Don't t. twice, it's all right | DYLAN 130:1 |
| For those who greatly t. | POPE 250:23 |
| In all I t. or speak or do | WESL 346:5 |
| I t., therefore I am | DESC 117:9 |
| know what I t. till I see what | WALL 341:11 |
| must do then, t. now before | DONNE 123:16 |
| not so t. as you drunk I am | SQUI 314:3 |
| people that t., and fox-hunters | SHEN 305:21 |
| something with them besides t. | LOOS 210:7 |
| so we've got to t. | RUTH 265:9 |
| then I don't t. much of it | STR 318:16 |
| t. of England | HILL 168:17 |
| T. of your forefathers | ADAMS 2:4 |
| t. only this of me | BROO 73:10 |
| t. on these things | BIBLE 56:9 |
| t. too little and who talk | DRYD 127:11 |
| whether machines t. | SKIN 308:5 |
| you can't make her t. | PARK 245:14 |
| thinking: It ain't t. about it | TROL 334:15 |
| Plain living and high t. | WORD 356:1 |
| t. for themselves is what | GILB 151:13 |
| t. makes it so | SHAK 275:14 |
| t. reed | PASC 246:6 |
| t. what nobody has thought | SZEN 322:3 |
| thought of t. for myself at all | GILB 152:19 |
| thinks: he t. no ill | SHAK 299:20 |
| He t. too much | SHAK 281:1 |
| Sometimes I sits and t. | PUNCH 256:21 |
| t. he knows everything | SHAW 301:13 |
| third: A t. event to the | DICK 120:11 |
| separately plunder a t. | BIER 59:2 |
| thirst: shall never t. | BIBLE 53:22 |
| neither t. any more | BIBLE 57:27 |
| t. after righteousness | BIBLE 48:19 |
| thirsty: As cold waters to a t. soul | BIBLE 43:37 |
| if he be t., give him water | BIBLE 43:36 |
| thirteen: clocks were striking t. | ORW 242:5 |
| thirty: At t. a man suspects himself | YOUNG 360:20 |
| past t., and three parts iced over | ARN 18:7 |
| T. days hath September | ANON 11:2 |
| t. pieces of silver | BEVAN 38:4 |

**thirty** (*cont.*):
t. pieces of silver — BIBLE 51:7
**thorn**: Oak, and Ash, and T. — KIPL 197:1
t. in the flesh — BIBLE 55:28
without t. the rose — MILT 229:8
**thorns**: crackling of t. under a pot — BIBLE 44:16
crown of t. *and* the thirty — BEVAN 38:4
fall upon the t. of life — SHEL 304:8
No t. go as deep as a rose's — SWIN 321:5
once was crowned with t. — KELLY 193:19
t. shall come up in her — BIBLE 46:3
**thou**: t. art not he or she — WAUGH 343:16
T. shalt have no other — BIBLE 40:3
T. swell! Thou witty — HART 163:11
**thought**: beautiful clean t. — LAWR 202:17
does not seem a moment's t. — YEATS 358:13
Expression is the dress of t. — POPE 252:2
father, Harry, to that t. — SHAK 278:27
forced into a state of t. — GALS 147:18
Grave without t. — CHUR 98:26
green t. in a green shade — MARV 220:16
I thought he t. I slept — PATM 246:17
Jesu, the very t. of Thee — CASW 92:17
Language is the dress of t. — JOHN 182:19
library is t. in cold storage — SAM 266:10
men use t. only to justify — VOLT 340:14
no t. for the morrow — BIBLE 49:5
One single grateful t. — LESS 206:5
one t. more steady — FORD 143:11
passion-wingèd Ministers of t. — SHEL 303:5
Perish the t. — CIBB 100:16
rear the tender t. — THOM 331:22
Religion is the frozen t. — KRIS 199:4
Restored to life, and power, and t. — KEBLE 193:16
Roman t. hath struck him — SHAK 271:6
sessions of sweet silent t. — SHAK 299:16
sinned exceedingly in t. — MISS 231:11
speech created t. — SHEL 304:20
Style is the dress of t. — WESL 346:18
t. charged with emotion — GIDE 151:1
T. is free — SHAK 296:7
T. is the child of Action — DISR 122:9
t. is viscous — ADAMS 1:21
T. shall be the harder — ANON 11:5
t.'s the slave of life — SHAK 278:14
thou pleasing, dreadful t. — ADD 2:18
through strange seas of T. — WORD 356:10
to have loved, to have t. — ARN 16:14
very life-blood of t. — FLAU 141:10
What oft was t., but ne'er — POPE 252:1
white, celestial t. — VAUG 337:7
with the pale cast of t. — SHAK 275:26
working-house of t. — SHAK 280:1
you sit alone with your t. — BOND 63:9
**thoughts**: generate misleading t. — SPEN 312:19
Good t. his only friends — CAMP 89:3
Hunter's waking t. — AUDEN 20:16
I do begin to have bloody t. — SHAK 296:11
only to conceal their t. — VOLT 340:14
pansies, that's for t. — SHAK 277:2
Secret t. and open countenance — ALB 3:13
sensations rather than of t. — KEATS 192:24
Staled are my t. — DYER 129:15
t. are not your thoughts — BIBLE 46:22
t. by England given — BROO 73:10
t. of a prisoner — SOLZ 311:1
t. of youth are long, long t. — LONG 209:21
T., that breathe, and words — GRAY 157:18
T. that do often lie too deep — WORD 355:24
t. unnatural — SHAK 292:13
Words without t. never — SHAK 276:18
**thousand**: better than a t. — BOOK 67:22
difference of forty t. men — WELL 345:13
end of a t. years of history — GAIT 147:12
good woman if I had five t. — THAC 329:21

**thousand** (*cont.*):
night has a t. eyes — BOUR 70:12
Night hath a t. eyes — LYLY 212:18
not in a t. years — SMITH 309:9
O for a t. tongues to sing — WESL 346:4
Ring in the t. years of peace — TENN 325:26
ten t. are their tongues — WATTS 343:3
Ten t. times ten thousand — BIBLE 47:15
t. ages in Thy sight — WATTS 343:14
t. thousand slimy things — COL 104:12
Would he had blotted a t. — JONS 187:32
**thousands**: limp father of t. — JOYCE 188:16
Where t. equally were meant — SWIFT 320:24
**thrall**: Thee hath in t. — KEATS 191:10
**thread**: t. of my own hand's weaving — KEATS 191:3
**threatened**: t. its life with a railway-share — CARR 92:9
**three**: married life t. is company — WILDE 349:17
quite a t.-pipe problem — DOYLE 125:15
tell you t. times is true — CARR 92:6
Though he was only t. — MILNE 225:20
t. events in his life — LA BR 199:14
t. gentlemen at once — SHER 306:2
T. hours a day will produce — TROL 334:12
T. in One and One in Three — ALEX 4:5
T. little maids from school — GILB 151:21
t. men, still hungry — CRANE 111:2
t. o'clock in the morning — FITZ 140:22
t. o'clock in the morning — THOR 332:10
T. quarks for Muster Mark — JOYCE 188:5
t. years old is half his height — LEON 205:23
When shall we t. meet again — SHAK 284:25
when two or t. are gathered — BOOK 64:10
whole is divided into t. — CAES 87:24
would give him t. sides — MONT 233:21
**threescore**: t. years and ten — BOOK 67:26
**thrice**: T. is he armed that hath — SHAK 280:8
**thrift**: Thrift, t., Horatio — SHAK 274:15
**thrive**: t. without one grain — DRYD 127:28
**throat**: feel the fog in my t. — BROW 77:2
fishbone in the city's t. — LOW 211:13
taking life by the t. — FROST 146:27
your t. 'tis hard to slit — KING 195:19
**throne**: Bust outlasts the t. — DOBS 122:25
Gehenna or up to the T. — KIPL 196:20
light which beats upon a t. — TENN 324:1
like a burnished t. — SHAK 271:14
Lord sitting upon a t. — BIBLE 45:10
royal t. of kings — SHAK 293:14
t. and thy kingly crown — ELL 136:1
t. he sits on, nor the tide of pomp — SHAK 279:16
t. of bayonets — INGE 178:14
t. of Denmark — SHAK 274:4
T. sent word to a Throne — KIPL 196:25
**through**: best way out is always t. — FROST 146:22
do *you* read books t.? — JOHN 184:26
T. all the changing scenes — TATE 322:17
T. them we pass out into — FORS 143:19
T. the night of doubt — BAR 29:2
**thrown**: t. out, as good for nothing — JOHN 183:19
**thrush**: aged t., frail, gaunt — HARDY 162:6
That's the wise t. — BROW 76:2
**thrust**: guardsman's cut and t. — HUXL 177:16
**Thule**: *Ultima* T. — VIRG 340:5
**thumb**: puts his t. in the scale — LAWR 202:12
**thumbs**: By the pricking of my t. — SHAK 287:18
his t. are off at last — HOFF 169:22
**thunder**: like t. outer China — KIPL 196:21
such sweet t. — SHAK 291:2
Glorious the t.'s roar — SMART 308:13
In t., lightning, or in rain — SHAK 284:25
surge and t. of the Odyssey — LANG 201:3
they steal my t. — DENN 117:2
t. of the captains — BIBLE 43:5
**thunderbolt**: like a t. he falls — TENN 323:21
**thunderbolts**: oak-cleaving t. — SHAK 283:6

time (cont.):

| | |
|---|---|
| T. shall throw a dart at thee | BROW 74:24 |
| T.'s noblest offspring | BERK 35:19 |
| T. spent on any item | PARK 245:22 |
| T.'s thievish progress | SHAK 299:26 |
| T.'s wingèd chariot | MARV 220:24 |
| t. that shall surely be | AING 3:9 |
| T. that's lost may all | BUCK 78:3 |
| t., that takes survey of all | SHAK 278:14 |
| T. the devourer of everything | OVID 243:16 |
| T. the subtle thief of youth | MILT 230:20 |
| t. to every purpose | BIBLE 44:11 |
| t. to win this game | DRAKE 126:13 |
| T. was away and somewhere | MACN 216:5 |
| t. was out of joint | STR 318:12 |
| t. will come when you will | DISR 121:5 |
| T. will run back, and fetch | MILT 227:27 |
| T. with a gift of tears | SWIN 321:3 |
| T., you old gipsy man | HODG 169:15 |
| T., you thief, who love to get | HUNT 176:15 |
| trencher-friends, t.'s flies | SHAK 296:20 |
| uncertain balance of proud t. | GREE 158:8 |
| unconscionable t. dying | CHAR 95:6 |
| unthinking t. | DRYD 128:15 |
| waste of t. and effort | VEBL 337:17 |
| week is a long t. in politics | WILS 351:15 |
| When t. is broke | SHAK 294:11 |
| which are the births of t. | BACON 24:30 |
| which are the rags of t. | DONNE 124:12 |
| while t. quietly kills them | BOUC 70:8 |
| With leaden foot t. creeps | JAGO 179:8 |
| with the productions of t. | BLAKE 61:5 |
| world enough, and t. | MARV 220:22 |

timely: by a t. compliance — FIEL 139:7
timeo: t. Danaos et dona ferentis — VIRG 339:5
times: And frew t. did I say to him — WORD 354:12
brisk and giddy-pacèd t. — SHAK 297:29

| | |
|---|---|
| discern the signs of the t. | BIBLE 50:12 |
| It was the best of t. | DICK 120:6 |
| most devilish thing is 8 t. 8 | FLEM 141:22 |
| Oh, the t.! Oh, the manners | CIC 100:25 |
| one year's experience 30 t. | CARR 90:30 |
| praiser of past t. | HOR 173:2 |
| Praise they that will t. past | HERR 167:21 |
| T. change, and we change | ANON 14:2 |
| T. go by turns, and chances | SOUT 312:9 |
| T. has made many ministries | BAG 26:7 |
| t. that try men's souls | PAINE 244:11 |
| t. they are a-changing | DYLAN 130:9 |
| t. will not mend | PARK 245:18 |

timetables: Europe by railway t. — TAYL 322:23
Timon: T. hath made his everlasting — SHAK 296:24
timor: T. mortis conturbat me — DUNB 129:8
Timothy: T. Winters — CAUS 93:9
tin: cheap t. trays — MAS 221:19
tincture: Actions receive their t. — DEFOE 115:19
left this t. in the blood — DEFOE 115:20
ting-a-ling-a-ling: bells of Hell go t. — ANON 9:21
tinker: expands to t. with his car — MACN 216:9
tinkling: talk but a t. cymbal — BACON 24:23
tinklings: t. lull the distant folds — GRAY 157:4
tinsel: vainly flapped its t. wing — MARV 220:12
tintinnabulation: t. that so musically wells — POE 250:4
tiny: My t. watching eye — DE L 116:23
tip: Within the nether t. — COL 104:10
tiptoe: Dance t., bull — BUNT 78:15
sweet-peas, on t. for a flight — KEATS 191:6
t. on the misty mountain — SHAK 295:18
t. when this day is named — SHAK 279:18
tired: and t. her head — BIBLE 42:14
Can mean to a t. heart — BOND 63:9
Give me your t., your poor — LAZ 203:2
I'm t. of Love — BELL 33:13
long process of getting t. — BUTL 84:13
Thou art t.; best be still — ARN 16:18

tired (cont.):

| | |
|---|---|
| T. of his dark dominion | MER 223:21 |
| t. the sun with talking | CORY 108:13 |
| When a man is t. of London | JOHN 185:15 |
| woman who always was t. | ANON 7:17 |

Tiresias: T., old man with wrinkled — ELIOT 134:28
tiring: Wooing, so t. — MITF 232:9
titanic: which t. wars had groined — OWEN 244:2
title: t. running 'fore the king — SHAK 279:16
titles: Conquering kings their t. — CHAN 94:6
that of the rich for t. — PEAR 246:26
T. are shadows, crowns — DEFOE 116:1
T. distinguish the mediocre — SHAW 301:31
titwillow: Sang 'Willow, t. — GILB 152:7
to: run-stealers flicker t. and fro — THOM 331:6
toad: I had rather be a t. — SHAK 292:17
Squat like a t., close — MILT 229:13
t. beneath the harrow knows — KIPL 196:26
t., ugly and venomous — SHAK 272:14
Why should I let the t. work — LARK 201:19
toads: Imaginary gardens with real t. — MOORE 234:8
toast: My t. would be — ADAMS 2:5
never had a piece of t. — PAYN 246:20
tobacco: that tawney weed t. — JONS 186:25
tocsin: t. of the soul — BYRON 86:20
today: do something t. which the world — COLL 105:4
if T. be sweet — FITZ 140:11
such a day to-morrow as t. — SHAK 298:21
these gave their t. — EDM 130:20
t. I am fifty-five — REED 258:14
T. shalt thou be with me — BIBLE 53:3
T. we have naming of parts — REED 258:15
toe: clerical, printless t. — BROO 73:5
toes: Pobble who has no t. — LEAR 203:14
toff: saunter along like a t. — HARG 162:20
together: persons acting t. — ARAB 14:18
toil: ambition mock their useful t. — GRAY 157:7
Bear the t., maintain — WHITE 347:16
bleared, smeared with t. — HOPK 172:4
blood, t., tears and sweat — CHUR 99:11
Double, double t. and trouble — SHAK 287:15
Horny-handed sons of t. — SAL 266:5
horny hands of t. — LOW 211:5
night in thought, the day in t. — QUAR 257:2
some men t. after virtue — LAMB 200:15
T., envy, want — JOHN 183:12
t. in other men's extremes — KYD 199:9
t. not, neither do they spin — BIBLE 49:4
To t. and not to seek for rest — IGN 178:8
token: t. of a covenant — BIBLE 39:10
tokens: Words are the t. current — BACON 23:23
told: I t. you so — BYRON 86:28
plato t. him — CUMM 112:19
They t. me, Heraclitus — CORY 108:19
t. you from the beginning — BIBLE 46:12
what we were formerly t. — BLUN 62:15
tolerable: Life would be t. — LEWIS 206:15
toleration: t. produced — GIBB 150:10
toll: T. for the brave — COWP 109:28
t. me back from thee — KEATS 192:6
tolle: T. lege, tolle lege — AUG 21:23
tolls: for whom the bell tolls — DONNE 124:20
Tom: lies poor T. Bowling — DIBD 117:19
Old Uncle T. Cobbleigh and all — BALL 28:11
Poor T.'s a-cold — SHAK 283:17
spurious brat, T. Jones — RICH 260:4
T. Pearse, lend me your grey mare — BALL 28:11
tomb: grave or t. of wit — CAV 93:13
My heart keeps empty in thy t. — KING 195:5
sea was made his t. — BARN 29:7
This side the t. — DAV 114:18
To fair Fidele's grassy t. — COLL 105:9
t. of a mediocre talent — SMITH 309:12
tombs: from the t. a doleful sound — WATTS 343:10
Tommy: T. this, an' T. that — KIPL 197:11

tomorrow: in next week t. — GRAH 156:6
Leave t. behind — COW 108:19
no t. hath, nor yesterday — DONNE 123:22
such a day t. as to-day — SHAK 298:21
T., and to-morrow — SHAK 288:5
t. is another day — MITC 232:7
t. we shall die — BIBLE 45:24
too late t. to be brave — ARMS 16:2
Unborn T., and dead YESTERDAY — FITZ 140:11
you can put off till t. — PUNCH 256:8
tomorrows: dividend from time's t. — SASS 267:10
For your t. these gave — EDM 130:20
tom-tit: by a river a little t. — GILB 152:7
tone: look at me in that t. of voice — PUNCH 256:17
t. of the company — CHES 97:7
tones: Sweet t. remembered not — SHEL 303:24
tongs: t. and the bones — SHAK 290:35
tongue: English t. a gallimaufry — SPEN 313:20
For God's sake hold your t. — DONNE 123:24
for I must hold my t. — SHAK 274:13
From lies of t. and pen — CHES 97:24
his t. dropped manna — MILT 228:23
his t. is the clapper — SHAK 291:21
Keep thy t. from evil — BOOK 66:25
Love's t. is in the eyes — FLET 142:9
My heart and t. employ — TATE 322:17
My t. is the pen — BOOK 67:5
My t. swore, but my mind's — EUR 137:22
nor t. to speak here — LENT 205:20
Now, my t., the mystery telling — THOM 330:3
obnoxious to each carping t. — BRAD 71:12
on every infant's t. — CALV 88:8
put a t. in every wound — SHAK 281:26
Silence is become his mother t. — GOLD 155:7
Sing, my t., the glorious — FORT 144:4
t. is the only edged tool — IRV 178:19
t. not understood — BOOK 69:18
t. of midnight hath told — SHAK 291:9
t. taking a trip of three — NAB 236:18
t. to persuade — CLAR 101:10
trippingly on the t. — SHAK 276:4
use of my oracular t. — SHER 305:29
would not yield to the t. — BIER 59:4
tongueless: t. vigil and all the pain — SWIN 321:1
tongues: Finds t. in trees — SHAK 272:14
He came in t. of living flame — AUBER 19:15
lack t. to praise — SHAK 300:5
O for a thousand t. to sing — WESL 346:4
silver-sweet sound lovers' t. — SHAK 295:3
Sweet the countless t. united — MANT 217:17
Though I speak with the t. — BIBLE 55:11
thousand thousand are their t. — WATTS 343:3
time in the t. — SHAK 297:16
tonight: Not t., Josephine — NAP 237:8
tonnage: New York swallowing the t. — MILL 225:5
too: T. kind, too kind — NIGH 240:1
T. small to live — ANON 11:8
took: 'E went an' t. — KIPL 197:14
person you and I t. me for — CARL 90:3
stranger, and ye t. me in — BIBLE 51:5
tool: Science is an edged t. — EDD 130:13
tongue is the only edged t. — IRV 178:19
tool-making: Man is a t. animal — FRAN 145:16
tools: For secrets are edged t. — DRYD 128:16
give us the t. and we will — CHUR 99:16
t. to him that can handle — CARL 90:8
Without t. he is nothing — CARL 90:21
tooth: danger of her former t. — SHAK 287:3
Eye for eye, t. for tooth — BIBLE 40:10
hadde alwey a coltes t. — CHAU 96:7
Nature, red in t. and claw — TENN 325:12
sharper than a serpent's t. — SHAK 282:25
where each t.-point goes — KIPL 196:26
toothache: Venerable Mother T. — HEAT 164:13

top: Life is a t. which whipping — GREV 158:18
There is always room at the t. — WEBS 344:12
t. thing in the world — KEATS 193:12
toper: t. whose untutored sense — CRAB 110:21
topless: t. towers of Ilium — MARL 218:11
torch: bright t., and a casement — KEATS 192:9
runners relay the t. of life — LUCR 212:5
t. borne in the wind — CHAP 94:15
t. has been passed — KENN 194:2
Truth, like a t. — HAM 160:17
torches: teach the t. to burn bright — SHAK 294:26
torchlight: t. procession — O'SUL 243:5
Tories: are T. born wicked — ANON 9:6
T. own no argument — BROW 74:25
torments: t. also may in length — MILT 228:26
t. lie in the small pique — CIBB 100:13
tornado: set off a t. in Texas — LOR 210:10
torrent: down the t. of his fate — JOHN 183:16
torrents: t. of her myriad universe — TENN 326:21
tortoise: t.-like, but not so slow — MARV 221:3
torture: t. one poor word — DRYD 128:6
torturer: life and the t.'s horse — AUDEN 21:2
Tory: burning hatred for the T. — BEVAN 37:18
T. men and Whig measures — DISR 121:25
T.'s secret weapon — KILM 195:2
tossed: t. you down into the field — FITZ 140:13
tossing: t. about in a steamer — GILB 151:16
total: t. solution of the Jewish — GOER 154:1
totter: charming to t. into vogue — WALP 341:19
totters: Who t. forth, wrapped — SHEL 305:15
touch: Can t. him further — SHAK 287:4
Do not t. me — BIBLE 58:22
He wants the natural t. — SHAK 287:23
One t. of nature makes — SHAK 297:6
T. me not — BIBLE 54:6
T. not the cat but a glove — SCOTT 268:25
t. of a vanished hand — TENN 323:11
t. of earthly years — WORD 356:25
t. of Harry in the night — SHAK 279:8
with gentle hand t. — WORD 355:16
touched: t. none that he did not adorn — JOHN 185:12
T. to the quick, he said — BROW 76:8
touches: silent t. of time — BURKE 81:10
t. of sweet harmony — SHAK 290:1
Who t. this touches a man — WHIT 348:14
toucheth: t. pitch shall be defiled — BIBLE 48:2
tough: t. get going — KENN 194:10
statements interesting, but t. — TWAIN 335:19
toujours: T. perdrix! — ANON 12:16
tourist: loathsome is the British t. — KILV 195:3
tous: T. pour un, un pour tous — DUMAS 129:4
tout: t. n'est qu'ordre et beauté — BAUD 30:4
toves: slithy t. — CARR 91:15
tow: thou shouldst t. me after — SHAK 271:18
tower: Child Roland to the dark t. — SHAK 283:18
Fighting in the captain's t. — DYLAN 129:20
from yonder ivy-mantled t. — GRAY 157:5
Giotto's t. — LONG 209:18
name is a t. of strength — SHAK 294:20
watchman on the lonely t. — SCOTT 268:16
with the blasted t. — NERV 238:8
towered: T. cities please us then — MILT 227:6
towers: cloud-capped t. — SHAK 296:10
spires, ye antique t. — GRAY 157:11
t. the last enchantments — ARN 18:2
With walls and t. were girdled — COL 103:22
towery: T. city and branchy — HOPK 172:2
town: Come sounding through the t. — BALL 27:5
Country in the t. — MART 220:8
destroy the t. to save it — ANON 8:10
down to the end of the t. — MILNE 225:20
each and every t. or city — HOLM 170:14
haunted t. it is to me — LANG 201:1
man made the t. — COWP 110:6

town (cont.):

| | |
|---|---|
| pretty how t. | CUMM 112:16 |
| spreading of the hideous t. | MORR 235:16 |
| There is a tavern in the t. | ANON 8:5 |
| town-crier: t. spoke my lines | SHAK 276:4 |
| towns: elephants for want of t. | SWIFT 320:21 |
| saw the t. of many men | HOMER 171:1 |
| Seven wealthy t. contend | ANON 10:10 |
| toy: foolish thing was but a t. | SHAK 298:15 |
| Or sells eternity to get a t. | SHAK 299:8 |
| toys: All is but t. | SHAK 286:26 |
| make you brooches and t. | STEV 317:19 |
| toyshop: moving t. of their heart | POPE 253:3 |
| trace: My hand delights to t. | WINC 352:3 |
| Projecting trait and t. | HARDY 162:10 |
| tracing: fitful t. of a portal | STEV 316:11 |
| track: ancient t. marched, rank | MER 223:22 |
| Come flying on our t. | THOM 332:2 |
| tracks: still hungry on the t. | CRANE 111:2 |
| trade: And all is seared with t. | HOPK 172:4 |
| autocrat: that's my t. | CATH 92:21 |
| God will pardon me, it is His t. | HEINE 165:3 |
| great t. will always | BURKE 79:24 |
| Irish poets, learn your t. | YEATS 360:6 |
| not your t. to make tables | JOHN 184:7 |
| There isn't any T. | HERB 166:14 |
| t. seldom meet together | SMITH 308:21 |
| traffic from the vulgar t. | MARL 219:1 |
| wheels of t. | HUME 176:6 |
| tradesmen: bow, ye t., bow | GILB 151:9 |
| Trade Unionism: T. of the married | SHAW 301:24 |
| trade unionist: T. when you want to change him | |
| | BEVIN 38:8 |
| tradition: t. approves all forms | CLOU 102:20 |
| T. means giving votes | CHES 98:13 |
| traditional: T. sanctity and loveliness | YEATS 358:18 |
| traffic: Hushing the latest t. | BRID 72:1 |
| mighty roar of London's t. | ANON 9:23 |
| t. from the vulgar trade | MARL 219:1 |
| two hours' t. of our stage | SHAK 294:23 |
| tragedies: t. are finished by a death | BYRON 86:12 |
| tragedy: be out of it simply a t. | WILDE 350:13 |
| blustering about Imperial T. | BROWN 73:16 |
| first time as t. | BARN 29:6 |
| first time as t. | MARX 221:10 |
| go, litel myn t. | CHAU 96:20 |
| so convenient in t. | ANOU 14:5 |
| That is their t. | WILDE 349:19 |
| That is what it means | STOP 318:5 |
| t., and she played it in tights | BEER 32:13 |
| T. is clean, it is restful | ANOU 14:6 |
| T. is thus a representation | ARIS 15:15 |
| t. of a man who could not | OLIV 241:8 |
| t. of a man who has found | BARR 29:18 |
| t. of the classical languages | MADAN 216:12 |
| T. ought to be a great kick | LAWR 202:25 |
| t. requires testicles | VOLT 340:25 |
| t. to those that feel | WALP 341:23 |
| t. which lies in frequency | ELIOT 132:11 |
| weak, washy way of true t. | KAV 190:7 |
| You may abuse a t. | JOHN 184:7 |
| tragic: acted so t. the house rose | HARG 162:21 |
| tragical: Merry and t. | SHAK 291:5 |
| trahit: T. sua quemque voluptas | VIRG 339:23 |
| trail: long, long t. awinding | KING 195:12 |
| t. has its own stern code | SERV 270:9 |
| trailing: t. clouds of glory | WORD 355:20 |
| train: And all her t. were hurled | VAUG 337:14 |
| as we rush in the t. | THOM 332:2 |
| express-t. drew up there | THOM 330:21 |
| headlight of an oncoming t. | DICK 120:19 |
| his t. filled the temple | BIBLE 45:10 |
| light of the oncoming t. | LOW 211:18 |
| Runs the red electric t. | BETJ 37:7 |
| who shaves and takes a t. | WHITE 347:14 |

train (cont.):

| | |
|---|---|
| will pack, and take a t. | BROO 73:6 |
| trait: Projecting t. and trace | HARDY 162:10 |
| traitors: Our fears do make us t. | SHAK 287:22 |
| tram: I'm not even a bus, I'm a t. | HARE 162:19 |
| trammel: t. up the consequence | SHAK 285:22 |
| tramp: lady is a t. | HART 163:9 |
| t. of the twenty-two men | BOWEN 70:16 |
| tranquil: Farewell the t. mind | SHAK 292:19 |
| tranquillity: emotion recollected in t. | WORD 357:12 |
| T. Base here | ALDR 3:18 |
| t. remembered in emotion | PARK 245:11 |
| t. which religion is powerless | FORB 143:2 |
| tranquillized: T. Fifties | LOW 211:14 |
| transcendental: chatter of a t. kind | GILB 152:10 |
| T. moonshine | CARL 90:19 |
| transgression: there is no t. | BIBLE 54:31 |
| transgressions: wounded for our t. | BIBLE 46:19 |
| transgressors: way of t. is hard | BIBLE 43:22 |
| transient: t. is the smile of fate | DYER 129:17 |
| transit: quam cito t. gloria mundi | THOM 329:28 |
| Sic t. gloria mundi | ANON 13:22 |
| transitory: Action is t. | WORD 354:13 |
| translated: T. Daughter | AUDEN 20:10 |
| t. into Italian for the clearer | WHAR 347:3 |
| translation: mistake in the t. | VANB 336:23 |
| Poetry is what is lost in t. | FROST 146:28 |
| unfaithful to the t. | BORG 69:22 |
| translations: t. not unlike to be | HOW 175:8 |
| transport: I wished to share the t. | WORD 357:4 |
| T. of Delight | FLAN 141:6 |
| trapeze: young man on the flying t. | LEYB 206:21 |
| trappings: t. and the suits of woe | SHAK 274:8 |
| trash: steals my purse steals t. | SHAK 292:11 |
| travail: had my labour for my t. | SHAK 296:28 |
| travel: But we'll t. along | WOODS 353:19 |
| goeth to school, and not to t. | BACON 25:17 |
| I t. for travel's sake | STEV 316:27 |
| preserve all that t. by land | SWIFT 320:8 |
| t. hopefully | STEV 317:6 |
| t. in the direction of our fear | BERR 36:12 |
| T. light and you can sing | JUV 189:11 |
| travelled: I took the one less t. | FROST 146:14 |
| I t. among unknown men | WORD 355:3 |
| t. a good deal in Concord | THOR 332:7 |
| traveller: from whose bourn no t. returns | SHAK 275:26 |
| Now spurs the lated t. apace | SHAK 287:7 |
| t. betwixt life and death | WORD 356:24 |
| t. from an antique land | SHEL 304:11 |
| T., knocking on the moonlit door | DE L 116:18 |
| t.'s dream under the hill | BLAKE 60:15 |
| travels: t. the fastest who travels | KIPL 196:20 |
| t. the world in search | MOORE 234:7 |
| treachery: t. of the intellectuals | BENDA 34:7 |
| tread: Doth close behind him t. | COL 104:15 |
| t. safely into the unknown | HASK 163:16 |
| T. softly because you t. | YEATS 359:7 |
| Were it ever so airy a t. | TENN 327:2 |
| treason: bloody t. flourished | SHAK 281:24 |
| [corporations] cannot commit t. | COKE 103:9 |
| If this be t., make the most of it | HENRY 166:5 |
| In trust I have found t. | ELIZ 135:5 |
| moderation is a sort of t. | BURKE 79:22 |
| none dare call it t. | HAR 162:22 |
| temptation is the greatest t. | ELIOT 134:7 |
| t. can but peep | SHAK 277:1 |
| T. has done his worst | SHAK 287:4 |
| t. is not owned when 'tis | DRYD 128:8 |
| treasons: fit for t., stratagems | SHAK 290:3 |
| treasure: purest t. mortal times afford | SHAK 293:7 |
| thou shalt have t. in heaven | BIBLE 50:21 |
| Where your t. is | BIBLE 49:2 |
| witty woman is a t. | MER 223:12 |
| yet liking his t. | THOM 331:1 |
| treasures: t. upon earth | BIBLE 49:1 |

| | | | |
|---|---|---|---|
| treasury: T. is the spring | BAG 26:4 | Trinity: strong name of the T. | ALEX 4:5 |
| T. were to fill old bottles | KEYN 194:16 | trip: Come, and t. it as ye go | MILT 227:2 |
| treat: Talk about a t. | COLL 105:6 | triple: t. cord, which no man | BURKE 79:21 |
| t. if met where any bar | HARDY 162:13 | trippingly: t. on the tongue | SHAK 276:4 |
| treaties: T. are like girls | DE G 116:4 | triste: jamais t. archy | MARQ 219:19 |
| treaty: not a peace t., an armistice | FOCH 142:15 | tristesse: Bonjour t. | ÉLUA 136:9 |
| signed the t. bred a fever | THOM 330:11 | Tristram: let call him T. | MAL 217:1 |
| tree: billboard lovely as a t. | NASH 237:17 | T. Shandy did not last | JOHN 185:7 |
| If he finds that this t. | KNOX 198:18 | Triton: this T. of the minnows | SHAK 273:18 |
| I shall be like that t. | SWIFT 320:26 | T. blow his wreathèd horn | WORD 357:11 |
| more to my mind than a t. | MORR 235:11 | triumph: for evil to t. | BURKE 81:13 |
| On a t. by a river a little | GILB 152:7 | in t. from the north | MAC 213:25 |
| only God can make a t. | KILM 195:1 | meet with t. and disaster | KIPL 197:6 |
| poem lovely as a t. | KILM 194:22 | Now is the Victor's t. won | POTT 253:28 |
| t. of actual life springs | GOET 154:5 | there is no glory in the t. | CORN 108:1 |
| t. of liberty must be refreshed | JEFF 180:21 | T. in God above | GURN 159:11 |
| t. of life | BIBLE 43:21 | t. of hope over experience | JOHN 184:24 |
| t. of the knowledge of good | BIBLE 38:19 | t. of modern science | WAUGH 344:1 |
| t. that a wise man sees | BLAKE 61:4 | t. of the embalmer's art | VIDAL 338:12 |
| t. were for the healing | BIBLE 58:7 | trivial: t. people should muse | LAWR 202:24 |
| Under the greenwood t. | SHAK 272:19 | T. personalities decomposing | WOOLF 353:20 |
| Woodman, spare that t. | MORR 235:13 | t. round, the common task | KEBLE 193:17 |
| woodman, spare the beechen t. | CAMP 88:17 | trivialities: t. where opposites | BOHR 63:1 |
| treen: t. priests and golden chalices | JEWEL 181:14 | Troilus: T. methinks mounted | SHAK 289:31 |
| trees: And all the t. are green | KING 195:17 | Trojan: T. 'orses will jump out | BEVIN 38:6 |
| die when the t. were green | CLARE 101:3 | troop: T. home to churchyards | SHAK 290:34 |
| I see men as t., walking | BIBLE 51:22 | troops: charged the t. of error | BROW 74:9 |
| Loveliest of t., the cherry now | HOUS 174:16 | trophies: her weedy t. | SHAK 277:7 |
| music of its t. at dawn | ARN 16:21 | tropical: night of t. splendour | PORT 253:18 |
| Orpheus with his lute made t. | SHAK 280:16 | trouble: Double, double toil and t. | SHAK 287:15 |
| Generations pass while some t. | BROW 74:6 | few days, and full of t. | BIBLE 42:33 |
| t. and the houses go wheeling | THOM 332:2 | Gold? a transient, shining t. | GRAI 156:7 |
| t. that grow so fair | KIPL 197:1 | has t. enough of its own | WILC 349:14 |
| T., where you sit | POPE 253:1 | In t. and in joy | TATE 322:17 |
| t. will never get across | FROST 146:16 | it is not our t. | MARQ 219:20 |
| With rocks, and stones, and t. | WORD 356:25 | Man is born unto t. | BIBLE 42:29 |
| Trelawny: And shall T. die | HAWK 163:17 | present help in time of t. | ANON 5:18 |
| tremble: t. for my country | JEFF 180:24 | There may be t. ahead | BERL 35:22 |
| trembled: T. the mariners | ANAT 5:10 | To-day the Roman and his t. | HOUS 174:23 |
| tremblers: boding t. learned to trace | GOLD 154:23 | transcendent capacity of taking t. | CARL 90:10 |
| trembling: salvation with fear and t. | BIBLE 56:6 | very present help in t. | BOOK 67:6 |
| T. in her soft and chilly nest | KEATS 190:19 | Wenlock Edge the wood's in t. | HOUS 174:22 |
| tremulous: postern behind my t. stay | HARDY 162:2 | When there's t. brewing | LYLE 198:13 |
| trencher-friends: t., time's flies | SHAK 296:20 | troubled: heart be t. | BIBLE 53:36 |
| trencher-man: very valiant t. | SHAK 291:12 | Like a bridge over t. water | SIMON 307:5 |
| trespass: And t. there and go | HOUS 174:14 | t. with her lonely life | PEPYS 247:16 |
| trespasses: And forgive us our t. | BOOK 63:16 | troubles: against a sea of t. | SHAK 275:25 |
| tress: A little stolen t. | YEATS 359:27 | From t. of the world | HARV 163:15 |
| tresses: t. man's imperial race insnare | POPE 253:4 | your t. in your old kit-bag | ASAF 18:17 |
| trial: T. by jury itself | DENM 116:27 | troubling: wicked cease from t. | BIBLE 42:27 |
| t. if I recognize it as such | KAFKA 189:17 | trousers: bottoms of my t. rolled | ELIOT 134:2 |
| t. is by what is contrary | MILT 230:31 | not a man, but—a cloud in t. | MAY 222:15 |
| triangle: The eternal t. | ANON 6:29 | t. on when you go out | IBSEN 178:3 |
| triangles: If t. were to make a God | MONT 233:21 | trout: grey t. lies asleep | HOGG 170:7 |
| tribe: badge of all our t. | SHAK 289:4 | you find a t. in the milk | THOR 332:5 |
| may his t. increase | HUNT 176:12 | trowel: should lay it on with a t. | DISR 122:20 |
| purify the dialect of the t. | ELIOT 133:9 | Troy: ringing plains of windy T. | TENN 328:21 |
| Richer than all his t. | SHAK 293:5 | sacked T.'s sacred city | HOMER 171:1 |
| tribeless: t., and nationless | SHEL 304:22 | T. came destined an exile | VIRG 338:23 |
| tribulation: came out of great t. | BIBLE 57:26 | Where's T., and where's | BRAM 71:13 |
| tribute: To his feet thy t. bring | LYTE 212:21 | truant: t. disposition, good my lord | SHAK 274:14 |
| trick: conjuring t. with bones | JENK 181:4 | trucks: lot to learn about t. | AWDRY 23:13 |
| dream when the long t.'s over | MAS 222:2 | true: And is it t? And is it true | BETJ 36:18 |
| T. that everyone abhors | BELL 33:10 | as t. a lover as ever sighed | SHAK 272:18 |
| When in doubt, win the t. | HOYLE 175:12 | by the people as equally t. | GIBB 150:10 |
| tricks: Frustrate their knavish t. | ANON 7:14 | dark and t. and tender | TENN 327:4 |
| t. are either knavish | JOHN 185:23 | England to itself do rest but t. | SHAK 282:15 |
| tried: Christian ideal not t. | CHES 98:15 | He said t. things, but called | BROW 75:16 |
| she for a little t. | WOTT 357:17 | in her ear, 'You are not t.' | WILB 349:10 |
| trifle: t. with the spoon | POPE 251:25 | Let God be t. | BIBLE 54:29 |
| trifles: She who t. with all | GAY 149:9 | my shape as t. | SHAK 282:20 |
| snapper-up of unconsidered t. | SHAK 298:27 | pessimist fears this is t. | CAB 87:23 |
| T. light as air | SHAK 292:18 | | |
| trigger: Whose finger do you want on the t. | | | |
| | ANON 11:21 | | |

tune (cont.):
Turn on, t. in and drop out | LEARY 203:19
tunes: Dance they to the t. of Handel | SITW 308:1
devil have all the good t. | HILL 168:14
tunic: closest, all-concealing t. | SHEL 304:14
tunnel: light at the end of the t. | DICK 120:19
light at the end of the t. | LOW 211:18
some profound dull t. | OWEN 244:2
time t. to the cultural cringe | KEAT 190:8
tuppence: t. for your old watch chain | COLL 105:6
tupping: Is t. your white ewe | SHAK 291:29
turbulent: rid me of this t. priest | HENR 165:23
turd: rymyng is nat worth a t. | CHAU 96:4
turf: blue ribbon of the t. | DISR 122:4
green t. beneath my feet | HAZL 164:8
Oft on the dappled t. at ease | WORD 357:8
t. in many a mouldering | GRAY 157:6
Turk: French, or T., or Proosian | GILB 152:21
Turkey: T. is a dying man | NICH 239:10
turkey: myrtle and t. part of it | AUST 22:20
Turkish: not the T. court | SHAK 278:29
Turks: [The T.] bag and baggage | GLAD 153:10
turn: And I t. the page | BROW 75:18
Because I do not hope to t. | ELIOT 132:18
goodnight and quickly t. | YEATS 359:5
I keep, and pass, and t. again | EMER 136:10
I t. to ducks | HARV 163:15
T. of the Screw | JAMES 180:3
T. on, tune in and drop out | LEARY 203:19
t. to him the other also | BIBLE 48:23
turned: having once t. round walks on | COL 104:15
in case anything t. up | DICK 118:11
t. my back upon Don or devil | TENN 328:12
we have t. every one | BIBLE 46:19
turning: still point of the t. world | ELIOT 132:28
turnip: candle in that great t. | CHUR 100:10
getting blood out of a t. | MARR 219:25
Have a t. than his father | JOHN 186:13
turnpike: consider supper as a t. | EDW 131:6
turns: Times go by t. | SOUT 312:9
turtle: t. lives 'twixt plated decks | NASH 237:9
voice of the t. is heard | BIBLE 44:32
Tuscany: even the ranks of T. | MAC 214:8
tu-whit: T., tu-who—a merry note | SHAK 284:23
twain: with t. he covered his face | BIBLE 45:10
twangs: t. and breaks at the end | MACN 216:4
Tweedledum: T. and Tweedledee | BYROM 84:24
twelve: ten or t. strokes of havoc | HOPK 171:24
T. for the twelve apostles | ANON 8:6
t. honest men have decided | PULT 256:4
twenty: kiss me, sweet and t. | SHAK 297:23
twenty-three: chaste, and t. | BYRON 85:23
twenty-twenty: Hindsight always t. | WILD 350:23
twice: do t. as well as men | WHIT 349:3
gives t. who gives soon | PUBL 256:1
it is t. blessed | SHAK 289:26
My life closed t. before | DICK 120:11
t. into the same river | HER 166:8
twilight: disastrous t. | MILT 228:17
full Surrey t.! importunate band! | BETJ 37:13
In a t. dim with rose | DE L 116:21
twilights: In ancient shadows and t. | Æ 3:4
twinkle: Twinkle, t., little bat | CARR 91:7
T., twinkle, little star | TAYL 323:3
twinkling: t. of an eye | BIBLE 55:21
t. of an eye | BOOK 66:22
twins: to have been born t. | MADAN 216:12
twirling: t. in thy hand a withered | ARN 17:8
twist: I have NO MORE T. | POTT 254:1
Let him t. slowly | EHRL 131:7
twisted: You silly t. boy | MILL 225:10
two: game at which t. can play | BEER 32:12
sweet t.-and-twenty | BYRON 87:10
that twice t. be not four | TURG 335:15
that t. and one are three | STEP 315:4

two (cont.):
t. and two unto Noah | BIBLE 39:8
t. and two would continue | WHIS 347:10
t. ears of corn or two | SWIFT 319:21
t. glasses and two chairs | MACN 216:5
T. loves I have of comfort | SHAK 300:13
T. nations | DISR 122:6
t. or three are gathered | BIBLE 50:18
t. or three are gathered | BOOK 64:10
t. people miserable instead | BUTL 84:12
t. things about the horse | ROYD 264:3
t. things believed of any man | TARK 322:14
T. voices are there | STEP 315:4
unfeathered t.-legged thing | DRYD 127:9
twopence: t. every day of my life | STEV 317:1
Tyne: from the Severn to the T. | KIPL 196:3
type: So careful of the t. | TENN 325:10
types: Seven t. of ambiguity | EMPS 137:7
T. and shadows have their | THOM 330:4
tyrannis: semper t. | BOOTH 69:20
tyrannous: t. to use it like a giant | SHAK 288:13
tyranny: against a monstrous t. | CHUR 99:12
Bad laws the worst sort of t. | BURKE 80:24
Ecclesiastic t.'s the worst | DEFOE 115:25
long dark night of t. | MURR 236:13
T. is always better organised | PÉGUY 247:4
tyrant: t. custom, most grave | SHAK 292:1
t. of his fields withstood | GRAY 157:9
tyrants: argument of t. | PITT 249:7
blood of patriots and t. | JEFF 180:21
intercourse between t. and slaves | GOLD 155:6
Kings will be t. from policy | BURKE 80:16
Rebellion to t. is obedience | BRAD 71:11
sceptre from t. | TURG 335:16
T. seldom want pretexts | BURKE 79:19
would be t. if they could | DEFOE 115:20
Tyre: one with Nineveh, and T. | KIPL 197:3
which men still call T. | FLEC 141:18
Tyrone: steeples of Fermanagh and T. | CHUR 99:7

# U

ubi: U. Petrus, ibi ergo ecclesia | AMBR 4:19
ubique: Quod u., quod semper | VINC 338:22
ubiquities: They are blazing u. | EMER 137:2
ugly: never saw an u. thing in my life | CONS 107:11
u., heavy and complex | FLAU 141:13
u. mathematics | HARDY 161:18
world's as u., ay, as sin | LOCK 208:22
Ulster: U. will fight | CHUR 99:2
ulterioris: ripae u. | VIRG 339:15
ultima: U. Thule | VIRG 340:5
Ulysses: Happy he who like U. | DU B 128:33
'umble: We are so very u. | DICK 118:14
umbrage: garden's u. mild | SMART 308:12
umbrella: steals the just's u. | BOWEN 70:14
umpire: u., the pavilion cat | LANG 201:2
unable: unwilling or u. | WILL 351:7
unacceptable: u. face of capitalism | HEATH 164:12
unaccommodated: u. man | SHAK 283:14
unadvised: too u., too sudden | SHAK 295:1
unadvisedly: taken in hand, u. | BOOK 65:26
unattempted: u. yet in prose or rhyme | MILT 228:8
unaware: And I was u. | HARDY 162:7
unbearable: in victory u. | CHUR 100:9
u. lightness of being | KUND 199:8
unbeatable: in defeat u. | CHUR 100:9
unbeautiful: furnished souls are u. | CUMM 113:5
unbecoming: conduct u. | ANON 6:2
u. men that strove | TENN 328:23
unbelief: help thou mine u. | BIBLE 51:24
unbidden: Singing hymns u. | SHEL 305:9
unborn: possible to talk to the u. | BARZ 29:22
unbowed: bloody, but u. | HENL 165:17

unbribed: what the man will do u. WOLFE 353:2
unburied: friendless bodies of u. WEBS 344:25
uncertain: U., coy, and hard to please SCOTT 268:22
  u. glory of an April day SHAK 298:18
uncharitableness: and from all u. BOOK 64:14
uncircumscribed: Sceptreless, free, u. SHEL 304:22
unclassed: Equal, u., tribeless SHEL 304:22
uncle: O my prophetic soul! My u. SHAK 274:32
  nor u. me no uncle SHAK 293:18
unclean: people of u. lips BIBLE 45:11
unclouded: u. blaze of living light BYRON 85:20
unclubbable: very u. man JOHN 184:18
uncoffined: u., and unknown BYRON 85:14
uncomfortable: moral when he is only u. SHAW 301:21
uncommon: and u. abilities BAG 26:2
unconquerable: nursing the u. hope ARN 17:12
unconscionable: u. time dying CHAR 95:6
unconscious: royal road to the u. FREUD 146:1
unconsidered: snapper-up of u. trifles SHAK 298:27
uncouth: find out his u. way MILT 228:29
  U. unkist, said the old poet SPEN 313:19
uncreated: wide womb of u. night MILT 228:24
uncreating: before thy u. word POPE 250:22
unction: Lay not that flattering u. SHAK 276:22
under: U. a spreading chestnut tree LONG 210:4
under-belly: u. of the Axis CHUR 99:19
under-dogs: Englishman among the u. WAUGH 343:21
underground: As Johnny u. PUDN 256:3
underlings: we are u. SHAK 280:27
underneath: U. the Arches FLAN 141:2
undersold: Never knowingly u. LEWIS 206:16
understand: don't criticize what you can't u.
  DYL 130:9
  grown-ups never u. anything DE S 265:15
  isn't confused doesn't really u. MURR 236:14
  Nor can anyone u. Ein ANON 8:2
  nor to hate them but to u. them SPIN 313:23
  remember, and u. BROW 75:29
  u. a little less MAJOR 216:19
  u. what is happening CHAM 93:24
understanded: tongue not u. of the people BOOK 69:18
understanding: not obliged to find you an u.
  JOHN 186:5
  shall light a candle of u. BIBLE 47:28
  sketchy u. of life itself CRICK 111:19
  spirit of wisdom and u. BIBLE 45:18
  they pass all u. JAM 179:13
  u. makes one very indulgent STAËL 314:5
  where is the place of u. BIBLE 43:1
  with all thy getting get u. BIBLE 43:10
understandings: cold hearts and muddy u.
  BURKE 80:15
understands: Reads verse and thinks she u.
  BROW 75:25
understood: something u. HERB 167:4
Underworld: way down to the U. VIRG 339:12
undevotional: Dirty, dark, and u. VICT 338:10
undiscovered: u. country from whose bourn
  SHAK 275:26
undo: for thee does she u. herself MIDD 224:9
  To u. the folded lie AUDEN 21:11
undone: death had u. so many ELIOT 134:21
  John Donne, Anne Donne, U. DONNE 124:23
  u. those things which we BOOK 63:14
  Weather and rain have u. KIPL 197:8
  What's done cannot be u. SHAK 287:31
  Woe is me! for I am u. BIBLE 45:11
undulating: and an u. throat BELL 33:19
unearned: u. increment of rent MILL 224:14
uneasy: U. lies the head that wears SHAK 278:23
uneatable: full pursuit of the u. WILDE 350:9
uneducated: government by the u. CHES 98:12
unemployment: need be no more u. KEYN 194:16
  u. and the recession have LAM 200:18
unespied: In the ocean's bosom u. MARV 220:9

unexamined: u. life not worth living SOCR 310:22
unexpected: Old age is the most u. TROT 334:22
unexplained: you're u. as yet HALL 160:14
unexpressive: chaste, and u. she SHAK 273:2
unfaithful: faith u. kept him falsely TENN 324:9
  u. to the translation BORG 69:22
unfathomable: The u. deep THOM 330:24
unfeeling: Th' u. for his own GRAY 157:13
unfinished: Liberty is always u. business ANON 8:19
unfit: chosen from the u. ANON 6:20
unforgiving: An u. eye SHER 306:7
  If you can fill the u. minute KIPL 197:7
unfortunate: u. man is the one BOET 62:17
ungirt: Song of the U. Runners SORL 311:15
ungodliness: tents of u. BOOK 67:22
ungodly: For the hope of the u. BIBLE 47:31
  fret not thyself because of the u. BOOK 66:26
  seen the u. in great power BOOK 66:28
unhappily: bad end u., the good STOP 318:5
unhappiness: loyalty we feel to u. GREE 158:5
  putting-off of u. GREE 158:3
  vocation of u. SIM 307:4
unhappy: can never be very u. GAY 149:16
  each u. family is u. in its own way TOLS 333:11
  For old, u., far-off things WORD 357:2
  in mourning for my life, I'm u. CHEK 96:25
  moral as soon as one is u. PROU 255:19
  soft, u. sex BEHN 32:24
unhasting: u., and silent as light SMITH 310:15
unheard: language of the u. KING 195:11
  those u. are sweeter KEATS 191:15
unholy: shrieks, and sights u. MILT 226:27
unhonoured: u., and unsung SCOTT 268:13
uniform: good u. must work its way DICK 120:1
  Should be more u. HOOD 171:6
uninitiated: you u. ones VIRG 339:13
union: Liberty and U. WEBS 344:9
  O U., strong and great LONG 209:11
  u. of hands and hearts TAYL 323:5
unions: u. and the industrialists NIEM 239:15
unite: Workers of the world, u.! MARX 221:15
United States: so close to the U. DIAZ 117:16
  U. . . . the greatest poem WHIT 348:25
uniting: By u. we stand DICK 120:18
unity: truth, u., and concord BOOK 65:9
universal: u. monarchy of wit CAREW 89:19
  wears one u. grin FIEL 139:13
universe: better ordering of the u. ALF 4:8
  cover the u. with mud FORS 143:18
  good u. next door CUMM 113:1
  Great Architect of the U. JEANS 180:17
  Life, the U. and Everything ADAMS 1:9
  Put back thy u. and give me JONES 186:20
  This u. is not hostile HOLM 170:13
  u. is not only queerer HALD 160:2
  u.'s very existence PENR 247:11
  visible u. was an illusion BORG 69:23
  Which is the measure of the u. SHEL 304:20
university: benefiting from u. AMIS 5:1
  gained in the U. of Life BOTT 70:7
  servant to be bred at an U. CONG 106:10
  U. of these days is a collection CARL 90:16
  We are the U. SPR 314:1
unjust: on the just and on the u. BIBLE 48:24
  u. steals the just's umbrella BOWEN 70:14
unjustly: They teach to talk u. ARIS 15:10
unkempt: U. about those hedges BROO 73:4
unkind: Tell me not, Sweet, I am u. LOV 210:20
unkindest: most u. cut of all SHAK 281:23
unkindness: you elements, with u. SHAK 283:7
unkist: Uncouth u. SPEN 313:19
  Unknowe, u. CHAU 96:14
unknowable: O world u. THOM 331:14
unknowe: U., unkist, and lost CHAU 96:14

| verse (cont.): | |
|---|---|
| flask of wine, a book of v. | FITZ 140:6 |
| indignation makes me write v. | JUV 189:2 |
| Let the v. the subject fit | CAREY 90:1 |
| Lies the subject of all v. | BROW 74:24 |
| No subject for immortal v. | DAY-L 115:6 |
| Not v. now, only prose | BROW 75:18 |
| Only with those in v. | CONG 106:18 |
| turnings intricate of v. | WORD 356:12 |
| unpolished rugged v. I chose | DRYD 128:14 |
| v. and thinks she understands | BROW 75:25 |
| v. is a measured speech | BACON 23:24 |
| v. may find him | HERB 166:21 |
| Voice, and I | MILT 226:4 |
| Who died to make v. free | PRES 255:5 |
| write free v. as play tennis | FROST 146:26 |
| verses: rhyme the rudder is of v. | BUTL 83:25 |
| Tear him for his bad v. | SHAK 281:27 |
| versions: hundred v. of it | SHAW 302:15 |
| verum: Ave v. corpus | ANON 13:14 |
| very: V. God of very God | BOOK 65:5 |
| vessel: gallant trim the gilded v. | GRAY 157:3 |
| Let the Irish v. lie | AUDEN 20:24 |
| unto the weaker v. | BIBLE 57:10 |
| v. with the pestle | FRANK 245:1 |
| wide v. of the universe | SHAK 279:7 |
| vesture: cast lots upon my v. | BOOK 66:16 |
| Mine outward v. be | LITT 208:2 |
| veterans: world its v. rewards | POPE 251:11 |
| vex: V. not thou the poet's mind | TENN 327:15 |
| vexation: Multiplication is v. | ANON 9:11 |
| vanity and v. of spirit | BIBLE 44:9 |
| vexes: The other v. it | KEATS 190:25 |
| vexing: V. the dull ear of a drowsy | SHAK 282:9 |
| vibrated: had better not be v. | DICK 117:21 |
| vibrates: V. in the memory | SHEL 305:4 |
| vice: Ambition, in a private man a v. | MASS 222:3 |
| Art is v. You don't marry it | DEGAS 116:2 |
| defence of liberty is no v. | GOLD 155:15 |
| distinction between virtue and v. | JOHN 184:11 |
| England but v. and religion | SMITH 310:12 |
| He lashed the v., but spared | SWIFT 320:24 |
| lost by not having been v. | WALP 342:3 |
| Prosperity doth best discover v. | BACON 24:11 |
| Public schools nurseries of all v. | FIEL 139:8 |
| raptures and roses of v. | SWIN 321:7 |
| render v. serviceable | BOL 63:7 |
| say there is no v. but beggary | SHAK 282:5 |
| sensual pleasure without v. | JOHN 186:10 |
| To sanction V., and hunt | BYRON 86:33 |
| tribute which v. pays to virtue | LA R 201:23 |
| V. came in always at the door | DEFOE 115:12 |
| When v. prevails | ADD 2:17 |
| vice-presidency: v. isn't worth a pitcher | GARN 148:7 |
| vices: By hating v. too much | BURKE 80:19 |
| most v. committed very genteelly | BOSW 70:5 |
| our pleasant v. | SHAK 284:2 |
| vicious: expect a boy to be v. till | SAKI 265:20 |
| vicissitude: This sad v. of things | STER 315:27 |
| vicisti: V., Galilaee | JUL 188:20 |
| victim: v. must be found | GILB 151:19 |
| v. to a big lie | HITL 169:3 |
| victims: its v. time to die | GUIB 159:8 |
| little v. play | GRAY 157:12 |
| v. who respect their executioners | SART 267:7 |
| victis: Vae v. | LIVY 208:5 |
| victor: to the v. belong the spoils | MARCY 218:2 |
| Victoria: ticket at V. Station | BEVIN 38:9 |
| victories: Peace hath her v. | MILT 230:27 |
| victorious: Make him v. | HOGG 170:8 |
| victory: But 'twas a famous v. | SOUT 311:20 |
| death in v. | BIBLE 45:25 |
| Dig for v. | DORM 124:24 |
| grave, where is thy v. | BIBLE 55:22 |
| In v.: magnanimity | CHUR 100:4 |

| victory (cont.): | |
|---|---|
| in v. unbearable | CHUR 100:9 |
| is only v. in him | DRYD 128:29 |
| not the v. but the contest | COUB 108:15 |
| V. has a hundred fathers | CIANO 100:12 |
| victuals: About their v. | CALV 88:9 |
| And the v. and the wine | CALV 88:10 |
| vie: Ah! que la v. est quotidienne | LAF 199:20 |
| Vienna: V. is nothing | METT 224:1 |
| view: lends enchantment to the v. | CAMP 88:19 |
| myself a motley to the v. | SHAK 300:6 |
| viewless: As v. too | AUBER 19:15 |
| vigil: tongueless v. and all the pain | SWIN 321:1 |
| vigilance: liberty to man is eternal v. | CURR 113:8 |
| vigilant: Be sober, be v. | BIBLE 57:12 |
| Vigny: Et V. plus secret | SAIN 265:14 |
| vile: And only man is v. | HEBER 164:16 |
| O v., intolerable | SHAK 295:29 |
| Things base and v. | SHAK 290:16 |
| V., but viler George II | LAND 200:24 |
| vilest: v. things become themselves | SHAK 271:17 |
| village: families in a country v. | AUST 23:9 |
| first in a v. than second | CAES 87:26 |
| image of a global v. | MCL 215:11 |
| loveliest v. of the plain | GOLD 154:17 |
| vegetate in a v. | COLT 105:18 |
| v.-Hampden | GRAY 157:9 |
| v. smithy stands | LONG 210:4 |
| villages: pleasant v. and farms | MILT 229:23 |
| villains: we were v. by necessity | SHAK 282:22 |
| villany: v. you teach me I will | SHAK 289:18 |
| Villon: V., our sad bad glad mad | SWIN 321:5 |
| Vinci: V. and pronounce it Vinchy | TWAIN 336:1 |
| vindicate: v. the ways of God to man | POPE 252:11 |
| vine: little prop best fits a little v. | HERR 167:22 |
| luscious clusters of the v. | MARV 220:15 |
| shall be as the fruitful v. | BOOK 68:32 |
| sweet grape who will the v. | SHAK 299:8 |
| thyme and the gadding v. | MILT 227:13 |
| vines: his client to plant v. | WRIG 357:23 |
| v. that round the thatch-eaves | KEATS 192:14 |
| vineyard: v. in a very fruitful | BIBLE 45:7 |
| vintage: draught of v. | KEATS 191:29 |
| v. where the grapes of wrath | HOWE 175:7 |
| violations: v. committed by children | BOWEN 70:17 |
| violence: In v., we forget who we are | MCC 214:11 |
| I say v. is necessary | BROWN 73:15 |
| Keep v. in the mind | ALD 3:16 |
| violent: v. feelings produce | RUSK 264:12 |
| v. hands upon themselves | BOOK 66:5 |
| violently: v. if they must | QUIN 257:9 |
| violet: At the v. hour | ELIOT 134:27 |
| bats with baby faces in the v. | ELIOT 134:30 |
| By v.-hooded Doctors | TENN 327:18 |
| in the v.-embroidered vale | MILT 226:10 |
| oxlips and the nodding v. | SHAK 290:26 |
| To throw a perfume on the v. | SHAK 282:10 |
| v. smells to him as it doth | SHAK 279:12 |
| v.'s reclining head | DONNE 124:2 |
| violets: By ashen roots the v. blow | TENN 325:29 |
| When daisies pied and v. blue | SHAK 284:21 |
| Who are the v. now | SHAK 294:8 |
| violins: v. wound my heart | VERL 337:21 |
| vipers: O generation of v. | BIBLE 48:14 |
| vir: Beatus v. qui timet Dominum | BIBLE 58:11 |
| virgin: poor v., sir, an ill-favoured | SHAK 273:11 |
| Every harlot was a v. once | BLAKE 60:5 |
| v.-choir to make delicious | KEATS 192:8 |
| v. goddess returns | VIRG 339:25 |
| v. renowned for ever | HOR 173:27 |
| v. shall conceive | BIBLE 45:14 |
| virginity: No, no; for my v. | PRIOR 255:12 |
| virgo: Iam redit et v. | VIRG 339:25 |
| virtue: accommodating sort of v. | MOL 232:20 |
| adversity doth best discover v. | BACON 24:11 |

| | | | |
|---|---|---|---|
| voted: always v. at my party's call | GILB 152:19 | walk (cont.): | |
| they v. cent per cent | BYRON 84:25 | w. o'er the western wave | SHEL 305:12 |
| votes: who uses his money as v. | SAM 266:11 | w. on the wild side | ALGR 4:9 |
| voting: v. that's democracy | STOP 317:28 | w. through the fields | CORN 108:6 |
| vow: I v. to thee, my country | SPR 313:26 | w. through the valley | BOOK 66:18 |
| vowels: v., some day I will tell | RIMB 260:11 | W. under his huge legs | SHAK 280:27 |
| vows: cancel all our v. | DRAY 126:13 | W. upon England's mountains | BLAKE 61:12 |
| vox: V. et praeterea nihil | ANON 14:3 | W., water, meditated wild | SMART 308:12 |
| V. populi, vox Dei | ALC 3:14 | w. within the purlieus | ETH 137:18 |
| voyage: about to take my last v. | HOBB 169:11 | was evident from her w. | VIRG 339:3 |
| all the v. of their life | SHAK 282:1 | Where'er you w., cool gales | POPE 253:1 |
| first to make the v. over | VIRG 339:15 | Will you w. a little faster | CARR 91:11 |
| voyages: v. of the starship *Enterprise* | RODD 261:12 | walked: He w. by himself | KIPL 197:20 |
| voyaging: V. through strange seas | WORD 356:10 | people that w. in darkness | BIBLE 45:15 |
| vulgar: takes place with the v. | BACON 24:7 | w. through the wilderness | BUNY 78:17 |
| work upon the v. with fine sense | POPE 253:12 | walkers: Six for the six proud w. | ANON 8:6 |
| worse than wicked, it's v. | PUNCH 256:15 | walking: from w. up and down | BIBLE 42:21 |
| vulgarity: v., concealing something | FORS 143:23 | I see men as trees, w. | BIBLE 51:22 |
| | | W., and leaping, and praising | BIBLE 54:10 |
| | | w. in the garden | BIBLE 38:26 |
| # W | | W. so early | SCOTT 269:1 |
| | | walks: I wish I liked the way it w. | RAL 258:6 |
| wabe: gyre and gimble in the w. | CARR 91:15 | She w. in beauty | BYRON 87:6 |
| waded: w. thro' red blude | BALL 28:8 | while Gibbon levelled w. | COLM 105:15 |
| waft: w. her love to come again | SHAK 289:32 | wall: Before I built a w. | FROST 146:17 |
| wage: home policy: I w. war | CLEM 101:8 | broken w., the burning roof | YEATS 359:14 |
| wages: better w. and shorter hours | ORW 242:13 | conclude against a w. of stone | WILB 349:11 |
| Home art gone and ta'en thy w. | SHAK 273:27 | Or close the w. up | SHAK 279:5 |
| w. of sin is death | BIBLE 54:36 | serves it in the office of a w. | SHAK 293:16 |
| Wagner: W. has lovely moments | ROSS 263:11 | standing like a stone w. | BEE 31:22 |
| W.'s music better than it sounds | NYE 240:15 | that doesn't love a w. | FROST 146:15 |
| wagon: Hitch your w. to a star | EMER 136:31 | that the w. fell down | BIBLE 40:27 |
| wail: mirth to w. a week | SHAK 299:8 | w. next door catches fire | HOR 173:14 |
| wailing: w. for her demon-lover | COL 103:23 | W. St lays an egg | ANON 11:10 |
| waist: arms went round her w. | MAS 221:20 | Watch the w., my darling | KIPL 196:28 |
| Then you live about her w. | SHAK 275:13 | weather on the outward w. | SHAK 289:13 |
| wait: serve who only stand and w. | MILT 230:23 | Without a city w. | ALEX 4:6 |
| Tomorrow, just you w. and see | BURT 83:3 | Wallace: wi' W. bled | BURNS 82:21 |
| w. for liberty till | MAC 213:8 | wallet: w. at his back | SHAK 297:4 |
| We had better w. and see | ASQ 19:2 | w., biform him in his lappe | CHAU 95:23 |
| We want eight, and we won't w. | ANON 11:17 | walling: w. in or walling out | FROST 146:17 |
| waiting: I was nearly kept w. | LOUI 210:13 | walls: close her from thy ancient w. | BLAKE 60:21 |
| So quickly, w. for a hand | TENN 324:26 | Stone w. do not a prison make | LOV 210:19 |
| W. for Godot | BECK 31:10 | these w. thy sphere | DONNE 124:13 |
| W. for the end, boys | EMPS 137:4 | walk the angels on the w. | MARL 219:11 |
| wake: do I w. or sleep | KEATS 192:7 | w. and towers were girdled | COL 103:22 |
| If I should die before I w. | ANON 9:20 | wooden w. are the best | COV 108:18 |
| sleep past, we w. eternally | DONNE 123:9 | walrus: W. and the Carpenter | CARR 91:21 |
| W. now, my love, awake | SPEN 313:5 | waltz: goes out of a beautiful w. | GREN 158:15 |
| W. up, England | GEOR 149:25 | Swoons to a w. | HUXL 177:12 |
| You will w., and remember | BROW 75:29 | waltzing: come a-w., Matilda | PAT 246:16 |
| waked: You have w. me too soon | WATTS 343:9 | waly: W., Waly | BALL 28:10 |
| waken: would w. the dead | GRAV 156:12 | wan: so w. with care | SHAK 277:21 |
| wakening: Our w. and uprising | KEBLE 193:16 | Why so pale and w., fond lover | SUCK 318:20 |
| wakes: Hock-cart wassails, the | HERR 167:12 | wand: bright gold ring on her w. | MOORE 234:17 |
| not breed one work that w. | HOPK 172:19 | wander: w. forth the sons of Belial | MILT 228:15 |
| Wordsworth sometimes w. | BYRON 86:17 | wandered: I w. lonely as a cloud | WORD 355:4 |
| waking: Be there at our w. | STR 318:17 | who w. far and wide | HOMER 171:1 |
| it is w. that kills us | BROW 74:22 | wandering: Or but a w. voice | WORD 357:7 |
| w., no such matter | SHAK 299:28 | W. between two worlds | ARN 17:16 |
| Wales: There is no present in W. | THOM 331:5 | wane: moons shall wax and w. | WATTS 343:12 |
| But for W.—! | BOLT 63:8 | want: envy, w., the patron | JOHN 183:12 |
| walk: Doth w. in fear and dread | COL 104:15 | freedom from w. | ROOS 262:13 |
| In a slow silent w. | HARDY 162:11 | must be in w. of a wife | AUST 23:2 |
| no spirit can w. abroad | SHAK 274:2 | my shepherd, I'll not w. | SCOT 269:8 |
| Oh! for a closer w. with God | COWP 109:27 | pleasantest preservative from w. | AUST 23:4 |
| Or w. with Kings | KIPL 197:7 | Ring out the w., the care | TENN 325:24 |
| Rise, take up thy bed, and w. | BIBLE 53:21 | something you probably won't w. | HOPE 171:19 |
| talk with you, w. with you | SHAK 288:31 | those who w. it most | CHES 97:9 |
| that ye w. circumspectly | BIBLE 56:1 | W. is one only of five giants | BEV 38:7 |
| This is the way, w. ye in it | BIBLE 46:2 | w. of decency is want of sense | DILL 120:23 |
| w. and live a Woolworth life | NIC 239:12 | w. of friends and empty purse | BRET 71:23 |
| W. cheerfully over the world | FOX 144:18 | want the world and we w. it now | MORR 235:20 |
| w. for walk's sake | KLEE 198:11 | w. which most would have | DYER 129:16 |
| w. humbly with thy God | BIBLE 47:23 | | |

**want** (*cont.*):

| | |
|---|---|
| What does a woman w. | FREUD 146:3 |
| **wanted**: no man is w. much | EMER 136:27 |
| wanting that have w. everything | HAZL 164:2 |
| **wanting**: and art found w. | BIBLE 47:12 |
| Nor w., nor wasting | SMITH 310:15 |
| **wanton**: wightly w. with a velvet | SHAK 284:14 |
| **wantonly**: lightly, on w. | BOOK 65:26 |
| **wantonness**: in clothes a w. | HERR 167:15 |
| **wantons**: play the w. with our woes | SHAK 294:3 |
| **wants**: supplying our w. by | SWIFT 320:12 |
| **wanwood**: worlds of w. leafmeal | HOPK 172:15 |
| **war**: after such a w. a little less democracy | ATK 19:10 |
| All the business of w. | WELL 345:6 |
| All the time I wage w. | CLEM 102:1 |
| Ancestral voices prophesying w. | COL 103:25 |
| As soon as w. is declared | GIR 153:5 |
| Austria is going to the w. | CHES 97:25 |
| blast of w. blows in our ears | SHAK 279:5 |
| book that made this great w. | LINC 207:13 |
| cold w. | BAR 29:20 |
| day w. broke out | WILT 351:23 |
| delays are dangerous in w. | DRYD 128:22 |
| done very well out of the w. | BALD 27:9 |
| except the British W. Office | SHAW 301:1 |
| First World W. had begun | TAYL 322:23 |
| flinty and steel couch of w. | SHAK 292:1 |
| France has not lost the w. | DE G 116:3 |
| garland of the w. | SHAK 271:25 |
| gave a w. & Nobody came | GINS 153:2 |
| give a w. and nobody will | SAND 266:16 |
| gone too long without a w. | BREC 71:20 |
| good w. makes a good peace | HERB 167:9 |
| Horses and Power and W. | KIPL 196:5 |
| Image of w., without its guilt | SOM 311:2 |
| image of w. without its guilt | SURT 319:8 |
| In a civil w., a general | REED 258:18 |
| In a pattern called a w. | LOW 211:2 |
| In w.: resolution | CHUR 100:4 |
| In w., whichever side may | CHAM 93:25 |
| It is easier to make w. | CLEM 102:2 |
| It is well that w. is so terrible | LEE 204:11 |
| jaw-jaw better than to w.-war | CHUR 100:3 |
| Laws are silent in time of w. | CIC 100:30 |
| learn w. any more | BIBLE 45:5 |
| Let w. yield to peace | CIC 100:23 |
| looks on w. as all glory | SHER 306:9 |
| lordship that this is w. | ADAMS 1:8 |
| magnificent, but it is not w. | BOSQ 69:28 |
| Minstrel Boy to the w. | MOORE 234:16 |
| My subject is W. | OWEN 243:19 |
| nature of w. consisteth | HOBB 169:9 |
| no declaration of w. | EDEN 130:14 |
| no discharge in that w. | BIBLE 44:17 |
| No w., nor prince's funeral | MARV 220:21 |
| No w., or battle's sound | MILT 227:26 |
| Now tell us all about the w. | SOUT 311:19 |
| Oh what a lovely w. | CHIL 208:3 |
| page 1 of the book of w. | MONT 233:2 |
| prepare for the last w. | TUCH 335:7 |
| prepare for w. | VEG 337:18 |
| quaint and curious w. | HARDY 162:13 |
| quickest way of ending a w. | ORW 242:12 |
| sinews of love, as of w. | FARQ 138:18 |
| sinews of w. | CIC 100:29 |
| so dauntless in w. | SCOTT 268:19 |
| stately tents of w. | MARL 219:4 |
| state of w. by nature | SWIFT 320:22 |
| testament of bleeding w. | SHAK 294:1 |
| that devil's madness—W. | SERV 270:12 |
| There never was a good w. | FRAN 145:14 |
| time of peace thinks of w. | ANON 7:16 |
| time of w., and a time | BIBLE 44:13 |
| To w. and arms I fly | LOV 210:20 |
| used to w.'s alarms | HOOD 171:4 |

**war** (*cont.*):

| | |
|---|---|
| w. against a monstrous | CHUR 99:12 |
| w. as is of every man against | HOBB 169:8 |
| w. between men and women | THUR 332:16 |
| w. drum throbbed no longer | TENN 326:12 |
| w. in Europe | BISM 59:20 |
| w. in heaven | BIBLE 57:31 |
| w. It panders to instincts | BENN 34:12 |
| W. hath no fury like a non-combatant | MONT 233:7 |
| W., he sung, is toil | DRYD 127:21 |
| W. is capitalism with the gloves off | STOP 318:7 |
| W. is peace | ORW 242:7 |
| W. is the continuation of politics | CLAU 101:16 |
| W. is the national industry | MIR 231:8 |
| w. is the necessary art | DULL 129:2 |
| W. is the trade of kings | DRYD 128:1 |
| W. is too serious a matter | CLEM 101:21 |
| W. makes rattling good history | HARDY 161:20 |
| W.'s annals will cloud | HARDY 162:12 |
| W.'s glorious art | YOUNG 360:15 |
| w. that we may live in peace | ARIS 15:14 |
| w. that will end war | WELLS 345:24 |
| W. That Would Not Boil | TAYL 323:2 |
| w. they kill you in a new way | ROG 262:2 |
| W. to the knife | PAL 244:16 |
| W. will cease when men refuse | ANON 11:11 |
| w. without bloodshed | MAO 217:18 |
| w. with women | SOUT 311:24 |
| waste of God, W.! | STUD 318:18 |
| weapons of w. | BIBLE 41:23 |
| what can w., but endless war | MILT 227:23 |
| When w. enters a country | ANON 13:3 |
| When w. is declared, Truth | JOHN 182:12 |
| which enable it to make w. | WEIL 345:3 |
| warble: W., child | SHAK 284:12 |
| wardrobe: silken dalliance in the w. | SHAK 279:2 |
| ware: Breath's a w. that will not keep | HOUS 174:18 |
| warfare: her w. is accomplished | BIBLE 46:7 |
| mother of arts, of w. | DU B 128:32 |
| warm: Her heart was w. and gay | HAMM 161:1 |
| O! she's w. | SHAK 299:4 |
| This is too w. work | NELS 238:4 |
| w. and still to be enjoyed | KEATS 191:21 |
| w. full blooded life | JOYCE 188:17 |
| w. kind world is all I know | CORY 108:14 |
| warmer: w. than after watry cloudes | LANG 201:9 |
| warming: w. his five wits | TENN 328:16 |
| warmth: His vigorous w. did | DRYD 127:3 |
| warn: All a poet can do today is w. | OWEN 243:20 |
| right to w. | BAG 26:14 |
| w. you not to be ordinary | KINN 196:1 |
| warning: w. to the world | SHAK 299:23 |
| warp: Weave the w., and weave | GRAY 157:2 |
| warrior: Home they brought her w. dead | TENN 327:26 |
| Who is the happy W.? | WORD 354:14 |
| wars: All skilful in the w. | VAUG 337:6 |
| All w. are planned by old men | RICE 259:18 |
| came to an end all w. | LLOY 208:10 |
| clucked thee to the w. | SHAK 273:22 |
| For all their w. are merry | CHES 97:20 |
| History is littered with the w. | POW 255:2 |
| I see w., horrible wars | VIRG 339:11 |
| my w. were global from the start | REED 258:17 |
| plumèd troop and the big w. | SHAK 292:19 |
| thousand w. of old | TENN 325:26 |
| w. and rumours of wars | BIBLE 50:33 |
| W. cannot be fought with | MOUN 236:4 |
| Warsaw: Order reigns in W. | ANON 12:12 |
| warts: and all | CROM 112:7 |
| was: picked the w. of shall | CUMM 113:2 |
| Thinks what ne'er w. | POPE 251:29 |
| w. when good Cinara was | HOR 173:30 |
| wash: And It-will-w.-no-more | TRAI 334:2 |
| Bid them w. their faces | SHAK 273:16 |
| Moab is my w.-pot | BOOK 67:14 |

wash (*cont.*):

| | |
|---|---|
| tears w. out a word of it | FITZ 140:14 |
| w. the balm from an anointed | SHAK 293:22 |
| w. their feet in soda water | ELIOT 134:26 |
| w. the wind | ELIOT 134:8 |

washed: have w. their robes

| | |
|---|---|
| | BIBLE 57:26 |
| W. by the rivers, blest by | BROO 73:10 |
| w. in the blood of the Lamb | LIND 207:16 |
| w. in the speechless real | BARZ 29:22 |

washing: and country w.

| | |
|---|---|
| | BRUM 77:24 |
| taking in one another's w. | ANON 6:28 |
| w. ain't done nor sweeping | ANON 7:17 |
| w. on the Siegfried Line | KENN 193:23 |

Washington: Government at W.

| | |
|---|---|
| | GARF 148:6 |

wassails: Hock-carts, w., wakes

| | |
|---|---|
| | HERR 167:12 |

waste: art of how to w. space

| | |
|---|---|
| | JOHN 182:2 |
| Don't w. any time in mourning | HILL 168:13 |
| I love all w. and solitary places | SHEL 303:20 |
| now doth time w. me | SHAK 294:12 |
| W. of Blood, and waste | STUD 318:18 |
| w. of breath the years behind | YEATS 359:11 |
| w. of goods | VEBL 337:17 |
| w. of shame | SHAK 300:10 |
| w. remains and kills | EMPS 137:6 |
| we lay w. our powers | WORD 357:10 |
| ye w. places of Jerusalem | BIBLE 46:16 |

wasted: W. his substance

| | |
|---|---|
| | BIBLE 52:29 |

wastes: W. without springs

| | |
|---|---|
| | CLARE 101:5 |

wasting: nor wanting, nor w.

| | |
|---|---|
| | SMITH 310:15 |

watch: as a w. in the night

| | |
|---|---|
| | BOOK 67:25 |
| done much better by a w. | BELL 33:26 |
| like a fat gold w. | PLATH 249:16 |
| like little w. springs | SPEN 313:2 |
| Lord w. between me and thee | BIBLE 39:23 |
| not w. with me one hour | BIBLE 51:12 |
| or my w. has stopped | MARX 221:6 |
| too large to hang on a w.-chain | ANON 11:8 |
| W. and pray, that ye enter | BIBLE 51:13 |
| w. over their flock | BIBLE 51:32 |
| W. therefore: for ye know not | BIBLE 50:38 |
| W. the wall, my darling | KIPL 196:28 |
| w., while some must sleep | SHAK 276:12 |
| Wear your learning like your w. | CHES 97:10 |

watched: w. the ads, and not the road

| | |
|---|---|
| | NASH 237:13 |

watcher: like some w. of the skies

| | |
|---|---|
| | KEATS 192:11 |
| posted presence of the w. | JAMES 179:25 |

watches: He w. from his mountain walls

| | |
|---|---|
| | TENN 323:21 |

watchful: And w. at his gate

| | |
|---|---|
| | DODD 122:30 |
| on occasion's forelock w. wait | MILT 230:4 |

watching: BIG BROTHER IS W. YOU

| | |
|---|---|
| | ORW 242:6 |
| My tiny w. eye | DE L 116:23 |

watchmaker: it is the *blind* w.

| | |
|---|---|
| | DAWK 115:2 |

watchman: w. on the lonely tower

| | |
|---|---|
| | SCOTT 268:16 |
| w. waketh but in vain | BOOK 68:30 |
| w. watches in vain | BIBLE 58:13 |
| W., what of the night | BIBLE 45:23 |

water: affliction and with w.

| | |
|---|---|
| | BIBLE 42:6 |
| By w. and the word | STONE 317:27 |
| Christ walking on the w. | THOM 331:17 |
| conscious w. saw its God | CRAS 111:6 |
| don't care where the w. goes | CHES 98:7 |
| ever-flowing w. near the house | HOR 174:4 |
| feet are always in the w. | AMES 4:22 |
| fountain of the w. of life | BIBLE 58:6 |
| hands than w. like Pilate | GREE 158:2 |
| hart desireth the w.-brooks | BOOK 67:3 |
| hewers of wood and drawers of w. | BIBLE 40:28 |
| if I were under w. | KEATS 193:7 |
| King over the w. | ANON 8:16 |
| Let the w. and the blood | TOPL 333:14 |
| Minnehaha, Laughing W. | LONG 210:2 |
| More w. glideth by the mill | SHAK 296:26 |
| noise of the w.-pipes | BOOK 67:4 |
| No more w., the fire next time | ANON 7:12 |
| ready by w. as by land | ELST 136:7 |

water (*cont.*):

| | |
|---|---|
| safe to go back in the w. | ANON 8:15 |
| [Tar w.] is of a nature | BERK 35:16 |
| w. clears us of this deed | SHAK 286:19 |
| w. hollows out a stone | OVID 243:12 |
| w. in the rough rude sea | SHAK 293:22 |
| W. like a stone | ROSS 263:2 |
| W., water, everywhere | COL 104:7 |
| We write in w. | SHAK 280:22 |
| whose name was writ in w. | KEATS 193:15 |
| with w. and a crust | KEATS 191:11 |

watered: Apollos w.

| | |
|---|---|
| | BIBLE 55:3 |
| w. our horses in Helicon | CHAP 94:17 |
| w. our houses in Helicon | CHAP 94:17 |

water-lily: She saw the w. bloom

| | |
|---|---|
| | TENN 326:3 |

Waterloo: at Austerlitz and W.

| | |
|---|---|
| | SAND 266:14 |
| That world-earthquake, W. | TENN 327:12 |
| W. *was* won on the playing | ORW 242:4 |
| W. was won on the playing | WELL 345:10 |

waterman: w., looking one way

| | |
|---|---|
| | BUNY 79:1 |

watermen: w., that row one way

| | |
|---|---|
| | BURT 83:7 |

waters: Across the waste of w. die

| | |
|---|---|
| | BETJ 37:1 |
| all that move in the W. | BOOK 64:2 |
| And the w. as they flow | ARMS 15:24 |
| beside the w. of comfort | BOOK 66:17 |
| Cast thy bread upon the w. | BIBLE 44:24 |
| cold w. to a thirsty soul | BIBLE 43:37 |
| Many w. cannot quench love | BIBLE 45:2 |
| moving w. at their priestlike | KEATS 190:10 |
| quiet w. by | SCOT 269:8 |
| Stolen w. are sweet | BIBLE 43:15 |
| their business in great w. | BOOK 68:12 |
| w. cover the sea | AING 3:9 |
| w. cover the sea | BIBLE 45:20 |
| w. of affliction | BIBLE 46:1 |
| w. of Babylon we sat down | BOOK 69:2 |
| w. of the heart | THOM 330:12 |
| w. were his winding sheet | BARN 29:7 |
| watery: pale swan in her w. nest | SHAK 299:9 |
| shoreless w. wild | ARN 17:22 |
| warmer than after w. cloudes | LANG 201:9 |

Watson: Elementary, my dear W.

| | |
|---|---|
| | DOYLE 125:19 |

Wattle: ever hear of Captain W.

| | |
|---|---|
| | DIBD 117:17 |

wattles: of clay and w. made

| | |
|---|---|
| | YEATS 359:12 |

wave: age is rocking the w.

| | |
|---|---|
| | MAND 217:10 |
| chin upon an orient w. | MILT 227:29 |
| cool, translucent w. | MILT 226:21 |
| Oh, lift me as a w. | SHEL 304:8 |
| w. rolls nightly on deep | BYRON 85:22 |

Waverley: W. pen

| | |
|---|---|
| | ANON 11:1 |

waves: all thy w. and storms

| | |
|---|---|
| | BOOK 67:4 |
| w. make towards the pebbled | SHAK 299:21 |
| w. of thy sweet singing | SHEL 304:21 |

waving: not w. but drowning

| | |
|---|---|
| | SMITH 309:19 |

wax: *didn't* w. his moustache

| | |
|---|---|
| | KIPL 198:3 |
| moons shall w. and wane | WATTS 343:12 |
| W. to receive, and marble | BYRON 84:28 |

way: Ask that your w. be long

| | |
|---|---|
| | CAV 93:10 |
| broad is the w. | BIBLE 49:12 |
| every one to his own w. | BIBLE 46:19 |
| Every which w. but loose | KRON 199:6 |
| flowers to strew Thy w. | HERB 166:24 |
| God moves in a mysterious w. | COWP 109:25 |
| gull's w. and the whale's w. | MAS 222:2 |
| I am the w., the truth | BIBLE 53:38 |
| Is there no w. out of the mind | PLATH 249:13 |
| known and common w. | WINC 352:3 |
| meet 'em on your w. down | MIZN 232:11 |
| more a w. of life | ANON 9:19 |
| Never *in* the w., and never *out* | CHAR 95:5 |
| Prepare ye the w. of the Lord | BIBLE 46:8 |
| Prepare ye the w. of the Lord | BIBLE 48:13 |
| Rebellion lay in his w. | SHAK 278:11 |
| Their w., however straight | THOM 330:24 |
| they kill you in a new w. | ROG 262:2 |

| | |
|---|---|
| **way** (cont.): | |
| This is the w., walk ye in it | BIBLE 46:2 |
| washy w. of true tragedy | KAV 190:7 |
| W. down upon the Swanee | FOST 144:12 |
| w. is commonly the foulest | BACON 24:3 |
| w. may be known upon earth | BOOK 67:16 |
| w. of all the earth | BIBLE 40:29 |
| w. of a man with a maid | BIBLE 44:4 |
| w. of transgressors is hard | BIBLE 43:22 |
| w. to dusty death | SHAK 288:5 |
| w. to the Better there be | HARDY 162:8 |
| **ways**: at the parting of the w. | BIBLE 47:7 |
| blood is nipped and w. be foul | SHAK 284:23 |
| her w. to roam | BROO 73:10 |
| in whose heart are thy w. | BOOK 67:21 |
| justify the w. of God to men | MILT 228:9 |
| keep thee in all thy w. | BOOK 67:30 |
| Let all her w. be unconfined | PRIOR 255:9 |
| Let me count the w. | BROW 75:5 |
| more w. of being dead | DAWK 115:3 |
| neither are your w. my ways | BIBLE 46:22 |
| vindicate the w. of God to man | POPE 252:11 |
| w. are ways of pleasantness | BIBLE 43:9 |
| w. deep and the weather sharp | ELIOT 133:21 |
| w. with men I find Him not | TENN 324:16 |
| **wayside**: some seeds fell by the w. | BIBLE 50:4 |
| **wayward**: w. is this foolish love | SHAK 298:17 |
| **we**: W. are the hollow men | ELIOT 133:17 |
| W. shall not be moved | ANON 11:15 |
| W. shall overcome | ANON 11:16 |
| **weak**: concessions of the w. | BURKE 79:27 |
| found him w. in chemistry | WELLS 345:16 |
| Made w. by time and fate | TENN 328:25 |
| refuge of w. minds | CHES 97:13 |
| Repentance is the virtue of w. | DRYD 127:34 |
| Strengthen ye the w. hands | BIBLE 46:5 |
| surely the W. shall perish | SERV 270:11 |
| w. always have to decide | BONH 63:11 |
| w. alone repent | BYRON 85:16 |
| w. from your loveliness | BETJ 37:11 |
| w. have one weapon | BID 59:1 |
| W. men must fall, for heaven | SHAK 293:23 |
| w. piping time of peace | SHAK 294:14 |
| **weaken**: great life if you don't w. | BUCH 77:26 |
| **weaker**: to the w. side inclined | BUTL 84:7 |
| w. sex, to piety more prone | ALEX 4:7 |
| w. vessel | BIBLE 57:10 |
| **weakness**: oh! w. of joy | BETJ 37:11 |
| **weal**: according to the common w. | JAM 179:12 |
| **wealth**: consume w. without producing | SHAW 300:26 |
| cunning purchase of my w. | JONS 187:12 |
| get w. and place | POPE 252:25 |
| greater the w., thicker the dirt | GALB 147:15 |
| His w. a well-spent age | CAMP 89:3 |
| insolence of w. will creep out | JOHN 185:19 |
| promoting the w., the number | BURKE 80:6 |
| There is no road to w. | TROL 334:14 |
| There is no w. but life | RUSK 264:20 |
| w. is a sacred thing | FRAN 145:1 |
| W. I seek not, hope nor love | STEV 317:25 |
| w. was his peculiar art | DRYD 127:13 |
| Where w. accumulates | GOLD 154:18 |
| **wealthy**: business of the w. man | BELL 33:22 |
| **weaned**: w. child | BIBLE 45:20 |
| w. on a pickle | ANON 11:4 |
| were we not w. till then | DONNE 124:5 |
| **weapon**: and his w. wit | HOPE 171:20 |
| bayonet is a w. with a worker | ANON 6:7 |
| Loyalty is the Tory's secret w. | KILM 195:2 |
| trusty shield and w. | LUTH 212:10 |
| weak have one w. | BID 59:1 |
| **weapons**: Spare us all word of the w. | WILB 349:8 |
| w. of war perished | BIBLE 41:23 |
| **wear**: w. him in my heart's core | SHAK 276:7 |
| Should so w. out to nought | SHAK 283:24 |

| | |
|---|---|
| **wear** (cont.): | |
| such qualities as would w. | GOLD 155:11 |
| w. out than to rust out | CUMB 112:15 |
| worth the w. of winning | BELL 34:3 |
| **weariness**: Art thou pale for w. | SHEL 305:14 |
| for w. of-walked | LANG 201:6 |
| much study is a w. | BIBLE 44:27 |
| w., the fever, and the fret | KEATS 191:31 |
| w. treads on desire | PETR 248:10 |
| **wearing**: w. armchairs tight about | WOD 352:22 |
| w. o' the Green | ANON 8:9 |
| w. such a conscience-stricken | HOUS 174:6 |
| **wearisome**: and make them w. | SHAK 293:17 |
| **wears**: so w. she to him | SHAK 297:30 |
| w. man's smudge and shares | HOPK 172:4 |
| **weary**: Age shall not w. them | BINY 59:12 |
| And I sae w. fu' o' care | BURNS 81:27 |
| For I'm w. wi' hunting | BALL 27:19 |
| How w., stale, flat | SHAK 274:10 |
| shall run, and not be w. | BIBLE 46:13 |
| there the w. be at rest | BIBLE 42:27 |
| w. warl goes round | BLAM 62:8 |
| **weasel**: w. under the cocktail cabinet | PINT 248:22 |
| **weather**: but the w. turned around | THOM 330:14 |
| But winter and rough w. | SHAK 272:19 |
| first talk is of the w. | JOHN 182:11 |
| Jolly boating w. | CORY 108:11 |
| Stormy w. | KOEH 198:22 |
| 'Tis the hard grey w. | KING 195:15 |
| W. and rain have undone | KIPL 197:8 |
| w. the cuckoo likes | HARDY 162:16 |
| w.-wise, some are otherwise | FRAN 145:9 |
| you won't hold up the w. | MACN 216:3 |
| **weave**: what a tangled web we w. | SCOTT 268:21 |
| W. the warp | GRAY 157:1 |
| **weaver**: swifter than a w.'s shuttle | BIBLE 42:30 |
| **weaving**: thread of my own hand's w. | KEATS 191:3 |
| **web**: cool w. of language | GRAV 156:14 |
| Out flew the w. | TENN 326:3 |
| O what a tangled w. we weave | SCOTT 268:21 |
| She left the w. | TENN 326:3 |
| **webs**: laws are like spider's w. | ANAC 5:9 |
| **Webster**: Like W.'s Dictionary | BURKE 81:15 |
| W. was much possessed by death | ELIOT 134:32 |
| **wed**: And think to w. it | SHAK 270:23 |
| December when they w. | SHAK 273:9 |
| w. the fair Ellen | SCOTT 268:20 |
| With this Ring I thee w. | BOOK 66:2 |
| **wedded**: thou art w. to calamity | SHAK 295:15 |
| **wedding**: small circle of a w.-ring | CIBB 100:13 |
| That earliest w.-day | KEBLE 193:18 |
| **wedlock**: W., indeed, hath oft compared | DAV 114:13 |
| yet w.'s the devil | BYRON 87:12 |
| **Wednesday**: He that died o' W. | SHAK 278:12 |
| **wee**: W., sleekit, cow'rin' | BURNS 82:26 |
| W. Willie Winkie | MILL 225:9 |
| **weed**: Pernicious w. | COWP 109:21 |
| w. that grows in every soil | BURKE 80:4 |
| What is a w.? | EMER 136:29 |
| **weeded**: W. and worn the ancient thatch | TENN 326:22 |
| **weeds**: her coronet w. | SHAK 277:7 |
| smell far worse than w. | SHAK 300:2 |
| w. and the wilderness yet | HOPK 172:8 |
| **weedy**: w. trophies and herself | SHAK 277:7 |
| **week**: minute's mirth to wail a w. | SHAK 299:8 |
| No admittance till the w. after | CARR 92:5 |
| w. is a long time in politics | WILS 351:15 |
| **weep**: But milk my ewes and w. | SHAK 299:1 |
| I w. for Adonais—he is dead | SHEL 303:3 |
| She must w. or she will die | TENN 327:26 |
| That he should w. for her | SHAK 275:22 |
| time to w., and a time to laugh | BIBLE 44:12 |
| W., and you weep alone | WILC 349:14 |
| W. me not dead | DONNE 124:16 |
| women must w. | KING 195:16 |

| | |
|---|---|
| **weeping**: Rachel w. for her children | BIBLE 48:11 |
| w. and gnashing of teeth | BIBLE 49:18 |
| **weigh**: more people see than w. | CHES 97:16 |
| **weighed**: w. in the balances | BIBLE 47:12 |
| **weight**: let us lay aside every w. | BIBLE 56:27 |
| to bear the w. of Antony | SHAK 271:10 |
| w. of rages will press | SPOO 313:25 |
| **weird**: w. sisters, hand in hand | SHAK 285:5 |
| **welcome**: Advice is seldom w. | CHES 97:9 |
| Love bade me w. | HERB 167:2 |
| W., all wonders in one sight | CRAS 111:11 |
| W. the coming, speed the | POPE 252:24 |
| W. to your gory bed | BURNS 82:21 |
| **welcomest**: w. when they are gone | SHAK 280:4 |
| **welfare**: w. of this realm | CHAR 95:1 |
| **welkin**: Hark! how all the w. rings | WESL 346:7 |
| **well**: alive and w. and living in | ANON 8:13 |
| And all shall be w. | ELIOT 133:13 |
| and all shall be w. | JUL 188:21 |
| being alive, but being w. | MART 220:6 |
| danger chiefly lies in acting w. | CHUR 98:20 |
| doing w. that which should | VIDAL 338:11 |
| foolish thing w. done | JOHN 184:25 |
| He does himself extremely w. | ANON 9:14 |
| Is it w. with the child | BIBLE 42:9 |
| It is not done w. | JOHN 184:16 |
| looking w. can't move her | SUCK 318:20 |
| loved not wisely but too w. | SHAK 293:5 |
| misery use it for a w. | BOOK 67:21 |
| spent one whole day w. | THOM 330:2 |
| 'tis not so deep as a w. | SHAK 295:7 |
| W. done, thou good and | BIBLE 51:1 |
| W. of Loneliness | HALL 160:14 |
| where nobody is w. | AUDEN 21:19 |
| **well-aired**: have the morning w. | BRUM 77:23 |
| **well-beloved**: bundle of myrrh is my w. | BIBLE 44:30 |
| w. hath a vineyard | BIBLE 45:7 |
| **well-bred**: Conscience is thoroughly w. | BUTL 84:20 |
| w. as if we were not married | CONG 106:20 |
| **well-content**: Stay-at-Home, sweet W. | DAV 114:22 |
| **well-dressed**: being w. gives a feeling | FORB 143:2 |
| **well-informed**: To come with a w. mind | AUST 22:23 |
| **wells**: spring of w. | NEWM 238:15 |
| **well-spent**: almost as rare as a w. one | CARL 90:7 |
| **well-written**: w. Life is almost as rare | CARL 90:7 |
| **Welsh**: devil understands W. | SHAK 278:5 |
| **Welshman**: care and valour in this W. | SHAK 279:11 |
| **welter**: w. to the parching wind | MILT 227:11 |
| **Weltgeschichte**: *Die W. ist das Weltgericht* | SCH 267:21 |
| **wen**: great w. of all | COBB 102:26 |
| **wench**: besides, the w. is dead | MARL 219:2 |
| **Wenlock**: On W. Edge the wood | HOUS 174:22 |
| **weoman**: oblidged to call it w. | FLEM 142:1 |
| **wept**: Babylon we sat down and w. | BOOK 69:2 |
| His big tears, for he w. well | SHEL 304:5 |
| Station I sat down and w. | SMART 308:15 |
| that I have sometimes w. | MUSS 236:16 |
| W. over her, carved in stone | TENN 324:6 |
| **wert**: Which w., and art, and evermore | HEBER 164:17 |
| **Werther**: W. had a love for Charlotte | THAC 329:23 |
| **Wesley**: W.'s conversation | JOHN 185:16 |
| **west**: Cincinnatus of the W. | BYRON 87:4 |
| closing time in the gardens of the W. | CONN 106:27 |
| East is East, and W. is West | KIPL 196:4 |
| from the east, nor from the w. | BOOK 67:18 |
| Go W., young man | GREE 157:20 |
| Go W., young man | SOULE 311:17 |
| Lochinvar is come out of the w. | SCOTT 268:18 |
| safeguard of the W. | WORD 356:2 |
| That's where the W. begins | CHAP 94:13 |
| W. of these out to seas | FLEC 141:14 |
| **wester**: rainy Pleiads w. | HOUS 174:15 |
| **western**: All quiet on the w. front | REM 259:4 |
| delivered by W. Union | GOLD 155:18 |
| **western** (cont.): | |
| Playboy of the W. world | SYNGE 321:22 |
| Swiftly walk o'er the w. wave | SHEL 305:12 |
| when you've seen one W. | WHIT 348:7 |
| **Westminster Abbey**: peerage, or W. | NELS 237:23 |
| **westward**: But w., look, the land | CLOU 102:24 |
| W. the course of empire | BERK 35:19 |
| What, you are stepping w.? | WORD 357:3 |
| **wet**: so w. you could shoot snipe | POW 254:26 |
| w. clothes and into a dry Martini | ANON 8:18 |
| w. sheet and a flowing sea | CUNN 113:7 |
| wildness and w. | HOPK 172:8 |
| **wether**: tainted w. of the flock | SHAK 289:24 |
| **whacks**: gave her mother forty w. | ANON 8:22 |
| **whales**: O ye W. | BOOK 64:2 |
| Where great w. come sailing by | ARN 16:17 |
| **whaleship**: w. was my Yale | MELV 223:3 |
| **what**: from the great united w. | ROCH 261:10 |
| He knew what's w. | BUTL 83:23 |
| W. is the matter with Mary Jane | MILNE 225:23 |
| W. is to be done | LENIN 205:3 |
| W. was he doing, the great | BROW 75:4 |
| **whatsoever**: W. things are true | BIBLE 56:9 |
| **wheat**: orient and immortal w. | TRAH 333:18 |
| separate the w. from the chaff | HUBB 175:15 |
| **wheel**: beneath thy Chariot w. | HOPE 171:23 |
| breaks a butterfly upon a w. | POPE 251:7 |
| depends upon a red w. barrow | WILL 351:8 |
| in thy w. there is a point | MARL 218:16 |
| w. broken at the cistern | BIBLE 44:26 |
| w. is come full circle | SHAK 284:3 |
| w. the sofa round | COWP 110:11 |
| **wheels**: all the w. of Being slow | TENN 325:7 |
| apparently rolled along on w. | HUXL 177:10 |
| none of the w. of trade | HUME 176:6 |
| tarry the w. of his chariots | BIBLE 40:34 |
| w. within w. | DICK 120:2 |
| **when**: had forgotten to say 'W.' | WOD 352:24 |
| w. a man should marry | BACON 25:3 |
| w. did you last see your father | YEAM 358:12 |
| W. I am dead, I hope it may be | BELL 33:27 |
| W. shall we three meet again | SHAK 284:25 |
| W. you go home, tell them | EDM 130:20 |
| **whence**: from w. cometh my help | BOOK 68:25 |
| W. did he whence | LENO 205:19 |
| **where**: But w.'s the bloody horse | CAMP 88:16 |
| fell earth, I knew not w. | LONG 209:10 |
| they fixed the w. and when | HAWK 163:17 |
| W. did you come from | MACD 214:18 |
| w. do they all come from | MCC 205:12 |
| **wherefore**: every why he had a w. | BUTL 83:22 |
| w. art thou Romeo | SHAK 294:30 |
| W. does he why | LENO 205:19 |
| **whereof**: w. one cannot speak | WITT 352:8 |
| **whetstone**: no such w. to sharpen | ASCH 18:19 |
| **whiff**: w. of grapeshot | CARL 90:11 |
| **Whig**: Tory men and W. measures | DISR 121:25 |
| **Whigs**: caught the W. bathing | DISR 121:9 |
| W. admit no force but argument | BROW 74:25 |
| **while**: But it's a long, long w. | AND 5:12 |
| **whimper**: Not with a bang but a w. | ELIOT 133:20 |
| **whine**: They do not sweat and w. | WHIT 348:19 |
| **whining**: w. of a door | DONNE 124:21 |
| **whip**: Do not forget the w. | NIET 239:17 |
| **whipped**: w. the offending Adam | SHAK 289:18 |
| **whipping**: top which w. Sorrow | GREV 158:18 |
| who should 'scape w. | SHAK 275:20 |
| **whips**: hath chastised you with w. | BIBLE 41:34 |
| **whirligig**: w. of time brings | SHAK 298:14 |
| **whirling**: by the w. rim I've found | BLAM 62:8 |
| **whirls**: expectation w. me round | SHAK 297:1 |
| **whirlwind**: Rides in the w. | ADD 2:11 |
| they shall reap the w. | BIBLE 47:17 |
| **whiskers**: Runcible Cat with crimson w. | LEAR 203:15 |
| **whisky**: drinkin' w. and rye | MCL 215:8 |

**whisky** (cont.):
Freedom and W. | BURNS 81:26
**whisper:** Hush! W. who dares | MILNE 226:1
w. of a faction | RUSS 265:5
w. softness in chambers | MILT 231:1
w. was already born | MAND 217:11
**whispered:** it's w. every where | CONG 106:9
**whispering:** W. sound of the cool colonnade | |
| COWP 109:30
**whispers:** W. the o'er-fraught heart | SHAK 287:25
**whist:** W. upon whist upon whist | BETJ 36:22
**whistle:** hir joly w. wel ywet | CHAU 96:3
until a shrimp learns to w. | KHR 194:18
W. and she'll come to you | FLET 142:6
w., an' I'll come to you | BURNS 82:19
w. her off and let her down | SHAK 292:14
**white:** always goes into w. satin | SHER 305:24
be the w. man's brother | KING 195:7
But a w., celestial thought | VAUG 337:7
Clothed in w. samite | TENN 324:3
Nor grew it w. in a single night | BYRON 87:5
no 'w.' or 'coloured' signs | KENN 194:7
see the w. of their eyes | PUTN 256:24
Take up the W. Man's burden | KIPL 197:15
Their w. it stays for ever | DOBS 122:27
Wearing w. for Eastertide | HOUS 174:16
w. and hairless as an egg | HERR 167:20
W. as an angel is the English | BLAKE 61:24
w. hairs become a fool | SHAK 278:32
w. in the blood | BIBLE 57:26
w. races are really pinko-grey | FORS 143:24
W. shall not neutralize | BROW 77:10
whose garment was w. | BIBLE 47:14
**whited:** like unto w. sepulchres | BIBLE 50:32
**Whitehall:** gentleman in W. | JAY 180:15
**White House:** Log-cabin to W. | THAY 329:27
no whitewash at the W. | NIXON 240:2
**whiter:** I shall be w. than snow | BOOK 67:9
Turned a w. shade of pale | REID 259:3
**whitewash:** no w. at the White House | NIXON 240:2
**whither:** W. is he withering | LENO 205:19
w. thou goest | BIBLE 41:8
**whiting:** said a w. to a snail | CARR 91:11
**whizzing:** W. them over the net | BETJ 37:8
**who:** that can tell me w. I am | SHAK 282:23
w. am I, that for my sake | CROS 112:13
W. is on my side? who? | BIBLE 42:15
W. is Silvia? what is she? | SHAK 298:19
W.? Whom? | LENIN 205:4
**whole:** nothing can be sole or w. | YEATS 358:20
Thy faith hath made thee w. | BIBLE 49:25
**wholly:** w. slaves or wholly free | DRYD 127:30
**whom:** Who? W.? | LENIN 205:4
**whooping:** out of all w. | SHAK 273:4
**whopping:** Latin for a w. | ANST 14:10
**whore:** Fortune's a right w. | WEBS 344:22
I am the Protestant w. | GWYN 159:13
I' the posture of a w. | SHAK 272:5
lash that w. | SHAK 283:25
Madhouses, prisons, w.-shops | CLARE 101:4
teach the morals of a w. | JOHN 184:1
'Tis Pity She's a W. | FORD 143:11
w. and gambler by the State | BLAKE 60:9
**whores:** flowing into second-rate w. | PLOM 250:1
no more w. to Paris | GEOR 149:26
to work, ye w., go spin | PEMB 247:5
**whoring:** w. with their own inventions | BOOK 68:11
**why:** and I can't tell you w. | MART 220:4
could he see you now, ask w. | AUDEN 20:17
for every w. he had a wherefore | BUTL 83:22
shall and finding only w. | CUMM 113:2
Their's not to reason w. | TENN 323:15
W., Edward, tell me why | WORD 354:12
**wibrated:** had better not be w. | DICK 117:21
**wicked:** and desperately w. | BIBLE 46:31

**wicked** (cont.):
August is a w. month | O'BR 240:18
make me sick and w. | AUST 23:12
no peace unto the w. | BIBLE 46:14
pomps and vanity of this w. | BOOK 65:21
Something w. this way comes | SHAK 287:18
tender mercies of the w. | BIBLE 43:20
Tories born w., and grow worse | ANON 9:6
w. cease from troubling | BIBLE 42:27
worse than w., it's vulgar | PUNCH 256:15
**wickedness:** manifold sins and w. | BOOK 63:12
spiritual w. in high places | BIBLE 56:4
That is the Path of W. | BALL 28:7
w. that he hath committed | BIBLE 47:6
**wicket:** flannelled fools at the w. | KIPL 196:18
**Widdicombe Fair:** for to go to W. | BALL 28:11
**wide:** nor so w. as a church | SHAK 295:7
Not deep the Poet sees, but w. | ARN 17:2
w. enough to wrap a fairy in | SHAK 290:27
W. is the gate, and broad | BIBLE 49:12
**wideness:** w. in God's mercy | FABER 138:5
**wider:** W. still and wider | BENS 34:20
**widow:** French w. in every bedroom | HOFF 170:5
Here's to the w. of fifty | SHER 306:6
or Molly Stark's a w. | STARK 314:12
virgin-w., and a *mourning bride* | DRYD 128:13
w. bird sat mourning | SHEL 303:14
W. The word consumes itself | PLATH 249:17
**widowhood:** comfortable estate of w. | GAY 149:4
**widows:** fatherless children, and w. | BOOK 64:17
**wife:** man who's untrue to his w. | AUDEN 21:3
And nobody's w. | HERB 166:13
Brutus' harlot, not his w. | SHAK 281:7
by degrees dwindle into a w. | CONG 106:21
chose my w., as she did her | GOLD 155:11
covet thy neighbour's w. | BIBLE 40:9
debauch his friend's w. | BOSW 70:5
either to look out for a w. | SURT 319:14
Giant Despair had a w. | BUNY 79:3
Giving honour unto the w. | BIBLE 57:10
health of his w. | CONN 106:29
hope that keeps up a w.'s | GAY 149:4
husband of one w. | BIBLE 56:16
isn't a moron; she is your w. | OGIL 241:2
I have a w., I have sons | LUCAN 211:26
I have married a w. | BIBLE 52:23
In every port a w. | DIBD 117:18
In riding to and from his w. | WHITE 347:14
kill a w. with kindness | SHAK 295:28
lay down his w. for his friend | JOYCE 188:18
married, but I'd have no w. | CRAS 111:13
Medicine is my lawful w. | CHEK 96:30
Matched with an agèd w. | TENN 328:19
monstrous animal, husband and w. | FIEL 139:12
must be in want of a w. | AUST 23:2
my w., and my name | SURT 319:11
My w., who, poor wretch | PEPYS 247:16
My w. won't let me | LEIGH 204:17
No casual mistress, but a w. | TENN 325:13
roaring of the wind is my w. | KEATS 193:9
shall cleave unto his w. | BIBLE 38:23
Thane of Fife had a w. | SHAK 287:29
There's my w.; look well on her | SPR 314:1
w. and children hostages to | BACON 25:1
w. must be above suspicion | CAES 87:25
w. or your servants to read | GRIF 159:2
w. shall be as the fruitful | BOOK 68:32
young w. and a good brain | JONS 186:23
**wigwam:** w. of Nokomis | LONG 210:1
**wild:** call of the w. | LOND 209:7
gone w. into his grave | SHAK 278:30
I never saw a w. thing | LAWR 202:21
Made us nobly w., not mad | HERR 167:19
O Caledonia! stern and w. | SCOTT 268:14
old, w., and incomprehensible | VICT 338:5

**wine** (*cont.*):

| | |
|---|---|
| not to be rinsed with w. | HOPK 172:6 |
| not woman, w., and song | LUTH 212:11 |
| Sans w., sans song | FITZ 140:9 |
| sweet white w. | MAS 221:18 |
| Sweet w. of youth | BROO 72:20 |
| upon the w. when it is red | BIBLE 43:33 |
| w. is in, the wit is out | BECON 31:18 |
| W. is a mocker | BIBLE 43:31 |
| W. maketh merry | BIBLE 44:23 |
| W., not water, binds the lover | SANS 266:20 |
| w. of life is drawn | SHAK 286:26 |
| w. of Shiraz into urine | DIN 121:2 |
| w. that tasted of the tar | BELL 34:1 |
| w. unto those that be of | BIBLE 44:5 |
| With seas of life, like w. | TRAH 334:1 |

**wing**: by Conquest's crimson w.

| | |
|---|---|
| by Conquest's crimson w. | GRAY 157:1 |
| Comin' in on a w. and a pray'r | ADAM 2:9 |
| flits by on leathern w. | COLL 105:10 |
| headlong joy is ever on the w. | MILT 230:9 |
| Nor knowst'ou w. from tail | POUND 254:21 |
| vainly flapped its tinsel w. | MARV 220:12 |

**winged**: Doth the w. life destroy

| | |
|---|---|
| Doth the w. life destroy | BLAKE 61:16 |
| W. words | HOMER 170:20 |

**wingèd**: w. squadrons of the sky  MILM 225:13

**wings**: Ill news hath w.

| | |
|---|---|
| Ill news hath w. | DRAY 126:15 |
| Love without his w. | BYRON 87:1 |
| mount up with w. as eagles | BIBLE 46:13 |
| On w. of song | HEINE 165:1 |
| take the w. of the morning | BOOK 69:6 |
| viewless w. of Poesy | KEATS 192:1 |
| void his luminous w. in vain | ARN 18:4 |
| w. like a dove | BOOK 67:11 |
| with healing in his w. | BIBLE 47:26 |

**wink**: And w. a reputation down  SWIFT 320:16

**winners**: no w., but all are losers  CHAM 93:25

**winning**: If the world be worth thy w.

| | |
|---|---|
| If the world be worth thy w. | DRYD 127:21 |
| lips ne'er act the w. part | HERR 167:17 |
| nothing worth the wear of w. | BELL 34:3 |
| O the glory of the w. | MER 223:20 |
| w. cause pleased the gods | LUCAN 211:23 |
| w. isn't everything | SAND 266:19 |

**wins**: Who dares w.  ANON 11:20

**winter**: blood reigns in the w.'s pale

| | |
|---|---|
| blood reigns in the w.'s pale | SHAK 298:26 |
| English w.—ending in July | BYRON 86:26 |
| go south in the w. | ELIOT 134:19 |
| hounds of spring are on w.'s | SWIN 321:1 |
| If W. comes, can Spring be | SHEL 304:10 |
| In w. I get up at night | STEV 317:12 |
| It was the w. wild | MILT 227:25 |
| Middle of W. | ADD 2:23 |
| mountains by the w. sea | TENN 324:17 |
| my age is as a lusty w. | SHAK 272:16 |
| Nor the furious w.'s rages | SHAK 273:27 |
| Now is the w. of our discontent | SHAK 294:13 |
| sad tale's best for w. | SHAK 298:22 |
| See, amid the w.'s snow | CASW 92:18 |
| Seeming and savour all the w. | SHAK 298:29 |
| very dead of W. | ANDR 5:15 |
| very dead of w. | ELIOT 133:21 |
| W. Afternoons | DICK 120:14 |
| w. and rough weather | SHAK 272:19 |
| W. is come and gone | SHEL 303:7 |
| W. is scummen in | POUND 254:8 |
| w.'s rains and ruins | SWIN 321:2 |
| W. suddenly was changed | SHEL 304:28 |

**wipe**: shall w. away all tears

| | |
|---|---|
| shall w. away all tears | BIBLE 57:28 |
| shall w. away all tears | BIBLE 58:5 |

**wire**: electric w. the message came  ANON 6:1

**wires**: If hairs be w., black wires  SHAK 300:11

**wisdom**: apply our hearts unto w.

| | |
|---|---|
| apply our hearts unto w. | BOOK 67:27 |
| beginning of w. | BOOK 68:15 |
| Can w. be put in a silver rod | BLAKE 60:10 |
| delight and ends in w. | FROST 146:24 |
| Here is w.; this is the royal Law | COR 108:10 |

**wisdom** (*cont.*):

| | |
|---|---|
| How can he get w. | BIBLE 48:6 |
| infallible criterion of w. | BURKE 79:18 |
| Knowledge comes, but w. lingers | TENN 326:14 |
| leads to the palace of w. | BLAKE 61:1 |
| Love is the w. of the fool | JOHN 186:9 |
| price of w. is above rubies | BIBLE 43:2 |
| privilege of w. to listen | HOLM 170:15 |
| spirit of w. and understanding | BIBLE 45:18 |
| teach his senators w. | BOOK 68:10 |
| those who love want w. | SHEL 304:17 |
| what is bettre than w.? | CHAU 95:28 |
| where shall w. be found | BIBLE 43:1 |
| W. and Wit are little seen | BRER 71:22 |
| W. denotes the pursuing | HUTC 177:1 |
| W. hath builded her house | BIBLE 43:14 |
| W. is the principal thing | BIBLE 43:10 |
| w. we have lost in knowledge | ELIOT 134:12 |
| with how little w. the world | OXEN 244:5 |

**wise**: All things w. and wonderful

| | |
|---|---|
| All things w. and wonderful | ALEX 4:2 |
| art of being w. | JAMES 180:9 |
| beacons of w. men | HUXL 177:20 |
| Be not w. in your own conceits | BIBLE 54:44 |
| be w. in his own conceit | BIBLE 43:38 |
| Be w. with speed | YOUNG 360:14 |
| consider her ways, and be w. | BIBLE 43:11 |
| deemed him wondrous w. | BEAT 30:13 |
| he is a w. man or a fool | BLAKE 60:22 |
| Nor ever did a w. one | ROCH 261:4 |
| So w. so young, they say | SHAK 294:17 |
| 'Tis folly to be w. | GRAY 157:14 |
| To be w., and love | SHAK 297:3 |
| tree that a w. man sees | BLAKE 61:4 |
| valorous than manly w. | MARL 219:13 |
| w. as serpents | BIBLE 49:29 |
| w. forgive but do not forget | SZASZ 321:24 |
| w. men from the east | BIBLE 48:9 |
| w. son maketh a glad father | BIBLE 43:16 |
| w. want love | SHEL 304:17 |
| word is enough for the w. | PLAU 249:22 |

**wisely**: Be w. worldly

| | |
|---|---|
| Be w. worldly | QUAR 257:3 |
| loved not w. but too well | SHAK 293:5 |

**wiser**: French w. than they seem

| | |
|---|---|
| French w. than they seem | BACON 25:12 |
| sadder and a w. man | COL 104:19 |
| w. than the children of light | BIBLE 52:33 |
| w. to-day than he was yesterday | POPE 253:13 |

**wisest**: gretteste clerkes been noght w.

| | |
|---|---|
| gretteste clerkes been noght w. | CHAU 96:2 |
| than the w. man can answer | COLT 105:17 |
| w. and justest and best | PLATO 249:20 |
| w. fool in Christendom | HENR 165:22 |
| w., virtuousest, discreetest | MILT 229:20 |

**wish**: If otherwise w. I

| | |
|---|---|
| If otherwise w. I | SHAW 303:1 |
| I w. I loved the Human Race | RAL 258:6 |
| Thy w. was father, Harry | SHAK 278:27 |
| Whoever hath her w. | SHAK 300:12 |
| w. for prayer is a prayer | BERN 36:7 |

**wishes**: exact to my w.  ANON 7:17

**wistful**: With such a w. eye  WILDE 350:15

**wit**: and fancy w. will come

| | |
|---|---|
| and fancy w. will come | POPE 250:27 |
| and his weapon w. | HOPE 171:20 |
| at their w.'s end | BOOK 68:13 |
| baiting place of w. | SIDN 306:20 |
| bin of wine, a spice of w. | STEV 317:17 |
| brevity, and w. its soul | COL 103:17 |
| Brevity is the soul of w. | SHAK 275:8 |
| deemed there but want of w. | SIDN 306:19 |
| grave or tomb of w. | CAV 93:13 |
| he shoots his w. | SHAK 273:14 |
| How the w. brightens | POPE 252:5 |
| Impropriety is the soul of w. | MAUG 222:9 |
| Little subject, little w. | CAREY 90:1 |
| mingled with a little w. | DRYD 127:31 |
| o'erflowing of unbounded w. | WINC 352:1 |
| only a w. among Lords | JOHN 183:28 |
| pick-purse of another's w. | SIDN 306:23 |

wit (cont.):

| | |
|---|---|
| pleasant smooth w. | AUBR 20:2 |
| sharpen a good w. | ASCH 18:19 |
| Staircase w. | DID 120:20 |
| too proud for a w. | GOLD 155:2 |
| universal monarchy of w. | CAREW 89:19 |
| use my w. as a pitchfork | LARK 201:19 |
| wine is in, the w. is out | BECON 31:18 |
| Wisdom and W. are little seen | BRER 71:22 |
| w. and humour are conveyed | AUST 22:22 |
| w. be like the coruscations | GOUL 155:26 |
| w. in all languages | DRYD 128:27 |
| w. invites you by his looks | COWP 109:22 |
| w. is Nature to advantage | POPE 252:1 |
| W. is the epitaph of an emotion | NIET 239:23 |
| w. on other souls may fall | DRYD 128:5 |
| w.'s the noblest frailty | SHAD 270:18 |
| W. will shine | DRYD 128:21 |
| w. with dunces, and a dunce | POPE 250:17 |
| witch: Aroint thee, w.! | SHAK 285:3 |
| witchcraft: Nor no w. charm thee | SHAK 273:28 |
| witching: w. time of night | SHAK 276:15 |
| with: I am w. you alway | BIBLE 51:17 |
| not w. me is against me | BIBLE 50:1 |
| wither: Age cannot w. her | SHAK 271:17 |
| w. slowly in thine arms | TENN 328:17 |
| withered: flowers of the forest are w. | COCK 102:27 |
| w. is the garland | SHAK 271:25 |
| withereth: Fast w. too | KEATS 191:8 |
| withers: it w. away | ENG 137:8 |
| our w. are unwrung | SHAK 276:10 |
| within: are w. would fain go out | DAV 114:13 |
| But, oh, he never went w. | COWL 109:14 |
| that w. which passeth show | SHAK 274:8 |
| without: are w. would fain go in | DAV 114:13 |
| forasmuch as w. thee | BOOK 64:26 |
| How many things I can do w. | SOCR 310:20 |
| live with you—or w. you | MART 220:7 |
| withstand: w. in the evil day | BIBLE 56:4 |
| witness: bear w. of that Light | BIBLE 53:9 |
| shalt not bear false w. | BIBLE 40:9 |
| witnesses: so great a cloud of w. | BIBLE 56:27 |
| wits: composed in their w. | ARN 18:5 |
| Great w. are sure to madness | DRYD 127:7 |
| in days when w. were fresh | ARN 17:11 |
| Some have at first for w. | POPE 251:27 |
| They have stolen his w. away | DE L 116:13 |
| warming his five w. | TENN 328:16 |
| youth have ever homely w. | SHAK 298:16 |
| wittles: I live on broken w. | DICK 118:10 |
| witty: am not only in myself | SHAK 278:16 |
| Thou swell! Thou w. | HART 163:11 |
| w. and it sha'n't be long | CHES 97:2 |
| w. beauty is a power | MER 223:12 |
| wives: And many, many w. | NAYL 237:20 |
| changes when they are w. | SHAK 273:9 |
| divides the w. of aldermen | SMITH 308:20 |
| Husbands, love your w. | BIBLE 56:11 |
| profane and old w.' fables | BIBLE 56:17 |
| Who married three w. at a time | MONK 232:26 |
| W. are young men's mistresses | BACON 25:2 |
| wizards: w. haste with odours sweet | MILT 227:24 |
| wobbles: good spelling but it W. | MILNE 225:17 |
| woe: and all our w. | MILT 228:7 |
| deep, unutterable w. | AYT 23:17 |
| discover sights of w. | MILT 228:10 |
| hideous notes of w. | BYRON 86:28 |
| life protracted is protracted w. | JOHN 183:15 |
| Oft in danger, oft in w. | WHITE 347:16 |
| rearward of a conquered w. | SHAK 300:1 |
| signs of w. that all was lost | MILT 229:26 |
| trappings and the suits of w. | SHAK 274:8 |
| wit, the balm of w. | SIDN 306:20 |
| W. is me | BIBLE 45:11 |
| w. that is in mariage | CHAU 96:5 |

woe (cont.):

| | |
|---|---|
| W. to her that is filthy | BIBLE 47:25 |
| W. to the bloody city | BIBLE 47:24 |
| W. to thee, O land | BIBLE 44:22 |
| W. to the land that's governed | SHAK 294:16 |
| W. unto them that join | BIBLE 45:8 |
| woes: th'exordium of our w. | DRAY 126:18 |
| wantons with our w. | SHAK 294:3 |
| Woking: playing for W. | BETJ 37:8 |
| wold: clothe the w. and meet the sky | TENN 325:34 |
| wolf: have the w. by the ears | JEFF 180:25 |
| like the w. on the fold | BYRON 85:22 |
| w. also shall dwell | BIBLE 45:19 |
| w. far thence that's foe | WEBS 344:26 |
| W. that shall keep it may | KIPL 198:1 |
| wolf's-bane: W., tight-rooted | KEATS 191:25 |
| Wolsey: Reno'd in W.'s Home Town | ANON 8:17 |
| wolves: lion to frighten the w. | MACH 215:3 |
| woman: artist man and the mother w. | SHAW 301:18 |
| As you are w., so be lovely | GRAV 156:16 |
| bloom on a w. | BARR 29:16 |
| body of a weak and feeble w. | ELIZ 135:6 |
| brawling w. in a wide house | BIBLE 43:32 |
| broken-hearted w. tends | HAYES 163:21 |
| called a w. in my own house | WAUGH 343:27 |
| changeable always is w. | VIRG 339:9 |
| clever w. to manage a fool | KIPL 197:28 |
| contentious w. are alike | BIBLE 44:1 |
| dead w. bites not | GRAY 156:19 |
| end to a w.'s liberty | BURN 81:19 |
| Eternal W. draws us upward | GOET 154:8 |
| Every w. adores a Fascist | PLATH 249:14 |
| excellent thing in w. | SHAK 284:5 |
| Fareweel dear, deluding w. | BURNS 82:28 |
| fat white w. whom nobody | CORN 108:6 |
| Frailty, thy name is w. | SHAK 274:12 |
| from man, made he a w. | BIBLE 38:21 |
| glory of a w. to be least talked | PER 248:3 |
| good w. if I had five thousand | THAC 329:21 |
| heart wrapped in a w.'s hide | SHAK 280:13 |
| help and support of the w. I love | EDW 131:2 |
| if a w. have long hair | BIBLE 55:10 |
| in a word, she's a w. | RAC 257:15 |
| inconstant w. | GAY 149:16 |
| large-brained w. | BROW 75:6 |
| Let us look for the w. | DUMAS 129:3 |
| like a w. scorned | CONG 106:12 |
| love a w. that she woot it not | CHAU 96:14 |
| lovely w. in a rural spot | HUNT 176:17 |
| make a man a w. | PEMB 247:6 |
| man that is born of a w. | BIBLE 42:33 |
| Man that is born of a w. | BOOK 66:6 |
| nor w. neither | SHAK 275:16 |
| One hair of a w. can draw | HOW 175:9 |
| One is not born a w. | DE B 115:8 |
| one w. differs from another | MENC 223:6 |
| O W.! in our hours of ease | SCOTT 268:22 |
| post-chaise with a pretty w. | JOHN 185:13 |
| scandal by a w. of easy virtue | HAIL 160:1 |
| She is a w., therefore may be | SHAK 296:25 |
| She is a w., therefore to be | SHAK 280:6 |
| speaks small like a w. | SHAK 290:8 |
| still able to have a w. | SOPH 311:14 |
| There shone one w. | SWIN 321:19 |
| this w. was full of good works | BIBLE 54:14 |
| 'Tis w.'s whole existence | BYRON 86:4 |
| unemancipated w. still had | LOW 211:11 |
| virtuous w. | BIBLE 43:19 |
| virtuous w. | BIBLE 44:6 |
| Vitality in a w. | SHAW 301:17 |
| way for a w. to hold a man | SPARK 312:10 |
| What does a w. want | FREUD 146:3 |
| What Every W. Knows | BARR 29:16 |
| what is bettre than a good w. | CHAU 95:28 |
| what's a play without a w. | KYD 199:11 |

**woman** (cont.):

| | |
|---|---|
| When lovely w. stoops to folly | GOLD 155:13 |
| while w. wakes to love | TENN 324:15 |
| Who loves not w., wine | LUTH 212:11 |
| will take some savage w. | TENN 326:15 |
| witty w. is a treasure | MER 223:12 |
| W., behold thy son | BIBLE 54:4 |
| w. be more like a man | LERN 205:26 |
| w. but she made mouths | SHAK 283:8 |
| w. can be a beauty without | FARQ 138:16 |
| w. can become a man's friend | CHEK 96:28 |
| w. can be proud and stiff | YEATS 358:20 |
| w. can forgive a man | MAUG 222:10 |
| w. can hardly ever choose | ELIOT 132:5 |
| w. clothed with the sun | BIBLE 57:30 |
| w. dictates before marriage | ELIOT 132:8 |
| w. has given you her heart | VANB 336:24 |
| w. in this humour wooed | SHAK 294:15 |
| w. is a sometime thing | GERS 168:7 |
| w. is his game | TENN 327:25 |
| w. is so hard upon the woman | TENN 328:1 |
| W. is the nigger of the world | ONO 241:13 |
| w. loves her lover | BYRON 86:9 |
| w. moved is like a fountain | SHAK 295:30 |
| W. much missed | HARDY 162:15 |
| w. must have money | WOOLF 354:1 |
| w. must submit to it | STAËL 314:6 |
| w. never smiled or wept | CLARE 101:7 |
| w. of so shining loveliness | YEATS 359:27 |
| W.'s at best a contradiction | POPE 251:12 |
| w.'s desire is rarely other | COL 104:27 |
| w. seldom writes her mind | STEE 314:15 |
| w.'s eye the unanswerable | BYRON 85:17 |
| w. should conceal it | AUST 22:23 |
| w.'s preaching is like | JOHN 184:16 |
| w.'s workhouse | SHAW 302:4 |
| w. take an elder than herself | SHAK 297:30 |
| w. taken in adultery | BIBLE 53:25 |
| w. that deliberates is lost | ADD 2:15 |
| w. to provide for herself | SHAW 302:11 |
| W. was God's second blunder | NIET 239:18 |
| W., what have I to do | BIBLE 53:16 |
| w. who always was tired | ANON 7:17 |
| w. who did not care | KIPL 197:12 |
| w. who lives for others | LEWIS 206:12 |
| w. who tells her real age | WILDE 350:10 |
| w. who wrote the book | LINC 207:13 |
| W. will be the last thing | MER 223:16 |
| w. with a slop-pail | HOPK 172:22 |
| w. with fair opportunities | THAC 329:14 |
| w. without a man is like | STEI 315:2 |
| w. yet think him an angel | THAC 329:11 |
| worser spirit a w. | SHAK 300:13 |
| **woman-head:** graves have learnt that w. | DONNE 124:9 |
| **womanhood:** Heroic w. | LONG 209:25 |
| **womankind:** packs off its w. | SHAW 301:23 |
| **womanly:** So w., her demeaning | SKEL 308:2 |
| **womb:** cloistered in thy dear w. | DONNE 123:18 |
| drew from the w. of time | HEINE 165:2 |
| from his mother's w. untimely | SHAK 288:7 |
| O w.! O bely! | CHAU 95:30 |
| teeming w. of royal kings | SHAK 293:16 |
| very w. and bed of enormity | JONS 186:24 |
| wide w. of uncreated night | MILT 228:24 |
| **women:** after the manner of w. | BIBLE 39:14 |
| Alexander w. | LEE 204:10 |
| all w. are born slaves | AST 19:7 |
| American w. shoot | FORS 143:14 |
| are not w. truly then | JONS 187:22 |
| apples, cherries, hops, and w. | DICK 119:26 |
| blessed art thou among w. | BIBLE 51:27 |
| Dream of Fair W. | TENN 323:20 |
| England is the paradise of w. | FLOR 142:13 |
| far from me, you grim w. | OVID 243:9 |
| girls turn into American w. | HAMP 161:5 |

**women** (cont.):

| | |
|---|---|
| Good w. always think | BROO 73:11 |
| Half the sorrows of w. | ELIOT 132:3 |
| happiest w. have no history | ELIOT 132:14 |
| hell for w., as the diverb | BURT 83:13 |
| In the room the w. come and go | ELIOT 133:25 |
| kill more w. and children | BALD 27:5 |
| Let us have wine and w. | BYRON 86:6 |
| married beneath me, all w. do | ASTOR 19:9 |
| men, w., and clergymen | SMITH 310:4 |
| Monstrous Regiment of W. | KNOX 198:16 |
| Music and w. I cannot but | PEPYS 247:19 |
| other w. cloy the appetites | SHAK 271:17 |
| our chilly w. | BYRON 84:29 |
| passing the love of w. | BIBLE 41:23 |
| revenge—especially to w. | BYRON 86:2 |
| Single w. have a dreadful | AUST 23:11 |
| Solomon loved many strange w. | BIBLE 41:32 |
| Some w.'ll stay in a man's | KIPL 198:4 |
| sung w. in three cities | POUND 254:11 |
| Though w. are angels | BYRON 87:12 |
| to w. Italian, to men French | CHAR 95:7 |
| 'Twixt w.'s love, and men's | DONNE 123:21 |
| war between men and w. | THUR 332:16 |
| Whatever w. do | WHIT 349:3 |
| with w. nor with priests | SOUT 311:24 |
| W., and Champagne | BELL 33:9 |
| W. and Horses and Power | KIPL 196:5 |
| w. are in furious secret | SHAW 301:4 |
| W. are really much nicer | AMIS 5:6 |
| w. become like their mothers | WILDE 349:19 |
| w. born slaves | WOLL 353:14 |
| W. can't forgive failure | CHEK 96:26 |
| W. desiren to have sovereynetee | CHAU 96:8 |
| w. do in men require | BLAKE 61:17 |
| w. from behind the vacuum | GREER 158:11 |
| W. have no wilderness | BOGAN 62:18 |
| W. have served all these | WOOLF 354:2 |
| w. in a drawing-room | WOOLF 354:3 |
| w. in a state of ignorance | KNOX 198:21 |
| w. must be half-workers | SHAK 273:26 |
| w. must weep | KING 196:16 |
| w. of that ever-fresh terrain | AMIS 5:8 |
| W.—one half the human race | BAG 26:11 |
| w. should be struck regularly | COW 109:11 |
| w.'s rights | FOUR 144:14 |
| W., then, are only children | CHES 97:11 |
| W. who love the same man | BEER 32:11 |
| work its way with the w. | DICK 120:1 |
| You are going to w. | NIET 239:17 |
| **won:** ground w. today | ARN 17:10 |
| I w. the count | SOM 311:4 |
| never lost till w. | CRAB 110:28 |
| not that you w. or lost | RICE 259:17 |
| prize we sought is w. | WHIT 349:8 |
| Things w. are done | SHAK 296:29 |
| who has w. it bear the palm | JORT 188:1 |
| woman in this humour w. | SHAK 294:15 |
| woman, therefore may be w. | SHAK 296:25 |
| woman, therefore to be w. | SHAK 280:6 |
| w. but to have fought well | COUB 108:15 |
| **wonder:** all a w. and a wild desire | BROW 77:5 |
| appeared a great w. in heaven | BIBLE 57:30 |
| Have eyes to w. | SHAK 300:5 |
| I w. by my troth, what thou | DONNE 124:5 |
| may w. at the workmanship | MILT 226:20 |
| One can only w. | BENT 35:7 |
| see the boneless w. | CHUR 99:8 |
| still the w. grew | GOLD 154:24 |
| w. at ourselves like men | WORD 354:13 |
| w. of our age | DYER 129:15 |
| w. of our stage | JONS 187:25 |
| **wondered:** I smiled and w. how | SHAK 288:16 |
| **wonderful:** All things wise and w. | ALEX 4:2 |
| most w. wonderful | SHAK 273:4 |

**world** (cont.):

| | |
|---|---|
| w. is so full of a number | STEV 317:13 |
| w. is still deceived | SHAK 289:21 |
| w. is the best of all possible | BRAD 71:8 |
| w. is too much with us | WORD 357:10 |
| w. knew him not | BIBLE 53:10 |
| w. made safe for democracy | WILS 351:21 |
| w. may end tonight | BROW 76:11 |
| w. only grasped by action | BRON 72:9 |
| w.'s a bubble | BACON 25:30 |
| w. safe for hypocrisy | WOLFE 353:6 |
| w.'s an inn, and death | DRYD 128:12 |
| w.'s as ugly, ay, as sin | LOCK 208:22 |
| w.'s at an end | D'AV 114:9 |
| w.'s great age begins anew | SHEL 303:18 |
| w.'s history is the w.'s judgement | SCH 267:21 |
| w. should be taxed | BIBLE 51:31 |
| w.'s last night | DONNE 123:13 |
| w.'s mine oyster | SHAK 290:9 |
| w. spin for ever down | TENN 326:17 |
| w.'s slow stain | SHEL 303:11 |
| w.'s storm-troubled sphere | BRON 72:16 |
| w.'s whole sap is sunk | DONNE 124:8 |
| w.'s worst wound | SASS 267:14 |
| w. was all before them | MILT 230:2 |
| w. will be in love | SHAK 295:14 |
| w. will end in fire | FROST 146:12 |
| w. without end | BOOK 63:17 |
| W., you have kept faith | HARDY 162:9 |
| **worldly**: be not w. wise | QUAR 257:3 |
| with all my w. goods | BOOK 66:2 |
| **worlds**: best of all possible w. | CAB 87:23 |
| best of all possible w. | VOLT 340:10 |
| in w. not realised | WORD 355:22 |
| Wandering between two w. | ARN 17:16 |
| what w. away | BROW 75:19 |
| w. of wanwood leafmeal | HOPK 172:15 |
| **worm**: I wish you all joy of the w. | SHAK 272:6 |
| like a w. i' the bud | SHAK 298:1 |
| invisible w. that flies | BLAKE 62:4 |
| w. at one end and a fool | JOHN 186:11 |
| **worms**: nor w. forget | DICK 119:9 |
| with vilest w. to dwell | SHAK 299:23 |
| **wormwood**: w. and the gall | BIBLE 47:1 |
| **worried**: w. into being | FROST 146:25 |
| **worry**: Leave your w. on the doorstep | FIEL 139:15 |
| **worrying**: What's the use of w. | ASAF 18:17 |
| W. the carcase of an old song | THOM 331:5 |
| **worse**: better day, the w. deed | HENRY 166:2 |
| Defend the bad against the w. | DAY-L 115:6 |
| even from w. to better | JOHN 182:3 |
| fear of finding something w. | BELL 33:5 |
| greater feeling to the w. | SHAK 293:14 |
| If my books had been any w. | CHAN 94:10 |
| I follow the w. | OVID 243:15 |
| I mean the W. one | ARIS 15:10 |
| It is w. than a crime | BOUL 70:9 |
| More will mean w. | AMIS 5:1 |
| one penny the w. | BARH 28:19 |
| w. appear the better reason | MILT 228:23 |
| w. to better hath in it | HOOK 171:15 |
| worst are no w. | SHAK 291:8 |
| **worship**: And we w. thy Name | BOOK 63:21 |
| are come to w. him | BIBLE 48:9 |
| earth doth w. thee | BOOK 63:18 |
| only object of w. | ANON 5:23 |
| O w. the King, all-glorious | GRANT 156:8 |
| O w. the Lord in the beauty | BOOK 68:2 |
| O w. the Lord in the beauty | MONS 233:3 |
| various modes of w. | GIBB 150:10 |
| with my body I thee w. | BOOK 66:2 |
| w. God in his own way | ROOS 262:13 |
| Your w. is your furnaces | BOTT 70:6 |
| **worshipped**: art w. by the names divine | BLAKE 60:15 |
| **worst**: And the best and the w. | SWIN 321:14 |

**worst** (cont.):

| | |
|---|---|
| be good to know the w. | BRAD 71:9 |
| Cheer up! the w. is yet to come | JOHN 182:1 |
| exacts a full look at the w. | HARDY 162:8 |
| it was the w. of times | DICK 120:6 |
| No w., there is none | HOPK 172:9 |
| so much good in the w. of us | ANON 10:20 |
| This is the w. | SHAK 283:20 |
| w. are full of passionate | YEATS 359:24 |
| w. is death | SHAK 293:25 |
| w. is better than any other | HAZL 164:6 |
| w. is better than none | JOHN 184:3 |
| world's w. wound | SASS 267:14 |
| w. time of the year | ANDR 5:15 |
| w. time of the year | ELIOT 133:21 |
| **worth**: but not w. going to see | JOHN 185:24 |
| calculate the w. of a man | FLAU 141:8 |
| charter of thy w. | SHAK 299:27 |
| it is w. doing badly | CHES 98:16 |
| Slow rises w., by poverty | JOHN 183:9 |
| **Worthington**: on the stage, Mrs W. | COW 109:5 |
| **worthy**: labourer is w. of his hire | BIBLE 52:10 |
| latchet I am not w. to unloose | BIBLE 53:12 |
| Lord, I am not w. | BIBLE 49:16 |
| w. to be called thy son | BIBLE 52:30 |
| **wotthehell**: w. archy | MARQ 219:19 |
| **would**: and what we w., we know | ARN 16:10 |
| evil which I w. not, that I do | BIBLE 54:38 |
| He w., wouldn't he? | RIC 259:20 |
| **wound**: Earth felt the w. | MILT 229:26 |
| first did help to w. itself | SHAK 282:15 |
| Hearts w. up with love | SPEN 313:2 |
| In every w. of Caesar | SHAK 281:26 |
| keen knife see not the w. | SHAK 285:19 |
| that never felt a w. | SHAK 294:29 |
| world's worst w. | SASS 267:14 |
| **wounded**: w. for our transgressions | BIBLE 46:19 |
| w. spirit who can bear | BIBLE 43:29 |
| You're w.! | BROW 76:8 |
| **Wounded Knee**: Bury my heart at W. | BENÉT 34:9 |
| **wounding**: wounded is the w. heart | CRAS 111:7 |
| **Wragg**: W. is in custody | ARN 18:3 |
| **wrang**: may gang a kennin w. | BURNS 81:21 |
| **wrapped**: All meanly w. | MILT 227:25 |
| w. him in swaddling clothes | BIBLE 51:32 |
| **wrath**: day of w. | MISS 231:23 |
| flee from the w. to come | BIBLE 48:14 |
| soft answer turneth away w. | BIBLE 43:24 |
| sun go down upon your w. | BIBLE 55:33 |
| tigers of w. are wiser | BLAKE 61:8 |
| w. endureth but the twinkling | BOOK 66:22 |
| **wreathed**: w. the rod of criticism | D'ISR 122:23 |
| **Wren**: Sir Christopher W. | BENT 35:9 |
| **wren**: Four Larks and a W. | LEAR 203:17 |
| robin-red-breast and the w. | WEBS 344:25 |
| w. goes to't | SHAK 283:23 |
| **wrest**: W. once the law | SHAK 289:28 |
| **wrestle**: w. not against flesh | BIBLE 56:4 |
| w. with words and meanings | ELIOT 133:3 |
| **wrestling**: w. with (my God!) | HOPK 172:1 |
| **wretch**: w. that dares not die | BURNS 82:15 |
| **wretched**: and yet a w. thing | DAV 114:14 |
| w. men are cradled into poetry | SHEL 303:22 |
| **wretches**: feel what w. feel | SHAK 283:12 |
| **wriggles**: He w. and giggles | HOFF 169:19 |
| **wriggle**: soon w. their hands | WALP 342:5 |
| **writ**: and, having w., moves on | FITZ 140:14 |
| I never w., nor no man ever | SHAK 300:9 |
| Presbyter is but old Priest w. | MILT 228:2 |
| **write**: But those who cannot w. | POPE 252:29 |
| comfortable I sit down to w. | KEATS 193:13 |
| I love to w. to the moment | RICH 260:3 |
| I w. like a distinguished | NAB 236:20 |
| look in thy heart and w. | SIDN 306:17 |
| much as a man ought to w. | TROL 334:12 |

**write** (*cont.*):
| people that w., people | SHEN 305:21 |
| people who can't w. | ZAPPA 361:1 |
| restraint with which they w. | CAMP 88:16 |
| Though an angel should w. | MOORE 234:10 |
| To make me w. too much | DAN 113:16 |
| W. me as one that loves | HUNT 176:13 |
| W. sorrow on the bosom | SHAK 293:26 |
| yet hate all who w. | WYCH 358:6 |
| You w. with ease | SHER 306:8 |

**writer**: every great and original w. | WORD 357:13
| modern hardback w. | TRIL 334:10 |
| pen: of a ready w. | BOOK 67:5 |
| plain, rude w. | BURT 83:6 |
| to protect the w. | ACH 1:4 |
| w.'s ambition should be | KOES 199:3 |

**writers**: W., like teeth, are divided | BAG 26:15
**writing**: All the rest is mere fine w. | VERL 337:20
| any style of w. untouched | JOHN 185:12 |
| God is love, but get it in w. | LEE 204:5 |
| incurable disease of w. | JUV 189:10 |
| sign the w., that it be not | BIBLE 47:13 |
| w. an exact man | BACON 25:15 |
| w. *at once* | GIDE 151:1 |
| w. increaseth rage | DYER 129:15 |
| w. is next to fine doing | KEATS 193:12 |
| W. is not a profession | SIM 307:4 |
| W., when properly managed | STER 315:17 |
**written**: Books are well w. or | WILDE 350:3
| in which anything may be w. | TRAH 333:17 |
| poetry should be *as well w. as prose* | POUND 254:24 |
| What I have written I have w. | BIBLE 54:3 |
| w. without effort | JOHN 186:15 |
| w. word as unlike the spoken | CONN 106:26 |
**wrong**: absent are always in the w. | DEST 117:10
| called them by w. names | BROW 75:16 |
| customer is never w. | RITZ 260:13 |
| different kinds of w. | COMP 106:5 |
| do a little w. | SHAK 289:28 |
| Eating people is w. | SWANN 141:5 |
| Ebenezer thought it w. to fight | BELL 33:28 |
| Englishman in the w. | SHAW 302:9 |
| gone w., however slightly | POTT 254:4 |
| Had anything been w. | AUDEN 21:17 |
| he done her w. | ANON 7:6 |
| he is very probably w. | CLAR 101:14 |
| I called the w. number | THUR 332:18 |
| idea, and that is a w. one | JOHN 184:23 |
| if w., to be set right | SCH 268:1 |
| keep himself from doing w. | BIBLE 48:3 |
| king can do no w. | BLAC 60:2 |
| Kings to govern w. | POPE 250:18 |
| million Frenchmen can't be w. | GUIN 159:9 |
| multitude is always in the w. | DILL 120:24 |
| On the w. side of the door | CHES 97:21 |
| Ran w. through all the land | MUIR 236:6 |
| rather be w. with Plato | CIC 101:1 |
| requite w. with wrong | SOCR 310:23 |
| right deed for the w. reason | ELIOT 134:7 |
| right of an excessive w. | BROW 77:8 |
| Should suffer w. no more | MAC 214:2 |
| suffering their wrongs were never w. | AUDEN 21:1 |
| thou hast seen my w. | BIBLE 47:3 |
| When everyone is w. | LA CH 199:15 |
| when I am in the w. | MELB 222:22 |
| w. because not all was right | CRAB 110:26 |
| W. but Wromantic | SELL 270:2 |
| w. could religion induce | LUCR 212:2 |
| w. extenuates not wrong | SHAK 296:33 |
| W. forever on the throne | LOW 211:8 |
| W. from the start | POUND 254:14 |
| w. side of a Turkey tapestry | HOW 175:8 |
| w. the poorest ploughman | CHAR 94:24 |
| w. with our bloody ships | BEAT 30:14 |
**wrongly**: And yet wouldst w. win | SHAK 285:15

**wrongs**: people's w. his own | DRYD 127:14
| Two w. don't make a right | SZASZ 322:2 |
**wrote**: ever w. except for money | JOHN 185:10
| Who w. like an angel | GARR 148:9 |
**wrought**: That first he w. | CHAU 95:21
| What hath God w. | BIBLE 40:19 |
**Wykehamist**: rather dirty W. | BETJ 37:15
**Wynken**: W., Blynken, and Nod | FIELD 139:2

# X

**Xanadu**: In X. did Kubla Khan | COL 103:22

# Y

**Yale**: whaleship was my Y. | MELV 223:3
**Yankee Doodle**: I'm a Y. Dandy | COHAN 103:5
| Y. came to town | ANON 11:24 |
**yawning**: like a man y. at a ball | LERM 205:25
**yawns**: grave y. for him | TREE 334:5
**yawp**: barbaric y. over the roofs | WHIT 348:22
**yea**: Let your y. be yea | BIBLE 57:5
**year**: beautiful and death-struck y. | HOUS 174:25
| next y. I shall be sixty-two | REED 258:14 |
| one y.'s experience 30 times | CARR 90:30 |
| sailed away for a y. and a day | LEAR 203:12 |
| stood at the gate of the y. | HASK 163:16 |
| thirtieth y. to heaven | THOM 330:13 |
| time of y. thou mayst in me | SHAK 299:24 |
| 'Tis the y.'s midnight | DONNE 124:7 |
| y. is going, let him go | TENN 325:23 |
| y.'s at the spring | BROW 76:28 |
**years**: breath the y. behind | YEATS 359:11
| down the arches of the y. | THOM 331:8 |
| end of a thousand y. of history | GAIT 147:12 |
| fleeting y. are slipping by | HOR 173:23 |
| gave up the y. to be | BROO 72:20 |
| Into the vale of y. | SHAK 292:16 |
| nor the y. condemn | BINY 59:12 |
| remember not past y. | NEWM 238:22 |
| Tell me, where all past y. are | DONNE 124:10 |
| thousand y. in thy sight | BOOK 67:25 |
| threescore y. and ten | BOOK 67:26 |
| touch of earthly y. | WORD 356:25 |
| y. of desolation pass over | JEFF 180:23 |
| y. that the locust hath eaten | BIBLE 47:19 |
| y. to come seemed waste | YEATS 359:11 |
**yeas**: russet y. and honest kersey | SHAK 284:19
**Yeats**: William Y. is laid to rest | AUDEN 20:24
**yellow**: Come unto these y. sands | SHAK 295:36
| fall'n into the sear, the y. leaf | SHAK 288:1 |
| falls into the y. leaf | BYRON 86:19 |
| paved with y. brick | BAUM 30:10 |
| silk-worm expend her y. | MIDD 224:9 |
| When y. leaves, or none | SHAK 299:24 |
| Y., and black, and pale | SHEL 304:6 |
| y. fog that rubs its back | ELIOT 133:26 |
| Y. God forever gazes down | HAYES 163:21 |
**yes**: place where y. may mean no | TOFF 333:7
| way of getting the answer y. | CAMUS 89:5 |
| Y., but not in the South | POTT 254:5 |
| Y.; I remember Adlestrop | THOM 330:21 |
| Y., Minister! No, Minister! | CROS 112:12 |
| Y.—oh dear yes, the novel | FORS 143:16 |
**yesterday**: art of keeping up with y. | MARQ 219:15
| call back y., bid time | SHAK 293:24 |
| in thy sight are but as y. | BOOK 67:25 |
| Jesus Christ the same y. | BIBLE 56:30 |
| universe and give me y. | HERM 186:20 |
| We were saying... | LUIS 212:7 |
| where leaves the rose of y. | FITZ 140:5 |
**yesterdays**: all our y. | SHAK 288:5

yesteryear: where are the snows of y.     VILL 338:20
yet: contingency—but not y.               AUG 21:22
  young man not y., an elder    BACON 25:3
yew: Gall of goat, and slips of y.        SHAK 287:17
yid: LET'S PUT THE ID BACK IN Y.          ROTH 263:15
yield: find, and not to y.                TENN 328:25
yoghurt: between the milk and the y.      TRIL 334:10
yo-ho-ho: Y., and a bottle of rum         STEV 317:2
yoke: bear the y. in his youth            BIBLE 47:2
  For my y. is easy             BIBLE 49:36
  savage bull doth bear the y.  SHAK 291:14
Yonghy-Bonghy-Bó: Lived the Y.            LEAR 203:7
Yorick: Alas, poor Y.                     SHAK 277:8
you: For y. but not for me                ANON 9:21
  I cannot live with y.         MART 220:7
  through y. but not from you   GIBR 150:19
young: America is a country of y. men     EMER 137:1
  But to be y. was very heaven  WORD 354:24
  crime of being a y. man       PITT 249:3
  dared be radical when y.      FROST 146:18
  for ever y.                    KEATS 191:21
  her six y. on the rail        BROW 76:10
  I, being y. and foolish       YEATS 359:1
  I have been y., and now       BLUN 62:15
  I have been y., and now       BOOK 66:27
  let me die a y.-man's death   MCG 214:21
  love's y. dream                MOORE 234:15
  Old and y., we are all        STEV 317:5
  O y., fresshe folkes          CHAU 96:22
  sight to make an old man y.    TENN 323:24
  So wise so y., they say        SHAK 294:17
  So y., and so untender        SHAK 282:17
  those that are with y.         BIBLE 46:11
  we that are y. shall never     SHAK 284:8
  When all the world is y., lad  KING 195:17
  Whom the gods love dies y.     MEN 223:5
  world and time were y.         RAL 257:20
  y. a body with so old a head   SHAK 289:25
  y. and easy in the mercy       THOM 330:9
  y. and easy under the apple    THOM 330:8
  Y., gifted and black           IRV 178:18
  y. in one another's arms       YEATS 359:20
  y. man not yet, an elder       BACON 25:3
  y. men glittering and sparkling  TRAH 333:19
  y. men shall see visions       BIBLE 47:20
  y. wife and a good brain       JONS 186:23
younger: I'm y. than that now             DYLAN 130:6
youngman: die a y.'s death                MCG 214:21
yours: Y. till Hell freezes               FISH 139:25
yourself: DO IT Y.                        BARH 28:22
youth: After the pleasures of y.          ANON 13:16

youth (cont.):
  All the flattering y. defy    ROCH 261:9
  April of your y.               HERB 166:19
  Ancient times the y. of the world  BACON 24:5
  bear the yoke in his y.        BIBLE 47:2
  Crabbed age and y.            SHAK 299:5
  Creator in the days of thy y.  BIBLE 44:25
  days of our y. are the days   BYRON 87:10
  flourish set on y.            SHAK 299:22
  flower of their y.            VIRG 340:1
  I do abhor thee, y.           SHAK 299:6
  If y. knew; if age could      EST 137:17
  I have y. and a little beauty  WEBS 344:14
  many a y., and many a maid    MILT 227:4
  sign of an ill-spent y.       ROUP 263:17
  sins and offences of my y.    BOOK 66:21
  spice-islands of Y. and Hope  COL 105:1
  thoughts of y. are long       LONG 209:21
  Time the subtle thief of y.   MILT 230:20
  very riband in the cap of y.   SHAK 277:5
  when Y. and Pleasure meet     BYRON 85:3
  Where y. grows pale           KEATS 191:32
  Y. is a blunder               DISR 121:26
  y. of England are on fire     SHAK 279:2
  y. of frolics, an old age of cards  POPE 251:11
  y. of labour with an age of ease  GOLD 154:19
  Y. on the prow, and Pleasure  GRAY 157:3
  Y.'s a stuff will not endure   SHAK 297:23
  Y.'s the season made for joys  GAY 149:6
  y. to the gallows              PAINE 244:13
  Y., what man's age is like to be  DENH 116:26
  Y., which is forgiven everything  SHAW 302:6
  Y. will be served             BORR 69:27

# Z

zany: mountebank and his z.               WALP 341:24
zeal: All z., Mr Easy                     MARR 220:1
  not the slightest z.          TALL 322:11
  tempering bigot z.            KNOX 198:17
  z. in politics as well        JUN 188:26
  z. of the Lord of hosts       BIBLE 45:17
zealous: relation is a z. citizen         BURKE 80:20
zed: Thou whoreson z.!                    SHAK 283:2
Zen: Z. and the Art of Motorcyle          PIRS 249:2
zenith: z. like a falling star            MILT 228:20
Zenocrate: Ah fair Z.                     MARL 219:10
zest: z. goes out of a beautiful          GREN 158:15
Zion: Z., city of our God                 NEWT 239:8
zoo: it is a human z.                     MORR 235:12
Zurich: little gnomes in Z.               WILS 351:12

# Sayings of the 90s

## Diane Abbott 1953–

**1** Being an MP is the sort of job all working-class parents want for their children—clean, indoors and no heavy lifting.

In *Independent* 18 January 1994

## Tony Benn 1925–

**2** If you file your waste-paper basket for 50 years, you have a public library.

In *Daily Telegraph* 5 March 1994

## John Biffen 1930–

Of Margaret Thatcher as Prime Minister

**3** She was a tigress surrounded by hamsters.

In *Observer* 9 December 1990

**4** In politics I think it is wiser to leave five minutes too soon than to continue for five years too long.

Resignation letter. In *Daily Telegraph* 5 January 1995

## James Black 1924–

**5** In the culture I grew up in you did your work and did not put your arm around it to stop other people from looking. You took the earliest possible opportunity to make knowledge available.

In *Daily Telegraph* 11 December 1995

## Tony Blair 1953–

**6** Labour is the party of law and order in Britain today. Tough on crime and tough on the causes of crime.

As Shadow Home Secretary. Speech at the Labour Party Conference, 30 September 1993

**7** The art of leadership is saying no, not yes. It is very easy to say yes.

In *Mail on Sunday* 2 October 1994

**8** Those who seriously believe we cannot improve on words written for the world of 1918 when we are now in 1995 are not learning from our history but living it.

On the proposed revision of Clause IV. In *Independent* 11 January 1995

## Betty Boothroyd 1929–

**9** My desire to get here [Parliament] was like miners' coal dust, it was under my fingers and I couldn't scrub it out.

Glenys Kinnock and Fiona Millar (eds.) *By Faith and Daring* (1993)

## Zbigniew Brzezinski 1928–

**10** Russia can be an empire or a democracy, but it cannot be both.

In *Foreign Affairs* March/April 1994 'The Premature Partnership'

## Barbara Bush 1925–

**11** Somewhere out in this audience may even be someone who will one day follow in my footsteps, and preside over the White House as the President's spouse. I wish him well!

At Wellesley College Commencement, 1 June 1990

Asked why she thought she was a popular First Lady.

**12** It was because I threatened no one. I was old, white-headed and large.

In *Independent on Sunday* 4 December 1994 'Quotes of the Week'

## Eric Cantona 1966–

**13** When seagulls follow a trawler, it is because they think sardines will be thrown into the sea.

*To the media at the end of a press conference, 31 March 1995.* In *The Times* 1 April 1995

## William Jefferson ('Bill') Clinton 1946–

**14** I experimented with marijuana a time or two. And I didn't like it, and I didn't inhale.

In *Washington Post* 30 March 1992

**15** The comeback kid!

Description of himself after coming second in the New Hampshire primary in the 1992 presidential election (since 1952, no presidential candidate had won the election without first winning in New Hampshire). Michael Barone and Grant Ujifusa *The Almanac of American Politics 1994*

1 The urgent question of our time is whether we can make change our friend and not our enemy.
   Inaugural address, 1993

## Denis Compton 1918–1997

2 I couldn't bat for the length of time required to score 500. I'd get bored and fall over.
   To Brian Lara. In *Daily Telegraph* 27 June 1994

## Robertson Davies 1913–95

3 It's an excellent life of somebody else. But I've really lived inside myself, and she can't get in there.
   On a biography of himself. Interview in *The Times* 4 April 1995

## Diana, Princess of Wales 1961–

4 There were three of us in this marriage, so it was a bit crowded.
   On her marriage breakdown. Interview on BBC1 TV 20 November 1995

5 I'd like to be a queen in people's hearts but I don't see myself being Queen of this country.
   Interview on BBC1 TV 20 November 1995

## Elizabeth II 1926–

6 In the words of one of my more sympathetic correspondents, it has turned out to be an 'annus horribilis'.
   Speech at Guildhall, London, 24 November 1992

## J. K. Galbraith 1908–

7 Trickle-down theory—the less than elegant metaphor that if one feeds the horse enough oats, some will pass through to the road for the sparrows.
   *The Culture of Contentment* (1992)

## Newton Gingrich 1943–

8 One of the greatest intellectual failures of the welfare state is the penchant for sacrifice, so long as the only people being asked to sacrifice are working, tax-paying Americans.
   In *USA Today* 16 January 1995

9 No society can survive, no civilization can survive, with 12-year-olds having babies, with 15-year-olds killing each other, with 17-year-olds dying of Aids, with 18-year-olds getting diplomas they can't read.
   In December 1994, after the Republican electoral victory. In *The Times* 9 February 1995

## Lord Gowrie 1939–

10 All the wrong bits are in and the right bits are out.
   Explaining why Vikram Seth's *A Suitable Boy* had not been shortlisted for the 1993 Booker Prize. In *Guardian* 9 March 1994

## Joseph Heller 1923–

11 When I read something saying I've not done anything as good as *Catch-22* I'm tempted to reply, 'Who has?'
   In *The Times* 9 June 1993

## David Hockney 1937–

12 The thing with high-tech is that you always end up using scissors.
   In *Observer* 10 July 1994 'Sayings of the Week'

## Geoffrey Howe 1926–

13 It is rather like sending your opening batsmen to the crease only for them to find the moment that the first balls are bowled that their bats have been broken before the game by the team captain.
   On the difficulties caused him as Foreign Secretary by the Prime Minister's anti-European views; resignation speech as Deputy Prime Minister. In the House of Commons 13 November 1990

## Alija Izetbegović 1925–

14 And to my people I say, this may not be a just peace, but it is more just than a continuation of war.
   After signing the Dayton accord with representatives of Serbia and Croatia. In Dayton, Ohio, 21 November 1995

## Paul Keating 1944–

15 Even as it [Great Britain] walked out on you and joined the Common Market, you were still looking for your MBEs and your knighthoods, and all the rest of the regalia that comes with it. You would take Australia right back down the time tunnel to the cultural cringe where you have always come from.
   Addressing Australian Conservative supporters of Great Britain. On 27 February 1992

## Garrison Keillor 1942–

**1** Years ago, manhood was an opportunity for achievement, and now it is a problem to be overcome.

*The Book of Guys* (1994)

## Helmut Kohl 1930–

**2** We Germans now have the historic chance to realize the unity of our fatherland.

On the reunification of Germany. In *Guardian* 15 February 1990

**3** The policy of European integration is in reality a question of war and peace in the 21st century.

Speech at Louvain University, 2 February 1996; in *Daily Telegraph* 3 February 1996

## Norman Lamont 1942–

**4** The green shoots of economic spring are appearing once again.

As Chancellor; often quoted as 'the green shoots of recovery'. Speech at Conservative Party Conference, 9 October 1991

**5** We give the impression of being in office but not in power.

As a backbencher. Speech in the House of Commons, 9 June 1993

## Fran Lebowitz 1946–

**6** The best fame is a writer's fame: it's enough to get a table at a good restaurant, but not enough that you get interrupted when you eat.

In *Observer* 30 May 1993 'Sayings of the Week'

## Paul McCartney 1942–

**7** Ballads and babies. That's what happened to me.

On reaching the age of 50. In *Time* 8 June 1992

## Lord McGregor 1921–

**8** An odious exhibition of journalists dabbling their fingers in the stuff of other people's souls.

On Press coverage of the marital difficulties of the Prince and Princess of Wales, speaking as Chairman of the Press Complaints Commission. In *The Times* 9 June 1992

## Candia McWilliam 1955–

**9** With the birth of each child, you lose two novels.

In *Guardian* 5 May 1993

## John Major 1943–

**10** Society needs to condemn a little more and understand a little less.

Interview with *Mail on Sunday* 21 February 1993

**11** It is time to get back to basics: to self-discipline and respect for the law, to consideration for others, to accepting responsibility for yourself and your family, and not shuffling it off on the state.

Speech to the Conservative Party Conference, 8 October 1993

## Matthew Parris 1949–

**12** Being an MP feeds your vanity and starves your self-respect.

In *The Times* 9 February 1994

## Frances Partridge 1900–

**13** Thirty years is a very long time to live alone and life doesn't get any nicer.

On widowhood, at the age of 92. In G. Kinnock and F. Miller (eds.) *By Faith and Daring* (1993)

## H. Ross Perot 1930–

After George Bush had laid stress on the value of experience in the 1992 presidential debates:

**14** I don't have any experience in running up a $4 trillion debt.

In *Newsweek* 19 October 1992

## Dennis Potter 1935–94

**15** Below my window ... the blossom is out in full now ... I *see* it is the whitest, frothiest, blossomiest blossom that there ever could be, and I can see it. Things are both more trivial than they ever were, and more important than they ever were, and the difference between the trivial and the important doesn't seem to matter. But the nowness of everything is absolutely wondrous.

On his heightened awareness of things, in the face of his imminent death. Interview with Melvyn Bragg on Channel 4, March 1994

**16** Religion to me has always been the wound, not the bandage.

Interview with Melvyn Bragg on Channel 4, March 1994

## Yitzhak Rabin 1922–95

**1** We say to you today in a loud and a clear voice: enough of blood and tears. Enough.

> To the Palestinians, at the signing of the Israel–Palestine Declaration. In Washington, 13 September 1993

## Gerald Ratner 1949–

**2** We even sell a pair of earrings for under £1, which is cheaper than a prawn sandwich from Marks & Spencers. But I have to say the earrings probably won't last as long.

> Speaking as Chief Executive of a High Street jewellery chain. Speech to the Institute of Directors, Albert Hall, 23 April 1991

## Claire Rayner 1931–

**3** I always say I don't think everyone has the right to happiness or to be loved. Even the Americans have written into their constitution that you have the right to the 'pursuit of happiness'. You have the right to try but that is all.

> G. Kinnock and F. Miller (eds.) *By Faith and Daring* (1993)

## Ronald Reagan 1911–

**4** I now begin the journey that will lead me into the sunset of my life.

> Statement to the American people revealing that he had Alzheimer's disease. In *Daily Telegraph* 5 January 1995

## Nicholas Ridley 1929–93

Of the European community:

**5** This is all a German racket, designed to take over the whole of Europe.

> In *Spectator* 14 July 1990

## Robert Shapiro 1942–

**6** Not only did we play the race card, we played it from the bottom of the deck.

> On O. J. Simpson's defence team's change of strategy after Shapiro was replaced as leader. In *The Times* 5 October 1995

## Margaret Thatcher 1925–

**7** I am naturally very sorry to see you go, but understand ... your wish to be able to spend more time with your family.

> Reply to Norman Fowler's resignation letter. In *Guardian* 4 January 1990

**8** I shan't be pulling the levers there but I shall be a very good back-seat driver.

> On the appointment of John Major as the next Prime Minister. In *Independent* 27 November 1990

**9** I think sometimes the Prime Minister should be intimidating. There's not much point being a weak, floppy thing in the chair, is there?

> On 'The Thatcher Years' (BBC 1), 21 October 1993

## John Tusa 1936–

**10** Management that wants to change an institution must first show it loves that institution.

> In *Observer* 27 February 1994 'Sayings of the Week'

## William Waldegrave 1946–

**11** In exceptional circumstances it is necessary to say something that is untrue in the House of Commons.

> In *Guardian* 9 March 1994

## Elie Wiesel 1928–

**12** God of forgiveness, do not forgive those murderers of Jewish children here.

> At an unofficial ceremony at Auschwitz on 26 January 1995, commemorating the 50th anniversary of the Soviet liberation of Auschwitz on 27 January 1945. In *The Times* 27 January 1995

## Terry Worrall

**13** It was the wrong kind of snow.

> Explaining disruption on British Rail. In *The Independent* 16 February 1991

## Boris Yeltsin 1931–

**14** Europe is in danger of plunging into a cold peace.

> At the summit meeting of the Conference on Security and Co-operation in Europe. In *Newsweek* 19 December 1994

**15** Today is the last day of an era past.

> At a Berlin ceremony to end the Soviet military presence. In *Guardian* 1 September 1994

# Popular Misquotations
## (Things They Didn't Quite Say)

**1** All is lost save honour.

> *After his defeat at Pavia, 1525, by the Emperor Charles V, the King of France wrote to his mother, 'Of all I had, only honour and life have been spared.'*

**Francis I of France** 1494–1547: in *Collections des Documents Inédits sur l'histoire de France* (1847) vol. 1

**2** All rowed fast, but none so fast as stroke.

> *Misquotation of a passage from the novel Sandford of Merton 'His blade struck the water a full second before any other: the lad had started well. Nor did he flag as the race wore on ... as the boats began to near the winning-post, his oar was dipping into the water nearly twice as often as any other.'*

**Desmond Coke** 1879–1931: *Sandford of Merton* (1903)

**3** All my possessions for a moment of time.

> *Often quoted as the last words of Queen Elizabeth, but not traced in any contemporary source and almost certainly apocryphal.*

**Elizabeth I of England** 1533–1603: attributed

**4** Beam me up, Scotty.

> *Supposedly the form in which Captain Kirk habitually requested to be returned from a planet to the Starship Enterprise; 'Beam us up, Mr Scott' is in fact the nearest equivalent found.*

**Gene Roddenberry** 1921–91: *Star Trek* ('Gamesters of Triskelion')

**5** The ballot is stronger than the bullet.

> *From a speech by Lincoln in 1858, 'To give victory to the right, not bloody bullets, but peaceful ballots only, are necessary.'*

**Abraham Lincoln** 1809–65: speech 18 May 1858; R. P. Basler (ed.) *Collected Works of Abraham Lincoln* (1953) vol. 2

**6** Crisis? What crisis?

> *Summarizing James Callaghan's remark of 10 January 1979, 'I don't think other people in the world would share the view there is mounting chaos.'*

**Anonymous** : *Sun* headline, 11 January 1979

**7** Dreams are the royal road to the unconscious.

> *Summary of Freud's view, 'The interpretation of dreams is the royal road to a knowledge of the unconscious activities of the mind.'*

**Sigmund Freud** 1856–1939: *The Interpretation of Dreams* (2nd ed., 1909)

**8** Elementary, my dear Watson.

> *Not found in any book by Conan Doyle, although a review of the film The Return of Sherlock Holmes in New York Times 19 October 1929 states: 'In the final scene Dr Watson is there with his "Amazing, Holmes", and Holmes comes forth with his "Elementary, my dear Watson, elementary"'; the nearest to this in Doyle's own work is, 'Excellent,' I cried. 'Elementary,' said he.*

**Arthur Conan Doyle** 1859–1930: *The Memoirs of Sherlock Holmes* (1894)

**9** England and America are two countries divided by a common language.

> *Attributed in this and other forms to George Bernard Shaw, but not found in Shaw's published writings.*

**George Bernard Shaw** 1856–1950: attributed

**10** Few die and none resign.

> *Thomas Jefferson had written in 1801, 'If a due participation of office is a matter of right, how are vacancies to be obtained? Those by death are few; by resignation none.'*

**Thomas Jefferson** 1743–1826: letter to E. Shipman and others, 12 July 1801; P. L. Ford (ed.) *Writings of Thomas Jefferson* vol. 8 (1897)

**11** The green shoots of recovery.

> *Popular misquotation of the Chancellor's upbeat assessment of the economic situation, 'The green shoots of economic spring are appearing once again.'*

**Norman Lamont** 1942– : speech at Conservative Party Conference, 9 October 1991

**1** In trust I have found treason.

> *Traditional concluding words of a speech given by Elizabeth I to a Parliamentary deputation at Richmond, 12 November 1586, from a report which the Queen is said to have corrected in her own hand, 'As for me, I assure you I find no great cause I should be fond to live. I take no such pleasure in it that I should much wish it, nor conceive such terror in death that I should greatly fear it ... I have had good experience and trial of this world. I know what it is to be a subject, what to be a Sovereign, what to have good neighbours, and sometimes meet evil-willers.'*

**Elizabeth I of England** 1533–1603: John Neale *Elizabeth I and her Parliaments, 1584–1601* (1957)

**2** I paint with my prick.

> *Possibly an inversion of 'It's with my brush I make love'.*

**Pierre Auguste Renoir** 1841–1919: A. André *Renoir* (1919)

**3** It is necessary only for the good man to do nothing for evil to triumph.

> *Attributed in a number of forms to Burke, but not traced in his writings.*

**Edmund Burke** 1729–97: attributed

**4** Man, if you gotta ask you'll never know.

> *When asked what jazz was, Louis Armstrong responded 'If you still have to ask ... shame on you.'*

**Louis Armstrong** 1901–71: Max Jones *et al. Salute to Satchmo* (1970)

**5** Me Tarzan, you Jane.

> *Summing up his role in Tarzan, the Ape Man (1932 film); the words occur neither in the film nor the original, by Edgar Rice Burroughs.*

**Johnny Weissmuller** 1904–84: in *Photoplay Magazine* June 1932

**6** Mind has no sex.

> *Summarizing the expressed view of the feminist Mary Wollstonecraft, 'To give a sex to mind was not very consistent with the principles of a man [Rousseau] who argued so warmly, and so well, for the immortality of the soul.'*

**Mary Wollstonecraft** 1759–97: *A Vindication of the Rights of Woman* (1792)

**7** My lips are sealed.

> *Misquotation from Stanley Baldwin's speech on the Abyssinian crisis in 1935, 'I shall be but a short time tonight. I have seldom spoken with greater regret, for my lips are not yet unsealed. Were these troubles over I would make a case, and I guarantee that not a man would go into the lobby against us.'*

**Stanley Baldwin** 1867–1947: speech in the House of Commons, 10 December 1935

**8** Play it again, Sam.

> *In the film Casablanca Humphrey Bogart says, 'If she can stand it, I can. Play it!'; earlier in the film Ingrid Bergman says, 'Play it, Sam. Play As Time Goes By.'*

**Julius J. Epstein** 1909– *et al.*: *Casablanca* (1942 film)

**9** Selling off the family silver.

> *Summary of Harold Macmillan's attack on privatization 'First of all the Georgian silver goes, and then all that nice furniture that used to be in the saloon. Then the Canalettos go.'*

**Harold Macmillan** 1894–1986: speech to the Tory Reform Group, 8 November 1985

**10** The soft under-belly of Europe.

> *Speaking in the House of Commons in 1942, Winston Churchill had said, 'We make this wide encircling movement in the Mediterranean, having for its primary object the recovery of the command of that vital sea, but also having for its object the exposure of the under-belly of the Axis, especially Italy, to heavy attack.'*

**Winston Churchill** 1874–1965: in the House of Commons, 11 November 1942

**11** Something must be done.

> *Speaking at the derelict Dowlais Iron and Steel Works, 18 November 1936, the King said, 'These works brought all these people here. Something should be done to get them at work again.'*

**Edward VIII (later Duke of Windsor)** 1894–1972: in *Western Mail* 19 November 1936

**12** Take away these baubles.

> *At the dismissal of the Rump Parliament in 1653, Cromwell gave the order, 'Take away that fool's bauble, the mace.'*

**Oliver Cromwell** 1599–1658: Bulstrode Whitelocke *Memorials of the English Affairs* (1732 ed.)

**1** Warts and all.

> From Cromwell's instructions to the court
> painter Peter Lely, 'Mr Lely, I desire you
> would use all your skill to paint my picture
> truly like me, and not flatter me at all; but
> remark all these roughnesses, pimples,
> warts, and everything as you see me;
> otherwise I will never pay a farthing for it.'

**Oliver Cromwell** 1599–1658: Horace Walpole
*Anecdotes of Painting in England* vol. 3 (1763)

**2** We are the masters now.

> From Hartley Shawcross's quotation from
> Lewis Carroll in asserting Labour's strength
> after winning the 1945 election, '"But," said
> Alice, "the question is whether you can make
> a word mean different things." "Not so,"
> said Humpty-Dumpty, "the question is which
> is to be master. That's all." We are the
> masters at the moment, and not only at the
> moment, but for a very long time to come."'

**Hartley Shawcross** 1902– : in the House of
Commons, 2 April 1946

*Was für plündern!*
**3** What a place to plunder!

> Misquotation of 'Was für plunder!' (What
> rubbish!), the reported comment of the
> Prussian Field Marshal on London as seen
> from the momument, in June 1814.

**Gebhard Lebrecht Blücher** 1742–1819:
Evelyn Princess Blücher *Memoirs of Prince
Blücher* (1932)

**4** When war is declared, truth is the first
casualty.

> Ultimately probably deriving from Samuel
> Johnson, 'Among the casualties of war may
> be jointly numbered the diminution of the
> love of truth, by the falsehoods which
> interest dictates and credulity encourages';
> in the shorter form, has also been attributed
> to Hiram Johnson, speaking in the US
> Senate in 1918, but is not recorded in his
> speech.

**Samuel Johnson** 1709–84: *The Idler* 11
November 1758

**5** The white heat of technology.

> From Harold Wilson's speech of 1963, 'The
> Britain that is going to be forged in the
> white heat of this revolution will be no place
> for restrictive practices or for outdated
> methods on either side of industry.'

**Harold Wilson** 1916– : speech at the Labour
Party Conference, 1 October 1963

**6** Why don't you come up and see me
sometime?

> Alteration of her invitation in the film She
> Done Him Wrong, 'Why don't you come
> up sometime, and see me?'

**Mae West** 1892–1980: *She Done Him Wrong*
(1933 film)

**7** You dirty rat!

> Associated with James Cagney, but not used
> by him in any film; in a speech at the
> American Film Institute banquet, 13 March
> 1974, Cagney said, 'I never said "Mmm, you
> dirty rat!"'

**James Cagney** 1899–1986: *Cagney by Cagney*
(1976)

# Slogans

1 **Access—your flexible friend.**
   Access credit card, 1981 onwards

2 **An ace caff with quite a nice museum attached.**
   advertising slogan for the Victoria & Albert Museum, February 1989

3 **Action this day.**
   annotation as used by Winston Churchill at the Admiralty in 1940

4 **All human life is there.**
   used by Maurice Smelt as an advertising slogan for the *News of the World* in the late 1950s

5 **All power to the Soviets.**
   workers in Petrograd, 1917

6 **All the news that's fit to print.**
   motto of the *New York Times*, from 1896; coined by Adolph S. Ochs (1858–1935)

7 **All the way with LBJ.**
   US Democratic Party campaign slogan, in *Washington Post* 4 June 1960

8 **American Express? ... That'll do nicely, sir.**
   advertisement for American Express credit card, 1970s

9 **And all because the lady loves Milk Tray.**
   Cadbury's Milk Tray chocolates, 1968 onwards

10 *Arbeit macht frei.*
   Work liberates; words inscribed on the gates of Dachau concentration camp, 1933, and subsequently on those of Auschwitz

11 **Australians wouldn't give a XXXX for anything else.**
   advertisement for Castlemaine lager, 1986 onwards

12 **Ban the bomb.**
   US anti-nuclear slogan, 1953 onwards, adopted by the Campaign for Nuclear Disarmament

13 **A bayonet is a weapon with a worker at each end.**
   British pacifist slogan (1940)

14 **Beanz meanz Heinz.**
   Heinz baked beans, *c.*1967

15 **Been there, done that, got the T-shirt.**
   *been there, done that* recorded from 1980s, expanded form from 1990s

16 **Be prepared.**
   motto of the Boy Scouts, 1909, founded on initials of Robert Baden-Powell 1857–1941

17 **Better red than dead.**
   slogan of nuclear disarmament campaigners, late 1950s

18 **Black is beautiful.**
   slogan of American civil rights campaigners, mid-1960s

19 **Bovril ... Prevents that sinking feeling.**
   Bovril beef essence, 1920

20 **Burn, baby, burn.**
   black extremist slogan in use during the Los Angeles riots, August 1965

21 **Burn your bra!**
   feminist slogan of the 1970s

22 **Can you tell Stork from butter?**
   advertisement for Stork margarine, from *c.*1956

23 **Careless talk costs lives.**
   Second World War security slogan

24 **Clunk, click, *every* trip.**
   Road safety campaign promoting the use of seat-belts, 1971

25 **Coughs and sneezes spread diseases. Trap the germs in your handkerchief.**
   Second World War health slogan (1942)

26 **Crime doesn't pay.**
   a slogan of the FBI and the cartoon detective Dick Tracy

27 **The customer is always right.**
   from French *Le client n'a jamais tort* (literally, 'The customer is never wrong', coined by César Ritz (1850–1918)

1 **Daddy, what did you do in the Great War?**
daughter to father in First World War recruiting poster

2 **The difficult we do immediately—the impossible takes a little longer.**
US Armed Forces slogan

3 **Dig for Victory.**
Reginald Dorman-Smith (1899–1977); radio broadcast, 3 October 1939

4 **Does she ... or doesn't she?**
Clairol hair colouring, 1950s

5 **Don't ask a man to drink and drive.**
UK road safety slogan, from 1964

6 **Don't be vague—ask for Haig.**
Haig whisky, c.1936

7 **Don't die of ignorance.**
slogan used in AIDS publicity campaign, 1987

8 **Don't forget the fruit gums, Mum!**
Rowntree's Fruit Gums, 1958–61

9 **Drinka Pinta Milka Day.**
slogan for the British Milk Marketing Board, 1958

10 *Ein Reich, ein Volk, ein Führer.*
One realm, one people, one leader; Nazi Party slogan, early 1930s

11 **Even your closest friends won't tell you.**
US advertisement for Listerine mouthwash, in *Woman's Home Companion* November 1923

12 **Every picture tells a story.**
advertisement for Doan's Backache Kidney Pills (early 1900s)

13 **Fair shares for all.**
Labour slogan devised for the North Battersea by-election, 1946, by Douglas Jay

14 **The family that prays together stays together.**
Al Scalpone motto devised for the Roman Catholic Family Rosary Crusade, 1947

15 **Full of Eastern promise.**
advertising slogan for Fry's Turkish Delight, 1950s onwards

16 **Garbage in, garbage out.**
incorrect or faulty input in computing will always cause poor output; often abbreviated to **gigo**

17 **Good to the last drop.**
said by Theodore Roosevelt to Joel Cheek in 1907 about Maxwell House coffee, and subsequently used as an advertising slogan

18 **Go to work on an egg.**
advertising slogan for the British Egg Marketing Board, from 1957; perhaps written by Fay Weldon or Mary Gowing

19 **The greatest show on earth.**
Barnum and Bailey's circus, 1880s

20 **Guinness is good for you.**
Guinness stout, 1930s

21 **Happiness is a cigar called Hamlet.**
Hamlet cigars, UK

22 **Have a break, have a Kit-Kat.**
Rowntree's Kit-Kat, from c.1955

23 **Heineken refreshes the parts other beers cannot reach.**
Heineken lager, 1975 onwards

24 **High o'er the fence leaps Sunny Jim 'Force' is the food that raises him.**
advertising slogan for breakfast cereal (1903)

25 **Horlicks guards against night starvation.**
Horlicks malted milk drink, 1930s

26 **I am a Marxist—of the Groucho tendency.**
slogan found at Nanterre in Paris, 1968

27 **I didn't get where I am today without—.**
managerial catch-phrase in BBC television series *The Fall and Rise of Reginald Perrin*, 1976–80)

28 **If you want to get ahead, get a hat.**
advertising slogan for the Hat Council, UK, 1965

29 **I like Ike.**
US button badge first used in 1947 when General Eisenhower was seen as a potential presidential nominee

30 *Ils ne passeront pas.*
They shall not pass; slogan used by French army at defence of Verdun in 1916;

variously attributed to Marshal Pétain and
to General Robert Nivelle

1 **I'm backing Britain.**
slogan coined by workers at the Colt
factory, Surbiton, Surrey and subsequently
used in a national campaign, in *The Times*
Jan. 1968

2 **I'm only here for the beer.**
Double Diamond beer, 1971 onwards

3 **Is your journey** *really* **necessary?**
1939 slogan, coined to discourage Civil
Servants from going home for Christmas

4 **It beats as it sweeps as it cleans.**
Hoover vacuum cleaners, 1919

5 **It'll play in Peoria.**
catch-phrase of the Nixon administration
(early 1970s) meaning 'it will be
acceptable to middle America', but
originating in a standard music hall joke
of the 1930s

6 **It's finger lickin' good.**
Kentucky Fried Chicken, 1958

7 **It's for you-hoo!**
slogan for British Telecom television
advertisements, *c.*1985

8 **It's good to talk.**
British Telecom, from 1994

9 **It's morning again in America.**
slogan for Ronald Reagan's election
campaign, 1984, coined by Hal Riney
(1932– )

10 **It's so bracing.**
tourist advertisement for Skegness, with
jolly fisherman symbol, from 1909

11 **I was a seven stone weakling.**
line from Charles Atlas body-building
advertising (originally in US)

12 **Just when you thought it was safe to go
back in the water.**
advertising copy for the film *Jaws 2* (1978),
featuring the return of the great white
shark

13 **Keep Britain tidy.**
issued by the Central Office of
Information, 1950s

14 **Keep on truckin'.**
slogan used in cartoons by Robert Crumb
(1943– ) from *c.*1972

15 **Keep that schoolgirl complexion.**
Palmolive soap, from 1917

16 **Kills all known germs.**
Domestos bleach, 1959

17 *Kraft durch Freude.*
Strength through joy; German Labour
Front slogan from 1933

18 **Labour isn't working.**
on a poster showing a long queue outside
an unemployment office; British
Conservative Party slogan, 1978

19 **Labour's Double Whammy.**
Conservative slogan, 1992 general election

20 **LBJ, LBJ, how many kids have you killed
today?**
anti-Vietnam marching slogan

21 **Let the train take the strain.**
British Rail, 1970 onwards

22 **Let your fingers do the walking.**
1960s advertisement for Bell system
Telephone Directory Yellow Pages

23 *Liberté! Égalité! Fraternité!*
Freedom! Equality! Brotherhood!; motto of
the French Revolution, 30 June 1793, but
of earlier origin

24 **Life's better with the Conservatives.
Don't let Labour ruin it.**
Conservative Party election slogan, 1959

25 **Lousy but loyal.**
London East End slogan at George V's
Jubilee (1935)

26 **Make do and mend.**
wartime slogan, 1940s

27 **Make love not war.**
student slogan, 1960s

28 **The man from Del Monte says 'Yes'.**
Del Monte tinned fruit, 1985

29 **A Mars a day helps you work, rest and
play.**
advertising slogan for Mars bar, *c.*1960
onwards

1 **Meet the challenge—make the change.**
Labour Party slogan, 1989

2 **The mint with the hole.**
Life-Savers, USA, 1920; Rowntree's Polo mints, UK from 1947

3 **My Goodness, My Guinness.**
Guinness stout, 1935

4 **Never knowingly undersold.**
motto, from c.1920, of the John Lewis Partnership

5 **Nice one, Cyril.**
1972 television advertising campaign for Wonderloaf; taken up by supporters of Cyril Knowles, Tottenham Hotspur footballer; the Spurs team later made a record featuring the line

6 **No manager ever got fired for buying IBM.**
IBM advertising slogan

7 **No surrender!**
adopted as a slogan of Protestant Ulster, recalling the siege of Derry by the Jacobite army of James II, April 1689

8 **Not a penny off the pay, not a second on the day.**
A. J. Cook (1885–1931); speech at York, 3 April 1926 (often quoted with 'minute' substituted for 'second')

9 **Nothing over sixpence.**
Woolworth stores, UK, from 1909

10 **One man, one vote.**
promoting the the policy that each individual should have a single vote: a slogan against plural voting originally coined in the nineteenth century, and more recently particularly associated with the 1993 debate in the British Labour Party on union block votes (the slogan being referred to by the acronym **omov**)

11 **Oxo gives a meal man-appeal.**
Oxo beef extract, c.1960

12 **Persil washes whiter—and it shows.**
Persil washing powder, 1970s

13 **Pile it high, sell it cheap.**
slogan associated with John Cohen (1898–1979) founder of Tesco, and his business

14 **Power to the people.**
slogan of the Black Panther movement, from c.1968 onwards

15 **P-p-p-pick up a Penguin.**
Penguin chocolate biscuits

16 **Put a tiger in your tank.**
Esso, USA, 1964

17 **The right one.**
Martini, UK, 1970

18 **Say it with flowers.**
slogan for the Society of American Florists

19 **Sch ... you know who.**
Schweppes mineral drinks, 1960s

20 **Smoking can seriously damage your health.**
government health warning now required by British law to be printed on cigarette packets

21 **Snap! Crackle! Pop!**
Kellogg's Rice Krispies, from c.1928

22 **Someone, somewhere, wants a letter from you.**
advertising slogan for the British Post Office in the 1960s

23 **Stop-look-listen.**
safety slogan current in the US from 1912

24 **Stop me and buy one.**
Wall's ice cream, from spring 1922

25 **Tell Sid.**
advertising slogan for the privatization of British Gas, 1986

26 **There's no such thing as a free lunch.**
colloquial axiom in US economics from the 1960s, much associated with Milton Friedman; first found in printed form in Robert Heinlein *The Moon is a Harsh Mistress* (1966)

27 **They come as a boon and a blessing to men,**
**The Pickwick, the Owl, and the Waverley pen.**
advertisement by MacNiven and H. Cameron Ltd., c.1920

**1 Things go better with Coke.**
Coca-Cola, 1963

**2 Thirteen years of Tory misrule.**
unofficial Labour party slogan for the 1964
election; also in the form *Thirteen wasted
years*

**3 Top breeders recommend it.**
Pedigree Chum dog food, UK, 1964

**4 Top people take *The Times*.**
advertising slogan for *The Times* newspaper
from January 1959

**5 Ulster says no.**
slogan coined in response to the Anglo-
Irish Agreement of 15 November 1985

**6 United we stand, divided we fall.**
a watchword of the American Revolution

**7 *Vorsprung durch Technik*.**
German = Progress through technology;
advertising slogan for Audi motors, from
1986

**8 Vote early and vote often.**
US election slogan, alluding to ballot-box
corruption, already current when quoted
by William Porcher Miles in the House of
Representatives, 31 March 1858

**9 Votes for Women.**
campaign slogan of the Suffragette
movement; Emmeline Pankhurst records
its coinage in 1905 from a banner
originally intended to read, 'Will the
Liberal Party Give Votes for Women?'

**10 War will cease when men refuse to
fight.**
pacifist slogan, from *c*.1936; often quoted
as 'Wars will cease ... '

**11 We are the Ovaltineys,
Happy girls and boys.**
in *We are the Ovaltineys*, song promoting
the drink Ovaltine, from *c*.1935

**12 We're number two. We try harder.**
Avis car rentals

**13 We shall not be moved.**
title of labour and civil rights song (1931),
adapted from an earlier gospel hymn

**14 We shall overcome.**
title of song, originating from before the
American Civil War, adapted as a Baptist
hymn ('I'll Overcome Some Day', 1901) by
C. Albert Tindley; revived in 1946 as a
protest song by black tobacco workers,
and in 1963 during the black Civil Rights
Campaign

**15 Where's the beef?**
advertising slogan for Wendy's
Hamburgers in campaign launched 9
January 1984 (taken up by Walter Mondale
in a televised debate with Gary Hart from
Atlanta, 11 March 1984: 'When I hear your
new ideas I'm reminded of that ad,
"Where's the beef?" ')

**16 Who dares wins.**
motto of the British Special Air Service
regiment, from 1942

**17 Worth a guinea a box.**
Beechams pills, *c*.1940

**18 Would you buy a used car from this
man?**
slogan (probably of earlier origin) directed
against Richard Nixon in 1968, in
response to a Nixon campaign poster

**19 Yesterday's men (they failed before!).**
advertising slogan for the Labour Party
(referring to the Conservatives), 1970

**20 You never had it so good.**
Democratic Party slogan during the 1952
US election campaign; later quoted by
Harold Macmillan 'Most of our people
have never had it so good', 20 July 1957

**21 You're never alone with a Strand.**
advertisement for Strand cigarettes, 1960;
the image of loneliness was so strongly
conveyed by the solitary smoker that sales
were in fact adversely affected

**22 Your King and Country need you.**
1914 recruiting advertisement

OXFORD

## MORE OXFORD PAPERBACKS

This book is just one of nearly 1000 Oxford Paperbacks currently in print. If you would like details of other Oxford Paperbacks, including titles in the World's Classics, Oxford Reference, Oxford Books, OPUS, Past Masters, Oxford Authors, and Oxford Shakespeare series, please write to:

**UK and Europe:** Oxford Paperbacks Publicity Manager, Arts and Reference Publicity Department, Oxford University Press, Walton Street, Oxford OX2 6DP.

Customers in UK and Europe will find Oxford Paperbacks available in all good bookshops. But in case of difficulty please send orders to the Cash-with-Order Department, Oxford University Press Distribution Services, Saxon Way West, Corby, Northants NN18 9ES. Tel: 01536 741519; Fax: 01536 746337. Please send a cheque for the total cost of the books, plus £1.75 postage and packing for orders under £20; £2.75 for orders over £20. Customers outside the UK should add 10% of the cost of the books for postage and packing.

**USA:** Oxford Paperbacks Marketing Manager, Oxford University Press, Inc., 200 Madison Avenue, New York, N.Y. 10016.

**Canada:** Trade Department, Oxford University Press, 70 Wynford Drive, Don Mills, Ontario M3C 1J9.

**Australia:** Trade Marketing Manager, Oxford University Press, G.P.O. Box 2784Y, Melbourne 3001, Victoria.

**South Africa:** Oxford University Press, P.O. Box 1141, Cape Town 8000.

OXFORD REFERENCE

# THE CONCISE OXFORD COMPANION TO ENGLISH LITERATURE

### Edited by Margaret Drabble and Jenny Stringer

Based on the immensely popular fifth edition of the *Oxford Companion to English Literature* this is an indispensable, compact guide to the central matter of English literature.

There are more than 5,000 entries on the lives and works of authors, poets, playwrights, essayists, philosophers, and historians; plot summaries of novels and plays; literary movements; fictional characters; legends; theatres; periodicals; and much more.

The book's sharpened focus on the English literature of the British Isles makes it especially convenient to use, but there is still generous coverage of the literature of other countries and of other disciplines which have influenced or been influenced by English literature.

From reviews of *The Oxford Companion to English Literature*:

'a book which one turns to with constant pleasure . . . a book with much style and little prejudice' Iain Gilchrist, *TLS*

'it is quite difficult to imagine, in this genre, a more useful publication' Frank Kermode, *London Review of Books*

'incarnates a living sense of tradition . . . sensitive not to fashion merely but to the spirit of the age' Christopher Ricks, *Sunday Times*